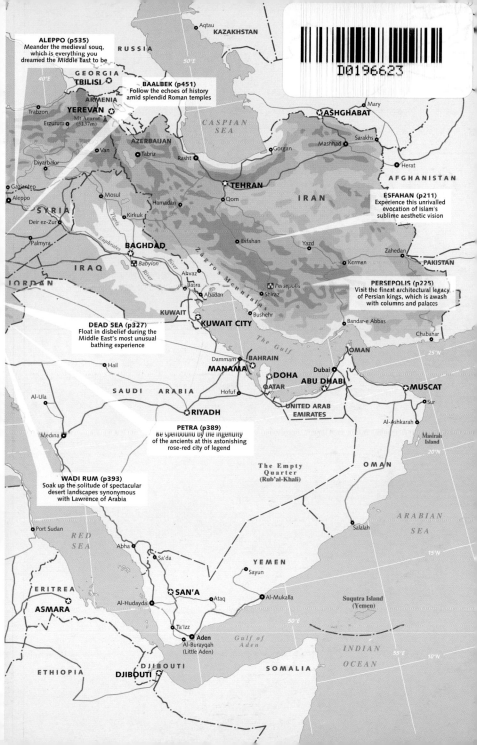

ALEPPO (p535)
Meander the medieval souq,
which is everything you
dreamed the Middle East to be

BAALBEK (p451)
Follow the echoes of history
amid splendid Roman temples

D0196623

ESFAHAN (p211)
Experience this unrivalled
evocation of Islam's
sublime aesthetic vision

PERSEPOLIS (p225)
Visit the finest architectural legacy
of Persian kings, which is awash
with columns and palaces

DEAD SEA (p327)
Float in disbelief during the
Middle East's most unusual
bathing experience

PETRA (p389)
Be spellbound by the ingenuity
of the ancients at this astonishing
rose-red city of legend

WADI RUM (p393)
Soak up the solitude of spectacular
desert landscapes synonymous
with Lawrence of Arabia

Aqtau
KAZAKHSTAN
RUSSIA
50°E
40°E
GEORGIA
TBILISI
ARMENIA
Trabzon
YEREVAN
Erzurum
Mt Ararat (5137m)
Van
AZERBAIJAN
Diyarbakır
Tabriz
Rasht
Gaziantep
Mosul
Aleppo
SYRIA
Kirkuk
Hamadan
Deir ez-Zur
Palmyra
Euphrates
Tigris River
BAGHDAD
JORDAN
IRAQ
Babylon
Ahvaz
Basra
Abadan
KUWAIT
KUWAIT CITY
Hail
Al-Ula
SAUDI ARABIA
Hofuf
Dammam
MANAMA
BAHRAIN
DOHA
QATAR
RIYADH
Medina
Port Sudan
RED SEA
Abha
Sa'da
The Empty Quarter (Rub'al-Khali)
YEMEN
Sayun
ERITREA
ASMARA
Al-Hudayda
SAN'A
Ataq
Al-Mukalla
Ta'Izz
Aden
Al-Burayqah (Little Aden)
Gulf of Aden
ETHIOPIA
DJIBOUTI
DJIBOUTI
SOMALIA
CASPIAN SEA
Gorgan
ASHGHABAT
Mary
Mashhad
Sarakhs
Herat
AFGHANISTAN
TEHRAN
Qom
IRAN
Esfahan
Yazd
Zahedan
Zagros Mountains
Persepolis
Shiraz
Kerman
PAKISTAN
Bushehr
Bandar-e Abbas
Chabahar
The Gulf
OMAN
Dubai
ABU DHABI
MUSCAT
UNITED ARAB EMIRATES
Al-Ashkarah
Sur
Masirah Island
OMAN
25°N
20°N
ARABIAN SEA
Salalah
Suqutra Island (Yemen)
INDIAN OCEAN
50°E
55°E
15°N
10°N

Destination Middle East

The Middle East is quite simply extraordinary, one of the world's most fascinating and reward-ing travel destinations. It was here that some of the most significant civilisations of antiquity rose and fell and where the three great monotheistic religions – Judaism, Christianity and Islam – were born. Left behind is an astonishing open-air museum of ancient cities and historic buildings, the stones of which still resonate with the sounds of the faithful.

The Middle East is home to some of the world's most significant cities – Jerusalem, Cairo, Damascus, Baghdad and İstanbul. The ruins of the once similarly epic cities of history – Petra, Persepolis, Ephesus, Palmyra, Baalbek, Leptis Magna and the bounty of ancient Egypt – also mark the passage of centuries in a region where the ancient world lives and breathes.

The landscapes of the region are equally spellbinding, from the unrivalled seas of sand dunes and palm-fringed lakes in Libya's Sahara desert to the stunning mountains of the north and the underwater world of the Red Sea.

Above all else, however, your most enduring memory of the Middle East is likely to be its people. Their gracious welcome, many kindnesses and boundless hospitality speak of an altogether more civilised age.

From the gravitas of the Sahara to the blue tiles of Esfahan, this is a region for discern-ing travellers, for those looking for the story behind the headline, and where the bridges between ancient and modern civilisations are everywhere evident. If you believe what the media tells you and decide not to visit, you'd be missing out on the journey of a lifetime.

Middle East

Anthony Ham
Andrew Burke, Jean-Bernard Carillet, Michael Kohn, Frances Linzee Gordon,
Virginia Maxwell, Bradley Mayhew

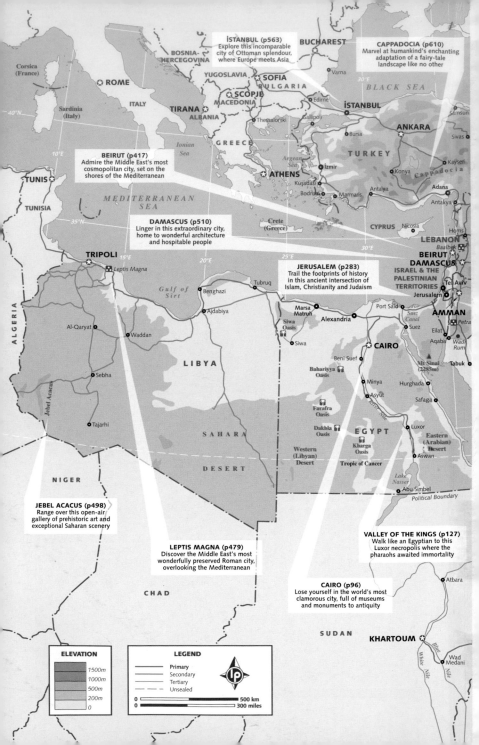

ISTANBUL (p563)
Explore this incomparable city of Ottoman splendour, where Europe meets Asia

CAPPADOCIA (p610)
Marvel at humankind's enchanting adaptation of a fairy-tale landscape like no other

BEIRUT (p417)
Admire the Middle East's most cosmopolitan city, set on the shores of the Mediterranean

DAMASCUS (p510)
Linger in this extraordinary city, home to wonderful architecture and hospitable people

JERUSALEM (p283)
Trail the footprints of history in this ancient intersection of Islam, Christianity and Judaism

JEBEL ACACUS (p498)
Range over this open-air gallery of prehistoric art and exceptional Saharan scenery

LEPTIS MAGNA (p479)
Discover the Middle East's most wonderfully preserved Roman city, overlooking the Mediterranean

VALLEY OF THE KINGS (p127)
Walk like an Egyptian to this Luxor necropolis where the pharaohs awaited immortality

CAIRO (p96)
Lose yourself in the world's most clamorous city, full of museums and monuments to antiquity

ELEVATION
1500m
1000m
500m
200m
0

LEGEND
Primary
Secondary
Tertiary
Unsealed

0   500 km
0   300 miles

Egypt

Survey mud-brick buildings and all that lies before them in beautiful Siwa Oasis (p148)

OTHER HIGHLIGHTS

- Size up the priceless treasures in Cairo's Egyptian Museum (p101).
- Probe the dark recesses of the royal rock-hewn tombs at Luxor's Valley of the Kings (p127).

Orbit the Bibliotheca Alexandrina (p120), on whose walls are symbols from every known alphabet

Take in the activity near the vast and ancient Pyramids of Giza (p106)

Iran

Admire the many gorgeous buildings and fine gardens that grace cultured Shiraz (p221)

CLINT LUCAS

MARK DAFFEY

Linger under the cool arches of luminous Khaju Bridge (p215) in exquisite Esfahan

OTHER HIGHLIGHTS

- Sleep over with the locals in Masuleh (p204), one of Iran's loveliest villages.
- Get lost in the old city of Yazd (p217), which is among the world's most ancient towns.

Cross-examine carved reliefs and ancient doorways in mysterious Persepolis (p225)

PHIL WEYMOUTH

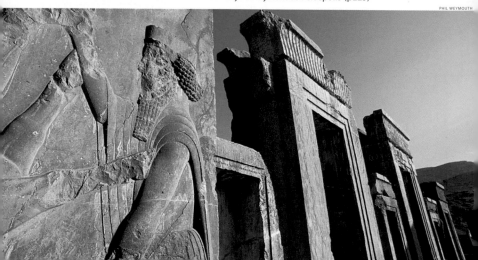

Israel & the Palestinian Territories

OLIVER STREWE

Get up close to Jerusalem's Dome of the Rock (p289), an enduring symbol of the city.

HANAN ISACHAR

Join the throngs at the festive Love Parade (p349) in Tel Aviv

ANTHONY PIDGEON

Feel the pressing aura at Masada (p328), site of the last Jewish stronghold during the First Revolt

OTHER HIGHLIGHTS

- Investigate timeless Akko (p313), a city that lives much as it has for thousands of years.
- Roll through verdant forests and emerald valleys in the lush area of Galilee (p316).

Jordan

Allow the echoes of ancient Rome to ring through your ears at remarkably well preserved Jerash (p377)

Join the locals for some outdoor activities (p399) in the wilds of Jordan

OTHER HIGHLIGHTS

- Delight in glorious desert scenery and pretend you're Lawrence of Arabia at Wadi Rum (p393).
- Indulge in some wild-at-heart adventure at Wadi Mujib Nature Reserve (p382), including repelling down a waterfall.

Take your breath away with a trip to towering, pink-hued Petra (p389), the impossible city of the Nabataeans

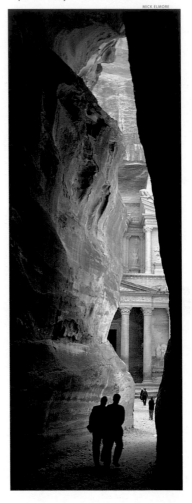

Lebanon

BETHUNE CARMICHAEL

Tickle your taste buds with sweet tempta-
tions (p416) from the Middle East's richest
cuisine

Peer at the majestic remains of the Temple
of Jupiter (p453) in Baalbek

BETHUNE CARMICHAEL

OTHER HIGHLIGHTS

- Dance till you can dance no more while
  enjoying Beirut's hip nightlife (p428).
- Feast your eyes on the magnificent
  Mamluk-era architecture of Tripoli
  (p437).

Fall under the spell of Byblos (p434), a city of great antiquity that's seen epic empires come and go

JANE SWEENEY

Libya

Walk like a Roman through the fascinating remnants of Leptis Magna (p479)

JANE SWEENEY

Open a door into an intricate culture by visiting Tripoli's mosques, including the elaborate Gurgi Mosque (p474)

PATRICK BEN LUKE SYDER

OTHER HIGHLIGHTS

- Marvel at the prehistoric rock art of the Jebel Acacus (p499), some of it 12,000 years old.
- Go off the beaten track to Waw al-Namus (p498), an extinct volcanic crater cupping blue, red and green lakes.

Get swept away by the beauty of the Idehan Ubari (p495), a land of immense sand dunes and stunning lakes

ANTHONY HAM

Syria

Succumb to the charms of Palmyra (p544), ancient city of the ambitious Zenobia

OTHER HIGHLIGHTS

- Follow the road to Damascus and spend your time exploring the streets and cafés of the Old City (p514).
- Poke around Qala'at Samaan (p544), the base of St Simeon Stylites who spent 36 years living atop pillars.

Let the souqs (p538) of Aleppo swallow you up as you wander their labyrinthine lengths

Peep around every corner while exploring Crac des Chevaliers (p529), a castle of childhood imaginings

Turkey

CHRIS BARTON

Be fascinated by the rock-cut buildings of Göreme (p611), rising from the earth like magic mushrooms

Face up to the gigantic fallen heads at Mt Nemrut (p626), site of the memorial sanctuary of a shadowy Commagene king

ANDREW BURKE

DALLAS STRIBLEY

Bow down to the glory of İstanbul's Aya Sofya (p567), one of the world's most splendid buildings

OTHER HIGHLIGHTS

- Dive into the deep blue of the shiny Mediterranean and relax in the seaside town of Kaş (p600).
- Kick back in Ottoman style at Safranbolu (p609), a World Heritage site boasting a multitude of 19th-century half-timbered houses.

Contents

Regional Map Contents

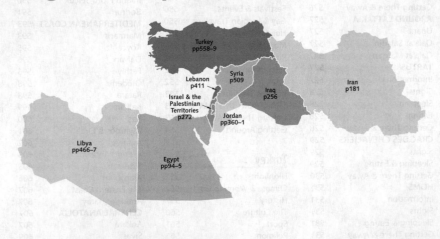

Turkey pp558–9

Lebanon p411

Syria p509

Israel & the Palestinian Territories p272

Jordan pp360–1

Iraq p256

Iran p181

Libya pp466–7

Egypt pp94–5

The Authors

ANTHONY HAM
Coordinating Author, Iraq, Libya

In another life Anthony was a refugee lawyer who represented clients from the Middle East – especially Iraq and Iran – and obtained a Masters degree in Middle Eastern politics. Then he went to the Middle East and really started learning. Now a full-time writer and photographer based in Madrid, he has written Lonely Planet's *Libya* and *Saudi Arabia* guides and has contributed to *Jordan*, *Iran* and previous editions of *Middle East*, as well as writing for numerous newspapers around the world. All of which provides him with an excuse (although none is needed) to return to the cities where he first fell irretrievably in love with the region, and to retreat to the silence of the desert.

My Favourite Trip

After plotting my journey from the idyllic seaside village of Kaş (p600), I would make a beeline for Damascus (p510), my favourite Middle Eastern city. When I could finally tear myself away from cafés filled with storytellers and hospitable Syrians, I'd drop in on old friends in Amman (p364). I'm always drawn to the wonder that is Petra (p389) and the silent beauty of Wadi Rum (p393). With my love of the desert rekindled, I'd head for Cairo (p96; one of the world's greatest cities) and sophisticated Alexandria (p117) before heading across Libya. En route to the desert oasis of Ghadames (p491), I wouldn't miss Cyrene (p485), Leptis Magna (p479) and the magical medina of Tripoli (p473). And then I'd leave the world behind and travel deep into the desert – the Idehan Ubari (p495), Jebel Acacus (p498) and the glorious isolation of Waw al-Namus (p498).

ANDREW BURKE
Iran

Andrew's long-held affection for Iran has seen him spend five months in the country in recent years, both working for Lonely Planet and as a photojournalist. Apart from enjoying endless tea and unforgettable hospitality, in 2003 he reported on the Bam earthquake and wrote much of Lonely Planet's *Iran* guide, and he's written about Iran's last two general elections for major newspapers. Andrew has twice been arrested while researching, but despite these 'misunderstandings' believes Iranians are among the most hospitable people on earth. During research he kept a blog featured on www.lonelyplanet.com. When he's not travelling Andrew lives in Phnom Penh, Cambodia.

LONELY PLANET AUTHORS

Why is our travel information the best in the world? It's simple: our authors are independent, dedicated travellers. They don't research using just the Internet or phone, and they don't take freebies in exchange for positive coverage. They travel widely, to all the popular spots and off the beaten track. They personally visit thousands of hotels, restaurants, cafés, bars, galleries, palaces, museums and more – and they take pride in getting all the details right, and telling it how it is. For more, see the authors section on www.lonelyplanet.com.

JEAN-BERNARD CARILLET   Turkey

Jean-Bernard's fervour for Turkey was first sparked by a train ride from Paris that ended in İstanbul during his teenage years. Since then, his attraction to the Middle East has never been tamed. For this book, he was too happy to travel the breadth and length of Turkey, from Edirne to Kars and from Trabzon to Gaziantep. He tried everything from puffing nargileh and relaxing in a *hamam* (bathhouse) to boutique hotels and sharing a cup of tea with Kurdish nomads in the mountains. As an incorrigible Frenchman and foodie, he also ate his way through more *fıstıklı baklava* (pistachio baklava) and kebabs than he now cares to remember.

MICHAEL KOHN   Israel & the Palestinian Territories

Michael's earliest exposure to Judaism and Israel came in his mother's kitchen, where the smell of matzo ball soup wafted through the air on Shabbat and toasted bagels were piled high on Sunday mornings. He made his first trip to Israel at the impressionable age of 15, when he and 50 schoolmates stormed the Old City markets by day and the Jerusalem Underground discotheque by night. A return to the Middle East half a lifetime later led him around Israel's neighbours Egypt, Jordan, Syria and Lebanon before finally plunging in to research this guide. Michael has worked on several other Lonely Planet guidebooks, including *Central Asia*, *Tibet* and *Mongolia*.

FRANCES LINZEE GORDON   Lebanon

Frances' fervour for travel was first sparked by a school scholarship to Venice aged 17. Since then she's travelled extensively in the Middle East, for which she has a special passion. Frances contributes travel articles and photos to a variety of publications, and recently completed an MA in African and Asian (Middle Eastern) Studies and Arabic. Her other work includes radio and TV appearances (including a slot as 'travel advisor' to BBC News 24). Frances believes passionately in the benefits of travel both for the tourist and for the country. She also encourages women to travel, considering her gender a help not a hindrance, particularly when negotiating hurdles on the road!

VIRGINIA MAXWELL   Food & Drink, Egypt, Syria

After working for many years as a publishing manager at Lonely Planet's Melbourne headquarters, Virginia decided that she'd be happier writing guidebooks than commissioning them. Since making this decision she's authored Lonely Planet's *İstanbul* city guide and covered Lebanon and the United Arab Emirates for other titles. With partner Peter and young son Max she travels regularly in the Middle East, and particularly loves spending time in İstanbul and Damascus.

BRADLEY MAYHEW

Jordan

Bradley has returned to the Middle East frequently since first visiting Jordan in the early 1990s as an adventure tour organiser. Since then he's travelled the breadth of the Islamic world from Morocco to Tajikistan as a guidebook writer.

He's the coauthor of Lonely Planet guides to Jordan, Central Asia, Tibet and Shanghai and has worked on Lonely Planet guides from *Morocco* to *Mongolia*. He's the coauthor and photographer of the *Odyssey guide to Uzbekistan* and has lectured on Central Asia at the Royal Geographic Society.

CONTRIBUTING AUTHORS

Roshan Muhammed Salih After two years of 'crowd control' (aka teaching) In a British inner-city school, Roshan started his journalism career in local papers. He then moved into documentary making, working on programmes about everything from politics to obesity. Since 2003 he has worked for Al-Jazeera in Qatar covering a tumultuous period in the Middle East. Roshan wrote the boxed texts 'Occupied or Liberated? Iraq Post-Saddam' (p258) and 'Prospects for an Iraqi Phoenix' (p257).

Will Gourlay Will has been a 'student' of the Muslim culture and history since encountering Islamic relics in Spain, Hungary and the Balkans. He has subsequently taught in Turkey, travelled widely in the Middle East and written about the region for Australian newspapers and magazines. A commissioning editor in Lonely Planet's Melbourne office, he is plotting an extended return to the eastern Mediterranean. Will wrote the chapter Islam & the West.

Getting Started

Apart from a few logistical matters, your pretrip planning will consist of the pleasurable pastimes of tracking down a great read, surfing the Net to learn other travellers' tales and the odd trip to your video store to find classic Middle Eastern movies. Most types of journey are possible regardless of your budget and can range from the highly active (see p638) to lazing by the sea. To whet your appetite and to survey possible routes, see p27.

Two issues to be aware of involve the thorny question of visas. Read carefully the information about Israeli visa stamps (see p353) and entering Libya on an organised tour (p503), and make the necessary advance preparations to avoid finding yourself at a border and being unable to cross it.

WHEN TO GO

When planning a trip to the Middle East, the two main things to bear in mind are the weather and the religious holidays.

Climate

Most of the Middle East is best visited in autumn and spring (September to November and March to May). December and January can be fairly bleak and overcast everywhere in the region; even in southern Egypt and Libya night-time desert temperatures can be bitterly cold. Unless you're an avid sun-worshipper or water-sports freak, the summer months of June through to September should definitely be avoided – it's just too hot to do anything. In July and August visitors to the Pharaonic sites at Aswan and Luxor in Egypt are obliged to get up at 5am to beat the heat and don't even think of an expedition into the Libyan Sahara at this time.

There are exceptions. The northeast of Turkey before May or after mid-October can be beset by snow, perhaps even enough to close roads and mountain passes. Parts of Syria and northern Iran also suffer from miserable weather between November and March or April.

For more details on weather conditions, see the Climate section in each individual country chapter and p644.

Religious Holidays & Festivals

Although non-Muslims are not bound by the rules of fasting during the month of Ramadan, many restaurants and cafés throughout the region will be closed and those who are fasting can be understandably taciturn, transport is on a go-slow and office hours are erratic to say the least. If you're visiting Turkey, you may also want to avoid Kurban Bayramı, which lasts a full week. Hotels are jam-packed, banks closed and transport booked up weeks ahead. Iran also has a couple of festivals to avoid including Moharram, the month of mourning, and the Persian New Year celebrations, while in Israel and the Palestinian Territories quite a few religious holidays, such as Passover and Easter, cause the country to fill up with pilgrims, prices to double and public transport to grind to a halt.

On the positive side, it's worth trying to time your visit to tie in with something like Eid al-Adha (the Feast of Sacrifice, which marks the Prophet's pilgrimage to Mecca) or the Prophet's Birthday, as these can be colourful occasions. See p647 for further details.

COSTS & MONEY

Libya, Lebanon and Israel and the Palestinian Territories aside, travel in the Middle East is cheap; the travel staples – accommodation, meals and transport (apart from flying) – are, thankfully, usually the cheapest items of your trip, although opportunities abound for spending a little more and travelling in considerable comfort.

If you're on a tight budget, stay at cheap hotels with shared bathrooms, eat street food and carry a student card with you to reduce entry fees at museums, you could easily get by on around US$10 to US$15 a day. Staying in comfortable midrange hotels, eating at quality restaurants to ensure a varied diet, the occasional private taxi ride and some shopping will push your daily expenses up to between US$30 and US$50. In Lebanon, US$20 a day is the barest minimum, while US$40 is more realistic. In Israel and the Palestinian Territories, budget travellers could keep things down to $US35 per day if they really tried hard, while a more comfortable journey would require up to US$60. Libya, the land of organised tours, can be done on the cheap (ie by staying in youth hostels and travelling in a large group), but can cost up to US$80 per day including good hotels and 4WD hire.

DON'T LEAVE HOME WITHOUT...

Ensure that you have the requisite vaccinations (p673) and visas (p653) before departure. Remember that anyone carrying an Israeli passport or an Israeli stamp in their passport will be denied entry to Iran, Iraq, Lebanon, Syria and Libya. Travel Insurance (p648) is strongly advised. If you're planning to drive, don't forget your licence and if you're bringing your own car make sure you get all the necessary documentation together (p662).

Other recommended items:

- basic medical kit
- mosquito repellent
- sleeping bag
- sunglasses, hat and sunscreen (as essential in the Sahara as on the beach)
- torch (flashlight) and spare batteries
- eight to 10 passport-sized photos for visas (if you plan to visit a number of countries and plan to obtain visas while there)
- Swiss Army knife with a bottle and/or can opener in case you buy a drink from a supermarket and want to actually drink it
- alarm clock (for early morning departures)
- universal washbasin plug
- washing powder and length of cord for drying clothes
- sanitary towels or tampons
- condoms
- toilet paper
- photocopies of your important documents (and leave a copy somewhere safe back home)
- a good book or 10 (the Middle East's night-time entertainment, or the absence thereof, may mean plenty of quiet nights in)
- a small size-three football (a great way to meet local kids and their families)
- a small sewing kit (useful for emergency repairs to backpacks stretched to bursting by souvenir shopping)
- a small cool pack (drinks are all much cheaper – and warmer – in supermarkets)
- a sense of perspective – persistent shopkeepers are just trying to make a living and can actually be nice people
- patience – most things do run on time, but the timetable may be elusive to the uninitiated
- an open mind

When estimating your own costs, take into account extra items such as visa fees (which can top US$50 depending on where you get them and what your nationality is), long-distance travel, and the cost of organised tours or activities, such as camel trekking, snorkelling or diving. And remember, some of the best travel experiences cost nothing: whiling away the hours taking on the locals in backgammon in Damascus, sleeping under the desert stars in the Sahara or watching the sun set over the Mediterranean.

More details of costs are given under the Money section in the Directory of each individual country chapter.

Travelling with a mixture of travellers cheques (relatively easy to replace and widely accepted), cash (super convenient) and credit cards (even more convenient, but of no use in Iran and little use in Libya) is the wisest way to stay liquid in the Middle East.

> 'Travelling with a mixture of travellers cheques, cash and credit cards is the easiest way to stay liquid in the Middle East.'

READING UP
Books

Lonely Planet has numerous guides to the countries of the Middle East, including *Egypt, Iran, Turkey, Libya, Jordan,* and *Syria & Lebanon*. There is also a city guide to *İstanbul*, a World Food guide to Turkey, and phrasebooks for Egyptian Arabic, Farsi, Hebrew and Turkish.

In *From the Holy Mountain*, William Dalrymple skips lightly but engagingly across the region's landscape of sacred and profane, travelling through Turkey, Syria and Israel and the Palestinian Territories in what could be an emblem for your own journey.

East is West, Valleys of the Assassins, and *Beyond the Euphrates,* by Freya Stark, are elegantly written accounts of Stark's intrepid 1930s journey through Persia. They are full of insight and highly sympathetic to the people and traditions of the region.

Travels with a Tangerine, by Tim Mackintosh-Smith, captures a modern journey in the footsteps of Ibn Battuta, a 13th-century Arab Marco Polo. It begins in Morocco and takes in several countries of the Middle East.

Eastward to Tartary: Travels in the Balkans, the Middle East, and the Caucasus, by Robert Kaplan, is confronting and occasionally sweeping in its generalisations, but the hard-headed narrative on Turkey, Syria and Iran will get you thinking.

The distinguished Islamic studies scholar CWR Long brings to life the people and history of most Middle Eastern countries, including, unusually, Libya, in *Bygone Heat: Travels of an Idealist in the Middle East*.

Bad Moon Rising: a Chronicle of the Middle East Today, by Gilles Kepel, is a master work by one of Islam's most compelling analysts. The scholar charts the history of radical Islam and its relationship with the West.

Websites

For specific country overviews, the lowdown on travel in the region and hundreds of useful links head to Lonely Planet's website (www.lonelyplanet .com), including the Thorn Tree, Lonely Planet's online bulletin board.

The following websites are an excellent way to get information about the Middle East.

Al-Bab (www.al-bab.com) Arab-world gateway that covers the entire Arab world with links to dozens of news services, country profiles, travel sites, maps, profiles, etc. A fantastic resource.

Al-Bawaba (www.albawaba.com) A good mix of news, entertainment and yellow pages directories, with everything from online forums to kids' pages.

Al-Mashriq (www.almashriq.hiof.no) A terrific repository for cultural information from the Levant (Israel, Jordan, Lebanon, Palestine, Syria, Turkey). Some of the information is a bit stale but its articles, ranging from ethnology to politics, are hard to beat.

Arabnet (www.arab.net) Excellent Saudi-run online encyclopedia of the Arab world, collecting together news and articles plus links to further resources organised by country.
BBC News (www.news.bbc.co.uk) Follow the links to the Middle East section for comprehensive and excellent regional news that's constantly updated.
Great Buildings Online (www.greatbuildings.com) Download then explore digital 3D models of the Pyramids and İstanbul's Aya Sofya, plus lots of other info and images of monuments throughout the Middle East.

MUST-SEE MOVIES

Lawrence of Arabia (1962) may be clichéd and may give TE Lawrence more prominence than his Arab companions, but David Lean's epic is a masterpiece that captures all the hopes for freedom and subsequent frustrations for the Arabs in the aftermath of WWI.

Arab Palestine (1948), directed by Mohammed Bakary, can be hard to find, but stands out because it contains conversations between Palestinians and Jewish settlers and is far more balanced than most films of its era.

Chronicle of a Disappearance (1996), by the Palestinian director Elie Suleiman, captures the despair and courageous survival of Palestinians living under occupation and its atmospheric sense of place is richly evocative of modern Palestine.

Secret Ballot (2001), by Babak Payami, is unrivalled in conjuring up the contradictions between revolutionary and democratic Iran by one of the country's most promising directors.

Yol (1982), by Yilmaz Guney, is epic in scale but at the same time allows the humanity of finely rendered characters to shine through as five Turkish prisoners on parole travel around their country.

FAVOURITE FESTIVALS & EVENTS

In addition to the various religious and national holidays (p647) common to all Middle Eastern countries, each country has its own festivals that can celebrate everything from classical Arabic music to the many and varied uses for the humble camel. For a full rundown, see the Directory section of each individual country chapter, but in the meantime, here are some of our favourites that you may want to factor in when planning your trip.
Arabic Music Festival (Cairo, Egypt) A sophisticated 10-day celebration of classical, traditional and orchestral Arabic music held in November.
Baalbek Festival (Baalbek, Lebanon) One of the Middle East's most famous arts festivals held against the backdrop of towering Roman ruins in July and August.
Bereshet Festival (Meggido Forest, Israel) This Bohemian gathering in September in the spiritual Megiddo Forest won't be to everyone's taste, but it boasts lots of live music and plenty of hedonism.
Bosra Festival (Bosra, Syria) Festival of music and theatre held in the town's spectacular Roman amphitheatre every second September or October in odd years.
Ghadames Festival (Ghadames, Libya) Excellent desert festival in October set in the enchanting ghost town of one of the Sahara's most significant oases with celebrations of traditional culture and weddings.
İstanbul International Music Festival (İstanbul, Turkey) Concerts are held in a wide variety of venues, including Aya İrini Kilisesi, in June and July.
Jerash Festival (Jerash, Jordan) Stunning setting in ancient Roman city for performances by local and overseas artists and displays of traditional handicrafts in July and August.
Mevlana Festival (Konya, Turkey) Ideal introduction to the whirling dervishes in one of their most important strongholds. Held from 10 to 17 December.
Nitaq Festival (Cairo, Egypt) Downtown Cairo's excellent arts festival with two weeks of exhibitions, theatre, poetry and music at galleries, cafés and a variety of other venues. Held in February or March.
Palmyra Festival (Palmyra, Syria) Another spectacular set amid Roman ruins, this popular folk festival, held in the desert in April and May, promises everything from camel races to music and dance performances.

West Beirut (1998) is Ziad Doueiri's powerful meditation on the scars and hopes of Christian and Muslim Lebanese, set against the backdrop of Lebanon's civil war about which there are few so superbly crafted films.

Nina's Tragedies (2005), by Savi Gabizon, begins with a Tel Aviv army unit telling a family that their son has been killed in a suicide bombing and ends with a disturbing but nuanced look at the alienation of modern Israel as it struggles for peace.

RESPONSIBLE TRAVEL

Tourism may have the potential to change for the better the relationship between the Middle East and the West, but the gradual erosion of traditional life is mass tourism's flipside. Sexual promiscuity, public drunkenness among tourists and the wearing of unsuitable clothing are all of concern. Please try to keep your impact as low as possible and create a good precedent for those who follow you by following the following tips:

'Try to learn some of the standard greetings – it will make a very good first impression.'

- Don't hand out sweets or pens to children on the streets, since it encourages begging. Similarly, doling out medicines can encourage people not to seek proper medical advice. A donation to a project, health centre or school is a far more constructive way to help.
- You can do more good by buying your snacks, cigarettes, bubble gum etc from the enterprising grannies trying to make ends meet rather than state-run stores. Also use locally owned hotels and restaurants and buy locally made products.
- Try to give people a balanced perspective of life in the West. Try also to point out the strong points of the local culture – strong family ties, comparatively low crime etc.
- Make yourself aware of the human-rights situation, history and current affairs in the countries you travel through.
- If you're in a frustrating situation, be patient, friendly and considerate. Never lose your temper as a confrontational attitude never goes down well and for many Arabs a loss of face is a serious and sensitive issue. If you have a problem with someone, just be polite, calm and persistent.
- Try to learn some of the standard greetings (p679) – it will make a very good first impression.
- Ask before taking close-up photos of people. Don't worry if you don't speak the language – a smile and gesture will be appreciated.
- Don't pay to take a photo of someone and don't photograph someone if they don't want you to. If you agree to send someone a photo, make sure you follow through on it.
- Be respectful of Islamic traditions and don't wear revealing clothing; loose lightweight clothing is preferable.
- Try not to waste water. Switch off lights and air-con when you go out.
- When visiting historical sites, consider the irreparable damage you inflict upon them when you climb to the top of a pyramid, or take home an unattached artefact as a souvenir.
- Resist the local tendency of indifference to littering.

For more specific advice, see Responsible Diving (p639) and Responsible Hiking (p640). For information on the etiquette of visiting mosques, see Mosques Not to Be Missed (p67).

A British organisation called **Tourism Concern** (☎ 020-7133 3330; www .tourismconcern.org.uk; Stapleton House, 277-281 Holloway Rd, London N7 8HN) is primarily concerned with tourism and its impact upon local cultures and the environment. It has a range of publications and contacts for community organisations, as well as advice on minimising the impact of your travels.

Itineraries

CLASSIC ROUTES

İSTANBUL TO CAIRO
Two Months

From that first moment in sophisticated **İstanbul** (p563), you know you're in for a fabulous ride. Cut through central Turkey to marvel at the other-worldly landscapes of **Cappadocia** (Kapadokya; p610) that seem to have sprung from a wonderfully childlike imagination.

For some, the Middle East starts at the Syrian border, just across which lies the enchanting city of **Aleppo** (p535). **Damascus** (p510) is incomparable, home to labyrinthine markets, hospitable people and a wealth of historical associations. Pass through **Amman** (p364) and on to **Jerusalem** (p283), a city like no other. Further south again, the extraordinary rose-red ruins of **Petra** (p389) lie hidden amid stunning rocky mountains, and are so well preserved that they leave you feeling as if the ancient Nabataeans must not be far away. **Wadi Rum** (p393) boasts beautiful rock formations, orange sand and Bedouin companions to guide the way. From **Aqaba** (p395), make your way across the Red Sea bound for **Cairo** (p96), which is everything you dreamed the Middle East would be.

On the route from İstanbul to Cairo (around 4000km) allow two to 2½ weeks for Turkey, 10 days in Syria, one week in Jordan, at least a week in Israel and the Palestinian Territories and another week in Cairo.

ESFAHAN TO İSTANBUL   Three to Four Weeks

The great overland journeys may be a thing of the past for all but the most hardy of travellers, but that doesn't mean you can't do a large (and, some would say, the best) chunk of it. **Esfahan** (p211) is like a Silk Road dream, home to dazzling blue-tiled architecture and teahouses spanning the river, reminiscent of *The Thousand and One Nights*. Esfahan also makes a great launching pad from which to explore other highlights of central and southern Iran, not least among them the mud-brick wonders of **Yazd** (p217) with its mazelike old town; the agreeable city of **Shiraz** (p221) with its pleasure gardens and fine mosques; and the antique city of **Persepolis** (Takht-e Jamshid; p225) where ancient Persia comes alive.

Tehran (p186) may not be the Middle East's most appealing metropolis, but it's a fascinating place and stands at the heart of modern Iran's struggle between Islamic conservatism and the country's liberal future; it has more than enough to keep you occupied for a few days.

As you head for Turkey, the historical resonance of **Tabriz** (p201) warrants an overnight stay. It's a long way east to the bright lights of modern Turkey, but don't fail to linger in enchanting little **Van** (p622) with its island church. Perhaps also detour north for a view of **Mt Ararat** (p621), thought by some to be the final resting place of Noah's Ark. The road to **İstanbul** (p563) – the one-time Constantinople and the place where Europe meets the Middle East – is long and lonely, but en route, you'll pass through dramatic landscapes and plenty of roads leading off to detours that you won't want to miss.

> With Esfahan as your base, you'll need two weeks to enjoy Yazd, Shiraz and Persepolis. Allow a week to get to the Turkish border and another to İstanbul. The 3900km journey can be done in three weeks if you keep up a cracking pace and don't stray from the path.

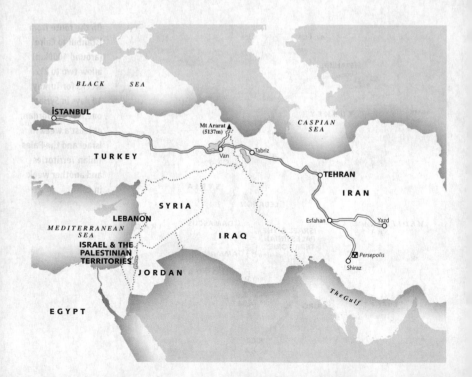

THE HEART OF THE MIDDLE EAST   One Month

The countries that lie at the heart of the Middle East – Syria, Lebanon, Jordan, Israel and the Palestinian Territories – will be well known to you from the news. Now it's time to discover what they're really like. **Beirut** (p417), the one-time 'Paris of the Middle East', is recovering its sophistication with elegant architecture, outdoor cafés by the Mediterranean and a fascinating social and religious mix of people. Beyond Beirut, Lebanon crams a lot in, with living history in **Byblos** (Jbail; p434), wonderful souqs in **Tripoli** (Trablous; p437), and evocative ruins from **Tyre** (Sour; p446) in the deep south to **Baalbek** (p451) in the Bekaa Valley.

Just across the border into Syria, **Damascus** (p510) is a glorious, hospitable city that at least one Lonely Planet author never wanted to leave. **Aleppo** (p535) is similarly friendly and enchanting and a base for visiting the wonderfully situated **Qala'at Samaan** (p544). The Jordanian capital of **Amman** (p364) can feel like an oasis and also makes a great base for exploring astonishing **Petra** (p389) and the solitude of **Wadi Rum** (p393).

Across the Jordan River, **Jerusalem** (p283) is where so much Middle Eastern history is written and it's so beguiling and loaded with significance that it can be difficult to believe you're actually there. From there, your ability to visit the biblical towns of **Bethlehem** (p339) and **Jericho** (p338) will depend entirely on the prevailing security situation. **Tel Aviv** (p297) is a lively place to let your hair down at the end of the journey, a chance to discover the other side of Israeli life that you rarely hear anything about. The world-class ruins of **Caesarea** (p313) and timeless **Akko** (p313) are worth as much time as you can give them.

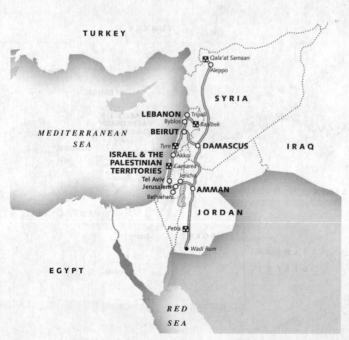

A week in each country will have you moving but the distance between sights is rarely long in this compact corner of the Middle East. In total you'll cover about 2500km. Leave Israel to last unless you want to be turned back at the Syrian or Lebanese borders.

EGYPT & LIBYA
One to Two Months

If you've already been on the road for a while, don't miss **Dahab** (p162), a travellers' hang-out, divers' paradise and one of the great places to rest from life on the Middle Eastern road. While there, schedule in an early morning climb to the summit of **Mt Sinai** (p167), which would be a glorious place to watch the sunrise even if Moses didn't bring down the Ten Commandments from here. They don't call **Cairo** (p96) the 'Mother of the World' for nothing. This crossroads of the Middle East and Africa has an endless capacity to surprise and is as at ease with its hip, young Egyptian middle class as with the age-old **Pyramids of Giza** (p106). Spend as long as you can making your way down the Nile and back up again, reserving most of your days for slow felucca trips to connect you with **Luxor** (p124) and **Aswan** (p137) – nowhere has the world of the pharaohs been so lovingly preserved.

After returning to Cairo, make your way up to **Alexandria** (p117), the height of Egyptian and Mediterranean chic, before following the coast all the way to Libya. Now you've left the crowds behind, allowing you to explore the evocative Graeco-Roman-Byzantine ruins of **Apollonia** (p488) and **Cyrene** (Shahat; p487), which perch by the Mediterranean like sentinels to another age. Further west, **Leptis Magna** (p479) is probably the finest Roman city still standing, while **Tripoli** (p471) buzzes with an outstanding medina, world-class museum and atmosphere that will make you wonder why you took so long to come here.

Egypt and Libya deserve a month each, but if you're pressed for time, count on three weeks for Egypt and 10 days to make your way across the Libyan coast. Remember to have your Libyan visa sorted well before you leave home. This route covers 4360km.

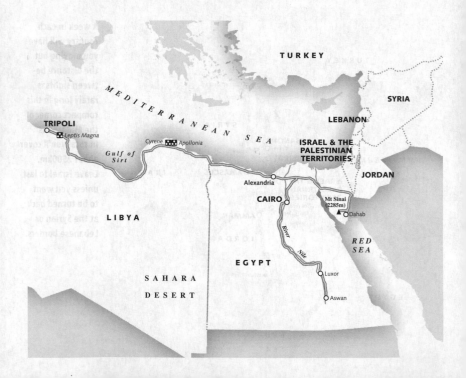

ROADS LESS TRAVELLED

THE MIDDLE EAST GRAND TOUR   Two Months

Most travellers who pass through the Middle East will visit many of the region's stand-out highlights, but how many can claim to have seen them all? Start in **Bam** (p234), then on to **Kerman** (p231), home to a fine bazaar and one of the region's premium teahouses. Mud-brick **Yazd** (p217), leafy **Shiraz** (p221) and ancient **Persepolis** (p225) should all be on your itinerary as you head for **Esfahan** (p211), one of the world's most beautiful cities.

Load up your backpack and steel yourself for the long journey ahead – en route to Turkey stop in **Tehran** (p186) or **Van** (p622), but keep going until you reach the improbable landscapes of **Cappadocia** (p610). Circle up to **İstanbul** (p563), down past **Ephesus** (p588) and the Mediterranean village of your choice – **Marmaris** (p593) is one highlight. You'll soon find yourself passing through some of the greatest cities in the world – **Aleppo** (p535), **Damascus** (p510), **Beirut** (p417) and **Jerusalem** (p283). **Petra** (p389) and **Wadi Rum** (p393) will leave you wondering how Jordan crams so much into such a small space. Dive the Red Sea at **Dahab** (p162) before forging on to **Cairo** (p96), the wonders of Ancient Egypt at **Luxor** (p124) and **Aswan** (p137), the rare pleasure of a felucca trip up the Nile and then a pause in **Alexandria** (p117), the beacon of the ancient world. Racing across Libya, don't miss **Cyrene** (p485), **Leptis Magna** (p479) and **Tripoli** (p471). If you're in this for the long haul, get to the **Jebel Acacus** (p498), deep in the Sahara. And then pause, hopefully not for the first time, to marvel at just how far you've come.

This epic 12,000km trip is really for those on extended career breaks or gap years as visiting every place will take at least two months. Get your Libyan visa before you set out and make sure an Israeli visa stamp doesn't limit your movement.

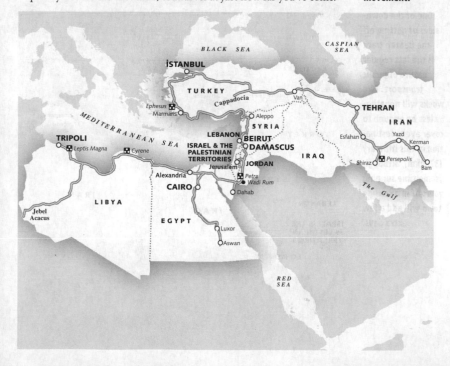

FROM THE CASPIAN TO THE BLACK SEA   Two Weeks

As long as the great Shiite pilgrimage centres of Najaf and Kerbala in Iraq remain off-limits, **Mashhad** (p238) is the place to go to understand the devotion, friendliness and architectural splendour of Shiite Islam's ancient past. The journey northwest from here begins in the steppes of Central Asia and winds close to the Turkmenistan border, taking you past the spectacular tomb tower at **Gonbad-e Kavus** (Gonbad-e Qabus; p238) and then down to the shores of the Caspian Sea. **Ramsar** (p204) is the Caspian's most appealing resort town, while the village of **Masuleh** (p204), near Rasht, is an enchanting little village of cream-coloured houses in the hills behind the Caspian.

After rejoining more-travelled routes at **Tabriz** (p201), cross into Turkey, pause long enough in **Doğubayazit** (p621) to marvel at the improbable beauty of **Mt Ararat** (p621), with a possible detour down to pretty **Van** (p622). While in the area, you'd kick yourself if you missed the fortress, *hammams* (bathhouses) and Russian houses of **Kars** (p620) or the Seljuk buildings of **Erzurum** (p618). **Trabzon** (p616), Turkey's most beautiful Black Sea port, feels more Eastern European than Turkish and promises a wealth of Byzantine buildings, most notable among them being the extraordinary Sumela Monastery. Hugging the coastline as you continue west, the beaches of **Ünye** (p616), the convenience of **Samsun** (p616), the time-worn feel of **Sinop** (p616), and the Roman and Byzantine ruins of **Amasra** (p616) are all recommended as a means of experiencing a Turkey that few Western travellers will ever get.

One of the downsides of getting off the beaten track is the less regular nature of public transport. Two weeks will nonetheless be enough to cover every destination in this itinerary (3700km), although some time sunning yourself in a seaside town will add a few extra days.

TAILORED TRIPS

CITIES OF ANTIQUITY

If the mere suggestion of toga-clad Romans or decadent Egyptians gets your heart racing, the Middle East is a dream for lovers of the ancient world – all of the places listed in this itinerary are inscribed on Unesco's World Heritage list (www.unesco.org). Long before Hollywood made it into a blockbuster, the ancient city of **Troy** (Truva; p581) was one of the greatest cities of ancient Greece. From the shores of the Aegean to an oasis in the Syrian desert, your next stop should be **Palmyra** (p544), an evocative site that is simply sublime at sunset. Across the border in Lebanon, **Baalbek** (p451) is similarly spectacular with its Phoenician origins and ample Roman ruins. In Jordan **Petra** (p389) is astonishing, hewn from the rose-red rock 2000 years ago by one of the Middle East's most enigmatic ancient peoples – the Nabataeans. A journey across the Red Sea and Sinai peninsula opens up the wonders of Ancient Egypt, primarily the **Pyramids of Giza** (p106), the less-visited **Memphis** and **Saqqara** (p117), and the incomparable tombs and temples around **Luxor** (p124). The ancient cities of Libya – **Apollonia** (p488), **Cyrene** (p485) and **Leptis Magna** (p479)

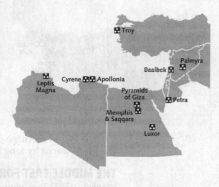

are quite possibly the Middle East's most impressive ruins to combine layers of Phoenician, Greek and Roman civilisations by the shores of the Mediterranean.

THE BEST OF THE BAZAARS

There are few experiences more unforgettable than a Middle Eastern bazaar (souq) – the ancient vaulted ceilings filtering sunlight into laby-rinthine lanes; the smell of spices; and everything from the kitsch of a Mecca wall clock to the finest carpets of Persia. If you're coming from the east, **Kerman** (p233) has a vaulted bazaar to whet your appetite. **Esfahan's** (p216) markets twist their way out across the city like a self-contained community, home to mosques, *hammams* and a discrete sales pitch. **Tehran** (p192) is another sprawling maze and the perfect place to take in the pulse of modern Iran. A long but beautiful journey across eastern Turkey will take you to **İstanbul** (p570), where the Covered Market is one of many highlights well worth the long haul to get here. The souqs of **Aleppo** (p538) are extensive, but it's the old-world charm that makes them perhaps the most evocative and rewarding bazaars in all the world. **Damascus** (p514) is similar, with the landmarks of the ancient world watching over the narrow laneways and the age-hold hospitality of traders who prefer tea to profits. Old **Cairo** (p106) can at times feel like one gigantic bazaar, but the clamour, aromas and endless array of goods serve as reminders that Middle Eastern markets are like no others.

DESERTS & DEEP-SEA DIVING

If you crave the solitude of a sand dune from which to watch the sun set over a blood-red sky, start your desert journey in **Wadi Rum** (p393), a world of myriad canyons, sand stretching to the horizon and ample reminders of the noble history of the once-nomadic Bedouin. To wash off the sand, the Red Sea is not far away, and home to an altogether different under-

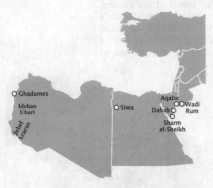

water world. Snorkelling off **Aqaba** (p395) is terrific, but donning your fins or oxygen tank and launching out from either **Dahab** (p162) or **Sharm el-Sheikh** (p158) is even better and an experience you'll never forget. If you still long for solitude, the oasis of **Siwa** (p148) is like an evocation of a fairy tale. It offers the chance to marvel at the sheer scale of what is known by some geographers as the 'Desert Continent'.

Across the border in Libya, you'll find the Sahara in all its glory. If you've come this far, keep going until you reach the **Idehan Ubari** (Ubari Sand Sea; p495), with its palm-fringed lakes amid the dunes, and then the towering cathedral of stones that is the **Jebel Acacus** (p498). To glimpse the other side of desert life, the Unesco World Heritage–listed oasis of **Ghadames** (p491) – connected to the Jebel Acacus by long but beautiful desert trails – is extraordinary.

THE MIDDLE EAST FOR KIDS

İstanbul (p563) is a wonderful introduction, at once markedly Middle Eastern and comfortably European. The human adaptations of the fairy-tale landscapes of **Cappadocia** (p610) will live long in the memory of most children, while the hospitality of the people of **Aleppo** (p535) and **Damascus** (p510) is a wonderful lesson in life that may just shape the perceptions of the next generation. Kids love castles and Syria and Jordan have them in abundance, from the **Crac des Chevaliers** (p529) to **Karak** (p387) and **Shobak** (p388). The **Dead Sea** (p381) will leave your kids giggling at the buoyancy of it all – yes, even Dad floats! **Petra** (p389) is the sort of place that kids will love to tell their friends about back home. **Jerusalem** (p292) has a host of

child-friendly activities, while diving in the Red Sea at **Dahab** (p162) will open up a whole new world that they never imagined, except when watching Nemo. **Cairo** (p96), with its diversity and endlessly interesting sights, is one of the world's great cities and the place to blow their minds. A felucca trip up the Nile from **Aswan** (p137) to **Luxor** (p124) offers an enjoyable break from sardine-can shared taxis. At journey's end in Luxor, the sound-and-light show at the temples of **Karnak** (p126) is a great alternative to learning history from a school textbook – a double-edged sword because they may acquire a new taste for learning, but never want to go to school again when they return home!

Current Events

Do you want the good news or the bad news first?

THE BAD NEWS

The more things change, the more they stay the same, or so it can seem when it comes to the Middle East's two major trouble spots.

In Israel and the Palestinian Territories, Israel's long-awaited withdrawal from the Gaza Strip is playing itself out to a familiar pattern, despite hopes for a new relationship following the death of Yasser Arafat. Israeli settlers are vowing to resist any moves towards a land handover by the government of Ariel Sharon. The Palestinian leadership of Mahmoud Abbas continues to struggle to rein in the suicide bombings and electoral popularity of Hamas. And the most contentious issues (the status of the West Bank and Jerusalem, the right of return for Palestinian refugees, and the ability of a future Palestinian state to guarantee security) are being postponed yet again. In the meantime, the division by the media of both Palestinians and Israelis into the stereotypical groupings of hardliners and moderates, despite many shades of grey in between, continues apace, as does the desperation of ordinary people on both sides.

In Iraq the morass that is the US-led occupation continues largely unabated – the most pressing problem is the perilous security situation for ordinary Iraqis – and will most likely do so until strong Iraqi institutions are built, Western soldiers leave the country and Iraqis feel that their future is their own to decide. Think years, not months.

Elsewhere there are other worrying signs that tensions won't be relieved anytime soon. The June 2005 election in Iran of the apparently conservative hardline president, Mahmoud Ahmadinejad, looks set to slow if not stall Iran's reform process. The election also signposted further tensions between Iran and the West over Iran's nuclear programme after the new president promised to continue it as a matter of national pride and necessity. Thinly veiled threats of military action by the US administration of George W Bush if Iran fails to comply are the most worrying component of this endgame between two countries that have come to symbolise the conflict between Islam and the West.

Syria, like Iran, has long suffered from a troubled relationship with the US. The latter claims that Syria has been less than wholehearted in its efforts to rein in insurgents operating in Iraq. US-Syrian relations seem to be perpetually on the verge of improvement, but expect no miraculous rapprochement as long as both sides play to their respective domestic audiences. Perhaps Syria's almost unfailingly hospitable people could show both governments the way.

If Syria has been waiting to become America's best friend for a while, that's nothing compared to Turkey's long wait for EU membership. The political sensitivity within Europe of having a Muslim (albeit secular) country as its largest member ensures that Turkey will most likely have to wait a few years more.

The suicide bombings in the Egyptian resort town of Sharm el-Sheikh in July 2005, in which 64 people died (most of them Egyptians), was a major blow to Egypt's tourism industry. Tourists in Egypt had been targeted before – most notably in 1997 – but Egyptian security forces had until recently been winning the battle.

NB The following figures do not include Iraq, for which accurate statistics are not available.

On most socioeconomic indicators, including GDP per capita, literacy, infant mortality and life expectancy, people living in the Palestinian Territories fare far worse than those covered by the statistics for the whole of Israel and the Palestinian Territories.

Israel and the Palestinian Territories have the highest life expectancy (79.02 years) with the lowest being Iran (69.35). Only in Israel (81.19) and Jordan (80.5) does the average woman live to over 80 and statistically, nowhere do men attain such an age.

Then, in November 2005, suicide bombings in three hotels in Amman, including one at a wedding party, sent shockwaves through Jordan. The Middle East's hitherto most stable country (long dubbed the 'Hashemite Kingdom of Boredom' by yawning journalists) turned overnight into a frontline of the war against terrorism.

THE GOOD NEWS

In Egypt, democracy normally advances at a becalmed felucca's pace, but there are increasing signs that the political system may be opened up to more dissenting voices and more widespread participation. The extension of this principle to the presidency of Hosni Mubarak is, however, highly unlikely.

Lebanon is a country that rarely does things by halves, so when the iconic Lebanese leader Rafiq Hariri was killed in a car bomb explosion in early 2005, the Lebanese did what they do best and ushered in fundamental change, taking to the streets during the so-called Cedar Revolution. The much-resented Syrian army – not known for yielding to people power and international pressure – left Lebanon after three decades of occupation. It leaves many to hope that, even as the Syrians continue to keep a watchful eye over their client politicians, Lebanon has its best opportunity in decades to finally determine its own future free from outside intervention.

Perhaps the most remarkable developments in the region have been those that have crossed borders. In the course of just a few years, the Qatar-based Al-Jazeera broadcasting company has transformed the flow of information to the extent that information is no longer something controlled solely by governments. Satellite TV is now almost universal across the region. While most sets are tuned to 24-hour music channels from Lebanon, the fact that Middle Easterners now have a choice is a potentially revolutionary change. When something happens in the Middle East, people from Libya to Iran can now make up their own mind as to what to watch and who to believe, rather than having to choose – as they did just a few years ago – between what the government tells them and the slanted infotainment that masquerades as truth on some Western channels. The Internet, too, has crossed borders and has denied dictators one of their hitherto most fiercely guarded weapons: the control over what their people read and watch.

If the younger generation of leaders now popping up across the Middle East (especially in Jordan and Syria) has offered hopes that the old conflicts may one day be put to rest, Libyans have no such luxury. That said, even as Mu'ammar Gaddafi continues to rule unchallenged – having ruled since 1969, he is the third-longest-serving ruler in the world – the wily old colonel has shown that change can come from the most unlikely of quarters. With his renunciation of weapons of mass destruction, the settling of all claims against Libya for past terrorist activities and the opening up of Libya's economy to foreign investment and greater liberalisation, Colonel Gaddafi has gone from Saddam Hussein–esque public enemy number one to the West's new best friend. Although issues remain in the critical area of human rights, Libya has never felt so optimistic, daring at last to believe that it stands on the cusp of a brighter future.

Iran's infant mortality rate (44.7 per 1000 live births) is the worst, with Turkey (44.2) and Egypt (35.26) not far behind. Israel and the Palestinian Territories (7.37) far outstrip the rest, of which Jordan (18.86), Lebanon (26.43) and Libya (26.8) come closest to shining.

The highest literacy rate is in Israel and the Palestinian Territories (93.6%), followed by Jordan (91.3%), Lebanon (87.4%), Turkey (86.5%), Libya (82.6%) and Iran (79.5%). Egypt has by far the lowest at 57.7%.

Israel and the Palestinian Territories have easily the highest GDP per capita (US$16,244), after which come Lebanon (US$4975), Turkey (US$3555) and Libya (US$3166). Egypt has the lowest at US$958.

History

The Middle East is a place where history is being remade daily. It has always been a battleground for empires seeking control over strategic riches, a constantly regenerating birthplace of civilisations and faiths, and home to the great myths of antiquity.

This section sketches out the broadest sweeps of Middle Eastern history – for further details see the more-specific history sections in the individual country chapters throughout this book.

CRADLE OF CIVILISATION

Although rock art dating back to 10,000 BC lies hidden amid the desert monoliths of the Jebel Acacus in Libya, little is known about the painters or their nomadic societies, which lived on the outermost rim of the Middle East.

The enduring shift from nomadism to more-sedentary organised societies began in the fertile crescent of Mesopotamia (ancient Iraq) and the Nile River Valley of Ancient Egypt.

In about 5000 BC a culture known as Al-Ubaid first appeared in Mesopotamia. We known little about it except that its influence eventually spread down what is now the coast of the Gulf. Stone-Age artefacts have also been found in Egypt's Western Desert, Israel's Negev Desert and in the West Bank town of Jericho.

Sometime around 3100 BC the kingdoms of Upper and Lower Egypt were unified under Menes, ushering in 3000 years of Pharaonic rule in the Nile Valley. The Levant (present-day Lebanon, Syria and Israel and the Palestinian Territories) was well settled by this time, and local powers included the Amorites and the Canaanites. In Mesopotamia it was the era

The Sumerians of Mesopotamia are credited with inventing cuneiform, the world's first form of writing.

The Epic of Gilgamesh was written in 2700 BC and was one of the first works of world literature; it tells the story of a Sumerian king from the ancient city of Uruk (which gave Iraq its name).

THE MIDDLE EAST'S INDIGENOUS EMPIRES AT A GLANCE

Few regions can match the Middle East for its wealth of ancient civilisations, all of which have left their mark upon history.

Sumerians (4000–2350 BC) Mesopotamia's first great civilisation developed advanced irrigation systems, produced surplus food and invented the earliest form of writing.

Egyptians (3100–400BC) The most enduring of ancient empires was a world of Pharaonic dynasties, exquisite art forms, the Pyramids and royal tombs. The monumental architecture of the empire reached new heights of aesthetic beauty.

Babylonians (1750–1180 BC) The empire further developed the cuneiform script and was one of the first civilisations to codify laws to govern the Tigris–Euphrates region from the capital at Bablyon, one of the great centres of the ancient world.

Assyrians (1600–609 BC) Conquerors of territories far and wide and shrewd administrators of their domains from their exquisite capital at Nineveh, the Assyrians also developed the forerunners of modern banking and accounting systems. Their heyday was the 9th century BC.

Garamantes (900 BC–AD 500) First mentioned by Herodotus, the Garamantes of southern Libya made the desert bloom, built cosmopolitan urban centres, controlled trade routes across the Sahara and introduced writing, camels and wheeled transport to the Sahara and further south.

Persians (6th–4th centuries BC) The relatively short-lived dynasties begun by Cyrus the Great ruled from India to the Aegean Sea and produced the stunning ancient city of Persepolis.

Ottomans (13th century AD–AD 1918) The last of the great indigenous empires to encompass most of the Middle East. From the opulent capital in Constantinople they governed from Iraq to Libya before the decadence of Ottoman rule (and the ungovernable size of their realm) got the better of them.

THE SEVEN WONDERS OF THE ANCIENT WORLD

The Middle East's dominance of ancient history is reflected in the fact that five out of the Seven Wonders of the Ancient World are to be found within the boundaries of the modern Middle East. Apart from the Pyramids, there's little left standing.

- Temple of Artemis (p586; 550 BC, Selçuk, Turkey) – once one of the most complex temples of the ancient world with a marble sanctuary and a tiled roof
- Mausoleum of Halicarnassus (p591; 353 BC, Bodrum, Turkey) – a white marble tomb, 135m-high, built by a provincial Persian king
- Hanging Gardens of Babylon (p262; 600 BC, Babylon, Iraq) – perhaps-mythical gardens built by King Nebuchadnezzar II for one of his wives, elevated high above the ground and irrigated by the waters of the Euphrates
- Pharos of Alexandria (p119; 270 BC, Alexandria, Egypt) – 120m-high lighthouse in Alexandria's harbour, which guided sailors for 1500 years using fires and sun-reflecting mirrors
- Pyramids of Giza (p106; 2700–2500 BC, Giza, Egypt) – the only ancient wonders to survive the test of time; the Great Pyramid was built over a period of 20 years by 100,000 workers using 2.3 million limestone blocks
- Statue of Zeus (457 BC, Olympia, Greece) – an ivory statue to the Greek god, seated on a throne and draped in gold
- Colossus of Rhodes (200 BC, Rhodes, Greece) – a 36m-high bronze statue to the sun god, Helios

Mesopotamia: The Invention of the City, by Gwendolyn Leick, takes a walk through the history of the great cities of Mesopotamia, including Babylon and Nineveh, and the civilisations that built them.

of Sumer, which had arisen in around 4000 BC and became arguably the world's first great civilisation.

In the late 24th and early 23rd centuries BC, Sargon of Akkad conquered much of the Levant and Mesopotamia. Other powers in the region at that time included the Hittite and Assyrian empires and, in Greece and Asia Minor, Mycenae and Troy.

By 900 BC the sophisticated Garamantes empire had arisen in Libya's Wadi al-Hayat, from where it controlled Saharan trade routes that connected central Africa to the Mediterranean rim. This facilitated the spread of Islam, many centuries later, along well-established livestock routes.

The 7th century BC saw both the conquest of Egypt by Assyria and far to the east, the rise of the Medes, the first of many great Persian empires. In 550 BC the Medes were conquered by Cyrus the Great, usually regarded as the first Persian shah (king). Over the next 60 years Cyrus and his successors Cambyses (r 525–522 BC) and Darius I (r 521–486 BC) swept west and north to conquer first Babylon and then Egypt, Asia Minor and parts of Greece. After the Greeks stemmed the Persian tide at the Battle of Marathon in 490 BC, Darius and Xerxes (r 486–466 BC) turned their attention to consolidating their empire.

The patriarch Abraham (a prophet in Judaism, Christianity and Islam) was born in Ur of the Chaldees on the Euphrates River; he migrated from Ur to Canaan in around 1800 BC.

Egypt won independence from the Persians in 401 BC only to be reconquered 60 years later. The second Persian occupation of Egypt was brief – little more than a decade after they arrived, the Persians were again driven out of Egypt, this time by the Greeks.

THE HELLENISTIC WORLD

In 336 BC Philip II of Macedonia, a warlord who had conquered much of mainland Greece, was murdered. His son Alexander assumed the throne and began a series of conquests that would eventually encompass most of Asia Minor, the Middle East, Persia and northern India.

Under Alexander, the Greeks were the first to impose any kind of order on the Middle East as a whole. Traces of their rule ring the eastern

Mediterranean from Ephesus in Turkey to the oasis of Siwa in Egypt's Western Desert. Perhaps the greatest remnants of Greek rule, however, lie on the outer boundaries of the former Greek empire, in the Cyrenaica region of Libya. The great cities of the Pentapolis (Five Cities), among them glorious Cyrene, bore the hallmarks of Greek sophistication and scholarship.

As important as the archaeological evidence is regarding Greek hegemony, it's the myths and legends – above all the *Iliad* and the *Odyssey* – and the descriptions left by historians such as Strabo, Herodotus and Pliny that present us with strong clues to the state of the Middle East 300 years before Christ and 900 years before the coming of Islam.

Upon Alexander's death, his empire was promptly carved up among his generals. This resulted in the founding of three new ruling dynasties: the Antigonids in Greece and Asia Minor; the Ptolemaic dynasty in Egypt; and the Seleucids. The Seleucids controlled the swath of land running from modern Israel and Lebanon through Mesopotamia to Persia.

That's not to say that peace reigned. Having finished off a host of lesser competitors, the heirs to Alexander's empire then proceeded to fight each other. The area of the eastern Mediterranean splintered into an array of different local dynasties with fluctuating borders. It took an army arriving from the west to again reunite the lands of the east – this time in the shape of the legions of Rome.

> Alexander the Great on the Web (www .isidore-of-seville.com /Alexanderama.html) contains good links to books and other references to the Middle East's youngest and most successful empire-builder.

> *Alexander the Great*, directed by Oliver Stone, made much of Alexander's supposed sexual ambiguity, but it's a spectacular Hollywood adaptation of the life of the great man.

ROMANS & CHRISTIANS

Rome's legionaries conquered most of Asia Minor in 188 BC, then Syria, Palestine and the North African territories of Carthage and Libya by 63 BC. When Cleopatra of Egypt, the last of the Ptolemaic dynasty, was defeated in 31 BC, the Romans controlled the entire Mediterranean world. This left the Middle East divided largely between two empires and their client states until the coming of Islam. Asia Minor, the Levant, Egypt and

---

ALEXANDER THE GREAT

One of the greatest figures to ever stride the Middle Eastern stage, Alexander (356–323 BC) was born into greatness. His father was King Philip II of Macedonia, who many people believed was a descendant of the god Hercules, and his mother was Princess Olympias of Epirus, who counted the legendary Achilles among her ancestors. For his part, the precocious young Alexander sometimes claimed that Zeus was his real father.

Alexander was the ultimate alpha male, as well versed in poetry as in the ways of war. At the age of 12, the young Alexander tamed Bucephalus, a horse that the most accomplished horsemen of Macedonia dared not ride. By 13 he had Aristotle as his personal tutor. His interests were diverse – he could play the lyre, but he also learned Homer's *Iliad* by heart and admired the Persian ruler Cyrus the Great for the respect he granted to the cultures he conquered.

He rode out of Macedonia in 334 BC to embark on a decade-long campaign of conquest and exploration. His first great victory was against the Persians at Issus in what is now southeast Turkey. He swept south, conquering Phoenician seaports and thence into Egypt where he founded the Mediterranean city that still bears his name. In 331 BC the armies of Alexander the Great made a triumphant entrance into Cyrenaica (modern Libya), although the great man himself stopped at the border after the Cyrenaicans greeted him with promises of loyalty. From Egypt he returned north, heading for Babylon. Crossing the Tigris and the Euphrates, he defeated another Persian army before driving his troops up into Central Asia and northern India. Eventually fatigue and disease brought the drive to a halt and the Greeks turned around and headed back home. En route, Alexander succumbed to illness (some say he was poisoned) and died at the tender age of 33 in Babylon. The whereabouts of his body and tomb remain unknown.

THE JEWISH REVOLTS

By the middle of the 1st century AD, Jews across the Roman Empire had had enough of Roman rule. Primary among their grievances were punitive taxes, the Roman decision to appoint Jewish high priests and Emperor Caligula's decision in AD 39 to declare himself a deity. The anti-Roman sentiment had been bubbling away for three decades, in part due to one rebellious orator – Jesus of Nazareth – and to a Jewish sect called the Zealots whose creed stated that all means were justified to liberate the Jews.

Led by the Zealots, the Jews of Jerusalem destroyed a small Roman garrison in the Holy City in AD 66. Infighting within the revolt and the burning of food stockpiles in order to force wavering Jews to participate had disastrous consequences. Jerusalem was razed to the ground and up to 100,000 Jews were killed in retaliation. Some Jewish historians claim that the number of dead over the four years of the revolt reached one million. Jerusalem was rebuilt as a Roman city and the Jews were sent into exile. It's an exile that many Jews believe ended only with the creation of the State of Israel in 1948. The Revolt, also known as the First Jewish-Roman War, was followed by further, equally unsuccessful uprisings in AD 115 to 118, when Jewish settlers sacked the ancient city of Cyrene in Libya, and AD 132 to 135.

Libya were dominated by Rome, while the Sassanids in Persia ruled the east. Only the nomads of the desert remained independent of the great powers of the day.

While the mighty empire of Rome suffered no great external threats to its eastern Mediterranean empire, there was plenty of trouble fomenting within, most notably a succession of rebellions by the Jewish inhabitants of the Roman dominions.

The Golden Age of Persia, by Richard N Frye, is a fine historical work that traces myriad Persian contributions to civilisation from the rise of Islam to the 11th century.

In AD 331 the newly converted Emperor Constantine declared Christianity the official religion of the 'Holy Roman Empire', with its capital not jaded, cynical Rome but the newly renamed city of Constantinople (formerly Byzantium, later to become İstanbul).

THE COMING OF ISLAM

Constantinople reached its apogee during the reign of Justinian (AD 527–65), when the Byzantine Empire consolidated its hold on the eastern Mediterranean, while also recapturing the lost domain of Italy. Meanwhile, the Sassanid empire to the east was cons tantly chipping away at poorly defended Byzantine holdings, creating a fault line between the two empires running down through what we know as the Middle East.

Far to the south, in lands that were independent of the two great empires, a new force was preparing to emerge. A merchant named Mohammed, born around AD 570 in the Arabian town of Mecca (now in Saudi Arabia), had begun preaching against the pagan religion of his fellow Meccans. For full details on the birth of Islam and Mohammed's emergence as its most revered prophet, see p53.

History of the Middle East Database (www .nmhschool.org/tthornton /mehistorydatabase /mideastindex.htm) has longish, informative essays on the great moments of Middle Eastern history and is especially good on the early Islamic period.

Mohammed died in 632 but under his successors, known as caliphs (from the Arabic word for 'follower'), the new religion continued its rapid spread, reaching all of Arabia by 634. Libya, Egypt, Syria and Palestine had been wrested from the Byzantines by 646, while most of Iraq, Iran and Afghanistan were taken from the Sassanids by 656.

Arguments over the leadership quickly arose and just 12 years after the Prophet's death a dispute over the caliphate opened a rift in Islam that grew into today's divide between Sunni and Shiite Muslims (see p53). Civil war broke out, ending with the rise to power of Mu'awiyah, the Muslim military governor of Syria and a distant relative of Mohammed.

EARLY ISLAM

Mu'awiyah moved the capital from Medina to Damascus and established the first great Muslim dynasty – the Umayyads.

The Umayyads were descended from a branch of the Quraysh, the Prophet's tribe, known more for expediency than piety. Mu'awiyah's father was one of the last people in Mecca to embrace Islam and had long been Mohammed's chief opponent in the city. By moving the capital to Damascus the Umayyads were symbolically declaring that they had aspirations far beyond the rather ascetic teachings of the Quran.

The Umayyads gave the Islamic world some of its greatest architectural treasures, including the Dome of the Rock (p289) in Jerusalem and the Umayyad Mosque (p514) in Damascus. History, however, has not been kind, remembering them largely for the high living, corruption, nepotism and tyranny that eventually proved to be their undoing.

In 750 the Umayyads were toppled in a revolt fuelled, predictably, by accusations of impiety. Their successors, and the strong arm behind the revolt, were the Abbasids. The Abbasid caliphate created a new capital in Baghdad and the early centuries of its rule constituted what's often regarded as the golden age of Islamic culture. The most famous of the Abbasid caliphs was Haroun ar-Rashid (r 786–809) of *The Thousand and One Nights* fame (see p75). Warrior king Haroun ar-Rashid led one of the most successful early Muslim invasions of Byzantium, almost reaching Constantinople. His name will forever be associated with Baghdad, which he transformed into a world centre of learning and sophistication.

After Haroun ar-Rashid's death the empire was effectively divided between two of his sons. Predictably, civil war ensued. In 813 one son Al-Maamun emerged triumphant and reigned as caliph for the next 20 years. But Al-Maamun's hold on power remained insecure and he felt compelled to surround himself with Turkish mercenaries.

By the middle of the 10th century the Abbasid caliphs were the prisoners of their Turkish guards, who spawned a dynasty of their own, known as the Seljuks (1038–1194). The Seljuks extended their reach throughout Persia, Central Asia, Afghanistan and Anatolia where the Seljuk Sultanate of Rum made its capital at Konya. The resulting pressure on the

The Court of the Calips, by Hugh Kennedy, is the definitive account of Abbasid Baghdad in its prime, blending careful scholarship using Arab sources with a lively and compelling style.

BAGHDAD THE BEAUTIFUL

When Haroun ar-Rashid came to power, Baghdad, on the western bank of the Tigris, had only been in existence for 24 years. By the time he died, Baghdad had become one of the world's preeminent cities.

Haroun ar-Rashid tried to rename the city Medinat as-Salaam (City of Peace). Although the name never caught on, everything else that Haroun ar-Rashid and his immediate successors did was an unqualified success. Baghdad was remade into a city of expansive pleasure gardens, vast libraries and distinguished seats of learning where the arts, medicine, literature and sciences all flourished. It was soon the richest city in the world. The crossroads of important trade routes to the east and west, it rapidly supplanted Damascus as the seat of power in the Islamic world, which stretched from Spain to India. Al-Maamun, Haroun's son and successor, founded the Beit al-Hikmah (House of Wisdom), a Baghdad-based academy dedicated to translating Greek and Roman works of science and philosophy into Arabic. It was only through these translations that most of the classical literature we know today was saved for posterity.

Although the city would later be much reduced by wars, civil and otherwise, and be sacked by the Mongols, the name of Baghdad has never lost its allure. It's a reminder of the time when Baghdad was the world's most beautiful and intellectually creative city on earth.

Byzantine Empire was intense enough to cause the emperor and the Greek Orthodox Church to swallow their pride and appeal to the rival Roman Catholic Church for help.

THE CRUSADES

In 1095 Pope Urban II called for a Western Christian military expedition – a 'Crusade' – to liberate the holy places of Jerusalem in response to the eastern empire's alarm. Rome's motives were not entirely benevolent: Urban was eager to assert Rome's primacy in the east over Constantinople.

The Crusades Through Arab Eyes, by Amin Maalouf, is brilliantly written and captures perfectly why the mere mention of the Crusades still evokes the anger of many Arabs today.

After linking up with the Byzantine army in 1097, the Crusaders successfully besieged Antioch (modern Antakya, in Turkey) and then marched south along the coast before turning inland, towards Jerusalem. A thousand Muslim troops held Jerusalem for six weeks against 15,000 Crusaders before the city fell on 15 July 1099. The victorious Crusaders then massacred the local population – Muslims, Jews and Christians alike – sacked the non-Christian religious sites and turned the Dome of the Rock into a church. For more information on the Crusades and their implications, see p61.

These successes were short-lived. It took less than 50 years for the tide to begin to turn against the Crusaders and only 200 before they were driven out of the region once and for all. The Muslim leader responsible for removing the Crusaders from Jerusalem (in 1187) was Salah ad-Din al-Ayyoub, better known in the West as Saladin.

Saladin and his successors (a fleeting dynasty known as the Ayyubids) battled the Crusaders for 60 years until they were unceremoniously removed by their own army, a strange soldier-slave caste, the Mamluks, who ran what would today be called a military dictatorship. The only way to join their army was to be press-ganged into it – non-Muslim boys were captured or bought outside the empire, converted to Islam and raised in the service of a single military commander. They were expected to give this commander total loyalty, in exchange for which their fortunes would rise (or fall) with his. Sultans were chosen from among the most senior Mamluk commanders, but it was a system that engendered vicious, bloody rivalries, and rare was the sultan who died of natural causes.

The Mamluks were to rule Egypt, Syria, Palestine and western Arabia for nearly 300 years (1250–1517) and it was they who succeeded in ejecting the Crusaders from the Near East, prising them out of their last stronghold of Acre (modern-day Akko in Israel) in 1291.

SALADIN – THE KURDISH HERO OF ARAB HISTORY

Saladin – Salah ad-Din (Restorer of the Faith) al-Ayyoub – was born to Kurdish parents in 1138 in what is modern-day Tikrit in Iraq. He joined other members of his family in the service of Nureddin (Nur ad-Din) of the ruling Zangi dynasty. By the time Nureddin died in 1174, Saladin had risen to the rank of general and had already taken possession of Egypt. He quickly took control of Syria and in the next 10 years extended his authority into parts of Mesopotamia, but was careful not to infringe too closely on the territory of the now largely powerless Abbasid caliphate in Baghdad. In 1187, Saladin crushed the Crusaders at the Battle of Hittin and captured Jerusalem, precipitating the Third Crusade and pitting himself against Richard I (the Lion-Heart) of England. After countless clashes the two rival warriors signed a peace treaty in 1192, giving the coastal territories to the Crusaders and the interior to the Muslims. Saladin died three months later in Damascus, where he is buried.

THE OTTOMAN TURKS

In 1258, just eight years after the Mamluks seized power in Cairo and began their bloody dynasty, a boy named Osman (Othman) was born to the chief of a Turkish tribe in western Anatolia. He converted to Islam in his youth and later began a military career by hiring out his tribe's army as mercenaries in the civil wars then besetting what was left of the Byzantine Empire. Payment came in the form of land.

Rather than taking on the Byzantines directly, Osman's successors (the Ottomans) deliberately picked off the bits and pieces of the empire that Constantinople could no longer control. By the end of the 14th century the Ottomans had conquered Bulgaria, Serbia, Bosnia, Hungary and most of present-day Turkey. They had also moved their capital across the Dardanelles to Adrianople, today the Turkish city of Edirne. In 1453 came their greatest victory when Sultan Mehmet II took Constantinople, the hitherto unachievable object of innumerable Muslim wars almost since the 7th century.

On a battlefield near Aleppo 64 years later, an army under the sultan Selim the Grim routed the Mamluks and, at one stroke, the whole of the eastern Mediterranean, including Egypt and coastal Libya, was absorbed into the Ottoman Empire.

The empire reached its peak, both politically and culturally, under Süleyman the Magnificent (r 1520–66), who led the Ottoman armies west to the gates of Vienna, east into Persia, and south through the holy cities of Mecca and Medina and into Yemen. His control also extended throughout North Africa.

After Süleyman, however, the Ottoman Empire went into a long, slow period of decline. Only five years after his death, Spain and Venice destroyed virtually the entire Ottoman navy at the Battle of Lepanto (in the Aegean Sea), thereby costing the Ottomans control over the western Mediterranean. North Africa soon fell under the sway of local dynasties. Conflict with the Safavids – Persia's rulers from the early 16th century to the early 18th century – was almost constant.

See p62 for further analysis of the Ottoman Empire.

ENTER EUROPE

Despite Portuguese interest around the southern Arabian Peninsula from the late 15th century, it was not until the late 18th century that the European powers truly began chiselling away at the ailing Ottoman Empire. In 1798 Napoleon invaded Egypt in what he planned as the first step towards building a French empire in the Middle East and India. The French occupation of Egypt lasted only three years, but left a lasting mark – even today, Egypt's legal system is based on a French model.

The British, protecting their own Indian interests, forced the French out of Egypt in 1801. Four years later, Mohammed Ali, an Albanian soldier in the Ottoman army, emerged as the country's strongman and he set about modernising the country. As time passed, it became increasingly obvious that Constantinople was becoming ever more dependent on Egypt for military backing rather then the reverse. Mohammed Ali's ambitions grew. In the 1830s he invaded and conquered Syria, and by 1839 he had effective control of most of the Ottoman Empire. The European powers, alarmed by the idea of the Ottoman government collapsing, forced him to withdraw to Egypt. In exchange, the Ottoman sultan gave long-overdue acknowledgment of Mohammed Ali's status as ruler of a virtually independent Egypt and bestowed the right of heredity rule on his heirs (who continued to rule Egypt until 1952).

Süleyman the Magnificent was responsible for achievements as diverse as building the gates of Jerusalem and introducing to Europe, via Constantinople, the joys of coffee.

Ottoman Centuries, by Lord Kinross, is perhaps the definitive history of the Ottoman Empire, covering everything from the key events of Ottoman rule to the extravagances of its royal court.

Lords of the Horizons: A History of the Ottoman Empire, by Jason Goodwin, is anecdotal and picaresque but still manages to illuminate the grand themes of Ottoman history.

In 1869 Mohammed Ali's grandson Ismail opened the Suez Canal. But within a few years his government was so deeply in debt that in 1882 the British, who already played a large role in Egyptian affairs, occupied the country.

At the same time, the Ottoman Empire was becoming increasingly dependent on the goodwill of the European powers. In 1860 the French sent troops to Lebanon after a massacre of Christians by the local Druze. Before withdrawing, the French forced the Ottomans to set up a new administrative system for the area guaranteeing the appointment of Christian governors, over whom the French came to have great influence. In 1911, after a short struggle between Rome and the Turks, Tripoli and Cyrenaica (Libya) went to the Italians.

A Peace to End All Peace: Creating the Modern Middle East, 1914–1922, by David Fromkin, is an intriguing account of how the map of the modern Middle East was drawn arbitrarily by European colonial governments.

THE COLONIAL MIDDLE EAST

With the outbreak of WWI in 1914, the Ottoman Empire sided with Germany, and Sultan Mohammed V declared a jihad (holy war), calling on Muslims everywhere to rise up against Britain, France and Russia.

World War II signalled the end of the Ottoman dynasty. Stripped of its Arab provinces, the Ottoman monarchy was overthrown and a Turkish Republic was declared under the leadership of Mustafa Kemal 'Atatürk' (p557), a soldier who became Turkey's first president in 1923.

His drive toward secularism (which he saw as synonymous with the modernisation necessary to drag Turkey into the 20th century) found an echo in Persia, where, in 1923, Reza Khan, the commander of a Cossack brigade who had risen to become war minister, overthrew the decrepit Ghajar dynasty. After changing his name from Khan to the more Persian-sounding Pahlavi (the language spoken in pre-Islamic Persia), he moved to set up a secular republic on the Turkish model. Protests from the country's religious establishment caused a change of heart and he had himself crowned shah instead. In 1934 he changed the country's name from Persia to Iran.

Lawrence of Arabia may overstate the role played by TE Lawrence (Peter O'Toole), but it's an epic that captures the atmosphere of Arab hope and colonial duplicity set against the stirring backdrop of Wadi Rum.

PROMISES ARE MADE TO BE BROKEN

When the British heard the Ottoman call to jihad, they performed a masterstroke – they negotiated an alliance with Hussein bin Ali, the grand sherif of Mecca who agreed to lead an Arab revolt against the Turks in return for a British promise to make him 'King of the Arabs' once the conflict was over. This alliance worked well in defeating the Ottomans, but it would plant the seeds for decades of conflict in the Middle East.

The British never had any serious intention of keeping their promise. Even as they were negotiating with Sherif Hussein, the British were talking with the French on how to carve up the Ottoman Empire. These talks yielded the Sykes-Picot Agreement – the secret Anglo-French accord that divided the Ottoman Empire into British and French spheres of influence. Britain had also given the Zionist movement a promise, known as the Balfour Declaration (named after the then-British foreign secretary), that it would 'view with favour the establishment in Palestine of a national home for the Jewish people' after the war. (For more on the background to Zionism and the Arab-Israeli conflict, see p271).

In the closing year of the war, the British occupied Palestine and Damascus. After the war, France took control of Syria and Lebanon. Britain retained Egypt and was given control of Palestine, Transjordan and Iraq, all of which bore the rubber-stamp approval of the newly created League of Nations.

The Arabs, who'd done so much to free themselves from Ottoman rule, suddenly found themselves under British or French colonial administration with the prospect of a Jewish state in their midst not far over the horizon.

GAMAL ABDEL NASSER: HERO OF THE ARAB STREET

Nasser's dreams weren't imperial, but his vision and pursuit of the ideal of a united Arab nation make him arguably the most important Arab world figure of the 20th century. The first president of the newly independent republic of Egypt was likened to a pharaoh with the self-confident swagger of Che Guevara. He stood defiantly against the old regional rulers of Britain and France, while playing the new superpowers – the Soviet Union and the USA – against each other.

Under Nasser, Egypt became a beacon for all those countries in Africa and Asia that had recently thrown off European colonial rule. His rousing pan-Arab speeches gave the people of the Middle East and North Africa the belief that together they might not only free themselves of Western dominance, but even achieve political and economic parity. From Libya to Iraq, Nasser was a bona fide hero.

But real attempts at any kind of political union failed and the brave new Egypt came crashing down on 5 June 1967 when Israel wiped out the Egyptian air force in a surprise attack. With it went the confidence and credibility of Nasser. He never recovered and died of heart failure three years later.

INDEPENDENCE & PAN-ARABISM

Although the Middle East was a persistent theatre of war throughout WWII – Egyptian and Libyan territory hosted decisive battles at Tobruk and El Alamein respectively – the region's problems began in earnest soon after the war was over.

Since taking control of Palestine in 1918, the British had been under pressure to allow unrestricted Jewish immigration to the territory. With tension rising between Palestine's Arab and Jewish residents, they had refused to do this and, in the late 1930s, had placed strict limits on the number of new Jewish immigrants.

Several plans to partition Palestine were proposed during the 1930s and '40s, but WWII (briefly) put an end to all such discussion. When the war ended, Britain again found itself under pressure to allow large-scale Jewish immigration, particularly in the wake of the Holocaust.

In early 1947 the British announced that they were turning the entire problem over to the newly created UN. The UN voted to partition Palestine, but this was rejected by the Arabs. Britain pulled out and the very next day the Jews declared the founding of the State of Israel. War broke out immediately, with Egypt, Jordan and Syria weighing in on the side of the Palestinian Arabs.

When Zionist and British policy makers were looking for a homeland for the Jewish people, sites they considered included northeastern Australia and the Jebel Akhdar in the Cyrenaica region of Libya.

The disastrous performance of the combined Arab armies in the 1948 Arab-Israeli War had far-reaching consequences for the region. Recriminations over the humiliating defeat and the refugee problem it created laid the groundwork for the 1951 assassination of King Abdullah of Jordan. Syria, which had gained its independence from France in 1946, became the field for a seemingly endless series of military coups in which disputes over how to handle the Palestine problem often played a large part. In Egypt, the army blamed the loss of the war on the country's corrupt and ineffective politicians. In July 1952 a group of young officers toppled the monarchy, with the real power residing with one of the coup plotters: Gamal Abdel Nasser. After facing down the combined powers of Israel, Britain and France over the Suez Crisis of 1956, Nasser also emerged as the preeminent figure in the Arab world. He was a central player in the politics of nationalism, socialism and decolonisation that gripped much of the developing world throughout the 1950s and '60s.

Middle East History & Resources (www.mideastweb.org/history) is a balanced examination of many of the region's thorniest political issues with a rare commitment to fairness and accuracy.

THE ARAB-ISRAELI WARS

Arab opposition to the creation of the State of Israel again came to a head (helped along by Nasser's fiery speeches) in 1967, with the formation of the Palestine Liberation Organisation (PLO) taking place around the same time. In May of that year the Egyptian army moved into key points in Sinai and announced a blockade of the Straits of Tiran, effectively closing the southern Israeli port of Eilat. The Egyptian army was mobilised and the country put on a war footing.

The Arab World: Forty Years of Change, by Elizabeth Fernea and Robert Warnock, is hard to beat as an accessible and balanced overview of the Israel-Palestine issue.

Israel responded on 5 June 1967 with a preemptive strike that wiped out virtually the entire Egyptian air force. The war lasted only six days (hence the 'Six Day War'), and when it was over Israel controlled all of the Sinai peninsula and the Gaza Strip. The West Bank, including Jerusalem's Old City, had been seized from Jordan and the Golan Heights from Syria. For the Arabs, it was an unmitigated disaster that sent shockwaves across the region.

The year 1970 saw the ascension of new leaders in both Egypt (Anwar Sadat) and Syria (Hafez al-Assad). Preparations were also well under way for the next Middle Eastern war, with these radical new leaders under constant pressure from their citizens to reclaim the land lost in 1967. On 6 October 1973, Egyptian troops crossed the Suez Canal, taking Israel (at a standstill, observing the holy day of Yom Kippur) almost entirely by surprise. After advancing a short distance into Sinai, however, the Egyptian army stopped, giving Israel the opportunity to concentrate its forces against the Syrians on the Golan Heights and then turn back towards Egypt.

Although the 1973 war is painted as a victory and reassertion of Arab pride by many historians, by the time the war ended the Israelis actually occupied more land than they had when it began.

When the war ended in late 1973, months of shuttle diplomacy by the US secretary of state, Henry Kissinger, followed. Pressure on the USA to broker a deal was fuelled when the Gulf States embargoed oil supplies to the West 10 days after the war began. The embargo was relatively short-lived but if the goal was to get the West's attention, it succeeded.

All of this shifted the balance of power in the Middle East. The oil states, rich but underpopulated and militarily weak, gained at the expense of poorer, more populous countries. Huge shifts of population followed the two oil booms of the 1970s as millions of Egyptians, Syrians, Jordanians, Palestinians and Yemenis went off to seek their fortunes in the oil states.

PEACE & REVOLUTION

Pity the Nation: Lebanon at War, by Robert Fisk, ranges far beyond Lebanon's borders and is a classic account of the issues that resonate throughout the region.

Anwar Sadat's dramatic visit to Jerusalem in 1977 opened the way for an Egyptian-Israeli peace process, which culminated, in March 1979, with the signing of a peace treaty between the two countries at Camp David in the USA. In response, Arab leaders meeting in Baghdad voted to expel Egypt from the Arab League.

Meanwhile, one of the few friends Sadat had left in the region had troubles of his own. Discontent with the shah of Iran's autocratic rule and his personal disregard for the country's Shiite Muslim religious traditions had been simmering for years. Political violence slowly increased throughout 1978. The turning point came in September of that year, when Iranian police fired on anti-shah demonstrators in Tehran, killing at least 300. The momentum of the protests quickly became unstoppable.

On 16 January 1979 the shah left Iran, never to return (he died in Egypt in 1980). The interim government set up after his departure was swept aside the following month when the revolution's leader, the hitherto obscure Ayatollah Ruhollah Khomeini, returned to Tehran from his exile in France. For more on Khomeini and the Islamic Revolution, see p182.

AFTER THE REVOLUTION

Iran's Islamic Revolution seemed to change everything in the Middle East, ushering in a period of instability that lasted until the end of the 1980s.

In 1979 militants seized the Grand Mosque in Mecca – Islam's holiest site – and were only ejected several weeks later after bloody gun battles inside the mosque itself. In November of that year student militants in Tehran overran the US embassy, taking the staff hostage. In 1980 Turkey's government was overthrown in a military coup, capping weeks of violence between left- and right-wing extremists. Further east, Iraq invaded Iran, launching what would become the longest, bloodiest and, arguably, most pointless war in modern history.

Tensions were further cranked up in 1981 when President Sadat of Egypt was assassinated by Muslim militants. The following year Israel invaded Lebanon, further exacerbating the cycle of chaos and destruction that had engulfed that country since 1975. In 1986 clashes between the USA and Libya, led by Colonel Mu'ammar Gaddafi, came to a head with the American air strikes on Tripoli. The following year saw an escalation in violence in Israel and the Palestinian Territories with the beginning of the intifada (the grass roots Palestinian uprising).

There were a few bright spots. Turkey returned to democratic rule in 1983, albeit with a new constitution barring from public office anyone who had been involved in politics prior to the 1980 coup. In 1988 Iran and Iraq grudgingly agreed to a cease-fire. The year after, Egypt was readmitted to the Arab League and Jordan held its first elections in more than 20 years.

THE PEACE DEFICIT

In August 1990 Iraq invaded Kuwait and King Fahd of Saudi Arabia requested help from the USA. The result was a US-led coalition whose air and ground offensive drove Iraq out of Kuwait. In the process Iraqi president Saddam Hussein (previously supported by the West in his war against Iran) became world public enemy number one.

While attempting to solicit Arab support for the anti-Iraq coalition, then-US president George Bush promised to make a new effort to achieve Arab-Israeli peace once the Iraqis were out of Kuwait. Endless shuttling between Middle Eastern capitals culminated in a US-sponsored peace conference in Madrid in October 1991. It achieved little, but by late summer 1993 it was revealed that Israel and the Palestinians had been holding secret talks in Norway for 18 months. The 'Oslo Accord' was cemented with a handshake between Yasser Arafat and Israeli prime minister Yitzhak Rabin on the White House lawn in September 1993.

A new era of hope for peace in the Middle East seemed on the horizon. Lebanon had just held its first democratic elections for 20 years and the mutually destructive fighting seemed at an end. In 1994 Jordan became the second Arab country to sign a formal peace treaty with Israel.

Tragically the nascent Arab-Israeli peace process was derailed by the November 1995 assassination of Rabin and the subsequent election to power of hardline candidate Binyamin Netanyahu. A blip of hope reemerged when Netanyahu lost office to Ehud Barak, a prime minister who pulled his troops out of occupied south Lebanon and promised to open negotiations with the Syrians and the Palestinians. When these talks came to nothing, the Palestinians launched an intifada that still continues and Israeli voters ousted Barak for the more hard-line (and, to many, frightening) figure of Ariel Sharon. Although the death of Yasser Arafat in November 2004 offered some signs for hope, the violent occupation of Palestinian land and bloody suicide bombings targeting Israeli citizens continues.

Libya's Colonel Gaddafi is the world's third-longest-serving leader, having come to power in 1969; only Fidel Castro (Cuba) and Omar Bongo (Gabon) have presided over their countries for longer.

Orientalism, by Edward Said, is dense and academic but is *the* seminal work on the history of Western misconceptions and stereotypes about the Middle East from colonial times to the present.

Mezzaterra, by the Egyptian writer Ahdaf Soueif, is an eloquent series of essays on the modern Middle East, challenging Western stereotypes about the region while being rooted in the lives of ordinary people.

People

The combined population of the Middle East is around 285 million, with Egypt (approximately 74 million), Iran (72 million) and Turkey (68 million) the most populous countries. Contrary to what you read in the media, the ethnic make-up of the Middle East is more than just Arabian and Jewish and is surprisingly diverse. Even within the two dominant ethnic groups, you'll find more Palestinians living beyond the borders of the Palestinian Territories than you will within. A significant proportion of Israeli Jews are quite recent immigrants from across the world, especially Eastern Europe and Africa. Other major groups include the Persians, Turks, Kurds, Berbers and Druze.

While these disparate groups now largely live at peace with each other, the ethnic dimension of Lebanon's civil war and the morass that is Iraq suggest that ethnic identity remains an important subject for peoples in the region.

Zones of aridity and fertility ensure that the Middle East is home both to clamorous cities and vast (usually desert) regions of emptiness. The country with the highest proportion of people living in urban areas is Israel and the Palestinian Territories (92%) while Lebanon has the highest population density (353.6 people per square kilometre), followed by Israel and the Palestinian Territories (290.3). By contrast, Libya has a population density of just 3.1 people per square kilometre.

> There is no finer work in English on the history of the Arabs from the Prophet Mohammed to modern times than *A History of the Arab Peoples*, by Albert Hourani, which is definitive, encyclopedic and highly readable.

ARABS

The question of who exactly the Arabs are is still widely debated. Are they all the people who speak Arabic, or only the residents of the Arabian Peninsula? Fourteen centuries ago, only the nomadic tribes wandering between the Euphrates River and the central Arabian Peninsula were considered Arabs, distinguished by their language. However, with the rapid expansion of Islam, the language of the Quran spread to vast areas.

Although the Arabs were relatively few in number in most of the countries they conquered, their culture quickly became established through language and intermarriage. The term 'Arab' came to apply to two groups: in addition to the original nomadic Arabs, the settled inhabitants of these newly conquered provinces also became known as Arabs.

In the 20th century rising Arab nationalism legitimised the current blanket usage of the term to apply to all the peoples of the Middle East – except the Persians, Israelis and Turks.

> The mass migration of two Arab tribes from the Arabian Peninsula – the Bani Hilal and Bani Salim – across North Africa in the 10th century cemented the Arabisation of the region, most notably in Libya.

Bedouin

The most romanticised group of Arabs is no doubt the Bedouin (Bedu in Arabic). While not an ethnic group, they are the archetypal Arabs – the camel-herding nomads who roam all over the deserts and semideserts in search of food for their cattle. From among their ranks came the warriors who spread Islam to North Africa and Persia 14 centuries ago.

Today, the Bedouin are found mainly in Jordan, Iraq, Egypt's Sinai peninsula, and the Gulf States. Their numbers are unknown due to their habit of wandering in regions where no census-takers venture.

While some have settled down to enjoy the facilities of modern life, many maintain semitraditional lifestyles. Their customs derive from the days of early Islam, and the hospitality towards strangers and love of poetry that Arabs are so famous for (and proud of) certainly takes its most genuine form among the Bedouin.

For more information see the boxed text on p394.

PERSIANS

The Persians are descendants of the Elamite and Aryan races (from southern Russia) who first settled in the central plateau of what is now Iran in the 2nd century BC. The Persians (Farsis), retained their own language even though they were among the first to adopt the new religion of Islam and welcomed the Arabic script for writing Persian.

TURKS

The Turkish peoples originated in Central Asia where they ruled several empires before being pushed westwards by the Mongols. At first they were shamanist nomads, but at times these early Turks followed each of the great religions of the region including Buddhism, Christianity and Judaism. During their western migrations they became familiar with Islam and it stuck. The Turks kept their own language even after conversion. During the 600-year Ottoman Empire, when Turks ruled most of the Middle East, they became known as Shimaliyya (Northerners) throughout the Arab world.

KURDS

The Kurds are spread across a large area of the Middle East, including a good part of eastern Turkey (with a Kurdish population of maybe 12 million), Iran, northeastern Iraq and Syria. Although they have been around longer than any other people in the region (since at least the 2nd century BC), the Kurds have never had a nation of their own. For more information on the Kurds see p265.

ARMENIANS

Another small group badly treated by history are the Armenians. They have lived in eastern Anatolia for millennia, almost always as subjects of some greater state such as the Byzantines, Persians, Seljuks or Ottomans. In the early 20th century the Orthodox Christian Armenian minority made the error of siding with the Russians against the Muslim Turk majority. The Armenians were massacred. Hundreds of thousands died and they were almost wiped out in Turkey. Elsewhere in the Middle East there are significant Armenian communities in Syria, Iran and Israel and the Palestinian Territories.

JEWS

The most high-profile non-Arab ethnic group in the Middle East are of course the Jewish people. Following their exile from Jerusalem at the hands of the Romans, the Jews spread far and wide, many settling in neighbouring countries. Until the middle of the 20th century and the creation of the Jewish home-state, Egypt, Libya, Syria, Iran and Iraq were all home to significant Jewish populations. For more background on the Jewish people in the Middle East see p276.

BERBERS

Believed to be the region's original inhabitants, the Berbers are North Africa's largest minority group and are spread from Libya to Morocco. When the Arab armies of Islam marched across the Maghreb, the Berbers retreated into the hills and desert oases keeping their culture intact.

A Modern History of the Kurds, by David McDowall, has been updated to 2004 (although the body of the work finishes in 1996) and it remains an excellent primer on the social and political history of the Kurds, focusing on Turkey and Iraq.

The key touchstones of Berber identity are language and culture. While almost all of Libya's Berbers speak Arabic and many have intermarried with Arabs over the centuries, most continue to speak Berber at home. 'Berber' is used as a loose term for native speakers of the various Berber dialects. In fact, many Berbers do not even use a word that unites them as a community, preferring instead to define themselves according to their tribe.

The name 'Tuareg' is thought to be an adaptation of the Arabic word *tawarek* (abandoned by God), a reference to their free-wheeling independence, inhospitable surrounds and less-than-orthodox adherence to Islamic tenets.

TUAREG

The Tuareg are the indigenous people of the Sahara. There are believed to be 1.5 million Tuareg across Africa. In Libya, this once-nomadic people are concentrated in the southwestern desert with a total population of 17,000. Although their origins are not fully understood, they are widely believed to be an offshoot of the Berbers. The name 'Tuareg' is a designation given to the community by outsiders and it's only recently that the Tuareg have called themselves by this name. The Tuareg previously defined themselves as 'Kel Tamashek' (speakers of the Tamashek language). Another name which the Tuareg sometimes call themselves is 'Imashaghen' – 'the noble and the free'.

DRUZE

The Druze have no homeland or language of their own and their nation is defined by their religion, an off-shoot of Islam. Like Muslims, the Druze believe in Allah and his prophets but they believe that Mohammed was succeeded by a further divine messenger, Al-Darazi – from whose name the term Druze is derived. The Druze also hold the non-Islamic belief of reincarnation.

The Druze, by Robert Betts, only covers up to 1990 but this is otherwise the most comprehensive work on this little-known people and essential to understanding their reputation for fierce independence.

Most of the Druze nation live in Lebanon and Syria and a few villages in the Galilee and Golan regions of Israel and the Palestinian Territories. The Druze people tend to give allegiance to whatever country they live in.

OTHER PEOPLES

At its southernmost fringes, the Middle East also includes various African peoples. Most notable of these are the dark-skinned people of Nubia, the region between Aswan in the south of Egypt and Khartoum in Sudan, which was known in ancient times as Kush. Since the creation of Egypt's High Dam, which caused the drowning of their homelands, many Nubians have migrated north to the cities of Cairo and Alexandria in search of a livelihood.

In southern Libya, the Muslim Toubou are, like the more numerous Tuareg, seminomadic. Although they display considerable cultural and linguistic similarities, many communities of Toubou speak related but mutually incomprehensible dialects of Tebu. One 19th-century explorer described Toubou society as 'the principle of freedom raised almost to the level of anarchy'. The Toubous' homeland is the Tibesti Mountains, a desert mountain range that straddles the Libya–Chad border.

DAILY LIFE

The Middle East is a region in transition, at once deeply traditional and experiencing newfound freedoms (eg the Internet and satellite TV) of which a previous generation never dared dream. High birth rates and, in the case of Israel, large-scale immigration have meant a population boom. An overwhelmingly youthful population has little memory of the causes for which their parents fought (eg Iran's Islamic Revolution, Libya's hostility to the West or Lebanon's civil war). Nor do they have sufficient

TIPS ON MEETING LOCALS

Etiquette plays a very important part in Arab culture. If you can follow a few simple rules (see also Responsible Travel on p26 for more advice) and play your part in a few set rituals, your path throughout the region is likely to be a lot smoother. That said, people are generally very forgiving of foreigners' social errors, but also very appreciative of any efforts you make towards complying with local etiquette. If you do make a faux pas, Arab etiquette is such that you will not even be permitted to know about it! Many of the following suggestions do not apply in Israel (other than in some Orthodox Jewish homes), nor many Western areas of Turkey.

- When entering a room, try to shake hands with everyone, even if you haven't been formally introduced. Touch your heart with the palm of your right hand after each handshake. This applies to both male and female visitors, although men finding themselves in the presence of Arab women should not offer to shake hands unless the woman extends her hand first. A devout Muslim man may prefer not to shake a woman's hand and will touch his heart instead.
- When meeting someone, greet them properly and inquire in detail about their health. If you know them a little, ask after their family (even if you've never met them). If you're a man, however, never inquire after another man's wife or daughters or any other female members of the family.
- Never eat, offer or accept anything with your left hand (which in the Middle East is reserved for ablutions only).
- Avoid displays of affection for your partner in public. Although it's OK for men to hold hands, it's taboo for couples to do so, and kissing and hugging is a definite no-no.
- Don't approach a woman or look at her until you've been introduced (though educated or 'Westernised' women may be more relaxed about this).
- Always stand up when someone enters the room.
- Never sit in a way that causes the soles of your feet to point at anyone else as the soles are considered unclean; shoes are usually removed before entering someone's house.
- Never beckon someone with your finger, as this is considered impolite.
- Avoid the subjects of politics, sex, women and religion (unless you're in private with trusted, long-standing friends or you're genuinely interested about Islam).

Dress

Wear long, loose clothing if you're a woman travelling in the Middle East. Dress should never be tight-fitting, transparent or low cut. Try always to cover the legs, cleavage and shoulders. Locals consider exposing the skin to the blistering sun at best odd and at worst silly or even offensive. No-one is going to stop a tourist for walking around in shorts and a sleeveless T-shirt, but it's about as appropriate as walking around wintry London in a thong. On the beach (apart from in Israel, the coastal Sinai region of Egypt, and Turkey) you will cause less of a local sensation if you wear shorts and a t-shirt rather than a swimming costume. Unless skirts are long, trousers are preferable. Men should avoid shorts and never appear bare-chested in public, except at the beach or swimming pool.

Men should choose their own dress over the local robes. Lawrence of Arabia aspirants should note that traditional dress has, in many places, acquired complex nationalist or cultural connotations. Women, by contrast, are welcome to wear local dress and it may even be appreciated. Bear in mind that in some countries locals tend to dress smartly if they can afford to. Scruffy clothes are often seen by locals as the mark of a traveller; look around you: the only people wearing shorts or tatty clothes are kids, labourers or the poor. Well-dressed travellers may also find that they are better received by Middle Eastern officialdom – from border police to the man who will decide whether you receive a visa extension.

jobs despite, in many cases, a university education, ensuring that old-style politicians are finding the formulae of the past simply doesn't work in appeasing their citizens.

For all such changes, families (immediate and extended) remain the bedrock of social life for most Middle Easterners, the one certainty in a changing world. Traditionally, the division of society into various, often competing tribes meant that the network of family members within a tribe were often the individual's only source of protection and hence loyalty. Although tribes remain significant (especially, for example, in Libya), the rise of nation-states in the region has ensured that family closeness is as much attributable to the fact that many, perhaps even most Middle Easterners live with their families until they are married. Often this is for purely economic reasons or because many simply wouldn't think of living any other way. The concept of independence from one's family is a Western idea that has yet to catch on. That said, the increasing trend towards university studies or military service away from a student's home town mean that more Middle Easterners than ever before are living away from home.

Nine Parts of Desire, by Geraldine Brooks, is one of most balanced investigations of the lives of women under Islam, with interviews with everyone from village women to Queen Noor of Jordan.

Even as women increasingly occupy positions of public responsibility and are entering the workforce in unprecedented numbers (most notably in the more traditional societies such as Iran and Libya), the division of the world into public (male) and private (female) realms remains largely intact. If you visit all but the most Westernised Middle Eastern homes, you may not even meet the women of the family although Western women have an advantage over men in this regard. Men and often Western women who seem to have the status of honorary men will eat with guests separately from the women. The situation is by no means monolithic but tradition retains a powerful hold and can appear in the most unlikely family settings.

The Hidden Face of Eve: Women in the Arab World, by Egyptian psychiatrist Nawal el-Sadaawi, is packed with insight and controlled anger in equal measure as she explores the role of women in Arab history and literature.

In Islam, a guest – whether Muslim or not – has a position of honour not very well understood in the West. Even if you visit a home where the inhabitants don't have much to offer, the Muslim code of hospitality – with its deep roots in desert societies where hospitality ensured survival among nomadic communities – demands that your host give to his or her guest all that they possess. Indeed, being treated with grace, generosity and absolute selflessness is likely to be one of your most treasured memories from your visit to the Middle East.

Religion

The Middle East is the birthplace of the three big monotheistic world religions: Judaism, Christianity and Islam. The followers of these religions worship the same God, the main difference between them being their understanding of when God's revelations ceased. While Judaism adheres to the Old Testament, Christianity adds on the teachings of the New Testament, and the Muslims claim that their holy book, the Quran, contains the final revelations of God, clearing up the points not made clear by earlier prophets.

For more information on the relationship between Islam and other monotheistic faiths, see p58.

Jerusalem: One City, Three Faiths, by Karen Armstrong, is a comprehensive history of a city believed to be holy by the three monotheistic religions; even better, she writes without prejudice.

ISLAM
The Birth of Islam
Abdul Qasim Mohammed ibn Abdullah ibn Abd al-Muttalib ibn Hashim (the Prophet Mohammed) was born in AD 570. Mohammed's family belonged to the Quraysh tribe, a trading family with links to Syria and Yemen. By the age of six, Mohammed's parents had both died and he came into the care of his grandfather, the custodian of the Kaaba in Mecca. When he was around 25 years old, Mohammed married Khadija, a widow and a merchant, and he worked in running her business.

At the age of 40, in AD 610, Mohammed retreated into the desert and began to receive divine revelations from Allah via the voice of the archangel Gabriel – the revelations would continue for the rest of Mohammed's life. Three years later, Mohammed began imparting Allah's message to the Meccans. Mohammed soon gathered a significant following in his campaign against Meccan idolaters and his movement appealed especially to the poorer, disenfranchised sections of society.

Islam provided a simpler alternative to the established faiths, which had become complicated by hierarchical orders, sects and complex rituals, offering instead a direct relationship with God based only on the believer's submission to God (Islam means 'submission').

Among Mecca's ruling families, however, there was a dawning recognition of the new faith's potential to sweep aside the old order. By AD 622 these families had forced Mohammed and his followers to flee north to the oasis town of Medina. There, Mohammed's supporters rapidly grew in number. By AD 630 Mohammed returned triumphantly to Mecca at the head of a 10,000-strong army to seize control of the city. Many of the surrounding tribes quickly swore allegiance to him and the new faith.

When Mohammed died in AD 632, the Arab tribes spread quickly across the Middle East with missionary zeal, conquering all of what now constitutes Jordan, Syria, Iraq, Lebanon and Israel and the Palestinian Territories. Persia and India soon found themselves confronted by the new army of believers and the unrelenting conquest also swept across North Africa. By the end of the 7th century, the Muslims had reached the Atlantic and marched on Spain in AD 710, an astonishing achievement given the religion's humble desert roots.

Muhammad: a Biography of the Prophet, by Karen Armstrong, is a sensitive, well-researched and highly readable biography of the Prophet Mohammed set against the backdrop of modern misconceptions and stereotypes about Islam.

The flight of Mohammed and his followers from Mecca to Medina (the Hejira) marks the birth of Islam and the first year of the Islamic calendar – 1 AH (AD 622).

Shiite & Sunni
Despite Mohammed's original intentions, Islam did not remain simple. The Prophet died leaving no sons, which led to a major dispute over the line of succession. Competing for power were Abu Bakr, the father

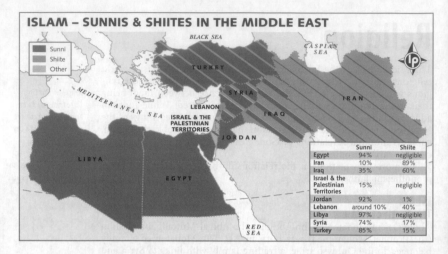

ISLAM – SUNNIS & SHIITES IN THE MIDDLE EAST

	Sunni	Shiite
Egypt	94%	negligible
Iran	10%	89%
Iraq	35%	60%
Israel & the Palestinian Territories	15%	negligible
Jordan	92%	1%
Lebanon	around 10%	40%
Libya	97%	negligible
Syria	74%	17%
Turkey	85%	15%

of Mohammed's second wife Aisha, and Ali, Mohammed's cousin and the husband of his daughter Fatima. Initially, the power was transferred to Abu Bakr, who became the first caliph (ruler), with Ali reluctantly agreeing.

Abu Bakr's lineage came to an abrupt halt when his successor was murdered. Ali reasserted his right to power and emerged victorious in the ensuing power struggle, moving his capital to Kufa (later renamed Najaf, in Iraq), only to be assassinated himself in AD 661. After defeating Ali's successor, Hussein, in AD 680 at Kerbala, the Umayyad dynasty rose to rule the vast majority of the Muslim world, marking the start of the Sunni sect. Those who continued to support the claims of the descendents of Ali became known as Shiites.

Beyond this early dynastic rivalry, there is little difference between Shiite Islam and Sunni Islam, but the division remains to this day. Sunnis comprise some 90% of the world's more than 800 million Muslims, but Shiites are believed to form a majority of the population in Iraq, Lebanon and Iran. There are also Shiite minorities in almost all Arab countries.

The Quran

For Muslims the Quran is the word of God, directly communicated to the Prophet Mohammed; unlike the Torah and Bible, which are the interpretive work of many individuals, the Quran is believed by Muslims to be the direct word of Allah. It comprises 114 suras (chapters), which govern all aspects of a Muslim's life from a Muslim's relationship to God to minute details about daily living.

In addition to drawing on moral ideas prevalent in 7th-century Arabia, some of the Quran's laws closely resemble those of the other monotheistic faiths, particularly the doctrinal elements of Judaism and the piety of early eastern Christianity. The suras contain many references to the earlier prophets – Adam, Abraham (Ibrahim), Noah, Moses (Moussa) and Jesus (although Muslims strictly deny his divinity) are all recognised as prophets in a line that ends definitively with the greatest of them all, the Prophet Mohammed. Muslims traditionally attribute a place of great respect to Christians and Jews as *ahl al-kitab* (the people of the book; sura 2:100–15). However, Muslims believe that the Quran is the final

The Quran is not only the sacred text for Muslims, but is also a classic of poetic Arabic literature – reading it is essential to understanding the Middle East's dominant faith.

expression of Allah's will and the ultimate and definitive guide to his intentions for humankind.

It's not known whether the revelations were written down during Mohammed's lifetime. The third caliph, Uthman (644–56), gathered together everything written by the scribes (parchments, stone tablets, the memories of Mohammed's followers) and gave them to a panel of editors under the caliph's aegis. A Quran printed today is identical to that agreed upon by Uthman's compilers 14 centuries ago.

Another important aspect of the Quran is the language in which it is written. Some Muslims believe that the Quran must be studied in its original classical Arabic form ('an Arabic Quran, wherein there is no crookedness'; sura 39:25) and that translations dilute the holiness of its sacred texts. For Muslims, the language of the Quran is known as *sihr halal* (lawful magic). Apart from its religious significance, the Quran, lyrical and poetic, is also considered one of the finest literary masterpieces in history.

Five Pillars of Islam

In order to live a devout life, Muslims are expected to observe, as a minimum, the Five Pillars of Islam.

Shahada This is the profession of faith, Islam's basic tenet; 'There is no god but Allah, and Mohammed is the Prophet of Allah'. This phrase forms an integral part of the call to prayer and is used at all important events in a Muslim's life.

Sala (sura 11:115) This is the obligation of prayer, ideally five times a day: at sunrise, noon, midafternoon, sunset and night. It's acceptable to pray at home or elsewhere, except for Friday noon prayers, which are performed at a mosque.

Zakat (sura 107) Muslims must give alms to the poor to the value of one-fortieth of a believer's annual income. This used to be the responsibility of the individual, but zakat now usually exists as a state-imposed welfare tax administered by a ministry of religious affairs.

Sawm (sura 2:180–5) Ramadan, the ninth month of the Muslim calendar, commemorates the revelation of the Quran to Mohammed. As Ramadan represents a Muslim's renewal of faith, nothing may pass their lips (food, cigarettes, drinks) and they must refrain from sex from dawn until dusk. For more details on Ramadan see p647.

Haj (sura 2:190–200) Every Muslim capable of affording it should perform the haj (pilgrimage) to the holiest of cities, Mecca, at least once in his or her lifetime. The reward is considerable: the forgiving of all past sins.

If Muslims wish to pray but are not in a mosque and there's no water available, clean sand (wholesome dust' according to the Quran) suffices; where there's no sand, they must go through the motions of washing (sura 5:5).

The Call to Prayer

Allahu akbar, Allahu akbar
Ashhadu an la Ilah ila Allah
Ashhadu an Mohammed rasul Allah
Haya ala as-sala
Haya ala as-sala

This haunting invocation will soon become the soundtrack to your visit to the Middle East, a ritual whose essential meaning and power remain largely unchanged in 14 centuries.

Five times a day, Muslims are called, if not actually to enter a mosque to pray, at least to take the time to do so where they are. The midday prayers on Friday, when the imam of the mosque delivers his weekly *khutba* (sermon), are considered the most important. For Muslims, prayer is less a petition to Allah (in the Christian sense) than a ritual reaffirmation of Allah's power and a reassertion of the brotherhood and equality of all believers.

The act of praying consists of a series of predefined movements of the body and recitals of prayers and passages of the Quran, all designed to express the believer's absolute humility and Allah's sovereignty.

Islamic Customs

In everyday life, Muslims are prohibited from drinking alcohol (sura 5:90–5) and eating carrion, blood products or pork, which are considered unclean (sura 2:165), the meat of animals not killed in the prescribed manner (sura 5:1–5) and food over which the name of Allah has not been said (sura 6:115). Adultery (sura 18:30–5), theft (sura 5:40–5) and gambling (sura 5:90–5) are also prohibited.

Islam is not just about prohibitions but also marks the important events of a Muslim's life. When a baby is born, the first words uttered to it are the call to prayer. A week later follows a ceremony in which the baby's head is shaved and an animal sacrificed in remembrance of Abraham's willingness to sacrifice his son to Allah. The major event of a boy's childhood is circumcision, which normally takes place between the ages of seven and 12. When a person dies, a burial service is held at the mosque and the body is buried with the feet facing Mecca.

Depending upon your interpretation, the charging of interest is prohibited by the Quran (sura 2: 275–80).

JUDAISM

The foundation of the Jewish religion is the Torah, the first five books of the Old Testament. The Torah contains the revelation from God via Moses from more than 3000 years ago, including, most importantly, God's commandments (of which there are 613 in all). The Torah is supplemented by the rest of the books of the Old Testament, of which the most important are the prophetic books, giving much of the substance to the religion.

Essential Judaism: a Complete Guide to Beliefs, Customs & Rituals, by George Robinson, is aimed more at Jews seeking to rediscover their traditions, but it covers everything from festivals and rituals to Jewish philosophy – the religion stripped of its political connotations.

These books are complemented by the Talmud, a collection of another 63 books, written in the early centuries AD and containing most of what separates Judaism from other religions. Included are plenty of rabbinical interpretations of the earlier scriptures, with a wealth of instructions and rulings for the daily life of a Jew.

The Talmud was written when the Jewish Diaspora began. After the Romans crushed the Jewish state and destroyed the Temple in Jerusalem in AD 70, many Jews were either exiled or sold into slavery abroad. The Jewish religion was kept intact, however, within families who passed the teachings from generation to generation. Until the foundation of the State of Israel and the subsequent backlash by many Arabs, Jewish communities lived peacefully alongside their Muslim neighbours in all countries of the Middle East covered by this book; Iraq was home to a particularly large Jewish community.

Unlike Christians or Muslims, Jews have never actively sought converts from the followers of other religions.

CHRISTIANITY

Jesus preached in what is present-day Israel and the Palestinian Territories, but Christians form only minority groups in all Middle Eastern countries, with Christians accounting for about 13% of the population of Egypt and Syria.

Lebanon and Jordan have sizable Christian populations too, and the former's one million Maronites also have followers all over the world. By far the biggest Christian sect in the region is formed by the Copts of Egypt, who make up most of that country's Christian population. Originally it was the apostle Mark who established Christianity in Egypt, and by the 4th century it had become the state religion. The Coptic Church split from the Byzantine Orthodox Church in the 5th century after a dispute about the human nature of Jesus, with Dioscurus, the patriarch of Alexandria, declaring Jesus to be totally divine. Internation-

THE BIBLE AS HISTORY

Unlike Egypt, where the wealth of tomb and temple texts and papyri has enabled historians to work out a detailed historical framework, the 'Holy Lands', where the earliest events as related in the Old Testament of the Bible are said to have taken place, have yielded little in the way of written archives. Historians cannot say for sure whether characters such as Abraham, Moses or even Solomon existed. The Old Testament was compiled from a variety of sources, and probably set down in script no earlier than the 6th century BC. The stories it contains might have some grain of truth in them, but then again they may have been no more than folk tales.

When it comes to the New Testament and episodes related in the Gospels by Matthew, Mark, Luke and John, we do have some means of corroboration. This was the Roman era and there are plenty of other sources in the form of written accounts, inscriptions and works of art so that we can say with certainty that figures such as Herod, Pontius Pilot and a man called Jesus, from Nazareth, did exist. Where history moves into the realm of conjecture again is in associating particular places with biblical events. Many sites commonly held to be of biblical significance were only fixed in the 4th century AD by the Empress Helena, some 300 years after the death of Christ. They owe their status more to tradition than historical veracity.

ally the most famous Egyptian Copt today is the former UN secretary-general, Boutros Boutros-Ghali.

Otherwise, the Arab Christians of the Middle East belong to many churches in all main branches of the religion – Orthodox, Catholic and Protestant. This richness reflects the region's location on major routes along which the religion spread to Europe and Asia, and by which people and ideas have flowed into the area for centuries.

However, the number of Christians in the Middle East is definitely in decline. The reasons are predominantly demographic. Over the centuries Christians, in Egypt and Syria in particular, have moved from the country to the city and this urbanisation has led to a fall in birth rates. Also traditionally Christian church schools have provided a better education than Muslim state schools, which again has had the effect of lowering the birth rate. The professional qualifications resulting from the better education and subsequent wealth have also meant that Middle East Christians are far more able to emigrate. Syrian and Egyptian churches have found it impossible to stem the flow of parishioners to Australia and the USA.

Islam & the West Will Gourlay

As the dust settled in Manhattan after 11 September 2001, an image emerged of the malevolent wagging finger of Osama bin Laden and his threats against the 'infidels'. Western puzzlement was replaced by dread. It was as if the West was suddenly aware of a restive element living in the modern world, biding its time and seeking an opportunity to bring it down.

Here, for some, was the realisation of American historian Samuel Huntington's 'clash of civilisations', a theory first propounded in the 1990s. And here, conveniently after the fizzling out of the Cold War, was a new enemy that the West could focus on. Gone was the stony-faced Soviet agent; neatly substituted was the Arab youth, reciting from the Quran and cradling a package of Semtex.

It was a seductive hypothesis that was supported by countless precedents: Palestinian terrorists at the Munich Olympics; Lebanon's internecine civil war; Saddam Hussein's ruthless invasion of Kuwait; Iranian mullahs berating the 'great Satan'; numerous hijackings and suicide bombings.

Hoary old clichés about the Middle East added weight: downtrodden women, erratic despots, public beheadings, massive oil wealth.

And through it all remained a perception that Islam was monolithic and all pervasive, not just a religion but a way of life, rigidly dictating all aspects of its adherents' existences. Such a philosophy and strictures were archaic to Western observers, for many of whom religion plays a negligible role.

For those who chose to subscribe to the 'clash of civilisations' theory, Islam and the West, with its inherently Judeo-Christian roots, were mutually irreconcilable and diametrically opposed antagonists – set to slog it out until only one victor emerged, eternally vindicated.

Western travellers, upon arriving in the Middle East, undoubtedly note a culture that feels different to the West. The fact that religion plays a more prominent role in the Middle East is undeniable. The call to prayer, five times a day, is the most noticeable indicator that the traveller is in a different milieu.

Nonetheless, travellers finding themselves in this milieu will not necessarily find it alien or confronting. The repeat visitor to the region will also know that there is no such thing as a single Muslim monolithic culture – daily life is played out to very different tunes across the region.

As well as professing faith in the same God, Arabs and Jews, as fellow Semites, are said to share a common ancestry. Legend has it that both peoples are descended from Isaac, Ishmael and Abraham.

However, many of the shared aspects of a broader Muslim culture are immediately appealing to the traveller: the generosity of everyday people; the immediate acceptance of visitors; great spontaneity and *joie de vivre* despite material hardship; and a willingness to take things easy, described rather patronisingly by the 19th-century traveller AW Kinglake as an 'Asiatic contentment'. Beyond which, any perceptive traveller will identify aspects of the symbiosis that exists between the Muslim world and the West and will discern the intricacy with which their histories are linked.

It may be that Islam and the West don't make for ideal bedfellows, but they have common concerns and shared interests, and to characterise them as sworn enemies is taking too simplistic an approach.

MONOTHEISM – SHARED FOUNDATIONS
In 2003 US general William Boykin, referring to a Muslim soldier, said, 'I knew that my God was real, and his was an idol,' provoking an outcry from the Muslim world. The protest wasn't a matter of an inferiority complex; it was because Muslims decried the statement as heretical.

The Muslim credo makes a nonsense of any such allusion to a pecking order of deities; it states categorically and unambiguously: 'There is no God but God'. The existence of a unique God is the central and defining tenet of the three great monotheistic religions.

As any Muslim will attest, the God who is invoked in Friday prayers across the Middle East is the selfsame God who is worshipped in synagogues and churches around the globe, albeit under different monikers. Muslims readily acknowledge that their faith is built on the foundations of Judaism and Christianity. They see their religion as the refinement – indeed the ultimate and perfect manifestation – of the monotheistic religions that preceded it. They believe that the Quran (from the Arabic for 'recitation') was the final word from God, delivered through the medium of Mohammed, the final prophet. But far from denouncing Christians and Jews, the Quran anoints them as *ahl al-kitab*, people of the book, and forbids their enslavement or persecution.

Beyond a shared foundation, Islam, Christianity and Judaism share rituals, traditions, parallels, interconnections and characteristics too many to mention. It is as if Christianity and Islam, as each has arisen, has adopted and adapted from its antecedents to establish its own structures and define its own identity. Islam, as the last of the three to arise, is flush with markers that are immediately identifiable to Jews and Christians.

The Quran never attempts to deny the debt it owes to the holy books that came before it. It is replete with characters, tales, anecdotes, terminology and symbolism that would be immediately recognisable to Jewish and Christian readers. Indeed the Quran itself was revealed to Mohammed by the archangel Gabriel.

Muslims look upon the font of Jewish and Christian religious learning and tradition as a heritage to which they too are privy. Islam venerates Jesus, but does not consider him the son of God. Eid al-Adha, the Muslim festival that marks the end of the haj, is based on the biblical tale of Abraham offering up his son for sacrifice. It is clear that the Muslim prohibition on the consumption of pork is based on the Jewish ruling. The Muslim month-long fast of Ramadan bears similarities to Lent. Osman, the Turkish founder of the Ottoman Empire, claimed descent from Noah.

The modern travel writer and historian William Dalrymple observed Syrian Orthodox Christians at prayer in the 1990s. He remarked that the series of genuflections and prostrations that these Eastern Christians performed was uncannily similar to the *salaat* (prayer) that Muslims perform, and he wondered aloud if the Muslim ritual could be based on the Christian.

It is here, in the Middle East, that the parallels between Islam and Christianity are most readily observed. When the Prophet's armies in the 7th century AD first engaged Byzantine armies in the Levant, the Byzantines believed that Islam was merely a newly arisen Christian sect. Similarly, the great theologian of the 8th century, St John of Damascus, contended that Islam was not a separate religion but a new offshoot of the Judeo-Christian tradition.

Where early Islam did depart from its precursors was in simplifying the relationship with God. With no priesthood, Islam allowed the individual to maintain a dialogue with God – a system ideal for nomads and merchants, perhaps explaining the speed with which the new faith spread. In doing so it allowed even the isolated individual to become part of a community, all members of which could communicate with God directly.

But Islam also had a peculiarly Arabic bent and the alacrity with which it moved and the realm into which it first spread are perhaps what brought it into confrontation with Christianity and the West.

All of the countries in this book, bar Libya, still have indigenous Christian populations. Most retained Jewish communities until the 1950s and mass emigration to Israel. There are still sizable Jewish communities in Turkey and Iran.

Much of the region covered in this book had sizable Christian populations before the coming of Islam in the 7th century.

Cultural Cross-Pollination

While Islam arose from the wellspring of the Judeo-Christian tradition, the interplay of the three monotheistic religions was not limited to matters theological. From the outset there has been a symbiosis and a two-way cultural exchange between Muslim cultures and Western Judeo-Christian cultures.

In the field of architecture, certain apparently archetypal characteristics of places of worship, both Christian and Muslim, owe much to the 'other'. The first Muslims prayed in mosques modelled on the house of the Prophet Mohammed, until the early Arabic armies encountered the domes of Byzantine churches. Thereupon the dome entered the repertoire of the Muslim architect, and the voluptuous skylines of the archetypal Islamic city were born – quintessentially Muslim, yet intrinsically European. Conversely, the pointed arch, beloved of European Gothic architects, was introduced to Europe by travellers returning from the Levant. The squared minaret, too, was a Muslim borrowing from the bell towers of the churches of Byzantine Syria. Centuries later St Francis of Assisi travelled through the Muslim realm and recognised the minaret and cry of the muezzin as a way of drumming up piety. On his return to Europe he instituted the practice of ringing church bells morning, noon and evening.

Earlier, the stalled engine of European intellectual thought was kick-started by Muslim catalysts. The heritage of classical Greek civilisation had been lost to Europe as the Roman Empire subsided. However, at the end of the first millennium, the intellectuals of Muslim Spain translated the classical works of medicine, astronomy, chemistry, philosophy and architecture, thus eventually bringing them to the attention of Christian Europe, and in turn laying the groundwork for the Renaissance. Words such as zenith, nadir, azimuth, algebra, algorithm – all of which have Arabic roots – are evidence of the legacy of Arabic scientists.

> The Middle Eastern influence on Western culture is clearly seen in words such as yogurt, saffron, sugar, caravan, bazaar and carafe, all of which come from Arabic, Persian or Turkish.

Undoubtedly the greatest contribution that the Arabs made to Europe was in mathematics. Until the 11th century Europe laboured under the strictures of Latin numerals. Europe was well aware of the wellspring of learning that existed in the Muslim realm, and what amounted to intellectuals' study tours from Europe to Muslim Spain were common. It was after one such foray that the 'Arabic' numeral system – the system still in use today – was introduced to Europe. Most crucial among this system was 'zero', a concept that had thus far eluded Europe's imagination. Without 'zero' the binary system – central to much modern technology – would never have been devised. Imagine trying to run a computer based on the Latin numeral system!

Some contend that it was first in the Muslim world that monarchs encouraged the learned to gather together and study a range of disciplines in one space, and it is from here that the concept of the university was conceived and spread to the West.

> The Ornament of the World, by Rosa Maria Menocal, is a vivid and inspiring portrait detailing the interaction of Muslims, Christians and Jews in medieval Spain and the heady cultural heights they achieved in concert.

Hedonism has also benefited from East–West interaction. When the Turks poured into Anatolia in the 11th century they discovered the bath-houses of Byzantium. The Turks, hardy nomads of the steppes, took to steamy ablutions with glee, making it part of the Turkish regimen, to the extent that a bathhouse experience is virtually mandatory for travellers to Turkey today. European caffeine junkies, too, owe much to the ebb and flow of Ottoman armies in Europe. Legend says that when the Turks abandoned the siege of Vienna in 1683 they left behind sacks of coffee beans, which were discovered by the relieved Viennese who promptly introduced the coffeehouse to Europe. Silk, spices, papermaking and chess also reached Europe from Asia, via the Middle East and Muslim middlemen.

Indeed, some historians argue that far from being mutually antagonistic, Christianity, Islam and Judaism, when given the opportunity, create a unique symbiosis. The greatest Muslim cultures arose where all three religions comingled and cross-pollinated – the Caliphate of Cordoba in Al-Andalus (the name given to the Iberian Peninsula by its Muslim conquerors; 756–1009), the Ottoman Empire under Süleyman (1520–66), and the Persian Safavid empire under Abbas I (1587–1629). The architectural legacies of these three are still to be seen in southern Spain, İstanbul and Esfahan. The cultural legacies of each are less tangible, but it may be argued that they are no less potent.

A HISTORY OF CONFLICT?

In the confrontation between Islam and Christianity there has always been a frontline that has shifted as the balance of power has shifted.

Infidels, by Andrew Wheatcroft, is a study of Islam and Christianity's troubled relationship from the birth of Islam to the 21st century.

Within only a few years of the death of Mohammed, the Umayyads moved their capital to Damascus, marking a shift in vision. Islam was no longer a religion of the Arabian Peninsula, but a world religion. In making this shift Islam encountered Christianity. Islam expanded, absorbing and assimilating, but also encountering Christian and Jewish communities the respect that the Quran specified the 'people of the book' should be accorded. The early Muslim armies also encountered other nations and civilisations – Hindu, Chinese, Persian – but in Christianity they recognised a rival. Christianity, like Islam a proselytising religion, also had an agenda.

Islam's First European Foray – Al-Andalus

The first successful Muslim expedition into Europe was launched from North Africa into Spain in 711. By 732 Muslim armies had taken the Iberian Peninsula and advanced as far north as Poitiers in France, before being pushed back across the Pyrenees. Muslim armies then consolidated in Spain, whereupon Christian and Muslim communities flirted, sized each other up and interacted productively for over seven centuries, only occasionally spilling into open conflict. This dalliance came to an end when the knights of the Spanish Reconquista expelled the last Muslim monarch from Spain in 1492, the very year that Columbus reached the Americas, setting in course a pendulum swing that would see the Christian West in the ascendant for centuries to come.

In *The Birth of Europe*, modern historian Jacques le Goff comments that the First Crusade was an unredeemed act of villainy that brought Europe only one benefit: the apricot.

The Crusaders Capture the Holy Land

Europe had earlier attempted to foil the Muslim advance and reclaim the Holy Land for Christendom. The monarchs and clerics of Europe attempted to portray the Crusades as 'just war', uncannily prefiguring advocates of the Iraq war in 2003. In the late 11th century such a battle cry attracted zealous support, and by 1099 the crusading rabble had taken Jerusalem, a victory marked by wanton and indiscriminate bloodletting, in significant contrast to the Muslim conquest of the region centuries earlier.

Curiously even after the gratuitous violence of the Crusades, Christians and Muslims assimilated in the Holy Land. European visitors to Palestine recorded with dismay that the original Crusaders who remained in the Holy Land had abandoned their European ways. They had become Arabised, taking on eastern habits and dress – perhaps it was not an unwise move to abandon chain mail and jerkins for flowing robes in the Levantine heat. It was at this time that what is thought of as the quintessentially Roman Catholic garment, the nun's habit, was adopted and adapted from the veils that Muslim women wore in Palestine.

In 1204 the armies of the Fourth Crusade sacked Constantinople, then the capital of the Byzantine Empire, and a fellow Christian power. The invaders visited more destruction on the city than any army before or since.

A series of Crusader 'statelets' arose through the Middle East during this period. Contemporary Arab observers noted these regimes were relatively stable in contrast to Muslim political entities, where matters of succession were always occasions of bloodshed and armed conflict. They described it as an inherent failing in the Muslim societies. Stable political institutions were very rarely created: a problem that continues in much of the Arab world to the modern day.

Ridley Scott's 2005 movie, the *Kingdom of Heaven*, which depicts the 12th-century battle for Jerusalem between Muslims and Crusaders, has been commended by Arab cinemagoers for challenging the stereotype of Arabs and Muslims as terrorists.

The Ottomans Push into Europe

Horse-borne, firing arrows from the saddle, the Ottoman Turks emerged from the Anatolian steppe in the 14th century and put Europe on the back foot again. The Ottomans advanced so swiftly – so seemingly miraculously – into Eastern Europe that Martin Luther wondered whether they should be opposed at all. The Ottoman Empire, at its greatest extent, reached from Ghadames in Libya to the steppes of Hungary and the shores of the Red Sea. Again, however, Christian and Jewish communities were accorded the respect the Quran outlines for them and were given special status. The Ottoman state was a truly multicultural and multilingual one and Christians and Muslims rose to positions of great power within the Ottoman hierarchy.

The end of Ottoman expansion is variously pinpointed to the failed Vienna campaign in 1683, or the treaty of Karlowitz in 1699 when the Ottomans sued for peace for the first time. Thereafter the Ottoman Empire went into a slow and enervating decline, making attempts to redefine itself along European lines. By the 19th century, however, a new Western concept, nationalism, rather than Muslim-Western aggression, spelt the ultimate undoing of the Ottoman state as Greeks and Balkan Slavs agitated for and achieved independence. Meanwhile in Arabia's arid Najd district in the 1760s, Abd al-Wahhab preached revolt against the Ottomans and a return to the core values of Islam. Wahhab's influence would, much later, prove to be of singular import.

Mark Mazower's *Salonica, City of Ghosts* is a lively social history of Salonica (modern-day Thessaloniki in Greece). Mazower poignantly evokes the last great multicultural Ottoman city wholly in Europe.

The Era of Colonialism

In 1798 Napoleon arrived in Egypt. Europe, by now industrialised and fresh from colonising the Americas and much of Asia, enjoyed economic and technological superiority over Muslim states. Napoleon's jaunt to the Pyramids marked the start of European meddling and interference in the Middle East that continues to the present. This was colonialism without grand conquest but rather colonialism by stealth. The Great Powers (largely Britain and France) apportioned much of the Middle East among themselves. And where there wasn't direct control there was behind-the-scenes manipulation. This was particularly the case in Iran, where Britain peddled influence but never came to colonise. Some Iranians lament this to this day, saying that because they were never 'really' colonised they were never 'really' liberated either – not until the revolution of 1979.

All the Shah's Men, by Stephen Kinzer, vividly details the CIA's 1953 coup to overthrow Iran's popularly elected leader, Mohammed Mossadegh. Gripping and insightful.

This era saw a wholly different dynamic to what had happened in earlier interactions between Islam and Western Christendom. Here was the haughty colonial administrator and the obsequious local Muslim: overlord and underling. This struck at the Muslim psyche – not only were they being technologically outstripped by the West, but resentment grew at foreign control and influence. The creation of the State of Israel in 1948 further fanned the flames of Muslim rancour. And a process that had earlier begun among the Wahhabis of Arabia gained momentum. Islam turned in on itself and looked to an idealised version of the past for inspiration.

Yet even at this time there was an exchange of ideas. At the end of the 19th century the concept of the 'desert-loving Englishman' arose, not least among them Lawrence of Arabia. And for the first time wealthy Muslims went to Europe to be educated. They returned to the Middle East bearing Western ideas, among them democracy.

European control of the Middle East diminished with the Suez Crisis of 1956 and the Algerian war of the 1960s. The 1950s and '60s became the decades of pan-Arabism as Nasser came to power in Egypt. Sayyid Qutb, an Egyptian radical, capitalised on resentments that had long simmered. He espoused a return to grassroots Islam, as Wahhab had almost 200 years earlier. But Qutb took it further. He prompted the creation of the Muslim Brotherhood, who would withdraw from society and prepare for violence and martyrdom in pursuit of a universal Muslim society. The meeting of Islam and the West was set to take another path entirely.

> Director Youssef Chahine's *Destiny* (1997) is a lavishly shot allegorical tale about the struggle within Islam against fundamentalism set in Al-Andalus, but it clearly resonates in the modern Middle East.

THE WAR ON TERROR

With the benefit of hindsight it is easy to remark that the War on Terror is the culmination of events that have been smouldering for years. Oil, particularly since the 1970s, has proved the lubricant for much of the interaction between the West and the Arab world. Ironically it is the West's appetite for oil that has provided Saudi Arabia, in particular, with immense wealth, with which it has attempted to spread its ascetic and puritan form of Islam, Wahhabism. Alongside this has voyaged the more apocalyptic, anti-Western vision of Sayyid Qutb.

Add to this Muslim resentment at the plight of the Palestinians and perceived Western bias towards Israel, the West's inability or unwillingness to protect Bosnian Muslims from Serbian ethnic cleansing, and Western support of various unsavoury regimes in the Middle East. Counterpoise this with Western alarm at the reign of terror of Saddam Hussein, the continuing anti-Western rants of Iranian hardliners and a succession of Palestinian suicide bombers. And all that was required was an apocalyptic event like 9/11 to get the conflagration started.

Nonetheless, portraying the War on Terror as a 'clash of civilisations' is overstating things markedly. Some on both sides (not least politicians) seek to portray it as such, and elements within both civilisations consider themselves besieged. The Lebanese writer and historian Amin Maalouf argues that the Crusades created within the Arab world a juxtaposed fear of and fascination with the West that persists to the modern day, such that many Muslims feel that their world is under constant threat of attack. At the same time many residents of Western cities find themselves understandably jittery at the prospect of terror attacks.

Yet, it remains that relatively small groups are spruiking for and prosecuting the war. The terrorists who seek to bring down the West are few, and the initial American enthusiasm for the invasion of Iraq appears to be waning. There is no doubt, in the light of the terror attacks on London in July 2005, that the West remains intent on removing the terrorist threat, but there appears to be a gradual but increasing recognition from many commentators that any war on terror must be a war of ideas rather than a war in the conventional sense.

Cynicism remains about the motivation for the US-led invasion of Iraq. Many see it as an abstraction little related to the campaign against terrorism and wholly related to the Bush family vendetta against Saddam Hussein. The degree to which the Saudi ruling family and the US oil lobby are in each others' pockets also raises eyebrows. Related to this is the alleged evacuation of members of the Bin Laden family from the US immediately after the terror attacks in Manhattan – this relationship is little understood but much speculated upon – much to the delight of conspiracy theorists.

But it is not only US interests that have used the War on Terror to push their own barrows. Uzbekistan and China have taken to branding much civilian unrest as Islamic extremism in order to shore up their own autocratic regimes. Meanwhile, Muslim radicals, in a ploy to enlist more jihadists, cite the recent invasions of Afghanistan and Iraq as evidence of a new crusade.

In fact, President Bush's use of the term 'crusade' in the early days of the campaign to combat terror was a fundamental tactical error. His decision to include Iran in his infamous 'Axis of Evil' speech only a short time after the Iranian government sent its condolences to the American people in the wake of 9/11 does not seem like a masterstroke either.

The Pentagon has since realised that the US is losing the battle for hearts and minds in the Middle East. A report by the Defence Science Board says that US claims to bring democracy to the region are viewed by many Muslims as self-serving and hypocritical. The report says that Muslims see the US-led invasions of Afghanistan and Iraq as resulting in chaos and misery rather than much-vaunted democracy. Not deigning to compile a toll of civilian dead in either conflict, the lack of weapons of mass destruction in Iraq and the appalling treatment of prisoners at Guantanamo Bay and Abu Ghraib jail have not helped the US cause. Meanwhile, the West's continued indulgence of unsavoury regimes throughout the Muslim world when it is politically expedient does little to make its championing of democracy appear heartfelt.

A Middle East Mosaic, by Bernard Lewis, is a fascinating miscellany compiled from many and varied sources, a grab bag of impressions of the 'other' by Muslim, Christian and Jewish observers through the ages.

To bring an end to terror and to solve the interconnected problems of the Middle East is a monumental task. It need not involve the obliteration of one civilisation by another. And there may be signs for optimism – Arab journalists' anguished recognition that most terrorists come from the Muslim world indicates that Muslims too are asking hard questions of themselves. And ever-larger numbers of Americans are demonstrating a desire to learn more about Islam and the Middle East; US universities report that since October 2001 demand for and enrolments in a range of courses from Arabic language to Persian mysticism have grown significantly. Recent elections in Iraq and Lebanon illustrate that the will of Muslim nations can be harnessed and their opinions canvassed in order to determine how they want to be ruled.

WHITHER THE CROSS & THE CRESCENT?

The frontline of the confrontation between Islam and the West continues to shift. Today that frontline may be in London, Madrid or New York…or Kabul or Baghdad. And misunderstandings and injustices continue on both sides. From the outset Islam and Christianity recognised in each other a rival for global hegemony. There has always been mutual wariness and scant attempt to engage in dialogue with the other side, but only rarely did that rivalry result in open conflict. That remains true in the era of the War on Terror.

History shows us that in the places where East and West have mingled, elements combine, retaining their intrinsic qualities while also creating a distinctive melange – as it was in Al-Andalus under the Cordoban caliphs and in Süleyman's Ottoman capital. It is happening again now: in glitzy Dubai, in İstanbul's hip Beyoğlu neighbourhood, in renascent Beirut, in the Moorish-styled cafés of Granada and in the in-vogue Lebanese restaurants of Melbourne. They stand as living proof that the fusion of Muslim and Western cultures brings about great things.

Arts

ARCHITECTURE

The journey through Middle Eastern architecture is an extraordinarily
rich one. It ranges from the enduring wonder of the towering monoliths
raised to the glory of Egypt's pharaohs to the enchanting simplicity of
Saharan mud-brick oasis towns in the Libyan Sahara, and from the lavish
Islamic legacy of Esfahan in Iran to the buildings that have served many
faiths in İstanbul and Jerusalem. Then there's the traditional indigenous
architecture perfectly adapted to local conditions, which is astonishing in
its childlike forms, most notably in Cappadocia (Kapadokya) in Turkey
and the Jebel Nafusa of northwestern Libya. When these are added to the
Phoenician, Roman, Greek and Nabataean cities of antiquity, it's hard not
to get excited about what's on offer.

Architectural Highlights

It's in the Middle East that you see the first transitions from the classical
column-and-lintel way of building (employed by the ancient Egyptians,
Greeks and Romans) to a more fluid architecture based on arches, vaults
and domes. This new style of construction, facilitated by the supplanting
of stone with the smaller and far more malleable unit of the brick, developed under the Byzantines based in Constantinople. Their legacy is best
illustrated by Justinian's great cathedral of Aya Sofya (p567) in İstanbul,
and a scattering of more-modest structures dotted throughout Syria,
most notably the 5th-century Qala'at Samaan (p544) north of Aleppo.

Byzantine forms carried through into the early Islamic period, and
some of the earliest Muslim monuments – the Dome of the Rock (p289)
in Jerusalem and the Umayyad Mosque (p514) in Damascus – owe their
form to eastern Christianity. Over time, Islam developed its own building vocabulary; for the best of the Middle Eastern mosques, see p67. An
egalitarian religion, its mosques simply required a single large, open space
with as little clutter as possible. A domed central chamber proved to be
the best way of achieving this. Slender minarets provided a platform for
the daily call to prayer.

In addition, a subsidiary set of buildings evolved including the madrassa (Quranic school), *khanqah* (monastery), *sabil* (fountain), *turba*
(mausoleum) and *hammam* (public bathhouse).

The Middle East's medieval architectural glory of accumulated great
mosques, palaces and old quarters is one of the region's greatest draws
and is best seen in the old cities of Aleppo, Cairo, Damascus and Jerusalem. For the most part, the finest structures were built before the 16th
or 17th centuries, including the Turkish architect Mimar Sinan's great
masterpieces in Edirne (p576) and İstanbul (see p570, p570 and p571),
and the shimmering complexes of Esfahan (p211).

From the 17th century, as the political clout of the Ottomans – the
overlords of much of the Middle East – declined, their buildings became
more modest. European influence also began to make itself felt. Europe
had flirted with baroque, so the simplicity of Arab and Turkish architecture was wedded to the decorative excesses of imported stylings. İstanbul's
palaces, the grand houses of Damascus and Aleppo, and numerous gaudy
Ottoman monuments in Cairo reflected the European trends.

European influence increased in the 19th century. Most Middle Eastern cities bear evidence of this with an assortment of churches, embassies

*Architecture & Polyphony:
Building in the Islamic
World Today,* is an exciting work stemming from
the Aga Khan Award for
Architecture. It's brimful
of the innovations of
modern Middle Eastern
architecture and an anti-
dote to the dominance of
mosques in the aesthetics
of Middle Eastern cities.

*Dictionary of Islamic
Architecture,* by Andrew
Petersen, is for those who
can't quite distinguish
a *sahn* (courtyard of a
mosque) from a *riwaq*
(arcade) and is useful
primarily if your journey
has whet your appetite
to learn more.

Islam: Art & Architecture, edited by Markus Hatt-stein and Peter Delius, is comprehensive, lavishly illustrated and one of those coffee-table books that you'll treasure and dip into time and again.

and public buildings fashioned in Gothic or Florentine or Slavic or some other such imported style, all examples of (rival) foreign powers asserting their presence in the region through architecture. Nowhere is this more evident than in Tripoli where Italianate architecture surrounds the earlier Ottoman medina. It was only in the mid-20th century that anything like a movement towards regional identity in architecture was to reemerge. And it was only at the close of the millennium that domes, courtyards, adobe and whitewash (all traditional elements of centuries past) once again returned to vogue.

Mosque Architecture
HISTORY
Embodying the Islamic faith, and representing its most predominant architectural feature is the masjid (mosque, also called a *jamaa*). The building, developed in the very early days of the religion, takes its form from the simple, private houses where the first believers gathered to worship.

The house belonging to the Prophet Mohammed is said to have provided the prototype for the mosque. It had an enclosed oblong courtyard with huts (housing Mohammed's wives) along one wall and a rough portico providing shade. This plan developed with the courtyard becoming the *sahn*, the portico the arcaded *riwaq* and the house the *haram* (prayer hall).

Islamic Art in Context: Art, Architecture and the Literary World, by Robert Irwin, one of the premier scholars on the Arab world, traces the development of Islamic arts from the 5th to the 17th centuries against the backdrop of prevailing social and political upheaval.

The prayer hall is typically divided into a series of aisles. The centre aisle is wider than the rest and leads to a vaulted niche in the wall called the mihrab; this indicates the direction of Mecca, towards which Muslims must face when they pray.

Before entering the prayer hall and participating in communal worship, Muslims must perform a ritual washing of the hands, forearms, neck and face (by washing themselves before prayer, the believer indicates a willingness to be purified). For this purpose mosques have traditionally had a large ablutions fountain at the centre of the courtyard, often fashioned from marble and worn by centuries of use. These days, modern mosques just have rows of taps.

The mosque also frequently serves the community in other ways: often you will find groups of small children or even adults receiving lessons (usually in the Quran), people in quiet prayer and others simply enjoying a peaceful nap – mosques provide wonderfully tranquil havens from the hustle and bustle of the streets outside.

STYLISTIC DEVELOPMENTS
The earliest of the grand mosques inherited much from Byzantine models (the Dome of the Rock is a converted basilica), but with the spread of the Muslim domain various styles soon developed, each influenced by local artistic traditions. The Umayyads of Damascus favoured square minarets, the Abbasids of Iraq built spiral minarets echoing the ziggurats of the Babylonians, and the Fatimid dynasty of North Africa made much use of decorative stucco work.

The vocabulary of mosque-building quickly became highly sophisticated and expressive, reaching its apotheosis under the Mamluks (1250–1517). A military dynasty of former slaves ruling out of Egypt, the Mamluks were great patrons of the arts. Their buildings are characterised by the banding of different coloured stone (a technique known as *ablaq*) and by the elaborate carvings and patterning around windows and in the recessed portals. The best examples of their patronage are found in Cairo, but impressive Mamluk monuments also grace the old cities of Damascus and Jerusalem.

MOSQUES NOT TO BE MISSED

With the exception of the Gulf countries, non-Muslims are generally quite welcome to visit mosques at any time other than during Friday prayers.

You must dress modestly. For men that means no shorts; for women that means no shorts, tight pants, shirts that aren't done up, or anything else that might be considered immodest. Some of the more frequently visited mosques provide wrap-around cloaks for anyone who is improperly dressed. Shoes have to be removed although some mosques will provide slip-on shoe covers for a small fee.

Azim-e Gohar Shad Mosque

This mosque (p240), in Mashhad in Iran, is the jewel at the heart of this pilgrimage city's holy shrine complex. It was built by the wife of the son of the Central Asian warlord Tamerlane in 1418. It shows a clear kinship with the Mongol-dynasty mosques of Samarkand and Bukhara (in modern-day Uzbekistan).

Dome of the Rock

The Dome of the Rock (p289), in Jerusalem in Israel and the Palestinian Territories, is one of the earliest-built mosques (691) and, with its octagonal plan and mosaic-encrusted exterior, one of the most unique of all Islamic structures.

Gurgi Mosque

The most recent of Tripoli's Ottoman mosques, the 19th-century Gurgi Mosque (p474) is compact but boasts a glorious interior incorporating marble pillars from Italy, ceramic tilework from Tunisia and stone carvings from Morocco.

Imam Mosque

The grandest and most ornate of the extravagant Persian mosques, almost every surface covered by shimmering turquoise-blue tiles and the whole thing topped by a great 51m-high dome, is the Imam Mosque (p213), in Esfahan in Iran, built in 1638.

Mosque of Ibn Tulun

The Mosque of Ibn Tulun (p105), built in 879 in Cairo, may be the first building to ever employ the pointed arch that has since come to typify Islamic architecture. It also has a wonderful spiral minaret based on the Iraqi model.

Mosque of Qaitbey

Built in 1474, the Mosque of Qaitbey (p105) is in Cairo. It's the most exquisite of the region's vast legacy of Mamluk buildings with perhaps the best carved-stone dome to be seen anywhere.

Selimiye Mosque

More modest and not as well known as his İstanbul mosques, but architectural historians rightly regard this, the most harmonious and elegant of Sinan's works, as his masterpiece. The Selimiye Mosque (p576) was built in 1575 in Edirne, Turkey.

Süleymaniye Camii

Sinan was the master builder of the Ottoman Empire and his work is found throughout the region. Fittingly, the grandest of his mosques, the Süleymaniye Camii (p570), built in 1557, dominates the skyline of the former Imperial capital of İstanbul.

Umayyad Mosque

An adaptation of a Christian cathedral (itself erected on the site of a Roman temple), the Umayyad Mosque (p514), built in 705, is notable for its age, size and the stunning Byzantine-style golden mosaics that cover the courtyard walls. It's in Damascus, Syria.

The Mamluks were eventually defeated by the Ottoman Turks, who followed up their military gains with an equally expansive campaign of construction. Designed on the basic principle of a dome on a square, and instantly recognisable by their slim pencil-shaped minarets, Ottoman mosques can be found throughout Egypt, Israel and the Palestinian Territories, Lebanon, Syria and Iraq. The most impressive monuments of this era, however, were built at the heart of the empire – the Süleymaniye Camii (p570) in İstanbul and the Selimiye Mosque (p576) in Edirne, both the work of the Turkish master architect Sinan.

Of all the non-Gulf regions of the Middle East, Persia was the one area that did not fall to the Turks. The Persian Safavid dynasty proved strong enough to hold the Ottomans at bay and thus Iran, and neighbouring Afghanistan, have a very different architectural tradition from elsewhere in the Middle East. Persian architecture has its roots not in Arab or Turkish forms, but in those of the eastern lands occupied by the Mongols who swept down from Central Asia. Their grand buildings are very simple in form but made startling by the sumptuous use of cobalt-blue and turquoise tiling, which often covers every available surface.

JUST LOOK, NO BUY

However averse you may be to the idea, you're likely at some stage to find yourself in a carpet shop. Resistance is futile. The secret is to accept the hospitality, enjoy the ceremony and not feel in the least obliged to buy – easier said than done if you're in Turkey and Egypt.

The process starts with a passing glance as you walk through one of the souq's lanes. You're invited inside and offered sweet tea or an adrenaline surge of coffee while you sit around and discuss the fact that the salesman (they're all men and all very charming) has a brother or uncle living in your country and indeed, what providence, sold a carpet, a very beautiful carpet, from his private collection, to one of your countrymen just last week.

While you wait for your drinks, why not look, looking is free, just for the pleasure of your eyes. Choices are unfurled by a boy, while another brings tea and coffee too hot to drink quickly. You ask a price and are told in a conspiratorial whisper that, because you have not come as part of a group, you will be offered a 30% discount. You're an honoured guest in their country and hospitality demands such things.

The carpets you don't like are rolled up and stacked against a wall. The designs are explained and more young men arrive to hold the carpets at viewing level. Suddenly the room is filled with young men at your service. Carpets are expertly rolled into tiny bundles to show how easily they will fit in your bag for carrying home.

This is the point at which you may decide that carpet buying is not for you. You say that you want to think about it. The salesman, possibly now casting furtive glances in the direction of the shop owner, is suddenly serious, knowing full well that the vast majority of tourists never return despite promises to do so. Prices drop. They may even do so dramatically. Looks of sadness will be exchanged that such beautiful carpets must be let go for such a price. As you walk out the door – you may be left to find your own way out as hospitality evaporates – you may hear dark mutterings and grim curses directed towards you. More likely, you'll look over your shoulder and see the salesman deflated on a chair, like a child who has lost his toy.

If you do decide to stay, bargain and buy, most of what the salesmen say about their carpets is true (apart from the price) – they are a wonderful keepsake to remember your journey. Your carpet is wrapped before you can reconsider. You hand over your credit card. The salesman looks aggrieved one last time. Cash is not possible, madam? Credit cards involve too much paperwork, sir.

You leave with your carpet under your arm and walk past all the other carpet dealers who'll tell you that you paid too much. You can't help but smile at the whole performance. Rest assured, the man who sold you the carpet is smiling too.

CARPETS

Although carpets can be admired and bought across the region, and Turkish carpets and kilims (double-sided flat-woven mats without knots) are highly regarded, there's no disputing the fact that Persian carpets are king.

Persian carpets are more than just a floor covering to an Iranian: they are a display of wealth, an investment, an integral part of religious and cultural festivals, and used in everyday life (eg as prayer mats). Most handmade carpets are made from wool and are distinguishable by the fact that the pattern is easily distinct on the underside. The wool is spun, and then rinsed, washed and dried. It's then dyed, either with natural dye or chemicals. Nomadic carpet weavers often use high-grade wool and create unique designs, but they use unsophisticated horizontal looms so the carpets are often less refined. In villages, small workshops use upright looms, which create carpets with more variety, but the designs are often uninspiring. City factories usually mass-produce carpets of monotonous design and variable quality.

Carpets are made with Persian knots, which loop around one horizontal thread and under the next; or Turkish knots, looped around two horizontal threads, with the yarn lifted between them. The higher the number of knots per square centimetre, the better the quality – and, of course, the higher the price. A normal carpet has up to 30 knots per square centimetre; a medium-grade piece 30 to 50 knots; and a fine one, 50 knots or more. A nomadic weaver can tie around 8000 knots each day; a weaver in a factory about 12,000 knots.

For information on taking your Persian carpet(s) home, see p243.

The Root of Wild Madder: Chasing the History, Mystery and Lore of the Persian Carpet, by Brian Murphy, is a travelogue through the countries of finest carpet production and a buyer's guide to quality, interwoven with stories told by individual designs.

Kilim: The Complete Guide: History, Pattern, Technique, Identification, by Alastair Hull et al, is for the would-be collector; this is the best book of its kind.

CINEMA

Egypt, Lebanon, Iran, Turkey and Israel and the Palestinian Territories have strong film-making traditions and the films from these countries are increasingly being distributed internationally to widespread acclaim. The fact remains, however, that many of the region's best films appeal more to an international audience (or are restricted from being shown in their own countries) and you're more likely to see the better work back home than in the Middle East itself.

Egypt

Egypt was once the Bollywood of the Middle East, but its film industry is widely perceived to be in serious decline. In its halcyon years, Cairo's film studios would be turning out more than 100 movies annually and filling cinemas throughout the Arab world. These days the average number of films made is around 20 per year. Most of these are genre movies relying on moronic slapstick humour and hysterics rather than acting, and usually a little belly-dancing thrown in for spice.

The one director of note is Yousef Chahine, a staple of international film festivals (which are virtually the only places you'll get to see his work) and recipient of a lifetime achievement award at Cannes in 1997. The Alexandria-born Chahine has directed over 40 films, the most notable of which have been the 1960s classic *The Choice* (the result of a collaboration with distinguished Egyptian novelist Naguib Mahfouz), *Sparrow* (1972), *An Egyptian Story* (1982) and the politically charged *Destiny* (1998).

The Encyclopedia of Arab Women Filmmakers, by Rebecca Hillauer, is one of few works to challenge the male dominance in Middle Eastern film making.

Lebanon

Lebanon's small film industry is showcased each year at the Mid East Film Festival Beirut. Some of the well-known film makers include Maroun Baghdadi (who won an award at the Cannes Film Festival), Samir

Nasri, Mohammed Sweid, and Paris-based Jocelyn Saab, who made *Sweet Adolescent Love* and the popular *Once Upon a Time in Beirut*. The critically acclaimed Randa Chahal-Sabbagh won the Venice Festival's Silver Lion award for her 2002 film *The Kite*. If you get a chance, see *West Beyrouth* (1998), the story of three teenagers. The film begins on 13 April 1975, the first day of the Lebanese civil war; the cinematography is supremely slick, which is not surprising given that first-time director Ziad Doueirim was formerly Quentin Tarantino's cameraman.

Randa Chahal-Sabbagh has won the Lebanese government's highest civilian honour, the Order of the Cedar, but her 1998 film *Civilised*, about the Lebanese civil war, was censored (47 out of 90 minutes were cut) and Chahal-Sabbagh refused to show the film in her country.

Iran
The real success story of the region is Iranian cinema. Despite serious straitjacketing by the authorities regarding content, Iranian directors have been turning out some extremely sophisticated and beautifully made films that have won tremendous plaudits on an international level. Their accent on character and story stands in refreshing contrast to much of modern cinema, particularly that of Hollywood. Such is the standing of Iranian cinema in Europe and America that new films by Iranian directors are regularly given first-run screenings in cities such as London, Paris and San Francisco.

Makhmalbaf Film House (www.makhmalbaf .com), the website of Iran's premier film family, hosts a full list of films, independent reviews and essays by the directors themselves.

Abbas Kiaorstami is widely regarded as Iran's preeminent film maker. His *The Taste of Cherry* won the Palme d'Or at Cannes in 1997 and his other works include *Close-Up* (1990), *Life and Nothing More* (1991), *Through the Olive Trees* (1994) and *The Wind Will Carry Us* (1999). The internationally acclaimed Mohsen Makhmalbaf is the best known of a prolific family of highly talented directors, among whom is his outstandingly talented, award-winning daughter Samira. Jafar Panahi's *The Circle* (2000), a brave and powerful account of the way women are oppressed in present-day Iran, and *Crimson Gold* (2003), a depressing tale of disillusionment with Iran's Islamic Revolution, are the most recent additions to an extraordinary body of work. A young documentary film maker of note is Nikki Karimi whose searing *To Have or Not to Have* explores the double standards applied to men and women when it comes to an inability to have children. Director Bahman Qobadi was honoured at Cannes in 2000 and Babak Paymi's *Secret Ballot* (2001) is another outstanding work.

Close Up: Iranian Cinema, Past, Present and Future, by Hamid Dabashi, is the definitive guide to the Middle East's most sophisticated film industry, surveying the major directors and the social context of the Islamic Revolution under which they operate.

Israel & the Palestinian Territories
The conflict between the Israelis and the Palestinians not surprisingly weighs heavily upon films from this troubled land, but some outstanding movies have emerged from both sides of the divide. There is rarely conflict between the directors from these two cultures, as most tend to belong to the liberal, more-moderate strands of Israeli and Palestinian society.

Amos Gitai has won plaudits for his sensitive and balanced portrayal of the conflict, while Avi Mograbi goes a step further with no-holds-barred depictions of the difficulties of life for the Palestinians under Israeli occupation. Savi Gabizon's multidimensional black comedy, *Nina's Tragedies*, has won numerous awards at home and abroad. Yeal Kipper Zaretzky's documentary study of the Holocaust, *Permission to Remember* (1993), is a fine work, as is anything by another documentary film maker Yoav Shamir. Daniel Wachsmann and Ilan Yagoda are two bright stars of Israeli cinema.

One Palestinian director who has made an international impact is the Hebron-born Michael Khalifa whose excellent *Images from Rich Memories*, *The Anthem of the Stone* and *Wedding in Galilee* (1998) were shot covertly inside the Palestinian Territories. Rasheed Masharawi has been rejected in some Palestinian circles for working with Israeli production companies, but the quality of his work is undeniable. Elie Suleiman's work – which includes *Cyber Palestine*, *Divine Intervention* and the notable *Chronicle of a Disappearance* – is a wonderful corpus of quietly angry and intensely powerful films. Azza al-Hassan is one of the finest Palestinian documentary film makers.

Turkey

Turkey is a shining light of the Middle Eastern film scene. Yilmaz Güney's Palme d'Or–winning *Yol* (The Road) was not initially shown in Turkish cinemas; its portrait of what happens to five prisoners on a week's release was too grim for the authorities to take. Güney's *The Herd* has also been shown in the West. More recently, Reis Çelik's *Hoşça Kal Yarın* (Goodbye Tomorrow) tells the story of the three student leaders of Turkey's revolutionary left in the 1970s.

The Companion Encyclopedia of Middle Eastern and North African Film, edited by Oliver Leaman, opens a window on the film industries in, among other countries, Egypt, Iran, Iraq, Lebanon, Libya, the Palestinian Territories, Syria and Turkey.

Other Countries

Although none of the other countries in the Middle East have major film industries, some outstanding directors have emerged from within their ranks. Syrian directors are little known beyond their own borders, with Nabil Maleh *(The Leopard and Mr Progressive)*, Omar Amiralay *(Daily Life in a Syrian Village)*, Mohammed Malass *(City Dreams)* and the up-and-coming Ziad Doueri *(West Beirut)* the most recognisable names.

At the 2005 Cannes Film Festival, Hiner Saleem marked the tentative resurgence of Iraqi cinema with the stirring *Kilometre Zero*.

TELEVISION

Middle Eastern TV has been transformed in recent years with the near-universal availability of satellite channels, although, it must be said, the quality of most drama and comedy is quite – how shall we put it? – lame to Western tastes. The only exception is Israel and, to a lesser extent Turkey and Lebanon. Maybe that's why so many TVs you'll encounter across the region are permanently tuned to 24-hour Gulf-based news or Lebanese music channels.

For information on the Al-Jazeera network, see p36.

DECORATIVE ARTS

The arts of the Middle East are largely the arts of Islam, typified in the minds of the non-Muslim by exotic curves and arabesques, and by intricate geometric patterning. The long-standing figurative art

ARAB BIG BROTHER

For the briefest of moments in 2004, Middle Eastern TV had an alternative to the standard fare of overwrought Egyptian soap operas, religious scholars arguing the merits of Quranic minutiae and government news broadcasts that celebrate diplomatic niceties as news. Indeed, few shows have captured the imagination of the Arab world quite like the Arab version of the worldwide *Big Brother* phenomenon.

For two weeks, the show *Al-Ra'is* (The Boss) – which was based in the Gulf emirate of Bahrain and offered prize money of US$100,000 – had viewers across the region glued to their TV sets agonising over how the Jordanian salsa-dancing jeweller would cope with the karate teacher from Kuwait, or whether romance would flourish between the Bahraini actress and the Iraqi musician. And few could quite understand why the Lebanese contestant thought that he would need 20 pairs of trousers to see him through his period of seclusion.

The show's producers made every effort to avoid controversy, including segregated sleeping areas for the show's 12 male and female contestants and providing a prayer room for the devout among them.

It didn't last long. During the first episode, only one of the female inhabitants wore a traditional black *abeyya* (full-length robe). By the second instalment, protesters were on the streets and conservative clerics were condemning the show as un-Islamic. For the first time since the reality-TV-show juggernaut was born, *Big Brother*, or rather *The Boss*, was tamed. The show went off the air, never to return.

Calligraphy is an expression of the belief that Arabic is a holy language revealed by Allah to the Prophet Mohammed in the Quran. Derived from the Greek words *kala* (beautiful) and *graphos* (writing), calligraphy was a way of glorifying the word of God.

traditions in Asia Minor, Persia and areas further east were never completely extinguished by Islam, which restricts the portrayal of living figures. The Turks and Iraqis continued to produce beautiful illuminated manuscripts, while the Persians retained their art of miniature painting, which is still practised today in places such as Esfahan in present-day Iran.

In the areas of calligraphy, metalwork, ceramics, glass, carpets and textiles, however, Islamic art has a cultural heritage of unsurpassable richness – one that in turn has had great influence on the West. Middle Eastern artisans and craftspeople (Armenians, Christians and Jews as well as Muslims) have for more than 1200 years applied complex and sumptuous decorations to often very practical objects to create items of extraordinary beauty. Plenty such items are on view in the region's museums, including the Topkapı Palace (p566) in İstanbul. However, to appreciate the achievements of Islamic art, just visit one of the older mosques in which tiling, wood carving, inlaid panelling and calligraphy are often combined in exaltation of Allah. Islamic art is, for a Muslim, foremost an expression of faith.

Artistic tradition in the Western sense of painting and sculpture has historically been largely absent in Islamic countries because Islam has always regarded the depiction of living beings as idolatrous.

Perhaps the most sophisticated of these decorative arts is calligraphy, a style of writing elevated to an art form of astonishing intricacy to accommodate Islam's restriction on portraying living figures. Early calligraphers used an angular script called Kufic that was perfect for stone carving. Modern calligraphy uses a flowing cursive style, more suited to working with pen and ink.

Another of the region's signature art forms is the mosaic, traditionally made from tiny squares called tesserae, chipped from larger rocks. The tesserae are naturally coloured, and carefully laid on a thick coating of wet lime. Mosaics depicting hunting, deities and scenes from daily life once adorned the floors and palaces of the Byzantine Middle East. The art of mosaic making continues in places such as Madaba in Jordan, while some of the finest ancient works are on display in the Jamahiriya Museum (p473) in Tripoli, Libya.

LITERATURE
Poetry

Poetry has traditionally been the preeminent literary form in the Middle East and all the best-known figures of classical Arabic and Persian literature are poets – men regarded as possessing knowledge forbidden to ordinary people, supposedly acquired from demons. The favourite demon seems to have been alcohol. Abu Nuwas, faithful companion to the 8th-century Baghdadi caliph Haroun ar-Rashid, and a rather debauched fellow, left behind countless odes to the wonders of wine, as did the Persian Omar Khayyam, famed 11th-century composer of *rub'ai* (quatrains). The current Iranian regime prefers to celebrate Khayyam for his work as a mathematician.

The tradition continues today, maintained by figures of international standing such as Syrian-born Adonis and Mahmoud Darwish. Darwish is the Arab world's bestselling poet and his public readings attract huge crowds. He has been translated into more than 20 languages and is the bestselling poet in France.

Modern Arabic Poetry, by Salma Khadra Jayyusi, can be a bit dense for the uninitiated, but there's no more comprehensive work about the Middle East's most enduring and popular literary form.

Novels & Short Stories

Arab literature in the form of novels and short stories is only as old as the 20th century. An increased exposure to European influences, combined with nascent Arab nationalism in the wake of the Ottoman Empire's decline, led to the first stirrings. The Egyptians and Lebanese have been the most active in the field, but much of the credit for the maturing of Arabic literature can be credited to one single author, Naguib Mahfouz, who was unquestionably the single most important writer of fiction in Arabic in the 20th century.

A life-long native of Cairo, Mahfouz began writing in the 1930s. From Western-copyist origins he went on to develop a voice that is uniquely of the Arab world and that draws its inspiration from storytelling in the coffeehouses and the dialect and slang of the streets. His achievements were recognised internationally when he was awarded the Nobel prize for literature in 1988. Much of his work has since been made available in English-language translations.

Nights and Horses and the Desert: An Anthology of Classical Arabic Literature, edited by Robert Irwin, traces the roots of Arabic poetry from the Quran to the modern day.

MIDDLE EASTERN SUPERHEROES

The Middle East has adapted many icons of Western culture to suit its own purposes, ranging from the novel to 24-hour news channels and McDonald's restaurants. Now it's the turn of the comic book.

Middle East Heroes is the brainchild of the Egypt-based AK Comics, which, instead of Superman, Batman and Wonder Woman, created Zein, the time-travelling pharaoh, Aya, who is turned into a Princess of Darkness after she is orphaned and adopted by an underground fighting group, and Rakan, a heroic warrior armed with a magic sword from ancient Arabia.

The age-old comic book formula of good struggling against evil is given a uniquely Middle Eastern twist as the comic entrusts the superheroes with the task of saving the region from evil after 55 years of war between two unnamed superpowers. Among those whom Zein and Rakan battle for control over the 'City of All Faiths' are shadowy forces that go by the name of the 'Zios Army' who are 'still clinging to their extreme views'. Nor do the cartoonists shirk from taking on the big issues of the day: they depict a female character, Jalila, who developed unrivalled superhuman powers as a result of a nuclear explosion, in full superhero equality with her male counterparts. The comic has thus far evaded the region's rigorous censors, save for the decision in some countries to black out Jalila's stomach. The comic is published in Arabic and English.

After Cairo, the other beacon for Arab literature is Beirut. As well as being the focus of Lebanese literary life, Beirut has been the refuge of Syrian writers escaping their own repressive regime and of refugee Palestinians. Of the latter category Liana Badr, who fled after the Israelis captured her home town of Jericho in 1967, has two books available in English: *The Eye of the Mirror* and the short-story collection *A Balcony over the Fakihani*. Both draw heavily on her first-hand experiences of upheaval.

Of the native Lebanese writers, the most famous is Hanan al-Shaykh, who writes extremely poignant but humorous novels *(Beirut Blues, The Story of Zahra* and *Women of Sand and Myrrh)* that resonate beyond the bounds of the Middle East.

THE BEST OF MIDDLE EASTERN LITERATURE

Given that the Arabic novel is largely a 20th-century phenomenon, most Middle Eastern novels are a fantastic companion to any journey through the region, charting as they do so many of the grand themes of the Middle East's recent political and social history. Here are our favourites:

- *Arabic Short Stories*, translated by Denys Johnson-Davies, is an excellent primer with tales from all over the Middle East gathered by the world's foremost translator of Arabic literature.
- *Beirut Blues*, by Hanan al-Shaykh, deals with the fallout from the Lebanese civil war, as seen through the eyes of a young woman trying to decide whether to stay or flee abroad following in the steps of friends and family.
- *The Black Book*, by Orhan Pamuk, is a Kafkaesque tale of an abandoned husband's search for his wife in İstanbul, written by Turkey's most outstanding writer.
- *The Harafish*, by Naguib Mahfouz, would be the desert-island choice if we were allowed only one work by Mahfouz, but everything he's written is worth reading.
- *The Map of Love*, by Ahdaf Soueif, is the Booker-nominated historical novel about love and clashing cultures by the London-based Anglo-Egyptian writer; any book by Soueif is epic and finely wrought.
- *Mehmet My Hawk*, by Yaşar Kemal, is the Nobel laureate's most famous (and very readable) work, which deals with near-feudal life in the villages of eastern Mediterranean Turkey.
- Although written in the 11th century and translated into English in the 19th century, the *Rubaiyat* of Omar Khayyam became a sensation throughout Europe and America, and a major influence on Western poetry ever since.
- Although Lebanese by birth, Amin Maalouf lives in Paris and writes in French. He's the author of several excellent historical novels, including *Samarkand*, a highly romantic tale that begins with Omar Khayyam and ends on the *Titanic*.
- *The Thousand and One Nights* is an anonymously written, mixed bag of colourful and fantastic tales that are widely regarded as the high point of historical storytelling, as appealing to adults as to children (see opposite).
- The Quran, Islam's holy book, is considered to be the highlight of classical Arabic literature.
- *Pillars of Salt*, by Fadia Faqir, is a skilfully conceived work exploring social divisions and the vulnerability of women against the backdrop of the British Mandate in Jordan.
- Amos Oz' fans will no doubt have their favourites but *My Michael* captures the turmoil of Jerusalem during the Suez Crisis of 1956 as reflected in the private torment of a woman in an unhappy marriage.
- *The Stone of Laughter*, by Hoda Barakat, is a lyrical work by a young Lebanese writer that beautifully charts Lebanon's civil war as seen through the eyes of a character torn apart by the issues of identity and sexuality.

> ### THE THOUSAND & ONE NIGHTS
>
> After the Bible, *The Thousand and One Nights* (in Arabic, 'Alf Layla w'Layla', also known as *The Arabian Nights*) must be one of the most familiar yet unread books in the English language. It owes its existence in the popular consciousness almost entirely to the Disneyfied tales of *Aladdin*, *Sinbad* and *Ali Baba & the 40 Thieves* that appear in children's books, animated films and Christmas pantomimes.
>
> That the actual text itself is largely ignored is unsurprising considering that in its most famous English-language edition (translated by the Victorian adventurer Sir Richard Burton), it runs to 16 volumes. In fact, an old Middle Eastern superstition has it that nobody can read the entire text of *The Thousand and One Nights* without dying.
>
> But what constitutes the entire text is a matter of academic debate. *The Thousand and One Nights* is a portmanteau title for a mixed bag of colourful and fantastic tales, and the many historical manuscripts that carry the famed title collectively contain many thousands of stories, sharing a core of exactly 271 common tales. They all, however, employ the same framing device – that of a succession of stories related nightly by the wily Sheherezade to save her neck from the misogynistic King Shahriyar.
>
> Sheherezade and her tales have their origins in pre-Islamic Persia, but over the ages (and in endless retellings and rewritings) they were adapted, expanded and updated, drawing on sources as far flung as Greece and India. As they're known to us now, the stories are mainly set in the semifabled Baghdad of Haroun ar-Rashid (r AD 786–809), and in Mamluk-era (1250–1517) Cairo and Damascus. In particular regarding the last two cities, *The Thousand and One Nights* provides a wealth of rich period detail, from shopping lists and prices of slaves, through to vivid descriptions of types and practices of assorted conjurers, harlots, thieves and mystics. *The Thousand and One Nights* is revered as much by medieval scholars as it is by Walt Disney's animators.

Turkey's best-known writer is probably Yaşar Kemal, winner of the 1998 Nobel prize for literature. Author of the moment is Orhan Pamuk whose books are walking out of bookshops in record numbers. He is widely published in a great number of languages, including English.

The most widely translated Israeli writer is the Jerusalem-born Amos Oz, whose name regularly appears as a candidate for the Nobel prize for literature. His work includes essays and award-winning novels with themes that go to the heart of the pride and angst at the centre of modern Israeli life.

The Libyan writer most widely read throughout the Arab world is Ibrahim al-Kouni, a native of Ghadames. His often disturbing depictions of life in the Sahara are particularly powerful, most notably *The Bleeding of the Stone*.

For the best literature from each country of the Middle East, see the Arts section of each individual country chapter.

An Introduction to Arabic Literature, by Roger Allen, is a worthy addition to the canon of literary criticism with extensive translations of seminal texts and lively analysis; it's especially good on *The Thousand and One Nights*.

MUSIC

If you're a music-lover, you'll adore the Middle East. Music is all pervasive, filling the narrow lanes of the souqs, with crooners and pop divas blasting out of seemingly every shop doorway and every taxi driver's cassette player.

The diversity of music is huge as in the West, and it's impossible to do it justice in such a brief space. Although we make the division here into three broad musical types – Arabic classical, pop and traditional music – there are many, many artists who fail to fit neatly under any of these headings or conversely cross over into all three.

Arabic Classical

Tonality and instrumentation aside, classical Arabic music differs from that of the West in one important respect: in the Middle East the orchestra is always there primarily to back the singer.

The kind of orchestra that backs such a singer is a curious cross-fertilisation of East and West. Western-style instruments, such as violins and many of the wind and percussion instruments, predominate, next to such local species as the oud (lute) and tabla (drum). The sounds that emanate from them are anything but Western – all the mellifluous seduction of Asia in the backing melodies alongside the vaguely melancholic, languid tones you would expect from a sun-drenched Middle Eastern summer.

Rumour has it that the coup that brought Libyan leader Colonel Mu'ammar Gaddafi to power on 1 September 1969 was delayed so as not to clash with an Umm Kolthum concert, thereby avoiding a public backlash against the coup leaders.

The all-time favourite voice of classical Arabic music is Egyptian-born songstress Umm Kolthum (see the boxed text below). The 1950s were the golden age of Arabic music and gave rise to a lesser pantheon of stars, although they never achieved the heights scaled by Umm Kolthum. Two male crooners who owed much of their popularity to their omnipresence on cinema screens in countless Cairo-produced romantic movies were Abdel Halim Hafez and Syrian-born Farid al-Atrache. As with Umm Kolthum, both of these male artists remain loved and widely listened to.

Of all these golden-era singers, only one is still active and that's Fairouz (see opposite).

Pop

Middle Eastern pop music is like its Western counterpart in that fashions change almost as regularly as the stars change hairstyles. Watch Arab MTV and you'll soon learn what's hot, although that doesn't necessarily mean that they'll be around tomorrow.

ARABIC

Characterised by a clattering, hand-clapping rhythm overlaid with synthesised twirlings and a catchy, repetitive vocal, the first true Arabic pop came out of Cairo in the 1970s. As the Arab nations experienced a population boom and the mean age decreased, a gap in popular culture had developed that the memory of the greats couldn't fill. Enter Arabic pop.

UMM KOLTHUM

The Egyptian singer Umm Kolthum was one of the towering figures of world 20th-century music and it's impossible to overestimate the breadth of her influence and popularity. A favourite of Egyptian president Gamal Abdel Nasser, Umm Kolthum had the ability to stop a nation whenever she performed. From the 1940s through to the '70s, her voice was that of the Arab world, a region that has never really fallen out of love with her voice nor with the fervour and hope of those tumultuous times that she represented. To the uninitiated she can sound rough and raucous, but the passion of her protracted love songs and *qasa'id* (long poems) was the very expression of the Arab world's collective identity. Egypt's love affair with Umm Kolthum (where she's known as Kawkab ash-Sharq, meaning 'Nightingale of the East') was such that on the afternoon of the first Thursday of each month, streets would become deserted as the whole country sat beside its radios to listen to her regular live-broadcast performance. When she died in 1975 her death caused havoc, with millions of mourners pouring out onto the streets of Cairo. Her appeal hasn't been purely confined to the Arab world either – former Led Zeppelin vocalist Robert Plant was reported as saying that one of his lifetime ambitions was to re-form the Middle Eastern Orchestra, Umm Kolthum's group of backing musicians.

FAIROUZ

A Lebanese torch singer with a voice memorably described as 'silk and flame in one', Fairouz has enjoyed star status throughout the Arab world since recording her first performances in Damascus in the 1950s. Along with her writers, the Rahbani brothers, Fairouz embraced a wide range of musical forms, blending Lebanese folk tales with flamenco and jazz. For all her experimentation, her lyrics embodied the recurring themes of love, loss, Lebanon and religious praise. During the 1960s and '70s her music – and three starring roles in Lebanese films – made her the embodiment of freewheeling Beirut, then referred to as the 'Paris of the Middle East'. During the Lebanese civil war she became a symbol of hope and an icon for Lebanese identity, resolutely refusing to sing inside Lebanon while her countrymen continued to kill each other.

After the war, and after a series of performances at church services, Fairouz returned to the Lebanese stage. In 1995 her concert in downtown Beirut drew a crowd of 40,000 newly hopeful Lebanese – surely one of the great concerts of all time. The fact that the concert took place in what was once a no-man's-land in formerly divided Beirut merely confirmed her iconic status and became a symbol of Lebanon's return to peace. Across the Arab world, 125 million tuned in and her record sales have now topped 80 million. Her appearance at the 1998 Baalbek Festival was also a landmark and confirmed her stunning return to form, while a 1999 concert in Las Vegas drew the biggest crowd since Frank Sinatra. Now in her seventies, Fairouz has shown that she remains a powerful figure in the life of the nation. After the former prime minister Rafik Hariri was assassinated in 2005, she refused to perform at Easter Mass, saying 'I will not sing to a divided people'.

The blueprint for the new youth sound (which became known as *al-jeel*, from the word for generation) was set by Egyptian Ahmed Adawiyya, the Arab world's first 'pop star'.

During the 1990s there was a calculated attempt to create a more up-market sound, with many musicians mimicking Western dance music. Tacky electronics were replaced with moody pianos, Spanish guitars and thunderous drums. Check out Amr Diab, whose heavily produced songs have made him the bestselling artist ever in the Arab world (achieved with his 1996 album *Nour al-Ain*).

Diab is Egyptian but in recent years the Egyptians have been beaten at their own game and many of the biggest-selling artists come from elsewhere. Heading the current crop of megastar singers (the Arabic music scene is totally dominated by solo vocalists, there are no groups) are Majida al-Rumi of Lebanon and Iraqi-born Kazem al-Saher. Unfortunately, in the largely shrink-wrapped world of pop, regional influences are minimised and most artists have a tendency to sound the same, no matter where they come from.

Amr Diab World (www.amrdiabworld.com) is the glitzy homepage of the Arab world's most famous modern pop star; it ranges across all the vacuousness and strangely compelling kitsch that is modern Arab celebrity.

Arab Gateway – Music (www.al-bab.com/arab/music/music.htm) has everything from clear explanations of the basics for the uninitiated to links and downloads of contemporary Arab music.

TURKISH

In Turkey there is a thriving indigenous pop culture, with some of the leading artists breaking out from the Turkish ghetto and making a splash in countries such as France as well. Tarkan, for example, first recorded 'Simarik', a track better known to Western audiences as 'Kiss Kiss', courtesy of a cover by chart popper Holly Valance. Other superpopular pop stars include 'arabesque' luminary İbrahim Tatlises (also a constant fixture on Turkish TV) and the more versatile female singer Sezen Aksu (writer of 'Simarik').

Turkish folk music has also undergone a revival in recent years, as 'Türkü' – an updated, modern version often using electronic instruments coupled with traditional songs.

Traditional Music

Each of the Arabic countries of the Middle East has its own minority groups – ethnic, regional or religious – and most of these groups have their own musical traditions. The most high profile is the Nubian music of southern Egypt.

Unlike much Arabic music, with its jarring use of quarter tones, the Nubian sound is extremely accessible, mixing simple melodies and soulful vocals, and having a rhythmical quality that's almost African and a brass sound that could be from New Orleans. Probably the biggest name is Ali Hassan Kuban, who has toured all over Europe as well as in Japan, Canada and the US. He has several CDs out on the German Piranha label, including *From Nubia to Cairo* and *Walk Like a Nubian*. There's also a loose grouping of musicians and vocalists recording under the name Salamat who have several CDs out, also on Piranha, including the highly recommended, explosively brassy *Mambo al-Soudani*.

Although not as high profile as the Nubians, other notable Arabic folk music comes from the Bedouin. Whether produced by the Bedouin of Egypt, Jordan or Syria, the music is raw and traditional with little or no use of electronic instruments. The sound is dominated by the *mismar*, a twin-pipe clarinet, and the *rabab*, a twin-stringed prototype cello.

Much more refined than the Bedouin sound, but equally dominated by traditional instrumentation, is what's known as Sufi music. Sufis are religious mystics who use music and dance to attain a trancelike state of divine ecstasy. The music is bewitchingly hypnotic – a simple repeated melody usually played on the *nai* (reed pipe) accompanied by recitations of Sufi poetry. Sufi music and dance can be experienced in Konya, Turkey.

Also worth mentioning is the Libyan music style of *malouf*, which draws strongly on the old songs of Andalusia and is performed publicly during religious holidays and at weddings.

One form of traditional music undergoing a major revival and taking the world music scene by storm is *klezmer*, which has its roots among the Jewish communities of Eastern Europe. Its fast-paced, vocal-free form was ideally suited to Jewish celebrations and it has sometimes been branded as the Jewish jazz in recognition of its divergence from established musical styles. The modern genre has added vocals – almost always in Yiddish.

Sterns World Music (www.sternsmusic.com) is a reputable and independent London-based seller of world music CDs that allows you to search by country, artist or even region.

Al-Mashriq – Music (www.wlmashriq.hiof .no/base/music.htnl) offers more links to Arabic music than you can poke a stick at, from Umm Kolthum to traditional folk music with plenty of detours into Arabic pop along the way.

ARAB POP IDOL

Big Brother may not have taken off in the Arab world (see p72), but *Superstar* – think *Pop Idol* or the Eurovision Song Contest beamed out of Beirut – certainly has. This 21-week epic, shown annually in August on the Lebanese satellite TV channel Future TV and voted for by a regionwide television audience, has rapidly become compulsory viewing. In Lebanon, the show captured 98% of the TV audience during the finals. Undaunted by Muslim clerics' condemnation of the show as an un-Islamic pandering to Western culture, contestants quickly become national celebrities in their home countries. It's safe to say that when Ayman al-Aathar of Libya won the 2004 competition, Tripoli had never seen anything like it with rock-star-like adulation showered upon the winner on his return to the country: he even scored an audience with Colonel Gaddafi, who was not, incidentally, a fan of such frivolities. Similar celebrations occurred in Amman when Jordan's Diana Karzon won in 2003. The flipside is, of course, disappointment when a newfound national hero loses. When the Lebanese contestant lost in 2003, the Beirut audience rioted and when the Palestinian finalist failed to win as expected in 2004 there were street demonstrations in the Palestinian Territories.

THE TOP 20 OF MIDDLE EASTERN MUSIC

You'll surely disagree with some of our selections, but these are the recordings that we think could provide a memorable soundtrack to your journey and that you're most likely to hear while there. Our selection takes in some of the best of the old as well as some visions of the future of Middle Eastern music.

Umm Kolthum, Al-Atlaal (Egypt) The epic Egyptian-born songstress at the height of her powers.

Abdel Halim Hafez, Banaat al-Yom (Egypt) Part of a superb series showcasing original soundtracks to Abdel Halim's films from the 1950s and '60s.

Amr Diab, Awedony (Egypt) As good as it gets in Arab pop with loads of chic.

Mohammed Munir, Al-Malek (Egypt) Nubian music sung in Arabic with a jazzy twist.

Hakim, Talakik (Egypt) Streetwise musicians that you'll find yourself dancing to.

Yeir Dalal, Asmar (Israel) A stunning blend of powerful voice, oud and violin by an Israeli artist keen to reclaim his Iraqi heritage; his *Silan* album is also outstanding.

Habrera Hativeet, Barefoot (Israel) Avant-garde group that's not afraid to look beyond Israel's borders for inspiration.

Chehade Brothers, Bridge over the Mediterranean (Palestinian Territories) Multidimensional and thoroughly modern take on Arabic, Ottoman, Christian and Jewish fusion.

Sabreen, Death of the Prophet (Palestinian Territories) Traditional instruments with an upbeat tempo.

El Funoun, Zaghareed (Palestinian Territories) The finest recording of traditional Palestinian music.

Abdullah Chhadeh & Nara, Seven Gates (Syria) At once groovy and melancholy.

Fairouz, The Lady and the Legend (Lebanon) A recent compilation that sends chills down your spine.

Mercan Dede, Nar with Secret Tribe (Turkey) Pioneering fusion between Turkish Sufi music and Western electronica.

Omar Faruk Tekbilek, Alif (Turkey) Another fusion of the contemporary with folk and Sufi music.

Ensemble Kudsi Erguner, The Ottoman Heritage (Turkey) Classical Ottoman music.

Kazem al-Sahir, Bare Footed (Iraq) Award-winning offering from one of the Arab world's most popular singers and one who's a touch classier than most in the genre.

Nasseer Shamma, Le Luth de Baghdad (Iraq) The oud has never sounded so good.

Googosh, Pol (Iran) A reminder of the talents of Iran's premier pop diva from the prerevolution days.

Camelspotting Excellent compilation of contemporary Arab pop.

Les Plus Grands Classiques de la Musique Arabe The best of Arabic music's heyday from the 1950s and '60s.

The Music Scene

Sadly, it's very difficult to see live music almost anywhere in the Middle East. Artists don't generally perform gigs and there are no live music clubs as such.

Other than the odd festival (see Festivals & Events in the Directory section of each individual country chapter for details), your best chance of catching a performance is at a wedding or party, which is the stage on which nearly all Arab singers and musicians get their start. Thursday night is the big wedding night and favoured venues are open-air restaurants or hotels. The exception to this is İstanbul, which has a vibrant live music scene centred on the backstreets of the Beyoğlu district.

In any event, when it comes to Arabic pop, its true home is not the stage but the cassette. Although the situation is changing as Middle Eastern music attracts a wider audience, artists traditionally had little regard for production values and the music was slapped down in the studio and mass produced on cheap tapes in their thousands. Every town and city has numerous kiosks and shops selling tapes of whoever's the flavour of the moment, plus a selection of the classics. Shopkeepers are usually only too happy to play cassettes (or, in some stores in larger cities, CDs) before you buy, although at only a dollar or two a pop you can afford to take risks.

Songlines (www.song lines.co.uk) is the premier world music magazine that features interviews with stars, extensive CD reviews and a host of other titbits that will broaden your horizons and prompt many additions to your CD collection.

Environment

The Middle East is geographically far more diverse than the reputation of its desert heartland would suggest. The region is also home to some of the most pressing environmental issues of our time, most notably the shortage of water and the ability of Middle Eastern countries to share meagre resources without going to war.

For more information on travelling responsibly in the region, see p26.

THE LAND

The Nile, by Michael Pollard, is aimed at children in its examination of the great river's history, geography, environmental future and the impact of tourism, but chances are that most adults will end up learning plenty about this grand old river.

The Middle East is where the three continents of the Old World – Europe, Africa and Asia – coincide. Indeed, so vast is the region that most of İstanbul is geographically part of Europe, eastern Iran is decidedly Central Asian, while southern Libya and Egypt are unmistakably African. Although there are some geographical features that define the limits of what can be called the Middle East – for example, the natural boundaries of the Black and Caspian Seas, the Caucasus Mountains and the Sahara – what unifies this diverse region and preserves it as a discrete entity is cultural. The area springs from the heartland of Islamic and/or Arabic culture, the boundaries of which are generally held to be Iran's border with Afghanistan, the Bosphorus, which divides İstanbul, and the mountains of northeastern Libya.

On hearing the term Middle East, many people immediately imagine vast deserts of sand dunes and arid plains. However, the reality is that sand deserts form only a tiny percentage of the whole area – mainly in Egypt and Libya. Mountains and high plateaus abound in many countries: in Turkey, Iran and parts of Lebanon much of the area rises above 1000m. The highest mountains in the Middle East include the 5671m-high Mt Damavand in Iran and the 5137m-high Ağrı Dağı (Mt Ararat) in Turkey.

The countries of the Middle East are home to 4.5% of the world's population and up to half of the world's oil supplies, but they only receive 2% of the world's rainfall and possess just 0.4% of the world's recoverable water supplies.

The biggest rivers in the area include the Nile, the world's longest at 6695km bringing African waters through Egypt, and the Euphrates and Tigris, flowing from the Anatolian highlands through Syria and Iraq to the Gulf. Otherwise, with the exception of those in Turkey and northwest Iran, rivers flowing year-round and reaching the sea are a rarity in the region, due to the arid climate.

WILDLIFE
Animals

Royal Society for the Conservation of Nature (www.rscn.org.jo) is the website of Jordan's impressive environmental watchdog and an example to the other countries in the region where such organisations are sadly lacking.

Due to its position at the junction of three natural zones, the Middle East was once a sanctuary for an amazing variety of mammals, including leopards, cheetahs, oryxes (see opposite), aardwolves, striped hyenas and caracals. Crocodiles used to inhabit the Nile River, and lions roamed the Iran of old. Unfortunately, all of these are either now extinct in the region or on the brink of extinction due to intense hunting and the spread of human settlement. These days you'll be lucky to see any mammals other than domesticated camels, donkeys and water buffaloes, although in Sinai, the southern desert regions of Israel and the Palestinian Territories, and southern Libya there are ibexes, gazelles, wolves and rock hyraxes.

Turkey and Iran have similar animal life to that in the Balkans and much of Europe (bears, deer, jackals, lynxes, wild boars and wolves). In Iran there is a small population of cheetahs that is considered highly endangered.

Desert regions are home to small rodents such as desert foxes, sand rats, hares and jerboas, but most of these are nocturnal. You may well spot lizards, possibly scorpions and the occasional snake.

SAVING THE ARABIAN ORYX

For many in the Middle East, the Arabian oryx is more than 'just' an endangered species. Thought by some to be the unicorn of historical legend, the herbivorous oryx is a remarkable creature.

Adapted well to their desert environment, wild oryxes once had an uncanny ability to sense rain on the wind. One herd is recorded as having travelled up to 155km, led by a dominant female, to rain. In times of drought, oryxes have been known to survive 22 months without water, obtaining moisture from plants and leaves.

Although their white coats traditionally offered camouflage in the searing heat of the desert, the oryxes and their long curved horns were highly prized by hunters. By 1972 the Arabian oryx – which once roamed across much of Jordan, Syria and the Arabian Peninsula – was declared extinct in the wild. Nine lonely oryxes left in captivity around the world were pooled and taken to the Arizona Zoo for a breeding programme. They became known as the 'World Oryx Herd'.

In 1978 four male and four female oryxes were transported to Jordan and three more were sent from Qatar the following year. In 1979 the first calf, Dusha, was born and the oryx began the precarious road to recovery. By 1983 there were 31 oryxes in Shaumari Wildlife Reserve in eastern Jordan, where large enclosures and their treatment as wild animals served to facilitate their eventual release into the wild. In a significant landmark for environmentalists the world over, five oryxes were released into the Wadi Rum Protected Area in 2002 – a small, tentative step in what is hoped will be the recovery of wild oryxes in Jordan and further afield.

Birds

In contrast to the region's paucity of high-profile wildlife, the variety of bird life in the Middle East is exceptionally rich. As well as being home to indigenous species, the Middle East serves as a way station on migration routes between Asia, Europe and Africa. Israel claims to be the world's second-largest fly way (after South America) for migratory birds and the **Society for the Protection of the Nature of Israel** (SPNI; Map p298; ☎ 03-638 8653; tourism@spni.org.il; 4 Hasfela St, Tel Aviv 66183) has an excellent map and guide, the *Bird Trails of Israel*, detailing 14 bird-watching centres.

Other organisations worth contacting:

International Birding & Research Centre (☎ 08-633 5319; ibrce@eilatcity.co.il; PO Box 774, Eilat 88106, Israel)

International Birdwatching Center of the Jordan Valley (☎ 04-606 8396; www.bird watching.org.il)

Egypt's Sinai peninsula and Al-Fayoum Oasis, and Wadi Araba in Jordan also receive an enormous and varied amount of ornithological traffic. Egypt alone has recorded sightings of over 400 different species.

Iranian Cheetah Society (ICS; www.iraniancheetah .org) opens a window on Iran's most endangered species and the programmes underway to ensure the cheetah's survival in Iran.

Marine Life

Coral exists in both hard and soft forms, their common denominator being they are made of polyps – tiny cylinders ringed by waving tentacles that sting their prey and draw it into the stomach. During the day corals retract into their tube and only at night do they display their real colours.

There are about 1000 fish species in the Red Sea, many of them endemic, living and breeding in the coral reefs or nearby beds of seagrass. These include groper, wrasses, parrotfish and snapper. Others, such as sharks and barracuda, live in open waters and usually only venture into the reefs to feed or breed.

When snorkelling or diving, the sharks you are most likely to encounter include white- or black-tipped reef sharks. Tiger sharks and the huge plankton-eating whale sharks are generally found in deeper waters only. No divers or snorkellers have ever been killed by sharks in the Red Sea.

Birdlife International Middle East (www.bird lifemed.org) has the lowdown on major issues facing the region's bird species and the best places to view the Middle East's rich bird life.

Plants

Middle Eastern flora tends to be at its lushest and most varied in the north, where the climate is less arid, although after millennia of wood-cutting much of Turkey and Syria are now largely denuded. Only the Mediterranean coast west of Antalya, the Black Sea area and northeast Anatolia and, to a lesser extent, the Jebel Akhdar (Green Mountains) of northeastern Libya still have forests of considerable size. Yew, lime and fir trees predominate in areas where vegetation has not been reduced to scrub. The Iranian landscape is far more pristine and large areas – especially the Alborz Mountains region – remain densely forested with broad-leaved deciduous trees.

In Lebanon the Horsh Ehden Forest Nature Reserve is the last archetype of the ancient natural forests of Lebanon and is home to several species of rare orchids and other flowering plants. The cedars that Lebanon is famous for are now confined to a few mountain-top sites, most notably at Bcharré and near Barouk in the Chouf Mountains. For more information on the cedars of Lebanon, see p415.

In the Jordan Valley cedar, olives and eucalyptus are dominant. South towards the Dead Sea the vegetation gives way to mud and salt flats. South and west of the Dead Sea the only other spread of greenery is Egypt's Nile Delta, a fertile agricultural region.

Climate Change: Environment and Civilization in the Middle East, by Arie Issar and Zohar Mattanyah, is a sobering study of how the rise and fall of civilisations in the Middle East has always been intricately tied to environmental issues.

Africa & the Middle East: a Continental Overview of Environmental Issues, by Kevin Hillstrom, contains an excellent exploration of the Middle East's environmental past and future, with a special focus on how human populations impact upon the environment.

NATIONAL PARKS & WILDLIFE RESERVES

Your best chance of spotting something lies in visiting a reserve, although in the Middle East these are few and far between. It's possible to see gazelles and oryxes, once common features of the desert landscape, at the Shaumari Wildlife Reserve (p384) in the east of Jordan.

In Lebanon there are about 30 different species of mammals at the **Al-Shouf Cedar Nature Reserve** (☎ 05-311 230; www.shoufcedar.org), including mountain gazelles, striped hyenas, lynxes and hyraxes. One of the best reserves to visit for wildlife in Israel is Ein Gedi (p328), on the shores of the Dead Sea.

ENVIRONMENTAL ISSUES

In relation to the environment, the Middle East has an ever-increasing litany of woes, but the greatest of these is water. Indeed it is often said that the next great Middle Eastern war will be fought not over land but over water. It's a problem that has great political ramifications: Syria and Iraq have protested to Turkey over that country's building of dams at the headwaters of the Tigris and Euphrates Rivers, while Egypt has threatened military action against Sudan or any other upstream country endangering its access to

---

TOURISM & THE ENVIRONMENT

As one of the Middle East's largest industries, tourism itself is a major environmental issue. **Greenpeace Mediterranean** (☎ 961 1 755 665; supporters@greenpeace.org.lb; PO Box 13-6590, 1102 2140, Beirut, Lebanon) considers tourism to be one of the major causes of coastal destruction in Lebanon, and that's certainly also the case in Egypt and Turkey. It cites the dozens of yacht ports, 'land reclamation' projects and hotels that have been established illegally along the coast.

Problems also arise when destinations cannot cope with the number of tourists they attract, so that natural and social environments quickly become damaged. The prime example of this is the Red Sea coral reefs, which are under enormous threat from irresponsible tourism and opportunistic development. Also sites such as Petra are now having to consider limiting the number of visitors to lessen the human wear and tear on the monuments and surrounding landscape.

For information on how to reduce your environmental impact, see p26.

LIBYA'S GREAT MAN-MADE RIVER

In a region where water is fast becoming as precious as oil, Libya's Colonel Gaddafi has come up with a typically novel and grandiose solution. The idea behind the An-Nahr Sinai (Great Man-Made River; GMR) is simple: to tap the Sahara's underground water and pipe it from hundreds of desert wells to Libya's thirsty coastal cities. It is one of the world's most ambitious (and expensive) development projects. Colonel Gaddafi has dubbed the GMR 'the eighth wonder of the world'.

The sheer scale of the project defies belief. Two wells in the Tazerbo and Sarir Basins of southeastern Libya alone have a storage capacity of 10,000 cu km, from which two million cubic metres of water per day are piped to Benghazi and Sirt. The Murzuq Basin (over 450,000 sq km in size, with a storage capacity of 4800 cu km) provides the Sahel al-Jefara of northwestern Libya and Tripoli with 2.5 million cu metres a day. The massive Al-Kufra Basin (capacity 20,000 cu km) is another source of water for Libya's coastal cities. By the time the project is completed, there will be over 4000km of prestressed concrete pipes crisscrossing the country, with a daily capacity of six million cubic metres.

Away from the impressive scale of the project, there are fears that the GMR is wholly unsustainable. Recent radiocarbon dating suggests that the water currently stored beneath the Saharan sands dates from periods of greater rainfall 14,000 and 38,000 years ago, with smaller deposits from 7000 years ago. It is estimated that these water sources, which took thousands of years to fill, could be emptied within 50 years. Already there is evidence to suggest that the GMR has begun to lower the ground-water table in northwestern Libya with potentially disastrous consequences for agriculture. The amount of money spent on the first stage of the project alone could have been used to fund five desalinisation plants. Neighbouring Sudan and Egypt have also weighed in, concerned over the threat to their own underground water supplies.

If the GMR succeeds, it will be hailed as one of the most visionary feats of modern engineering. If it fails, the GMR promises to leave Libya without any freshwater supply at about the same time as its other underground resource, oil, runs out – a prospect that doesn't bear thinking about.

the waters of the Nile. Israel and the Palestinian Territories has outstanding water disputes with all of its neighbours. Demand far exceeds supply, and wastage on the land and in the cities exacerbates the situation.

In Jordan the virtual disappearance of water from the wetlands of the Azraq oasis (p383) has seen more than 20 species of fauna disappear from the country in the last two decades with even more threatened with extinction. Meanwhile Saddam Hussein's draining of the marshes (p263) in southern Iraq has been devastating for the region's bird life and people alike.

Beyond the water-shortage problem, air pollution (already critical in Cairo and Tehran), water pollution, deforestation, soil erosion, habitat and wildlife destruction, and conservation of natural resources are all becoming increasingly pertinent.

None of these issues can be viewed in isolation from the wider economic, social and political situations that prevail in the Middle East. Nor are the solutions simple. For example, in Egypt an ever-increasing human population puts great demands on the land and other natural resources. One possible solution would be to lower the rate of population growth. And yet, because such growth is closely linked to poor living conditions and issues such as a lack of education and health care, many conservationists argue that it is not reasonable to expect people with little money or food to worry about conservation in its widest sense. The root of the problem – poverty – desperately needs to be addressed. The problem is that few governments in the region have demonstrated the political will to tackle either problem. At the same time, Israel, which is by no means a poor country, has been criticised by Greenpeace for fouling the Jordan River with industrial sewage.

The Middle East Water Question: Hydropolitics and the Global Economy, by Tony Allan, can be hard to track down, but it's well worth it for the insight into the coming conflicts over water in the Middle East and beyond.

Water in the Middle East (www.columbia.edu/cu /lweb/indiv/mideast /cuvlm/water.html) hosts numerous links to articles on the Middle East's most pressing environmental issue.

Food & Drink

The countries of the Middle East may have their political and cultural differences, but there's one thing they have in common: an emphatic belief in the importance of good food. Travelling through the region you'll quickly realise that the regional cuisine is about celebrating friends, family, conversation and life itself. When travelling here, make sure you throw yourself wholeheartedly into the celebration.

STAPLES & SPECIALITIES

Mezze

Mezze isn't just a type of dish: it's a whole performance. The headline act when it comes to Levantine cuisine, it's the understudy to kebabs in Turkey and the trusted warm-up act to the region's other cuisines, guaranteed to get the audience enthusiastic for what's next on the culinary bill. Largely vegetable-based and bursting with colour and flavour, it's the region's most compelling culinary flourish.

The Spice Routes, by Chris and Carolyn Caldicott, is a fascinating overview of the history of the international spice trade and includes a number of recipes from the Middle East region.

It's usually perfectly acceptable for diners to construct an entire meal from the mezze list and forego the mains on offer. You will probably encounter the following dishes throughout the region (spellings on menus differ from country to country).

baba ghanooj – purée of grilled aubergines (eggplants) with tahini and olive oil

basturma – a cold, sliced meat cured with fenugreek

borek – pastry stuffed with salty white cheese or spicy minced meat with pine nuts; also known as *sambousek*

fatayer – triangular deep-fried pastries stuffed with spinach, meat or cheese

hummus bi tahina – cooked chickpeas ground into a paste and mixed with tahini, lemon and garlic; sometimes served with meat on top

kibbeh – minced lamb, burghul wheat and pine nuts made into a lemon-shaped patty and deep-fried

labneh – thick yogurt flavoured with garlic and sometimes with mint

loobieh – French bean salad with tomatoes, onions and garlic

mouhamarra – walnut and pomegranate syrup dip

muttabal – purée of aubergine mixed with tahini, yogurt and olive oil; similar to but creamier than *baba ghanooj*

shanklish – tangy, eye-wateringly strong goat's cheese served with onions, oil and tomatoes

tahini – paste made of sesame seeds and served as a dip

wara ainab – stuffed vine leaves, served both hot and cold; in Egypt also called *mahshi*

Bread

Bread *(khobz* or *'aish)* appears in a multiplicity of forms. Often unleavened and cooked over an open flame, it's used in lieu of cutlery to scoop up dips and ripped into pieces to wrap around morsels of meat. Depending on where you are, your day may start with a French-style croissant filled with zaatar (a fragrant mix of sun-dried thyme and sesame seeds with olive oil) or a crusty white loaf to accompany white cheese, tomatoes, cucumbers and olives. In Iran you'll be served thin and crisp *lavash* straight from the oven, and in Turkey, Egypt and Jordan you'll encounter a chewy, sesame-encrusted bread ring known respectively as a *simit, semit* or *ka'ik.* Lunch could be a felafel or shwarma stuffed into a freshly baked bread pocket *(shammy),* or a zaatar-smeared type of pizza known as a *manaeesh.* Other lunch or snack dishes include the Turkish *gözleme* (a thin pancake baked on a concave griddle over an open fire and filled with cheese, potato, spinach or mushrooms) or the Levantine equivalent, *saj*. Dinner is always served with baskets of bread to mop up mezze, and kebabs are often served with a tasty canopy of *lavash*. In all, bread is considered a gift from God and the essential accompaniment to any Middle Eastern meal.

Salads

Simplicity is the key to Middle Eastern salads, with crunchy fresh ingredients (including herbs) often being caressed by a shake of oil and vinegar at the table and eaten with relish as a mezze or as an accompaniment to a meat or fish main course. Three salads are found throughout the region and form an integral part of the local diet: fattoosh (toasted *khobz*, tomatoes, onions and mint leaves, sometimes served with a smattering of tangy pomegranate syrup); shepherd's salad (also known as oriental salad, a colourful mix of chopped tomatoes, cucumber, onion and pepper; extremely popular in Turkey, where it's known as *çoban salatası*); and the region's signature salad, tabbouleh (burghul wheat, parsley and tomato, with a tangy sprinkling of sesame seeds, lemon and garlic).

> Parsley was mentioned by Homer in the *Odyssey*. It's now the main ingredient in the region's most famous salad, tabbouleh.

Snack Food

Forget the bland international snack food served up by the global chains; once you've sampled the joys of Middle Eastern street food you'll never again be able to face dining under the golden arches or with the colonel.

The regional stars of the snack food line-up are shwarma and felafel, and they are both things of joy when served and eaten fresh. Shwarma is the Arabic equivalent of the Greek *gyros* sandwich or the Turkish döner kebap – strips are sliced from a vertical spit of compressed lamb or chicken, sizzled on a hot plate with chopped tomatoes and garnish, and then stuffed into a pocket of bread. Felafel is mashed chickpeas and spices formed into balls and deep-fried; a variation known as *ta'amiyya*, made with dried fava beans, is served in Egypt. The felafel balls are stuffed into a pocket of bread that's been smeared with tahini and then the whole thing is topped with some fresh salad, or sometimes with pickled vegetables. Delicious!

> The earliest physical evidence of an international spice trade is found in the wall reliefs of the Funerary Temple of Hatshepsut in Luxor, Egypt.

Of course, each country has its particular snack food speciality. In Egypt look out for shops sporting large metal tureens in the window: these specialise in the vegetarian delight *kushari*, a delicate mix of noodles, rice, black lentils and dried onions, served with an accompanying tomato sauce that's sometimes fiery with chilli. In neighbouring Libya, the local version is called *rishda*.

In Lebanon, nothing beats grabbing a freshly baked *fatayer bi sbanikh* (spinach pastry) from one of the hole-in-the-wall bakeries that dot city streets. In Turkey, visitors inevitably fall deeply in love with melt-in-the-mouth *su böreği*, a noodle-like pastry oozing cheese and butter. Variations of the pizza abound, one of the most delicious being Egypt's fiteer, featuring a base of thin, filo-style pastry. Try it topped with salty haloumi cheese, or even with a mixture of sugar-dusted fruit.

> *Duqqa* (Arabic for 'to pound') is an ancient mixture of spices used as a condiment in Egyptian kitchens. It combines dry roasted cumin, coriander, sesame and nigella seeds, as well as salt, pepper, nuts and mint.

The most unassuming of all Middle Eastern fast foods is also one of the most popular. Fuul (a peasant dish of long-cooked fava beans cooked with garlic and garnished with parsley, olive oil, lemon, salt, black pepper and cumin) is mopped up by bread for breakfast and ladled into a pocket of bread for a snack on the run. You'll find it in Egypt (where it's the national dish), Syria, Jordan, Lebanon and Iraq.

Kebabs

A New Book of Middle Eastern Food, by Claudia Roden, brought the cuisines of the region to the attention of Western cooks when it was released in 1968. It's still an essential reference, as fascinating for its cultural insights as for its great recipes.

There are more variations on the kebab in this part of the world than you could poke a skewer at. Every country has its specialities – Syria has the delicious *kebab Halebi* (Aleppan kebab, served with a spicy tomato sauce), Turkey is understandably proud of its luscious *İskender kebap* and Lebanon has an unswerving devotion to *shish tawooq* (grilled chicken kebab, often served with a garlic sauce) – but if you're serious about the skewered stuff you need to make your way to Iran, where the kebab is the national dish. When there, make sure you try *chelow kebab*, a succulent lamb shish served on a fluffy mound of buttery *chelow* (rice).

Other Meats

The kebab might be king, but when it comes to meat dishes there are a number of courtiers waiting in the wings. *Kibbeh*-lovers will be in seventh heaven when they taste the examples on offer in Lebanon, Syria and Turkey, some of which are raw *(kibbeh nayye)* and others cooked. *Kofta* (spiced ground meat formed into balls) is served in innumerable ways in Turkey, and are the signature element of the Egyptian favourite *daood basha* (meat balls cooked in a *tagen* pot with pine nuts and tomato sauce). In Syria and Egypt *fatta* (an oven-baked dish of bread soaked in tahini, chickpeas and minced meat or chicken) is a favourite breakfast dish. Even more common than these dishes is one simple but delicious meal that you'll find throughout the region: roast chicken accompanied by salad, bread and hummus or tahini.

In the 17th century 1300 workers slaved away in the kitchens of İstanbul's Topkapı Palace, producing food for around 10,000 people every day.

Regional differences abound when it comes to meat dishes, and are far too numerous to be listed here. Of particular note is the Bedouin dish *mensaf* (lamb served on a bed of rice and pine nuts and accompanied by a tangy yogurt sauce), which, in its true Bedouin form, comes complete with a gaping sheep's head. You can find this in the Palestinian Territories, Jordan and Syria (around Palmyra).

Seafood

When on the Mediterranean and Black Sea coasts (particularly in İstanbul, Alexandria and both Tripolis), you'll undoubtedly join the locals in falling hook, line and sinker for the marvellous array of fresh seafood on offer. Local favourites are calamari, red mullet, sea bass and sole. Oddly enough, it's difficult to access good seafood in other parts of the region.

Vegetables

The Complete Middle East Cookbook, by Tess Mallos, is full of easy-to-follow recipes and devotes individual chapters to national cuisines including those of Turkey, Iraq, Iran, Egypt and Israel.

If it weren't for the regional obsession with the kebab, the locals would probably all be vegetarian. There's none of the silly Western fixation with preparing vegetables that are out of season; here tomatoes are eaten when they're almost bursting out of their skins with sweet juices, corn is picked when it's golden and plentiful, and cucumbers are munched when they're crispy and sweet. There are a number of vegetables that are particular to Middle Eastern cuisine, including *molokhiyya* (aka *moolookhiye* or *melokhia*), a slimy but surprisingly sexy green leafy vegetable known in the West as mallow. In Egypt it's made into an earthy garlic-flavoured soup that has a glutinous texture and inspires an almost religious devotion among the locals. In Syria and Lebanon molokhiyya is used to make highly spiced lamb and chicken stews.

The region also has a particularly distinctive way of serving vegetables, known as dolma (stuffed with rice or meat and slow cooked in olive oil; also called *dolmeh* or *mahshi*). The most famous example of this style of cooking is the Turkish dish *ımam bayıldı* (literally 'the imam fainted'). A simple dish of aubergine stuffed with onion and garlic, slow cooked in olive oil and served cold, it is so named because legend has it that an imam fainted with pleasure on first tasting it.

Desserts & Sweets

If you have a sweet tooth, be prepared to put it to good use on your travels in this part of the world. The prince of the regional puds is undoubtedly *muhalabiyya* (also known as *mahallabiye*), a blancmange-like concoction made of ground rice, milk, sugar and rose or orange water and topped with chopped pistachios and almonds. Almost as popular is *ruz bi laban* (rice pudding, also known as *fırın sütlaç* in Turkey). Seasonal fresh fruit is just as commonly served, and provides a refreshing light finale to a mezze-and-kebab-laden feast.

Best of all are the pastries, including kunafa, a vermicelli-like pastry over a vanilla base soaked in syrup; and the famous baklava, made from delicate filo drenched in honey or syrup. Variations on baklava are flavoured with fresh nuts or stuffed with wickedly rich clotted cream (called *kaymak* in Turkey, *eishta* elsewhere).

> The popular Egyptian dessert of *umm ali* is said to have been introduced into the country by Miss O'Malley, an Irish mistress of Khedive Ismail, the viceroy of Egypt.

DRINKS
Alcoholic Drinks

Though the region is predominantly Muslim, and thus abstemious, most of its countries have a local beer. The best are Turkey's Efes; Egypt's Stella and Sakkara; Jordan's Amstel; and Lebanon's famous Almaza. Less impressive are Syria's Barada and Al-Charq and Israel's Maccabee, Gold Star and Nesher. The most interesting ale is Taybeh, the product of the Arab world's first microbrewery, which comes from Ramallah.

Good wine is harder to access, with the one exception being the excellent vintages produced in Lebanon. Try the products of its Chateaux Musar, Ksara and Kefraya – we particularly recommend Ksara's Reserve du Couvent. In Egypt, there's a growing viticulture industry but the product is pretty unimpressive – Grand de Marquise is the best of a lacklustre bunch. In Turkey, the two largest producers are Doluca and Kavaklıdere. Doluca's best wines are its Özel Kav (Special Reserve) red and white; its Antik red and white are its second-string wines (but are still quite drinkable). Kavaklıdere's most popular wines are the quaffable Yakut red and Çankaya white. Syrian wine is diabolically bad, and most of the local tipplers stick to the Lebanese drops, which are locally available. Israeli wine is improving, and Carmel, Golan, Barchan, Tishbi and Tzora all have reasonable reputations.

> Shiraz (aka Syrah) was first produced in Iran more than 1000 years ago, and is believed to have been taken to France by the Crusaders. Needless to say, it's no longer produced in its namesake city.

If there is a regional drink, it would have to be the aniseed firewater known as raki in Turkey and as arak in the rest of the region. The aniseed taste of these two powerful tipples perfectly complements mezze.

Alcohol is banned in Libya and Iran.

> You can drink arak neat, but most devotees first pour about two fingers of arak, then add water and finish off with one ice cube.

Nonalcoholic drinks

Juice stalls selling cheap and delicious freshly squeezed *asiir* (juices) are common throughout the region. Popular juices include lemon (which is often blended with sugar syrup and ice, and sometimes with mint), orange, pomegranate, mango, carrot and sugar cane, and you can order combinations of any or all of these. For health reasons, steer clear of stalls that add milk to their drinks.

Other traditional drinks include *aryan*, a refreshing yogurt drink made by whipping yogurt with water and salt to the consistency of pouring cream. This is widely available throughout the region and is a ubiquitous accompaniment to kebabs. It's known as *dugh* in Iran. Another favourite is the delicious and unusual sahlab (sahlep in Turkey), a drink made from crushed tapioca-root extract and served with milk, coconut, sugar, raisins, chopped nuts and rosewater. Famed for its aphrodisiacal properties, it is served hot in winter and cold in summer.

> The Turks love *boza*, a viscous mucus-coloured beverage made from fermented burghul with water and sugar that has a reputation for building up strength and virility.

WATER

Many locals don't drink the tap water and we recommend that you follow their lead. If you do decide to risk the local stuff, the safest places to do this are in Iran, Israel and Syria. Don't even *think* of drinking from the tap in Egypt, Iraq or Lebanon. Cheap bottled water is readily available throughout the region.

Tea & Coffee

> When drinking Turkish-style coffee, you should never drink the grounds in the bottom of your cup. You may want to read your fortune in them, though – check out the website of İstanbul's longest-established purveyor of coffee, Kuru-kahveci Mehmet Efendi (www.mehmetefendi .com) for a guide.

Drinking tea (*shai*, *chai* or *çay*) is the signature pastime of the region and it is seen as strange and decidedly antisocial not to swig the tannin-laden beverage at regular intervals throughout the day. The tea will either come in the form of a tea bag plonked in a cup or glass of hot water (Lipton is the usual brand) or a strong brew of the local leaves. Sometimes it's served with mint (*na'ama*) and it always comes with sugar. Be warned that you'll risk severe embarrassment if you ask for milk if you're anywhere other than a tourist hotel or restaurant.

Surprisingly, Turkish or Arabic coffee (*qahwa*) is not widely consumed in the region, with instant coffee (always called Nescafé) being far more common. If you do find the real stuff, it's likely to be a thick and powerful Turkish-style brew that's served in small cups and drunk in a couple of short sips. It is usually served very sweet; if you want less sugar ask for it to be served *wassat* (medium sweet) or *sada* (without sugar).

CELEBRATIONS

The people of this region love nothing more than a celebration, and food plays an important role when it comes to giving thanks for a birth, bringing in a harvest or marking a significant religious holiday.

Many dishes owe their derivation and popularity to the celebration of particular religious events or stories. One of these is Turkey's *aşure Bayramı*. The story goes that when the flood waters were subsiding, Noah asked his wife to cook up all the food left in the pantry. She formulated a bizarre 40-ingredient pudding that included beans, barley, chickpeas, cinnamon, sultanas and burghul, and called it *aşure*. These days Turks

---

QUALITY QAHWAS

There's absolutely nothing more satisfying than spending an hour or so soaking up the ambience and fragrant nargileh smoke at a *qahwa* (coffeehouse; *ahwa* in Egypt). Most serve up more tea than coffee – in Turkey they're called *çay bahçesi* (tea gardens) and in Iran they're known as *chaykhana* (teahouses) – and all have loyal, predominantly male, clients who enjoy nothing more than a daily natter and a game of dominoes. Some of our favourites:

Fishawi's (p113) Khan al-Khalili, Cairo, Egypt.
An-Nafura (p520) Old City, Damascus, Syria.
Al-Kahwa (p426) Beirut, Lebanon.
Leale-al Sultan (p315) Akko, Israel.
Papirüs Cafeteria (p629) Gaziantep, Turkey.
Qeysarieh Tea Shop (p216) Esfahan, Iran.

OUTSTANDING DINING EXPERIENCES

Our favourite restaurants in the region:

Sabaya (p112) Cairo, Egypt. World-class Lebanese restaurant.
Yord Restaurant (p224) Shiraz, Iran. Fabulous Iranian cuisine served in a colourful tent.
Ticho House (p294) Jerusalem, Israel. Bohemian eatery set in a 19th-century home.
Fakhr el-Din (p374) Amman, Jordan. Delicious Lebanese cuisine.
Kasr Fakhredine (p431) Broummana, Lebanon. Possibly the best classic Lebanese food in the country.
Mat'am Obaya (p475) Tripoli, Libya. Wonderful home-cocked seafood.
Beit Wakil (p542) Aleppo, Syria. Aleppo's best restaurant set in a glorious building.
Sofyali 9 (p573) İstanbul, Turkey. The best tavern food in İstanbul.

---

eat *aşure* on the 10th day of Muharram (the first month of the Muslim calendar) to celebrate Noah, his ark and the great glory of God.

A staple that owes its name to another story from religious history is the bread known as *challah* (Sabbath bread). This bread is baked each week by Jewish householders in Israel and the Palestinian Territories to commemorate the Israelites being given a double portion of manna on the sixth day that they were in the wilderness to provide for the succeeding seventh day.

The region's most important religious feasts occur during Ramadan, the Muslim holy month. There are two substantial meals a day during this period. The first, *imsak* (or *sahur*), is a breakfast eaten before daylight. Tea, bread, dates, olives and pastries are scoffed to give energy for the day ahead. *Iftar*, the evening meal prepared to break the fast, is a special feast calling for substantial soups, rice dishes topped with almond-scattered grilled meats and other delicacies. It's often enjoyed communally in the street or in large, specially erected tents. The end of Ramadan (Eid al-Fitr) is also celebrated in great culinary style. In Turkey, locals mark this important time with Şeker Bayramı (Sugar Festival), a three-day feast in which sweet foods occupy centre stage. Varieties of baklava turn up at many religious feasts; in Iran the delicious local version uses a greater proportion of nuts to pastry than most of its regional equivalents, and is widely prepared to celebrate No Ruz (the Iranian New Year).

Family milestones are also celebrated with food. Egyptians mark the birth of a son by serving an aromatic rice pudding with aniseed called *meghlie*; in Syria and Lebanon a pudding also celebrates the same event, but this is called *mighlay* and is made of rice flour and cinnamon.

WHERE & WHEN TO EAT & DRINK

Eating patterns and styles differ throughout the region, but one rule stands firm in each and every country: the best food is always served in private homes. If you are fortunate enough to be invited to share a home-cooked meal, make sure you take up the offer.

The quality of food served in restaurants differs greatly from country to country. While it can be disappointing in Egypt, Israel, Iran and Jordan, it can soar to the culinary heavens in Lebanon, Syria and Turkey, particularly in the big cities. See above for a list of some of region's best restaurants.

Though there are restaurants in every country serving up a variety of international cuisines (and even the dreaded fusion), it's a much safer bet to eat the local cuisine. The only times we'd recommend travelling your tastebuds out of the region's indigenous cuisines are in İstanbul

Syrians believe that seeing in the New Year with white dishes brings good luck; *labanieh* (chicken and lamb cooked in yogurt) is a favourite.

The common name of the famous Spice Bazaar in İstanbul is the Mısır Çarşısı (Egyptian Market), commemorating the fact that Egypt was once the centre of the world's spice trade.

(at the likes of the world-class Vogue in Beşiktaş); in Beirut (where the food is uniformly excellent whatever its geographical derivation); and in Cairo (where we have no hesitation in highly recommending eateries such as the excellent Thai and Lebanese restaurants at the Semiramis Intercontinental, see p112). When you do eat out, you'll find that the locals usually dine at a later hour than is the norm in the West (it's usual to see diners arrive at a restaurant at 10pm or even later in the big cities, particularly in summer). They also dine as large family groups, order up big, smoke like chimneys and linger over their meals. The main meal of the day is usually lunch, which is enjoyed at around 2pm. See under Business Hours in each country Directory section for the usual opening hours for restaurants.

Seductive Flavours of the Levant, by Nada Daleh, is a lavishly illustrated guide to the regional specialities of Syria and Lebanon.

VEGETARIANS & VEGANS

Though it's quite usual for the people of the Middle East to eat a vegetarian meal, the concept of vegetarianism is quite foreign. Say you're a vegan and they will either look mystified or assume that you're 'fessing up to some strain of socially aberrant behaviour. There is a sprinkling of vegetarian restaurants in big cities such as Beirut and İstanbul, but the travelling vegetarian certainly can't rely on finding them in most cities and towns.

To ask 'Do you have any vegetarian dishes?' in Egypt say '*andak akla nabateeyya?*'. In Iran, ask '*in ghaza gusht dare?*' (Does this dish have meat?) and in Turkey ask '*Etsiz yemekler var mı?*' (Is there something to eat that has no meat?). In other countries ask for dishes that are '*bidoon lahem*' (without meat).

Fortunately, it's not difficult to find vegetable-based dishes. You'll find that you eat loads of mezze and salads, fuul, tasty cheese and spinach pastries, the occasional omelette or oven-baked vegetable *tagens* (stews baked in a terracotta pot) featuring okra (ladies' fingers) and aubergine.

The main source of inadvertent meat-eating is meat stock, which is often used to make otherwise vegetarian pilafs, soups and vegetable dishes. Your hosts may not even consider such stock to be meat, so they will reassure you that the dish is vegetarian. Chicken and mutton are the biggest hide-and-seekers in the region's food, often lurking in vegetable dishes and mezze. Be careful.

The best country for vegetarians is Israel, where kosher laws don't permit the mixing of meat and dairy products, resulting in a lot of 'dairy' restaurants where no meat in any form is served. The most challenging destination is Iran, where kebabs dominate the menus and meat stock is often used to cook rice.

EATING WITH KIDS

It's usual to eat out as a family group in the region, and you'll often see young children dining with their parents and friends in restaurants until the early hours. Waiters are uniformly accepting of children and will

---

DOS & DON'TS

- Remember to always remove your shoes before sitting down on a rug to eat or drink tea.
- Always avoid putting your left hand into a communal dish if you're eating Bedouin style.
- Be sure to leave the dining area and go outside or to the toilet before blowing your nose in a restaurant.
- Make sure you refrain from eating, drinking or smoking in public during the daytime in the holy month of Ramadan (international hotels are an exception to this rule).
- Always sit at the dinner table next to a person of the same sex unless your host(ess) suggests otherwise.

THAT HUBBLY-BUBBLY FEELING

Called a nargileh in Turkey, Lebanon, Jordan and Syria, a *sheesha* in Egypt, and a *qalyan* in Iran, the water pipe is a tradition, an indulgence and a slightly naughty habit all wrapped into the one gloriously fragrant and relaxing package. A feature of coffeehouses from Ankara to Aswan, it's a pastime that's as addictive as it is magical. Consider yourselves warned.

When you order a water pipe you'll need to specify the type of tobacco and molasses mix you would like. Most people opt for tobacco soaked in apple juice (known as *elma* in Turkey and *tufah* in Egypt), but it's also possible to order strawberry, melon, cherry or mixed-fruit flavours. Some purists order their tobacco unadulterated, but in doing this they miss out on the wonderfully sweet and fragrant aroma that makes the experience so memorable. Once you've specified your flavour, a decorated bulbous glass pipe filled with water will be brought to your table, hot coals will be placed in it to get it started and you will be given a disposable plastic mouthpiece to slip over the pipe's stem. Just draw back and you're off. The only secret to a good smoke is to take a puff every now and again to keep the coals hot; when they start to lose their heat the waiter (or dedicated water-pipe minder) will replace them. Bliss!

usually go out of their way to make them feel welcome (offerings of fried potato chips being a tried and true method). Best of all, the cuisine of the region is very child-friendly, being simple and varied.

Some places have high chairs, but they're in the minority. Kids' menus are usually only seen at Western-style hotel restaurants.

For more information on travelling with children, see p643.

Egypt

A land of magnificent World Heritage sites and a thousand tourist clichés, Egypt was enticing visitors millennia before Mr Cook sailed his first steamers up the Nile and Ms Christie caused a couple of passengers to be stabbed along the way. It was in Egypt that the Holy Family sheltered, Alexander conquered and Mark Antony flirted. Napoleon stopped long enough to nick a few obelisks, the Ottomans paused to prop up the great and barbarous pasha Mohammed Ali, and the British stayed around to get the train system running and to furnish every empty nook and cranny of the British Museum. And all this was long, long after Menes (Narmer) united the two states of Upper and Lower Egypt and set the scene for the unfolding of the greatest civilisation the world has ever known.

The pointed perfection of the Pyramids, the magical minarets of Cairo's skyline and the tantalising tombs and temples of Luxor are just a few of the wonders these and millions of other visitors have admired during jaunts up and down the Nile and camelback trips through spectacularly stark desert landscapes.

As all travellers to this ancient land swiftly realise, Howard Carter's discovery of Tutankhamun's tomb did a lot more than raise the boy pharaoh's previously negligible profile and set off a craze for Egyptology among the chattering classes of the Western world – it confirmed once and for all that Egypt's discoveries are ongoing and her treasures limitless.

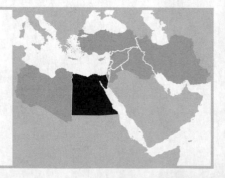

FAST FACTS

- **Area** 997,739 sq km
- **Capital** Cairo
- **Country code** ☎ 20
- **Language** Arabic
- **Money** Egyptian pound (E£); US$1 = E£5.75; €1 = E£6.79
- **Official name** Arab Republic of Egypt
- **Population** 74.9 million

HIGHLIGHTS

- **Cairo** (p96) The 'Mother of the World' is home to a big museum, even bigger Pyramids and a bigger-still local population.
- **Luxor** (p124) The many glories of ancient Thebes and the persistence of the local touts never fail to impress.
- **Abu Simbel** (p143) Ramses II's most magnificent monument is worth the trek through the desert.
- **Alexandria** (p117) This very cosmopolitan Mediterranean city is Egypt's hidden treasure – don't miss it.
- **Dahab** (p162) A backpackers' nirvana where you can kick back and recover from chronic Pharaonic fatigue.

CLIMATE & WHEN TO GO

Egypt's climate is easy to summarise. Except for the winter months of December, January and February, it is hot and dry. Temperatures increase as you travel south from Alexandria. Alexandria receives the most rain – approximately 190mm a year – while in Aswan, in the far south, rain is rare.

Summer temperatures range from 31°C on the Mediterranean coast to a scorching 50°C in Aswan. At night in winter, the temperatures sometimes plummet to as low as 8°C, even in the south of the country. In the mountains of Sinai, night-time temperatures in winter can fall well below zero.

June to August is unbearable in Upper Egypt (the area extending south of Cairo to the Sudan), with daytime temperatures soaring to 40°C or more. Summer in Cairo is almost as hot, and the combination of heat, dust, pollution, noise and crowds makes walking the city streets a real test of endurance.

For visiting Upper Egypt, winter is easily the most comfortable time – though hotel rates are at a premium. In Cairo from December to February, skies are often overcast and evenings can be colder than you'd think, while up on the Mediterranean coast, Alexandria is subject to frequent downpours.

The happiest compromise for an all-Egypt trip is to visit in spring (March to May) or autumn (October and November). See Climate Charts p643.

In this chapter, we have used 'summer' and 'winter' hours for museums and other attractions. Summer generally means May to September and winter October to April.

HOW MUCH?

- **Cup of tea** E£2 to E£4
- **Newspaper** 50pt
- **One-minute phone call to the UK** E£3.50
- **Internet connection per hour** E£5 to E£10
- **Museum admission** E£40

LONELY PLANET INDEX

- **Litre of petrol** 18pt
- **Litre of bottled water** E£2.50
- **Bottle of Stella** E£10
- **Souvenir T-shirt** E£30
- **Fuul or ta'amiyya sandwich** 50pt

HISTORY

About 5000 years ago an Egyptian pharaoh named Menes (Narmer) unified Upper and Lower Egypt for the first time. For centuries before, communities had been developing along the Nile. The small kingdoms eventually developed into two important states, one covering the valley as far as the Delta, the other consisting of the Delta itself. The unification of these two states in about 3100 BC set the scene for the greatest era of ancient Egyptian civilisation.

Little is known of the immediate successors of Menes except that, attributed with divine ancestry, they promoted the development of a highly stratified society, patronised the arts and built many temples and public works. In the 27th century BC, Egypt's pyramids began to appear. The Pharaoh Zoser and his chief architect, Imhotep, built what may have been the first, the Step Pyramid at Saqqara. Zoser ruled from the nearby capital of Memphis.

For the next three dynasties and 500 years (a period called the Old Kingdom), the power of Egypt's pharaohs and the size and scale of their pyramids and temples greatly increased. The size of such buildings symbolised the pharaoh's importance and power over his people. The last three pharaohs of the 4th dynasty, Khufu (Cheops), Khafre (Chephren) and Menkaure (Mycerinus), built the three Great Pyramids of Giza.

EGYPT

It is evident that the pharaohs had ceded some of their power to a rising class of nobles by the beginning of the 5th dynasty (about 2494–2345 BC). In the following centuries Egypt broke down into several squabbling principalities. The rise of Thebes (Luxor) saw an end to the turmoil, and Egypt was reunited under Montuhotep II, marking the beginning of the Middle Kingdom. For 250 years all went well, but more internal fighting and 100 years of occupation by the Hyksos, invaders from the northeast, cast a shadow over the country.

The New Kingdom, its capital at Thebes and later Memphis, represented a blossoming of culture and empire in Pharaonic Egypt. For almost 400 years, from the 18th to the 20th dynasties (1550–1069 BC), Egypt was a great power in northeast Africa and the eastern Mediterranean. But by the time Ramses III came to power (1184 BC) as the second pharaoh of the 20th dynasty, disunity had again set in. This was the state of affairs when the army of Alexander the Great took control of Egypt in the 4th century BC.

Alexander founded a new capital, Alexandria, on the Mediterranean coast, and for the next 300 years the land of the Nile was ruled by a dynasty established by one of the Macedonian's generals, Ptolemy. Romans followed the Ptolemaic dynasty, and then came Islam and the Arabs, conquering Egypt in AD 640. In due course, rule by the Ottoman Turks and the Europeans

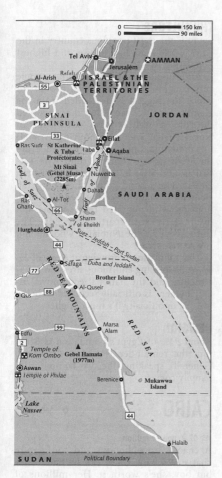

followed (the French under Napoleon, then the British) – shifts of power common to much of the Middle East (see p37).

Self-rule was finally restored to the Egyptians as a result of the Revolution of 1952. Colonel Gamal Abdel Nasser, leader of the revolutionary Free Officers, ascended to power and was confirmed as president in elections held in 1956. That same year, the colonial legacy was finally and dramatically shaken off in full world view when Nasser successfully faced down Britain, France and Israel over the Suez Canal. Nasser was unsuccessful, however, in the 1967 war with Israel, dying shortly after of a heart failure. Anwar Sadat, his successor, also fought Israel in 1973, a war that paved the way for a

peace settlement, culminating in the Camp David Agreement in 1979. In certain quarters, Camp David was viewed as a traitorous abandonment of Nasser's pan-Arabist principles and it ultimately cost Sadat his life at the hands of an assassin in 1981.

Sadat's murderer was a member of Islamic Jihad, an uncompromising terrorist organisation that aimed to establish an Islamic state in Egypt. Mass roundups of Islamists were immediately carried out on the orders of Sadat's successor, Hosni Mubarak, the vice president and a former air-force general, who declared a state of emergency when he assumed power. This state of emergency continues today.

Mubarak was able to rehabilitate Egypt in the eyes of the Arab world without abandoning the treaty with Israel. For almost a decade, he and his National Democratic Party (NDP) managed to keep the domestic political situation calm – with the constant presence of the armed forces always in the background. Things started to change in the late 1980s. Discontent brewed among the poorer sections of society as the country's economic situation worsened. With a repressive political system that allowed little or no chance to legitimately voice opposition, it was almost inevitable that the Islamist opposition would resort to extreme action.

Frequent attempts were made on the life of the president and his ministers, and regular clashes with the security forces occurred. The government responded with a heavy-handed crackdown, arresting thousands and continuing to outlaw the most popular Islamist opposition group, the Muslim Brotherhood. By the mid-1990s, the violence had receded from the capital, retreating to the religious heartland of middle Egypt where, in 1997, members of the Gama'a al-Islamiyya (Islamic Group), a Muslim Brotherhood splinter group, carried out a bloody massacre of 58 holidaymakers at the Funerary Temple of Hatshepsut in Luxor.

The massacre destroyed grass-roots support for militant groups and the Muslim Brotherhood declared a cease-fire the following year. Things were relatively quiet until October 2004, when a bomb at Taba, on the border with Israel, killed 34 and signalled the start of an unsettled 12 months. In early 2005, President Mubarak bowed to growing international pressure to bring the country's political system in line with Western-style democracy, and proposed a constitutional amendment (subsequently approved by parliament and ratified at a national referendum) that aimed to introduce direct and competitive presidential elections in September that year. While some pundits saw this as a step in the right direction, others saw it as a sham, particularly as popular opposition groups such as the Muslim Brotherhood were still banned and other independent candidates were required to have the backing of at least 65 members of the overwhelmingly NDP-dominated lower house of parliament. When the Kifaya! (Enough!) coalition of opposition groups loudly voiced its unhappiness with these restrictions, security forces cracked down. Ayman Nour, the leader of the popular Ghad (Tomorrow) party, was thrown into jail on what many thought were trumped-up charges and opposition rallies around the country were violently dispersed. At this stage the banned Muslim Brotherhood began holding its own rallies, and in Cairo there were two isolated terrorist incidents aimed at foreign tourists, both carried out by members of the same pro-Islamist family. Soon after, three bombs at the popular beach resort of Sharm el-Sheikh claimed the lives of 64 people, most of them Egyptian. Various groups claimed responsibility, tourism took an immediate hit and Egyptians braced themselves for the possibility of further terrorist incursions and domestic unrest.

Egypt Today

Despite the ever-present – though slim – threat of an Islamist uprising, the major challenge facing President Mubarak as this book goes to print isn't associated with religious extremism or global terrorism. Nor is it related to the constant international and opposition denunciation of press censorship and other infringements on human rights. The biggest threat to the NDP's hold on power is the irrefutable fact that Egypt is in serious economic crisis, and has been for many years. The national economy is best described as a basket case, and when the ever-burgeoning growth in population, rise in unemployment, and decline in tourism resulting from the July 2005 Sharm el-Sheikh bombs are considered, a prosperous national future looks increasingly unlikely.

THE CULTURE

Egypt is the most populous country in the Arab world and has the second-highest population in Africa.

Anthropologists divide Egyptian people very roughly into three racial groups, of which the biggest is descended from the Hamito-Semitic race that has peopled the Nile (as well as many other parts of North Africa and neighbouring Arabia) for millennia. Included in this race are the Berbers, a minority group who settled around Siwa in the country's Western Desert. The second group, the truly Arab element, is made up of the Bedouin Arab nomads, who migrated from Arabia and live in desert areas, particularly Sinai. The third group is the Nubians, who inhabit the Aswan area.

The population is growing at a rate of 2% annually, placing enormous stress on infrastructure and the national economy. Unemployment is officially recorded as being at 10%; unofficially it's much higher.

RELIGION

About 94% of Egypt's population is Muslim; the remainder is Coptic Christian. Generally speaking, the two communities happily coexist.

CAIRO القاهرة

☎ 02 / pop 11 million

A chaotic, cacophonous and confidently charismatic city, Cairo can be hard work but boy, she's worth it. Her millions of children live in the shadow of the Pyramids, along the banks of the Nile, alongside the mausoleums of the dead and on the edges of her voracious urban sprawl. All have their complaints about pollution, traffic and overcrowding, but none of them would dream of leaving. This is, after all, the capital of the Arab world and Egypt's greatest city. Tutankhamun's treasure and the Khan al-Khalili are obvious – and wonderful – diversions for the visitor, but it's the everyday rituals of life here that prove most enticing. Once you've dodged the gladiatorial traffic a few times, promenaded along the Corniche, grown attuned to the multitudinous calls to prayer and listened to the new Amr Diab song time after time, you'll forget that you're filthy and exhausted, and will throw yourself willingly into the madness.

HISTORY

Cairo is not a Pharaonic city, though the presence of the Pyramids leads many to believe otherwise. At the time the Pyramids were built, the capital of ancient Egypt was Memphis, 22km south of the Giza plateau.

The core foundations of the city of Cairo were laid in AD 969 by the early Islamic Fatimid dynasty. There had been earlier settlements, notably the Roman fortress of Babylon and the early-Islamic city of Fustat, established by Amr ibn al-As, the general who conquered Egypt for Islam in AD 640. Much of the city that the Fatimids built remains today: the great Fatimid mosque and university of Al Azhar is still Egypt's main centre of Islamic study, while the three great gates of Bab an-Nasr, Bab al-Futuh and Bab Zuweila still straddle two of Islamic Cairo's main thoroughfares.

Under the rule of subsequent dynasties, Cairo swelled and burst its walls, but at heart it remained a medieval city for 900 years. It wasn't until the mid-19th century that Cairo started to change in any significant way.

Before the 1860s, Cairo extended west only as far as what is today Midan Opera. The future site of modern central Cairo was then a swampy plain subject to the annual flooding of the Nile. In 1863, when the French-educated Ismail came to power, he was determined to upgrade the image of his capital, which he believed could only be done by dismissing what had gone before and starting afresh. For 10 years the former marsh became one vast building site as Ismail invited architects from Belgium, France and Italy to design and build a brand-new European-style Cairo beside the old Islamic city. This building boom has continued until the present day, with the city's boundaries constantly expanding into the surrounding desert.

ORIENTATION

Finding your way around the vast sprawl of Cairo is not as difficult as it may first seem. Midan Tahrir is the centre. Northeast of Tahrir is Downtown, a noisy, busy com-

CAIRO IN TWO DAYS

On day one, brave the crowds to view the magnificent exhibits at the **Egyptian Museum** (p101), then take a wander around the Downtown area, stopping to grab a cheap and delicious lunch at **At-Tabie ad-Dumyati** (p112). In the afternoon, make your way to **Khan al-Khalili** (p104) and practise your haggling skills with the cheerful stall owners. When there, don't forget to have a tea and *sheesha* (water pipe) at **Fishawi's** (p113). Return to Downtown to eat a simple but delicious Levantine meal at the long-running **Greek Club** (p111) or dine like a pasha at Zamalek's glamorous **Abou El Sid** (p112).

Your second day is devoted to the **Pyramids** (p106). You'll need at least four hours here, and should explore the interior of at least one of the massive stone structures. After you've had a late outdoor lunch at **Andrea's** (p108), it's back to the centre of town for a sunset **felucca cruise** (p108). On your last night in town, a splurge is on the cards – **Sabaya** (p112), at the Semiramis Intercontinental on the Corniche, will fit the bill perfectly.

mercial district centred on Sharia Talaat Harb. This is where you'll find most of the cheap eateries and budget hotels. Midan Ramses, location of the city's main train station, marks the northernmost extent of Downtown.

Heading east, Downtown ends at Midan Ataba and Islamic Cairo takes over. This is the medieval heart of the city, and is still very much alive today. At its centre is the great bazaar of Khan al-Khalili.

Sitting in the middle of the Nile is the island neighbourhood of Zamalek, historically favoured by ruling colonials and still a relatively upmarket enclave with many foreign residents, a few midrange hotels and innumerable restaurants and bars.

The west bank of the Nile is less historical and much more residential than areas along the east bank. The primary districts, north to south, are Mohandiseen, Agouza, Doqqi and Giza, all of which are heavy on concrete and light on charm. Giza covers by far the largest area of the four, stretching some 20km west either side of one long,

EGYPT

CAIRO

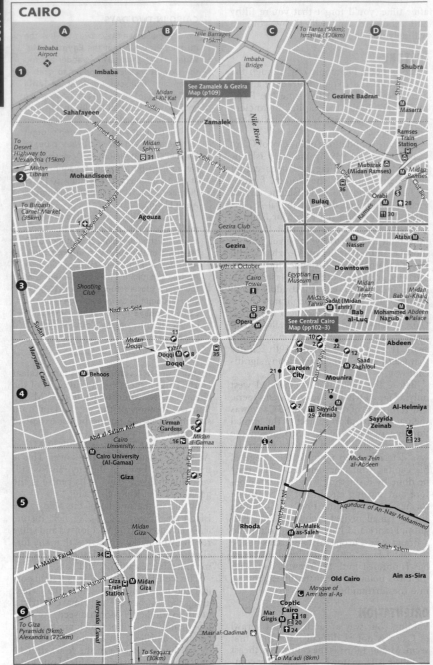

A   B   C   D

To Nile Barrages
(15km)

To Tanta (58km);
Ismailia (120km)

Imbaba
Airport

Imbaba

Imbaba
Bridge

Shubra

Midan
al-Kit Kat

Sudan

Geziret Badran

Masarra

Sahafayeen

Zamalek

Nile River

Ramses
Train
Station

Ahmed Orabi

Midan
Sphinx
31

26th of July

El-Nil

Mubarak
(Midan Ramses)

Al-Gish

Midan
Ramses

To Desert
Highway to
Alexandria (15km)

Midan
Libnan

Mohandiseen

Agouza

36

Bulaq

Orabi

28

Gamal at-Dowal al-Arabiya

To Birqash
Camel Market
(35km)

Gezira Club

30

Ramses

Sudan

Shooting
Club

Nadi as-Seid

Gezira

6th of October

Cairo
Tower

Nasser

Ataba

Egyptian
Museum

Downtown

Midan
Talaat
Harb

Midan
Bab al-Khalq

Maryutia Canal

Midan
Doqqi

Tahrir
Doqqi   8

Doqqi

11

32

Opera

35

Midan
Tahrir

Sadat (Midan
Tahrir)

Bab
al-Luq

Mohammed
Naguib

Abdeen
Palace

Behoos

10
13   2
22   12

Saad
Zaghloul

Abdeen

21

Garden
City

Qasr al-Aini

17

Mounira

Al-Helmiya

Urman
Gardens

9

7

Sayyida
Zeinab

Sayyida
Zeinab

25

Cairo
University

16

Midan
al-Gamaa

Manial

29

23

Cairo University
(Al-Gamaa)

Giza

Shara al-Giza

5

4

Midan Zein
al-Abdeen

Abd al-Salam Arif

Midan
Giza

Rhoda

Corniche el-Nil

Aqueduct of An-Nasr Mohammed

Al-Malek Faisal

34

Salah Salem

Al-Malek
as-Saleh

Pyramids Rd (Al-Haram)

Giza
Train
Station

Midan
Giza

Old Cairo

Ain as-Sira

Maryutia Canal

To Giza
Pyramids (9km);
Alexandria (220km)

Mosque of
Amr ibn al-As

Coptic
Cairo

Mar
Girgis

18

20

24

To Saqqara
(30km)

Masr al-Qadimah

To Ma'adi (8km)

See Zamalek & Gezira
Map (p109)

See Central Cairo
Map (pp102-3)

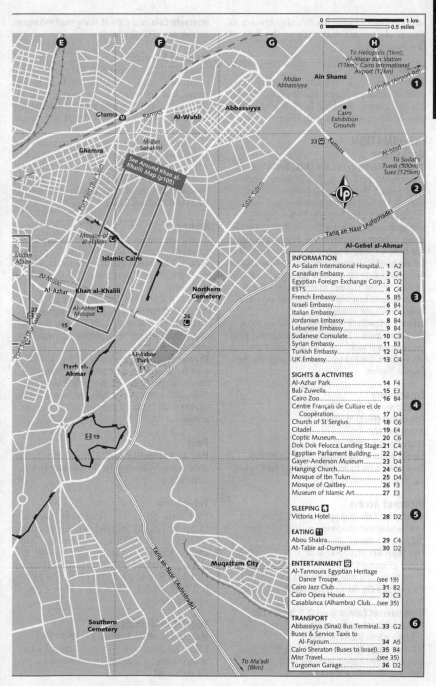

straight road (Pyramids Rd, also known as Sharia al-Haram) that ends at the foot of the Pyramids.

Maps

The American University in Cairo Press publishes *Cairo Maps: the Practical Guide* (E£30), a book-sized but lightweight collection of 40 street maps with index.

INFORMATION
Bookshops

American University in Cairo (AUC) bookshop
Downtown (Map pp102-3; ☎ 797 5370; Sharia Mohammed Mahmoud; ⏱ 9am-6pm Sat-Thu); Zamalek (Map p109; ☎ 739 7045; 16 Sharia Mohammed ibn Thakeb; ⏱ 10am-7pm Sat-Thu, 1-7pm Fri) The best English-language bookshop in Egypt, with stacks of material on the politics, sociology and history of Cairo, Egypt and the Middle East. It also has plenty of guidebooks and some fiction. The Zamalek branch is smaller than the main Downtown branch.
Diwan (Map p109; ☎ 736 2578; 159 Sharia 26th of July, Zamalek; ⏱ 9am-11.30pm) An excellent English- and French-language bookshop with its own café and a wide range of novels and guidebooks.
Lehnert & Landrock (Map pp102-3; 44 Sharia Sherif; ⏱ 9.30am-2pm & 4-7.30pm Mon-Fri, Sat morning) Very good selection of books about Cairo and Egypt. It also sells postcards. There's a convenient branch opposite the Egyptian Museum.

Emergency

Ambulance (☎ 123)
Fire department (☎ 180)
Police (☎ 122)
Tourist police (☎ 126)
Tourist police office (Map pp102-3; ☎ 390 6028; Downtown) On the 1st floor of a building in the alley just left of the main tourist office.

Internet Access

4U Internet Café (Map pp102-3; ☎ 575 9304; 1st fl, 8 Midan Talaat Harb, Downtown; per hr E£5; ⏱ 24hr) Under the Lialy Hostel.
Five St@rs Net (Map pp102-3; ☎ 574 7881; ⏱ 24hr) Next to 4U Internet Café. Offers an almost-identical service for the same price, the only difference being that it doesn't burn CDs. There's another branch near Midan Tahrir.
Hany Internet Cafe (Map pp102-3; ☎ 395 1985; 16 Sharia Abdel Khalek Sarwat, Downtown; per hr E£3; ⏱ 24hr) In front of El-Tahrir Kushari.
Internet Egypt (Map pp102-3; per hr E£10; ⏱ 9am-midnight) In the basement of the Nile Hilton shopping mall. Students receive a 20% discount.

Internet@Cafe (Map p109; 25 Sharia Ismail Mohammed, Zamalek; per hr E£5; ⏱ 9am-1am)

Medical Services

Many of Cairo's hospitals have antiquated equipment and a cavalier attitude to hygiene, but there are some exceptions, including the **As-Salam International Hospital** (Map pp98-9; ☎ 524 0250, emergency ☎ 524 0077; Corniche el-Nil, Ma'adi).

There is no shortage of pharmacies in Cairo and almost anything can be obtained without a prescription. Pharmacies that operate 24 hours and deliver include **Al-Ezaby** (Bulaq Map p109; Arcadia Mall, Corniche el-Nil; Heliopolis ☎ 414 8467; 1 Sharia Tayseer).

Money

There are banks and forex bureaus all over town; the Banque Misr branches at the Nile Hilton and Mena House Oberoi hotels are open 24 hours. There are ATMs throughout the city.
Amex (⏱ 9am-4.30pm) Midan Tahrir (Map pp102-3; ☎ 578 5001; Nile Hilton, Midan Tahrir, Downtown); Sharia Qasr el-Nil (Map pp102-3; ☎ 574 7991; 15 Sharia Qasr el-Nil, Downtown) Exchanges travellers cheques and supplies US dollars.
Thomas Cook (emergency hotline ☎ 010 140 1367) Downtown (Map pp102-3; ☎ 574 3955; 17 Sharia Mahmoud Bassiouni; ⏱ 9am-4.30pm Sat-Thu); Garden City (Map pp102-3; ☎ 795 8544; Semiramis Intercontinental, Corniche el-Nil; ⏱ 8am-4.30pm Sat-Thu) Same services as Amex.

Post

Main post office (Map pp102-3; ☎ 391 2615; Midan Ataba; ⏱ 8am-6pm Sat-Thu, 8am-noon Fri & public holidays)

Telephone

In Cairo, there are telephone centrales (Map pp102-3) located on the northern side of Midan Tahrir (in central Cairo) and on Sharia Mohammed Mahmoud, Bab al-Luq, Sharia Adly, next to the Windsor Hotel off Sharia Alfy, and on Sharia 26th of July in Zamalek. All of these have a couple of cardphones.

Tourist Information

Main tourist office (Map pp102-3; ☎ 391 3454; 5 Sharia Adly, Downtown; ⏱ 8.30am-7pm) Staff seem totally uninterested in supplying tourist information. It's not worth a visit.

Visa Extensions

All visa business is carried out at the **Mogamma** (Map pp102-3; Midan Tahrir, Downtown; ⊙ 8am-1.30pm Sat-Wed), a 14-storey Egypto-Stalinist monolith. Foreigners go up to the 1st floor, turn right and proceed straight down the corridor ahead. Go to window 12 for a form, fill it out and then buy stamps from window 43 before returning to window 12 and submitting your form with the stamps, one photograph, and photocopies of the photo and visa pages of your passport (photos and photocopies can be organised on the ground floor). The visa extension will be processed overnight and available for collection from 9am the next day.

SIGHTS

Egyptian Museum

More than 100,000 relics and antiquities from almost every period of ancient Egyptian history are housed in the **Egyptian Museum** (Map p104; ☎ 575 4319; Midan Tahrir, Downtown; adult/student E£60/30; ⊙ 9am-6.15pm). To put that in perspective, if you spent only one minute at each exhibit it would take more than nine months to see everything. Some of the museum's exhibits will be moved to the new 'Great Museum', close to the Pyramids in Giza, but this isn't scheduled to open until 2008 at the earliest.

Guides costs E£50 per hour and congregate outside the ticket box. You must check your cameras into the baggage room before entering the museum. Access to the Royal Mummy Room costs an additional E£80/40; tickets for this are bought at the 1st-floor entrance to the room.

There are many rooms to see, but those that are particularly noteworthy are described here.

GROUND FLOOR

Rooms 32, 37 & 42 – Old Kingdom Rooms

Room 32 is dominated by the **double statue of Rahotep and Nofret**. The simple lines of this limestone sculpture make the figures seem almost contemporary, despite having been around for a staggering 4600 years. Also in here are the panels known as the **Meidum Geese**, part of a frieze that originates from a mud-brick mastaba at Meidum, near Al-Fayoum (to this day, the lakes there are still

host to a great variety of bird life). Room 37 contains the **tomb of Queen Hetepheres**, mother of Khufu, builder of the Great Pyramid at Giza. Room 42 holds what some consider to be the museum's masterpiece – a larger-than-life-size **statue of Khafre**, builder of the second Pyramid at Giza.

Room 3 – Amarna Room

This room is devoted to **Akhenaten** (1352–1336 BC), the 'heretic pharaoh' who set up ancient Egypt's first and last monotheistic faith. Compare the bulbous bellies, hips and thighs, and the elongated heads and thick, Mick Jagger–like lips of these statues with the sleek, hard-edged norm of typical Pharaonic sculpture. Also very striking is the delicate, but unfinished, **head of Nefertiti**, Akhenaten's wife.

1ST FLOOR

Room 2 – Royal Tombs of Tanis

This is a glittering collection of gold- and silver-encrusted amulets, gold funerary masks, daggers, bracelets, collars, gold sandals, and finger and toe coverings from five intact New Kingdom tombs found at the Delta site of Tanis.

EGYPT

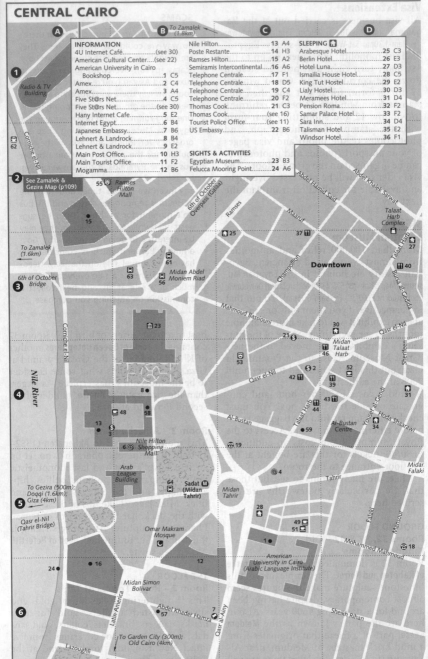

CENTRAL CAIRO

INFORMATION
4U Internet Café	(see 30)
American Cultural Center	(see 22)
American University in Cairo Bookshop	1 C5
Amex	2 C4
Amex	3 A4
Five St@rs Net	4 C5
Five St@rs Net	(see 30)
Hany Internet Cafe	5 E2
Internet Egypt	6 B4
Japanese Embassy	7 B6
Lehnert & Landrock	8 B4
Lehnert & Landrock	9 E2
Main Post Office	10 H3
Main Tourist Office	11 F2
Mogamma	12 B6
Nile Hilton	13 A4
Poste Restante	14 H3
Ramses Hilton	15 A2
Semiramis Intercontinental	16 A6
Telephone Centrale	17 F1
Telephone Centrale	18 D5
Telephone Centrale	19 C4
Telephone Centrale	20 F2
Thomas Cook	21 C3
Thomas Cook	(see 16)
Tourist Police Office	(see 11)
US Embassy	22 B6

SIGHTS & ACTIVITIES
Egyptian Museum	23 B3
Felucca Mooring Point	24 A6

SLEEPING 🏠
Arabesque Hotel	25 C3
Berlin Hotel	26 E3
Hotel Luna	27 D3
Ismailia House Hotel	28 C5
King Tut Hostel	29 E2
Lialy Hostel	30 D3
Meramees Hotel	31 D4
Pension Roma	32 F2
Samar Palace Hotel	33 F2
Sara Inn	34 D4
Talisman Hotel	35 E2
Windsor Hotel	36 F1

Radio & TV Building

See Zamalek & Gezira Map (p109)

Ramses Hilton Mall

To Zamalek (1.6km)

6th of October Bridge

Nile River

Corniche el-Nil

To Zamalek (1.8km)

6th of October Overpass (Galaa)

Ramses

Maaruf

Abdel Hamid Said

Abdel Khalek Sarwat

Talaat Harb Complex

Downtown

Midan Abdel Moniem Riad

Champollion

Mahmoud Bassiouni

Talaat Harb

Busta al-Gedida

Qasr el-Nil

Midan Talaat Harb

Qasr el-Nil

Sherifeen

Youssef al-Gendi

Hoda Shaarawi

Al-Bustan

Al-Bustan Centre

Midan Falaki

Nile Hilton Shopping Mall

Arab League Building

Sadat (Midan Tahrir)

Midan Tahrir

Tahrir

To Gezira (500m); Doqqi (1.6km); Giza (4km)

Qasr el-Nil (Tahrir Bridge)

Falaki

Mansour

Omar Makram Mosque

American University in Cairo (Arabic Language Institute)

Mohammed Mahmoud

Midan Simon Bolivar

Abdel Khader Hamza

Latin America

Qasr al-Ainy

Sheikh Rihan

To Garden City (300m); Old Cairo (4km)

Lazoughli

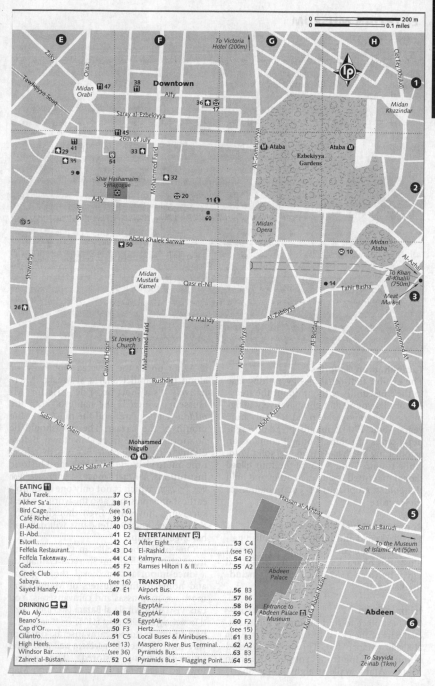

EGYPT

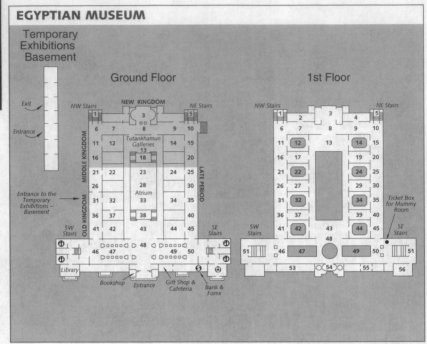

Tutankhamun Galleries

The exhibit that outshines everything else in the museum is without doubt the treasure of this young and comparatively insignificant pharaoh, who ruled for only nine years. About 1700 items are spread throughout a series of rooms. Room 3 contains an astonishing **death mask** made of solid gold, while rooms 7 and 8 house the four **gilded shrines** that fitted inside each other and held the gold sarcophagus of Tutankhamun at their centre.

Room 56 – Royal Mummy Room

This darkened and somewhat ghoulish gallery houses the bodies of 11 of Egypt's most illustrious pharaohs and queens, who ruled Egypt between 1552 and 1069 BC, including **Ramses II**.

Islamic Cairo   مصر الاسلامية

The best place to start exploring this medieval part of the city is the great bazaar, **Khan al-Khalili** (Map p105). This is easy to find if you're walking from central Cairo: from Midan Ataba walk straight along Sharia

al-Azhar under the elevated motorway, or along the parallel Sharia al-Muski. Alternatively it's a short taxi ride – ask for 'Al-Hussein', which is the name of both the *midan* (city square) and the mosque at the mouth of the bazaar. The fare should be no more than E£5 from Downtown. Before diving into the bazaar, it's worth taking time out to visit one of Cairo's most historic institutions, **Al-Azhar Mosque** (Map p105; admission free; 24hr), which is not only one of Cairo's earliest mosques, but also the world's oldest surviving university. Even though admission is free, pushy attendants will demand baksheesh (a tip).

One of the best walks in Cairo is north from Khan al-Khalili up Sharia al-Gamaliyya, a once-important medieval thoroughfare and home to fine clusters of Mamluk-era mosques, madrassas and caravanserais. You can visit the **Wikala al-Bazara** (Map p105; Sharia al-Tombakshiyya; adult/student E£10/5; 10am-5pm), a beautifully restored caravanserai, on your way towards the old **northern wall** and **gates** (currently being restored). The square-towered **Bab an-Nasr** (Gate of Victory; Map p105) and the rounded **Bab al-Futuh** (Gate of Conquests; Map p105) were built in 1087 as the two main northern entrances to the new walled Fatimid city of Al-Qahira. Returning to the bazaar via Sharia al-Muizz li-Din Allah, don't miss the spectacular **Beit el-Suhaymi** (Darb al-Asfar; Map p105; adult/student E£20/10; 9am-5pm), a beautifully restored complex of three houses. You'll find it tucked down a small alley. This part of Islamic Cairo is home to the city's most historic and architecturally significant madrassas, including the **Madrassa & Mausoleum of Barquq** (Map p105; baksheesh requested; 6am-9pm) and the **Madrassa & Mausoleum of Qalaun** (Map p105), which was closed for restoration at the time of research.

If you walk east from Al-Hussein along Sharia al-Azhar and bear right after breasting the top of the hill, walking under the overpass and straight on, you'll come to the fascinating **Northern Cemetery** (commonly known as the 'City of the Dead'; Map pp98–9), home to the splendid **Mosque of Qaitbey** (Map pp98–9).

South of Khan al-Khalili, a busy market street runs down past the **Mausoleum of Al-Ghouri** (Map p105; closed for renovation at the time of research) and the exquisite **Mosque & Madrassa of Al-Ghouri** (Map p105; admission free) to the twin minarets of **Bab Zuwella** (Map pp98–9), the sole surviving gate from the old city's southern wall. The view from the minarets is about the best in Cairo. Continuing south from Bab Zuweila, you pass through the **Street of the Tentmakers**, a covered bazaar filled by craftsmen specialising in appliqué work. From here you can turn right to make your way to the **Museum of Islamic Art** (Map pp98–9; also closed at the time of research), home to one of the world's finest collections of Islamic applied arts, or go left to the Citadel (a long walk).

Commenced by Saladin (Salah ad-Din al-Ayyoub) back in the 12th century, the **Citadel** (Map pp98–9; 512 1735; Midan al-Qala'a; adult/student E£50/25; 8am-5pm winter, 8am-6pm summer) is one of the city's busiest tourist attractions – but we're not quite sure why. Its walls encircle an assortment of three very different and not terribly impressive mosques, and several palaces housing some fairly indifferent museums. The best part of any visit is marvelling at the view from the two terraces; on a clear day you can see all the way to the Giza Pyramids.

Don't miss the **Mosque of ibn Tulun** (Beit al-Kritliyya; Map pp98–9; 364 7822; www.gawp.org; Sharia ibn Tulun; admission E£6; 8am-6pm), 800m southwest of the Citadel. It's quite unlike any other mosque in Cairo, mainly because the inspiration is almost entirely Iraqi – the closest things to it are the ancient mosques of Samarra. Right next door to Ibn Tulun is

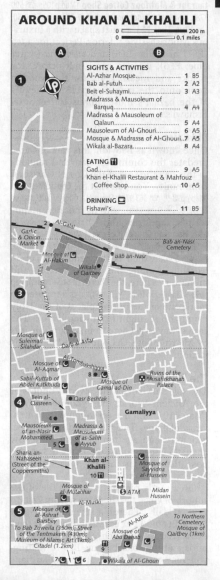

AROUND KHAN AL-KHALILI

0 ____ 200 m
0 ____ 0.1 miles

SIGHTS & ACTIVITIES
Al-Azhar Mosque................................1 B5
Bab al-Futuh.......................................2 A2
Beit el-Suhaymi.................................3 A3
Madrassa & Mausoleum of
  Barquq...4 A4
Madrassa & Mausoleum of
  Qalaun...5 A4
Mausoleum of Al-Ghouri.................6 A5
Mosque & Madrassa of Al-Ghouri..7 A5
Wikala al-Bazara................................8 A4

EATING
Gad...9 A5
Khan el-Khalili Restaurant & Mahfouz
  Coffee Shop...................................10 A5

DRINKING
Fishawi's..11 B5

Garlic & Onion Market
Al-Galal
Bab an-Nasr Cemetery
Mosque of Al-Hakim
Bab an-Nasr
Wikala of Qaitbey
Al-Muizz li-Din Allah
Al-Gamaliyya
Mosque of Suleiman Silahdar
Darb al-Asfar
Mosque of Al-Aqmar
Al-Tombakshiyya
Sabil-Kuttab of Abdel Katkhuda
Mosque of Gamal ad-Din
Ruins of the Musafirkhanah Palace
Bein al-Qasreen
Qasr Beshtak
Gamaliyya
Mausoleum of an-Nasir Mohammed
Madrassa & Mausoleum of as-Salih Ayyub
Mosque of Sayyidna al-Hussein
Sharia an-Nahaseen (Street of the Coppersmiths)
Khan al-Khalili
ATM
Midan Hussein
Mosque of al-Mutahar
Al-Muski
Mosque of al-Ashraf Barsbey
Al-Azhar
To Northern Cemetery; Mosque of Qaitbey (1km)
To Bab Zuweila (350m); Street of the Tentmakers (430m); Museum of Islamic Art (1km); Citadel (1.2km)
Mosque of Abu Dahab
Wikala of Al-Ghouri

the **Gayer-Anderson Museum** (Map pp98-9; Sharia ibn Tulun; adult/student E£30/15, video E£20; ☉ 8am-4pm), two 16th-century houses restored and furnished by a British major between 1935 and 1942. It's well worth a visit.

After wandering the bazaar and dealing with its touts there's nothing better than sheltering for a while in **Khan el-Khalili Restaurant & Mahfouz Coffee Shop** (Map p105; ☎ 590 3788; 5 Sikket el-Baddistan; snacks E£9-20, mains E£30-50; ☉ 10am-2am; ⊠), a quiet space with a luxurious Moorish-style interior. Perfect for a tea (E£7) or Stella (E£8) and a *sheesha* (water pipe; E£6), it's also good (but pricey) for snacks and meals. Look for the wooden door onto the lane. See p113 for details of the bazaar's most famous coffeehouse, Fishawi's.

Old Cairo مصر القاديمة

Once known as Babylon, this part of Cairo predates the coming of Islam and remains to this day the seat of the Coptic Christian community. You can visit the **Coptic Museum** (Map pp98-9; ☎ 363 9742; Sharia Mar Girgis; adult/student E£35/20; ☉ 9am-4pm), with its mosaics, manuscripts, tapestries and Christian artwork, and **Hanging Church** (Kineeset al-Muallaqa; Map pp98-9; Sharia Mar Girgis; admission free; ☉ mass 8-11am Fri, 7-10am Sun), which is the centre of Coptic worship. Among the other churches and monasteries here, the **Church of St Sergius** (Map pp98-9; admission free; ☉ 8am-4pm) is supposed to mark one of the resting places of the Holy Family on its flight from King Herod. The easiest way to get here from Midan Tahrir is by Metro (50pt). Get out at the Mar Girgis station.

The Pyramids

The sole survivor of the Seven Wonders of the Ancient World, the Pyramids of Giza (Map p107) still live up to more than 4000 years of hype. Their extraordinary shape, geometry and age render them somehow alien; they seem to rise out of the desert and pose the ever-fascinating question 'How were we built, and why?'.

On a sandy plateau in the middle of the suburb of Giza, the site is open from 7am to 7.30pm daily. There's a general admission fee of E£60/30 per adult/student, and then extra charges for each of the three Pyramids and the solar barque. Before visiting, you may want to look at www.guardians

.net/hawass, the official website of Dr Zahi Hawass, secretary general of the Supreme Council of Antiquities and director of the Giza Pyramids Excavation.

If you're keen to ride around the site on a horse, donkey or camel, or in a carriage, there are stables encircling the plateau. Rates range from E£10 per hour for a donkey to E£30 for a carriage.

GREAT PYRAMID OF KHUFU (CHEOPS)

The oldest pyramid at Giza and the largest in Egypt, the Great Pyramid of Khufu stood 146.5m high when it was completed in around 2600 BC. Although there isn't much to see inside the pyramid, the experience of climbing through such an ancient structure is unforgettable, though completely impossible if you suffer from even the tiniest degree of claustrophobia. The elderly and the unfit shouldn't attempt it either, as it is very steep.

Entry to the Great Pyramid costs an extortionate E£150/75 per adult/student. Only Egyptian pounds are accepted. Tickets are limited to 300 per day – 150 in the morning and 150 in the afternoon. These go on sale at 8am and 1pm at the dedicated ticket box in front of and slightly to the east (city side) of the pyramid and you'll need to queue ahead of time. Cameras are not allowed into the pyramid – you must surrender them to the guards at the entrance, who will ask for baksheesh before returning them.

PYRAMID OF KHAFRE (CHEPHREN)

Southwest of the Great Pyramid, and with almost the same dimensions, is the Pyramid of Khafre. At first it seems larger than that of Khufu, his father, because it stands on higher ground and its peak still has part of the original limestone casing that once covered the entire structure. Among the most interesting features of this pyramid are the substantial remains of Khafre's funerary temple, located outside to the east. Entry costs E£30/15 per adult/student and tickets are obtained from the ticket box in front of the pyramid.

PYRAMID OF MENKAURE (MYCERINUS)

At a height of 62m (originally 66.5m), this is the smallest of the three Pyramids. Extensive damage was done to the exterior by a 16th-century caliph who wanted to demol-

THE GIZA PLATEAU

INFORMATION
Giza Tourist Office.....................1 C1

SIGHTS & ACTIVITIES
Eastern Cemetery.......................2 C2
Great Pyramid of Khufu (Cheops)..3 C2
Khafre's Funerary Temple............4 C3
Khafre's Valley Temple................5 D3
Menkaure's Funerary Temple......6 B3
Menkaure's Valley Temple.........7 C3
Pyramid of Khafre (Chephren).....8 B3
Pyramid of Menkaure (Mycerinus) 9 B3
Pyramid of Queen Hetepheres...10 C2
Queens' Pyramids......................11 C2
Queens' Pyramids......................12 B3
Solar Barque Museum...............13 C2
Solar Barque Pits......................14 C2
Sound-&-Light Auditorium.......15 D3
Sound-&-Light Ticket Office.....16 D3
Sphinx......................................17 C3
Stables.....................................18 C1
Ticket Box for Great Pyramid....19 C2
Ticket Box for Pyramids of Khafre &
  Menkaure.............................20 B2
Ticket Office.............................21 C1
Ticket Office.............................22 D3
Tomb of Khenthawes...............23 C3
Tomb of Seshemnufer IV...........24 C2
Western Cemetery....................25 B2

EATING
Khan el-Khalili Restaurant & Hotel
  Bar..26 C1

DRINKING
Coffee Shop.............................27 D3

TRANSPORT
355/357 Bus Stop.....................28 C1

ish all the Pyramids. Entry costs E£25/15 per adult/student and tickets are obtained from the ticket box in front of the Pyramid of Khafre.

THE SPHINX
Known in Arabic as Abu al-Hol (Father of Terror), the Sphinx is carved almost entirely from one huge piece of limestone left over from the carving of the stones for the Great Pyramid of Khufu. It is not known when it was carved, but one theory is that it was Khafre who thought of shaping the rock into a lion's body with a god's face, wearing the royal headdress of Egypt. Another theory is that it is the likeness of Khafre himself that has been staring out over the desert sands for so many centuries.

SOLAR BARQUE MUSEUM
Along the eastern and southern sides of the Great Pyramid are five long pits that once contained the pharaoh's funerary barques. One of these ancient wooden vessels, possibly the oldest boat in existence, was unearthed in 1954. It was restored and a glass

museum (adult/student E£35/20, 9am-4pm winter, 9am-5pm summer) was built over it to protect it from the elements. It's well worth a look.

SOUND-&-LIGHT SHOW
Hordes of tour groups converge on an area below the Sphinx for the nightly **sound-and-light show** (386 3469; www.sound-light.egypt.com; adult/child 6-12 E£60/30; 6.30pm, 7.30pm & 8.30pm winter, 1hr later in summer). There are three performances in a variety of languages. Check with the Giza tourist office for the schedule or check the website. Though there's officially no student discount, we have heard from travellers who have managed to negotiate one.

EATING & DRINKING
Just below the Sphinx there's an expensive **coffee shop** (Map p107; tea E£10, fresh juice E£15) with an outdoor terrace and truly amazing view. It's just outside the site, but as long as you have your ticket, the guards will let you come in again. If you're in need of something stronger, the bar and the Khan el-Khalili Restaurant (Map p107) at the nearby

Mena House Oberoi serve up Stella (E£19) in fabulous c1960s Arabesque surrounds. For meals, try the Peace II seafood restaurant, Christo Nile View Fish Restaurant or the local branch of Felfela, all of which are around the corner from Mena House. A short taxi ride away (no more than E£5), on the road to Saqqara, is the extremely popular **Andrea's** (☎ 381 0938; ☽ 10am-8pm), which serves a great set meal of roast chicken, hummus, salad and bread (E£45) in a garden setting on the Maryoutia Canal. A Stella costs E£15.

GETTING THERE & AROUND

Bus 355/357 runs from Heliopolis to the Pyramids via Midan Tahrir every 20 minutes. It picks up from the road (not the island) under the overpass at Midan Abdel Moniem Riad (Map pp102–3) and can sometimes be flagged down from the side of the road near the northwestern Metro stairs on Midan Tahrir. You'll recognise it by the 'CTA' sign on its side. It costs E£2 and takes 45 minutes.

Expect to pay about E£20 one way for a taxi. Returning to Cairo, these leave from outside the Mena House Oberoi hotel. They'll try for E£40, so you'll need to bargain hard.

ACTIVITIES

You can hire a **felucca** (Map pp102–3) for about E£30 per hour from the mooring point by the Semiramis Intercontinental, on the Corniche. However, the best place to hire feluccas is about 800m to the south at the Dok Dok landing stage (Map pp98–9), just short of the bridge over to Le Meridien hotel.

CAIRO FOR CHILDREN

There is plenty to keep children entertained in Cairo. If the **Pyramids** and **Egyptian Museum** aren't enough to keep them happy, they can feed the animals (25pt per feeding) at the **Cairo Zoo** (Guineenat al-Haywanet; Map pp98–9; ☎ 570 8895; Midan al-Gamaa, Giza; admission 25pt; ☽ 9am-4pm); pretend to be a pirate on a **felucca ride**; or investigate the new **Al-Azhar Park** (Map pp98–9; ☽ 10am-10pm), home to one of the few children's playgrounds in the city. If the situation is serious and only bribery will help, try **Top Toys** (Map p109; ☎ 736 3741; 13 Sharia Brazil, Zamalek; ☽ 10am-11pm).

TOURS

Myriad companies and individuals offer tours of sights within and around Cairo. We recommend Salah Muhammad's **Noga Tours** (☎ 205 7908, 012 313 8446; www.first24hours.com), as he employs excellent English-speaking guides, Egyptologists and drivers. His vehicles are also properly maintained. If you're keen to dispense with a guide and hire a taxi for the day, friendly **Fathy el-Menesy** (☎ 259 3218, 012 278 1572) owns a well-maintained Peugeot and speaks English. Otherwise, ask at your hotel. To give you an idea of cost, the Berlin Hotel can organise a local taxi to visit Dahshur, Memphis and Saqqara for E£40 per person; Fathy el-Menesy charges between E£200 and E£250 for a full day; and Noga Tours charges US$22.50 plus entry fees per person for a full-day trip to the Giza Pyramids, Memphis and Saqqara. Its half-day tour of Dahshur costs US$19 plus entry fees per person.

SLEEPING
Budget

Inexpensive hostels, hotels and pensions are concentrated in Downtown, mainly on the higher floors of office buildings on and around Sharia Talaat Harb. All tend to be very hot in summer. If you're a light sleeper, request a rear room rather than one facing a busy street.

Hotel Luna (Map pp102–3; ☎ 396 1020; www.hotel lunacairo.com; 5th fl, 27 Sharia Talaat Harb, Downtown; s/d with shared bathroom E£60/80, with private bathroom E£80/100; ☒ ☐) The Luna is one of the best budget hotels in Egypt. Its large rooms have crisp, clean linen and air-con; seven offer private bathrooms and the others have hand basins. Shared bathrooms are so clean they gleam. There's a sitting area near reception where you can relax, and guests have free use of the kitchen. Guests staying four or more nights get a free airport pickup. Fantastic.

Lialy Hostel (Map pp102–3; ☎ 575 2802; www .lialyhostel.com; 3rd fl, 8 Midan Talaat Harb, Downtown; dm/s/d E£25/50/60, s/d with air-con E£70/80; ☒) One of the friendliest hostels in the city, right in the thick of the action. Eleven rooms share three bathrooms; everything is clean but the hot water sometimes runs out. Some rooms have double beds and air-con. There's a small collection of books to read, a large breakfast room with satellite TV, and free use of the kitchen. Also fantastic.

ZAMALEK & GEZIRA

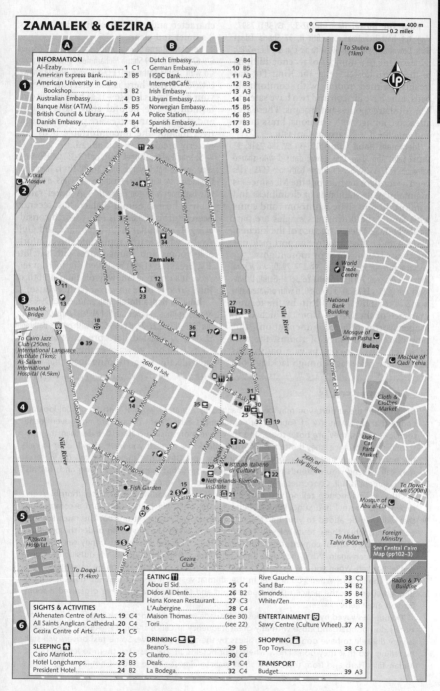

0 — 400 m
0 — 0.2 miles

INFORMATION
Al-Ezaby............................1 C1
American Express Bank.........2 B5
American University in Cairo
  Bookshop........................3 B2
Australian Embassy..............4 D3
Banque Misr (ATM)..............5 B5
British Council & Library........6 A4
Danish Embassy..................7 B4
Diwan.............................8 C4
Dutch Embassy...................9 B4
German Embassy.................10 B5
HSBC Bank.......................11 A3
Internet@Café...................12 B3
Irish Embassy....................13 A3
Libyan Embassy.................14 B4
Norwegian Embassy.............15 B5
Police Station....................16 B5
Spanish Embassy................17 B3
Telephone Centrale.............18 A3

SIGHTS & ACTIVITIES
Akhenaten Centre of Arts......19 C4
All Saints Anglican Cathedral..20 C4
Gezira Centre of Arts...........21 C5

SLEEPING
Cairo Marriott....................22 C5
Hotel Longchamps..............23 B3
President Hotel...................24 B2

EATING
Abou El Sid......................25 C4
Didos Al Dente..................26 B2
Hana Korean Restaurant......27 C3
L'Aubergine......................28 C4
Maison Thomas.............(see 30)
Torii...........................(see 22)

DRINKING
Beano's...........................29 B5
Cilantro...........................30 C4
Deals.............................31 C4
La Bodega........................32 C4

Rive Gauche......................33 C3
Sand Bar.........................34 B2
Simonds..........................35 B4
White/Zen........................36 B3

ENTERTAINMENT
Sawy Centre (Culture Wheel)..37 A3

SHOPPING
Top Toys.........................38 C3

TRANSPORT
Budget............................39 A3

EGYPT

King Tut Hostel (Map pp102-3; ☎ 391 7897; king_tut_hostel@hotmail.com; 8th fl, 37 Sharia Talaat Harb, Downtown; s/d E£40/60, with air-con & TV E£45/80; ✂ ▣) One of a number of recent additions to the Cairo hostel scene, the King Tut has freshly painted rooms with comfortable beds; nine have air-con and two have satellite TV. All share spotless bathrooms. There's an attractive lounge with cushions, brass tables and satellite TV. Nearly as fantastic.

Meramees Hotel (Map pp102-3; ☎ 396 2318; 32 Sharia Sabri Abu Alam, Downtown; dm/s/d with shared bathroom E£17/35/50, d with private bathroom E£75) It's been around for a while, but the Meramees is maintaining its standards of cleanliness and comfort. Rooms share bathrooms and come with fans – the downstairs singles are particularly nice. There's free use of the kitchen, free tea and coffee, and free airport pick-ups for guests staying three or more nights.

Sara Inn (Map pp102-3; ☎ 392 2940; www.sarainnhostel.2ya.com; 7th fl, 21 Sharia Yousef el-Gendi, Downtown; dm E£25, s E£25-50, d E£40-60, d with private bathroom & air-con E£120; ✂ ▣) Run by the former manager of the Dahab Hotel (which is no longer worthy of a recommendation), this new place has a range of rooms, the best of which have air-con, private bathrooms and a hefty price tag. Though lacking both

character and enough shared bathrooms, it's quiet and clean.

Pension Roma (Map pp102-3; ☎ 391 1088; fax 579 6243; 4th fl, 169 Sharia Mohammed Farid, Downtown; s/d with shared bathroom E£37/69, with private shower E£40/78) Staying here is like sleeping over at your grandma's house – it's charmingly old-fashioned. The helpful staff, large rooms and elegant lounge area are positives; negatives include the uncomfortable beds and miserly breakfast. Book ahead.

Samar Palace Hotel (Map pp102-3; ☎ 390 1093; samar-palace-hotel@yahoo.com; 3rd fl, Sharia Magharipi, Downtown; s/d with shared bathroom E£35/65, d with private bathroom & air-con E£75; ✂) A hotel rather than a hostel, Samar Palace has recently been refurbished and is really worth considering. It's popular with Egyptians and Gulf Arabs, who clearly appreciate the comfortable rooms and lounge area with satellite TV. Breakfast (E£5) is served on the roof terrace. It's down a laneway off Sharia 26th of July, directly over an *ahwa* (coffeehouse).

Ismailia House Hotel (Map pp102-3; ☎ 796 3122; ismahouse@hotmail.com; 8th fl, 1 Midan Tahrir, Downtown; dm E£16-17, s E£22-27, d E£48-50, d with private bathroom E£60-65; ▣) Listed here predominantly due to its fabulous views over the *midan* and to the Nile, this long-running hostel has rooms

---

CAIRO HOTEL SCAMS

On arrival at the airport, you may be approached by a man or woman with an official-looking badge that says 'Ministry of Tourism' or something similar. These people are not government tourism officials, they are hotel touts, and they have more tricks up their sleeves than they do scruples. For instance, they'll often ask if you've booked a hotel. If you have, they'll offer to call the hotel to make sure that a room is waiting for you. Of course, they don't call the hotel – they call a friend who pretends to be the hotel and says that there is no booking and that his establishment is full. Concerned, the tout will offer to find you an alternative…

Other scams include telling you that the hotel you're heading for is closed/horrible/very expensive/a brothel and suggesting a 'better' place, from which they will earn a commission that will then be added to your bill. Many taxi drivers will also try it on too. The most innovative scam is when these touts ask you your name and where you're staying under the pretence of striking up a casual conversation. After a chat (often on the airport bus), they say goodbye and aren't seen again. What they next do is call a friend, who goes and stands outside the hotel you've booked. When you arrive, he or she will ask 'Are you…?', using the name you volunteered back at the airport. When you answer in the affirmative, you'll be told that the hotel has been flooded/closed by the police/totally booked out and that the owners have organised a room for you elsewhere.

Do not be swayed by anyone who tries to dissuade you from going to the hotel of your choice. Hotels do not open and close with any great frequency in Cairo, and if it's listed in this book it is very unlikely to have gone out of business by the time you arrive. Some taxi drivers will stall by telling you that they don't know where your hotel is. In that case tell them to let you out at Midan Talat Harb and from there it's a short walk to almost all the budget hotels.

that could benefit from a good scrub. Ask for rooms 805, 810 or 820, all of which come with balcony and amazing views. There's a pleasant lounge with satellite TV.

Berlin Hotel (Map pp102-3; ☎ 395 7502; berlin hotelcairo@hotmail.com; 4th fl, 2 Sharia Shawarby, Downtown; s/d E£77/97; ☒ ☐) This small place, just off Sharia Qasr el-Nil, is pricey, but is worth considering due to its very helpful management. Rooms come with comfortable beds, air-con and shower cubicles.

Midrange

Hotel Longchamps (Map p109; ☎ 735 2311; www .hotellongchamps.com; 21 Sharia Ismail Mohammed, Zamalek; s US$42-46, d US$56-62; ☒ ☒) This place is probably the best midrange option in Cairo. Pristine rooms feature extremely comfortable beds, private bathrooms and satellite TV. There's a generous breakfast buffet, as well as a restaurant (alcohol served) and a blissfully peaceful rear balcony where guests can relax with a tea. Owner Hebba Bakri is an excellent host.

Victoria Hotel (Map pp98-9; ☎ 589 2290; info@ victoria.com.eg; 66 Sharia al-Gomhuriyya; s/d US$28/37; ☒ ☐) It's a shame the Victoria's location isn't better. Near Ramses train station, it offers large rooms with comfortable beds, satellite TV and private bathrooms. Though lacking atmosphere, it offers four-star amenities for two-star prices and that's a pretty attractive proposition.

Arabesque Hotel (Map pp102-3; ☎ 579 9679; arabesque_hotel@yahoo.com; 11 Sharia Ramses, Downtown; s/d with shared bathroom E£60/80, with private bathroom & air-con Ff100/150; ☒) Midrange hotels are thin on the ground, so the Arabesque is destined to do well. Rooms have a bland fit out but are comfortable and clean; avoid those at the front, which overlook one of the city's busiest and noisiest motorways. The lounge has great views over the Nile, comfortable seating and a satellite TV.

President Hotel (Map p109; ☎ 735 0718; preshotl@ thewayout.net; 22 Sharia Taha Hussein, Zamalek; s/d US$70/55; ☒ ☐) The President's in-house patisserie, Le Bec Sucré, is one of the best in the city, and breakfasts are a highlight of any stay. The mouldy bathrooms provide the downside. Rooms come with three-star accoutrements, including satellite TV.

Windsor Hotel (Map pp102-3; ☎ 591 5277; www .windsorcairo.com; 19 Sharia Alfy, Downtown; s/d with shower & hand basin US$30/38, with private bathroom

US$37/46; ☒ ☐) This ageing edifice was the British Officers' Club before 1952 and retains a colonial air. Rooms have more atmosphere than comfort, though all come with air-con. The large deluxe rooms (single/double US$47/57) also have satellite TV. The hotel's best feature is its charming lounge-bar.

Top End

Cairo Marriott (Map p109; ☎ 735 8888; www.marriott .com/CAIEG; Sharia al-Saray al-Gezira, Zamalek; r from US$157; ☒ ☒ ☐ ☒) Despite the addition of two very modern towers that house all the rooms, this is one of the few historic hotels left in the city. It has a popular garden café, loads of restaurants, large rooms with all the mod cons and a health club. Breakfast costs an extra US$16.

EATING
Restaurants

In central Cairo, most places to eat are centred around Midan Talaat Harb. The city's most interesting eateries are over the river in the neighbourhood of Zamalek. In this section and other Eating sections throughout this chapter, we have noted when alcohol is available. All the other restaurants reviewed are booze-free.

Greek Club (Map pp102-3; ☎ 577 4999; 3 Sharia Qasr el-Nil, Downtown; mains E£9-16; ☼ 7am-2am) With its

EGYPT

great neoclassical interior, soaring ceilings and outdoor terrace, this Cairene institution oozes faded charm. There's no menu, but the waiter will reel off the dishes of the day, likely to include well-cooked Levantine choices such as shish tawooq (kebab made with marinated, spiced chicken, E£30) and excellent Greek salad (E£15). A Stella costs E£10. You'll find it above the Groppi Patisserie (entrance on the side).

Estoril (Map pp102-3; ☎ 574 3102; 12 Sharia Talaat Harb, Downtown; mezze E£6, mains E£29-56; ✖) Tucked down an alley opposite Amex, this eatery has been serving up traditional Egyptian and French dishes since 1959. It claims to offer its diners an intro into 'the esoteric Cairene's world of art, literature, journalism and the rest', and though we're not sure it delivers on this, we always like to linger over a beer and a few mezze dishes.

Hana Korean Restaurant (Map p109; ☎ 738 2972; 21 Sharia Aziz Abaza, Zamalek; dishes E£30-40; ✖) You'll feel as if you're in Seoul when you eat at this bustling Zamalek restaurant. The kimchi (pickled vegetables) is authentic and the Stella is ice cold – what more could you ask for?

Abou El Sid (Map p109; ☎ 735 9640; 157 Sharia 26th of July, Zamalek; mezze E£6-24, mains E£20-50; ✖ noon-2am; ✖) A sumptuous Orientalist fantasy of a restaurant-bar, Abou El Sid serves traditional Egyptian food to wannabe pashas, amid hanging lamps, large cushions and brass tables. Reservations are necessary. A beer costs E£20.

Felfela Restaurant (Map pp102-3; ☎ 392 2833; 15 Sharia Hoda Shaarawi, Downtown; mezze E£2-5, mains E£20-35; ✖ 8am-midnight; ✖) Perpetually packed with tourists, coach parties and locals, Felfela deserves its popularity. A

THE AUTHOR'S CHOICE

At-Tabie ad-Dumyati (Map pp98-9; ☎ 575 4211; 31 Sharia Orabi, Downtown; dishes E£2-8; ✖ 6am-1am) About 200m north of Midan Ramses, this highly recommended place offers the best cheap meals in Cairo. Your choice of four salads from a large array costs E£3.25, and a small plate of shwarma costs E£5.75. A fresh juice is E£2.50. You can sit down or take away. Highly recommended. There's also a branch in the food court of the Talaat Harb Commercial Centre.

bizarre jungle theme rules when it comes to the décor, but the food is straight-down-the-line Egyptian and consistently good, especially the mezze. A Stella costs E£12.

Maison Thomas (Map p109; ☎ 735 7057; 157 Sharia 26th of July, Zamalek; sandwiches E£16-26, pizzas E£19-28; ✖ 24hr; ✖) Is this the best pizza in Cairo? Many locals think it is, and they can be seen lining up to perch on the high stools and grab a quick pizza fix. You can eat in or take away (alcohol is sold only with takeaway).

Didos Al Dente (Map p109; ☎ 735 9117; 26 Sharia Bahgat Ali, Zamalek; pasta E£5-19; ✖) A pasta joint popular with students from the nearby AUC, Didos comes pretty close to living up to its claim of making the best pasta in town. It's tiny, so be prepared to wait on the street for a table.

Abou Shakra (Map pp98-9; ☎ 531 6111; 69 Sharia Qasr al-Aini, Garden City; ✖ 9am-2am; ✖) Abou Shakra is where to come for a skewer or two. It's been serving up its plates of kofta (mincemeat and spices grilled on a skewer) and kebabs (E£28), and shwarma sandwiches (E£6 to E£12) at this main branch since 1947 and locals love it to bits. There's takeaway at the front and a dining room behind it. Believe it or not, an imam reading from the Quran is posted next to the toilets on Friday.

L'Aubergine (Map p109; ☎ 738 0080; 5 Sharia Sayed al-Bakry, Zamalek; mains E£16-30; ✖ noon-2am; ✖) This dimly lit Western-style bistro isn't as glam as it used to be, but it still serves up a wide range of dishes, lots of which are vegetarian. Its upstairs bar (Stella E£14) is popular, and often has a DJ.

Café Riche (Map pp102-3; ☎ 392 9793; 17 Sharia Talaat Harb, Downtown; dishes E£12-25; ✖ 8am-midnight; ✖) This Cairo institution was being renovated when we visited. Once the favoured drinking spot of Cairo's intelligentsia, in recent years it's been a reliable spot to enjoy a meal and a glass of wine.

The city's best restaurants are found in its five-star hotels. Our favourites are both at the Semiramis Intercontinental: **Sabaya** (Map pp102-3; ☎ 795 7171; mains E£40-60; ✖), a world-class Lebanese restaurant, and its Thai neighbour **Bird Cage** (Map pp102-3; ☎ 795 7171; mains E£40-60; ✖) are both excellent. **Torii** (Map p109; ☎ 739 4691; set menus E£120-140, noodles E£53-88; ✖) at the Cairo Marriott is also worth a mention for its theatrical interior, fresh fish and promotional material, in which it claims to be 'the gateway to sushi and self-discovery'! All sell alcohol.

Quick Eats

Akher Sa'a (Map pp102-3; 8 Sharia Alfy, Downtown; meals E£3-4; ⏰ 24hr) A frantically busy fuul and ta'amiyya takeaway joint with a no-frills cafeteria next door, Akher Sa'a has a limited menu but its food is fresh and good.

Gad (Map pp102-3; ☎ 576 3583; 13 Sharia 26th of July, Downtown; ⏰ 7am-1am; ❄) This Western-style fast-food eatery is usually packed to the rafters with a constant stream of young Cairenes sampling its fresh, well-priced food. The fiteer with Greek cheese (E£9.50) is scrumptious, and the quarter chicken with rice and salad (E£10) is both flavoursome and great value. You can sit upstairs or take away from the street-front counters. There are also branches opposite Khan al-Khalili (Map p105) and on Sharia Mourad, Midan Giza (☎ 569 0250).

We recommend two Downtown joints that specialise in kushari: **Abu Tarek** (Map pp102-3; 40 Sharia Champollion, Downtown; small/large E£3/4; ⏰ 24hr), which has been serving up the stuff to locals for nearly as long as touts have been working the Ramses train station; and **Sayed Hanafy** (Map pp102-3; Midan Orabi, Downtown; small/medium/large E£2/3/4, ⏰ 24hr), which is relatively new, but building a big, well-deserved reputation.

Felfela takeaway (Map pp102-3; Sharia Talaat Harb, Downtown) sells excellent fuul and ta'amiyya sandwiches, and try the phenomenally popular **El-Abd** (Map pp102-3; ⏰ 8am-midnight; Sharia 26th of July, Downtown; Sharia Talaat Harb cnr Sharias Talaat Harb & Bursa al-Gedida, Downtown) for the best Oriental pastries in town (takeaway only).

DRINKING
Cafés

Italian-style coffee is very popular in Cairo, and there's an ever-growing number of stylish cafés serving up decent café latte for around E£6 (regular). The most popular are those of the Cilantro and Beano's chains. **Cilantro** (Downtown Map pp102-3; ☎ 792 4571; 31 Sharia Mohammed Mahmoud; Heliopolis ☎ 415 0167; 4 Sharia Ibrahim Korba; Ma'adi ☎ 521 1190; 17 Rd 219; Ma'adi City Centre ☎ 520 4410; Carrefour; Zamalek Map p109; ☎ 736 1115; 157 Sharia 26th of July) outlets are small and clean, with open fridges displaying packaged sandwiches, cakes and salads (E£5.50

to E£14) to eat in or take away. The brownies (E£3.50) are particularly delicious. Most of the outlets are nonsmoking (although the Downtown branch near the AUC isn't) and have wi-fi. **Beano's** (Downtown Map pp102-3; ☎ 792 2328; 49 Sharia al-Falaky; Heliopolis ☎ 690 3484; 15 Sharia Baghdad; Zamalek Map p109; ☎ 736 2388; 8 Midan al-Marsafy) branches offer more of the same. At Zamalek's famous **Simonds** (Map p109; ☎ 735 9436; 112 Sharia 26th of July, Zamalek), the barista has been frothing cappuccino (E£5) for over half a century, and the croissants (E£2.50) are as good as any served up in Paris.

Ahwas

Fishawi's (Map p105; Khan al-Khalili; tea E£3, sheesha E£4.50; ⏰ 24hr) One of Cairo's oldest and most famous coffeehouses, and an essential stop on every Cairo itinerary. It's a few steps off Midan Hussein.

Middle-aged and moneyed Cairenes frequent the popular *sheesha* courtyard and tent at the Nile Hilton's **Abu Aly** (Map pp102-3; sheesha E£7-8, tea E£9.50; ⏰ 10am-4am). The younger set tends to congregate at the bustling **Zahret al-Bustan** (Map pp102-3; Khan al-Khalili; tea E£3, sheesha E£4.50; ⏰ 24hr), in a laneway off Talaat Harb.

Bars

The best Downtown bars are **Estoril** (Map pp102-3; ☎ 574 3102; 12 Sharia Talaat Harb; ❄), which also has a restaurant (opposite) that serves good mezze; the **Cap d'Or** (Map pp102-3; Sharia Abdel Khalek Sarwat, Downtown); and the appallingly monikered **High Heels** (Map pp102-3; ☎ 578 0444; Corniche el-Nil, Downtown) at the Nile Hilton. If you want a quiet drink, you could do worse than colonise an armchair at the **Windsor Bar** (Map pp102-3; ☎ 591 5277; 19 Sharia Alfy, Downtown) at the Windsor Hotel (p111).

There's more choice in Zamalek. Cashed-up locals and expats prop up the bar at the stylish **La Bodega** (Map p109; ☎ 736 6761; 157 Sharia 26th of July, Zamalek; ⏰ noon-2am), and at **Abou El Sid** (Map p109; ☎ 735 9640; 157 Sharia 26th of July, Zamalek; ⏰ noon-2am), where you can order a *sheesha* with your drinks or eat in the restaurant (opposite). For a more casual alternative, try the bar above **L'Aubergine** (Map p109; ☎ 738 0800; 5 Sharia Sayed al-Bakry, Zamalek; ⏰ noon-2am; ❄), a Western-style restaurant (opposite); the rowdy **Deals** (Map p109; ☎ 736 0502; 2 Sharia Sayed al-Bakry, Zamalek; ⏰ 6pm-2am), off Sharia

26th of July; or the more laid-back **Sand Bar** (Map p109; ☎ 736 3558; 13a Sharia al-Marashly, Zamalek; ☼ 4pm-3am). Those who want to listen to music congregate at the likes of **White/Zen** (Map p109; ☎ 012 230 4404; 25 Sharia Hassan Assem, Zamalek), an *über*-glam bar that serves Thai food and noodles, hosts a DJ and sells two-for-one Heinekens at its Wednesday happy hour. They then move on to colonise the large dance floor and outdoor terrace at **Rive Gauche** (Map p109; ☎ 012 210 0129; Sharia Maahad el-Swissry, Zamalek).

ENTERTAINMENT
Sufi Dancing
There are regular displays of Sufi dancing by the **Al-Tannoura Egyptian Heritage Dance Troupe** (Map pp98-9; ☎ 512 1735; admission free; ☼ 7pm Mon, Wed & Sat winter, 8pm summer) at the El-Gawhara Theatre in the Citadel. Go to the exit gate rather than the main entrance gate of the Citadel and make sure you're there at least one hour before the performance.

Belly-Dancing
The best belly dancers perform at Cairo's five-star hotels. Current favourites are **Haroun El-Rashid nightclub** (Map pp102-3; ☎ 795 7171, ext 8011; Corniche el-Nil, Downtown; ☼ 11pm-3.30am Tue-Sun) at the Semiramis Intercontinental, where the famous Dina undulates; and the Cairo Sheraton's **Casablanca Club** (Alhambra; Map pp98-9; ☎ 336 9700; Midan al-Galaa, Doqqi; ☼ 7pm-4am Tue-Sun), where Soraya stars. Performances at these places begin late (around 1am). **Palmyra** (Map pp102-3; admission E£5.50 ☼ 10pm-4am), off Sharia 26th of July in Downtown, is a cavernous, dilapidated 1950s dance hall. It has a full Arab musical contingent, belly dancers who get better the more money is thrown at them, and an occasional singer or acrobat. The Stella here costs a very reasonable E£11, but the *sheeshas* are expensive (E£20 for apple). There's a minimum charge of E£35, which basically covers the entrance fee, a beer and a *sheesha*.

Live Music
For live music try the **Cairo Jazz Club** (Map pp98-9; ☎ 345 9939; 197 Sharia 26th of July, Agouza) or **After Eight** (Map pp102-3; ☎ 574 0855; 6 Sharia Qasr el-Nil, Downtown; minimum charge Fri-Wed E£60, Thu E£90; ☼ noon-2am). Several nights a week, concerts of everything from electronic fusion to classical to Nubian music are

held at the **Sawy Centre** (Culture Wheel; Map p109; ☎ 736 6178; www.culturewheel.com; Sharia 26th of July, Zamalek). The **Cairo Opera House** (Map pp98-9; ☎ 739 8132, 739 8144; www.operahouse.gov.eg; Gezira Exhibition Grounds) has two auditoriums hosting performances by the Cairo Opera and the Cairo Symphony Orchestra, as well as recitals and concerts by local and international jazz and classical musicians.

Cinemas
If you're keen to see an English-language film, try the **Ramses Hilton I & II cinemas** (Map pp102-3; ☎ 574 7435) at the Ramses Hilton shopping mall. Tickets at the 10.30am and 1.30pm sessions cost E£10; at the 6.30pm, 9.30pm and midnight sessions they're E£25.

GETTING THERE & AWAY
Air
EgyptAir (Corniche el-Nil Map pp102-3; ☎ 577 2410; Nile Hilton, Corniche el-Nil, Downtown; Sharia Adly Map pp102-3; ☎ 392 7649; 6 Sharia Adly, Downtown; Sharia Talaat Harb Map pp102-3; ☎ 393 2836; 9 Sharia Talaat Harb, Downtown) has a number of offices. The main sales office is on Sharia Adly.

Bus
Cairo's main bus station is **Turgoman Garage** (Map pp98-9; Sharia al-Gisr, Bulaq), 1km northwest of the intersection of Sharias Galaa and 26th of July. It's too far to walk from central Cairo and the only way to get here is by taxi (E£5 from Downtown). The station was being redeveloped at the time of research, so its confusing split into two sections will soon be a thing of the past. There are two other bus stations: Al-Mazar, near the airport, where international services depart and where most other services stop en route out of Cairo; and **Abbassiyya (Sinai) Bus Terminal** (Map pp98-9; Sharia Ramses, Abbassiyya), where all of the services from Sinai arrive (confusingly, these leave from Turgoman).

For details of international bus services from Cairo, see p176.

ALEXANDRIA & THE MEDITERRANEAN COAST
All services leave from Turgoman. **West Delta Bus Co** (☎ 576 5582) travels to Alexandria (E£16, 2½ hours) on the hour between 5am and 1am. Services to Marsa Matruh (E£32 to E£40, 5½ hours) leave at 6.45am, 8.15am, 1.15pm and 9.30pm.

LUXOR & ASWAN
Upper Egypt Travel (☎ 576 0261) buses depart from Turgoman. There's one daily service going to Luxor (E£85, 10 to 11 hours) at 9pm and one service to Aswan (E£85, 12 to 13 hours) at 5pm. You're much better off getting the train.

RED SEA
Superjet (☎ 579 8181) leaves from Turgoman, going to Hurghada (E£57 to E£60, 6½ hours), at 7.30am, 2.30pm and 11.15pm. Upper Egypt Travel services to Hurghada (E£55) depart at 7.30am, 9am, noon, 3pm, 10pm and 11.30pm. The 9am and 10pm services go on to Safaga (E£65, 7½ hours).

There are Upper Egypt Travel services to Marsa Alam (E£80, 12 hours) via Al-Quseir (E£70, nine hours) at 1.30pm, 6.30pm and 11pm. There's an additional service to Al-Quseir at 9pm.

SINAI
All Sinai buses leave from Turgoman, but return to Abbassiyya.

East Delta Bus Co (☎ 574 2814) has services going to Sharm el-Sheikh (E£55 to E£65, seven hours) at 6.30am, 7.15am, 10am, 1pm, 3pm, 5pm, 7pm, 11pm, 11.30pm, midnight and 12.15am. The 7.15am, 1pm, 5pm and 12.15am services go on to Dahab (E£62 to E£75, nine hours).

There are three daily buses to Nuweiba (E£55 to E£75, eight hours) and Taba (E£55 to E£75, nine hours), leaving at 6.30am, 9.30am and 10.15pm. A daily service to St Katherine's Monastery (E£37, 7½ hours) leaves at 10.30am.

Superjet has services to Sharm el-Sheikh (E£68) at 7.30am, 3.15pm and 11.15pm.

SUEZ CANAL
All Suez buses leave from Turgoman Garage. East Delta Bus Co travels to Ismailia (E£7.25, 2½ hours) and Suez (E£7.25, 1½ hours) every 30 minutes between 6am and 8pm. Buses to Port Said (E£16, three hours) leave every 30 minutes between 6am and 9.30am, and then every hour until 9.30pm.

WESTERN OASES
All Western Oases buses leave from Turgoman. Note that to get to Siwa you must take a bus to Alexandria or Marsa Matruh, and then another onwards.

There are two Upper Egypt Bus Co services per day to Bahariyya (E£20, five hours), Farafra (E£40, eight hours) and Dakhla (E£50 to E£55, 10 to 12 hours) at 7am and 6pm. Two extra services travel to Dakhla via Asyut and Al-Kharga (E£50), leaving at 9.30pm and 10pm.

Service Taxi
Most service taxis depart from taxi stands around Ramses train station and Midan Ulali. Service taxis depart for Alexandria (E£12, three hours), Ismailia (E£8, 1½ hours), Port Said (E£14, two hours) and Suez (E£7.50, one hour).

Train
Ramses train station (Mahatta Ramses; Map pp98-9; ☎ 575 3555; Midan Ramses, Downtown) is Cairo's main train station. It has a left-luggage office charging E£2.50 per piece per day, a **post office** (⏰ 8am-8pm), a pharmacy and a **tourist information office** (⏰ 9am-7pm).

The closest place to access US dollars or euros is **Egyptian Foreign Exchange Corp** (Map pp98-9; Sharia Emad ad-Din, Downtown), a 10-minute walk away.

LUXOR & ASWAN
The **Abela Egypt Sleeping Train** (☎ 574 9274; www.sleepingtrains.com) leaves for Upper Egypt at 8pm. It arrives in Luxor at 5.05am the next morning and in Aswan at 8.15am. It costs US$53/74 per person one way in a double/single cabin. Children four to nine years of age pay US$40. There are no student discounts and tickets must be paid for in US dollars or euros (cash only). The price includes dinner and breakfast. The ticket office is next to the tourist information office near the station's main entrance.

Aside from the sleeping train, foreigners can only travel to Luxor and Aswan on train 980, departing Cairo daily at 7am; train 996, departing at 10pm; and train 1902, departing at 12.30am. To Luxor, 1st-/2nd-class fares are E£67/45 on the night trains, and E£62/40 on the morning train. To Aswan they're E£81/47 on the night trains, E£77/43 on the morning train. The trip to Luxor takes 10 hours; to Aswan it's around 13. Student discounts are available on tickets for both classes.

Tickets can be bought from the ticket office beside platform 11, which is on the other side of the tracks from the main hall. You must buy your tickets at least a couple of days in advance.

ALEXANDRIA

The best trains running between Cairo and Alexandria are the *Turbini* (E£36/28 in 1st/2nd class, two hours). They depart from Cairo at 8am, 2pm and 7pm. The next best trains are the *Espani* (Spanish) services, which cost the same as the *Turbini* and leave at 9am, noon, 6pm and 10.30pm. Slower trains, known as *Francese* (French; E£26/16 in 1st/2nd class, three hours), leave at 6am, 8.30am, 11am, 3.10pm, 4pm and 8pm. Student discounts are available on all tickets.

PORT SAID

Trains to Port Said (E£20, four hours) and Ismailia (E£14, three hours) leave at 8.45am, 11.30am, 2.30pm, 7pm and 10pm.

GETTING AROUND
To/From the Airport
Cairo International Airport (Terminal 1 ☎ 265 5000; Terminal 2 ☎ 265 2222) is 20km northeast of Cairo. There are four terminals in all, but two terminals about 3km apart handle most passenger traffic: Terminal 1 services EgyptAir's international and domestic flights and Terminal 2 services all international airlines except Saudi Arabian Airlines. You'll find ATMs and exchange booths in the arrivals halls.

Bus 356 is air-conditioned, and runs at 20-minute intervals from 7am to midnight between both terminals of the airport and Midan Abdel Moniem Riad (Map pp102–3),

---

PLAYING CHICKEN IN CAIRO

It may sound silly, but the greatest challenge most travellers face when travelling through Egypt is crossing the street in Cairo. Roads are always frantically busy and road rules are something that the average Cairene has heard of, but only in jokes. Our advice is to position yourself so that one or more locals form a buffer between you and oncoming traffic, and then cross when they cross – they usually don't mind being used as human shields! Basically, it's a game of chicken. Never, ever hesitate once you've stepped off the sidewalk; cross as if you own the road. And do it fast.

---

behind the Egyptian Museum in central Cairo (E£2, plus E£1 per large luggage item, one hour). There is a far less comfortable 24-hour service on bus 400 (50pt), which leaves from the same places. Note that between the hours of midnight and 6am, this bus only stops at Terminal 1.

If you arrive at Terminal 1, you'll see the bus-parking area to the side of the arrivals hall. If you arrive at Terminal 2, walk out of the arrivals hall, cross the road, go down the stairs or escalator, cross through the car park and wait on the opposite side of the street at the end of the car park to flag the bus down. There's no marked stop.

If you decide to grab a black-and-white taxi, the going rate to central Cairo is around E£45 to E£60 (it's around E£30 to E£35 *to* the airport). You'll get the best rate if you walk down to the car park rather than relying on the taxis right outside the arrivals hall. Limousines cost anything from E£50 to E£85.

Bus & Minibus
Cairo's main local bus and minibus stations are at Midan Abdel Moniem Riad (Map pp102–3). From there, services leave for just about everywhere in the city.

Metro
The Metro system is startlingly efficient, and the stations are cleaner than any other public places in Cairo. It's also surprisingly inexpensive. You're most likely to use the Metro if you're going down to Old Cairo (served by a station called Mar Girgis). A short-hop ticket (up to nine stations) costs 50pt. The first and (sometimes) second carriages are reserved for women only.

Microbus
Destinations are not marked, so microbuses are hard to use unless you're familiar with their routes. Position yourself beside the road that leads where you want to go and when a microbus passes, yell out your destination – if it's going where you want to go and there are seats free, it'll stop.

River Bus
The Maspero river bus terminal (Map pp102–3) is on the Corniche in front of the big round Radio & TV Building. From here boats depart every 15 minutes between 7am

and 10pm for Doqqi, Manial, Giza and Misr al-Qadima (Old Cairo). The trip takes 50 minutes and the fare is 50pt. From 7am to 3pm, some boats go only to Doqqi. There's also a service between Zamalek and Imbaba (25pt).

Taxi

If a destination is too far to walk, the easiest way of getting there is to take a taxi. They're cheap enough to make buses, with their attendant hassles, redundant. Use the following table as a rough guide as to what you should be paying for a taxi ride around Cairo. It's best to hail a Peugeot 504 rather than one of the diabolically unroadworthy Fiats.

TAXI FARES FROM DOWNTOWN	
Destination	**Fare (E£)**
Abbassiyya (Sinai) Bus Terminal	15
Airport	30-35
Citadel	5
Heliopolis	10-15
Khan al-Khalili	5
Midan Ramses	3
Pyramids	20
Turgoman Garage	5
Zamalek	5

AROUND CAIRO

MEMPHIS, SAQQARA & DAHSHUR
دهشور & سقارة ممفيس

There's little left of the former Pharaonic capital of **Memphis**, 24km south of Cairo. It's only worth visiting for its **museum** (adult/student E£25/15; 🕙 8am-4pm winter, 8am-5pm summer), which contains an impressive statue of Ramses II.

A few kilometres away is **Saqqara** (adult/student E£50/25; 🕙 8am-4pm winter, 8am-5pm summer), a massive necropolis covering 7 sq km of desert and strewn with pyramids, temples and tombs. Deceased pharaohs and their families, administrators, generals and sacred animals were interred here. The star attraction is the **Step Pyramid of Zoser**, the world's oldest stone monument and the first decent attempt at a pyramid. Surrounding it is Zoser's pyramid complex, which includes shrines and a huge court.

Other attractions include the **Mastaba of Ti** and the **Pyramid of Teti**.

Ten kilometres south of Saqqara is **Dahshur** (adult/student E£20/10; 🕙 8am-4pm winter, 8am-5pm summer), an impressive 3.5km-long field of 4th- and 12th-dynasty pyramids, like the **Bent Pyramid** (unfortunately off limits to visitors) and the wonderful **Red Pyramid**. If you're on a tight budget, there's a lot to be said for visiting Dahshur and exploring the interior of this, the oldest true pyramid in Egypt, rather than spending a fortune at Giza.

It's possible to visit Memphis, Saqqara and Dahshur in five hours, but you will need your own transport to get you here, take you around the sites (parking at each site costs E£5) and bring you back to Cairo. A taxi will cost about E£140 shared among a maximum of seven people. Stipulate the sights you want to see and how long you want to be out, and bargain hard. Otherwise, organise a day tour (p108).

MEDITERRANEAN COAST

ALEXANDRIA   الاسكندرية
🕾 03 / pop 3.8 million

For a city with such a glorious past, Alexandria (Al-Iskendariyya) is surprisingly low-key – and this is its greatest charm. Arranged necklace-style around the coastline, it has a very different feel to the rest of Egypt. If the *belle époque* buildings, excellent food and efficient public transport system aren't enough to convince you of this fact, the European-like allegiance to good espresso coffee and the total lack of touts will. All we can say is *'Vive la différence!'*

History

Established in 332 BC by Alexander the Great, the city became a major trade centre and focal point of learning for the entire Mediterranean world. Its ancient library held 500,000 volumes and the Pharos lighthouse was one of the Seven Wonders of the Ancient World. Alexandria continued as the capital of Egypt under the Roman Empire and its eastern offshoot, the Byzantine Empire. From the 4th century onwards, the city declined into insignificance. Napoleon's arrival and Alexandria's subsequent

EGYPT

CENTRAL ALEXANDRIA

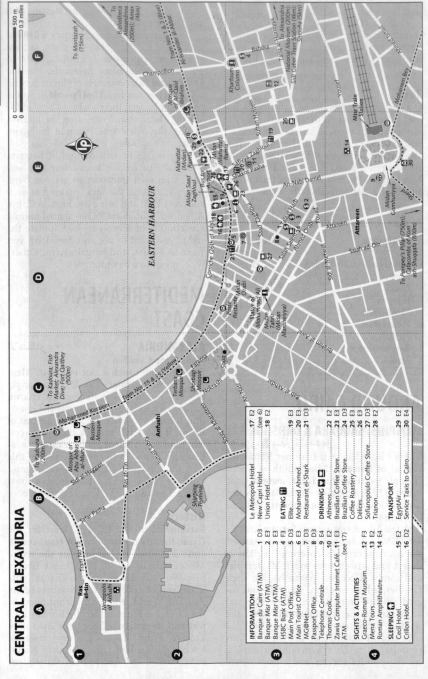

INFORMATION	
Banque du Caire (ATM)...............	1 D3
Banque Misr (ATM).....................	2 E3
Banque Misr (ATM).....................	3 E3
HSBC Bank (ATM).......................	4 E3
Main Post Office........................	5 D3
Main Tourist Office....................	6 E3
MG@Net....................................	7 D3
Passport Office..........................	8 D3
Telephone Centrale.....................	9 E4
Thomas Cook.............................	10 E2
Zawia Computer Internet Café...11 E3
ATM.................................(see 17)

SIGHTS & ACTIVITIES	
Graeco-Roman Museum..............	12 F3
Mena Tours...............................	13 E2
Roman Amphitheatre.................	14 E4

SLEEPING 🛏	
Cecil Hotel...............................	15 E2
Crillon Hotel............................	16 D2

| Le Metropole Hotel.................. | 17 E2 |
| New Capri Hotel.............(see 6) |
| Union Hotel............................. | 18 E2 |

EATING 🍴	
Elite...	19 E3
Mohamed Ahmed.......................	20 E3
Restaurant el-Shark..................	21 D3

DRINKING 🍷 🍸	
Athineos...................................	22 E2
Brazilian Coffee Store................	23 E3
Brazilian Coffee Store................	24 D3
Coffee Roastery........................	25 E3
Délices.....................................	26 E3
Sofianopoulo Coffee Store.........	27 D3
Trianon....................................	28 E2

TRANSPORT	
EgyptAir...................................	29 E2
Service Taxis to Cairo................	30 E4

redevelopment as a major port attracted people from all over the world, but the 1952 Revolution put an end to much of the city's pluralistic charm.

Orientation

Alexandria is a true waterfront city, nearly 20km long from east to west and only about 3km wide. The focal point of the city is Midan Ramla, also known as Mahattat Ramla (Ramla station) because it is the central terminus for the city's tramlines. Immediately adjacent is Midan Saad Zaghloul, a large square running back from the seafront and joining Midan Ramla at the corner. Around these two *midans*, and in the streets to the south and west, are the central shopping area, the main tourist office, restaurants, cafés and most of the cheaper hotels. To the west of this central area are the older quarters of the city, such as Anfushi. To the east are new suburbs stretching 15km along the coastline to Montazah, and its palace and gardens. Most of the city's five-star hotels and restaurants are either in this part of town or near the popular Green Plaza Mall, beyond the southern suburb of Smouha on the agricultural road to Cairo.

Information

INTERNET ACCESS

Internet cafés are frustratingly thin on the ground. Other than the two central cafés mentioned here, you are entitled to one hour of free Internet access as part of the entry price to the Bibliotheca Alexandrina.

MG@Net (per hr E£2; ☼ 10am-midnight) Conveniently located near Midan Saad Zaghloul.

Zawia Computer Internet Café (☎ 484 8014; Sharia Dr Hassan Fadaly; per hr E£4; ☼ 11am-11pm) Off Sharia Safiyya Zaghloul.

MONEY

For changing cash, the simplest option is to use one of the many exchange bureaus on the side streets between Midan Ramla and the Corniche. There are also dozens of currency-exchange offices along Sharia Talaat Harb. There's an ATM at the **HSBC Bank** (47 Sharia Sultan Hussein), a five-minute walk east of the centre, and another in the foyer of Le Metropole Hotel. There's also one at Misr train station, but it's often out of order. Go to **Thomas Cook** (☎ 484 7830; 15 Sharia Saad Zaghloul; ☼ 8am-5pm) if

you want to cash travellers cheques, as **Amex** (☎ 541 0177; 5 Sharia Toudor, Mina Roman Mall, Rushdy) is a long way from the centre.

POST & TELEPHONE

The main post office is two blocks east of Midan Orabi. There is a 24-hour telephone centrale on Midan Gomhurriya.

TOURIST INFORMATION

Main tourist office (☎ 485 1556; Midan Saad Zaghloul; ☼ 8.30am-6pm) This very helpful office is in the southwest corner of the *midan*, beneath the tourist police station.

Tourist office (☼ 8.30am-6pm) At Misr train station.

VISA EXTENSIONS

Passport office (28 Sharia Talaat Harb; ☼ 8am-1.30pm Sat-Thu) Off Sharia Salah Salem.

Sights

GRAECO-ROMAN MUSEUM

Ancient Alexandria is almost as intangible to us as Atlantis, but the 40,000 artefacts collected in the 24 rooms of this excellent **museum** (☎ 483 6434; 5 Sharia al-Mathaf ar-Romani; adult/student E£30/15; ☼ 9am-4pm) go some way towards bringing it to life. Objects to look out for include three carved heads of Alexander (the city's founder); an extraordinary wooden statue of Serapis in human form; a carved head of Cleopatra; and several small terracotta lanterns, the only historical depictions of the ancient Pharos lighthouse in existence. The central courtyard has an unassuming cafeteria where you can sip tea while sitting in a plastic chair among a plethora of Roman columns.

ALEXANDRIA NATIONAL MUSEUM

This recently opened **museum** (Sharia Tariq al-Horreyya; adult/student E£30/15; ☼ 9am-4pm) is housed in an elegant villa and features an impressive collection of pieces showcasing various stages in the city's development. Interpretive labels are clear and informative, but the lighting is very poor. Make sure you see the heads of Akhenaten and Hatshepsut in the ground floor Pharaonic section, and the coins and statuary retrieved from the Mediterranean on the 1st floor.

ROMAN AMPHITHEATRE (KOM AL-DIKKA)

The 13 white marble terraces of the only **Roman theatre** (Sharia Yousef; adult/student E£15/10;

EGYPT

9am-5pm) in Egypt were discovered in 1964. Also worth seeing is the 'Villa of the Birds' **mosaic** (adult/student E£10/5) in the grounds.

CATACOMBS OF KOM ASH-SHUQQAFA

Dating back to the 2nd century AD, these eerily fascinating **tombs** (Carmous; adult/student E£20/10; 8am-5pm) would have held about 300 corpses. The centrepiece of the catacombs, the **principal tomb**, is the prototype for a Hammer horror-film set, with a miniature funerary temple decorated with a weird synthesis of ancient Egyptian, Greek and Roman death iconography. No cameras are allowed. You'll find the catacombs in the southwest of the city, a five-minute walk from the famed, misnamed and disappointing **Pompey's Pillar** (adult/student E£10/5, tripod E£20; 8am-5pm).

BIBLIOTHECA ALEXANDRINA

Resembling the Death Star from *Star Wars*, this architecturally splendid **library** (483 9999; www.bibalex.org; Corniche al-Bahr; adult/student main library E£10/5, antiquities museum E£20/10, manuscript collection E£20/10; 11am-7pm Sun, Mon, Wed & Thu, 3-7pm Fri & Sat) is an attempt to put the city back on the world's cultural map. Inspired by the original great library, which was founded in the early 3rd century BC and acclaimed as the greatest of all classical institutions, this modern version has been designed to hold eight million books in its vast rotunda space. The ancient wealth of learning is lyrically evoked on its curved exterior walls, which are carved with giant letters, pictograms, hieroglyphs and symbols from every known alphabet.

Activities

In recent years Alexandria has been giving up some of her hidden treasures. Underwater excavations have been carried out in the eastern harbour and around Fort Qaitbey, dredging up pavements, platforms, statues and red-granite columns – remnants from what is being described as 'Cleopatra's Palace'. **Alexandra Dive** (483 2042; www.alexandra-dive.com) offers diving tours of the submerged harbour sites when the water is clear. You'll find its office in the grounds of the Grand Café/Tikka Grill/Fish Market complex on the Corniche near Fort Qaitbey.

Sleeping

Alexandria is one of the few Egyptian cities where hotel rates stay the same year-round.

We counsel against staying at the New Hotel Welcome House near Midan Saad Zaghloul, as the tourist office has no hesitation in reporting that it receives on average one complaint per day from travellers saying that personal items have gone missing during their stay at this extremely dodgy place.

Union Hotel (480 7312; fax 480 7350; 5th fl, 164 Corniche; s/d with shared bathroom E£46/64, with private bathroom E£52/70, with private bathroom & air-con E£171/196;) This is the best of the budget options, offering clean and comfortable rooms with satellite TV for more-or-less budget rates. Front rooms have balconies overlooking the harbour and are very light (singles/doubles E£62/67). Upstairs rooms have been freshly painted. Breakfast is E£8 extra.

New Capri Hotel (/fax 480 9703, 480 9310; 8th fl, 23 Sharia el-Mina el-Sharkia; s/d E£39/56) You'll find the New Capri by taking the frighteningly creaky lift to the 8th floor of the building housing the tourist office. The hotel is run-down but reasonably clean, with one shared bathroom for every two bedrooms. Half the rooms have fans; the remaining rooms would be sweatboxes in summer. There's a lovely breakfast room with great views over the harbour. Enter from the side street.

Crillon Hotel (480 0330; 3rd fl, 5 Sharia Adib Ishaq; s/d with private bathroom or view E£60/90) Two blocks back from Midan Saad Zaghloul, this old-fashioned place runs a close second to the Union in the cleanliness and comfort stakes, and most of the freshly painted rooms have balconies with harbour views. Twelve of the 36 rooms have private bathrooms, but these don't have views. To find it, look for the brass plaque next to the building entrance.

Le Metropole Hotel (484 0910; resamet@paradiseinegypt.com; 52 Sharia Saad Zaghloul; s US$100-135, d US$120-155;) An excellent, centrally located four-star hotel with high ceilings and ornate cornices that hint at Alexandria's early-20th-century heyday. Rooms are well appointed and extremely comfortable.

Cecil Hotel (487 7173; h1726@accor-hotels.com; 16 Midan Saad Zaghloul; s/d/ste from US$144/170/291;) Run by the Sofitel chain, the Cecil is a local institution, as famous for its progression of famous guests as it is for the Moorish whimsy of its architecture.

A recent renovation has endowed rooms with reproduction antique furniture, marble bathrooms, work desks and extremely comfortable beds. It's worth paying extra for one with a harbour or *midan* view.

Eating

The place for cheap eating is around the area where Sharia Safiyya Zaghloul meets Midan Ramla, and along Sharia Shakor Pasha, one street over to the west. There are plenty of little fuul and ta'amiyya places here, as well as sandwich shops and the odd kushari joint.

Mohamed Ahmed (☎ 483 3576; 17 Sharia Shakor Pasha; dishes E£1-10) This basic eatery is usually full to the brim with locals ordering tasty ta'amiyya, fuul, omelettes and fried cheese. It's fantastic value – a filling meal for two will cost around E£8. You can sit down or take away. Recommended.

Restaurant el-Shark (Sharia Hassan ash-Seikh) If you're in the mood for edgy local special-

ities such as grilled dove (E£8) or gizzard soup (E£3), this friendly local eatery could be for you. It also serves staples such as roast chicken (E£15) and *fatta* (rice and bread soaked in a garlicky-vinegar sauce with lamb or chicken; E£3.50 to E£15.50) in its plant-filled dining room. A fresh lemon juice costs E£2.

Elite (☎ 486 3592; 43 Sharia Safiyya Zaghloul; dishes E£3.50-31; ✗) Another of those Alexandrian time warps, the Elite faintly resembles a Left Bank café c1960, with the additional (and discordant) feature of diner-style booths. The menu contains everything from cheese on toast to *tournedos aux champignons* (fillet streak with mushrooms) and is extremely popular with locals. Alcohol is available.

Kadoura (per person around E£50; ✗ 9am-3am; ✗) Famed for serving huge, ultrafresh seafood dishes, Kadoura is an essential stop on any Alex itinerary. Diners choose from the outdoor display of the catch of the day, specify whether they want it grilled or fried, and

---

COFFEE À GO-GO

Those travellers who come to Alex to discover the sophisticated city immortalised in Lawrence Durrell's The Alexandria Quartet inevitably end up whiling away hour upon hour in the city's wonderful array of coffeehouses and patisseries. Most of these institutions date back to first half of the 20th century and have retained their wonderful interiors and European flavoured (mainly Greek) atmospheres – fortunately most have also retained loyal clienteles. We love the fact that most of the men behind the coffee machines look as if they've been honing their coffee-making skills for the full life of the cafés.

Though the famous Pastroudi's has sadly closed, you can still discuss Camus novels over an espresso at the following, which are generally open from 9am till 11pm daily.

Sofianopoulo Coffee Store (Sharia Saad Zaghloul; espresso E£2.50) It's stand-up service only at this atmospheric and extremely attractive coffee bar. Vies with the Brazilian Coffee Store for the 'best coffee in town' award; we think it's the winner.

Brazilian Coffee Store (Sharia Saad Zaghloul; espresso E£2) The Brazilian makes a damn fine espresso and is always packed with locals grabbing a quick caffeine fix and discussing the day's news. There is no seating at this branch, but you'll find a few tables at the branch on Sharia Salah Salem.

Délices (Sharia Saad Zaghloul; cappuccino E£7.50, cakes E£4) The best cakes in town are served up at this venerable tearoom. The coffee's so-so, but the outdoor tables overlooking Midan Saad Zaghloul are wonderful spots to spend an hour or so watching the world go by.

Trianon (Midan Ramla; cappuccino E£7, gateaux E£4) The Trianon's *salon de thé* was a favourite of the Alexandrian-Greek poet Cavafy, who worked in offices above it. It's still immensely popular despite its coffee and food being of only average quality. There's a minimum charge of E£10.

Athineos (Midan Ramla; cappuccino E£4, pastries E£2.50) The wonderful interior in the half that faces the tramline features soaring ceilings, mint-green walls and gilded columns but is inevitably empty, unlike the modernised sea-facing side. The coffee here is disappointing, but the pastries are good.

Coffee Roastery (48 Sharia Tariq al-Horreyya; cappuccino E£6) This Hard Rock Café–style place is the modern heir to Alex coffeehouse heritage. Nostalgia-lovers will hate it; local youths love it to bits. The coffee is good and there's free wi-fi.

EGYPT

take a seat in the utilitarian interior along-side the many local families who treat this place as a home away from home. It's then eaten with side dishes of dips, salads, bread and delicious pickles. Kadoura is at the end of a laneway inland from Sharia Moham-med Koraiem. There's a second branch on the Corniche near Fort Qaitbey. Highly recommended.

Fish Market (☎ 480 5114; per person around E£70; ✂) The seafood here is nearly as good as the catch served up at Kadoura, and this place has the added bonuses of great views of the harbour and a licence to sell alcohol. Service can be a bit surly and the muzak is wrist-slashingly bad. The mezze (E£4 per person) that comes with your choice of fresh seafood is excellent, as is the freshly baked bread that accompanies it.

Getting There & Away
BUS
Long-distance buses all leave from the 15th of May bus station, behind Sidi Gaber train station. The tram trip from Midan Ramla takes 30 minutes.

Between them, Superjet and the West Delta Bus Co run services to Cairo every 30 minutes from 5.30am to 10pm.

Superjet goes to Cairo (E£24 to E£28, 2½ hours) and Cairo airport (E£26 to E£32, three hours). It also has VIP services at 8am and 4pm (E£32 to Cairo, E£37 to Cairo air-port), and an extra service to Cairo airport at 1am (E£37).

West Delta Bus Co has cheaper (E£20 to Cairo, E£25 to Cairo airport) less-comfy services. It also has VIP services at 8am and 3pm (E£27 to Cairo, E£35 to Cairo airport) and early-morning services to Cairo airport at 12.30am and 1.30am (E£33).

West Delta Bus Co runs buses to Marsa Matruh (E£20 to E£23, 4½ hours) every hour between 7am and 1am. These go via El Alamein (E£15, two hours). Superjet only travels to Marsa Matruh between June and September (E£24); it leaves at 7.15am.

There are West Delta Bus Co buses to Siwa (E£27, nine hours) at 8.30am, 11am and 2pm.

To Sallum (E£23, eight hours), there are West Delta Bus Co services at 9.30am, 10.30am, noon, 1.30pm, 3.30pm and 6pm.

To Sharm el-Sheikh, there's one Superjet service (E£88, 10½ hours) at 7.30pm and

one West Delta Bus Co service (E£70) at 9pm. To Port Said, there's one daily Super-jet service (E£24, four hours) and five daily West Delta Bus Co services (E£20 to E£22), which leaves at 6am, 8am, 1pm, 4pm and 7pm. West Delta Bus Co buses travel to Ismailia (E£28, five hours) at 7am and 2.30pm.

Superjet travels to Hurghada (E£85, nine hours) at 8pm; West Delta Bus Co some-times has a service (E£70) at 8am but you shouldn't bank on it.

SERVICE TAXI
Most service taxis in Alexandria are mini-vans. The main station is Moharrem Bey taxi station in the city's south. From here minivans travel to destinations includ-ing Cairo (around E£10, three hours) and Marsa Matruh (around E£12, four hours). A taxi from Moharrem Bey to Midan Ramla costs E£5, or you can catch tram 6.

TRAIN
Cairo-bound trains depart from Misr train station (Mahatta Misr), Alexandria's main train terminal. They stop five minutes later at the equally busy Sidi Gaber train station, which serves the populous eastern suburbs and is next to the main bus station. The fastest and most comfortable trains are the express *Turbini* (E£36/28 in 1st/2nd class, 2¼ hours), which leave at 8am, 2pm and 7pm. Next best are the express *Espani* (Spanish) trains (E£34/25 in 1st/2nd class), which depart at 8.15am, 3pm, 7.30pm and 10pm. There's also one *Espani* service (E£30 in 1st class) at 11pm that stops once en route. The cheaper and far less comfort-able *Francese* (French) trains (E£26/16 in 1st/2nd class, three hours) leave at 6am, 10am, 11am, 1pm, 3.30pm, 5pm, 6pm, 8pm and 9.30pm. To be assured of seats on the *Turbini* and *Espani* services it is essential to book ahead. Student discounts are available on all trains.

The **Abela Egypt Sleeping Train** (☎ 393 2430; www.sleepingtrains.com) travels daily to Aswan, via Cairo and Luxor. It leaves Alexandria at 5.20pm and arrives in Luxor at 5.25am the next day, terminating in Aswan at 8.50am. It costs US$56/74 per person one way in a double/single cabin. There are no student discounts and tickets must be paid for in US dollars or euros. The price includes a basic dinner and breakfast. Between June and September, the sleeping train also travels three times per week to Marsa Matruh. Contact the office for prices and departure times.

There are local services to Marsa Matruh (E£37/23 in 1st/2nd class) at 1.30pm and 6.45pm, but these trains are so dirty and old that both the tourist office and train-station staff give them the big thumbs down. The 1st-class service only operates in summer.

It costs E£5 for a taxi from the Misr train station to Midan Ramla, or E£10 if you catch a taxi that's waiting in the parking area.

Getting Around
TO/FROM THE AIRPORT
The **international airport** (☎ 425 0527) is at Burg al-Arab, 60km west of the city. To get there, take bus 555 (E£6, one hour) from near the Cecil Hotel. A taxi should cost no more than E£80.

EgyptAir flights sometimes land at the city's smaller **airport** (☎ 427 1036), at Nouzha. To get there, catch minibus 711 or 703 (50pt) from Midan Orabi or Ramla. A taxi should cost no more than E£10.

BUS & MINIBUS
As a visitor to Alexandria, you won't use the buses much – the trams are a much better way of getting around. The only routes worth considering are bus 1 (75pt), which runs from Midan Sa'ad Zaghloul to 15th of May Bus Station (Sidi Gaber); bus 4 (75pt), which runs from Ramla to Kilo 21 (northwest coast); and bus 11 (E£1.50), which runs from Ras el-Tin to Ramla to Mamoura via the Corniche.

There are a couple of minibuses (all tickets 50pt) that travellers sometimes use: minibus 735 runs from Ramla to Montazah via the Corniche; and minibus 736 runs from Ras el-Tin to Mamoura via the Corniche.

TAXI
A short trip within town (eg Midan Ramla to Misr train station) will cost E£5. Midan Ramla to Sidi Gaber will cost E£10; to the eastern beaches will cost around E£15.

TRAM
Midan Ramla is the main tram station; from here, yellow-coloured trams go west

and blue-coloured ones go east. All tickets cost 25pt. The most useful routes:

Tram No	Route
1 & 2	Ramla to Victoria, via the sporting club & Rushdy
6	Moharrem Bey to Ras el-Tin
15	Ramla to Ras el-Tin via El-Gomruk & Anfushi
16	Midan St Katerina to Pompey's Pillar
25	Ras el-Tin to Sidi Gaber, via Ramla
36	Ras el-Tin to San Stefano & Sidi Gaber

EL ALAMEIN   العلمين
The beginning of General Montgomery's offensive on 23 October 1942 ruined forever Field Marshall Rommel's hopes of pushing his Afrika Korps from Tobruk, Libya, through Allied lines to Alexandria and the Suez Canal, so winning North Africa. Within two weeks he was on the run, and the battle at El Alamein, 105km west of Alexandria, went down as a turning point of WWII. Today a **war museum** (admission E£5, camera/video E£5/20; ☑ 9am-4pm winter, 8am-6pm summer) and the Commonwealth, German and Italian **war cemeteries** mark the scene of one of the biggest tank battles in history.

To get here, catch any of the West Delta Bus Co services (E£15, two hours) to Marsa Matruh from the 15th of May bus station in Alexandria, and ask to be let off outside the museum. The spot is marked by a tank in the middle of the highway, so you can't miss it. Alternatively, minivans leave from the Moharrem Bey taxi station and cost around E£5.

Returning to Alexandria is a bit more difficult, as you'll need to flag down a minivan by the side of the highway. If you're lucky it will go all the way to Moharrem Bey, but sometimes it will stop in an outlying suburb and you'll need to find another minivan to take you into town.

The easiest way to visit El Alamein is to organise a car and English-speaking driver through **Mena Tours** (☎ 480 9676; fax 486 5827; Midan Saad Zaghloul; ☑ 9am-6pm Sat-Thu), which is based next to the Cecil Hotel in Alexandria. This will cost approximately E£350. A private taxi will charge between E£150 to E£200 to take you to the museum, ferry you around the cemeteries and bring you back to Alexandria.

EGYPT

NILE VALLEY وادى النيل

In this part of Egypt, the world's longest river is fringed by fertile farmland and scattered with remains from the country's ancient past.

LUXOR الأقصر
☎ 095 / pop 422,400

Built on and around the 4000-year-old site of ancient Thebes, contemporary Luxor is a curious but comfortable mix of provincial country town and staggering ancient splendour. The concentration of monuments is extraordinary: they tower incongruously above the buzz of everyday life and make this the most compelling of all Egyptian destinations.

History

Following the collapse of centralised power at the end of the Old Kingdom period, the small village of Thebes emerged as the main power in Upper Egypt under the 11th- and 12th-dynasty pharaohs. Rising against the northern capital of Heracleopolis, Thebes reunited the country under its political, religious and administrative control and ushered in the Middle Kingdom period. The strength of Thebes' government also enabled it to re-establish control after a second period of decline, liberate the country from foreign rule and bring in the New Kingdom dynasties.

At the height of their glory and opulence, from 1550 to 1069 BC, all the New Kingdom pharaohs (with the exception of Akhenaten, who moved to Tell al-Amarna) made Thebes their permanent residence. The city had a population of nearly one million, and the architectural activity was astounding.

Orientation

What most visitors today know as Luxor is actually three separate areas: the town of Luxor itself on the east bank of the Nile; the village of Karnak, 2km to the north-east; and the towns of Gurna, New Gurna and Al-Gezira near the monuments and necropolis of ancient Thebes on the west bank of the Nile.

In Luxor town there are three main thoroughfares: Sharia al-Mahatt, which runs from the train station down to Luxor

Temple; Sharia al-Karnak, which runs from Luxor Temple past the souq and up towards the Temples of Karnak; and the Corniche. Most of the package-tour hotels are at the southern end of town, on Sharia Khalid ibn al-Walid. The majority of budget hotels are located between the train station and Sharia Televizyon, down near Sharia Khalid ibn al-Walid. Banks, the main tourist office and other services are clustered around the Old Winter Palace Hotel on the Corniche.

Information

INTERNET ACCESS

East Bank

Aboudi (Map p125; ☎ 237 2390; Corniche el-Nil; per hr E£10; ☽ 9am-10pm, closed noon-1pm Fri) On the cramped 1st floor above the bookshop.

Friends Internet Café (Map p125; ☎ 236 7260; Sharia Salah ad-Din; per hr E£10; ☽ 9am-midnight) This air-conditioned café is the best place in town to check your email; it boasts fast ADSL connections and a comfortable setup. A cappuccino costs E£2.50.

Rainbow Net (Map p125; ☎ 238 7938; Sharia Yousef Hassan; per hr E£6; ☽ 9am-midnight) You'll find it up the laneway – it's well posted from the street.

West Bank

Nile Centre Internet (Map p128; Main Rd, Al-Gezira; per hr E£5; ☽ 9am-midnight) Conveniently located near the ferry stop.

Ramoza Internet (Map p128; Main Rd, New Gurna; per hr E£3; ☽ 8am-midnight) Inconveniently located and has dodgy connections, but it's the cheapest place in Luxor.

MONEY

There are ATMs at the Banque du Caire and National Bank of Egypt branches on the Corniche near the Old Winter Palace Hotel, and at the Egyptian American Bank in front of the Novotel. The National Bank of Egypt also has a foreign exchange desk open between 8.30am and 9pm.

Amex (Map p125; ☎ 237 8333; ☽ 9am-4.30pm) and **Thomas Cook** (Map p125; ☎ 237 2196; ☽ 8am-2pm & 3-8pm) both have offices at the Old Winter Palace Hotel. They will usually change money and travellers cheques to Egyptian pounds or US dollars. There's also a conveniently located exchange office in the Tourist Bazaar.

POST

Main post office (Map p125; Sharia al-Mahatta) There's also a branch in the Tourist Bazaar on the Corniche.

EGYPT

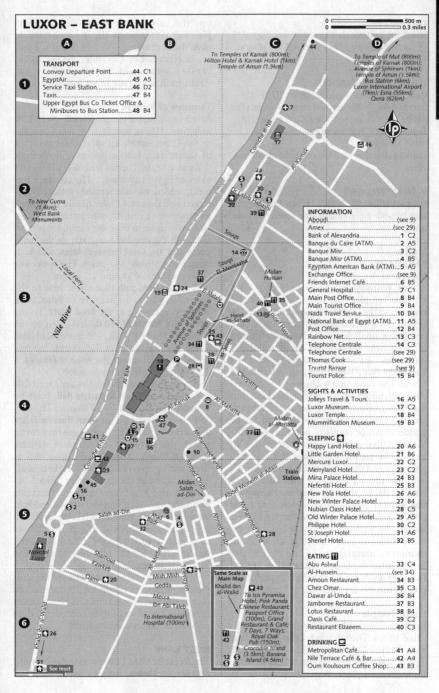

LUXOR – EAST BANK

0 _____ 500 m
0 _____ 0.3 miles

TRANSPORT
Convoy Departure Point............**44** C1
EgyptAir..................................**45** A5
Service Taxi Station..................**46** D2
Taxis.....................................**47** B4
Upper Egypt Bus Co Ticket Office &
 Minibuses to Bus Station........**48** B4

To Temples of Karnak (800m);
Hilton Hotel & Karnak Hotel (1km);
Temple of Amun (1.9km)

To Temple of Mut (800m);
Temples of Karnak (800m);
Avenue of Sphinxes (1km);
Temple of Amun (1.5km);
Bus Station (6km);
Luxor International Airport
(7km); Esna (55km);
Qena (62km)

To New Gurna
(1.4km);
West Bank
Monuments

Souqs

Souqs
El-Montazha

Midan
Hussan

Dr Labib Habashi

Local Ferry

Nile River

El-Matafi

Avenue of Sphinxes

Haret
es-Sahabi

Souqs

Oust Hassan

Al-Bahr

Al-Karnak

Al-Mahatta

Cleopatra

Midan
al-Mahatta

Mohammed Farid

Train
Station

Corniche el-Nil

Midan
Salah
ad-Din

Ahmed Orabi

Abdel Monem al-Adasi

Salah ad-Din

Ahad
Badr

Mohammed Farid

Shamoui

Kawkeb

Qamr

Mish Mish

Gedda

Mecca

Ibn Abi Taleb

Al-Medina

Cleopatra

Ahmed Orabi

Khalid ibn al-Walid

To International
Hospital (100m)

Novotel
Luxor

Khalid Ibn al-Walid

See Inset

Same Scale as
Main Map

Khalid Ibn
al-Walid

To Isis Pyramisa
Hotel; Pink Panda
Chinese Restaurant;
Passport Office
(100m); Grand
Restaurant & Café;
7 Days, 7 Ways;
Royal Oak
Pub (150m);
Crocodile Island
(3.5km); Banana
Island (4.5km)

INFORMATION
Aboudi..(see 9)
Amex...(see 29)
Bank of Alexandria.............................**1** C2
Banque du Caire (ATM).......................**2** A5
Banque Misr.....................................**3** C2
Banque Misr (ATM)............................**4** B5
Egyptian American Bank (ATM)..............**5** A5
Exchange Office................................(see 9)
Friends Internet Café..........................**6** B5
General Hospital.................................**7** C1
Main Post Office................................**8** B4
Main Tourist Office.............................**9** B4
Nada Travel Service...........................**10** B4
National Bank of Egypt (ATM)..............**11** A5
Post Office.....................................**12** B4
Rainbow Net...................................**13** C3
Telephone Centrale............................**14** C3
Telephone Centrale..........................(see 29)
Thomas Cook.................................(see 29)
Tourist Bazaar.................................(see 9)
Tourist Police..................................**15** B4

SIGHTS & ACTIVITIES
Jolleys Travel & Tours.........................**16** A5
Luxor Museum..................................**17** C2
Luxor Temple...................................**18** B4
Mummification Museum.......................**19** B3

SLEEPING
Happy Land Hotel.............................**20** A6
Little Garden Hotel............................**21** B6
Mercure Luxor.................................**22** C2
Merryland Hotel...............................**23** C2
Mina Palace Hotel.............................**24** B3
Nefertiti Hotel.................................**25** B3
New Pola Hotel................................**26** A6
New Winter Palace Hotel....................**27** B4
Nubian Oasis Hotel...........................**28** C5
Old Winter Palace Hotel.....................**29** A5
Philippe Hotel..................................**30** C2
St Joseph Hotel................................**31** A6
Sherief Hotel...................................**32** B5

EATING
Abu Ashraf....................................**33** C4
Al-Hussein..................................(see 34)
Amoun Restaurant............................**34** B3
Chez Omar....................................**35** C3
Dawar al-Umda...............................**36** B4
Jamboree Restaurant.........................**37** B3
Lotus Restaurant..............................**38** B4
Oasis Café.....................................**39** C2
Restaurant Elzaeem..........................**40** C3

DRINKING
Metropolitan Café............................**41** A4
Nile Terrace Café & Bar......................**42** A4
Oum Koulsoum Coffee Shop.............**43** B3

EGYPT

TELEPHONE
Telephone centrale Old Winter Palace Hotel (Map p125; ☾ 8am-10pm); Sharia al-Karnak (Map p125; ☾ 24hr); train station (☾ 8am-8pm)

TOURIST INFORMATION
Main tourist office (Map p125; ☎ /fax 237 2215; Corniche el-Nil; ☾ 8am-8pm) The extremely helpful office is in the Tourist Bazaar, next to New Winter Palace Hotel.
Tourist office (☾ 8am-8pm) Branches at the train station and airport.
Tourist police (Map p125) Next door to the main tourist office.

VISA EXTENSIONS
Passport office (☎ 238 0885; ☾ 8am-2pm Sat-Thu) Almost opposite the Isis Pyramisa Hotel, south of the town centre.

Sights
EAST BANK
Museums
About halfway between the Luxor and Karnak Temples, the impressive **Luxor Museum** (Map p125; Corniche el-Nil; adult/student E£55/30; ☾ 9am-2pm & 4-9pm winter, 9am-2pm & 5-10pm summer) has a small but well-chosen collection of relics from the Theban temples and necropolises. All are impressively conserved and displayed, with excellent interpretive labels. The collection includes pottery, jewellery, furniture, statues and stelae. Look out for the exquisitely carved statue of Tuthmosis III and the gorgeous gilded head of the goddess Hathor depicted as the cow Mehit-Werit. A five-minute video presentation in English in the theatrette near the entrance gives a useful overview of the collection.

Down the steps opposite the Mina Palace Hotel is the small but fascinating **Mummification Museum** (Map p125; Corniche el-Nil; adult/student E£40/20; ☾ 9am-1pm & 4-9pm winter, 9am-1pm & 5-10pm summer). Its well-presented displays tell you everything you ever wanted to know about mummies, mummification and the journey to the afterlife. During excavation season (January to March), visiting Egyptologists give lectures every Saturday at 7pm.

Luxor Temple
Built on the site of an older sanctuary dedicated to the Theban triad, **Luxor Temple** (Map p125; ☎ 237 2408; adult/student E£50/25, tripod E£20; ☾ 6am-9pm winter, 6am-10pm summer) is a strikingly graceful piece of architecture close to the Nile. Largely built by the New Kingdom pharaoh Amenhotep III, it was added to over the centuries by Tutankhamun, Ramses II, Nectanebo, Alexander the Great and various Romans. In the 13th century, the Arabs built a mosque in an interior court.

Temples of Karnak
Much more than a temple, **Karnak** (☎ 238 0270; adult/student E£60/30, tripod E£20; ☾ 6am-5.30pm winter, 6am-6.30pm summer) is a spectacular complex of sanctuaries, kiosks, pylons and obelisks, dedicated to the Theban gods and the greater glory of Egypt's pharaohs. The complex was built, added to, dismantled, restored, enlarged and decorated over nearly 1500 years and today it's a major tourist attraction. Most work was done in the New Kingdom period, although the original sanctuary of the main enclosure, the **Great Temple of Amun**, was built during the Middle Kingdom. The entire site covers an area of around 1.2 sq km.

A **sphinx-lined path** that once went to the Nile takes you to the massive **1st Pylon**, from where you end up in the **Great Court**. To the left is the **Temple of Seti II**, dedicated to the triad of Theban gods – Amun, Mut and Khons. In the centre of the court is the one remaining column of the **Kiosk of Taharqa**, a 25th-dynasty Ethiopian pharaoh.

Beyond the **2nd Pylon** is the unforgettable 6000-sq-metre **Great Hypostyle Hall**, built by Amenhotep III, Seti I and Ramses II.

You can also visit an **Open Museum** (adult/student E£20/10) off to the left of the first court, where you can see a collection of statuary found throughout the complex, as well as three well-preserved chapels. Tickets must be purchased at the main ticket office.

A stampede of tour groups descends upon the site for the nightly **sound-and-light show** (☎ 237 2241; adult/student E£55/44, video camera E£35). There are three or four performances in a variety of languages. Check with the tourist office for the schedule or see www .sound-light.egypt.com.

Microbuses make the short run to the temples from Luxor's centre for 50pt. A *calèche* (horse-drawn carriage) costs E£7 from Luxor Temple; a taxi costs E£10 to E£15, depending on where you are coming from.

WEST BANK
The West Bank of Luxor was the necropolis of ancient **Thebes**, a vast city of the dead

where magnificent temples were raised to honour the cults of pharaohs entombed in the nearby cliffs, and where queens, royal children, nobles, priests, artisans and even workers had tombs built, ranging from spectacular to ordinary in design and décor.

To see every site would cost about E£320 (without student card), and take days. Except for Deir al-Bahri (commonly known as the Funerary Temple of Hatshepsut) and the tombs in the Valleys of the Kings and Queens, you can't pay for admission at the individual sites. Instead you must go to the **Antiquities Inspectorate Ticket Office** (Map p128; ☯ 6am-4pm winter, 6am-5pm summer) on Main Rd, 500m west of the Colossi of Memnon. Plan exactly which sites you wish to visit, as you must purchase individual tickets for each one. Tickets are valid only for the day of purchase; no refunds are given. Students pay half price. Note that photography is strictly forbidden in all the West Bank tombs; if you're caught using a camera, guards will confiscate the film or memory card.

To give you an idea of the distances involved, from the local ferry landing it is 3km straight ahead to the Antiquities Inspectorate Ticket Office, past the Colossi of Memnon. From there it's 1km to the Valley of the Queens and 5km to the Valley of the Kings.

It should cost around E£100 to hire a taxi to bring you here from the East Bank

and transport you from site to site. Alternatively, you can hire a bicycle on the East Bank and bring it over on the ferry, or you can catch a ferry, take a local pick-up truck (25pt; ask for 'Gurna') to the Antiquities Inspectorate Ticket Office, and then hire a rattletrap bike from the **bike hire place** (Map p128; per day E£10) next to the Nour al-Gurna hotel and pedal yourself around.

Before you visit, you may like to look at www.thebanmappingproject.com, Professor Kent Week's fascinating website focusing on the monuments of the West Bank, particularly the Valley of the Kings.

Colossi of Memnon
These 18m-high statues (Map p128) are all that remain of a temple built by Amenhotep III. The Greeks believed that they were statues of Memnon, who was slain by Achilles in the Trojan War.

Temple of Seti I
This pharaoh expanded the Egyptian empire to include Cyprus and parts of Mesopotamia. The temple (Map p128) is seldom visited, but is well worth a look.

Valley of the Kings
Once called the Gates of the Kings and the Place of Truth, this famous **royal necropolis** (Map p128; ☎ 231 1662; adult/student E£70/35; ☯ 6am-

---

WEST BANK SITES

Tickets to the following sites must be purchased at the Antiquities Inspectorate Ticket Office. Opening hours are from 7am to 5pm daily in winter, and 6am to 7pm in summer. Deir al-Bahri and the Valleys of the Kings and Queens have dedicated ticket offices and opening hours. All sites are shown on the map on p128.

Site	Adult/student (E£)
Assasif Tombs (Tombs of Kheruef & Ankhor)	20/10
Assasif Tombs (Tomb of Pabasa)	20/10
Deir al-Medina Temple & Tombs	20/10
Deir al-Medina (Tomb of Peshedu)	10/5
Medinat Habu (Funerary Temple of Ramses III)	30/15
Ramesseum	30/15
Temple of Seti I	30/15
Tombs of the Nobles (Tombs of Khonsu, Userhet & Benia)	12/6
Tombs of the Nobles (Tombs of Menna & Nakht)	20/10
Tombs of the Nobles (Tombs of Neferronpet, Dhutmosi & Nefersekheru)	20/10
Tombs of the Nobles (Tombs of Ramose, Userhet & Khaemhet)	20/10
Tombs of the Nobles (Tombs of Sennofer & Rekhmire)	20/10

EGYPT

LUXOR – WEST BANK

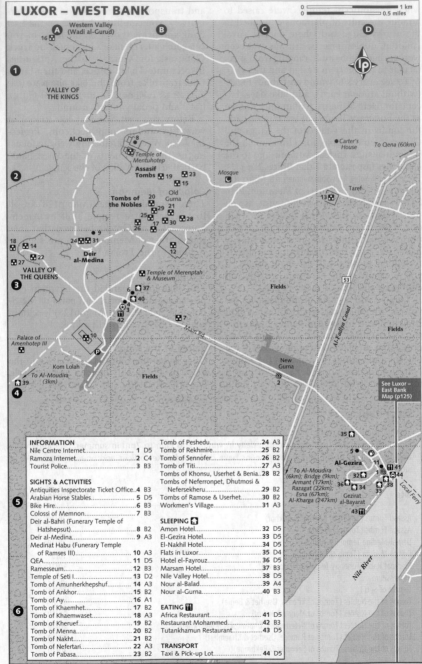

4pm winter, 6am-5pm summer) is dominated by the barren **Al-Qurn** (Horn) mountain. The tombs were designed to resemble the underworld; a long, inclined, rock-hewn corridor descends into either an antechamber or a series of halls, and ends in a burial chamber. Over 60 tombs have been excavated here, but not all belong to pharaohs. At the time of research, a disappointingly small array of tombs was open to visitors, including the tombs of **Ramses III**, **Ramses V/VI**, **Ramses IX**, **Amenhotep II**, **Queen Tawosret/Sethnakht** and **Siptah**.

The **tomb of Tutankhamun**, found in 1922 by Howard Carter and far from the most interesting, needs an extra ticket (adult/student E£100/50). This is bought at the second ticket box when you enter the site, where the ludicrous toy train (E£1) stops. It's only worth paying the exorbitant entry fee if you've been to Cairo's Egyptian Museum and wish to see where the extraordinary collection of objects from the tomb was found.

Hiking across the **Theban Hills** from the Valley of the Kings to Deir al-Bahri is one of the most rewarding activities in Luxor. To do this, ascend the steep cliff opposite the closed tomb of Seti I. Ask a guard to point you in the right direction, as the official path is sometimes blocked by restoration work and there's no signage here or at any point along the route. When you start climbing, souvenir vendors will offer to guide you to the ridge in return for a tip; it's up to you whether you take them up on their offer but be prepared for them to also try to sell you bits and pieces of tourist tat along the way. Once on the ridge, follow the path to the left and continue left when you come to a fork in the path. Follow the path around the ridge, passing a police post on your distant left, until you eventually see Deir al-Bahri down the sheer cliff to your right. Continue along the ridge, ignoring the steep trail that plunges down the cliff face, and almost complete a circle to descend in front of the ticket office to Hatshepsut's magnificent temple. The walk takes 50 minutes and is extremely steep in parts. Make sure you have water and are wearing decent walking shoes.

Deir al-Bahri (Funerary Temple of Hatshepsut)
Rising out of the desert plain in a series of terraces, the **Funerary Temple of Hatshepsut** (Map p128; adult/student E£30/15; 🕙 6am-4.30pm winter,

6am-5pm summer) merges with the sheer limestone cliffs of the eastern face of the Theban mountain. It was desecrated and vandalised by her bitter successor, Tuthmosis III, but retains much of its original magnificence, including some fascinating reliefs.

Assasif Tombs
Three of these 18th-dynasty tombs (Map p128) are open to the public – those of **Pabasa**, **Kheruef** and **Ankhor**. Like the Tombs of the Nobles further south, the artwork concentrates on events from everyday life such as fishing and hunting. You can buy admission tickets at the Antiquities Inspectorate Ticket Office or at Deir al-Bahri.

Tombs of the Nobles
There are at least 12 tombs (Map p128) in this group worth visiting; the most colourful are those of **Ramose**, **Rekhmire** and **Nakht**. Tickets are sold for groups of two or three tombs.

Ramesseum
Ramses II was keen to leave behind monuments to his greatness, and his funerary temple (Map p128) was to be the masterpiece. Sadly, it lies mostly in ruins.

Deir al-Medina
This small Ptolemaic temple (Map p128), dedicated to the goddesses Hathor and Maat, was later occupied by Christian monks – hence its name, literally 'the monastery of the city'. Near the temple are the tombs of some of the workers and artists who created the royal tombs.

Valley of the Queens
The 70-odd **tombs** (Map p128; adult/student E£30/15; 🕙 6am-4.30pm winter, 6am-5pm summer) in this valley belong to queens and other royal family members from the 19th and 20th dynasties. Only three – the tombs of **Titi**, **Amunherkhepshuf** and **Khaemwaset** – are currently open to the public. The crowning glory of the site, the **Tomb of Nefertari**, was closed to the public at the time of research; authorities weren't giving any clues as to when or if it will reopen.

Medinat Habu
The temple complex of Medinat Habu is dominated by the enormous **Funerary Temple of Ramses III** (Map p128), inspired by the

temple of his father, Ramses II. The largest temple after Karnak, it has a stunning mountain backdrop and some fascinating reliefs. The best time to visit is in the late afternoon, when the setting sun interacts amazingly with the golden stone.

Activities

FELUCCA RIDES

Feluccas cruise the Nile throughout the day, and cost between E£30 and E£50 per hour per boat, depending on your bargaining skills. Captains will regularly accost you along the Corniche, so it's easy to shop around for the best boat and price. The most popular trip is 5km upriver to Banana Island, a tiny, palm-dotted isle where locals grow fruit and vegetables. The trip takes between two and three hours, and is best timed so that you are on your way back in time to watch the sunset over Luxor from the boat.

HORSE RIDING

A ride around the West Bank temples is an unforgettable experience, particularly near sunset. Two West Bank stables offer guided rides, the best being **Arabian Horse Stables** (Map p128; ☎ 231 0024, 010 504 8558; ☾ 7am-sunset), which is known for its well-maintained horses and tackle. If you phone ahead to book, staff will collect you from the East Bank in a launch. Rides usually take three hours and cost E£25 per hour. The stable also offers guided camel rides (E£20 per hour) and donkey rides (E£15 per hour).

The Khalifa family, which owns the Nile Valley Hotel, runs **donkey treks** to the Valley of the Kings and Deir el-Bahri for E£35. For more information see www.nile-valley.nl.

Tours

Travel restrictions for foreigners in the Nile Valley make independent travel challenging, so you may want to visit sites outside Luxor on an arranged day tour.

Jolleys Travel & Tours (Map p125; ☎ 010 183 8894; ☾ 9am-10pm) Has a good reputation for its day trips. Located next to the Old Winter Palace Hotel.

QEA (Map p128; ☎ 231 1667; www.questfortheegyptian adventure.com; Main Rd, Al-Gezira) A newly opened British-and-Egyptian-run agency based on the West Bank. It can tailor tours around and in Luxor, as well as in the Western Desert. A percentage of its profits go towards charitable projects in Egypt.

Sleeping

Perhaps more than at any tourist destination in Egypt, the cost of accommodation in Luxor fluctuates seasonally. Some hotels drop their charges by 50% in the low season (May to September), although others don't bother altering them at all. The second half of January is Luxor's busiest season, as Egyptians travel here over the school holiday break. You'll need to book ahead at this time.

Whether to stay on the East or West Bank is a hard call to make. The West Bank is quieter, has fewer touts and is closer to the tombs and temples that are Luxor's major attraction. There is a good array of midrange accommodation choices here, but not so many budget or top-end alternatives. Eating options are also limited. The East Bank is where most of the shopping and entertainment action is based, as well as the majority of Luxor's budget hotels and cheap eateries. It's home to the Karnak and Luxor Temples, Luxor Museum and a battery of *calèche* drivers, hotel touts and shop owners who see all foreigners as walking wallets.

Try to avoid the dodgy hotel touts who pounce on travellers as they get off the train and bus – these guys get a 25% to 40% commission for taking you to hotels who work with them, a cost which ends up being factored into your bill. They're also renowned for telling fibs about hotels that refuse to pay them commission. Always check for yourself.

EAST BANK
Budget

Happy Land Hotel (Map p125; ☎ 237 1828; www.luxor happyland.com; Sharia Qamr; dm with air-con E£10, s/d with shared bathroom E£15/21, with private bathroom & air-con E£22.50/30; ✉ ▣) A large and extremely popular hostel run by the enthusiastic Mr Ibrahim Abdul, Happy Land has spotless, freshly painted rooms, half of which have air-con and private bathrooms. Generous breakfasts, soap and mosquito coils are included in the price. There's a rooftop lounge with satellite TV, bikes for hire (E£10 per day) and free laundry facilities. It's about a 10-minute walk from the train station.

Nubian Oasis Hotel (Map p125; ☎ 292 9445; Sharia Mohammed Farid; dm E£10, s/d E£10/20, with air-con E£20/35; ✉) A newcomer to the budget-accommodation scene in Luxor, this place is sure to become a permanent fixture. The 24 rooms have private bathrooms, hard beds and clean linen; 18 have air-con and some have double beds and satellite TV. It offers a generous breakfast, bike hire (E£6 per day) and free use of two kitchens and a washing machine. Tea (E£1) and Stella (E£6) can be enjoyed on the roof terrace. You'll find it in a residential street five minutes' walk from the train station.

Nefertiti Hotel (Map p125; ☎ 237 2386; www.nefertitihotel.com; btwn Sharia al-Karnak & Sharia as-Souq; s/d E£40/60; ❄) Budget hotels don't come much better than the Nefertiti. Its simple but spotlessly clean rooms all have small private bathrooms and air-con; some have double beds. The roof terrace has good views over to the West Bank, and the top-floor lounge has a pool table and satellite TV. A generous breakfast is included in the price. Recommended.

Merryland Hotel (Map p125; ☎ 238 1746; s/d E£50/80; ❄ 🖳) This quiet three-star choice, just near the Luxor Museum, has an old-fashioned, institutional feel but offers bargain rooms that come complete with satellite TV and private bathrooms. All are clean and have small balconies. The roof terrace has a bar, breakfast area and great views over to the West Bank.

Sherief Hotel (Map p125; ☎ 237 0757; sheriefhotel@yahoo.co.uk; Sharia Badr; s/d with shared bathroom E£25/50, with private bathroom E£40/60; ❄ 🖳) Owner Abdul took over this small place in 2004 and is trying hard to give it a homely feel. It has 12 rooms, five with their own bathroom and six with air-con. Lila the cat holds court in the comfortable downstairs restaurant and there's a sunny roof terrace. Service is impressive, but the prices are a tad steep for what's on offer.

Mina Palace Hotel (Map p125; ☎ 237 2074; fax 238 2194; Corniche el-Nil; s/d E£80/100; ❄) If you want to be in the thick of the Luxor scene and you travel with earplugs to ensure a good night's sleep, this long-running hotel could be for you. The corner rooms sport two balconies and have extraordinary views of the West Bank and the avenue of sphinxes at the Luxor Temple. Rooms have satellite TV, comfortable beds and very clean bathrooms, though all could do with a lick of paint. There's a roof terrace where you can enjoy a beer while watching the sun set over the Nile.

Midrange
Little Garden Hotel (Map p125; ☎ 238 9038; www.littlegardenhotel.com; Sharia Radwan; s/d US$18/24; ❄) This hotel is without doubt the best midrange choice on the East Bank. Its location isn't attractive, but the charming secluded courtyard garden at the front makes amends. The owner worked in hotel management in Germany and has brought European standards of service and cleanliness with him. There's a rooftop restaurant serving Oriental food, including a set menu of soup, salad, *tagen* (stew), rice, pastry and tea or coffee (E£29.50); it also has *majlis* seating where you can relax over a tea and *sheesha* (no alcohol or views). A 10% student discount is offered.

New Pola Hotel (Map p125; ☎ 236 5081; www.newpolahotel.com; Sharia Khalid ibn al-Walid; s/d US$30/40; ❄ 🖳 🍺) The newest addition to Luxor's hotel scene is officially only a three-star hotel, but its amenities are definitely four-star standard. These include a rooftop swimming pool, 24-hour room service and a pleasant downstairs restaurant and bar. Half of the 80 rooms have Nile views; all have satellite TV and comfortable beds.

Philippe Hotel (Map p125; ☎ /fax 238 0050; Sharia Dr Labib Habashi; s/d US$30/40; ❄ 🍺) A large place near the Luxor Museum, the Philippe has recently undergone a renovation and its motel-style rooms are comfortable, if characterless. Each has satellite TV and a private bathroom. There's a roof terrace with a decent-sized pool. It's worth trying to negotiate a discount.

St Joseph Hotel (Map p125; ☎ 238 1707; stjoseph2@hotmail.com; off Sharia Khalid ibn al-Walid; s/d US$25/35; 🍺) This place, at the package-tour end of town, is another decent three-star option, with a small rooftop pool (heated) and rooms featuring satellite TV, comfortable beds and private bathrooms. Ask for a room with a Nile view.

Top End
Old Winter Palace Hotel (Map p125; ☎ 238 0422; h1661@accor-hotels.com; Corniche el-Nil; r Pavilion Bldg US$125-375, old wing US$235-1125; ❄ ❄ 🍺) This Victorian pile on the Corniche is a significant monument in its own right. The spectacular foyer and luxurious rear garden are the stuff of which lasting memories are made, but rooms in the old wing aren't quite as impressive, as most are small and

only half have Nile views. The new Pavilion Building in the garden is home to 118 comfortable rooms overlooking the large pool area. The adjoining New Winter Palace Hotel is real package-tour territory, offering 136 rooms (US$88 to US$126) that are sorely in need of a refit; half have Nile views. Breakfast costs an extra E£72 to E£85.

Mercure Luxor (Map p125; ☎ 238 0944; h1800-gm@accor-hotels.com; Corniche el-Nil; s US$85-124, d US$104-156, ste $374; ✖ ✖ ✖) If you make your way past the usual kitsch gilt-and-marble foyer beloved by tour-group operators, the Mercure offers some pleasant surprises. Nileside rooms (US$105 to US$124) are large and very light, with extremely comfortable beds and furnished balconies. The suites are knockouts, featuring Nile-facing terraces and Jacuzzis. The hotel has a bar, two restaurants, coffee shop, tennis court and large pool. Avoid the cheaper garden- or pool-facing rooms at the rear – it's worth paying a bit extra for a Nile view. The hotel's location is possibly the best on the East Bank.

WEST BANK
Budget
Marsam Hotel (Map p128; ☎ 237 2403; marsam@africamail.com; Gurna; s/d with shared bathroom E£45/90, with private bathroom E£65/130) This is the best budget place on the West Bank. It has 27 simple but spotless rooms (four with private bathrooms) with ceiling fans and traditional palm-reed beds. Owned by a member of the Abdul Rasul family (of tomb-robbing fame),

---

it was originally built for American archaeologists in the 1920s. Atmospheric and quiet, it's an old favourite with archaeologists, so it can be difficult to get rooms during the dig season (January to March).

El-Gezira Hotel (Map p128; ☎ 231 0034; www.el-gezira.com; Al-Gezira; s/d E£60/80; ✖) Though showing its age, this place offers clean rooms for bargain prices. All rooms have air-con, private bathrooms and comfortable beds; some have screened balconies overlooking the Nile. There's also a pleasant rooftop restaurant where you can enjoy a Stella (E£8) and a filling Egyptian meal (E£25). The hotel's only downside is its proximity to a small, mosquito-infested lake.

Midrange
Nour al-Gurna (Map p128; ☎ 231 1430; Gurna; s E£100, d E£120-150, ste E£200) A small mud-brick house with a family feel, the Nour al-Gurna is notable for its stylish rooms and its excellent indoor-outdoor restaurant, which serves up food made from home-grown ingredients to locals and travellers. It's located near the Antiquities Inspectorate Ticket Office, and pick-ups regularly run between the hotel and the river.

Nour al-Balad (Map p128; ☎ 242 6111; s/d/ste E£120/150/500) Run by the same family as the Nour al-Gurna, the Nour al-Balad is an extremely attractive boutique hotel in an isolated location near Medinat Habu.

Hotel el-Fayrouz (Map p128; ☎ 231 2709; www.elfayrouz.com; Al-Gezira; s/d E£70/100; ✖ ✖) A relatively recent addition to the West Bank's hotel scene, the German-run Fayrouz is worth considering due to its quiet but central location, pleasant garden and panoramic roof terrace. Very clean rooms have balconies and hard beds; some have air-con. The restaurant serves good-quality Egyptian and European dishes (E£7 to E£19).

El-Nakhil Hotel (Map p128; ☎ /fax 231 3922; Al-Gezira; s/d US$24/33; ✖) This attractive new hotel offers an array of well-appointed rooms, including garden villas modelled on traditional Nubian housing. One of these is fully set up to cater to wheelchair-bound guests.

Nile Valley Hotel (Map p128; ☎ 231 1477; www.nilevalley.nl; Main Rd, Al-Gezira; s/d E£75/110; ✖) This large pink hacienda-style block, near the ferry dock, is a good midrange choice. All rooms have clean private bathrooms and air-con; those overlooking the garden at the rear

---

THE AUTHOR'S CHOICE

Amon Hotel (Map p128; ☎ 231 0912; fax 231 1353; Al-Gezira; s/d in old wing E£80/120, in new wing E£100/160; ✖) This family-run place is a favourite haunt of foreign archaeological missions, and no wonder. It offers great food, friendly service and spotlessly clean rooms for bargain prices. The comfortable rooms in the new wing have private bathrooms and balconies overlooking the attractive central courtyard garden. Five old-wing rooms have air-con, and some also have private bathrooms. The triple rooms on the top floor of the old wing (E£230) and adjoining roof terrace offer breathtaking views over to the Theban Hills and back to the East Bank.

are the best. The rooftop restaurant has great Nile views and is a good place to grab a *shee-sha*, tea or meal (E£13 to E£28). On Sunday nights it hosts a buffet (E£40) accompanied by Sufi dancing and local music.

Top End

Al-Moudira (☎ 2325 1307; moudirahotel@yahoo.com; Daba'iyya; r/ste US$200/275; ☒ ☒ ☐ ☒) Built to resemble a Damascene courtyard house, this gorgeous hotel features luxurious rooms, whimsical interiors, a wonderful pool area and a stylish bar and restaurant. Some guests revel in its seclusion (it's a 15-minute taxi ride from the ferry landing), others end up feeling as if they're trapped in a gilded cage. We're of the former opinion, highly recommended.

Flats in Luxor (Map p128; ☎ 010 356 4540; www .flatsinluxor.com; per week Jun-Sep E£1900, Oct-May E£2500; ☒ ☐ ☒) If you're planning a longish stay in Luxor, you need look no further than these impressive flats. Located between Al-Gezira and New Gurna, they're run by a British-Egyptian couple and feature three bedrooms (sleeping six), large sitting/dining areas, satellite TV and fully equipped kitchens. The two upper-floor flats have balconies with views over to the Thoban Hills. There's a panoramic roof terrace with a pool table and sun lounges, and a downstairs area with a pool and Jacuzzi.

Eating
EAST BANK

Sharia al-Mahatta has a number of good sandwich stands and other cheap-eat possibilities, as well as a few juice stands at its Luxor Temple end. One of the most popular fast-food joints in town is **Restaurant Elzaeem** (Map p125; ☒ 24hr), where you can grab a table and enjoy tasty kushari (small/medium/large E£4/7/10) or spaghetti (E£6 to E£11). Other decent cheap eats can be found around Sharia Televizyon.

Abu Ashraf (Map p125; Sharia al-Mahatta; dishes E£2-9) This popular restaurant and takeaway near the station has a terrace on the street and an air-con dining room behind. It serves up decent kushari (medium/large E£4/6), as well as pizza (from E£12) and kebabs (E£14).

Grand Restaurant & Café (☒ 8am-1am; ☒) It may be a favourite of tour groups, but this doesn't mean that the Grand should be dismissed out of hand. The outdoor terrace is

a pleasant spot to enjoy everything from soup (E£5) to a sandwich (E£9 to E£15) or a *sheesha* (E£5). It also serves mezze and salads (E£5).

Chez Omar (Map p125; ☎ 236 7678; Midan Youssif Hassan; salads E£3.50; ☒ 24hr) The friendly Chez Omar, in a small oasis of green, is a pleasant spot to enjoy a casual meal. It serves up good basic Egyptian dishes, including kebabs and pigeon. You can get an under-the-counter Stella here for E£10.

Lotus Restaurant (Map p125; ☎ 238 0419; Sharia As-Souq; ☒) You can observe the goings-on in the souq from the windows of this spotlessly clean 1st-floor restaurant. The Egyptian dishes are good – try the delicious lentil soup (E£5) or tasty chicken *tagen* (E£22) – or order European dishes such as spaghetti napolitana (E£12). The owners also run the Ritz Restaurant (Map p125) near Le Meridien Hotel. Credit cards are accepted.

Amoun Restaurant (Map p125; Sharia al-Karnak; mezze E£2.50-7, mains E£7-19; ☒ 7am-10pm) At the end of the souq near the Luxor Temple, this long-standing travellers' favourite serves up bland Oriental dishes, pizzas and pastas in clean surrounds. You can sit on the outdoor terrace or in the air-con dining room. The neighbouring Al-Hussein is a carbon copy, with identical menu and prices. Both offer a student discount.

7 Days, 7 Ways (Sharia Khalid ibn al-Walid; ☒) This 1st-floor eatery is keeping the British

EGYPT

colonial spirit alive and well by serving up affronts to the Egyptian palate, such as roast beef and Yorkshire pudding (E£29.50, Sunday only) and chip butties (E£11). A Stella costs E£10.50, renditions of 'Rule Britannia' come free.

Jamboree Restaurant (Map p125; ☎ 235 5827, 012 781 3149; Sharia al-Montazah; 🕙 10.30am-2.30pm for snacks & Oriental dishes, 6-10.30pm for full menu; 🍴) If you're feeling like a jacket potato (E£10 to E£16), spaghetti carbonara (E£22.50) or something similarly non-Egyptian, this British-run place could be just the thing. Relax on the pleasant rooftop terrace or dine in air-con comfort in the character-less but spotlessly clean dining room. A selection from the (safe) salad bar costs E£14.50.

The town's five-star hotels are home to myriad pricey restaurants. Among the best are **Dawar al-Umda** (Map p125; ☎ 238 0721; Sharia al-Karnak), a *Thousand and One Nights*–style outdoor restaurant in the garden of the Mercure Inn that hosts a popular Oriental buffet (E£85) on Thursday evenings, featuring performances by Sufi and belly dancers; and the **Pink Panda Chinese Restaurant** (☎ 237 2750) at the Isis Pyramisa Hotel.

WEST BANK
Restaurant Mohammed (Map p128; ☎ 231 1014; Gurna; meals E£8-20; 🕙 24hr) This laid-back restaurant is set in and around the peaceful courtyard of Mohammed Abdel Lahi's mud-brick house, just along from the Antiquities Inspectorate Ticket Office. Mohammed's mum cooks up a delicious *kofta tagen* (E£20), served with home-grown salad leaves; it goes down a treat with a cold Stella (E£8) or fresh lemon juice (E£3).

Nour al-Gurna (Map p128; ☎ 2311 430; Gurna; set meal E£20) The restaurant of this boutique hotel serves up delicious Egyptian food in a pleasant courtyard or a cool room, depending on the season. The food is made using fresh home-grown ingredients and is quite excellent.

Africa Restaurant (Map p128; set menu E£25; 🕙 10am-11pm) In a pleasant courtyard space close to the ferry landing, the Africa serves up large and very tasty set meals of chicken, fish, *kebab hala* (kebabs in a tomato sauce) or *kofta* with an avalanche of side dishes. If you ask nicely, the waiter can usually find a cold Stella (E£9) under the counter.

Tutankhamun Restaurant (Map p128; ☎ 231 0118; fixed menu E£35) Just south of the ferry dock, this outdoor terrace restaurant is run by a cook who once worked on one of the French archaeological missions in Luxor. He serves up decent set meals of roast chicken, duck *à l'òrange, kebab hala* or chicken curry, accompanied by a generous array of vegetable dishes, bread, soup, salad and tahini. The view of the Luxor Temple is great, but the restaurant's overall standard of hygiene leaves a lot to be desired.

Drinking
Nile Terrace Café & Bar (Map p125; Corniche el-Nil; beer E£23; 🕙 9am-7pm) At the front of the Old Winter Palace Hotel, this is a wonderful, if pricey, place to enjoy a sunset apéritif.

Metropolitan Café (Map p125; Stella small/large E£8/12) Its Nile-side terrace is a cheaper alternative to the Old Winter Palace Hotel, but its views are often obscured by moored cruise ships. Don't bother eating here.

Oum Koulsoum Coffee Shop (Map p125; sheesha & coffee E£4) Off the souq next to the Nefertiti Hotel, this is the most popular *ahwa* in town.

The **Royal Oak Pub** (Sharia Khalid ibn al-Walid; 🕙 4pm-2am) and the **Kings Head Pub** (Map p125; Sharia Khalid ibn al-Walid; 🕙 10am-2am) are British-style watering holes where you can watch English football or Sky News (an oxymoron if ever we heard one) on the satellite TV. You can even score some Indian food at the Kings Head. A beer costs around E£12 at both.

Getting There & Away
AIR
The **EgyptAir office** (Map p125; ☎ 238 0580; Corniche el-Nil; 🕙 8am-8pm) is next to Amex. There are regular connections with Cairo (E£714 one way) and Aswan (E£360 one way), and thrice-weekly flights to Sharm el-Sheikh (E£537 one way). Flights to Abu Simbel operate only in the high season, when there are one or two departures a day via Aswan. These entail ridiculously long transits, so you're much better off organising transport from Aswan.

BUS
The new **bus station** (Sharia al-Karnak) is located near the airport. There's an Upper Egypt Bus Co ticket office in front of the Horus

Hotel, near the Luxor Temple, and from here minibuses transfer passengers to the bus station for E£5. Note that this transfer service doesn't commence until 9am each day – if you wish to catch an earlier bus you'll need to catch a taxi to the station (E£25). There are two daily Upper Egypt Bus Co services to Cairo (E£85, 10 to 11 hours), departing at 7pm and 9pm. Eight daily buses run to Hurghada (E£25 to E£30, five hours) between 6.30am and 9pm. From Hurghada, the service goes on to Suez (E£46 to E£55, eight to nine hours). There's one bus per day to Port Said (E£70), which leaves at 8pm. One daily bus leaves at 5pm, travelling to Sharm el-Sheikh (E£100, 14 to 16 hours) and Dahab (E£110, 14 to 16 hours).

There is sometimes a bus to Aswan at 3.30pm (E£15), but it's often cancelled. You are much better off catching the train.

There is a service to Al-Kharga (E£40, four hours) on Saturday and Tuesday at 7:15am, and on Sunday and Wednesday at 1pm.

If you are travelling to Al-Quseir (E£8) or Marsa Alam(E£15), you'll need to make your way to the bus station at Qift, which is minutes before Qena, and catch a bus there. These leave at 11am, 2.30pm and 5pm.

CONVOY

It is often, but not always, compulsory for foreigners to travel out of Luxor by convoy. At the time of our research, you could make your own way to the Western Desert, Minya, Tell al-Amarna and Asyut, but were forced to travel in the convoy when going to Aswan, Esna, Edfu, Kom Ombo, Hurghada, Dendara, Abydos, Qena, Marsa Alam, Al-Quseir and Safaga. There are 10 checkpoints between Luxor and Hurghada and nine between Luxor and Aswan, so your chances of travelling outside the convoys are somewhere between slim and impossible.

There are convoys to Hurghada at 8am, 2pm and 6pm daily, travelling via Qena and Safaga. The 8am convoy also stops at Dendara and Abydos, and the 2pm stops at Dendara but not Abydos. If you're travelling to Al-Quseir, you need to travel the first part of the trip with the Hurghada convoy.

Convoys to Aswan leave at 7am, 11am and 3pm. The 7am convoy travels via Esna, Edfu and Kom Ombo. If you're travelling

to Marsa Alam, you need to travel the first part of the trip with the Aswan convoy.

All convoys leave Luxor from a road off the Corniche, north of the general hospital and Luxor Museum (Map p125).

CRUISES

The best times of the year for cruising are October/November and April/May. During the high season (October to May), an armada of cruise boats travels the Nile between Aswan and Esna (for Luxor), stopping at Edfu and Kom Ombo en route. You should be able to negotiate a decent discount on the usually high cruise price if you make your way to Esna and deal directly with the boat captains rather than booking through a travel agency. Feluccas can also be organised from Esna, but most travellers prefer to travel the other way (Aswan to Luxor), as this is how the current runs. See p142 for more information.

SERVICE TAXI

The service taxi station (Map p125) is on a street off Sharia al-Karnak, a couple of blocks inland from the Luxor Museum, but because of police restrictions you will have to take an entire car and go in convoy, which means paying about E£300 for Hurghada and E£200 for Aswan. Be at the taxi stand 30 minutes before the convoy is due to leave.

TRAIN

Luxor's **train station** (Map p125; Midan al-Mahatta) is conveniently located in the centre of town.

Abela Egypt Sleeping Train (☎ 237 2015; www .sleepingtrains.com) services leave at 8.30pm and 9.30pm daily, arriving in Cairo at 5.45am and 6.45am the next morning. The first service travels on to Alexandria. The trip costs US$53/74 per person one way in a double/single cabin. Children four to nine years old pay US$40. There are no student discounts and tickets must be paid for in US dollars or euros. The price includes breakfast.

The only other Cairo trains that foreigners are allowed to take are train 981 (E£62/40 in 1st/2nd class), departing at 9.15am; train 1903 (E£67/45), departing at 9.15pm; and train 997 (E£67/45), departing at 11.10pm. The trip takes approximately 10 hours and student discounts are available on both classes for all three services. All trains have air-conditioning.

Train 981 to Cairo stops at Al-Balyana (for Abydos; E£26/16 in 1st/2nd class, three hours), Asyut (for Tell al-Amarna; E£36/22, four hours) and Minya (for Tell al-Amarna or Beni Hasan; E£49/32, 4½ hours). Be warned that the authorities are not keen on foreigners getting off at these destinations, and usually insist on a tourist police escort for everyone who does.

Foreigners are permitted to take three daily services to Aswan. These are train 996 (E£30/21 in 1st/2nd class), leaving at 7.15am; train 1902 (E£30/21), leaving at 9.30am; and train 980 (E£26/16), departing at 5pm. The trip takes three hours and a student discount is available on tickets for both classes.

All three of the Aswan trains stop at Esna (E£14/12 in 1st/2nd class, 45 minutes), Edfu (E£19/15, 1½ hours) and Kom Ombo (E£25/18, 2½ hours).

There's a train from Luxor to Al-Kharga every Thursday (E£11/10.25 in 2nd/3rd class, seven hours) at 6am or 7am, depending on the time of year.

Getting Around
TO/FROM THE AIRPORT
Luxor International Airport (☎ 237 4655) is 7km east of town. A taxi will cost around E£25 to East Bank destinations and E£50 to West Bank destinations. There are no buses between the airport and town.

CALÈCHE
For about E£20 per hour you can get around town by *calèche*. Rates are subject to haggling, squabbling and – occasionally – screaming. You can usually bargain a short trip down to E£5. When the time to pay arrives, drivers have been known to demand 'Nubian pounds', which – surprise, surprise – they maintain are worth more than Egyptian pounds. Tell them where they can park their carriages (you get the picture...) if they try this scam on you.

FERRY & BOAT
Regular *baladi* (municipal) ferries carry passengers between the East and West Banks. You'll find the East Bank stop down a flight of stone stairs in front of the Luxor Temple, and the West Bank stop in front

(to the left) of the dusty car park where the pick-ups congregate. A ticket costs E£1 each way. Private launches charge E£5 each way for the same trip.

PICK-UP
On the West Bank, colourful pick-up trucks shuttle passengers from the ferry dock to various destinations for 25pt. To catch one, flag it down from the side of the street; when you want to alight, push the bell on the inside of the partition between the driver and passengers. You can also hire one of these as a private taxi for E£5.

NORTH OF LUXOR
Dendara   دندرة
☎ 096
The wonderfully preserved **Temple of Hathor** (adult/student E£30/15; ☯ 7am-6pm), at her cult site of Dendara, is one of the most impressive temples in Egypt. Built at the very end of the Pharaonic period, its main building is still virtually intact, with a great stone roof and columns, dark chambers, underground crypts and twisting staircases, all carved with hieroglyphs. Hathor, the goddess of pleasure and love, is figured on the 24 columns of the Outer Hypostyle Hall, and on the walls are scenes of Roman emperors as pharaohs. The views from the roof are magnificent.

Dendara is 4km southwest of Qena on the west side of the Nile. It's an easy day trip from Luxor.

The tourist police in the Nile Valley do everything possible to discourage independent travel to Dendara, preferring travellers to take a day cruise from Luxor, or to travel by taxi or tour bus in the daily 8am and 2pm convoys. A taxi from Luxor costs E£100 to E£130 return; to Dendara and Abydos it will cost E£225 to E£250. If you decide to try your luck getting here under your own steam, your best bet is the bus to Qena, and a taxi from there to the site. You'll have to put up with a tourist police escort. See p134 for details.

The Novotel Hotel's **M/S Le Lotus** (☎ 238 0925; h1083@accor-hotels.com; adult/child E£260/130) cruises to Dendara each day during the winter tourist season. Tickets include lunch and entry fees. *Le Lotus* also sometimes offers a dinner cruise. Contact the company for further details.

SOUTH OF LUXOR
Esna أسنا
The hypostyle hall, with its 24 columns still supporting a roof, is all that remains of the **Temple of Khnum** (adult/student E£15/10; ☼ 6am-4pm winter, 6am-5pm summer), constructed by Egypt's Ptolemaic rulers. Dedicated to the ram-headed creator god who fashioned humankind on his potter's wheel using Nile clay, its pillars are decorated with hieroglyphic accounts of the temple rituals.

Trains running between Luxor and Aswan stop here (see p135 and p142), but the station is on the opposite side of the Nile, making a visit in this way complicated. It's much easier to take a day tour or travel in a private taxi (E£100 return) in the 7am daily convoy from Luxor.

Edfu أدفو
The attraction in this town, 53km south of Esna, is the **Temple of Horus** (adult/student E£50/25; ☼ 6am-4pm winter, 6am-5pm summer), the most completely preserved Egyptian temple in Egypt. Built by the Ptolemies, it was one of the last great Egyptian attempts at monument building on the grand scale, and was dedicated to the falcon-headed son of Osiris. It took about 200 years to complete. Excavation of the temple from beneath the sand, rubble and structures that had been built on its roof was conducted by Auguste Mariette in the mid-19th century.

Trains running between Luxor and Aswan stop here (p135 and p142); the station is approximately 4km from the temple. Pick-up trucks travel between the station and town for E£5 (for the whole truck). Again, it's easier to take a day tour or travel in a private taxi (E£130 to E£150 return) in the 7am daily convoy from Luxor.

Kom Ombo كوم أمبو
The dual **Temple of Sobek & Haroeris** (adult/student E£30/15; ☼ 6am-4pm winter, 6am-5pm summer) is dedicated to the local crocodile god and the falcon-headed sky god, respectively. One of the most spectacularly sited temples in the country, it stands on a promontory at a bend in the Nile near the village of Kom Ombo. In ancient times sacred crocodiles basked in the sun on the river bank here.

Kom Ombo is closer to Aswan than to Luxor. If you're travelling from Luxor you can stop here on the train (p135) and catch a pick-up from the station to the town (25pt), and then another from the town to the boat landing near the temple (25pt, 4km). If you're coming from Aswan you can catch the train (p142) or bus (p142). The easiest way to visit is to take a day tour or travel by private taxi in the morning convoys between Luxor and Aswan. A return taxi from Luxor to Edfu and Kom Ombo costs E£225 to E£250.

ASWAN أسوان
☎ 097 / pop 241,000
Egypt's southernmost city sits on the banks of a particularly beautiful stretch of the Nile. Here, the river's dark blue water is fringed by dense palms, gentle hills of sand rise in the background and flocks of local feluccas are ever present. This is Egypt at its most photogenic, the stuff of picture books and postcards galore.

Orientation
The train station (Map p138) is at the northern end of town, three blocks east of the river. The bus station is a few kilometres further north. The lively souq (Sharia as-Souq) runs south from the square in front of the train station, parallel to the Corniche, which is home to banks, restaurants, shops and most of the public utilities. The southern end of the Corniche is marked by the distinctive form of the Archangel Michael Coptic Orthodox Cathedral, and is where you'll find the Nubia Museum and a number of the city's better hotels.

Information
INTERNET ACCESS
Aswan Internet Cafe (Map p140; ☎ 231 4472; Corniche el-Nil; per hr E£10; ☼ 9am-midnight) In the oddly shaped El-Tagdiffe (Rowing) Club building on the Corniche.
Aswanet (Map p140; ☎ 231 7332; Keylany Hotel; per hr E£10; ☼ 9am 1am)

MONEY
The main banks all have branches on the Corniche; there are ATMs at the Banque Misr, Banque du Caire and the National Bank of Egypt. Banque Misr has a **foreign-exchange booth** (☼ 8am-3pm & 5-8pm) beside its main building. **Amex** (Map p138; ☎ 230 6983; Corniche el-Nil; ☼ 9am-5pm) and **Thomas Cook** (Map p140; ☎ 304 011; Corniche el-Nil; ☼ 8am-2pm & 5-9pm) also have offices here. Both cash travellers

EGYPT

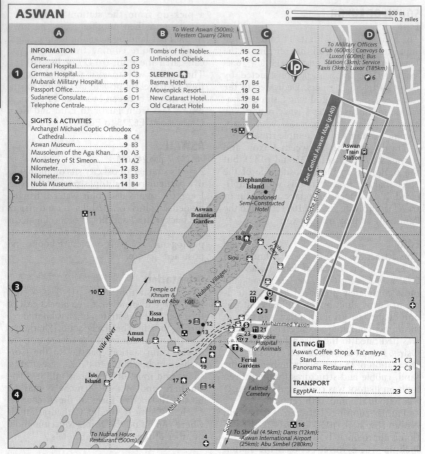

ASWAN

0 ————————— 300 m
0 ————————— 0.2 miles

INFORMATION
Amex...1 C3
General Hospital..........................2 D3
German Hospital..........................3 C3
Mubarak Military Hospital..............4 B4
Passport Office.............................5 C3
Sudanese Consulate......................6 D1
Telephone Centrale.......................7 C3

SIGHTS & ACTIVITIES
Archangel Michael Coptic Orthodox
    Cathedral................................8 C4
Aswan Museum.............................9 B3
Mausoleum of the Aga Khan......10 A3
Monastery of St Simeon..............11 A2
Nilometer..................................12 B3
Nilometer..................................13 B3
Nubia Museum...........................14 B4

Tombs of the Nobles..................15 C2
Unfinished Obelisk.....................16 C4

SLEEPING
Basma Hotel..............................17 B4
Movenpick Resort......................18 C3
New Cataract Hotel....................19 B4
Old Cataract Hotel.....................20 B4

To West Aswan (500m);
Western Quarry (2km)

To Military Officers
Club (600m); Convoys to
Luxor (600m); Bus
Station (3km); Service
Taxis (3km); Luxor (185km)

Aswan
Train
Station

Elephantine
Island
Abandoned
Semi-Constructed
Hotel

Aswan
Botanical
Garden

Siou

Temple of
Khnum &
Ruins of Abu
Koti

Nubian Villages

Essa
Island

Amun
Island

Muhammed Yassin

Brooke
Hospital
for Animals

EATING
Aswan Coffee Shop & Ta'amiyya
    Stand...................................21 C3
Panorama Restaurant.................22 C3

TRANSPORT
EgyptAir...................................23 C3

Ferial
Gardens

Isis
Island

Fatimid
Cemetery

To Nubian House
Restaurant (500m)

To Shellal (4.5km); Dams (12km);
Aswan International Airport
(25km); Abu Simbel (280km)

Nile River

cheques and will sell US dollars if they have them in stock. There's an Egypt Exchange office (Map p140) on the Corniche.

POST
Main post office (Map p140; Corniche el-Nil; 8am-2pm Sat-Thu) Next to the Rowing Club.

TELEPHONE
Telephone centrale (Map p138; Corniche el-Nil; 24hr) You can make international calls from this office, located towards the southern end of town, just past the EgyptAir office.

TOURIST INFORMATION
Main tourist office (Map p140; 231 2811; Midan al-Mahatta; 8am-3pm & 6-8pm) Next to the train station.

Tourist office (232 3297; 8am-3pm) On a side street one block in from the West Bank ferry landing.

VISA EXTENSIONS
Passport office (Map p138; 8.30am-1pm Sat-Thu) On the 1st floor of the police building on the Corniche.

Sights
NUBIA MUSEUM
This fascinating **museum** (Map p138; Sharia Abtal at-Tahrir; adult/student E£50/25; 9am-1pm & 5-9pm) showcases the history, art and culture of Nubia from prehistoric times to the present day. The impressive and well-labelled collection is housed in a building that has been designed to reference traditional Nubian architecture. Make sure you have a look at

the 'Nubia Submerged' exhibition, which includes photographs of Philae, Abu Simbel and Kalabsha before they were resited. The entrance is opposite the Basma Hotel, a 15-minute walk from the town centre.

UNFINISHED OBELISK

This huge discarded **obelisk** (Map p138; adult/student E£30/15; ☾ 7am-5pm winter, 8am-6pm summer) lies southeast of the Fatimid Cemetery, on the edge of the northern granite quarries that supplied the ancient Egyptians with most of the hard stone used in pyramids and temples. Three sides of the shaft, which is nearly 42m long, were completed, except for the inscriptions; it would have been the largest single piece of stone ever handled if a flaw had not appeared in the granite. Private taxis will charge E£5 to bring you here from the centre of town.

ELEPHANTINE ISLAND

The ruins of the ancient town of Yebu and two impressive **Nilometers** (Map p138) lie at the southern end of this island, within the grounds of the small and decidedly underwhelming **Aswan Museum** (Map p138; adult/student E£20/10; ☾ 8am-5pm winter, 8.30am-6pm summer). If you're keen to visit the museum or the two small Nubian villages on the island (and to be frank, we're not sure it's worth the effort), go down the stairs opposite the telephone centrale or the Thomas Cook office and wait on the pontoon landing for one of the regular ferries (E£1). Note that women sit up front, men at the back.

ASWAN BOTANICAL GARDEN

Lord Kitchener turned this island into a verdant **botanical garden** (Map p138; admission E£10; ☾ 8am-5pm winter, 8am-6pm summer) and you can admire the product of his labours today. You'll need to hire a boat or felucca to get here.

MONASTERY OF ST SIMEON

To reach this well-preserved, 6th-century mud-brick Coptic Christian **monastery** (Map p138; adult/student E£20/10; ☾ 7am-4pm winter, 8am-5pm summer), it's a half-hour hike from the felucca dock near the Mausoleum of the Aga Khan. If you decide to take a camel or donkey instead of walking, bargain hard – a return trip with a 45-minute waiting period should cost no more than E£30.

TOMBS OF THE NOBLES

A few of the Old and Middle Kingdom **tombs** (Map p138; adult/student E£20/10; ☾ 8am-4pm winter, 8am-5pm summer) of local dignitaries are worth exploring.

Activities

No visit to Aswan would be complete without at least an hour spent sailing around the islands in a felucca. Late afternoon is probably the best time of day to do this. The official government price for hiring a felucca capable of seating one to eight people is E£25 per hour, but with a bit of bargaining you should be able to hire a boat for three hours for about E£60 – enough time to sail to Seheyl Island and back.

Sleeping

Be warned that hotels in the centre of town, particularly those on the Corniche, can be noisy at night.

BUDGET

Keylany Hotel (Map p140; ☎ /fax 231 7332; www .keylanyhotel.com; Sharia Keylany; s/d E£50/70; ✸) The best budget option in town, this place is noteworthy for its extremely professional staff and its delicious breakfasts (filter coffee, fresh juice and pancakes). Rooms are freshly painted and very clean; all have private bathrooms. The owner is planning to add a pool, a Jacuzzi and new Nile-view rooms, so prices may rise.

Nuba Nile Hotel (Map p140; ☎ 231 3267; hamdi _abed@hotmail.com; s/d E£50/70; ✸ ⬚) This clean and comfortable place is a short walk from the train station, next to a popular *ahwa*. Rooms have tiny private bathrooms; most have air-con and a few have 'honeymoon' (king-sized) beds. Some rooms have no windows, others have balconies overlooking the street. The friendly owner has plans to put a pool and coffee shop upstairs in the future.

Nubian Oasis Hotel (Map p140; ☎ 231 2123/6; nubianoasis_hotel_aswan@hotmail.com; Sharia as-Souq; s/ d E£20/25; ✸ ⬚) When we visited this popular backpacker haunt, threadbare carpets, grotty bathrooms and lumpy beds featured. We've since heard that the place has been refurbished, which is good news. There's a terrace café where you can relax over a Stella (E£7), free Internet access, and air-con and private bathrooms in all rooms.

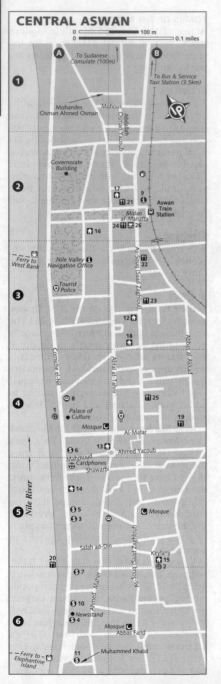

CENTRAL ASWAN

Hathor Hotel (Map p140; ☎ 231 4223; fax 230 3462; Corniche el-Nil; s/d E£35/55; 🛏 🖥) A slightly grubby place on the Corniche, Hathor has a friendlier feel than neighbouring Horus Hotel, but is nowhere near as nice as Keylany. There's a tiny pool and outdoor furniture on the rooftop. Most rooms have air-con; all have cramped private bathrooms.

Happi Hotel (Map p140; ☎ 231 4115; fax 230 7572; Sharia Abtal at-Tahrir; s/d E£50/70; 🛏 🖥) If you can ignore the spectacularly rude reception staff, the Happi comes close to living up to its name, offering clean rooms with private bathrooms and satellite TV. Guests have free use of the pool at the Cleopatra Hotel.

MIDRANGE & TOP END

Marhaba Palace Hotel (Map p140; ☎ 233 0102; marhabaaswan@yahoo.com; Corniche el-Nil; s/d US$50/60; 🛏) Aswan's dearth of decent midrange hotels means any new place is good news, but the Marhaba overshadows the competition. Rooms are small but well appointed, with comfortable beds, tasteful décor, luxurious bathrooms and satellite TV. Bright and welcoming, it has two restaurants, friendly staff and a roof terrace with excellent Nile views. Recommended.

INFORMATION	
Aswan Internet Cafe	1 A4
Aswanet	2 B5
Bank of Alexandria	3 A5
Banque du Caire	4 A6
Banque du Caire (ATM)	5 A5
Banque Misr (ATM)	6 A4
Egyptian Exchange (Forex)	7 A6
Main Post Office	8 A4
Main Tourist Office	9 B2
National Bank of Egypt (ATM)	10 A6
Thomas Cook	11 A6

SLEEPING 🏠	
Cleopatra Hotel	12 B3
Happi Hotel	13 A4
Hathor Hotel	14 A5
Keylany Hotel	15 B5
Marhaba Palace Hotel	16 A2
Nuba Nile Hotel	17 B2
Nubian Oasis Hotel	18 B3

EATING 🍴	
Al-Masry Restaurant	19 B4
Aswan Moon Restaurant	20 A5
Biti Pizza	21 B2
Chief Khalil	22 B3
El Madena	23 B3
Fiteer Stand	24 B2
Kushari Store	25 B4

DRINKING 🍹	
Cafés	26 B2

Cleopatra Hotel (Map p140; ☎ 231 4001; fax 231 4002; Sharia as-Souq; s/d US$32/45; ❂ ▢ ▣) This attractive hotel in the souq is one of Aswan's few real midrange hotels. It has friendly staff, and clean rooms with satellite TV and private bathrooms. The best feature is its small rooftop pool.

Basma Hotel (Map p138; ☎ 231 0901; basma@roc ketmail.com; Sharia Abtal at-Tahrir; s/d US$108/141; ❌ ❂ ▢ ▣) An extremely comfortable four-star place, opposite the Nubia Museum. Basma has a nice garden and pool, and some good Nile views, especially from the terrace rooms at the end of the building. Breakfast costs E£27.

New Cataract Hotel (Map p138; ☎ 231 6000/1; h1666@accor.com; Sharia Abtal at-Tahrir; s/d US$96/124, with Nile view US$124/149; ❂ ▣) If you're keen to share the views and amenities of the Old Cataract but don't have the budget, its modern, adjoining neighbour may be worth considering. Usually full of tour groups, it offers 144 large rooms, half of which have Nile views. Ask for one on the 7th or 8th floor. Breakfast, which is obligatory, costs an extra E£41.

Movenpick Resort (Map p138; ☎ 230 3455; www .moevenpick-aswan.com; s/d US$183/236; ❂ ▣) This five-star resort on Elephantine Island is a great place for a relaxing Egyptian break. Rooms are large and comfortable, and all have a balcony with Nile views. Resort facilities are impressive – an enormous pool, tennis courts, and a spa and health club with well-equipped gym. A free 24-hour ferry shuttles guests between the island and the Corniche. Breakfast costs E£37.

Old Cataract Hotel (Map p138; ☎ 231 6000; www .sofitel.com; Sharia Abtal at-Tahrir; r US$168-1500; ❂ ▣) This world-famous hotel is where Agatha Christie wrote and where presidents and potentates have watched the Nile flow by. It offers fabulous views and great Moorish architecture. If you decide to stay here, it's worth paying extra for a deluxe room with a balcony overlooking the Nile (US$265).

Eating

The most popular snack stand in town is next to the Aswan Coffee Shop (Map p138), in the street housing the Brook Hospital for Animals. It's opposite a public oven and uses freshly baked bread in its ta'amiyya sandwiches. For good, cheap fiteer, try the fiteer stand (Map p140) on the southern side of Midan al-Mahatta, opposite Biti Pizza. For kushari, try the kushari store (Map p140) with the couple of outdoor tables on Sharia as-Souq, just around the corner from Sharia al-Matar.

Nubian House Restaurant (☎ 232 6226; mezze E£4-5, mains E£7-20) The afternoon views of the First Cataract from the terrace of this friendly place are utterly breathtaking and shouldn't be missed. As well as serving authentic Nubian dishes, it is very welcoming to guests who choose to linger over a tea (E£4) and a *sheesha* (E£3). The only downside to a visit is the presence of tour groups, which often book out the tables with the best views. To get here, follow the road from the Basma Hotel and veer right after 15 minutes, when it comes to a fork past a development of upmarket housing. There's no street lighting at all, so don't attempt the walk at night   catch a taxi. Not to be confused with the far less impressive Nubian House on Elephantine Island.

Panorama Restaurant (Map p138; ☎ 231 6108; Corniche el-Nil; mains E£8-15) Our favourite of the Nile-side terrace restaurants, the Panorama serves up a delicious fish *tagen* (E£15) as well as offering a wide range of herbal and medicinal teas (E£2). Pristine toilets, a laid-back feel, all-day breakfasts and great views over to Elephantine Island are added bonuses.

Al-Masry Restaurant (Map p140; ☎ 230 2576; Sharia al-Matar; meals around E£25) A local institution, Al-Masry produces tasty kebabs and *kofta*, served with bread, salad and tahini.

Biti Pizza (Map p140; Midan al-Mahatta; pizzas E£20; ☯ 24hr) A good but pricey pizza joint, Biti serves up Egyptian- and Italian-style pizzas in refreshingly clean surrounds. Sitting on the roof terrace and watching the frenetic goings-on in the square below is great fun.

El Madena (Map p140; Sharia as-Souq) This unpretentious place in the souq serves a meal of *kofta*, tahini, rice, bread and salad for E£20, and a vegetarian meal for E£12.

Aswan Moon Restaurant (Map p140; ☎ 231 6108; Corniche el-Nil; mezze E£4-9, mains E£12-30) A pontoon with brightly coloured awnings and views over to Elephantine, this popular place serves up lacklustre food to hoards of tourists. The pizzas (E£17 to E£23) are unimpressive, but the *daood basha* (meatballs in a tomato sauce, E£10) is quite tasty. Stella (E£8) is served. This is one of the best places in town to meet up with felucca captains.

Chief Khalil (Map p140; ☎ 231 0142; Sharia as-Souq; meals E£25-50; ☒) This tiny but popular seafood restaurant grills delicious fresh fish from Lake Nasser and the Red Sea over coals and serves it up with salads, and rice or french fries.

Drinking

Old Cataract Hotel (Map p138; ☒ 8am-11pm) Enjoying tea or an apéritif on the Nile-side terrace at the Old Cataract is on many a traveller's 'must-do' list. The hotel discourages an inundation of tourists by charging E£55 per person for this privilege, which goes towards the price of afternoon tea (E£43 to E£55), a Stella (E£17), open sandwiches (E£24 to E£29) or a cappuccino (E£9).

Nubian House Restaurant (☎ 232 6226) The most atmospheric tea-and-*sheesha* spot in town.

The cafés (Map p140) on the busy corner of Midan al-Mahatta and Sharia as-Souq are great places to linger over a honeydrenched baklava and a glass of tea.

Getting There & Away

AIR

EgyptAir (Map p138; ☎ 231 5000; Corniche el-Nil; ☒ 8am-8pm) offers six flights between Aswan and the Egyptian capital (E£1037 one way, 1¼ hours). The one-way hop to Luxor is E£364 (30 minutes) and leaves daily at 9am. A service taxi between the airport and the centre of town costs E£1.

BOAT TO SUDAN

See p664 for details of the weekly ferry to Wadi Halfa.

BUS

The new bus station is north of the town centre. A taxi to the town centre (including the hotels near the Nubia Museum) will cost E£5; a seat in one of the regular service taxis costs 50pt. Buses leave for Cairo (E£85, 13 hours) at 3.30pm. There are 6am, 8am, 12.30pm, 2pm, 3.30pm and 5pm services to Luxor (E£15, four to five hours) via Kom Ombo and Esna. To Suez (E£85, 13 hours) buses leave at 6am, 8am, 3.30pm and 5pm, travelling via Hurghada (E£45, seven hours). There is one 6.30am service to Marsa Alam (E£15, six hours).

CONVOY

It is compulsory for foreigners to travel between Luxor and Aswan by convoy, and the nine checkpoints along the way mean that it is impossible to get around this rule. Two daily convoys leave Aswan from the front of the Military Officers Club near the bus station. The 8am convoy travels via Esna, Edfu and Kom Ombo, allowing stops at each of these sites. The 1.30pm convoy travels direct to Luxor and only allows one brief toilet stop en route. The trip to Luxor takes three hours. From Luxor, the convoy continues to Hurghada.

See p144 for details of the daily convoys to Abu Simbel.

FELUCCA

Aswan is the best place to arrange overnight felucca trips because even if the winds fail, the Nile's strong currents will propel you north. The most popular trips are to Kom Ombo (one night, two days) or Edfu (two nights, three days), but some people go on to Esna (three nights, four days).

Prices are usually based on six people travelling on the felucca; if there are fewer passengers the price per person will be higher. The standard cost is E£31.50 per person to Kom Ombo, E£56.50 to Edfu and E£62.50 to Esna. Feluccas rarely travel all the way to Luxor, as winds are hard to catch on the final Esna–Luxor stretch. All passengers must pay an extra E£5 per person for a permit, plus the cost of food and drink supplies.

SERVICE TAXI

At the time of writing, the police in Aswan were forbidding foreigners from taking service taxis between Aswan and Luxor, often turning them back at the checkpoint just north of town. As with all such directives, people do get around the rules, but in general it's better to take the bus or train, or else get a group of people together and hire a private taxi. A taxi to Luxor will cost between E£150 to E£200; E£200 to E£250 if you stop at Kom Ombo, Edfu and Esna en route.

TRAIN

Air-conditioned tourist trains to Cairo (E£77 to E£81 in 1st class, E£43 to E£47 in 2nd class, 13 hours) via Luxor (E£26 to E£30 in

1st class, E£16 to E£21 in 2nd class, three hours) leave at 6am, 6pm and 8pm. Tickets can be booked in advance. A student discount is available on tickets for both classes.

All three of these trains stop at Kom Ombo (E£15/12 in 1st/2nd class, 45 minutes), Edfu (E£19/10, 1¾ hours) and Esna (E£22/14, 2½ hours).

Abela Egypt Sleeping Train (☎ 230 2124; www .sleepingtrains.com) services leave at 5pm and 6.30pm, arriving in Cairo at 5.45am and 6.45am the next morning. The first service travels on to Alexandria. Tickets cost US$53/74 per person one way in a double/single cabin. Children four to nine years old pay US$40. There are no student discounts and tickets must be paid for in US dollars or euros. The price includes a basic dinner and breakfast.

Getting Around

TO/FROM THE AIRPORT
Aswan International Airport (☎ 248 0333) lies about 25km southwest of town; the taxi fare into town should be no more than E£25.

CALÈCHE
A *calèche* trip along the Corniche will cost E£10.

TAXI
A 3½-hour taxi tour to the Temple of Philae, High Dam and Unfinished Obelisk costs around E£30. A taxi anywhere within town costs E£5.

AROUND ASWAN
Philae (Aglikia Island)   معبد فيله
South of Aswan and relocated to another island to save it from being flooded during the building of the High Dam in the 1960s, the **Temple of Philae** (adult/student E£50/25; ☽ 7am-4pm winter, 7am-5pm summer) was dedicated to Isis, who found the heart of her slain brother, Osiris, on Philae Island (now submerged). Most of the temple was built by the Ptolemaic dynasty and the Romans. Early Christians later turned the hypostyle hall into a chapel.

Tickets are purchased from the small office before the boat landing at Shellal, south of the Old Dam. You'll pay E£25 (maximum) for a taxi to bring you here, wait for an hour or so and then bring you back to town. You'll need to negotiate a price for

a boat to take you between the ticket box and the island – the captains have formed a cartel, so it's very hard indeed to organise a return trip for less than E£30 to E£35 per boat, particularly at night.

A nightly **sound-and-light show** (☎ 230 5376; admission E£55), lasting 1½ hours, is held at the temple. Though there is officially no student discount, we have seen ISIC holders negotiate tickets for E£44. Check with the tourist office in Aswan for performance times and languages.

Abu Simbel   أبو سمبل
☎ 097
Ramses II, never one to do things by half, surpassed even himself when he caused the magnificent **Great Temple of Abu Simbel** (☎ 400 325; adult/student E£70/35; ☽ 5am-5pm winter, 5am-6pm summer) to be carved out of a mountainside. The temple was dedicated to the gods Ra-Harakhty, Amun, Ptah and the deified pharaoh himself. Guarding the entrance, the four famous colossal statues of Ramses II sit majestically, each more than 20m tall, with smaller statues of the pharaoh's mother, Queen Tuya, his beloved wife, Nefertari, and some of their children.

The other temple at the Abu Simbel complex is the rock-cut **Temple of Hathor**, fronted by six massive 10m-high standing statues. Four represent Ramses and the other two Nefertari. Both temples were moved out of the way of the rising waters of Lake Nasser in the 1960s and relocated here.

Sound-and-light shows (E£60) are performed here each night. The tourist office in Aswan has the latest schedule.

There are banks in town, but no ATMs. You can eat at the Seti Abu Simbel or at a clutch of ramshackle eateries (including ta'amiyya and shwarma stands) on the main street.

SLEEPING
Abu Simbel Village (☎ /fax 400 092, ☎ 012 363 9794; r E£110; ☒) Also known as Hotel Abbas, this is the cheapest option in town. Basic but clean rooms are arranged around a concrete courtyard and come with wheezing air-con units, intermittent hot water and small private bathrooms.

Eskaleh (☎ 012 368 0521; fikrykachif@genevalink .com; s €30-35, d €40-50; ☐) This recently opened cultural centre is housed in a traditionally constructed mud-brick building and offers comfortable accommodation in five rooms. There's an attractive restaurant-lounge and a roof terrace with views over the lake. Rooms are simple but stylish, with modern tiled bathrooms. The friendly owners serve meals (breakfast/lunch/dinner E£15/30/40) featuring produce grown in their organic vegetable garden and host regular performances of Nubian music and dance.

GETTING THERE & AWAY
Most foreigners travel to Abu Simbel in one of the two official daily convoys from Aswan. These leave at 4am and 11am, take 3½ hours to get to the site and allow two hours before returning. No taxis are allowed to travel in the convoy, so your only options are luxury coach (if you're part of a tour group) or cramped minibus (if you've paid for a tour through one of Aswan's hotels or travel agencies). You'll need to shop around to get the best deal for a day tour – Thomas Cook charges E£240 for a seat on its minibus; most of the budget hotels in town sell seats for E£50 to E£90. These prices don't include admission costs, but most include stops at the Unfinished Obelisk, High Dam and Philae on the return trip. To pay for your seat on the bus and to see all four sites you'll be looking at a minimum cost of E£190/140 per adult/student for the day, plus food and drink.

The only way to avoid the convoy is to travel on the services offered by the Upper Egypt and El Gouna Bus Cos. These leave from the Aswan bus station at 8am, 9am, 11.30am, 4pm and 5pm, take four hours and cost E£20 one way. Some of these buses are comfortable and offer air-con, others are filthy old rust buckets on wheels; you'll have to rely on the luck of the draw as to which type you get. Officially, a maximum of four foreign tourists are allowed on each of these services, so arrive at the bus station well ahead of time to be sure of getting a seat. Check return times when you purchase your tickets. Bring your passport, as there are two checkpoint stops. In Abu Simbel the buses depart from the front of the Wady El Nile Restaurant on the main street. Tickets are purchased from the conductor.

EgyptAir has two daily flights from Aswan to Abu Simbel (E£640 return), leaving at 6.30am and 9am.

WESTERN OASES
الواحات الغربية

Forming the northeast section of the great Sahara, the Western (Libyan) Desert starts on the banks of the Nile and continues into Libya, covering 2.8 million sq km. The stark landscape is bizarre and beautiful in equal measure, and the five major oases provide unique pit stops for the growing number of adventurers and travellers making their way here. Asphalt roads link all the oases, four of them in a long loop from Asyut around to Cairo. Siwa, out near the Libyan frontier, is linked to Bahariyya, but permits are needed to use the road. The easiest access is via Marsa Matruh on the Mediterranean coast.

If you want to know more about travelling in this part of Egypt, the best reference is *The Western Desert of Egypt: An Explorer's Handbook* by Cassandra Vivian. This is widely available in Egypt.

KHARGA OASIS   الواحات الخرجة
☎ 092
The largest of the oases, Kharga is currently blighted by overexuberant tourist police who stick to foreigners like superglue. It's one of those places that hides many of its treasures under a veneer of provincial insignificance.

The town itself, **Al-Kharga**, is of little interest; its only real tourist attraction is the impressive **Antiquities Museum** (Sharia Gamal Abdel Nasser; adult/student E£20/10; ☒ 9am-4pm), but 2km to the north you'll find the well-preserved **Temple of Hibis** (admission E£10; ☒ 8am-5pm winter, 8am-6pm summer), built in honour of the god Amun by the Persian emperor Darius I. To the east are the remains of the **Temple of An-Nadura**, built by the Romans, and just north is the Coptic **Necropolis of Al-Bagawat**, dating as far back as the 4th century. South of the town are the fortified Roman temples of **Qasr al-Ghueita** and **Qasr az-Zayyan**.

Information
There's a helpful **tourist office** (☎ 792 1206; Midan Nasser; ☒ 8am-3pm, variable evening hr Sat-Thu). The **Banque du Caire** (off Sharia Gamal Abdel Nasser) has an ATM and will change cash and travellers cheques.

Sleeping & Eating

El-Radwan Hotel (☎ 792 9897; s/d E£50/80; 🅿) The freshly painted rooms in this budget choice, on the street behind the museum, are quite comfortable, if slightly on the pricey side. All come with air-con and pristine private bathrooms.

El Dar el-Bidaa Hotel (☎ 792 1717; Midan Sho'ala; s/d with shared bathroom E£30/40, with private bathroom E£35/45; 🅿) A noisy, dirty and generally depressing place, El Dar el-Bidaa should only be considered by those down to their last few piastres (it's the only low-budget option around). The best rooms come with air-con and satellite TV. No breakfast is served and the hot water shouldn't be counted on.

Kharga Oasis Hotel (☎ 792 1500; Midan Nasser; s/d with fan E£63/88, with air-con E£70/95; 🅿) The quiet corridors of this large and perennially empty concrete building are eerily reminiscent of the hotel in Kubrick's *The Shining*. The rooms come with private bathrooms, screened windows and comfortable beds. No scary Jack Nicholson types were spotted. You can camp in the palm-filled garden for E£7.50 per person, but you'll be charged E£25 per group to use a bathroom.

Sol Y Mar Pioneer (☎ 792 7982; www.solymar -hotels.com; Sharia Gamal Abdel Nasser; s/d with half board E£530/701; 🅿 🖥 🏊) This ridiculously overpriced option has all the amenities and blandness of a standard international four-star hotel. Dinner here costs E£55 and alcohol is available.

Restaurants are few and far between in Kharga and the best places to eat are the hotels. Otherwise, try Al-Ahram, at the front of the Waha Hotel on Sharia an-Nabawi, which sells cheap roast chicken and salads.

Getting There & Away

It's important to note that the checkpoints at either end of the road between Al-Kharga and Luxor close at 4pm, which means that you must start your trip in either direction before midday.

EgyptAir flights from Cairo to Al-Kharga had been suspended at the time of research due to a lack of demand.

Buses leave from the new bus station behind Midan Basateen. Three buses leave Al-Kharga daily for Cairo (E£40 to E£45, eight hours) at 7pm, 9.30pm and 11pm. These travel via Asyut. There are extra services to Asyut (E£8, three hours) at 6am, 7am, 11am and 9pm.

Buses to Dakhla (E£8, two hours) leave at 11am, 2pm, 11pm, 1am and 3am. The 2pm and 1am buses connect with the 6pm and 6am buses to Farafra, Bahariyya and Cairo (see p146).

There are bus services to Luxor (E£35, five hours) on Tuesday and Saturday at 1pm, and on Sunday and Wednesday at 7am.

Minibuses to Asyut and Dakhla cost E£9 and leave from the bus station.

There's a train from Al-Kharga to Luxor every Friday at 6am or 7am, depending on the time of year. The trip takes about

---

TAKING A DESERT SAFARI

The oases are chock-full of operators eagerly offering camel and 4WD desert safaris. Needless to say, these vary dramatically in terms of cost and quality. A few companies have been running desert treks for years and can be trusted to supply roadworthy vehicles, healthy camels and Bedouin guides who know the desert like the back of their hands, but there are also a fair number of fly-by-night operations that are more interested in making a quick buck than providing a quality service. Before signing up, check vehicles to make sure they're roadworthy, confirm how much food and drink is supplied (and what this will be), ask how long the operators have been conducting safaris, confirm start and end times (some shifty types start late in the afternoon and return early in the morning but charge for full days) and try to get feedback from travellers who have just returned from a trip. If you're planning on exploring remote parts of the desert such as the Gilf Kebir, Oweynat or the Great Sand Sea it is absolutely imperative that you go with an outfit that supplies new 4WDs travelling in convoy, GPS, satellite phones and experienced Bedouin guides. You'll need an official permit for the Great Sand Sea (US$100, 14 days to process). To give an idea of prices, a one-night camping trip into the White Desert will cost between E£150 and E£400 per person per day, with the average price being E£230. If you're travelling into the remote corners of the desert, you'll be looking at between E£550 and E£650 per day.

EGYPT

seven hours and tickets cost E£11/10.25 in 2nd/3rd class.

DAKHLA OASIS الواحات الدخلة
☎ 092

The verdant and very easy-going oasis of Dakhla contains two small towns, **Mut** and **Al-Qasr**. Mut is the bigger and has most of the hotels and public utilities. The towns' signature, and their unifying element, are their 600 **hot springs** – make sure you investigate a few. Also be sure to visit the remarkable mud-brick citadel at Al-Qasr, which is home to a small **Ethnographic Museum** (admission E£3; ☺ variable). Local guides are happy to take you through the citadel's narrow winding lanes and into its half-hidden buildings in exchange for some baksheesh.

Information

The **tourist office** (☎ 782 1685/6; Sharia as-Sawra al-Khadra; ☺ 8am-3pm) is on Mut's main road. The Abu Mohamed Restaurant, opposite the tourist office, offers **Internet access** (per hr E£10; ☺ 7am-midnight). The **Bank Misr** (Sharia Al-Wadi) in Mut will change cash and travellers cheques and give advances on Visa and MasterCard, but it doesn't have an ATM.

Sleeping

El-Kasr Hotel (☎ 787 6013; Al-Qasr; to sleep on roof E£3, beds E£10) Conveniently located on the main road near the entry to the old town, the friendly El-Kasr is the best backpacker option in town. It has four big, screened rooms with hard beds, narrow balconies and one reasonably clean shared bathroom with hot water from a nearby spring. There's a relaxing roof terrace with great views and a busy downstairs café where you can watch satellite TV, play backgammon, and enjoy a Stella (E£7) and good simple food. Breakfast is included in the room price, and costs E£3 for those sleeping on the roof.

Beir Elgabal Camp (☎ 787 6600; elgabalcamp@ hotmail.com; s/d with shared bathroom E£35/70, with private bathroom E£50/100) A clean and very attractive camp located at the foot of a dramatic mountain range, this place is isolated (it's 5km off the main road between Al-Qasr and Mut) and wonderfully peaceful. Run by Bedouin (no English is spoken), it offers a mix of concrete and mud-brick rooms arranged around a grassed courtyard with

palm-shaded seating. All rooms have mosquito nets, soft mattresses and fans. You can pitch a tent and use a bathroom for E£20. Hot water isn't always assured. Dinner costs E£20 and Stella (E£15) is served.

Bedouin Oasis Village (☎ 782 0070; bedouin_oasis _village@hotmail.com; Mut; s/d with shared bathroom E£30/50, with private bathroom E£50/60; 🖵) On the crest of a hill on the main road into Mut, this recently opened and very stylish hotel offers extraordinary value for money. A central mud-brick building houses a restaurant with outdoor terrace; the nearby Fort-style annexe has rooms with screened windows and comfortable beds.

Desert Lodge (☎ 734 5960; www.desertlodge.net; s/d half board US$45/60; 🗷 🖵) Crowning a hill near Al-Qasr, this fort-style ecolodge is a wonderful place to stay. The building's design is nearly as impressive as its spectacular setting – the common areas are extremely attractive, the outdoor terraces have theatrical lighting and comfortable seating, and rooms have four-star appointments (no TVs). The lodge has a billiard room, giant outdoor chess set, licensed restaurant, and Bedouin tent for evening *sheeshas*. It offers an array of desert-safari options.

Eating

Ahmed Hamdy's Restaurant (☎ 782 0767; Sharia as-Sawra al-Khadra) Popular with travellers, this restaurant's official name is 'Ahmed Hamdy's Restaurant for Delicious Food' and it lives up to its claim. Hearty set meals of chicken, rice, bread, salad, beans and tea cost a bargain E£16.

Abu Mohamed Restaurant (☎ 782 1431; Sharia as-Sawra al-Khadra; dishes E£8-10) Another excellent main-street eatery, Abu Mohamed has been serving up good-value meals for 18 years. A very large set meal costs E£25 and includes a delicious dessert. Stella costs E£15.

Getting There & Around

All buses leave from near the new mosque on the main square in Mut.

Buses leave at 6am and 6pm travelling to Farafra (E£20, 4½ hours), Bahariyya (E£20, seven hours) and Cairo (E£45, eight to 10 hours).

Buses leave at 7pm and 8.30pm travelling to Al-Kharga (E£10, 2½ hours), Asyut (E£20, six hours) and Cairo (E£50 to E£55, 11 hours).

Three daily services travel to Asyut (E£20 to E£21, six hours) via Al-Kharga (E£10, 2½ hours) at 6am, 8.30am and 10pm.

Service taxis (Peugeots and microbuses) travel to Farafra, Al-Kharga and Asyut for the same ticket costs. All depart from near the new mosque when full.

Local pick-ups depart from near the police station in Mut and travel to Al-Qasr for 75pt.

Abu Mohamed Restaurant hires out bikes for E£10 per day.

FARAFRA OASIS الواحات فرافرا
☎ 092

The smallest and least attractive of the oases, Farafra makes a good setting-off point for trips into the spectacular **White Desert** but isn't worth visiting otherwise. The only tourist attraction in the town is **Badr's Museum** (☎ 751 0091; admission redeemable with any purchase E£5; ☽ 8.30am-sunset), a gallery designed and run by enthusiastic local artist, Badr Abdel Moghny.

Sleeping & Eating
El-Waha (Oasis) Hotel (☎ 751 0040; hamdyhamoud@hotmail.com; s/d with shared bathroom E£15/30, with private bathroom E£20/40) This budget place is basic but bearable. Rooms have screened windows and fans; some have private bathrooms. There's a dirt garden and 'Bedouin-style' meal shack in the rear garden. The smelly shared bathrooms have no hot water. By the time this book hits the shops, the friendly owners should have opened a new place in town called Arabia Safari Camp.

Al-Badawiya Hotel (☎ 751 0060; www.badawiya.com; s/d with private bathroom US$18/$26; ☒) The Al-Badawiya is constructed from mud bricks and built around a central courtyard. Rooms are clean and light and have beds sporting pristine linen and filmy mosquito nets. There's a lovely swimming pool with a children's pool and poolside seating. Breakfast costs E£15. The Bedouin owners have years of experience in conducting desert safaris.

Dining choices are limited. The restaurant in the **Al-Badawiya Hotel** (lunch E£35, dinner E£45) serves meals and has a good reputation. You'll find a shack on the main road called Al-Tamawy that serves up tea and stodge at a few tables. Alcohol isn't available in Farafra.

Getting There & Away
Buses travel to Cairo (E£40, seven to nine hours) via Bahariyya (E£20, 2½ hours) daily at 10.30am and 10.30pm. Buses coming from Cairo travel on to Dakhla (E£20, 4½ hours, two daily). Buses leave from outside the shops at the Dakhla end of the main street. Tickets are issued on board.

Occasional microbuses travel to Dakhla and Bahariyya for the same prices.

BAHARIYYA OASIS الواحات البحرية
☎ 011

The hilly oasis of Bahariyya is dotted with palm trees and mineral-rich springs. Buses will bring you to **Bawiti**, the dusty main village. Attractions include the **Temple of Alexander**, 26th-dynasty tombs at **Qarat Qasr Salim** and the 10 famous Graeco-Roman **Golden Mummies** on show near the **Antiquities Inspectorate Ticket Office** (admission to 6 local antiquities sites E£30; ☽ 8.30am-4pm), just south of the main road in Bawiti.

Information
The **tourist office** (☎ 847 3039; Main St, Bawiti; ☽ 8am-2pm & 7-9pm Sat-Thu) is on the roundabout on the right-hand side of the main road coming from Cairo. When we visited, the staff had closed for the day to take tourists on a safari, so take the opening hours with a grain of salt. There are two small grocery stores, a small bookshop and a phone office in the main group of shops, which you'll find around the Western Desert Hotel. The **National Bank of Development** (☽ 8am-2pm Sun-Thu), in the first street on the right after the tourist office, will change money, but not travellers cheques.

Sleeping & Eating
Ahmed's Safari Camp (☎ /fax 847 2090; ahmed_safari@hotmail.com; camping per person E£10, huts per person E£10, s/d with private bathroom E£40/80, with air-con & private bathroom E£70/100; ☒ ▢ ☒) This popular travellers' haunt is 4km outside Bawiti, on the road to Farafra; you'll need your own transport to get here. It's got almost as many facilities as Bawiti itself, with a 24-hour restaurant, farm and kitchen garden, safari company, bakery, and swimming pool fed by a hot spring. There is a range of accommodation options, all of which are basic and only just clean enough to pass muster. Dinner costs E£10 and a

EGYPT

Stella will set you back the same amount. Genial owner Abd Elrahem is a font of local knowledge and runs popular desert safaris.

Alpenblick Hotel (☎ 847 2184; alpenblick@hotmail .com; Bawiti; s E£45, d with shared/private bathroom E£60/90) The 30-year-old Alpenblick is not-able for its bizarre concrete architecture and its attractive courtyard garden. Though simple, rooms are clean and light, with screened windows and fans.

Paradise Hotel (☎ 847 2600; Main St, Bawiti; tr per person E£10) We can't imagine a more inap-propriate name for this squalid place. It's the cheapest place around, but we guar-antee that you'll commence a meaningful and protracted relationship with a derma-tologist if you sleep in the filthy beds here. Breakfast costs an extra E£5.

Western Desert Hotel (☎ 847 1600; www.western deserthotel.com; Bawiti; s/d US$17/25; ✂ ▣) A new and very clean midrange hotel, opposite the Popular Restaurant in the centre of town, this place has a pleasant roof terrace and a restaurant serving home-style Egyptian dishes. Eighteen rooms have white walls, balconies and private bathrooms; some have air-con and all have fans.

International Hot Springs Hotel (☎ 847 3014; www.whitedeserttours.com; s/d with half board US$45/70; ✂ ▣) It may not be the most attractive hotel in the Western Desert, but this profes-sionally run place, 1km outside Bawiti on the Cairo Rd in the shadow of Black Mountain, is undoubtedly one of the best. The spring that gives the hotel its name is in a private sheltered courtyard and is extremely hot – wonderful for relaxing after a hard day in the desert. Chalet rooms feature comfortable beds, private bathrooms, fans and screened windows. A restaurant serves excellent food and alcohol. Owner Peter Wirth is an old Western Desert hand and organises pricey but highly regarded tours throughout the area and further afield. Highly recommended.

Food options are limited to the hotels, a basic cafeteria near the petrol station or the town's one restaurant, **Popular Restaur-ant** (☎ 847 2239; set meal E£20; ⌚ 5am-midnight). The decent set meal here comprises soup, roast chicken, rice, pickles, salad, vegetable dishes and bread. Beer is available.

Getting There & Away
Buses travel to Cairo (E£20, four hours) daily at 1pm and 1am.

Heading to Farafra (E£20, two hours) or Dakhla (E£30, five hours) you can pick up one of the buses from Cairo. These leave from the front of the Paradise Hotel op-posite the Upper Egypt Bus Co ticket office on the main road.

Occasional microbuses travel to Farafra and Cairo for the same ticket costs.

See p150 for information about permits for travel between Bahariyya and Siwa.

SIWA OASIS   الواحات سيوه
☎ 046

With its donkey-slow pace of life and distinc-tive Berber culture, Siwa offers the traveller a unique Egyptian experience. Cut off from the rest of the country for centuries – an as-phalt road to the coast was only constructed in the 1980s – it retains a detached, almost mystical, air and is considered by many to be the most beautiful of all the oases.

Information
To the north of the main square you'll find a branch of the **Banque du Caire** (⌚ 8.30am-2pm & 5-8pm) with ATM, as well as a post office and a helpful **tourist office** (⌚ 9am-5pm Sat-Thu). **El Negma Internet Centre** (☎ 460 0761; per hr E£10; ⌚ 9am-midnight) is near the Fortress of Shali.

Sights & Activities
Apart from date-palm groves, Siwa's major attractions include a couple of **springs** where you can swim, the remains of the **temple of Amun** and some Graeco-Roman **tombs**. The town centre is marked by the jagged rem-nants of the medieval mud-brick **Fortress of Shali**. At the edge of town are the towering dunes of the **Great Sand Sea**.

There are innumerable safari companies in Siwa, most of which charge around E£80 per person to visit Abu Shufuf, E£100 to visit the Great Sand Sea and E£120 for an overnight camping trip to White Mountain and Lubbaq Oasis. You can hire **sand boards** at the Nour el-Wahaa Restaurant.

Several shops around town sell local crafts, such as basketware and jewellery, but the quality is pretty disappointing. The local dates and olives on sale throughout town are delicious.

Women need to be very careful if wan-dering alone among the palm groves or bathing in the springs. There have been a number of reports of assaults.

Sleeping

Make sure your hotel room has screened windows – the mosquitoes in Siwa are extremely vicious.

Palm Trees Hotel (☎ 460 1703; salahali2@yahoo .com; s/d with shared bathroom E£15/25, d with private bathroom E£35) Just off the main square, this popular but knocked-around backpacker place has rooms with grotty bathrooms, screened windows and fans. The hotel's redeeming feature is the shady, palm-filled garden at the rear. Single women wouldn't feel comfortable here. Breakfast is extra (around E£5).

Yousef Hotel (☎ 460 0678; s/d with shared bathroom E£8/16, with private bathroom E£10/20) Smack in the centre of town, this long-standing backpacker favourite offers very simple and reasonably clean rooms. Front rooms have balconies and all windows are screened. The hotel doesn't provide breakfast.

Kilany Hotel (☎ 460 1052; zaltsafari@yahoo.com; d E£50) The Kilany has 10 small twin rooms with screened windows (some with balcony), fans and private bathrooms. There's a roof terrace overlooking the palm groves and fortress. Its position near the mosque and on the main street means that noise can be a problem. Breakfast costs an extra E£10.

Shali Lodge (☎ 460 1299; info@eqi.com.eg; Sharia el-Seboukha; s/d E£200/260; ❄) Siwa's only boutique hotel is an absolutely charming place to stay. A tiny but beautiful mud-brick building in a lush palm grove a couple of hundred metres from the main square, it offers eight large suite-style rooms with satellite TV, screened windows and private bathrooms. Reservations are necessary and breakfast costs an extra E£12 or so. Recommended.

Eating

No alcohol is served in Siwan restaurants. There are cheap chicken-and-salad joints on the central market square, including Elahrar Chicken Restaurant, which has been recommended by travellers.

Abdo Restaurant (☎ 460 1243; ❍ 8.30am-midnight) The type of place that is beloved by backpackers, Abdo is unusual in that it is equally popular with locals. The food is both good and well priced – try the vegetable couscous (E£10) or the half chicken and salad (E£13); we'd suggest avoiding the fiteer and the meat dishes. A fresh lemon juice costs E£4, tea is E£2 and breakfast pancakes are E£6.

Sahara Café & Restaurant (Sharia Batoukhi; salads E£1.50-3, mains E£4.50-11) This sprawling and highly attractive garden restaurant is on the road to the bus office. It offers a limited and very cheap array of mezze, kebabs, fuul and omelettes. We visited twice – the first time to be comprehensively ignored, the second time only to be told that the cook hadn't turned up to work. Hmm.

Nour el-Wahaa Restaurant (☎ 460 0293; dishes E£5-15) In the palm groves near the Shali Lodge hotel, this attractive garden restaurant is a great place to relax over a *sheesha* (E£4.50) and mint tea (E£3). It serves up an array of simple Egyptian dishes including molokhiyya (stewed leaf soup, E£5), lentils with rice (E£7) or half a roast chicken (E£16). Breakfast here costs E£3 to E£5.

Kenooz Siwa (☎ 460 1299; Shali Lodge, Sharia el-Seboukha; dips E£5, pastas E£10-15, pizzas E£10-20, mains E£20) The setting on a rooftop among the palms next to Shali Lodge is fabulous, but when we visited the food was absolutely inedible. The only reason we list the place is that locals have told us that our experience wasn't representative, and that the food is usually the best in town.

There are several places dotted around the square where you can have a *sheesha* or a cup of coffee and play some backgammon. Bakri's Café, next to Abdo Restaurant, is one of the most popular.

Getting There & Around

There's no bus station in Siwa. When you arrive, you'll be let off the bus in the central market square. To purchase tickets to Marsa Matruh or Alexandria you'll need to visit the West Delta Bus Co office at the southern end of town, near the Sports Centre. To get there walk down Sharia Sadat past the mosque and the Cleopatra Hotel. The road divides just past the mosque; take the right fork and you'll soon come to a residential block of apartments, which is part of a housing estate, on the right-hand side of the street. Look for the ground floor window with a blue shutter – this is the ticket office. It's sensible to buy your ticket ahead of time, as buses are often full. You can board from here, or from the central market square.

There are three daily buses to Alexandria (E£27, eight hours), stopping at Marsa Matruh (E£12, four hours). These services leave at 7am, 10am and 10pm. The 7am and 10am buses connect with buses to Cairo at Marsa Matruh (1½-hour transit). There is an additional daily service to Marsa Matruh at 1pm.

Microbuses going to Marsa Matruh leave from the main square near the King Fuad Mosque. They are more frequent but not as comfortable as the West Delta Bus Co bus. Tickets cost the same.

Although there is a road linking the oases of Siwa and Bahariyya, no public transport travels along it. Some 4WD owners in town will take you if you can manage the hefty prices they charge (approximately E£1300, 10 hours). At present the road is in an appalling state, but it is due to be fully asphalted by the end of 2006, meaning that many more people will use it. To get a permit to drive to Bahariyya (US$10 per person), contact the tourist office. This can take quite a while, as it must be processed in Cairo.

A trip on a donkey cart within town costs E£5. You can hire bone-rattling bikes on the main square or in a shop near Palm Trees Hotel for E£10 per day.

SUEZ CANAL

قناة السويس

The Suez Canal severs Africa from Asia and links the Mediterranean with the Red Sea. It's an extraordinary sight to see the supertankers appear to glide through the desert as they ply its waters. One of the greatest feats of modern engineering, the canal opened in 1869 and remains one of the world's busiest shipping routes.

PORT SAID بور سعيد

☎ 066 / pop 539,000

Like many port cities, Port Said has a slightly seedy but undeniable charm. Its grand but faded New Orleans–style wooden buildings hint at its prosperous past, and its long and bustling Corniche attests to the fact that its locals enjoy life and enjoy sharing it with the thousands of Egyptians who come here for summer holidays.

The town is effectively built as an island, connected to the mainland by a bridge to the south and a causeway to the west.

Information

Most financial services are on Sharia al-Gomhuriyya. The Banque du Caire and the National Bank of Egypt have ATMs, and the **Thomas Cook** (☎ 322 7559; 🕑 8am-4.30pm), next to the petrol station will change travellers cheques. The main **American Express Bank** (🕑 9am-2pm & 6.30-8pm Sun-Thu) is on Sharia Palestine near the tourist office, and there's another one on Sharia Gomhuriyya, opposite the mosque; both have ATMs.

Compu.Net (per hr E£3; 🕑 9am-midnight) Just opposite the main post office.

Main post office (🕑 8.30am-2.30pm) Opposite Ferial Gardens, one block north of Sharia al-Gomhuriyya.

Telephone centrales (🕑 24hr) One is on Sharia Palestine two blocks northwest of the tourist office; the other is behind the governorate building.

Tourist office (☎ 323 5289; 8 Sharia Palestine; 🕑 9am-6pm Sat-Thu, 9am-2pm Fri) This helpful office supplies maps.

Sights & Activities

The **National Museum** (☎ 323 7419), at the top end of Sharia Palestine, was closed for renovation at the time of research. The small **Military Museum** (☎ 322 4657; Sharia 23rd of July; admission E£5; 🕑 9am-4pm Fri-Wed, 9am-10pm Thu, closed for Fri prayers) has some interesting relics from the 1956 Anglo-French War, and the 1967 and 1973 wars with Israel.

The easiest way to explore the canal is to take the free public ferry from near the tourist office across to Port Fuad and back.

Sleeping

Youth Hostel (☎ 322 8702; port-said-y.h@hotmail .com; Sharia 23rd of July; dm HI members/nonmembers E£13.25/15.25, f per person E£30.25; 🗶 🖵) You'll find this enormous, friendly hostel opposite the stadium, just near the public beach at the end of the New Corniche. Though it's mainly geared towards school groups, there are large and ridiculously pricey family rooms that come complete with private bathroom and air-con. Dorms are worn but clean.

Hotel de la Poste (☎ /fax 322 4048; 42 Sharia al-Gomhuriyya; s/d E£39/49; 🗶) The owners of this faded but elegant hotel make a real effort to keep it clean and well maintained, and it's undoubtedly the best-value option in town. Freshly painted rooms are comfortable, and some offer satellite TV, private bathrooms and air-con. You can buy breakfast in the popular downstairs patisserie. Rooms with balconies cost slightly more.

Sonesta (☎ 332 5511; sonesta@iec.egnet.net; s/d city view US$137/186, canal view US$186/230; 🖭 🖳) This excellent four-star choice is wonderfully positioned right at the entrance to the canal, and its poolside terrace café is a fabulous spot from which to watch the ships make their majestic passage through the water. Rooms have the usual business-hotel amenities, and the hotel has an English pub and Egyptian and Italian restaurants. Breakfast costs US$5.

Eating & Drinking

There's a swathe of fast-food joints on the New Corniche up from the Helnan Port Said hotel. This is also where most of the night-time action is.

El-Borg (☎ 332 3442; New Corniche; meals E£25-50; 🕑 10am-3am) This cavernous place is located at the top end of the New Corniche, a 30-minute walk from the roundabout, and offers up the best seafood in town. The waiter will show you the display of the day's catch so that you can make your choice, and it will then be served with a large, very tasty array of side dishes, as well as a small *muhalabiyya* (a combination of ground rice, milk, sugar and rose or orange water, topped with chopped pistachios and almonds) for dessert. Credit cards are accepted.

Pizza Pino (☎ 323 9949; cnr Sharias 23rd of July & al-Gomhuriyya; pasta E£7-22, pizza E£11-25) Port Said's version of Pizza Express, this bright and friendly place overlooking the seashell fountain serves good food, fresh juice and a wide range of ice-cream sundaes in an interior sporting the colours of the Italian flag. It offers kids' meals and accepts credit cards.

There's a popular terrace *ahwa* at the front of the Grand Albatross Building on the New Corniche where locals linger over *sheeshas*.

Getting There & Away

BOAT

For details of boats from Port Said to Cyprus and Israel, see p664 and p177.

BUS

The bus station is 3km from the centre of town.

Two companies travel to Cairo: East Delta Bus Co has buses (E£13.50 to E£16,

three hours) hourly between 6am and 10pm. Superjet buses (E£17, three hours) leave hourly between 7am and 8pm.

To Alexandria, East Delta Bus Co has services (E£20 to E£22, four hours) at 7am, 11am, 3.30pm and 7pm. Superjet has a bus (E£22, four hours) departing every day except Friday at 3.30pm or 4.30pm.

There are buses to Ismailia (E£4 to E£5.50, one hour) on the hour between 6am and 6pm, and services to Suez (E£10.50, three hours) at 10am and 3.30pm. A daily 5pm bus travels to Luxor (E£60) via Hurghada (E£45).

A taxi from the bus station into town costs E£5. Taxis within town cost E£2.

SERVICE TAXI

These leave from an area in the bus station. Fares include Cairo (E£15), Qantara (E£5), Ismailia (E£7) and Suez (E£10).

TRAIN

Slow and uncomfortable trains to Cairo leave daily at 5.30am, 9.45am, 1pm, 5.30pm and 7.30pm (E£14 to E£18 in 2nd class, five hours).

SUEZ   السويس

☎ 062 / pop 488,000

Watching the constant procession of massive cargo ships and tankers make their way in and out of the canal is surprisingly hypnotic. Many travellers, discovering in themselves a strange and hitherto submerged fascination with this maritime equivalent of trainspotting, end up extending by a day or two what was originally intended as only a transit stop en route between Cairo and the Sinai peninsula. Consider yourself warned.

The town is in two parts: Suez proper and Port Tawfiq, at the mouth of the canal. There's nothing to do other than watch the maritime traffic.

Information

There are ATMs at the National Bank of Egypt and Banque Misr on Sharia Saad Zaghloul, and at the Commercial International Bank, opposite the entrance to the Corniche.

CACE (Sharia al-Geish; per hr E£2; 🕑 9am-8pm) Internet access. Has branches near Midan Nesima and next to the Green House Hotel.

Main post office (Sharia Hoda Shaarawi) In Suez.

Telephone centrale (Sharia Saad Zaghloul) In Suez.

Tourist office (☎ 333 1141; ⏰ 8am-8pm Sat-Thu, 8am-3pm Fri) The extremely helpful tourist office in Port Tawfiq overlooks the canal.

Sleeping

All hotels are fully booked during the month of the haj.

Sina Hotel (☎ 333 4181; Sharia Bank Misr, Suez; s/d with shared bathroom E£23/35, d with private bathroom E£45; 🗲) A slightly grubby place that's very popular with Egyptian tourists, the Sina has certainly seen better days. Beds are hard and though some rooms have air-con, we're not convinced it works. It's located smack-bang in the centre of Suez and is surrounded by shops and cheap eateries. No breakfast is served.

Arafat Hotel (☎ 333 8355; 7 Sharia Arafat, Port Tawfiq; s/d with shared bathroom E£27/34, with private bathroom E£33/43) This quiet place offers basic but clean rooms with fans, satellite TV and extremely hard beds. A few rooms have private bathrooms and balconies. Little English is spoken and no breakfast is available.

Red Sea Hotel (☎ 333 4302; www.redseahotel.com; 13 Sharia Riad, Port Tawfiq; s/d with city view E£271/332, with canal view E£313/374; 🗲) A very good three-star hotel that's popular with international mariners, the Red Sea offers spotlessly clean rooms with satellite TV and air-con; half of these have balconies overlooking the canal. The 6th-floor restaurant has a panoramic view and serves decent fresh seafood meals (E£25 to E£40).

Eating & Drinking

The main cheap-eats area is in the street between the Al-Khalifa Fish Centre and the White House Hotel, off Sharia as-Salaam. The best of these is probably **Koshary Palace** (Sharia Saad Zaghloul, Suez; meals E£1.50-5), just around the corner from the Al-Khalifa Fish Centre.

Pizza Pronto (☎ 330 4443; Sharia as-Salaam; pizzas E£7-22) Locals dote on the pizzas served at this welcoming fast-food outlet. It's in the main drag, opposite the White House Hotel.

Al-Khalifa Fish Centre (☎ 333 7303; Sharia as-Salaam; salads E£1.50-2, mains E£15-35; 🗲) A no-nonsense place that sells the day's catch by weight and then cooks it according to your preference. You'll find it close by the White House Hotel – look for the big glass windows and fishy décor.

Safsafa Seafood Restaurant (☎ 366 0474; mains around E£18-48; 🗲) You can choose between the air-conditioned dining room and the outdoor tent at this popular eatery. It serves up fresh seafood and a wide range of pastas (E£10 to E£30). There's no view, but locals rate the food highly. You'll find it at the end of the Corniche, opposite the stadium.

Alf Lila Italian Restaurant & Coffee Shop (Sharia al-Marwa; dishes E£5-25) One of several cafés in Port Tawfiq, this is a decent spot to while away a few hours sipping a drink or puffing on a *sheesha*, and watching ships on the canal.

Getting There & Away

BOAT

For details of international boats from Suez, see p664.

BUS

The New Bus Station is 5km from central Suez, on the road to Cairo. Arriving by bus, it's possible to get off before the bus station at the highway on the edge of the centre. Taxis (E£10) and microbuses (50pt to E£1) congregate here to take passengers into the centre of town or Port Tawfiq – it's cheaper than going all the way to the bus station. A taxi between the New Bus Station and Suez costs E£15.

Upper Egypt Bus Co buses to Cairo (E£8, 1½ hours) leave every 15 minutes from 6am to 9pm. Four services travel to Alexandria (E£25, three to four hours) at 7am, 9am, 2.30pm and 5pm. To Hurghada (E£33 to E£40, four to five hours), buses depart almost every hour from 5am to 11pm. Services to Luxor (E£46 to E£55, seven to eight hours) via Safaga (E£35 to E£43) and Qena (E£43 to E£50) depart at 8am, 2pm and 8pm. Buses to Aswan (E£54 to E£62, 11 to 12 hours) leave at 5am, 11am and 5pm. There are two services to Qena via Hurghada and Safaga at 6am and 6.30pm. Buses leave at 10am and 2.30pm for Al-Quseir (E£40, seven hours).

East Delta Bus Co services to Ismailia (E£5, 1½ hours) depart every 30 minutes between 6am and 4pm. There are five buses to Port Said (E£10, 2¼ hours) at 7am, 9am, 11am, 12.15pm and 3.30pm.

East Delta Bus Co buses travel along the direct route down the Gulf of Suez to Sharm el-Sheikh (E£30, 5½ hours) at 8.30am,

11am, 1.30pm, 3pm, 4.30pm, 5.15pm and 6pm. The 11am bus goes on to Dahab (E£35, 6½ hours) and Nuweiba (E£35, 7½ hours). Two extra services travel to Nuweiba (E£35) at 3pm and 5pm. To Taba, (E£35) there is a bus at 3pm via Dahab and a direct service at 5pm. A bus leaves for St Katherine's Monastery (E£25, five hours) via Wadi Feiran at 2pm.

MICROBUS & TAXI
Small blue microbuses travel between Port Tawfiq and Suez (50pt). A taxi will cost E£3 to E£5.

SERVICE TAXI
Microbuses and clapped out taxis depart from beside the bus station to Cairo (E£7), Ismailia (E£5), Port Said (E£10) and Nuweiba (E£30). There is an occasional service to Hurghada (E£30). To get to Sharm el-Sheikh you'll need to travel to Al-Tor (E£16) and catch an onward service.

TRAIN
Six trains depart for Cairo (E£3.50/1.25 in 2nd/3rd class, 2¼ hours) daily between 5.45am and 9.25pm, but they only make it as far as Ain Shams, 10km northeast of central Cairo. There is also one daily slow train (E£5.50) to Cairo's Ramses train station at 3.20pm.

RED SEA COAST
ساحل البحر الاحمر

Stretching from Suez in the north to the disputed border with Sudan in the south, the once-idyllic Red Sea Coast is suffering from the curse of unfettered overdevelopment. The coast around its main city, Hurghada, is the Egyptian version of Spain's Costa del Sol, full of package tourists from eastern and central Europe, and afflicted with the ugliest construction projects you could possibly imagine. Up till now, the villages of Al-Quseir and Marsa Alam have avoided the same fate, and offered a welcome refuge to those interested in world-class diving or in getting away from the tourist madness. Unfortunately, recent developments hint that this might change, with the rash of resorts to the north starting to spread down

south. If you are keen to explore the area before this happens, contact **Red Sea Desert Adventures** (☎ 012 399 3860; www.redseadesertadventures.com; Marsa Shagra), a highly recommended safari outfit offering tailored walking, camel and jeep safaris, or **Shagara Eco-Lodge** (in Cairo ☎ 02-337 1833; www.redsea-divingsafari.com; Marsa Shagra; d in tents/huts/chalets full board US$88/100/125), a simple place offering first-rate diving.

HURGHADA
الغردقة
☎ 065 / pop 96,000
It's incumbent on travel writers to tell it like it really is, and to this end we've vowed to spare no punches when describing this ever-sprawling tourist enclave on the Red Sea Coast. The Egyptian Tourist Authority might see it as the jewel in Egypt's crown, the place where 'the sun always shines, every day', but we see it differently. In short, if there's a holiday hell on earth, Hurghada is it. Visit at your peril and avoid it if you can.

Little more than 20 years ago, Hurghada (an anglicised version of it's Arabic name Al-Gharadaka) had two hotels separated by nothing more than virgin beach. Once an isolated and modest fishing village, it's now home to more than 96,000 people – most of them drunk package tourists – and is crammed with hundreds of tacky and environmentally disastrous resorts, overpriced souvenir shops and money-grubbing con men. Even its once-glorious coral reefs have been degraded. This is tourism gone terribly, terribly wrong.

Orientation
Most budget hotels are in the main town area, Ad-Dahar. This is at the northern end of the stretch of resorts that makes up the whole area. A main road connects Ad-Dahar with Sigala, where the town's port is. South of Sigala, a road winds 15km down along the coast through the glitzy 'resort strip', which is the town's upmarket tourism enclave.

Information
Most banks in Hurghada have ATMs.
El Baroudy Internet (Sharia Sheikh Sabak, Ad-Dahar; per hr E£4; ⏱ 24hr; ✦)
Express.Net (☎ 012 316 2770; per hr E£12; ⏱ noon-midnight) In Kotta's West Side Mall on the resort strip.
Main post office (Sharia an-Nasr) Towards the southern end of Ad-Dahar.

Oznet (Sharia Sheraton; per hr E£5; 24hr) Opposite the Seagull Resort in Sigala.

Telephone centrale (Sharia an-Nasr; 24hr) Further northwest from the main post office, along the same road.

Thomas Cook Ad-Dahar (☎ 354 1870/1; Sharia an-Nasr; 9am-2pm & 6-10pm); resort strip (☎ 344 6830; 9am-5pm); Sigala (☎ 344 3338; Sharia Sheraton; 9am-3pm & 4-10pm) Changes travellers cheques.

Tourist office (☎ 344 4421; 8am-8pm) On the resort strip.

Activities

There's nothing to do in Hurghada itself other than sit on a beach and wish you were elsewhere. Besides the less-than-appealing **public beach** in Sigala, the main option for enjoying sand and sea is to go to one of the resorts, most of which charge nonguests between E£20 and E£60 for beach access.

If you decide to go diving or snorkelling, there are innumerable operators. We've heard good things about the following:

Dive Too (☎ 340 8414; www.divetoo.net; Seagull Resort, Sharia Sheraton, Sigala)

Easy Divers (☎ 354 7816; www.easydivers-redsea.com; Triton Empire Beach Hotel, Corniche, Ad-Dahar)

Red Sea Scuba Schools/Emperor Divers (☎ 344 4854; www.emperordivers.com; Hilton Hurghada Resort, resort strip)

Sleeping

AD-DAHAR

Al-Arosa Hotel (☎ 354 8434; elarosahotel@yahoo.com; s/d US$25/40;) This faded but spotless place, off the Corniche, has views to the sea in the distance and offers air-con rooms with private bathrooms, satellite TV and sea-facing balconies. There's a roof garden serving Stella (E£10) and an indoor pool.

Snafer Hotel (☎ /fax 354 0260; s/d E£55/85;) A friendly place, behind the National Hospital off Sharia Sayyed al-Qorayem, offering clean and large rooms. Some have balconies and views to the water.

SIGALA

Royal City Hotel (☎ 344 7729; fax 344 7195; s/d E£80/120;) It doesn't have too many frills, but this long-running option, near the port off Sharia Sheraton, charges reasonable prices for its clean, freshly painted rooms. All come with private bathroom, satellite TV and comfortable bed.

Zak Royal Wings Hotel (☎ 344 6012; www.zakhotel.com; Sharia al-Hadaba; s/d US$21/32;) This

small, good-value place is next to Papas Bar and offers clean rooms clustered around a pool.

RESORT STRIP

Giftun Beach Resort (☎ 346 3040; www.giftunbeachresort.com; s/d all-inclusive US$52/81;) If you're keen on sampling the full resort-hotel shebang at a reasonable price, this is a good option. It offers pleasant chalet-style rooms, a popular diving centre and excellent windsurfing facilities (from E£25 per hour).

Oberoi Sahl Hasheesh (☎ 344 0777; www.oberoihotels.com; Sahl Hasheesh; ste from US$310;) This utterly indulgent hotel features stunning suites decorated in minimalist Moorish style that come complete with sunken marble baths, walled private courtyards, and panoramic sea views. Some even have private pools.

Eating

AD-DAHAR

Cheap eateries include **Pizza Tarboush** (☎ 354 8456; Sharia Abdel Aziz Mustafa; pizzas E£10-20), on the edge of the souq, and **Taibeen** (☎ 354 7260; Sharia Soliman Mazhar; dishes E£3-15), which serves up good kebabs and *kofta*.

Portofino (☎ 354 6250; Sharia Sayyed al-Qorayem;) An old-fashioned trattoria serving up generous homemade pasta and meat dishes to a constant stream of tourists. The food is good (the local salad, *insalata baladi*, was fabulous), and it's made from fresh local ingredients. With its very clean toilets and three-course set menus of E£26.50 or E£34.50, it's one of Hurghada's best eating options. Stella is E£8.

SIGALA

The best cheap eats are found in Sharia Sheery, off Sharia Sheraton in Sigala, close to McDonald's.

Abu Khadigah (☎ 344 3768; Sharia Sheraton; meals E£3-15) This no-frills place is known for its *kofta*, stuffed cabbage leaves and other Egyptian staples.

Moby Dick (Sharia Sheraton; noon-2am;) Once you've recovered from the shock of finding a faux-Austrian chalet in the middle of Sigala, this laid-back place is sure to appeal. Dine under the bougainvillea-laden trellis or in the pleasant and very clean air-conditioned dining room. The lentil soup (E£6) is excellent, and though the rest of the dishes are on the bland side, they're better and a lot cheaper than those you'll find elsewhere. A spaghetti bolognese or napoli costs E£8 to E£10. Stella is E£6.

Rossi Restaurant (☎ 344 7676; Sharia Sheraton; mains E£17-50) This popular hang-out for divers and expat residents serves a variety of pizza toppings on crispy crusts, as well as pasta dishes. The service is laid-back, and women on their own can relax without being hassled.

RESORT STRIP

Felfela Restaurant (☎ 344 2410/1; Sharia Sheraton; dishes E£10-60; ⏲ 8.30am-midnight) Perched on the coastline and overlooking the turquoise sea, this branch of the Felfela chain wins a prize for its view, which you can enjoy while dining on serviceable Egyptian classics at reasonable prices. If you're on a tight budget, be prepared for the extra charges (bread E£1 per piece).

Shanghai Chinese Restaurant (☎ 012 239 6840; Esplanada Bay Mall; mains E£30-40; 🗷) About as stylish as Hurghada comes, the Shanghai manages to transcend its mall location with a minimalist interior and sea-fronting terrace. BBQ fish with ginger (E£35) and a glass of wine (E£18) almost made us forget we were trapped in holiday hellsville.

Drinking

Papas Bar (www.papasbar.com; Sharia Sheraton) This popular, Dutch-run place is attached to Rossi Restaurant in Sigala. Filled with diving instructors and other foreign residents, it has a great atmosphere most nights. The same management team runs the equally popular Liquid Lounge and Papas II. All three places feature a constantly changing entertainment programme – watch for the flyers around town, or check the website.

Look out for information about the Chill, a popular and laid-back bar that was about to be re-housed when we visited town.

If you can overlook the affront of its misspelt name, the Shakespear Coffee Shop, on the *midan* at the end of Sharia Soliman Mazhar, is a good spot to enjoy a tea and *sheesha*.

The El-Arabi Coffee Shop, situated opposite Seagull Resort, is a popular local tea-and-*sheesha* spot.

Getting There & Away

AIR

Hurghada International Airport (☎ 344 2592) is located 6km southwest of town. **EgyptAir** (☎ 344 3592/3; resort strip) has daily flights to Cairo (E£740 one way). There are no buses between the airport and town; a taxi costs somewhere between E£10 and E£20.

BOAT

A luxury high speed ferry operated by **International Fast Ferries Co** (☎ 344 7571; www.international fastferries.com; one way adult E£250 or US$40, child 3-12 half price) plies the waters of the Red Sea between Hurghada and Sharm el-Sheikh, departing at 5am each Monday and 8am each Tuesday, Thursday and Saturday from the port in Sigala. The trip takes 1½ hours, but can be cancelled or take longer when seas are rough (particularly in January and February). There is no student discount on tickets.

It's sensible to buy a ticket ahead of time, preferably the day before the trip, and you'll need to make your way to the ticket box at the harbour at least 30 minutes before the official departure time so as to obtain a boarding pass. You'll find the ticket office in the Fantasia building opposite the Hurghada Touristic Port entrance. The rate of the dollar against the Egyptian pound and the whim of the ferry officials determine which currency you'll need to use to purchase the ticket. Come prepared with dollars, as they're not available at banks in Hurghada, but be prepared to convert them to pounds.

For details of boats to Duba in Saudi Arabia see p664.

BUS

Three bus companies operate services from Hurghada.

Superjet's bus station is near the main mosque in Ad-Dahar. It offers services to Cairo (E£55 to E£57, six hours) at noon, 2pm, 5pm and midnight; and a 2.30pm service to Alexandria (E£83, nine hours).

The Upper Egypt Bus Co bus station is at the southern end of Ad-Dahar. There are 10 daily buses to Cairo (E£55) between 10am and 2am; the 7.30pm service goes on to Alexandria (E£75). There are four buses per day to Luxor (E£30, five hours) at 10am, 1pm, 10.30pm and midnight, all of which travel on to Aswan (E£35 to E£40, seven to eight hours). There's also an occasional

Luxor service (E£30, five hours) at 7.30pm. There are three daily buses to Marsa Alam (E£30, five hours) via Safaga (E£5, one hour) and Al-Quseir (E£20, three hours), leaving at 5am, 3pm and 8pm. To Suez (E£35, four to five hours), buses depart every two hours between 11.30am and midnight.

The newly established El Gouna Bus Co has a bus station next to the Red Sea Hospital on Sharia Al-Nasr in Ad-Dahar. It has 10 daily services to Cairo (E£40 to E£55) between 9am and 3am.

CONVOY
It is officially compulsory for foreigners to travel from Hurghada to Cairo and Luxor by convoy. Although we have met many travellers who have had no problems driving themselves independently to Cairo, it's not possible to dodge the convoy to Luxor (there are 10 checkpoints). The convoys to Cairo leave from the first checkpoint on the road to Cairo in Al-Gouna, 20km outside Hurghada, at 2.30am, 11am and 5pm. Convoys to Luxor depart from Safaga, 53km south of Hurghada, at 7am, 9am and 4pm.

SERVICE TAXI
The service taxi station is near the telephone centrale in Ad-Dahar. Taxis go to Cairo (E£35), Safaga (E£5) Al-Quseir (E£15 to E£20), Marsa Alam (E£20 to E£25) and Suez (E£27). They cannot take you to Luxor or Aswan except on a private basis in a police convoy. With bargaining, it costs about E£200 per vehicle (up to seven passengers) to Luxor.

Getting Around
Local minibuses function as service taxis in Hurghada. These can be hailed from the side of the road. To travel from the resort strip to Sigala costs E£1, and E£2 to Ad-Dahar. The trip between Sigala and Ad-Dahar costs 50pt. A taxi from Sigala to Ad-Dahar or the resort strip costs E£5; it costs E£10 between Ad-Dahar and the resort strip. You'll need to bargain to get these prices.

El Gouna Bus Co operates a more comfortable service (E£5) between Al-Gouna, Ad-Dahar and the end of Sharia Sheraton in Sigala about every half hour, beginning at 9am. You can flag the bus down at any point along the way and pay on board.

AL-QUSEIR القصير
☎ 065 / pop 25,000
Until the 10th century, Al-Quseir was one of the most important exit points for pilgrims travelling to Mecca. Later it became an important entrepôt for Indian spices destined for Europe. These days, its long history and sleepy present lend it a charm absent from Egypt's other Red Sea towns.

There's a 24-hour telephone centrale, a National Bank of Egypt branch (no ATM) and a post office. For Internet access try **Hot Line Internet Café** (Sharia Port Said; per hr E£10; ☼ 9am-3am).

Sights & Activities
You'll find an **Ottoman fortress** (admission E£5; ☼ 9am-5pm), and old coral-block buildings line the waterfront. Mixed in among these are the domed tombs of various saints – mostly pious pilgrims who died en route to or from Mecca.

Arrange diving trips and excursions into the Eastern Desert with **Mazenar Tours** (☎ 333 5247, 012 265 5044; rockyvalleycamp@yahoo.dk; Sharia Port Said), located along the waterfront.

Sleeping & Eating
Sea Princess Hotel (☎ 333 1880; Sharia al- Gomhuriyya; s/tw/tr E£27/44/67) The only shoestring choice in Al-Quseir offers cubicle-like rooms and slightly dodgy shared bathrooms. Breakfast costs E£5 extra.

Al-Quseir Hotel (☎ 333 2301; Sharia Port Said; s/d E£112/157; ☒) This charming hotel has six simple but spacious rooms in a renovated 1920s merchant's house on the seafront. Bathrooms are shared between three rooms, but are large and clean. Sea-facing rooms have good views.

Mövenpick Sirena Beach (☎ 333 2100; www.movenpick-quseir.com; r from US$200; ☒ ☐ ☒) This low-set, domed ensemble, 7km north of the town centre, is top of the line in Al-Quseir, and one of the best resorts along the coast. There are restaurants, a Subex diving centre and a refreshing absence of the glitz so common in other resort hotels. The hotel management is known for its environmentally conscious approach.

Dining options are limited. There are the usual ta'amiyya and fish joints around the seafront and the bus station. Locals hang out at the **Sahraya Coffeehouse** (Sharia Port Said) on the waterfront, which also serves snacks.

Diagonally opposite is **Restaurant Marianne** (☎ 333 4386; Sharia Port Said; dishes E£15-50), which serves grilled fish and other simple but filling meals.

Getting There & Around
The bus and service-taxi stations are next to each other, about 1.5km northwest of the Safaga road, and about 3km from the telephone centrale (E£2 to E£3 in a taxi).

BUS
There are daily buses to Cairo (E£57, 11 hours) via Safaga (E£5, two hours) and Hurghada (E£15, three hours), departing at 6am, 7.30am, 9am, 7pm and 8.30pm. The 6am bus continues to Suez (E£40, seven hours). Services to Marsa Alam (E£5, two hours) depart at 5am, 9am, 7pm and 8pm.

MICROBUS
You'll find that microbuses run along Sharia Al-Gomhuriyya from the roundabout near Sea Princess Hotel north to the administrative buildings on the road to Safaga. Some also go to the bus and service taxi stations. Fares are between 50pt and E£1, depending on the distance travelled.

SERVICE TAXI
Destinations include Cairo (E£43), Suez (E£30), Qena (E£20), Hurghada (E£10) and Safaga (E£6). As in Hurghada, you have to hire the entire taxi for the trip to Luxor, Qena or Aswan (all routes via Safaga). Expect to pay from E£250 after negotiating.

MARSA ALAM   مرسى علم
☎ 065
If you're keen on diving and/or desert safaris, this little-visited corner of Egypt is sure to appeal.

Marsa Alam itself is not much more than a T-junction where the road from Edfu meets the coastal road. Just south of the junction is a modest collection of shops, a pharmacy, a telephone centrale and a bustling market. The coast to the south and north is sprinkled with resorts.

Activities
Trips to the many fascinating sites of the Eastern Desert can be organised with **Red Sea Desert Adventures** (☎ 012 399 3860; www.red seadesertadventures.com; Marsa Shagra), a highly rec-

ommended safari outfit offering tailored walking, camel and jeep safaris throughout the area. Camel safaris cost approximately US$100 per person per day; other prices are available on its website. In order that the necessary permits can be organised for multiday desert safaris, try to book at least one month in advance.

Sleeping & Eating
There is nowhere to stay in Marsa Alam village itself, but along the coast is an ever-expanding array of resorts, plus a handful of simple, diver-oriented 'ecolodges' (diving camps). These usually consist of no-frills reed or stone bungalows with generator-provided electricity and a common area for meals. They are run together with a dive centre, and offer a more down-to-earth alternative to the resort scene. In addition to diving, most of these places can also arrange desert excursions. If you're travelling during the winter and planning to stay in a tent or hut at one of the ecolodges, ask if they provide blankets; if not, it's a good idea to bring a sleeping bag along for warmth.

Shagara Eco-Lodge (in Cairo ☎ 02-337 1833; www .redsea-divingsafari.com; Marsa Shagra; d in tents/huts/ chalets full board US$88/100/125) The best of the camps is Shagara, a simple place owned by lawyer, committed environmentalist and diving enthusiast Hossam Helmi. It offers simple, spotless and comfortable accommodation designed to be as kind to the environment as possible – plus first-rate diving. It's along the main road, 24km north of Marsa Alam.

There are a couple of cafés at the junction of town where you can find ta'amiyya and similar fare, and there's a small supermarket with a modest selection of basics.

Getting There & Away
AIR
Marsa Alam International Airport (☎ 370 0005) is 67km north of Marsa Alam along the Al-Quseir road. There is no public transport, so you'll need to arrange a transfer in advance with your hotel. EgyptAir has indefinitely suspended flights to and from Cairo, and the airport is currently used only by charters.

BUS
There is no bus station in Marsa Alam. For transport to the Nile Valley, wait at the

petrol station in Marsa Alam, or at the T-junction about 1km further along on the Edfu road. Buses from Shalatein pass Marsa Alam en route to Aswan (E£15, six hours), via Edfu (E£12, four hours), at around 7am and 9am daily. Buses to Shalatein (E£20, four hours) come from Hurghada and depart Marsa Alam at around 5am, 7am, noon and 8.30pm.

There are four daily buses to Al-Quseir (E£5, two hours) and Hurghada (E£20, five hours), departing at 5am, 12.30pm, 2.30pm and 5pm. There's a direct bus to Cairo (E£80, 11 to 12 hours).

SINAI   سيناء

A region of extraordinary beauty and great historical significance, Sinai is the most atypically 'Egyptian' part of the country. This is no surprise, of course, as it bears the physical and psychological legacies of Israeli occupation from 1967 to 1982. Before this, though, it was the place where Moses received the Ten Commandments, where ancient armies fought and where members of the very proud local Bedouin tribes established their homes. These days, it's the meeting spot of choice for the world's political leaders, a booming package-tour destination and nirvana for the members of the international diving fraternity, who make regular pilgrimages to its superb coral reefs.

In recent years Sinai resorts have been the targets of terrorist bombs. In October 2004 a bomb in Taba, on the border with Israel, killed 34 people; and in July 2005 three bombs in Sharm el-Sheikh and Na'ama Bay claimed 64 lives. Though tourism arrivals were relatively unaffected by the Taba bomb (the notable exception being tourism from Israel), international arrivals immediately dropped as a result of the Sharm el-Sheikh/Na'ama Bay bombings, taking a few months to stabilise.

RAS MOHAMMED NATIONAL PARK
محمية رأس محمد

Declared a **national marine park** (admission per person/vehicle US$5/5; ☉ 8am-5pm) in 1988, the headland of Ras Mohammed is about 20km west of Sharm el-Sheikh. The waters surrounding the peninsula are considered the jewel in the crown of the Red Sea, and the

park is inundated with more than 50,000 visitors annually, enticed by the prospect of marvelling at some of the world's most spectacular coral-reef ecosystems. Camping permits cost US$5 per person per night and are available from the visitors centre inside the park, but camping is allowed only in designated areas. Take your passport with you, and remember that it is not possible to go to Ras Mohammed National Park if you only have a Sinai permit in your passport.

You can hire a taxi from Sharm el-Sheikh to bring you here, but expect to pay at least E£150 for the day. If you don't mind company, the easiest option is to join one of the many day tours by jeep or bus from Sharm el-Sheikh and Na'ama Bay, most of which will drop you at the beaches and snorkelling sites. Expect to pay from E£150.

To move around the park you'll need a vehicle. Access is restricted to certain parts of the park and, for conservation reasons, it's forbidden to leave the official tracks.

SHARM EL-SHEIKH & NA'AMA BAY
شرم الشيخ & خليج نعمة
☎ 069
If you want to visit Egypt's version of Vegas, make your way to these settlements on the southern coast of the Gulf of Aqaba. These are the types of places where the gals from *Desperate Housewives* would choose to holiday – full of manicured estates, glitzy malls and overpriced brasseries and hotels. The best advice we can give most independent travellers is to move on as soon as possible, the only caveat being that the diving on offer around here is some of the best in the world.

Na'ama Bay is a throbbing resort that has grown from virtually nothing since the early 1980s, while Sharm el-Sheikh, initially developed by the Israelis, is a long-standing settlement. They are 6km apart, but are joining together with fast-growing, American-style suburban sprawl. Around 12km northeast of Na'ama Bay is Shark's Bay, home to the area's best budget accommodation.

Information
There are ATMs every few metres in Na'ama Bay. Most major banks have branches in Sharm; the National Bank of Egypt and the Banque Misr both have ATMs. **Thomas Cook** (☎ 360 1808; Gafy Mall, Sharm-Na'ama Bay Rd, Na'ama Bay; ☉ 9am-2pm & 6-10pm), near Pigeon's House

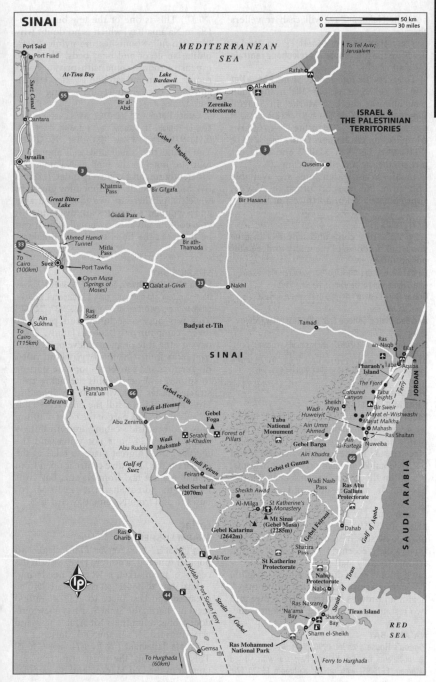

SINAI

0 — 50 km
0 — 30 miles

MEDITERRANEAN SEA

At-Tina Bay
Lake Bardawil

Port Said
Port Fuad

Rafah
To Tel Aviv; Jerusalem

Al-Arish

55

Bir al-Abd

Zerenike Protectorate

ISRAEL & THE PALESTINIAN TERRITORIES

Qantara

Gebel Maghara

3

Quseima

Ismailia

3

Khatmia Pass

Bir Gifgafa

Bir Hasana

Great Bitter Lake

Giddi Pass

Ahmed Hamdi Tunnel

Mitla Pass

Bir ath-Thamada

33

To Cairo (100km)

Suez

Port Tawfiq

Oyun Musa (Springs of Moses)

Qalat al-Gindi

33

Nakhl

Ain Sukhna

Ras Sudr

Badyat et-Tih

Tamad

Ras an-Naqb

Eilat

To Cairo (115km)

SINAI

Taba

Aqaba

JORDAN

Pharaoh's Island

The Fjord

Hammam Fara'un

66

Gebel et-Tih

Coloured Canyon

Taba Heights

Zafarana

Wadi al-Homur

Sheikh Atiya

Bir Sweir

Wadi Huweiyit

Mayat el-Wishwashi

Gebel Foga

Abu Zenima

Taba National Monument

Ain Umm Ahmed

Mayat Malkha

Mahash

Forest of Pillars

Serabit al-Khadim

Ras Shaitan

Wadi Mukattab

Gebel Barga

Ain al-Furtega

Nuweiba

Abu Rudeis

Ain Khudra

66

Gulf of Suez

Wadi Feiran

Gebel el Gunna

Feiran

Wadi Nasb Pass

Ras Abu Galum Protectorate

Gebel Serbal (2070m)

Sheikh Awad

Al-Milga

St Katherine's Monastery

Mt Sinai (Gebel Musa) (2285m)

Gebel Feirani

Dahab

Gulf of Aqaba

SAUDI ARABIA

Ras Gharib

Gebel Katarina (2642m)

Al-Tor

Shatira Pass

St Katherine Protectorate

Nabq Protectorate

Nabq

44

Suez-Jeddah Ferry

Port-Sudan Ferry

Straits of Gubal

Ras Nasrany

'Na'ama Bay

Shark's Bay

Sharm el-Sheikh

Tiran Island

Straits of Tiran

RED SEA

To Hurghada (60km)

Gemsa

Ras Mohammed National Park

Ferry to Hurghada

hotel in Na'ama Bay, will cash travellers cheques.

The **post office** (Sharm el-Sheikh; � 8am-3pm Sat-Thu) is on the hill. There's a **telephone centrale** (� 24hr) nearby.

To access the Internet try **Sharm Phone Net Café** (☎ 366 4725; per hr E£7; � 24hr) in the small mall opposite the Old Market in Sharm; **Speednet Internet Café** (Sharm-Na'ama Bay rd, Sharm el-Sheikh; per hr E£5; � 24hr) in the Delta Sharm complex; or **Yes Business Centre** (per hr E£12; � 11am-1am) between Mall 7 and Avis car hire on the main road in Na'ama Bay.

In Sinai, visa extensions are available only from the passport office in Al-Tor, approximately 90km northwest of here.

Activities
Any of the dive clubs and schools can give you a full rundown of the many underwater possibilities.

Camel Dive Club (☎ 360 0700; www.cameldive.com; Camel Hotel, King of Bahrain St, Na'ama Bay)
Oonas Dive Centre (☎ 360 0581; www.oonasdivers .com; Na'ama Bay)
Red Sea Diving College (☎ 360 0145; www.redsea college.com; Na'ama Bay)
Sinai Divers (☎ 360 0697; www.sinaidivers.com; Na'ama Bay)
Subex (☎ 360 0122; www.subex.org; Na'ama Bay)

Sleeping
SHARM EL-SHEIKH
Youth Hostel (☎ /fax 366 0317; City Council St, Hadaba; per person member/nonmember E£25/56; ☒) The main attraction here is that it's the cheapest place to stay in the area. Rooms are bland but acceptable; all have private bathrooms. It's up on the hill in Hadaba, near the police station and mosque, and away from the beach.

Amar Sina (☎ 366 2222; www.minasegypt.com; Hadaba; s/d US$35/40; ☒ 🖥 🛏) In the middle of the new subdivision above Ras Um Sid, this vaguely eccentric place has a garden setting, friendly staff and attractively decorated rooms with domed ceilings, satellite TV, sitting areas and private bathrooms. A health-and-fitness centre, a dive centre and two restaurants are on site. Excellent value.

NA'AMA BAY
Pigeon's House (☎ 360 0996; pigeon@access.com.eg; Sharm-Na'ama Bay Rd, Na'ama Bay; s/d with shared bathroom E£75/95, with private bathroom E£120/170;

☒ 🖥) This is one of the few budget hotels in Na'ama Bay, which is no doubt why it's often full. Rooms feature nylon sheets, utilitarian décor and hard beds. The more expensive rooms come with private bathrooms, air-con and satellite TV. It's cleanish and has a central courtyard serving meals and drinks.

Camel Hotel (☎ 360 0700; www.cameldive.com; King of Bahrain St, Na'ama Bay; s/d with street view US$103/126, with pool view US$120/143; ☒ 🖥 🛏) You'll find this small and well-appointed four-star hotel in the mall at Na'ama Bay. Efficiently run and relatively quiet, it offers five rooms specially equipped for guests in wheelchairs. There are two good restaurants and a popular bar. Rates are discounted if you book in advance by email, which can be done via the hotel's website. Breakfast costs extra.

SHARK'S BAY
Shark's Bay Umbi Diving & Camp (☎ 360 0942; www .sharksbay.com; s/d huts with shared bathroom US$15/19, cabins with private bathroom & air-con US$25/37; ☒ 🖥) This was once a secluded and primitive divers' camp run by a Bedouin family. These days it's the core of an overdeveloped small bay, 6km from Na'ama Bay, where cafés, dive centres and souvenir shops are starting to sprout, and new cabins are being constructed faster than you can say 'paradise lost'. That said, it's still the only truly laid-back camp on this part of the coast. Clifftop huts and beachside cabins are refreshingly clean, there's 24-hour hot water and the *sheesha* café is a great place to relax at the end of the day. The dive centre is open from 8am to 6pm. A taxi from Na'ama Bay costs E£25; to the port at Sharm, it's E£50. Microbuses to and from Na'ama Bay cost E£3.

Eating
SHARM EL-SHEIKH
King (dishes E£2-7; � from 7am) This clean and popular fuul and ta'amiyya takeaway, in the centre of the market, is worth considering.

Sinai Star (☎ 366 0323; set meals around E£20) The cheapest and best place to grab a seafood meal in Sharm, the Sinai Star has a few outdoor tables, a fondness for Arabic pop and very fresh fish. It's in the Old Market.

Safsafa Restaurant (☎ 366 0474; meals E£10-45) This is probably the most attractive restaurant in the Old Market, and it's popular with locals. An intimate space filled with a few tables sporting white tablecloths, it serves good fresh seafood (1kg Red Sea fish E£85), as well as seafood pastas (spaghetti with shrimps E£30).

The reasonably priced **Sharm Express Supermarket** (8am-2am), in front of the Old Market, sells a limited range of toiletries, drinks and food.

NA'AMA BAY

Gado (24hr) This 'nouvelle Egyptian' fast-food place, at the start of the mall, has a pleasant outdoor terrace and a refreshingly cheap (for Sharm) price list. Felafel sandwiches cost E£1.75, shwarma sandwiches E£7 and fuul E£3.50 to E£4.25. You can also enjoy a tea (E£4) and *sheesha* (E£5) here.

Tam Tam Oriental Café (☎ 360 0150; mezze E£12, sandwiches E£8-14, mains E£29-66) On the beach strip of the main mall, this place offers a range of Egyptian fare at inflated prices, but its roof terrace is a decent spot to enjoy a *sheesha* (E£8) and Stella (E£20).

Tandoori Indian Restaurant (☎ 360 0700; mains E£24-110, set menus E£145-185; 6.30-11.30pm) In a courtyard within the Camel Hotel, Sharm's best Indian restaurant serves up an aromatic array of tandoori and North Indian dishes. It's inevitably full – make sure you book ahead. A Stella costs E£16.

La Rustichella (☎ 360 1154; meals E£35-60;) Off the main strip and scandalously empty considering the quality of its food, this large and friendly trattoria has an outdoor terrace and an air-conditioned dining room and bar (Stella E£12). There's often live jazz to accompany your pasta, pizza or meat dishes. You'll find it on a hilly winding road that runs between the main road and the mall.

Drinking & Entertainment

Popular watering holes include the ubiquitous Hard Rock Café, in the mall at Na'ama Bay; the **Camel Roof Bar** (☎ 360 0700; Camel Hotel, Na'ama Bay); the pricey and very glam **Little Buddha** (☎ 360 1030; Na'ama Bay; 1pm-3am); and the **Pirates' Bar** (☎ 360 0137; Hilton Fayrouz Village, Na'ama Bay), which has a popular happy hour from 5.30pm to 7.30pm.

If you're keen to go clubbing, the most popular option is **Pacha** (☎ 012 399 5020; www .pachasharm.com; Sanafir Hotel; admission Fri-Wed E£100, Thu E£175; 10pm-4am), which absolutely heaves on Thursday nights.

THE AUTHOR'S CHOICE

Ristorante & Beach Club El-Fanar (☎ 366 2218; www.elfanar.net; Ras Um Sid; pastas E£35-50, seafood mains E£60-90; 10.30am-midnight) Imagine yourself relaxing in a place away from Sharm's mall madness. You've ordered a pizza with a perfectly crisp base that's topped with a simple but delectable mix of fresh mozzarella, capers, anchovies and tomato (E£40), and you're enjoying this while sipping a chilled glass of white wine (E£30) and looking over the Red Sea's turquoise waters. After your meal, you relax over a great espresso (E£10) and then, feeling reinvigorated, decide to snorkel in the reef below. After that, it's back to the beach bar and another glass of wine…

Fortunately you can do all of this in the Italian-run El-Fanar beach compound, perched on the edge of a cliff next to the lighthouse in the quiet resort area of Ras Um Sid. Comprising a restaurant, beach bar and beach club (E£40 for beach entrance, umbrella, lounge and soft drink), it's a wonderful place to spend the day and watch the sunset. There is even a beach party (admission US$25, from 11.30am till 3am Wednesday) in summer.

Getting There & Away

AIR

Sharm el-Sheikh International Airport (☎ 360 1140) is about 10km north of Na'ama Bay at Ras Nasrany. **EgyptAir** (☎ 366 1056; Sharm el-Sheikh; 9am-9pm), at the beginning of the road to Na'ama Bay, has four daily flights to Cairo (E£733 one way) and two flights per week to Luxor (Tuesday and Thursday, E£530 one way). Microbuses charge E£2 for the trip between the airport and Na'ama Bay or Sharm el-Sheikh; taxis charge E£20/40.

BOAT

A luxury high-speed ferry operated by **International Fast Ferries Co** (www.internationalfast ferries.com; one way adult E£250 or US$40, child 3-12 half price) runs between Sharm el-Sheikh and Hurghada, departing at 6pm each Saturday, Monday, Tuesday and Thursday from the port west of Sharm el-Maya. The trip takes 1½ hours, but can be cancelled or take longer when seas are rough, particularly in January and February. There is no student discount on tickets and you need to be at the port one hour ahead of departure time to organise your boarding ticket.

Ferry tickets can be bought from various travel agencies in town. They are also sold at the ferry office at the port on days that the ferry runs, beginning at 4pm (two hours before departure time).

If you're arriving by ferry, don't be pressured into getting one of the overpriced taxis close to the ferry building's exit. If you walk up the hill to where the gates are, you'll be able to pick up a taxi for half the price (E£15 to the bus station, E£25 to Na'ama Bay).

BUS & SERVICE TAXI

The bus station is behind the Mobil Station, halfway between Na'ama Bay and Sharm el-Sheikh. Superjet has services to Cairo (E£68, six hours) at noon, 1pm, 3pm, 7pm, 11pm and 11.30pm. The 3pm service travels on to Alexandria (E£88, nine hours); there's also an East Delta Bus Co service to Alexandria (E£80) at 9pm. East Delta Bus Co has 11 daily services to Cairo (E£55 to E£65, seven hours), starting at 7.30am and ending at midnight. It travels to Suez (E£30, five hours) at 7am, 9am, 10am and 1pm daily.

East Delta Bus Co goes to Dahab (E£11, one hour) at 9am, 2.30pm, 5pm, 8.30pm, 9pm and 12.30am. The 2.30pm and 5pm services go on to Nuweiba (E£21.50, 2½ hours), and the 9am bus then continues all the way to Taba (E£26.50, three to four hours). If enough travellers get off the ferry from Hurghada and want to transfer directly to Dahab, an extra service may be provided. A bus to St Katherine's Monastery (E£28, 3½ hours) departs at 7.30am, but you may have to change at Dahab. To Luxor (E£95, 12 to 15 hours), there's one daily East Delta Bus Co service at 6pm.

Service taxis congregate around the bus station and charge slightly more per ticket than the bus. A private taxi to Dahab will cost around E£150.

Getting Around

The prices of local taxis and microbuses are regulated by the municipality. Microbuses travel regularly between Sharm el-Sheikh and Na'ama Bay for E£1. A taxi costs E£15, with larger Peugeots being slightly more expensive.

DAHAB   دهب
☎ 069

Galaxies away from the somnolent hippy haven it was a decade or so ago, Dahab (literally 'Gold') has managed to preserve its laid-back charm against the odds. There are plenty of touts, a highly competitive scene among the camp operators and the usual shops selling tourist tat, but somehow this unassuming village on a windy promontory has avoided the ignoble fate of those other once-idyllic diving destinations, Sharm el-Sheik and Hurghada. It's a perfect place to chill out after exploring the rest of Egypt, particularly if diving and snorkelling are your things.

Orientation

There are two parts to Dahab: Dahab City is home to five-star hotels and the bus station; Assalah, once a Bedouin village, is about 2.5km north of here. It now has more budget travellers and Egyptian entrepreneurs than Bedouin in residence and is divided into two sections, Masbat and Mashraba.

Information

INTERNET ACCESS

Download.Net (per hr E£5; ☉ 24hr) Next to the Nesima Resort in Mashraba.

Felopater Internet (per hr E£5; ☉ 10am-midnight) There are three branches in Mashraba: next to Penguin Village, behind Nesima Resort and on the main street just down from Nesima Resort.

Seven Heaven Internet Café (per hr E£4; ☉ 8am-midnight) In the camp of the same name.

MONEY

Banque du Caire (☉ 9am-2pm & 6-9pm Sat-Thu, 9-11am & 6-9pm Fri) The Mashraba branch doesn't have an ATM, but it will change cash and give advances on Visa and MasterCards.

National Bank of Egypt (☉ 9am-10pm) Has a branch on the promenade in Masbat that has an ATM and will change cash and travellers cheques. It has another ATM just up the road in front of the Ghazala Market, and a third in Dahab City.

POST & TELEPHONE

The post office and **telephone centrale** (☉ 24hr) are in Dahab City. The latter has a Menatel cardphone, and there are also a number of cardphones next to the Ghazala Market in Masbat. There's a postbox here, too.

Activities

After loafing around and developing a milk-shake addiction, diving is the most popular activity in Dahab. The town's various dive clubs all offer a full range of diving possibilities, including camel/dive safaris. However, you should choose your club carefully because some places have lousy reputations when it comes to safety standards. The following are among the best:

Fantasea Dive Centre (☎ 364 0483; www.fantasea diving.net; Masbat)

Inmo (☎ 364 0370; www.inmodivers.de; Inmo Divers Home, Mashraba)

Nesima Dive Centre (☎ 364 0320; www.nesima -resort.com; Nesima Resort, Mashraba)

Orca Dive Club (☎ /fax 364 0020; Masbat)

In the morning, camel drivers and their charges congregate along the waterfront to organise camel trips into the dry interior of Sinai. Prices for a three-day trip, including food, are between E£600 and E£900.

Sleeping

BUDGET

Bish Bishi Village (☎ 364 0727; www.bishbishi.com; Mashraba; s/d with shared bathroom E£25/35, with private bathroom E£45/60, with private bathroom & air-con E£60/80; ✷) Despite the fact that it's removed from the seafront, this simple camp has a lot going for it. Freshly painted rooms are arranged around a well-maintained palm-filled courtyard and feature comfortable beds and screened windows; some have private bathrooms and air-con. It's extremely clean and offers free use of a washing machine and outdoor kitchen. No breakfast.

Penguin Village (☎ 364 1047; www.penguindivers .com; Mashraba; s/d E£60/80, with air-con E£75/100, with view E£80/120; ✷ 🖳) With its great position right on the beach, attractive courtyard, dive centre and popular beachfront restaurant, the Penguin is hard to beat. Once a basic camp, it's gone upmarket and rooms now have private bathrooms; some also have air-con. The four beach-fronting rooms with balconies (singles/doubles E£100/140) are worth the splurge. Our only criticism is that the place is a tad grubby. Breakfast costs E£12.

Seven Heaven (☎ 364 0080; www.7heavenhotel .com; Masbat; huts E£10, concrete cabins E£15, r with private bathroom E£50, with private bathroom & air-con E£60; ✷ 🖳) A bustling camp right on the promenade but set back from the beach, Seven Heaven elicits praise from the many backpackers who stay here. There are four types of accommodation, friendly management, a cheap restaurant and a dive centre. Breakfast costs E£8 to E£10.

Deep Blue Hotel & Camp (☎ 012 722 5126; info@ octopusdivers.net; Mashraba; huts per person E£5, s/d E£20/30, with air-con E£30/40; ✷) Deep Blue doesn't have the atmosphere of the other camps in town, but it's certainly cheap. Concrete-floored fibro huts come with filthy shared bathrooms. Much better value is offered by the rooms with private bathrooms, which are clean and comfortable. Breakfast costs E£8.

Bedouin Lodge (☎ 364 0317; bedouinlodgehotel@ hotmail.com; Mashraba; s/d E£50/70; ✷) In a premier position on the beach, this place has a pleasant restaurant with Bedouin seating and offers 26 rooms with private bathrooms; half have double beds and air-con. If it were cleaner our recommendation would be more enthusiastic. Ask for one of the three rooms with balconies and sea views (E£120 to E£150).

Jasmine Pension (☎ 364 0852; webmaster@jasmine pension.com; Mashraba; s & d E£60, s/d with view E£80/90; 🖳) Shoestringers who don't want to stay at one of the larger camps may be attracted by this tiny pension on the promenade. Rooms are minute and pretty basic, albeit with private bathrooms; four have balconies with sea views. The excellent Jasmine Restaurant is based here. Breakfast costs E£13.

MIDRANGE & TOP END

Inmo Divers Home (☎ 364 0370; www.inmodivers .de; Mashraba; s/d US$37/46; ✷ 🖳) You must be a diver to stay at this excellent midrange hotel and it's always fully booked. Rooms are comfortable, attractively decorated and very clean; terrace rooms (singles/doubles US$45/60) have balconies with good sea views. Backpacker rooms (singles/doubles US$17/22) are tiny but they have good mattresses and screened windows. The shared bathrooms come with 24-hour hot water. The hotel houses a restaurant, a children's playground and a small pool.

Nesima Resort (☎ 364 0320; www.nesima-resort .com; Mashraba; s/d E£385/501; ✷ 🖳) This comfortable hotel has an attractive garden setting and the best beachfront pool (day use E£30) in Dahab. Rooms don't offer views and are a

EGYPT

bit dark, but they are extremely clean. There are two pleasant restaurant-bars.

Blue Beach Club (☎ 364 0411; www.bluebeachclub .com; Mashraba; s/d E£240/300; ⌗ ⌗) Blue Beach's twenty attractively decorated rooms come with private bathrooms and plump white continental quilts; some upstairs ones have sea-fronting balconies. Features include the

freshwater pool, a stylish restaurant with great views, Arabic classes, a dive centre, regular yoga workshops and Dahab's most popular bar, the Furry Cup. It's windy at this end of town.

Sunsplash Divers (☎ 364 0932; www.sunsplash -divers.com; Mashraba; cabanas E£40, s/d cabins E£60/120) The small wooden cabins here are utilitarian

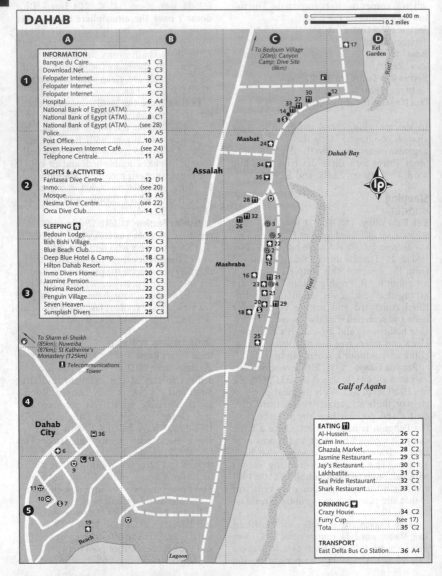

DAHAB

To Bedouin Village (20m); Canyon Camp; Dive Site (8km)

Eel Garden

Reef

Masbat

Assalah

Dahab Bay

Mashraba

Reef

To Sharm el-Sheikh (85km); Nuweiba (87km); St Katherine's Monastery (125km)

Telecommunications Tower

Dahab City

Gulf of Aqaba

Beach

Lagoon

and very clean, with mosquito nets, cotton mattresses and private bathrooms. Cabanas offer a foam mattress on the floor and use of pristine shared bathrooms. There's a restaurant, rooftop lounge, dive centre and small garden. Buffet breakfast costs E£15.

Hilton Dahab Resort (☎ 364 0310; www.hilton .com/worldwideresorts; Dahab City; s US$65-76, d US$90-101, ste US$97-132; ✗ ✗ ☐ ☎) Far away from the Assalah action, this resort is designed around a garden-and-lagoon concept and has a tranquil atmosphere. Leisure facilities are impressive: a large pool area, a sand beach on the (real) lagoon where you can windsurf ($41 for two hours), a kids club and the highly regarded Sinai Divers Dive Centre (open 8am to 1pm, and 2pm to 5.30pm). Rooms are extremely comfortable and the suites come with hammock-equipped terraces.

Eating

Jasmine Restaurant (☎ 364 0852; Mashraba; ☉ 7am-1am) Serving enormous and delicious dishes right at the water's edge, this casual eatery is understandably popular with locals and travellers. The chicken satay (E£35) is excellent and the chocolate brownie with ice cream (E£19) goes down a treat. A Stella costs E£10, a *sheesha* is E£7 and there's a wide variety of fresh fruit juices (E£11).

Shark Restaurant (Masbat; pastas E£12-25, pizzas E£18-20; ☉ 6pm-midnight) If you can't find the local diving fraternity sinking a few pints at the Furry Cup, they're likely to be on the rooftop terrace of this popular eatery on the promenade. Food is fresh and served in generous portions. Though no alcohol is sold, management doesn't mind if you bring your own.

Lakhbatita (☎ 364 1306; Mashraba; mains E£15-60) Dahab's best restaurant is at the Mashraba end of the promenade. Its charming interior features *mashrabiyya* (wooden lattice screens), rich red cushions and shelves of home-bottled preserves. The menu mixes traditional Egyptian food with the influences of Asia and Europe, and includes daily specials and a lavish salad/antipasto bar (small/medium/large plate E£8/15/22). Its beach bar opens at 6am and is a good place for breakfast.

Carm Inn (☎ 364 1300; Masbat; dishes E£25-65) Vegetarians will be happy indeed when they peruse the menu at this stylish restaurant.

The owners claim that their food is all about 'vitality, building a strong body, muscular development and fun', and while this might be overstating the case, there's no doubt that dishes such as the veggieburger (E£8) and nasi goreng (E£30) are healthy and tasty in equal measure. Herbal teas are E£4.50.

Jay's Restaurant (☎ 364 1228; Masbat; dishes E£7-10; ☉ 11am-3pm & 5pm-10pm) This perennial favourite serves the usual mixture of Egyptian and Western fare at very cheap prices. The dinner menu changes daily, but lunch is limited to pizzas, pastas and salads.

The **Ghazala Market** (☉ 24hr) in Masbat stocks a good range of food and toiletries. The restaurant at **Seven Heaven** (☎ 364 0080; Masbat; meals E£10-25) is famous for its spaghetti bolognese, which is enormous and costs only E£10. Other recommended cheap eateries include **Sea Pride Restaurant** (☎ 364 0891), which serves a set meal of fresh fish, salad, soup, tahini. aubergine, bread and soup for E£20 to E£25; and the neighbouring Al-Hussein, which has a set chicken meal for E£11. Both are near the taxi set-down in Masbat.

Drinking

Furry Cup (Blue Beach Club, Mashraba; ☉ noon-2am) Divers decompress every evening at the Furry Cup. It has a happy hour from 6pm to 8pm (Stella E£6, spirits E£15) and serves up non-Egyptian nosh such as bangers and mash.

Other popular watering holes include Tota and Crazy House (Stella E£10 at both), on the Masbat stretch of the promenade.

Entertainment

Gold Soul Productions organises **full moon parties** (☎ 012 370 7774; admission E£100; ☉ 6pm-6am) at a canyon outside town. These feature overseas DJs and live music. The price covers music and a transfer from town.

Getting There & Around
BUS

The new **East Delta Bus Co station and ticket office** (☉ 7.30am-11pm) is located in Dahab City, close to the mosque. The most regular connection is to Sharm el-Sheikh (E£11 to E£16, one hour), with buses at 8am, 8.30am, 10am, 11.30am, 12.30pm, 2.30pm, 4pm, 5.30pm, 8.30pm and 10pm. There are four daily buses to Nuweiba (E£11, one hour)

EGYPT

at 10.30am, 3pm, 4pm and 6.30pm. The 10.30am service goes on to Taba (E£22). There is a bus at 9.30am going to St Katherine's Monastery (E£16, 1½ hours). Buses to Cairo (E£62 to E£75, 10 hours) leave at 8.30am, 12.30pm, 2.30pm and 10pm. Buses for Suez (E£35 to E£47, 6½ hours) depart at 8am and 4pm, and there's one daily service to Hurghada (E£90) and Luxor (E£110) at 4pm. If you're going to Luxor, this is a cheaper and faster (but less comfortable) option than the bus-ferry-bus alternative.

Tickets for a battered old bus from the bus station to Assalah cost E£1.50. It's always there to pick up passengers arriving in Dahab by scheduled bus service, but it only provides a one-way service (it doesn't take passengers back from Assalah to the bus station).

TAXI
A taxi (usually a pick-up) between Assalah and Dahab City costs E£5.

ST KATHERINE'S MONASTERY
دير القديسة كاترينا

☎ 069

There are 22 Greek Orthodox monks living in this ancient monastery at the foot of Mt Sinai. The monastic order was founded in the 4th century AD by the Byzantine empress Helena, who had a small chapel built beside what was believed to be the burning bush from which God spoke to Moses. The chapel is dedicated to St Katherine, the legendary martyr of Alexandria, who was tortured on a spiked wheel and then beheaded.

In the 6th century, Emperor Justinian ordered the building of a fortress with a basilica and a monastery, as well as the original chapel. It served as a secure home for the monks of St Katherine's and as a refuge for the Christians of southern Sinai. There's no charge to visit the **monastery** (🕙 9am-noon Mon-Thu & Sat, except religious holidays), but you'll need to pay to see the wonderful collection of manuscripts and icons in the **Sacred Sacristy** (adult/student E£25/10). Be warned that the monastery is inevitably overrun by tour groups and can be unpleasantly crowded.

St Katherine Protectorate is a 4350-sq-km national park that encompasses Mt Sinai and the monastery. You will need to pur-

chase a **ticket** (US$3) at the entrance to the park, 10km before the monastery. The local camps offer all-inclusive camel safaris for around E£150 per person per day.

Information
In the village of Al-Milga, about 3.5km from the monastery, there's a post office, centrale, bank and variety of shops and cafés. The **Banque Misr** (🕙 10am-1pm & 5-8pm Sat-Thu) will change cash and give Visa and MasterCard advances. There's no Internet café and no ATM.

Sleeping & Eating
Monastery Guesthouse (☎/fax 347 0353; s/d half board US$180/320) If you fancy a taste of monastic life, this hotel, inside the monastery walls, could be just the thing. Rooms aren't too spartan, with clean private bathrooms, comfortable beds and plenty of blankets for cold mountain nights. There's also a reasonable restaurant that serves beer and wine. Nonguests can leave baggage here (E£5) while they hike up Mt Sinai.

El-Malga Bedouin Camp (☎ 347 0042; sheik mousa@yahoo.com; tent per person E£10, dm E£10-15, r with 2 beds E£30; 🖳) This new and very friendly camp offers mattresses on straw floors in stone buildings. Three rooms have sagging beds. Shared bathrooms are extremely clean, there's 24-hour hot water, and free Internet and kitchen use. The Bedouin owners organise popular desert safaris. The camp is a 10-minute walk from the bus station.

In Al-Milga there's a bakery opposite the mosque and a couple of well-stocked supermarkets in the shopping arcade. A few small restaurants are just behind the bakery.

Getting There & Away
BUS
All buses leave from the East Delta Bus Co office behind the mosque in Al-Milga. A daily bus at 6am travels to Cairo (E£37, seven hours) via Suez (E£27, four hours) and another Suez service leaves at 1pm. To Dahab (E£16, two hours) and Nuweiba (E£21, three hours), there's one bus at 1pm.

SERVICE TAXI
Taxis travel in and out of Al-Milga village irregularly and infrequently, although there are plenty available if you are willing to pay

for the extra places to fill the vehicle (up to seven people). Per person fares are E£30/45 to Dahab/Sharm el-Sheikh.

NUWEIBA   نويبع
☎ 069

By rights, Nuweiba should be a tourist hot spot. Its location is true picture-postcard stuff, with turquoise waters lapping long sandy beaches, and craggy pink mountains providing a dramatic backdrop. It's also far more peaceful than nearby Dahab, and offers similar opportunities for desert and diving safaris. If you want to avoid the scenes at Sharm and Dahab and just relax in a basic beach camp while gazing over to Saudi Arabia (only 13km away), it could well be the place for you. But go soon – if

---

CLIMBING MT SINAI   *Mary Fitzpatrick*

Rising up out of the desert and jutting above the other peaks surrounding the monastery is the towering 2285m Mt Sinai, known locally as Gebel Musa – and not to be confused with the far-lower mountain directly up the valley behind the monastery. Although some archaeologists and historians dispute Mt Sinai's biblical claim to fame, it is revered by Christians, Muslims and Jews, all of whom believe that God delivered his Ten Commandments to Moses at the summit. The mountain is beautiful, easy to climb, and – except at the summit, where you'll invariably be overwhelmed by crowds of other visitors – it offers a taste of the serenity and magnificence of southern Sinai's high mountain region. For those visiting as part of a pilgrimage, it also provides a moving glimpse into Biblical times.

There are two well-defined routes – the camel trail and the Steps of Repentance – that meet about 300m below the summit at a plateau known as Elijah's Basin. Here, everyone must take a steep series of 750 rocky and uneven steps to the top. Both the climb and the summit offer spectacular views. Most people make the climb in the predawn hours to take in the magnificence of the sun rising over the surrounding peaks, and then arrive back at the base before 9am, when the monastery opens for visitors.

The **camel trail** is the easier route, and takes about two hours to ascend, moving at a steady pace. En route are several kiosks selling tea and soda, and vendors hiring out blankets (E£5) to ward off the chill at the summit. The trail is wide, clear and gently sloping as it moves up a series of switchbacks, with the only potential difficulty – apart from the sometimes-fierce winds – being gravelly patches that can be slippery on the descent. Most people walk up, but it's also possible to hire a camel at the base, just behind the monastery, to take you all or part of the way to where the camel trail meets the steps. If you decide to try a camel, it's easier on the anatomy to ride up the mountain, rather than down.

The alternative path to the summit, the taxing 3750 **Steps of Repentance**, was laid by one monk as a form of penance. The steps – 3000 up to Elijah's Basin, and then the final 750 to the summit – are made of roughly hewn rock and are steep and uneven in many places, requiring strong knees and concentration in placing your feet. If you want to try both routes, it's best to take the path on the way up and the steps on the way back down.

During the summer, try to avoid the heat by beginning your hike by 3am. Although stone signs have been placed on the trail as guides, it can be a bit difficult in parts and a torch is essential. The start of the camel trail is reached by walking along the northern wall of the monastery, past the end of the compound. The Steps of Repentance begin outside the southeastern corner of the compound.

Due to the sanctity of the area and the tremendous pressure that large groups place on the environment, the Egyptian National Parks Office has instituted various regulations. Apart from creating a basic hikers code (see p640 for information on responsible hiking), the office asks that you sleep below the summit at the small Elijah's Basin plateau. Here, you'll find several composting toilets, and a 500-year-old cypress tree that marks the spot where the prophet Elijah heard the voice of God. Bring sufficient food and water, warm clothes and a sleeping bag; there is no space to pitch a tent. It gets cold and windy, even in summer, and light snows are common in winter. Even as late as mid-May, be prepared to share the summit with up to 500 other visitors, some carrying stereos, others Bibles and hymn books.

an end is called to the intifada, Nuweiba's previous popularity among young Israelis may well be resurrected, and its peaceful, almost catatonic, ambience farewelled.

Orientation

The town is divided into three parts. To the south is the ugly port, with the bus station and banks. About 8km further north is Nuweiba City, a small but spread-out settlement with a variety of accommodation options, a small bazaar and several cheap places to eat. About a 10-minute walk further north along the beach is Tarabin, which models itself on Dahab's Assalah backpacker colony.

Information

The post and telephone offices are next to the bus station. There are Menatel cardphones in the port building opposite the Misr Travel office. The Banque Misr, Banque du Caire and National Bank of Egypt branches near the bus station have ATMs but will not always supply US dollars, meaning that you should bring these with you if you intend on purchasing ferry tickets to Aqaba. Neither will they change Jordanian dinars. The National Bank of Egypt and Banque du Caire will change travellers cheques. There's also a branch of the **National Bank of Egypt** (9am-1pm & 7-9pm Sat-Thu, 9-11am Fri) in front of the Nuweiba Village hotel. The **Almostakbal Internet Café** (☎ 350 0090; per hr E£6; 10am-midnight) is behind Dr Sheesh Kebab in Nuweiba City.

Activities

Once again, underwater delights are the feature attraction, and scuba diving and snorkelling the prime activities. **Diving Camp Nuweiba** (☎ 012 249 6002; www.scuba-college.com), in the Nuweiba Village hotel, and **Emperor Divers** (☎ 352 0321; www.emperordivers.com), which operates out of the Nuweiba Coral Hilton Resort, have good reputations.

Nuweiba is the place to organise Jeeps or camel treks to sights such as **Coloured Canyon**, **Khudra Oasis**, **Ain Umm Ahmed** (the largest oasis in eastern Sinai) and **Ain al-Furtaga** (another palm-filled oasis). Try your luck with the Bedouin people of Tarabin or head to the camps at Mahash or Ras Shaitan, further up the coast. All-inclusive camel treks cost around E£150 per day.

Sleeping

Soft Beach Camp (☎ 364 7586; info@softbeachcamp .com; s/d E£15/20;) Soft Beach, the best camp in Sinai, has a very enthusiastic owner who is trying hard to create a slice of paradise in Nuweiba. He's succeeding, too. Hammocks and chairs are placed along the camp's large and tranquil stretch of sand beach, and there's a palm-frond beachside restaurant serving fresh food (spaghetti bolognese E£15) and Stella (E£10). Forty-five huts come with padlocks; some have mosquito nets. Shared bathrooms are basic but clean. Breakfast costs E£15. If you ring ahead, the owner will pick you up from the bus.

Fayrouza Village (☎ 350 1133; fayrouza@sinai4you .com; s/d US$10/14) On the beach at the edge of Nuweiba City and in front of a good reef, Fayrouza offers simple but spotless huts, all with fans, window screens and good beds. The shared bathrooms have hot water, and the restaurant serves up filling, tasty meals.

Sababa Camp (☎ 350 0382; sababa_sinai@hotmail .com; huts E£15) On a quiet stretch of the promenade in Tarabin, this well-maintained Bedouin-run place offers palm-frond huts set around a grassed garden. All have fans and mosquito nets; some have beds. There's a restaurant right on the water, and a Bedouin tent for *sheesha* and tea at the rear of the camp. The shared bathrooms have cold water only.

Habiba Village (☎ 350 0770; www.sinai4you.com /habiba; cabins with shared bathroom per person US$11, bungalows with private bathroom s/d US$22.50/55;) Though it's attractive and very well run, this beachside hotel in Nuweiba City is a less-than-restful proposition due to an expensive restaurant in its central courtyard that serves loads of tour groups every lunchtime. It's a great place to come for a meal, though, with fresh and delicious food cooked in clean surrounds (buffet lunch E£50, tea E£7).

Nuweiba Village (☎ 350 0401; www.nuweiba resort.com; s/d huts US$15/20, r from US$40/50;) A good four-star choice in Nuweiba City, with a private beach, comfortable rooms, a large pool and children's playground.

Eating

Eating options in Nuweiba are limited.

Dr Sheesh Kebab (☎ 350 0273; 7am-11pm) This welcoming eatery in Nuweiba City offers *kofta* (E£20) and kebabs (E£25), as well as ta'amiyya with salad and bread (E£8), and can usually supply a beer under-the-counter.

Cleopatra Restaurant (☎ 350 0503; ⌚ 8am-midnight) Opposite the Nuweiba Domina Resort, Cleopatra serves staples such as grilled chicken (E£22) and mezze (E£5 to E£20) in a small courtyard and offers Stella (E£10) to go with it.

There are a couple of supermarkets and a sprinkling of open-air eateries among the camps on Tarabin's promenade, including the ever-popular Blue Bus and the well-located Ilaa.

Getting There & Away

BOAT

For information about ferries to Aqaba in Jordan, see p177.

BUS

Buses going to or from Taba stop at both the port and the nearby bus station. You can also request that they stop outside the hospital in Nuweiba City, but this is on the whim of the driver. They don't stop at Tarabin. A seat in a service taxi from the bus station to Tarabin costs E£5; the whole taxi will cost E£15. The drivers will always try to charge more, so be ready to haggle.

There are three daily buses to Cairo (E£60, nine hours) via Taba (E£11, one hour) at 9am, 11am and 3pm. There is an extra service to Taba at 6.30am. Buses to Sharm el-Sheikh (E£21, 2½ hours) via Dahab (E£11, one hour) leave at 6.30am, 9.30am and 4pm. There's one daily service to St Katherine's (E£21, three hours) at 8.30am.

SERVICE TAXI

There is a service taxi station by the port, but unless you get there when the ferry has arrived from Aqaba, you'll have to wait a long time for the car to fill up. Per person fares (multiply by seven for the entire car) average about E£30 to Sharm el-Sheikh, E£15 to Dahab and E£60 to Cairo (usually changing vehicles in Suez).

TABA طابا

☎ 069

This busy border crossing between Egypt and Israel is open 24 hours. There's a small post and telephone office opposite the New Taba Beach Resort in the 'town', along with a few shops. You can change money at the 24-hour Banque Misr booth in the arrivals hall, and there's an ATM just outside the border. The Taba Hilton will usually change travellers cheques.

When you exit the arrivals hall, the bus station is a 10-minute walk straight ahead on the left-hand side of the road. East Delta Bus Co has a 7am service that goes to St Katherine's Monastery (E£26, four hours) via Nuweiba (E£11, one hour) and Dahab (E£21, 2½ hours). Services at 9am and 3pm travel to Sharm el-Sheikh (E£26, 3½ hours) via Nuweiba and Dahab, and a 7.15am service goes to Suez (E£35, four hours). Buses travel to Cairo (E£55 to E£60, six to seven hours) at 10.30am, 12.30pm and 4.30pm.

Peugeot taxis and minibuses function as service taxis but are really expensive. You're much better off getting the bus. To Nuweiba they charge E£50 per person, to Dahab E£70, to Sharm el-Sheikh E£120 and to Cairo E£100 to E£120.

AL-ARISH العريش

☎ 068 / pop 129,000

Al-Arish boasts a long, palm-fringed beach, a collection of holiday villages and chalets, and a small town centre bustling with Bedouin traders. The town comes alive during the height of summer, when vacationing Cairenes arrive en masse. Otherwise, it's rarely visited. In the winter months, the waterside areas resemble a ghost town, and you're likely to have the windswept beach to yourself.

Information

There's a **National Bank of Egypt ATM** (Sharia Tahrir), a telephone centrale and a post office (both just off Sharia Tahrir) in town. **El Basha.Net** (per hr E£2; ⌚ 11am-3am) is just off Midan al-Gamma at the southern edge of town, signposted on the second storey of a small white building.

Sights & Activities

There's a lively **Bedouin market** (signposted in Arabic as Souq al-Hamis) every Thursday between about 9am and 2pm at the southern edge of town, near the main market. The **Sinai Heritage Museum** (Coast Rd; admission E£1, camera/video E£5/25; ⌚ 9.30am-2pm Sat-Thu) is on the outskirts of town along the coastal road to Rafah.

Sleeping

Hotel Sinai Sun (☎ /fax 336 1855; Sharia 23rd of July; s/d from E£60/70; ☒) The rooms at this ageing yet respectable hotel are quite faded, but linen is clean, and overall it's a reasonable deal for the price. Most rooms have TV and phone; breakfast costs extra.

El-Arish Resort (☎ 335 1321; Sharia Fuad Zikry; s/d US$60/80; ☒ ☒) This faded but pleasant five-star establishment (formerly the Oberoi) is well located on a good stretch of beach. All rooms have sea views, balconies and the usual amenities.

Eating

Try the good-value **El-Arish Resort restaurant** (☎ 335 1321; Sharia Fuad Zikry; dishes E£25-75; ☒) or **Aziz Restaurant** (☎ 335 4345; Sharia Tahrir; dishes E£5-25), which serves fuul and ta'amiyya, as well as grilled chicken, *kofta*, rice and spaghetti.

Getting There & Away

The main bus and service taxi stations are next to each other, about 3km southeast of the town centre (about E£2 in a taxi).

BUS

Superjet has buses for Cairo (E£21 to E£25.50, five hours) departing at 8am and 4pm. The similarly priced East Delta Bus Co has buses to Cairo (E£18 to E£25) at 8am, 4pm and 5pm, and departures to Ismailia (E£10, three to four hours) at 7am, 10.30am, 11.30am, 1pm, 2pm, 3pm and 4pm.

SERVICE TAXI

Service taxis to Cairo cost about E£15 per person. Service taxis to Qantara cost E£7, to Ismailia E£8, and to the border (or vice versa) for anywhere between E£10 and E£20.

EGYPT DIRECTORY

ACCOMMODATION

There are a few youth hostels in Egypt, and many excellent budget hotels. In Sinai the most popular budget choices are beachside camps – all have electricity and 24-hour hot water unless noted in our reviews. Good midrange hotels are much harder to find. When it comes to the top end, travellers are spoilt for choice, with the major inter-national chains represented in most of the larger cities.

Generally speaking, winter (December to February) is the tourist high season and summer (June to August) the low season in all parts of the country except on the coasts, and to a lesser degree in Cairo. Hotel prices reflect this distinction. Prices cited in this chapter are for rooms in the high season and include taxes. Breakfast and private bathrooms are included in the price unless indicated otherwise in the review. We have defined budget hotels as any that charge up to E£100 (US$17) for a double room; mid-range as any that charge between E£100 and E£580 (US$17 to US$100) and top end as any that charge more than E£580 (US$100) for a room. In the low season you should be able to negotiate significant discounts at all hotels, including those at the top end.

Hotels rated three-star and up generally require payment in US dollars. They are increasingly accepting credit-card payments but you shouldn't take this for granted.

ACTIVITIES

As the tourism-advertisement mantra goes, Egypt is 'more than just monuments'. There are plenty of nonarchaeological pursuits on offer. These include desert safaris, horse riding, and world-class diving and snorkelling. Opportunities for these are mentioned throughout the chapter.

BUSINESS HOURS

The following information is a guide only. The official weekend is Friday and Saturday. Note that during Ramadan, all banks, offices, shops, museums and tourist sites keep shorter hours.

Banks Open 8.30am to 1.30pm Sunday to Thursday. Many banks in Cairo and other cities open again from 5pm or 6pm for two or three hours, largely for foreign-exchange transactions. Some also open on Friday and Saturday for the same purpose. Exchange booths are open as late as 8pm.

Government offices Open 8am to 2pm Sunday to Thursday. Tourist offices are generally open longer.

Post offices Generally open from 8.30am to 2pm Saturday to Thursday.

Private offices Open 10am to 2pm and 4pm to 9pm, except Friday and holidays.

Restaurants Open between noon and midnight daily. Cafés tend to open earlier and close a bit later.

Shops Open 9am to 2pm and 5pm to 10pm summer, 10am to 7pm winter. Most large shops tend to close on Sunday and holidays.

CHILDREN

Though Egyptians are extraordinarily welcoming to children, Egypt's budget and midrange hotels almost never have child-friendly facilities (the five-star chains do). Towns and cities don't have easily accessible public gardens with playground equipment, or shopping malls with amusement centres. Fortunately, there are other things kids find cool: felucca and camel rides, exploring the interiors of pyramids and snorkelling on Sinai reefs are only a few. Restaurants everywhere are very welcoming to families.

Formula is readily available in pharmacies, and supermarkets stock disposable nappies. Highchairs are often available in restaurants. Baby-sitting facilities are usually available in top-end hotels.

COURSES

If you're serious about learning Arabic, the best option is to sign up at the **Arabic Language Institute** (☎ 02-797 5055; www.aucegypt .edu; 113 Sharia Qasr al-Ainy, Downtown, Cairo), a department of the American University in Cairo. It offers intensive instruction in both modern standard Arabic and Egyptian colloquial Arabic at elementary, intermediate and advanced levels in semester courses (US$7024) running over five months. The institute also offers intensive summer programmes (US$3475).

One less expensive option is studying at the **International Language Institute** (ILI; Map p109; ☎ 02-346 3087; www.arabicegypt.com; 4 Sharia Mahmoud Azmy, Sahafayeen, Cairo). This offers courses in modern standard Arabic and Egyptian colloquial Arabic over eight levels. Prices start at US$240 for 32 hours over four weeks.

DISABLED TRAVELLERS

Egypt for All (☎ 02-311 3988; www.egyptforall.com; 334 Sharia Sudan, Mohandiseen, Cairo) specialises in organising travel arrangements for travellers who are mobility-impaired.

DISCOUNT CARDS

If you have an officially recognised student card you'll be eligible for major discounts to museums and sites throughout Egypt. The best is the International Student Identity Card (ISIC), and it's possible to organise this in Egypt if you didn't get a chance before you left home. You'll need one photo, proof of being a student, a photocopy of the front page of your passport and E£65. There are no age limits. In Luxor you can do this at the **Nada Travel Service** (NTS; Map p125; ☎ 095 238 2163; elnada91@hotmail.com, Petra Travel Agency Bldg, Sharia Ahmed Orabi; ☺ 8am-11pm), near Luxor Temple. In Cairo, go to **ESTS** (☎ 02-531 0330; www.estsegypt.com; 23 Sharia Manial, Midan el-Mammalek, El-Roda).

PRACTICALITIES

- *Egyptian Gazette* (50pt) is Egypt's flimsy and embarrassingly bad daily English-language newspaper. **Al-Ahram Weekly** (www.ahram.org.eg/weekly; E£1) appears every Thursday and does a much better job of keeping English readers informed of what's going on. *Egypt Today* (E£12) is an ad-saturated general-interest glossy with good listings.

- You can pick up the **BBC World Service** (www.bbc.co.uk/worldservice) on various frequencies, including AM 1323 in Alexandria, the Europe short-wave schedule in Cairo and the Middle East short-wave schedule in Upper Egypt. In Cairo, FM95 broadcasts on 557kHz between 7am and midnight daily, including news in English at 7.30am, 2.30pm and 8pm. Nile FM (104.2kHz) is an English-language music station broadcasting out of Cairo.

- Satellite dishes are common in Egypt, and international English-language news services such as CNN and BBC World can be accessed in hotel rooms throughout the country.

- Electrical current is 220V AC, 50Hz in most parts of the country. Exceptions are Alexandria, and Heliopolis and Ma'adi in Cairo, which have currents of 110V AC, 50Hz. Wall sockets are the round, two-pin European type.

- Egypt uses the metric system for weights and measures.

EGYPT

EMBASSIES & CONSULATES
Egyptian Embassies & Consulates
There is a comprehensive listing of Egyptian diplomatic and consular missions overseas at www.mfa.gov.eg. For the addresses of Egyptian embassies and consulates in the Middle East, see the relevant country chapter.

Australia Canberra (☎ 02-6273 4437/8; fax 02-6273 4279; 1 Darwin Ave, Yarralumla 2600, ACT); Melbourne (☎ 03-9654 8869, 03-9654 8634; consgened@primus .com.au; 9th fl, 124 Exhibition St, Melbourne 3000, Vic); Sydney (☎ 02-9281 4844; www.egypt.org.au; 3rd fl, 241 Commonwealth St, Surry Hills 2010, NSW)

Canada Montreal (☎ 514-866 8455; www.egyptiancon sulatemontreal.org; 1 Place Sainte Marie, 2617 Montreal, Quebec H3B 4S3); Ottawa (☎ 613-234 4931-5; www.egypt embassy.ca; 454 Laurier Ave E, Ottawa, Ontario K1N 6R3)

France Marseilles (☎ 04 91 25 04 04; 166 Ave d'Hambourg, 13008); Paris (☎ 01 53 67 88 30/2; www .ambassade-egypte.com; 56 Ave d'Iena, 75116)

Germany Berlin (☎ 30-477 5470; www.egyptian -embassy.de; Stauffenberg Str 6-7, 10785); Frankfurt-am-Main (☎ 69-955 1340/1; Eysseneckstrasse 34, 60322)

Ireland (☎ 01-660 6566; www.embegyptireland.ie; 12 Clyde Rd, Ballsbridge, Dublin 4)

Israel Eilat (☎ 08-637 6882; 68 HaAfroni St); Tel Aviv (☎ 03-546 4151; fax 03-544 1615; 54 Basel St, 64239)

Italy Milan (☎ 02 951 63 60; fax 02 951 81 94; Via Gustavo Modena 3/5); Rome (☎ 06 84 24 18 96; fax 06 85 30 11 75; Villa Savoia, Via Salaria 267)

Japan (☎ 813-37 70 80 22; www.embassy-avenue.jp /egypt; 1-5-4 Aobadai, Meguro-ku, Tokyo 153-0042)

Netherlands (☎ 70-354 4535; ambegnl@wanadoo.nl; Badhuisweg 92, 2587 CL, The Hague)

Spain (☎ 3491-577 6308/9/10; fax 3491-578 1732; Velazquez 69, 28006, Madrid)

UK London (☎ 020-7499 2401; www.egyptianconsulate .co.uk; 26 South St, Mayfair W1); London (☎ 020-7235 9777; 2 Lowndes St, SW1)

USA Chicago (☎ 312-828 9162/4/3; Suite 1900, 500 N Michigan Ave, IL 60611); Houston (☎ 713-961 4915/6; Suite 2180, 1990 Post Oak Blvd, TX 77056); New York City (☎ 212-759 7120/1/2; 1110 2nd Ave, NY 10022); San Francisco (☎ 415-346 9700/2; 3001 Pacific Ave, CA 94115); Washington, DC (☎ 202-895 5400; www.egypt embassy.us; 3521 International Court NW, Washington, DC, 20008)

Embassies & Consulates in Egypt
Most foreign embassies and consulates are open from around 8am to 2pm Sunday to Thursday.

Australia (Map p109; ☎ 02-575 0444; fax 02-578 1638; 11th fl, World Trade Centre, 1191 Corniche el-Nil, Bulaq, Cairo)

Canada (Map pp98-9; ☎ 02-794 3110; fax 02-796 3548; 26 Sharia Kamal el-Shenawy, Garden City, Cairo)

France Alexandria (☎ 03-480 9038; 2 Midan Orabi, Man-sheyya); Cairo (Map pp98-9; ☎ 02-570 3916; fax 02-571 0276; 29 Sharia al-Giza, Giza)

Germany Alexandria (☎ 03-545 7025; 5 Sharia Mena, Rushdy); Cairo (Map p109; ☎ 02-735 3687; fax 02-736 0530; 8 Hassan Sabry, Zamalek)

Iran (☎ 02-748 6400; fax 02-748 6495; 12 Sharia Rifa'a, Doqqi, Cairo) Off Midan al-Misaha.

Ireland (☎ 03-484 3320; 9 Sharia el-Fawateem); Cairo (Map p109; ☎ 02-735 8547; 3 Sharia Abu el-Feda, Zamalek)

Israel Alexandria (☎ 03-544 9501; 10 Sharia Mena, Kafer Abdou); Cairo (Map pp98-9; ☎ 02-761 0545; fax 761 0414; 6 Sharia ibn Malek, Giza)

Italy Alexandria (☎ 03-487 9470; 25 Sharia Saad Zaghloul); Cairo (Map pp98-9; ☎ 02-794 3194; 15 Sharia Abdel Rahman Fahmy, Garden City)

Japan Alexandria (☎ 03-583 1859; 41 Sharia Mostafa Abou Heif); Cairo (☎ 02-795 3962; 106 Sharia Qasr el-Aini, Garden City)

Jordan (Map pp102-3; ☎ 02-748 5566; fax 02-760 1027; 6 Sharia Gohainy, Doqqi, Cairo)

Lebanon Alexandria (☎ 03-484 6589; 64 Sharia el-Horreya); Cairo (Map pp98-9; ☎ 02-361 0623; fax 02-361 0463; Sharia Ahmad Nasim, Giza)

Libya Alexandria (☎ 03-494 0877; fax 03-494 0297; 4 Sharia Batris Lumomba, Bab Shark); Cairo (Map p109; ☎ 02-735 1269; fax 02-735 0072; 7 Sharia el-Saleh Ayoub, Zamalek)

Netherlands (Map p109; ☎ 02-739 5500; fax 02-735 5959; 18 Hassan Sabry, Zamalek, Cairo)

New Zealand (☎ 02-574 9360; emeco@attmail.com; 4th fl, 2 Sharia Talaat Harb, Downtown, Cairo)

Spain (Map p109; ☎ 02-735 6462; embespeg@mail.mae .es; 41 Sharia Ismail Mohammed, Zamalek, Cairo)

Sudan (Map pp98-9; ☎ 02-794 9661; fax 02-354 2693; 3 Sharia al-Ibrahimy, Garden City, Cairo)

Syria (Map pp98-9; ☎ 02-335 8806; fax 02-749 4560; 18 Abdel Rahim Sabry, Doqqi, Cairo)

Turkey Alexandria (☎ 03-393 9086; 11 Sharia Kamel el-Kilany); Cairo (Map pp102-3; ☎ 02-794 8364; 25 Sharia al-Falaky, Downtown)

UK Alexandria (☎ 03-546 7002; 3 Sharia Mena, Rushdy); Cairo (Map pp98-9; ☎ 02-794 0852; 7 Sharia Ahmed Ragheb, Garden City)

USA (Map pp102-3; ☎ 02-797 3300; fax 02-797 3200; 8 Sharia Kamal el-Din Salah, Garden City, Cairo)

FESTIVALS & EVENTS
Surprisingly, there aren't very many head-line events on the national cultural calendar. The most notable are the **Cairo International Book Fair** in January/February, the **Ascension**

of Ramses II at Abu Simbel on 22 February and 22 October each year, and the **Egyptian Marathon** (egyptianmarathon@egypt.net) in February, when competitors race around the monuments on Luxor's West Bank.

GAY & LESBIAN TRAVELLERS

While homosexuality is not actually illegal according to Egypt's penal code, arrests on the charge of 'debauchery and contempt of religion' do occur. The website www.gayegypt.com is a good source of information.

HOLIDAYS

In addition to the main Islamic holidays (p648), Egypt celebrates the following public holidays:

New Year's Day 1 January
Coptic Christmas 7 January – only Coptic businesses are closed for the day
Coptic Easter March/April
Sham an-Nessim (The Smell of the Breeze) First Monday after Coptic Easter
Sinai Liberation Day 25 April
May Day 1 May
Liberation Day 18 June
Revolution Day 23 July
Wafa'a el-Nil (The Flooding of the Nile) 15 August
Coptic New Year 11 September (12 September in leap years)
Armed Forces Day 6 October
Suez Victory Day 24 October
Victory Day 23 December

MONEY

The official currency is the Egyptian pound (E£) – in Arabic, a *guinay*. One pound consists of 100 piastres (pt). There are notes in denominations of 5pt, 10pt, 25pt and 50pt, and one, five, 10, 20, 50, 100 and 200 *guinay*. Coins in circulation have denominations of five, 10, 20 and 25 piastres. You should try to hoard as many E£1 and E£5 notes as you possibly can, as these come in very handy for baksheesh and taxi fares.

See the table for the rates for a range of currencies at the time of going to press.

ATMs

These have spread rapidly throughout the country; you'll find them everywhere in Cairo, Hurghada and Sharm el-Sheikh, and less commonly in Alexandria, Luxor, Aswan and Dahab. They are very rare in the Western Desert and in smaller towns

Country	Unit	Egyptian pound (E£)
Australia	A$1	4.21
Canada	C$1	4.87
euro zone	€1	6.79
Israel & the Palestinian Territories	1NIS	1.23
Japan	¥100	4.93
Libya	1LD	4.58
New Zealand	NZ$1	3.95
UK	UK£1	10.03
USA	US$1	5.75

throughout the country. ATMs are run by a number of different banks and not all are compatible with credit cards issued outside Egypt. In general, those belonging to Banque Misr, Egyptian American Bank, Banque du Caire, the National Bank of Egypt and HSBC will accept Visa and MasterCard and any Cirrus- or Maestro-compatible cards.

Credit Cards

These have become widely accepted in Egypt over recent years, but keep in mind that they usually aren't accepted in budget hotels and restaurants, nor in remote areas such as Siwa and the Western Oases. Visa and MasterCard can be used for cash advances at Banque Misr, the National Bank of Egypt and Thomas Cook offices. To report lost cards in Egypt:

Amex (in Cairo ☎ 02-870 3152)
Diners Club (in Cairo ☎ 02-578 3355)
MasterCard (in Cairo ☎ 02-797 1179, 796 2844)
Visa (in Cairo ☎ 02-796-2877, 797 1149)

Moneychangers

Money can be officially changed at commercial banks, foreign exchange (forex) bureaus and some hotels. Rates don't tend to vary much but forex bureaus generally offer marginally better rates than the banks and they usually don't charge a commission fee.

Look at the money you're given when exchanging and don't accept any badly defaced, shabby or torn notes as you'll have great difficulty off-loading them.

Taxes

Taxes of up to 25% will be added to your bill in most restaurants. There are also hefty taxes levied on upmarket accommodation;

these have been factored into the prices we have quoted.

Tipping & Bargaining

Bargaining is a part of everyday life in Egypt and people haggle for everything from hotel rooms to clothes. There are rare instances where it's not worth wasting your breath (supermarkets, for example), but in any tourist-type shop, even marked prices can be fair game.

Tipping, called baksheesh, is another fact of life in Egypt. Salaries are extremely low and are supplemented by tips. In hotels and restaurants the 12% service charge goes into the till; an additional tip of between 10% and 15% is expected for the waiter. A guard who shows you something off the track at an archaeological site should be given a pound or two.

Travellers Cheques

There is no problem cashing well-known brands of travellers cheques at major banks and at Amex and Thomas Cook offices, but most forex bureaus don't take them. Most banks charge a small commission per cheque plus E£2 or E£3 for stamps. You must have your passport with you.

POST

Postcards cost E£1.15 to post and will take four or five days to get to Europe and around a week to 10 days to the USA and Australia. Letters of 20g cost between E£1.60 and E£2.20 (depending on the destination) and 1kg parcels cost between E£65.40 and E£88.40 to send by surface mail. If you use postboxes, blue is for international airmail, red is for internal mail and green is for internal express mail.

TELEPHONE & FAX
Fax

Fax services are available at the main centrales in the big cities. A one-page fax costs E£7.65 to send.

Mobile Phones

Egypt's mobile-phone network runs on the GSM system.

There are two mobile-phone companies operating in Egypt: **MobiNil** (in Cairo ☎ 02-760 9090; www.mobinil.com) and **Vodafone** (in Cairo ☎ 02-529 2000; www.vodafone.com.eg, www.mobileconnect

.vodafone.com). Both sell convenient prepaid cards from their many retail outlets across the country. MobiNil sells its 'Alo Magic Scratch Card' in denominations of E£10, E£25, E£50, E£100, E£200 and E£300; these have a validity period of 30 days and airtime credit is carried over if you recharge the card before the end of the validity period. Vodafone has a similar card, available to Vodafone customers only, as well as a Mobile Connect card that enables wi-fi connection to the Internet through your laptop.

Phone Cards

Two companies have card phones in Egypt. Menatel has booths that are yellow-and-green, while Nile Tel's are red and blue. Cards are sold at shops and kiosks and come in units of E£10, E£15, E£20 and E£30. Once you insert the card into the telephone, press the flag in the top left corner to get instructions in English.

There are different rates for peak (8am to 8pm Sunday to Thursday) and off-peak (8pm to 8am Sunday to Thursday and all day Friday and Saturday) calls. Rates average E£3 per minute to the USA and Canada (E£2.25 off-peak); E£3.50 per minute to Europe (E£3 off-peak); and E£4.50 per minute to Australasia (E£3 off-peak).

Phone Codes

The country code for Egypt is ☎ 20, followed by the local area code (minus the zero), then the subscriber number. Local area codes are given at the start of each city or town section. The international access code (to call abroad from Egypt) is ☎ 00. For directory assistance call ☎ 140 or ☎ 141.

Telephone Centrales

Alternatively, there are the old telephone offices, known as centrales, where you can book a call at the desk, which must be paid for in advance (there is a three-minute minimum). The operator directs you to a booth when a connection is made.

VISAS

Most foreigners entering Egypt must obtain a visa. The only exceptions are citizens of Guinea, Hong Kong and Macau. There are three ways of doing this: in advance from the Egyptian embassy or consulate in your home country; at an Egyptian embassy abroad; or, for certain nationalities, on arrival at the airport. This last option is the cheapest and easiest of the three.

The processing times and the costs for visa applications vary according to your nationality and the country in which you apply. Visas at the airport are available for nationals of all western European countries, the UK, the USA, Australia, all Arab countries, New Zealand, Japan and Korea. Nationals from other countries must obtain visas in their countries of residence. At Cairo airport the entire process takes only 20 minutes or so and costs US$15 or €15. If you are travelling overland you can get a visa at the port in Aqaba, Jordan, before getting the ferry to Nuweiba, but if you are coming from Israel, you *cannot* get a visa at the border unless you are guaranteed by an Egyptian travel agency. Instead, you have to get the visa beforehand at either the embassy in Tel Aviv or the consulate in Eilat.

A single-entry visa is valid for three months and entitles the holder to stay in Egypt for one month. Multiple-entry visas (for three visits) are also available, but although good for presentation for six months, they still only entitle the bearer to a total of one month in the country.

Sinai Entry Stamps

It is not necessary to get a full visa if your visit is confined to the area of Sinai between Sharm el-Sheikh and Taba (on the Israeli border), including St Katherine's Monastery. Instead you are issued with an entry stamp, free of charge, allowing you a 15-day stay. Note that this does not allow you to visit Ras Mohammed National Park. Points of entry where such visa-free stamps are issued are Taba, Nuweiba (port), St Katherine's (airport) and Sharm el-Sheikh (airport or port).

Travel Permits

Military permits issued by either the Ministry of the Interior or the border police are needed to travel in the Eastern Desert south of Shams Allam (50km south of Marsa Alam), on or around Lake Nasser, off-road in the Western Desert, or on the road between the oases of Bahariyya and Siwa. These can be obtained through a safari company or travel agency at least a fortnight in advance of the trip.

Visa Extensions & Re-entry Visas

Extensions of your tourist visa can easily be obtained. These cost E£11 for an extension of less than six months, E£16 for less than one year and E£46 for one year, and are obtained at passport offices. You'll need one photograph and photocopies of the photo and visa pages of your passport. You have a short period of grace (usually 14 days) to apply for an extension after your visa has expired. If you neglect to do this there's a fine of approximately E£100 and you'll require a letter of apology from your embassy.

If you don't have a multiple-entry visa, it's possible to get a re-entry visa that's valid to the expiry date of your visa and any extensions. Re-entry visas for one/two/several entries cost E£13.10/15.10/16.10.

WOMEN TRAVELLERS

Egypt is a conservative society and a woman's sexuality is, by and large, controlled by her family. Not only are most Western women outside these strictures but, thanks to a steady diet of Western films and soap operas, they are perceived as sexually voracious and available. The comparatively liberal behaviour of some tourists reinforces these prejudices.

As a result, while the country is generally safe for women, hassling is more or less constant. Sometimes it is in the form of hissing or barely audible whispers; usually it is a lewd phrase. Very occasionally there is physical harassment. Rape is rare. Commonsense tips to avoid problems include wearing a wedding ring, dressing conservatively (ie no shorts, tank tops or above-the-knee skirts except in beach resorts), ignoring verbal comments, trying to sit beside women on public transport and avoiding eye-contact with men unless you know them. Take care not to get yourself into a situation of close proximity with men and stay alert in large crowds, particularly at *moulids* (religious festivals).

A couple of useful Arabic phrases for getting rid of unwanted attention are: *la tilmasni* (don't touch me); *ihtirim nafsak* (behave yourself); or *haasib eedak* (watch your hand). Swearing at would-be Romeos will only make matters worse.

EGYPT

TRANSPORT IN EGYPT

GETTING THERE & AWAY
Entering Egypt
If you enter the country via Cairo airport, there are a few formalities. After walking past the dusty-looking duty-free shops you'll come to a row of exchange booths, including a Thomas Cook booth. If you haven't already organised a visa, you'll need to pay US$15 or €15 here to receive a visa stamp. You then fill in one of the pink forms available on the benches in front of the immigration officials before queuing to be processed.

Air
Egypt has a few airports, but only seven are international ports of entry: Cairo, Alexandria, Luxor, Aswan, Hurghada, Sharm el-Sheikh and Marsa Alam. Most air travellers enter Egypt through Cairo, Alexandria or Sharm el-Sheikh. The other airports tend to be used by charter and package-deal flights only.

Egypt's international and national carrier is **EgyptAir** (☎ 0900 70000; ✆ 8am-8pm). Its service isn't particularly good and its fleet is in need of an upgrade. You'll do better flying with a different airline.

Air tickets bought in Egypt are subject to hefty government taxes, which make them extremely expensive. Always try to fly in on a return or onward ticket.

Land
Egypt has land borders with Israel and the Palestinian Territories, Libya and Sudan, but for the latter there is no open crossing point. The only way to travel between Egypt and Sudan is to fly or take the Wadi Halfa ferry (p664).

Note that almost all international bus and ferry tickets must be paid for in US dollars.

DEPARTURE TAX

If you're leaving Egypt by air your departure tax will usually have been prepaid with your ticket. If you're departing by land, you'll need to pay E£2 (travellers who entered Egypt on a Sinai-only visa are exempt).

ISRAEL & THE PALESTINIAN TERRITORIES
There are officially two border crossings with Israel: Rafah and Taba.

Rafah
At the time of research, the Rafah border crossing, which services a direct route from Cairo to Tel Aviv through the Gaza Strip, was closed to individual travellers. Responsibility for policing the border was relinquished by the Israelis after their withdrawal from Gaza in September 2005, and the border is now jointly policed by the Palestinian Authority and the Egyptian government. At the time of research, there were problems with border security. The situation is unsettled and foreigners are unlikely to be able to use the border crossing in the near future.

Taba
This border crossing is used for the vast majority of travel between Egypt and Israel. Travellers make their way to Taba from destinations across Egypt and then walk across the border (open 24 hours) into Israel. Once the border is crossed, taxis or buses can be taken to Eilat (4km from the border), from where there are frequent buses onwards to Jerusalem and Tel Aviv.

Coming from Israel to Egypt, you must have a visa in advance unless your visit is limited to eastern Sinai (p175) or you have prearranged your entry with an Egyptian tour operator. Once you've crossed the border you'll need to pay an Egyptian entry tax of E£30 at a booth about 1km south of the border on the main road.

Vehicles can be brought into Egypt from Eilat; the amount of entry duty depends on the type of vehicle, but averages about E£100.

At the time of research, **Misr Travel** (Map pp98-9; ☎ 02-335 5470; Cairo Sheraton, Midan al-Galaa, Doqqi) and the Israeli travel company **Mazada Tours** (Map p298; ☎ 03-544 4454; www.mazada.co.il; 141 Ibn Gvirol St, Tel Aviv, Israel) were running an express service (US$55, 12 to 14 hours) that left the Cairo Sheraton on Sunday, Monday and Thursday at 9am, travelling via Taba to Tel Aviv and then on to Jerusalem. Contact them for details.

JORDAN
From Cairo, there's a twice-weekly Superjet service to Amman (US$70), leaving Al-

Mazar Garage on Sunday and Thursday at 5am. There is also a daily East Delta Bus Co service to Aqaba (US$41) at 8pm.

From Alexandria, there's one daily Superjet service to Amman (US$72) at 4pm and one service to Aqaba (US$34) at 6pm.

These services use the ferry between Nuweiba and Aqaba, so you will be liable for the port tax.

LIBYA

The border crossing point of Amsaad, just north of the Halfaya Pass, is 12km west of Sallum. The bus from Marsa Matruh costs E£12; a service taxi costs E£15. Service taxis run up the mountain between the town and the Egyptian side of the crossing for E£3 to E£4. Once through passport control and customs on both sides (you walk through), you can get a Libyan service taxi on to Al-Burdi. From there you can get buses on to Tobruk and Benghazi. Note that Libyan visas are not issued at the border.

From Cairo, one Superjet service leaves Al-Mazar Garage for Benghazi (E£140) at 7.30am daily. East Delta Bus Co services also travel to Benghazi (E£114), leaving on Sunday, Tuesday, Wednesday and Friday at 8am. East Delta Bus Co services leave for Tripoli (E£255) on Monday, Wednesday, Thursday and Saturday at 8am.

From Alexandria, there's one daily Superjet service to Benghazi and Tripoli (US$60), leaving at 8.30am.

Sea & Lake

For information on ferries between Egypt and Cyprus, Saudi Arabia or Sudan, see p664.

ISRAEL

There's been talk about resuming the boat service from Port Said to Haifa in Israel; ask **Canal Tours** (in Port Said ☎ 066-332 1874, 012 798 6338; canaltours@bec.com.eg) for the latest information on this.

JORDAN

There's an excellent fast-ferry service between Nuweiba in Egypt and Aqaba in Jordan that leaves Nuweiba at 2pm and only takes one hour. One-way tickets cost US$55 for adults, US$39 for children aged three to 12 years old. You must be at the port at least two hours before departure so as to go

---

> **PORT TAX**
>
> All Egyptian international ferries charge E£50 port tax per person on top of the ticket price.

---

through the shambolic departure formalities in the main ferry terminal building.

Tickets must be paid for in US dollars (note that these are not always available at the banks in Nuweiba) and can be purchased on the day of departure only at the **ticket office** (⊙ 9am), which is in a small sand-coloured building near the port. To find the office turn right when you exit the bus station, walking towards the water, and turn right again after the National Bank of Egypt. Continue one long block, and you'll see the ticket-office building ahead to your left. The office stops selling tickets approximately one hour before the ferry leaves.

There's also a slow ferry (US$41/29 per adult/child, 2½ hours) leaving at noon daily.

No student discounts are available on these ferry services. Note that boats are always full during the haj, and you'll need to purchase your ticket through a travel agency a long way in advance.

Free Jordanian visas can be obtained on the ferry if you have an EU, US, Canadian, Australian or New Zealand passport. Fill out a green form on board, give it and your passport to the immigration officers and – hey presto – your passport and visa are collected when you pass through Jordanian immigration at Aqaba. Other nationalities will need to organise a visa in advance.

GETTING AROUND
Air

EgyptAir (☎ 0900 70000; ⊙ 8am-8pm) is the main domestic carrier. Air Sinai, which to all intents and purposes is EgyptAir by another name, is virtually the only other operator. Fares are expensive and there are no student discounts.

During the high season (October to May), many flights are full so it's wise to book as far in advance as possible.

Bus

Buses service just about every city, town and village in Egypt. Deluxe buses travel between some of the main towns such as Cairo and Alexandria, and around Sinai. These buses are reasonably comfortable, with decent seats, air-con and loud Arabic videos. The best of the deluxe bus companies is Superjet – try to travel with it whenever possible. The bulk of buses servicing other routes are horribly uncomfortable, dirty and noisy. Arabic pop or Quranic dirges are played at ear-splittingly loud levels – it's a good idea to take earplugs.

Often the prices of tickets for buses on the same route will vary according to whether or not they have air-con and video, how old the bus is and how long it takes to make the journey – the more you pay, the more comfort you travel in and the quicker you get there.

Tickets can be bought at the bus stations or often on the bus. Hang on to your ticket until you get off, as inspectors almost always board the bus to check fares. There are no student discounts on bus fares.

Car & Motorcycle

Driving in Cairo is a crazy affair, but in other parts of the country, at least in daylight, it isn't so bad. You should avoid intercity driving at night. Driving is on the right-hand side and you'll need an International Driving Permit. When travelling out of Cairo, remember that petrol stations are not always that plentiful; when you see one, fill up.

The official speed limit outside Cairo is 90km/h and 100km/h on major motorways. If you are caught speeding, your driving licence will be confiscated and you'll have to pick it up (and also pay a fine) at the nearest traffic police station several days later. Roads throughout the country have checkpoints, so make sure you have all of your documents with you, including your passport.

Several car-hire agencies have offices in Egypt. The following are all in Cairo.

Avis (www.avisegypt.com) Airport (☎ 02-291 4288); Nile Hilton (Map pp102-3; ☎ 02-579 2400; Corniche el-Nil, Downtown)

Budget Airport (☎ 02-265 2395); Zamalek (Map p109; ☎ 02-340 0070; 5 Sharia Makrizy)
Hertz (www.hertzegypt.com) Airport (☎ 02-265 2430); Ramses Hilton (Map pp102-3; ☎ 02-575 8914; Corniche el-Nil, Downtown)

Their rates match international charges and finding a cheap deal with local dealers is virtually impossible. You are much better off organising cheap car hire via the Web before you arrive in Egypt. Of the locals, **Max Rent A Car** (in Cairo ☎ 02-303 5630; maxrent@max.com.eg; 22 Sharia el-Kods el-Sherif, Mohandiseen; ☻ 9am-5pm Sun-Thu) has a good reputation. It also has a booth in the arrivals hall at the Taba border crossing.

As a rough guide, rates are around US$50 a day for a small Toyota (100km included, US$0.25 per km after this) to US$90 a day for a Cherokee 4WD (US$0.40 for the extra kilometres). This doesn't include taxes.

Local Transport

Travelling by *servees* is one of the fastest ways to get from city to city. Service taxis are either microbuses or big Peugeot 504 cars that run intercity routes. Drivers congregate near bus and train stations and tout for passengers by shouting their destination. When the car's full, it's off. A driver won't leave before his car is full unless you and/or the other passengers pay for all of the seats.

Train

Although trains travel along more than 5000km of track to almost every major city and town in Egypt, the system is badly in need of modernisation (it's a relic of the British occupation) and most services are grimy and battered and a poor second option to the deluxe buses. The exceptions are some of the trains to Alexandria, and the tourist and sleeping trains down to Luxor and Aswan – on these routes the train is the preferred option rather than the bus.

Students with an ISIC card can get discounts of about 33% on all fares except the sleeping-car services.

Iran

IRAN

You're going to Iran? Why? The misconceptions about Iran are so many and so misleading that the majority of the Western world sees it as a mysterious, dangerous wasteland full of hostile, crazy Arabs. How wrong they are.

Iran is a fascinating mix of modern and ancient, of East and West, of the exotic and the mundane. It's far more developed than you'd imagine, and far less dangerous. And the people are Persians, not Arabs. In fact, spending a few weeks with the Iranian people will probably redefine hospitality as you know it. The key is to open up to the people and just go with it. When someone you've barely met asks you to eat in their home, accept the invitation. You will be in their care, and that care is warmer than you can imagine – and yes, that includes the kindness shown towards Americans.

While the rich and ancient Persian culture will ensure you are treated well, it also provides a stunning architectural and archaeological backdrop. The wonders of Persepolis, Esfahan and Yazd are the big-ticket items, but wandering through labyrinthine bazaars, shopping for carpets and just sitting, sipping tea and chatting with ordinary Iranians are just as memorable. There is also some good trekking and skiing in the northern mountains.

From a practical point of view, Iran is one of the cheapest countries in the Middle East and, despite its size, transport is both cheap and efficient. Getting a visa can be a hassle, which contributes to Iran being relatively undiscovered by travellers – making it all the more worthwhile to visit.

FAST FACTS

- **Area** 1,648,000 sq km
- **Capital** Tehran
- **Country code** ☎ 98
- **Languages** Farsi, Arabic
- **Money** Iranian rial (IR); US$1 = IR8970; €1 = IR10,980
- **Official name** Islamic Republic of Iran
- **Population** 72 million

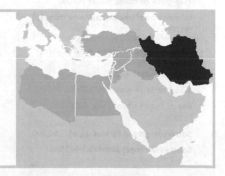

HIGHLIGHTS

- **Esfahan** (p211) The most beautiful city in Iran, set around the stunning Imam Khomeini Sq and its exquisite Safavid mosques.
- **Persepolis** (p225) Built by Darius the Great, destroyed by Alexander the Great – the artistry of the ancient Persians in all its monumental glory.
- **Yazd** (p217) A forest of tall, brown wind towers dotted with atmospheric hotels and restaurants.
- **Masuleh** (p204) A gorgeous stepped mountain village where you can sleep over with the locals.
- **Garmeh** (p217) Classic desert oasis, far off the beaten track.

CLIMATE & WHEN TO GO

Iran is hot and dry in summer and cold and dry in winter. In the desert and along the Gulf coast, summer (June to August) temperatures regularly top 40°C and the humidity is draining. In midwinter (December to February), places such as Tehran, Mashhad and Tabriz are quite cold and snow is common in the higher regions, particularly the northwest. However, the rest of the country is usually quite pleasant – clear skies and about 15°C during the day.

The best times to visit Iran are mid-April to early June, and late September to early November. Winter is definitely the best time to visit the southern coast and the Gulf islands. Some prefer not to visit during Ramazan (Ramadan), though it won't affect your travels too much. For about 10 days either side of No Ruz (Iranian New Year, March 21), transport and accommodation are at a premium – book ahead if possible.

HISTORY

The Achaemenids & the First Persian Empire

In 550 BC 29-year-old Cyrus the Great defeated the Medians and within a century he and his successors, Darius I and Xerxes, had made the Achaemenid empire (550–331 BC) into the greatest the world had seen. The Persians expanded their rule all the way to India in the east and the Aegean Sea in the west, but Xerxes' defeat by the Greeks at Marathon began a slow decline. The end came in 330 BC when Alexander the Great invaded Persia and sacked the greatest of all Achaemenid monuments, Persepolis.

After Alexander's death his empire split, with Persia being controlled by the Macedonian Seleucids who gradually introduced a Hellenistic culture. The Parthians, under King Mithridates, took over in the 2nd century BC and in turn were replaced by the Sassanids, a local dynasty from the Fars province. The Sassanids ruled from AD 224 to AD 638 but suffered continuing conflict with the Roman and, later, the Byzantine Empires.

Islam & Other Arrivals

Weakened by this scrapping, the Persians, whose religion was Zoroastrianism, fell easy prey to the spread of Islam and the Arabs (see p40). Persia was controlled by an assortment of rulers before the Turkish Seljuk dynasty established itself in the 11th century, heralding a new era of Persian art, literature and science marked by such thinkers as the mathematician-poet Omar Khayyam. The Seljuk era ended abruptly in 1194 when Genghis Khan's Mongol hordes swept into Persia devastating all before them. At the end of the 14th century the Mongols' crumbling Ilkhanid dynasty were themselves routed, this time by bloodthirsty Tamerlane after he rode in from the east.

HOW MUCH?

- **Internet connection (one hour)** IR10,000
- **Short taxi ride** IR5000
- **Museum admission** IR4000
- **Two-pack of toilet paper** IR7000
- **International phone call (one minute)** IR1700

LONELY PLANET INDEX

- **Litre of petrol** IR800
- **1.5L bottle of water** IR2500
- **Pot of tea in a teahouse** IR4000 to IR6000
- **Souvenir qalyan (water pipe)** IR60,000
- **Sausis (sausage) sandwich** IR3500

IRAN

IRAN

From Safavids to Pahlavis

Beginning in 1502, the Safavid era heralded a great Persian renaissance. Under the rule of Shah Abbas I (1587–1629) foreign influences were purged from the country, and architectural works such as those in Imam Sq (p213) in Esfahan have left a permanent reminder. The Safavid decline was hastened by an invasion from Afghanistan in 1722. A few years later Nader Shah, a tribal leader from the northeast, threw out the Afghans and went on to antagonize Persia's neighbours until he was assassinated in 1747.

The brief Zand period, in which Karim Khan-e Zand ruled from Shiraz, was followed by a longer period of decline under the corrupt and incompetent Qajar rulers (1779–1925). It ended in 1925 when Reza Khan Pahlavi, an officer in the imperial army, founded the Pahlavi dynasty. Foreign influence – and oil – soon became an important element in Iran's story. During WWII, Iran was officially neutral, but Reza Khan was exiled to South Africa because he was thought to be too friendly with the Axis powers. His 22-year-old son, Mohammed Reza, succeeded him. The government of Shah Mohammed Reza was repressive, but Iran was rapidly modernised. Illiteracy was reduced, women emancipated, land holdings redistributed, health services improved and a major industrialisation programme embarked upon.

The Islamic Revolution

Since the early days of the Pahlavi era there had been a smouldering resistance that occasionally flared into violence. Students wanted faster reform, devout Muslims wanted reforms rolled back, and everybody attacked the Pahlavis' conspicuous consumption. As the economy deteriorated following the 1970s oil-price spike the growing opposition made its presence felt with sabotage and massive street demonstrations. The shah introduced martial law, and hundreds of demonstrators were killed in street battles in Tehran before the shah fled in January 1979. He died a year later.

Exiled cleric Ayatollah Ruhollah Khomeini returned on 1 February 1979 and was greeted by adoring millions. His fiery brew of nationalism and fundamentalism had been at the forefront of the revolt, and he achieved his goal of establishing a clergy-dominated Islamic Republic (the first true Islamic state in modern times) with brutal efficiency. Opposition disappeared, executions took place after meaningless trials and minor officials took the law into their own hands.

In 1980 Saddam Hussein, looking to take advantage of the postrevolutionary chaos, invaded Khuzestan, in southwest Iran, on the pretext that the oil-rich province was historically part of Iraq. The resulting war lasted until 1988 and claimed hundreds of thousands of lives as trench warfare and poison gas were used for the first time since WWI.

Iran Today

Khomeini died in 1989, leaving an uncertain legacy to the country he had dominated for a decade. Ayatollah Ali Khamenei succeeded him as Iran's Supreme Leader, but inherited little of his predecessor's popular appeal.

In 1997 moderate cleric Mohammed Khatami was elected president by a huge majority, most voters hoping he could liberalise some of the social restrictions of the Islamic Republic. Virtually overnight Iran became a different, far more liberal place, and in 2000 the reform movement won a sizable majority in the Majlis (parliament). However, while the religious police disappeared and couples could be seen courting openly, the public wanted more. The reformers were keen to deliver, but about a third of all the legislation passed during their 2000 to 2004 term was subsequently vetoed by the Guardians Council, a hardline body appointed by Ayatollah Khamenei.

People began to feel that the reformers were impotent and during the 2004 Majlis elections many voters stayed away. The result was a conservative victory and Khatami served his last 16 months as virtually a lame-duck president. The 2005 presidential election shocked not only the world, but many Iranians too. Outsider Mahmoud Ahmadinejad, the hardline mayor of Tehran, came out of the blue to win a clear majority from voters interested as much in rejecting what was perceived as a network

---

MOHAMMAD MOSSADEGH & THE CIA'S FIRST COUP

Iranian prime minister Mohammad Mossadegh was the first democratically elected leader toppled by a CIA coup. Mossadegh, a highly educated lawyer, paid the price for seeking a better deal for Iran from the hugely profitable oilfields run by the Anglo-Iranian Oil Company. When the British refused, he nationalised the company and expelled British diplomats whom he rightly suspected of plotting to overthrow him.

The British were desperate to get 'their' oil back. They encouraged a worldwide boycott of Iranian oil and worked hard to muddy Mossadegh's name both at home and abroad. Eventually, Winston Churchill managed to persuade the new Eisenhower administration that Mossadegh had to go. The CIA's Operation Ajax was the result. Kermit Roosevelt, grandson of Theodore Roosevelt and one of the agency's top operatives, established a team in the basement of the US embassy in Tehran (p193) and soon won the shah's support. As much as US$2 million was spent buying support from senior clerics, military officers, newspaper editors and thugs.

At first it seemed the operation had failed when Mossadegh loyalists arrested the coup leaders on 16 August 1953. The shah fled to Rome, but three days later Roosevelt engineered a second, ultimately successful, attempt. The shah returned and the oil industry was denationalised, but the British monopoly was broken and the US now held a 40% stake.

The 96-page CIA history of the coup can be viewed at www.payk.net.

of political elites as a vote to turn back reforms. Economic progress and a reduction in the high unemployment rates are what most Iranians now want.

Meanwhile Iran's relationship with the USA has retreated from the relative warmth generated during their collaboration to rid Afghanistan of the Taliban to mutual sabre-rattling over Iran's seemingly inevitable pursuit of nuclear power, weapons, or both, depending on who you believe. As unpredictable as Iranian politics can be, it seems a fairly safe bet Iran will remain a member of the USA's 'Axis of Evil' for some time to come.

THE CULTURE
The National Psyche
The one newspaper headline you won't read about Iran is 'Iranians Redefine Hospitality!'. But for the vast majority of Iranians that's the truth. They are deeply curious about foreigners, their welcome is warm and even the most religiously conservative are generous hosts. Through long experience, they are adept at differentiating the actions of governments from those of individuals; Americans are at least as welcome as anyone else. Iranians take their role as hosts very seriously, and ta'arof (right) notwithstanding, their generosity is usually genuine.

Throughout their history, Iranians have managed to maintain their own culture by subtly assimilating those of the many foreign invaders who have come and gone. Iranians are proud of their Aryan roots and hate being classed as Arabs.

The Iranian way is to bend to the prevailing wind only to spring back in time with regained poise. Ever-changing fortunes have also taught Iranians to be indirect people, unwilling to answer with a bald negative and unable to countenance rudeness or public displays of anger.

Daily Life
Family is at the heart of Iranian life, providing an essential support unit in a country with no state benefit system and sometimes trying social conditions. On weekends you'll see the typical multigenerational Iranian family out together, walking, laughing and picnicking in the countryside and parks.

The majority of Iran's urban dwellers live in flats. As population has grown land prices

---

TA'AROF

Ta'arof is a system of formalised politeness that might seem to have people say or offer something merely out of politeness. In reality, ta'arof gives everyone the chance to be on equal terms. For example, an offer of food will be turned down several times first, giving the person making the offer the chance to save face if in reality they don't have the ability to provide a meal. A good rule is to refuse any offer three times but, if they continue to insist, do accept.

However, when a taxi driver or shopkeeper refuses payment, do remember that this is just ta'arof and insist on paying: your rials will soon be accepted.

---

have risen, and in Tehran the monthly rent for a two bedroom flat is about US$450. Compare that with the US$120 a midranking civil servant earns each month, and you begin to understand why almost all single people and many young couples still live with their parents.

There is a small but conspicuous wealthy class in larger cities – in northern Tehran some of the homes are palatial. In contrast, a typical middle-class couple lives in a modest apartment and both partners work. Small children are looked after by grandparents and evening meals are often eaten with the wider family. In poorer or more traditional families women often stay at home, spending much of the day preparing meals.

Education is highly regarded and literacy is well above average for the region at around 80%. University places are scarce, however, and competition is fierce. More than 60% of university students are women.

Meeting members of the opposite sex is difficult and Iranians have become masters of the art of flirting. You'll see the flirtatious young in shopping malls and parks or cruising in cars, and Internet cafés are packed with expectant youngsters on messenger services.

Population
Iran's population is around 72 million – and rising fast. More than 60% of inhabitants can be classified as Persians, descendants of the Aryans who first settled in the central plateau of Iran in about 2000 BC. About 25% of the population are Azerbaijanis, who live in the

northwesternmost region of Iran. Turkmen (2%) are a fierce race of horse people and warriors who inhabit Iran's far northeast.

Other inhabitants include: the Lors (2%) – thought to be part Persian, part Arab – a seminomadic people who live in the western mountains south of Kermanshah; Kurds (5%) who mostly inhabit the western mountains between Orumiyeh and Kermanshah; and Arabs (4%) who mostly live on the south coast and Gulf islands, and in Khuzestan.

More than 300,000 nomads still roam the plains and mountains. The Baluchis are seminomadic and inhabit Baluchestan, a formerly semi-autonomous territory now divided between Iran and Pakistan. The Qashghars of southwest Iran are traditionally wandering herders.

RELIGION

Iran is the only Shiite Muslim regime on earth, with official figures saying about 89% of the population is Shiite. About 10% is Sunni, made up of Kurds, Baluchis, Turkmen and about half the Arabs. For more on Islam, see p53. The other 1% comprises Christians, Jews and Zoroastrians, though these numbers might well be higher as many followers of minority faiths call themselves Muslims in official documents.

Most Iranian Christians are Armenians, predominantly members of the Gregorian Church; the rest are mainly Assyrians. Iran is a centre of Zoroastrianism, and followers are found mainly in Yazd, Tehran and Kerman. Freedom of worship is guaranteed in the constitution, but the 300,000 or so Baha'is are routinely persecuted and discriminated against; the religion is not recognised by the Iranian authorities.

ARTS

Most Iranian artforms predate the Arab conquest but, since nearly all of them reached their peak within the Islamic era, religious influences are rarely completely absent.

Architecture

Iran's most obvious art form is architecture, and it is often regarded as the field in which Persia made its greatest contribution to world culture. Iranian architecture has influenced building throughout much of the Islamic world, especially in Central Asia, Afghanistan, Pakistan and India. Most of the greatest buildings were built for a religious purpose and marvelling at mosques such as the Imam Mosque (p213) in Esfahan will be among the highlights of your trip.

Music

Traditional Persian music is poetry set to music. The instruments used include the *tar,* similar to the Indian sitar; the *dahol* and *zarb* drums; and the *daf* and *daryereh,* outsized tambourines. Ethnic minorities are responsible for the most appealing traditional music, and the distinctive Kurdish rhythms have gained some recognition through the success of The Kamkars.

Pop and rock are slowly emerging despite being less than encouraged. Popular pop artists include Shadmehr Aghili and clarinet-playing Farhad, while Arian are the first mixed band to be allowed to play publicly; women are banned from performing for men. For rock, underground band O-Hum is one of the most popular.

While pirated music is everywhere, the government is slowly approving the legal release of cutting-edge Western artists like…Queen, Elton John and the hugely popular Gypsy Kings.

Literature

All over Iran you're likely to encounter four of its greatest poets: Ferdosi, Hafez, Omar Khayyam and Sa'di. Street names and statues abound, and their mausoleums are among the most-visited places in the country.

More contemporary literature is relatively easily accessible in the West.

Paper (2005), by Bahiyyih Nakhjavani, has been described as one of the most exquisitely written books in years, full of imagery weaving together the story of a 19th-century scribe.

Reading Lolita in Tehran (2003), by Azar Nafisi, analyses life in Iran through the banned books she and her students read in an underground book club. It's a bit dated now, but worth it.

Persepolis: The Story of a Childhood (2003), by Marjane Satrapi, is not traditional literature, but it is very readable. It's a funny, moving, Art Spiegelman–style graphic autobiography of growing up in Iran in the '80s. It was so popular that *Persepolis 2: The Story of a Return* (2005) has also been published. Highly recommended!

See p242 for books about Iran by non-Iranian authors.

Cinema

Iranian film makers are hugely popular in the Western art-house scene, though you're unlikely to see much of their work while in Iran, where locally made action films and dubbed Bollywood are the most popular flicks. However, seeing some Iranian films before you leave home is a great way to get in touch with the country. Some worth looking for include: *10* by Abbas Kiarostami, *Time For Love*, *Kandahar* or *Gabbeh* by Mohsen Makhmalbaf; *Blackboards* or *Apple* by his daughter Samira Makhmalbaf; *Children of Heaven* or *The Willow Tree* by Majid Majidi; or *The Lizard* (Marmulak) by Kamal Tabrizi. Check out the **Iranian Film Society** (www.irfilms.com) for the latest releases.

ENVIRONMENT
The Land

Iran covers 1,648,195 sq km, with the two great deserts, Dasht-e Kavir and Dasht-e Lut, occupying most of the northeast and east of the central plain. There are three dominant mountain ranges: the volcanic Sabalan and Talesh ranges in the northwest; the vast, ancient and virtually inourmountable Zagros range in the central west; and the Alborz range, which skirts the Caspian Sea and is home to Iran's highest peak, Mt Damavand (5671m; p198).

Most Iranian rivers drain into the Gulf, the Caspian Sea, or one of a number of salty and swampy lakes, such as Orumiyeh, Iran's largest lake.

Wildlife

Iran is not blessed with an enormous amount of wildlife and that which is especially notable, such as the Asiatic cheetah (www.iraniancheetah.org), is often on the endangered list. National parks are rarely set up for visitors, so few visit Iran solely to look at flora and fauna.

Environmental Issues

Air pollution is the biggest of Iran's environmental problems. All cities suffer to a certain degree, and in Tehran it has reached crisis point. More than 70% of it comes from frighteningly inefficient vehicles. A culture of waste, which has developed because petrol and gas are virtually free, doesn't help. With the population growing so quickly, the energy and pollution issues (if not the desire for weapons) are at the heart of Iran's push for nuclear fuel. Dozens of dams are also being built.

Unrestrained urban and industrial development (look for it on the road skirting the Caspian Sea), deforestation, erosion and overgrazing are also evident.

FOOD & DRINK
Food

Iranian food varies considerably from the Middle Eastern norm, but you'll soon discover that the main dish on most menus is kebabs. This lack of variety can be tiresome, but it's an extra reason to say 'yes' if you're invited to eat in someone's home, a real Iranian experience – invitations flow freely.

Almost every meal in Iran is accompanied by *nun* (bread) or *berenj* (rice) or both. *Nun* is dirt cheap and comes in four main varieties: thin *lavash* is great fresh but quickly turns cardboardy; crisp, salty *barbari* is more like Turkish bread; wonderful *sangak* is long, thick and baked on a bed of stones; and *taftun* is crisp with a ribbed surface. Boiled rice is called *chelow*, and dishes include *chelow zereshk* (chicken and rice) and the ubiquitous *chelow kebab*.

A standard Iranian meal starts with a prefabricated green salad, radioactive-pink dressing and soup (*sup*), usually pearl barley. It's often served with kebab, though unlike the greasy doner kebabs so often inhaled after alcohol in the West, Iranian kebabs are tasty, healthy and cooked over hot charcoals. The cheapest, standard version is *kubide* (ground) kebab, made of minced meat. *Makhsus* (special) kebabs use better quality lamb, *kabab-e barg* (literally, 'leaf kebab') is thinner and more variable in quality, *fille kabab* uses lamb fillet while *juje kabab* are chunks of marinated chicken. Kebabs are usually sprinkled with spicy *somaq* (sumach) and accompanied by raw onion and, for a small extra fee, a bowl of delicious *mast* (yogurt).

If you're sick of kebab, keep an eye out for *zereshk polo ba morq* (chicken on rice made tangy with barberry fruit), *ghorme sabzi* (stewed beans, greens and mince); *khoresht* (any kind of meaty stew with vegetables); *bademjun* (aubergine served in various styles); and the divine *fesenjun* (a sauce of pomegranate juice, walnuts, aubergine and cardamom served over roast chicken, duck or goose). In Western Iran *chelow mahi* (fried fish on rice) is quite common in season. Many teahouses specialise in the underrated *dizi* (or *abgusht*), a cheap and delicious soup-stew combination that involves an age-old eating process.

Fast food is widely available, and usually consists of felafel, sausage or hamburger meat loaded into a fresh roll and topped with tomato and pickles – usually about IR3500 to IR5000 with a soft drink. Pizza (IR13,000 to IR20,000) is also common, though usually not very good.

Sweets are an important Iranian institution. Most cities or provinces have their own particular type of sweet, usually available from shops in the bazaar. Probably the best known is *gaz*, a type of nougat with pistachio, from Esfahan. In Shiraz try *koloche masqati*, a combination biscuit and jelly sweet; in Kerman and Bam *kolompeh* (date cookies) are unbeatable; in Qom you can't miss the tins of *sohun,* a delicious pistachio brittle.

VEGETARIANS
Vegetarianism as a concept is foreign to most Iranians. Solace can be found in the felafels, samosas and potatoes sold in street stalls, and in the wonderful *mirza ghasemi* (mashed aubergine, squash, garlic and egg); the various *kuku* dishes – thick omelettes with mixed herbs, aubergine or cauliflower; and the common *ash* (a filling thick soup).

Self-catering is also an option: nuts, fruits, and vegetables such as cucumbers, tomatoes and pickles are commonly available and cheap.

Drinks
Drinking in Iran inevitably involves *chay* (tea). According to the rules of Iranian hospitality, a host is honour-bound to offer a guest at least one cup of tea, and the guest is expected to drink it. It is customary to dip the sugar provided into the tea, place the cube between the front teeth and suck the brew through it. Iranian coffee is often called 'Turkish coffee' – it's thick and black. However, Nescafé is more common.

Delicious fresh fruit juices and shakes (about IR4000) are found in shopfronts festooned with oranges, bananas, carrots, pomegranates…and electric blenders.

Sour-tasting but refreshing *dugh* is made of churned sour milk or yogurt, mixed with either sparkling or still water and is often served with meals. Tap water is usually drinkable and bottled water is widely available. Soft drinks come as standard with most Iranian meals.

Alcohol is strictly prohibited and officially unavailable in Iran, so forget about a glass of Shiraz in Shiraz. Iranian beer, often labelled as 'nonalcoholic malt beverage', tastes more like cider; it's best not to think of it as beer.

TEHRAN   تهران

☎ 021 / pop 14 million

Tehran is the social and economic heart of Iran and it is here that change begins and ends in the Islamic Republic. It's a fascinating place to feel and see the transformations unfold. It also has the country's finest museums and restaurants, a good range of hotels and it's an easy day trip into the Alborz Mountains from here.

The downsides are terrible pollution, chronic overcrowding and a lack of any responsible planning, so don't expect an exotic crossroads steeped in Oriental splendour.

Give the capital a chance – at least a couple of days spent exploring Tehran is an essential part of the Iranian experience.

HISTORY
In the 13th century writer Yaqoot Hamavi described Tehran as a village of Rey, then the major centre in the region, where 'rebellious inhabitants' lived in underground dwellings. The Safavid kings helped develop Tehran through the 16th and 17th centuries and it became famous for its enchanting vineyards and gardens. Tehran's real expansion began in 1795, when newly victorious Qajar shah Agha Mohammed Khan declared this dusty town of around 15,000 souls his capital. In the past 100 years or so Tehran has grown into the megalopolis you see today. It was the setting for the CIA's first coup in 1953 (see p182) and pronouncements from Tehran have been the driving force behind the growth of radical Islam since 1979.

Today it is fascinating to walk in the footsteps of that modern history; you can see the White Palace, where the last shah hosted the CIA's Kermit Roosevelt as they plotted the overthrow of Prime Minister Moham-mad Mossadegh; gaze up at the Azadi Monument, where hundreds of thousands of people gathered to mark the 1979 revolution; or visit the haunting Behesht-e Zahra cemetery (p198), resting place of thousands of dead from the Iran-Iraq War.

ORIENTATION

Tehran is vast and, with its maze of freeways, can be confusing. But take comfort in knowing that most of the streets you'll use have English signs and follow a rough north–south grid – the Alborz Mountains are in the north. Tehran's Metro is growing and, combined with countless shared taxis, makes getting around relatively simple. If you're using public transport, get to know the names and locations of the main squares (vital for shared-taxi navigation).

South Tehran is cheaper, more congested and generally less appealing than the wealthy north. However, it is home to many of the sights, good transport links and all the budget hotels. The north is more inviting, more expensive, has cleaner air and better hotels and restaurants.

If you're flying in, see p197. Travellers arriving by bus will be dropped at one of four bus stations: most will come to the western bus station or the southern bus station, near the train station; fewer to the Arzhantin station in the city centre or the eastern bus station. At the time of writing only the southern bus station connected to the Tehran Metro; elsewhere you're best taking a taxi.

Maps

If you're staying a while, the **Gita Shenasi Map shop** (☎ 6670 9335; www.gitashenasi.com; 15 Ostad Shahrivar St, Razi St, Valiasr Crossroads, Enqelab Ave) has several maps of Tehran.

INFORMATION
Bookshops

Book City Hafez Store (Map pp190-1; ☎ 8880 5733; www.ourbooksite.com; 743 Hafez St) The biggest store of the best chain of bookstores.
Jahanelm Institute (Map pp190-1; ☎ 6695 0324; Enqelab Ave) Huge range of foreign magazines. It's below qround level in a large arcade.

Emergency

Ambulance (☎ 115)
Fire brigade (☎ 125)
Iran Emdad (☎ 643 6662) Private ambulance service.
Police (☎ 110)

Internet Access

Internet cafés (coffeenets) open and close at a remarkable rate in Tehran. There are many more in northern Tehran, around Valiasr and Vanak Sqs in particular.
Ferdosi Coffeenet (Map pp190-1; ☎ 6673 0499; 1st fl, Ferdosi Sq, Enqelab Ave; per hr IR8000; ◷ 9am-10pm)
Gad Internet (Map pp190-1; ☎ 6648 9004; Valiasr Sq; per hr IR8000; ◷ 10am-10pm) One of several in the Iranian Shopping Centre.

TEHRAN IN...

Two Days
Start early in the **Tehran Bazar** (p192) watching the hustling, bustling and haggling of the country's biggest market. Stop in the **Imam Khomeini Mosque** (p192) at prayer-time for a taste of Islam in action, then head over to Park-e Shahr for some headspace and lunch at the **Sofre Khane Sonnati Sangalag** (p195). Spend the afternoon in the **National Museum of Iran** (p192), then wander down Khayyam St to the **Iranian Traditional Restaurant** (p194) for a traditional meal. On day two check out the **Golestan Palace** (p192) then, after a coffee with the paper in **Café Naderi** (p195), head down for the 2pm viewing of the **National Jewels Museum** (p192). Round the day out with some alternative cuisine in northern Tehran.

Four Days
Follow the two-day plan, then head north to check out the **S'ad Abad Museum Complex** (p193) and for a hike around the trails of **Darband** (p198). Duck across to **Park-e Jamshidiyeh** (p194) for an ethnic dinner and spectacular views of Tehran by night. Use your last day to take in the relaxed **Tehran Museum of Contemporary Art** (p193) before chilling out in the cafés of northern Tehran and feasting at **Monsoon** (p195).

TEHRAN

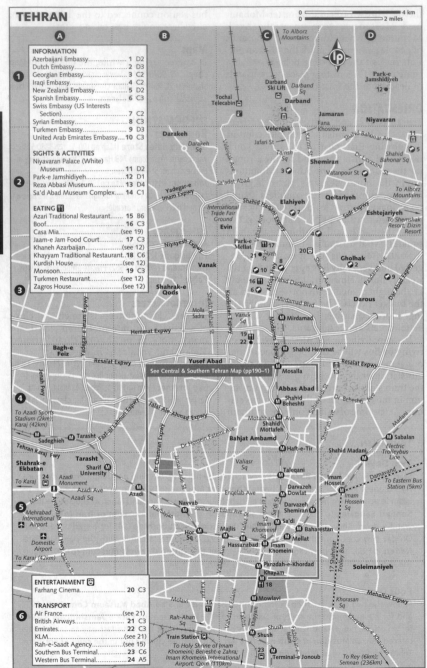

0 — 4 km
0 — 2 miles

INFORMATION
Azerbaijani Embassy.................... 1 D2
Dutch Embassy............................ 2 D3
Georgian Embassy....................... 3 C2
Iraqi Embassy.............................. 4 C2
New Zealand Embassy................. 5 D2
Spanish Embassy......................... 6 C3
Swiss Embassy (US Interests
   Section)................................... 7 C2
Syrian Embassy........................... 8 C3
Turkmen Embassy....................... 9 D3
United Arab Emirates Embassy... 10 C3

SIGHTS & ACTIVITIES
Niyavaran Palace (White)
   Museum................................. 11 D2
Park-e Jamshidiyeh..................... 12 D1
Reza Abbasi Museum................... 13 D4
Sa'd Abad Museum Complex..... 14 C1

EATING 🍴
Azari Traditional Restaurant...... 15 B6
Boof.. 16 C3
Casa Mia................................(see 19)
Jaam-e Jam Food Court.............. 17 C3
Khaneh Azarbaijan..................(see 12)
Khayyam Traditional Restaurant.18 C6
Kurdish House..........................(see 12)
Monsoon................................... 19 C3
Turkmen Restaurant................(see 12)
Zagros House..........................(see 12)

ENTERTAINMENT 🎭
Farhang Cinema.......................... 20 C3

TRANSPORT
Air France..............................(see 21)
British Airways.......................... 21 C3
Emirates.................................... 22 C3
KLM.......................................(see 21)
Rah-e-Saadt Agency................(see 15)
Southern Bus Terminal.............. 23 C6
Western Bus Terminal............... 24 A5

Pars Internet (Map pp190-1; ☎ 3392 4173; 369 Ferdosi St; per hr IR9000; ◷ 9am-9pm) Can burn photos to CD, has webcams, headphones and international calls at about IR900 per minute.

Sepanta Internet (Map pp190-1; ☎ 6676 0418; Sl Tir St; per hr IR2000; ◷ 9am-9pm) Slowish but cheap.

Medical Services

The quality of medical care is reasonably high in Tehran. For 24-hour pharmacies, get your hotel to phone the **pharmacy line** (☎ 191). The following are accessible, clean and reputable hospitals:

Arad Hospital (Map pp190-1; ☎ 7760 1001; Somayyeh St) Between Shari'ati Ave and Bahar St.

Day Hospital (Map pp190-1; ☎ 8801 7111; cnr Valiasr Ave & Tavanir St)

Tehran Clinic (Map pp190-1; ☎ 8872 8113; Farahani St)

Money

The airport bank has fair rates. Banks along Ferdosi St and around Ferdosi Sq change cash but won't touch travellers cheques or credit cards (see p246). **Bank Melli** (Map pp190-1; Central Branch; Ferdosi St) is the best bank.

It's much quicker to use the exchange shops (or, if you count your money carefully, the freelance moneychangers waving wads of rials) along Ferdosi St.

Post

Main post office (Map pp190-1; Sa'di St) Southeast of Imam Khomeini Sq.

Telephone

Phone cards are available from newsstands. Independent telephone offices are often found near the major squares, including the **telephone office** (Map pp190-1; Ferdosi St, Imam Khomeini Sq; ◷ 7.30am-10pm). Internet calls are cheaper.

Tourist Information

Iran Touring & Tourism Organisation (Map pp190-1; ITTO; ☎ 8896 7065; 154 Keshavarz Blvd) More tour operator than information office. Has a few brochures.

Travel Agencies

Nejatollahi St in central Tehran is packed with agencies selling flight and train tickets, including the following:

Asia2000 Travel Agency (Map pp190-1; ☎ 8889 6947-58; asia2000@sanapardaz.com; Nejatollahi St)

Taban Travel & Tourism (Map pp190-1; ☎ 3395 5660-61; Sarcheshmeh Cross, Amir Kabir St; taban@sanapardaz.com)

> ### NEW NUMBERS
>
> In mid-2005 most Tehran phone numbers expanded from seven to eight digits. All numbers, except those beginning with 5 or 9, grew by repeating the first digit. For example, 123 4567 became 1123 4567. Numbers in this guide were accurate at the time of publication, but if you come across a seven-digit Tehrani number, you'll know what to do.

Visa Extensions

If at all possible, *do not* get your visa extended in Tehran. If it's unavoidable, go to the **Disciplinary Force for Islamic Republic of Iran Department for Aliens Affairs** (Map pp190-1; ☎ 8880 0000; Valiasr Ave; ◷ 7.45am-1.30pm Sat-Wed, 7.45am-noon Thu); yes, it's as bad as it sounds. The nominated **Bank Melli** (Map pp190-1; Valiasr Ave) is about 300m south.

DANGERS & ANNOYANCES

The traffic in Tehran can be both dangerous and annoying. The sheer volume of traffic makes crossing the street seem like a game of Russian roulette. Take some comfort, however, in knowing that, despite most drivers having no regard for little things like road rules, they're actually pretty good at steering their cars and it's too much paperwork to run you over. As a pedestrian, until you get used to it, the best way to safely cross the street is to wait for one or two other roadcrossers to appear and put them between you and the oncoming traffic. And be aware of the contra-flow bus lanes, running the wrong way along one-way streets.

Tehran is one of the most polluted cities on earth. When pollution levels reach crisis point – usually during summer – head north to the hills of Darband or Park-e Jamshidiyeh.

As far as crime is concerned, very few travellers report any problems but those who do have usually been stung in the bogus police scam (p243).

SIGHTS

Tehran doesn't have much to show for its history, but there are some good museums and the various Qajar and Pahlavi-era palaces are worth a look. The following sights begin with the Tehran Bazar in the south and head north from there. If you're pushed

IRAN

CENTRAL & SOUTHERN TEHRAN

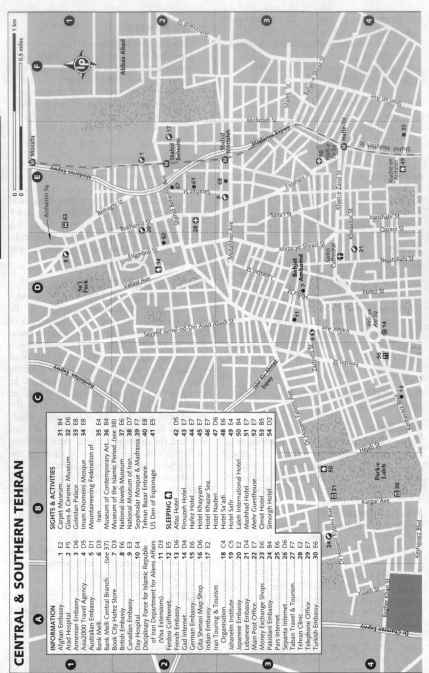

INFORMATION
Afghan Embassy	1 E2
Arad Hospital	2 F5
Armenian Embassy	3 D6
Asia2000 Travel Agency	4 D5
Australian Embassy	5 D1
Bank Melli	6 D3
Bank Melli Central Branch	(see 37)
Book City Hafez Store	7 D3
British Embassy	8 E6
Canadian Embassy	9 E3
Day Hospital	10 E4
Disciplinary Force for Islamic Republic	
of Iran Department for Aliens Affairs	
(Visa Extensions)	11 D3
Ferdosi Coffeenet	12 E5
French Embassy	13 D6
Gad Internet	14 D4
German Embassy	15 E6
Gita Shenasi Map Shop	16 D3
Indian Embassy	17 E2
Iran Touring & Tourism	
Organisation	18 C4
Jahanelm Institute	19 C5
Japanese Embassy	20 E2
Lebanese Embassy	21 D4
Main Post Office	22 E7
Money Exchange Shops	23 E6
Pakistani Embassy	24 B4
Pars Internet	25 E6
Sepanta Internet	26 D6
Taban Travel & Tourism	27 F7
Tehran Clinic	28 E2
Telephone Office	29 E7
Turkish Embassy	30 E6

SIGHTS & ACTIVITIES
Carpet Museum	31 B4
Glass & Ceramic Museum	32 D6
Golestan Palace	33 E8
Imam Khomeini Mosque	34 E8
Mountaineering Federation of	
Iran	35 E4
Museum of Contemporary Art	36 B4
Museum of the Islamic Period	(see 38)
National Jewels Museum	37 E6
National Museum of Iran	38 D7
Sepahsalar Mosque & Madrassa	39 F7
Tehran Bazar Entrance	40 E8
US Den of Espionage	41 E5

SLEEPING
Atlas Hotel	42 D5
Firouzeh Hotel	43 E7
Hafez Hotel	44 E7
Hotel Khayyam	45 E7
Hotel Khazar Sea	46 E7
Hotel Naderi	47 D6
Hotel Sa'adi	48 E6
Hotel Safir	49 E4
Laleh International Hotel	50 B4
Mashhad Hotel	51 E7
Mehr Guesthouse	52 E7
Omid Hotel	53 B5
Simorgh Hotel	54 D2

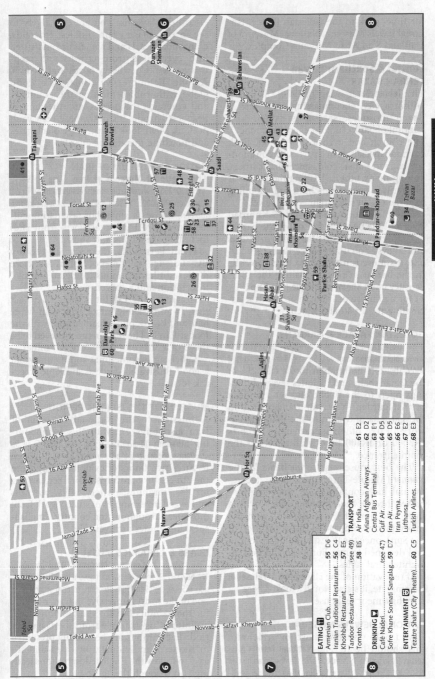

IRAN

for time, stick to the Golestan Palace, National Jewels Museum, National Museum of Iran and S'ad Abad Museum Complex.

Central & Southern Tehran

TEHRAN BAZAR

The **Tehran Bazar** (Map pp190-1) is a city within a city, encompassing more than a dozen mosques, several guesthouses, a handful of banks (not for changing money), one church and even a fire station. Each corridor specialises in a particular commodity: copper, paper, gold, spices and carpets, among many others. Visiting the bazaar is primarily a people-watching and shopping experience – it's no architectural jewel.

The main entrance is from 15 Khordad Ave, and the best way to explore the bazaar is simply to wander its labyrinth of streets and alleys. You'll almost certainly get lost and it's more fun to just go with it. While in the bazaar, it's worth visiting the 18th-century **Imam Khomeini Mosque** (Map pp190–1) for a glimpse of Islam in action. It's fascinating to just sit and watch.

GOLESTAN PALACE & GARDENS

The **Golestan Palace** (Map pp190-1; ☎ 3311 8335; www.golestanpalace.org; Ark Sq; ⏰ 9am-3pm, closed Sun & Thu) is a monument to the excesses of the Qajar shahs and includes several buildings open to the public and set around a formal garden. You can wander around the gardens and admire the painted tilework for free, otherwise each museum costs IR3000 or IR4000 – buy all tickets at the main entrance.

The best museums are the **Ivan-e Takht-e Marmar** (Marble Throne Verandah), a ceremonial hall containing an imposing alabaster throne; **Negar Khane**, a gallery with a fine collection of Qajar artworks; and the many-mirrored **Shams-Al Emarat** (Edifice of the Sun), once the tallest building in Tehran and designed to mix European and Persian architectural styles.

If renovation of the **Ethnographical Museum** is complete, it's also worth a look. There's a cosy basement teahouse.

NATIONAL JEWELS MUSEUM

If you only visit one museum in Tehran, this should be it. The **National Jewels Museum** (Map pp190-1; ☎ 6446 3785; Ferdosi St; admission IR30,000; ⏰ 2pm-4.30pm Sat-Tue) has more jew-els on display than you are ever likely to see in one place again. Rubies, emeralds, diamonds, pearls and spinels are encrusted into everything from crowns and sceptres to cloaks, jewellery boxes and swords. Among the impressive displays is a world globe with rubies forming the countries and emeralds the oceans, and the famous Peacock Throne. It's in the basement vault of Bank Melli; look for the huge black gates and machine-gun-toting guards.

NATIONAL MUSEUM OF IRAN

The **National Museum of Iran** (Map pp190-1; ☎ 6670 2061; www.nationalmuseumofiran.ir; Si Tir St; admission IR10,000; ⏰ 9am-4.45pm, to 5.45pm summer, Tue-Sun) houses a small but fascinating collection of pre-Islamic artefacts from sites including Persepolis and Shush.

From Persepolis, there's a 6th-century BC audience-hall relief of Darius I, a frieze of glazed tiles, a famous trilingual Darius I inscription and a carved staircase.

An intriguing exhibit is the grizzly 'salt man', a remarkably intact skull with white hair and beard, plus a leather boot with the foot still in it. The remains are believed to be those of a 3rd- or 4th-century salt miner.

Labelling is sometimes rudimentary but a good illustrated guide is available free – ask for it.

MUSEUM OF THE ISLAMIC PERIOD

Admission to the National Museum of Iran also buys entry to this neighbouring **museum** (Map pp190-1; ☎ 6670 2655; Si Tir St; ⏰ 9am-4.45pm, to 5.45pm summer, Tue-Sun), which features two floors of exhibits dating from the 7th century onwards. You'll see carpets, textiles, ceramics, pottery, silks, portraits and excellent examples of stucco work from mosques throughout the country. English-speaking guides are available.

GLASS & CERAMICS MUSEUM

The **Glass & Ceramic Museum** (Map pp190-1; ☎ 6670 8153; www.glasswaremuseum.ir; Si Tir St; admission IR5000; ⏰ 9am-5pm Tue-Sun, to 6pm summer) is one of the most impressive in Iran, not only for the exhibits but for the building itself, an interesting example from the Qajar period. The exhibits are beautifully presented in modern, individually lit cases and it's easy to follow the English descriptions leading you through the ages.

SEPAHSALAR MOSQUE & MADRASSA
The **Sepahsalar Mosque & Madrassa** (Map pp190-1; Mostafa Khomeini St) is Tehran's largest and most important Islamic building. It was built between 1878 and 1890 and its eight minarets are impressive. The poetry, inscribed in several ancient scripts in the tiling, is famous.

US DEN OF ESPIONAGE
The only indications that this vast complex was once the US embassy are a vandalised symbol of the bald eagle outside the main entrance and the anti-American murals daubed along the southern wall. Now called the **US Den of Espionage** (Map pp190-1; Taleqani Ave) and used by the military, the building is closed to visitors, though occasionally it opens, usually around No Ruz (March 21). Be discreet about taking any photos in the area.

TEHRAN MUSEUM OF CONTEMPORARY ART
This **museum** (Map pp190-1; ☎ 8896 5411; www.tehranmoca.com/en; admission IR2000; ☽ 9am-6pm Sat-Thu, 2-6pm Fri), near the Carpet Museum, contains interesting paintings from modern Iranian artists, as well as temporary exhibitions featuring Iranian and foreign photographers and calligraphers.

CARPET MUSEUM
The **Carpet Museum** (Map pp190-1; ☎ 8896 7707; www.carpetmuseum.ir; cnr Fatemi St & Kargar Ave; admission IR5000; ☽ 9am-5pm Tue-Sun, to 6pm summer) contains more than 100 high-quality pieces from all over Iran and is a must if you're interested in Persian rugs. There's a decent café inside.

North Tehran
REZA ABBASI MUSEUM
The **Reza Abbasi Museum** (Map p188; ☎ 8851 3001; www.rezaabbasimuseum.org; Shari'ati Ave; admission IR2500; ☽ 9am-5pm Tue-Sun) contains fine examples of Islamic painting and calligraphy from ancient Qurans, and galleries with delicate pottery and exquisite jewellery. If you're short of time, the Sa'd Abad and Niyavaran palaces are better.

SA'D ABAD MUSEUM COMPLEX
In the pretty and extensive grounds of the former shah's summer residence, the **Sa'd Abad Museum Complex** (Map p188; ☎ 2228 2031; www.saadabadpalace.org in Arabic; Taheri St, Valiasr Ave; ☽ 8.30am-4pm, to 5pm summer) consists of several

small museums. These include the **National Palace (White) Museum**, the last shah's palace (with 54 rooms); the interesting **Military Museum**, with a collection of armoury; the **Green (Shahvand) Palace**, with its collection of carpets, furniture and other oddments; and the **Museum of Fine Arts**, with some charming Persian oil paintings.

The grounds are open daily and each museum has a separate entrance fee – between IR3000 and IR5000. Take a shared (or private) taxi from Tajrish Sq, or walk about 1.5km from Tajrish, along Shahid Ja'afar.

SLEEPING
Tehran has a good range of accommodation, though inspiration can be hard to find and it's usually more expensive than elsewhere in Iran. Most hotels tend to be concentrated in a couple of areas, making comparisons relatively easy. Tehran's traffic can be deafening, so if you're a light sleeper look for something away from a main road, or at the back of the building.

Budget
Most cheap places are within a 1km radius of Imam Khomeini Sq and conveniently near the museums, bazaar and train station. However, it's also the noisiest and grubbiest part of the city and pretty dead after dark.

Hafez Hotel (Map pp190-1; ☎ 6670 9063; hafez hotel@yahoo.com; Bank Melli Alley; s/d with breakfast US$17.55/23.40; ✷ ▣) Off Ferdosi St, the Hafez' quiet, clean and relatively modern rooms with fridges, soft beds and poky Western bathrooms are pretty good value. There's a small restaurant and English is spoken.

Mashhad Hotel (Map pp190-1; ☎ 3311 3062; mashhadhotel@yahoo.com; 416 Amir Kabir St; dm/s/tw IR25,000/50,000/75,000; ▣) The Mashhad's tiny and often noisy rooms with share bathrooms are simplicity itself, though management can be helpful. Don't confuse this with the Mashad Hotel, near the former US embassy.

Hotel Sa'adi (Map pp190-1; ☎ 3311 7653; Lalehzar St; s/tw IR70,000/110,000) The family-run Sa'adi has rudimentary but clean rooms with showers, but toilets are shared. There's a low-key restaurant serving Iranian food.

Mehr Guesthouse (Map pp190-1; ☎ 3311 0133; s/tw with shower IR40,000/50,000; ✷) Off Amir Kabir St, Mehr could use a facelift but its rooms with firm mattresses are cheap and management is obliging, though little English is spoken. The squat toilets are shared and singles without shower are IR30,000.

Midrange

Prices in this range start at about US$25 for a twin or double room. All rooms have bathrooms, some with squat toilets, and most will have a fridge, TV and air-con.

Atlas Hotel (Map pp190-1; ☎ 8890 6058; www.atlas -hotel.com; 206 Taleqani St; s/tw US$38/58; ⊠ ☐) This quiet, tastefully decorated place in the centre of Tehran is fair value. The rooms overlooking the courtyard are best. Rates are negotiable and the Indian/Pakistani restaurant (meals IR45,000 to IR65,000, open noon to 4pm and 7pm to 11pm) isn't bad.

Omid Hotel (Map pp190-1; ☎ 6641 4564; www .omid-hotel.com; 20 East Nosrat St; s/d with breakfast US$52/70; ⊠) Well-located near Park-e Laleh, the welcoming staff and large rooms with fridge, TV and video are easy to return to. Best to book ahead.

Hotel Naderi (Map pp190-1; ☎ 6670 1872; naderi hotel@yahoo.com; Jomhuri-ye Eslami Ave; s/d US$15/30; ⊠) The atmospheric Naderi has large, airy rooms with a '50s ambience, right down to the bakelite telephones. Rooms are large, but those at the front are noisy. The adjoining café is great.

Hotel Safir (Map pp190-1; ☎ 8830 0873; www .indianhotelsafir.com; 10 Ardalan St; s/d with breakfast US$35/45-53; ⊠ ☐) Above the famous Tandoor Restaurant off Mofatteh Ave, the Safir is small, clean and has comfortable rooms with satellite TV. Good value.

Hotel Khayyam (Map pp190-1; ☎ 3311 3757; hotel khayyam@hotmail.com; 3 Navidy Alley; s/tw US$18/25 with

---

THE AUTHOR'S CHOICE

Firouzeh Hotel (Map pp190-1; ☎ 3311 3508; www.firouzehhotel.com; Dolat Abadi Alley; s/d IR90,000/120,000; ⊠ ☐) The Firouzeh is easily the best budget option, thanks mainly to the efforts of the genuinely friendly English-speaking manager Mr Musavi. It's far enough off Amir Kabir St to be quiet, and the spotless rooms have a fridge, satellite TV and a shower; toilets are shared. The communal area is a good place to meet travellers, and Mr Musavi can arrange everything from bus tickets and vegetarian meals to US$20 ski trips. There's also a great guestbook. Highly recommended.

---

breakfast; ℗ ⊠ ☐) The Khayyam, off Amir Kabir St, is quiet but tired. Discounts are probable.

Top End

Simorgh Hotel (Map pp190-1; ☎ 8871 9911; www .simorghhotel.com; 1069 Valiasr Ave; s/d with breakfast US$119/129; ⊠ ☐ ☒) The most professionally run hotel in Tehran, rates for the stylish rooms include use of the gym, Jacuzzi and pool. It's well set up for business.

Laleh International Hotel (Map pp190-1; ☎ 8896 5021; www.lalehhotel.com; Dr Hossein Fatemi Ave; s/d US$130/152; ℗ ⊠ ☐) The former InterContinental has fine rooms, a great location and panoramic views. The restaurants here are pretty good.

EATING

Tehran boasts plenty of good Iranian restaurants plus a refreshing range of international cuisines: make the most of them.

Azari Traditional Restaurant (Azari Coffeehouse; Map p188; ☎ 5537 6702; Valiasr Ave, Rah-Ahan Sq; meals IR25,000; ⏰ 7am-4.30pm & 8pm-midnight) About 250m north of Rah-Ahan Sq, this restored coffeehouse serves top-notch *dizi* and chicken kebabs and is wonderfully atmospheric. There's traditional music most nights.

Iranian Traditional Restaurant (Agha Bozorg; Map pp190-1; ☎ 8890 0522, 28 Keshavarz Blvd; meals IR20,000-35,000; ⏰ noon-midnight) Full of flirting young Tehranis, this attractive underground lair successfully combines old and new – *dizi* and kebabs on the menu and an eclectic nightly music scene.

Khoshbin Restaurant (Map pp190-1; ☎ 3390 2194; Sa'di St; meals IR15,000-35,000; ⏰ 11.30am-3.30pm & 7.30-10.30pm) Cheap, cheerful place with mouthwatering Caspian cuisine including several fish dishes and, vegetarians take note, the divine *mirza ghasemi* and *baghli*, a vegetable *khoresht* that's only available at lunchtime. There's no English sign so look for the fish in the window.

Armenian Club (Map pp190-1; ☎ 6670 0521-2; 68 Khark St, cnr France Ave; meals IR50,000; ⏰ noon-3pm & 8pm-midnight Sat-Thu; noon-3pm Fri) This Christian club is an escape where women can take off their scarves. The barbecued sturgeon, chicken schnitzel and Iranian dishes aren't bad. Look for a yellow awning. Muslims cannot enter.

Tandoor Restaurant (Map pp190-1; ☎ 8830 0873; Ardalan St; meals IR45,000-65,000; ⏰ noon-3pm &

7-11pm) Under the Hotel Safir, the curries and daals are reliably good, and there are several vegetarian dishes.

There are four popular themed restaurants in **Park-e Jamshidiyeh** (Stone Park; Map p188; Feizieh Ave, Niyavaran St, Tajrish), in the far north of Tehran, where the spectacular mountain and city views are worth the trip alone. All the restaurants here are open from about 9am to midnight. Starting from the bottom of the hill, you'll come to the **Khaneh Azarbaijan** (☎ 2229 7540; meals IR40,000); then the **Kurdish House** (☎ 2280 1309; meals IR50,000), the **Turkmen Restaurant** (☎ 2281 0106; meals IR35,000), which has the best and cheapest food, including *mirza ghasemi* (IR15,000), and finally **Zagros House** (☎ 2281 0107; meals IR50,000).

From sushi to a divine yellow curry, **Monsoon** (Map p188; ☎ 8879 1982; Gandhi Shopping Centre, Gandhi Ave; meals IR50,000-90,000; ☺ noon-3pm & 7-11.30pm Sat-Thu) is one of Tehran's best restaurants. The all-Asian menu changes regularly. In the same complex, **Casa Mia** (Map p188; ☎ 8879 1959; meals IR75,000-130,000) is an excellent Italian option.

Quick Eats
You won't have to look too hard to find a kababi (basic kebab shop) or pizza joint in Tehran.

Boof (Map p188; ☎ 2225 3262; Valiasr Ave; meal IR20,000) The closest Iran comes to McDonald's, but with far superior burgers.

Tomato (Map pp190-1; ☎ 6671 1579; Jomhuri-ye Eslami Ave; pizzas IR20,000; ☺ 9am-11pm) Good pizzas, better lamb sandwiches and decent coffee.

Jaam-e Jam Food Court (Map p188; Jaam-e Jam Shopping Centre; cnr Valiasr Ave & Taheri St) A food court? Yes indeed! The food here is not cheap and not necessarily the best in town. But this is as close to a Western-style pick-up bar as you'll find in Tehran. The choice of food – Chinese, Greek, French, British, Italian, Mexican and BBQ – is wide, but this is more about looking hot than eating. So practise raised eyebrows and meaningful looks, and settle in for some flirtatious fun.

DRINKING
Most of the traditional restaurants mentioned above are also good places to just hang out and drink tea.

Café Naderi (Map pp190-1; Jomhuri-ye Eslami Ave; ☺ 8am-7pm, Sat-Thu) Attached to the Hotel Naderi in southern Tehran, Naderi is famous

---

> **THE AUTHOR'S CHOICE**
>
> **Khayyam Traditional Restaurant** (Map p188; ☎ 5580 0760; Khayyam St; meals IR40,000-60,000; ☺ 11am-midnight) Just south of Khayyam Metro station, this beautifully restored restaurant serves a wide variety of Iranian dishes (though some aren't on the menu), including juicy kebabs and various *bademjun* (aubergine or eggplant) options. It's also a great place to just relax with tea and *qalyan*.

---

not only for its coffee but as a meeting place of intellectuals and artists – there are lots of berets and goatees here.

Sofre Khane Sonnati Sanqalaq (Map pp190-1; ☎ 6673 1075; Park-e Shahr; meals IR45,000; ☺ 9am-10pm) A relaxing stop on the museum circuit. Musicians sometimes play at lunchtime.

Tehranis love the walking trails of Darband and Darekeh (Map p188) and the numerous teahouses and restaurants that line them. It's a great place to walk, talk and sip tea in cosy teahouses.

ENTERTAINMENT
Cinema
Tehran has plenty of cinemas, but most show (often violent) Iranian films. If you want Hollywood or better-quality Iranian flicks, head to the trendy **Farhang Cinema** (Map p188; ☎ 2200 2088; www.fcf-ir.com; Shari'ati Ave, Gholhak; tickets IR10,000) where relatively recent releases can be seen, some in English.

Theatre
One of the few inner-city theatres featuring cultural events and traditional performances that foreigners are welcome to attend is the **Tezatre Shahr** (City Theatre; Map pp190-1; ☎ 6646 0595; Daneshju Park, cnr Valiasr & Enqelab Aves). Check the English-language newspapers or www.tehranavenue.com for upcoming events.

SHOPPING
In **Tehran Bazar** (main entrance 15 Khordad Ave) you'll find everything from carpets and tacky souvenirs to intricate glassware. See p192.

Other good shopping strips are the endless Valiasr Ave, particularly around Valiasr and Vanak Sqs, where scarves and manteaus can be bought, while Ferdosi St around Ferdosi Sq and Taleqani St just west of the US Den of Espionage have plenty of souvenir shops.

IRAN

GETTING THERE & AWAY

See p657 for details about international air and bus services to/from Tehran.

Air

Iran Air flies daily between Tehran and most cities and larger towns in Iran. Services are less frequent on the smaller airlines, including Iran Aseman and Mahan Air. Tehran is full of travel agencies (see p189), which are easier to deal with than airline offices.

Iran Air services from Tehran include the following:

To/from	One-way fare (IR)	Duration (hr)
Bandar Abbas	480,000	2
Esfahan	195,000	¾
Kerman	364,000	1½
Mashhad	344,000	1½
Rasht	195,000	¾
Shiraz	315,000	1½
Tabriz	256,000	1
Yazd	320,000	1

There are some international airlines represented in Tehran.

Air France (Map p188; ☎ 2204 4498; Sayyeh Tower, Valiasr Ave)

Air India (Map pp190-1; ☎ 8873 9762; Serafraz St)

Ariana Afghan Airlines (Map pp190-1; ☎ 8855 0156-60; 29 Khalid St)

British Airways (Map p188; ☎ 2204 4552, 10th fl, Sayyeh Tower, Sayeh St, Valiasr Ave)

Emirates (Map p188; ☎ 8879 6786; 1211 Valiasr Ave)

Gulf Air (Map pp190-1; ☎ 2225 3284-7; Nejatollahi St)

KLM (Map p188; ☎ 2204 4757; 12th fl, Sayeh Tower, Sayyeh St, Valiasr Ave)

Lufthansa (Map pp190-1; ☎ 8873 8701; Beheshti Ave, 2 Sarafraz St) Also represents Austrian Airlines.

Turkish Airlines (Map pp190-1; ☎ 8874 8450; 239 Motahhari Ave)

Bus

There are four bus terminals in Tehran but most travellers should only need the western and southern bus terminals. Tickets can be prebooked at the **Iran Peyma office** (Map pp190-1; ☎ 6670 9964; Ferdosi St) but it's just as easy to turn up at the appropriate terminal and ask around the bus company offices.

The western bus terminal (terminal-e gharb) caters for all places west of Tehran, and anywhere along the Caspian Sea west of, and including, Chalus. Mercedes/Volvo services include Rasht (IR16,500/33,000, eight hours), Ramsar (IR15,500/56,000, six hours), Chalus (IR19,000/35,000, five hours), Tabriz (IR35,000/50,000, 10 hours), Qazvin (IR8000/20,000, three hours), Hamadan (IR18,500/35,000, six hours), Kermanshah (IR27,500/48,000, eight hours, mornings only). International buses to Turkey, Armenia and Azerbaijan also leave from here (see p250 and p660). To get to the terminal, take a shared taxi (IR4000) to Azadi Sq, from where it's a 10-minute walk, or a private taxi (IR20,000).

The southern bus terminal (terminal-e jonoub) has Mercedes/Volvo buses to the south and east of Tehran, such as Mashhad (IR39,000/75,000, 14 hours), Esfahan (IR20,000/33,000, seven hours), Shiraz (IR38,000/66,000, 12 to 16 hours), Yazd (IR27,000/52,000, around 10 hours), Kerman (IR41,000/65,000, 18 hours) and Bandar Abbas (IR62,000/110,000, 20 hours). The Metro stop here (terminal-e jonoub) makes it easy to reach from Imam Khomeini Sq.

The small eastern bus terminal (terminal-e shargh) has buses to anywhere east, and anywhere along the Caspian Sea east of Chalus. Take a shared taxi to Imam Hossein Sq and another from there.

The central bus terminal (Seiro Safar or Arzhantin terminal) has buses to Esfahan, Kerman, Mashhad, Rasht, Shiraz and Yazd, but the southern bus terminal is better for all these destinations.

Savari

Most towns within about three hours by car from Tehran are linked by savari (long-distance taxi). They leave from inside, or just outside, the appropriate bus terminals. For instance, savaris to Qazvin (IR20,000) or Chalus (IR60,000) leave from the western bus terminal or nearby Azadi Sq, and savaris to Qom (IR30,000) leave from outside the southern bus terminal.

Train

Almost all train services in Iran start and finish at the **train station** (Map p188; Rah-Ahan Sq) in southern Tehran. Arrival and departure times are listed in English and the staff at the **information booth** (☎ 5565 1415) speak English.

There are services (daily unless specified) between Tehran and Ahvaz (IR113,800/ 18,350 in 1st/2nd class, 15 hours, twice daily), Gorgan (IR39,750/17,200, 10½ hours), Tabriz (IR57,750/27,200, 13 hours), Esfahan (IR31,000 1st class only, seven hours), Mashhad (IR60,200/37,800, 12 to 16 hours, 11 daily), Bandar Abbas (IR88,700 1st class only, 20 hours), Yazd (IR35,950 1st class only, eight hours, twice daily), and Kerman (IR39,750/63,150, 13 hours, twice daily). See p253 for more on trains.

Incredibly, you can't buy tickets at the station. Instead, you'll be sent to **Rah-e-Saadt Agency** (Map p188; ☎ 538 2939; 270 Moktari, Valisar Ave), about 200m north of the station.

To get there, take any bus or shared taxi heading down Valiasr or Hafez streets.

GETTING AROUND
To/From the Airport
If you're arriving in Tehran for the first time, it's wise to pay for a private taxi to your hotel. Whether you fly into Mehrabad International Airport or, as seems more likely, the new Imam Khomeini International Airport (see right), avoid the taxi drivers who approach you outside the terminals and head for the taxi booth, which has set prices. From Mehrabad to most parts of Tehran it's IR30,000, though this rises in peak hour. From the domestic terminal you could catch a bus to Vanak Sq or to the train station.

You can also take the Metro out as far as Sadeghieh near Azadi Sq and get a taxi from there.

Bus
Buses cover virtually all of Tehran but, as they're often crowded and slow, most travellers end up using shared taxis instead. However, buses are dirt cheap – IR200 for most trips – and since they often use dedicated bus lanes they can actually be faster than a taxi in heavy traffic. Some useful routes include: bus 145 between Imam Khomeini Sq and Tajrish; bus 18 between Tajrish Sq and Arzhantin Sq; bus I-22 between Imam Khomeini Sq and Arzhantin Sq; and the I-33 between Tajrish Sq and Valiasr Sq. Buy tickets at booths near major bus stops. Numbers tend to change frequently, so ask around before getting on.

Metro
The ever-expanding **Tehran Metro** (www.tehran metro.com) is cheap and relatively fast, even if it is a frotteur's paradise because it's so packed. The north–south Line 1 (red line)

IMAM KHOMEINI INTERNATIONAL AIRPORT

More than 30 years after work began, Tehran's huge **Imam Khomeini International Airport** (IKIA; www.ikia.com) finally began taking regular flights in mid-2005. However, at the time of writing many flights were still arriving at the old Mehrabad International Airport. If you land at IKIA, taxis are going to be much more expensive than from Mehrabad. The Metro is supposed to run to IKIA, but you'll probably need to take a taxi to or from the last stop.

is quite handy for travellers. It runs from Haram-e Motahar (for the Holy Shrine of Imam Khomeini) in the south, and useful stops include the southern bus terminal (terminal-e jonoub), the bazaar (Pamzdah-e Khordad), Imam Khomeini Sq and Taleqani for the US Den of Espionage. It finishes now at Mirdamad, near Vanak Sq, though it will eventually run all the way to Tajrish Sq.

Line 2 (blue line) runs from Dardasht in the east, crossing Line 1 at Imam Khomeini Sq, and on to Sadeghieh, near the western bus terminal. A single trip on either line costs IR650. Line 5 (green line) runs from Sadeghieh out to Karaj. Trips cost IR1000.

Taxi
Taxis *dah baste* (closed door) and shared taxis travel every nanosecond linking the main squares: Imam Khomeini, Vanak, Valiasr, Tajrish, Arzhantin, Azadi, Ferdosi, Enqelab, Haft-e Tir, Rah-Ahan and Imam Hossein. Any taxi can be chartered for a private trip but you'll have to negotiate a fare. Prices are usually about 30% to 50% higher during peak hour. Sample *dah baste* fares include: Imam Khomeini Sq to Tajrish IR30,000 and Imam Khomeini Sq to Valiasr Sq IR17,000. Bargain hard.

AROUND TEHRAN

TOCHAL & DARBAND   توچال & در بند
To get a complete picture of Tehran and its people, you need to venture into the affluent, leafy northern suburbs at the very foot of the Alborz Mountains – a perfect antidote to busy, working-class southern Tehran.

From Tajrish Sq minibuses and taxis run to **Tochal telecabin** (Map p188; www.tochalcomplex .com), where rather battered cable cars take you up Mt Tochal (3957m). It operates from 8am to 3pm daily (until 5pm Thursday and Friday) and costs IR20,000 (each way) to Station 5, where there's a restaurant, and another IR15,000 each way to Station 7, where you can go skiing between about November and May. Hire skis at Station 5.

At **Darband** (Map p188), reached by foot or shared taxi from Tajrish Sq, a series of walking trails lead into the foothills. The scenery here is better than at Tochal and the trails near Darband village have something of a carnival atmosphere with food and drink stalls, good teahouses and shops. Both Tochal and Darband get crowded on Fridays, but are peaceful during the week.

ALBORZ SKI RESORTS   تفریحگاه اسکی البرز

Skiing in the Alborz Mountains above Tehran can be one of the most unexpected pleasures of a trip to Iran. There are four resorts within day-trip distance, all of which have good facilities, equipment for hire and are pretty cheap. Tochal is the nearest, but **Shemshak Resort** (☎ 0221-355 2912; IR40,000; ☽ 8.30am-3.30pm Jan-Mar) has the most challenging slopes, and **Dizin Resort** (☎ 0262-254 2449; IR50,000; ☽ 8.30am-3.30pm Nov-Apr) is *the* place to be seen. Dizin usually has decent snow from about November to April. As a rough guide to cost, a day's ski-hire starts at about IR75,000 but can climb as high as IR250,000 – you should be able to get a decent pair of carve skis, boots and poles for about IR140,000.

All the resorts have hotels, with prices starting at about US$35/50 per single/twin. Rooms at the **Dizin Hotel** (☎ 0262-254 2449; tw US$50; ℗) are adequate.

Getting there can be a big hassle on public transport, so unless you have friends with a vehicle and chains it's better to use a day tour. Mr Musavi at the Firouzeh Hotel (p194) in Tehran can arrange inexpensive but reliable day trips. Or, try a travel agency or check the English-language newspapers.

MT DAMAVAND   کوه دماوند

This magnificent conical volcano (5671m) is the highest in the country. It's possible to climb it in two or three days, starting from the pretty village of **Reyneh**, but if you intend to go mountain climbing, first contact the **Mountaineering Federation of Iran** (☎ 021-883 9928; www.iranmountfed.com; irmountfed@neda.net; 15 Varzandeh, Moffateh Ave, Tehran). Even if you're not a mountain climber, there are plenty of gentle hiking trails in the area.

THE HOLY SHRINE OF IMAM KHOMEINI   مرقد مطهر امام خمینی

The resting place of **Imam Khomeini** (admission free; ☽ 24hr), about 35km south of Tehran on the main road to Qom, is one of the largest Islamic complexes in the world. It's not, however, particularly attractive. The shrine itself is in the aircraft-hangar-sized main building. To get there take the Metro to Haram-e Motahar station.

BEHESHT-E ZAHRA   بهشت زهرا

The main military cemetery for those who died in the Iran-Iraq War is an extraordinary, but eerie, place. It can easily be combined with a trip to the Holy Shrine of Imam Khomeini. The cemetery is about 500m east from the back of the shrine, past a huge civilian cemetery and over the main road.

NOSHAHR/CHALUS & AROUND   نوشهر / چالوس

☎ 0191

The twin towns of Noshahr and Chalus are set where the spectacular road from Tehran (via Karaj) meets the coast, so they're easily reached. These classic resort towns have some decent hotels and other facilities, but not much character. Noshahr is nicer, while Chalus has better transport connections. Regular shared taxis (IR2000) link the two.

Sights

At **Namak Abrud**, about 12km west along the road from Chalus, there's a **telecabin** (return IR30,000; ☽ 10am-4pm) to the top of Mt Medovin (1050m). Get here early to avoid the queues and the clouds that roll in later in the day.

The small **Sisangan National Park**, 31km east of Noshahr, is a lovely pocket of rare forest with a few walking trails. Take any transport between Chalus and Nur and get off at the sign saying 'Jungle Park'.

Sleeping & Eating

Shalizar Hotel (☎ 325 0001; Azadi Sq; s IR150,000-200,000, d IR250,000-300,000; ✗) In the heart of Noshahr, the Shalizar has clean, comfortable rooms, some with balconies and views; rates are very negotiable. The excellent underground restaurant (meals IR35,000 to IR50,000, open noon to 4pm and 7pm to 1am) is in a former nightclub.

Hotel Malek (☎ 222 4107; Noshahr Blvd; d/ste IR200,000/350,000; ◷ noon-3.30pm & 8-11pm; ⓟ ✗ ▯ ☎) Between Chalus and Noshahr, Malek is a modern, great-value place with satellite TV, fridge, 'minibar' and Western bathrooms. The attached and misnamed Malek Burger (meals IR25,000 to IR60,000, open 7am to midnight) has some of the best food on the coast; steak, schnitzel, fish, *mirza ghasemi* and, yes, burgers.

WESTERN IRAN
غرب ایران

For thousands of years western Iran played host to the rise and fall of civilisation's earliest empires. Standing at the frontiers with Mesopotamia and Turkey, the region's fortunes have been mixed; the trading riches it enjoyed due to its position on the Silk Road were offset by bloody episodes on the battlefield, most recently during the Iran-Iraq War (p182).

Western Iran extends from the border with Armenia and Azerbaijan in the north to the industrial city of Ahvaz near the Gulf. Culturally, it is the most diverse part of Iran, with Azaris, Armenians, Loris, Bakhtiaris, and Kurds among the distinct ethnic groups you'll encounter. Despite this and a wealth of historical, religious and cultural sights, stunning mountain scenery and great trekking possibilities, few travellers see more than Tabriz. Pity them, then take advantage of the unspoilt expanses and go yourself.

This section starts with Bazargan, the main overland border crossing from Turkey.

BAZARGAN
بازرگان
☎ 0462

Bazargan is a one-street town on the Iran-Turkey border but there's little reason to stop here. For border crossing details see p250. The best sleeping option is the **Hotel Hamid** (☎ 337 2435; Imam St; tw IR65,000), just beyond the outer border gate.

Avoid the rip-off taxis outside immigration and take the shuttle bus (IR500)

to Bazargan village, where the main taxi stand is in front of the Hotel Jafapoor. From here, savaris to Maku (IR4000) and Tabriz (IR25,000) leave regularly.

MAKU
ماکو
☎ 0462 / pop 40,000

Many travellers stop in Maku just before, or after, crossing the border with Turkey. The town is attractively set in a rocky canyon and the essentials are either side of the Tabriz highway.

Friendly and helpful **Hotel Alvand** (☎ 322 3491; Imam Ave; s/d IR35,000/46,000), just west of the main square, has clean rooms and shared bathrooms – the hot shower is downstairs.

Buses to Tabriz (IR12,000, four hours) and Orumiyeh (IR12,000, 4½ hours) leave in the morning from the terminal at the east end of town, from where savaris make the same trips. Savaris to Bazargan (IR4000) leave from outside Hotel Alvand.

QAREH KALISA
قره کلیسا

Set in lonely, rolling hills **Qareh Kalisa** (Black Church; admission IR3000; ◷ 8am-1pm & 2-7pm) is one of the best-preserved Christian monuments in Iran. It's more accurately known as Kalisa-ye Tad – the Church of St Thaddaeus. Poor St Thaddaeus is believed to have founded a church here in AD 43 before his success led to him and his converts being massacred by the jealous Armenian king in AD 66.

The church was largely rebuilt after extensive earthquake damage in the 13th century. More was added in 1810. Its one service a year, on the feast day of St Thaddaeus (around 19 June), is well attended by Armenian pilgrims from all over Iran.

There is no scheduled public transport and the best access is from Maku, from where you can charter a taxi for about IR80,000 return, including waiting time.

JOLFA
جلفا
☎ 0492

Sleepy Jolfa is on the border with the little-visited Azeri enclave of Nakhchivan, and is a waypoint en route to the border crossing to Armenia (see p660 for border details). Jolfa also serves as a base from which to visit the picturesque Aras River Valley and the **Church of St Stephanos** (Kalisa Darreh Sham; admission IR2000), an impressive Armenian monastery 16km west of Jolfa.

In Jolfa, the best hotel is above the famous **Haj Ali Kababi** (☎ 302 2207; r IR80,000; ⊠) at the west end of town.

Infrequent savaris (IR20,000, two hours) and rare buses (IR8000, 3½ hours) run to and from Tabriz, but if you're a group it's better value to take a half-day tour to Jolfa and St Stephanos with Nasser or Mansour Khan from the Tabriz **tourist information office** (☎ 525 2501, 0914-116 0149; Qods St).

ORUMIYEH (URMIEH)   ارومیه
☎ 0441 / pop 500,000

Orumiyeh lies to the west of the lake of the same name and boasts a long and deep-rooted Azari heritage, with liberal doses of Christianity and Judaism thrown into the ethnic mix. Today about a third of the population is Christian, the highest of any Iranian city. There is little of visual interest for the traveller but, if you're passing through, don't miss the bustling bazaar.

Most essentials are on or near Imam Ave, between Faqiyeh Sq and Enqelab Sq, including the **Wisiaynet Coffeenet** (☎ 224 1400; Khayyam St; per hr IR8000).

Sights
The **bazaar**, off Imam Ave, between Besat St and Faqiyeh Sq, is full of life and worth rambling around for an hour or so. While you're there, look for the hidden entrance to the partly Seljuk-era, brick-domed **Jameh Mosque**, which has some fine plaster mouldings.

Orumiyeh Museum (☎ 224 6520; Beheshti St; admission IR3000; ⊙ 9am-2pm Tue-Sun) has a new, English-speaking director and some more lively exhibits – worth a quick look.

Sleeping & Eating
Hotel Tak Setareh (☎ 223 1861; Sardar Camii Lane; s/tw IR60,000/80,000) In a lane leading northwest from Imam Ave, about 150m south of Besat St, this helpful, English-speaking place is excellent value. Rooms have Eastern bathrooms and fridge and discounts are possible.

Reza Hotel (☎ 222 6580; Besat St; s/d IR80,000/120,000; P ⊠) Centrally located near the corner of Imam Ave, Reza has Western toilets, satellite TV and a passable restaurant. Fair value.

Flamingo (☎ 346 1177; Kashani St; meals IR35,000; ⊙ noon-3pm & 5-10.30pm) Central and serves the best Iranian food. Stalls around town sell delicious baked potatoes for IR1000.

Getting There & Away
Iran Air (☎ 344 0520) flies to Tehran (IR272,000, twice a day).

Several bus companies have offices along Imam Ave. The terminal for buses, minibuses and savaris is northeast of the centre – catch a shared taxi along Imam Khomeini St. There are buses to Kermanshah (IR27,000, 11 hours), Maku (IR10,000, five hours), Tabriz (IR12,500, 4½ hours), Sanandaj (IR25,400, seven hours) and Tehran (IR55,000, 13 hours). Savaris to Tabriz (IR25,000, three hours) are faster, crossing the lake by ferry. A new bridge should cut the trip for all transport. To Sero, take a savari (IR10,000) from the Sero terminal (off Raja'i Blvd) or a direct taxi (IR40,000). For other destinations, get connections in Tabriz or Kermanshah.

SERO   سرو
Miniscule Sero is 4km east of a secondary border-crossing point between Iran and Turkey. It's quieter and quicker than Bazargan. There is nowhere to stay. Smiling-assassin taxi drivers want IR50,000 per car for the 45-minute trip to Orumiyeh – wait for fellow passengers.

TAKHT-E SOLEIMAN   تخت سلیمان
In a bowl of mountains ringed by 1500-year-old fortress walls, **Takht-e Soleiman** (Throne of Soleiman; admission IR4000; ⊙ 8am-sunset) is a World Heritage–listed site and one of the most memorable experiences in western Iran. Once the spiritual centre of Zoroastrianism, the site has been used since the Achaemenid period (550–330 BC). However, the oldest remaining structures are the ruined **Sassanian palace** and **fire temples**. It's well worth walking to the top of the conical **Prison of Soleiman** mountain, about 2.5km west of the ruins, for spectacular views.

The easiest way to get there is by charter taxi (about IR200,000 for the day) from Zanjan, stopping in Dandy en route. Alternatively, get to Takab on a series of minibuses from Tabriz, via Meyando'ab and Shahn Dezh, or from Zanjan by direct bus. From Takab, where there are a couple of hotels, rare minibuses (IR1500) and savaris (IR4000) run to Nostrabad village, from where you walk to the ruins. Chartering a taxi from Takab (IR40,000 return, plus waiting time) is a good idea.

TABRIZ   تبریز

☎ 0411 / pop 1,400,000

Tabriz had a spell as the Persian capital during the Safavid period (AD 1502–1736), although most of its inhabitants are now Azaris. The city fills a sprawling low depression between red hills and from afar can seem like an impenetrable maze of low-rise apartments. However, the central bazaar area is lively and, with a good range of sleeping options and exceptionally helpful local guides, Tabriz makes the ideal base for exploring northwestern Iran.

Information

INTERNET ACCESS

There are several other Internet cafés in the electronics malls off Imam Khomeini St.

Kral Coffeenet (☎ 0914-311 3992; per hr IR5000; ☾ 8.30am-11pm)

Sabs Coffeenet (☎ 554 0577; Tarbeyat Shopping Mall; per hr IR6000; ☾ 9am-10pm; Sat-Thu) The mall is off Imam Khomeini St.

MONEY

Exchange offices in the bazaar and the tourist office (see below) both change money much faster and at good rates.

Bank Melli (Shohada Sq)

TELEPHONE

Telephone office (Miyar Miyar Alley; ☾ 8am-9pm) Small place, hidden in a lane off Imam Khomeini St.

TOURIST INFORMATION

Tourist office (☎ 525 2501, 0914-116 0149; amico nasser@yahoo.com; Shohada St; ☾ 9am-1pm & 4.30pm-7.30pm Sat-Thu) Upstairs in a building straddling the main bazaar entrance is where you'll find the best tourist office in Iran. Brothers Nasser and Mansour Khan speak several languages and are full of helpful advice, without hassle. They have maps, tea, a book exchange and offer fairly priced tours to surrounding areas. Make this your first stop.

VISA EXTENSIONS

Passport office (☎ 477 6666; Saeb St; ☾ 7.30am-1.30pm Sat-Wed, 7.30am-11.30pm Thu) Good place to extend your visa – often done on the same day.

Sights

Tabriz has the largest, oldest and some say most interesting **bazaar** in Iran. Built more than 1000 years ago, it was damaged several times by earthquakes and most of the 35km of covered, often brick-vaulted passageways

and 7000 shops you see today date to the 15th century. There are several local teahouses, usually full of *qalyans* (water pipes) with men attached, which make great places to soak up the atmosphere. Tabriz is renowned for carpets, silverware, jewellery, silk and spices such as henna. At the western end you can walk through the **Jameh Mosque**, with its impressive brick-vaulted interior, and on to **Constitution House** (Motahhari St; admission IR3000; ☾ 9am-3pm winter, 9am-1.30pm & 4.30-7.30pm summer), which is where the 1906 constitution was signed.

Although badly damaged by earthquakes, the 15th-century **Blue Mosque** (Kabud; admission IR2000; ☾ 9am-7pm Sat-Thu, 9am-1pm Fri) is still notable for the extremely intricate tilework. A sensitive restoration is ongoing: walls painted to resemble the missing tiled areas work quite well.

Azarbayjan Museum (Imam Khomeini St; admission IR2000; ☾ 8am-5pm Sat-Thu, to 8pm summer) has a worthwhile collection of exhibits from regional archaeological digs. Look for the copy of the famous Chelsea carpet, thought to be one of the best ever weaved, and the stone 'handbags', an ancient symbol of wealth.

The remains of the large, crumbling **Arg-e-Tabriz** (citadel; Imam Khomeini St), built in the early 14th century, are impressive in their enormity but don't warrant further exploration.

Elgoli is a large, pleasant park and a good place to get away from the city – as many locals do on summer evenings. Take a shared taxi (IR2000) from Shahrdari Sq.

Sleeping

Most accommodation is centrally located on or not far off Imam Khomeini St.

Kosar Hotel (☎ 553 7691-3; info@kosarhotel.com; Imam Khomeini St; s/d IR110,000/142,000; 🍴) The best value in town, this new and professionally managed midrange place has clean, well-furnished rooms with satellite TV and fridge; most have Western bathrooms. Rooms at the back are quieter.

Hotel Sina (☎ 551 6211; Fajr Sq; s/tw IR150,000/250,000; P 🍴) Spacious, clean, bright rooms and friendly English-speaking service make this a good bet.

Morvarid Hotel (☎ 551 3336-7; morvarid_hotel@yahoo.com; Fajr Sq; s/d/tr IR99,000/136,000/152,000) Rooms with private Western bathroom and fridge are reasonable value.

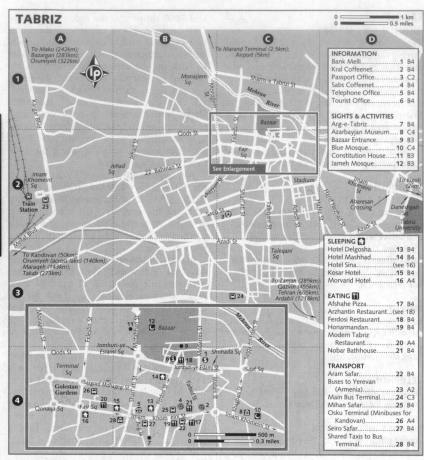

TABRIZ

INFORMATION
Bank Melli..............1 B4
Kral Coffeenet.........2 B4
Passport Office........3 C2
Sabs Coffeenet.........4 B4
Telephone Office.......5 B4
Tourist Office.........6 B4

SIGHTS & ACTIVITIES
Arg-e-Tabriz...........7 B4
Azarbayjan Museum......8 C4
Bazaar Entrance........9 B3
Blue Mosque...........10 C4
Constitution House....11 B3
Jameh Mosque..........12 B3

SLEEPING
Hotel Delgosha........13 B4
Hotel Mashhad.........14 B4
Hotel Sina.........(see 16)
Kosar Hotel...........15 B4
Morvarid Hotel........16 A4

EATING
Afshahe Pizza.........17 B4
Arzhantin Restaurant..(see 18)
Ferdosi Restaurant....18 B4
Honarmandan...........19 B4
Modern Tabriz
  Restaurant..........20 A4
Nobar Bathhouse.......21 B4

TRANSPORT
Aram Safar............22 B4
Buses to Yerevan
  (Armenia)...........23 A2
Main Bus Terminal.....24 C3
Mihan Safar...........25 B4
Osku Terminal (Minibuses for
  Kandovan)...........26 A4
Seiro Safar...........27 B4
Shared Taxis to Bus
  Terminal............28 B4

Hotel Mashhad (☎ 555 8255; Ferdosi St; dm/s/tw IR15,000/34,300/47,200) Simple, cheap and popular with backpackers, clean rooms have basin and table. The share showers cost IR5000 a wash and there's a no-frills restaurant downstairs.

Hotel Delgosha (☎ 554 3362; Ferdosi St; s/d/tr IR34,300/47,200/55,600; ✗) Beds are crammed into these basic but clean rooms. It's IR5000 to use the shared showers.

Eating

Tabriz' most famous dish is the cheap and hearty *dizi* (*abgusht*, meat stew).

Ferdosi Restaurant (dizi IR10,000) Down a small lane off Jomhuri-ye Eslami St, this unsigned and earthy eatery is a great place to sample it with the locals; look for the yellow doors.

Afshahe Pizza (Imam Khomeini St; pizzas IR15,000; ✗ 11am-10pm) A popular fast-food option.

Modern Tabriz Restaurant (☎ 556 7411; Imam Khomeini St; meals IR20,000-35,000; ✗ 8am-10pm) It's no longer modern, but the food, service and retro, mirrored interior will impress nonetheless. There are several fish options.

Honarmandan (☎ 553 4594; Imam Khomeini St; meals IR15,000-30,000; noon-11.30pm Sat-Thu) The décor might be tacky, but dishes such as *dizi* (IR10,000) and *chelow ghimeh* (rice and minced meat, IR15,000) are hard to beat for taste and value.

Arzhantin Restaurant (meals IR12,000; ✗ 1-4pm Sat-Thu) In the same lane as the Ferdosi, off

Jomhuri-ye Eslami and just behind the tourist office, this tiny lunchtime place serves tasty vegetarian dishes including *chelow khoresht*.

Renovation of the **Nobar Bathhouse** (Imam Khomeini St) is finally nearing completion and it should be worth a look for tea or food.

Getting There & Away

Whatever mode of transport you're using, the **tourist office** (☎ 525 2501, 0914-116 0149; amiconasser@yahoo.com; Shohada St; ☺ 9am-1pm & 4.30pm-7.30pm Sat-Thu) can help with schedules and tickets.

AIR

Iran Air (☎ 334 9038) flies to Tehran (IR256,000, several daily), Mashhad (IR508,000, twice weekly) and İstanbul (twice weekly).

BUS & SAVARI

Take a shared taxi from the corner of Imam Khomeini and Shari'ati Sts south to the terminal. Services run (Mercedes unless stated, not always regularly) to Jolfa (IR8000, 3½ hours), Kermanshah (IR33,000, 11 hours, 5pm), Maku (IR8500, about four hours), Orumiyeh (IR12,000, 4½ hours), Ardabil (IR15,000, four hours), Rasht (IR28,000, eight hours, 8.30pm), and Tehran (IR35,000/50,000 in Mercedes/Volvo, nine hours). For Qazvin and Zanjan take any Tehran-bound bus.

Savaris leave from the bus terminal for Orumiyeh (IR30,000), Maku and Bazargan (IR40,000), Jolfa (IR20,000, two hours) and Ardabil (IR30,000).

International buses leave from Imam Khomeini Sq near the train station for Yerevan (Armenia; IR150,000, four times weekly); buy tickets from **Seiro Safar** (☎ 555 7797; Imam Khomeini Sq). To both Baku (Azerbaijan; IR150,000, eight hours) and İstanbul (Turkey; IR200,000) buses leave nightly at about 10pm from outside the relevant bus office on Imam Khomeini St, notably **Aram Safar** (☎ 552 3724) and **Mihan Safar** (☎ 555 4908).

TRAIN

There are two overnight trains to Tehran (IR51,000/23,000 in 1st/2nd class, 13 hours). Trains also travel west to Turkey (Van, Ankara and İstanbul) and to Damascus (Syria). The **train station** (☎ 444 4419; Imam Khomeini Sq) is about 5km west of the town centre, acces-

sible by shared taxi along Imam Khomeini and 22 Bahman Sts.

AROUND TABRIZ

The remarkable village of **Kandovan** (Chandovan; admission IR2500), 50km southwest of Tabriz, is built around and inside volcanic rock formations similar to those found in Cappadocia in central Turkey. Many of the cave homes are still inhabited. Catch a minibus from Tabriz to Osku, then a savari to Kandovan; or charter a taxi from Tabriz for around IR90,000, including one-hour waiting time.

Maraghe was a capital of the Mongol Il-khanid dynasty (1220–1380) and is famous for its four ancient brick tomb towers. It's 150km southeast of Tabriz and can easily be visited as a day trip in combination with Kandovan.

ARDABIL   اردبيل
☎ 0451

Sprawling below Mt Sabalan, historic Ardabil is a logical stopping point if you're heading to Azarbayjan or the Caspian Sea coast from Tabriz. Its main attraction is the impressive **Sheikh Safi od-Din Mausoleum** (Sheikh Safi St; admission IR4000; ☺ 8.30am-5pm, 8.30am-noon & 3.30-7pm summer, Tue-Thu), where the founder of the Safavid dynasty is buried. It also has an interesting **bazaar**, and the hot mineral springs at **Sareiyn** are 27km away. A few doors southwest of the Sabalan Hotel is **Tak Taz Cafe Net** (Sheikh Safi St; per hr IR8000).

Sabalan Hotel (☎ 223 2857; fax 223 2877; Sheiki Safi St; s/tw US$15/25) is in a good location virtually opposite the mausoleum and has clean, quiet rooms, some with Western bathroom and fridge. Negotiate breakfast into the price. The restaurant is decent.

Cheaper is the simple **Hotel Goolshan** (☎ 224 6644; r IR60,000), which has clean, bright rooms with firm beds and share bathrooms about 50m east of Imam Khomeini Sq.

Iran Air (☎ 223 8600) offers flights to Tehran (IR221,000) at least once a day. Regular buses service Tabriz (via Bostan Abad, IR7,600, four hours), and leave for Tehran via Astara (IR4000, two hours), Rasht (IR12,000, five hours) and Qazvin (IR18,500, eight hours). More frequent savaris run to Tabriz (IR30,000, 2½ hours) from Bahonar Sq and to Astara (IR10,000, 70 minutes) from the bus terminal, which is 3km northeast of the centre.

IRAN

ASTARA   آستارا
☎ 0182

This busy border town on the Caspian coast is the main crossing point between Iran and Azerbaijan; see p661.

Caspian Coffeenet (☎ 521 3747; per hr IR8000; ☺ 9am-10pm Sat-Thu & 1-9pm Fri) can occupy some time. **Bilal Hotel** (☎ 521 5586; Mo'allem Sq; s/d IR100,000/172,000; ⊠ ▢) is central, the clean rooms have Western bathrooms and the manager speaks English.

Plenty of savaris and minibuses head towards Rasht, Bandar-e Anzali and Ardabil.

RASHT   رشت
☎ 0131

Fast-growing Rasht is the largest city in the Shomal (Caspian littoral) and despite the near-constant rain is a popular weekend and holiday destination for Tehranis. The city itself has little to offer travellers, but it's a transport hub and the jumping-off point for Masuleh.

Information

The city centre is chaotic Shohada Sq (known as Shahrdari Sq), where you'll find the post office and police headquarters, which can extend your visa within 24 hours. Stretching southeast from Shohada Sq, Imam Khomeini St is the main thoroughfare and home to most of the accommodation.

The major banks will change money, but it's quicker at **Mehrpouya Exchange** (☎ 222 7826; ☺ 9am-1.30pm & 4.30-8pm) down a lane off Imam Khomeini St (near Hotel Golestan).

Get online at **Violet Coffeenet** (☎ 224 7172; Imam Khomeini St; per hr IR10,000; ☺ 9am-9pm), upstairs just southeast of the Carvan Hotel.

Sleeping & Eating

Except Bijan's, all these places are a short walk from Shohada Sq.

Carvan Hotel (☎ 222 2613; Imam Khomeini St; s/tw IR70,000/80,000) The best of the budget hotels, with clean rooms and shared bathrooms and friendly management.

Ordibehesht Hotel (☎ 222 9210; Shohada Sq; s/d US$25/30; ⓟ ⊠) This clean, quiet midrange hotel is just west of the square. The quaint, comfortable rooms have a Western bathroom and fridge.

Kourosh Restaurant (☎ 222 0890; Erkhtesat Lane; meals IR30,000; ☺ 10am-4pm & 6pm-midnight) Kourosh serves *fesenjun* and several difficult-to-find

Gilani dishes. It's down an alley off Sa'di St, about 50m north of Shohada Sq.

Bijan's (☎ 323 3099; Namju Blvd; meals IR25,000; ☺ 6-11pm Sun-Fri) Offering a cosy taste of Tuscany in provincial Iran, Bijan's Sheffield-trained chef cooks up authentic pastas served in his tiny trattoria. Take a taxi *dah baste* (IR5000).

Getting There & Away

Iran Air (☎ 772 4444; Golsar Ave) flies daily to Tehran (IR195,000).

Buses head in all directions from the main bus terminal, accessible by shared taxi heading southeast along Imam Khomeini St. Several bus companies have offices just north of Shohada Sq. Mercedes/Volvo buses run to Tehran (IR16,500/33,000, six hours), Tabriz (IR28,000/50,000, nine hours) and Gorgan (IR26,500/40,000, nine hours). For destinations along the Caspian coast, take any bus, minibus or savari going your way. Savaris to Qazvin, Tehran, Ramsar and Bandar-e Anzali leave from around Shohada Sq.

MASULEH   ماسوله
☎ 0132

This is one of the most beautiful villages in Iran, with its earth-coloured houses stacked on top of one another and clinging to the mountainsides. The locals are interested to meet travellers who don't arrive on buses and it's a great place to stay in an Iranian home. The mountains around the village are ideal for hiking. The **Cultural Heritage Organization** (☎ 757 2066; www.masooleh.ir) welcome visitors.

The two hotels in Masuleh, the **Monfared Masooleh Hotel** (☎ 757 3250; s/d IR150,000/250,000) at the bottom of the village, and **Mehran Suites** (☎ 757 2096; apt IR120,000-200,000) at the top, are alright, but staying in one of the 70 rooms in local homes (some with private bathroom) for about IR60,000 to IR80,000 a double (more in summer and if you include food) is a far richer experience. Just walk into town and the offers will come.

From Sabzi Sq in Rasht, take a savari (IR3000) to Fuman, then another past stunning scenery to Masuleh (IR4000). A taxi *dah baste* is about IR35,000.

RAMSAR   رامسر
☎ 0192

Backed by forested hills, Ramsar is a relatively attractive Iranian 'beach resort' even though the beaches are rubbish and women can't use them. The main road is Motah-hari, and the centre is Enqelab Sq, where you can change money at Bank Melli.

For travellers, the **Caspian Museum** (☎ 522 5374; admission IR4000; ⏱ 8am-3pm, 8am-1pm & 4-8pm summer) is housed in Reza Shah's small but extravagantly furnished 1937 summer palace and is worth a look.

More interesting is the nearby **Ramsar Grand Hotel** (☎ 522 3592; www.ramsarparsianhotels .ir; Old Wing s/d/ste US$53/75/100; P ⏱ ☐ ☐), a neocolonial wonder that dominates the town. The hotel now has two wings; the old wing's '40s-era rooms are small but attractive while the newer, less expensive main building is a monument to all things '60s. Neither is worth the money.

Ramsar also has several apartment hotels near Enqelab Sq, of which the **Caspian Suites** (☎ 522 0520; apt IR250,000; P ⏱) and **Nazia Suites** (☎ 522 4588; apt IR150,000-200,000; P ⏱) are best. Prices fall sharply in winter.

Golesorkh Restaurant (☎ 522 2463; Motahhari St; meals IR20,000-40,000; ⏱ 10am-midnight), west of Enqelab Sq, Golesorkh serves delicious Caspian fish dishes (about IR35,000) and the to-die-for *mirza ghasemi*.

Minibuses run the whole Rasht–Chalus route, but short-hop savaris are much faster. They both stop at the terminal in western Ramsar, or take any bus heading your way. Buses to Tehran leave from a terminal about 500m north of the Ramsar Grand Hotel.

QAZVIN   قزوين
☎ 0281

Qazvin is a pleasant stopover and a good base from which to visit the Castles of the Assassins (p206).

Most of the life-support services are on or near the central Azadi Sq, including the **post office** and **Bank Sepah**. Unsigned **Paez Internet** (Taleqani St; per hr IR6000; ⏱ 9am-9pm) is handy; look for the green gates on the north side of the street, about 150m east of Azadi Sq.

Sights
The 16th-century **Chehel Sotun Palace** (Azadi Sq) is set in attractive gardens and has a mildly interesting **museum** (admission IR2000; ⏱ 8am-2pm & 4-8pm) inside. The ancient **Jameh Mosque**, 700m south of Azadi Sq, has some features dating back to the Arab period (AD 637–

1050), including an exquisitely decorated prayer hall. About 300m further south, the 16th-century **Imamzadeh-ye Hossein** shrine has a well-proportioned blue dome framed by fountains. The covered **bazaar** amply repays idle wandering.

Sleeping & Eating
The following are on Azadi Sq or Taleqani St, which heads east from that square.

Hotel Iran (☎ 222 8877; Shohada St, Azadi Sq; s/tw IR100,000/150,000; P ⏱) Popular Hotel Iran has a range of rooms, most with private facilities. The manager speaks English and can arrange trips into the Alamut region.

Alborz Hotel (☎ /fax 222 6631; Taleqani St; hotel _alborz_q@yahoo.com; s/d IR190,000/280,000; ⏱ ☐) This modern European-style place has small, well-appointed rooms with Western bathroom and satellite TV. Staff are helpful and there's a good coffee shop.

Khasar Hotel (☎ /fax 222 4239; Khaleqi Alley; tw IR55,000) Down a lane virtually opposite the Alborz, the Khasar is cheap but the rooms and shared bathrooms are pretty grim.

Eghbali Restaurant (☎ 222 4990; Taleqani St; meals IR25,000-50,000; ⏱ 11am-4pm & 7-11pm) About 200m east of Azadi Sq, the large menu includes local specialities like *gheymeh nasar* (lamb stew, IR15,000).

Yas (☎ 222 2853; Yasa Alley; meals IR20,000; ⏱ 7am-10pm) With fewer menu options but much more atmosphere, this eatery is a local favourite famous for its excellent *gheymeh nasar*. It's off the north side of Taleqani St, just east of Khayyam St.

Getting There & Away
The main bus and minibus terminal is at Darvazeh Sq (Tehran Gate), where buses go regularly to Tehran (IR8500, three hours), and occasionally to Hamadan (IR14,000, 3½ hours) and Kermanshah (IR19,000, six hours). Savaris to Tehran (IR20,000, 90 minutes) leave from outside.

If you're heading west, go to the Dorah-e Hamadan junction where buses stop momentarily on their way to Zanjan (IR10,000, 2½ hours), Tabriz (IR31,000, seven hours) and Hamadan. For Rasht, go to Enqelab Sq (Darbaza Rasht).

Trains to Tehran, Zanjan and Tabriz depart several times a day. The train station is about 2km south of Azadi Sq; call ☎ 223 0001 to check the schedule.

AROUND QAZVIN
Alamut & the Castles of the Assassins
الموت & لعه حشاشیون

Scattered through the valleys and hilltops
of the Alborz Mountains are the shattered
remnants of over 50 fortresses, collectively
known as the Castles of the Assassins
(Dezha-ye Hashish-iyun). The castles were
the heavily fortified lairs of the adherents
of a bizarre religious cult whose followers
kidnapped and murdered leading political and religious figures. Today, the castles
are mostly rubble and the stunning views,
mountain villages and opportunities for
hiking are the main attractions.

The most famous castle is **Alamut**, once
occupied by Hasan Sabah, founder of the Assassins, and reached by a paved road about
110km northeast of Qazvin. **Lamiasar** (aka
Lam Besar, Lamsar) is the most extensive
ruined site and is only 65km from Qazvin. A
guide is recommended, but not essential.

You can charter a taxi in Qazvin that
will drive you to the beginning of the track
to Lamiasar, wait while you climb around
the ruins and bring you back for about
IR150,000 plus IR10,000 per hour for waiting. Hotel Iran in Qazvin also organises trips
to Lamiasar, with English-speaking guides,
for a pricey US$35. To Alamut costs more.
A daily minibus leaves Qazvin's Tehran Gate
at about 11.30am for Gazor Khan (three
hours), from where you can walk to Alamut,
and returns the following morning. You'll
need to negotiate a bed in the village.

Soltaniyeh
سلطانیه

This place is dominated by the **Oljeitu
Mausoleum** (Gonbad-e Soltaniyeh; admission IR5000;
🕑 7am-7pm, to 9pm summer), resting place of the
Mongol sultan Oljeitu Khodabande. With
the largest brick dome in the world – 48m
high, and 25m in diameter – it was originally built as the final resting place of Ali,
the son-in-law of the Prophet Mohammed,
but the sultan inconveniently converted to
Sunnism so Ali stayed in Najaf. Much of the
interior is covered by scaffolding.

The mausoleum is not far from the old
road (not the expressway) between Qazvin
and Zanjan, but is much closer to Zanjan
(36km). Take any bus (IR8000) or savari
(IR40,000) between the two towns, get
off at the junction and catch a shared taxi
(IR3000) to Soltaniyeh village.

KERMANSHAH
کرمانشاه
☎ 0431 / pop 800,000

This is the largest and busiest city in the central west and has long traded on its location
on the Royal Road to Baghdad. The city is a
rich mix of Kurds, Lori and other Iranians,
but with its oil refineries and other major
industries, it's decidedly lacking in charm.

The vast Azadi Sq marks the north edge
of central Kermanshah. From here, the
main drag is called Beheshti St as it runs
north and turns into Sheikh Shoodi St before ending at Taq-e Bostan. South of Azadi
Sq, it's called Modarres St and then Kashani
St and is home to a relatively uninteresting
bazaar, the **Bank Melli** (Modarres St), opposite the
mosque, and **Padideh Coffeenet** (☎ 727 0120; per
hr IR5000; 🕑 8am-10pm), which is off Kashani St
about 200m south of Gohad Sq. There's a
telephone office (Beheshti St; 🕑 7am-10pm) about
100m north of Azadi Sq on the west side.

Sights
The Sassanian-era (AD 224–642) bas-reliefs
and carved alcoves at **Taq-e Bostan** (admission
IR5000; 🕑 8am-8pm) are Kermanshah's star attraction. The figures in the large grotto are
believed to represent Khosro II while, in the
small arched recess, Shapur II and his grandson, Shapur III, can be seen. From Azadi Sq
take a shared taxi to 15 Khordad Sq (IR1500)
and another to Taq-e Bostan (IR1500), or
charter one for about IR10,000.

In the centre of town, the colourful
Qajar-era **Takieh Mo'aven ol-Molk** (Hadid Abil St;
admission IR4000; 🕑 8am-noon & 2-5.30pm, 8am-noon
& 4-8pm summer) is used to commemorate the
death of Imam Hossein.

Sleeping & Eating
Hotel Nabovat (☎ 823 1018; Azadi Sq; s/tw/tr IR40,000/
60,000/90,000; 🍴) Very basic but mostly clean
rooms and share bathrooms. The triple has
a private bathroom.

Until the **Bisotun Hotel** (☎ 772 3792; Kashani St)
reopens; the soulless and overpriced **Hotel
Karbala** (☎ 727 3665; Parking Shaderi; s/tw US$20/30;
🍴), just off Modarres St, is the best midrange option. That doesn't mean it's much
good; most of the small rooms have fridge,
basin and shower; some have squat toilets.

Food in Kermanshah includes a lot of
offal or sliced fat kebabs – not good. The
best places to eat are the **restaurants** (🕑 about
noon-3.30pm & 6-10pm) around Taq-e Bostan.

Getting There & Away

There are several **Iran Air** (☎ 824 8610; Beheshti St) flights each day to Tehran (IR218,000).

The huge bus and minibus terminals are side by side about 8km north of Azadi Sq – shared taxis to the terminal (IR1500) leave from the northeastern corner of the square. Buses leave regularly for Esfahan (IR25,000, nine hours), Tabriz (IR33,000, eight hours), Ahvaz (IR40,000 in Volvo), and Tehran (IR27,500, nine hours). For Hamadan take a minibus (IR6000, three hours) or a savari via Kangavar. For Khorramabad, Taavoni No 7 has an 8.30am bus (IR15,000, five hours), or take any bus heading to Ahvaz.

BISOTUN   بیستون

Overlooking the main road to Hamadan, about 2km west of Bisotun village, are two eroded **bas-relief carvings**. Access is via a rusty scaffold (not always open) that affords views of a 480 BC Darius receiving sup-plicants, with a winged Zoroastrian angel overhead. It's surrounded by entertaining cuneiform inscriptions (translations are available from the shop just west of here). Come in the morning for the best view. Savaris (IR5000) run from 15 Khordad Sq in Kermanshah.

HAMADAN   همدان
☎ 0261

Hamadan has for millennia been an impor-tant trading city and is the site of Ecbatana, one of the ancient world's greatest cities when it was the fortified capital of the Me-dian empire (750–550 BC). Pitifully little remains, and these days Hamadan is notable for its European-style street plan, designed in 1929 by German engineer Karl Frisch.

The centre of town is the huge Imam Khomeini Sq, from which streets fan out cartwheel-style. Change money at **Bank Melli** (Imam Khomeini Sq) and check email at **Net Gostar** (☎ 252 9929; Bu Ali Sina Sq; per hr IR8000; ☉ 8.30am-9.30pm Sat-Thu & 10.30am-1.30pm Fri).

Sights

The **Aramgah-e Ester va Mordekhay** (☉ 8am-3pm winter, 9am-4pm summer) is the most important Jewish pilgrimage site in Iran. Jews believe that it contains the body of Esther, the Jew-ish wife of Xerxes I, who is credited with organising the first Jewish emigration to Persia in the 5th century BC.

Just north of the main square, the **Jameh Mosque** (off Ekbatan St) has 55 columns, and was built during the Qajar period.

The distinctive **BuAli Sina (Avicenna) Mauso-leum** (admission IR4000; ☉ 8am-7pm), is Hamadan city's icon. BuAli Sina, known in the West as Avicenna, was a famous philosopher and physician, whose 11th century works were used in European universities until the 1600s. It is a rare triumph of modern Iranian design.

Some ruins of **ancient Ecbatana** (☎ 822 4005; admission IR4000; ☉ 9am-1pm & 3-5pm, to 8pm summer) can be seen around the archaeological site at Hekmetaneh Hill, about 750m north of Imam Khomeini Sq. Most items of inter-est are in the National Museum of Iran in Tehran.

Sleeping & Eating

The cheapest hotels are around Imam Kho-meini Sq.

Arian Hotel (☎ 826 1266; fax 826 7329; Takhti St; s/d/tr US$35/40/45; ☒ P) A comfortable mid-range option, the sizable rooms have West-ern bathroom, fridge and satellite TV, and management are helpful. US$10 discounts are possible.

Hamadan Guest House (☎ 252 7577; Ekbatan St; r IR70,000; P) Just north of Imam Khomeini Sq, the clean, three- and four-bed rooms here are very simple and the smelly bathrooms can be a long walk, but it's still the pick of the budget joints. The adjoining teahouse/restaurant is both cheap and atmospheric.

Hezaroyek Shab (☎ 822 7569; meals IR25,000-50,000; ☉ 11.30am-3.30pm & 7-11pm Sat-Thu) A huge var-iety of Iranian dishes, plus Western fare and a charming English-speaking owner. It's 2km south of town but taxi drivers know it.

Chaykhuneh Baharestan (☎ 254 2777; Shohada St; meals IR10,000-15,000; ☉ 6am-7pm) Just off Imam Khomeini Sq, it serves great *dizi*.

Getting There & Away

The bus terminal is about 1.2km north of the main square and easily reached along Ekbatan St. Buses regularly go to Esfahan (IR19,500, eight hours), Orumiyeh (via Sanandaj, IR37,000, 12 to 14 hours); and Teh-ran (IR15,000, five hours). Bus companies have offices around Imam Khomeini Sq.

The main minibus terminal is about 200m northeast of the bus terminal and serves Kermanshah (via Bisotun, IR7000),

Lalejin and Qorveh for Sanandaj (IR2500) and other local destinations. For Khorramabad minibuses/savaris go first to Borujerd (IR3000/30,000), then go on to Khorramabad (IR1800/15,000). Savaris to Kermanshah (IR30,000) and Qazvin (IR40,000) leave from Sepah Sq, near the bus terminal.

AROUND HAMADAN

The village of **Lalejin**, 32km north of Hamadan, is famous for its pottery and turquoise glazing. You can browse the showrooms, visit workshops and fend off endless entreaties to purchase a souvenir.

KHORRAMABAD   خرم آباد

☎ 0661 / pop 300,000

Set in a long, steep-sided valley, the scenic capital of Lorestan is famous for, and dominated by, the imposing hilltop citadel, the **Falak-ol-Aflak** (☎ 220 4090; www.lorestanmiras.org; admission IR4000; ☼ 9am-noon & 3-5pm, to 7pm summer). Views from the top are breathtaking and the museum inside is interesting and well presented. **Bank Melli** (Imam Khomeini St) changes money, and **Khoram Pardos** (☎ 220 0006; Kashani St; per hr IR8000; ☼ 10am-1pm & 6-9pm) has Internet connections; it's on the east side of the river, in the street that has the last bridge before the river bends, as you head north.

Sleeping & Eating

Hotel Karoon (☎ 220 5408; Shari'ati St; s/tw/tr US$15/20/24) Musty but relatively clean, with eastern bathrooms and English-speaking management. Bargain hard.

Mehmunpazir Sahel (☎ 220 3260; Shari'ati St; s/tw IR55,000/75,000) You probably won't be allowed to stay, which is probably a good thing. It's grim, and has no shower.

Some decent kababis can be found just west of the bridge leading to the citadel, and juice bars are plentiful on Imam Khomeini St.

Getting There & Away

Buses leave from outside the relevant bus company offices along Shari'ati St. Services to Tehran (IR35,000 in Volvo, seven hours) and Esfahan (IR18,000, seven hours) usually leave in the morning and evening, and buses to Ahvaz (IR18,000, six hours) at night. Taavoni 17 has a 2pm bus to Kermanshah (IR13,000, 3½ hours). For Hamadan, see p207 and take a savari/minibus in reverse.

Minibuses (IR9500, 4½ hours) and savaris (IR40,000, three hours) to Andimeshk depart from south of Imam Hossein Sq.

ANDIMESHK   اندیمشک

☎ 0642 / pop 140,000

Andimeshk is not unattractive but it is boring and is mainly useful as a transport hub en route to Shush and Choqa Zanbil. The town centre is, surprise surprise, Imam Khomeini St where you'll find **Hotel Rostam** (☎ 424 1818; s/d IR80,000/105,000), 300m north of Beheshti Sq, where rooms have private bathrooms. The only alternative is the mid-range **Hotel Bozorg** (☎ 422 2100; Azadegan Sq; s/d IR175,000,000/250,000; ☒ P), where you can arrange taxis to Shush and Choqa Zanbil for about IR100,000 per half day.

The blue-glass bus terminal has irregular services to Tehran (IR27,000, 12 hours), Esfahan (IR27,000, 11 hours) and Ahvaz (IR10,000). For Shush, frequent minibuses (IR1500, one hour) and savaris leave from the terminal. Savaris run to Khorramabad from a terminal 2km north of town.

SHUSH (SUSA)   شوش (سوسا)

☎ 0642 / pop 68,000

Settled since about the 4000 BC, Shush (Susa) reached its peak as one of the grand capitals of the Achaemenid empire (550–330 BC). Little of that grandeur remains, but Shush is easily the best and most relaxed base from which to explore the area and visit Choqa Zanbil. Apart from the limited remains of the Ancient City, Shush is home to the **Tomb of Daniel** (Aramgah-e Danyal), the resting place of a Jewish figure best known for his exploits in lions' dens. Odd!

The best-value place to stay and eat is the **Apadana Hotel** (☎ /fax 522 3131; s/tw with breakfast IR170,000/190,000; P ☒), centrally located on the river. Rooms have Western bathrooms, fans and a fridge. Prices are negotiable by about IR20,000.

Ancient City

Work at the **archaeological site** (admission IR4000; ☼ 8am-dusk) has uncovered the remains of four mounds, which formed the centre of ancient Shush. The **Royal Town**, once the quarter of the court officials, is nearest the entrance. Northwest of this is the **Apadana**, where Darius I built his residence and two other palaces. Two well-preserved foundation tablets found beneath the site of **Darius' Palace** record the noble ancestry of its founder. The imposing **Chateau de Morgan**, near the entrance, was built by the French Archaeological Service at the end of the 19th century as a defence against marauding Arab and Lori tribesmen. It's not open to the public.

CHOQA ZANBIL   چغا زنبيل

A Unesco World Heritage–listed site, the 13th-century-BC **ziggurat** (admission IR5000; ☼ guarded 24hr) at Choqa Zanbil is the best surviving example of Elamite architecture anywhere. Its pure size combined with its age can't fail to impress. The ziggurat and surrounding town were sacked and abandoned in about 640 BC, and it incredibly became 'lost' under the desert sands for more than 2500 years. It was accidentally rediscovered during a 1935 aerial survey by the Anglo-Iranian Oil Company, forerunner of BP.

Originally it had five concentric storeys but only three remain, reaching a total height of about 25m. There was originally a complex of chambers, tombs, tunnels and water channels on the lowest level, as well as two temples to Inshushinak on the southeastern side. The rest of the city is not well preserved.

There's no public transport to Choqa Zanbil, so a taxi from Shush (IR80,000 return) or between Shush and Ahvaz, (about IR140,000 plus IR15,000 per hour waiting time) is the best option.

AHVAZ   اهواز
☎ 0611

This place is big and ugly and you'll probably only use it as a transit point to or from Shush and Choqa Zanbil. The city was heavily bombed throughout the Iran-Iraq War and has since been ruined by uncontrolled redevelopment.

If you must stay, the **Iran Hotel** (☎ 221 7200; Shari'ati St; s/tw IR150,000/250,000; ✖) is reliable if uninspiring. Budgeteers might consider **Tulu** (☎ 222 2221; Shari'ati St; r IR60,000), which is central and cheap but, critically, has no fans.

Iran Air (☎ 365 680) flies every day to Tehran (IR264,000) and Esfahan (IR195,000), and less often to Mashhad and Shiraz. The main bus terminal is about 5km west of the river. Services include Bushehr (IR20,000, seven hours), Esfahan (IR37,500, 14 hours), Khorramabad (IR18,000, six hours), Ker-

manshah (IR24,000, nine hours) and Shiraz (IR26,000, 10 hours).

There are three trains a day to Tehran (IR113,800/18,350 in sleeper/2nd class, 17 hours).

CENTRAL IRAN   مركز ايران

As home to three of Iran's most interesting, attractive and contrasting cities – Esfahan, Shiraz and Yazd – central Iran will be on almost every traveller's itinerary. But it's not just about the big three. Although relatively sparsely populated, especially in the east where Iran's two great deserts meet, there are several lesser-known but equally appealing towns to occupy your time.

QOM   قم
☎ 0251

Iran's second-holiest city after Mashhad, Qom (Ghom) is home to both the magnificent **Hazrat-e Masumeh** (☼ 24hr) shrine and many of the hardline clerics who rule the country. The shrine is dedicated to Fatima (sister of Imam Reza), who died and was buried here in the 9th century. This extensive and ever-growing complex was initiated by Shah Abbas I and expanded by other Safavid rulers anxious to establish their Shiite credentials. Non-Muslims are not permitted to enter the shrine itself but you can enter the courtyards and observe the pilgrims, mullahs and Shiite devotees. Be discreet if taking photographs. A few hours is enough in Qom, which is best visited as a stop between Tehran and Kashan.

There is a huddle of cheap guesthouses in Haramnema Lane, over the Ahanchi Bridge from the shrine complex.

Etminan Hotel (☎ 660 9640; Haramnema Lane; s/d IR80,000/100,000) has tiny, tidy rooms with private bathroom; front rooms have views but are terribly noisy.

Safa Apartment Hotel (☎ 773 2499; Mo'allem St; d/ste US$30/40; Ⓟ ✖), about 600m south of the shrine, has rooms with satellite TV and Western bathrooms. They're as good as you'll find in Qom and offer great value.

Buses and savaris from Tehran's southern bus terminal stop momentarily at a large roundabout north of town before continuing to Kashan and all points beyond. Savaris to Tehran (IR30,000) or Kashan (IR20,000) leave from near the Ahanchi Bridge opposite the shrine.

KASHAN   کاشان
☎ 0361

Historic Kashan is a large but tranquil oasis town well worth a stop between Tehran and Esfahan. The centre of town is the stretch of Mohtasham between Imam Khomeini Sq and Kamal-ol-Molk Sq, about 700m to the south, though many of the life-support services are found on Shahid Mohammad Ali-ye-Raja'i St, which becomes Ayatollah Kashani St and Amir Kabir St as it heads south towards Fin.

Bank Melli (Amir Ahmad St), just west of the bazaar, changes money, and **Central City Cafenet** (☎ 0912-261 0911; Shahid Mohammad Ali-ye-Raja'i St; per hr IR10,000; ☼ 8am-11pm) has fast Internet service; it's just north of the intersection with Baba Afzal St.

Sights
The main reason to visit Kashan is to see the beautifully restored Qajar-era mansions just off Alavi St in the southeast of town. To get there, wander south through the lively **bazaar**, stopping for sweets and tea, and then another 700m or so further south from Kamal-ol-Molk Sq.

The magnificent **Khan-e Ameriha** (☎ 422 4008; admission IR2000; ☼ 1-5pm, 7.30am-7pm summer), with its dizzying seven courtyards, is a living work of art. Restoration is ongoing and it will likely become a hotel when completed. You'll still be able to visit; ask to see the roof.

On the opposite side of Alavi St, the **Khan-e Borujerdi** (☎ 422 3777; admission IR2000; ☼ 8am-5pm, to 7pm summer) was once home to a wealthy handicrafts merchant and contains charming wall paintings and a lovely courtyard flanked by summer and winter houses. About 100m further south, the **Khan-e Tabatabai** (☎ 422 0032; admission IR20,000; ☼ 8am-6pm, to 8pm summer) was the home of a carpet merchant and is famous for its carved reliefs, mirror and stained-glass work. The entrance is adjacent to the conical-roofed shrine.

Khan-e Abbasi (☎ 422 4070; admission IR20,000; ☼ 8am-dusk) boasts exceptional three-storey courtyards and fine stained-glass windows.

Sleeping & Eating
Sleeping options are limited. Both these places are within a few metres of the northern entrance to the bazaar.

Golestan Inn (☎ 444 6793; Abazar St; s/d/tr IR60,000/70,000/90,000) On Motahari Sq, the Golestan's no-frills rooms and clean shared bathrooms make it the best budget option, despite the wafer-thin mattresses.

Sayyah Hotel (☎ 444 4535; Abazar St; s/d IR120,000/ 160,000, with bathroom IR180,000/240,000; P ⌗ ☐) About 150m east of the Golestan, Sayyah is the best midrange option where clean rooms have fridge and, if you ask, views over the city. There's a decent restaurant (open 7am to 9pm) downstairs.

Delpazir Restaurant (☎ 455 322; Ayatollah Kashani St; meals IR40,000; ☼ noon-3pm & 7-11pm) Run by an English lady, her Iranian husband and their sons, Delpazir has a wide range of Iranian dishes, such as a very rich *fesenjun* (chicken marinated in pomegranate and walnut sauce) and excellent *bademjun* (aubergine).

Sultan Amir Ahmad Hammam (☎ 422 0038; Alavi St; ☼ 10am-3pm & 7-11pm Sat-Thu) Next to Khan-e Borujerdi, this beautifully restored *hammam*-turned-restaurant is a great place to stop for tea or lunch. If you don't eat or drink, there is an admission fee.

Getting There & Away
Dozens of buses leave Kashan for Esfahan (IR9000/15,000 in Mercedes/Volvo, three hours) and Tehran (IR10,500/18,000) every day, leaving from 15 Khordad Sq or the terminal, 1km north. Minibuses/savaris run to Qom (IR5000/20,000). Trains pass through between Tehran and Esfahan or Kerman, but the hours are unsociable.

AROUND KASHAN
Fin Garden   باغ فین
About 8km southwest of Kashan, this beautiful **garden** (admission IR2500; ☼ 8.30am-5pm, 7.30am-10.30pm summer) has buildings from the Safavid (1502–1736) and Qajar periods, as well as pools, natural springs, orchards and a charming **teahouse**. The gardens are famous as the site of the murder of Mirza Taghi Khan – commonly known as Amir Kabir – in 1851; you can check out the serene-looking waxwork re-enactment. If you've visited formal gardens in Shiraz, Fin is probably not worth a special trip. Take a shared taxi (IR2000) from Kashan.

Abyaneh ابیانه

☎ 0362

Nestled in a mountain valley 82km south of Kashan, this ancient red-mud village makes a fascinating day trip. Recognised for its antiquity and uniqueness by Unesco, most of the original structures date to the Safavid period. Villagers still wear distinctive clothing and speak Middle Persian, a dialect long-since disappeared elsewhere.

The only sleeping option is the **Abyaneh Hotel Restaurant** (☎ 436 2223; bed per person with breakfast US$20; P 🗙), where construction work has been proceeding slowly for years. Prices are outrageous, especially considering most rooms are dorms. Meals (about IR40,000) aren't bad.

Rare minibuses run from Kashan, but it's possible you'll be dropped near a nuclear site and need to wait for an equally rare connection. Easier is chartering a taxi for a full day from Kashan for around IR150,000, or arrange to stop in Abyaneh between Kashan and Esfahan (about IR200,000 for the taxi).

ESFAHAN اصفهان

☎ 0311

Of all Iran's cities, don't miss Esfahan. The cool blue tiles of its Islamic buildings, and the city's majestic bridges, contrast perfectly with the hot, dry Iranian countryside around it. The architecture is superb and there's a relaxed atmosphere compared with other Iranian towns. It's a city in which to walk, get lost in the bazaar, shop for handicrafts, doze in beautiful gardens, and meet people.

Esfahan reached its peak when Shah Abbas I came to power in 1587. He set out to make Esfahan a great city, and the famous half-rhyme *Esfahan nesf-e jahan* (Esfahan is half the world) was coined at this time to express its grandeur.

Information

BOOKSHOPS

Naqshe Jahan Bookshop (Map p214; ☎ 0931-310 7901; Imam Sq; 🕙 9am-9pm) Good range of English-language books and postcards.

EMERGENCY

Ambulance (☎ 229 2222, 115)
Tourist police (Map p212; ☎ 668 0046-7; 🕙 24hr) Outside the Madraseh-ye Chahar Bagh.

INTERNET ACCESS

Central Library of Esfahan (Map p212; ☎ 222 3698; Goldasteh Ave; per hr IR5000; 🕙 8am-8pm Sat-Thu) Friendly, English-speaking staff and loads of fast terminals.
Rose Internet (Map p212; ☎ 221 1222; Imam Sq; per hr IR10,000; 🕙 8am-9pm Sat-Thu & 10am-6pm Fri)

MEDICAL SERVICES

Al Zahra Hospital (Map p212; ☎ 669 2180; Soffeh St) English-speaking doctors.
Dr Hosseini Pharmacy (Map p212; ☎ 222 3511; Shahid Madani St; 🕙 24hr)

MONEY

Bank Melli (Map p212; Sepah St)
Money exchange office (Map p212; ☎ 222 2592; Sepah St; 🕙 8.30am-4.30pm Sat-Thu) Much faster and competitive rates.

POST

Main post office (Map p212; Neshat St) For parcels.
Post office (Map p214; Imam Sq)

TRAVEL AGENCIES

Iran Travel & Tourism (Map p212; ☎ 222 3010; irantravel1964@hotmail.com; Shahid Medani St) Tickets and tours.

VISA EXTENSIONS

Esfahan is the best place in Iran to get your visa extended. Staff at the **Department of Foreign Affairs office** (Map p212; ☎ 668 8166; 2nd Lane, Chahar Bagh Baia; 🕙 7am-1.30pm Sat-Wed, 7am-noon Thu) will take your money on the spot and usually issue the visa inside an hour. Head south from Si-o-Seh Bridge, pass the enormous Azadi Sq roundabout and 2nd Lane is 50m south of a pedestrian overpass.

Sights & Activities

Sights here are organised north to south.

JAMEH MOSQUE

The **Jameh Mosque** (Map p212; Masjed-e Jameh; admission IR3000; 🕙 8-11am & 1.15-4.30pm, 8am-noon & 2-6pm summer) is a virtual museum of Islamic architecture and is the biggest mosque in Iran. On display are 800 years' worth of Islamic design, from the simplicity of the Seljuk period (1051–1194), through the Mongol Ikhanid period (1220–1380) and on to the more baroque Safavid period (1502–1736). To fully appreciate this mosque you must go into the fine interior rooms, including the **Room of Sultan Uljaitu,** with its exquisite stucco mihrab, the room beneath the grand **Nezam al-Molk Dome** and the Seljuk-era hypostyle **prayer halls** either side, and the **Taj al-Molk Dome,** widely considered the finest brick dome ever built.

BAZAR-E BOZORG

The **Bazar-e Bozorg** (Great Bazaar; ⏱ Sat-Thu) is one of the highlights of Esfahan, linking Imam Sq with the Jameh Mosque, about 2km away. The covered bazaar, one of the largest in the country, was mostly built during the early 16th century, although some of it dates back almost 1300 years. Of the dozens of entrances, the main one is the elaborately decorated **Qeysarieh Portal** at the north end of Imam Sq. In the bazaar

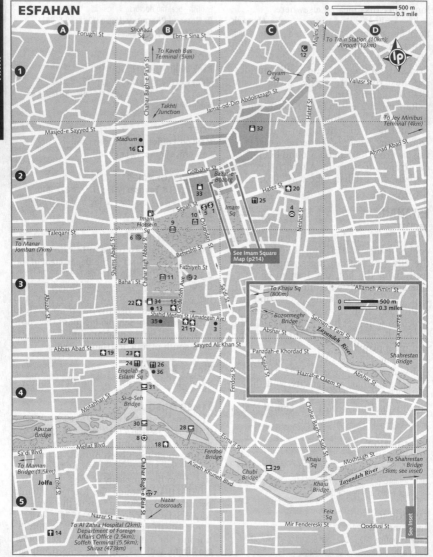

itself, the distinctive domed and vaulted ceilings usually culminate in an opening, sometimes star-shaped, allowing shafts of light to spill in on the commerce below. See also p216.

IMAM SQUARE (NAQSH-E JAHAN)
When French poet Renier described Esfahan as 'half of the world' in the early 17th century, it was the myriad wonders of the square called Naqsh-e Jahan that inspired him. While the name has changed it is still the home of arguably the most majestic collection of buildings in the Islamic world.

Naqsh-e Jahan means 'pattern of the world', and it's a world that owes much to the vision of Shah Abbas the Great. Begun in 1602 as the centrepiece of Abbas' new capital, the square was designed as home to the finest architectural jewels of the Safavid empire. At 512m long and 163m wide, this immense space is the second-largest square on earth after Tiananmen Sq.

The square is best visited in the late afternoon and early evening when the fountains are on and the splendid architecture is illuminated; you can't beat the view from the Qeysarieh Tea Shop (p216).

IMAM MOSQUE
One of the most beautiful mosques in the world is the **Imam Mosque** (Map p214; Masjed-e Imam; admission IR2500; ⏰ 8am-11.30am & 1-5pm Sat-Thu 1-5pm Fri, to 7pm summer). The richness of its blue-tiled mosaic designs and its perfectly proportioned Safavid-era architecture form a visually stunning monument to the im-

agination of Shah Abbas I, who had it built over 27 years from 1611 to 1638.

The 30m-high entrance portal was built largely as an ornamental counterpoint to the entrance to the Bazar-e Bozorg. Although the portal faces the square, the mosque itself is angled in the direction of Mecca. A short corridor winds into the inner courtyard, which has a pool for ritual ablutions surrounded by four *iwans* (vaulted halls). The walls of the courtyard contain the most exquisite sunken porches, framed by mosaics of deep blue and yellow. The main sanctuary is entered via the south *iwan* and the black paving stones under the dome create seven clear echoes when stamped upon. The interior ceiling is 36.3m high, although the exterior reaches up to 51m due to the double-layering used in construction.

SHEIKH LOTFOLLAH MOSQUE
It isn't as grand as the nearby Imam Mosque, but the **Sheikh Lotfollah Mosque** (Map p214; admission IR2500; ⏰ 8.30am-4.30pm, to 7pm summer) is an exquisite study in harmony. Built between 1602 and 1619, also by Shah Abbas I, the mosque is unusual because it has neither a minaret nor a courtyard, and because steps lead up to the entrance. This was probably because the mosque was never intended for public use, but rather served as the worship place for the women of the shah's harem. It is named after the ruler's father-in-law, Sheikh Lotfollah, a revered Lebanese scholar.

The pale dome makes extensive use of delicate cream-coloured tiles that change colour throughout the day from cream to pink; sunset is usually best. Photography is allowed but flashes are not.

ALI QAPU PALACE

The six-storey **Ali Qapu Palace** (Map p214; admission IR2500; ⏱ 8.30am-sunset Sat-Thu & 2.30pm-sunset Fri) was built in the late 16th century, it is believed, as a residence for Shah Abbas I.

IMAM SQUARE

EATING 🍴
Aboozar Restaurant..............7 B1
Bastani Traditional
  Restaurant.....................8 B4
Only Kabab Kababi..............9 B2
Restaurant Traditional
  Banquet Hall..................10 B3

INFORMATION
Naqshe Jahan Bookshop....1 A3
Post Office.........................2 A3

SIGHTS & ACTIVITIES
Ali Qapu Palace.................3 A3
Imam Mosque....................4 A4
Qeysarieh Portal................5 A2
Sheikh Lotfollah Mosque...6 B3

DRINKING 🍷
Azadegan Teahouse.........11 B2
Qeysarieh Tea Shop.........12 A1

SHOPPING 🛍
Aladdin Carpets...............13 B2
Bazar-e Bozorg................14 A1
Fallahi Miniatures............15 A4
Nomad Carpet Shop........16 A3

Many of the murals and mosaics have been destroyed, but the fretwork stalactites on the top floor, chiselled out in the shapes of musical instruments, are beautiful. The views of the square from the top floor are superb, so don't miss it.

CHEHEL SOTUN PALACE

This marvellously decorated **palace** (Map p214; Ostandari St; admission IR2000; ⏱ 8am-5pm, 8am-noon & 2-8pm summer) was built as a pleasure pavilion and reception hall sometime in the first half of the 17th century; though its exact age is unknown, what you see today was built after a fire in 1706. Its 20 columns, when reflected in the pool, become 40, hence the name, which means 'forty columns'. The main hall features a stunning series of frescoes showing the decadence of palace life and horror of war, including a gory battle with the Uzbeks. There is a miniscule museum inside.

The extensive gardens are a pleasant place to sit and chill, and there's a small teahouse. Early morning is best for photos.

MUSEUMS

The **Decorative Arts Museum of Iran** (Map p212; Ostandari St; admission IR2500; ⏱ 7am-2pm Wed-Mon) contains some wonderful miniatures, lacquerwork, calligraphy, ceramics, brasswork, woodcarvings and traditional costumes. It's in a building that was once stables for the nearby Chehel Sotun Palace. Nearby, the **Museum of Contemporary Art** (Ostandari St; admission IR10,000; ⏱ 9am-noon & 4-7pm, 5-8pm summer, Sat-Thu) sometimes has interesting exhibitions.

HASHT BEHESHT PALACE

Built in the 1660s, the small **Hasht Behesht Palace** (Map p212; admission IR2000; ⏱ 8am-5pm, to 7pm summer) was once the most luxurious in Esfahan. It has been damaged over the years but retains a seductive tranquillity that comes from its setting amid the tall trees of the surrounding garden. The Hasht Behesht (meaning Eight Paradises) blends in perfectly, with the soaring wooden columns on its open-sided terrace seeming to mirror the trees in the surrounding park. Inside are some impressive mosaics and stalactite mouldings, most of which can be seen from outside.

MADRASEH-YE CHAHAR BAGH

Part of an expansive complex built at the end of the Safavid dynasty, the **Madraseh-ye**

Chahar Bagh (Madraseh-ye Madar-e Shah; Map p212; Chahar Bagh Abbasi St; admission IR30,000; ☾ 8am-7pm Thu & Fri) is extraordinarily beautiful and restful. The complex contains a prayer hall with a lovely mihrab, two of the finest Safavid-era minarets in Esfahan, some exquisite mosaics and a particularly attractive dome.

ZAYANDEH RIVER BRIDGES

There are few better ways to spend an afternoon than strolling along the **Zayandeh River**, crossing back and forth using the fairytale old bridges, stopping in their cosy teahouses and just relaxing with the Esfahanis. In total, 11 bridges (six are new) cross the Zayandeh, the most interesting being east of Chahar Bagh St.

The pedestrian **Si-o-Seh Bridge** links the upper and lower halves of Chahar Bagh St, and was so-named because it has 33 arches. It was completed in 1602 and has simple teahouses at either end. **Chubi Bridge** was built for Shah Abbas II, primarily to help irrigate palace gardens in the area; its cosy teahouse is one of the best in Esfahan.

Khaju Bridge is the largest and doubles as a dam. On hot summer days, Iranians lounge around under the cool arches here, making this a great place to meet people.

Shahrestan Bridge is the oldest – most of its present stone-and-brick structure is believed to date from the 12th century – but it's a good 3km from Khaju.

ARMENIAN QUARTER

The lively and liberal Armenian quarter of **Jolfa** dates from the time of Shah Abbas I. The 17th-century **Vank Cathedral** (Kelisa-ye Vank; Map p212; Kelisa St; adult/student IR30,000/15,000; ☾ 8am-12.30pm & 2-5.30pm, to 6.30pm summer) is the historic focal point of the Armenian church in Iran. The exterior of the church is a little dull, but the interior is richly decorated, and shows a fascinating mixture of Islamic and Christian styles, with a domed ceiling. The attached **museum** (☾ 8am-noon & 2-5pm Mon-Sat) contains over 700 handwritten books, and other ethnological displays, including a moving pictorial display on the Armenian genocide in Turkey.

MANAR JOMBAN

In Kaladyn, about 7km west of the city centre, is the tomb of Abu Abdollah, known as **Manar Jomban** (Shaking Minarets; Map p212; admission IR2000; ☾ 8.30am-4pm, to 8pm summer) because if you lean hard against one minaret it will start to sway back and forth – and so will its twin. If it's crowded you won't be able to climb the minaret, but an attendant will shake it so you can see the effect. Frequently, however, it's closed due to concerns that the minarets are being shaken too hard, too often.

Buses (IR250, 20 minutes) go west along Bahai St from near the corner of Chahar Bagh Abbasi St and run past Manar Jomban.

Sleeping

There's a good range of accommodation in Esfahan, though prices can be higher than you'd pay elsewhere.

BUDGET

Amir Kabir Hostel (Map p212; ☎ 222 7273; mrziaee@ hotmail.com; Chahar Bagh Abbasi St; dm/s/tw/tr IR30,000/ 55,000/80,000/120,000; ☐) A cheap, popular backpacker hangout, the rooms and shared bathrooms here are decidedly basic. However, the Ziaee brothers speak good English and can sort out bus tickets. There's a guestbook and a cheap laundry.

Aria Hotel (Map p212; ☎ 222 7224; fax 233 2441; Shahid Medani St; s/d incl breakfast US$15/20; ✺) While the questionable plumbing can be a problem, for the money the centrally located Aria is still good value. Rooms are cleaned daily and have soft beds, fridge, Iranian TV and Western bathrooms (some with baths). Guests can use the kitchen.

Shad Hotel (Map p212; ☎ 221 8621; fax 220 4264; Chahar Bagh Abbasi St; s/tw/tr IR68,800/85,000/95,000; ✺) Central and fair value, Shad has small, clean two- and three-bed rooms and share bathrooms, and there's a kitchen. Front rooms are noisy.

Tous Hotel (Map p212; ☎ 222 1599; tous@yahoo .com; Chahar Bagh Abbasi St; s/d IR100,000/170,000; ✺) Fun staff, clean rooms with bathrooms and a great location.

MIDRANGE & TOP END

All the rooms in this range have bathrooms and air-con, and most will have a TV and fridge as well.

Sadaf Hotel (Map p212; ☎ /fax 220 2988; Hafez St; s/d US$45/65; ✺ ☐) The hotel is well managed and located, and the spotless rooms with fridge and satellite TV are about the best in the midrange. Discounts are available and the rooftop restaurant is a delight in summer.

IRAN

Pol & Park Hotel (Map p212; ☎ 667 4785; fax 667 4788; A'ineh Khuneh Blvd; s/d US$21/31; P ✸) Although the rooms are a little tired, the Western bathrooms and balconies with views over the Si-oh-Seh Bridge make them great value. The English-speaking management is helpful, and prices are negotiable.

Safir Hotel (Map p212; ☎ /fax 221 9931; www.safir hotel.com; Shahid Medani St; s/d US$45/60; ✸ 💻) Diagonally opposite the Abbasi, this is a busy but welcoming place with modern rooms and a handy café. English and French are spoken by the obliging management. Discounts are possible.

Saadi Hotel (Map p212; ☎ 220 3881; saadi_hotel@ yahoo.com; Abbas Abad St; d/tr IR185,000/215,000; ✸ 💻) Central but in a relatively quiet street, Saadi is a solid option with large rooms and a kitchen open to guests.

Abbasi Hotel (Map p212; ☎ 222 6010; www.abbasi hotel.com; Shahid Medani St; s/d incl breakfast US$94/141; P ✸ 💻 ☎) Built in the shell of a Safavid-era caravanserai and set around a gorgeous garden, the Abbasi's probably the best hotel in Esfahan. Still, the rooms and service can be a little disappointing, considering the price. Ask for a room overlooking the courtyard.

Eating

There is not much culinary variety in Esfahani restaurants.

Bastani Traditional Restaurant (Map p214; ☎ 220 0374-5; Imam Sq; meals IR30,000-45,000; ☽ 11.30am-10.30pm) The great location and traditional food, including several types of *khoresht*, make it worth braving the lunchtime tour groups. Evenings are much quieter.

Restaurant Traditional Banquet Hall (Map p214; ☎ 221 9068; Imam Sq; meals IR35,000; ☽ 11.30am-10pm) This modern-traditional teahouse-cum-restaurant was described by one reader as the best place he ate at in Iran. The Iranian food, atmosphere, service, and regular evening music are all good.

Aboozar Restaurant (Map p214; ☎ 222 0654; meals IR13,000-25,000; ☽ noon-3pm) This bustling little place is where the *bazaris* eat fast, cheap meals. Arrive early or you'll miss the best food.

Restaurant Shahrzad (Map p212; ☎ 220 4490; Abbas Abad St; meals IR50,000; ☽ noon-10.30pm) Among Esfahan's best restaurants, the period wall-paintings, stained-glass windows and mirrorwork make Shahrzad an experience worthy of the fine food.

Bame Sahel Teahouse (Map p212; Chahar Bagh Abbasi St; ☽ 8am-11pm) On the top floor of the Sahel Hotel, the *dizi* (IR14,000) is good and the character raw.

Maharaja Restaurant (Map p212; ☎ 222 4985; Enqelab Sq; meals IR25,000-40,000) If you can deal with the dire service, the Maharaja's Indian food, including yellow daal, makes a welcome change.

Chahar Bagh Abbasi St is where you'll find the greatest concentration of pizza, sandwich, burger, ice-cream and, occasionally, real kebab joints, especially near Sayyed Ali Khan St. Near the Amir Kabir Hostel there are a couple of kababis and an excellent all-day **ash-e reshte place** (Chahar Bagh Abbasi St; ☽ 7am-9pm), great for breakfast; look for the huge pot inside the doorway. A bowl with bread is IR5000.

Elsewhere, the **Only Kabab Kababi** (Map p214; Hafez St), just east of Imam Sq, makes a fast, tasty kebab, and further along **Fereni Hafez** (Map p212; Hafez St; ☽ 8am-midnight) serves delicious *fereni*, made of rice-flour, milk, sugar and rose-water, for IR1000; look for the red sign.

Drinking

Esfahan has some of the most atmospheric teahouses in Iran. The most famous are in the pillars of bridges spanning the Zayandeh River – the tiny, richly decorated teahouse in the **Chubi Bridge** (Map p212; ☽ 8am-8pm) should not be missed, while the **Si-o-Seh Bridge** (Map p212; ☽ 8am-11pm) has teahouses underneath both ends.

There are two good teahouses on Imam Sq. **Qeysarieh Tea Shop** (Map p214; ☽ 8am-11pm), upstairs at the north end of the square, is quite simply the best place to sit on the terrace and watch the square, especially at sunset. Cheap tea, too. Tucked away in the northeastern corner, the more local **Azadegan Teahouse** (Map p214; Chaykhuneh-ye Azadegan; ☎ 221 1225; ☽ 10am-10pm) is cluttered with statues, bells, weapons, ceramics, and lines of men smoking *qalyan*. Good fun!

On a small island on the river, **Agig Restaurant & Teahouse** (Map p212; ☽ 11am-midnight) is a good place to meet flirting students, or perhaps flirt with students meeting...

Shopping

Esfahan has probably the widest selection of handicrafts anywhere in the country. The best buys are carpets (from all over Iran), miniatures hand-painted on camel bone, inlaid boxes and intricate copper, brass and silver work. Prices can be higher than elsewhere but for the vast range of price and quality, and the pleasure of shopping in the **Bazar-e Bozorg** and the wonderful arcades of **Imam Square**, it's worth it.

Most carpet shops are on or just off Imam Sq. For gold, head directly to the **Bazar-e Honar** (Map p212; Chahar Bagh Abbasi St; ☉ 8.30am-1pm & 4-9pm Sat-Thu). Bargain hard. Recommended, reputable shops:

Aladdin Carpets (Map p214; ☎ 221 1461; Imam Sq; ☉ 8am-8pm)

Fallahi Miniatures (Map p214; ☎ 220 4613; Imam Sq; ☉ 8.30am-12.30pm & 3-7.30pm) There's also a branch opposite the Abbasi Hotel.

Nomad Carpet Shop (Map p214; ☎ 221 9275; nomad shop@yahoo.com; Imam Sq; ☉ 9am-8pm Sat-Thu)

Getting There & Away
AIR
Iran Air (Map p212; ☎ 222 8200; Shahid Medani St) has flights to Tehran (IR195,000 one way, several daily), Shiraz (IR196,000, daily), Ahvaz (IR195,000, daily), Mashhad (IR379,000, five weekly), Bandar Abbas (IR361,000, three weekly), Kerman (IR267,000, twice weekly), Bushehr (IR220,000, weekly) and Zahedan (IR407,000, weekly).

BUS
There are two major bus terminals – **Soffeh** (Map p212; ☎ 668 8341), 5km south of the river, and the larger and more convenient **Kaveh bus terminal** (☎ 441 4375), about the same distance north. From Kaveh Mercedes/Volvo buses depart regularly going to Tehran (IR20,000/33,000, seven hours); Shiraz (IR19,000/33,000, eight hours); Yazd (IR12,600/24,000, five hours); Hamadan (IR18,000/32,000, seven hours); Kermanshah (IR25,000/48,000, nine hours); Kerman (IR19,000/40,000, 12 hours); and Kashan (IR9000/15,000, three hours). City buses and shared taxis (IR3000) to Chahar-Bagh Abbasi St pass by regularly on the main road outside the terminal; a taxi *dah baste* should cost about IR12,000 – not IR30,000.

TRAIN
Trains run to Tehran (IR31,000, seven hours, 10pm daily) via Kashan (IR18,000, 3½ hours); and to Bandar Abbas (IR66,000) via Yazd (IR15,000 in 1st-class sleeper, three

times weekly). For tickets, head to the convenient **Raja ticket office** (Map p212; ☎ 222 4425; Enqelab Sq; ☉ 8am-4pm Sat-Thu).

The **train station** (☎ 668 8001) is about 6km south of town but if you have a prebooked ticket you can catch a shuttle bus from outside the Kowsar International Hotel at the southern end of Si-o-Seh Bridge – ask at the ticket office.

Getting Around
You can happily walk around most of Esfahan's sights. The airport is about 12km from the city centre. To get there catch a shared taxi from Takhti Sq and another from Qods or Laleh Sqs. A taxi *dah baste* costs about IR30,000.

Bus 301 runs along Chahar Bagh Abbasi St linking the Kaveh and Soffeh bus terminals (IR500).

GARMEH   گرمه
☎ 0324 / pop about 300 and a few camels
The tiny oasis village of Garmeh is everything you'd imagine an oasis village to be. More than 50 varieties of date palm spread out from a small spring, and where the palms finish the ancient mud-brick village begins. In the midst of this village is **Ateshoni** (☎ 443 3356, in Tehran ☎ 021-273 1983; www.ateshoni.com; per person US$20), where Tehrani artist Maziar Ale Davoud has fled the fumes to renovate the family home. The US$20 includes all the food (and wonderful dates and pomegranates) you can eat. It gets ridiculously hot in summer.

Getting to Garmeh is not easy. From Esfahan, a Seiro Safar bus (IR18,000, about seven hours) leaves at 1pm. Get off at Khur, and if you've called ahead someone will be waiting to drive you (IR30,000) the last 37km into the desert. From Yazd, the Mashhad bus leaves about 1pm every day, passing Na'in about 5pm and reaching Khur about 9pm. From Garmeh, a direct bus to Yazd via the desert road leaves on Monday, Wednesday and Friday at 1pm. From Khur, daily buses run to Esfahan via Na'in at 1pm or 2pm (IR18,000).

YAZD   یزد
☎ 0351 / pop 450,000
With its winding lanes, wind towers and mud-brick old town, Yazd is one of the highlights of any trip to Iran. Wedged between

the northern Dasht-e Kavir and southern Dasht-e Lut deserts, Yazd boasts the best old – and still inhabited – city in the country. Yazd was an important centre for the pre-Islamic religion, Zoroastrianism, and still has the largest Zoroastrian community in the country. It's also famous for its *badgirs*, the wind towers designed to catch and

circulate the merest breath of wind and funnel it to underground living rooms, which dominate the city's roofscape.

Yazd is planned around a very loose northeast–southwest grid, with Beheshti Sq at its centre. If you stay within walking distance of this square, most sights and restaurants can be visited on foot. Expect to

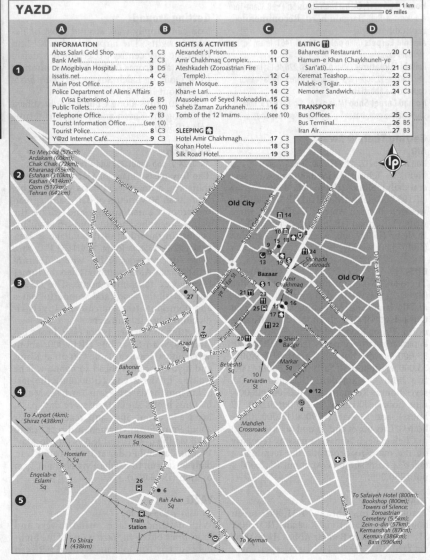

YAZD

0 _____ 1 km
0 _____ 05 miles

INFORMATION
Abas Salari Gold Shop...................**1** C3
Bank Melli.....................................**2** C3
Dr Mogibiyan Hospital..................**3** D5
Issatis.net.....................................**4** C4
Main Post Office............................**5** B5
Police Department of Aliens Affairs
 (Visa Extensions).......................**6** B5
Public Toilets..........................(see 10)
Telephone Office...........................**7** B3
Tourist Information Office.........(see 10)
Tourist Police...............................**8** C3
Y@zd Internet Café........................**9** C3

SIGHTS & ACTIVITIES
Alexander's Prison........................**10** C3
Amir Chakhmaq Complex...........**11** C3
Ateshkadeh (Zoroastrian Fire
 Temple)...................................**12** C4
Jameh Mosque..............................**13** C3
Khan-e Lari...................................**14** C2
Mausoleum of Seyed Roknaddin..**15** C3
Saheb Zaman Zurkhaneh.............**16** C3
Tomb of the 12 Imams...............(see 10)

SLEEPING
Hotel Amir Chakhmagh...............**17** C3
Kohan Hotel.................................**18** C3
Silk Road Hotel............................**19** C3

EATING
Baharestan Restaurant..................**20** C4
Hamum-e Khan (Chaykhuneh-ye
 San'ati).....................................**21** C3
Keremat Teashop..........................**22** C3
Malek-o Tojjar..............................**23** C3
Nemoner Sandwich......................**24** C3

TRANSPORT
Bus Offices...................................**25** C3
Bus Terminal................................**26** B5
Iran Air..**27** B3

To Meybod (57km);
Ardakam (60km);
Chak Chak (72km);
Kharanaq (85km);
Esfahan (310km);
Kashan (414km);
Qom (517km);
Tehran (642km)

Engelab St

Navaab-e Safavi Blvd

Tomhidye Eslami Blvd

Moahhad St

Old City

Sayyid Golsorkhi St

Imam Khomeini St

22 Bahman Blvd

Shahid Rajai St

Dr Nezhad Blvd

Shahrivar Blvd

Shahid Nezhad Blvd

Imamzadeh Ja'far St
Panjeh Ali Bazar
Qiyam St

Bazaar

Amir Chakhmaq Sq

Hazrati Mahari St

Seliman Fahal St

Dehe Parirokh St

Old City

Azadi Sq

Farrokhi St

Beheshti Sq

Sadughi Blvd

Bahonar Sq

Taleqan Blvd

Shesh Badgir

Markar Sq

10
Farvardin St

Shahid Cha'em Blvd

● 12

Bahonar Blvd

To Airport (4km);
Shiraz (438km)

Imam Hossein Sq

Beheshti Blvd

Mahdieh Crossroads

Dr Chamran St

@ 4

Homafer Sq

Jadde-ye Taft

Engelab-e Eslami Sq

26

● 6

Rah Ahan Sq

Train Station

Rah Ahan Blvd

Daneshju Blvd

Kashan St

To Safaiyeh Hotel (800m);
Bookshop (800m);
Towers of Silence;
Zoroastrian
Cemetery (5.5km);
Zein-o-din (57km);
Kermanshah (87km);
Kerman (386km);
Bam (590km)

To Shiraz
(438km)

5 ☎

To Kerman

Shonada Crossroads

get delightfully lost when walking around the old city.

Information

EMERGENCY
Dr Mogibiyan Hospital (☎ 624 0061; Kashani St)
Tourist police (☎ 621 4444)

INTERNET ACCESS
Issatis.net (☎ 623 1425; www.issatis.net; Kashani St; per hr IR6000; 🕙 9am-1.30pm & 5-9.30pm Sat-Thu) International phone calls for about IR1000 per minute.
Y@zd Internet Café (☎ 622 3832; yazd.internet.cafe@gmail.com; per hr IR8,000; 🕙 9am-10pm) Outside the Jameh Mosque entrance. Can arrange trips to the Jameh Mosque roof!

MONEY
Abas Salari Gold Shop (Qeyam St) Green corner store; fast with no commission.
Bank Melli (Shohada Crossroads) Takes a commission of US$2.

POST & TELEPHONE
Main post office (Ghasem Abad St)
Telephone office (Taleqani Blvd)

TOURIST INFORMATION
Recommended local guides include **Hossain Bagharian** (☎ 0913-352 0370) and the endlessly enthusiastic **Hadi Safaeian** (☎ 523 8037, 0913-353 1894; hadiinyazd@hotmail.com).
Tourist information office (☎ 621 6542-5; Ziaee Sq; 🕙 8am-1pm & 3.30-6pm, 8.30am-1.30pm & 4.30-7pm summer) Maps and brochures available; can arrange tours.

VISA EXTENSIONS
Police Department of Aliens Affairs (Rah Ahan Blvd; 🕙 7am-2pm Sat-Wed, 7am-noon Thu) Opposite the bus terminal, not as reliable as Esfahan or Shiraz. The relevant Bank Melli is around the corner.

Sights

OLD CITY
According to Unesco, the old city in Yazd is one of the oldest towns in the world. Almost everything is made from sun-dried mud bricks, and the resulting brown skyline is dominated by tall *badgirs*. The best way to see it is simply to wander, get lost and feel the history oozing out of the baked-brown labyrinth of lanes. Ask locals to direct you to one of the restored traditional houses, notably **Khan-e Lari** (admission IR1500; 🕙 7.30am-3pm Sat-Thu).

MOSQUES & SHRINES
Conservative Yazd has dozens of mosques but the most magnificent is undoubtedly the 14th-century **Jameh Mosque** (🕙 5am-10pm). Its 48m-high minarets dominate the old city and the elaborately tiled 15th-century entrance portal is among the tallest in Iran. The beautiful mosaics covering the dome, and on the mehrab (the niche indicating the direction of Mecca), are also quite special.

Not far away, the 14th-century **Mausoleum of Seyed Roknaddin** (Bogheh-ye Seyed Roknaddin; 🕙 8am-7pm Wed) is easily recognised by the beautiful tile-adorned dome. **Alexander's Prison** (Zaiee Sq; admission incl entry to the Tomb of the 12 Imams IR1500; 🕙 7.30am-dark) probably wasn't a prison and definitely wasn't built by Alexander the Great, as often claimed, but is worth a look and there are clean public toilets inside. Nearby is the 11th-century **Tomb of the 12 Imams**, which boasts fine inscriptions but no actual tombs.

The stunning three-storey façade of the *takieh* (the building used to commemorate the death of Imam Hossein) in the **Amir Chakhmaq Complex** (to climb IR1500; 🕙 8am-2pm & 4pm-6pm) is one of the most recognisable and unusual buildings in Iran. Views from the top are superb.

ZOROASTRIAN SITES
The **Ateshkadeh** (Zoroastrian Fire Temple; Kashani St; 🕙 nominally open 7-11am & 5-7pm Sat-Thu) attracts followers from around the world. Its sacred flame has apparently burned since about AD 470 and was transferred here in 1940.

On barren hilltops on the outskirts of Yazd, the **Towers of Silence** (Dakhmeh-ye Zartoshtiyun) were until recently used as burial sites where corpses were picked clean by vultures. The best way to get there is to charter a taxi (about IR20,000 including one-hour waiting time).

Activities
The **Saheb Zaman Zurkhaneh** (Amir Chakhmaq Sq; admission IR10,000; 🕙 6-8am & 6-10pm Sat-Thu) is a great place to see a *zurkhaneh* (traditional gym) in action. The equipment is rather unorthodox, including huge bowling-pin-style weights to wave around. All of this is done to a drumbeat and the words of Hafez. This particular *zurkhaneh* is under the five *badgirs* of a now-disused *moazedi* (ice-house). Check out the cavernous area downstairs.

IRAN

Sleeping

Yazd has some of the most atmospheric and good-value hotels in Iran.

Silk Road Hotel (☎ 625 2730; www.silkroadhotel .ir; dm/s/d IR30,000/100,000/150,000; P ⬚ ⬚) In the heart of the old city off Masjed Jameh Ave, attractive and comfortable rooms with Western bathrooms in this restored traditional house have made the Silk Road the most popular place in Yazd. The courtyard restaurant is good and management can help with tickets, tours and other information. Excellent value!

Malek-o Tojjar (☎ 626 1479; info@malekhotel .com; Panjeh-ali Bazar, Qeyam St; dm/s/d US$3/35/55; ⬚) Atmosphere pours out of this Qajar-era home-cum-restaurant and hotel. The rooms, set around a covered courtyard, are not huge and the bathrooms are tiny, but the setting, courtyard restaurant and location easily compensate. The underground dorm, with attached bathroom, is the best in Iran. Prices are negotiable.

Kohan Hotel (☎ 621 2485; dm/r per person €3/10; P ⬚ ⬚) This renovated traditional house, off Imam Khomeini St in the midst of the old city, has rooms with Western bathroom, TV and fridge. Management is friendly and there are great views from the roof. Prices are negotiable. Follow the signs from Imam Khomeini St.

Hotel Amir Chakhmagh (☎ 626 9823; Amir Chakhmaq Sq; s/tw/tr IR35,000/60,000/80,000; ⬚ ⬚) Previously the most popular backpacker haunt, this friendly place is ultrabasic. Rooms are noisy and bathrooms shared, but the views are super.

Eating

Yazd has several atmospheric teahouses-cum-restaurants in restored homes, mills and *hammams*.

Hamum-e Khan (Chaykhuneh-ye San'ati; ☎ 627 0366; meals IR35,000; ⬚ 11.30am-3.30pm & 7.30-11pm) This elegantly restored underground *hammam* now serves an extensive menu of Iranian food, including trout (IR24,000), around tranquil pools. Or you can drink tea here at any time between 10am and 11pm. It's in the Meydan-e Khan Bazaar, off Qeyam St.

Malek-o Tojjar (☎ 626 1479; Panjeh-ali Bazar; meals IR35,000) In the courtyard of the hotel of the same name, this is one of the most romantic places in Iran. Fountains and traditional furniture are bathed in soft light and music,

and the reasonably priced food is excellent, including a few vegetarian dishes.

Silk Road Hotel (☎ 625 2730; meals IR25,000-30,000; ⬚ 11am-10.30pm) Another serene courtyard restaurant, this one boasts the usual Iranian dishes plus Indian curries, pizzas, some Mediterranean meals and genuine meat-free vegetarian options. Off Masjed Jameh Ave.

Less formal eateries include the rustic **Keremat Teashop** (Imam Khomeini St), which serves tea, *qalyan*, kebabs and breakfasts of ineffable sheep offal; the unsophisticated **Baharestan Restaurant** (☎ 622 5107; Beheshti Sq; meals IR20,000; ⬚ 11.30am-10pm); and the **Nemoner Sandwich** (⬚ Sat-Thu), opposite the camel butchery, which can whip up a fresh and tasty camel burger (IR5000) in no time.

Shopping

The bazaars in the old city are the best places in Iran to buy silk (known locally as *tirma*), brocade, glassware and cloth – products that brought the town its prosperity in centuries past.

Getting There & Away

AIR

Iran Air (☎ 622 2080; Motahhari St) flies to Mashhad, (IR320,000, twice weekly) and Tehran (IR250,000, twice daily).

BUS & MINIBUS

Many bus companies have convenient offices along Imam Khomeini St. Buses leave from the bus terminal, accessible by shared taxi from Beheshti Sq and Azadi Sq. Mercedes buses run reasonably frequently to Tehran (IR27,000, 10 hours), Esfahan (IR12,600, five hours), Kerman (IR15,000, five hours) and Bandar Abbas (IR30,750, 10 hours), and much less often to Shiraz (IR18,000, seven hours), Mashhad (IR45,500, 16 hours, 4pm), Bam (IR24,600, nine hours) and Zahedan (IR 34,500, 14 hours); the 4pm Zahedan bus gets you to the border just as it opens.

TRAIN

Depending on the season, three or four trains pass through Yazd on the way to and from Tehran each day – one going to Bandar Abbas and the others to Kerman. Relatively convenient trains include a 6am service to Kerman (IR13,750 in 2nd class, five hours) and an 8pm sleeper train to Tehran (IR35,950, eight hours). The **train station** (☎ 139) is south of town near the bus terminal.

A new line linking Yazd and Mashhad, via Meybod and vast tracts of desert, was due to open in 2005. Ask around in Yazd for details or check www.rajatrains.com.

AROUND YAZD
Desert Loop Day Trip

An enjoyable day trip from Yazd involves a loop along quiet roads to the ancient mud-brick village of Kharanaq, the Zoroastrian shrine of Chak Chak and the desert cities of Ardakan and Meybod. It's a long day (about 7am to 6pm) and, without sprouting wings, the only way to do this in a day is by chartering a taxi (about IR250,000) or taking a guided tour. There's no public transport to Chak Chak.

Kharanaq (خرانق; admission IR10,000; ☉ 7.30am-2pm Sat-Thu) is a crumbling village about 85km northeast of Yazd, parts of which are believed to be more than 1000 years old. Wandering through the Qajar-era mosque, 17th-century shaking minaret, restored caravanserai and ancient aqueduct is a great way to spend an hour or so. Buy tickets in the caravanserai.

In a dramatic desert-mountain landscape, **Chak Chak** (چک چک) is the most important Zoroastrian pilgrimage site in Iran. The buildings are uninspiring, but the views from the Pir-e-Sabz fire temple make it worthwhile.

Meybod (میبد) and **Ardakan** (اردکان) are busy cities with a few sites worth a look. Meybod is more interesting, with the old post office, caravanserai and Safavid-era *moazedi* all adjacent to each other. There's also a bizarre circular bird tower as you enter town from Yazd – avoid mind-altering drugs before entering this taxidermists' delight!

SHIRAZ   شیراز
☎ 071

Shiraz was one of the most important cities in the medieval Islamic world, and was the Iranian capital during the Zand period (1747–79), when many of its most beautiful buildings were built or restored. Through its many artists and scholars, Shiraz has been synonymous with learning, poetry, roses and, at one time, red wine.

Shiraz is a relaxed and cultured city, with wide tree-lined avenues, and enough monuments, gardens and mosques to keep most visitors happy for several days. It's also the

base for visiting Persepolis – making this one of Iran's most visited cities.

Orientation & Information

Most of the sights and tourist facilities are along or near Karim Khan-e Zand Blvd – simply called 'Zand'. The city centre is Shohada Sq, still widely known as Shahrdari Sq.

EMERGENCY
Dr Faqihi Hospital (☎ 235 1091; Karim Khan-e Zand Blvd)
Police headquarters (☎ 236 4998; Shohada Sq)
Tourist police (Karim Khan-e Zand Blvd)

INTERNET ACCESS
Ferdous Internet (☎ 222 5014; per hr IR8000; ☉ 9am-9pm)
Max Coffee Net (☎ 628 6081; Mollasadra Passage, Molla Sadra St; per hr IR8000; ☉ 9am-10pm, closed Fri) In a small complex of computer stores 50m south of the western end of Zand.

MONEY
Bank Melli (Karim Khan-e Zand Blvd) Changes money.
Zand Exchange (☎ 222 2854; ☉ 9am-8pm Sat-Thu) Much quicker than Bank Melli.

POST
Main post office (Taleqani St)

TELEPHONE
Telephone office (Park Hotel Lane; ☉ 8am-10pm)

TOURIST INFORMATION
Tourist information office (☎ 0917-302 2966; Zand Blvd; ☉ 9am-noon & 4-7pm) English-speaking staff provide free maps in English and French, postcards and directions.

VISA EXTENSIONS
Aliens office (Valiasr Sq; ☉ 7.30am-1.30pm Sat-Wed, 7.30am-noon Thu) A good place to extend visas – you usually get 30 days, delivered the same day. Walk or take a shared taxi (about IR800) along Zand to Valiasr Sq, where it's on the southeast corner.

Sights & Activities
ARG-E KARIM KHANI

The walls and 14m-high circular towers of the **Arg-e Karim Khani** (☎ 222 1423; Citadel of Karim Khan; Shohada Sq; admission IR3000; ☉ 8am-4pm, to 7pm summer) dominate the city centre. This well-preserved fortress was, in the time of the Zand dynasty, part of a royal courtyard

SHIRAZ

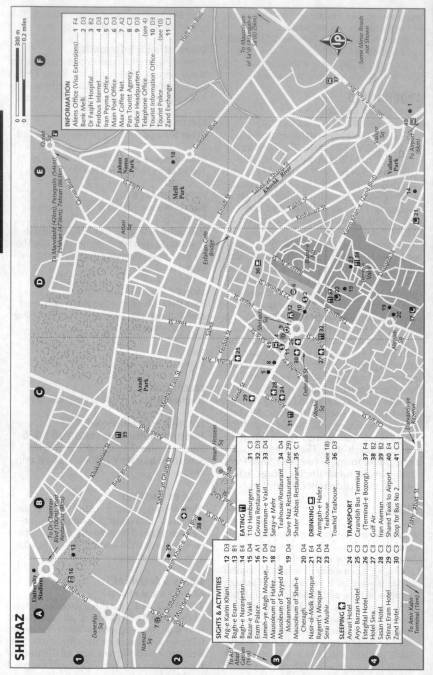

INFORMATION	
Aliens Office (Visa Extensions)	1 F4
Bank Melli	2 D3
Dr Faghi Hospital	3 B2
Ferdous Internet	4 D3
Iran Peyma Office	5 C3
Main Post Office	6 D3
Max Coffee Net	7 A2
Pars Tourist Agency	8 C3
Police Headquarters	9 D3
Telephone Office	(see 4)
Tourist Information Office	10 D3
Tourist Police	(see 10)
Zand Exchange	11 C3

SIGHTS & ACTIVITIES	
Arg-e Karim Khani	12 D3
Bagh-e Eram	13 B1
Bagh-e Naranjestan	14 E4
Bazar-e Vakil	15 D4
Eram Palace	16 A1
Jameh-ye Atigh Mosque	17 D4
Mausoleum of Hafez	18 E2
Mausoleum of Sayyed Mir Mohammad	19 D4
Mausoleum of Shah-e Cheragh	20 D4
Nasir-ol-Molk Mosque	21 E4
Regent's Mosque	22 D4
Serai Mushir	23 D4

SLEEPING	
Anvari Hotel	24 C3
Aryo Barzan Hotel	25 C3
Esteghlal Hotel	26 C3
Hotel Sina	27 C3
Sasan Hotel	28 C3
Shiraz Eram Hotel	29 C3
Zand Hotel	30 D4

EATING	
110 Hamburgers	31 C3
Govara Restaurant	32 D3
Hammam-e Vakil	33 D4
Saray-e Mehr Teahouse/Restaurant	34 D4
Sarve Naz Restaurant	(see 29)
Shater Abbas Restaurant	35 C1

DRINKING	
Aramgah-e Hafez	(see 18)
Teahouse	36 D3
Towhid Teahouse	

TRANSPORT	
Carandish Bus Terminal (Terminal-e Bozorg)	37 F4
Gulf Air	38 B2
Iran Aseman	39 B2
Shared Taxis to Airport	40 E4
Stop for Bus No 2	41 C3

which Karim Khan hoped would rival that of Esfahan. The courtyard is filled with citrus trees, but that's about it.

REGENT'S MOSQUE (VAKIL MOSQUE)

The beautiful **Regent's Mosque** (Masjed-e Vakil; admission IR2500; 8am-noon & 3.30pm-sunset, Sat-Thu) was built in 1773 by Karim Khan. It has two vast *iwans* to the north and south, and a magnificent inner courtyard surrounded by beautifully tiled alcoves and porches. Although the structure of the mosque dates from 1773, most of the tiling, with its predominantly floral motifs, was added in the early Qajar era (about 1820).

The best time for a look is during noon prayers. Women should wear a manteau that reaches below the knee and a dark scarf.

BAZAR-E VAKIL

Shiraz' atmospheric bazaar has been described as the most architecturally impressive in the country. It was constructed by Karim Khan as part of a plan to make Shiraz into a great trading centre. The vaulted brick ceilings ensure that the interior is cool in summer and warm in winter. In the best traditions of Persian bazaars, the **Bazar-e Vakil** (dawn-dusk Sat-Thu) is best explored by wandering without concern for time or direction, soaking up the atmosphere in the labyrinthine lanes.

Chances are you'll stumble across **Serai Mushir**, off the southern end of the main bazaar lane coming from Zand. This tastefully restored two-storey caravanserai is a pleasant place to gather your breath and do a bit of souvenir shopping.

MAUSOLEUM OF SHAH-E CHERAGH

The famous **Mausoleum of Shah-e Cheragh** (Mausoleum of the King of the Lamp, Bogh'e-ye Shah-e Cheragh; Ahamadi Sq; 222 2158; 7am-6pm, to 9pm summer) houses the remains of Sayyed Mir Ahmad, a brother of Imam Reza of Mashhad fame who died, or was killed, in Shiraz in 835. A mausoleum was originally erected over the grave in the mid-14th century, and it's now an important Shiite place of pilgrimage. The intricate mirror tiling inside the shrine is dazzling. At the mausoleum there is a separate entrance for men and women. Women must wear a chador (available from a desk at the entrance).

At the southeast corner of the courtyard is the **Mausoleum of Sayyed Mir Mohammad** (Bogh'e-ye Sayyed Mir Mohammad), a brother of Mir Ahmad. And through the southeast entrance to the courtyard is the 9th-century **Jameh-ye Atigh Mosque**.

NASIR-OL-MOLK MOSQUE

The 19th-century **Nasir-ol-Molk Mosque** (admission IR15,000; 7.30am-6.30pm, to 8pm summer), off Dastqeib St, is one of the most elegant in southern Iran. The stunning stained glass and exquisitely carved pillars of the winter prayer hall are worth the admission.

MAUSOLEUM OF HAFEZ

Hafez the poet is an Iranian folk-hero; loved, revered and as popular as many a modern pop star. And there is no better place to try and understand Hafez' eternal hold on Iran than here, at the **Mausoleum of Hafez** (Armagah-e Hafez; Golestan Blvd; admission IR3000; 8am-9.30pm).

Set in a charming garden, the marble tombstone was placed here by Karim Khan in 1773. In 1935 an octagonal pavilion was erected above it. There is a wonderfully atmospheric teahouse (p225) in a walled garden inside the grounds. Spend an hour sitting in a discreet corner, at sunset if possible, watching Iranians react to what is, for many, a pilgrimage to Hafez. Take a shared taxi from Shohada Sq, or take bus 2.

MAUSOLEUM OF SA'DI

The **mausoleum** (Aramgah-e Sa'di; Bustan Blvd; admission IR3000; 9.30am-8.30pm, to 10pm summer) commemorates another famous Persian poet, Sa'di. It's tranquil, but not as impressive as the Hafez mausoleum. The plain marble tomb, which dates from the 1860s, is inscribed with various verses from Sa'di. The underground teahouse set around a fish pond can get a bit too atmospheric – ie stinky. Take a shared taxi from Shohada Sq, and another from Valiasr Sq, or bus 2 all the way from Karim Khan-e Zand Blvd.

FORMAL GARDENS

Apart from those surrounding the mausoleums of Hafez and Sa'di, Shiraz has several formal gardens, though the hefty admission fees mean seeing one is probably enough.

Famous for its cypress trees, **Bagh-e Eram** (Garden of Paradise; Daneshju Blvd; admission IR40,000; 8am-noon & 2-5pm, to 7pm summer) is one of the most famous gardens in Iran. Alongside a pretty pool is the charming 19th-century

IRAN

Eram Palace, though it's not open to visitors. Take any shared taxi along Zand heading towards the university.

Picturesque **Afif Abad Garden** (admission IR30,000; ☾ 5-8pm) holds the **Afif Abad Palace**, once owned by the shah. The palace, built in 1863 and influenced by the Qajar style of architecture, has a lower floor that's now an interesting military museum. The gardens are a fair way from the city centre, so charter a taxi.

The smaller **Bagh-e Naranjestan** (Orange Garden; Dastqeib St; admission IR30,000; ☾ 8am-sunset), east of the bazaar, features a mirror-filled pavilion that was a governor's residence during the Qajar period.

Tours

Pars Tourist Agency (☎ 222 3163; www.key2persia .com; Zand Blvd; ☾ 8am-10pm Sat-Thu, 10am-1pm Fri) has good-value group tours to Persepolis and Naqsh-e Rostam (US$8 per person) and dozens of other professionally organised trips elsewhere in Fars Province. They also hire bikes (US$4 a day).

Sleeping

Shiraz is well stocked with good-value hotels, all an easy walk to the centre. Midrangers should head for Rudaki St, and budgeteers to Dehnadi St or neighbouring Piruzi St. Rates are negotiable in most places.

BUDGET

Zand Hotel (☎ 222 2949; alvanch@yahoo.com; Dehnadi St; s/tw/tr IR55,000/75,000/95,000; P ⌘) The best-value budget option, with a friendly, well-informed manager and clean rooms with private bathroom downstairs, showers only upstairs; specify! Guests can use the kitchen.

Anvari Hotel (☎ 233 7591; Anvari St; d/tr 90,000/ 130,000; ⌘) At the 'luxury' end of the budget range, rooms here have bathrooms and guests can use the kitchen. The IR8000 breakfast is good.

Hotel Sina (☎ 222 5665; Piruzi St; s/d IR120,000/ 140,000; ⌘) Rooms with eastern bathrooms, TV and fridge are clean and management is helpful. Knock IR20,000 off in low season.

Esteghlal Hotel (☎ 222 5383; Dehnadi St; s/d/tr IR54,000/72,000/86,000, with shower IR63,000/92,000/ 110,000) A reasonable back-up if Zand is full.

MIDRANGE

Aryo Barzan Hotel (☎ 224 1222; www.aryohotel.com; Rudaki Ave; s/d/ste incl breakfast US$37/50/$75; ⌘ ▣)

The classy Aryo Barzan offers top-end quality for a midrange price. The comfortable rooms have Mini Me–sized baths. The restaurant and café are good.

Shiraz Eram Hotel (☎ 230 0814; www.eramhotel .com; Zand Blvd; s/d incl breakfast US$30/40; P ⌘ ▣) The welcoming, knowledgeable staff are a highlight here, and large rooms with satellite TV and fridge aren't bad either. It's getting a makeover, so prices might rise. The buffet breakfast (IR30,000 for nonguests) is great, and food in the Sarve Naz Restaurant (meals IR35,000) is pretty good.

Sasan Hotel (☎ 230 2028; sasanhotel@shirazsport .com; Anvari St; s/d IR135,000/185,000; ▣) Lower midrange rooms here are small but clean and management is obliging.

Eating

Yord Restaurant (☎ 625 6774; meals IR45,000; ☾ 8pm-midnight, call first for lunch) About 8km northwest of the city, Yord serves up fantastic Iranian food and fresh bread along with liberal doses of nomadic Qashqa'i culture in a huge, wonderfully colourful *yord* (tent). There's live music most nights. It's almost impossible to find without a taxi (IR25,000, ask for Yord in Dinakan); the restaurant will call one for the return journey. Worth every rial!

Hammam-e Vakil (☎ 222 6467; Taleqani St; meals IR40,000; ☾ 11am-11pm) In the marvellously restored baths of the Bazar-e Vakil, this teahouse and restaurant serves good *dizi* and kebab with live music. It's a bit touristy, but still a must-see in Shiraz.

Shater Abbas Restaurant (☎ 227 1612; Khakshenasi St; meals IR40,000; ☾ lunch & dinner) The open-sided kitchen and tasty food make this a popular place with Shirazis. The lari kabab (a speciality of southern Iran, IR28,000) is recommended for carnivores. Look for the flame torches outside.

Govara Restaurant (☎ 222 7211; Piruzi St; meals IR20,000; ☾ 11am-11pm) No frills, subterranean place serving good, cheap kebabs, *khoreshts* and fish dishes.

Saray-e Mehr Teahouse/Restaurant (☎ 222 9572; meals IR25,000-35,000; ☾ 8am-10pm) Deep in the bazaar, near the Serai Mushir, this ambient old place is great for tea or lunch.

Zand and the nearby streets are home to numerous cheap kababis and pizza joints; we liked the shwarmas (IR8000) at **110 Hamburgers** (Anvari St).

Drinking

You can also sit with tea and a *qalyan* in most of the places to eat.

Aramgah-e Hafez (Golestan Blvd; 🕑 8am-9.30pm) In the grounds of Hafez' tomb, this delightful garden teahouse is the perfect place to sit, contemplate and listen to traditional music.

Towhid Teahouse (Ferdosi St; 🕑 7am-11pm) This teahouse, packed with a mesmerising array of lovingly collected 'stuff', is far from touristy. The (mostly male) patrons banter animatedly and the *dizi* (IR7000) and kebabs, grilled on the sidewalk, are super cheap.

Shopping

The Vakil Bazaar was constructed by Karim Khan as part of a plan to make Shiraz into a great trading centre. With vaulted brick ceilings and a range of stores catering to tourists and locals alike, it's one of the finest bazaars in Iran. There are a few teahouses and the Serai Mushi is a pleasant courtyard in a two-storey caravanserai. Shiraz is a good place to buy printed fabrics, tea sets and *qalyan* pipes made from copper and bronze.

Getting There & Away

AIR

Iran Air (☎ 233 0041; cnr Zand Blvd & Faqihi St) flies to Tehran (IR315,000, several daily), Esfahan (IR117,000, daily), Bandar Abbas (IR230,000, seven weekly), Mashhad (IR450,000, daily) and Ahvaz (IR229,000, twice weekly). **Iran Aseman** (☎ 230 8841; Zand Blvd) flies similar routes for the same prices.

Iran Air flies to Dubai, Doha, Bahrain and Kuwait and **Gulf Air** (☎ 230 1962; Zand Blvd) has twice-weekly flights to Bahrain.

BUS & MINIBUS

Shiraz' main bus/minibus station is **Carandish bus terminal** (Terminal-e Bozorg; ☎ 730 1654), though you can buy tickets to many destinations at the convenient **Iran Peyma** (Taavoni No. 1; ☎ 222 3888; Zand) office. Mercedes/Volvo buses and minibuses leave frequently for cities including Bandar Abbas (IR28,500/55,000, 10 hours), Bushehr (IR18,000/32,000, five hours), Esfahan (IR19,000/33,000, eight hours) and Tehran (IR38,000/66,000, 12 to 16 hours), and less frequently for Kerman (IR23,500/37,000, eight hours), Yazd (IR18,000/28,500, seven hours), Ahvaz (IR26,000/40,000, 10 hours) and Kermanshah (IR44,000/65,000, 16 hours).

Minibuses to Marvdasht (for Persepolis, IR2000) leave regularly from behind the terminal.

Getting Around

TO/FROM THE AIRPORT

Shared taxis to the airport leave from Valiasr Sq. A taxi *dah baste* will cost about IR10,000 to most hotels.

BICYCLE

Shiraz is one of the few places in Iran where it's easy to hire a bicycle and the traffic is certainly manageable. Pars Tourist Travel Agency hires out decent mountain bikes for US$4 a day and also has guided bike tours for IR55,000/80,000 a half/full day.

AROUND SHIRAZ
Persepolis (Takht-e Jamshid)

پرسپولیس (تخت جمشید)

Magnificent **Persepolis** (Takht-e Jamshid; admission IR5000; 🕑 8am-5pm Nov-Mar; 6am-6pm Mar-Jun & Sep-Oct, 6am-8pm Jul & Aug) is the embodiment of the greatest successes of the ancient Achaemenid empire (see p180). Begun in about 518 BC by King Darius I (the Great), this massive and magnificent palace complex was built as the Achaemenids' spring capital. It was added to by a host of subsequent kings over the following 200 years.

The original name was Parsa, but the Greeks, who invaded and destroyed the city in 331 BC, named it Persepolis.

THE SITE

Entrance to the site is via the monumental **Grand Stairway**, carved from massive blocks of stone but with shallow steps so Persians in long elegant robes could walk gracefully up into the palace. At the top of the stairway is **Xerxes' Gateway** (Gate of All Nations), with three separate doors and a hallway. The remaining doors are covered with inscriptions, graffiti and carvings in the ancient Elamite language. Continuing east, you pass some double-headed capitals that once topped the columns in the Apadana Palace before reaching the **Unfinished Gate**.

The southern door of Xerxes' Gateway leads to the immense **Apadana Palace**, where the kings received visitors. Inside, the **Court of Apadana** was built from stone somehow excavated from nearby mountains. The roof of the **central hall** was supported by 36 towering stone columns, each 20m high. The stairways are decorated with superb reliefs, and the Apadana Stairway, at the eastern entrance, is considered a master work. As you look at the reliefs depicting people from the Achaemenids' ancient subject nationalities, it's not hard to see why.

Behind the central hall, and connected by another stairway, is the **Palace of Darius I**. Once the private residence of Darius I, it was filled with statues covered with jewels, but only the carvings along the staircase remain.

The **Palace of 100 Columns** was probably one of the largest buildings constructed during the Achaemenid period (559–330 BC), and contained 100 columns about 14m high, each with reliefs showing Darius struggling

with evil spirits. **Darius' Treasury** was a large collection of rooms housing the wealth of the city. Overlooking all of this are the **Tomb of Artaxerxes II**, and the larger **Tomb of Artaxerxes III**, which are carved into the rocky hills overlooking the site.

The restored **Haramsara** (Persepolis Museum; admission IR5000) is believed to have housed the king's harem. Today it's a modest museum, with a few ceramics, carvings, cloths and coins.

An impressive sound-and-light show (in Farsi only) is supposed to play at 8.30pm on Thursday and Friday evenings from March to September (and daily during No Ruz, Iranian New Year), though check it's definitely on before heading out for it.

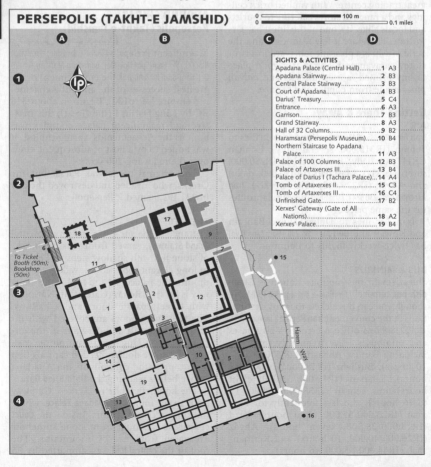

PERSEPOLIS (TAKHT-E JAMSHID)

SIGHTS & ACTIVITIES
Apadana Palace (Central Hall)............**1**	A3
Apadana Stairway..............................**2**	B3
Central Palace Stairway....................**3**	B3
Court of Apadana..............................**4**	B3
Darius' Treasury................................**5**	C4
Entrance...**6**	A3
Garrison..**7**	B3
Grand Stairway.................................**8**	A3
Hall of 32 Columns............................**9**	B2
Haramsara (Persepolis Museum)......**10**	B4
Northern Staircase to Apadana	
Palace..**11**	A3
Palace of 100 Columns....................**12**	B3
Palace of Artaxerxes III...................**13**	B4
Palace of Darius I (Tachara Palace)...**14**	A4
Tomb of Artaxerxes II......................**15**	C3
Tomb of Artaxerxes III.....................**16**	C4
Unfinished Gate...............................**17**	B2
Xerxes' Gateway (Gate of All	
Nations)...**18**	A2
Xerxes' Palace.................................**19**	B4

GETTING THERE & AWAY

By public transport, take a minibus from the south side of the Carandish bus terminal in Shiraz to Marvdasht. From the last stop, walk about 1km along the main road to Imam Khomeini Sq, from where a shared taxi (IR2000, 12km) or private taxi (about IR10,000) will take you to Persepolis.

Easier is a charter taxi from Shiraz; expect to pay about IR120,000 for a six-hour trip to Persepolis and Naqsh-e Rostam and IR220,000 for an 11-hour day including Pasargad. **Pars Tourist Agency** (☎ 222 3163; www .key2persia.com; Karim Khan-e Zand Blvd) in Shiraz organises daily tours to Persepolis for US$8 per person, leaving at 8am.

Naqsh-e Rostam   نقش رستم

Hewn out of a cliff, the four tombs of **Naqsh-e Rostam** (admission IR3000; ⏲ 7.30am-5pm, to 7pm summer) are believed to be those of Darius II, Artaxerxes I, Darius I and Xerxes I (from left to right). There are also several **reliefs** from the Sassanian period depicting scenes of imperial conquests and royal investitures. Facing the cliff is the **Kaba Zartosht**, which is believed to be an Achaemenid fire temple, although the walls are marked with inscriptions cataloguing Sassanian victories. Photographers should get there before mid-afternoon.

Naqsh-e Rostam is 6km north from Persepolis. If you charter a taxi to Persepolis, this site can be visited along the way, otherwise shared taxis usually link the two (IR2000).

Pasargad   پاسارگاد

Begun under Cyrus (Kouroush) the Great in about 546 BC, the city of **Pasargad** (admission IR3000; ⏲ 8am-5pm, 7am-6pm summer) was superseded by Persepolis soon after Cyrus' death. It's not as visually stimulating as Persepolis, though the scattered ruins and plains are beautiful in a lonely kind of way.

The first and most impressive structure you'll see is the six-tiered **Tomb of Cyrus**. Within walking distance are the insubstantial remains of three **Achaemenid Palaces**; the ruins of a tower on a plinth, known as the **Prison of Solomon**; and a large stone platform on a hill known as the **Throne of the Mother of Solomon** (Takht-e Madar-e Soleiman), which affords panoramic views.

Pasargad is 130km north of Shiraz (80km north of Persepolis) so if you really need to see it the best option is to charter a taxi (or take an organised tour) and combine it with a visit to Persepolis. By public transport, take a bus (IR8500) from the Carandish bus terminal in Shiraz to Sa'adatshahr (Sa'adat Abad), and a taxi the remaining 30km.

Firuz Abad   فيروز آباد

The remains of the Sassanian-era cities of Firuz and Gur are about 6km before Firuz. On the road from Shiraz, an abandoned chairlift leads to the ruins of the three-storey **Doktar Palace**.

About 2km further towards Firuz, an unsignposted rocky trail leads to the **Ardeshir Fire Temple** (admission IR3000).

At least one bus and several minibuses run between Shiraz and Firuz every day.

THE PERSIAN GULF
خليج فارس

The Persian Gulf is one of the least visited parts of Iran and that in itself is a great attraction. It's different from the rest of the country, with its Bandari culture and architecture blending Persian and Arab roots, and a laid-back way of life that suits the climate perfectly – it gets diabolically hot in summer. Increasing numbers of travellers are using the Gulf ports to enter or leave Iran.

BUSHEHR   بوشهر
☎ 0771

Set on a peninsula jutting out into the ocean, Bushehr is perhaps the most relaxed town along the Gulf. The Bandari architecture and dress provide the flavour but, as it's five hours from Shiraz and not really on the way to anywhere, you need plenty of time to devote some of it to Bushehr.

The highlight is the easily explored **old city**, a kind of living museum of traditional Bandari architecture that has yet to be flattened to make way for development. Much of it is, however, terribly run down – one reader described it as looking like 'Grozny after the third Russian war'.

Information

Bank Melli (Leyan St)
Coffeenet Baharrayanehlian (☎ 252 1505; Leyan St; per hr IR5000; ⏲ 8am-10pm) Opposite Bank Melli; look for the red sign.

Main hospital (☎ 252 6591; Siraf St)
Police headquarters (☎ 253 0799; Qods Sq; ☺ 8am-2pm) Can extend visas, including transit visas; ask for English-speaking Saeed Iranzad.
Post office (Valiasr St)
Telephone office (Novvab-e Safavi St; ☺ 7am-10pm) Just south of Enqelab Sq.

Sleeping & Eating

Getting a cheap room in Bushehr was a nightmare of red tape, but in theory permits are no longer required. Yippee! The cheap options are near Enqelab Sq, just northeast of the terminal. Bushehr's waterfront and around the bazaar are the places to find food.

Hotel Sadi (☎ 252 2605; Nader St; tw IR40,000) The pick of the budget options, where small, clean rooms have their own bathrooms!

Mosaferkhune-ye Pars (☎ 252 2479; Enqelab Sq; tr IR60,000) Simple rooms and share bathrooms and a friendly atmosphere in a great location overlooking Enqelab Sq.

Sadra Tourist Inn (☎ 252 2346; cnr Valiasr St & Khalij-e Fars Sts; d $30; ⓟ ⌘) Well-located on the seafront, rooms here are tired but still the cheapest in the midrange.

Ghavam Restaurant (☎ 252 1790; Khalij-e Fars St; meals IR40,000; ☺ noon-3.30pm & 7-11.30pm) The seaside location, vaulted ceilings and traditional music (Thursday and Friday) of this former underground cistern make this the best place to eat on the coast. Consider the tasty fish kebab and surprisingly spicy dizi. Tea and *qalyan* on the roof are great at sunset.

Salon Ghaza Khoreid Faghid (☎ 252 5755; Novvab-e Safavi St; meals IR20,000; ☺ lunch & dinner) Just south of the bazaar, there is no English sign and zero frills but the local speciality *ghalye mahi*, a richly flavoured fish stew, is worth finding.

Getting There & Away

Iran Air (☎ 252 2041; Valiasr St) flights include Tehran (IR225,000, twice daily) and Esfahan (IR220,000, twice weekly). Iran Aseman flies to/from Dubai three times a week.

The town's bus terminal is just west of the bazaar. Relatively infrequent Mercedes/Volvo services depart for Bandar Abbas (IR49,000/85,000, about 14 hours), Bandar Lengeh (IR29,000/50,000, about nine hours, 4.30pm), Ahvaz (IR31,000, seven hours), Shiraz (IR18,000/32,000, five hours) and Esfahan (IR35,000/63,000, 16 hours).

Valfajre-8 Shipping Company (☎ 252 2188; www .vesc.net; Solhabad St) has passenger ferries to Kuwait, Bahrain and Qatar.

KISH ISLAND   جزیره کیش
☎ 0764

Kish is Iran's Hawaii, without the bars and bikinis. And while Iranians not familiar with such decadence simply love the place, it's of little interest to most foreigners. If you do come here, perhaps as a back-door entry point from Dubai, the diving isn't bad and there's a fun bike path around the edge of the island. That path passes all the sights, the pick of which are the ruins of ancient **Harireh**, the rusted and haunting **Greek Ship**, and the **Men's Beach** and **Ladies Beach** – don't get them confused!

Divers should head to the professionally run **Kish Dive Centre** (☎ 442 2757) on the beach outside the Shayan Hotel. A one-hour dive with equipment is about US$35. Bikes can be hired from vendors near here for about IR15,000 an hour. For brochures and other information, drop into the **Kish Tourism Organisation** (KTO; ☎ 442 2434; Sanaee Sq; ☺ 7.30am-5pm Sat-Thu).

You can fly into Kish from Dubai without a visa, get a 14-day pass at the airport and then head down to the **Ministry of Foreign Affairs** (☎ 442 0734; Ferdous Villas, Complex 2, Ferdosi St), where they can grant you a full tourist visa within 48 hours.

Sleeping & Eating

There are dozens of hotels on Kish, but cheap ones are like needles in haystacks. The KTO might be able to help, or check www.irantour.org/kishisland-hotels.html. Almost all hotels have restaurants.

Hotel Khatam (☎ 443 1520; khatamhotel@hotmail .com; Khatam Blvd; tw IR200,000; ⓟ ⌘) In the village of Saffein, these comfortable rooms are good value for Kish.

Asia Hotel (☎ 443 0774; Saffain St) Around the corner from the Khatam, it has similar rooms and rates. Bargain in both.

Shayan International Hotel (☎ 442 2771; Sahel Sq; s/d incl breakfast US$80/110; ⓟ ⌘) This prerevolution edifice mixes quality with a suggestion of '70s kitsch. Ask for a room facing east.

If the prices of the above places are too much, the proprietors of the **Salar Kish Hotel** (☎ 442 0111; Sanaee Sq; dm IR60,000; ⌘) might let you share an apartment.

Kish has a curious mix of Western-style fast-food places and try-hard theme restaurants, mostly in the northeast. One standout is **Payab Restaurant** (☎ 0914-769 1213; Olympic Blvd; meals IR50,000; ☑ 7-11pm), located in an underground water reservoir. The fish dishes are mouthwatering.

Getting There & Away

Iran Air (☎ 442 2274; Sanaee Sq) flies to and from Tehran (IR452,000) and Shiraz, and **Kish Airlines** (☎ 442 3922; Sanaee Sq) flies more regularly to Tehran, Shiraz, Esfahan and Mashhad. Kish Airlines also flies to Bahrain, Sharjah, Abu Dhabi and Bahrain.

Valfajre-8 sails daily between Kish and Bandar Lengeh (IR65,000); catamarans take two hours but the bigger ferries take close to five. Buy tickets at the port.

The alternative is to take the speedboat from Bandar-e Charak; see below. Note that speedboats stop in high winds.

BANDAR LENGEH   بندر لنگه
☎ 0762

Bandar Lengeh is an infectiously lethargic place, and a pleasant overnight stop to or from Kish Island. There is not much to do except wander around, taking in the different dress (look for the distinctive Bandari burkas worn by some women) and the bazaar.

Hotel Amir (☎ 224 2311; Enqelab St; r IR52,000), not far north of the port entrance, is the only hotel in the town centre and the simple rooms are fair value. Bathrooms are shared and some English is spoken.

The **Amir Restaurant** (☎ 224 1370; Enqelab St; ☑ 11am-3.30pm & 6-10pm; meals IR20,000-30,000), a few doors south of Hotel Amir, serves good *sabzi* and rice (IR15,000) and *meigu* (battered prawns or shrimps, IR20,000).

From the bus terminal, about 2km east of the docks, buses go to Bandar Abbas (IR15,000, four hours) about every hour, and twice daily to Bushehr (IR31,000, nine hours). Savaris also go to Bandar Abbas (IR30,000, 2½ hours).

Ferries and catamarans sail from the **Valfajre 8 terminal** (☎ 222 0252; Imam Khomeini St) to Kish Island (IR65,000 one way, two to five hours, twice daily). For international services, see p664. Alternatively, take an early morning (about 6am) savari to Bandar-e Charak (IR15,000, one hour) and a speedboat from Charak to Kish (IR30,000, 45 minutes).

BANDAR ABBAS   بندر عباس
☎ 0761

Bandar Abbas is the busiest port in Iran and the major city along the Gulf. Sights are few, but the city – universally known as Bandar – is the ideal base from which to explore the nearby islands and Minab. Bandar's population is a fascinating mix of Arabs, Persians and African Iranians, with a large Sunni minority. The best place to see it all come together is in the **bazaar**.

Orientation & Information

The city centre is 17 Shahrivar Sq, where the **police headquarters** (☎ 222 7676) and **Bank Melli** are located. **Morvarid Money Exchange** (☎ 222 7446; Imam Khomeini St; ☑ 8am-1pm & 4.30-9pm Sat-Thu), in a small arcade west of the square, is a better place to change money. The **main post office** (Shahrivar St) and the **telephone office** (Mahan Alley; ☑ 7am-9pm) are near the square.

Get online at **Intel Coffeenet** (Imam Khomeini St; per hr IR10,000; ☑ 8am-noon & 4-10pm), or **Coffee Net Sorena** (Imam Khomeini St; per hr IR9000; ☑ 5pm-9pm Sat-Thu), on the 3rd floor just west of 17 Shahrivar Sq.

Sleeping

If these places don't suit, there are several more on or just off Imam Khomeini St.

Mema Pazir Bouali (☎ 222 2516; Shari'ati St; dm/r IR15,000/50,000) Family-run and ideal for solo women, this infectiously friendly place has clean if noisy rooms, shared bathrooms and a great little teahouse. Look for the yellow awning; it's upstairs.

Mosaferkhuneh-ye-Bazar (☎ 222 2303; Taleqani Blvd; s/d/tr IR44,000/60,000/71,000) Luxury it ain't, but this popular *mosaferkhuneh* (cheap hotel) is perfectly located on top of the bazaar, overlooking the Gulf.

Hotel Ghods (☎ 222 2344; Imam Khomeini St; s/d IR450,000/550,000; ☒ ☐) Ghods is the best midrange choice, with large, relatively quiet and well-equipped rooms.

Eating

For 'modern Iranian' fast food – pizza and burgers – head west to Sayyadan St, where such establishments pull crowds of chatty students. **Tanuri Pizza** (pizzas IR20,000) uses real mozzarella, making it the pick of the bunch.

Persian Restaurant (☎ 224 4147; Imam Khomeini St; meals IR30,000; ☑ 11am-3.30pm & 7-10pm) A longtime favourite, this central, busy little

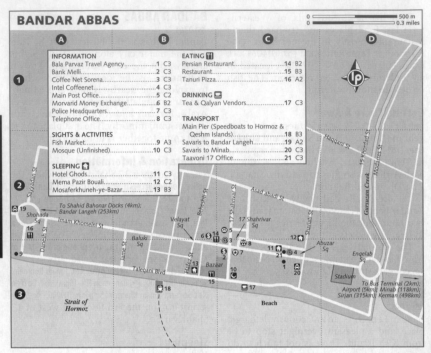

BANDAR ABBAS

0 _____ 500 m
0 _____ 0.3 miles

INFORMATION	
Bala Parvaz Travel Agency	1 C3
Bank Melli	2 C3
Coffee Net Sorena	3 C3
Intel Coffeenet	4 C3
Main Post Office	5 C2
Morvarid Money Exchange	6 B2
Police Headquarters	7 C3
Telephone Office	8 C3

SIGHTS & ACTIVITIES	
Fish Market	9 A3
Mosque (Unfinished)	10 C3

SLEEPING	
Hotel Ghods	11 C3
Mema Pazir Bouali	12 C2
Mosaferkhuneh-ye-Bazar	13 B3

EATING	
Persian Restaurant	14 B2
Restaurant	15 B3
Tanuri Pizza	16 A2

DRINKING	
Tea & Qalyan Vendors	17 C3

TRANSPORT	
Main Pier (Speedboats to Hormoz &	
Qeshm Islands)	18 B3
Savaris to Bandar Langeh	19 A2
Savaris to Minab	20 C3
Taavoni 17 Office	21 C3

place whips up decent fish dishes, kebabs and *chelow khoresht* (stew and rice).

Restaurant (☎ 222 3413; Taleqani Blvd; meals IR25,000-30,000; ☽ 11am-11pm Sat-Thu) There's no English menu in this unnamed place, but the Iranian dishes are fresh and the location above the bazaar is perfect as the sun sets into the Gulf.

Drinking
Bandar is short on atmospheric teahouses. Instead, locals head down to the seafront in the late afternoon and buy tea and *qalyan* from vendors spaced along the sea wall.

Getting There & Away
The city is well connected to the rest of Iran by road, rail and air but, if you're travelling overland, it's a long ride. For international ferry services, see p664. Helpful staff at **Bala Parvaz Travel Agency** (☎ 222 4500; Imam Khomeini St) can sort out plane, ferry and train tickets.

AIR
Iran Air flies to Tehran (IR480,000, several times daily), Shiraz (IR230,000, five per

week), Esfahan (IR361,000 thrice weekly) and Mashhad (IR468,000, twice weekly). Kish Air flies to Kish Island (IR195,000, daily).

BOAT
Speedboats to Hormoz (IR9000) and Qeshm (IR12,000, or IR18,000 by covered launch) islands leave when full from the main jetty, opposite the bazaar. International ferries leave from the Shahid Bahonar docks, about 6km west of the city centre.

BUS
The bus terminal is in the far east of the city – a taxi *dah baste* costs about IR9000. Mercedes/Volvo buses run to cities including Bandar Lengeh (IR9,000/15,000, 3½ hours), Bushehr (IR45,000/85,000, around 14 hours), Bam (IR20,000/34,000, about eight hours), Kerman (IR29,500/43,600, eight hours), Shiraz (IR28,500/55,000, 10 hours), Yazd (IR30,750/55,000, 10 hours) and Esfahan (IR37,500/73,000, 16 to 18 hours). **Taavoni 17** (Imam Khomeini St) has a handy office in town.

TRAIN

The daily train to Tehran leaves at 1pm (IR87,000 in 1st class, 21 hours), travelling via Sirjan and Yazd (IR53,000). Trains to Esfahan (IR55,750, 15 hours) run three times a week. The station is in the far north of the city so you'll need to charter a taxi to get here.

AROUND BANDAR ABBAS
Hormoz Island　جزیره هرمز

Historic Hormoz Island is worth a quick visit, and is easily accessible from Bandar Abbas. About 750m northeast of the jetty are the ruins of a 16th-century **Portuguese castle** (admission IR2000). It's the most impressive colonial fortress in Iran, but is badly neglected. Get the caretaker to open the subterranean parts.

Speedboats travel between the jetty (opposite the bazaar) in Bandar Abbas and Hormoz village (IR9000, 30 minutes) at least every hour, the last returning about 4pm.

Qeshm Island　جزیره قشم
☎ 0763

Mountainous Qeshm is the largest island (1335 sq km) in the Gulf and, if you have the time both literally and mentally, is a great place to just wander around. It's dotted with villages and mangrove forests and is gradually being developed as a duty-free zone – a sort of poor man's Kish. The main town is Qeshm, which is well equipped with hotels and the usual life-support services, but elsewhere you'll need to make friends to find a bed.

The undoubted highlight of Qeshm is **Laft**, a beautiful Bandari fishing village 58km west of Qeshm town. The *badgirs*, wells, dhows and chilled-out locals make this a great place to spend an afternoon and well worth the taxi from Qeshm town (about IR100,000 for five hours).

There are plenty of hotels in Qeshm town, including the **Hotel Sahel** (☎ 522 4723; Imam Khomeini Ave; tw IR70,000), close to Sangi pier (where the boats from Bandar arrive) with reasonable twins and share bathrooms; and the excellent value **Qeshm International Hotel** (☎/fax 255 4905; 22 Bahman Blvd; s/d/tr US$30/35/50; P ⊠ ▯), a semiluxurious place at the southern end of town.

For information about boat transport to Qeshm see opposite.

Minab　میناب
☎ 0765

Surrounded by date palms and with a crumbling fortress overlooking the town, Minab is an easy and pleasant day trip from Bandar Abbas – or an alternative base. The region is famous for ceramics and mosaic tiles, and the **Thursday market** is one of the most colourful in Iran; it's held about 500m downstream from the bridge as you enter town.

Sadaf Hotel (☎ 222 5999; s/d IR100,000/153,000; ⊠) is about 500m before the main bridge into town. Its large, spotless rooms with TV, fridge, and Eastern bathroom are fair value, and the restaurant is decent.

Savaris from Bandar (IR15,000, 75 minutes) leave from a roadside known as 'garage' just south of Abuzar Sq.

SOUTHEASTERN IRAN
جنوب شرق ایران

Southeastern Iran is frontier territory. From historic Kerman, on the cusp of the cultural divide between the central plateau's ethnic Persians and the more eastern-oriented Baluchis, the exotic is never far away as you skirt the southern reaches of the blistering hot Dasht-e Lut and on to Zahedan. While earthquake damage means the Arg-e Bam citadel is not quite the draw it was, it's still worth a visit. And a stop in relaxed Rayen to wander through its own little-visited mud-brick citadel is worth the effort.

KERMAN　کرمان
☎ 0341 / pop 508,000

Kerman sits near the edge of the Dasht-e Lut desert on the road to Pakistan (and Bam) and is an agreeable place to spend a day or two. It's the capital of Kerman province and for many centuries thrived on its position along the Asian trade routes. These days it's famous for its carpets and industry, and infamous as a major transshipment centre for opium from Pakistan and Afghanistan.

The two main squares in Kerman are Azadi Sq to the west and Shohada Sq to the east. Most of the important offices and things to see are on or close to the road between these two squares, or in the bazaar near Shohada Sq.

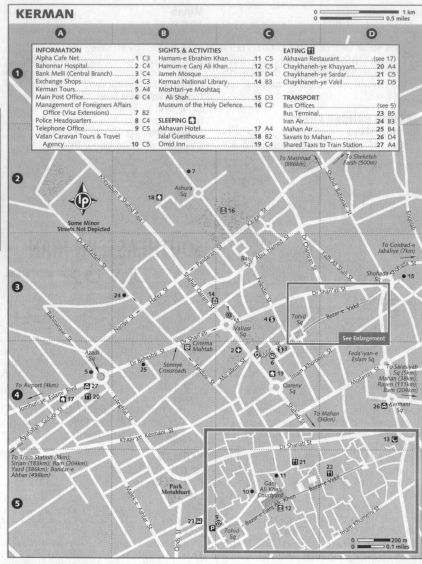

KERMAN

0 — 1 km
0 — 0.5 miles

INFORMATION
Alpha Cafe Net...........................1 C3
Bahonnar Hospital.....................2 C4
Bank Melli (Central Branch)........3 C4
Exchange Shops.........................4 C3
Kerman Tours............................5 A4
Main Post Office........................6 C4
Management of Foreigners Affairs
  Office (Visa Extensions)............7 B2
Police Headquarters..................8 C4
Telephone Office.......................9 C5
Vatan Caravan Tours & Travel
  Agency..................................10 C5

SIGHTS & ACTIVITIES
Hamam-e Ebrahim Khan............11 C5
Hamum-e Ganj Ali Khan............12 C5
Jameh Mosque.........................13 D4
Kerman National Library............14 B3
Moshtari-ye Moshtaq
  Ali Shah................................15 D3
Museum of the Holy Defence....16 C2

SLEEPING
Akhavan Hotel..........................17 A4
Jalal Guesthouse.......................18 B2
Omid Inn.................................19 C4

EATING
Akhavan Restaurant................(see 17)
Chaykhaneh-ye Khayyam.........20 A4
Chaykhaneh-ye Sardar.............21 C5
Chaykhaneh-ye Vakil...............22 D5

TRANSPORT
Bus Offices..............................(see 5)
Bus Terminal............................23 B5
Iran Air....................................24 B3
Mahan Air................................25 B4
Savaris to Mahan......................26 D4
Shared Taxis to Train Station.......27 A4

Information

EMERGENCY

Bahonnar Hospital (☎ 223 5011-8; Shahid Qarani St)
Police headquarters (☎ 110, 211 3068; Adalat St)

INTERNET ACCESS

Alpha Cafe Net (☎ 226 7270; Valiasr Sq; ⏲ 8am-10pm, closed Fri)

MONEY

Bank Melli central branch (Adalat St) Avoid it…or prepare for a blizzard of paperwork.
Exchange shops (Felestin St) Much faster.

POST & TELEPHONE

Main post office (Adalat St)
Telephone office (Tohid Sq; ⏲ 7am-10pm)

TOURS & GUIDES

For small, personal and fairly priced tours of the desert and other regional highlights, **Jalal Mehdizadeh** (☎ 271 0185, 0913-142 3174; jalal guesthouse@yahoo.de) and **Vatan Caravan Tours and Travel Agency** (vatan_caravan@yahoo.com; Ganj Ali Khan St) are worth investigating.

VISA EXTENSIONS

Management of Foreigners Affairs office (☎ 272 5798; Police Building No 14, Abbas Pour St; ⊗ 7am-1.30pm, Sat-Thu) Reported to extend visas, including transit visas, within two days.

Sights & Activities

BAZAR-E VAKIL

Kerman's 1km-long covered bazaar, running from Tohid Sq to the Jameh Mosque, is one of the best in Iran. Within it, the **Hamum-e Ganj Ali Khan** (☎ 222 5577; Gang Ali Khan Sq; admission IR3000; ⊗ 8.30am-noon, to 7.30pm summer) was once Kerman's largest bathhouse and has been transformed into a museum where tacky wax dummies illustrate the workings of a traditional bathhouse. **Hamam-e Ebrahim Khan** (⊗ 7am-5pm, to 7pm summer), at the end of the gold bazaar, is the real thing and men, but not women, can still be rubbed, scrubbed and beaten, all for the fun of it and IR20,000.

MOSQUES & MAUSOLEUMS

Built in 1349 but extensively modernised by the Safavids, the **Jameh Mosque**, off Shohada Sq in the bazaar district, has four lofty *iwans*, shimmering blue tiles and a handy English explanation at the main entrance; the back entrance leads into the bazaar. The twin-domed **Moshtari-ye Moshtaq Ali Shah** (Shohada Sq), mausoleum to a renowned Sufi mystic, is worth a quick look.

KERMAN NATIONAL LIBRARY

The **Kerman National Library** (Shahid Qarani St; ⊗ 7am-midnight) is a particularly harmonious example of Qajar-era architecture. Wandering through the forest of finely carved columns supporting vaulted ceilings, it's hard to imagine it was once a textile factory.

MUSEUM OF THE HOLY DEFENCE

The **Museum of the Holy Defence** (Felestin St; admission IR3000; ⊗ 7am-12.30pm & 3.30-6pm) commemorates the Iran-Iraq War. Symbolism abounds, although much of it won't be obvious without an English-speaking guide.

Inside is a gallery of gruesome photos and an animated model of a famous battle. Outside are tanks, missile launchers and a battlefield complete with bunkers, minefield and sound effects. Well worth a look.

Sleeping

Akhavan Hotel (☎ 244 1411-2; akhavanhotel@yahoo .com; Ayatollah Saduqi St; s/d incl breakfast US$24/34; P ⊠ 💻) The modern and semiluxurious rooms here are excellent value, even better once the jovial Akhavan brothers knock up to US$10 off during quieter times. These guys speak English and can arrange tours and tickets, and the restaurant is great value.

Omid Inn (☎ 222 0571; Shahid Qarani St; s/tw/tr IR35,000/50,000/60,000; P) The simple but welcoming family-run Omid is the pick of the budget options. The manager speaks English and the rooms, shared bathrooms and kitchen are clean. Ideal for lone women.

Jalal Guesthouse (☎ 271 0185, 0913-142 3174; jalalguesthouse@yahoo.de; 11 Imam Reza St; per person incl breakfast US$12; P ⊠ 💻) In the comfortable home of English- and German-speaking guide Jalal Mehdizadeh, this three-room traveller's homestay is not central but has a kitchen, washing machine and satellite TV.

Eating

Chaykhaneh-ye Sardar (☎ 226 4016; meals IR45,000; ⊗ 11.30am-4pm & 6pm-midnight) Popular with locals who enjoy the live traditional music (extra IR5000) from 8.30pm. Try the *borsgone*, a do-it-yourself mixture of *dizi* and the aubergine-based *kashke bademjun*.

Chaykhaneh-ye Khayyam (☎ 245 1417; Ayatollah Saduqi St; meals IR35,000; ⊗ 11am-11pm, closed Fri) Near Azadi Sq, this faux-traditional place serves reliably good and diverse local food.

Akhavan Hotel (☎ 244 1411-2; Ayatollah Saduqi St; meals IR30,000) Huge portions of tasty Iranian food (including several vegetarian options) more than make up for the less-than-atmospheric surrounds.

Drinking

Chaykhaneh-ye Vakil (☎ 222 5989; Bazar-e Vakil; admission IR5000, meals IR30,000; ⊗ 9am-8pm Sat-Thu & 9am-2pm Fri) This architecturally magnificent subterranean teahouse and restaurant is the most atmospheric in Kerman. It's more about sipping tea and smoking *qalyan* under the vaulted ceilings than eating, but the *dizi* (noon to 3pm) isn't bad.

Getting There & Away

AIR
Iran Air (☎ 245 8871; Dr Mafatteh St) has flights to Esfahan (IR267,000 one way, twice weekly), Tehran (IR364,000, daily) and Zahedan (IR205,000, weekly). **Mahan Air** (☎ 245 0423; Dr Beheshti St) also flies to Tehran and Mashhad.

BUS & SAVARI
Regular Volvo buses leave the terminal for Bam (IR13,000, three hours); Bandar Abbas (IR38,000, eight hours); Esfahan (IR40,000, 12 hours); Shiraz (IR37,000, eight hours); Tehran (IR65,000, 18 hours); Yazd (IR25,000, five hours); and Zahedan (IR21,000M, six hours). Mercedes buses are less frequent, but cheaper. Savaris to Bam (IR20,000, two hours) and Rayen (IR15,000, 75 minutes) leave from Sarasiyab Sq (about 5km east of Kermani Sq). Savaris to Mahan (IR4000) leave from Kermani Sq and occasionally from Azadi Sq.

TRAIN
The train to Tehran (IR63,150/39,750 in 1st/2nd class, 13 hours, twice daily) stops at Yazd, Kashan and Qom, but not Esfahan. There's also a daily train to Bam and the line through to Zahedan should be finished during the life of this book. Tickets can be bought from **Kerman Tours** (☎ 245 0465; Azadi Sq) or arranged through Akhavan Hotel, saving you the trip to the **train station** (☎ 211 0762) 8km southwest of town – take a shared taxi from Azadi Sq.

AROUND KERMAN
Mahan   ماهان
☎ 0342
Mahan is a relaxed town 38km southeast of Kerman. The highlight is the 15th-century **Aramgah-e Shah Ne'matollah Vali** (admission IR3000; ☿ 8am-5pm, to 8pm summer), the mausoleum of a well-known local poet, mystic and founder of the Ne'matollah order of dervishes.

About 5km up the main road from the mausoleum is the charming and famous **Bagh-e Shahzade** (admission IR3000; ☿ 9am-6pm, 8am-11pm summer) gardens, with a collection of pools leading to a large palace, part of which has been converted into a teahouse and restaurant (meals IR35,000).

Mahan is easily visited on a day (or half-day) trip from Kerman, but you could stay and eat in the good-value **Mahan Inn** (☎ 622 2700; Gharani Sq; d/ste US$15/25; P ☼).

Regular savaris (IR4000, 20 minutes) and minibuses (IR800, 35 minutes, approximately hourly) to Kerman leave from outside the mausoleum.

RAYEN   راين
☎ 0342
With the demise of Bam, several other ancient adobe structures are challenging for the title of 'new Arg'. The pick of them is the **Arg-e Rayen** (☿ 8am-noon & 2-6pm) in Rayen, halfway between Kerman and Bam. About a quarter the size of its Bam cousin, the hotchpotch of architectural styles suggests the Arg-e Rayen is over 1000 years old. The imposing outer walls are 3m thick at the base and 1m thick at the top, and support most of the Arg's 15 towers. Caretaker **Hamid Reza** (☎ 662 3644) will unlock the various doors for you for a small tip.

The **Restaurant Arg** (☎ 662 3931; meals IR30,000), 30m downhill from the Arg, serves large portions of tasty food and has a few simple rooms for a negotiable IR30,000 per bed.

Buses (IR5500, two hours) run to and from Kerman terminal every hour or so; Taavonis No. 3 and No. 16 are your best bet. Savaris (IR15,000) from Kerman's Sarasiyab Sq are usually more frequent. Private taxis cost about IR150,000 for a half-day trip from Kerman.

BAM   بم
☎ 0344
This ancient oasis town famed for its magnificent citadel, the Arg-e Bam, was all but flattened by a powerful earthquake that killed more than 31,000 people on 26 December 2003. Rebuilding work has slowly returned some normality, though signs of the destruction will be around for years to come. It's a long haul to get to Bam, but travellers who have made the trip invariably think it worthwhile. Although badly damaged, the Arg remains a truly impressive structure and the hospitality of locals, who are desperate for you to come, is memorable. If you don't want to stay, it's possible to make a long day trip from Kerman.

The **Bank Sepah** (Shahid Sadoqi St) can change money and **Internet access** (Pasdaran St; per hr IR15,000; ☿ 8am-12.30pm & 3.30-8pm Sat-Thu) can be found between the Bank Tejarat and a shop selling motorbikes.

Arg-e Bam

The ancient mud city of Bam was one of the jewels in Iran's tourism crown. Dating from at least as far back as the Sassanian period, the city was a staging post on the trade routes between India and Pakistan at one end and the Gulf and Europe at the other. Marco Polo was one of the visitors awestruck by the city's 38 towers, huge mud walls and fairy-tale citadel, the **Arg-e Bam** (admission free; ☺ dawn-dusk).

Today the 9th-century walls, mud-brick ramparts and monumental entrance gateway are crumbling, but are still far more impressive than many other ruined sights you'll see across the Middle East. A gangway has been built to allow visitors to enter and leads through the collapsed main gate and up to the foot of the citadel itself. Reconstruction has begun but it's going to be slow – estimates range from 20 to 50 years. The focus is on using traditional materials.

Sleeping & Eating

Akbar Tourist Guest House (☎ 231 4843, 0913-144 4146; mr_panjali@yahoo.com; Sayyeh Jamal od-Din St; dm/s/d IR30,000/50,000/80,000) Panjalizadeh Akbar and his family have rebuilt this landmark on the overland trail and their warm hospitality and courtyard communal area are attracting travellers. Facilities are adequate if simple (bathrooms are shared), but a restaurant and several air-con doubles are expected soon.

Azadi Hotel (☎ 222 2097-9; r/ste US$65/75; ⓟ ⌘) Left of the main road into Bam from Kerman, this has large, comfy rooms and helpful service. The restaurant (meals IR40,000) is probably the best sit-down option in Bam.

Bami dates are fantastic, but the restaurants are less inspirational. Among the simple eateries along Imam Khomeini St, the pink-painted **Maroof** (☎ 0913-320 8291; meals IR20,000; ⓨ 11am-2pm & 6-11pm) serves tasty kebabs plus a few more exotic dishes; virtually opposite is the **Shandiz Pizza** (pizzas IR20,000; ⓨ 11am-11pm).

Getting There & Away

Iran Aseman flies between Bam and Tehran (IR420,000, at least daily).

Bam's terminal is just south of Arg Sq, but most buses are going to or from Zahedan and stop instead at the square itself; when we passed bus offices were located in shipping containers on the northwest corner. A taxi from Arg Sq to the town centre costs around

IR5000, a shared taxi is IR1000. Mercedes buses from Bam include: Bandar Abbas (IR20,000, nine hours); Kerman (IR9,500, three hours); Yazd (IR18,000, eight hours); Esfahan (IR45,000, 11 hours) and Zahedan (IR12,000, five hours). The 6.30am Zahedan bus is good if you want to cross the border the same day. Savaris to Kerman (IR20,000, two hours) leave Arg Sq several times an hour. For Rayen, ask to be dropped at the turn-off and take any transport from there.

The train to Tehran (20 hours) leaves at 4pm on Sunday, Tuesday and Thursday, stopping at Kerman, Yazd and Kashan. The line to Zahedan should be finished in the next couple of years.

ZAHEDAN   زاهدان
☎ 0541

Zahedan is a dusty, featureless frontier desert town with virtually zero attractions but, since it's the nearest major town to the border with Pakistan, most overland travellers spend time here – either at the terminal or overnight.

The **Institute for Internet Services** (☎ 321 4180; Azadi Sq; per hr IR14,000; ⓨ 8am-10pm Sat-Thu) has decent connections; the **Bank Melli central branch** (Azadi St) changes US dollars but head to the bazaar (or better, wait until Taftan) to change Pakistani rupees. Head to the **Khatam hospital** (☎ 322 7067) in an emergency. The **Police Department of Alien Affairs** (☎ 323 1182; Motahhari Blvd; ⓨ 7am-2pm, closed Fri) handles visa extensions. See p244 for details of the Indian and Pakistani consulates.

If you do end up in Zahedan, the **Bazar-e Ruz** is the most interesting part of town. It has a definite Pakistani and Afghani flavour, with the *salwar kameez* (a long tunic worn over baggy pants) being the dominant form of dress among men.

Sleeping

Hotel Momtzahirmand (☎ 322 2313; Bazar-e Ruz; s/tw IR35,000/50,000; ⌘) Right in the bazaar, most rooms have a sink and the shared showers and toilets are clean. It's along the first laneway on the left off Shari'ati (look for a brown door with coloured glass panels).

Abuzar Hotel (☎ 451 2132; 40 Metri-e Kamarbandi St; r without/with bathroom IR40,000/60,000; ⓟ) Away from the centre, this friendly place is good value and has a decent restaurant downstairs.

Kavir Hotel (☎ 321 1840; Motahhari Blvd; s/d IR90,000/120,000; ⓟ ⌘) It's the pick of the mid-

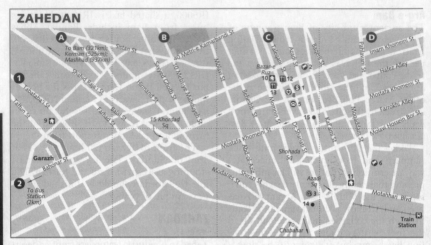

range but it's a long way from opulent. The bordello-like interiors could be cleaner, so could the bathrooms. The restaurant is fair.

Eating
There are plenty of fast-food outlets on Dr Shari'ati St, including kababis and good barbecue chicken (IR12,000 for half a chook, tomatoes and bread) places. Apart from the hotel restaurants, the **Esteghlal Restaurant** (☎ 322 2250; Imam Khomeini St; meals IR15,000) does a filling *khoresht*.

Getting There & Away
Iran Air (☎ 322 0813-4; near Azadi Sq) has flights to Tehran (IR477,000, 12 per week), Esfahan (IR407,000, weekly), Kerman (IR205,000, weekly), Mashhad (IR347,000, three weekly) and Chabahar (IR226,000). Mahan Air flies to Tehran daily except Friday; buy tickets at **Khaterat Zahedan Travel** (☎ 322 9113; Azadi St).

Regular Mercedes/Volvo buses leave the sprawling terminal in the west of town to just about everywhere. Destinations include Bam (IR12,000, five hours), Kerman (IR21,000/35,000, six hours), Yazd (IR34,500/55,000, 14 hours), Esfahan (IR44,800/75,000, 21 hours), Shiraz (IR49,200/75,000, 17 hours), Bandar Abbas (IR42,200/65,000, 17 hours), Mashhad (IR70,000/100,000, 15 hours) and Tehran (IR63,300/95,000, 22 hours). A taxi from the terminal to town should cost about IR6000, or IR1500 shared.

To the Pakistan border or Mirjaveh, savaris and the odd pick-up (about IR15,000)

leave Forudgarh Sq (also known as Meydan-e Mirjaveh). Occasionally buses (IR5500, 1½ hours) leave the terminal, where smiling-assassin taxi drivers also ask IR100,000 for the trip – bargain hard. Diehard trainspotters with wide masochistic streaks might consider the twice-monthly train to the border, and thence on to Quetta.

MIRJAVEH   میرجاوه
☎ 0543
Mirjaveh is the closest town to the border with Pakistan, although it's not necessary to come here as pick-ups and shared taxis run directly between Zahedan and the border – see p660. Coming from Pakistan, buses run to Zahedan for an outrageous IR20,000, savaris cost about IR100,000 for the whole vehicle. If you get stuck, **Mirjaveh Tourist Inn** (Hotel Ali; ☎ 322 2486; s/tw IR40,000/75,000; P ☒) isn't bad, but isn't that secure, either.

NORTHEASTERN IRAN
شمال شرق ایران

Northeastern Iran encompasses the eastern part of the Alborz Mountains and the wide, flat steppes and desert further south. It's a region full of history, with the Gonbad-e Kavus tower and the vast Islamic complex around the shrine to Imam Reza in Mashhad among the highlights. The borders with Afghanistan and Turkmenistan are open.

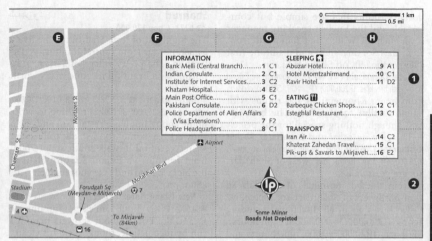

INFORMATION
Bank Melli (Central Branch).........1 C1
Indian Consulate.........................2 C1
Institute for Internet Services.......3 C2
Khatam Hospital.........................4 E2
Main Post Office.........................5 C1
Pakistani Consulate.....................6 D2
Police Department of Alien Affairs
  (Visa Extensions)......................7 F2
Police Headquarters.....................8 C1

SLEEPING
Abuzar Hotel..............................9 A1
Hotel Momtzahirmand...............10 C1
Kavir Hotel................................11 D2

EATING
Barbeque Chicken Shops...........12 C1
Esteghlal Restaurant..................13 C1

TRANSPORT
Iran Air.....................................14 C2
Khaterat Zahedan Travel............15 C1
Pik-ups & Savaris to Mirjaveh.....16 E2

SARI
سارى

☎ 0151

Sari is a busy but attractive town some distance back from the Caspian coast. The centre is little Haft-e Tir Sq (usually called Sa'at Sq because of the clock), from where streets radiate in all directions. Sights include the 15th-century **Shrine of Yahya**, tucked in behind the **bazaar**, and the nearby **Soltan Zein-ol-Abedin Tower**; and the **Shrine of Abbas**, about 2km east of Clock Sq. All three are active places of worship but none is unmissable.

Three Internet cafés surround Sa'at Sq, including **Safanet** (per hr IR10,000; 8am-3pm & 4-8pm).

Sleeping & Eating
Sarouyeh Guesthouse (☎ 324 5600; Danesh St; s/d IR80,000/85,000; P) Located just off Taleqani St, east of Shohada Sq, this good-value place has rooms with eastern bathrooms and fans.

Sarouyeh Hotel (s/d IR170,000/260,000; P) Across the courtyard from its sister guesthouse, the spacious rooms are better here.

Mosaferkhuneh (Modares St; dm/tw/tr IR15,000/50,000/55,000) Ultrabasic rooms and shared toilets. There's no shower. Head upstairs, 5m from the corner of Sa'at Sq.

Sorena Restaurant (☎ 222 7069; Jomhuri-ye Eslami St; meals IR40,000; 11am-3.30pm & 7pm-midnight) About 1km from Sa'at Sq, this trendy upstairs restaurant has plenty of kebabs and some tasty fish dishes.

Getting There & Away
Iran Air flies to Tehran (IR195,000) and Mashhad (IR275,000).

The bus terminal is about 3km northeast of Sa'at Sq (take a shared taxi along 18 Dei St). Buses run to Tehran (IR14,000, five hours), Rasht (IR19,000, seven hours) and Mashhad (IR30,000, 11 hours, mostly morning and evening). For Gorgan, minibuses (IR5000) leave from a separate terminal, 2km east of Sa'at Sq, or take a savari (IR20,000) from the office opposite.

Trains to Tehran (IR13,750 in 2nd class, eight hours) and Gorgan depart daily. The train station is about 1km south of Sa'at Sq.

GORGAN
گرگان

☎ 0171

Gorgan is a reasonable place to break up a journey between the Caspian and Mashhad. In the bazaar, **Jameh Mosque**, off Aftab 27 Lane, has a traditional sloping, tiled roof and an unusual minaret. About 200m west, the **Shrine of Nur** is mildly interesting.

About 6km east of Gorgan, **Nahar Khoran** is an unspoilt forest area with plenty of hiking trails.

The centre of Gorgan is huge Valiasr Sq, usually known as Shahrdari Sq. **Pasargad Coffeenet** (☎ 222 7001; Edalat St; per hr IR5000; 10am-10pm) is in the Laleh Arcade; and there's a **phone office** (Behesht 2nd Alley; 7am-10pm) about 40m east of Shahrdari Sq.

Pars Hotel (☎ 222 9550; s/tw/tr IR45,000/55,000/65,000), set around a quiet courtyard, has upstairs rooms that are simple but comfortable and the English-speaking manager is very helpful. Walk about 20m north from Shahrdari Sq, turn right and it's in the first alley on the left, off Shohada St.

Hotel Tahmasebi (☎ 442 2780; Jomhuri-ye Eslami St; tw with breakfast IR200,000; P 🞰), 500m down from Imam Khomeini Sq, has rooms with (some smelly) squat toilets. The best option, though nothing special for the price.

The *ghorme sabzi* and kebabs at **Abshar Restaurant** (☎ 222 2993; Imam Khomeini St; meals IR20,000; 🕙 noon-10pm), just west of Shahrdari Sq, are great value.

From the bus terminal, at Enqelab Sq 2km northwest of Shahrdari Sq, Mercedes/Volvo buses go in all directions including Tehran (IR20,000/36,000, about eight hours), Mashhad (IR30,000/40,000, nine hours) and Shahrud (IR12,000/18,000, four hours). Minibuses for Sari (IR5000, 2½ hours) leave from a separate terminal 3km southwest of Imam Khomeini Sq. Savaris and minibuses also serve Shahrud; change at Azadshahr for the scenic drive across the Alborz Mountains.

The train to Tehran (IR39,750/17,200 in 1st/2nd class) departs daily; the station is about 300m west of the bus terminal.

AROUND GORGAN
Gonbad-e Kavus (Gonbad-e Qabus)
گنبد کاووس

This chilled-out Turkmen town, 93km west of Gorgan, is named after its most famous asset – the spectacular **Mil-e Gonbad tower** (admission IR3000; 🕙 7.30am-dusk) and its sponsor, Qabus ebn-e Vashmgir. Completed in 1006, the circular tower is 55m tall and has 12m-deep foundations. Minibuses from Gorgan run every hour or so, but savaris are much faster; you'll need to change at Azadshahr, 17km nearer to Gorgan, from where savaris also run to Shahrud (IR25,000). It's well worth stopping en route to Mashhad or along the mountain pass road to Shahrud.

TEHRAN TO MASHHAD

Flying or taking the overnight train at least one way to Mashhad is a good idea, but if you decide to go by road there are a few interesting stops along the way. Semnan is the first major town, about five hours by bus from Tehran. Damghan is three hours further, but Shahrud and nearby Bastam are prettier than both.

Shahrud
شاهرود
☎ 0273 / pop 120,000

The highlight of leafy Shahrud is the lively **bazaar**, not far from central Jomhuri-ye Eslami Sq. The pretty village of **Bastam**, 7km north, has a beautiful mosque that's worth a visit.

Hotel Nader (☎ 333 2835; s/d IR70,000/120,000, with shower IR85,000/130,000) is nothing to write home about, but has a restaurant and clean showers in some rooms; all toilets are shared. To find it, walk south about 700m from Jomhuri-ye Eslami Sq, turn right at the biggish road and take your first left – it's 250m on.

New Islami Hotel (☎ 222 2335; Shohada St; tw IR50,000; P) is about 15m east of Jomhuri-ye Eslami Sq. Forget about showers here. It's run by nice people, though, and it's clean.

The bus/minibus terminal is about 5km south of Jomhuri-ye Eslami Sq, where bus agents have offices. Buses go to Tehran (IR19,000), Mashhad (IR21,000), Gorgan (IR12,000) and Sari (IR18,000).

Neishabur
نیشابور
☎ 0551

Neishabur, 114km west of Mashhad, is most famous as the home town of poet and all-round genius Omar Khayyam (see p73). The **Mausoleum of Omar Khayyam** (admission IR4000, 🕙 8am-sunset) is designed to reflect his mathematical as well as poetic achievements, and sits in attractive gardens that also contain the fine 16th-century **Mausoleum of Mohammed Mahrugh**. In the town centre, a partially restored Safavid-era **caravanserai** (🕙 8am-5pm, to 7pm summer) houses a small museum.

Neishabur can be visited as a day trip from Mashhad. Alternatively, the **Tourist Hotel** (☎ 33445; s/d US$20/25; P 🞰), in the centre of town, is reliable and has a good restaurant.

Minibuses from Mashhad (IR7000, 2½ hours) leave in the morning, or take any bus heading towards Tehran. If you charter a taxi it's easy to visit Neishabur along with the 17th-century **Qadamgah Mausoleum**, just off the main Mashhad–Neishabur road, the ancient minaret and dome at **Sang Bast**, and the Timurud-era caravanserai at **Binolud**.

MASHHAD
مشهد
☎ 0511 / pop 3.1 million

As the place where the eighth Shiite Imam and direct descendant of the Prophet Mo-

MASHHAD

hammed, Imam Reza, died in 817, Mash-had (Place of Martyrdom) is the most holy city in the country. Here you'll see tears, wailing and selfless devotion in full frame, as more than 12 million pilgrims journey to the city each year. Particularly around No Ruz (late March) and in summer, Mashhad is packed.

Mashhad is the capital of vast Khorasan province, which, despite being largely made up of desert plains, does have several attractions within easy reach of Mashhad.

Information
EMERGENCY
Imam Reza Hospital (☎ 854 3031-9; Ebn-e Sina St)
Tourist police (☎ 841 8236; Beit-ol-Moqqadas Sq)

INTERNET ACCESS
Khayyam Internet Cafe (☎ 851 7272; Imam Reza St; per hr IR6000; ☒ 24hr) Offers IR800 per minute international calls and fast connections.
Toos Internet Cafe (Imam Reza St; per hr IR5000; ☒ 8.30am-midnight Sat-Thu, 4pm-midnight Fri)

MONEY
You'll find that there are a number of banks in Mashhad that will change money, including **Bank Melli central branch** (Imam Khomeini St). However, **Sepehri Exchange** (Pasdaran Ave; ☒ 9am-6pm Sat-Wed & 9am-2pm Thu) is a much faster option.

POST
Main post office (Imam Khomeini St)

TOURIST INFORMATION

ITTO Khorasan (☎ 726 9501; 2nd fl, Saheb al-Zaman Ave, Molavi St; ◷ 8am-4pm) Has simple maps and a few brochures. The office at the train station is just as good.

TRAVEL AGENCIES

Adibian Travel Agency (☎ 859 8151; www.adibian tours.com; 56 Pasdaran Ave; ◷ 7.30am-8pm) For tickets, visa renewals and city and regional tours including Neishabur, Kalat, Torbet-e Jam and Sarakhs.

VISA EXTENSIONS

Police Department of Aliens Affairs (☎ 876 0603; 45 Metri-ye Reza Blvd) Near Piroozy Blvd. Not the best place to apply, but it's there if you're desperate. A taxi *dah baste* should cost about IR6000 from the Holy Shrine; ask for *Edari-ye Atbareh Khariji* (Aliens' Office).

Sights

ASTAN-E QODS-E RAZAVI

The Holy Shrine of Imam Reza, and the surrounding buildings, are known collectively as the **Astan-e Qods-e Razavi** (◷ 24hr) and comprise one of the marvels of the Islamic world. The original tomb chamber of Imam Reza was built in the early 9th century, but later destroyed, restored and destroyed again.

The present **Holy Shrine**, with its golden dome, was built under the orders of Shah Abbas I at the beginning of the 17th century. Since 1983, continuous construction has ensured the architects (both literal and metaphorical) of the Islamic Republic will be remembered long after they're gone. The main entrances are at the end of Imam Reza Ave and Shirazi St.

As well as the shrine, the complex contains two mosques, museums, 12 lofty *iwans* (two of them coated entirely with gold), six theological colleges, several libraries, a post office and a bookshop. The remarkable **Azim-e Gohar Shad Mosque** has a 50m blue dome and cavernous golden portal.

Three museums are entered from the southern courtyard. The **Muze-ye Markazi** (Central Museum; admission IR4000; ◷ 8am-4pm) houses an eccentric collection including Olympic medals, stamps, paintings, shells, a huge 800-year-old wooden door and a one-tonne stone drinking vessel made in the 12th century. The **Muze-ye Quran** (Quran Museum) has a collection of more than 100 hand-inscribed Qurans, and the attached **Carpet Museum** (admission for both IR3000; ◷ 8am-1pm) has an impressive collection of carpets dating back 500 years.

The Holy Shrine, the Azim-e Gohar Shad Mosque and the courtyards outside are off-limits to non-Muslims. If you're not with a guide, you're supposed to report first to the friendly **International Relations Office** (◷ 7am-5pm) in the far west of the complex and are assigned a guide. Evenings are a good time to wander about unaccompanied. Women must wear a chador, available at the entrance. Bags and cameras are not permitted inside.

Sleeping

Mashhad is full of hotels, most within a few minutes' walk of the shrine complex. Some will not accept foreigners. Outside No Ruz and the June-to-September pilgrimage season, prices are very negotiable.

Karim Khan Hotel (☎ 0912-307 8414; www.karim khanhotel.8k.com; Imam Reza St; d/apt IR300,000/450,000; P ✗ 🖳 🖳) The classy Karim Khan boasts stylish rooms and professional service for a very reasonable price; apartments sleep four. There's a good restaurant downstairs.

Razi Hotel (☎ 854 1122; Razi St; s/d incl breakfast IR98,200/148,900; ✗) The Razi is a comfy, good-value budget option, although it's a decent walk to the shrine.

Atlas Hotel (☎ 854 5061; Beit-ol-Moqaddas Sq; s/d US$30/45; P ✗) Ideally located for views of the shrine and access to the bustling bazaar, comfortable rooms here have recently been renovated. Fair value.

Taranom Apartment Hotel (☎ 859 5761; Tavakoli Lane; d IR120,000; ✗) Top-value place where affable staff complement the clean rooms with private bathrooms. The hotel is off Imam Reza St.

Eating

There are lots of cheap eating houses around the shrine complex, especially on Imam Reza St. Most hotels also have restaurants.

Pars Restaurant (☎ 222 5331; cnr Imam Khomeini & Pasdaran Sts; meals IR18,000-25,000; ◷ noon-3pm & 6-10pm Sat-Thu) This unpretentious place serves cheap but tasty *khoresht*, *ghorme sabzi* and kebab meals.

Emam Reza Restaurant (☎ 851 4658; Imam Reza St; meals IR15,000-25,000; ◷ 11am-4pm & 7pm-1am Sat-Thu) Typically characterless for Mashhad, but the hearty servings of the usual Iranian fare are welcome.

Moein Darbary (☎ 878 5248; Kalantari Hwy; meals IR60,000; ◷ noon-3pm & 7-11pm) Considered one of the best restaurants in Mashhad, Moein

Darbary serves top-notch Iranian fare. Take a taxi (IR7000) – most drivers know it.

Drinking

The teahouses also serve food, but drinking and smoking is the primary pastime.

Hezardestan Traditional Teahouse (☎ 222 2943; Jannat Mall; meals IR45,000-60,000; ⏰ noon-3pm & 5pm-midnight) Atmosphere oozes out of the subterranean Hezardastan but, while the tea and sweets (IR15,000), *qalyan* (IR15,000), meals and live music are all pretty good, it gets pricey when you add a IR20,000 service charge.

Bagh-e Sabz (1st fl, cnr Imam Khomeini & Shahid Raja'i Sts) At Bagh-e Sabz, overlooking the corner, watching the young couples and groups flirting shamelessly can be fun.

Vitamin Sara (☎ 222 7998; Shahid Raja'i St) Don't miss the banana and pistachio shakes (IR6000) – awesome!

Shopping

Mashhad has several bazaars, including the 700m-long Reza Bazaar. The city is famous for turquoise (but beware of fakes), saffron and rugs.

Tours

Towhid Foroozanfar (☎ 0915-313 2960; towhid@imam reza.net) is a well-informed, engaging and passionate guide offering tours within Mashhad and also to Kalat, Torbet-e Jam, Neishabur, Tus and other regional highlights. Prices are negotiable but very reasonable.

Getting There & Away

AIR

Iran Air (☎ 225 2080; Modarres St) flies several times daily to Tehran (IR344,000); daily to Esfahan (IR379,000) and Shiraz (IR430,000); and less often to Bandar Abbas (IR468,000), Tabriz (IR508,000), Yazd (IR319,000) and Zahedan (IR347,000). **Iran Aseman** (☎ 752 8200; Andarzgu St) also flies to Tehran and Esfahan, and **Mahan Airlines** (☎ 221 9294) flies to Kerman.

BUS

The bus terminal is about 2km southwest of the Holy Shrine (reached by shared taxi along Imam Reza Ave), and from here a plethora of buses go to every major city and regional town. Long-distance routes by Mercedes/Volvo include: Shahrud (IR25,000/40,000, 10 hours), Tehran (IR39,000/75,000, 14 hours), Yazd (IR45,500/79,000, 16 hours), Esfahan (IR60,000/85,000, about 22 hours) and Zahedan (IR57,000/90,000, 15 hours).

To Afghanistan, the fastest way is a bus or savari to Taybad, another savari the last 20km to the border and another from there to Herat. Easier is the direct bus to Herat (IR55,000, eight to 12 hours), which has delays aplenty but assures you an exit registration. For details, see p661.

TRAIN

Several trains run daily between Tehran and Mashhad, mostly overnight services (around 13 hours). Fares range from IR27,250 in 2nd class to IR122,700 in the four-berth sleeper 'green class', which includes dinner and breakfast.

AROUND MASHHAD

Tus (Ferdosi)   طوس (فردوسی)

Tus (also known as Ferdosi) is a former regional capital. After being razed by the Mongols, it was abandoned and is now better known for the **Mausoleum of Ferdosi** (admission IR3000; ⏰ 8am-4pm, to 7pm summer), dedicated to one of Iran's most famous poets, Abolqasem Ferdosi, who wrote the epic *Shahnamah* (Book of Kings). Beneath the stone mausoleum (completed in 1965) is a simple marble tomb and reliefs depicting scenes from the Book of Kings. The small **Tus Museum** (admission IR2000) in the gardens contains a 73kg copy of the *Shahnamah,* and a café inside the gardens serves drinks and simple meals. Minibuses and savaris leave regularly from Shohada Sq in Mashhad.

Sarakhs   سرخس

Sarakhs is on the border with Turkmenistan; see p661 for details on crossing the border. The town is remarkable mainly for the **Gonbad Sheikh Loghman Baba** tower on the outskirts of town.

If you're coming this way, don't miss the fantastically remote **Rubat Sharaf Caravanserai**, reached by a 6km road south from Shorleq, about 130km from Mashhad. You'll need to hitch from Shorleq, likely by motorbike.

Several buses (IR7000, 2½ hours) and savaris (IR20,000, two hours) travel daily from Mashhad to Sarakhs. There are also two trains (IR6000; three hours) daily, the best leaving Mashhad at 10.30am and returning at 3pm.

IRAN

IRAN DIRECTORY

ACCOMMODATION

Accommodation in Iran is generally cheap and there is a reasonable choice, from a tiny cell in a noisy *mosaferkhuneh* (basic lodging house) right through to a few world-class luxury hotels. Camping facilities, however, are almost nonexistent.

In this chapter a 'budget' room will be a *mosaferkhuneh* or other basic hotel. Except in Tehran, where prices are higher, in this chapter a budget room is a double/twin costing less than US$20. Probably the cheapest rooms will be small and just have a bed and access to a grotty shared bathroom sans toilet paper – these cost about IR60,000 a twin (budget places seldom have double beds). If you add a private bathroom, usually with squat toilet, you're looking at between about IR90,000 and IR180,000. Almost every room in Iran is heated, though some go without fans. Some *mosaferkhunehs* won't accept foreigners, though this is increasingly rare.

PRACTICALITIES

■ The following daily newspapers are available at newsstands in Tehran and other large cities: *Iran Daily* (balanced and generally liberal); *Iran News* (most liberal; good international coverage); *Kayhan International* (somewhere right of Genghis Khan) and *Tehran Times* (thorough; the government line).

■ All Iranian broadcasters are controlled by the state, though many Iranians watch satellite stations from California. On Iranian TV, channels 1 to 4 are national, 5 and 6 province-based. Channel 4 has 15 minutes of English news at 11.30pm.

■ You can pick up the BBC World Service. Frequencies include 11760kHz, 15575kHz and 17640kHz; and, for VOA, 11760kHz and 15205kHz.

■ Electric current is 220V AC, 50Hz. Wall sockets are the European, two-round-pin type.

■ Iran uses the metric system for weights and measures.

'Midrange' hotels in this chapter range from about US$20 to US$70 a twin/double. All will have private bathrooms – many with Western toilets – and often they'll have air-conditioning, a fridge and TV (some with satellite).

Prices are set by the government and most midrange and top-end places charge foreigners more than Iranians, though prices can be negotiated outside peak times (see No Ruz, The Peak Season p245). Prices are often quoted in US dollars, though they accept (and usually prefer) rials. All guests must fill out a registration form and hotel management will usually want to keep your passport because police/security officers check to see who's staying. Check-out is usually 2pm.

Top-end hotels are few and far between, and in this chapter they cost more than US$70. There are also 'homestays' (a room in someone's home) and 'suites' (fully equipped apartments), mainly in the Caspian provinces.

ACTIVITIES

Growing numbers of travellers are combining activities such as skiing in the mountains north of Tehran (p198), trekking, and even diving off Kish Island (p228) with the more well known cultural attractions of Iran. There are reasonably easy hiking trails in the Alborz Mountains north of Tehran, and around places such as Masuleh (p204) and Alamut (p206). For the more adventurous, Mt Damavand (p198) can be climbed in three days.

For mountaineers and trekkers, more information can be obtained from **Araz Adventure Tours** (☎ 021-760 9292; www.araz.org), **Kassa Mountaineering & Tourism** (☎ 021-751 0463; www.kassaco.com) and the **Mountaineering Federation of Iran** (☎ 021-830 6641).

BOOKS

As well as this book, Lonely Planet publishes a comprehensive country guide, *Iran*.

New travel literature, social and political commentaries about Iran have been racing off the presses in recent years. These are some of the best.

All The Shah's Men (2003) is journalist Stephen Kinzer's thoroughly researched and thrilling account of the CIA coup that ousted Mohammad Mossadegh in 1953. Highly recommended!

Persian Pilgrimages (2002), by Afshin Molavi, sees the US-educated Iranian journalist explore his homeland through a series of 'pilgrimages' to cities and historical sites. This is a well-balanced read, full of insight into Iranian culture.

The Persian Puzzle: The Conflict Between Iran and America (2004), by Kenneth Pollack, looks at the history of Iran's path towards nuclear weapons – and argues against a US invasion.

Shah of Shahs (1985), by journalist Ryszard Kapuscinski, is a fast-paced yet perceptive account of Iran in the decade leading to the revolution.

Journeys in Persia and Kurdistan, by Isabella Bird, is a classic travelogue from Bird's time in Iran during the 1890s.

See p184 for books by Iranian authors, and p24 for general titles on the Middle East.

BUSINESS HOURS

Few places have uniform opening and closing times, but most businesses close early on Thursday and all day Friday. Many businesses close for a siesta (from about 1pm to 3pm or 4pm); along the hot Gulf this siesta stretches until about 5pm.

In this chapter hours will accord with the following list unless stated otherwise.

Banks Open 7.30am to 1.30pm Saturday to Wednesday, 7.30am to 12.30pm Thursday.

Government offices Open 8am to 2pm Saturday to Wednesday, 8am to noon Thursday.

Museums Open 8.30am to 6pm in summer (4pm or 5pm in winter), with one day off, usually Monday or Tuesday.

Post offices Open 7.30am to 3pm Saturday to Thursday. Some main offices open until 9pm.

Private businesses Open 8am or 9am till 5pm or 6pm Saturday to Wednesday, till noon Thursday.

Shops Open 9am to 8pm, but more likely to have a siesta.

Telephone offices Open daily 8am to 9pm. In smaller towns they can close at 5pm.

CHILDREN

Nappies (diapers), baby formula, most simple medications and so on are available in the big cities. Parents will need to explain to their daughters aged nine or older that they'll have to wear a scarf, and make sure they do. High chairs, child-care agencies, baby seats in cars and nappy-changing facilities are as rare as rocking-horse shit. Breastfeeding in public is not a good idea.

CUSTOMS

Iranian officialdom is fairly relaxed about what foreigners take into and out of the country; you're unlikely to be searched. However, don't take this to mean you can load your luggage with vodka, bacon, or magazines featuring semiclad women that might provoke 'moral outrage'.

On arrival, you'll fill out a form declaring what you have, and get a yellow copy – keep this until you leave; it's a big hassle if you lose it. You'll probably get away with almost any book, no matter how critical of the government, as long as it doesn't have too much female skin or hair visible on the cover. Visitors are supposed to declare cash worth more than US$1000, but no-one really cares.

Export Restrictions

You can leave with handicrafts other than carpets or rugs up to the value of US$160 (keep receipts). Many traders are willing to undervalue goods on receipts issued to foreigners. You can take out Persian carpets or rugs up to a total of 20 sq metres in size, 150g of gold and 3kg of silver, without gemstones. To exceed these limits, you need an export permit from the customs office. Officially, you need permission to export anything 'antique' (ie more than 50 years old). Staff are not trained in antique identification, so there is always a slight risk that anything vaguely antique-looking could be confiscated.

DANGERS & ANNOYANCES

Open hostility towards Western visitors – including Americans – is extremely rare and violent crime almost unheard of. Many travellers regard Iran as one of the safest and most hospitable countries in the world. Uniformed men are a common sight but, as long as you dress appropriately and don't point your camera at anything you shouldn't, they'll likely be as courteous as other Iranians. And while the notorious *komite* (religious police) are no longer, the change of presidency in 2005 could see a tightening of interpretations. If you are arrested, insist on seeing identification, telephone your embassy and remain deferential at all times.

Scams

A few travellers have been stopped in the street by bogus plain-clothes policemen. Never show or give important documents, money or cameras to any policeman in the street. If they insist, tell them you'll walk to the police station or that your passport and valuables are at your hotel. At the time of writing, Tehran was the place where you needed to be most wary of bogus police. If they try this scam on you and you send them away, be aware a bag snatch might follow you.

DISCOUNT CARDS

With admission prices now virtually free, the ISIC (International Student Identity Card) are pretty useless.

EMBASSIES & CONSULATES
Iranian Embassies & Consulates

Following are Iranian embassies and consulates in major cities around the world. For addresses of Iranian embassies in other Middle Eastern countries see the relevant country chapter. If your country isn't here, try **Netiran** (www.netiran.com).

Afghanistan (☎ 017-24700; Solh Ave, Gharar Rah Shir Pour, Kabul)

Australia (☎ 02-6290 2421; www.iranembassy.org.au; 25 Culgoa Crt, O'Malley, ACT 2606)

Azerbaijan (☎ 12-921932; Cafar Cabbarli 10) Opposite Nizami Metro station. For visas.

Canada (☎ 613-233 4726; www.salamiran.org; 245 Metcalfe St, Ottawa, Ontario K2P 2K2)

Denmark (☎ 3916 0073; www.iran-embassy.dk; Svanemøllevej 48, 2100 Copenhagen)

France (☎ 01 4069 7900; www.amb-iran.fr; 4 Ave d'Iena, 75116, Paris)

Germany (☎ 030-8419 1835; www.iranembassy.de; Podbielskiallee 67, D-14195, Berlin)

Ireland (☎ 01-288 5881; iranembassy@indigo.ie; 72 Mount Merrion Ave, Blackrock, Dublin)

Japan (☎ 3-3446 8011; www.iranembassyjp.com; 10-32-3 Chome Minami Aazabu, Minato-ku, Tokyo)

Netherlands (☎ 070-354 8483; www.iranian embassy.nl; Duinweg 20, 2585JX, The Hague)

New Zealand (☎ 04-386 2976; www.iranembassy.org.nz; 151 Te Anau Rd, Hataitai, Wellington)

Pakistan Islamabad (☎ 051-2276270; House 222-238, St 2, G-5/1, Islamabad); Karachi (☎ 021-5874371; 81 Shahrah-i-Iran, Clifton, Karachi); Lahore (☎ 042-7590926; asran@worldcall.net.pk; 55 Shadman II, Lahore); Quetta (☎ 081-843098, 2/33 Hili Rd)

UK (☎ 020-7225 3000; www.iran-embassy.org.uk; 27 Princes Gate, London SW7 IPX)

USA (☎ 202-965 4990; www.daftar.org; 2209 Wisconsin Ave, NW, Washington, 20007) The Iranian Interests Section is in the Pakistan embassy.

Embassies in Iran

Embassies in Tehran generally open from about 9am to noon for visa applications and from 2pm to 4pm for collecting visas, although much shorter hours are possible. Western missions are usually closed on Friday and Saturday, others on Thursday afternoon and Friday.

Afghanistan Mashhad (Map p239; ☎ 859 7551; Do Shahid St); Tehran (Map pp190-1; ☎ 8873 5040; fax 8873 5600; Beheshti Ave, cnr 4th St & Pakistan St; ☽ 9am-2pm Sat-Wed, 9am-noon Thu) In both places, 30-day tourist visas cost US$30 and are issued in two days.

Armenia (Map pp190-1; ☎ 6670 4833; emarteh@ yahoo.com; 1 Ostad Shahriar St, Razi St, Jomhuri-ye Eslami Ave, Tehran) Tourist visas issued in nine to 11 days for US$50, in three to five days for $80.

Australia (Map pp190-1; ☎ 8872 4456; www.iran .embassy.gov.au; 13 Eslamboli St, 23rd St, Tehran)

Azerbaijan (Map p188; ☎ 2223 5197; Nader Sq, 15 Golbarg St, Chizar, Tehran; ☽ 9am-noon Sun, Tue, Thu) Single-entry tourist visas issued in three days for US$40.

Canada (Map pp190-1; ☎ 8873 2623; www.iran.gc.ca; 57 Shahid Sarafraz St, Motahhari Ave, Tehran)

France (Map pp190-1; ☎ 2228 0372; www.amba france-ir.org; 85 Nofl Loshato St, Tehran)

Georgia (Map pp190-1; ☎ 2221 1470; Agha Bozorgi St, Fereshti St, Tehran; ☽ 9.15am-1.30pm Sun, Tue, Thu) Two-week tourist visas cost US$40 and take four days (US$60 for two-day service).

Germany (Map pp190-1; ☎ 3999 0000; www.teheran .diplo.de; 324 Ferdosi St, Tehran)

India Tehran (Map pp190-1; ☎ 8875 5103-5; www .indianembassy-tehran.com; 46 Mir-emad Ave, cnr Ninth St & Dr Beheshti St; ☽ 8.30am-5pm Sun-Thu); Zahedan (Map pp236-7; ☎ 0541-322 2337; off Imam Khomeini St) Visas issued in four days with a letter from your embassy; IR460,000.

Iraq (Map p188; ☎ 2221 1154; 20 Karamian Alley, Dr Shari'ati Ave, Tehran) Not issuing tourist visas.

Japan (Map pp190-1; ☎ 8871 3974; fax 8872 1792; cnr Bucharest & Fifth Sts, Arzhantin Sq, Tehran)

Lebanon (Map pp190-1; ☎ 8890 8451; 30 Afshin St, Tehran) Visas issued for IR31,500 with letter from your embassy.

Netherlands (Map pp190-1; ☎ 2256 7005-7; 1st E Lane, 22 Sharzad Blvd, Darous, Tehran)

New Zealand (Map p188; ☎ 2280 0289; newzealand@ mavara.com; 34, cnr 2nd Park Alley, Sosan St, Nth Golestan Complex, Aghdasiyeh St, Niavaran, Tehran)

Pakistan Mashhad (Map p239; ☎ 222 9845; Imam Khomeini St; ☽ 9am-noon Sat-Wed); Tehran (Map pp190-1; ☎ 6694 4888; fax 6694 4898; Block 1, Etemadzadeh Ave, Jamshidabad, Dr Hossein Fatemi Ave); Zahedan (Map pp236-7; ☎ 0541-322 3389; Pahlavani St) Single-entry visas (US$35) issued in Mashhad and Tehran in two to seven days with letter of introduction from your embassy. No visas are issued in Zahedan!

Spain (Map p188; ☎ 8871 4575; fax 8878 7082; 76 Sarv St, Afriqa Hwy, Tehran)

Syria (Map p188; ☎ 2205 9031; fax 2205 9409; Afriqa Hwy, Arash Blvd, Tehran) Visas same day.

Turkey Orumiyeh (☎ 0441-222 8974, Beheshti St); Tehran (Map pp190-1; ☎ 3311 5299; 314 Ferdosi St)

Turkmenistan Mashhad (Map p239; ☎ 854 7066; Do Shahid St; ◷ 8.30-noon Sat, Tue, Wed); Tehran (Map p188; ☎ 2254 2178; fax 2258 0432; 39 Fifth Golestan St, Pasdaran Ave; ◷ 9.30am-noon Sun-Thu) Bring an invite and US$51 for overnight processing, US$31 for 10 days later.

UK (Map pp190-1; ☎ 6670 5011; www.britishembassy .gov.uk/iran; 143 Ferdosi St, Tehran)

United Arab Emirates Bandar Abbas (☎ 222 4229; Nasr Blvd); Tehran (Map p188; ☎ 8678 1333; 355 Vahid Dastjerdi Ave)

USA (Map p188; ☎ 2200 8333; Sharifi Manesh, Elahieh, Tehran) The Swiss embassy has a US Interests Section. It might be able to help in an emergency but cannot offer full consular services.

GAY & LESBIAN TRAVELLERS

Homosexuality is illegal and, in theory, punishable by hundreds of lashes and even death (although foreigners would probably be deported instead). Barbaric laws aside, there is no reason why gay and lesbian travellers shouldn't visit Iran. There are no questions of sexuality on visa application forms, and we have not heard of any homosexual travellers being treated badly as long as they refrained from overt displays of affection in public.

Meeting Iranian gays and lesbians is difficult. Gays could try www.homanla.org, while www.khanaye-doost.com is an Iranian lesbian site.

HOLIDAYS

Iran always seems to be mourning the death of some religious figure or a more recent revolutionary victory.

Religious Holidays

In addition to the main Islamic holidays (p648), Iran observes the following, which change with the lunar calendar (check out http://www.payvand.com/calendar/, which can convert Persian dates, which are different to other lunar calendar dates, to Gregorian calendar dates).

NO RUZ – THE PEAK SEASON

No Ruz, the Iranian New Year, has been celebrated by Persians, Kurds and others for thousands of years. Today, it's the main annual holiday in Iran and a huge family celebration. Starting on the spring equinox (around 21 March), Iranians traditionally return to their home villages and towns to celebrate with friends and relatives.

For the traveller, visiting Iran during No Ruz has good and bad points. It is more sociable than other times, but also requires more forward planning. Accommodation and public transport are heavily booked in the week before 21 March and, especially, in the 10 days following No Ruz. Both hotel and transport costs rise by about 30% as a matter of course. You're strongly advised to book your hotel ahead. Most businesses (but not hotels), including many restaurants, close for about five days from 21 March.

No Ruz also marks the beginning of the 'high' season. Hotel rates rise by about 20% and don't fall again until October. In busier places such as the Gulf and Caspian coasts, prices often double.

Ashura (10 Moharram) Anniversary of the martyrdom of Imam Hossein at Karbala; celebrated with religious dramas and sombre, chain-flailing street parades. Intense.

Arba'een (20 Safar) The 40th day after Ashura

Death of Imam Reza (30 Safar)

Birthday of Imam Mahdi (15 Shaban)

Death of Imam Ali (21 Ramazan)

Death of Imam Jafar Sadegh (25 Shawwal)

Qadir-e Khom (18 Zu-l-Hejjeh) The day Prophet Mohammed appointed Imam Ali as his successor

National Holidays

These holidays follow the Persian calendar, meaning their Western calendar dates are usually the same each year.

Magnificent Victory of the Islamic Revolution of Iran (11 February; 22 Bahman) Anniversary of Khomeini's coming to power in 1979

Oil Nationalisation Day (20 March; 29 Esfand) Commemorates the 1951 nationalisation of the Anglo-Iranian Oil Company

Eid-e No Ruz (21 to 24 March; 1-4 Farvardin) Iranian New Year

Islamic Republic Day (1 April; 12 Farvardin) Anniversary of the establishment of the Islamic Republic of Iran in 1979

Sizdah Bedar (2 April; 13 Farvardin) The 13th day of the Iranian New Year; Iranians traditionally leave their houses for the day

Heart-Rending Departure of the Great Leader of the Islamic Republic of Iran (4 June; 14 Khordad) Anniversary of the death of Ayatollah Khomeini in 1989

Anniversary of the Arrest of Ayatollah Khomeini (5 June; 15 Khordad)

Anniversary of the Death of Dr Seyed Beheshti (28 June; 7 Tir)

Day of the Martyrs of the Revolution (8 September; 17 Shahrivar)

INTERNET ACCESS

Many young Iranians are addicted to Internet messaging and you can get online in all Iranian cities and big towns, and quite a few smaller centres. Internet cafés are known as 'coffeenets', though getting a coffee is about as likely as getting a stiff whisky. Costs range from about IR5000 to IR15,000 an hour. Note that Yahoo! Messenger is much more common than MSN Messenger.

INTERNET RESOURCES

Some Iran-specific websites:

Cultural Heritage Organisation (www.chn.ir/english /index.asp) News on Iranian cultural activities, archaeological finds and great links.

Iran Chamber Society (www.iranchamber.com) Historical, cultural and background information galore.

Iran Mania (www.iranmania.com) Links to just about everything about Iran.

Iran Touring & Tourism Organisation (www.itto .org) Useful summary of facts and figures about Iran and its various regions.

Iran Traveling Center (www.irantravelingcenter.com) For travellers.

Net Iran (www.netiran.com) News, facts and figures, covering politics, law and government structure.

LANGUAGE

The vast majority of Iranians speak the national language, Farsi (Persian), but it's the mother tongue of only about 60% of the population. The most important minority languages are Turkish/Azerbaijani, Kurdish, Arabic, Baluchi and Lori.

English is understood by many of the educated middle-class, university students, most employees of midrange and top-end hotels and restaurants, and most staff in travel agencies and tourist offices.

The Language chapter (p679) lists some important Farsi words and phrases, and Lonely Planet's *Farsi Phrasebook* can get you through most difficulties.

LEGAL MATTERS

Iran's legal system is based on Islamic principles. For most minor crimes, including having sex with an Iranian woman or, if you're a woman, deliberate refusal to comply with the hejab (the Islamic dress code for women), foreigners will probably get deported, though more serious punishments are possible. The penalties for drug use and smuggling are extremely harsh. See p243 for advice on dealing with bogus police.

MAPS

Maps are hard to find outside Tehran, so visit the **Gita Shenasi office** (Map pp190-1; ☎ 021-670 9335; www.gitashenasi.com) in Tehran. Gita Shenasi's *Iran 2004* (1:2,250,000) is the best country map.

MONEY

The official unit of currency is the rial (IR), but in conversation Iranians almost always refer to the *toman*, a unit of 10 rials. It is essential when asking the price of anything to think in *tomans* – that way you won't find yourself in a situation where the vendor is demanding 10 times more than you thought you had agreed on. Often the unit of currency is omitted when discussing prices, so be aware and don't assume you are deliberately being ripped off. There are coins for 500, 250, 100 and 50 rials, and notes for 50,000, 20,000, 10,000, 5000, 1000, 500 and 200 rials.

Iran is a cash economy. No credit cards. No travellers cheques. Just cold, hard cash, preferably in US dollars or euros. You can change cash in some bank branches but it's easier and rates are the same in moneychanging shops, jewellers, carpet shops or on the street. There is no currency black market.

ATMs & Credit Cards

While there are ATMs in Iran, they are of no use to travellers because none are linked to international banking networks. Credit cards are similarly useless; you can't use them to pay for a hotels, plane tickets, anything. You cannot draw cash on your credit card. There is constant talk that Iran will be linked into the international credit card and ATM networks, but don't bank on it happening before you get there.

Cash

Bring as much cash in US dollars or euros as you are likely to need. You can change these two almost everywhere, though the greenback is still the most widely accepted, especially in remote areas. British pounds can be changed in some places, but it can be a hassle. US notes should be undamaged and should have been printed since 1996.

'Official' Interbank rates are artificially low, so don't believe the rates you see on Oanda or other currency converters. The www.iranmania.com/dcfaultenglish.asp page has up-to-date conversions.

Country	Unit	Iranian rial (IR)
Australia	A$1	6890
Canada	C$1	7270
euro zone	€1	10,980
Japan	¥100	8280
UK	UK£1	16,420
USA	US$1	8970

International Transfers

If you've been robbed, lost your wallet or maybe bought one too many carpets and are out of cash, it is possible to have money transferred from overseas to a bank or an individual's account in Iran.

The easiest way to do this is go to the nearest Bank Melli (BMI) central branch, preferably in Tehran where Mr Abdollahi at counter 14 speaks English. Get the Swift code for this particular BMI branch (eg Tehran central branch is MELIIR THA060); and ask whether there is a BMI branch in your home country (these are listed at www.bmi.ir), or which bank in your country is affiliated with BMI (eg in Australia, it's Westpac bank). Get someone at home to go to a branch of the nominated bank (eg Westpac) with your full name, passport number and the Swift code, and deposit the money. A few days later, the cash should arrive.

Tipping

Tipping is not expected in Iran, but it's usual to round up a bill or add 10% at good restaurants. You'll also be expected to offer a small tip to anyone who guides you or opens a door that is usually closed, but Iran doesn't have the baksheesh mentality of much of the Arab world.

DUAL PRICING

The officially sanctioned practice of charging foreigners more than Iranians for the same service is annoying. All but the cheapest hotels charge foreigners about 30 to 50% more than Iranian guests, though this is sometimes negotiable. The good news, however, is that where you used to pay 10 times as much to enter tourist sights, most now have the same low prices for everyone.

Travellers Cheques

American Express. Leave home without them! Like credit cards, travellers cheques are useless in Iran. No matter what currency or who issues them, Iranian banks will not change travellers cheques.

POST

Postage is cheap. The cost of sending a postcard to Europe, North America and Australasia is IR1000. The cost for a normal-sized letter by airmail to anywhere outside Iran should be IR4000. The service is reliable and reasonably swift. Postcards usually reach Europe in four or five days. Rates for parcels tend to vary, but a 5kg parcel to anywhere by surface mail should cost less than US$20. Carpets cannot be posted but kilims (flat, woven mats) can.

Poste restante is little used and, according to readers, quite unreliable. You're far more likely to receive your goods if you get them posted to a particular hotel or home.

TELEPHONE

Making telephone calls within Iran and internationally is both cheap and easy. For domestic calls, modern cardphones and older coin phones (which are only good for local calls) can be found in most cities, often outside post offices. Phone cards (carte telefon) are available from newsstands and telephone offices in denominations of IR5000, IR10,000 and IR20,000, and can be used to make local or long-distance calls in Iran, but not international calls.

Local calls are almost free in Iran so your hotel should let you make them for nothing.

International calls can be made at private telephone offices. International calls are dirt cheap at IR1700 per minute to anywhere;

there's a minimum charge of three minutes. International calling cards are also available from newsstands, though telephone offices usually work out cheaper. Some coffeenets offer international calls through the Internet for about IR1000 a minute to Europe, Australasia and North America.

You can't make reverse-charge calls to or from Iran.

Mobile Phones

Mobile phone use is booming in Iran, but while SIM cards from about 30 foreign countries are supposed to work in Iran, they often don't. Things are changing fast and the network is due to be upgraded, so check with your phone company to see if there is a reciprocal agreement.

Getting hooked up to the domestic network short-term is an expensive hassle. SIM cards cost about US$500 from the government, or double that on the black market. You can resell your SIM once you've finished with it, but it hardly seems worthwhile. There was talk of cheaper SIM cards becoming available – ask around in the major cities.

TOILETS

Iranian toilets are often the squat kind; even if you pay a royal US$50 for a hotel room, it might not be fitted with a throne. Mosques, petrol stations, bus and train stations and airport terminals always have toilets, and they're usually survivable. Toilet paper is only reliably provided in top-end hotels, but is available in most grocery shops in major cities.

VISAS

It's definitely worth it, but getting an Iranian visa is inevitably a hassle. Turkish passport-holders can get a three-month tourist visa on arrival. Everyone else will need to apply well ahead of departure; to be safe that means months in the US and at least five weeks in most other countries. Americans and Brits will need to jump

---

STAMPED OUT

Israeli passport holders and anyone with evidence of a visit to Israel in their passport will not be able to get a visa to enter Iran. For more on Israeli stamps, see p353.

---

through a frustrating set of hoops. US citizens are welcome, but unless you have an Iranian sponsor or are prepared to badger the Iranian interests section in Washington, you'll probably only get a visa if you join an organised tour or arrange a private guide.

Regulations seem to change all the time. They also vary from one Iranian embassy to another so check Lonely Planet's **Thorn Tree bulletin board** (thorntree.lonelyplanet.com) to learn which consuls are hot, and which not. The best issue 30- or 45-day tourist visas virtually on the spot (if you've got the right passport). The worst demand you have local contacts, then leave you waiting for weeks or months – don't be afraid to call them, but be nice. Some will only issue transit visas.

It's best to apply for a tourist visa in your home country. It's possible, but harder, to get tourist visas while you're on the road. These days transit visas have become a last resort.

Many Iranian embassies have their own websites so you can often download the appropriate forms and check prices and other requirements. In most cases you must complete two or three application forms (in English); provide up to four passport-sized photos – women should check if they need to have their hair covered in the photo – and pay a fee, often by money order, which varies according to nationality but is rarely less than the equivalent of US$50.

In mid-2005 Iran announced it would issue seven-day tourist visas to people flying into the airports in Tehran, Shiraz, Mashhad, Tabriz and Esfahan. They cost US$50 and are available to citizens from 68 countries – but not Americans or British. Whether or not these can be extended was not explained.

Increasing numbers of travellers are biting the bullet and using agencies to arrange their visas. Agents can usually get you a visa even if you've already been rejected. They apply on your behalf and send you an approval number, which you then take to the Iranian mission in a city you have previously nominated. For example, you can apply in Europe then travel overland and pick up your visa in İstanbul without needing to wait weeks for it. The agency fee is separate from the normal fee you pay at the embassy.

THE BIG COVER UP – DRESSING FOR SUCCESS IN IRAN

From the moment you enter Iran, you are legally obliged to observe its rigid dress code. So what exactly does this mean? The letter of the Islamic law says all females aged nine or older must wear hejab (modest dress) in the actual or potential sight of any man who isn't a close relative. All parts of the body except hands, feet and the face above the neckline and below the hairline should be covered, and the shape of the body must be disguised.

In practice, as a foreigner you'll be cut quite a lot of slack on your interpretation of the hejab. In most situations a perfectly acceptable outfit would include a scarf (as colourful as you like); a loose-fitting, long-sleeved shirt that covers your bottom; jeans or pants; and shoes – sandals in summer. Some women choose to buy a manteau (or *roupush*), an overcoat of varying lengths, and wear that over everything. In summer, a lightweight manteau makes sense because if you bring safety pins to close the gaps, you can get away with wearing it with nothing but a bra beneath on your top half. Carry a blouse with you in case you're invited into someone's home – Iranian women often lose their scarves and overcoats once indoors, but sitting around in a bra would probably be pushing the limits a bit too far.

Many Iranian women still wear the chador, a tent-like cloak (normally black), draped loosely over the head, legs and arms. For foreigners it's not necessary – nor advisable – to wear one unless you need to, such as entering a particularly holy site. And forget about dowdy long skirts – the vast majority of Iranian women wear pants.

Iranian women have pushed the hejab to its very limit in recent years. In Tehran, in particular, capri pants, inches of make-up and vast tracts of coiffured hair are not uncommon. But, all this could change with hardliners again controlling both the Majlis (parliament) and presidency.

To avoid offending anyone, just keep your eyes open and watch what the women around you are wearing and doing. If your clothing is offensive, you'll soon enough be told – usually by an older woman. Unless you go out of your way to make a statement, that will be as bad as it gets.

It's easier for men. Pants must be long, but short-sleeve shirts are usually OK unless you're visiting a particularly holy place. During Ramazan, it's recommended that you wear long sleeves.

Iran Traveling Center (www.irantravelingcenter.com) US$70 charge. Good feedback from users.

Iranianvisa.com (www.iranianvisa.com) Charges €30 to arrange a visa number through a simple website.

Pars Tour & Travel (www.key2persia.com) Charges US$30 but will often drop this if you use its efficient Shiraz-based agency once you arrive.

A final option is to enter through the 'back door' – Kish Island. You can fly from Dubai to Kish without a visa, get stamped in for a stay of 14 days on the island, then head to the **Ministry of Foreign Affairs office** (☎ 0764-442 0734; Ferdous Villas, Complex 2, Ferdosi St, Kish Island), which can issue 30-day tourist visas to most foreign nationals within two working days. From here, the mainland is a short boat or plane ride away.

Tourist Visas

Clearly, a tourist visa is the best option. Like transit visas, you must enter Iran within three months of the issuing date. If you're arranging your tourist visa through a rela-tive, visa agency, travel agency or other contact in Iran, they will need your full personal and passport details and a brief itinerary. A week or so later your sponsor will send you an authorisation number from the Ministry of Foreign Affairs in Tehran, which you then take, with your cash, to collect your visa from the relevant embassy.

Double-entry tourist visas are available from some embassies – a good excuse is that you want to visit the mosques of Herat, in Afghanistan, then return to Iran.

Transit Visas

Unfortunately, new Iranian policy says transit visas cannot be extended. However, it is sometimes possible to extend your five-, seven- or 10-day transit visa – try Bushehr and Shiraz. In theory, transit visas should be issued within a few days, but it often takes two or three weeks and you might still need a (sometimes expensive) letter of recommendation from your embassy if you apply from outside your home country.

Visa Extensions

The secret to extending your visa simply is to plan your itinerary so you're in Esfahan, Shiraz or Tabriz just before your first visa expires. The locations of visa offices are provided in the relevant sections. You usually cannot extend more than three days before your existing visa expires, and your new visa begins from the date it's issued, not the date your old visa expires. If you're in the cities mentioned, you can expect to get one 30-day extension within a few hours. In theory you can extend to a total stay of three months, though the second extension is usually shorter.

To get an extension arrive early (most offices close at 1pm), then obtain and fill out the visa extension form. In most cities you'll then be directed to a branch of Bank Melli where you pay IR100,000 and receive a receipt. Take this back to the visa office, pay a further IR2500 for paperwork, provide one or two photocopies of your passport and original Iranian visa, and two passport-sized photos (women might need be wearing hejab in the pictures). In Tabriz, Esfahan and Shiraz the extension is issued on the spot; in other places it can take up to two days.

Yazd, Kerman, Zahedan, Bushehr and Rasht are second-string cities for extensions, but avoid Mashhad, Bandar Abbas and especially Tehran, which can be a nightmare.

WOMEN TRAVELLERS

Despite having the hassle of wearing a scarf every time you step outside – see p249 – most women find the sexual harassment and constant come-ons common in other Middle Eastern countries are largely absent in Iran.

By comparison, women enjoy considerably more independence in Iran than elsewhere in the Middle East. One welcome consequence of this is that female visitors will find it quite easy to meet and chat with Iranian women, particularly in large cities such as Esfahan, Shiraz and Tehran where educational standards are higher.

Unwanted attention does occur, though, especially in remote or untouristed areas, and some women will feel more comfortable travelling with a male companion or in a group.

TRANSPORT IN IRAN

GETTING THERE & AWAY

Entering Iran

For anyone with an Israeli stamp in their passport, there won't be any entering Iran. For everyone else, assuming you've managed to somehow get a visa, you shouldn't have any problems (see also Customs, p243). Just remember not to lose that little yellow customs form they give you – you'll need it when you leave.

Air

Iran's main international airport is in the western suburbs of Tehran, though by the time you read this more flights might be using the new Imam Khomeini International Airport, about 35km south of the city. Shiraz, Esfahan, Tabriz, Mashhad, Bandar Abbas, Bushehr and even Zahedan also see infrequent international services, usually from elsewhere in the Middle East.

The national carrier is **Iran Air** (www.iranair .com), with smaller Iranian airlines including **Iran Aseman** (www.iaa.ir) and **Mahan Air** (www .mahanairlines.com) also offering a handful of international flights. Iran Air has a vast network of direct flights between Tehran and Europe, Asia, the Middle East and Central Asia. On Iranian airlines female passengers must wear hejab and no alcohol is served.

European airlines including **Air France** (www.airfrance.com), **British Airways** (www.britishair ways.com), **KLM** (www.klm.com) and **Lufthansa** (www .lufthansa.com) fly into Tehran, while Middle Eastern airlines including **Gulf Air** (www.gulf air.com), **Emirates** (www.emirates.com) and **Kuwait Airways** (www.kuwait-airways.com) service the Gulf and further.

Land

Iran is bordered by seven countries, but most overland travellers enter or exit via Turkey or Pakistan. For details of travel between Iran and Afghanistan, Armenia, Azerbaijan, Pakistan and Turkmenistan, see p660. The Iraqi frontier was closed at the time of writing.

TURKEY

Road

There are two border crossings. The easiest and most popular is at Bazargan/Gürbulak (open 24 hours, see p199), reached via Tabriz. Most long-distance buses between Tehran and İstanbul use this route, but it is far quicker to catch a bus, minibus or savari to either border, cross independently and then catch onward transport, rather than wait hours for the rest of the bus to clear customs and immigration.

Further south, a useful alternative for travellers heading to or from Orumiyeh is Sero (Iran)–Esendere (Turkey; open 8am till 10.30pm Iran time; see p200). There are buses most days from Orumiyeh to İstanbul via Van.

Train
International trains run from Tehran to İstanbul and Damascus. The *Trans-Asia Express* to İstanbul (IR499,500, about 66 hours) via Ankara departs on Thursday evenings. The Damascus (IR722,250, about 65 hours) train leaves on Monday evenings. Both trains have deluxe four-bed couchettes. Check www.rajatrains.com for up-to-date timetables.

Sea
Ferries sail across the Gulf from Bushehr, Bandar Abbas and Bandar Lengeh to Kuwait, Qatar and the UAE. The ferries are operated by the **Valfajre-8 Shipping Company** (www.vesc.net) and schedules are published on its website. See p663 for details.

GETTING AROUND
Air
Iran's once ludicrously cheap domestic airfares are no more, but they're still very reasonable. Fares are set by the government, so are the same irrespective of the airline. It's worth booking ahead a couple of days as flights are often full. Around No Ruz, a couple of weeks is wiser.

Iran Air offers a free domestic flight to passengers who fly into Iran with the airline. Otherwise, buying inside Iran is often cheaper.

AIRLINES IN IRAN
The main domestic airline, Iran Air, has regular services to just about anywhere you want to go. The airline is reliable, safe and efficient. Ask for a pocket-sized timetable from any Iran Air office. Other smaller airlines, such as **Iran Aseman** (www.iaa.com),

Mahan Air (www.mahanairlines.com) and **Kish Airlines** (www.kishairline.com), have more erratic schedules but are useful for specific destinations. Fares for domestic flights are the same whether booked at a travel agency or directly at the airline office.

Bus
Like Turkey, Iran is extremely well covered by bus and minibus services. Fares are dirt cheap, services are frequent and most buses are comfortable – standing is not normally allowed.

The best companies, with the most extensive networks, are Iran Peyma (Taavoni No 1), Hamsafar and Seiro Safar, which has the most modern fleet (mostly air-con Volvos).

You rarely need to book ahead – just ask around at the bus company offices in the terminal and get on the next bus going your way. From one major city to another, say Shiraz to Esfahan, buses from one company or another leave at least every hour. But departures are much less frequent in more remote places and between smaller towns.

What you pay depends on the type of bus you take. Prices tend to vary from one

---

KNOW YOUR IRANIAN BUSES

There are three main species of bus in Iran, all of which are reasonably comfortable and very cheap. Confusingly, their names differ from region to region.

Mercedes (Aliases: normal, super, old and, in western Iran, RD. Cost: about half a Volvo) These ancient but funky-looking Mercedes buses are dirt cheap and often have more legroom than their newer cousins, but the air-con won't work and they're slower. Prices in this chapter are for Mercedes buses unless stated.

Super-luxe (Aliases: lux, super-lux, several others. Cost: about 30% to 45% more than Mercedes) This class doesn't always exist and standards are variable, to put it mildly. Buses look more modern but are usually 10-20 years old and, despite the 'Arctic Winter' sign on the roof, the air-con never works.

Volvo (Aliases: deluxe, super-deluxe, air-con. Cost: about twice a Mercedes) We call these Volvo because that is usually what they are; new coaches similar to those in Europe. The air-con should work and you'll get a snack and a sweet drink.

Taavoni to another, but the amounts are so small it's barely worth shopping around.

While roads are generally good you'll be lucky to average more than about 65km/h on most routes because all buses are speed-limited and must make regular stops at police checkpoints to show their trip log.

Cramped minibuses are often used for travel over shorter distances and between less-populated places.

Car & Motorcycle

A good number of travellers drive the overland route between Turkey and Pakistan. The flexibility is unbeatable and, with petrol virtually free, it's pretty cheap. However, the distances are great, the countryside is often boring and the traffic is truly horrendous.

If you're bringing in a vehicle you'll need a *carnet de passage* (see p662) and an international driving licence. In Iran, the main automobile organisation is the **Touring & Automobile Club of the Islamic Republic of Iran** (☎ 021-874 0411; 12 Shahid Arabali, Khorramshahr Ave, Tehran).

Leaded petrol (called *benzin*) costs IR800 per litre and diesel is a ridiculous IR150 a litre. The quality, however, is often poor. Some travellers have reported being charged a hefty 'fuel tax' at the border. In 2005 there was talk this would be formalised, making it much more costly than it is now. Petrol stations are found on the outskirts of cities and towns, though diesel can be hard to find.

In theory, you're supposed to drive on the right in Iran. Road surfaces are generally good, but the roads are poor or unpaved in remote desert and mountainous regions. Never drive off the main road near the Pakistani, Iraqi or Afghani borders.

Although it is possible to hire your own car in Tehran (check the *Tehran Times*), there's really no point. It's much easier to hire a taxi with a driver for about IR200,000 to IR300,000 per day, and let the driver deal with the traffic, the parking and the navigation.

Local Transport

Almost any car in Iran is potentially a taxi. In towns, shared taxis are used for short trips, constantly plying set routes between designated points (usually major squares) for between IR500 and IR4000 a trip. The taxis are usually white or orange Paykans and will cram in five passengers – two in the front and three in the back. Prices are fixed in shared taxis.

There are no meters and if you hire a taxi privately you'll need to negotiate the fare before you get in. In this chapter a private taxi is referred to as a taxi *dah baste*, which literally means 'closed door'. If you stop an empty taxi but want to hire it on a share basis, tell the driver *nah dah baste* (no closed door).

Savari

Savaris are shared taxis that run between major towns less than four hours away by car. This form of transport is more useful for the short hops in western Iran and the Caspian provinces, rather than the sparsely populated central desert areas.

Savaris cost about three times more than buses, but are still cheap at about IR10,000 to IR15,000 per hour. They are less comfortable than buses so speed is their main advantage.

If you wish to speed up a departure, or crave a little extra comfort, pay for an empty seat or simply charter the vehicle (about four times the single fare). Savaris normally leave from inside, or just outside, the relevant bus terminal, or from a designated point (usually a roundabout) on the outskirts of town.

Tours

Iranian agencies operate group tours for foreigners and also offer more flexible private tours. These can usually be arranged online, and services range from booking hotels to fully organised and catered tours; expect to pay about US$130 per person per day for the latter. Many travellers, particularly from the USA and UK, use Iran-based agencies at least as a starting point to facilitate or speed up the visa process (see p248). If you book a tour the agency will generally organise your visa as part of the cost of a tour.

The following are reputable, Iran-based operators.

Arg-e-Jadid Travel (in Tehran ☎ 021-8881 1072; www.atc.ir)

Azadi International Tourism Organisation (AITO; in Tehran ☎ 021-8873 2191; www.aitotours.com)

Caravan Sahra (in Tehran ☎ 021-8884 8672; www.caravansahra.com)

Pars Tourist Agency (in Shiraz ☎ 071-222 3163;
www.key2persia.com) Welcomes groups of any size on
any budget.
Persepolis Tour & Travel Agency (in Tehran ☎ 021-
8880 5266; www.persepolistour.com)
Poonel Tour & Travel (in Tehran ☎ 021-8876 8563;
www.poonel.com)

Train

Tehran is the hub of Iran's growing network of trains and almost all services begin
or end there. Trains from Tehran head to
Tabriz, Ahvaz, Esfahan, Bandar Abbas,
Bam and Mashhad, stopping at points in

between. Although trains don't run everywhere, they are efficient, reasonably fast,
much more comfortable than buses and ridiculously cheap. Taking a 1st-class sleeper
overnight to Mashhad, for example, makes
a lot of sense and it's a great way to meet
Iranians.

It's always worth paying a little more
for 1st-class compartments. If you buy a
ticket from any town along a route (ie not
at the starting point), you may only be able
to get a 2nd-class ticket. Overnight trains
usually have comfortable four- or six-bed
couchettes, with bedding provided.

IRAN

Iraq

Long ago in the fertile valleys between the Tigris and Euphrates Rivers, the great civilisations of the age were born. Modern Iraq was ancient Mesopotamia, from the Greek meaning 'between two rivers', and it was here that human beings first began to cultivate their land, where writing was invented and where the Assyrians, Sumerians and Babylonians all made Iraq the centre of the ancient world.

With the arrival of Islam, Iraq again took centre stage. Islam's most enduring schism – between Sunnis and Shiites – was first played out on Iraqi soil. Baghdad also became one of Islam's greatest capitals, home to the Abbasid caliphs whose reign has become a byword for Islam's golden age of learning and sophistication.

The country remains rich with the resonance of a glorious history, but recent history has dealt less kindly with Iraq. Under Saddam Hussein, widespread political repression and conflicts with Iran, Kuwait and the West earned Iraq international infamy and also drew the attention of international human-rights organisations and Western armies in equal measure. Indeed in recent years, few countries have experienced such external interference as Iraq has, culminating in the 2003 American-led invasion of the country.

Iraq has now dominated international news headlines for more than a decade for all the wrong reasons, just as Vietnam did three decades before it. The country's future is uncertain, with Iraqis struggling to eke out an existence and build the institutions of a democratic Iraq against the backdrop of political and religious tension, and amid the numbing constancy of terrorist attacks.

Iraq is now one of the most dangerous countries on earth, but few countries can boast such a rich history. When the country gets back on its feet, it will be one of the great travel destinations of the Middle East.

FAST FACTS

- **Area** 434,924 sq km
- **Capital** Baghdad
- **Country code** ☎ 964
- **Languages** Arabic, Kurdish (Kurmanji and Sorani)
- **Money** Iraqi dinar (ID); US$1 = ID1469.20; €1 = ID1734.83
- **Official name** Republic of Iraq
- **Population** 26.07 million

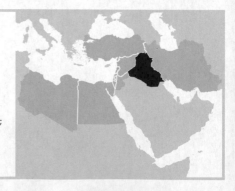

WARNING

At the time of writing, Iraq was one of the most dangerous places on earth, with Westerners the targets for kidnapping and suicide attacks and at risk from the generalised violence sweeping the country. Until the situation stabilises, Iraq must be considered off-limits to tourists. For this reason, we did not visit the country for the purposes of updating this chapter.

CLIMATE

Iraq is fiercely hot in summer (May to September); the average summer temperature in Baghdad is 34°C and in Basra 37°C, but daytime temperatures can soar well above that. The north is slightly cooler, while in the south there's debilitatingly high humidity. Winter can be cold and the mountains can become covered with snow. The average winter temperature in Baghdad is 11°C and in Basra 14°C.

HISTORY
Ancient Mesopotamia

Iraq's story begins with the Sumerians who flourished in the rich agricultural lands surrounding the Tigris and Euphrates Rivers from around 4000 BC. In 1750 BC Hammurabi seized power and went on to dominate the annals of the Babylonian empire. Despite constant attacks from the Hittites and other neighbouring powers, Babylon would dominate the region until the 12th century BC, after which it went into a slow decline. It survived in a much reduced state, and Babylon remained an important cultural centre, but it was not until 626 BC that the New Babylonian Empire regained the extent of power that the Babylonians had enjoyed under Hammurabi.

By the 7th century BC, Assyrian civilisation had reached its high point under Ashurbanipal, whose capital at Nineveh was one of the great capitals of the world with cuneiform libraries, luxurious royal courts and magnificent bas-reliefs that survive to this day. And yet, it was the extravagance of Ashurbanipal's court and the debilitating military expenditure needed to keep his disparate empire together that sowed the seeds of Assyrian decline. Nineveh fell to the Medes in 612 BC. In 539 BC Babylon finally fell to

the Persian Empire of Cyrus the Great into whose empire Nineveh was also absorbed.

For the next 1200 years, Mesopotamia would be ruled by a string of empires, among them the Achaemenid, Seleucid, Parthian and Sassanid.

For more information on Iraq's early history, see p37.

Islamic Iraq

In AD 637 the Arab armies of Islam swept north from the Arabian Peninsula and occupied Iraq. Their most important centres became Al-Kufa, Baghdad and Mosul.

In 749 the first Abbasid caliph was proclaimed at Al-Kufa and the Abbasids would go on to make Iraq their own. The founding of Baghdad by Al-Mansur saw the city become, by some accounts, the greatest city in the world (see p41). In 1258 Hulagu – a grandson of the feared Mongol ruler Genghis Khan – laid waste to Baghdad, and killed the last Abbasid caliph. Political power in the Muslim world shifted elsewhere.

By 1638 Iraq had come under Ottoman rule. After a period of relative autonomy, the Ottomans centralised their rule in the 19th century, whereafter Iraqi resentment against foreign occupation crystallised even as the Ottomans undertook a massive programme of modernisation. The Ottomans held on until 1920, when the arrival of the British saw Iraq come under the power of yet another occupying force, which was at first welcomed then resented by Iraqis.

Independent Iraq

Iraq became independent in 1932 and the period that followed was distinguished by a succession of coups, counter-coups and by the discovery of massive reserves of oil. On 14 July 1958 the monarchy was overthrown in a military coup and Iraq became a republic.

The 1967 Arab-Israeli War caused Iraq to turn to the Soviet Union for support, accusing the USA and UK of supporting Israel. On 17 July 1968 a bloodless coup by the Ba'ath Party put General Ahmad Hassan al-Bakr in power.

In 1979 Saddam Hussein replaced Al-Bakr as president, the revolution in Iran took place and relations between the two countries sank to an all-time low. Saddam, increasingly concerned about the threat of a Shiite revolution in his own country, declared

IRAQ

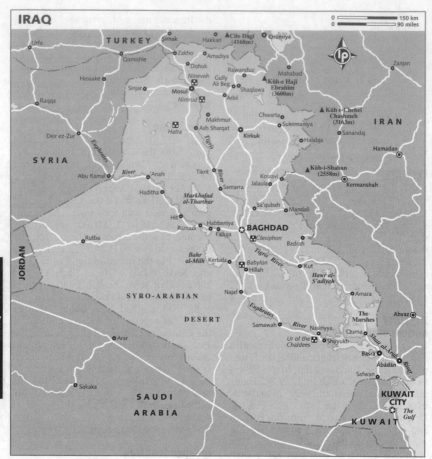

IRAQ

that Iraq wanted a return to exclusive control over the Shatt al-Arab River. Full-scale war broke out on 22 September 1980, with Iraqi forces entering Iran along a 500km front. The eight years of war that followed were characterised by human-wave infantry advances and the deliberate targeting of urban residential areas by enemy artillery, all for little territorial gain. A million lives were lost and the economic cost to Iraq alone is estimated at more than US$100 billion.

In March 1988, just prior to the war's end, the Iraqi government responded to the occupation of northern Iraq by Kurdish guerrillas by killing thousands of civilians, most infamously in Halabja where chemical weapons were used to devastating effect.

Confrontation with the West

Saddam Hussein soon turned his attention to Kuwait. In July 1990 Saddam accused the Kuwaitis (with some justification) of waging 'economic warfare' against Iraq by attempting to artificially hold down the price of oil, and of stealing oil from the Iraqi portion of an oilfield straddling the border. On 2 August 1990 Iraq sent its troops and tanks into Kuwait and six days later annexed Kuwait as Iraq's 19th province. It was a costly miscalculation.

An international coalition – including a number of Arab states – gathered on Iraq's borders before launching a five-week bombing campaign followed by a ground offensive that drove Iraqi forces from Kuwait.

PROSPECTS FOR AN IRAQI PHOENIX   Roshan Muhammed Salih

When Iraqis are asked about a possible democratic future they often respond with a sceptical sigh – by and large, their main preoccupations are getting regular electricity and water supplies rather than casting votes.

To ordinary Iraqis the prospect of a peaceful and democratic future remains little more than a pipe dream, the chatter of elites and powerful politicians, the minority who have so far benefited from foreign occupation. The stark reality is that there is a major insurgency in the country that affects the lives of everyone and is hindering the political process.

The failure to incorporate the country's once all-powerful Sunnis into the new Iraq and the occupation itself are fuelling this insurgency. It's reasonable to assume that foreign Islamic fighters, Saddam loyalists and Arab nationalists will always oppose what they consider an occupation. It therefore seems that more bombings and chaos are likely as long as foreign forces remain and the political process is sponsored by outsiders.

Moreover, the fact that the lives of ordinary people have not improved post-invasion means that those who were willing to give the political process a chance are increasingly losing patience with the situation.

Yet in the face of all the death and destruction most Iraqis remain optimistic and show a resilience that is nothing short of heroic.

Foreigners are always surprised to observe how calm Iraqis appear in the face of constant danger, and how they can laugh at their harrowing plight. When a bomb rips through a Baghdad night, residents hardly bother to rouse themselves from their slumber any more. The next morning, they laugh and joke with foreign journalists who were paralysed with fright.

The country's cafés are full of storytellers who crack vicious jokes about the alleged crimes and treacheries of certain religious and ethnic groups, before reminding listeners that 'we must learn to get along, we are all Iraqis'.

Perhaps repression, war and upheaval have become such a way of life that if they didn't laugh they'd be crying. It sometimes seems that a strong sense of religious solidarity and national identity, as well as a good dose of humour, are all that is preventing a full scale civil war from breaking out.

But despite the country's current dire predicament there are some reasons for hope. Notwithstanding all the scepticism about peace and democracy, there is no doubt that Iraqis would like more of a say in the running of their country, and many see the current political process as the only way of achieving that – a fact evidenced by the 58% turnout in national elections in January 2005.

And the new Iraq is not without its winners. The Shiite leadership has astutely manoeuvred itself into political pole position and the Kurds are consolidating their gains. If US plans come to fruition the future Iraq will probably be run by people who represent the majority of the population.

In addition, and contrary to many Iraqis' expectations, the US has not bailed out after achieving its short-term goals and continues to pump in large amounts of money for the country's reconstruction.

The success of the new Iraq is central to the stability of the whole region.

Turkey is rather wary of the ambitions of the Iraqi Kurds. They fear that if the Iraqi Kurds achieve independence, this result will embolden restive elements within Turkey's own Kurdish population.

Iran, meanwhile, is keen that a Shiite-led government, with whom it may wield political clout, and by whom it would not be threatened, should control Iraq.

Nevertheless, the Iraqi conundrum remains stark: if US-led forces stay for the long term the country is doomed to a prolonged guerrilla war that will derail the political process and destroy any hope of a peaceful and democratic future for Iraq; and if the US-led forces leave there is a real prospect of civil war that could split the nation into three and draw Iraq's neighbours into a regional conflict.

IRAQ

Controversy has persisted over the number of civilian and military deaths in Iraq and Kuwait: estimates range from 10,000 to more than 100,000.

As part of the ceasefire signed on 28 February 1991, Iraq agreed to comply fully with all UN Security Council resolutions, including full disclosure, inspection and destruction of the country's biological, chemical, ballistic and nuclear weapons stockpiles and development programmes.

Kuwait was free but the moral support offered by US president George Bush in calling on the Iraqi people to rise up was not backed by Allied military support and rebellions in the Shiite south and Kurdish north were brutally put down.

UN sanctions caused widespread malnutrition and medical care became inadequate throughout Iraq. Despite the much-abused UN oil-for-food programme, according to the World Health Organization (WHO) over half a million children died as a direct result of sanctions that did little – if anything – to undermine Saddam and his regime.

In early August 1998, weapons inspectors were denied access to a number of sites and the Iraqi government announced the suspension of all cooperation until the sanctions were removed. The USA, with British backing, responded with four days of air strikes in December.

On 20 March 2003, despite a lack of UN authority, the US launched missile attacks on Iraqi targets, followed soon after by a ground offensive that would sweep American forces into Baghdad, Saddam Hussein from power and most members of his regime into hiding. Tikrit, Saddam's home town, was one of the last cities to fall.

In July 2003 Saddam's feared sons, Uday and Qusay, were killed in a shoot-out with US troops. In December of the same year, a bedraggled Saddam Hussein was found cowering in a hole in Tikrit. Few Iraqis mourned his or his family's demise.

OCCUPIED OR LIBERATED? IRAQ POST-SADDAM   Roshan Muhammed Salih

Iraq is not a place for the faint-hearted. For foreigners danger and risk are constant companions and for Iraqis hardship has become second nature.

I first travelled to the country in March 2004 to report on the anniversary of the US-led invasion. When I arrived in my Baghdad hotel there was debris everywhere – the result of a massive explosion the previous night that killed 49 people nearby. This remains the reality of occupied Baghdad and the area that surrounds it, often referred to as the Sunni Triangle.

Iraq's capital has become a living hell for its residents – the worst place in the world to live, according to a 2005 survey by Mercer Human Resource Consulting. It is a place where a journey of around a kilometre can take over an hour because of traffic jams caused by heavily fortified US bases and countless checkpoints.

More seriously, Baghdad has become a breeding ground for criminals, gun-runners and drug addicts – anything from an AK-47 to hard drugs is available in broad daylight for knockdown prices. Gangs terrorise the city's residents in a spree of robberies, and newspapers are full of stories about children being abducted at gunpoint outside schools.

Most people in central and southern Iraq are very critical of the US-led foreign presence. This criticism ranges from outright hostility and demands for immediate withdrawal to complaints about how they have handled the post-Saddam era. Irregular water and electricity supplies are major sore points.

Tempers seem to particularly fray during the stiflingly hot summers, when a lack of essentials can be deadly. Despite the national obsession with politics, it is the difficulties of everyday life that have turned many Iraqis against foreign occupation.

As a result of the continuing insurgency, occupier and occupied have little normal interaction. American soldiers barricade themselves behind the high walls and barbed wire of their bases. They are mostly young, have little understanding of Muslim and Arab culture, and can't understand why they are getting shot at all the time.

On the other hand, many Iraqis seem to acknowledge that foreign forces must stay until the appalling security situation is under control. Most people also seem grateful that Saddam Hussein was toppled and that they now have the right to express themselves relatively freely.

Iraq Today

Euphoria on the streets of Iraq over Saddam's demise quickly turned to anger at the inept early days of the US administration. riceless antiquities were looted, the Iraqi army was disbanded leaving massive bands of armed and suddenly unemployed men on the streets, and the process of de-Ba'athification stripped the country of many capable administrators who had joined the Ba'ath Party only under threat of death. Up to 100,000 Iraqi civilians (and more than 1500 US troops) are believed to have died as a direct result of the invasion and its aftermath.

Iraq descended into chaos, the country transformed from one of the most repressive states in the world to its most dangerous, as insurgents – primarily Iraqi Sunnis and foreign fighters – sustained a campaign of suicide bombings, high-profile kidnappings and executions of hostages, and missile attacks on US and civilian targets. The US failure to find the alleged stockpiles of weapons

of mass destruction led many to question the real motives behind the US invasion. When photographic evidence that US soldiers abused and tortured Iraqi prisoners in Baghdad's Abu Ghraib prison emerged in May 2004, it was eerily reminiscent of the Saddam era and much of the remnant support for the US occupation evaporated.

For all the devastation, there are small signs of hope. On 30 January 2005 eight million Iraqis cast their vote in elections for a Transitional National Assembly. The government that finally emerged from the elections after months of negotiations granted the most powerful position of prime minister to the Shiites and the post of president to the Kurds. Although the position of speaker of the parliament went to the Sunnis, the majority of Iraq's Sunnis continue to believe that they have been sidelined in the new Iraq. This was particularly apparent in August 2005 when the Shiites and Kurds decided to press ahead with a draft Iraqi constitution

A plethora of newspapers, and TV and radio stations have appeared since the fall of Saddam, expressing every opinion in the political spectrum – perhaps the freest media in the Middle East. This would have been simply unthinkable under Saddam when owning a satellite dish was a criminal offence.

Most of the new media are low quality and a mouthpiece for interest groups, and some have been controversially shut down by the Americans. But in general Iraqis seem to be revelling in their newly discovered ability to talk freely without the risk of being imprisoned, tortured or worse.

Although Iraq's unstable centre grabs most of the headlines, the situation in the country as a whole is far from black and white.

The Shiite-dominated south has been relatively stable since the US-led invasion. Heavily influenced by the clergy, most people have not fought occupation because Shia leaders have bargained that tacit cooperation with foreign forces is their best means of attaining political power after decades of repression under Saddam.

This is probably the reason why British forces stationed in the south have suffered relatively few casualties, and have established a working relationship with local leaders. Ordinary people, however, remain deeply resentful of and humiliated by foreign occupation. This has occasionally spilled over into outright hostility and confrontation, such as during the bloody battle of Najaf in August 2004 when hundreds were killed and injured.

The Kurdish north of the country, meanwhile, seems like a different world entirely, a haven of relative stability and prosperity where many openly laud American forces as 'liberators'. When I visited the Kurdish town of Arbil in April 2004, my Arab companions said they felt like foreigners in their own country.

Unlike other parts of Iraq, the Kurdish north does not feel the strains of occupation and has not been as affected by insurgent activity. It has effectively enjoyed de facto autonomy under UN protection since 1991 and is set to cement that status in the new Iraq. This attitude and success, however, causes deep resentment in many Iraqis, who accuse the Kurds of collaboration.

Nevertheless, for the moment Kurdistan remains the only undoubted success story the US can boast of. But repeating the formula in the rest of Iraq will be a lot tougher.

despite widespread dissatisfaction and even outright rejection among Sunnis.

Although violence continues to be reported across the country, the guerrilla warfare of the insurgency remains largely restricted to the so-called Sunni Triangle centred around Fallujah, Tikrit and Mosul, and Baghdad where the Iraqi government and the greatest concentration of Coalition troops are based.

THE CULTURE
Population
Iraq's population is one of the most multicultural in the Middle East. Around 75% of the population is Arab, 15% is Kurdish, while there are smaller communities of Persians (3%), Turkomans (2%), Yezidis, Assyrians, Chaldeans and the Jezira Bedouin who live in the highlands of the north. Iraq is also a predominantly urban society with 74% living in urban centres. Population density is 54.9 persons per square kilometre.

RELIGION
The official religion in Iraq is Islam: Muslims make up 97% of the population. Shiites account for more than 60% of the population and Sunnis around 35%. There are also small but historically significant communities of Christians who belong to various sects, including Chaldeans, Assyrians, Syrian and Roman Catholics, Orthodox Armenians and Jacobites. Other religious minorities are the Yezidis, often erroneously called devil worshippers, and the Sabaeans (Mandeans), who are followers of John the Baptist.

ARTS
Iraqi cinema – largely a wasteland under Saddam – made a spectacular debut at the 2005 Cannes Film Festival with Hiner Saleem presenting his critically acclaimed *Kilometre Zero*. Set in Iraq's Kurdish north during Iraq's war with Iran, the film follows the journey of a Kurd and an Arab returning the body of a dead soldier to his family.

Iraqi musicians have been much more prolific. Kazem al-Sahir, the current biggest-selling singer in the Arab world, capped a remarkable career by winning the 2004 BBC World Music Award for best Middle Eastern and North African artist for his song 'Hal Endak Shak' from the album *Bare Footed*. He has been fêted across the region since 1996 when he began his collaborations with the

Syrian poet Nizar Qabbani, who once wrote songs for Egyptian diva Umm Kolthum. Other well-known Iraqi musicians include Ilham al-Madfai (renowned for giving traditional Iraqi folk music a contemporary twist) and Nasseer Shamma whose *Le Luth de Baghdad* (released by Institute du Monde Arabe) is sublime.

ENVIRONMENT
The Land
Iraq's upper plain stretches northwest from Hit and Samarra to the Turkish border between the Euphrates and Tigris Rivers and is the most fertile region, although high soil salinity reduces the cultivable potential to 12% of arable land. The lower plain stretches from Hit and Samarra southeast to the Gulf and contains the marshes, an area of swamps, lakes and narrow waterways, flanked by high reeds. Iraq's northeast is different again, with towering mountains, while Iraq's deserts lie to the west of the Euphrates, stretching to the borders of Syria, Jordan and Saudi Arabia. The Tigris and Euphrates converge near Baghdad, then diverge again, before meeting at Qurna to form the wide Shatt al-Arab River, flowing through Basra into the Gulf.

Environmental Issues
Iraq faces a looming catastrophe in water supplies, primarily because of pollution of its rivers. The draining of the marshes (p263) by Saddam Hussein precipitated the decline of numerous species – particularly wetland bird species – and the indigenous culture of the Marsh Arabs. Turkish dams on the Euphrates River have also threatened Iraq's precarious water supplies. Pollution from oil wells, the ongoing threats to public health from uranium-enriched weapons used by all sides during Iraq's various wars, soil salinity, erosion and the encroaching trend towards desertification are other problems in urgent need of attention.

BAGHDAD
بغداد

pop 5.672 million
Baghdad, the one-time city of caliphs, pleasure gardens and vast libraries of scholarship, has fallen on hard times, the repository of a nation's anger against yet another occupation by a foreign power. The old

Baghdad, the very name of which conjures up vivid images of golden domes and shafts of sunlight filtering through exotic bazaars, has all but disappeared and the Iran-Iraq and Gulf Wars have destroyed much of the modern city. But since the 13th century, Baghdad has been as much an idea as a place bearing any correspondence to its glorious past and the one thing its resilient inhabitants cling to amid the uncertain daily realities of modern Iraq is the hope that the Baghdad of legend will once again rise from the ashes.

HISTORY

Baghdad was founded in AD 762 by Al-Mansur, the second caliph of the Abbasid dynasty, on the western bank of the Tigris River and enclosed within a circular wall. Known as the Round City or Medinat as-Salaam (City of Peace), the Baghdad of the caliphs was home to their palace and the main mosque at its centre, and was surrounded by forbidding walls entered by four gates. In AD 800 Baghdad had a population of 500,000.

From the mid-9th century onwards, the Abbasid caliphate became weakened by internal conflict, and civil war between Haroun ar-Rashid's two sons resulted in the partial destruction of the Round City. Total destruction came about in 1258 when the Mongols sacked Baghdad, killed the caliph and up to 800,000 Baghdad residents, and destroyed the irrigation system. In 1534 it became part of the Ottoman Empire and centuries of neglect followed.

Although attempts were made to improve the city in the early years of the 20th century, Baghdad's greatest modern developments occurred when large oil revenues began to flow in after 1973.

ORIENTATION

Baghdad extends along both sides of the Tigris River. The eastern side is known as Rusafah and the western as Karkh. The core of the city is a 3.5km by 2km area in Rusafah, extending from Midan Muadham in the north to Midan Tahrir in the south. Sharia Rashid is the main street of this area and contains the city's financial district, and the copper, textile and gold bazaars.

The controversial and fortress-like Green Zone lies on the west bank of the Tigris,

south of Sharia Port Said. The road from here to the airport has the unenviable distinction of being one of the most dangerous stretches of tarmac in the world.

From the 1950s the city expanded enormously, and planned, middle-class neighbourhoods grew between the city centre and the Army Canal. On the western bank are a number of residential areas, including the relatively affluent Mansour district. The grim Shiite suburbs of Sadr City trail away to the south of Greater Baghdad.

SIGHTS
Museums

One the many tragedies to beset Iraq in the aftermath of the 2003 war was the looting and subsequent disappearance of countless priceless archaeological treasures and manuscripts. Worst hit was the **Iraqi Museum** (Sharia Damascus); remember that as impressive as the collection still is, it's a fraction of what was there before. Exhibits included Sumerian, Babylonian and Assyrian artefacts and pieces from the Abbasid period.

Other worthwhile museums that may or may not still be open include: the **Baghdad Museum** (Sharia Mamoun) with life-sized models depicting traditional Baghdadi life; the **Museum of Pioneer Arts** (Sharia Rashid) with pre-1950s works by Iraqi artists and housed in a wonderful old Baghdadi house; the **Museum of Popular Heritage** (Sharia Haifa), another fine traditional home; and the **Museum of Modern Art** (Midan Nafura).

Mosques

The **Kadhimain Mosque** is the most important in Iraq after those at Kerbala and Najaf. Inside are the shrines of the two imams (religious teachers) Musa al-Kadhim and Mohammed al-Jawad. The very large and elaborate mosque has gold-coated domes and minarets and was built in 1515. Built 40 years ago, the **14th Ramadan Mosque** (Midan Fardous, Sharia Sadoun) has lovely arabesques and glazed wall tiles. Another attractive mosque is the **Ibn Bunnieh Mosque**, in front of Alawi al-Hilla bus station.

The **Marjan Mosque** (Sharia Rashid), on the eastern side of the street, was built in 1357, and in its early days served as the Murjaniyya School. In the early 20th century, most of it was pulled down and rebuilt as a mosque.

Mustansiriyya School

Not far northwest of the Baghdad Museum, Mustansiriyya School was built in the reign of the 36th Abbasid caliph, Mustansir Billah, and was the most highly esteemed university of that time. It was completed in 1232 and in its heyday it was renowned for its extensive library and for its enlightened approach of teaching all four schools of Islamic law, rather than one, which had hitherto been the case. It was one of the few structures to survive the Mongol invasion of 1258 relatively intact and, as such, stands as a landmark example of Abbasid architecture.

Abbasid Palace

Another fine remnant of the city's Abbasid architectural glories, the 13th-century Abbasid Palace stands about 750m northeast of the Baghdad Museum. Overlooking the Tigris, it has a fine arch and its resemblance in style and structure to the Mustansiriyya School has led some scholars to believe that it is the Sharabiyya School mentioned by old Arab historians.

AROUND BAGHDAD

THE ARCH OF CTESIPHON   سلمان بك

Little is left of the ancient city of Ctesiphon, 30km southeast of Baghdad and east of the Tigris, but its 3rd-century-BC arch is a remarkable feat of engineering for its time. Constructed by the Parthian Persians, the arch was part of a great banqueting hall and is the largest single-span brick arch in the world. It survived the disastrous flooding of the Tigris in 1887, which destroyed much of the rest of the building, although a fine relief façade stands alongside.

SOUTHERN IRAQ

Southern Iraq is the spiritual homeland of the Shiites and the cities of Najaf and Kerbala are like all sacred cities the world over – clamorous, devout and brought alive by pilgrims from across the world. The region is also awash with the legends of the past, from the intriguing southern city of Basra – from where Sinbad the Sailor set out on his epic journeys – to the ancient sites of Baby-

lon and Ur of the Chaldees, which are rich with Biblical and Quranic resonance.

BABYLON   بابل

Perhaps the most famous of Iraq's archaeological sites, Babylon, 90km south of Baghdad and 10km north of Hillah, has at once become a byword for the sophistication of ancient Mesopotamia and a symbol of modern Iraq's difficulties. Although a small settlement was first built on the site in 2350 BC, its days of pre-eminence did not begin until the 18th century BC when Hammurabi made it the capital of Babylonia. After centuries of decline, the city's golden age occurred during the reign of Nebuchadnezzar II (605–563 BC). With its high walls and magnificent palaces and temples, it was regarded as one of the most beautiful cities in the world. Visiting today, there's little to suggest such an extravagant past to anyone except expert archaeologists, although the trace outlines of Nebuchadnezzar's Summer Palace (sections of which are believed to be all that remain of the Hanging Gardens, one of the Seven Wonders of the Ancient World) have been reconstructed. The replica Ishtar gate, temples and amphitheatre give an idea of the city's outline, although the modern brickwork used to reconstruct the structures leaves little sense of the city's antiquity. For those seeking a small reminder of ancient Babylon, the huge and magnificent lion, eroded by time and the weather, offers an enticing glimpse.

KERBALA   كربلا
pop 434,457

Kerbala, 108km southwest of Baghdad, is one of Shiite Islam's holiest sites and of great religious significance to all Muslims because of the Battle of Kerbala that took place in AD 680 (p53), whereafter Islam would forever be divided between the Sunni and Shiite sects. Hussein ibn Ali, who has become revered as leader of the Shiites, and his brother Abbas, grandsons of the Prophet Mohammed, were killed in the battle, and their shrines are contained in the two mosques here, thereby making Kerbala one of the greatest pilgrimage centres in the Islamic world. In the centre of town, the mosques have stunning domes of gold, exquisitely tiled archways and a buzzing atmosphere that spreads into the surrounding streets – testament to the fact that Shiite Muslims (including from Iran) are once again permitted to make the pilgrimage unlike during the rule of Saddam Hussein. Non-Muslims are not allowed to enter the shrines but, with the permission of an attendant, may be able to walk around the surrounding courtyards.

NAJAF   النجف
pop 482,583

Najaf, 160km south of Baghdad, is another sacred city for Shiites and was once the centre of Shiite scholarship, home to philosophers, powerful ayatollahs, Quranic schools and extraordinary libraries. It also has the distinction of being founded by Haroun ar-Rashid in AD 791. In the city centre the mosque containing the tomb of the revered Ali ibn Abi Talib (600–61), cousin and son-in-law of Mohammed and founder of the Shiites, is today the reason why Najaf possesses such a powerful hold over Shiites across the world. Its desecration by Saddam's troops during the 1991 uprising further cemented Najaf as a centre of Shiite opposition to the Saddam regime. There is no higher honour for Shiite Muslims than to be buried in graveyards in either Kerbala or Najaf. The latter especially seems to have graveyards all over the place and it's fascinating, if a little macabre, to wander around them. Many of the graves are small shrines.

NASIRIYYA   النصرية
pop 400,254

Nasiriyya, 375km southeast of Baghdad on the northern bank of the Euphrates, is an attractive if unexciting riverside town, which once served as a base for travellers wanting to visit Ur of the Chaldees. In its prewar days, it had a good museum with an accessible collection from Sumerian, Assyrian, Babylonian and Abbasid times.

AROUND NASIRIYYA
Ur of the Chaldees   أور الكادانية

The ancient Sumerian city of Ur is one of the most impressive archaeological sites in Iraq. Mentioned in the Bible as being the birthplace of Abraham, its earliest buildings date from 4000 BC, although the earliest settlements here may predate that by 2000 years. For three successive dynasties it was

the capital of Sumeria, although it reached its height during the third and last dynasty (2113–2095 BC).

The city's showpiece is its remarkably well preserved ziggurat, one of the finest still standing anywhere in the world and whose current form owes much to Nebuchadnezzar II who made Babylon such a great city. Also impressive are the expansive royal tombs and Sumerian temples.

The Marshes   الأهوار

The marshes originally covered an area of approximately 10,000 sq km between the Tigris and Euphrates Rivers, stretching from Basra in the south, Nasiriyya in the west and Kut in the north. Some parts were permanent, and others were temporary marshland, changing with the seasons. The marshes were a world of vast expanses of water and shallow lagoons. Here it is sometimes possible to see sarifas (Marsh Arab dwellings) with their ornate latticework entrances. The people row mashufs (long, slender canoes) through the high reeds. There is archaeological evidence that life has continued here, almost unchanged, for 6000 years and the marshes are also home to many species of water birds.

Sadly, much of the marshes were drained in the late 1980s after Saddam Hussein claimed that Iranian soldiers were using the marshes as a cover for attacks on Iraqi forces. Most Marsh Arabs, who were immortalised in Wilfred Thesiger's The Marsh Arabs (p268), had no option but to flee to refugee camps, mainly in Iran, thereby spelling an end to one of Iraq's most enduring and fascinating cultures. In the post-Saddam era, there are plans to re-establish the marshes, although it's unlikely they will ever revert to their former state.

BASRA   البصرة
pop 2.016 million

Iraq's second-largest city, 550km southeast of Baghdad and 130km from the Gulf, once went by the romantic epithet of the 'Venice of the East', famed for its canals and strategic location at the headwaters of the Shatt al-Arab River. The modern reality is somewhat less inspiring, as the city bears many scars of war and its once-bustling port (Iraq's most important) has yet to fully revive after the long years of sanctions and war. There are extensive palm groves on the outskirts of the city and most of Iraq's dates are grown in and around Basra. Although the city remains on edge, its occupation by predominantly British troops has yet to attract the violence experienced in Baghdad or elsewhere.

History
Basra was founded by the caliph Omar in AD 637 as a military base but the city rapidly grew into a major Islamic city. It became the focal point of Arab sea trade during the 16th century, when ships left its port for distant lands in the East. Its strategic position has made it the scene of many battles, sometimes between the Marsh Arabs and the Turks and sometimes between invading Persians and Turks. In 1624 Ali Pasha repulsed a Persian attack and, in the period of peace that followed, Basra became a mecca for poets, scientists and artists. The peace was short-lived; Ali Pasha's son imposed a buffalo tax upon the Marsh Arabs and the fighting and instability resumed.

Orientation & Information
The city comprises three main areas – Ashar, Margil and Basra proper. Ashar is the old commercial area and includes the Corniche, which runs alongside the Shatt al-Arab River, Sharia al-Kuwait, and Sharia ath-Thawra, where banks and the old Iraqi Airways office are found. Basra's bazaars are also here. Margil includes the port and a modern residential area to the northwest of Ashar. Basra proper is the old residential area to the west of Ashar.

Sights
In the Basra proper area you'll find the lovely **19th-century houses** called *shenashils* by the canal that flows into the Shatt al-Arab River. For most visitors, these houses with their high, pointed windows and ornate, wooden overhanging balconies are the highlights of a visit to Basra and a reminder that Basra's past was far more elegant than its present. In one of the few old houses to have been restored, **Basra Museum** contains a few objects from the Sumerian, Babylonian, and Islamic eras. Not far from the museum is the derelict **St Thomas Chaldean Church**.

The **Floating Navy Museum**, in Ashar at the northern corner of the Corniche, exhibits military hardware from both sides in the Iran-Iraq War, while the **Museum for the Martyrs of the Persian Aggression** (Sharia Istiklal) contains heart-rending displays of the sufferings of the ordinary local people of Basra during the war with Iran.

Basra's **bazaar** in Ashar is one of the most atmospheric in Iraq, a treasure-trove of gold, jewellery and palm products made by the Marsh Arabs. It's a shadow of its former self, but it's propelled by Basra's ever-optimistic merchants and you'll find it's hard not to get caught up in the energy. In parts of the bazaar you'll see old houses with wooden façades and balconies tilting at such precarious angles that it's amazing they manage to stand at all.

Sinbad Island was the home port for the sailor of legend and it was from here that Sinbad is supposed to have begun his voyages. The island used to be attractive, with outdoor restaurants and gardens, but it suffered extensive bombing and now is a little dreary, although like most things in Iraq, there are plans to rebuild.

NORTHERN IRAQ

Northern Iraq is considered by some to be the Switzerland of the Middle East with towering mountain ranges and abundant greenery. It's a stunning area and home to Iraq's most complicated ethnic mix – the northeast is the Iraqi homeland of the Kurds who are in the majority, but the region is also home to communities of Turkomans, Yezidis and Assyrian and Chaldean Christians, not to mention a large proportion of Arabs. Although part of Iraq, its people and its scenery have many connections to neighbouring Turkey and Iran. The north also boasts some of Iraq's most significant archaeological sights, among them Nimrud, Hatra and the legendary Nineveh, while Mosul is a charming city. All in all, it's probably Iraq's most fascinating corner.

ZAKHO   زاخو
pop 95,336

Zakho, near the Turkish border, is Iraq's most northerly town and is famous for its evocative **stone bridge**, which is well pre-

THE KURDS

Iraq is home to over four million Kurds, who are the descendants of the Medes and have inhabited northern Iraq since Parthian times (247 BC to AD 224). The overwhelming majority of Kurds are Sunni Muslim and live in the northern provinces of the country. These provinces form part of the ancient Kurdish homeland of Kurdistan, which extends across the modern-day territories of Iraq, Iran, Turkey and Syria.

The 1961 Kurdish campaign to secure independence from Iraq laid the foundations for an uneasy relationship between the Kurds and the Iraqi state. Cycles of conflict and détente have consistently characterised the relationship ever since, as greater official recognition and freedom have alternately been offered and denied, culminating frequently in brutal repression.

This sad process was tragically reenacted after the 1991 Gulf War when more than two million Kurds were forced to flee across the mountains from Iraq to the relative safety of Turkey and Iran, countries with their own restive Kurdish populations. Under UN protection, the Kurdish Autonomous Region was set up in northern Iraq. Although ongoing Iraqi incursions and the bitter rivalry between the region's two main parties – the Patriotic Union of Kurdistan (PUK) and the Kurdistan Democratic Party (KDP) – frequently threatened the north, Kurdish Iraq became a model for a future federal Iraqi system, characterised as it was by good governance and relative peace.

After the fall of Saddam, there were fears that the Kurds would take the opportunity and go their own way. However, after the Kurds won 17% of the vote in the 2005 elections, Kurdish leaders restated their commitment to a federal but unified Iraq and have, along with Shiite leaders, been at the forefront of moves to build a democratic and plural Iraq.

served and still in constant use. Its age is unknown but it's reputed to have been built by a local Abbasid ruler and is at the far side of town. There's also a stone **castle** with a fine tower. Like any border town worth its salt, Zakho lives and breathes cross-border trade, and the busyness of its markets – Zakho has thrived since the 1990s when Iraq's Kurdish north enjoyed a large measure of autonomy and the town suffered little damage during Iraq's wars – stands in stark contrast to many Iraqi cities further south. The approaches to Zakho are spectacular, crossing many high mountain ridges.

AMADIYA   العمادية

Like Zakho, Amadiya stands amid some awe-inspiring landscapes and the village itself is breathtakingly picturesque, located high on a plateau 1985m above sea level and surrounded by magnificent mountains and endless green valleys. Coming from Dohuk, 90km away to the southwest, the road passes through scenery that, as the road unfolds, becomes more and more spectacular. It winds through several villages – firstly Zawila, then Suara Tuga, which has a wonderful view of the plain of Sarsang, then through Anshki to Sulaf,

a village with waterfalls and plenty of cafés where it was possible to sit and enjoy the magnificent views.

DOHUK   دهوك
pop 129,127

Dohuk is a small Kurdish town, 73km north of Mosul. It's a pleasant place, with an interesting market and some extant remnants of a castle wall, but otherwise it serves mainly as a base from which to explore the surrounding mountains.

MOSUL   الموصل
pop 2.066 million

When peace returns to Iraq, Mosul, 396km north of Baghdad and Iraq's third-largest city, will be a magnet for travellers. It's Iraq's most ethnically mixed city, with Arabs, Kurds, Assyrians and Turkomans. It's a fascinating town, a meeting place of the peoples of the region, with a polyglot history to match, all of which is reflected in the city's myriad sites just longing to be explored.

After the fall of Fallujah to American forces in late 2004, the centre of the insurgency shifted to Mosul, which is where Kurdish-controlled areas meet the Sunni Triangle.

History

There has been a settlement here since Assyrian times. By the time the Abbasids were in town, Mosul achieved commercial importance because of its position on the caravan route from India and Persia to the Mediterranean. Its most important export was cotton. The word 'muslin' is derived from Mosul, and cotton is still produced here today. Mosul was devastated by the Mongols in the 13th century but began to revive under the Ottomans.

Orientation

Mosul's main street and commercial area is Sharia Nineveh. The city centre is Midan Babatub, a huge open area with a fountain in the middle. The bazaar is between here and Sharia Nineveh. Sharia Duwasa runs south from Midan Babatub.

Sights & Activities

Along Sharia Nineveh in the town centre you'll find some delightful old houses that represent fine examples of 19th-century Mosul architecture. The exceptional **Mosul House**, built around a central courtyard, has a façade of Mosul marble and hosts life-sized models depicting traditional Mosul life. It has a large wooden entrance. The **old city** is a maze of narrow streets off both sides of Sharia Nineveh, west of the bazaar.

On the western side of the river, **Mosul Museum** once housed a large collection of finds from the successive civilisations of Iraq, from prehistoric to Islamic times, with an emphasis on finds from Nineveh to Nimrud. It's not known how much has survived.

Believed to be the burial place of Jonah, the **Mosque of Nebi Yunus**, on the eastern side of the Tigris, is built on a mound beneath which are buried some ruins of Nineveh, but because of the sanctity of the site, excavation is impossible. A little community of mud-brick houses and narrow, winding streets has grown up around the mosque.

The **Great Nur ad-Din Mosque** was built in 1172 by Nur ad-Din Zanqi and is famed for its remarkably bent minaret, which stands 52m high and has elaborate brickwork.

An essential part of Mosul's multicultural mix is the fact that the city has a higher proportion of Christians than any other Iraqi city. The **Clock & Latin Church** (Sharia Nineveh) is a good place to start as its interior is awash with blue Mosul marble, lovely brickwork in blue, brown and cream, and stained-glass windows of abstract patterns. Many of the churches are near this one, but hidden away in the labyrinth of old Mosul's fascinating backstreets.

The imposing ruins of **Bash Tapia Castle**, rising high above the Tigris on its western bank, are now the only part of Mosul's city wall still in existence. Just a few minutes away, a little further south on the river bank, are the remnants of the 13th-century palace of the sultan Badr ad-Din called the **Qara Saray** (Black Palace).

Between the two ruins is the **Chaldean Catholic Church of At-Tahira** (Church of the Upper Monastery). The oldest part was built in AD 300 as a monastery, and in 1600 was added to and became a church. In the street running parallel to this is the Syrian Orthodox **Al-Tahira Church** (1210).

AROUND MOSUL

Nineveh   نينوى

The ancient city of Nineveh, on the eastern bank of the Tigris and on the outskirts of modern Mosul, was the third capital of Assyria and one of Assyria's greatest cities – many of the Assyrian bas reliefs and other artefacts in museums around the world (eg the British Museum and the Louvre) came from here.

Up until King Hammurabi's death it was a province of Babylonia, but after this time it developed as an independent kingdom. By 1400 BC it had become one of the most powerful city states in the Middle East, but by 500 BC it had been destroyed by the Medes of northern Persia. For 200 years prior to this, however, Nineveh was the centre of the civilised world and Ashurbanipal's 25,000-text cuneiform library was sited here.

There are a few reliefs left *in situ* but Nineveh's charm lies in its historical significance rather than the state of its monuments – few ancient cities in the world have been as extensively looted as Nineveh. In its heyday, Nineveh's walls measured 12km in circumference and there were 15 gates, each named after an Assyrian god. Several have been reconstructed. The **Shamash gate** is just beyond the Ash-Shamal bus station. The **Nergal gate** is about 2km from the university and it has a small **museum** with some Assyrian reliefs and a model of the city of

Khorsabad, which was the fourth capital of Assyria.

Nimrud   نمرود

Nimrud, the second capital of Assyria, is 37km southeast of Mosul and one of the best preserved of Iraq's ancient sites. The city wall has an 8km circumference containing several buildings, the most impressive being **King Ashurnasirpal II's Palace**. On either side of the entrance are two huge sculptures of human-headed lions with hawk wings. Inside are some beautiful bas-relief slabs. Two 2800-year-old **Assyrian tombs** were discovered shortly before the Gulf War. They included large quantities of gold and jewellery from what archaeologists believe are two 9th- and 8th-century-BC tombs of princesses or consorts – possibly of the court of Ashurnasirpal II. One tomb held three bronze coffins containing the remains of 13 people. In one coffin, a woman in her twenties was buried with a foetus, four children and 449 objects. The **Temple of Nabu**, the God of Writing, is also impressive.

Hatra   حترا

Hatra, located 110km southwest of Mosul, is another impressive site, although it's of much more recent vintage (1st century AD) than Nimrud or Nineveh. In architecture, sculpture, metalwork and military expertise, Parthian Hatra was no less advanced than Rome. The ruins, most notably the preponderance of temples and tombs, contain many fine pieces of sculpture.

Sinjar   سنجار
pop 38,437

Sinjar, 160km west of Mosul on the slopes of the Jebel Sinjar mountain range near the Syrian border, is most renowned as the town of the Yezidis, the so-called devil worshippers who are of Kurdish stock. What they actually believe is that the devil is a fallen angel, bringing evil to the world, and must be appeased so he will once again take up his rightful place among the angels. The Yezidis will never say his name, Shaitan, or any similar-sounding word. Their religion contains elements of nature worship, Islam and Christianity. In October a festival is held at the shrine of Sheikh Adi, the sect's founder. Like the Kurds, the Yezidis are friendly and hospitable.

ARBIL   أربيل
pop 932,854

Arbil (also written Irbil; Kurdish: Hewler), 84km east of Mosul, is one of the oldest continuously inhabited cities in the world, and headquarters of the Kurdish Autonomous Region. Its beginnings are buried in the mists of antiquity, but there is archaeological evidence that Neolithic peoples roamed the area 10,000 years ago.

The modern town, atop a mound formed by successive building over centuries, is dominated by a **fortress**, behind which are three large **19th-century Kurdish houses** that, along with the fortress, have been turned into **museums**. The houses have ceilings decorated with floral patterns and coloured-glass windows. One has a room with an interesting collection of everyday Kurdish objects and handicrafts, another an art gallery showing works by contemporary Iraqi artists. Nearby is a large *hammam* (bathhouse), also part of the house.

Arbil Museum was opened in 1989 and, prior to the 2003 war, housed a comprehensive collection from Sumerian to Abbasid times.

Arbil is also renowned throughout the Middle East for the quality of its carpets and there are few more atmospheric bazaars in the whole region than Arbil's wonderful **covered souq**.

SHAQLAWA & GULLY ALI BEG
شقلاوة & قلي علي بيك

The road from Arbil winds steeply upwards to Salahuddin at 1090m above sea level, and then on to Shaqlawa, 50km northeast from Arbil. This is an idyllic town surrounded by mountains and orchards where pears, apples, grapes, pomegranates, almonds and walnuts grow in abundance. From Shaqlawa the mountain ranges begin to close in and the scenery becomes more rugged and dramatic. Gully Ali Beg, 60km from Shaqlawa, is a narrow 10km-long pass with a lovely 80m-high waterfall tumbling into it.

KIRKUK
pop 601,442

Although Kirkuk traces its origins to Sumerian times and was occupied by the Assyrians, the modern city is dominated by the surrounding oil fields – some of Iraq's most prolific. There's little to see and the city does replicate the 'Wild West' feel of oil towns across the world, but there's a **castle**, some fine **old houses** and a bustling **bazaar**.

IRAQ DIRECTORY

BOOKS

For a comprehensive but highly readable history of Mesopotamia, encompassing the Sumerians, Assyrians and Babylonians among others, *Ancient Iraq*, by Georges Roux, is hard to beat.

Essential reading for anyone hoping to catch a glimpse of the marshes is the excellent *The Marsh Arabs*, written by Wilfred Thesiger who felt a great affinity with the Marsh Arabs and lived with them for five years in the 1950s. Gavin Young also visited the marshes in the 1950s at the instigation of Thesiger. He returned again in the '70s to see how much the Marsh Arabs' lives had changed. *Return to the Marshes* is an account of this visit.

The Longest War, by Dilip Hiro, is a detailed account of the Iran-Iraq War. Hiro offers a similarly dispassionate study of the 1991 Gulf War in *Desert Shield to Desert Storm*.

Yitzhak Nakash's *The Shi'is of Iraq* is the definitive study of Iraq's majority community and essential reading for understanding the sense of historical grievance felt by Iraq's Shiites.

Andrew and Patrick Cockburn's *Saddam Hussein – An American Obsession* is a clearheaded exploration of Saddam's shift from friend of the West to one of its greatest enemies.

To get a sense of how the key players viewed the invasion of Iraq, Bob Woodward's *Plan of Attack* offers unfettered insights into views within the Bush administration, while *Disarming Iraq* by Hans Blix, former UN chief weapons inspector, is similarly enlightening.

The accounts of the 2003 US-led invasion of Iraq and the aftermath are legion, but two of the best are Asne Seierstad's *A Hundred and One Days: a Baghdad Journal*, and *Salam Pax – the Baghdad Blog*, a sobering but often grimly humorous series of reports from arguably Iraq's most famous blogger.

For a journey back to 1960s Baghdad and a window into Iraq's Jewish community, Mona Yahia's fictional work *When the Grey Beetles Took Over Baghdad* is definitely worth tracking down.

A Sky So Close, by the young Iraqi writer Betool Khedairi, is a moving coming-of-age journey through Saddam Hussein's Iraq as penned by one of Iraq's most promising young writers.

EMBASSIES & CONSULATES
Iraqi Embassies & Consulates
Australia (☎ 02-6286 9952; 48 Culgoa Circuit, O'Malley, ACT 2606)
France (☎ 01 45 01 51 00; 53 rue de la Faisanderie, Paris 75016)
UK (☎ 020-7581 2264; 169 Knightsbridge, London SW7 1DW)
USA (☎ 202-483 7500; Iraqi Interests Section, c/o Embassy of Algeria, 1801 Peter St NW, Washington, DC 20036)

Embassies & Consulates in Iraq
Australia (☎ 01-778 2210; austemb.baghdad@dfat .gov.au)
France (☎ 01-719 6061)
Germany (☎ 01-541 3032)
Jordan (☎ 01-542 9065)
Turkey (☎ 01-422 0021)
UK (☎ 01-703 270 0254; www.britishembassy.gov.uk /iraq)
USA (☎ 01-240 553 0584)

INTERNET RESOURCES
Institute for War and Peace Reporting (www.iwpr .net) Independent reporting on the latest Iraqi news by local journalists.
Iraq Net (www.iraq.net) Everything from chat rooms to the latest news.

LANGUAGE
Arabic, the official language, is spoken by 80% of the population. The Kurds speak a language that is widely known as Kurdish, but in reality Kurds speak either of two Indo-European languages – Kurmanji or Sorani. The Turkomans, who live in villages along the Baghdad to Mosul highway, speak a Turkish dialect. Persian is spoken by minorities near the Iranian border, while similar numbers speak Assyrian and Chaldean. English is quite widely spoken in urban centres.

For a list of Arabic words and phrases see p679.

MONEY

A new Iraqi dinar came into circulation in October 2003 although its value continues to fluctuate widely. For the record, the exchange rate at the time of going to print was as set out in the table.

Country	Unit	Iraqi dinar (ID)
Australia	A$1	1077.31
Canada	C$1	1239.46
euro zone	€1	1734.83
Iran	IR100	16.14
Japan	¥100	1254.37
Jordan	JD1	2059.15
Syria	S£1	27.98
Turkey	YTL1	1080.00
UK	UK£1	2563.46
USA	US$1	1469.20

SOLO TRAVELLERS

You'd have to be mad.

VISAS

At the time of writing, Iraqi embassies overseas were extremely reluctant to issue visas to anyone other than journalists, aid workers and others with contracts for the reconstruction of the country.

TRANSPORT IN IRAQ

Iraq has a good network of roads and a rail line connecting Mosul, Baghdad and Basra, but at the time of writing, Iraq was not safe for independent travel or travel by public transport.

GETTING THERE & AWAY

Both Royal Jordanian Airlines and Iraqi Airways have resumed their flights into Baghdad from Amman in Jordan, but the spiralling descent into Baghdad International Airport, necessitated by constant insurgent attacks on aircraft, means that only those who absolutely *must* fly into Baghdad do so.

GETTING AROUND

At the time of writing, shared taxis and a few buses were operating between Baghdad and Damascus (Syria) or Amman (Jordan), while cross-border traffic between Turkey and relatively peaceful northern Iraq was also possible. Iraqi Airways is also planning to operate domestic flights connecting Baghdad to Basra, Suleimaniya and Arbil.

IRAQ

Israel & the Palestinian Territories

Israel, or Palestine depending on your politics, defies the logic that size equals importance. A tiny finger of land hugging the eastern Mediterranean, no bigger than the US state of New Jersey, the biblical lands of Judea and Samaria bear as much significance for the modern world today as they have for the past one or two millennia.

The same land that St John predicted would host Armageddon is today the land frequented by heads of state, each armed with ideas to prevent that event from occurring. It's the land of the Bible and Talmud, still considered by millions as the basis of Western law, ethics and religion. And for many, it's a spiritual centre *par excellence:* the Promised Land of the Jews, the last place touched by Mohammed on his journey to Heaven, and the birthplace of Christ.

Israel and the Palestinian Territories may be renowned for their mystical past, disputed present and uncertain future, but there is more than what meets the international headlines. Fascinating archaeological sites, a wealth of natural beauty spots and a cultural diversity matching anywhere else in the Middle East are enough for a trip in their own right. The modern state of Israel, developed for tourism and equipped with stringent security, makes travel both safe and easy to explore its sites and commune with its people.

Your religious, cultural and political baggage is best left at home – any militant preconceptions picked up during a lifetime of media exposure are bound to leave you off balance. So clear the slate. Then plunge in, stay informed, ask questions and listen to the voices around you. Most surprising are not the opinions you'll be bombarded with, but the effects that this speck of land leaves you with long after you've left.

ISRAEL & THE PALESTINIAN TERRITORIES

FAST FACTS

- **Area** 20,770 sq km; Gaza Strip and the West Bank 6220 sq km
- **Capital** Jerusalem (disputed)
- **Country code** ☎ 972
- **Languages** Hebrew and Arabic
- **Money** new Israeli shekel (NIS); US$1 = 4.68NIS; €1 = 5.52NIS
- **Official name** Medinat Yisra'el (State of Israel)
- **Population** 6.9 million; Gaza Strip and the West Bank 3.8 million.

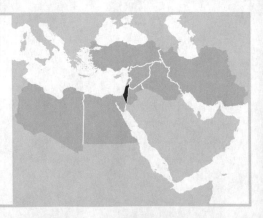

HIGHLIGHTS

- **Jerusalem** (p283) The Holy City, bursting with architectural, historical and spiritual wonders that have been drawing pilgrims for millennia.
- **Tel Aviv** (p297) Jerusalem's antithesis, a modern, European-styled metropolis with a fantastic café culture and the Middle East's best nightlife.
- **The Dead Sea** (p327) At the lowest spot on Earth, the Dead Sea lures with promises of health restoration and a relaxing float on water.
- **The Golan Heights** (p326) An area of spectacular natural beauty, with scope for leisurely hiking, cycling and skiing.
- **Nakhal Gishron** (p336) Off the beaten track to magnificent desert scenery along the Israel National Trail.

HOW MUCH?

- **Newspaper** 8NIS
- **Dorm bed in guesthouse** 25NIS to 50NIS
- **Internet connection per hour** 12NIS
- **City bus ticket** 5.3NIS
- **Museum admission** 25NIS to 40NIS

LONELY PLANET INDEX

- **Litre of petrol** 5.4NIS
- **Litre of bottled water** 6NIS
- **Bottle of Maccabee beer** 18NIS
- **Souvenir T-shirt** 15NIS to 20NIS
- **Shwarma** 15NIS

CLIMATE & WHEN TO GO

Israel and the Palestinian Territories enjoy a warm Mediterranean climate for much of the year, although winter (November to March) sees plenty of rain and cool temperatures in coastal areas and even snow in the highlands, including Jerusalem. Summer (April to October) is hot and dry with the peak months in July and August, when daytime temperatures of 45°C aren't uncommon. In the evenings – especially in the highlands and deserts – temperatures may drop as much as 30°C to 40°C below the daytime highs. See Climate Charts, p643. If possible, avoid visiting Israel during the Jewish religious holidays (see p350 for details) when businesses close, public transport is limited and accommodation prices double or triple.

HISTORY

The first inhabitants of modern Israel, the West Bank and the Gaza Strip were probably the Canaanites, who had migrated to the productive coastal areas from Arabia and Mesopotamia as early as the 20th century BC. (It's believed that these Canaanites were Semitic – that is, descended from Shem, the son of Noah of diluvial fame, but that seriously strains the biblical time line.) Around 2800 BC, Egypt claimed Canaan as part of its empire, and in a period of famine, the Israelites (descendants of Israel, grandson of the patriarch Abraham) migrated to the Nile Valley for work. According to the Book of Genesis, God had promised that there,

Israel would be made a great nation. After a period of prosperity in exile, the pharaoh Ramses forced the 'migrant workers' into servitude. Some time around the 13th century BC, Moses led the descendants of the Israelites for 40 years through the Sinai (as reported by the Book of Exodus) and across the Jordan River back into their Promised Land. At this point, the lands were divided between the 12 tribes of Israel – descendants of the 12 sons of Israel.

Around 1200 BC, the Semitic civilisation known as the Philistines arrived and established a coastal government between present-day Ashdod and Gaza. The Israelites, threatened by the Philistines' political superiority, consolidated their disparate tribes under one king, Saul. Upon Saul's death, some Israelites supported his son Ishbaal as successor, but the tribe of Judah supported King David, who became a local hero when he killed the Philistine Goliath and eventually conquered the city-state of Jerusalem. There, in the 10th century BC, David's son Solomon built the First Temple.

This is at least one version of history. However, the history of the region is just as much a battleground as any present-day West Bank or Gaza refugee camp, and millennia-old events are constantly being requestioned, reinterpreted and fresh claims made. This is a part of the world where archaeology and scholarship have serious political implications.

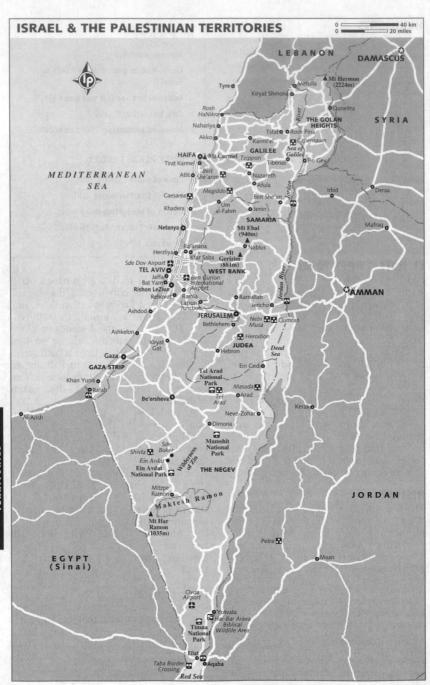

ISRAEL & THE PALESTINIAN TERRITORIES

| 0 | 40 km |
| 0 | 20 miles |

LEBANON

DAMASCUS

Tyre

Metulla

Mt Hermon (2224m)

Kiryat Shmona

Quneitra

Rosh HaNikra

THE GOLAN HEIGHTS

SYRIA

Nahariya

Tsfat

Rosh Pina

Akko

Karmi'el

Capernaum

Sea of Galilee

HAIFA

Mt Carmel

GALILEE

Tzippori

Tiberias

Ein Gev

Tirat Karmel

Beit She'arim

Nazareth

MEDITERRANEAN SEA

Atlit

Afula

Beit She'an

Irbid

Deraa

Caesarea

Megiddo

Khadera

Um al-Fahm

Jenin

Netanya

SAMARIA

Mafraq

Mt Ebal (940m)

Ra'anana

Nablus

Herzliya

Kfar Saba

Mt Gerizim (881m)

Sde Dov Airport

TEL AVIV

WEST BANK

Jaffa

Bat Yam

Ben Gurion International Airport

Rishon LeZion

Rehovot

Ramallah

Jericho

Jordan River

AMMAN

Ramla

Latrun Junction

Ashdod

JERUSALEM

Nebi Musa

Qumran

Bethlehem

Ashkelon

Herodion

Kiryat Gat

JUDEA

Dead Sea

Gaza

Hebron

GAZA STRIP

Ein Gedi

Khan Yunis

Tel Arad National Park

Masada

Rafah

Be'ersheva

Tel Arad

Arad

Al-Arish

Kerak

Neve-Zohar

Dimona

JORDAN

Mamshit National Park

Shivta

Sde Boker

Ein Avdat

Ein Avdat National Park

Wilderness of Zin

THE NEGEV

Mitzpe Ramon

Maktesh Ramon

Mt Har Ramon (1035m)

Petra

EGYPT (Sinai)

Maan

Ovda Airport

Yotvata

Hai-Bar Arava Biblical Wildlife Area

Timna National Park

Eilat

Taba Border Crossing

Aqaba

Red Sea

Few accounts written prior to the Roman era can be considered absolute fact (see p57), and millennia-old events are constantly being reinterpreted to fit current political agendas.

Fast-forward a few thousand years, to the modern Middle Eastern conflict between the Jews (said to be the tribe of Judah and remnants of the scattered Diaspora or 'lost tribes') and the Palestinians (who argue descent from the Philistines). Many Jews claim the right to live in the lands now known as Israel based on a historical lineage stretching back to the kingdoms of Solomon and David and, before that, to the rule of the 12 tribes. Taking this perspective to its extreme, some Israelis claim (based on Old Testament writings) that 'God gave Israel to the Jews', and that the land is theirs by divine right.

The Palestinian claim is based on centuries of occupancy. Whether they are descendants of the Philistines or not, Arabs formed the majority inhabitants of Palestine from soon after the ascendancy of Islam in the 7th century until the 20th century.

For centuries Jews dreamed of returning to their ancestral homeland ('next year in Jerusalem' being a phrase uttered since the fall of the second temple). But the idea was never really stoked into serious action until Austrian journalist Theodore Herzl surmised in his 1896 book Der Judenstaat that the Jews had to establish their own homeland or risk further persecution in Europe. The following year he organised the first International Zionist Congress in Basel, Switzerland, which resolved to 'find a small piece of the Earth's surface' where Jews could establish a homeland. In 1903 London offered Uganda, which the Zionists accepted but then threw out the following year in their ultimate pursuit of a state in Israel.

Waves of Jewish immigrants began making their way to Palestine, which was then a part of the Ottoman Empire. In the wake of WWI, these lands passed into the British sphere of influence (see p43). The increasing numbers of Jews arriving at the ports of Haifa and Jaffa had been causing unrest among the Arabs of Palestine, sparking fighting and rioting, and Britain determined it had to take a stance. In November 1917 the British cabinet announced the Balfour Declaration, which promised a homeland for the Jews in Palestine. However, the controversial document never determined the status or extent of this homeland, and from an Arab perspective it contradicted the McMahon White Paper for Arab Independence, signed two years earlier, which guaranteed an Arab Kingdom to the Sharif of Mecca.

In the 1930s Adolf Hitler rose to power in Germany and set about fulfilling his twofold dream of establishing a Third Reich and exterminating the Jewish race, which he considered the root of the world's problems. By the end of WWII, six million Jews (1.5 million of them children) had been murdered in the death camps of Eastern Europe.

Hundreds of thousands of Holocaust survivors moved to British-controlled Palestine, knowing now more than ever the importance of Herzl's Zionist dream. Palestinian Arabs felt ever more threatened and resented having to bear the brunt of what they saw as a European problem. In February 1947 the British decided to turn the issue over to the UN, which voted to partition the region into Arab and Jewish states, and make Jerusalem an international city. Ironically, it was Hitler's Holocaust that did more to create the hope for a Jewish state than any other factor.

While the Jews accepted the proposal, the Arabs rejected it outright. Britain washed its hands of the whole affair and withdrew from Palestine in 1948; the Jews declared the independent state of Israel, and war broke out. The combined armies of Egypt, Jordan, Iraq and Syria invaded, but backed with arms from Czechoslovakia, the Tsahal (Israeli army) held its ground until a ceasefire was declared.

An armistice of 1949 delimited the Jewish state, leaving the Gaza Strip under Egyptian mandate and the West Bank under Jordanian control. A 'Green Line' determined the border with Jordan largely on the basis of where soldiers dropped their weapons.

Hundreds of thousands of Arabs fled the fighting (their house keys and land deeds would become a symbol for their right of return), and became refugees in Syria, Lebanon, Jordan and Egypt. The Palestinian desire to return would be later echoed with Yasser Arafat's rallying cry: 'Next year in Al-Quds (Jerusalem)!' But Arab governments neither engaged in dialogue with Israel nor would they offer amnesty to the Palestinian refugees, causing an instability that would haunt the Middle East for the next 50 years.

Tensions came to a head again in 1967 with Egypt's blockade of the Strait of Tiran, a move that ended with Israel's pre-emptive strike against Syria, Jordan and Egypt. After six days of fighting, Israel had tripled in size with its occupation of the West Bank, Gaza and the Sinai. However, early defeats in the Yom Kippur War of 1973 left Israel less certain of its defences. Subsequent negotiations resulted in the 1978 Camp David Agreement, which brought peace between Egypt and Israel – for which Egypt was ostracised by the rest of the Arab world.

During the 1970s and '80s, under the spearhead of Yasser Arafat's Palestine Liberation Organisation (PLO), a terrorist campaign brought the Palestinian plight to international attention. Initially, much of the world watched in horror, condemning the Palestinians for their ruthlessness, but in 1987 the intifada (popular uprising) pitted stone-throwing Arab youths against well-equipped Israeli soldiers and the resulting images seen worldwide on TV news did a great deal to resurrect international sympathy for the Palestinians.

The peace talks to follow appeared to offer little fruit until news broke in August 1993 that Israel and the PLO had been holding secret talks for some 18 months in Norway, resulting in mutual recognition. Now, PLO leader Yasser Arafat and the Israeli prime minister Yitzhak Rabin made their (prematurely) Nobel Prize–winning handshake on the White House lawn in Washington, DC. As a result, the Gaza Strip and most of the West Bank were handed over to Palestinian Authority rule (see opposite), with Yasser Arafat ostensibly at the helm.

Despite the Washington show, mutual trust between Rabin and Arafat wasn't exactly solid, and there remained quite a few details to be hashed out, not least of which were the status of Jerusalem and the future of the four million Palestinian refugees spread across the Arab world. Added to that was a fractious relationship with Syria, centred on the disputed Golan Heights, not to mention the continued confrontation with Hezbollah (Party of God) in southern Lebanon.

Any progress forward, such as the Israeli troop withdrawal from most of the West Bank, was set back once again with the assassination of Yitzhak Rabin by a disgruntled Jewish extremist on 4 November 1995.

Rabin's death marked the beginning of several years of stalled negotiations that came to an ultimate collapse when a deal for a two-state solution (known as the Wye II Accord), brokered by Bill Clinton in 2000, was rejected by Arafat despite support by Israel and much of the Arab world. Meanwhile, tit-for-tat violence escalated to a fever pitch in September of that year when Israel's Defence Minister Ariel Sharon paid a controversial visit to the Temple Mount. Within months the fighting grew into a fully fledged intifada, and when Jewish voters got their chance they chose Sharon to lead them through the storm.

While most moderate Israelis and Palestinians continued to support the cause of peace and the creation of a Palestinian state, Sharon and Arafat got down to what they do best. Blows were exchanged in the form of Palestinian suicide attacks and Israel Defence Force (IDF) aggression that ranged from bulldozing Palestinian homes and dragnet arrests to full-scale aerial and ground assaults.

By late 2004 the number of deaths stood at nearly 3500 Palestinians and over 1000 Israelis. The intifada was also taxing national morale as Sharon's hardball tactics were threatening to make Israel a pariah state among European governments. The economy suffered too: Israel's tourist industry collapsed and the Palestinian economy suffered US$14 billion in losses. But the war was to be Arafat's swan song; despite a lifetime of fighting for an independent state, he never realised this achievement, dying of an unknown disease in a Paris hospital on 11 November 2004.

Arafat's passing sparked a mood for change that fell on the shoulders of longtime PLO bureaucrat Mahmoud Abbas (aka Abu Mazen). Three months after Arafat's death, Sharon, known as 'the bulldozer' in reference to his strong-arm tactics in campaigns that stretched back more than 50 years, shook hands with his new Palestinian counterpart at a summit for peace in Sharm el-Sheikh.

Encouraged by the internationally supported 'Road Map for Peace', the Palestinian Authority and Israeli cabinet resumed talks and took several encouraging steps, including the withdrawal of Jewish settlers from Gaza and four West Bank towns in August 2005 and the release of hundreds of Palestinian prisoners from Israeli jails.

YASSER ARAFAT & THE PLO

'Don't forget Palestine' was the simple petition, written in blood, which a young Yasser Arafat handed to Egyptian military leader General Neguib back in 1953. It was an ominous start to a long career that would evolve from student dissident to revolutionary and terrorist and finally, statesman.

The petition, though, had little effect and five years later Arafat and like-minded Palestinian youth decided to go it alone by forming the first Palestinian resistance group – Fatah (meaning 'Conquest'), which later joined with other groups to form the Palestine Liberation Organisation (PLO).

In the mid-1960s, the PLO began a campaign of brash acts of sabotage, murder and hijackings in Israel and the Middle East. But it was not until the killing of 11 Israeli athletes at the 1972 Munich Olympics, and the assassination of US ambassador Cleo Noel a year later, that the world's attention started to focus on the Palestinian cause.

PLO militancy was also a growing threat to Jordan's King Hussein and the resulting confrontation culminated in the 1971 massacre of Palestinian refugees, an incident that became known as 'Black September'. The PLO was forced to seek refuge in Lebanon where it created a mini state within a state. There too the PLO presence proved disastrous for the host country, leading to Israel's 1982 invasion and occupation. On the verge of collapse, Arafat and the PLO decamped to a new base in Tunisia. These setbacks brought about a more conciliatory tone and in 1988 Arafat changed tactics by explicitly recognising Israel and accepting the principle of a two-state solution.

From then on Arafat attempted to play the dual role of statesman in the international spotlight, and resistance leader in front of his people. These two sides often collided, notably at the UN when he had to check his gun at the door before talking peace.

Negotiations paved the way for the PLO leadership to set up shop in the West Bank and Gaza under the auspices of the newly created Palestinian Authority (PA). Here Arafat continued to oscillate between reconciliation and terror – funding suicide bombers while attending peace conferences. By greasing the palms of his allies with the millions of dollars made from a secret business empire (mostly built on the largesse of foreign governments), Arafat stayed in control despite rising competition from the Islamist group Hamas.

In 1992 Arafat secretly married his economics advisor, a Palestinian-Christian named Suha Daoud Tawil. Suha, 30 years younger than Arafat, worked diligently in Gaza to establish an aid organisation, but during the second intifada she retreated to Paris where her shopping sprees took on legendary proportions, thanks to a US$100,000-a-month allowance from the PA.

Arafat's signing of the Oslo peace accords won him a Nobel Peace prize, but he was never able to seal the deal and in the end rejected Clinton's best offer in 2000, a decision that ultimately led to a second intifada.

In their parting exchange following the collapse of the Wye II deal, Arafat called Clinton a 'great man', to which Clinton responded: 'Mr Chairman, I am not a great man. I am a failure, and you have made me one'.

When the second intifada hit its stride, Arafat found himself under siege in his Ramallah compound, a virtual prisoner of Israeli tanks and mortar fire. His 40-year war ended, though not from an assassin's bullet but his own failing health; in November 2004 he slipped into a coma and died in a Paris hospital.

Israel denied Arafat's request to be buried in Jerusalem and, after lying in state in Cairo, he was interred at his Ramallah compound.

No official statement has been made on the cause of Arafat's death, but rumours range from the pedestrian (liver disease or blood disorder) to the more sensational (AIDS or poisoning).

The cause of Arafat's passing is, of course, less of a concern in the eyes of ordinary Palestinians compared to the legacy that he left behind. Despite his years of mismanagement in the Chairman's seat, they'd still rather remember the image of Yasser Arafat – his scraggly beard and trademark keffiyeh – as Palestine's most prolific leader in its longstanding fight for freedom.

Yet the path to peace moves slowly. IDF disengagement has stalled in the West Bank and Israel continues to build its controversial 'Security Fence' (see the boxed text, p340). Sharon has repeatedly called for Abbas to disarm rogue militant groups, but so far the PA has refused to confront Islamic Jihad and Hamas, fearing a civil war.

The stalemate has put off final status talks that would finalise issues like settlements, refugees, water, borders and most importantly, Jerusalem. The wait-and-see period has only caused added strain for ordinary Palestinians and Israelis, as attacks from both sides still occur, despite the 'ceasefire'. The lack of significant progress has soured public opinion of both Abbas and Sharon. The former took a beating in 2005 when Hamas and Islamic Jihad rolled over the leading Fatah party in local elections.

Mainstream Israelis and Palestinians, mainly those living in the bigger cities, are visibly tired of war and the enormous economic and emotional toll it has wrought on them. But with peace still hanging in the balance it may not be up to the mainstream to decide the fate of the conflict. As ever, violence on the part of extremists – Jewish or Arab, even in small numbers – can have a lasting impact on the still fragile peace plan.

THE CULTURE
The National Psyche

As the only Jewish state, Israel and its society are unique in the Middle East – and in the world. However, it's impossible to generalise about characteristics, mainly because Jewish society is so diverse, and ranges from secular (nonreligious) to conservative ultra-Orthodox.

The one thing that binds all Israelis – be they Jerusalem Hasidim, Tel Aviv peaceniks, or new immigrants from Russia, Yemen or Ethiopia – is a tribal sense of community based on their Jewish roots. While Jews may argue fervently about the best diplomatic path to forge for the country, it is their religion, and belief in Zionism, that has united them in the face of danger.

The army, to which most young men and women are drafted at the age of 18, both unifies the nation and gives it a link that connects the first three generations of Israelis. The effects of the holocaust and over 50 years of almost constant military conflict (not to mention centuries of persecution and anti-Semitism) are more difficult to gauge nationally and can really only be broken down to the individual level.

Despite this unique position from which to view the world, Israelis still see them-

---

BIG BIRD, PEACE ENVOY

While Ariel Sharon and Mahmoud Abbas struggle to forge a lasting peace, it may be Big Bird and Snuffleupagus who ultimately resolve the Arab-Israeli conflict. Sesame Street (or Sesame Stories as it's known here, streets not necessarily being the safest of places) is just one of several 're-education' programmes promoting peace among the youngest members of society.

The method for fostering such tolerance is being developed in joint Arab-Jewish schools where the playground serves as a tool for integration and dialogue. On TV, specially designed kids programmes like Sesame Stories, in both Arabic and Hebrew language, focus on ethnic tolerance and unity. In Israel children are also brought together for Arab-Jew dance clubs, theatre groups and sports leagues. In May 2005 football superstar Ronaldo, a special 'peace envoy' to the UN, gave a clinic at an interethnic football league.

Both Arab and Jewish adults have also used the film and media as a path towards peace. The 1982 film *Ghandi* (translated into Arabic) has been shown to Palestinian audiences throughout the West Bank and Gaza, in the hope of showing Palestinians the positive effects of nonviolent resistance. Likewise, themes of tolerance directed at Jewish audiences are played out on the theatrical stages of Tel Aviv and Jerusalem.

Some meet face to face; the Berethian Circle Families builds dialogue among families grieving for relatives killed in IDF attacks and suicide bombings.

For more information, check out www.pinv.org – the website for Palestinians and Israelis for Non-violence. Also see **Givat Haviva** (www.givathaviva.org), another organisation promoting peace and solidarity, or www.handinhand12.org, a website for a joint Arab-Jewish school. Another worthwhile source is the Museum on the Seam (p291).

selves as being essentially European. They are global travellers, leaders in the high-tech world, proficient in the English language, and connected closely to the United States through family ties. Ties to Europe are clear in the cultural sense – Israel, for example, participates in the Eurovision song contest and the Euroleague basketball championships.

Palestinians have a national psyche that's all their own. While Islam plays a major role in their worldview, the struggle for independence has made politics of equal importance. This is no more noticeable than on Israel's Independence Day, known in the Palestinian Territories as *Al-Naqba*, the Great Catastrophe. A day for celebration in Israel, this is a day of mourning for Palestinians.

For Palestinians or Israelis, it is above all the Holy Land itself that creates a psychological bridge across cultures and religions. 'It (the conflict) is in God's hands' is a phrase often uttered by the religious right, a fatalistic approach for both Muslims and Jews which shows that no matter how far the conflict is stretched, acceptance of their future together is undeniable.

Daily Life

Although most of Israel was founded on the principles of socialism and the shared community life on the kibbutz, many contemporary Israelis have converted to a two-cars-in-the-garage, white-picket-fence suburban existence. A boom in Israel's economy has helped to increase the independence of individual families – per capita GDP is US$20,800. New-found wealth and a love of the outdoors have made them an active lot: sports, outdoor pursuits, travel and other leisure activities take the edge off an otherwise stressful position in the Middle East.

Orthodox Jews, by the nature of their relatively large families and religious commitments, are more involved with domestic affairs. While Tel Avivans are out clubbing on Friday nights, the Jerusalem Orthodox are maintaining strict kosher laws – they observe dietary rules and avoid any form of work during Shabbat. Similarly, while gays and lesbians live an open lifestyle in Tel Aviv and other cities, their lifestyle in Jerusalem is more cautious and conservative.

Israeli women enjoy a freedom and prestige on par with their European coun-

---

CULTURAL CONSIDERATIONS

While mainstream Israeli society is quite similar to that found in southern Europe, due care should be taken when interacting with Orthodox people – or even walking through Orthodox areas, such as the Jerusalem neighbourhood of Me'a She'arim. Women must wear modest clothing that covers their arms and legs, and outsiders should avoid these areas during Shabbat, unless invited by a local resident.

While a handshake is a common greeting in Israel, Jewish rabbis don't usually shake hands; in Palestinian communities, men should avoid shaking hands with women.

Cultural guidelines for interacting with Arabs outlined on p26 apply to both Christian and Muslim Arabs.

---

terparts and have historically played significant roles in the economy, the military and politics. (Israel was one of the first countries to elect a female prime minister, Golda Meir). But a number of challenges remain: domestic violence is on the rise and a level of inequality still exists in the workforce. Most troubling for feminists are obsolete divorce laws that technically give a husband the right to prevent his ex-wife from remarrying.

Palestinians earn far less than the average Israeli (an annual per-capita income of just US$1100), a troublesome statistic that has done much to keep the Arab-Jewish conflict simmering. With an unemployment rate of around 30% (in some places over 60%), and a spectacular birth rate (around 7.5 children per woman), the Palestinian home is both overcrowded and poor. These days, *any* home has become something of a luxury – in the Gaza Strip alone, the IDF was destroying 120 Palestinian houses per month during the second intifada.

While poverty may keep Palestinians hungry for a homeland it is has also driven them to mosque. Traditionally, Palestinians have proven no more religious than secular Jews (women are encouraged to go to work and school), but in recent years, as trust in the Palestinian Authority fades away, more and more people are turning towards the Islamic militants and their fiery faith, hoping to find a better future.

Population

For more than 50 years Israel has served as a melting pot for the Jewish faithful. Economic opportunities and spiritual commitments have seen the entrance of Russians to Haifa, Moroccans to Tiberias, Yemenites to Tel Aviv, and ultra-Orthodox Ashkenazi to Jerusalem. Other arrivals include Syrian, Ethiopian and Iraqi Jews, among others, all of whom have taken advantage of the *Aliyah* law, which gives full citizenship (and the accompanying benefits) to any Jew who requests it.

But while Arab birth rates are some of the highest in the world (see p277), Israelis have proven mediocre in child production, sporting a growth rate of just 1.2%. For this reason the Israeli government continues to encourage immigration – offering cash incentives to young Russian and American Jews who move to Israel. It's a move with overtones that are as economic as they are political, because, for the moment, maintaining a solid workforce is as important as keeping up with the growing Arab population; demographers report that in 20 years the Arab minority will increase from 20% to 30%.

Many of the newly arrived Jews take up residence in settlements which, for obvious reasons, offer excellent housing at a low cost. The obvious risk in this is the peace process. Some 9000 Gazan settlers were forced to move from their homes in 2005 and, in time, it's likely that 20% of West Bank settlers (who number some 280,000) will be subject to a similar fate.

The Arab population in the West Bank and Gaza is around 3.8 million, 90% of whom are Muslim. This fact, many believe, is why Israel never attempted to annex these areas; had they done so it would have meant giving Israeli citizenship to 3.8 million Arabs, thereby ending the Jewish majority in Israel and negating its status as a 'Jewish state'. As it stands, West Bank and Gaza citizens are, for all intents and purposes, stateless, although many still carry a Jordanian passport.

SPORT

Football (soccer) is the national obsession, with a number of clubs representing various cities across the country. Beitar Jerusalem FC has the biggest following and hooliganism among their fans is not uncommon. Football crosses cultural boundaries, and several Arabs play on Israel's national side. After star strikers Abbas Suan and Walid Badir scored key goals for Israel during the 2005 World Cup qualifiers, an Arab member of the Knesset (Israeli parliament) suggested changing the popular slogan of the Jewish right from 'No Arabs, no terrorism' to 'No Arabs, no goals'.

Palestine also has its own national football squad, although in qualifying matches it is grouped in Asia while Israel is grouped in Europe. In 2002 it made a surprising debut in the World Cup qualifiers, finishing second in its opening-round group ahead of Malaysia and Hong Kong.

Basketball is the second favourite sport and professional teams are a combination of local talent and American imports. The country's best club, Tel Aviv Maccabee has also enjoyed international success, winning several EuroLeague titles including back-to-back championships in 2004 and 2005.

RELIGION

Around 80% of Israel's population is Jewish, with Muslims making up 15% of the total and Christians and other sects 5%. Church and state are not separate in Israel, so everything from the justice system, holidays and education, right down to the national anthem, is based on Judaism. A special government arm – the Ministry for Religious Affairs – ensures no breaching of Jewish law, although the finer details, like businesses keeping kosher for Passover, tend to be overlooked.

Jewish doctrine states that Jews exist as a conduit between God and the rest of mankind. As God's 'chosen people', Jews have recorded his law in the Torah, the first five books of the Old Testament. The Torah contains 613 commandments, which cover fundamental issues like the prohibition of theft, murder and idolatry. The remainder of the Old Testament (the prophetic books), along with the Talmud (commentary on the laws of the Torah, written around AD 200), make up the teachings that form the cornerstone of Jewish study.

Judaism includes several sects of varying piousness, the most religious being the Hasidim (Haredim) ultra-Orthodox Jews, easily identified by their black hats, long black coats, collared white shirts, beards, and *peyot* (side curls). Hasidic women, like Muslim women, act and dress modestly, covering up exposed

---

THE MESSIAH COMMETH

It won't take long before you start wondering about a particular bearded fellow peering at you from billboards, flyers, posters and bookmarks. With his right arm raised and eyes beaming under a black hat, Rabbi Manachem Mendel Schneerson (1902–94) will soon become a familiar sight on your travels.

A Ukrainian by birth, Schneerson later moved to Berlin and then Paris where he joined the **Chabad movement** (www.chabad.org), a Jewish outreach organisation. During WWII he emigrated to the USA and settled in Brooklyn, where he built up the Chabad empire that rapidly spread across the USA, Canada, Israel and North Africa. Schneerson later succeeded his father-in-law as 'The Rebbe', the head of the Lubavitch, an ultra-Orthodox sect that founded Chabad in 1772. In this role Schneerson gathered a worldwide following and everyone from political leaders to corporate magnates sought his blessing and wise counsel.

Schneerson's ultraright beliefs came to the fore during the 1967 Six Day War when he called for the capture of Damascus and Cairo; he later voiced strong objections to any return of Palestinian land.

Towards the end of his life Schneerson imparted on his followers that the coming of the Messiah was imminent. Full page ads in the *New York Times* were taken out to make the public aware of this momentous event. In 1992 The Rebbe suffered a serious stroke. It was during this time of sickness that the many Lubavitchers believed Schneerson himself to be the Messiah, a theory that led to much controversy within the ultra-Orthodox community.

Despite much encouragement from his followers, The Rebbe never set foot in Israel, probably because it is halachically forbidden to leave Israel upon entry. By staying outside of Israel he could wield more influence over the worldwide Jewish community, as well as visit the graves of his predecessors, as is customary of Chabad Rebbes.

---

hair and skin (except hands and face). Many Jews, both Secular and Orthodox, wear a *kippa* (skullcap), generally thought to be more of a tradition than a commandment.

Because of their common roots, Islam and Judaism share holy sites (the Temple Mount in Jerusalem and the Cave of Machpelah in Hebron) as well as prophets and ancestors (Adam, Noah, Abraham, Isaac, Jacob and Joseph and Moses). Although historically Palestinians have been moderate Muslims, the strongest centre of Islam is Gaza, where militant Islamic groups have found ready ears among those disenchanted with false promises of peace. For more on the Islamic faith, see p53.

Despite its origins in Israel, Christianity remains relatively small, and most of the holy sites are administered by overseas churches. The balance of power lies with the Greek Orthodox Church, which has jurisdiction over more than half of Jerusalem's Church of the Holy Sepulchre and a large proportion of Bethlehem's Church of the Nativity. The Armenians, Copts, Assyrians, Roman Catholics and Protestants also lay claim to various holy sites, and disputes arise frequently over how to share their stewardship.

Smaller faiths include the Druze, an offshoot of Islam, whose small communities are based mainly in northern Israel, especially Haifa and Mt Carmel. Haifa is also the centre of the fast growing Baha'i faith, a development of a Muslim mystical movement, founded in Persia in 1844.

ARTS

Israel's struggle for independence – and the conflicts endured since attaining that goal – has been the inspiration for three generations of artists, film makers, musicians and writers. A strong Ashkenazi influence means that most work is European in style.

Not surprisingly, the Palestinian world of art shares a similar passion for freedom, independence and justice. A lack of funding often means less exposure, but Palestinian artists, especially musicians, are slowly making a name for themselves.

Literature

Israel's most celebrated writer is Amos Oz, whose contemporary fiction involving ordinary Israeli characters and settings has been translated into 30 languages. His most recent work, *A Tale of Love and Darkness*

(2004), is a touching autobiography of his childhood that many reviewers are calling his best work to date.

Across the Green Line, it's worth getting hold of some Emile Habibi, a long-time Arab member of the Israeli Knesset, who took up the pen in 1967 when an Israeli counterpart censured Palestine for its lack of literature. His work *The Pesoptimist* was translated into 16 languages including Hebrew. Palestine's most eminent lyricist is Mahmoud Darwish; a highly political poet and member of the PLO in the 1970s he wrote, among other works, Palestine's Declaration of Independence.

Music

Much of Israel's political dialogue is shouted on band stages and in recording studios by its young, mostly left-wing musicians. The biggest act of the moment is Jerusalem-based Hadag Nahash (Snake Fish), an anti-establishment, antigovernment funk outfit that sings about the inevitability of a Palestinian state. Rapper Mook E broke into the Israeli charts with his hit single *Talking About Peace*, while on the right side of the political spectrum, Subliminal and Shadow rap for Israeli nationalism. Elizabeth Nord's documentary film *Jericho's Echo: Punk Rock in the Holy Land* (2005) is an investigative look into complex issues confronted by Israeli punk rockers.

Palestinian hip hop is similarly loaded with political overtones. *Slingshot Hip Hop* (2005), a documentary about Arab rap in Israel, the West Bank and Gaza, gives a powerful perspective on Arab youth culture and the use of rap, instead of weapons, as a means of protest. For a more traditional sound, listen to **El-Funoun** (www.el-funoun.org), a Palestinian folk music and dance group that has toured in a dozen of countries since its inception in 1979.

While Tel Aviv may lead the way in experimental, cutting-edge music, another worthy testing ground for young musicians is Jerusalem's appropriately named Lab (p296).

Theatre & Dance

Unsurprisingly, politics are also played out on stage by all of Israel's main repertory theatres, coming a long way since *Fiddler on the Roof*. The Cameri Theatre in Tel Aviv is the leader in this field, recently performing controversial works like *Plonter*, by 29-year-old Yael Ronon, which challenges the relationships between Palestinians and Israelis.

Also well received is *Milano,* which describes how various people live under the threat of terrorism and suicide bombings. *Eyewitness,* another fascinating production, is the story of Austrian farmer Franz Jagerstatter's refusal to serve in the Wehrmacht during WWII and the last day of his life before his execution. The story alludes to Israelis who refuse to serve mandatory service in the IDF.

Ramallah-based Al Kasaba Theatre has produced a number of equally stirring theatrical productions, including *Alive From Palestine,* a series of monologues and scenes that the actors have drawn from personal experience. The Palestine National Theatre, based in Jerusalem, has also run racy themes, including the 2004 production *A Happy Woman,* which challenges Arab women to demand equal rights.

Overseas, look out for David Hare's *Via Dolorosa,* a monologue reflecting on his travels in Israel and the conversations he incurs with Jews and Arabs.

Cinema

Historically, Israeli films have never enjoyed much international success. Prior to independence they were mainly Zionist propaganda pieces designed to raise funds for the young nation. Post-independence films were largely overshadowed by British and Hollywood productions filmed on-site, such as Otto Preminger's classic *Exodus.* Only in recent years has there been some success at the box office, including *Six Days to Eternity,* a film about the 1967 Six Day War which includes the first release of documentary clips shot by the Arab army. Meanwhile, Palestinian dramatic cinema is still developing stages, although some of its documentaries have enjoyed international success.

In recent years a slew of films and documentaries about the Arab-Israeli conflict have hit the market, earning accolades at film festivals worldwide. Unmissable is Academy Award–winning *One Day in September* (1999), a play-by-play account of the 1972 Olympic hostage crisis that ended with the deaths of 11 Israeli athletes.

One of the more austere documentaries, *Death in Gaza* (2004), chronicles the lives of children being trained as resistance fighters, but then changes dramatically when its producer, 34-year-old James Miller, is shot and killed by Israeli tank fire.

Among other documentaries, Hany Abu-Assad's film *Paradise Now* (2005) is a gripping account of two Palestinian suicide bombers during the final 48 hours before their mission. *Checkpoint* (1997) discusses the effect of the Oslo Peace Accords on Palestinian lives. And the somewhat more up-to-date *Wall* (2004), by Simone Bitton, is a sensitive investigation of the Security Fence and the effects of its construction on the Palestinian people. To take the edge off these tension-filled flicks, check out Ari Sandel's zany **West Bank Story** (2005; www.westbankstory.com), a modern spoof on the musical *West Side Story*.

ENVIRONMENT

With an area of nearly 28,000 sq km, Israel and the Palestinian Territories are geographically dominated by the Great Rift Valley (also known as the Syrian–African Rift), which stretches from Southern Turkey to Lake Kariba on the Zambia–Zimbabwe border.

Between the mountain-fringed rift and the Mediterranean Sea stretches the fertile, but sandy, coastal plain where the bulk of the population and agriculture is concentrated. The lightly populated Negev, the country's southern wedge, is characterised by mountains, plains and wadis, and punctuated by military bases and desert-transforming irrigation schemes.

Due to its position at the junction of three natural zones, Israel and the Palestinian Territories support a diverse wealth of plant and animal life. In the wet, mountainous Upper Galilee, otters dive in highland streams and Golden eagles circle dense laurel forests, while in the southern desert landscapes, ibex water at date palm-shaded wadis.

Of the 58 national parks run by the Israel Nature & National Parks Protection Authority, just two (Herodian and Qumran National Parks) are located in the West Bank and none are in the Gaza Strip. Many of the protected areas actually double as large archaeological complexes, including Masada, Beit She'an, Nimrod Fortress and Caeasaria. If you plan to visit a lot of national parks, its worth investing in an all-access 'Green Card' for 102NIS. It's valid for one year and available at most national park visitor centres.

Environmental Issues

When Theodore Herzl suggested planting 10 million trees in Palestine, his colleagues thought he was nuts. But 100 years later the people of Israel proved that they could indeed 'make the desert bloom'. Unfortunately, the Zionists' zeal to populate the land has had a much greater environmental impact than the afforestation project. The demands on the land from increased urbanisation have resulted in the same problems found in many parts of the world – air and water pollution, over-extension of natural resources and poor waste management. Israel's 197km of coastline is particularly threatened: 56km are already urbanised and construction is zoned for a further 103km.

GREEN TEAMS

The **Society for the Protection of Nature in Israel** (SPNI; tourism@spni.org.il; www.teva.org.il), which is charged with the conservation and protection of antiquities, wildlife and the environment, is an excellent source of information for travellers. At the main offices in Tel Aviv and Jerusalem you'll find outdoor shops selling a range of nature and wildlife publications. The Tel Aviv shop also stocks camping and outdoor equipment.

The SPNI also runs field trips and tours, and operates 10 field schools, where enthusiastic specialists can provide information on local hikes, wildlife and accommodation. For a complete list of addresses, contact either of the two main offices, **SPNI Jerusalem** (Map p286; ☎ 02-624 4605; 13 Heleni HaMalka St, PO Box 930, Jerusalem 96101) or **SPNI Tel Aviv** (Map p298; ☎ 03-638 8674; 4 Hashfela St, Tel Aviv 66183).

The network of managed forests in Israel is overseen by the government-sponsored Kakal. The numerous national parks and archaeological sites are managed by the **Israel Nature & National Parks Protection Authority** (☎ 02-500 5444; www.parks.org.il; Am Ve'olamo St, Givat Shaul, Jerusalem 95463).

Israel and the West Bank's most obvious environmental threat is the drying up of the Dead Sea, which has continued unabated for 30 years – the direct result of overuse of its main water source, the Jordan River. The 20m drop in the Dead Sea water level threatens not only Israel, but also Jordan and Palestine, and in recognition of this the three sides have entered into talks on how to reverse the problem. A number of solutions have been proposed, including one plan to build a canal that would bring water from the Red Sea to the Dead Sea. Whether or not the plan gets off the ground · depends as much on finances as it does on political will.

FOOD & DRINK

In the street markets and supermarkets of Israel and the Palestinian Territories, you can choose from an appealing range of quality fruit and vegetables. Alternatively, follow the locals to the pervasive felafel and shwarma stands; for a 6NIS-to-19NIS filled pitta, you'll also be able to heap on a selection of salads, pickles and sauces. Hummus is regarded more as a national obsession than a mere condiment and when prompted,

many Israelis and Palestinians can wax lyrical about the various kinds of hummus and which local joint produces the best stuff.

Much of the best sit-down fare varies little from that in other Middle Eastern countries – kosher and halal fare is quite similar. On workdays, most fully fledged restaurants offer a good-value 'business lunch', a set lunch special that typically costs 33% to 50% less than other options.

Certified kosher restaurants can't prepare meat and dairy products in the same kitchen, so they'll have either a meat format or a dairy, fish and pasta format. Vegetarians will find joy in the latter, which generally focuses on vegetarian dishes. Meat-oriented places typically include steakhouses, Chinese restaurants and traditional Ashkenazi restaurants serving such Eastern European fare as schnitzel, goulash, liver and gefilte fish.

A real treat is the variety of juices, which are freshly squeezed and sold in juice bars all over the country. Coffee is generally either instant or of the gritty Turkish variety (*qahwa bi-hel*; or in Hebrew: *kafé turki*) with cardamom. Another local favourite is tea with spearmint (*shai bi-naana*; or in Hebrew: *tey im naana*).

FOR SALE: THE BREAD OF A NATION

The Orthodox, ultrareligious Jews call it their 'Passover Telephone'. Used once a year during the week of Passover, this special 'kosher telephone' is sealed off for the remaining 51 weeks to keep it protected from the elements, lest some rogue breadcrumb falls into its cracks (to keep kosher, you cannot touch bread during Passover, or anything that has touched bread).

Is it an extreme form of devotion? Or is it a clever marketing ploy? However you see it, the Passover Phone is but one of many oddities facing the visitor to Israel during this holy week.

Travellers browsing the supermarket aisles during Passover are confronted with huge plastic tarps blanketing large sections of the store, effectively covering up any form of bread product, from pretzels right down to wheat grain.

Snackers find soft matzo (unleavened bread) used in place of pita at falafel stands. McDonald's gets into the act too: using buns made from, of all things, mashed potatoes.

On farms across Israel, livestock are given kosher feed for weeks before Passover so that Israel's milk won't have any trace of grain. Because their handlers can't touch bread, gorillas and other zoo animals also stay kosher for Passover. Jewish babies do their part by sucking on kosher pacifiers.

Israel's Ministry for Religious Affairs, responsible for ensuring the grain lockdown, symbolically sells off all of Israel's grain reserves to a non-Jew for a few shekels. This temporary grain baron then (hopefully) sells his newfound wealth back to the state when the holiday is over.

On the ground, everybody has their own interpretations of how far they'll go without bread. Since beer contains *chametz* (prohibited food) there is a certain element of society that quickly violates the no-bread rule. Try as they might, other folk simply can't go a week without a proper felafel; the result is covert trips to Akko, Nazareth and Jaffa: Arab towns where felafel addicts can get their fix.

Alcohol is available everywhere, but observant Muslims don't drink at all and Jewish Israelis drink very little. Although Israelis use wine mainly for ceremonial purposes (eg during Shabbat and Pesah), the country now produces a range of very nice red and white wines, including Carmel, Golan, Tishbi and Tzora. To learn more of the wines in this growing industry, pick up a copy of Daniel Rogov's *Guide to Israeli Wines* (Toby Press), which includes a map of the wine regions.

These days, younger people prefer the appeal of beer as a nightlife accompaniment. The national brewery produces Maccabee, Gold Star and Nesher, which are acceptable (in descending order). In the Palestinian Territories, you can try the tasty but rather expensive boutique (micro) brew Taybeh.

JERUSALEM

ירושלים القدس

☎ 02 / pop 693,000

Jerusalem, Israel's ancient and enigmatic capital, is certainly one of the world's most fascinating cities, as well as one of the holiest, most beautiful – and most disputed.

HISTORY

Jerusalem, originally a small Jebusite settlement, occupied the slopes of Mt Moriah, where according to the Old Testament Abraham offered his son Isaac as a sacrifice. In 997 BC King David captured the city and made it his capital, and his son and successor, Solomon, built the great First Temple. The temple was destroyed by the Babylonian king Nebuchadnezzar in 586 BC and the Jews were exiled into the wilderness.

After 50 short years, the Babylonians were pushed off the land by the Persians and it was under Cyrus the Great that the Jews were allowed to return and reconstruct a 'Second Temple', which was completed in 515 BC. Power shifted hands between subsequent invading armies until the Romans marched on Jerusalem in 63 BC, and installed Herod the Great as the king of Judea. Herod launched a massive building campaign in Jerusalem, and the city was thereafter ruled by a series of procurators. It was the fifth of these, the renowned Pontius Pilate, who ordered the crucifixion of Jesus.

The swell of Jewish discontent with Roman rule escalated into the First Revolt in AD 66, resulting in the destruction of the Temple. A Second Revolt in AD 132 took the Romans four years to quell. The Jews were banished from Jerusalem and the Emperor Hadrian razed the city and rebuilt it as Aelia Capitolina, which is the basis of today's Old City. For more information, see p40.

Christianity became the official state religion after Emperor Constantine's mother St Helena visited Jerusalem, causing the conversion of many local Jews and Samaritans. This sparked a building campaign of churches and basilicas atop Christian holy places; most notably, the first work on the Church of the Holy Sepulchre commenced in AD 326. The importance of Jerusalem as a centre of Christian worship spread through the Eastern Roman Empire and was recognised as one of the five patriarchal cities (the others being Antioch, Rome, Alexandria and Constantinople).

In 638 AD, however, after weathering a short-lived Persian invasion and occupation, Byzantine Jerusalem fell to a new power, Islam.

The Umayyad Caliph paid tribute to the place associated with Muhammed's *miraj* (ascension to heaven) and the Dome of the Rock was completed in AD 691 to commemorate the event. But despite its significance to Islam, Jerusalem's political and economic fortunes fell into decline, the result of its distance from the imperial capitals Damascus and Cairo.

For a time all faiths were free to live and practise in the city, but in the 11th century Palestine fell to the Seljuk Turks, who stopped Christian pilgrims from visiting Jerusalem. Hence, between 1095 and 1270, Western Christians led a series of Crusades to deliver the Holy Land from Arab occupation. The Crusaders took Jerusalem in 1099 but lost it in 1187, to Saladin.

In 1250 the city came under the influence of the Mamluks, successors to Saladin's Ayyubid dynasty, who ruled out of Egypt. They endowed the holy city with much fine architecture and turned it into a centre of Islamic learning. In 1517 the Ottoman Turks under Selim I defeated the Mamluks in battle near Aleppo, and thereby absorbed Jerusalem into their expanding empire. The

ISRAEL & THE PALESTINIAN TERRITORIES

JERUSALEM

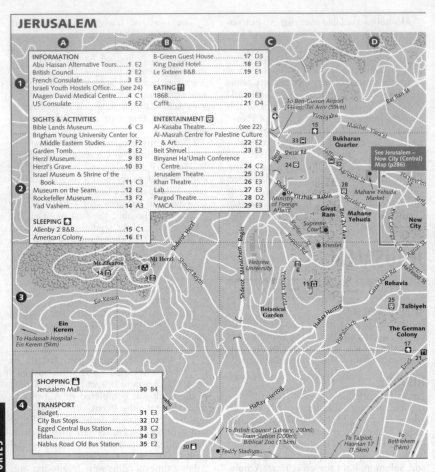

INFORMATION
Abu Hassan Alternative Tours......1 E2
British Council..............................2 E2
French Consulate...........................3 E3
Israeli Youth Hostels Office......(see 24)
Magen David Medical Centre......4 C1
US Consulate.................................5 E2

SIGHTS & ACTIVITIES
Bible Lands Museum.....................6 C3
Brigham Young University Center for
    Middle Eastern Studies...........7 F2
Garden Tomb.................................8 E2
Herzl Museum...............................9 B3
Herzl's Grave...............................10 B3
Israel Museum & Shrine of the
    Book.....................................11 C3
Museum on the Seam..................12 F2
Rockefeller Museum.....................13 F2
Yad Vashem.................................14 A3

SLEEPING
Allenby 2 B&B.............................15 C1
American Colony..........................16 E1

B-Green Guest House.................17 D3
King David Hotel.........................18 E3
Le Sixteen B&B...........................19 E1

EATING
1868..20 E3
Caffit..21 D4

ENTERTAINMENT
Al-Kasaba Theatre...................(see 22)
Al-Masrah Centre for Palestine Culture
    & Art....................................22 E2
Beit Shmuel................................23 E3
Binyanei Ha'Umah Conference
    Centre..................................24 C2
Jerusalem Theatre......................25 D3
Khan Theatre..............................26 E3
Lab...27 E3
Pargod Theatre...........................28 D2
YMCA..29 E3

SHOPPING
Jerusalem Mall............................30 B4

TRANSPORT
Budget..31 E3
City Bus Stops.............................32 D2
Egged Central Bus Station...........33 C2
Eldan..34 E3
Nablus Road Old Bus Station.......35 E2

To Ben-Gurion Airport
(44km); Tel Aviv (59km)

Yirmiyahu
Bar Ilan St
Malchei Yisra'el
Bukharan Quarter
See Jerusalem – New City (Central) Map (p286)
Shezar Rd
Jaffa St
Agrippas St
Ha Nevi'im
Mahane Yehuda Market
Shmu'el
Mahane Yehuda
New City
King George
Agron St
Keren HaYesod St

To Ben-Gurion Airport

Shderot Herzl
Shderot Herzl
Mt Zikaron
Mt Herzl
Shmuel Beyth

Shderot Menachem Begin

Hebrew University

Yitzhak Rabin
Ministry of Foreign Affairs
Givat Ram
Ruppin Rd
Supreme Court
Knesset
Ben Zvi Ave
Rehavia

Ein Kerem

Yehuda Burla
Yehuda Herzog

Botanical Garden

HaRav Herzog

Hatzanim St
Gaza ('Azza) Rd
Talbiyeh

The German Colony

Ein Kerem
To Hadassah Hospital – Ein Kerem (5km)

To British Council (Library; 200m);
Train Station (200m);
Biblical Zoo (1.5km)

To Talpiot;
Haoman 17
(1.5km)

To Bethlehem
(5km)

HaRav Herzog

Teddy Stadium

city remained under loose Turkish rule from İstanbul for 400 years.

A lack of central authority from the 18th century on resulted in squabbles between landowners, and in the mid-19th century the power vacuum seemed to invite portions of the Jewish Diaspora to return to their ancestral homeland.

Subsequently, Jerusalem became a hotbed of Arab and Jewish rivalry. The Ottomans rejected a British proposal to create an international enclave in the city, a decision that made the city a battleground again in 1948. When the fighting ended, a ceasefire, or Green Line, divided the city, with Israel on the west and Jordan to the east. After the Six Day War of 1967, Jeru-

salem was reunified under Israeli rule, but the control of the Holy City remains a bone of contention with the Palestinians, who also claim it as their capital.

ORIENTATION

Jerusalem is conveniently divided into three parts: the walled Old City with its four Quarters – Jewish, Muslim, Christian and Armenian; the predominantly Arab enclave of East Jerusalem; and the Israeli New City, also known as West Jerusalem. The main street in the New City, Jaffa Rd, connects the bus station and the Old City; the main shopping area is concentrated on King George V, Ben Yehuda and Ben Hillel Sts. Bus No 99, which makes a loop around

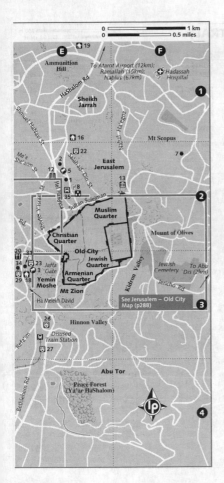

JERUSALEM IN...

Two Days

Line up early (around 7.30am) on day one for a visit to the **Temple Mount** (p289), followed by a visit to the **Western Wall tunnels** (p289). The tunnel tour terminates conveniently at the start of the Via Dolorosa (Stations of the Cross), which you can follow to the **Church of the Holy Sepulchre** (p289). There are several first-rate places to break for lunch in the Christian Quarter, including **Papa Andrea's** (see the boxed text, p294).

After lunch, wander through the historic Cardo and the busy David St before capping the day with a tour of the **Citadel & Tower of David** (p290).

Spend day two exploring the new city's major sites, including the **Israel Museum** (p291) and the **Shrine of the Book** (p291), the **Bible Lands Museum** (p291) and **Yad Vashem** (p291). Spend your evening around the shops and cafés of Ben Yehuda St.

Three Days

With one extra day you could visit East Jerusalem, touring the **Museum on the Seam** (p291), the **Garden Tomb** (p291) and the **Rockefeller Museum** (p291), before ambling over to the **Mount of Olives** (p290). Continuing south around the Old City, check out the **City of David** (p290) and, if time allows, **King David's tomb** (p290) on Mt Zion.

---

the city while providing commentary in English, is a good way to orient yourself upon arrival.

INFORMATION
Bookshops
Sefer VeSefel (Map p286; ☎ 624 8237; 2 Ya'Avetz St; ☽ 8am-8pm Sun-Thu, 8am-2.30pm Fri, 8.30-11.30pm Sat) This Jerusalem institution houses floor-to-ceiling new and secondhand fiction and nonfiction titles. It's upstairs in an alley linking Jaffa Rd with Mordechai Ben Hillel St.
Steimatzky (Map p286; ☎ 625 0155; 39 Jaffa Rd; ☽ 10am-7pm Sun-Thu, 10am-3pm Fri) Other locations include 7 Ben Yehuda St and the Jerusalem Mall.
Tmol Shilshom (Map p286; ☎ 623 2758; www .tmol-shilshom.co.il; 5 Yoel Salomon St; ☽ 8.30am-midnight Sun-Thu, 8.30am-4pm Fri, 8pm-midnight Sat)

Bohemian café and used bookshop, this place often hosts poetry readings or lectures by authors and journalists.

Emergency
Central police station (emergency ☎ 100) Near the Russian Compound in the New City.
Fire department (☎ 102)
First aid (☎ 101)
Police (☎ 100)

Internet Access
Laptop carriers can find wi-fi 'hot spots' on Ben Yehuda St (on the benches outside Burger King), in Tmol Shilshom bookshop and in the lobbies of several main hotels. If you are hanging around the central bus

JERUSALEM – NEW CITY (CENTRAL)

0 ━━━━━━━ 200 m
0 ━━━━━━━ 0.1 miles

INFORMATION	
Amex..................................1	C4
Central Police Station...........2	C3
Internet Café.....................3	C3
ISSTA................................4	B3
ISSTA................................5	C2
Laundry Place....................6	B3
Main Post Office.................7	C3
Sefer VeSefel.....................8	B2
SPNI Office and Bookshop....9	C3
Steimatzky.......................10	A3
Steimatzky.......................11	B3
Steimatzky.......................12	B3
Tmol Shilshom...................13	B3

SIGHTS & ACTIVITIES	
Time Elevator....................14	B4
SLEEPING	
Hotel Habira.....................15	B3
Hotel Palatin.....................16	A2
Kaplan Hotel.....................17	B3
EATING	
El Toro.............................18	B3
King of Felafel & Shwarma...19	A3
Ticho House.......................20	B2
Ticho House.......................21	B2
Village Green.....................22	B3

DRINKING	
Gong................................23	B3
Yankees Bar......................24	B3
Zolli's...............................25	B3
ENTERTAINMENT	
Glasnost...........................26	C2
Mike's Place......................27	B3
Shoshan...........................28	C4
Underground.....................29	B3
TRANSPORT	
Arkia Airlines.....................30	C3
El Al.................................31	A3
Sheruts to Tel Aviv.............32	B3

station, Internet terminals (9NIS per 30 minutes) are located on the 4th floor.

Freeline (Map p288; ☎ 627 1959; 8th station, 51 Aqabat al-Khanqah; per hr 8NIS; 🕑 10am-midnight)

Internet Café (Map p286; ☎ 622 3377; 31 Jaffa Rd; per hr 12NIS; 🕑 9.30am-4am) Located beside the main post office.

Mike's Centre (Map p288; ☎ 628 2486; www.mikes centre.com; 9th Station, 172 Souq Khan al-Zeit; per hr 8NIS; 🕑 9am-10pm) In the Old City, with Internet and laundry services.

St Raphael@Internet (Map p288; Jaffa Gate; per hr 15NIS; 🕑 10am-midnight Mon-Sat)

Laundry

Laundry Place (Map p286; ☎ 625 7714; 12 Shamai St; 🕑 8.30am-8pm Sun-Thu, 8.30am-3pm Fri)

Mike's Centre (Map p288; ☎ 628 2486; www.mikes

centre.com; 9th Station, 172 Souq Khan al-Zeit; 🕑 9am-10pm) In the Old City.

Libraries

British Council (Map p286; ☎ 640 3900; Agudat Sport Maccabee St; 🕑 2-7pm Mon-Tue & Thu, 11am-4pm Wed, 10am-1pm Fri) Large collection of DVDs, videos and books. Located opposite the Jerusalem Mall.

Media

Jerusalem Post (www.jpost.com) This is an excellent source of local news and events listings. On Friday, the *Post* includes an extensive 'What's On' weekend supplement.

Medical Services

Magen David Medical Centre (Map pp284-5; ☎ 652 3133; 7 Himem Gimel St, Romema; 🕑 24hr) This place is located approximately five minutes' walk from the central bus station.

Orthodox Society (Map p288; ☎ 627 1958; Greek Orthodox Patriarchate Rd; ☟ 8am-3pm Mon-Fri, 8am-1pm Sat) In the Old City's Christian Quarter, the Orthodox Society operates a low-cost medical and dental clinic that welcomes travellers.

Money
The best deals for changing money are at the private, commission-free change offices all over the New City, Old City and East Jerusalem. Many, especially around Ben Yehuda St, will also change traveller's cheques. Note that they close early on Friday and remain closed all day Saturday.

Amex (Map p286; ☎ 624 0830; 18 Shlomzion HaMalka St) Replaces lost travellers cheques.

Post
Main post office (Map p286; ☎ 624 4745; 23 Jaffa Rd ☟ 7am-7pm Sun-Thu, 7am-noon Fri) The place to pick up poste restante.

Tourist Information
Christian Information Centre (Map p288; ☎ 627 2692; fax 628 6417; Omar Ibn al-Khattab Sq; ☟ 8.30am-noon Mon-Sat) Opposite the entrance to the Citadel; provides information on the city's Catholic sites.

Jaffa Gate Tourist Office (Map p288; ☎ 627 1422; www.tourism.gov.il; Jaffa Gate; ☟ 8.30am-5pm Sun-Thu) Offers free maps and can arrange informal meetings with Christian, Orthodox Jewish and Muslim families.

Jewish Student Information Centre (Map p288; ☎ 628 2634, 052 2867795; www.jeffseidel.com; 5 Beit El St) Committed to giving young Jews an appreciation of their heritage, this centre organises free walking tours of Jewish sites around the Old City. (And it's got a great website!)

Travel Agencies
ISSTA New City (Map p286; ☎ 625 7257; 31 HaNevi'im St); Old City (☎ 621 1888; 4 Herbert Samuel St, Zion Sq) Organises inexpensive flight tickets.

Mazada Tours (Map p288; ☎ 623 5777; www.mazada.co.il; Pearl Hotel Bldg, 15 Jaffa Rd) Operates tours and buses to Cairo.

SIGHTS
The Old City
Bound by stone ramparts, the Old City is divided into Jewish, Muslim, Christian and Armenian Quarters. Sites of interest include the Haram ash-Sharif (Temple Mount to the Jews), the site of the Dome of the Rock; the Western Wall; and the Church of the Holy Sepulchre, built over what's claimed to be the traditional site of the Crucifixion.

WALLS & GATES
The Old City walls are the legacy of Süleyman the Magnificent who built them between 1537 and 1542, although they've since been extensively renovated. The **Ramparts Walk** (Map p288; adult/child 16/8NIS; ☟ 9am-4.30pm) is a 1km jaunt along the top of the city wall – from Jaffa Gate north to Lion's Gate (also called St Stephen's Gate), via New, Damascus and Herod's Gates, and Jaffa Gate south to Dung Gate (also called Gate of the Moors), via Zion Gate.

There are seven open gates. The **Jaffa Gate** (Map p288), so named because it was the beginning of the old road to Jaffa, is now the main entrance to the Old City from the New City. Moving clockwise, the 1887 **New Gate** (Map p288) also gives access from the New City. Down the hill, **Damascus Gate** (Map p288), the most attractive and crowded of all the city gates, opens into bustling East Jerusalem. **Herod's Gate** (Map p288) also faces Arab East Jerusalem, and it was near here in 1099 that the Crusaders first breached Jerusalem's walls.

Lion's Gate (Map p288), facing the Mount of Olives, has also been called St Stephen's Gate after the first Christian martyr, who was stoned to death nearby. **Zion Gate** (Map p288) became known as the Gate of the Jewish Quarter in late medieval times and is still pocked with reminders of the fierce fighting here in the 1948 war.

JEWISH QUARTER
Flattened during the 1948 fighting, the Jewish Quarter has been almost entirely reconstructed since its recapture by the Israelis in 1967. There are few historic monuments above ground level but the excavations during reconstruction unearthed a number of archaeological sites. The most significant is the **Cardo** (Map p288), the main north–south street of the Roman Aelia Capitolina and, later, of Byzantine Jerusalem. Part of it has been restored to what may have been its original appearance, while another part has been reconstructed as a shopping arcade with expensive gift shops and galleries of Judaica. The Cardo also includes the **Last Ditch Battle of the Jewish Quarter Museum** (Map p288; admission free; ☟ 10am-3pm Sun-Thu, 9am-1pm

JERUSALEM – OLD CITY

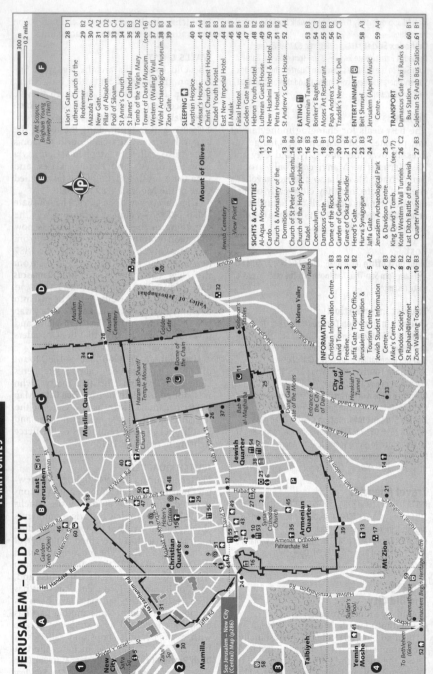

ISRAEL & THE PALESTINIAN TERRITORIES

Fri), which documents the 1948 campaign for control over the city.

At Hurva Sq, east of the Cardo, a graceful brick arch is the most prominent remnant of the **Hurva Synagogue** (Map p288). Down a narrow alleyway east of the Sq is the impressive **Wohl Archaeological Museum** (Map p288; ☎ 628 8141; admission 15NIS; ☼ 9am-5pm Sun-Thu, 9am-1pm Fri), which features a 1st-century home and several Herodian archaeological sites, plus interpretive displays.

The **Western (Wailing) Wall** (Map p288), the only remnant of Judaism's holiest shrine, is part of the retaining wall built by Herod in 20 BC to support the temple esplanade (the 'wailing' moniker stems from Jewish sorrow over the destruction of the temple). The area immediately in front of the wall now serves as an open-air synagogue; the right side is open to women (who must dress modestly, covering their arms and legs), and the left side to men. It's accessible 24 hours a day, and up-to-the-minute live shots can be viewed in cyberspace at: www.aish.com/wallcam.

A Jerusalem highlight is the **Kotel Western Wall Tunnels** (Map p288; ☎ 627 1333; www.thekotel .org; adult/child 18/10NIS), a 488m passage that follows the northern extension of the Western Wall. One-hour tours operate several times daily, but must be booked in advance.

On the southern side of the Western Wall, the recently renovated **Jerusalem Archaeological Park & Davidson Centre** (Map p288; ☎ 627 7550; www .archpark.org.il; Dung Gate; adult/child 30/16NIS; ☼ 8am-5pm Sun-Thu) includes an excellent multimedia presentation and virtual tour of the Temple Mount as it looked 2000 years ago.

The Jewish Quarter is the only part of the Old City that is fully equipped to accommodate wheelchair users.

MUSLIM QUARTER

This is the most bustling and densely populated area of the Old City, and while it's undeniably claustrophobic and hassle-plagued, it's also exhilarating. Clustered around the district of narrow medieval alleys are some fine examples of **Mamluk architecture**. At the Lion's/St Stephen's Gate is **St Anne's Church** (Map p288), perhaps the finest example of Crusader architecture in Jerusalem.

The road leading from the Lion's/St Stephen's Gate into the heart of the Old City is known as **Via Dolorosa** (Sorrowful Way) or

Stations of the Cross, the route that tradition claims was taken by the condemned Jesus as he lugged his cross to Calvary. While this was probably not the actual route taken, the notion does appear to promote faith in believers and at 3pm on Fridays, the Franciscan Fathers lead a solemn procession here.

Haram ash-Sharif, the **Temple Mount** (Map p288; ☼ 7.30-11am & 1.30-2.30pm Sat-Thu) is one of the most instantly recognisable icons of the Middle East, and not to be missed. The massive stone platform was built over the biblical Mt Moriah, the site of Solomon's First and Herod's Second Temples and the place where Abraham was instructed by God to sacrifice his son Isaac in a test of his faith. The sacred altar of the First and Second Temples (aka the 'Holy of Holies') was here, making it one of Judaism's most holy places. For Muslims, the Temple Mount is revered for its association with Mohammed's mystical night journey *(isra)*, in which the Prophet dreamed of flying to heaven from the mount to take his place alongside Allah. In more recent years, the Temple Mount has been thrust into the centre of controversy as Arabs and Jews attempt to stake their sovereignty over it. Plans by Jewish groups to destroy the Muslim sites and build a **Third Temple** (www .thirdtemple.com) have only increased tensions at the now heavily guarded site.

The gold-plated **Dome of the Rock** (Map p288), completed in AD 691, is the centrepiece of the Temple Mount, but actually serves more as a figurehead than a mosque, while the nearby **Al-Aqsa Mosque** (Map p288) is a functioning house of worship. Entrance to the Temple Mount is through the Bab al-Magharba gate, at the Western Wall. Non-Muslims can walk around the Temple Mount, but are barred from entering the Dome of the Rock or the Al-Aqsa Mosque. It's closed to visitors on Islamic holidays. Conservative dress, including a headscarf for women, is required.

CHRISTIAN QUARTER

The Christian Quarter revolves around the **Church of the Holy Sepulchre** (Map p288), the site where the Catholic, Greek Orthodox, Ethiopian and Coptic churches believe that Jesus was crucified, buried and resurrected. The church itself represents a collision of architectural traditions. The original

Byzantine structure was extensively rebuilt by the Crusaders and tweaked by numerous others over the years, but it remains quite a sombre place. It's open daily to anyone who's modestly dressed. It's also worth visiting the tower of the neighbouring **Lutheran Church of the Redeemer** (Map p288) for excellent views over the Old City.

The Jaffa Gate area is dominated by the Crusader **Citadel** (Map p288), which includes Herod's Tower and the Tower of David minaret. It's occupied by the highly worthwhile **Tower of David Museum** (Map p288; ☎ 626 5333; www.towerofdavid.org.il; Jaffa Gate; adult/student/child 30/20/15NIS; ☒ 10am-4pm Mon-Thu & Sat, 10am-2pm Fri), which tells the entire history of Jerusalem in a concise and easily digestible format. Revolving art exhibits in the halls and gardens add an especially pleasant angle. For blind visitors, there is also a series of relief aluminium models of the city at several stages of its history.

ARMENIAN QUARTER & MT ZION

A worthwhile visit is the Armenian **St James' Cathedral** (Map p288; Armenian Orthodox Patriarchate Rd; ☒ 8.30am-5pm Mon-Sat), which has a sensuous aura of ritual and mystery. There's also the **Church of St Peter in Gallicantu** (Map p288; adult/student 6/4NIS; ☒ 8.30am-5pm Mon-Sat), which commemorates the crowing of the cock that Jesus had predicted would reveal Peter's three denials of him.

From the Armenian Quarter, Zion Gate leads out to Mt Zion, site of the **Coenaculum** (Cenacle; Map p288), traditionally held to be the site of the Last Supper. At the back of the same building is the traditional site of **King David's Tomb** (Map p288; ☎ 671 9767; Mt Zion; ☒ 8am-6pm Sun-Thu, 8am-2pm Fri), and around the corner, the **Church & Monastery of the Dormition** (Map p288), where Jesus' mother Mary fell into 'eternal sleep'.

Just south of King David's Tomb is a small cemetery containing the unelaborate **grave of Oskar Schindler** (Map p288); ask the caretaker to the point the way.

Mount of Olives, Mt Scopus & the Kidron Valley

To the east of the Old City, outside Lion's/St Stephen's Gate, the land drops away into the lovely Kidron Valley, then rises again up the slopes of the Mount of Olives. For Christians, this hillside holds special significance as the site where Jesus took on the sins of the world, was arrested and later ascended into heaven. Predictably, several churches have been built here, and visitors can still see the olive grove in the **Garden of Gethsemane** (Map p288) and the **Tomb of the Virgin Mary** (Map p288). Equally impressive is the panorama of the Old City from the summit – visit early in the morning for the best light.

On Mt Scopus, between the Mount of Olives and Hebrew University, is the Mormon **Brigham Young University Center for Middle Eastern Studies** (Map pp284-5; Martin Buber St, Mt Scopus; ☎ 626 5621; ☒ tours 10am-3.30pm Tue-Fri). Free guided tours explain the centre's wonderful architecture and include a demonstration of the incredible pipe organ in the main assembly hall. On Sunday evenings, it hosts free public concerts; a list is available on request (from concerts@jc.byu.ac.il).

The **Kidron Valley**, between the City of David/Mt Ophel (the original Jerusalem) and the Mount of Olives, presents an enigmatic set of historical sites. At the top of the valley sits the 1st-century **Pillar of Absalom** (Map p288), which is almost certainly not Absalom's tomb, as claimed.

Below Jerusalem's current city walls sits the remains of the **City of David** (Map p288; ☎ 1-800-252423; www.cityofdavid.org.il; ☒ 9am-5pm Sun-Thu, 9am-1pm Fri), the Canaanite settlement captured by Kind David some 3000 years ago. The main attraction is the extraordinary 500m-long **Hezekiah's Tunnel** (Map p288; ☎ 626 2341; adult/child 12/6NIS; ☒ 9am-4pm Sun-Thu, 9am-2pm Fri), an underground passage of waist-deep water that ends at the **Pool of Siloam** (Map p288), where it is said a blind man was healed after Jesus instructed him to wash in it. You'll need sandals, a strong torch (flashlight) and a sense of adventure. The City of David is not well set up for tourists so a guided tour in English (11am Monday and Thursday) does wonders to improve your understanding of the place.

Note that quite a few women have reported unpleasant experiences while walking around the Mount of Olives and Kidron Valley, and we strongly advise women not to visit these areas alone.

East Jerusalem

The modern, blaring, fume-hazed Palestinian part of Jerusalem is characterised by small shops, businesses and ageing hotels.

On Sultan Suleiman St, just outside the Old City walls, the **Rockefeller Museum** (Map pp284-5; ☎ 628 2251; http://www.imj.org.il/rockerfeller/; cnr Jericho Rd & Sultan Suleiman St; adult/student 26/16NIS; ☻ 10am-3pm Sun-Thu, 10am-2pm Fri & Sat) has some impressive archaeological and architectural exhibits, although the presentation is a bit musty (your Israel Museum ticket is also good here).

Behind a heavy stone wall on Nablus Rd is the beautiful **Garden Tomb** (Map pp284-5; ☎ 627 2745; ☻ 2-5.30pm Mon-Sat), which contains a 2000-year-old stone tomb and garden that are believed to have once been the property of Joseph of Arimathaea. The site also provides a view of what some claim to be the hill Golgotha (The Place of the Skull), also known as Gordon's Calvary. For the many reasons outlined on the free guided tour, it's believed by most Protestants to be the site of Jesus' crucifixion and resurrection.

Located on the former Green Line that once divided East and West Jerusalem (and the Arab and Jewish armies) is the **Museum on the Seam** (Map pp284-5; ☎ 628 1278; www.coexlstence.art .museum; 4 Hel Handasa; adult/senior/student 25/10/20NIS; ☻ 9am-5pm Sun-Thu, 9am-3pm Fri), a powerful multimedia exposition that deals with conflict and coexistence through the use of art.

The New City
The New City is roughly centred on the triangle formed by Jaffa Rd, King George V St and the pedestrianised Ben Yehuda St. However, the most colourful and bustling district is **Mahane Yehuda**, the Jewish food market. Possibly one of the world's most reluctant tourist attractions, the ultra-Orthodox Jewish district of **Me'a She'arim** is reminiscent of a *shtetl* (ghetto) in pre-Holocaust Eastern Europe. Dress conservatively, don't take photos without permission and avoid the area during Shabbat.

MUSEUMS
The Holocaust museum **Yad Vashem** (Map pp284-5; ☎ 644 3565; www.yadvashem.org; Mt Zikaron; admission free; ☻ 9am-5pm Sun-Thu, 9am-2pm Fri) is a moving memorial to the six million victims of the Nazi Holocaust. An impressive US$56 million history museum, completed in 2005, includes the tear-jerking 'Hall of Names'. This rotunda is the physical repository for the Pages of Testimony – forms filled out by friends and family of Holocaust victims;

three million have so far been collected. The hole dug out of the floor honours those victims whose names will never be known. Equally moving, the solitary flame reflected infinitely inside the Children's Memorial remembers the 1.5 million Jewish children exterminated in the Holocaust.

Next to Yad Vashem is the grave of Theodore Herzl and the **Herzl Museum** (Map pp284-5; ☎ 643 3266; adult/child 20/15NIS; ☻ 8am-5pm Sun-Thu) dedicated to the Zionist movement that he founded. Bus Nos 13, 17, 18, 20 or 27 drop you off near the Herzl Museum.

The **Bible Lands Museum** (Map pp284-5; ☎ 561 1066; www.blmj.org; 25 Granot St, Givat Ram; adult/child/student 28/15/15NIS; ☻ 9.30am-5.30pm Sun-Tue & Thu, 9.30am-9.30pm Wed in summer, 1.30-9.30pm Wed in winter, 9.30am-2pm Fri, 11am-3pm Sat) chronologically reveals the history of the Holy Land with a wealth of well-displayed artefacts and background information.

The country's major museum complex is the **Israel Museum** (Map pp284-5; ☎ 670 8811; www.imj .org.il; Rupin St, Givat Ram; adult/child/student 40/20/30NIS; ☻ 10am-4pm Mon, Wed & Sat, 4-9pm Tue, 10am-9pm Thu, 10am-2pm Fri), just west of the New City. An assemblage of several major collections of national historical and artistic significance, it also includes a peaceful sculpture garden and the jar-shaped and architecturally inspiring **Shrine of the Book**. Here you'll see background displays and examples of the Dead Sea Scrolls, which were uncovered at Qumran between 1947 and 1956. Your ticket is also good for seven days to visit the Rockefeller Museum in East Jerusalem.

A cross between a museum, a theatre and a carnival ride is the **Time Elevator** (Map p286; ☎ 625 2228; www.time-elevator-jerusalem.co.il; Beit Agron, 37 Hillel St; admission 48NIS; ☻ 1-5.30pm). Spectators are jolted around in their seats along with the on-screen action as Chaim Topol (star of Fiddler on the Roof) leads them through Jerusalem's equally moving history.

COURSES
Language
British Council (Map pp284-5; ☎ 626 7111; issa .faltas@ps.britishcouncil.org; 31 Nablus Rd) Offers Arabic language courses beginning in September, January and April. Classes meet at the East Jerusalem branch twice weekly for 10 weeks and cost 900NIS.
YMCA (Map pp284-5; ☎ 569 2692; fax 623 5192; 26 HaMelekh David St) A three-month Hebrew language course is available at the YMCA *ulpan* for 900NIS.

ISRAEL & THE PALESTINIAN TERRITORIES

JERUSALEM FOR CHILDREN

The list of kid-friendly sites around Jerusalem begins with the excellent **Biblical Zoo** (☎ 675 0111; www.jerusalemzoo.org.il; Masua Rd; adult/child 3-8/senior 40/32/32NIS; ☼ 9am-6pm Sun-Thu, 9am-4.30pm Fri, 10am-5pm Sat) in the southwest of the city, which includes just about every pair of animals that Noah could fit in his ark. Other obvious attractions for kids are the **Time Elevator** (p291), the **Kotel Western Walls** (p289) and **Hezekiah's Tunnel** (p290) where they can make like Indiana Jones and wade through an ancient water channel. Also try the **Tower of David Museum** (p290), which often has special exhibitions for kids – recently featured was a giant model train set snaking its way around the ruins. Outside Jerusalem, **Mini Israel** (☎ 08-921 4121; www.minisrael.co.il; ☼ 10am-6pm Nov-Mar, 10am-8pm Apr-Oct) shrinks 330 of Israel's famed attractions down to scale-model size. It's near the Latrun Junction, halfway to Tel Aviv if you're headed that way.

TOURS

A good introduction to the city is Egged's **Route 99 Circular Line** (ticket 9.90NIS; ☼ 10am & noon Sun-Fri). This coach service, which departs from Safra Sq, cruises past 36 of Jerusalem's major sites, with basic commentary that's more or less in English.

Zion Walking Tours (Map p288; ☎ 050 530 5552; Omar Ibn al-Khattab Sq) operates a three-hour Old City walking tour (US$15 per person) at 10am, 11am and 2pm Sunday to Thursday (when there are at least four participants).

David Tours (Map p288; ☎ 052 863 8550; www.davidstours.com; 24 Cardo, Jewish Quarter) does a variety of city tours including one of the Temple Mount (US$25/23 per adult/student).

SLEEPING

A lack of tourism during the last intifada closed down most budget places in the New City, forcing backpackers to take refuge in East Jerusalem and the Old City. Midrange travellers have many more options in the New and Old Cities, including friendly B&Bs, historic Christian hospices and boutique hotels, among others. Top-end hotels are mostly located in the posh neighbourhoods of Yemin Moshe and Mamila in the New City. Better-value business-style hotels are clustered in the Sheikh Jarrah neighbourhood of East Jerusalem.

For a list of B&Bs, contact the **Home Accommodation Association of Jerusalem** (☎ 645 2198; www.bnb.co.il; PO Box 7547, Jerusalem 91074).

Old City
BUDGET

Citadel Youth Hostel (Map p288; ☎ 628 5253; www.citadelhostel.com; 20 Mark St; dm 30NIS, d with bathroom 150-190NIS, without bathroom 70-120NIS; ☐) This Palestinian-run guesthouse, with a cave-like entrance, has a mix of scruffy dorms and better private rooms decorated along traditional Arabic lines. Bathroom facilities are mediocre but the rooftop views are dramatic and the management is excellent. Free wi-fi available.

Hebron Youth Hostel (Map p288; ☎ 628 1101; ashraftabasco@hotmail.com; 8 Aqabat at-Takiya St; dm 25NIS, d with/without bathroom 100/70NIS; ☐) This venerable old hostel, with a magnificent stone interior, is buried inside the Muslim Quarter's Souq Khan al-Zeit. Facilities include a billiards table and lockers to protect your valuables.

Petra Hostel (Map p288; ☎ 628 6618; www.inisrael.com/petra; Omar Ibn al-Khattab Sq; roof mattresses/dm 25/35NIS, d with/without bathroom 150/120NIS; ☐) Converted from a grand old hotel (which has housed Mark Twain and Herman Melville), the Petra is starting to come apart at the seams but still retains a friendly atmosphere and first-class management. A big attraction is the Jaffa Gate location and spectacular views over the Old City. Laundry services are available, as well as airport shuttle and 24-hour hot water.

New Hashimi Hotel & Hostel (Map p288; ☎ 628 4410; www.hashimihotel.com; 73 Souq Khan al-Zeit; dm/s/d/ste US$8/30/35/120; ✄ ✄ ☐) Down the souq from the Golden Gate, the Hashimi has a variety of rooms built around a sunny atrium. Strict Islamic house rules prevent unmarried couples from sleeping in the same room. A variety of services includes laundry, a gift shop and café.

Golden Gate Inn (Map p288; ☎ 628 4317; goldengate442000@yahoo.com; 10 Souq Khan al-Zeit; dm/s/d/tr 30/100/120/150NIS) Just off a busy souq in the Muslim quarter, the Golden Gate is an underrated option with a large kitchen, friendly management and cool rooms protected from the heat and noise by thick walls.

El Malak (Map p288; ☎ 628 5382, 054 567 8044; 18 El-Malak & 27 Ararat; dm/s/d 50/100/150NIS) This B&B-style place, located in the Jewish Quarter, has

several partitioned rooms in the cool basement of an Armenian home. The dorms are
overpriced but the private rooms are good
value. Two better rooms are also available
in the house upstairs. Ask for Claire Ghawi.

MIDRANGE

East New Imperial Hotel (Map p288; ☎ 628 2261;
www.newimperial.com; Jaffa Gate; s/d/tr US$35/55/75;
⊠ ▣) This rambling old hotel was built
in 1885 on the site of Bath Shebiye, where
King David supposedly saw the wife of
Uriah bathing in a pool. It's got loads of
character, and the common rooms are decorated with lovely Palestinian embroidered
clothing and an incredible hand-drawn
family tree.

Christ Church Guest House (Map p288; ☎ 627
7727; www.itac-israel.org; Omar Ibn al-Khattab Sq; Jaffa
Gate; s/d US$50/80, extra person US$25) This is in the
Anglican compound near Jaffa Gate and
enjoys a quiet and comfortable atmosphere.
Attached are the Christian Heritage Centre
and an Anglican church that's built in the
form of a synagogue for Messianic Jews.
Prices include breakfast.

Austrian Hospice (Map p288; ☎ 627 1466; www.aus
trianhospice.com; 37 Via Dolorosa; dm/s/d/tr €14/42/66/93;
⊠) Looking like a prime location to shoot a
film about chain-rattling ghosts or Christian
crusaders, this castle-like guesthouse offers
clean rooms off cavernous hallways. The
front porch and leafy garden are nice places
to share a beer with your fellow guests.

THE AUTHOR'S CHOICE

Lutheran Guest House (Map p288; ☎ 626
6888; www.luth-guesthouse-jerusalem.com; Marks
St; dm/s/d US$9/49.50/80; ⊠) The Lutheran
Guest House offers the best dormitory
rooms in the Old City, with clean, airy
rooms with traditional stone walls, and
comfortable bunk beds. A bonus is access to a wonderfully medieval kitchen
with plenty of room to spread out, cook
and socialise. Likewise, the private rooms
are some of the best around, on par with
rooms you'd find in the New City, albeit
with slightly higher prices. The backyard
rose garden and antique sitting room add
to the atmosphere. It's located right on the
crossroads between the Jewish, Christian
and Armenian quarters.

East Jerusalem

BUDGET

Faisal Hostel (Map p288; ☎ 628 7502; faisalsam@
hotmail.com; 4 HaNevi'im St; dm/d 25/80NIS; ▣) Political tensions run high in this very Palestinian
guesthouse, making it a popular meeting
point for freelance journalists, political activists and wannabe anarchists. Hisham, the
owner, provides free Internet, free tea and
free dialogue. Although Faisal is somewhat
dishevelled, no guesthouse in Israel offers
character quite like this place.

Palm Hostel (Map p288; ☎ 627 3189; 6 HaNevi'im St;
dm/d 25/80NIS; ▣) The Palm, reached through
a small vegetable stand, is cleaner than its
neighbour Faisal, but dimly lit and with less
character. Free Internet.

TOP END

American Colony (Map pp284-5; ☎ 627 9777; www.amcol
.co.il; 23 Nablus Rd, East Jerusalem; s US$175-340, d US$230-
700; Ⓟ ⊠ ⊠ ▣ ◉) Offering luxury and
class like no other hotel in Israel, this hotel
is in a league of its own. Despite its high-
brow status, it remains an unpretentious
place, a rendezvous point for journalists and
scholars as well as a temporary home for visiting celebrities. Former guests include Winston Churchill, Mikhail Gorbechov, Jimmy
Carter, Ingrid Bergman and John Steinbeck.

West Jerusalem

If you prefer to stay in West Jerusalem, plan
on spending double the price for similar
quality in other areas.

TOP END

King David Hotel (Map pp284-5; ☎ 620 8888; www.dan
hotels.com; 7 King David St; s US$228-488, d US$298-508;
Ⓟ ⊠ ⊠ ▣ ◉) Like a hangover from the
British mandate, the King David offers
old-world atmosphere, lush gardens and a
grand dining room. Note that some standard rooms are smaller than others, so if you
are given something resembling a janitor's
closet, ask to see another.

New City

BUDGET

At the time of writing, Mike's Place (p296)
was planning to set up a dormitory-only
guesthouse above the bar on Jaffa Rd.

Kaplan Hotel (Map p286; ☎ 625 4591; www.mznet
.org/kaplanhotel; 1 HaHavatzelet St, Zion Sq; s US$35-45,
d US$45-65; ⊠ ▣) With a very convenient

location next to Zion Sq, this small budget hotel has basic rooms with private bathroom and kitchen facilities.

MIDRANGE
Allenby 2 B&B (Map pp284-5; ☎ 052 578493; www.bnb.co .il/allenby; Allenby Sq 2, Romema; s US$20-55, d US$30-70; ☒ ☒ ▣) A comfortable, friendly B&B two minutes' walk from the central bus station. The irrepressible owner is a font of knowledge on the city and a delightful host. Rates include breakfast and use of the communal kitchen. Long-term rates are available.

St Andrew's Guest House (Map p288; ☎ 673 2401; www.scotsguesthouse.com; 1 David Remez St, Yemin Moshe; s/d/tr US$55/80/100; ℗ ☒) This charming hospice is not as gloomy as its counterparts in the Old City, but still retains a quaint feel, thanks to the fireplace, novel-stuffed reading room and old-world café. Rooms, most with balconies that overlook the Old City, are equipped with heater, fan and phone.

B-Green Guest House (Map pp284-5; ☎ 566 4220; www.bnb.co.il/green/index.htm; 4 Rachel Imeinu Rd, German Colony; s/d US$40/50; ☒) In a lively area 20 minutes' walk or a short bus ride from the Old City. Each fan-cooled room has private facilities and a kitchenette. Futons are available for a third guest at no extra charge.

Avissar's House (Map p288; ☎ 625 5447; www .jeru-avisar-house.co.il; 12 Hame-vasser St, Yemin Moshe; s US$63-118, d US$73-120; ☒ ☒) Owner Yossi offers a variety of well-kept suites and studio guest flats. It's one of the closest midrange places to the Old City, but unfortunately it imposes a minimum three-night stay.

Other recommended midrange places:
Le Sixteen B&B (Map pp284-5; ☎ 532 8008; www.bnb .co.il/le16/index.htm; 16 Midbar Sinai St, Givat Hamivtar;

s US$35-40, d US$55-60; ☒ ☒) Rates include breakfast and wi-fi access.
Hotel Palatin (Map p286; ☎ 623 1141; www.hotel -palatin.co.il; 4 Agrippas St; s/d US$60/70; ☒ ▣) Central location near Ben Yehuda St. Rates include breakfast and wi-fi access.
Hotel Habira (Map p286; ☎ 625 5754; jhabira@netvision .net.il; 4 HaHavatzelet St; s/d/tr US$40/50/60; ☒) Central location off Zion Sq. Competitive ates include breakfast.

EATING
Most of the fine dining places are in the New City, with a concentration of ethnic restaurants along Yoel Salomon St.

Old City
Moses Art Restaurant (Map p288; ☎ 628 0975; Omar Ibn al-Khattab Sq; ☯ 7.30am-1am) A friendly and informal Lebanese choice just inside Jaffa Gate in the Old City. The friendly owner Moses is always up for engaging political debate.

Armenian Tavern (Map p288; ☎ 627 3854; 79 Armenian Patriarchate Rd; meat dishes 35-45NIS; ☯ 11am-10.30pm Tue-Sun) In the Jaffa Gate area, this place attracts diners with its beautiful stone-and-tile interior and a gently splashing fountain. The strongly flavoured meat dishes are excellent, including *khaghoghi derev*, a spiced minced-meat mixture bundled in vine leaves.

Bonker's Bagels (Map p288; ☎ 627 2590; Tiferet Israel St; bagels 3-13NIS) This is a friendly little place where you can munch on the original Jewish snack with a choice of fillings.

Tzaddik's New York Deli (Map p288; ☎ 627 2148; Tiferet Israel St; hot dishes 20-29NIS, sandwiches 16-32NIS) A clone of a New York deli, this place is best known for its attached Internet café and convenient location near the Western Wall.

THE AUTHOR'S CHOICE
Papa Andrea's (Map p288; ☎ 628 4433; Aftemeos Market No 4; meals 35-60NIS; ☯ 11am-10.30pm) Head up the stairs at this old Christian-quarter building, down the street from the Church of the Holy Sepulchre, to Papa Andrea's, a wonderful rooftop restaurant that guarantees spectacular views from all angles. The food is hot, fresh and excellent, with a selection of soups and salads for starters, followed by platters of grilled meat and chips. The friendly staff and management are eager to please and not shy in lending an opinion to all matters political – apropos as you gaze over the Muslim, Jewish and Christian quarters below.

Ticho House (Map p286; ☎ 624 4186; Ticho House Museum, 9 Harav Kook St; meals 30-60NIS; ☯ 10am-midnight Sun-Thu, 10am-3pm Fri, 8pm-midnight Sat) This renowned bohemian café and restaurant is housed in the 19th-century home of artist Anna Ticho. You can eat a late breakfast from 10am to noon and for lunch and dinner the speciality is fish and vegetarian pasta dishes. On Tuesday at 8pm it holds a cheese-and-wine evening (75NIS) with live jazz music, for which bookings are required.

New City

1868 (Map pp284-5; ☎ 622 2312; 10 King David St; starters 35-70NIS, mains 80-120NIS; ☘ noon-midnight) This French-Italian gourmet restaurant is set in one of the oldest buildings in West Jerusalem, built (obviously) in 1868. It offers a choice of wines to complement a menu of lamb chops, roast beef and other meat-based dishes.

Village Green (Map p286; ☎ 625 3065; 33 Jaffa Rd; dishes 21-25NIS; ☘ 9am-10pm Sun-Thu, 9am-3pm Fri) This clean, kosher vegetarian place serves up a range of vegetable soups, quiches, veggie burgers, pizza, stuffed vegetables, blintzes, savoury pies and lasagne dishes, all served with home-baked bread. It has a well-stocked salad bar.

El Toro (Map p286; ☎ 623 3982; 23 Hillel St; ☘ noon-2am Sun-Thu, noon-5pm Fri, 8pm-2am Sat) Slick little bar-restaurant offering Latin American fare including burritos (25NIS) and 400g Argentinean steaks (75NIS). Try the 'cinco element' (55NIS) with five kinds of grilled meat. The first shot of vodka is free.

Caffit (Map pp284-5; ☎ 563 3584; 35 Emek Refa'im St; ☘ 7am-2am Sun-Thu, 7am-3pm Fri, 8pm-2am Sat) A buzzing atmosphere, candle-lit tables, healthy light meals and a lovely street-side patio make this a fine choice if you're in the trendy German Colony.

Quick Eats

There are surprisingly few felafel places in the Old City, and even fewer are especially good. For decent felafel, try the unnamed stall as you enter from Damascus Gate, in the narrow frontage between the two forking roads. Shwarma stands around the Church of the Holy Sepulchre and Jaffa Gate cater mostly to foreign tourists lured by the location. Walk down a back street or two, especially towards the Muslim Quarter, and you'll find cheaper, more authentic places.

The best value snack shops are in East Jerusalem; try the joint a few doors down from Faisal Guesthouse (shwarmas 12NIS).

In the New City, one of the most popular stands with locals is **King of Felafel & Shwarma** (Map p286; ☘ 8am-midnight), on the corner of King George V and Agrippas Sts, which serves Israeli and Ethiopian food.

Self-Catering

Mahane Yehuda market (Map pp284-5; btwn Jaffa & Agrippas Sts; ☘ Sun-Fri) Offers Jerusalem's best-value food shopping. For the best deals, stroll in just as it's winding down for the day (5.30pm to 6.30pm Sunday to Thursday in winter, 7.30pm to 8.30pm Sunday to Thursday in summer, and 3pm to 4pm Friday year-round), when stallholders are clearing out the day's produce.

DRINKING

East Jerusalem and the Old City roll up their pavements at sundown and only a hike into the New City will provide an alternative to beer and a book in your room. Yoel Salomon and Rivlin, the two parallel main streets in the New City, are lined with enough late-night bars and cafés to defeat even the most ardent pub-crawlers. The Russian compound is also a safe bet for drinks and late-night dancing.

Gong (Map p286; ☎ 625 0818; 33 Jaffa St; ☘ 7pm-2am) Dimly lit Japanese-influenced place with black lacquer furniture, blood-red lighting and blaring hip-hop sounds. It's mostly a bar but it also serves excellent appetizers such as sushi and chicken wings, as well as main dishes.

Yankee's Bar (Map p286; ☎ 625 6488; 12 Yoel Salomon St; ☘ 4pm-9.30am) This beer bar puts on a variety of events: Monday is all you can drink beer night (49NIS), jam sessions are held on Wednesday, outdoor concerts are held on Saturday and a DJ is in-house on Sunday.

Zolli's (Map p286; ☎ 054 812 4200; 5 Rivlin St; ☘ 4.30pm-late) Located down a narrow alley, this popular sports bar offers 12 draught beers, 15 flavours of tobacco for the nargileh (water pipe) and 50 types of whiskey.

ENTERTAINMENT
Nightclubs

Haoman 17 (☎ 678 1658; 17 Haoman St, Talpiot; admission 50-80NIS; ☘ 11pm-late Thu & Fri) With its warehouse location, booming sound system and great lighting, Haoman 17 is one of the ultimate clubbing venues. When you get down to Haoman St, it's opposite the Anjril Grill, under the Philips sign.

Glasnost (Map p286; ☎ 054 443 3153; 15 Heleni Ha-Malka St; ☘ 9pm-3am Thu & Sat, 2.30pm-2am Fri, 9pm-2am Mon) In the middle of a strip of grumpy Russian bars, this offers a lighter mood, especially on Friday when it hosts a salsa lesson (40NIS) from 2.30pm to 8pm. Monday is salsa night, when students put their moves on the floor. The bar is also open on Thursday and Saturday when it hosts DJs or live music.

ISRAEL & THE PALESTINIAN TERRITORIES

Underground (Map p286; ☎ 054 677 2856; 1 Yoel Salomon St; ☼ 9pm-6am) Cavelike bar and disco floor that reels in Jerusalem's teenage tearaways and first-time tourists.

Live Music

Mike's Place (Map p286; ☎ 052 267 0965; 37 Jaffa St; ☼ 4pm-5am) Nightly live music, pool tables and a 4pm to 9pm happy hour make this one of the most popular night spots in town.

Lab (Map pp284-5; ☎ 673 4116; adult/student 65/40NIS; 28 Hebron St; ☼ 10pm-3am Mon-Sat) Crafted out of a disused railroad warehouse, this innovative bar and theatre hosts young artists, musicians and dancers mainly interested in alternative and 'experimental' arts, hence the name. Call ahead for upcoming events.

Pargod Theatre (Map pp284-5; ☎ 625 8819; 94 Bezalel St) Great for jazz; jam sessions take place every Friday from 2.30pm to 5.30pm.

Gay & Lesbian Venues

Shoshan (Map p286; ☎ 623 3366; 4 Shoshan St; ☼ 9.30pm-2am) Gay places come and go. At the time of writing the main hangout was this small, slick bar at the end of a quiet alley south of Safra Sq. Dance parties are held Thursday and Friday, while Sunday is lesbian night.

Theatre & Classical Music

Jerusalem Theatre (Map pp284-5; ☎ 561 7167; 20 David Marcus St) The theatre offers simultaneous English-language translation headsets for certain performances. It's also home to the Jerusalem Symphony Orchestra.

Khan Theatre (Map pp284-5; ☎ 671 8281; www.khan .co.il; 2 David Remez Sq; adult/student 150/120NIS) Occasional English-language performances.

Binyanei Ha'Umah Conference Centre (Map pp284-5; 1 Shezar Rd; ☎ 622 2481) Is the residence of the Israel Philharmonic Orchestra.

Al-Masrah Centre for Palestine Culture & Art and Al-Kasaba Theatre (Map pp284-5; ☎ 628 0957; Abu Obeida St) Off Salah ad-Din St in East Jerusalem, these places stage plays, musicals, operettas and folk dancing in Arabic, often with an English synopsis.

Classical performances are held at the **YMCA** (Map pp284-5; ☎ 569 2692; 26 HaMelekh David St); at the **Jerusalem (Alpert) Music Centre** (Map p288; ☎ 623 4347; Mishkenot Sha'ananim), on alternate Fridays; and at **Beit Shmuel** (Map p288; ☎ 620 3435; www. beitshmuel.com; 6 Shema St), part of Hebrew Union College, on Saturday morning.

GETTING THERE & AWAY

Air

Jerusalem's Atarot airport is used mainly by international charter flights. When demand is high, domestic carriers Arkia and Israir will connect Jerusalem with Eilat and Haifa. These airlines have offices in Jerusalem:

Arkia (☎ 621 8444; fax 623 5758; 4th fl, 42 Agrippas St)
El Al (Map p286; ☎ 677 0207; fax 677 0255; 12 Hillel St)

Bus

From the sparkling **Egged central bus station** (Map pp284-5; ☎ 694 4888; Jaffa Rd), buses connect to all major cities and towns around Israel. Buses to Tel Aviv (17.70NIS, one hour) depart every 15 minutes; to Haifa (39NIS; 2½ hours), Tiberias (42NIS, 2½ hours) and Be'ersheva (32NIS, 1½ hours) depart roughly hourly; and to Eilat (65NIS, 4½ hours) buses depart four times daily. For day trips to the Dead Sea, including Ein Gedi (32NIS, two hours) or Masada (39NIS, 2½ hours), be sure to leave on the first service of the day (8.45am) or you'll be pressed to get back the same day. There is also service to Rachel's Tomb (3.80NIS, 25 minutes) near Bethlehem, departing every two hours.

For info on buses to Egypt, see p355.

Sherut

Sheruts (service taxis) are much faster than buses, depart more frequently and cost only a few shekels more; they're also the only way to travel during Shabbat. *Sheruts* for Tel Aviv (20NIS per person on weekdays, 30NIS on Friday and Saturday) depart from the corner of Harav Kook St and Jaffa Rd (Map p286).

Sheruts for all destinations on the West Bank and Gaza depart from the ranks opposite Damascus Gate in East Jerusalem.

Train

Trains to Tel Aviv's Arlosoroff station (adult/child 19/17NIS) leave hourly from 6.10am to 9.10pm Sunday to Thursday. The last train on Friday is at 3pm. A combo train/bus ticket saves a few shekels. Reach the station on bus No 6 from Jaffa Rd or the central bus station. Ring ☎ *5770 for more details.

GETTING AROUND

To/From the Airport

Bus No 947 departs from the central bus station for Ben-Gurion airport (20NIS, 40 minutes) at least hourly from 6.30am to

8.30pm Sunday to Thursday, 6am to 4.30pm Friday, 8.20pm to 10pm Saturday. Alternatively, **Nesher service taxis** (☎ 625 3233, 625 5332) picks up booked passengers from their accommodation 24 hours a day for 40NIS.

Bus
Jerusalem is laced with a very good network of city bus routes (5.30NIS per ride). Pick up a colour-coded route map (in Hebrew) from the Jaffa Gate tourist office. Or for the latest route information, call ☎ *2800.

Taxi
Plan on spending 20NIS to 25NIS for trips anywhere within the central area of town. Always ask to use the meter, or risk getting ripped off.

MEDITERRANEAN COAST

The Israeli coast from Ashkelon to Rosh HaNikra is a long band of white sand backed up by a flat, fertile coastal plain interrupted by low coastal hills. Most of Israel's growing population is concentrated in this area, particularly in Tel Aviv, Netanya, Haifa and a host of sprouting new suburbs and communities.

TEL AVIV   תל-אביב   תל אביב
☎ 03 / pop 1,160,000

Tel Aviv, barely a century old, is a greatly underrated Mediterranean city that proclaims a modern, tolerant, laissez-faire attitude while thumbing its nose at Jerusalem's piety and 3000-year history. Forsaking spirituality for the stock exchange, and tradition for the latest fads, this modern, secular city concerns itself with finance, commerce and, above all else, fun.

For visitors, Tel Aviv shows off an absorbing array of distinctive faces – a result of mass immigration from all over the Jewish world, along with its piles of intact cultural baggage. These days, a short walk connects the exotic orientalism of the Yemenite Quarter with the seedy cafés of Russified lower Allenby St and the Miami chic of the pastel, glass-fronted condos along the glitzy beachfront.

Orientation
Tel Aviv's bustling central area focuses on four roughly parallel north–south streets that follow 6km of seafront from the Yarkon in the north to the Yemenite Quarter (the 1930s town centre) in the south. Nearest the sand is Herbert Samuel Esplanade, while the hotel-lined HaYarkon St lies a block inland. The next main street to the east is backpacker-central Ben Yehuda St. The trendy shopping zone, Dizengoff St, is the geographic centre of the city. Allenby St, effectively a continuation of Ben Yehuda St, is lined with bars, cafés and second-hand bookshops.

MAPS
The English-language *Tel Aviv-Jaffa Tourist* map is an excellent resource and available for from the Tourist Information Centre (see p299). Most hotels also have the free *Tourist Map of Tel Aviv. Tel Aviv – The White City* (40NIS), published by editions de l'eclat, produces a (1:3000) map indicating where to find the various styles of Bauhaus architecture across the city. It is available at the **Bauhaus Centre** (Map p300;

TEL AVIV IN TWO DAYS
Begin day one with a visit to the **Nahum Goldman Museum of the Jewish Diaspora** (p300) at Tel Aviv University, followed by a wander around the **Tel Aviv Museum of Art** (p301). Have lunch downtown before exploring the **Yemenite Quarter** (p301) and **Carmel Market** (p301). Tuesday and Friday are best for these neighbourhoods, as nearby **Nahalat Binyamin Street** (p301) comes alive with a crafts fair. End the day with dinner and dancing at the Old Port.

Start out day two with an outdoor breakfast and wander through the **junk stalls** (p306) of Jaffa, buying up trinkets or any other discarded gems that catch your fancy. Spend the rest of your morning around **Old Jaffa** (p306), peeking into the **Ilana Goor museum** (p306) and Visitor's Centre. Relax after lunch in the arty neighbourhood of **Neve Tsedek** (p301), from where you can join the sunworshippers at Tel Aviv's **main beach** (p301). Dinner and a pub crawl around posh Rothschild and Lilienblum Sts is a fine way to cap of the southern part of the city.

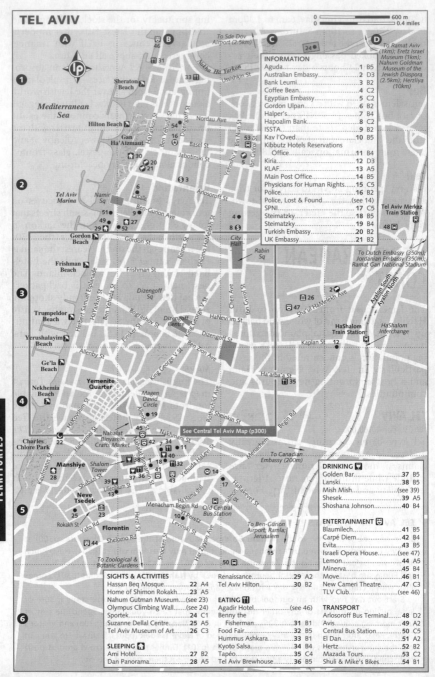

TEL AVIV

Mediterranean Sea

0 _____ 600 m
0 _____ 0.4 miles

To Sde Dov Airport (2.5km)

To Ramat Aviv (1km); Eretz Israel Museum (1km); Nahum Goldman Museum of the Jewish Diaspora (2.5km); Herzliya (10km)

Sheraton Beach
Hilton Beach
Gan Ha'Atzmaut
Tel Aviv Marina
Namir Sq
Gordon Beach
Frishman Beach
Trumpeldor Beach
Yerushalayim Beach
Ge'la Beach
Nekhemia Beach
Charles Chlore Park
Manshiye
Neve Tsedek
Florentin

Nordau Ave
Basel St
Jabotinsky St
Arlosoroff St
Gordon St
Frishman St
Dizengoff Sq
Dizengoff Centre
Dizengoff St
Allenby St
Yemenite Quarter
Magen David Circle
Nahalat Binyamin Crafts Market
Shalom Tower
Rabin Sq
City Hall
Kaplan St
HaShalom Train Station
HaShalom Interchange
Ayalon South
Ayalon North
Tel Aviv Merkaz Train Station

See Central Tel Aviv Map (p300)

To Dutch Embassy (350m); Jordanian Embassy (350m); Ramat Gan National Stadium

To Canadian Embassy (200m)

Menacham Begin Rd
Old Central Bus Station

To Ben-Gurion Airport; Ramla; Jerusalem

To Zoological & Botanic Gardens

INFORMATION
Aguda	1	B5
Australian Embassy	2	D3
Bank Leumi	3	B2
Coffee Bean	4	C2
Egyptian Embassy	5	C2
Gordon Ulpan	6	B2
Halper's	7	B4
Hapoalim Bank	8	C2
ISSTA	9	B2
Kav l'Oved	10	B5
Kibbutz Hotels Reservations Office	11	B4
Kiria	12	D3
KLAF	13	A5
Main Post Office	14	B5
Physicians for Human Rights	15	C5
Police	16	B2
Police, Lost & Found	(see 14)	
SPNI	17	C5
Steimatzky	18	B5
Steimatzky	19	B2
Turkish Embassy	20	B2
UK Embassy	21	B2

SIGHTS & ACTIVITIES
Hassan Beq Mosque	22	A4
Home of Shimon Rokakh	23	A5
Nahum Gutman Museum	(see 23)	
Olympus Climbing Wall	(see 24)	
Sportek	24	C1
Suzanne Dellal Centre	25	A5
Tel Aviv Museum of Art	26	C3

SLEEPING
Ami Hotel	27	B2
Dan Panorama	28	A5
Renaissance	29	A2
Tel Aviv Hilton	30	B2

EATING
Agadir Hotel	(see 46)	
Benny the Fisherman	31	B1
Food Fair	32	B5
Hummus Ashkara	33	B1
Kyoto Salsa	34	B4
Tapéo	35	C4
Tel Aviv Brewhouse	36	B5

DRINKING
Golden Bar	37	B5
Lanski	38	B5
Mish Mish	(see 39)	
Shesek	39	A5
Shoshana Johnson	40	B4

ENTERTAINMENT
Blaumilech	41	B5
Carpé Diem	42	B4
Evita	43	B5
Israeli Opera House	(see 47)	
Lemon	44	A5
Minerva	45	B4
Move	46	B1
New Cameri Theatre	47	C3
TLV Club	(see 46)	

TRANSPORT
Arlosoroff Bus Terminal	48	D2
Avis	49	B5
Central Bus Station	50	C5
El Dan	51	A2
Hertz	52	C2
Mazada Tours	53	C2
Shuli & Mike's Bikes	54	B1

☎ 522 0249; www.bauhaus-center.com; 99 Dizengoff St; 🕒 10am-7.30pm Sun-Thu, 10am-2.30pm Fri).

Information

BOOKSHOPS

Halper's (Map p298; ☎ /fax 629 9710; halpbook@netvision.net.il; 87 Allenby St) Specialist in English-language titles.

Lametayel (Map p300; ☎ 616 3411; www.lametayel.com; Dizengoff Centre) Specialist shop for travel books and maps.

Steimatzky (Map p300; ☎ 522 1513; 109 Dizengoff St) Chain bookstore. The company's other locations include the Central Bus Station, the Dizengoff Centre, the Opera Tower Centre, and at 71 and 103 Allenby St (Map p298).

EMERGENCY

Emergency ambulance (☎ 101)
Fire department (☎ 102)
Police (☎ 100)
Tourist police (Map p300; ☎ 516 5832; cnr Herbert Samuel Esplanade & Geula St) There is also a police booth at the main post office that will record lost items.

INTERNET ACCESS

If you have your own laptop, wi-fi access is available at the Old Port restaurant strip.
Coffee Bean (Map p298; ☎ 579 8669; 73 Ibn Gvirol St; 🕒 7.45am-12.30am Sun-Thu, 7.45am-3.30am Fri, 8.45am-1am Sat) Wired café, which will even let you borrow a wi-fi card if you don't have one (upon deposit of picture ID).

Masarik (Map p300; ☎ 527 2411; 🕒 7am-1am Sun-Fri, 9am-2am Sat) Wi-fi access.

Private Link (Map p300; ☎ 529 9889; private_link@hotmail.com; 78 Ben Yehuda St; per hr 13NIS)

Surf-Drink-Play (Map p300; per hr 10NIS; 🕒 24hr) 112 Dizengoff St (☎ 529 1618); 65 Ibn Gvirol St (☎ 695 8750); 77 King George V St (☎ 629 1311) Three locations with Internet access.

Web Stop (Map p300; ☎ 620 2682; 28 Bograshov St; per hr 12NIS)

INTERNET RESOURCES

www.tel-aviv.gov.il/english Official website for the municipality.
www.tel-aviv-insider.com Excellent tips on activities, dining and nightlife.

LAUNDRY

Nameless self-serve laundromats (12NIS washing machine, 5NIS dryer; open 24 hours) are widespread. A relatively clean one is at 104 Ben Yehuda St.

Momo's Bar (Map p300; 28 Ben Yehuda St) also has self-service laundry, affording you the chance to start your pub crawl in sparkling attire.

LEFT LUGGAGE

Left-luggage facilities are available at Ben-Gurion airport for a pricey US$4 per day. Most guesthouses and hotels in Tel Aviv have a left-luggage room, charging between 2NIS to 10NIS per day.

MEDIA

Time Out Tel Aviv, produced bi-monthly, is a great resource for what's on in the city. It's available at the Tel Aviv Tourist Information Centre.

MEDICAL SERVICES

Dr Ayaldan (Map p300; ☎ 525 4186) For dental services, try this doctor in the Dizengoff shopping centre.

Physicians for Human Rights (Map p298; ☎ 687 3718, 687 3027; fax 687 3029; 52 Golomb St; 🕒 5-7pm Sun, Tue & Wed) This clinic provides free medical assistance for visitors who aren't covered by health insurance in Israel.

MONEY

The best currency-exchange deals are at the private bureaus that don't charge commission, and there are plenty of them. Try the change bureau at the foot of the Opera Tower escalator. Most post offices also change traveller's cheques. ATMs are similarly widespread. Note that the Amex office in Tel Aviv will not change travellers cheques. ATMs are available at major banks – Bank Leumi, Mizrahi Bank and Hapoalim Bank.

POST

Main post office (Map p298; HaRakevet St; 🕒 7am-6pm Sun-Thu, 7am-noon Fri) On the corner of Yehuda HaLevi St. This is the place to pick up poste restante.

TOURIST INFORMATION

Tourist Information Centre (Map p300) City Hall (☎ 521 8214; 69 Ibn Gvirol St, Lobby, City Hall); Downtown (☎ 516 6188; 46 Herbert Samuel Esplanade)

TRAVEL AGENCIES

American Express (Map p298; ☎ 777 8880; fax 777 8801; Beit El Al Bldg, cnr Ben Yehuda & Shalom Aleichem Sts; 🕒 9am-5pm Sun-Thu, 9am-1pm Fri) Can book tours and flights.

ISSTA (Map p300; ☎ 521 0555; www.issta.co.il; 109 Ben Yehuda St; 🕒 9am-6pm Sun-Thu, 8.30am-1pm Fri) Student

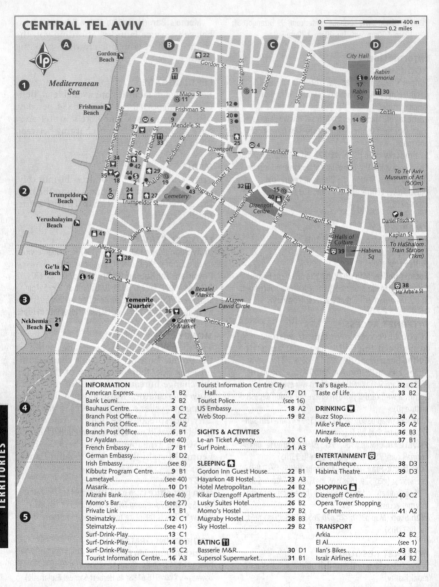

CENTRAL TEL AVIV

INFORMATION	
American Express	1 B2
Bank Leumi	2 B2
Bauhaus Centre	3 C1
Branch Post Office	4 C2
Branch Post Office	5 A2
Branch Post Office	6 B1
Dr Ayaldan	(see 40)
French Embassy	7 B1
German Embassy	8 D2
Irish Embassy	(see 8)
Kibbutz Program Centre	9 B1
Lametayel	(see 40)
Masarik	10 D1
Mizrahi Bank	(see 40)
Momo's Bar	(see 27)
Private Link	11 B1
Steimatzky	12 C1
Steimatzky	(see 41)
Surf-Drink-Play	13 C1
Surf-Drink-Play	14 D1
Surf-Drink-Play	15 C2
Tourist Information Centre	16 A3

Tourist Information Centre City Hall	17 D1
Tourist Police	(see 16)
US Embassy	18 A2
Web Stop	19 B2

SIGHTS & ACTIVITIES	
Le-an Ticket Agency	20 C1
Surf Point	21 A3

SLEEPING	
Gordon Inn Guest House	22 B1
Hayarkon 48 Hostel	23 A3
Hotel Metropolitan	24 B2
Kikar Dizengoff Apartments	25 C2
Lusky Suites Hotel	26 B2
Momo's Hostel	27 B2
Mugraby Hostel	28 B3
Sky Hostel	29 B2

EATING	
Basserie M&R	30 D1
Supersol Supermarket	31 B1

Tal's Bagels	32 C2
Taste of Life	33 B2

DRINKING	
Buzz Stop	34 A2
Mike's Place	35 A2
Minzar	36 B3
Molly Bloom's	37 B1

ENTERTAINMENT	
Cinematheque	38 D3
Habima Theatre	39 D3

SHOPPING	
Dizengoff Centre	40 C2
Opera Tower Shopping Centre	41 A2

TRANSPORT	
Arkia	42 B2
El Al	(see 1)
Ilan's Bikes	43 B2
Israir Airlines	44 B2

travel agency that can sometimes come up with very well-priced airline tickets. It's on the corner with Ben-Gurion.

UNIVERSITIES

Tel Aviv University (☎ 642 2752; www.tau.ac.il; Ramat Aviv 69978) Israel's biggest university is located on a leafy campus a couple of kilometres north of the Yarkon River. Worthy of a wander if you've come up here

to see the on-site Nahum Goldman Museum of the Jewish Diaspora (see below).

Sights
MUSEUMS

The recommended **Nahum Goldman Museum of the Jewish Diaspora** (☎ 646 2020; www.bh.org.il; Beit Hatefutsoth, 2 Klausner St, Matiyahu Gate, Ramat Aviv;

adult/student 34/24NIS; ☾ 10am-4pm Sun-Tue, 10am-6pm Wed) has dioramas, films and displays chronicling 2500 years of Jewish culture in exile. It's on the grounds of Tel Aviv University, 2.5km north of the Yarkon River. Take bus No 25 from King George V St or bus No 27 from the central bus station.

Eretz Israel Museum (☎ 641 5244; 2 Chaim Levanon St, Ramat Aviv; adult/student 33/22NIS; ☾ 9am-3pm Sun-Thu, 10am-2pm Fri & Sat), south of the Diaspora museum, consists of 11 themed collections (glass, ceramics, folklore etc) constructed around the Tel Qasile archaeological site.

Tel Aviv Museum of Art (Map p298; ☎ 607 7000; www.tamuseum.com; 27 Shaul HaMelekh Ave; adult/student 40/32NIS; ☾ 10am-4pm Mon & Wed, 10am-8pm Tue & Thu, 10am-2pm Fri, 10am-4pm Sat) is home to a superb permanent collection of Impressionist and post-Impressionist works, as well as some fine 20th century avant-garde. Works by Picasso, Matisse, Gauguin, Degas and Pollock feature prominently, though the gem of the collection is van Gogh's *The Shepherdess* (1889).

YEMENITE QUARTER
The Yemenite Quarter's maze of narrow, cobbled streets and crumbling buildings seems at odds with the clean-cut modernism of the rest of Tel Aviv. Imbued with an oriental flavour, the **Carmel Market** is one of the few places in the city that reminds visitors of Tel Aviv's Middle Eastern location. Push past the first few metres of knock-off brand-name clothing and trainers to reach the more aromatic and enticing stalls of fresh fruits and vegetables, hot breads and spices. Nearby **Nahalat Binyamin Street** is a busy pedestrianised precinct full of fashionable cafés and arty shops. On Tuesday afternoon and Friday midday, it hosts a crafts market and fills with buskers and other street performers.

NEVE TSEDEK
Lovely Neve Tsedek, with its narrow streets and historic houses, is one of Tel Aviv's most upmarket and character-filled neighbourhoods. In the late 19th century it was the choice area for intellectual Jews looking for a prestigious address.

The **Suzanne Dellal Centre** (Map p298; ☎ 510 5656; www.suzannedellal.org.il; 5 Yechieli St), a former school and cultural centre, serves as a venue for festivals, exhibits and cultural events, as

well as a relaxing place to look at artistic murals and spend a sunny afternoon. On weekends, you can visit the historic 1887 **home of Shimon Rokakh** (Map p298; ☎ 516 8042; www.rokach-house.co.il; 36 Rokakh St; admission 10NIS; ☾ 10am-4pm Sun-Thu, 10am-2pm Fri & Sat), with a video and exhibits outlining life in 19th-century Tel Aviv. On the same street is the **Nahum Gutman Museum** (Map p298; ☎ 516 1970; www.gutmanmuseum.co.il; 21 Rokakh St; admission adult/child 20/10NIS; ☾ 10am-4pm Sun, Mon, Wed, Thu, 10am-7pm Tue, 10am-2pm Fri, 10am-5pm Sat), which displays 200 lively and fanciful works by the 20th-century Israeli artist.

Activities
The **Olympus Climbing Wall** (Map p298; ☎ 699 0910; 42 Rokakh Ave; www.kir.co.il; admission & harness 50NIS, shoe rental 12NIS; ☾ 5-10pm Sun-Thu, 2-8pm Fri, 11am-9pm Sat) is located in the Sportek, along the Yarkon river. Avoid overcrowded Saturdays.

The **Sportek** (Map p298) also has basketball courts, a skate park and trampolines. Ultimate Frisbee matches are held here every Friday at 4.45pm and Saturday at 4.30pm.

Tel Avivans are passionate about their football team, the Maccabee Tel Aviv. Big matches are played October to June at Ramat Gan National Stadium, reached from downtown bus Nos 20, 42 or 67. Buy your ticket at the stadium on game day for 40NIS to 120NIS or in advance from **Le-an ticket agency** (Map p300; ☎ 524 7373; 101 Dizengoff St).

Budding yachties may want to contact **Danit Tours** (☎ 052 3400128; www.danit.co.il), which runs sailing and motorboat trips from the Tel Aviv Port. For a group of up to 13 people it costs 1500NIS for two hours at sea.

At Tel Aviv's main beach is a fine place for swimming and surfing. Windsurfers can rent equipment from **Surf Point** (Map p300 ☎ 517 0099; www.surf-point.co.il; Nekhemia Beach) for a pricey 100NIS per hour.

Courses
Gordon Ulpan (Map p298; ☎ 522 3095; hadas.goren@012.net.il; LaSalle 7, Tel Aviv) Hebrew-language programme that charges around 500NIS per month, plus 70NIS registration fee.

Sleeping
If you have your own car, ask your hotel if it offers parking. Otherwise, you'll need to pay around 45 to 50NIS per day to keep your car in a car park.

BUDGET

Tel Aviv's lively budget hostels are concentrated near the central beaches, trendy restaurants, shopping centres and nightspots. Those who prefer solitude may want to consider staying in nearby Jaffa.

Hayarkon 48 Hostel (Map p300; ☎ 516 8989; www .hayarkon48.com; 48 HaYarkon St; dm 47NIS, d 185-225NIS; ⊠ ▣) Renovated from a converted school, this hostel sits just two blocks from the beach and has excellent facilities including a clean kitchen, great showers and a free breakfast. Booking through its website could net you a small discount on double rooms.

Momo's Hostel (Map p300; ☎ 528 7471; www.momos hostel.com; 28 Ben Yehuda St; dm 40NIS, d 100-130NIS; ⊠) This colourful, character-filled place has an attached bar-café and a central location. Rates include a light breakfast and use of the kitchen. Men and women (including married couples), and travellers and long-term workers, have separate dorms. In summer you can sleep on the roof for 35NIS.

Sky Hostel (Map p300; ☎ 620 0044; skyhostel@ walla.com; 34 Ben Yehuda St; dm/d 45/100NIS; ⊠ ▣) One block north of Momo's, this place is rather more staid than its neighbour, but with a touch more privacy.

Mugraby Hostel (Map p300; ☎ 510 2443; www .mugraby-hostel.com; 30 Allenby St; dm 43NIS, s with/without shower 170/150NIS, d with/without shower 190/170NIS; ▣) Grubby fallback should the aforementioned have suffered some ignoble fate.

MIDRANGE

Note that prices for these places vary according to the season; the highest rates apply mainly to the summer high season and Jewish holidays.

Kikar Dizengoff Apartments (Map p300; ☎ 524 1151; www.hotel-apt.com; 89 Dizengoff St; s US$60-90, d US$75-90, ste US$140; ℗ ⊠ ⊠ ▣) Overlooking Dizengoff Sq, these comfortable self-contained units are hard to beat for price and quality. All four types of units have cable TV, safes and kitchenettes. Book through the Internet for discounted price.

Gordon Inn Guest House (Map p300; ☎ 523 8239; www.sleepinisrael.com; 17 Gordon St; s US$30-40, d US$40-55; ℗ ⊠ ⊠) This hybrid hostel/hotel is a well-kept and friendly downtown option. Cheaper shared rooms have a shared bathroom. All rates include breakfast. Take bus No 4 from the central bus station.

Lusky Suites Hotel (Map p300; ☎ 516 3030; www .luskysuites-htl.co.il; 84 HaYarkon St; d/ste US$70/110; ℗ ⊠ ⊠) A smart lobby leads up to well-appointed rooms, some with an en suite and kitchenette. The 'penthouse' could even squeeze into the top-end category.

Ami Hotel (Map p298; ☎ 524 9141; www.inisrael.com /ami; 152 HaYarkon St; s/d/ste US$50/65/80; ℗ ⊠ ⊠) This friendly, rambling option near the cluster of luxury hotels has decent rooms, some with sea views, others with balconies.

Hotel Metropolitan (Map p300; ☎ 519 2727; www .hotelmetropolitan.co.il; 11-15 Trumpeldor St; s/d US$105/ 127; ℗ ⊠ ⊠) Clean and central; the Met has a few suites that cost about 50% more than the standard rooms.

TOP END

Most of Tel Aviv's top-end palaces rise just a quick shuffle from the beach and, as with the midrange places, rates change with the season. Generally, a good travel agent will get a better deal than you'll manage on your own. All have Internet wi-fi access.

Tel Aviv Hilton (Map p298; ☎ 520 2222; hiltonisrael sales.telaviv@hilton.com; Gan HaAtzma'ut or Independence Park; d US$260-355; ℗ ⊠ ⊠ ▣ ▣) With its parkland setting and beach access, this is one of the best choices.

Renaissance (Map p298; ☎ 521 5555; www.renais sancehotels.com; 121 HaYarkon St; d US$145-165; ℗ ⊠ ⊠ ▣ ▣) Set amid other high-rise luxury hotels, this one distinguishes itself by having a slightly better location overlooking a sandy beach.

Dan Panorama (Map p298; ☎ 519 0190; www.dan hotels.com; 10 Kaufmann St; d US$166-214; ℗ ⊠ ⊠ ▣ ▣) Reasonably comfortable and well known, but a long walk from the centre of things.

Eating

RESTAURANTS

Despite its small size Tel Aviv can rival even the biggest European cities for its diversity and quality of restaurants. Spanish tapas bars are *en vogue*, but you'll also find everything from sheikh Japanese fusion joints to American-style brew-pubs.

Brasserie M&R (Map p300; ☎ 696 7111; 70 Ibn Gvi-rol St; dishes 50-100NIS; ◷ noon-5am; ⊠) Wannabe French 'matradies' (complete with surly attitude) serve up mouth-watering steak and chicken dishes, in a dimly lit brasserie that stays busy even until the wee hours. It's quietly known as a meeting place for local celebrities, but still maintains a neighbourhood atmosphere.

Benny the Fisherman (Map p298; ☎ 544 0764; Old Port; dishes 70-90NIS; ☺ noon-midnight) Serving up large portions of grilled fish, shrimp and calamari, with an excellent location overlooking the harbour, this is arguably the best fish restaurant in Tel Aviv.

Agadir Hotel (Map p298; ☎ 544 4045; Old Port; burgers 30-40NIS; ☺ noon-6am; ☒) About 500m north of Benny the Fisherman is another swanky restaurant with fine food offerings, mostly steaks and burgers. This one is done up like a Moroccan hotel lobby from the 1920s.

Kyoto Salsa (Map p298; ☎ 566 1234; 31 Montefiore St; dishes 50-100NIS ☺ noon-midnight; ☒) Tel Aviv's answer to Sushi Samba of Manhattan fame, this fuses sushi and margaritas into a winning combination. The excellent menu ranges from Latin-spiced seafood casserole to Japanese business set lunch for 59NIS.

Tel Aviv Brewhouse (Map p298; ☎ 516 8666; 11 Rothschild Ave; dishes 50-100NIS; 12.30pm-1am; ☒ ☒) Just south of the Shalom Tower, this is Tel Aviv's poshest bar-restaurant. Here, yuppies sip four kinds of designer lagers (26NIS for 500ml). Try the Masters, a 7% alcohol dark ale. The food is excellent, but doesn't stray much from the usual beer accompaniments.

Tapéo (Map p298; ☎ 624 0484; 16 Ha'arba'a St; dishes 15-40NIS; ☺ 7pm-1am; ☒) Salsa rhythms beat slowly in the background of this glossy tapas bar, located near the Cinemateque. Carefully prepared meat, veggie and fish selections go well with a bottle (or two) of Israeli wine (100NIS).

Taste of Life (Map p300; ☎ 620 3151; 60 Ben Yehuda St; dishes 30-45NIS; ☺ 9am-9pm Sun-Thu, 9am-2pm Fri) This place, run by African-Americans, does vegan cuisine that includes tasty veggie shwarma, steamed vegetables, vegetarian hot dogs, *tamali* (vegetables steamed in masa dough), *tofu-lafel* (felafel with tofu), barbecue twist burgers (veggie burgers with barbecue sauce), yogurts and shakes.

QUICK EATS

The heaviest concentration of Middle Eastern fast food is found along the busy reaches of Ben Yehuda and Allenby Sts.

The city's many cafés, most serving excellent salads and sandwiches, provide ringside seating for its continuous pavement carnival-cum-fashion show. Bakeries and nut stalls are common for people on the go. On Saturday afternoon, you can sample all sorts of fare when local restaurants set up an informal food fair along Rothschild Ave.

Hummus Ashkara (Map p298; 45 Yirmiyahu St; dishes 18NIS) This is where locals go when they are after excellent hummus and fuul (fava bean paste). Further credibility was earned when a national newspaper recently voted its hummus the best in Israel. The sign is in Hebrew only, so look out for the Coca-Cola sign and the tables on the street.

Tal's Bagels (Map p300; 69 Dizengoff St; bagel with toppings 18NIS) New York–style bagels served up with your choice of cream cheese or veggie toppings.

SELF-CATERING

Some of the best fresh fruit and vegetables anywhere are sold at the Carmel Market. For one-stop shopping, try the convenient **Supersol supermarket** (Map p300; 79 Ben Yehuda St; ☺ 7am-midnight Sun-Thu, 7am-4pm Fri, 8.30pm-midnight Sat).

Drinking

The bars clustered around the intersection of Allenby and Lilienblum Sts, and those along Sheinkin St, are considered locally to be the most fashionable. Travellers' bars and the dive spots on upper Allenby St remain the least-expensive option for serious beer aficionados, but it's hard to keep track of what's hot, what's not and what's gone.

Golden Bar (Map p298; ☎ 516 9194; 9 Rothschild Ave; ☺ 6pm-late) Even after the neighbouring Allenby-area bars have closed, this raucous yuppie bar is going strong. DJs play a strong mix of rock, blues and rap for patrons on the street-side patio or the small indoor dance floor. There is also a decent choice of pub grub scrawled onto a blackboard, including chicken wings, burgers and fries.

Shoshana Johnson (Map p298; ☎ 506 7443; 97 Allenby St; ☺ 6pm-late) A curious find in downtown Tel Aviv: where most places are all sleek chrome and neon lights, this one belongs in the Latin quarter of some other continent. Reels in a 30s crowd. There is no sign in English, so look for the 'Libros en Español' sign.

Lanski (Map p298; ☎ 517 0043; 1st fl, Shalom Tower; 6 Montefiore St; ☺ 9pm-late Sat-Thu, 10pm-late Fri) Built in the shape of an 'H' for maximum eye-contact opportunities, this bar makes claim to being the biggest in the Middle

East, an assertion we won't try to dispute. Sunday is bartender's night, when Tel Aviv's barmen come in to swap war stories.

Minzar (Map p300; ☎ 517 3015; 60 Allenby St; ☻ 24hr) Set back from the main street, this is a bohemian-style coffee bar that actually specialises in beer. Happy hour extends from 5pm to 10pm.

Mike's Place (Map p300; ☎ 052-267 0753; 86 Herbert Samuel Esplanade; ☻ 4pm-late) On the beach, this is the place to go for live music. Blues and rock bands play nightly from 10.30pm. There's also a sizable menu of grill-style meals, cocktails and, especially, beer. Happy hour lasts from 4pm to 9pm, and all day on Saturday.

Buzz Stop (Map p300; ☎ 510 0869; 86 Herbert Samuel Esplanade; ☻ 24hr) At the beach beside the US embassy, this place caters to night owls and dawn watchers who appreciate pub grub, a wide choice of beer and full English breakfasts (which are often administered as a hangover cure).

Shesek (Map p298; ☎ 516 9520; 17b Lilienblum St; ☻ 9pm-late) This rough-around-the-edges scenester bar is well known for pumping out a variety of music (smash-ups and punk to trance and avant-garde hip hop) and quality beer (including Taybeh, a microbrew manufactured in Ramallah).

Mish Mish (Map p298; ☎ 516 8178; 17a Lilienblum St; ☻ 8pm-late) Next door to Shesek, this place attracts a more upmarket crowd.

Molly Bloom's (Map p300; ☎ 522 1558; 2 Mendele St; ☻ 4pm-late Sat-Thu, noon-late Fri) One of only a handful of Irish pubs in Israel, Molly Bloom's is popular with both locals and diplomats that work at nearby embassies. The decent bar menu features such Gaelic options as Irish stew and shepherd's pie. Happy hour lasts from 4pm to 8pm nightly.

Entertainment

Tel Aviv is well known for its nightlife, and the mind-boggling variety of spots can keep you crawling all night long. The funkiest café district is undoubtedly Sheinkin St, which is a great place to meet people and soak up the atmosphere.

NIGHTCLUBS

Tel Aviv has a number of excellent, party-till-dawn clubs but it's essential that you dress to impress. Cover charges for dedicated discotheques range from 50NIS to 100NIS. Bars, many of which double as dance clubs, are free. For a full listing, pick up a copy of Time Out Tel Aviv, available at kiosks and hotels.

Move (Map p298; ☎ 602 0426; Old Port; admission 60NIS; ☻ 11pm-late Mon-Sat) If you only have the time (and money) for one club in Tel Aviv, make it this place. Bursting at the seams with young Israelis, the quandary of how so many people fit into such a small space is a sight to behold. Tuesday is gay night.

TLV Club (Map p298; ☎ 544 4194; Old Port; admission 50-100NIS ☻ midnight-late Mon, Fri, Sat) This large discotheque often has Israeli rock and pop stars; call to find out what's on. Admission prices vary depending on who's performing.

Blaumilech (Map p298; ☎ 560 8852; 32 Rothschild Ave; ☻ 7pm-late) Fashionable, low-lit lounge-bar with a small dance floor. Rather swanky clientele, mostly in their late 20s and 30s.

Lemon (Map p298; ☎ 681 3313; 17 HaNagarim St; ☻ Fri & Sat nights) Lemon holds house parties every Friday and Saturday, and is located in Florentin.

CINEMAS

In summertime, free films are sometimes screened on the beach near Allenby St.

Cinematheque (Map p300; ☎ 606 0800; 1 Ha'Arba'a St; admission 35NIS; ☻ 11am-late) This is the flagship in a chain of Israeli cinemas that feature classic, retro, foreign, avant-garde, new-wave, and off-beat films. Alternatively, choose a film from the video library and pay 20NIS for a private screening.

GAY & LESBIAN VENUES

Tel Aviv has the Middle East's most vibrant gay community, and even plays host to an annual Gay Pride Parade. Most of the nightlife is focused on Sheinkin and Nahalat Binyamin Sts, where you'll find plenty of rainbow flags, but the best gay night out in town is surely Tuesday at the Move (see above) in the Old Port. **Plug & Play** (☎ 527 5631; admission 30-60NIS), a suggestively named gay party, is held Thursday, Friday and Saturday. Call for the location.

Evita (Map p298; ☎ 566 9559; 31 Yavne St; ☻ noon-late) This preppy café mutates into a saucy gay lounge-bar by night. There's plenty of pelvic shaking and free-flowing alcohol. It's located on a quiet alley a half block south of Rothschild Ave.

Carpé Diem (Map p298; ☎ 560 2006; 17 Montefiore St; ☻ 8pm-late) A relaxed atmosphere pervades this place, aided by the back lounge deck which has floor seating on cushions. There are occasional professional strip performances: Monday for men and Tuesday for women.

Minerva (Map p298; ☎ 560 3801; 98 Allenby St; ☉ 10pm-late) Dedicated lesbian bar that was supposedly renovated, though it's still quite the seedy dive, which may appeal to some. DJ dance parties are held every Thursday.

THEATRE
New Cameri Theatre (Map p298; ☎ 606 0900; www .cameri.co.il; Golda Meir Centre, cnr Leonardo da Vinci & Sha'ul HaMelekh Sts) The new Cameri hosts theatre performances in Hebrew, with simultaneous English translation on Thursdays only. The theatre is in the **Israeli Opera House** (☎ 692 7777).

Habima Theatre (Map p300; ☎ 629 5555; Tarsat Blvd, Habima Sq) Home to Israel's national theatre company, Habima stages performances on Thursday, with simultaneous English-language translation.

Getting There & Away
AIR
Most travellers fly in and out of Ben-Gurion airport, usually on **El Al** (Map p300; ☎ 629 2312; www.elal.co.il; 32 Ben Yehuda St) but **Arkia** (Map p300; ☎ 699 2222; telavivb@arkia.co.il; 74 HaYarkon St) also has flights to Eilat (370NIS, 50 minutes, daily) and Haifa (442NIS, 20 minutes, daily except Saturday) from Sde Dov airport, north of the Yarkon River. The other domestic airline is **Israir** (Map p300; ☎ 795 5777; 23 Ben Yehuda St).

Travellers leaving Israel on El Al flights from Ben-Gurion airport can pre-check bags the day before their flight at the **Arlosoroff bus terminal** (Map p298; ☎ 695 8614; cnr Arlosoroff & AP Derakhim Sts; ☉ 4-9pm Sun-Thu, 11am-3pm Fri, 6-11pm Sat). At the time of writing no other airline offered this service, but it's worth asking.

BUS
From Tel Aviv's enormous **central bus station** (Map p298; ☎ 694 8888; Levinski St) outgoing intercity buses depart from the 6th floor, where there's also an efficient information desk. Suburban and city buses use the poorly signposted stalls on the 4th floor. Note that during Shabbat you'll have to resort to service taxis.

Buses leave for Jerusalem (17.70NIS, one hour) roughly every 10 minutes; for Haifa (23NIS, 1½ hours) every 15 to 20 minutes; Tiberias (42NIS, 2½ hours) once or twice hourly from 6am to 9pm; and Eilat (65NIS, five hours), more or less hourly from 6.30am to 5pm (an overnight service departs at 12.30am).

Tel Aviv's second bus station, the Arlosoroff terminal, adjoins the central train station northeast of the centre. To get there, take bus No 61, which travels along Allenby, King George V, Dizengoff and Arlosoroff Sts.

For information on buses to Egypt, see p355.

SHERUT
The *sheruts* outside the central bus station run to Jerusalem (20NIS) and Haifa (25NIS). On Saturday, they leave from HaHamashal St just east of Allenby St and charge about 20% more than the weekday fare.

TRAIN
Tel Aviv has two train stations: the main station, **Tel Aviv Merkaz** (Map p298; ☎ 577 4000, *5770; www.israrail.org.il/english), and the smaller **HaShalom station** (Map p298; HaShalom Interchange). From Tel Aviv Merkaz, you can travel to Haifa (24.50NIS, one hour), via Netanya (12.50NIS, 25 minutes), more or less hourly from 6am to 8pm Sunday to Friday, and on to Akko (34NIS, 1½ hours) and Nahariya (38NIS, 1¾ hours). Heading south, you can travel as far as Be'ersheva (25.50NIS, 1¼ hours, hourly). To reach Tel Aviv Merkaz from the centre, take bus Nos 61 or 62 north from Dizengoff St to the Arlosoroff bus terminal, which is a two-minute walk from the station.

Getting Around
TO/FROM THE AIRPORT
Bus No 222 runs hourly on the hour from the Dan Panorama hotel (p302) to Ben-Gurion airport (18NIS, 45 minutes) from 6am to 11pm Sunday to Thursday, 6am to 7pm Friday and noon to 11pm Saturday. En route the bus makes stops at the Sheraton Moriah and the Arlosoroff bus terminal (near Tel Aviv Merkaz train station). It also runs hourly in the opposite direction. From the central bus station, take bus No 475 (11.70NIS), departing every 20 to 30 minutes.

At least two trains per hour also service the airport from Tel Aviv Merkaz station (12NIS, 3.30am to 11pm daily).

BICYCLE

Tel Aviv is flat and traffic relatively light so it's easy to get around by bike. For rentals, try **Shuli & Mike's Bikes** (Map p298; ☎ 544 2292; www.shvoong.co.il; 245 Dizengoff St) or **Ilan's Bikes** (Map p300; ☎ 629 9901; 44 Bograshov St). A 24-hour rental costs around 50NIS.

BUS

Tel Aviv city buses follow an efficient network of routes. The single fare is 5.20NIS, but for 12NIS you can buy a red pass *(hofshi yomi)* which allows one day of unlimited bus travel around Tel Aviv and its suburbs. The city centre is well covered by bus No 4, which travels from the central bus station to the Reading Terminal via Allenby, Ben Yehuda and northern Dizengoff Sts. Bus No 5 also reaches Dizengoff Centre from the **central bus station** (☎ 639 4444).

TAXI

Tel Aviv special taxis suffer from the same rip-off tendencies that pervade the entire country (see p357). Plan on 20NIS to 25NIS for trips anywhere within the central city.

JAFFA   יפו יאפا
☎ 03 / pop 46,400

After Noah was catapulted to fame in a flood of worldwide proportions, one of his sons, Japheth, headed for the coast and founded a new city that was humbly named Jaffa (Yafo in Hebrew) in his own honour. During Solomon's time, it came to prominence as a major port city, but this largely Arab town has now been superseded – and swallowed up – by its neighbouring upstart Tel Aviv.

Today, it's a quaint and mostly Christian harbourside suburb where you'll get a taste of both the enigmatic Middle East and the fruits of the adjacent sea.

Sights & Activities

The central attraction is **Old Jaffa**, for thousands of years a thriving, tumble-down commercial port, now restored and preserved as an outdoor museum and tourist attraction. The once active residential community of longshoremen and market traders have long since been replaced by art studios, galleries and a sprinkling of outdoor cafés, making for a pleasant if somewhat staid one-hour stroll.

As you enter from Roslan St, walk past the boarded up Museum of Jaffa Antiquities (which may reopen pending an increase in visitors), to a grassy knoll called **HaPisgah Gardens**, where an **amphitheatre** affords a panorama of the Tel Aviv beachfront; ongoing archaeological excavations reveal Egyptian ruins dating back at least 3300 years.

From the gardens, a footpath leads to **Kikar Kedumim** (Kedumim Sq), which is ringed by restaurants and galleries but dominated by the orange-painted **St Peter's Monastery**. The small gift shop on the square acts as Old Jaffa's de facto **Tourist Information Centre**, offering up tourist information and free maps of the area.

Close by, in an underground chamber, the well-designed **Visitors Centre** (⌚ 10am-6pm) describes the history of Jaffa from its beginnings as a Canaanite settlement nearly 4000 years ago, through its development by and submission to various foreign armies, until its 1948 liberation from British rule by Jewish underground forces. The display is centred on some partially excavated dwellings from the Hellenistic and Roman eras; a guide *might* be on hand to provide some commentary.

A worthwhile stop is the **Ilana Goor Museum** (☎ 683 7676; www.ilanagoor.com; 4 Mazal Dagim St; admission adult/child/student/senior 24/14/20/20NIS; ⌚ 10am-4pm Sat-Thu, 10am-6pm Fri), housed in an 18th-century stone hostel for Jewish pilgrims. It features the design and wooden, stone, glass, bronze and iron sculpture of its namesake and owner, Ilana Goor.

Fancy an old boot or rusty xylophone? How about a six-foot tall grinning plastic monkey in a top hat and trench coat? Such treasures and more are waiting for new owners at a desultory marketlike expanse locally known as the **flea market** (junk market), which makes up the heart of new Jaffa. The market also has an array of shops with a more exotic, Oriental flavour, selling nargilehs and silver jewellery.

Normally, a free three-hour **Old Jaffa walking tour** departs from the **clock tower** at 9.30am Wednesday. Also worthwhile is a **boat tour** (☎ 682 9070; admission 20NIS) running every 30 minutes on Saturdays from 11am to 7pm.

Sleeping

Old Jaffa Hostel (☎ 682 2370; www.inisrael.com/old jaffahostel; 8 Olei Zion St; dm 40NIS, s 147-226NIS, d 168-246NIS) In a beautiful old Turkish home, the

ISRAEL & THE PALESTINIAN TERRITORIES

Jaffa is both friendly and atmospheric. The large bar and common room, as well as the airy dorms and comfortable private rooms, are decorated with historic Arabic furniture and *objets d'art*. The *Independent* recently included this place in a list of top 50 guesthouses worldwide (it ranked No 15). Enter from Ami'ad St.

Eating

For Israelis, Jaffa's main culinary attraction is fish, and both Mifraz Shlomo St and the port area boast numerous outdoor restaurants. Around the flea market you'll find plenty of hole-in-the-wall tamiya and felafel stands.

Itzik Bar (☎ 518 4882; 5 Olei Zion) Try this popular stand, which serves up two eggs, chips, salad and hummus for 20NIS.

Said Abu Elafia & Sons (☎ 681 2340; 7 Yefet St; 24hr) This is a bakery that has become a legend in Israel. In addition to all sorts of breads, pastries and *samosas* (locally called *sambusas*), it does a spinach-and-egg pitta and a uniquely Arab pizzalike concoction which involves cracking a couple of eggs on a pitta, stirring in tomato, cheese and olives, and baking it in the oven.

Dr Shakshuka (☎ 682 2842; 3 Beit Eshal St; meals 35-50NIS) This is a culinary highlight in the Tel Aviv area. Along with the eponymous *shakshuka* (a skillet concoction featuring egg, capsicum, tomato sauce and spices), the Gabso family whips up a range of Libyan and North African delights. For an enormous business lunch, you'll pay 64NIS; a massive 'complete couscous' spread with couscous, bread, salads, lamb and a stuffed potato will set you back just 44NIS. Don't miss it!

Puaa (☎ 682 3821; 3 Rabbi Yohanan St; mains from 45NIS) Part retro-style café and part flea market, this place specialises in lunchtime soups and salads, but dabbles in fish and chicken dishes. The beverage selection includes an excellent lassi yogurt drink with cardamom. In the unlikely event that you have a room that needs furnishing, you could also take home the plates, tables, chairs, silverware and wall hangings – everything is for sale.

Bernhardt Show (☎ 681 3898; 10 Kikar Kedumim; mains from 75NIS) This is an upmarket seafood blast, serving calamari, sea trout, mullet, mussels and other *fruits-de-mer* (including lobster from 220NIS). Those on a tight budget can stick to the starters and salads, which average 35NIS to 40NIS.

Getting There & Away

From the centre of Tel Aviv, it's a pleasant 2.5km seafront stroll to Old Jaffa. Alternatively, take bus No 46 from the central bus station, bus No 10 from Ben Yehuda St (or the train station), bus No 26 from Ibn Gvirol St, bus No 18 from Dizengoff St or bus Nos 18 or 25 from Allenby St, and get off

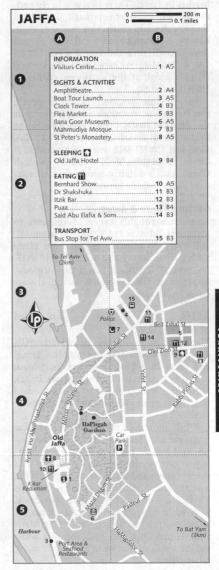

at the clock tower. To return to the centre, take bus No 10 from immediately north of the clock tower.

NETANYA　　　　　　נתניה נتانيا
☎ 09 / pop 167,000

As a sun-and-sand resort, Netanya offers approximately 11km of the finest **free beaches** in Israel. There is also a lively pedestrianised main street that's lined with shops, cafés and patisseries, many of them run by Netanya's recent influx of French Jews. You'll find the **tourist office** (☎ 882 7286; fax 884 1348; 8.30am-4pm Sun-Thu, 9am-noon Fri) in a kiosk at the southwest corner of Ha'Atzma'ut Sq.

In a prime position near the beach, the budget accommodation of choice is the **Atzma'ut Hostel** (☎ 862 1315; 2 Ussishkin St, Ha'Atzma'ut Sq; dm/s/d US$10/25/30; P ❸ ▣). **Hotel Orit** (☎ 861 6818; www.israelsvan.com/orit; 21 Chen St; s/d US$40/56; P ❌), run by Swedish Christians, is a fairly good-value alternative. Rates include breakfast.

Getting There & Away

Buses run roughly every 15 minutes to and from Tel Aviv (14.80NIS, 30 minutes), and every 30 minutes to and from Haifa (20NIS, one hour) and Jerusalem (32NIS, 1¼ hours). To reach Caesarea, Megiddo, Nazareth or Tiberias, you'll need to change buses in Khadera.

HAIFA　　　　　　חיפה حيفا
☎ 04 / pop 270,400

The attractive multilevel city of Haifa spills down the wooded slopes of Mt Carmel and takes in a busy industrial port area, a trendy German Colony, the landmark Baha'i Gardens, and a host of white-sand beaches, promenades and panoramic views.

While Jerusalem is swathed in historical mystique and Tel Aviv buzzes with hedonism and *joie de vivre*, Haifa, Israel's third-largest city, seems content with its lot as a student town and a solid cornerstone of the country's technological industry. Perhaps it's this air of prosperity that provides it with what appears to be Israel's most relaxed attitude, in which Jews, Christians and Muslims live and work together without the tensions that seem to pervade many other cities.

Orientation

Haifa occupies three main tiers on the slopes of Mt Carmel. New arrivals by bus, train or boat are ushered into Haifa in the Port Area, also known as downtown. Uphill lie the busy Arab commercial district of Wadi Nisnas and the predominantly Russian Hadar district. The Carmel Centre district at the top of the mountain is home to the university, exclusive residences and trendy Carmel Centre bars and eateries.

Information

The Bank Leumi and Hapoalim Bank main branches are both on Jaffa Rd, and you'll find lots of change places around Hadar and other shopping districts. Post offices on MaPalyam and Ben-Gurion will change travellers cheques.

Aldara (Map p310; ☎ 852 0222; 47 Ben Gurion Ave; per hr 10NIS; 10am-8pm) Coffee shop with on-line computers and wi-fi for laptop users.

Haifa Tourism Development Association (Map p310; ☎ 853 5605, toll free ☎ 1 800 305-090; www .tour-haifa.co.il; 48 Ben-Gurion Ave) Immediately at the foot of the Baha'i Gardens, this tourist office distributes several useful publications, including *A Guide to Haifa Tourism* and a city map (4NIS), which outlines four themed walking tours.

ISSTA (Map p310; ☎ 868 2227; www.issta.co.il; Bei Hakranot Bldg, 20 Herzl St) Books air tickets and sells student ID cards.

Main post office (Map p310; 19 HaPalyam Ave; 8am-12.30pm & 3.30-6pm Sun-Tue & Thu, 8am-1pm Wed, 8am-noon Fri)

Rambam Medical Centre (Map p309; ☎ 1-700-505-150; Bat Galim)

Steimatzky Bookshop (Map p310; ☎ 866 4058; 16 Herzl St; 10am-7pm Sun-Thu, 10am-3pm Fri)

Sights
BAHA'I GARDENS

The 19 immaculately kept terraces of the dizzily sloped **Baha'i Gardens** (Map p310; ☎ 831 3131; admission free; 9am-5pm) are truly a wonder. Apart from the top two tiers, the gardens are accessible to the general public only on guided tours (daily except Wednesday), which must be pre-booked well in advance. Baha'i pilgrims, however, can organise individual entry.

Amid the perfectly manicured gardens, fountains and walkways rises Haifa's most imposing landmark, the golden-domed **Shrine of the Bab** (Map p310; 9am-noon). Completed in 1953, this tomb of the Baha'i prophet, Al-Bab, integrates both European and Oriental design, and is considered one of the two most sacred sites for the world's five million Baha'is (the other is the tomb of Mizra Hussein Ali; see p315) outside nearby Akko. Visitors to the shrine must remove their shoes and dress modestly (no shorts or bare shoulders).

Near the upper entrance to the Baha'i Gardens is the **Ursula Malbin Sculpture Garden** (Gan HaPesalim; HaZiyonut Blvd), a small park filled with 'hands-on' sculptures, where families come to relax amid the greenery.

STELLA MARIS MONASTERY & ELIJAH'S CAVE

The neo-Gothic **Stella Maris Carmelite Church & Monastery** (Map p309; ☎ 833 7748; ☙ 6am-1.30pm & 3-6pm), with its wonderful painted ceiling, was originally established as a 12th-century Crusader stronghold. It was later used as a hospital for the troops of Napoleon in 1799, but was subsequently destroyed by the Turks. In 1836, it was replaced by the present structure. The easiest access to Stella Maris is via

the **cable car** (Map p309; ☎ 833 5970; one way/return 16/22NIS; ☙ 10am-6pm) from the highway below.

Below Stella Maris, close to the highway, is the grotto known as **Elijah's Cave** (Map p309; admission free; ☙ 8am-5pm Sun-Thu, 8.30am-12.45pm Fri). Here the prophet Elijah hid from King Ahab and Queen Jezebel after slaying the 450 priests of Ba'al, as reported in 1 Kings XVIII.20–40 It now attracts pilgrims of all three monotheistic faiths, and the adjacent garden is a favoured picnic site for local Christian Arabs. Take bus No 44 or 45 from downtown.

MUSEUMS

The **Haifa Art Museum** (Map p310; ☎ 852 3255; www.hms.org.il; 26 Shabtai Levi St; adult/senior/child/student 22/11/16/16NIS; ☙ 10am-4pm Mon & Wed-Thu, 4-8pm Tue, 10am-1pm Fri, 10am-3pm Sat) is three museums in one – ancient art, modern art, and music and ethnology. The same ticket (good for three days) also admits you to the following museums, all with the same opening hours: **Haifa City Museum** (Map p310; ☎ 851 2030; 11 Ben-Gurion Ave), with revolving exhibitions by local artists; the wonderful **Tikotin Museum of Japanese Art** (Map p310; ☎ 838 3554; 89 HaNassi

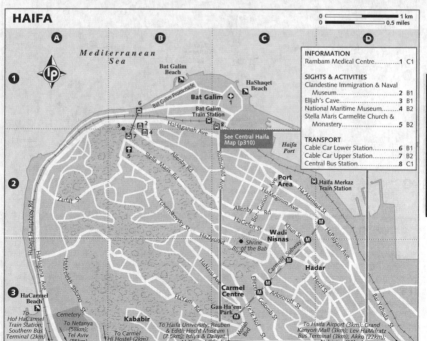

CENTRAL HAIFA

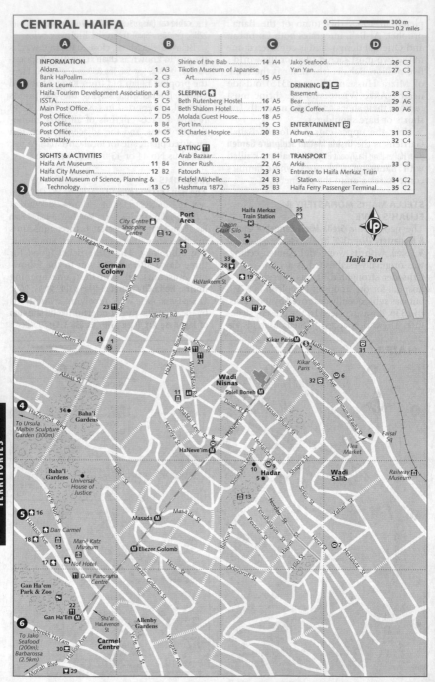

INFORMATION
Aldara	1	A3
Bank HaPoalim	2	C3
Bank Leumi	3	C3
Haifa Tourism Development Association	4	A3
ISSTA	5	C5
Main Post Office	6	D4
Post Office	7	D5
Post Office	8	B4
Post Office	9	C5
Steimatzky	10	C5

SIGHTS & ACTIVITIES
Haifa Art Museum	11	B4
Haifa City Museum	12	B2
National Museum of Science, Planning & Technology	13	C5
Shrine of the Bab	14	A4
Tikotin Museum of Japanese Art	15	A5

SLEEPING
Beth Rutenberg Hostel	16	A5
Beth Shalom Hotel	17	A5
Molada Guest House	18	A5
Port Inn	19	C3
St Charles Hospice	20	B3

EATING
Arab Bazaar	21	B4
Dinner Rush	22	A6
Fatoush	23	A3
Felafel Michelle	24	B3
Hashmura 1872	25	B3
Jako Seafood	26	C3
Yan Yan	27	C3

DRINKING
Basement	28	C3
Bear	29	A6
Greg Coffee	30	A6

ENTERTAINMENT
Achurva	31	D3
Luna	32	C4

TRANSPORT
Arkia	33	C3
Entrance to Haifa Merkaz Train Station	34	C2
Haifa Ferry Passenger Terminal	35	C2

ISRAEL & THE PALESTINIAN TERRITORIES

Ave) and its unique collection of Far Eastern works; and the **National Maritime Museum** (Map p309; ☎ 853 6622; 198 Allenby Rd), which presents the history of Mediterranean shipping.

The **Clandestine Immigration & Naval Museum** (Map p309; ☎ 853 6249; 204 Allenby Rd; adult/child 10/5NIS; ⊗ 8.30am-4pm Sun-Thu) commemorates Israel's naval history and the Zionists' 1930s and '40s attempts to migrate into British-blockaded Palestine.

The **Reuben & Edith Hecht Museum** (☎ 825 7773; http://research.haifa.ac.il/~hecht/; Eshkol Tower, Haifa University; admission free; ⊗ 10am-4pm Sun, Mon, Wed & Thu, 10am-7pm Tue, 10am-1pm Fri, 10am-2pm Sat) features Israeli archaeology and a collection of French Impressionist art. The museum was donated by Belgian philanthropist, Dr Reuben Hecht, who migrated to Israel in 1939.

A great place to take kids is the hands-on **National Museum of Science, Planning & Technology** (Map p310; ☎ 862 8111; www.netvision.net.il/inmos; Technion Bldg, Shmaryahu Levin St, Hadar; adult/senior/child/student 35/17.50/20/25NIS; ⊗ 9am-4pm Sun, Mon, Wed & Thu, 9am-7.30pm Tue, 10am-2pm Fri, 10am-6pm Sat).

Tours
The Haifa Tourism Development Association organises a free guided walking tour on Saturday at 10.30am; meet behind the **Nof Hotel** (101 HaNassi Ave) in Carmel Centre.

Sleeping
Port Inn (Map p310; ☎ 852 4401; www.portinn.co.il; 34 Jaffa Rd; dm/s/d 55/180/250NIS; ⊠ ⊗ ▦) Haifa's best budget option is this friendly and central family-run place that's more like a hotel than a hostel. There's a communal kitchen and sitting room, breakfast is an extra 20NIS and laundry service is available for 40NIS.

St Charles Hospice (Map p310; ☎ 855 3705; stcharls@netvision.net.il; 105 Jaffa Rd; s/d/tr US$35/60/75) With a lovely garden, this place is owned by the Latin Patriarchate and run by the Catholic Rosary Sisters. Rooms all have fans and private showers and rates include a filling breakfast. The gate is often locked so you'll need to ring the bell to enter.

Beth Shalom Hotel (Map p310; ☎ 837 7481; www.beth-shalom.co.il; 110 HaNassi Ave; s/d/tr US$60/84/108; ⊠ ⊗) In the Carmel Centre district, this is a basic but comfortable Lutheran 'evangelical guesthouse'. Rates include breakfast, and dinner is available for an additional US$10. From downtown take the metro.

Carmel HI Hostel (☎ 853 1944; www.iyha.org.il; dm/s/d US$20/37.50/56; ℗ ⊠ ⊗) Comfortable and friendly, this place is close to the Hof HaCarmel train and bus station, but less convenient for Haifa's main tourist attractions. Take bus No 3 or 114 from the Hof HaCarmel station or No 43 or 45 from downtown.

Molada Guest House (Map p310; ☎ 838 7958; www.rutenberg.org.il; 82 HaNassi Ave; s/d US$40/60; ⊗) Run by the Rutenberg Institute for Youth Education, this welcoming guesthouse has clean comfortable rooms, some with balconies that offer sea views. It is opposite the Dan Carmel hotel.

Beth Rutenberg Hostel (Map p310; ☎ 838 7958; 77 HaNassi Ave; dm US$22; ℗ ⊠ ⊗) Close to Molada Guesthouse is this cheaper hostel, which is run by the same institute. Phone ahead during normal working hours to secure a bed.

Eating
RESTAURANTS
Hashmura 1872 (Map p310; ☎ 855 1872; 15 Ben-Gurion Ave; dishes 39-105NIS; ⊗ noon-midnight Sun-Thu, noon-8pm Fri & Sat) This is a classy and recommended splurge in the German Colony. It does a range of pasta, chicken, steak and lamb dishes, but the speciality is seafood. Shrimp, *carpaccio* (thinly sliced raw fish) or squid starters cost 39NIS to 55NIS, and salmon, bream or mussel mains are 72NIS to 80NIS. A glass floor reveals the extensive wine cellar in the historic 1872 basement, where there's also an atmospheric pub.

Jako Seafood (Map p310; ☎ 866 8813; 12 Qehilat Saloniki St; dishes 55-65NIS; ⊗ noon-midnight Sun-Thu, noon-8pm Fri & Sat) Offers an excellent variety of fish (including salmon, bream, bass, shark, triggerfish and St Peter's fish) and seafood (calamari, crab or shrimp). There's a second location at 11 Moriah in Carmel Centre.

Fatoush (Map p310; ☎ 852 4930; 38 Ben-Gurion Ave; dishes 25-45NIS; ⊗ 8am-1am) Set up like a medieval Arabic house, complete with burgundy cushions, nargilehs and candle lamps, Fatoush is an atmospheric and popular restaurant serving a fusion of Western and Middle Eastern cuisine. In pleasant weather it's just as nice to eat on the street-side patio.

Dinner Rush (Map p310; ☎ 836 1908; 122 HaNassi Ave; dishes 25NIS; ⊗ noon-1am) A concept bar, this one has the bartenders doubling as chefs who serve up American diner–style food – pasta, burgers and chicken wings. It's right next to the Gan Ha'em metro station.

Yan Yan (Map p310; ☎ 855 7878; 28 HaMeganim Ave; main dishes 35-50NIS; ☺ noon-11pm) Friendly downtown place serving excellent Chinese and Vietnamese fare. The Chinese business lunch costs 39.50NIS and in the evening there's a 49NIS all-you-can-eat special.

QUICK EATS

Felafel Michelle (Map p310; 21 Wadi Nisas Rd; ☺ 8am-6pm Mon-Sat) Serves up what many locals claim to be the best felafel in Haifa. As you are walking east on Wadi Nisnas Rd, look for the hole-in-the-wall on the left side of the road.

Around the HaNevi'im St end of HeHalutz St, you'll find a wide range of excellent felafel and shwarma, as well as bakeries selling sweet pastries, sticky buns and other delights. The other prime shwarma area is Allenby Rd, around HaZiyonut Blvd. For fruit and vegetables, shop at the great little Arab bazaar in Wadi Nisnas.

Drinking & Entertainment

For an evening out, locals head for the trendy bars and cafés along Moriah St and the environs of Carmel Centre. A handful of bars and nightclubs are clustered around downtown.

Bear (Map p310; ☎ 838 1703; 135 HaNassi Ave; meals 35-75NIS; ☺ 6pm-3am Sun-Wed, 11am-4am Thu-Fri, 5pm-3am Sat) The Bear, Haifa's only Irish-style pub, is regarded as the city's main expat hang-out and sports bar. For meals, you can choose between salads, sandwiches, chicken, steak and seafood, washed down with your choice of 12 different draught beers.

Barbarossa (☎ 811 4010; 8 Pica St; ☺ 5.30pm-3am) Haifa's most popular singles bar is located just off Moriah St, about 2.5km south of Carmel Centre. Two-for-one drinks offered during happy hour, 6.30pm to 9pm.

Basement (Map p310; ☎ 853 2367; 2 HaVankeem St; ☺ 9pm-3am) Dim, hedonistic and rowdy, this alternative rock bar is popular with young Haifans. Live music is featured on Saturdays while Sunday is open-mike night; aspiring rock stars will have a captive audience.

Greg Coffee (Map p310; 3 Derekh HaYam St; ☺ 7am-1am) If it's a good cup of joe you're after, or some fantastic brownies, try this stylish little café in Carmel Centre.

Downtown dance places, such as **Luna** (Map p310; HaPalyam St) and **Achurva** (Map p310; admission 50NIS; Captain Steve St; ☺ midnight-sunrise Thu night) only open on weekends.

Getting There & Away

AIR

Arkia (Map p310; ☎ 861 1600; 80 Ha'Atzma'ut St) connects Haifa with Eilat (422NIS, 1¼ hours).

BUS

Arriving from the south, passengers are dropped off at the new Hof HaCarmel bus station (adjacent to the train station of the same name) from where you can take bus No 103 downtown. The old **central bus station** (HaHaganah Ave) handles city buses. Buses to Akko, Nahariya and Galilee use the eastern bus terminal at Lev HaMifratz.

During the day, buses depart every 20 minutes for Tel Aviv (23NIS, 1½ hours), while there's an hourly service to Jerusalem (39NIS, two hours). Heading north, bus Nos 271 and 272 (express) go to Nahariya (13.50NIS, 45 to 70 minutes, every 15 minutes) via Akko, and bus Nos 251 and 252 (express) stop at Akko (11.50NIS, 30 to 50 minutes). Eastbound, bus No 430 goes to Tiberias (28NIS, 1½ hours) and bus No 332 goes to Nazareth (17.50NIS, 45 minutes).

FERRY

For information on travelling to and from Cyprus and Greece by ferry, see p663.

TRAIN

Haifa has three train stations: Haifa Merkaz, near the port; Bat Galim, adjacent to the central bus station (accessible via the passage from platform 34); and Hof HaCarmel, at the new southern bus terminal. From Haifa Merkaz, trains depart roughly hourly for Tel Aviv (27.50NIS, 1½ hours) via Netanya (23NIS, one hour), and north to Nahariya (16NIS, 45 minutes) via Akko (12.50NIS, 30 minutes).

Getting Around

The only underground in Israel, the **Carmelit** (☎ 837 6861; per person 5.50NIS; ☺ 6am-10pm Sun-Thu, 6am-3pm Fri, 7pm-midnight Sat), connects Kikar Paris with Carmel Centre, via the Hadar district. Visitors can ride to the top and see the city sights on a leisurely downhill stroll.

DRUZE VILLAGES

The dusty but friendly Druze villages of **Isfiya** and **Daliyat al-Karmel**, on the slopes of Mt Carmel, have popular high-street bazaars where you'll find inexpensive Indian clothing, trinkets and handmade Druze handbags. The best way to get there is by *sherut* (11NIS, 30 minutes) departing when full from Hadar. Alternatively, bus No 192 (11NIS, 45 minutes) departs from the central bus station three times daily except Saturday.

CAESAREA   קיסריה قيصريا

☎ 04 / pop 3400

First developed by the Persians in the 6th century BC, Caesarea never amounted to much until about 30 BC when Herod the Great made it the headquarters of the Roman government in Palestine. The palaces, temples, churches and mosques built by Herod and subsequent conquerors have all but disappeared, but their ruins, stretching along the Mediterranean for over 1km, are now considered a world-class archaeological site.

Sights & Activities

The central attraction of **Caesarea National Park** (☎ 636 1358; basic ticket adult/child 23/12NIS, with interactive tour 40/33NIS; ☺ 8am-5pm) is the walled **Crusader city**, with its citadel and harbour. Beyond the walls to the north stretch the beachfront remains of an impressive Roman aqueduct. A hippodrome lies to the south, and beyond this, a reconstructed **Roman amphitheatre**, which serves as a modern-day concert venue.

The recommended **interactive tour** features the latest in digital technology, complete with a holographic Herod the Great who answers your questions, a high definition movie, and an interactive panoramic display that lets you explore the city during different historical periods, all with a few taps of a touch screen.

For a more hands-on experience, **Caesarea Diving** (☎ 626 5898; www.caesarea-diving.com), at the national park, by the waterfront, does scuba trips in the area, allowing you to explore the foundations of Herod's ancient harbour.

Sleeping

Grushka B&B (☎ 638 9810; www.grushka.co.il; 28 Hameyasdim St, Binyamina; d 525NIS, per child extra 125NIS; P ⊠ ⌷) This friendly Dutch-and-Israeli-run B&B offers several comfortable rooms as well as a quiet cottage and a fully equipped villa for families. It's just a seven-minute walk from the Binyamina train station, or call for a pick up.

Getting There & Away

From Tel Aviv or Netanya, take any bus along the coastal road towards Khadera, where you can disembark and connect with bus No 76 to Caesarea, the best of which depart at 8.20am, 11.25am, 1.10pm and 2.45pm. Coming from Haifa, get off at the Caesarea intersection and hike the last 3.5km to the site. Alternatively, take the train to Binyamina from Tel Aviv (21NIS, 45 minutes) or Haifa (17.50NIS, 30 minutes) and look for a taxi to take you the last 7km.

BEIT SHE'ARIM   בית שערים شعاريم بيت

☎ 04

A pleasant day trip from Haifa, the archaeological site of **Beit She'arim** (☎ 983-1643; adult/child 18/8NIS; ☺ 8am-5pm), 19km southeast of Haifa, includes a network of burial caves and 2nd-century ruins. To get there, use bus No 338 from Haifa to Kiryat Tivon.

AKKO   עכו عكا

☎ 04 / pop 45,800

Few of the world's cities are as timeless as Akko, the stonewalled fortress by the sea. After enjoying a long and varied history under Alexander the Great, the Egyptians and the Romans, Akko came to prominence as the Crusader city of Acre. Among the many people of prominence to breach its gates was a young Marco Polo who used this city as a staging point on his journey to the court of Khublai Khan.

During the Jewish immigration of the 1930s, it served as a hotbed of Arab hostility, and in the end the Jews left Old Akko to the Arabs and set about developing a 'new city' outside its historic walls. As a result, Akko has avoided modern development, and while the rest of Israel scrambles to package its history for tourists, Akko soldiers on as an oblivious – and genuine – remnant from the past. Akko's historic homes house families rather than artists, and in the souq and on the quays, merchants and fisher-folk carry on pretty much as they have for several thousand years.

Orientation

From the bus and train stations, it's roughly a 20-minute walk to Old Akko. From the bus station, exit to the left on Derekh

HaArba'a St and continue one long block to the traffic lights. There, turn right (west) onto Ben Ami St. After two blocks turn left onto Weizmann St and you'll see the city walls ahead. The train station is about 300m further east from the bus station.

Information

Public Library (per 30min 7NIS; 9am-7pm Sun-Thu, 9am-3pm Fri) Located 200m north of the old city walls, the library offers Internet access.

Tourist office (995 6707; www.akko.org.il; 1 Weizmann St; 8.30am-5.30pm Apr-Oct, 8.30am-4.30pm Nov-Mar) Located north of the 'Festival Garden', inside the Crusader Citadel.

Sights

OLD AKKO

You enter the predominantly Arab enclave of Old Akko through walls built by Ahmed Pasha al-Jazzar in 1799. Its northwestern corner is secured by Al-Jazzar's Citadel, which was reconstructed on the foundations laid out by the 13th-century Crusaders.

The **Al-Jazzar Mosque** (admission 3NIS; 8am-6pm Sat-Thu), with its green, distinctly Turkish dome and minaret, is the dominant element on the Akko skyline. North of the mosque is the **Citadel**, entered from the car park to the east. To the right is the tourist office where you buy a ticket for the Citadel or the better value **combination ticket** (adult/student/senior 44/37/37NIS), which allows admission to Knight's Halls, Hammam al-Pasha, Okashi Museum and the Templar Crusader Tunnel. For about 20NIS extra you can add on the Rosh HaNikra sea caves (p316) if you are headed that way. After a short film about the city, grab an audio headset and visit the **Knight's Halls** (adult/child 25/22NIS; 8.30am-5pm Sun-Thu, 8.30am-2pm Fri), a haunting series of vaulted halls that lie 8m below the street level. At one time, they served as the headquarters of the crusading Knights Hospitallers.

At the back end of the Citadel, look for the tunnel (hard to spot) and follow it through a winding series of passages to the **Turkish Baazar**. Then turn right to reach the **Hammam al-Pasha** (Turkish Bath), housed in the 1780 bathhouse built by Al-Jazzar, which remained in use until the 1940s. The *hammam* now contains a 30-minute **multi-media show**

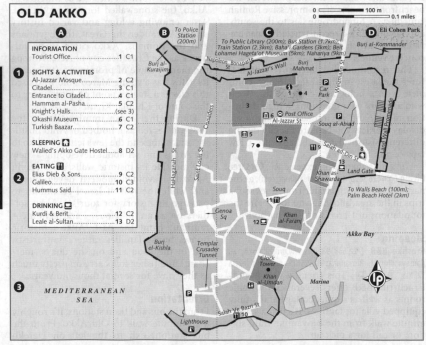

OLD AKKO

INFORMATION
Tourist Office.....................1 C1

SIGHTS & ACTIVITIES
Al-Jazzar Mosque.................2 C2
Citadel.............................3 C1
Entrance to Citadel..............4 C1
Hammam al-Pasha...............5 C2
Knight's Halls..................(see 3)
Okashi Museum..................6 C1
Turkish Baazar...................7 C2

SLEEPING
Walied's Akko Gate Hostel.....8 D2

EATING
Elias Dieb & Sons...............9 C2
Galileo...........................10 C3
Hummus Said.....................11 C2

DRINKING
Kurdi & Berit....................12 C2
Leale al-Sultan..................13 D2

(adult/child 25/21NIS; 8.30am-5pm Sun-Thu, 8.30am-2pm Fri) called 'The Story of the Last Bath Attendant'. From the *hammam* walk back towards the Citadel to the **Okashi Museum** (adult/child 10/7NIS; 8.30am 5pm Sun-Thu, 8.30am-2pm Fri), an incongruous modern art gallery.

From the Citadel, follow the alley south into the souq, which is the Old City's main marketplace. Beyond it lies the **Khan al-Umdan**, once a grand khan (caravanserai) that served the camel trains carrying grain from the hinterlands, and above its courtyard rises an Ottoman **clock tower**. En route to the harbour, don't miss the amazing **Templar Crusader Tunnel** (adult/child 10/7NIS; 8.30am-5pm Sun-Thu, 8.30am-4pm Fri), an underground passageway that connected the Port to a Templar palace.

The original **land walls** date from the 12th century, but the sea walls were only put in place in the 18th century, their construction ordered by Al-Jazzar. Throughout the day and evening, **Malkat Akko** (991 0606, 050-5551136) runs tourist cruises from the Marina.

NEW AKKO

Travellers with an interest in the Baha'i faith may want to check out the wonderful **Baha'i Gardens** (admission free; 9am-4pm), 3km northeast of central New Akko. The gardens contain the Mansion of Bahji, where the founder of the Baha'i faith, Mizra Hussein Ali (Baha'u'llah) lived until his death in 1892. He is buried in the adjacent **shrine** (9am-noon Fri-Mon), considered the holiest place on Earth for the Baha'i.

Another worthwhile site just outside new Akko is the **Beit Lohamei HaGeta'ot Museum** (995 8052; www.gfh.org.il; adult/child 20/18NIS; 9am-4pm Sun-Thu), which commemorates the ghetto uprisings, Jewish resistance and Allied assistance during the Nazi Holocaust. Despite the depressing theme, it presents a hopeful picture of this tragic period. Your ticket is also good for **Yad Layeled** (9am-4pm Sun-Thu, 10am-5pm Sat) a moving museum dedicated to children of the Holocaust, located in an adjacent circular structure.

Sleeping

Walied's Akko Gate Hostel (991 0410; fax 981 5530; Salah ad-Din St; dm 30NIS; s with/without bathroom 200/120NIS, d with/without bathroom 220/140NIS;) In this split personality guesthouse, you have got a choice of fine-looking street-side rooms with attached bathrooms, or stuffy nonattached rooms that overlook a grubby yard filled with discarded metal bunk beds. Owner Walied can arrange trips to the Golan Heights (200NIS) and Rosh HaNikra (35NIS) when there is enough demand. Call for a free pick up from the station.

Palm Beach Hotel (987 7777; www.palmbeach.co.il; s/d US$105/130;) Located 2km east of the old city, the Palm Beach offers four-star quality rooms and fine facilities, including a pool, sauna, health spa and water sports. Book through the Internet for a 10% discount. To get to the hotel, head east from the Land Gate along the coastal road.

Eating & Drinking

For cheap eating there are several **felafel places** around the junction of Salah ad-Din and Al-Jazzar Sts. Self-catering supplies are available at **Elias Dieb & Sons** (Salah ad-Din St), a great little cavelike supermarket opposite Souq al-Abiad; there's no English sign. For spices or coffee, try the atmospheric **Kurdi & Berit** (991 6188), located in the souq.

Hummus Said (6am-2pm) Very much entrenched in the souq, this place has become something of an institution, doling up that much-loved Middle Eastern dip to throngs of visitors from around the country. For 15NIS, you'll get salads, pickles, pitta and a big glob of hummus with fuul or garlic.

Galileo (991 4617; 176/11 Salah Ve Bazri St; dishes 45-80NIS; 10am-midnight) Conjuring up images of Arabian nights, this charming restaurant is actually built into the sea wall that divides Akko from the Mediterranean. Not surprisingly, the main menu option is fish.

Leale-al Sultan (Khan as-Shawarda; 9am-midnight) Traditional Middle Eastern coffeehouse sporting sequined cushions, colourful wall hangings and backgammon tables. A Turkish coffee costs 5NIS while a nargileh is 10NIS.

Getting There & Away

Akko's bus terminal and train station lie about a 20-minute walk from the main entrance to the Old City. From Haifa (11.70NIS, 30 to 50 minutes, every 15 minutes), bus Nos 252 and 272 depart frequently, as do the slower bus Nos 251 and 271. From Akko, bus Nos 270, 271 and 272 (express) run north to Nahariya (7.60NIS, 15 to 25 minutes, every 15 minutes). The most pleasant way to travel between Akko and Haifa (12.50NIS, 30 minutes, every 30 minutes) or on to Nahariya (7.50NIS, 15 minutes), however, is by train along the beachfront railway.

NAHARIYA נהריה نهاريا
☎ 04 / pop 47,400

The appeal of the quiet seaside resort of Nahariya lies solely in its lovely beaches, though most travellers come here to simply catch onward transport for Rosh HaNikra. A **tourist office** (☎ 987 98301; 19 HaGa'aton Blvd; ☿ 8am-4.45pm Sun-Thu, 8am-12.30pm Fri) is on the ground floor of the municipality building, a block east of the bus station.

If you feel like staying, try the quiet **Hotel Rosenblatt** (☎ 992 3469; jael@walla.co.il; 59 Weizmann St; s/d 170/200; P ☒ ☒), on the corner of HaGa'aton Blvd.

Bus Nos 270, 271 and 272 (express) run roughly every 25 minutes (until 10.30pm) to Akko (7.50NIS, 15 to 25 minutes), with the 271 and 272 services continuing to Haifa (10.50NIS, 45 to 70 minutes).

ROSH HANIKRA
ראש הניקרה رأس الناقورة
☎ 04

Right on the Lebanese border, the wondrous **sea caves** at Rosh HaNikra were originally carved by nature but were enlarged by the British for a railway and by the Israelis to improve visitor access. The 10km road from Nahariya ends at the **Rosh HaNikra Tourist Centre** (☎ 985 7109; www.rosh-hanikra.com; ☿ 8.30am-4pm Sep-Mar, 8.30am-6pm Apr-Jun, 11pm Jul-Aug) from where a **cable car** (adult/child 38/30NIS; ☿ 8.30am-4pm Sep-Mar, 8.30am-6pm Apr-Jun, 8.30am-11pm Jul & Aug) descends steeply to the caves. Alternatively, find the dim walking track that leaves the main highway about 300m south of the tourist centre; it leads through a former rail tunnel to the caves. Ticket price includes admission to a 15-minute film presentation.

Sleeping & Eating
Rosh HaNikra Holiday Village (☎ 982 3112; www .kfar-rosh-hanikra.co.il; camp sites/r per person 40/180NIS; P ☒ ☒) This is housed in the old British Customs Post about 700m south of the cable car. This self-styled health spa also offers a pool, gym (40NIS) and massage (165 to 195NIS). Rates include breakfast, but add 50NIS for half board.

Eli Avivi (☎ 982 3219; 1avivi@walla.com; camp sites per person 80NIS, r 150-175NIS) A rustic 'lost-hippie' hideaway, Eli Avivi claims to be a separate state – you'll even get a passport stamp upon entry. The rambling property takes in not only a beautiful stretch of Akhziv Beach (national park fee 25NIS), but also a desultory museum (admission 15NIS) of archaeological finds from all over Israel. You'll find it 5km south of Rosh HaNikra.

For meals, there's a tourist café at the top of the cable car offering a buffet lunch with drink for 45NIS.

Getting There & Away
From Nahariya, bus Nos 20 and 32 run four times daily to Rosh HaNikra (6.50NIS, 15 minutes, noon, 2.30pm, 5.30pm and 6pm). Only one bus comes back to Nahariya, at 3pm. You could also get there by shared taxi or hitching.

GALILEE הגליל الجليل

With its lush scenery and religious heritage, Galilee's green valleys, verdant forests, fertile farmland and, of course, the Sea of Galilee, all provide relief from the drier lands to the south. For Christians, the Galilee area is serious Bible territory: it was here that Jesus grew up, gathered his disciples, preached one of the most enigmatic sermons in history, multiplied loaves and fishes, walked on water – and even turned water into wine, when it was necessary.

NAZARETH נצרת الناصرة
☎ 04 / pop 61,700

As the childhood home of Jesus, and the place where he preached, taught and worked in his father's carpentry shop, the timeless but scruffy Arab town of Nazareth is one of the most revered sites in Christendom. Although modern Nazareth may not fulfil everyone's expectations, it is certainly worth a visit, even if only for half a day.

Orientation & Information
Most sites of pilgrim interest are concentrated on Paul VI St and El-Bishara St (also called Annunciation or Casa Nova St). On El-

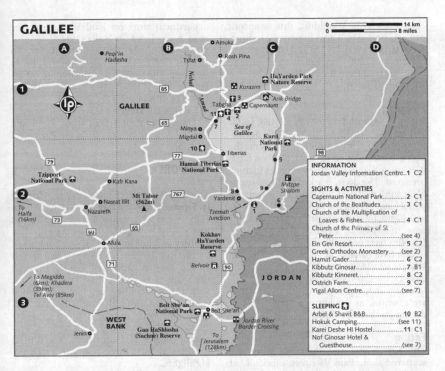

GALILEE

0 ————— 14 km
0 ————— 8 miles

Peqi'in Hadasha
Amuka
Rosh Pina
Tsfat
HaYarden Park Nature Reserve
Korazim
Arik Bridge
GALILEE
Tabgha
Capernaum
85
Nahal
Amud
Minya
Sea of Galilee
Migdal
Kursi National Park
79
Tiberias
77
Hamat Tiberias National Park
98
Tzippori National Park
Kafr Kana
Mt Tabor (562m)
767
Yardenit
Mitzpe Shalom
Ein Gev
Nasrat Illit
Nazareth
Tzemah Junction
Hamat Gader
To Haifa (16km)
73
65
Kokhav HaYarden Reserve
Afula
71
Belvoir
90
JORDAN
To Megiddo (6km); Khadera (39km); Tel Aviv (85km)
Beit She'an National Park
Beit She'an
Jordan River Border Crossing
WEST BANK
Gan HaShlosha (Sachne) Reserve
Jenin
To Jerusalem (128km)

INFORMATION
Jordan Valley Information Centre..**1** C2

SIGHTS & ACTIVITIES
Capernaum National Park............**2** C1
Church of the Beatitudes.............**3** C1
Church of the Multiplication of Loaves & Fishes.....................**4** C1
Church of the Primacy of St Peter..(see 4)
Ein Gev Resort...............................**5** C2
Greek Orthodox Monastery.......(see 2)
Hamat Gader................................**6** C2
Kibbutz Ginosar............................**7** B1
Kibbutz Kinneret...........................**8** C2
Ostrich Farm.................................**9** C2
Yigal Allon Centre......................(see 7)

SLEEPING
Arbel & Shavit B&B.....................**10** B2
Hokuk Camping.........................(see 11)
Karei Deshe HI Hostel................**11** C1
Nof Ginosar Hotel & Guesthouse.............................(see 7)

Bishara St, just above the Paul VI intersection, is the helpful **tourist office** (☎ 657 0555; nazrat@int.gov.il; ☽ 8.30am-5pm Mon-Fri, 8.30am-2pm Sat).

Sights

Nazareth's revered **Basilica of the Annunciation** (El-Bishara St; ☽ 8.30-11.45am & 2-5pm Mon-Sat) stands on the site where Catholics believe the Angel Gabriel announced to the Virgin Mary that she would bear the Son of God. Its rather bland 1969 exterior is redeemed by remnants of earlier Crusader and Byzantine churches inside, and the outdoor collection of 'Madonna and Child' artwork donated by Catholic communities around the world.

At the **Sisters of Nazareth Convent** (☎ 655 4304; ☽ 8.30-11.45am & 2-5pm Mon-Sat), up the street, you can see one of the best examples of an ancient stone-sealed tomb; it lies under the present courtyard and can only be viewed by appointment. The nearby **Church of St Joseph** (Al-Bishara St; ☽ 8.30-11.45am & 2-5pm Mon-Sat), built in 1914, occupies the traditional site of Joseph's carpentry shop, over the remains of a medieval church. In

pre-Byzantine times, the underground cavern was probably used for grain storage.

The **Al-Balda al-Qadima souq**, west of upper Al-Bishara St, occupies a maze of narrow streets. In its midst sits the **Greek Catholic Church** (☽ 8.30-11.45am & 2-5pm Mon-Sat), on the site of the synagogue where the young Jesus prayed and taught. The attractive **St Gabriel's Greek Orthodox Church** (Mary's Well Sq; ☽ 8am-6pm Mon-Sat) lies about 10 minutes' walk northeast of the basilica, two blocks off Paul VI St. Across Well Sq from here is **Mary's Well** (Paul VI St), which the Greek Orthodox Church claims is the site of the Annunciation. Beside it at the **Cactus gift shop** is a wonderful **ancient bathhouse** (☎ 050 538 4343; admission per group US$25; ☽ 10am-7pm Mon-Sat), which utilised water from Mary's Well. A 40-minute guided tour of the bathhouse includes excellent commentary and refreshments, including fresh juice and Turkish delights.

Those who just can't imagine Jesus amid Nazareth's modern bustle may want to head for the worthwhile **Nazareth Village** (☎ 645 6042; www.nazarethvillage.com; St 5079; admission 50NIS; ☽ 9am-5pm Mon-Sat). Located in

Nazareth's YMCA building, this nonprofit project, staffed by actors in period clothing, reconstructs everyday life and commerce in Nazareth of 2000 years ago. It's a 15-minute walk due west from the basilica, just beyond Al-Wadi al-Jawani St.

Sleeping

Sisters of Nazareth Convent (☎ 655 4304; fax 646 0741; dm US$8, s/d US$28/46; 🖭 🗶) With dormitories and 30 private rooms, this is by far the best accommodation in town. Kitchen facilities are available, private room rates include breakfast. The door, marked 'Réligieuses de Nazareth', is closed for security reasons, so you'll have to ring the bell. Reception closes at 9.30pm, but if you're prebooked (which is wise, in any case), they may wait a bit later. It's 50m west of the basilica.

Casa Nova Hospice (☎ 645 6660; fax 657 9630; El-Bishara St; s/d/tr US$40/54/68; 🖭 🗶) Opposite the basilica, the Casa Nova caters mainly for Italian pilgrimage groups. Advance bookings are essential, as the hospice may not open during low periods. Breakfast is included.

Eating

The best felafel and shwarma joints are scattered along Paul VI street, especially at the intersection below the tourist office.

Tishreen (☎ 608 4666; 56 El-Bishara St; meals 30-75NIS; 🕙 11am-midnight) This recent addition to Nazareth is dressed up to look like the interior of a medieval storehouse with scattered wine bottles and antiques clipped to the straw-encrusted walls. The menu is replete with Middle Eastern fare: try the excellent *muhammar,* an Arabic pizza topped with chicken and slices of onion baked in a brick oven. Chicken, seafood, steak and pasta dishes are also available. It's located 200m southwest of Mary's Well.

Holy Land Restaurant (☎ 657 5415; 6168 Casa Nova St; set menus US$10) With exotic handmade tiles and lots of old artefacts, Holy Land is set in a cavelike 1860 building that served as Nazareth's first sesame mill and, during WWI, as a German and Turkish supply depot. It's friendly but caters mainly for tour groups, so you're normally limited to a set menu.

Getting There & Away

There's no main bus terminal in Nazareth. Bus No 431 for Tiberias (21.50NIS, 45 minutes) departs hourly from the Hamishbir

department store on Paul VI St; over the road, buses leave for Haifa (19NIS, 45 minutes) with about the same regularity. To Akko (25NIS, 45 minutes, hourly), buses stop opposite the Egged information office. For Tel Aviv (36NIS, two hours), take bus Nos 823 or 824.

Sheruts to Tiberias leave from in front of Hamishbir department store. For Haifa and Tel Aviv, they leave from the Paz petrol station.

TZIPPORI   ציפורי
☎ 04

The impressive archaeological site **Tzippori (or Sepphoris) National Park** (☎ 656 8262; admission 23NIS; 🕙 8am-5pm in summer, 8am-4pm in winter) was first settled by the Hasmoneans in the 2nd century BC, but in 63 BC it was conquered by the Roman general Pompeii and served as the Roman capital of Galilee through the reign of Herod. Today Tzippori brims with ruins, including original colonnaded roadways, an amphitheatre, a Roman villa with some lovely mosaic floors, a Crusader citadel and a haunting underground system of cisterns and aqueducts. You'll need to allow at least three hours to catch the highlights.

Buses between Nazareth and Akko stop at Tzippori Junction, about 4km from the site. From there you'll have to walk or hitch – there's no public transport.

MEGIDDO   מגידו ميچنْدَّوْ هَظْبه
☎ 04

Better known as Armageddon (in Hebrew Har Megiddo, or Mt Megiddo), the site that St John predicted would host the last great battle on earth is now preserved in **Megiddo National Park** (☎ 659 0316; adult/child 23/12NIS; 🕙 8am-5pm Sat-Thu, 8am-4pm Fri). Ongoing excavations at the site have unearthed evidence of 20 distinct historical phases dating from 10,000 to 400 BC. The most enigmatic ruins are those of the 10th-century-BC fortified city, which was originally built by King Solomon, and the 9th-century-BC water system, which connected the city with a natural spring. The several excellent visitor-centre models depict how it must have looked.

The site lies 2km north of Megiddo Junction, west of the Haifa road, and is best accessed on the Haifa–Afula bus. Alternatively, take the half-hourly Tel Aviv–Tiberias bus, get off at Megiddo Junction and walk the last 2km up the hill.

BEIT SHE'AN   בית שאן بيت سبان
☎ 04 / pop 15,300

The tidy town of Beit She'an makes a great stop along the scenic Jordan River Hwy route between Jerusalem and Tiberias, but check the latest security situation before following this route.

Beit She'an National Park (adult/child 23/12NIS; ☽ 8am-4pm winter, 8am-5pm summer) features Israel's best-preserved Roman amphitheatre, as well as extensive and ongoing excavations, which so far have revealed a temple, basilica, nymphaeum, a colonnaded Roman street and 0.5 hectare of elaborate, mosaic-floored Byzantine baths. There's also a smaller amphitheatre in the town centre, and several inviting walking tracks along the lush riverfront.

Buses run frequently between Jerusalem and Tiberias, via Beit She'an, and there are also regular bus services to and from Afula.

TIBERIAS   טבריה طبريا
☎ 04 / pop 35,000

As the only town beside the Sea of Galilee, Tiberias is the obvious base for visiting the lakeside beauty spots and points of interest. With its mix of natural spas and tombs of venerated sages, the town invites observant Jews to combine treatment of the body with purification of the soul, while the less observant can partake of the town's lakeside wining, dining and nightlife. If possible, try to avoid visiting Tiberias and the Sea of Galilee on weekends when hotel prices can rise by 25% to 50%.

Information

Exchange Office (HaBanim St; ☽ 10am-7pm) No-commission money changer. Bank Leumi and Mizrahi Bank charge a 4% commission. The post office changes travellers cheques.

Internet Café (☎ 672 4672; per hr 20NIS; ☽ 10am-3am) Located behind Al-Omri Mosque.

Main post office (cnr HaYarden & HaBanim Sts; ☽ 7am-6pm Sun-Thu, 7am-noon Fri)

Solnan Communication (☎ 672 6470; 3 Midrahov; per hr 20NIS; ☽ 8am-11pm) Internet café and international phone office.

Tourist office (☎ 672 5666; 9 HaBanim St; ☽ 9am-1pm & 2-4pm Sun-Thu, 8.30am-12.30pm Fri) Located in the 'archaeological park', this office has free maps of Tiberias, Nazareth and the Galilee area. A free city walking tour departs from the Sheraton Tiberias Hotel on Saturday at 10.30am.

Sights

The dignified but incongruous mid-18th-century **Al-Omri Mosque** is one of the few historic structures in Tiberias' Old Town; a second mosque, **Jama al-Bahr** (1880), now stands forlorn and abandoned. The enigmatic **St Peter's Church** (☽ mass 6pm Mon-Sat, 8.30pm Sun), on the waterfront promenade, was originally built by 12th-century Crusaders, but the present structure dates from 1870. The boat-shaped nave is a nod to St Peter's piscatorial profession.

The **Galilee Experience** (☎ 672 3620; adult/student US$6/5; ☽ 9-10pm Sun-Thu, 9-4pm Fri), part of a modern waterfront development, presents an hourly audiovisual programme in 12 languages, recounting the historical, geographical and political story of Galilee from Abraham to Jesus, Napoleon and the Israeli General Moshe Dayan.

Uphill from the centre, the **Tomb of Rabbi Moshe Ben Maimon** (Ben Zakkai St) is the final resting place of the Spanish physician, also known as Maimonides or Rambam, who worked in the court of the Muslim ruler Saladin. This revered rabbi, who died in 1204, was one of 12th-century Egypt's most highly regarded sages. Legend has it that before his death in Cairo, he instructed followers to load his remains onto a camel and bury him wherever the camel expired. The beast was apparently drawn to Tiberias.

Around 2km south of town, the **Tiberias Hot Springs** (☎ 672 8500; Elizer Kaplan Blvd; admission 60NIS; ☽ 8am-8pm Sun, Mon & Wed, 8am-11pm Tue & Thu, 8.30am-8pm Sat) promises physical rejuvenation after a dip in one of its mineral pools. Swedish massage (125NIS) and mud wrap (115NIS) are also available. Don't mistake this for the older facility on the mountain side of the street.

Just past the modern bathhouse, the archaeological site **Hamat Tiberias National Park** (adult/senior/child 12/6/6NIS; ☽ 8am-5pm) dates back to Roman times, though its major feature is a small synagogue dating to the 3rd to 5th centuries CE. A small museum is housed in the reconstructed hammam,

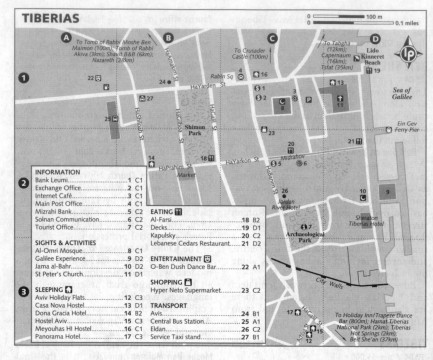

INFORMATION
Bank Leumi.....................1	C1
Exchange Office..............2	C1
Internet Café..................3	C1
Main Post Office.............4	C1
Mizrahi Bank..................5	C2
Solnan Communication....6	C2
Tourist Office.................7	C2

SIGHTS & ACTIVITIES
Al-Omri Mosque.............8	C1
Galilee Experience..........9	D2
Jama al-Bahr................10	D2
St Peter's Church..........11	D1

SLEEPING
Aviv Holiday Flats.........12	C3
Casa Nova Hostel..........13	D1
Dona Gracia Hotel.........14	B2
Hostel Aviv.................15	C3
Meyouhas HI Hostel......16	C1
Panorama Hotel............17	C3

EATING
Al-Farsi.....................18	B2
Decks........................19	D1
Kapulsky....................20	C2
Lebanese Cedars Restaurant......21	D2

ENTERTAINMENT
O-Ben Dush Dance Bar............22	A1

SHOPPING
Hyper Neto Supermarket........23	C2

TRANSPORT
Avis..........................24	B1
Central Bus Station........25	A1
Eldan.........................26	C2
Service Taxi stand.........27	B1

in use as a bathhouse from 1780 until its closure in 1944.

Tours

Holy Land Sailing (☎ 672 3007, 050 217416) Offers sightseeing cruises on the Sea of Galilee and for prebooked groups, providing ferry services between Tiberias, Tabgha and Ein Gev.

Lido Boats (☎ 672 1538) Has party cruises complete with full bar and music for 20NIS per person. The cruises are not always open to the public so call first.

Sleeping

Hostel Aviv (☎ 671 2272; fax 671 2272; cnr HaGalil & Achiva Sts; dm/s/d 40/90/120NIS; holiday flats 280-350NIS; P X X) This is probably the best budget option in town. Both the dorms and private rooms have showers, fridges, and cable TV, and some have private balconies with lake views. The Aviv holiday flats in the adjacent building (to the west) also feature kitchenettes and some have Jacuzzi tubs. Top-quality bicycles can be hired for 40NIS per day.

Meyouhas HI Hostel (☎ 672 1775; www.iyha.org .il; 2 HaYarden St; dm/s US$19/37, d US$48-56; X X)

In a 110-year-old stone building, formerly a Scottish hospital, this is one of Israel's most pleasant HI hostels. All rates include breakfast. Students and HI card holders receive a small discount.

Casa Nova Hostel (☎ 671 2281; 1 HaYarden St; dm/s/d US$15/32/50; P X X) Adjacent to St Peter's Church, this is a clean and quiet 100-year-old pilgrims' hostel. All rates include breakfast as well as use of the kitchen facilities and satellite-TV lounge.

Dona Gracia Hotel (☎ 671 7176; www.donagracia .com; 3 HaPrahim; s/d US$70/90; X ▢ X) This midrange theme hotel is built around the legend of a 16th-century Portuguese-Jewish woman revered across Europe for her wealth and political influence. There is a museum dedicated to Dona Gracia, free if you are staying here, or 45NIS if you are not. Rates include breakfast.

Shavit B&B (☎ 679 4919; www.members.tripod .com/~shavit/; s/d US$30/60; P X X) Located in Arbel village, this B&B makes for a pleasant treat for those who prefer relaxation in a tranquil garden setting to the bustle of central Tiberias. All units have kitchenettes and cable TV; meals are also available. Call for a free pick up.

Panorama Hotel (☎ 679 1004; 56 HaGalil St; s/d/tr 100/150/200NIS; ✗ ✵) This friendly hotel offers clean, airy but basic rooms, a communal kitchen and a dining area.

Eating

The cheapest sit-down dining options are cafés at the top end of the *midrahov* (pedestrian mall). More upmarket places are along the waterfront. The small **market** (✵ Sun-Fri), off HaYarkon St south of Gan Shimon Park, sells a range of fruits and vegetables. There's also the convenient Hyper Neto supermarket behind the Al-Omri Mosque.

Decks (☎ 672 1538; Lido Beach; mains 70-120NIS; ✵ noon-midnight; ✗) Just to whet your appetite, the enormous grills for this legendary steakhouse are set by the door as you walk inside. Everything on the menu is tempting, from the spare ribs and tuna steak, right down to the garlic fries and heavenly desserts. This is not a good place if you're on a diet. In summer it opens from 6pm.

Kapulsky (☎ 672 0341; Midrahov; dishes 35-55NIS; ✵ 8am-1am; ✗ ✵) This is part of a nationwide chain of kosher vegetarian restaurants, specialising in pasta, salad, crepes and a range of omelettes and baked potatoes. It also whips up starters, extensive Israeli breakfasts (until noon) and stir-fries.

Lebanese Cedars Restaurant (☎ 651 0314; Promenade; dishes 30-70NIS; ✵ 8am-10pm; ✗ ✵) This authentic Lebanese restaurant, on the waterfront, is designed to look like the interior of a ship. Try the excellent hummus with lamb (30NIS) or the kebab with tahini (49NIS).

Al-Farsi (cnr HaGalil & HaYarkon Sts; snacks 14NIS) Lively late-night fast food place with low prices and a range of local staples, including shashlik, liver and shwarma.

Entertainment

The cafés and bars around the *midrahov* attract crowds on weekend evenings, especially in summer.

O-Ben Dush Dance Bar (☎ 050 451133; ✵ 10.30am-late Thu-Sat in summer) Features salsa, techno, rumba, samba and disco dancing. It's near HaYarden St.

From the Lido Kinneret Beach, **disco cruises** (☎ 672 1538; 20NIS) depart according to demand throughout the year. There is some-

thing on most nights, especially in summer, but you'll need to phone to confirm.

Getting There & Away

Egged buses (☎ 672 9222) depart for Tel Aviv (42NIS, 2½ hours) and Jerusalem (42NIS, three hours) at least hourly from the central bus station. There are also several daily (except Saturday) services to Haifa (28NIS, 1½ hours), Nazareth (21.50NIS, 45 minutes), Tsfat (20NIS, one hour), Beit She'an (21.50NIS, 40 minutes) and Kiryat Shmona (25NIS, 1½ hours).

Outside the bus station and across the street, *sheruts* leave throughout the day, mostly to Tel Aviv (35NIS, two hours) and occasionally Haifa (20NIS, one hour), and to other destinations like Nazareth.

SEA OF GALILEE ים כנרת البحر الجليل

Around 21km long and 55km in circumference, the Sea of Galilee (Kinneret in Hebrew), fed by the Jordan River, is both a natural beauty site and the main source of Israel's water supply. For foreign visitors, it is better known as home base for the preaching Jesus – the area where he gathered followers and worked miracles. Using Tiberias as a base, travellers can readily explore the Galilee in a couple of days. Short of walking on water, the best way around is by hired bike.

Information

The **Jordan Valley Information Centre** (☎ 675 2727; ✵ 8.30am-4pm Mon-Thu, 8.30am-2pm Fri & Sat), at the shopping centre in Tzemah Junction, provides free maps and regional information.

Northwestern Shore

Migdal, 6km north of Tiberias, was the birthplace of Mary Magdalene. The connection is commemorated with a tiny white-domed shrine, overgrown with vegetation, beside a fetid canal near junky Restal Beach.

On Kibbutz Ginosar is the **Yigal Allon Centre** (☎ 672 1495; adult/child 20/15NIS; ✵ 8.30am-5pm Sat-Thu, 8.30am-1pm Fri), a museum devoted to the theme 'man in the Galilee'. Its most celebrated exhibit is the skeletal remains of an 8.2m fishing vessel that shrewd tour operators have dubbed 'the Jesus boat'. Discovered in 1986, it has been dated to the time of Christ's ministry.

Tabgha & Capernaum

كفر نحوم & طبحة & تبخأ & كبرنحيم

Generally considered to be the most beautiful and serene of the Christian holy places, **Tabgha** (an Arabic rendition of the Greek *hepta pega*, meaning 'seven springs') is associated with three salient episodes from the New Testament. Modest dress (no shorts or tank tops) is required when visiting the following sites.

The **Church of the Beatitudes** (admission per car 5NIS; 8-11am & 2.30-4.40pm), which commemorates the Sermon on the Mount, sits in a lovely garden about 100m above the lake. The Beatitudes of Jesus are commemorated in stained glass around the dome. The altar of the **Church of the Multiplication of Loaves & Fishes** (8.30am-5pm Mon-Sat, 9.45am-5pm Sun), also called the Heptapagon Church, is thought to include the rock where Jesus laid the five loaves and two fishes that multiplied to feed 5000 faithful listeners. In 1932, excavations uncovered some beautiful mosaic floors, including the ubiquitous 'loaves-and-fishes' mosaic. The wonderfully serene **Church of the Primacy of St Peter** (8am-noon & 2-5pm), with its lovely stained glass, was built by Franciscans in 1933 at the site called Mensa Christi. In the 4th century, a now-ruined church was constructed here to commemorate the spot where the resurrected Jesus conferred the church leadership on St Peter.

Capernaum (Kfar Nahum; admission 3NIS; 8am-4.40pm) was the home base of Jesus during the most influential period of his Galilean ministry. An octagonal church hovers over the ruins of a 3rd- or 4th-century synagogue that was built over his lodgings. Further east along the shoreline rises the very pink, domed **Greek Orthodox Monastery**. Just beyond it lies the tranquil **Capernaum National Park**, which has a souvenir shop, lakeside gardens and a boat terminal. **Lake cruises** (25NIS) to Tiberias, Ein Gev and Ginosar are available when there's sufficient demand.

Buses from Tiberias pass by Capernaum Junction (12NIS, 30 minutes, twice hourly), which is a 5km hike or hitch to any of the major sites.

Eastern Shore

There are plenty of scenic, uncrowded swimming spots along the eastern shore, highlighted by the **Ein Gev Resort** (see opposite), with its secluded beach and renowned seafood restaurant. Another diversion, great for kids, is the **ostrich farm** (adult/child 18/15NIS; 9am-3pm) at Kibbutz Ha'On.

Kursi National Park (673 1983; adult/child 12/6NIS; 8am-5pm), designated by the Jewish Talmud as a site for idol worship, was also the place where Jesus cast a contingent of demon spirits into a herd of swine. The beautiful, recently excavated ruins feature an impressive 5th-century Byzantine-era monastery.

Hamat Gader

חמת גדר

Hamat Gader (675 1039; www.hamat-gader.com; admission Sun-Thu 69NIS, Fri & Sat 79NIS; 7am-10pm Mon-Sat, 7am-4pm Sun), which is actually in the Golan Heights, is a resort complex occupying the bottom of a deep valley split by the Jordanian border. Retirees in beach gear and tots spilling ice cream over themselves hang around Hamat Gadar's luxury mineral pools. Mineral saturation complete, try one of several ethnic restaurants, or check out the alligator farm and zoo park.

From Tiberias, bus 24 departs Sunday to Thursday at 8.45am and 10.30am, and Friday at 8.30am and 9.30am. Returning, buses leave Hamat Gader Sunday to Thursday at noon and 3pm, and Friday at noon and 1pm.

Sleeping

CAMPING

Camping is often expensive as most sites are run by kibbutzim or private resorts, but you do get something for your money – security, a decent shower block and toilet facilities. For a free camping spot, try the bank of the Jordan, near the Arik Bridge.

Hokuk Camping (671 5440, 057 740 0242; camp sites 100NIS; P) Around the bend from Karei Deshe, this is one of the few camping grounds with a grassy pitch. It's open from April to October.

HOSTELS & GUESTHOUSES

Karei Deshe HI Hostel (672 0601; dm/s/d 91.50/171/240NIS; P 🗶 🐾) In Tabgha, this is a sparkling white facility set in attractive grounds with date palms, eucalyptus trees, a rocky beach and a few peacocks. Meals are available for 42NIS. To get here, take bus No 52 from Tiberias.

Nof Ginosar Hotel & Guesthouse (670 0311; www.ginosar.co.il; s US$66-110, d US$80-130; P 🗶 🐾)

 ⊞ ⊠) On Kibbutz Ginosar, this place provides comfortable lakeside accommodation flanked by gardens and a private beach. The lower rates are for the guesthouse and the higher are for the hotel; add 50% to all rates in summer and during Jewish holidays. Rates include breakfast and a visit to the Yigdal Allon Centre (see p321). Nonguests can use the beach for 30NIS.

Ein Gev Resort (☎ 665 9800; www.eingev.org.il; s/d weekdays US$70/90, weekends US$80/95; P ⊠ ⊠ ⊠) Set on a working agricultural and dairy kibbutz, Ein Gev has 166 units with kitchenettes and cable TV. Price includes breakfast but a tour of the kibbutz will cost an extra 16NIS. The site also features an acclaimed garden restaurant specialising in grilled fish. Note that a two-night minimum booking is required for weekends.

Getting There & Around
All long-distance access to the Sea of Galilee is via Tiberias. There's a shortage of buses from town to other parts of the lakeshore, but the main sites along the relatively level road around the Sea of Galilee are accessible to cyclists in an easy two-day circuit. In Tiberias, anyone can rent an 18-speed mountain bike (30NIS to 40NIS per day) from Hotel Aviv. If you're in a hurry, hire a car and make the circuit on a day trip.

TSFAT   צפת تصفد
☎ 04 / pop 26,400
The attractive hilltop town of Tsfat (also spelt Zefat, Tzfat or Safed) enjoys a temperate, high-altitude setting and a rich heritage of Jewish mysticism. It makes a pleasant visit on weekdays, but don't under any circumstances turn up during Shabbat, when even the birds are grounded.

Orientation & Information
Tsfat is spread over a single hilltop, with the bus station on the east side and the old town centre directly opposite on the west side – the hill is scored by the restaurant-studded Yerushalayim (Jerusalem) St, which makes a complete loop between the two.

Sights
At the hilltop, the pleasant breeze-cooled park and viewpoint **Gan HaMetsuda** was once the site of a Crusader citadel. Central Tsfat's old quarters slither down from Yerusha-

layim St, divided by the broad, stiff stairway of **Ma'alot Olei HaGardom St**. This sector was developed by the British after the 1929 riots that divided the Arab and Jewish communities.

The **Synagogue Quarter**, accessed via the stairway north of the City Hall, is a traditional Jewish neighbourhood that focuses on **Kikar HaMaganim** (Defenders' Sq). Two of the synagogues are worth a visit: the **Ha'Ari Ashkenazi Synagogue** and the **Cairo Synagogue**. Prospective visitors should dress modestly; women should avoid bare ankles or shoulders and cardboard yarmulkes are available to male visitors. Photography is permitted except during Shabbat.

Courses
Courses in Torah teachings, the Kabbalah and general Jewish mysticism are available at the well-known **Ascent of Safed** (☎ 692 1364; www.ascentofsafed.com). Classes are open to anyone; for an introduction to the concept, check out the websites www.kabalaonline .org and www.thirtysevenbooks.com.

Sleeping
Beit Binyamin HI Hostel (☎ 697 3514; fax 692 1086; 1 Lohamei HaGeta'ot St; dm/s/d 89/153/224NIS; P ⊠ ⊠) Sitting at the edge of town, this hostel is about 2km (and a stiff slog) from the town centre. All rates include breakfast. This place is more than a little institutional, but at the time of writing it was the cheapest option in Tsfat. Take bus Nos 6 or 7 from the central bus station.

Ascent of Safed Hostel (☎ 692 1364; www.ascent ofsafed.com; dm/d 60/180NIS; ⊠) This hostel is open to Jews who are studying at Ascent of Safed. It's a five-minute walk from the centre of Yerushalayim St.

Eating
Tsfat's main attraction is a range of eating establishments on pedestrianised Yerushalayim St, which are accompanied by some of Israel's most inspiring views. There's a fruit-and-vegetable market on Wednesday; there's also a supermarket at the eastern end of Yerushalayim St near the Javits St steps.

California Felafel (Yerushalayim St; snacks 5-10NIS) An excellent felafel and shwarma option; it's just below the HaPalmach St overpass.

Art Café (☎ 682 0928; Yerushalayim St; dishes 30-40NIS; ⏳ 9.30am-midnight) Poking over the edge of the cliff face, this café offers sweeping views and a dairy menu of pizzas and pastas.

Café Baghdad (☎ 697 4065; 61 Yerushalayim St; dishes 32-55NIS; ☺ 9am-midnight) This dairy and vegetarian restaurant serves up breakfasts, blintzes, soup, salad and sandwiches, as well as dinner entrées. It also enjoys a great terrace view.

Getting There & Away
Buses run to Haifa (34NIS, two hours) every 30 minutes until 9pm (5.45pm on Friday), hourly to Tiberias (20NIS, one hour) until 7pm (4pm on Friday), and twice daily to Tel Aviv (51NIS).

UPPER GALILEE & THE GOLAN HEIGHTS
الجليل & الجولان
הגולן & הגליל העליון

The Upper Galilee is an area of lush greenery watered by runoff from the surrounding mountains. These streams flow together in the Hula Valley to form the Jordan River, which provides most of Israel's fresh water. The chain of high peaks known as the Golan Heights rises to form a tense barrier between the fertile Jordan Valley and the more arid plains of Syria, to the east.

A shortage of public transport makes the Upper Galilee and the Golan Heights more difficult to explore than the rest of Israel. Independent travellers with a vehicle should plan at least two days in the area, especially if they include hiking in the national parks and nature reserves.

Those with limited time and money may prefer a guided tour of the regional highlights, which will cost an average of US$38 per day. Hostels in Tiberias can provide information and details on the latest operators.

ROSH PINA   ראש פינה راس بنيا
☎ 04 / pop 2300
Recent years have seen a rush of artists make their way to Rosh Pina, reinvigorating its former reputation as a laid-back bohemian colony. The 1882 **Rosh Pina Pioneer Settlement Site** (☎ 693 6603), about 1.5km up the hill west of the main road junction, was the first Jewish settlement in Galilee. Here

you'll find cobbled streets and several historic buildings that have been renovated to serve as restaurants, galleries and pubs. You may also want to check out the bizarre **Chocolate Café** (☎ 686 0647; HaRishonim St; ☺ 9am-11pm), which specialises in X-rated chocolate confections (a whole new twist on the sinful nature of that medium!).

The idiosyncratic luxury guesthouse **Villa Tehila** (☎ 693 5336; www.villa-tehila.co.il; 10 Mabat Lachermon Hacholotzim St; d 380-680NIS; P ☒ ☒ ☒ ☒) gets our vote for Israel's most unique accommodation option. Once you get past the various enclosures for rabbits, chickens, ducks, turtles and ponies, the inner courtyard leads to antique-filled reading rooms and a billiards hall. The upstairs guest rooms are beautifully decorated with local art, hand-sewn quilts, brass fittings and wood cabinets. In the basement, the colourful **Blues Brothers Pub** (☺ 9am-late Thu-Sat) is worth visiting on the weekend even if you aren't staying here. Both the hotel and pub are run by a jolly retired journalist who bears a striking resemblance to Charlton Heston in his portrayal of Moses in *Ten Commandments*. A two-night minimum stay is required on weekends. It's located on the main road just below the Pioneer Settlement.

Rosh Pina lies on the bus routes between Tiberias, Tsfat and Kiryat Shmona.

HULA VALLEY   עמק החולה وادي الحولة
☎ 04
Thanks to a reflooding project along the upper Jordan River, the beautiful Hula Valley attracts lots of migratory birds and nesting waterfowl. The best wildlife-viewing spot is **Hula Lake** in the HaHula Reflooding Site, 12km south of Kiryat Shmona then 3km east on an unmarked side road. Here, an elevated hide overlooks ponds and wetlands that attract ducks, coots, moorhens and other waterfowl. You'll also see nutrias ploughing through the incongruous water holes.

The **Hula Nature Reserve** (☎ 693 7069; adult/child 23/14NIS; ☺ 8am-5pm Sat-Thu, 8am-4pm Fri), best known for its migrating flocks of storks and pelicans, has a visitors centre that explains its eucalyptus forest and wetland environment. Free guided tours are conducted between 9.30am and 1.30pm on Saturday, Sunday, Tuesday and Thursday (call ahead). Buses

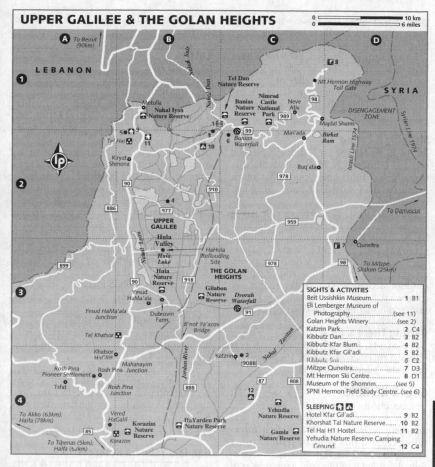

UPPER GALILEE & THE GOLAN HEIGHTS

SIGHTS & ACTIVITIES	
Beit Ussishkin Museum	1 B1
Eli Lemberger Museum of	
Photography	(see 11)
Golan Heights Winery	(see 2)
Katzrin Park	2 C4
Kibbutz Dan	3 B2
Kibbutz Kfar Blum	4 B2
Kibbutz Kfar Gil'adi	5 B2
Kibbutz Snir	6 C2
Mitzpe Quneitra	7 D3
Mt Hermon Ski Centre	8 D1
Museum of the Shomrim	(see 5)
SPNI Hermon Field Study Centre	(see 6)

SLEEPING	
Hotel Kfar Gil'adi	9 B2
Khorshat Tal Nature Reserve	10 B2
Tel Hai H1 Hostel	11 B2
Yehudia Nature Reserve Camping	
Ground	12 C4

between Rosh Pina and Kiryat Shmona will drop you at the signposted junction 2.5km west of the reserve.

Kibbutz Kfar Blum (☎ 694 8409; www.kfarblum-hotel .co.il; s US$80-100, d US$120-160), with a comfortable guesthouse, lies 3km east of the main road between Kiryat Shmona and Rosh Pina.

KIRYAT SHMONA
קרית שמונה كريات شمونة

☎ 04 / pop 22,000

Kiryat Shmona, the 'town of the eight', was named for the eight Jewish settlers killed at nearby Tel Hai in 1920. Since then, its proximity to the Lebanese border has made it a target for Hezbollah (Party of God) attacks, resulting in more casualties. At Tel

Hai, the original watchtower and stockade have been converted into the **Settlement Museum**, but this was under renovation at the time of research. Immediately north, at Kibbutz Kfar Gil'adi, the **Museum of the Shomrim** (adult/child 10/5NIS; ⏱ 10am-5pm Sun-Thu, 10am-2pm Fri) documents the history of WWI Zionist regiments in the British Army.

Near Tel Hai, but west of the highway, you may want to see the **Eli Lemberger Museum of Photography** (☎ 695 0769; www.open-museums.co.il; admission 15NIS; ⏱ 8am-4pm Sun-Thu, 10am-5pm Sat), which displays the work of many renowned Israeli and international photographers.

Above the frontier town of Metulla, you can saunter up to the **Good Fence** (HaGader Ha Tova), which proverbially makes for good neighbours. The place was deserted when we visited, but there is nothing stopping you from looking around.

East of the Metulla road, **Nahal Iyon Nature Reserve** (adult/child 18/8NIS; 8am-5pm Sun-Thu 8am-4pm Fri) encompasses the valley of the Iyon River and several impressive waterfalls, including 18m **Tanur Falls**. It's a great place for a quick leg stretch.

Sleeping & Eating

Tel Hai HI Hostel (☎ 694 0043; telhai@iyha.org.il; dm/s/d 95/195/260NIS; P ⊠ ☒) This place is friendly and functional option, but more expensive than most HI hostels. Breakfast is included.

Hotel Kfar Gil'adi (☎ 690 0000; www.kfar-giladi.co .il; s US$70-90, d US$90-110) Located on Kibbutz Kfar Gil'adi, this is a beautifully situated getaway with a range of amenities, including indoor and outdoor swimming pools, a sauna, gym, tennis courts and organised outdoor activities. The deluxe rooms are somewhat newer. All rates include breakfast, additional meals are US$18 each.

Getting There & Away

Bus Nos 541, 841 and 963 connect Kiryat Shmona to Tiberias (26NIS, 1½ hours) via the Hula Valley and Rosh Pina.

GOLAN HEIGHTS   הגולן الجولان

The beautiful Golan Heights, between the Jordan River and the Syrian border, was annexed by Israel in 1981, after it forcefully occupied this former Syrian territory during the 1967 Six Day War and successfully defended it in the Yom Kippur War of 1973. Despite negotiations during the 1990s (mediated by the United States), Syria and Israel remained at loggerheads and still today the Golan is a major stumbling block in normalising relations between the two countries. Despite the conflicts, it remains a lovely area of rich agricultural developments, traditional Druze villages and wonderful national parks and nature reserves. You'll also see trenches, bomb shelters, bunkers, bombed-out villages, minefields and a host of modern ruins.

Mitzpe Shalom   מצפה שלום

From the dramatic **Mitzpe Shalom** (☎ 676 1991; ☼ 9am-5pm) lookout at Haruv you'll have a view across all of the Sea of Galilee, and

see Tiberias spilling down the slopes in the distance.

Katzrin   קצרין كترين

☎ 04 / pop 7000

The planned community of Katzrin, the Golan Heights' 'capital', makes a decent if soporific regional base. Highly worthwhile is the ancient Talmudic village at **Katzrin Park** (☎ 696 2412; adult/child 22/14NIS; ☼ 8am-5pm Sun-Thu, 8am-3pm Fri, 10am-4pm Sat), which includes the remains of a 3rd-century synagogue, two reconstructed houses and an audiovisual programme, the **Talmudic Experience** (admission 10NIS). This also serves as the local tourist office.

Another highlight is the **Golan Archaeological Museum** (☎ 696 1350; adult/student 15/12NIS; ☼ 9am-4pm Mon-Thu, 9am-1.30pm Fri, 10.30am-1.30pm Sat), in the town centre, which features discoveries from Gamla and Katzrin Park. The laudable **Golan Heights Winery** (☎ 696 8420; www .golanwines.co.il), on the west side of Katzrin, conducts tours (20NIS including wine tasting) during business hours from Sunday to Thursday.

SPNI Field School (☎ 696 1234; Daliyat St; d 245NIS; P ⊠ ☒) has a clean and comfortable guesthouse and staff that can recommend hikes in the area.

Three buses per day (except Saturday, 25NIS, 6am, 7am and 2pm, 45 minutes), connect Katzrin with Tiberias (25NIS, 6am, 7am and 2pm). A daily bus (except Saturday) also follows the scenic route via Mas'ada to Kiryat Shmona (32NIS, 11.15am, 1½ hours).

Gamla & Yehudia Reserves
          גמלא & שמורת הטבע של נחל יהודיה

South of Katzrin, a large wild area presents some terrific hiking along deep canyons and past lovely, feathery waterfalls and freshwater pools. **Gamla Nature Reserve** (adult/child 23/14NIS; ☼ 8am-4pm Sun-Thu, 8am-3pm Fri) preserves both a large natural area and the ruins of the ancient Jewish stronghold, **Gamla**, overlooking the Sea of Galilee. In a Roman siege on 12 October, in the year AD 67, three legions of the Roman army killed 4000 Jewish inhabitants; the historian Flavius Josephus reports that another 5000 leapt off the cliff face rather than submit.

Between Gamla and Katzrin lies the fantastic 66-sq-km **Yehudia Nature Reserve** (adult/child 23/14NIS), where there's a camping ground and a large network of hiking tracks. The popular five-hour Nahal Zavitan hike leads past some interesting hexagonal basalt formations, as well as canyons, waterfalls and swimmable pools. If you are going to be doing a lot of walking, pick up a 1:50,000 'Golan Heights' map available at the SPNI Field School in Katzrin (see opposite).

Majdal Shams & Mas'ada
מסעדה & מג'דל שאמס   مجدل شمس و مسعده

The Druze villages of Majdal Shams and Mas'ada, on the slopes of Mt Hermon, maintain their autonomy from Israeli authority and continue to protest the Israeli occupation of the Golan Heights. At the **Mitzpe Quneitra** viewpoint, 15km south of Mas'ada, you can look across the border to the Syrian ghost town of **Quneitra**, flattened by the IDF before it retreated after the 1967 Six Day War. Along the road here, sample the unleavened bread with goat cheese sold by local Druze villagers at roadside stalls.

Mt Hermon
הר הרמון   هرمن جبل

In the northeastern corner of the Golan Heights rises 2224m Mt Hermon, the highest peak in Israel, which is shared with Syria and Lebanon. Limited ski facilities are available from late December to early April. To reach the **ski lifts** (adult/child Sun-Fri 27/24NIS; Sat 31/26NIS), drivers must use the Mt Hermon toll road (30NIS per vehicle). For information, visit the **ski centre** (☎ 04-698 1337; www.skihermon.co.il), down the mountain in the tourist settlement of Neve Ativ, where there are also a few places to stay.

Banias Nature Reserve & Nimrod Castle
בניאס & קלעת נמרוד

One of the most spectacular spots in the region, **Banias Nature Reserve** (adult/child 23/14NIS; 8am-4pm Sun-Thu, 8am-2pm Fri), which is also known as the Nahal Hermon Reserve, takes in the Banias Cave sanctuary as well as the lovely **Banias waterfall**, about 1km away (and accessed by a separate gate – one ticket is good for both sites). On a hill above the cave, the grave of the prophet Elijah is marked by a white cliffside memorial. Less than 2km east of Banias, the best-preserved Crusader fortress in Israel rises above its hilltop surroundings in **Nimrod Castle National Park** (☎ 04-694 9277; adult/child 18/9NIS; 8am-4pm). Bus No 55 from Kiryat Shmona passes

by Banias twice daily and bus Nos 25, 26 and 36 pass by Kibbutz Dan, which is 6km to the west.

Tel Dan
תל דן   تيل دان هظلبه

East of Kiryat Shmona, an appealing forested area of natural springs and ancient Canaanite ruins (2700–2400 BC) are preserved in **Tel Dan Nature Reserve** (adult/child 23/12NIS; 8am-4pm Sun-Thu, 8am-3pm Fri). The site was first settled in the 5th century BC as the city of Leshem, but was conquered in the 12th century BC by the tribe of Dan and became the northernmost Israelite outpost.

This popular and often crowded picnic spot is best known for its walking tracks, bubbling waters and ancient stands of oak and ash trees. From Kiryat Shmona, take bus No 25, 26 or 36. The adjacent **Beit Ussishkin Museum** (☎ 694 1704; adult/child 18/15NIS; 9am-4pm Sun-Thu, 9am-3pm Fri, 10am-4pm Sat) features an audiovisual programme, dioramas and extensive natural-history exhibits.

Camping is available at nearby **Khorshat Tal Nature Reserve** (☎ 694 2360; camp sites 15NIS), which also offers basic bungalows. The **SPNI Hermon Field Study Centre** (☎ 694 1091; fax 695 1480; d 245NIS), at Kibbutz Snir, has guest cottages set on oak-shaded lawns.

DEAD SEA
ים המלח   البحر الميت

At an elevation of 400m below sea level, the Dead Sea shoreline is the lowest bit of dry real estate in the world. After the obligatory float, don't miss the ruins at Masada, which is probably Israel's most enigmatic attraction. Though not as well frequented by travellers, the hiking tracks and springs of Ein Gedi National Park also merit some exploration.

QUMRAN
קומרן   قمران
☎ 02

Described as 'the most important discovery in the history of the Jewish people', the **Dead Sea Scrolls**, now on display at the Israel Museum in Jerusalem, were discovered at Qumran in 1947. The site includes the settlement and caves of the Essenes, the Jewish sect that authored the scrolls from 150 BC to AD 68,

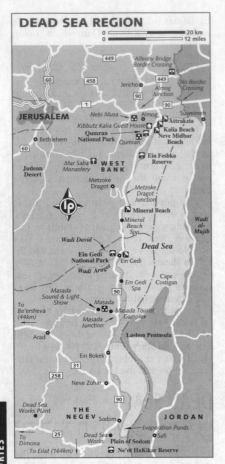

DEAD SEA REGION

when the Essenes were disbanded by the Roman invaders. **Qumran National Park** (☎ 994 2235; adult/child 18/8NIS) includes a seven-minute multimedia programme, a small museum and shops selling books, souvenirs, Dead Sea mineral creams and beauty products.

There are also a couple of beaches at Qumran. **Neve Midbar Beach** (☎ 994 2781; adult/child 35/30NIS, camp sites/huts per person 45/60NIS), located 1.5km off the highway, has a bar and a simple restaurant. **Kalia Beach** (☎ 994 2391; admission 25NIS) is slightly better value.

Kibbutz Kalia Guest House (☎ 993 6333; www .kalia.org.il; s/d incl breakfast 250/320NIS; ☒☒☒☒) is located 1km from Qumran National Park. This kibbutz-hotel occupies a beautiful oasis of gardens and date palms. It offers

a heated pool and horse riding. Meals are available for US$7 to US$10.

EIN GEDI   עין גדי عين جدي
☎ 08

Ein Gedi National Park (☎ 658 4285; adult/child 23/12NIS) is a paradise of dramatic canyons, freshwater springs, waterfalls, and lush tropical vegetation. Despite the busloads of rampaging school groups that descend on it daily, it continues to provide a haven for desert wildlife. In the winter months, hikers can enter Wadi David from 8am to 3pm and Wadi Aragot from 8am to 2pm; in summer, the trails are open one hour later. The neighbouring **Ein Gedi National Antiquities Park** (adult/child 12/6NIS; ☺ 8am-4pm) includes the ruins of an ancient trapezoid synagogue with an especially inspiring mosaic floor, which was used from the 3rd to 6th centuries AD.

South of the reserve, you'll find the **Ein Gedi spa bathing beach** (admission free; showers 8NIS), petrol station, restaurant and camping ground, and the turnoff for Kibbutz Ein Gedi. One of the best places to bathe is the **Mineral Beach spa complex** (☎ 02-994 4888; www.dead-sea .co.il; admission 35NIS), located 15km north of Ein Gedi, with its pools, mud and sulphur baths.

Sleeping & Eating
Beit Sarah Hostel (☎ 658 4165; eingedi@iyha.org .il; dm/s/d US$21/39.50/60; ☒☒☒) Uphill and 250m from the bus stop, this hostel occupies the finest setting of any Israeli hostel. Rates include breakfast.

SPNI Field School (☎ 658 4288; www.teva.org.il; dm/s 75/130NIS, d 190-305NIS; ☒☒☒) Perched on the hillside above Beit Sarah, this place enjoys great views and is an excellent launch point for early hikes. Stay a few days and watch the magical light and changing scene over the lake. Rates include breakfast and dinner is 38NIS to 45NIS.

Kibbutz Ein Gedi (☎ 659 4222; www.ein-gedi.co.il; s US$122-143, d US$174-204) Has a guesthouse surrounded by lush gardens, with a pool and hot spa. Rates include half board.

MASADA   מצדה مسعدأ
☎ 08
Masada, a desert mesa rising high above the Dead Sea, figures prominently in the Israeli psyche. In 150 BC, a fortress was built atop

THE DEAD SEA

The water in the Dead Sea, while surprisingly clear, is deceptively laden with microscopic solids that virtually overwhelm the two parts hydrogen, one part oxygen that make up fresh water, creating an oily broth in which people can float.

The ingredients that make up the Dead Sea read like a science experiment: compared to ocean water, the Dead Sea has 20 times more bromine, 15 times more magnesium and 10 times more iodine. Bromine, a component of many sedatives, relaxes the nerves; magnesium counteracts skin allergies and clears bronchial passages; iodine, which is essential to good health, has a beneficial effect on thyroid functions. Not surprisingly, this is all loudly proclaimed by local health-spa owners and cosmetic companies.

Healthy or not, wading into the Dead Sea may seem distinctly unhealthy if you have exposed cuts or grazes – in fact, you'd instantly assimilate the phrase 'to rub salt into the wound'.

Similarly, swallowing even a drop of this foul-tasting brew will induce retching and may well burn your throat for half an hour. It goes without saying that if you splash this water in your eyes, you must immediately flush them with fresh water.

this superb natural lookout, and was re-fortified and improved in 43 BC by Herod the Great, who used it as a retreat. During the Jewish First Revolt against the Romans in AD 66, after the sacking and burning of Jerusalem, the Zealots fled to Masada, which became the last outpost of Jewish Resistance. Faced with imminent attack as the Romans constructed an earthen ramp to invade the fortress, 10 Jewish men were elected to slay the rest of their men. In the end, one of these killed the rest before committing suicide himself. When the Romans stormed the fortress, they discovered 960 bodies; only seven people, who'd hidden in a water cistern, survived to relay the tale to the world.

Once a dusty outpost, Masada is now guarded by a massive **tourist complex** (☎ 658 4207; gl.masada@nautre-parks.org.il), including a restaurant and theatre that shows a short introductory video on the history of Masada. The summit ruins are accessible on foot via the steep and sinuous **'Snake Path'** (adult/child 19/12NIS) or on the considerably more popular **cable car** (adult one way/return 45/61NIS, child one way/return 22/34NIS). For a hand-held audio guide add 15NIS. From March to October, the Masada **Sound-and-Light show** (☎ 995 9333) is presented on the Arad side.

Sleeping & Eating

Isaac H Taylor HI Hostel (☎ 658 4349; fax 658 4650; dm/s/d 78/162/224NIS; P ☒ ☒) By the Masada bus stop this hostel provides college-style dorms with breakfast included. Sleeping

out on Masada is no longer permitted, but the hostel will let you set up a tent in its garden.

Getting There & Away

You can approach Masada from either the Dead Sea (for the youth hostel, tourist complex and summit access) or Arad (for the Sound-and-Light show). For the former, there are about nine daily Jerusalem buses (39NIS, two hours) and four Eilat buses (55NIS, four hours).

THE NEGEV

הנגב   ألعقبة سحرأ

The Negev, the sparsely inhabited southern wedge of Israel, takes in nearly half the national area, but the only towns of any size are Be'ersheva, Arad, Mitzpe Ramon and Israel's subtropical toehold of Eilat. In addition to numerous military bases, this desert area supports a number of experimental agricultural projects, as well as 75,000 semi-nomadic tent-dwelling Bedouin.

Not surprisingly, the Negev presents some of Israel's best hiking venues, including the recommended Sde Boker, the Wilderness of Zin, En Avedat, Maktesh Ramon, Timna National Park and the Eilat Mountains. For route information and maps, visit the SPNI field schools at Sde Boker, Mitzpe Ramon or Eilat. Note that much of the Negev is a firing zone for the area's numerous military bases; for the latest

330 THE NEGEV •• Be'ersheva

information, phone the **army co-ordination office** (☎ 08-990 2294).

BE'ERSHEVA   באר שבע بير السبع
☎ 08 / pop 183,200

Scruffy and dusty, Be'ersheva won't impress many, and although it's the 'capital' of Negev, the most satisfaction it's likely to offer is the view from the rear window as you leave.

The **main post office** (cnr HaNessi'im & Ben Zvi Sts) is just north of the central bus station. There are plenty of banks in the adjacent Kanyon shopping centre.

Sights & Activities
The much-vaunted **Bedouin market** (☼ 6am-4pm Thu) provides evidence that the Israeli Bedouin are as interested in Nike and Yves St-Laurent knock-offs as anyone in the world. You may see the odd camel, but it's definitely less than a cultural than a commercial experience. While that's fair enough, it's not an especially interesting visit.

Be'ersheva's most worthwhile attraction is the **Israeli Air Force Museum** (☎ 690 6855; www .iaf-museum.org.il; admission 26NIS; ☼ 8am-5pm Sun-Thu, 8am-1pm Fri), at the Khatserim IAF base 6km west of the centre. From the central bus station take bus No 31 (9.80NIS, 10 minutes, once or twice per hour).

On Kibbutz Lahav, off the Be'ersheva to Kiryat Gat road, the Joe Allon Centre features the **Museum of Bedouin Culture** (☎ 991 3322; admission 20NIS; ☼ 9am-5pm Sun-Thu, 8am-2pm Fri). Bus No 42 runs directly to the kibbutz once daily, but immediately heads back to Be'ersheva without allowing time for a visit. Alternatively, use bus No 369 towards Tel Aviv, which will drop you at the junction 8km from the kibbutz.

Sleeping & Eating
Beit Yatziv HI Hostel (☎ 627 7444, 627 5735; beit _yatziv@silverbyte.com; 79 Ha'Atzma'ut St; dm/s/d 102/ 185/280NIS; ℗ ✗ ✗ ✗) It isn't all that cheap, but this hostel has a garden and no curfew. Rates include breakfast and other meals cost US$11.

Yitzhak's Bulgarian Restaurant (☎ 623 8504; 112 Keren Kayemet Le-Y'israel St; dishes 40NIS; ☼ 10am-10pm Sun-Thu, 11am-7pm Sat) This restaurant does meat-oriented sit-down meals. The focus is on Ashkenazi specialities: kebabs, schnitzel, liver etc.

Getting There & Away
On business days, buses run every 20 minutes to Tel Aviv (13.80NIS, 1½ hours) and at least half-hourly to Jerusalem (32NIS, 1½ hours). For Eilat (55NIS, three hours), buses depart more or less every hour via Mitzpe Ramon (23NIS, 1¼ hours). Bus services for Dimona (9.80NIS, 30 minutes) and for Arad (14.80NIS, 45 minutes) run at least every half-hour.

From Be'ersheva's central train station, which is adjacent to the central bus station, you can travel comfortably to Tel Aviv (25.50NIS, 1½ hours) roughly hourly on business days.

ARAD   ערד اراد
☎ 08 / pop 24,500

More appealing than Be'ersheva or Dimona is Arad, a lethargic eastern Negev community that benefits from its surrounding wealth of mineral deposits. An attractive addition to the city is Eshet Lot Artist's Quarter, being developed in an abandoned industrial zone, 2km southwest of town. Nearly 20 artists have transformed the old hangers, garages and factories into gift shops, studios and workshops. Check out the **Glass Museum** (www.warmglassil.com; Sadan Rd; ☼ 10am-5pm Sat-Thu, 10am-3pm Fri) opened by artist Gideon Fridman, and **Studio 11** (☎ 054 554 0002; Sadan Unit 4) a bar and concert hall featuring live music on weekends.

Tel Arad National Park (adult/child 18/9NIS; ☼ 8am-4pm Sun-Thu, 8am-3pm Fri), 8km west of town, includes the ruins of a Bronze Age city from the 3rd century BC. Take any bus towards Be'ersheva, get off at the Tel Arad junction and walk the final 2km to the site. East of Dimona, on the road to Arad lies **Mamshit National Park** (☎ 659 1543; adult/child 18/9NIS), which features a complex of extensive and impressive 1st-century Nabataean ruins.

Sleeping & Eating
Blau-Weiss HI Hostel (☎ 995 7150; arad@iyha.org.il; 4 HaAtad St; dm/s/d/tr 63/164/198/248NIS) Typically comfortable rooms in a distinctly institutional atmosphere. For breakfast add another 31NIS.

Zimmer Paz B&B (☎ 054 470 8694; rivkapaz@hot mail.com; 37 HaGilad St; s/d 180/200NIS; ℗ ✗ ✗) Offers four private suites, each with their own sitting room and kitchen. Breakfast costs an additional 40NIS. Weekend prices jump by around 50NIS.

Muza Pub (☎ 997 5555; ◷ noon-5am) A curious mix of Texas roadhouse and British pub, this charming local watering hole is an Arad institution. It's next to the Alon gas station as you enter the town on the road from Be'ersheva.

Getting There & Away
From the central bus terminal on Rehov Yehuda, buses run twice per hour to and from Be'ersheva (14.80NIS, 45 minutes). Buses depart for Ein Gedi (20.50NIS) at 10.15am, 1pm and 3.45pm.

DIMONA   דימונה ديمونه
☎ 08 / pop 29,300
Unless you're involved in espionage (Dimona is the site of Israel's no-longer-secret nuclear weapons facility), the main interest in this bleak desert town is the African Hebrew Israelite Community. In one small enclave, this motivated and self-contained group of around 2000 people operates its own school, and members make their own jewellery and natural-fibre clothing. Dietary restrictions are a variation on veganism, as African Hebrew Israelis don't eat meat, dairy products, fish, eggs, or refined sugar or flour. Visitors are welcome, but you'll get better attention by calling first (☎ 657 3286). The African Hebrew Israelites run a small **guesthouse** (beds with half board 100NIS) and an adjacent vegan restaurant (meals 25NIS). For more information, consult their website: www.kingdomofyah.com.

From the central bus terminal, buses run frequently to and from Be'ersheva (9.80NIS, 30 minutes).

SDE BOKER & AVDAT
שדה בוקר سدبوكار
☎ 08
These stops along the route between Be'ersheva and Mitzpe Ramon merit anything from a few hours to a couple of days.

Sde Boker Kibbutz, a popular stopping point for Jewish history buffs, contains the modest **home of David Ben-Gurion** (☎ 656 0469; adult/child 10/7NIS; ◷ 8.30am-4pm Sun-Thu, 8.30am-2pm Fri, 9am-3pm Sat), preserved as it was at the time of his death in 1973. At the entrance to the Sde Boker, a **visitor centre** shows a 20-minute film (7NIS) about the kibbutz. Around 3km south of the kibbutz, at a spectacular clifftop setting, are the graves of Ben-Gurion and his wife Paula. The gravesite is close to the northern entrance of **En Avedat National Park** (☎ 655 5684; adult/child 23/12; 8am-5pm Sun-Thu, 8am-4pm Fri) where day-hikers can amble through the **Wilderness of Zin** to the bizarrely chilly desert spring, **En Avedat**. The starting point for the 2½-hour walk is at the end of a 3km paved road. Note that this is a one-way hike, so if you need to return to the northern entrance you'll need to hitch or wait for a bus (one every 1½ hours). Ask for a bus schedule before heading off, to help time your hike.

A great place to stay is the British-run **Krivine's** (☎ 052 712304; krivjohn@netvision.net.il; dm/s/d 75/145/215NIS), which provides excellent tourist information, meals, mountain-bike rental and transport from the Sde Boker bus stop. Advance booking is essential.

Avdat National Park (☎ 655 1511; adult/child 23/12NIS; ◷ 8am-5pm Sun-Thu, 8am-4pm Fri), a ruins complex with Nabataean, Roman and Byzantine elements, is best known for the camel-caravan sculpture on the crest of the hill. Constructed by Nabataeans in the 2nd century BC, it served as a *caravanserai* along the trade route between Petra and the Mediterranean coast.

MITZPE RAMON
מצפה רמון متسزبئ رآمون
☎ 08 / pop 6000
Mitzpe is Hebrew for 'watchtower', and accordingly, this small but engaging desert town enjoys an impressive vista across the dramatic **Maktesh Ramon** crater, which measures 300m deep, 8km wide and 40km long. All along this dramatic 'watchtower', you'll find far-ranging views and an extensive network of hiking routes. Pick up a Makhtesh Ramon Nature Reserve map at the visitors centre and set off into the desert on foot; this wild wonderland is good for days of wandering – but be sure to carry lots of water.

Information
The ammonite-shaped **visitors centre** (☎ 658 8691; adult/child 23/12NIS; ◷ 8am-5pm Sun-Thu, 8am-4pm Fri), perched on the crater rim, has a tourist office and presents an overview of Maktesh Ramon's intriguing natural history, along with a film about the park.

Sights

Downhill from the visitors centre, the **Bio-Ramon** (☎ 658 8755; adult/child 12/6NIS; ◷ 9am-6pm Sun-Thu, 9am-4pm Fri, 9am-5pm Sat) complex displays a collection of desert flora and fauna. East of town, the **Alpaca Farm** (☎ 658 8047; www .alpaca.co.il; adult/child 25/23NIS; ◷ 8.30am-4.30pm Sat-Thu) is a labour of love for its owners, who spin wool and keep a variety of South American camelids (ie llamas and alpacas).

Tours

Lots of companies run rugged jeep tours, but they come and go with the desert wind and you may need to muster a group; see the visitors centre for the latest offerings.

Guide Horizon (☎ 659 5333; www.guidehorizon .com; 27 Har Boker St) hires out desert dune buggies for excursions into the Negev; a three-hour trip with breakfast goes for 350NIS while an overnight trip, including cook out and sauna upon return to the home base, goes for 800NIS.

Negevland Tours (☎ 659 5555; www.negevland.co .il; 6 Gvanim St) is an adventure company offering crater tours (US$25 per person) and abseiling (US$14 for two descents). It has a bike repair shop and will hire out mountain bikes (US$25 per day).

Peter Bugel Tours (☎ 658 8958; www.shunra.net /peter.html; PO Box 327 Mitzpe Ramon) caters for travellers who are interested in desert culture, geology and botany. It's a sophisticated outfit run by a fellow who speaks Dutch, German, English and Swiss-German. Overnight trips cost US$350 for a group of seven.

Sleeping

Mitzpe Ramon HI Hostel (☎ 658 8443; fax 658 8074; dm/s/d 100/195/280NIS) This is a short downhill walk from the visitors centre. Most rooms have a great crater view. Rates include a continental breakfast.

Chez Alexis (☎ 658 8258, 056 432627; 7 En Saharonim St; r per person US$12) This is probably the friendliest place in town, thanks to the French-Algerian owner, who speaks French, English and Hebrew. Guests have access to the kitchen facilities.

Succah in the Desert (Succah HaMidbar; ☎ 658 6280; www.succah.co.il; PO Box 272, Mitzpe Ramon; s/d Sat-Thu 240/400NIS, Fri 450/550NIS) Set 7km from town on a poor track, this is the place to stay if you're intrigued by any sort of mysticism. Although short on creature comforts, the point is integration with the desert; so if you can't live without modern plumbing, forget it. Advance bookings, which are essential, will avail you of free transport from Mitzpe Ramon.

Be'erot Camping (☎ 658 6713; www.beerot.com; camp sites/Bedouin tent beds per person 25/40NIS) This is camping in a dramatic setting, with local tents, Bedouin cuisine, clean bathrooms and a modern shower block. It's 12km south of Mitzpe Ramon on the highway to Eilat, and then 5km down a bumpy access road. Meals are available for 30NIS but call ahead.

Eating

Pangea (☎ 653 9222; 5 Oded St; dishes 35-40NIS; ◷ 8am-midnight) This kosher restaurant, situated next to the bus stop at the northern entrance to the town, specialises in grilled meats and cheeseless pasta dishes.

HaHavit (☎ 658 8226; dishes 28-45NIS; ◷ 9-2am) Located at the visitors centre, HaHavit (Barrel) serves business lunches and set meals all day, while the pub operates until late.

Self-caterers will find joy at the Hyper Neto and Supersol supermarkets, both in the town centre.

Getting There & Away

From Sunday to Thursday bus No 392 travels to Eilat (42NIS, 2½ hours) at 8.55am, 10.25am, 1.10pm and 4.45pm. The lone Friday bus departs at 9.10am. From 6am to 9.30pm, bus No 60 shuttles hourly to and from Be'ersheva (26NIS, one hour), via Sde Boker and Ein Avdat.

EILAT   אילת آيلات
☎ 08 / pop 50,000

Wedged between Jordan and Egypt, and separated from the Israel of international headlines by 200km of desert, Eilat is a resort town where glitzy, ziggurat-like hotels line an artificial lagoon and glass-bottomed boats ply deteriorating coral reefs. Its founding fathers – convicts sent here in the 1950s to build the city – now mix with tie-dyed beach bums selling trinkets from India and weekend holidaymakers in search of sin.

The Miami-style scene is somewhat diminished by coarse and cluttered beaches and for most visitors Eilat's real appeal is in its surrounding desert mountains and canyons. Divers, snorkellers, sunbathers and anyone else searching for the Red Sea's

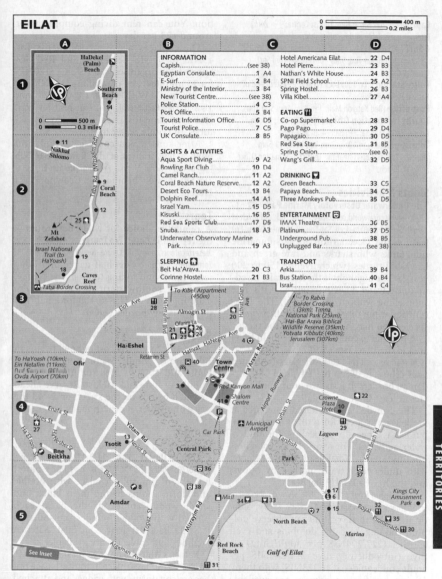

EILAT

0 —————— 400 m
0 —————— 0.2 miles

INFORMATION
Capish	(see 38)
Egyptian Consulate	1 A4
E-Surf	2 B4
Ministry of the Interior	3 B4
New Tourist Centre	(see 38)
Police Station	4 C3
Post Office	5 B4
Tourist Information Office	6 D5
Tourist Police	7 C5
UK Consulate	8 B5

SIGHTS & ACTIVITIES
Aqua Sport Diving	9 A2
Bowling Bar Club	10 D4
Camel Ranch	11 A2
Coral Beach Nature Reserve	12 A2
Desert Eco Tours	13 B4
Dolphin Reef	14 A1
Israel Yam	15 D5
Kisuski	16 B5
Red Sea Sports Club	17 D6
Snuba	18 A3
Underwater Observatory Marine Park	19 A3

SLEEPING
Beit Ha'Arava	20 C3
Corinne Hostel	21 B3

Hotel Americana Eilat	22 D4
Hotel Pierre	23 B3
Nathan's White House	24 B3
SPNI Field School	25 A2
Spring Hostel	26 B3
Villa Kibel	27 A4

EATING
Co-op Supermarket	28 B3
Pago Pago	29 D4
Papagaio	30 D5
Red Sea Star	31 B5
Spring Onion	(see 6)
Wang's Grill	32 D5

DRINKING
Green Beach	33 C5
Papaya Beach	34 C5
Three Monkeys Pub	35 D5

ENTERTAINMENT
IMAX Theatre	36 B5
Platinum	37 D5
Underground Pub	38 B5
Unplugged Bar	(see 38)

TRANSPORT
Arkia	39 B4
Bus Station	40 B4
Israir	41 C4

ISRAEL & THE PALESTINIAN TERRITORIES

magical underwater world should head posthaste for the Egyptian Sinai.

Orientation

Eilat consists of a town centre, the hotel-fringed lagoon and beaches, and the 5km coastal strip between the town centre and the Egyptian border. The massive Jordanian flag down the coast to the east marks the town of Aqaba; on clear days it's possible to see King Hussein's mansion.

Information

To change money, head for the many no-commission change bureaus in the town centre. ATMs are widespread.

Capish (☎ 632 5977; New Tourist Centre; ◷ 24hr) Internet is available at this coffee shop.

E-Surf (☎ 634 4331; central bus station; per hr 15NIS; ◷ 9am-11pm Sun-Thu, 9am-4pm Fri, 4-11pm Sat) Internet café.

Police station (☎ 100) Located at the eastern end of Hativat HaNegev Ave.

Post office (Red Kanyon Mall; ◷ 8am-4pm Sun-Thu)

Tourist Information Office (☎ 630 9111; Bridge House, Yacht Marina; ◷ 8am-4pm Sun-Thu)

Tourist police (◷ 10am-3am Sun-Wed, 10-6am Thu-Sat) This station is near the Tourist Information Office at North Beach.

Sights & Activities

The **Underwater Observatory Marine Park** (☎ 636 4200; www.coralworld.com/eilat; Taba Rd; adult/child 79/69NIS; ◷ 8.30am-4pm Sat-Thu, 8.30am-3.30pm Fri) features the 'Oceanarium' mock submarine ride, tanks with sharks and rare green and hawksbill turtles (which live for 150 to 200 years!). The highlight is the magical glassed-in underwater viewing centre – it's like snorkelling without getting wet. The adjacent aquarium displays many of the tropical species you may have missed on the reef.

A popular excursion from the main hotel area is the **Israel Yam** (☎ 637 5528, 050 531 0090; Yacht Marina; adult/child 60/40NIS) glass-bottomed boat cruise, between the Egyptian and Jordanian borders. It lasts two hours and operates at least three times daily.

The crowded and cluttered hotel area at **North Beach** is great for a drink in the sun, but isn't especially appealing for underwater activities. For snorkelling, your best options are the **Coral Beach Nature Reserve**, with underwater trails marked by buoys, and the free **HaDekel (Palm) Beach**.

At **Dolphin Reef** (☎ 637 1846; www.dolphinreef.co .il; Southern Beach; adult/child 42/28NIS; ◷ 9am-5pm), on the Taba road, visitors can observe dolphin training, feed the dolphins and even snorkel (227/204NIS per adult/child) or dive (introductory dive 274/246NIS per adult/child, guided dive 223NIS) with them. Diving certification courses are available from 1400NIS.

You can also dive with one of Eilat's other operators: **Red Sea Sports Club** (☎ 633 3666; www.redseasports.co.il; Bridge House); **Snuba** (☎ 637 2722; www.snuba.co.il; Caves Reef); or **Aqua Sport** (☎ 633 4404; www.aqua-sport.com; Coral Beach). All charge around €41 for an introductory dive, or €315 for a five-day PADI certifica-

tion. You can rent diving equipment for around €23 per day.

These places also rent sailboards for 45NIS to 55NIS per hour, and Red Sea Sports Club organises water-skiing (120NIS for 15 minutes) and parasailing (120NIS for 10 minutes). With **Kisuski** (☎ 637 2088; www .kisos.co.il; Red Rock Beach), you can rent jet skis, jet boats, parasails, pedal boats, kayaks, ski tubes and other water toys.

After sunset, you could get drunk and bowl a few frames at the **Bowling Bar Club** (☎ 631 6797; Eilat Marina; ◷ 3pm-2am Sun-Fri, 6pm-2am Sat) located behind the Crowne Plaza Hotel.

Tours

A reputable choice for wilderness tours is the reputable **Desert Eco Tours** (☎ 637 4259; www .desertecotours.com; Zofit Centre, Neviot St, PO Box 4113, Zofit Centre), which does half-day to multi-day jeep, camel and hiking tours in the Negev, Sinai and southwestern Jordan. If you're camping, plan on US$40/100 for a half/full day (plus any border taxes).

Sleeping

As a resort town, the cost of hotel rooms in Eilat rise by about 25% or more on weekends, and 25% to 50% (or more) in the months of June and August. Reserve ahead or you'll be out on the street, or avoid the place altogether at peak holiday times.

BUDGET

Camping isn't permitted on most beaches.

Corinne Hostel (☎ 637 1472; 127 Retamim St; dm/ s/d 40/70/120NIS; ✕ ✿) This is Eilat's oldest hostel, an atmospheric place with double and dorm rooms in the main block and small wood cabins out the back, each topped with wooden reindeer cut-outs, as if Santa had just arrived in Eilat. Kitchen facilities and cable TV are available.

Nathan's White House (☎ 637 6572; Retamim St; s/d 100/120NIS) This place is quite basic, but has air-con dorms with fridges and attached bathrooms.

Spring Hostel (☎ 637 4660; www.avivhostels.co .il; 126 Ofarim Lane; dm/s/d/ste 40/120/150/200NIS; ✕ ✿ ▣ ✿) This small hotel has very clean doubles and handy little two room suites that come with kitchenette. Breakfast is served in the high season and kitchen facilities are available. The small pool on the second floor is a rare commodity among places in this range.

Beit Ha'Arava (☎ 637 4687; 106 Almogin St; dm/s/d/tr 40/100/120/150NIS; P ⊠ ⊠ ⊠) Considered by many travellers the cleanest and best value guesthouse among several others in this area, the Beit Ha'Arava consists of 27 rooms, a well-lit common room and a pleasant patio garden. Breakfast costs an additional 12NIS to 20NIS.

MIDRANGE

Villa Kibel (☎ /fax 637 6911; ☎ 050 534 5366; www .villakibel.co.il; 18 Peres St; flats 160NIS; P ⊠ ⊠) This is a friendly and quiet private home divided into a collection of comfortable holiday flats with kitchenettes and cable TV. The same management also offers a 13-bed house for 760NIS. It tends to fill up, so bookings are highly recommended. If you have a lot of luggage, the owner will pick you up at the bus station.

Hotel Pierre (☎ 632 6601; www.eilat-guide.com /pierre; 123 Ofarim Lane; s/d US$50/80; P ⊠ ⊠) This place is friendly, quiet, unassuming and very French. The small-but-comfortable rooms all have fridges, phones and cable TV.

Hotel Americana Eilat (☎ 633 3777; www.america nahotel.co.il; Kaman Rd; s/d 200/250NIS) Attracting the Israeli blue-collar set, this place is not the best place to meet the party crowd, but it's got a well-placed location near the marina, a five-minute walk from the heart of North Beach. Amenities include tennis courts, a large swimming pool and the Flintstone-style Cave Bar. Breakfast is included.

Eating & Drinking

Spring Onion (☎ 637 7434; Bridge House; dishes 45-65NIS; ⊙ 9am-3am) This is a popular dairy and vegetarian place beside the lagoon bridge in the hotel area. In addition to a great Israeli breakfast (38NIS), you'll find fruit shakes, salads, pizza, and fish dishes.

Pago Pago (☎ 633 6660; Eilat Marina; dishes 45-100NIS; ⊙ 1pm-midnight) On a boat in the marina, this is the place to go for an atmospheric seafood dinner or grilled speciality in nice watery surroundings. It's best known for sushi combos (from 49NIS), seafood platters (from 78NIS), and fish, beef, chicken, ostrich and duck grills.

Red Sea Star (☎ 634 7777; Mizrayim Rd; dishes 64-109NIS; ⊙ 6pm-midnight Mon-Thu, noon-midnight Fri & Sat) This is the place to go for underwater

dining – that is, if you don't mind eating your fish dinner while accusing eyes glare at you through the windows. In the evening, there's a dance bar on the upstairs deck.

Papagaio (☎ 633 2217; Dan Hotel, Royal Promenade; all you can eat 110NIS; ⊙ noon-midnight) Bring an empty gut and a lot of cash and gorge on greasy grilled meat until your shirt buttons pop open. This Brazilian-style restaurant serves 12 kinds of meat and seven salads in a chic restaurant-bar combo, enlivened by periodic Carnival-style song and dance routines.

Wang's Grill (☎ 636 8989; Royal Promenade; dishes 45-95NIS; ⊙ 7-11pm Sat-Thu) 'Kosher Asian food' might sound a bit out of the ordinary, but it works here, combining a Japanese steak-house, Chinese noodle bar and strict Jewish cooking law approved by the rabbinate of Jerusalem.

A number of small restaurants, cafés and shwarma stands can be found in the New Tourist Centre, opposite the IMAX theatre, as well as the Food Court inside the Mall. If a sandwich is sufficient – and it probably will be given Eilat's appetite-busting temperatures – try the **Co-op supermarket** (cnr Elot Ave & HaTemarim Blvd), or the one in the Shalom Centre.

Three Monkeys Pub (☎ 636 8888; Royal Beach Hotel, Royal Promenade; ⊙ 9pm-late) This recommended watering hole on the promenade does a plying trade in fruity cocktails.

The beach bars are fashionable with Eilat's beautiful people, but there's not much between them. Try **Green Beach** (☎ 637 7032; North Beach) and **Papaya Beach** (☎ 634 0804; North Beach) and think DJs and tanned, bikini-clad bods partying until sunrise.

Entertainment

Eilat's nightlife is firmly bar-based, and the action focuses on the New Tourist Centre. This compact little area is packed with frequently changing options.

Underground Pub (☎ 637 0239; www.under ground-pub.com; New Tourist Centre; ⊙ noon-4am) This is the travellers favourite, with cheap pub grub and beer, easy music and nightly live entertainment.

Unplugged (☎ 632 6299; New Tourist Centre; ⊙ 7pm-3am) Next door to the Underground Pub, this place attracts a younger crowd with a dance-bar atmosphere.

Platinum (☎ 636 3444; Antibes Rd; admission 60-100NIS; ⊙ 11pm-6am) Located in King Solomon hotel, this was, at the time of writing, the most popular disco in town. Monday is Hebrew music only, Thursday is reserved for 25-and-overs, and on Friday the club hosts a gay party.

For a more family-friendly activity, or if the temperatures reach unbearable heights, take cool respite in the pyramid-shaped **IMAX theatre** (☎ 634 8080; www.imaxeilat.co.il; admission 55NIS; ✆ 4-11pm Sun-Thu, 11am-5pm Fri, 9pm-midnight Sat).

Getting There & Away
AIR
Step outside of Eilat's **municipal airport** (☎ 637 3553) and you are already downtown. Both **Arkia** (☎ 638 4888; Red Kanyon Mall) and **Israir** (☎ 634 0666; Shalom Centre) fly several times daily between the municipal airport and Tel Aviv (US$72), and to Haifa three times per week (US$87).

BUS
The **central bus station** (☎ 636 5120; HaTemarim St) offers service to Tel Aviv (65NIS, five hours) with buses departing every 1½ hours from 5am to 7pm, with an additional overnight service at 1am. The last Friday bus is at 3pm and the first Saturday bus at 11.30am; this bus also stops in Be'ersheva (55NIS, three hours). To Mitzpe Ramon (45NIS, 2½ hours), buses run more or less hourly on weekdays and at least twice on Saturday. To Jerusalem (65NIS, 4½ hours), there are buses Sunday to Thursday (7am, 10am, 1.30pm and 4.30pm), Friday (7am, 10am and 1pm) Saturday (4.30pm and 9.30pm).

Getting Around
The town centre is walkable, but you'll need a bus or taxi for locations along the Taba road. The hourly bus No 15 connects the central bus station with the Egyptian border at Taba (6.40NIS) from 8am to 6pm Sunday to Thursday, 8am to 3pm Friday and 9am to 7pm Saturday. To reach the Rabin border crossing into Jordan, you'll have to get a taxi (25NIS).

AROUND EILAT
Hikers will want to head for the Eilat Mountains, but be sure to pick up a copy of the 1:50,000 SPNI *Eilat Mountains* hiking map (82NIS), which is sold at the SPNI Field School in Eilat. Any of the following

places is accessible on a 38NIS to 50NIS taxi ride from Eilat.

The small spring and 30m **waterfall** (✆ running Apr, May, Oct & Nov) at Ein Netafim, which attract wildlife with their perennial water, lie less than 1km off the main road. From here, hikers can follow the Israel National Trail to the spectacular **Shehoret Canyon**, 15km away; make arrangements with a tour operator to pick you up at the trailhead at the finish. Near the mouth of Shehoret Canyon lie the impressive **Amram Pillars**, also along the Israel National Trail, where there's an official camp site (no water).

An excellent six- to seven-hour day hike will take you through the spectacular **Nakhal Gishron** (part of the Israel National Trail) from HaYoash to the Egyptian border. In the early 1990s the Dalai Lama walked part of this route, lecturing to a small collection of adherents atop one of its upper crests. Get an early start and carry at least 3L of water per person.

Further north, the 600m-long **Red Canyon**, a slot canyon 1m to 3m wide and 10m to 20m deep, is readily accessed on foot via a 1.5km walking track from the car park. It makes a great short hike.

If you'd prefer to take to the mountains under an alternative form of transport, **Camel Ranch** (☎ 637 0022; www.camel-ranch.co.il; Nakhal Shlomo; ✆ 9am-1pm & 4-8pm) organises 90-minute (98NIS per person) and four-hour (180NIS per person) camel treks from its base, less that 2km inland from the Eilat–Taba road.

Timna National Park
תמנע פארק تمنه حديقه

About 25km north of Eilat and accessible by public bus, **Timna National Park** (☎ 631 6756; www.timna-park.co.il; adult/child 38/33NIS) is the site of some stunning desert landscapes, enlivened with multicoloured rock formations. It's best known as a source of copper for 5th-century-BC Egyptian miners – the park is dotted with ancient mine shafts – but it also includes a wonderland of geological phenomena. The most intriguing are the **Natural Arch**, the eroded monolith known as the **Mushroom** and the photogenic **Solomon's Pillars**. There is also a range of excellent day hikes through one of Israel's wildest desert landscapes.

Overnight **accommodation** (Bedouin tents per person 25NIS) is available at the artificial **Timna**

Lake. Camping is sometimes possible but call ahead to the park. For meals, try the adjacent **restaurant** (dishes 30-45NIS; 🕙 9am-5pm).

Buses between Eilat and Jerusalem pass the park turn-off, 2.5km from the park entrance. From there, it's a long walk to anything of interest. This is one place where it really makes sense to hire a car.

Hai-Bar Arava Biblical Wildlife Reserve
שמורת חי-בר
Located 35km north of Eilat, the **Hai-Bar Arava Biblical Wildlife Reserve** (☎ 637 3057; per person 23NIS; 🕙 8.30am-5pm Sun-Thu, 8.30am-4pm Fri & Sat) was created to establish breeding groups of threatened Negev wildlife. A private car is needed to navigate its gravelled roads, from where you can observe the animals in their 'natural state'. Just behind the ticket office is the **Predator Centre** (☎ 637 3057; per person 23NIS), a modest zoo housing animals endemic to the Negev. A combined ticket for both the Wildlife Reserve and the Predator Centre is 40NIS.

Camp sites (per person 20NIS) with shower block and toilets are available at Hai-Bar Arava. Around 5km north of here, the caféteria at **Yotvata Kibbutz** (☎ 635 7449; yotvata -office@yotvata.ardom.co.il), offers simple meals and fresh dairy products.

THE WEST BANK & GAZA STRIP
أضفة & غزة
רצועת עזה & הגדה
(המערבית) יו"ש

The West Bank and the Gaza Strip, predominantly Palestinian territories captured by Israel in 1967 during the Six Day War, have been neither annexed by Israel (as were East Jerusalem and the Golan Heights), nor granted outright autonomy. Security around both territories is extraordinarily tight, with hundreds of checkpoints, fences, walls and road blocks built around them to monitor the movement of Palestinians.

IDF control over Palestinian cities, and their surrounding roads, has waxed and waned with the political tide. The 1993

Oslo Accords brought Palestinians limited self rule in the Gaza Strip and West Bank, but the IDF took back most urban areas during the second intifada. Under the 2005 ceasefire agreement, Israel promised to pull back from five West Bank towns – Ramallah, Qalqiyla, Bethlehem, Jericho and Tulkarem. At the time of writing it had only pulled back from the latter two.

The biggest disengagement plan yet occurred in August 2005 when some 9000 Israeli settlers were pulled out of their homes in Gush Katif and forced to relocate in Israel proper. They left behind a US$200 million a year hothouse industry and 1500 homes, which were demolished to make way for low-cost housing.

The IDF pullout includes Rafah, the scene of some of the most appalling atrocities committed by the IDF against ordinary Palestinians. In May 2004, a six-day siege on Rafah left 42 dead, 180 homes destroyed and a swathe of urban destruction that prompted international outrage and a strong rebuke from inside Sharon's own cabinet. Rafah is a hotbed of violence largely because of the secret tunnels that connect to Egypt, allowing the trafficking of weapons, drugs and people.

If you feel uneasy about travelling to the West Bank on your own, **Abu Hassan Alternative Tours** (Map pp284-5; ☎ 052 286 4205; www.jrshotel .com; Jerusalem Hotel) organises custom tours to the Palestinian Territories for around US$25 per person – if you can muster a group. Another excellent resource is the snazzy **This Week In Palestine** (www.thisweekin palestine.com) brochure, available in upmarket Arab hotels.

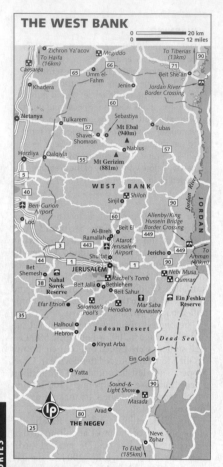

THE WEST BANK

0 20 km
0 12 miles

Zichron Ya'acov
Megiddo
To Tiberias
(13km)
To Haifa
(16km)
Caesarea
Umm el-
Fahm
Beit She'an
Khadera
Jenin
Jordan River
Border Crossing
Netanya
Tulkarem
Sebastiya
Tubas
Shavei-
Shomron
Mt Ebal
(940m)
Herzliya
Qalqilya
Nablus
Mt Gerizim
(881m)
WEST BANK
Ben-Gurion
Airport
Sinjil
Shiloh
Lod
Al-Bireh
Beit El
Allenby/King
Hussein Bridge
Border Crossing
Ramallah
Atarot
Jerusalem
Airport
Shu'fat
Jericho
To
Amman
(40km)
Bet
Shemesh
JERUSALEM
Nahal
Sorek
Reserve
Rachel's Tomb
Nebi Musa
Beit Jalla
Bethlehem
Qumran
Beit Sahur
Efar Etzion
Solomon's
Pool's
Herodion
Mar Saba
Monastery
Ein Feshka
Reserve
Halhoul
Judean Desert
Dead Sea
Hebron
Kiryat Arba
Ein Gedi
Yatta
Sound-&-
Light Show
Masada
Arad
THE NEGEV
Neve
Zohar
To Eilat
(185km)

RAMALLAH

רמאללה رام الله

☎ 02 / pop 40,000

Once a Christian religious centre and later
a resort town for wealthy Arabs, Ramallah
is now better known as the administrative
headquarters for the Palestinian Authority
and the centre for culture and arts in the
West Bank.

There is little left to remind the visitor
of old Ramallah, much of it having been
torn down to make way for modern shops
and malls. However, the city does have
the feel of prosperity and youthful energy
that's lacking in other West Bank towns.
Apart from catching onward transport to
Nablus, the main reason to come here is to
view **Yasser Arafat's tomb** (admission free; ⏱ 8am-

9pm), which is located inside the compound
of the partially destroyed headquarters of
the Palestinian Authority (bullet holes still
clearly visible).

Duar al-Manara Sq marks the centre of
Ramallah; Arafat's compound (Muqata) is
900m east, access is from the south side.

To get to Ramallah, take Arab bus No
78 from the Nablus Road old bus station
in East Jerusalem (Map pp284–5) to the
Calandia checkpoint. From the checkpost,
frequent *sheruts (servees)* run to central
Ramallah for 2.50NIS.

JERICHO

יריחו أريحا

☎ 02 / pop 32,000

Jericho is best known for the biblical account of Joshua, his army's seven circuits
with its trumpets and the subsequently
tumbling walls. Unfortunately, precious
little remains of this legacy, but Jericho still
claims the title of the oldest town in the
world. At 260m below sea level it's also the
lowest town in the world. While Jericho's
archaeological sites remain impressive, they
are readily surpassed by the surrounding
desert landscapes and the views across the
Dead Sea to the mysterious Mountains of
Moab.

Ancient Jericho

Ancient Jericho's main sites are best accessed on the 6km anticlockwise loop
formed by Qasr Hisham St and Ein as-
Sultan St. Heading north out of the centre,
the first site of interest is the **Mount & Monastery of Temptation**, a 12th-century Greek
Orthodox monastery, rebuilt in the 19th
century, which clings to the rocks at the
traditional site where Jesus was tempted by
Satan. You could walk there in 30 minutes
or take the 1.3km-long **cable car** (☎ 232 1590;
www.jericho-cablecar.com; adult/child 40/30NIS; ⏱ 9am-
6pm Mon-Sat), triumphantly advertised as the
'world's longest cable car under sea level'.

Across the street from the cable car is
the Ahava Temptation tourist complex with
souvenir stalls, shops and restaurants, and
the archaeological site of **Tel Yericho** (adult/child
10/7NIS; ⏱ 8am-5pm), otherwise known as Tel
as-Sultan, which has little more than signposted trenches and mounds of dirt.

Around 3km past the tourist complex,
the road winds to the ruins of a 5th- or 6th-
century synagogue and **Hisham's Palace** (adult/

child 10/7NIS; 8am-5pm) – the impressive ruins of a 7th-century hunting lodge, replete with a beautiful Byzantine mosaic floor.

Back in town, look out for the **Zacchaeus Tree**, said to be the very same that Zacchaeus climbed for a better view of the preaching Jesus (Luke 19:1–10).

Sleeping & Eating

Jericho Resort Village (232 1255; fax 232 2189; s/d 250/320NIS; P X X X) A surprisingly well-run operation, catering for well-heeled Jordanian tourists. It's 2km past the Mount of Temptation cable car.

Intercontinental Hotel (231 1200; jericho@ interconti.com; s/d US$80/90; P X X X) An odd place for a five-star hotel, this 180-room operation closed its casino and limped through the last intifada, but there are renewed hopes for a business boom if peace prevails. It's located southeast of Jericho on the road to Jerusalem.

Hisham's Palace Hotel (052 275 6990; Ein as-Sultan St; r 100NIS) This place is so neglected that floorboards have started to sprout vegetation. Shabby rooms with three beds have private bathrooms and dodgy plumbing.

There are a few cafés and felafel/shwarma joints around the main square, and a proper sit-down restaurant at the Ahava Temptation tourist complex, opposite the cable car.

Getting There & Away

At present, no buses service Jericho. Shared taxis and *sheruts* depart from Abu-Dis, an eastern suburb of Jerusalem. A private taxi will cost 50NIS. There are buses to/from the Allenby border crossing for 10NIS from the bus station, a 20-minute walk east of downtown.

AROUND JERICHO

About 8km before Jericho a road leads right to **Nebi Musa**, a small monastic complex built in 1269 and revered by Muslims as the tomb of Moses, with the Judean Desert as a dramatic backdrop.

Wadi Qelt is a nature reserve with a natural spring where you can swim in a pool under a waterfall and hike along an aqueduct to **St George's Monastery**, built into the cliff face of a canyon on the Mount of Temptation. The hike takes about four hours. The starting point is the Wadi Qelt turn-off on the Jerusalem–Jericho road (get the bus driver

to drop you off here) and the finishing point is Jericho, from where you can continue sightseeing in the town or easily find transport back to Jerusalem.

BETHLEHEM   بيت لحم   בית לחם
 02 / pop 61,000

The Christian Arab town of Bethlehem no longer resembles the cosy Middle Eastern village portrayed on Christmas cards, but even worse, much of it has been bombed and otherwise damaged in conflicts dating back to the intifada. Christian visitors will probably still want to see Bethlehem, but those hoping for a spiritual experience may be disappointed by the blatant commercialism and the unheavenly host of kitsch that surfaces here. If it's all too much for you, head out to the Shepherds' Fields early in the morning, before the tour groups arrive, and gaze back at the town from a contemplative distance.

Besides the pilgrimage sites, there are also some excellent excursions to places just outside the town, such as the Mar Saba Monastery and the Herodion.

Orientation & Information

Around Manger Sq, right in the centre, are the Church of the Nativity, police station, post office and various shops. The **tourist office** (276 6677; Manger Sq; 10am-4pm) has maps of the town.

Milk Grotto St heads off to the southeast, past the Milk Grotto Chapel; uphill to the northeast Paul VI St leads to the museum, the outdoor market and more shops and hotels. The winding Manger St, running off the east side of the square, is the main street through the new town; it eventually brings you close to the security fence, from where you can walk to the Jerusalem–Hebron road.

Sights

The venerable **Church of the Nativity**, which is one of the world's oldest functioning churches, is built like a citadel over the cave cited by tradition as Jesus' birthplace. In April 2002 it suffered damage as 200 Palestinian troops sought sanctuary there from the IDF.

Down Milk Grotto St is **Milk Grotto Chapel**, a shrine that commemorates the lactation of the Virgin Mary. North of the square

A WALL BETWEEN THEM

When crossing into the West Bank from Jerusalem, either to Bethlehem or Ramallah, the most noticeable feature is no longer the change of cultures from Israeli to Palestinian, but the wall that divides them.

A Berlin Wall for the 21st century, this 'Security Fence', as its known by Israelis, cuts through farmers' fields, town centres and between the homes of onetime neighbours. In the case of one unfortunate Palestinian in Elkana, the 6m wall and its supporting fences actually encircles his home, caging him between Israel and Palestine.

This vast barricade's construction began during the second intifada and is part of a 704km security project to halt the movement of Palestinian weapon smugglers and suicide bombers (leading supporters to compare it not to the divisive Berlin wall but the defensive Great Wall of China). The IDF claims an 80% drop in the rate of terror attacks since its construction.

But Palestinians argue that the wall, because it cuts well beyond the 1949 Green Line armistice, is an Israeli attempt to grab land before an official border is established between the territories. In July 2004, the International Court of Justice in the Hague sided with the Palestinians, claiming the wall violated international law.

The wall, along with its fences, barricades, earth mounds and watchtowers, is costly beyond its US$3-billion price tag. Neighbourhoods around the wall have been turned into virtual ghost towns as people have been uprooted from their homes and road blocks have halted trade between customers and clients. Case in point is Rachel's Tomb (below), a holy site outside Bethlehem, which has seen the closure of 72 of 80 surrounding businesses since the barrier went up in June 2002.

Equally traumatic is the political fallout caused by the Security Fence, or as its known by Palestinians and political activists, the 'Apartheid Wall'. For Arabs worldwide, this is the new symbol of Israeli domination of Palestinian land, central to Islam's conflict with the Judeo-Christian West.

Locally, this sentiment is reflected on the wall itself in the form of graffiti. 'American Money, Israel Apartheid', a common rally cry among graffiti artists, refers to America's US$2.5 billion in economic and military aid to Israel per year; strong support that deepens the divide confronting Americans, Europeans, Israelis and the Arab world.

For more information on the Wall, see the IDF-sponsored www.securityfence.mod.gov.il. For details from the Palestinian side, click on www.stopthewall.org. Also contact **Machsom Watch** (www.machsomwatch.org), an NGO that monitors Israeli checkpoints.

on Paul VI St, the **Bethlehem Museum** (☎ 274 2589; admission 8NIS; 🕙 10am-noon & 2.30-5pm Mon-Sat, closed Thu afternoon) exhibits traditional Palestinian crafts and costumes. In the gift shop you can buy handmade crafts produced by a local NGO, the **Arab Women's Union** (www.arab womenunion.org).

Around 1km south of the Gilo (Bethlehem) checkpost, and 400m past the security fence, is **Rachel's Tomb**, revered by Jews but also considered holy by Christians and Muslims. Every two hours a bus travels here direct from the Jerusalem central bus station (3.80NIS, 30 minutes). For security reasons, Jewish pilgrims are ferried to the site from the checkpost.

Sleeping & Eating

Accommodation in Bethlehem is limited, especially at Christmas and Easter, and it makes more sense to stay in nearby Jerusalem.

Casa Nova Hospice (☎ 274 2798; www.cnop-beth .org; s/d US$25/50; ☒ ☒ 🖳) This Franciscan-run guesthouse beside the Church of the Nativity has reasonable facilities and a dining room. Price includes breakfast and additional meals cost US$5.

Alexander Hotel (☎ 277 0780; ahotel@p-ol.com; s/d US$30/45; 🄿 ☒ ☒) Tastefully furnished rooms with a scenic view over the valley, a 20-minute walk from Manger Sq on the road to Jerusalem.

You'll find plenty of felafel and shwarma merchants around Manger Sq, and the **St George Restaurant** (☎ 274 3780; Paul VI St; dishes 35-50NIS; 🕙 8am-11pm), which serves up grilled chicken, fish and meat dishes.

Getting There & Away

Bethlehem *sheruts* (3NIS, 40 minutes) run from East Jerusalem's Sultan Suleiman station, passing Jaffa Gate (they are often full when leaving so it's difficult to pick one up at Jaffa Gate). Shared taxis (5NIS, 20 minutes) sometimes leave from the taxi stand outside Faisal's Guesthouse (Damascus Gate). All vehicles stop at the Gilo checkpoint, from where you can take a taxi (15NIS) the final 3km.

Alternatively, follow the pilgrims' option and walk from Jerusalem (at Christmas, there's an official procession). Unfortunately, the 2½-hour up-and-downhill trek attracts heavy traffic all the way.

AROUND BETHLEHEM

Various biblical events are associated with the **Field of Ruth** and the **Shepherds' Fields**, 2km from Beit Sahur (1km east of Bethlehem). The ruined Byzantine monastery here was destroyed by the Persians in AD 614, and there's also a 5th-century church built over a mosaic-floored cave. From Manger St in Bethlehem, take Arab bus No 47 to Beit Sahur and walk for 20 minutes to the fields. The **Herodion** (☎ 776 2251; adult/child 23/12NIS; ☽ 8am-5pm Sun-Thu, 8am-4pm Fri), the amazing volcano-shaped remains of the palace complex built by Herod between 24 and 15 BC, lies 8km south of Beit Sahur. Buses run infrequently from Bethlehem and your best bet is to take a taxi or walk.

Splendid architecture and a superb location combine to make the Greek Orthodox Monastery of **Mar Saba**, on the steep Kidron banks, one of the Holy Land's most impressive structures. The interior is open only to men, but the exterior is also quite amazing. Without a private vehicle you'll have to walk the 6km from the bus stop at Abu Diye (accessible on Arab bus 60 from Bethlehem).

The large reservoir and Turkish fort at **Solomon's Pools** lie 8km south of Beit Jalla. To get there from Bethlehem, take Arab bus No 23 or Arab minibus No 1 to Dashit. From here it's possible to continue to Hebron by shared taxi.

HEBRON   هبرون   חברון
☎ 02 / pop 120,000
A major flashpoint of the Israeli-Arab conflict, Hebron maintains a palpable sense of tension, even when a ceasefire is in place. Visitors to the old city and marketplace should strive to look like a tourist – avoid wearing a yarmulke, Star of David or any other suggestion of Judaism.

The main stress point is the disputed **Cave of Machpelah**, which is the presumed burial site of father Abraham, and the **Ibrahimi Mosque**, which overlays it. For Jews, it's a highly revered site and to Muslims, its importance in the region is second only to that of Jerusalem's Dome of the Rock.

In the early 1970s, Jewish settlers established a community on the fringes of this largely Arab town, and their incursion inflamed strong – and often violent – passions. The result was an IDF guard posted to protect the 500 settlers from their unhappy Palestinian neighbours. Tragically, in February 1994, a Jewish settler stepped into the mosque and opened fire on the Muslims at prayer. The building is now segregated into Muslim and Jewish sections, and security is tight.

Hebron's souq is a blend of Crusader and Mamluk façades, vaulted ceilings and narrow alleyways; but repeated violence has cleared out its shops and residents, making the place a virtual ghost town. Most commerce has moved to the adjoining new town, centred on a vibrant outdoor market. Also, don't miss the Ein Sara St factories that produce Hebron's fabulous blue glass.

Located 3km from the bazaar, the modern hotel complex of **Regency Al Mezan** (☎ 225 7389; regency@palnet.com; s/d U$333/77, P ☒ ☒ ☐), with plush rooms and mod cons, is an island of luxury in scruffy old Hebron.

Arab bus No 23 operates between Jerusalem and Hebron (10NIS), via Bethlehem, but service taxis (12NIS) from Damascus Gate (outside Faisal's guesthouse) are faster and more frequent. Public transport will drop you on HaMelekh David St, at the northern edge of the market. To the south lies the aforementioned Ibrahimi Mosque.

NABLUS   نابلس   שכם
☎ 09 / pop 260,000
The typically bustling and quite attractive Arab town of Nablus, which is scenically situated between the Gerizim and Ebal peaks, is the largest West Bank population centre and is known for its production of soap, olive wood and olive oil. In the central Palestine/Al-Hussein Sq, you'll find the bus stops, the service taxi ranks and a small market. Immediately to the south, the Old Town stretches eastward along Nasir St.

Sights

From Al-Hussein Sq head south toward the minaret of **An-Nasir Mosque** (Nasir St) – one of 30 minarets punctuating the Nablus skyline. Nearby is the privately owned old Turkish mansion known as **Touqan Castle**, where visitors will normally be able to admire the architecture and garden. From Nasir St walk south through Al-Beik Gate and the entrance is up the slope on your left.

East of the An-Nasir Mosque on An-Nasir St is **Al-Shifa** (☎ 09-838 1176; ☺ men only 8am-10pm daily, women only 8am-5pm Tue), the country's oldest functioning Turkish bath. Built around 1480 at the start of the Ottoman period, Al-Shifa has been lovingly restored, and along with the hot rooms, you can enjoy the cushion-strewn central hall where guests can recline, sip black coffee or mint tea and puff on a nargileh. A bath costs 10NIS and a massage goes for 20NIS.

The nearby Arab village of **Sebastiya** stands about 15km northwest of Nablus up on the scenic slopes of the Samarian hills. Just above it on the summit of the peak lie the impressive ruins of Samaria, the capital of the ancient Israelite kingdom.

Sleeping & Eating

Crystal Hotel (☎ 233 2485; Faisal St; s/d with air-con 100/150NIS; s/d without air-con 120/170NIS, P ✖) A reasonable option in Nablus, this place has a central location, clean rooms and English-speaking staff.

Al Qasr Hotel (☎ 238 5444; alqasr@alqasr.com; Sharia Omar Ibn al-Khatib; s/d incl breakfast US$75/85; P ✖ 💻) Visiting journalists and aid workers often make this their temporary home. It's about as luxurious as you can get in the West Bank with all the mod cons.

Al-Istiqlal Pension (☎ 238 3618; 11 Sharia Hitteen; dm 30NIS) At the bottom of the scale, this pension offers basic dormitory accommodation.

Along with soap, the Nablus speciality is sweets, including Arabic pastries, halvah, Turkish delights, and especially *kunafa* (cheese topped with orange wheat threads soaked in honey). The best bakery at which to try this delicious delicacy is **Al-Aqsa** (Nasir St), in the Old City beside the An-Nasir Mosque.

Getting There & Away

Sherut taxis run to Nablus from Al-Nahda St. in central Ramallah (13NIS, one hour) or from Calandia check point (16NIS, 1¼

hours) just south of Ramallah. Taxis stop at Huwwara check point outside Nablus from where you can catch a *sherut* to central Nablus (3NIS).

GAZA CITY   عزه غزة

☎ 08 / pop 469,000

Historically, Gaza has been one of the most strategically important eastern Mediterranean towns, and has long served as a staging post on the major trade routes linking Central Asia and Persia with Arabia, Egypt and sub-Saharan Africa. In fact, it's believed that Gaza has been captured and destroyed more than any other town in the world – and that tradition lives on. After the establishment of limited self-rule in 1994, Gaza became a respectable place, but closed up once again during the second intifada.

Despite the ceasefire and pullout of all Israeli settlers in August 2005, Gaza remains unstable. The Palestinian Authority has put little effort into disarming militant groups and Islamic fundamentalism is on the rise.

Sights & Activities

Palestine Sq holds most of the city's sites of historical interest. The most distinguished structure is the converted Crusader-era church, **Jama'a al-Akbar (Great Mosque)**. Along its southern wall runs the short, vaulted **Goldsmiths' Alley**, which served as a lively souq during the Mamluk era. A short walk from here, across Palestine Sq, **Fras Market** is a photogenic menagerie of donkey carts, mounds of fruit and tables overflowing with seafood.

In 1799, during his Egyptian campaign, Napoleon Bonaparte camped in Gaza and established his base on Al-Wahida St in the attractive Mamluk-era building now called **Napoleon's Citadel**, which is currently a girls' school. From the citadel, head west and take

---

WARNING

At the time of research, tourists were barred from visiting Gaza. For this reason, we did not visit the area for the purposes of updating this chapter. If the situation changes and the area opens up, exercise caution and take a trusted guide. For further information on Gaza and a map of the city, see www.mogaza.org.

the second right to reach the **Mosque of Said Hashim**, which was built on the grave of the Prophet Mohammed's great-grandfather.

An **Arts and Craft Village** (☎ 284 6405; artvlg@ palnet.com; Jamal Abdel Nasser St) produces and then sells a range of local art and craft, which includes embroidery, copperware and glasswork. You'll find the village about 800m south of the Islamic University on El-Khartoum St.

INDEPENDENT PALESTINE?

Depending on your level of optimism, Independent Palestine is either a pipe dream or a near reality. But how would a future Palestinian state look? A few of the essentials are already there. They have a flag, a national football squad, a motto (May God Protect My Country) and there's even a currency lined up – the Palestinian Pound. More sticky discussions revolve around population movements and borders.

Helping with the complexities are the EU, Russia, the UN, the USA – the 'quartet' of groups which devised the current 'Road Map for Peace'. First outlined in June 2002 by US president George W Bush, the Road Map called for an independent Palestinian state living side by side with Israel, in peace, by 2005. The second intifada caused delays in implementation and the new target date is 2008, conspicuously set prior to the next US and Palestinian elections.

In April 2004, Bush announced two key revisions to the Road Map. The first declared that Israel would retain major Israeli settlement blocs inside the Green Line (the 1949 Armistice). The second announced that Palestinian refugees would not be allowed to return to Israel, but that they could be re-settled in Palestine. The latter would comply with the two-state solution – one state for Jews and one for Arabs. Both of his amendments were, of course, part of Clinton's parameters in the Wye II deal rejected by Arafat.

Any progress forward, though, hinges on Israel stopping further settlement build up (particularly around East Jerusalem which the Palestinians plan to make their future capital), and the Palestinian Authority dismantling militant groups. Little progress has been made on either account.

If and when independent Palestine is born, numerous challenges will stand in the way of security, prosperity and peace – simple geography being the most obvious. With just 6220 sq km (smaller than the US state of Maryland), Palestine would have little land to stand on. The Gaza enclave would be separated from 'mainland Palestine' by around 50km of Israeli territory which would probably require the construction of a secure highway linking the two. Already overcrowded Gaza and West Bank cities could become even more impacted if a significant proportion of the four million Palestinians abroad decide to return. An estimated 400,000 to 800,000 are expected to do just that.

These small portions of land are of grave concern to Israel as well – the heavily populated coastal corridor between the West Bank and Netanya will be narrowed to just 14km, posing an obvious security threat for the country.

Palestine's economy, crippled in recent years by high-level corruption and Israeli occupation, is another big question mark. Certainly tourism will come to the fore as the country would contain a number of historical sights associated with the Bible, including the Church of the Nativity in Bethlehem, the Cave of Machpelah in Hebron and the Mount & Monastery of Temptation in Jericho. Trade opportunities would improve with the departure of the IDF, but Palestine's likely trading partners are to be found not in Israel but elsewhere in the Arab world.

For international negotiators, Jerusalem remains the elephant in the room. Should a final resolution go back to the parameters of the Wye II deal, East Jerusalem will become the capital of Palestine and West Jerusalem the capital of Israel. As for the Old City, Palestine would control the Muslim and Christian quarters while Israel would take the Armenian and Jewish quarters. Also to Palestine would go the Temple Mount while the Western Wall would remain with Israel. A 10-minute stroll through the tightly knit alleys of the Old City, and the proximity of these areas, displays the complexities of such a plan.

Suggestions by mediators to internationalise Jerusalem (ie putting its authority in the hands of a multinational force of observers) have been given a thumbs-down by both Jews and Arabs.

For a first-hand account of the peace negotiations, read *The Missing Peace* by former US Envoy to the Middle East Dennis Ross.

The best **surfing** in the Gaza Strip can reportedly be found along the stretch of beach between the Al-Deira hotel and Chalehut beach, 1km to the south.

Sleeping

Marna House (☎ 282 3322; marna_house_hotel@yahoo.com; Ahmed Abdel Aziz St; s/d US$50/70; ✗ ✗) Located two blocks north of Omar al-Mukhtar St, just west of An-Nasser St, this place has 16 clean and spacious rooms with satellite TV, private bathrooms and balconies. Rates include breakfast.

Al Deira (☎ 283 8100; adeira@p-i-s.com; Rashid St; s/d US$90/110; P ✗ ✗) An island of luxury in Gaza, the Al Deira has 12 swish rooms, all with excellent sea views plus minibar and cable TV. Local expats report that the seafood restaurant here is the best in town.

Getting There & Away

The only entry/exit point at the time of writing was Erez. At the time of writing, access was only allowed to visitors with special permits given by the IDF or Ministry of the Internal Affairs (ie journalists, aid workers and diplomats). Erez is reached by *sherut* from Damascus Gate in East Jerusalem (50NIS per person), but allow lots of time to await other passengers. A private taxi will cost around 300NIS.

Or, take an Egged bus from Tel Aviv to Ashkelon (21NIS, one hour, every 30 minutes) and find a southbound bus to Yad Mordechai junction; taxis (10NIS, five minutes) run the last 5km to the Erez border.

ISRAEL & THE PALESTINIAN TERRITORIES DIRECTORY

ACCOMMODATION

Accommodation in Israel and the Palestinian Territories is varied and caters to all budgets, although travellers coming from Egypt or Jordan will need to modify their pricing scale somewhat, as Israel is one of the most expensive destinations in the Middle East (although the Palestinian Territories is somewhat cheaper). Note that accommodation costs in both Israel and the Palestinian Territories can change quickly with the seasons or influx of tourists. Prices are even more volatile in resort areas such as the Galilee and Eilat.

B&Bs

All over Israel you'll find accommodation in private homes, ranging mostly from US$25 to US$70 for a single or double. Facilities vary from simple rooms with shared facilities to self-contained studio apartments with kitchenettes and cable TV. You'll find them by looking for signs posted in the street or check the website of the **Home Accommodation Association** (www.bnb.co.il). More often than not tourist information offices will also keep a list of B&Bs in their city.

Camping

Camping grounds with all the usual amenities are found all over Israel, but they don't offer the sort of cheap alternative most people would expect; in fact, hostels cost only a bit more. On a few public beaches, you can pitch a tent free of charge; but this is not so on the Dead Sea shore, much of the Sea of Galilee or the Mediterranean coast north of Nahariya. Note that theft is a big problem on beaches, particularly around Eilat, Tel Aviv and Haifa. Wilderness camping is possible in many places along major hiking tracks (except in national parks), but water may not be available, especially in the Negev region.

Hostels

Israel has an extensive network of roughly 30 official HI hostels, all of which are clean and well appointed. In most cities and towns, though, private hostels charge a third to half the prices of the official hostels and they're generally more amenable to socialising – but also louder. For more on HI hostels, contact the **Israel Youth Hostels Association** (Map pp284-5; ☎ 02-655 8405; www.iyha.org.il; 6th fl, Binyanei Ha'Umah Conference Centre, PO Box 6001, Jerusalem 91060; ☾ 8.30am-3pm Sun-Thu, 9am-noon Fri).

Hotels & Guesthouses

Even the grimmest of Jerusalem flea pits will charge US$6 to US$7 per night for a dorm bed while a slightly better guesthouse might charge US$8 to US$10. The cheapest double room in a backpacker-orientated guesthouse starts at around US$25. Guesthouses are great places to meet other travellers, as they usually have a common kitchen

PRACTICALITIES

- English-language daily (except Saturday) newspapers include, **Ha'aretz** (www.haaretzdaily.com) and the **Jerusalem Post** (www.jpost.com). In East Jerusalem you can pick up the weekly, Palestinian-produced *Jerusalem Times*.

- Tel Aviv's best station for English- and Hebrew-language rock music is 102FM. In Jerusalem, English news can be heard at 10pm on 88.2FM. English news and music is played sporadically on 100.7FM (Tel Aviv), 98.4FM (Jerusalem), 97.2FM (Haifa) and 94.4FM (Tiberias). The short-wave BBC World Service (1323kHz) broadcasts news in English, as does the Voice of America broadcasts (1260kHz).

- Israel's two state TV channels feature plenty of English-language programming with Hebrew subtitles. These are supplemented by the Arabic-language Jordan TV. Nearly all hotels and guesthouses also have cable TV, which carries CNN, Sky and BBC World.

- The predominant video format in Israel is PAL.

- Electric power is 230 volts AC, 50Hz. The sockets are designed to accommodate two- and three pin, round plugs (European standard).

- Israel and the Palestinian Territories follow the international metric system.

and TV room where guests lounge around for hours, swapping travel info.

In the midrange category, for a European standard hotel room with reasonable facilities, expect to pay around US$65 to US$80 for a double room. An Israeli breakfast (yogurt, cheese, toast, vegetables and a fried egg) is sometimes included with the room.

You don't get any better service with top-of-the-range hotels, which are often soulless and filled with package tour groups from the USA and Europe. Room rates usually start from around US$90 and you can expect a full breakfast plus other amenities like a swimming pool and fitness centre. Many hotels in this range are kosher, which means you'll have to deal with a few quirky restrictions; for example, the swimming pool will have separate hours for men and women; guest services will be limited during Shabbat; and the elevators will automatically stop on every floor during Shabbat.

All hotels and guesthouses listed in this chapter will have private bathrooms unless stated otherwise.

Kibbutz Guesthouses

In a bid to diversify their income, quite a few kibbutzim have turned to the guesthouse concept. They fit mostly into the midrange category and facilities may include swimming pools, beach access, and renowned dining and guest activities. The **Kibbutz Hotels Reservations Office** (Map p298; ☎ 03-

560 8118; www.kibbutz.co.il; 41 Montefiore St, Tel Aviv) publishes a booklet listing all of its hotels, restaurants and camp sites, with prices, amenities and a map.

ACTIVITIES
Hiking

With its range of terrain, Israel offers a wealth of superb hiking opportunities. The most popular venues include Maktesh Ramon, the Wilderness of Zin, Ein Gedi, the Eilat Mountains and the Golan Heights. For guidelines and detailed route information, visit the Society for the Protection of Nature in Israel (SPNI) in Jerusalem or Tel Aviv, or any of its field schools around the country (see p281). The SPNI also sells detailed sectional hiking maps (60NIS, laminated 82NIS).

Long-distance hikers may want to attempt all or part of the Israel National Trail, which rambles for over 1200km through Israel's least-populated and most scenic areas, from Tel Dan in the north to Taba in the south. This remarkably varied and beautiful route is marked with red, white and blue blazes.

Note that due to the security situation, hiking in the West Bank is not recommended. In 2001 two Israeli teenagers were murdered while hiking in the Judean Desert. The only area considered safe for hiking is Wadi Qelt (p339). For an armchair read, check out *Walks in Palestine: Including the*

Nativity Trail, written by Nabeel Kassis and published by Cicerone Press (2002).

Water Sports

Eilat's beaches are rather overrated, despite its subtropical climate, but the beaches at Bat Yam, Tel Aviv, Netanya, Carmel (near Haifa), and most intervening areas are excellent. These, along with the Sea of Galilee, all offer ample opportunities to swim, windsurf and sail, while the Dead Sea provides a unique and therapeutic 'floating' experience, and the water-sports capital of Eilat offers everything from parasailing to water-skiing.

While many privately owned beaches along the Sea of Galilee, the Dead Sea and the Mediterranean and Red Sea coasts charge admission fees (or are restricted for military reasons), some remote, marginal and/or undeveloped beaches are accessible to the public free of charge.

Eilat is Israel's major scuba-diving and snorkelling venue, but if you're headed for the world-class reefs of Sinai, it's hardly worth a stop. An alternative is to dive amid the underwater ruins of Herod's city at Caesarea (see p313).

BOOKS

To catch up on the causes, effects and possible solutions for the Israeli-Palestinian conflict, read Richard Ben Cramer's *How Israel Lost* (2004). You may develop a love-hate relationship with Cramer's brash writing style, but his points are valid and clear.

Leaning further to right is Alan Dershowitz's book *The Case for Israel* (2003), in which the author responds to 32 particular criticisms chronically made of Israel's defence, domestic and foreign policies.

For something less political and more sentimental, try *If a Place Can Make You Cry* (2002), the compilation of emails and letters sent by the author, Daniel Gordis, to friends and family in the US following his move to Jerusalem with his family. A line of similar stories mixed with politics is the excellent *Elvis in Jerusalem* (2003), written by longtime *Ha'aretz* columnist Tom Segev. *The Innocents Abroad* by Mark Twain, written in 1871, is still one of the best accounts of the tourist experience in the Holy Land.

Well-known novelist Amos Oz deals in Israeli history and peace efforts in his collections of essays: *In the Land of Israel* (2003); *The Slopes of Lebanon* (1989); and *Israel, Palestine and Peace* (1989). The BBC's *The Fifty Year War: Israel & the Arabs* (2000) was published to accompany the TV series of the same name. This largely balanced account of the conflict was cowritten by the Jewish Israeli Ahron Bregman and the Arab Jihan al-Tahri, and contains hitherto unpublished interviews with key players on both sides.

The list of popular historical novels is topped by James Michener's *The Source* (1965), and Ernest K Gann's *The Antagonists* (1970; later published as *Masada*); both have enjoyed enormous international success.

For a Palestinian perspective on the conflict, see Edward Said's *The Question of Palestine* (1977). Said's famous, influential and controversial work, *Orientalism* (1978), investigates how the Western world views the Arab world. In similar fashion, his book *Covering Islam* (1997) describes the adverse image of Islam and Arabs propagated in the American media.

More emotive and gritty is *Gaza: Legacy of Occupation* (1995) by Dick Doughty and Mohammed al-Aydi, in which the authors put in print the images and words of Palestinian refugees living in Gaza and Egypt. For an academic approach, try Nur Masalha's *The Politics of Denial* (2003) and *Imperial Israel and the Palestinians* (2000). For a moving personal story, read Mourid Barghouti's *I Saw Ramallah* (2003), in which the author describes his heart-breaking return to his home city after a 30-year absence.

The Jewish and Christian Bibles are also logical texts for anyone interested in the historical significance of Israel and the Palestinian Territories. The Jewish Bible includes the Pentateuch (the five books of Moses), and most of the rest of the Christian Old Testament. Among the many translations of the Christian Bible, which includes the Old and New Testaments, the King James Version is the most literary and the Septuagint (the Greek version) is generally considered the most historically sound. One of the best English translations of the Quran is by Abdullah Yusuf Ali.

BUSINESS HOURS

Israeli shopping hours are 9am to 6pm (or later) Sunday to Thursday, and 9am to 3pm Friday, with some places opening after sundown on Saturday.

Bear in mind that in most parts of the country, things grind to a halt during Shabbat, the Jewish Sabbath, which starts at sundown on Friday and ends one hour after sundown on Saturday. In Jerusalem and most other parts of the country, businesses close down around 3pm on Friday.

In largely secular Tel Aviv, most shops and offices close at around 2pm on Friday afternoon, but at the same time, street markets and cafés spring to life. In fact, Friday is the biggest night out of the week.

In predominantly Muslim areas – East Jerusalem, Akko, Jaffa, the West Bank and Gaza – businesses are closed all day Friday but remain open on Saturday. Christian-owned businesses (concentrated in Nazareth, Bethlehem and the Armenian and Christian Quarters of Jerusalem's Old City) are closed on Sunday.

CHILDREN

Travel in Israel shouldn't be too rough on children as distances are short and roads are in good nick. Baby food and nappies are readily available in shopping centres, but if any special medicines are necessary it's best to bring what you need from your own country, as labels are often in Hebrew.

Many of Israel's museums and historical sites are geared for children as much they are for adults, complete with learning centres, games and activities. Notable attractions aimed at kids include the National Museum of Science, Planning & Technology (p311) in Haifa, the multimedia adventure (p313) at Caesarea and the Tower of David Museum (p290) in Jerusalem.

Public parks are common in Israeli cities, as are activity centres like miniature golf, bowling alleys and cinemas. If they are still bored, a trip to the beach works every time.

The tense situation in the West Bank – and the checkpoints between towns – makes places like Hebron and Nablus less kid-friendly.

COURSES

Some Israeli universities operate overseas programmes for students of Hebrew, Arabic and Middle Eastern studies. Participants don't necessarily need to speak Hebrew, but may be required to study it as part of their curriculum. **Bir Zeit University** (www.birzeit.edu), 7km north of Ramallah, runs both beginners

and advanced courses in Arabic language and literature for US$650 per course.

Travellers wishing to learn Hebrew will probably want to look for an *ulpan* – a language school catering mainly to new Jewish immigrants – but will have to find one that also welcomes nonimmigrant students. Most programmes cost under 500NIS per month.

For those who prefer not to study too hard, there are also kibbutz *ulpanim,* where you can take-on study in a rural atmosphere and work at the same time. The website www.kibbutzprogramcenter.org/kibulpan .htm is an excellent source of information.

CUSTOMS

Israel allows travellers to import duty free up to 1L of spirits and 2L of wine for each person over 17 years of age, as well as 250g of tobacco or 250 cigarettes. Animals, plants, firearms or fresh meat may not be imported at all. Any video, computer or diving equipment may need to be declared on arrival, and a deposit paid to prevent its sale in Israel (however, this regulation is rarely applied).

DANGERS & ANNOYANCES
Theft

Theft is as much a problem in Israel and the Palestinian Territories as it is in any other country, so take the usual precautions: don't leave valuables in your room or vehicle and use a money belt. In hostels, it's wise to check your most valuable belongings into the desk safe. On intercity buses, it's fine to stow large bags in the luggage hold, but keep valuables with you inside. Crowded tourist spots and markets are obvious haunts for pickpockets, so stay aware of what's happening around you.

Terrorism & Military Action

Streets in the West Bank, Gaza and Israel proper have been relatively quiet since a formal ceasefire was declared in February 2005. Still, it's a good idea to keep abreast of the situation as sporadic violence still occurs. Register with your embassy for email updates and pay attention to the local media.

Even in the best of times, both Jews and Arabs still hold demonstrations. These are mostly peaceful, but are also potential flashpoints for violence and you're best off keeping a safe distance. In the spring of 2003, three foreign nationals were killed in Gaza at the hands of the IDF; one of them, 23-year-old activist Rachel Corrie, died shortly after being steamrolled by an IDF house bulldozer as she attempted to block its path. See www.rachelcorrie.org for details.

Security Measures

When it comes to security, travellers won't be able to ignore Israel's justifiably paranoid – but almost universally welcomed – measures. Suspiciously parked vehicles are towed and/or destroyed by police; abandoned parcels and packages are blown up; and streets, markets and public facilities are spontaneously closed at the vaguest rumour of a threat. When entering bus or rail terminals, shopping malls, government buildings and any place else that might conceivably be a terrorist target, your bags will be searched – and in some cases X-rayed. You will also be checked with a metal detector or body search and probably asked the question: 'do you have a gun?'. Flashing a foreign passport can quicken the process.

Roads into most West Bank towns have army roadblocks where you'll need to show a passport and answer questions about your reason for travel. Similarly, those leaving the country from Ben-Gurion airport are likely to be grilled about their stay and have their luggage thoroughly scrutinised. As annoying as they may be, such measures have thwarted countless terrorist attacks and aren't likely to be relaxed anytime soon.

DISABLED TRAVELLERS

For information on accessible facilities, contact **Access Israel** (☎ 04-632 0748, 054-287702; www.access-israel.com). The **Yad Sarah Organisation** (☎ 02-624 4242; www.yadsarah.org) loans wheelchairs, crutches and other mobility aids free of charge (a deposit is required). You may also want to look for the guidebook *Access in Israel & the Palestinian Authority* by Gordon Couch (www.accessinisrael.org), which provides the lowdown for travellers with mobility restrictions.

DISCOUNT CARDS

A Hostelling International (HI) card is useful for obtaining discounts at HI hostels and an ISIC card entitles bearers to a 10% student discount on Egged buses, a 20% discount on Israel State Railways as well as reductions on admissions to most museums and archaeo-

logical sites. Having said that, many places offer student discounts only to those studying in Israel, and cards issued by individual universities may not be recognised.

EMBASSIES & CONSULATES
Israeli Embassies & Consulates

Following are the Israeli embassies and consulates in major cities around the world. For addresses of the Israeli embassy in Amman see p400 and in Cairo see p172. Note: there is no Israeli embassy in Lebanon or Syria.

Australia (☎ 02-6273 1309; http://canberra.mfa.gov.il; 6 Turrana St Yarralumla, Canberra, ACT 2600)

Canada Montreal (☎ 514-940 8500; http://montreal.mfa.gov.il; Suite 2620, 1155 Blvd Rene Levesque Ouest Montreal, PQ H3B 4S5); Ottawa (☎ 613-567 6450; http://ottawa.mfa.gov.il; 50 O'Conner St Ottawa, Ont K1P 6L2)

France Marseille (☎ 04 91 53 39 90; fax 04 91 53 39 94; 146 rue Paradis Marseille F-13006); Paris (☎ 01 40 76 55 00; http://paris.mfa.gov.il; 3 rue Rabelais F-75008 Paris)

Germany (☎ 30-8904 5500; http://berlin.mfa.gov.il; Auguste Victoriastr 74-75, D-14193 Berlin)

Ireland (☎ 01-230 9400; http://dublin.mfa.gov.il; Carrisbrook House, 122 Pembroke Rd Ballsbridge, Dublin)

Netherlands (☎ 070-376 0500; cons@hague.mfa.gov.il; Buitenhof 47, 2513AH Den Hague)

UK (☎ 020-7957 9500; http://london.mfa.gov.il; 2 Palace Green, London W8 4QB)

USA New York (☎ 212-499 5400; http://newyork.mfa.gov.il; 800 Second Ave New York NY10017); Washington, DC (☎ 202-364 5500; www.israelemb.org; 3514 International Drive NW, Washington DC 20008) Israel has nine consulates in the USA – the listed contacts can provide details.

Embassies & Consulates in Israel

Jerusalem may be Israel's capital, but the vagaries of international politics have led most diplomatic missions to locate in Tel Aviv; some also maintain consulates in Jerusalem, Haifa and/or Eilat.

Most diplomatic missions are open in the morning from Monday to Thursday, and some for longer hours. The only Middle Eastern countries with diplomatic representation in Israel are Jordan, Egypt and Turkey. There is no Lebanese or Syrian embassy in Israel.

Australia (☎ 03-695 0451; www.australianembassy.org.il; 37 Sha'ul HaMelekh St, Tel Aviv 64928)

Canada (☎ 03-636 3300; fax 03-636 3380; 3 Nirim St, Tel Aviv 67060)

Egypt Eilat (☎ 08-637 6882; 68 HaAfroni St 88119); Tel Aviv (☎ 03-546 4151; fax 03-544 1615; 54 Basel St, 64239)

France Haifa (☎ 04-813 8811; fax 04-813 8800; 37 HaGefen St); Jerusalem (☎ 02-625 9481, fax 02-625 9178;

5 Paul-Émile Botta St 91076); Tel Aviv (☎ 03-520 8300; fax 03-520 8340; 112 Herbert Samuel Esplanade, 63572)
Germany Haifa (☎ 04-838 1408; fax 04-837 1353; 98 HaNassi Ave); Tel Aviv (☎ 03-693 1313; www.tel-aviv .diplo.de; 3 Daniel Frisch St, 64731)
Ireland (☎ 03-696 4166; fax 03-696 4160; 17th fl, 3 Daniel Frisch St, Tel Aviv 64731)
Jordan (☎ 03-751 7722; fax 03-751 7712; 14 Abbe Hillel St, Ramat Gan, Tel Aviv 52506)
Netherlands (☎ 03-752 3150; www.netherlands -embassy.co.il; 14 Abbe Hillel St, Ramat Gan, Tel Aviv 52506)
Turkey Jerusalem (☎ 02-532 1087; fax 02-582 0214; 20 Nashashibi St); Tel Aviv (☎ 03-524 1101; fax 03-524 0499; 202 HaYarkon St, 63405)
UK Jerusalem (☎ 02-671 7724; fax 02-532 5629; 19 Nashashibi St, 97200); Tel Aviv (☎ 03-725 1222; fax 03-527 1572; 192 HaYarkon St, 64505)
USA Jerusalem (☎ 02 622 7200; fax 02 625 9270; 27 Nablus Rd, 94190); Tel Aviv (☎ 03-519 7575; www.us embassy-israel.org.il; 71 HaYarkon St, 63903)

FESTIVALS & EVENTS

The specific dates of Jewish festivals may vary from year to year. For the latest dates, ask at tourist offices.

March

Boombamela Festival (www.boombamela.co.il; Netzanim Beach, Ashkelon) Very popular and lots of fun! Naked bodies painted in rainbow colours, beach bonfires, bongo drums, art and hedonism. It's one of the wildest parties in the Middle East.
Haifa International Youth Theatre (Haifa)
International Judaica Fair (Jerusalem)
International Poets Festival (Jerusalem)

April

Ein Gev Music Festival (Ein Gev, Galilee)

May

Abu Ghosh Vocal Music Festival (Abu Ghosh, near Jerusalem)
Israel Festival (Jerusalem)
Jacob's Ladder Anglo-Saxon Folk Music Festival (Sea of Galilee) Draws artists from around the world.
Jerusalem International Book Fair (Jerusalem)
Shantipi New Age Festival (Kibbutz Lehavot Haviva, Pardesh Hanna) A gathering in the spirit of Glastonbury.
Tribal Dance Experience (Barkai Forest)

July

Cherry Festival (the Golan Heights)
Dead Sea Water Festival (Dead Sea)
International Street Theatre (Bat Yam)
Jerusalem Film Festival (Jerusalem)

Karmi'el Dance Festival (Karmi'el)
Kol Israel Music Days (Kfar Blum, Upper Galilee)
Oriental Soul Music Festival (Sea of Galilee)

August

Full Moon Desert Festival (Negev)
Klezmer Dance Festival (Tsfat)
Red Sea Jazz Festival (Eilat)

September

Beresheet Festival (Meggido Forest) A Bohemian gathering in the spiritual Megiddo Forest, with lots of live music.
Wigstock (Independence Park, Tel Aviv) Tel Aviv's answer to a gay Woodstock.

October

Fringe Theatre Festival (Akko)
Haifa International Film Festival (Haifa)
Jerusalem Marathon (Jerusalem)
Love Parade (Tel Aviv)

December

International Christmas Choir Assembly (Nazareth)

GAY & LESBIAN TRAVELLERS

Undoubtedly, freewheeling Tel Aviv is the gay capital of Israel, and nearly all of those bars and nightspots that don't specifically cater to gays are at least gay-friendly. Jerusalem, Haifa and Eilat also have gay-oriented entertainment venues. For details, see the coverage for those cities in this chapter or contact the **Gay Hotline** (☎ 03-516 7234; ☽ 7.30-10.30pm Sun, Tue & Thu) in Tel Aviv or the **Jerusalem Infoline** (☎ 02-537 3906; ☽ 8pm-10pm Tue) in Jerusalem. Gay culture is non-existent in the Palestinian Territories and many gay Palestinians have taken refuge in Israel (although this has become increasingly difficult with tight border controls). To better understand the difficult plight of gay and lesbian Palestinians, click on www .globalgayz.com/g-palestine.html.

Several local organisations may also be useful:
Association of Gay Men, Lesbians, Bisexuals & Transgenders (Agudah; ☎ 03-516 7234; www.aguda -ta.org.il; 18 Nahalat Binyamin; ☽ 10.30am-4pm Sun, Tue & Thu)
CLAF (☎ 03-516 5606; www.gay.org.il/claf; 22 Lilienblum St, Tel Aviv; ☽ 11am-4pm Mon & Wed) Lesbian organisation.
Jerusalem Open House (JOH; ☎ 02-625 3191; www .gay.org.il/joh; 7 Ben Yehuda St, Jerusalem; ☽ 10am-5pm Mon-Wed, 10am-11pm Sun & Thu)

HOLIDAYS

Dates of Jewish holidays may vary from year to year, as they're based on the Jewish lunar calendar. The Orthodox Union website (www.ou.org/chagim) has links to a calendar of Jewish holidays. For a list of Islamic holidays, see p648.

January

Eastern Orthodox Christmas 5 and 6 January
Armenian Christmas 19 January
Tu Bishvat (Arbour Day) The new year for trees. On this day different types of fruit and nuts are eaten and trees planted.

February

Black Hebrew Day of Appreciation & Love Festivities include art, music, food and dancing.

March/April

Purim The Feast of Lots commemorates the Persian Queen Esther's deliverance of her Jewish subjects from the despicable secular politician, Haman. Kids and adults alike dress up in costume and enjoy an evening of revelry. This is the time for the typically nondrinking Israelis to atone; according to tradition they get so plastered that they can't distinguish between 'bless Mordecai' and 'curse Haman'.
Good Friday Christian holiday commemorating the crucifixion of Jesus.
International Women's Day Palestinians celebrate this day on 8 March.
Easter Sunday Celebrated first by the Roman Catholics and Protestants and about two weeks later by the Armenian and Eastern Orthodox churches, Easter commemorates the resurrection of Jesus on the third day after the crucifixion. When times are calm, Catholic pilgrims throng the Via Dolorosa and Church of the Holy Sepulchre in the Old City, while many Protestants gather at the Garden Tomb for religious services.
Land Day (30 March) A Palestinian day of protest against the Israeli government's take over of Palestinian lands.
Pesah The Feast of Passover celebrates the exodus of the Children of Israel from Egypt, led by Moses. On the first and last days of this week-long festival, most businesses (including shops and markets) are closed and public transport shuts down; on other days of the festival, businesses may open for limited hours. Passover dinner, or Seder, consists of several prescribed dishes, each commemorating a different event, and during the entire period, bread is replaced with matzo, an unleavened wafer up to 1m in diameter.
Omer (Pesah to Shevuot) This is a Lent-like period solemnly commemorating the various trials of the Jewish people.
Soldiers Memorial Day This day commemorates fallen soldiers in various Israeli conflicts.
The Armenian Holocaust Memorial Day 24 April

Mimouna North African Jewish festival.
Eastern Orthodox & Armenian Good Friday Takes place two weeks after the Protestant and Catholic Good Friday.
Eastern Orthodox & Armenian Easter This falls two weeks after the Protestant and Catholic Easter.

May

Yom HaSho'ah On Holocaust Day (22nd day of Omer) Sirens sound periodically throughout the day signalling two minutes of silence in memory of the six million Jewish victims of the Nazi Holocaust.
Labor Day (1 May) Day for Palestinian workers to celebrate their achievements.
Lag B'Omer Picnics Sports matches and bonfires and a permissible feast on the 33rd day of Omer commemorate the 2nd-century break in the plague that killed Rabbi Akiva's students (in some years, it may fall in late April).
Yom HaAtzma'ut This day commemorates 14 May 1948, when Israel became an independent state. The day before, Yom Hazikaron, is a memorial day dedicated to soldiers lost in Israel's various conflicts. For Palestinians, this day is called Al-Naqba, the Great Catastrophe.

June

Liberation of Jerusalem Day (4 June) This is a commemoration of the reunification of Jerusalem in June 1967.
Shevuot (Pentecost) Seven weeks after Pesah, this day celebrates the delivery of the Torah to Moses on Mt Sinai.

August

Tish'a BeAv This is a commemoration of the 'Destruction of the Temples'.

September

Rosh HaShanah This is the 'head of the Year' (Jewish New Year) and prayer services begin on the eve of the holiday.

October

Independence Day (15 November) Marks the signing of the Palestine Declaration of Independence (signed in 1988).
Yom Kippur The Day of Atonement ends the 10 days of penitence that begin on Rosh HaShanah. The observant spend 25 hours in prayer and contemplation, confessing sins and abstaining from food, drink, sex, cosmetics (including soap and toothpaste) and animal products.
Sukkot On Sukkot (Tabernacles Festival) people erect homemade *sukkotim* (shelters) in commemoration of the 40 years which the ancient Israelites spent in the wilderness after the Exodus. The *sukkotim* walls are constructed of plywood with a roof of loose branches (so the sky is visible from inside); these sit on apartment balconies, gardens and even in hotels and restaurants.
Simhat Torah This falls seven days after Sukkot.

Yitzhak Rabin Memorial Day This day honours the assassinated prime minister, Yitzak Rabin (sometimes held in November).

December

Hanukkah Also called the Festival of Lights, Hanukkah celebrates the re-dedication of the Temple after the triumphant Maccabean revolt against the Seleucids. Each night for a week, families light a candle on a menorah (an eight-branched candelabrum) and exchange gifts.

Christmas Commemorating the humble birth of Jesus in Bethlehem, Christmas is celebrated by Catholics and Protestants on 25 December, while the Eastern Orthodox churches celebrate it on 7 January and the Armenians on 19 January. When things are calm on the West Bank, the event to attend is the Christmas Eve (24 December) midnight mass on Bethlehem's Manger Sq outside the Church of the Nativity. Note that space inside the church is reserved for observant Catholics who hold tickets (distributed free at the Christian Information Centre in Jerusalem's Old City).

INTERNET ACCESS

Most cities and towns have Internet cafés, which typically keep very long hours and charge anywhere from 12NIS to 30NIS per hour. Visitors carrying laptops can find wi-fi hot spots in Tel Aviv (p299), Jerusalem (p285) and Haifa (p308). To sign up for you own ISP account, contact the well-known **Netvision** (04-830 0000, www.netvision.net.il/services).

Israeli phone networks are now 100% digital. Phone plugs look similar to those used in the UK, but they employ a different wiring polarity, so either bring an Israel-specific adaptor or buy one locally.

LANGUAGE

Israel's national language is Hebrew, and the first language of most of the Arab population is the Syrian dialect of Arabic. Most Israelis and Palestinians speak some English – or will attempt to – and many speak other European languages, especially in the tourist centres.

Because Israelis are largely immigrant stock, various other languages are also represented. Some Ashkenazim still speak Yiddish (medieval German using the Hebrew alphabet) in everyday conversation, but due to an influx of over a million Russian Jews from the former Soviet Union, Russian has now emerged as Israel's fourth major language. A very small number of Sephardic people still speak their traditional – but dying – language, Ladino, a blend of Hebrew and Spanish written in the Hebrew alphabet.

Most road signs appear in all three alphabets, but often with baffling transliterations – Caesarea, for example, may be rendered Qisariyya, Kesarya, Qasarya, and so on; and Tsfat may appear as Zefat, Zfat, Safed and other renditions. In other cases, signs may use Hebrew names, such as Yerushalayim for Jerusalem or Tverya for Tiberias.

MONEY

The official currency is the new Israeli shekel (NIS), which is divided into 100 agorot. Coins come in denominations of 10 and 50 agorot (actually marked ½ shekel) and one and five new Israeli shekels, and notes in 10, 20, 50, 100 and 200NIS. The Palestinian pound only exists in theory. If and when a Palestinian state is created you can expect this currency to be put into use.

To make things easier for travellers, most top-end hotels, HI hostels, car-hire companies and many airlines quote their rates and accept payment in US dollars, and paying in US dollars will save you the 17% Value Added Tax (VAT). Euros are also widely accepted by money changers.

Tourists who pay in foreign currency are exempt the VAT, and others are entitled to a refund on most items purchased in shops registered with the Ministry of Tourism (there'll be a sign in the window or at the till). Purchases must be wrapped in sealed, partially transparent plastic, and the original invoice must be legible without opening the parcel. Claim your refund from Bank Leumi in the departure lounge at Ben-Gurion airport.

ATMs are widespread and almost everywhere accepts Visa. Bank Leumi accepts Visa and several other bank cards, but with MasterCard or a Cirrus or Plus format ATM card, you'll have to use Hapoalim Bank.

Exchange rates vary little from place to place, but banks may charge voracious commissions and the best deals are the independent exchange bureaus dotted around every major city and town. Typically, they charge no commission at all.

Banks function from 8.30am to 12.30pm and 4pm to 5.30pm on Sunday, Tuesday and Thursday, from 8.30am to 12.30pm on Monday and Wednesday, and 8.30am to 11.30am on Friday and holiday eves. Most exchange bureaus keep longer hours.

Until recently, tipping wasn't an issue, but these days, restaurant bills arrive with a

10% to 12% addition for service, or a notice that service is not included. Note that taxi drivers do not expect tips – they're usually content just to overcharge.

Travellers cheques may be changed at most banks, but commission can be as high as 20NIS, regardless of the cheque amount. It's better to change them at a no-commission exchange bureau or the post office. Post offices also operate instant Western Union international money transfer services.

Below are the rates for a range of currencies when this book went to print.

Country	Unit	New Israeli shekel (NIS)
Australia	A$1	3.43
Canada	C$1	3.95
Egypt	E£1	0.81
euro zone	€1	5.52
Japan	¥100	4.00
Jordan	JD1	6.55
Lebanon	LL100	0.31
New Zealand	NZ$1	3.20
Syria	S£100	9.03
UK	UK£1	8.16
USA	US$1	4.68

POST

Letters and postcards to North America and Australasia take seven to 10 days to arrive, and to Europe, a bit less. Incoming mail takes three or four days from Europe and around a week from other places. Small postcards to anywhere in the world cost 1.40NIS, while large postcards and airmail letters are 1.90NIS to Europe and 2.30NIS to North America.

For poste restante, have correspondents send mail or packages to the main post office in the city or town where you'll pick up post. Note that the Amex offices in Jerusalem and Tel Aviv will receive mail for card holders or travellers-cheque customers.

TELEPHONE & FAX

Standard rates (14NIS per minute) to anywhere in the country, including local calls, apply between 7am and 7pm. Between 7pm and 7am and on weekends, calls cost considerably less.

Fax

At post offices, you can send a local or international fax for 12NIS for the first sheet and 5.20NIS for subsequent sheets, regard-

less of the destination. At most Internet cafés, you can send or receive faxes for 7NIS to 10NIS for the first page and 5NIS for each page thereafter.

Mobile Phones

Cellular phones are extremely popular in both Israel and the Palestinian Territories, and most foreign providers operate here (but it may be worth checking with your provider before you leave home). In Israel Nokia, Pelefon, Cellcom and Orange all offer both fixed-line (local user) and pay-as-you-go services. Pelefon allows phone rentals for a charge of 12NIS per day. A minimum charge is 185NIS which allows about three hours of domestic talk time and free incoming calls. If you have your own phone, the best deal is with Cellcom, which sells a SIM card for 46.80NIS. Calls run around 1.20NIS per minute. With Orange, SIM card purchase and activation costs 109NIS.

Phone Codes

The country code for Israel and the Palestinian Territories is ☎ 972, followed by the local area code (minus the zero), then the subscriber number. Local area codes are given at the start of each city or town section. The international access code (to call abroad from Israel and the Palestinian Territories) is ☎ 013 with Barak, ☎ 011 with Golden Lines and ☎ 001 with Bezeq, all of which offer comparable international rates.

Phonecards

Local and international calls can be made from cardphones, which are found at post offices and other public places. The best-value telephone cards are sold at post offices, but are also available from lottery kiosks, newsstands and bookshops. A 20NIS international card allows you to talk for 60 minutes.

TOILETS

Most Israeli towns have clean (and often free) public toilets in such prominent places as town squares, pedestrian underpasses, and bus and train stations. Alternatively, a 'McBathroom' is never too far away. In an emergency, do as the Israelis do and just ask at any restaurant – most Israelis are sympathetic to such plights and will normally let you use the facilities without expecting you to buy anything. Public facilities it the West

Bank and Gaza are usually not as good or are hard to find. If you do find something, toilet paper probably won't be available, so it's a good idea to carry some of your own. If there is nothing available, again the best thing to do is ask politely at a restaurant or hotel if you can use their facilities.

VISAS

With a few exceptions, visitors to Israel and the Palestinian Territories need only a passport valid for at least six months from the date of entry. Nationals of most Central American and African countries (but not South Africa), India, Singapore and some ex-Soviet republics also require a pre-issued visa.

Visas given at the border are valid for 90 days. But (very important here) you will be asked how long you plan to stay in Israel and what you state is generally what you get. So even if you don't plan on staying the full three months, ask for it anyway, on the chance that you'll stay longer than you intended. Kibbutz and moshav volunteers must secure a volunteer's visa, which can be arranged with the assistance of the kibbutz or moshav.

Anyone who appears 'undesirable' or is suspected of looking for illegal employment may be questioned by immigration officials about the purpose of their visit and asked to provide evidence of a return ticket and sufficient funds for their intended length of stay. Those who can't comply may find themselves on the next flight home.

For details on how an Israeli stamp can blight your passport, see the boxed text, below.

Visa Extensions

To stay more than three months, visitors must apply for a visa through the **Ministry of the Interior** (Eilat ☎ 08-637 6332; HaTemarim Blvd; Jerusalem ☎ 02-629 0222; 1 Schlomzion HaMalka St; Tel Aviv ☎ 03-736 2534; 3rd fl, Tel Aviv Government Complex, aka: Kiria), with offices in most cities and towns. Join the queue by 8am or you could be waiting all day. You'll need 145NIS for the visa extension (plus 75NIS if you take the multi-entry visa option) and one passport-sized photo. You must also present evidence of sufficient funds for the extended stay. The Tel Aviv office is so backed up with applications that your first day of waiting in line is only to make an appointment to come back another day (usually one month later). For faster service try a smaller branch office.

Note that overstaying your allotted time elicits a fine of 135NIS per month – this can be sorted out at Ministry of the Interior offices or Ben-Gurion airport, but not at land borders. Travellers who overstay by just a few days report no hassles or fines.

WOMEN TRAVELLERS

Female travellers can expect the same sort of treatment they'd receive in most European countries. Women wanting to blend in and respect local customs should dress modestly

ISRAEL & THE PALESTINIAN TERRITORIES

THE ISRAELI STAMP STIGMA

The game of wits played between travellers and diplomatic consulars across the Middle East is ratcheted up by what's known as the 'Israeli Stamp Stigma'. In the Middle East, only Turkey, Egypt and Jordan recognise Israel – all other countries refuse to admit anyone whose passport has been tainted by evidence of a visit to the Jewish state. Israeli immigration officials will, *if asked*, stamp only a separate entry card and not your passport. This is fine for travellers flying into and out of Israel, but if you are crossing into Jordan or Egypt overland, the entry/exit stamps into those countries (marked, for example: 'Taba' or 'Aqaba') will be no less incriminating than an Israeli stamp.

Travellers can ask the Jordanians and Egyptians not to stamp their passport when entering/ leaving Israel (instead stamping a separate piece of paper), but further down the track those missing stamps may raise questions in the eyes of consuls when you apply for visas in other parts of the Middle East. We had no trouble getting into Lebanon, Syria and Jordan after visiting Egypt and Israel (avoiding Egypt exit and Israel entry stamps), but maybe we were just lucky.

A safer option includes returning to the country (Jordan or Egypt) from where you started. This will negate the need for a new entry stamp (it will seem like you never left). Even better, arrange your itinerary so that a visit to Israel is that final stop on your tour in the Middle East.

For information on possible new regulations related to organised group travel from Israel to Syria via Jordan, see p553.

in conservative areas like Tsfat and parts of Jerusalem (including the Old City and M'ea She'arim). A long-sleeve shirt, ankle-length skirt and head scarf are par for the course in these areas. Western women won't blend in as well in Arab areas, but the same precautions apply. Take particular care when walking on the Mount of Olives, where reports of harassment are not uncommon.

WORK

While it isn't difficult to find casual work in Israel, to work legally you'll need a work permit from the Ministry of the Interior and they aren't easy to get. Unfortunately, unscrupulous employers often take advantage of illegal workers, assuming the workers have no recourse. They're wrong. The *pro bono publico* service **Kav l'Oved** (☎ 03-688 3766; www .kavlaoved.org.il; 3rd fl, 17 Yl Peretz St, Tel Aviv; ☉ 9.30am-4.30pm Sun, Tue & Wed, noon-6pm Thu) provides legal services on behalf of workers – legal or not – who have not been paid by employers.

In good times, eager international volunteers descend on Israel for a stint on a kibbutz or moshav. By definition, a kibbutz (plural kibbutzim) is a communal farm or other rural project staffed by volunteers, who trade their labour for food, lodging and a small stipend. After a short stint, though, quite a few volunteers are disappointed with what they encounter, and Tel Aviv hostels are crowded with dropouts who found things less utopian than anticipated. Before committing yourself to a volunteer programme, be sure to balance agency propaganda with testimonials from previous volunteers to get a realistic idea of what to expect. Note that kibbutz volunteers must be between the ages of 18 and 32 and moshav volunteers 20 to 35.

On a moshav, which is a community of small, individually worked farms, the work is typically more strenuous and more interesting than on a kibbutz. It also pays better and allows more privacy and independence.

Some volunteers organise a kibbutz stay through a kibbutz representative office in their own country. After collecting a basic registration fee (around US$50), the kibbutz representative will arrange flights and visas (individuals may make their own travel arrangements, which is generally cheaper). Alternatively, would-be volunteers can apply in person at the kibbutz agent in Tel Aviv. Your chances of success will increase dramatically

if you can convince the officials that you're not a drug-crazed, beer-guzzling layabout.

For more information, contact one of the following offices:

Australia
Kibbutz Program Centre (☎ 02-9360 2368; fax 02-9380 5124; 140 Darlinghurst Rd, Darlinghurst, NSW 2010)
Kibbutz Program Desk (☎ 03-9272 5688; fax 03-9272 5640; 306 Hawthorn Rd, Caulfield South, Victoria 3162)

Canada
Kibbutz Aliyah Desk Montreal (☎ 514-486 9526; fax 514-483 6392; Suite 206, 1 Carre Cumming Sq, Montreal, PQ H3X 2H9); Ontario (☎ 416-633 4766; fax 416-633 2758; Suite 100, 3995 Bathurst St, North York, Ont M3H 5V3); Vancouver (☎ 604-257 5100; israelmatters@jfgv .com; 950 W 41st Ave, Vancouver, BC V5Z 2N7)

Israel
Kibbutz Program Centre (Map p300; ☎ 03-527 8874; www.kibbutz.org.il; 18 Frishman St, cnr Ben Yehuda St, Tel Aviv; ☉ 8am-2pm Sun-Thu)

New Zealand
Kibbutz Program Desk (☎ 04-384 4229; fax 04-384 2159; 80 Webb St, Wellington 6001)

UK
Kibbutz Representatives (☎ 0181-458 9235; fax 0181-455 7930; 1A Accommodation Rd, London NW11 8ED)

USA
Israel Aliyah Centre (☎ 305-573 7631; aliyahmiami@ gmjf.org; 4200 Biscayne Blvd, Miami, FL 33137)
Kibbutz Program Centre (☎ 800-247 7852; www .kibbutzprogramcenter.org; 21st fl, 633 3rd Ave, New York, NY 10017)

TRANSPORT IN ISRAEL & THE PALESTINIAN TERRITORIES

GETTING THERE & AWAY
Entering Israel & the Palestinian Territories

A frequent topic of conversation among travellers (a great source of annoyance for some and a breeze for others) is the entrance procedures for Israel and the Palestinian Territories. It's rigorous even at the best of times, and you can expect a barrage of questions about your recent travels, occupation, any acquaintances in Israel and possibly your religious or family background. If you are meeting friends in Israel, have their phone number handy. Anyone planning to work in Israel can expect delays. A passport full of stamps from neighbouring Islamic countries will likewise be circumspect. When immigration asks how long you plan to stay in the country, and you say 'two weeks', that is exactly what they will write on your entry card. For the maximum time allowed, you must specifically ask for three months.

Air

Israel's main gateway, Ben-Gurion airport, is 20km southeast of Tel Aviv and 50km west of Jerusalem. An ultramodern US$1 billion international terminal, unveiled in 2004, handles 16 million passengers a year. Only a handful of international charter flights may touch down at Ovda airport, outside Eilat. Israel's national carrier El Al operates flights to and from Ben-Gurion (except on Saturday). To check on international flights, phone **Ben-Gurion airport information** (TLV; ☎ 03-972 3388; www.ben-gurion-airport.co.il).

Last Minute Tickets (☎ 03-636 6808), on the 2nd floor of the international terminal, has reasonably priced tickets to Europe (eg London one way for US$260), but you'll pay well over the odds here for a ticket to the USA or Australia.

Note that airport security is tight, especially on El Al services, and international travellers should check in at least three hours prior to their flight. In Tel Aviv, passengers can check in downtown on the day before their flight and avoid lugging baggage to the airport (see p305).

Fares into Israel aren't especially cheap and it's rarely an allowable stop on round-the-world itineraries. The best deals are normally available on the Internet (try www.travelocity.com), or with a discount travel agent or consolidator. At the time of writing, the lowest return fare from New York to Tel Aviv was US$880 on LOT Polish Airlines, via Warsaw. From London Heathrow, return fares on El Al go for US$535, nonstop. From Sydney, the lowest current return fare is US$1250 on Qantas to London Heathrow, then with British Airways to Tel Aviv.

Apart from neighbouring Jordan and Egypt, which may be visited overland, Tur-

key is the only Middle Eastern country that may be visited from Israel, and lots of Israelis take advantage of the great airfare deals that are available between Tel Aviv and İstanbul.

Airlines that fly to Israel:

Air Canada (AC; ☎ 03-607 2111; www.aircanda.com) Hub: Pearson International Airport, Toronto.
Air France (AF; ☎ 03-511 0000; www.airfrance.com) Hub: Charles de Gaulle Airport, Paris.
Alitalia (AZ; ☎ 03-971 1047; www.alitalia.it) Hub: Fiumicino Airport, Rome.
American Airlines (AA; ☎ 03-795 2122; www.aa.com) Hub: O'Hare Airport, Chicago.
Austrian Airlines (OS; ☎ 03-511 6700; www.aua.com) Hub: Vienna Airport.
British Airways (BA; ☎ 03-606 1555; www.britishair ways.com) Hub: Heathrow Airport, London.
KLM (KL; ☎ 03-971 1138; www.klm.com) Hub: Schiphol Airport, Amsterdam.

The Israel Student Travel Association (ISSTA; p299) offers competitive fares, though it's worth getting quotes from other travel agents in downtown Tel Aviv or Jerusalem. Alternatively, check around the hostels and night spots for cut-price flight advertising.

Land

If you're planning to visit Lebanon or Syria, try to do so before arriving in Israel or the Palestinian Territories. Not only are borders with these countries closed, but any evidence in your passport showing a visit to Israel will bar you from visiting them (see p353).

On the other hand, Egypt and Jordan both have open land borders with Israel and the Palestinian Territories, and you may cross on foot or by private vehicle, but not in a taxi or rental car. Drivers and motorcyclists will need the vehicle's registration papers and proof of liability insurance, plus a driving licence from home (but not necessarily an international driving licence).

EGYPT

The **Taba crossing** (☎ 08-637 2104, 08-636 0999; ⊙ 24hr) is currently the only open border between Israel and Egypt. Here, travellers pay a 68NIS fee to leave Israel, plus around E£20 to enter Egypt. Driving your own vehicle across, you'll pay a fee of 32NIS on the Israeli side and a whopping E£180 on the Egyptian side.

For safety and security reasons, the **Rafah crossing** (☎ 08-673 4080), on a 'safe' road in the Gaza Strip, is currently closed to individual travellers. Tour operators, though, are still allowed to ferry paying clients across on organised trips; contact Mazada Tours (below) for details.

Nearly all visitors require visas to enter Egypt, which cost 65NIS for US and German citizens and 100NIS for everyone else. They're available at the **Egyptian embassy** (☎ 03-546 4151; 54 Basel St, Tel Aviv; ☿ for applications 9-11am Sun-Thu) and the **Egyptian consulate** (☎ 08-637 6882; 68 HaAfroni St, Eilat; ☿ for applications 9-11am Sun-Thu). Deliver your passport, application and one passport-sized photo during opening hours in the morning and pick up the visa around 2pm the same day.

Alternatively, at the Taba border you can pick up a free Sinai-only entry permit, which is valid for 14 days and allows travel between Taba and Sharm el-Sheikh, and to Mt Sinai and St Katherine's Monastery; however, it is not valid for diving at Ras Mohammed National Park near Sharm el-Sheikh.

Access to the Taba border from Eilat is on city bus No 15. From the Egyptian side, buses and shared taxis leave for Sinai; for details, see p176.

If you are trying to get to Cairo in a hurry, the best way is to hop on the **Mazada Tours** (Jerusalem Map p288; ☎ 02-623 5777; 15 Jaffa Rd, Pearl Hotel; Tel Aviv Map p298; ☎ 03-544 4454; www.mazada.co.il; 141 Ibn Gvirol St) direct bus service between Tel Aviv or Jerusalem and Cairo via Rafah (US$84, 12 hours). Buses leave Jerusalem/Tel Aviv at 9am/11am Sunday, Monday and Thursday. After picking up passengers in Cairo, they head back. Mazada is represented in Cairo by **Misr Travel** (☎ /fax 02-335 5470; Cairo Sheraton, Midan al-Galaa, Doqqi).

JORDAN

There are three border crossing points with Jordan.

The least used of the three is the **Jordan River crossing** (☎ 04-648 0018; ☿ 8am-10pm), which is 6km east of Beit She'an in Galilee. It's not particularly convenient for anywhere. Exit tax here is 70NIS.

More popular is the **Allenby/King Hussein Bridge crossing** (☎ 02-548 2600; ☿ 8am-6pm Sun-Thu, 8am-2pm Fri & Sat), which is only 30km from Jerusalem and 40km from Amman. Traffic can be heavy here, especially between 11am and 3pm. Exit tax here is 127NIS.

In the south the **Yitzhak Rabin crossing** (☎ 08-630 0530; ☿ 6.30am-10pm Sun-Thu, 8am-8pm Fri & Sat), called Wadi Araba by Jordanians, lies just 2km northeast of central Eilat, making it handy for day trips from Eilat to Aqaba, Petra and Wadi Rum. Exit tax here is 68NIS, entry to Jordan is free and exit from Jordan is JD5.

Nearly all travellers require visas to enter Jordan; for details see p403. Visas can be purchased at both the Rabin (formerly called Arava) and Jordan River border crossings, but not at Allenby Bridge. If you're going that way, get a visa at the **Jordanian embassy** (☎ 03-751 7722; fax 03-751 7712; 14 Abbe Hillel St, Ramat Gan, Tel Aviv), in the Tel Aviv suburb of Ramat Gan (take bus No 66 from Ben Yehuda St). You can apply in the morning and pick the visa up around 2pm the same day; bring one passport-sized photo.

Sea

For details of sailings between Haifa and Piraeus (the port for Athens) see p663.

GETTING AROUND

Air

Israir (www.israir.co.il) flies at least once daily (including Saturday) between Ben-Gurion, Tel Aviv Sde Dov, Eilat and Haifa. **Arkia** (www.arkia.co.il), which also runs international charters, operates flights between the same cities, as well as international charters to Jerusalem.

Bicycle

Cycle tourists should bear in mind the hot climate, winter rainfall and steep hills. Israeli drivers can be aggressive at times, but generally respect a cyclist's right of way. The best place for a leisurely cycle trip is around the Sea of Galilee; for such purposes, several Tiberias hostels hire out bicycles for quite reasonable rates.

Bus

Israel's small size and excellent road system combine to make bus travel the public transport of choice. The network is dominated by **Egged** (☎ 03-694 8888), which runs

ISRAEL & THE PALESTINIAN TERRITORIES

fast and modern air-con buses on both long-distance and city bus routes; call for information on schedules and prices, including city buses.

In Nazareth, East Jerusalem and the West Bank, a number of small Arab-run bus companies provide public transport on typically slow and antiquated vehicles. Fares are quite cheap and ISIC holders are entitled to a discount of about 10% on interurban fares.

Note that Egged bus schedules are affected by public holidays and usually don't run during Shabbat, while Arab buses operate daily.

Car & Motorcycle

Drivers won't need an international driving licence, but must have their home driving licence in order to rent a car or drive a private vehicle.

Because buses are less frequent in the Golan Heights and the Negev areas, these places are best seen with a rental car, and those on a budget will find that sharing a vehicle can be quite economical (unless you're staying in Tel Aviv, where parking costs at least US$10 per day).

Car hire companies include:

Avis Ben-Gurion airport (☎ 03-971 2315); Tel Aviv (Map p298; ☎ 02-527 2314; 113 HaYarkon St); Tiberias (☎ 04-672 2766; cnr HaAmakim & HaYarden)

Budget Ben-Gurion airport (☎ 03-971 1504); Jerusalem (Map pp284-5; ☎ 02-624 8991; 23 HaMelekh David St)

Eldan Ben-Gurion airport (☎ 03-977 3400); Jerusalem (Map pp284-5; ☎ 02-625 2151; 24 HaMelekh David St); Tel Aviv (Map p298; ☎ 03 527 1166; 114 HaYarkon St); Tiberias (☎ 04-679 1822; 1 HaBanim)

Hertz Ben-Gurion airport (☎ 03-977 2444); Tel Aviv (Map p298; ☎ 03-522 3332; 144 HaYarkon St)

With most of these companies you can hire a car with insurance and unlimited kilometres for as little as US$250 per week or US$600 per month. Just make sure your designated driver is good on both the offence and defence, and has a long fuse, especially when tackling Jerusalem or Tel Aviv.

Hitching

Although hitching was once a common way of getting around Israel, increasing reports of violent crime make this a risky business. Women should not hitch without male companions and all travellers should be circumspect of the cars they get into. The local method of soliciting a lift is to simply point an index finger at the road, but the fact that we tell you how it works doesn't mean we recommend you do it.

Local Transport
SHERUT

As in neighbouring Middle Eastern countries, the shared taxi (*sherut*) rules the roads of both Israel and the Palestinian Territories. The Arabs call it a service taxi (pronounced 'ser-*vees*'). During Shabbat, *sheruts* provide the only transport on certain major intercity routes, and on the West Bank, where Egged is limited to Jewish towns, the *sheruts* save hours of travelling time over the typically spluttering, smoke-belching Arab buses.

SPECIAL TAXI

Drivers of 'special' (ie nonshared) taxis are renowned for overcharging (sometimes spectacularly!). If you can't negotiate a reasonable fare – trips around central Jerusalem or Tel Aviv should run between 20NIS and 25NIS – insist that the driver use the meter, and watch your progress on a map to ensure that the shortest route is followed. Tariffs rise between 9pm and 5.30am.

Note that taxi drivers are not normally tipped, but in the absence of an attempted rip-off, it's fine to refuse a shekel or two in change.

Tours

Several local companies offer day tours to sites of interest around Israel. The following options operate only when demand is sufficient, so it helps to turn up with a motivated group. These are some of the more useful ones:

Ben Harim Tours (☎ 03-546 8870; www.beinharim .co.il)

United Tours (☎ 03-693 3412; www.unitedtours.co.il)

Train

Israel State Railways (ISR; ☎ 03-577 4000; www.isra rail.org.il) runs a limited but convenient, efficient and inexpensive network of passenger rail services between Be'ersheva and Nahariya, as well as a new spur to Jerusalem. It is especially recommended for travel between Tel Aviv and Haifa or Akko. ISIC holders get a 20% discount. For the latest details, see its website.

Jordan

Ahlan wa sahlan! – 'Welcome to Jordan!' It's the first and sometimes only piece of English most Jordanians learn, and from the Bedouin of Wadi Rum to the taxi drivers of Amman you'll be on the receiving end of this mantra every day. The thing is, it really is genuine, and it's this open-armed welcome that makes travel in Jordan such a delight. In the midst of a very tough neighbourhood, Jordan retains a calmer air; a peacefulness not prevalent in surrounding countries.

One thing that overwhelms travellers in Jordan is the sense of history, with every stone seemingly carrying some historical significance. Amman, Jerash and Umm Qais were cities of the ancient Roman Decapolis, while biblical sites range from Bethany-Beyond-the-Jordan, where Jesus was baptised, to Mt Nebo, where Moses is said to have looked out over the Promised Land. Grandest of all, before Christ was born Nabataean stonemasons carved out their awe-inspiring capital at Petra from dramatic towering sandstone walls.

Jordan is also a great place to put down the history books and get active, whether it be diving off the coast of Aqaba, trekking with the Bedouin in the camelprints of Lawrence of Arabia, or hiking through stunning river gorges. Jordan's excellent nature reserves in particular offer some of the most exciting adventure options in the Middle East.

Like much of the Arab world, Jordan is trying to balance its tribal traditions and its cherished values of Islam with a push towards the global lifestyle; it's a tricky balancing act. In the meantime travellers in Jordan can still manage to combine the best of both worlds.

In comparison with other Middle Eastern countries, Jordan can be a little expensive for travellers, but it's very compact and has enough compelling attractions (including some spectacular landscapes) to keep you interested for a couple of weeks. On no account should you miss it.

FAST FACTS

- **Area** 89,206 sq km
- **Capital** Amman
- **Country code** ☎ 962
- **Language** Arabic
- **Money** Jordanian dinar (JD); US$1 = JD0.704; €1 = JD0.831
- **Official Name** Hashemite Kingdom of Jordan
- **Population** 5.8 million

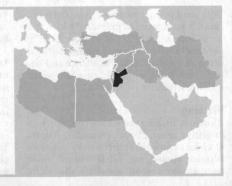

JORDAN

HIGHLIGHTS

- **Petra** (p389) From the labyrinthine canyon of the Siq to the spectacular high places, ancient Petra is simply unmissable.
- **Wadi Rum** (p393) Enjoy camel rides, Bedouin camps, and experience the ghosts of Lawrence of Arabia in this stunning desert landscape.
- **Jerash** (p377) The echoes of Rome still linger in the columns, amphitheatres and chariot races of this magnificently preserved city.
- **Mt Nebo** (p386) Christian pilgrims flock to this site where Moses finally cast eyes on the Promised Land.
- **Wadi Mujib Nature Reserve** (p382) High adventure by the Dead Sea means splashing down a slot canyon or rappelling down a 20m waterfall in this ecotourism venture.

HOW MUCH?

- **Souvenir keffiyeh** from JD2
- **Cup of tea** 200 to 400 fils
- **Midrange dinner** JD7
- **Daily rate for budget travellers** US$15 to US$20
- **Midrange hotel room** JD15 to JD35

LONELY PLANET INDEX

- **Litre of petrol** 350 to 450 fils
- **1.5L bottle of water** 350 fils
- **Bottle of Amstel beer (in restaurant)** JD2.50
- **Souvenir T-shirt** JD5
- **Street stall felafel** 250 fils

CLIMATE & WHEN TO GO

Average daily maximum temperatures in Amman range from 12°C in January to 32°C in August. Weatherwise April/May and September/October are probably the best times to visit Jordan and these months are considered peak season.

Summer is an uncomfortable time to visit the Jordan Valley, Desert Castles and Wadi Rum: daily temperatures are well in excess of 36°C and can peak at 49°C. At the other extreme, snow in Amman and Petra is not unheard of in winter, when desert nights can be very cold. Even during winter Aqaba remains balmy.

Note that most nature reserve facilities are closed from November until 1 April. One date for the calendar is the excellent Jerash Festival (p377), staged at the end of July.

See Climate Charts p643.

HISTORY

Jordan has always been a crossroads for the Middle East's great civilisations, although most invaders have simply passed through en route to more prized possessions.

In 333 BC, Alexander the Great stormed through Jordan on his way to Egypt. After Alexander's death in 323 BC, Ptolemy I gained Egypt, Jordan and parts of Syria. In southern Jordan, the Nabataeans, a semi-nomadic Arabian tribe that controlled lucrative trade routes, built its splendid capital at Petra, while the Roman Empire controlled much of the rest of the country.

After periods of occupation by the Seleucids, Sassanians and Byzantines, Jordan was the site of several initial key battles between the Byzantines and Arabs, before it was overrun by the armies of Islam in the 7th century AD. In the late 7th century, Jordan came under the control of the Umayyad Empire centred in Damascus.

In AD 747 an earthquake devastated much of Jordan, ushering in the rule of the Abbasids, who were in turn followed by the Cairo-based Fatimids in AD 969, and then, from 1037, by the Seljuk Turks.

In the 11th century, Pope Urban II launched the Crusades, capturing Jerusalem in 1099, slaughtering countless inhabitants and devastating the area. The Crusaders took control of most of Jordan by about 1115, and built fortresses at Karak, Shobak and Petra.

In the 12th century, the armies of Nur ad-Din, and later Salah ad-Din (Saladin), reunited the Arab and Islamic world and occupied most of the Crusader strongholds in Jordan. The Mamluks, former soldier-slaves, finally expelled the Crusaders in 1250. The Ottoman Turks defeated the Mamluks in 1516 and ruled until WWI.

In June 1916 the Arabs, with the assistance of TE Lawrence ('Lawrence of Arabia'), launched the Arab Revolt and helped the British drive the Turks from the region. In return, the Arabs were given British assurances that they would be allowed to establish an independent Arab state.

JORDAN

MEDITERRANEAN SEA

LEBANON

SYRIA

Qatana

DAMASCUS

Tyre

Quneitra

Akko

Golan
Heights

Ezra'a

Haifa

Sea of
Galilee

Tiberias   Fiq

Suweida

Jebel al-'Arab

Umm
Qais

Der'a

Jebel Druze
(1735m)

Netanya

Sheikh Hussein
Bridge

Irbid   Ramtha

Nasib   Bosra

Pella

Jabir

Qala'at
ar-Rabad

Mafraq

*Jordan
River*

Ajlun

Umm
al-Jimal

Jerash

10

TEL AVIV

West Bank

Deir Alla

Zarqa River

Safawi

Zarqa

King Hussein/
Allenby Bridge

Salt

Zarqal

15

Qasr al-Hallabat

65

Suweileh

JERUSALEM

Wadi as-Seer

AMMAN

30

Qala'at
al-Azraq

Jericho

Shuneh al-
Janubiyyeh
(South Shuna)

Qasr al-
Mushatta

40

Qusayr
Amra

Azraq

Azraq
Wetland
Reserve

Suweimeh

Bethany-
Beyond-
the-Jordan

Mt Nebo
(802m)   Madaba

Gaza

To Cairo

Ein Gedi

Gaza Strip

*Dead
Sea*

Hammamat Ma'in

Machaerus
(Mukawir)

Dhiban

Ariha

Queen Alia
International
Airport

Dhab'a

Umm ar-Rasas

Qasr
al-Kharana

Shaumari
Wildlife
Reserve

Al-Umari

30

Al-Haditha

Wadi Mujib
Nature Reserve

Wadi Mujib

Al-Qurayat

King's Hwy

50

Qatranah

Karak

Mu'tah

15

Safi

Wadi Hasa

Dead Sea Hwy

ISRAEL
& THE PALESTINIAN
TERRITORIES

Fifa

Tafila

Bayir

5

Jebel
al-Adhriyat
(986m)

The Negev

Dana Nature
Reserve
Wadi Finan

Qadsiyya

Shobak

35

Wadi Araba

Wadi
Musa

Petra

Udruh

Al-Jafr

Ma'an

Desert Hwy

Qa'al Jafr

Jebel
al-'Unnab
(1022m)

65

Jebel
Haroun

Ras an-Naqb

5

15

Jebel 'Atrah
(1382m)

Quweira

EGYPT

Eilat

Wadi Araba
Crossing

Taba

Aqaba

66

Ad-Durra

Haqi

Nuweiba

Gulf of Aqaba

Rum   *Wadi
Rum*   Diseh

Jebel
Umm Adaami
(1830m)

Al-Mudawwara

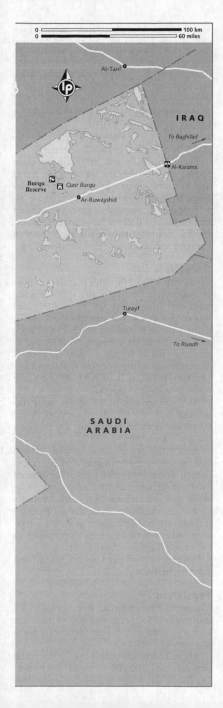

The newly formed League of Nations instead gave Britain a mandate over Palestine, and shortly afterwards the state of Transjordan, lying between Iraq and the East Bank of the Jordan River, was made a separate entity under King Abdullah. What remained of Palestine corresponded more or less to present-day Israel and the Palestinian Territories.

Directly after WWII, the British threw in the towel and handed over the mess to the UN, which voted in favour of the partition of Palestine into separate Arab and Jewish states. But, agreement could not be reached and the Arab-Israeli War broke out in 1948, prompting many Palestinians to flee to Transjordan and ending with a comprehensive victory for Israel; it ensured Jewish occupation of the zones allocated to them under the UN partition plan as well as almost all those assigned to the Palestinian Arabs. Transjordan exploited the situation and occupied the West Bank and part of Jerusalem. This done, King Abdullah shortened his fledgling country's name to Jordan.

King Abdullah was assassinated in 1951. He was succeeded the following year by his grandson Hussein, who took the throne at the age of just 17 and managed to hold it for 48 years through insurrection attempts, two wars with the Israelis and a virtual civil war with the Palestinians. He reigned until his death in 1999.

In the 1960s aid poured in from the USA and Jordan enjoyed a boom in tourism, mainly in Jerusalem's old city. The situation was radically altered by the Six Day War of 1967, in which Jordan lost the West Bank and its half of Jerusalem to occupying Israeli forces. In return it gained a huge influx of Palestinian refugees.

As the Palestinians, particularly the Palestine Liberation Organisation (PLO), became more militant against the Israeli occupation in the early 1970s they also posed a danger to King Hussein, given that most operated from Jordanian territory. They came to contest power in the kingdom, angered in part by Hussein's claim to be the leader of the Palestinian people. After some bloody fighting in 1971, the bulk of the radicals were forced to cross the border to Lebanon, where they would later become one part among many of that country's woes.

King Hussein's diplomatic skills were stretched to the fullest when, during the

1991 Gulf War, he refused to side against Iraq, fearing unrest among Jordan's Palestinian populace. For the third time in 45 years, Jordan experienced a massive refugee inflow, with as many as 500,000 Palestinians previously working in the Gulf states fleeing to Jordan.

Jordan recovered remarkably well from that conflict and, despite fears of the threat of Islamic extremism, King Hussein went ahead and signed a full peace treaty with Israel in 1994.

When King Hussein finally succumbed in February 1999 to the cancer that had been ailing him for so long, his son and nominated heir, Abdullah II, became king of a comparatively stable and prosperous country.

Jordan Today

King Abdullah has impressed most observers with his ability to protect the moderate and largely democratic legacy of his diplomatically adept father, though some grumble about the pace of change. Like much of the Middle East, Jordan faces tensions between tradition and modernity, and dilemmas between Islamisation and Westernisation that remain to be resolved.

The Palestinian intifada (uprising) and the US invasion of Iraq has hit Jordan's tourism industry hard and has stirred deep passions among Jordan's population, suggesting that Jordan's future stability may hinge on events largely beyond its borders.

This last point was brought home with a bang in November 2005 when a series of suicide bombings killed 60 people at Amman's Grand Hyatt, Radisson SAS and Days Inn hotels.

Whether King Abdullah responds to the attacks with an increased rate of reform or a security crackdown remains to be seen.

THE CULTURE
The National Psyche

Jordanian people are extremely hospitable with initial conversation inevitably leading to a heartfelt 'welcome'. This traditional sense of hospitality is mixed with an easy modernity and wonderful sense of humour that make Jordanians easy to get along with.

In many ways the modern Western outlook of Amman's young middle and upper classes contrasts strongly with the conservative Bedouin morality of the country-side. This tension, along with the rapid social change linked to the rise of tourism has led to a clash of values in places such as Wadi Musa.

Shared values include a deep respect for the Jordanian royal family, which is part of the ingrained tribal respect for elders. Islam dominates Jordanian views of the world, of course, as does the Palestinian experience, which is hardly surprising when you consider that 65% of Jordanians are Palestinian.

Being physically and ethnically so close to Iraq, most Jordanians are often frustrated and at times angered by American policies towards Palestine and Iraq but they are always able to differentiate a government from its people. You'll never be greeted with animosity, regardless of your nationality, only a courtesy and hospitality that are humbling.

Daily Life

More than 40% of Jordan's population lives in Amman, reflecting a big split between rural and urban lifestyles. The middle and upper classes of Amman shop in malls, drink lattes in mixed-sex Starbucks and obsess over the latest fashions. Mobile phones dominate life in Jordan as they do abroad. Yet urban unemployment is high, and entire neighbourhoods of Amman are made up of Palestinian refugees.

At the other end of the spectrum is traditional Bedouin life, deeply rooted in the desert and centred on herding. For more on the Bedouin see p394.

Family ties are essential to both groups and the sexes are often segregated. Most Jordanian women socialise with other women only and often inside the family group only, while men chat in male-only cafés. Attitudes to women remain quite traditional. 'Honour killings' are not infrequent and the Jordanian judicial process seems unprepared to take a stand against them.

Women were allowed to vote for the first time in the 1989 elections.

Population

The population of Jordan stood at about 5.8 million in 2005. Some 900,000 of these are still registered as refugees (primarily from the wars of 1948 and 1967).

About 1.8 million people live in the capital Amman, and 700,000 more in neighbouring Zarqa. The majority (98%) of Jordanians are Arab (which includes Bedouin); about two thirds of these are Palestinians. There are also small communities of Circassians, Chechens and Armenians who moved to the region during the Ottoman period.

SPORT

Jordanians are football crazy, and watching football in the bars and coffeehouses is free and can be lots of fun. Amman's two main teams are Wahadat (generally supported by Palestinians) and Faisaly (supported by other Jordanians). Games are mostly played on Friday at the Amman International Stadium near Sports City in Shmeisani (JD2).

RELIGION

Over 92% of the population are Sunni Muslims. A further 6% are Christians living mainly in Amman, Madaba, Karak and Salt. There are tiny Shiite and Druze groups.

Most Christians belong to the Greek Orthodox Church, but there are also some Greek Catholics, a small Roman Catholic community, and Syrian, Coptic and Armenian Orthodox communities.

ARTS

In general Jordanian arts, especially literature and music, are dominated by Egyptian and Lebanese artists, as well as Western imports. Palestinian artists are an influential force and much of their inspiration comes from the often first-hand tragedy of recent Palestinian history.

Literature

Mounis al-Razzaz, who died in 2002, was regarded by many as the driving force behind modern Jordanian literature. His works spoke of wider turmoil in the Arab world, notably in his satirical final work *Sweetest Night,* and of Amman's transition from a small village to a modern metropolis.

Diana Abu-Jaber, a celebrated Jordanian-American author, draws on her family's memories of Jordanian cultural identity, a love of Jordanian food and her life as an immigrant in the USA. Her works include *Arabian Jazz, Crescent* and *The Language of Baklava.*

Other modern novels include the Palestinian Yasmin Zahran's *A Beggar at Damascus Gate,* and *Pillars of Salt* by Fadia Faqir, the tale of two women in a Jordanian asylum.

Cinema & TV

David Lean's epic masterpiece *Lawrence of Arabia* was partially filmed in Wadi Rum. Everyone headed to Petra will get to see *Indiana Jones and the Last Crusade* with its famous parting shots of Petra's Siq and Treasury.

Most Jordanians have access to satellite TV, which shows programmes from across the Arab world. Most of Jordan went berserk in August 2003 when a Jordanian singer won the first ever *Superstar* competition, an Arab version of *Pop Idol.*

Music

In general the airwaves are dominated by Egyptian and Lebanese superstars but Jordan's traditional Bedouin music remains distinctive and vibrant. The most popular instrument is the *rubaba,* a melancholy one-stringed violin.

Painting

The 7th-century Umayyad frescoes at the desert castle, Qusayr Amra, in Jordan's eastern *badia* (basalt desert) and the Byzantine mosaics of the Madaba region are high points of Jordan's historical visual arts.

To check out Jordan's contemporary art scene, visit the Darat al-Funun (p371) and the Jordan National Gallery of Fine Arts (p371) in Amman.

Traditional Crafts

In Jordan, jewellery is an important indicator of wealth and status, especially among the Bedouin, who also produce wonderful weavings. Today more than 2000 Palestinian and Bedouin women produce rugs, carpets and camel bags under the guidance of several Jordanian organisations such as Beni Hamida. Palestinian embroidery is another important craft, and most visible on the Palestinian dresses known as *roza.*

ENVIRONMENT
The Land

Jordan can be divided into three major geographic regions: the Jordan Valley, the East Bank plateau and the desert. The fertile valley of the Jordan River is the dominant physical feature of the country's western region, running from the Syrian border in the north, down the border with Israel and the Palestinian Territories and into the Dead Sea. The valley (part of the larger African Rift Valley) continues under the name Wadi Araba down to the Gulf of Aqaba. The majority of the population lives in a 70km-wide strip running the length of the country on the East Bank plateau. The remaining 80% of the country is desert, stretching to Syria, Iraq and Saudi Arabia.

Wildlife

Spring is the best time to see some of Jordan's two thousand flowers and plants, including the black iris, the national flower.

Two of Jordan's most impressive animals are the Arabian oryx and Nubian ibex which can be spotted at the Shaumari (p384) and Wadi Mujib (p382) nature reserves, respectively. Jordan is an important corridor for migratory birds en route to Africa and southern Arabia.

Nature Reserves

The **Royal Society for the Conservation of Nature** (RSCN; www.rscn.org.jo) operates six reserves in Jordan, of which Wadi Mujib (p382) and Dana (p387) are the undoubted highlights. The Azraq Wetland Reserve (p383) in eastern Jordan is a good place for bird-watching.

Environmental Issues

According to the Environmental Sustainability Index for 2005, Jordan ranked higher than any other Arab country. Still, a chronic lack of water and increasing desertification remain pressing environmental problems. There are ambitious plans to build a pipeline connecting the Red and Dead Seas to provide desalinated water and also raise the dropping levels of the Dead Sea.

The RSCN was a pioneer in reintroducing several endemic animals in Jordan and creating sustainable tourism programmes.

FOOD & DRINK

For those on a tight budget, there are the normal street eats – felafel, shwarma, fuul, roast chicken and hummus. In midrange restaurants, the most common way for a group to eat is to order mezze – a variety of small starters followed by several mains to be shared by all present.

The Bedouin speciality is *mensaf*, delicious spit-roasted lamb that is basted with spices until it takes on a yellow appearance. It is served on a bed of rice and pine nuts, some-

times with the head of the lamb plonked in the centre and the cooking fat mixed into the rice. Honoured guests get the eyes, less honoured guests the tongue. The dish is served with a sauce of cooked yogurt that has been mixed with the leftover cooking fat.

Another local favourite is *maqlubbeh* (sometimes called 'upside down') – steamed rice topped with grilled slices of eggplant or meat, grilled tomato and pine nuts.

In Wadi Rum you might be lucky enough to be offered a Bedouin barbecue from the *zarb*, a pit oven buried in the desert sand.

Dessert here, as in many parts of the Middle East, may be kunafa or *muhalabiyya* (a milk custard containing pistachio nuts).

The universal drink of choice is sweet black tea (coffee comes a close second); as soon as you enter a compound you are sat down on the floor and offered tea, then tea, then more tea. Other options include yansoon (aniseed herbal tea) and zaatar (thyme-flavoured tea).

Bottled mineral water (350 fils) is widely available, as are the usual soft drinks, Amstel beer and locally produced wines.

AMMAN عمان

☎ 06 / pop 1.8 million

Amman is not one of the great cities of antiquity. Indeed for those arriving from Damascus or Cairo, it can feel disappointingly (or refreshingly) modern and Westernised. Its obvious tourist attractions – the 6000-seat Roman Theatre, Odeon and Citadel with its great views – can easily be visited in a few hours.

But Amman has lots to offer the visitor, not least the balance it strikes between the demands of the past and the vision of its next generation. Residents talk openly of two Ammans, although in truth there are many. Eastern Amman (which includes Downtown) is home to the urbanised poor; conservative, more Islamic in its sympathies and with vast Palestinian refugee camps on its fringe. Western Amman is a world apart, the preserve of leafy residential districts, trendy cafés and bars, impressive contemporary art galleries and young men and women openly walking arm in arm.

Don't come to Amman looking for medieval bazaars or grand mosques. But do come to Amman to catch a glimpse of a tolerant and thoroughly modern Arab city, embracing an international and culturally diverse vision of the future. It's also a great base from which to visit Jerash, the Dead Sea and the Desert Castles of the east. Whatever your reason for visiting, the welcome is sure to be warm.

HISTORY

The site of Amman has been continuously occupied since 3500 BC. Biblical references to the city are numerous and indicate that by 1200 BC 'Rabbath Ammon' was the capital of the powerful Ammonites. When King David was insulted by the Ammonite king, Nahash, he sent Joab, commanding the Israelite armies, to besiege Rabbath. After taking the town, David burnt alive many inhabitants in a brick kiln.

Amman was taken by Herod around 30 BC, and fell under the sway of Rome.

Philadelphia (as it was then known) was the seat of Christian bishops in the early Byzantine period, but the city declined and fell to the Sassanians (from Persia) in about AD 614. At the time of the Muslim invasion in about AD 636, the town was again thriving as a staging post of the caravan trade.

Amman was nothing more than a little village when a colony of Circassians resettled there in 1878. In 1900 it was estimated to have just 2000 residents. In 1921 it became the centre of Transjordan when King Abdullah made it his headquarters.

ORIENTATION

Built originally on seven hills (like Rome), Amman now spreads across 19 hills. This is not a city to explore on foot, apart from the Downtown area – known locally as *il-balad* – with its cheap hotels and restaurants, banks, post offices and Amman's ancient sites.

The main hill is Jebel Amman, home to embassies and midrange/top-end hotels and restaurants. The traffic roundabouts (some now replaced with tunnels and major intersections) on Jebel Amman are numbered west of Downtown from 1st Circle to 8th Circle. The Jebel Weibdeh and Abdali areas have more hotels, the distinctive blue dome of the King Abdullah Mosque, and the JETT and Abdali bus stations. West and south of these areas are glamorous Shmeisani and Abdoun, the most upmarket areas of Amman and the places to go for nightlife.

Maps

If you plan to stay for some time or intend to visit places out of the centre, *Maps of Jordan, Amman and Aqaba*, published by Luma Khalaf, is reliable and worth picking up from bookshops in Amman.

INFORMATION
Bookshops

Al-Aulama Bookshop (Map p368; ☎ 4636192; 44 Al-Amir Mohammed St; ☽ 8am-8pm Sat-Thu)
Amman Bookshop (Map p370; ☎ 4644013; Al-Amir Mohammed St; ☽ 9am-2pm & 3.30-6.30pm Sat-Thu) The city's biggest.

AMMAN IN...

One Day

Take a taxi to the **Citadel** (p369) and check out the **National Archaeological Museum** (p369) and the views. Head east and navigate the steps down to aptly named Downtown to check out the area around the **Roman Theatre** (p369). Depending on time, shop the souqs around the **King Hussein Mosque** (p371), the most interesting part of Downtown, before grabbing a cheap lunch of hummus and mint tea at **Hashem Restaurant** (p373).

In the late afternoon get a sugar hit at **Habibah's** (map p368) and savour a coffee on the balcony of the **Al-Rashid Court Café** (p374), before heading on to Abdoun Circle or the **Blue Fig Café** (p373) for dinner and drinks.

Two Days

Make a half-day excursion to **Wadi as-Seer** (p376), then buy some souvenirs at an Amman nonprofit shop like **Jordan River Foundation** (p375). If you're short on time, make a day trip to **Jerash** (p377), the **desert castles** (p383) or the **Dead Sea** (p381). Enjoy a Lebanese dinner at **Fakhr el-Din** (p374). After a busy couple of days say *salaam* to the city in the relaxing **Al-Pasha Hammam** (p371).

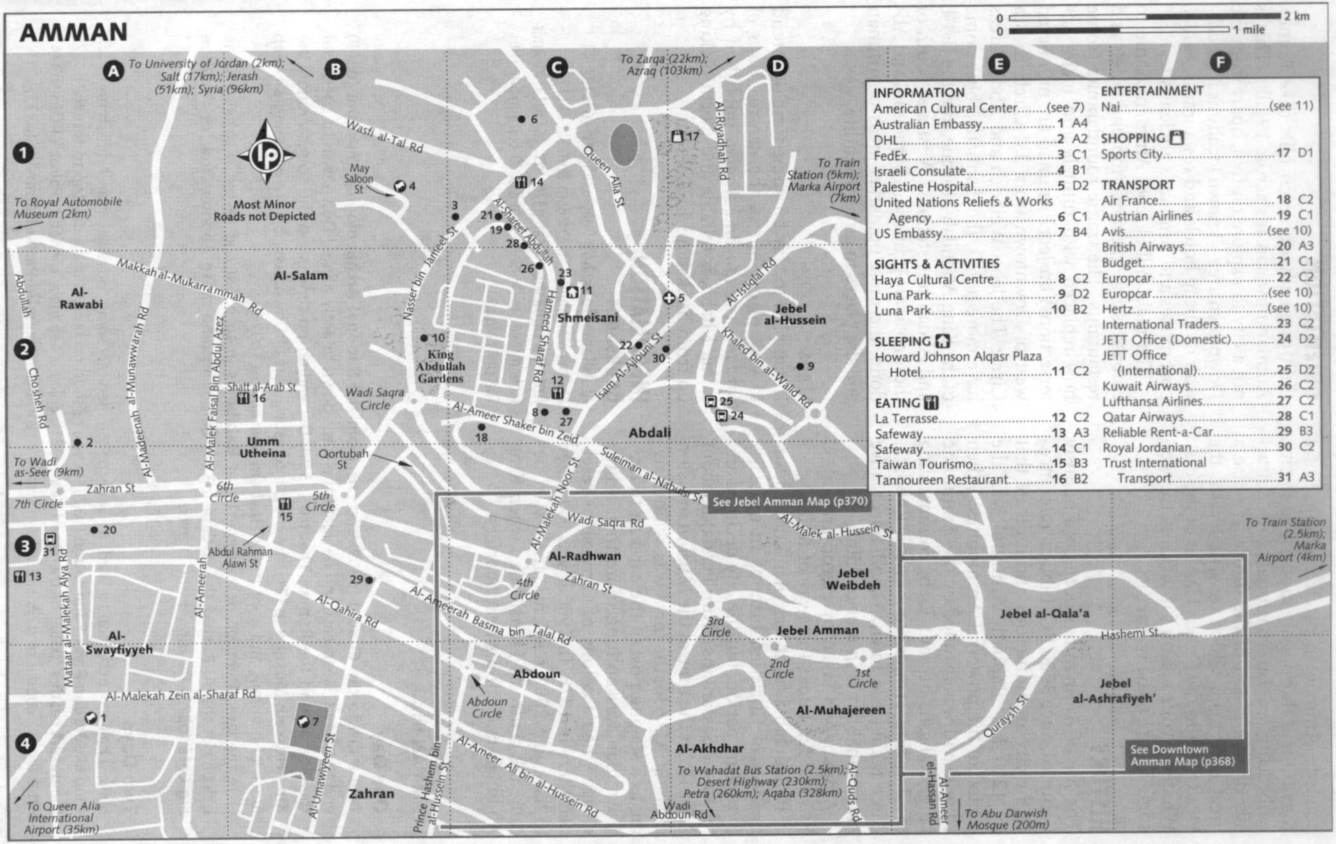
AMMAN
0 2 km
0 1 mile
INFORMATION
American Cultural Center........(see 7)
Australian Embassy........1 A4
DHL........2 A2
FedEx........3 C1
Israeli Consulate........4 B1
Palestine Hospital........5 D2
United Nations Reliefs & Works Agency........6 C1
US Embassy........7 B4
SIGHTS & ACTIVITIES
Haya Cultural Centre........8 C2
Luna Park........9 D2
Luna Park........10 B2
SLEEPING
Howard Johnson Alqasr Plaza Hotel........11 C2
EATING
La Terrasse........12 C2
Safeway........13 A3
Safeway........14 C1
Taiwan Tourismo........15 B3
Tannoureen Restaurant........16 B2
ENTERTAINMENT
Nai........(see 11)
SHOPPING
Sports City........17 D1
TRANSPORT
Air France........18 C2
Austrian Airlines........19 C1
Avis........(see 10)
British Airways........20 A3
Budget........21 C1
Europcar........22 C2
Europcar........(see 10)
Hertz........(see 10)
International Traders........23 C2
JETT Office (Domestic)........24 D2
JETT Office (International)........25 D2
Kuwait Airways........26 C2
Lufthansa Airlines........27 C2
Qatar Airways........28 C1
Reliable Rent-a-Car........29 B3
Royal Jordanian........30 C2
Trust International Transport........31 A3
To University of Jordan (2km); Salt (17km); Jerash (51km); Syria (96km)
To Zarqa (22km); Azraq (103km)
To Train Station (5km); Marka Airport (7km)
To Royal Automobile Museum (2km)
Most Minor Roads not Depicted
To Wadi as-Seer (9km)
To Queen Alia International Airport (35km)
To Train Station (2.5km); Marka Airport (4km)
To Wahadat Bus Station (2.5km); Desert Highway (230km); Petra (260km); Aqaba (328km)
To Abu Darwish Mosque (200m)
See Jebel Amman Map (p370)
See Downtown Amman Map (p368)
Al-Rawabi
Al-Salam
Umm Utheina
Al-Swayfiyyeh
Zahran
Abdoun
Al-Radhwan
Shmeisani
Abdali
King Abdullah Gardens
Jebel al-Hussein
Jebel Weibdeh
Jebel Amman
Al-Muhajereen
Al-Akhdhar
Jebel al-Qala'a
Jebel al-Ashrafiyeh'
7th Circle
6th Circle
5th Circle
4th Circle
3rd Circle
2nd Circle
1st Circle
Wadi Saqra Circle
Abdoun Circle
Wasfi al-Tal Rd
Queen Alia St
Al-Riyadhah Rd
Al-Istiqlal Rd
Khaled bin al-Walid Rd
Makkah al-Mukarrammah Rd
Al-Madeenah al-Munawwarah Rd
Al-Malek Faisal Bin Abdul Azez
Zahran St
Al-Ameer Shaker bin Zeid
Suleiman al-Nabulsi St
Al-Malekah Noor St
Wadi Saqra Rd
Al-Malek al-Hussein St
Al-Qahira Rd
Al-Ameerah Basma bin Talal Rd
Al-Malekah Zein al-Sharaf Rd
Al-Ameer Ali bin al-Hussein Rd
Prince Hashem bin al-Hussein St
Al-Quds Rd
Al-Ameer el-Hassan Rd
Hashemi St
Quraysh St
Al-Umawiyeen St
Mataar al-Malekah Alya Rd
Choshe Rd
Abdullah
Al-Ameerah
Hameed Sharaf Rd
Isam Al-Ajlouni St
Al-Shareef Abdullah
Nasser bin Jameel St
Shatt al-Arab St
Abdul Rahman Alawi St
Qortubah St
May Saloon St
Wadi Abdoun Rd

www.lonelyplanet.com
AMMAN •• Information 367

Books@cafe (Map p368; ☎ 4650457; contact@books
-cafe.com; Omar bin al-Khattab St; ☒ 10am-11.30pm)
Grab a bite to eat (p373) while browsing for books.
Bustami's Library (Map p368; ☎ 4622649; Al-Amir
Mohammed St; ☒ 5am-6pm Sat-Thu) Good for
international newspapers.

Cultural Centres

The following cultural centres have a library
and regularly organise film nights, exhibitions and concerts.
American Cultural Center (Map p366; ☎ 5859102;
US Embassy, Al-Umawiyeen St; ☒ 1-4.30pm Sat-Wed,
9am-4pm Thu)
British Council (Map p370; ☎ 4636147; www.british
council.org.jo; Abu Bakr as-Siddiq St; ☒ 9am-6.30pm
Sun-Wed, 9am-3.30pm Thu) Southeast of 1st Circle. Has
a library with current English newspapers, and a pleasant
outdoor café. Library hours are noon to 6.30pm Sunday to
Wednesday, 11am to 3.30pm Thursday.
Centre Culturel Français (Map p368; ☎ 4612658;
www.cccljor-jo.org; Kulliyat al-Sharee'ah St; ☒ 8.30am-
2pm & 4-6pm Sat-Thu)
Goethe Institut (Map p370; ☎ 4641993; www.goethe
.de/na/amm/; 5 Abdul Mun'im al-Rifa'l St; ☒ 8.30am-
2pm & 4.30-6.30pm Sun-Wed, 8.30am-2pm Thu)
Northwest of 3rd Circle.

Emergency

Ambulance (☎ 193)
Fire department (☎ 4617101, 199)
Police (☎ 192, 191)
Tourism police (toll-free ☎ 0800-22228)
Traffic police/accidents (☎ 4896390, 190)

Internet Access

Books@cafe (Map p368; ☎ 4650457; Omar bin
al-Khattab St; per hr JD2; ☒ 10am-11.30pm)
A professional set-up (see p373) with fast connections.
Internet Yard (Map p368; ☎ 079-5509569; Al-Amir
Mohammed St; per hr JD1; ☒ 9.30am-midnight)
Welcome Internet (Map p368; ☎ 4620206; Al-Amir
Mohammed St; per hr JD1; ☒ 10.30am-1am)

Media

The *Jordan Times* and the *Star* are the two
English-language newspapers and both are
worth a read.
   Jordan Today (www.jordantoday.com.jo) is a free
monthly booklet that includes a yellow
pages listing of embassies, airlines and the
like. **Where to Go** (www.w2go.com) is similar and
includes a useful collection of Amman restaurant menus. Pick them up in the better
hotels and restaurants.

Medical Services

The two English-language daily newspa-
pers list the current telephone numbers
of doctors and pharmacies on night duty
throughout the capital.
Al-Khalidi Medical Centre (Map p370; ☎ 4644281;
www.kmc.jo; Bin Khaldoun St, southwest of 3rd Circle)
Italian Hospital (Map p368; ☎ 4777101; Italian St,
Downtown)
Jacob's Pharmacy (Map p370; ☎ 4644945; 3rd Circle;
☒ 9am-3am)
Palestine Hospital (Map p366; ☎ 5607071; Queen
Alia St)
University Hospital (☎ 5353444) Situated in the Uni-
versity of Jordan complex, northwestern Amman.

Money

Changing money is easy and the Downtown area especially is awash with banks,
ATMs and moneychangers. See p402 for
information, and the Downtown map for
locations.

Post

Central post office (Map p368; ☎ 4624120; Al-Amir
Mohammed St, Downtown; ☒ 7.30am-5pm Sat-Thu,
8am-1.30pm Fri)
Customs office (Map p368; Omar al-Khayyam St,
Downtown; ☒ 8am-2pm Sat-Thu) Diagonally opposite
the parcel post office. Come here to send a parcel overseas.
Parcel post office (Map p368; Omar al-Khayyam St,
Downtown; ☒ 8am-3pm Sun-Thu, 8am-2pm Sat)

Telephone

The private telephone agencies around the
Downtown area are the cheapest places for
international and domestic calls.
Communication International (Map p368; Nimer bin
Adwan St, Downtown) Charges 150 fils a minute to the
US or UK.

Tourist Information

Jordan is one country where tourism complaints are taken seriously. If you have a
question or problem call the toll free **Halla
Line** (☎ 800-22228).
Ministry of Tourism & Antiquities (Map p370;
☎ 4642311; Al-Mutanabbi St; ☒ 8am-9pm) The information office on the ground floor can answer most queries,
or call the Halla Line.
Wild Jordan Centre (Map p368; ☎ 4616523; www
.rscn.org.jo; Othman bin Affan St) The place for information
and bookings for Jordan's nature reserves, including Dana
and Wadi Mujib. There's also a good shop (p375) and café
(p373).

JORDAN

DOWNTOWN AMMAN

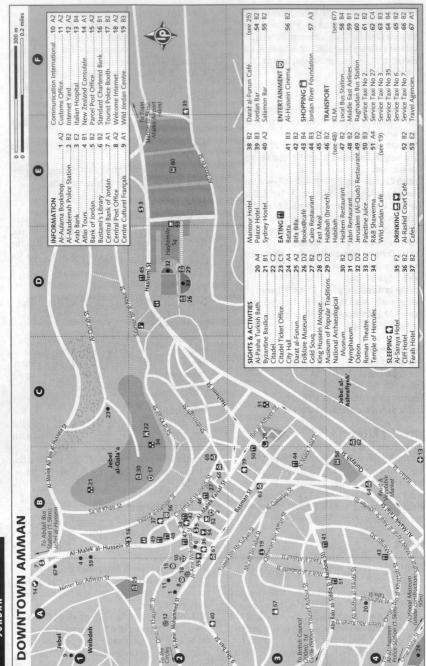

INFORMATION	
Al-Aulama Bookshop	1 A2
Al-Madeenah Police Station	2 B1
Arab Bank	3 E2
Atlas Tours	4 B1
Bank of Jordan	5 B2
Bustani's Library	6 B2
Central Bank of Jordan	7 A1
Central Post Office	8 A2
Centre Culturel Français	9 A1
Communication International	10 A2
Customs Office	11 A2
Internet Yard	12 A2
Italian Consulate	13 B4
New Zealand Consulate	14 A1
Parcel Post Office	15 A2
Standard Chartered Bank	16 B1
Tourist Police Booth	17 B2
Welcome Internet	18 A2
Wild Jordan Centre	19 B3

SIGHTS & ACTIVITIES	
Al-Pasha Turkish Bath	20 A4
Byzantine Basilica	21 B1
Citadel	22 C2
Citadel Ticket Office	23 C1
City Hall	24 A4
Darat al-Funun	25 A2
Folklore Museum	26 D2
Gold Souq	27 B2
King Hussein Mosque	28 C3
Museum of Popular Traditions	29 D2
National Archaeological Museum	30 B2
Nymphaeum	31 C3
Odeon	32 D2
Roman Theatre	33 D2
Temple of Hercules	34 C2

SLEEPING	
Al-Saraya Hotel	35 F2
Cliff Hotel	36 B2
Farah Hotel	37 B2

Mansour Hotel	38 B2
Palace Hotel	39 B3
Sydney Hostel	40 A2

EATING	
Batata	41 B3
Bifa Billa	42 B2
Books@café	43 B4
Cairo Restaurant	44 B3
Fast Meal	45 D2
Habibah	46 B2
Habibah (branch)	(see 48)
Hashem Restaurant	47 B2
Jabri Restaurant	48 B2
Jerusalem (Al-Quds) Restaurant	49 B2
Palestine Juice	50 B3
R&B Shawerma	51 A4
Wild Jordan Café	(see 19)

DRINKING	
Al-Rashid Court Café	52 B2
Cafes	53 E2

Darat al-Funun Café	(see 25)
Jordan Bar	54 B2
Salamon Bar	55 B2

ENTERTAINMENT	
Al-Hussein Cinema	56 B2

SHOPPING	
Jordan River Foundation	57 A3

TRANSPORT	
KLM	(see 67)
Local Bus Station	58 B4
Middle East Airlines	59 B1
Raghadan Bus Station	60 E2
Service Taxi No 2	61 B2
Service Taxi No 27	62 C4
Service Taxi No 3	63 B4
Service Taxi No 35	64 B4
Service Taxi No 6	65 B2
Service Taxi No 7	66 B2
Travel Agencies	67 A1

SCAMS

Be wary of taxi drivers who claim that your chosen hotel is closed, dirty or 'burnt down', only to recommend another hotel – where they get commission.

Travel Agencies

There is a string of travel agencies along Al-Malek al-Hussein St, near the flyover, in Downtown.

Atlas Tours (Map p368; ☎ 4624262; www.atlastours .net; Al-Malek al-Hussein St) Reliable for airline tickets.

Visa Extensions

If you are staying in Jordan for longer than one month, you must obtain a (free) visa extension. First you will need to get your hotel to write a short letter confirming where you are staying. Your hotel will also need to fill out two copies of a small card which states all its details. On the back is the application form for an extension which you must fill out. That done, take the form, the letter, a photocopy of the page in your passport with your personal details, your Jordanian visa page and your passport to the relevant police station (depending on which area of Amman you're staying in; ask at your hotel). If you're staying Downtown, go to the 1st floor of the **Al-Madeenah Police Station** (Map p368; ☎ 4657788; upstairs, Al-Malek Faisal St), opposite the Arab Bank.

After getting a stamp, take your passport to the **Al-Muhajireen Police Station** (Markez al-Muhajireen; Map p370; Al-Ameera Basma bin Talal Rd), west of Downtown, where you'll be granted a stay of up to three months. From Downtown take a taxi (600 fils) or take service taxi No 35 from along Quraysh St. Police stations are usually open for visa extensions from 10am to 3pm Saturday to Thursday, although it's better if you go in the morning.

SIGHTS & ACTIVITIES

The restored **Roman Theatre** (Map p368; admission JD1; 8am-4pm Sat-Thu, 10am-4pm Fri Oct-Mar, 8.30am-7pm Apr-Sep) is the most obvious and impressive remnant of ancient Philadelphia. The theatre is cut into the northern side of a hill that once served as a necropolis, and can hold 6000 people. The theatre was built in the 2nd century AD during the reign of Antoninus Pius, who ruled

the Roman Empire from AD 138 to 161. Performances are sometimes staged here in summer. The wings of the theatre are home to two fairly interesting **museums** (admission incl in theatre ticket), with well-presented displays of traditional costumes and jewellery as well as a mosaic collection.

The row of columns immediately in front of the theatre is all that's left of the **Forum**, once one of the largest public squares (about 100m by 50m) in Imperial Rome. On the eastern side of what was the Forum stands the 500-seat **Odeon**. Built about the same time as the Roman Theatre, it served mainly as a venue for musical performances.

Hashemite Square, between the Roman Theatre and Raghadan station, is an ideal place to stroll, sip tea, smoke the nargileh (water pipe) and simply watch the world go by.

Philadelphia's chief fountain or **nymphaeum** (Map p368; admission free; daylight Sat-Thu) dates from AD 191 and stands with its back to Quraysh St, west of the theatre and not far from King Hussein Mosque.

The **Citadel** (Map p368; ☎ 4638795; admission JD2; 8am-4pm Sat-Thu Oct-Mar, 8am-7pm Sat-Thu Apr-Sep, 10am-4pm Fri year-round), on Jebel al-Qala'a, has some excavated ruins of an Umayyad palace, dating from about AD 720, of which the domed audience hall is the most impressive. There is also an Umayyad Cistern; a Byzantine Basilica from the 6th or 7th century AD; and the pillars of the Temple of Hercules which was constructed during the reign of Marcus Aurelius (AD 161 to AD 80). Next to the temple is a lookout with great views of the Downtown area.

Included in the Citadel's admission fee is the **National Archaeological Museum**, one of the best museums in Jordan. Exhibits include three 8500-year-old statues from Ain

GETTING A FACE-LIFT

Amman's interesting and earthy Downtown area is set for some changes. A Japanese-funded redevelopment project has already cleaned up many buildings, reoriented some roads, built panoramic stairways and lookouts, and rebuilt Raghadan bus station. The US$33 million development also includes impressive plans for a new national museum (currently under construction next to City Hall) and several shopping plazas.

JORDAN

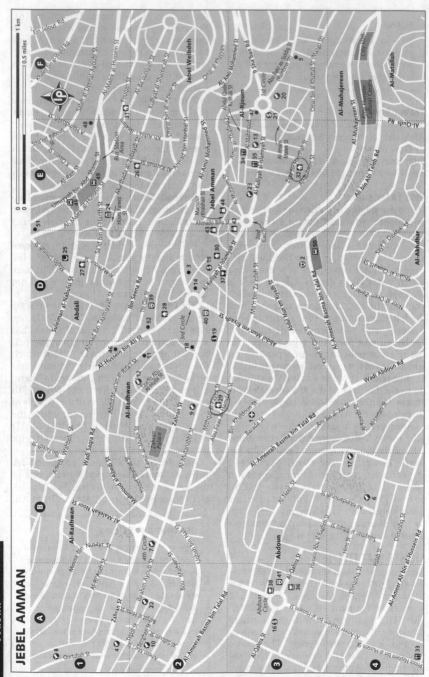

JEBEL AMMAN

JORDAN

INFORMATION			
Al-Khalidi Medical Centre.......... **1** C3	Syrian Embassy...................... **22** A2	Living Room.......................... **37** D2	
Al-Muhajireen Police Station...... **2** D3	Turkish Embassy.....................**23** E3	Tche Tche Cafe.......................**38** A3	
Amman Bookshop...................... **3** D2	**SIGHTS & ACTIVITIES**		
Australian Embassy.................... **4** A1	Jordan National Gallery of Fine	**ENTERTAINMENT**	
British Council........................**5** F3	Arts............................**24** E1	Century Cinemas..................... **39** D2	
UK Embassy............................ **6** B4	King Abdullah Mosque.............**25** D1	Cine Le Royal......................... **40** D2	
Citibank...............................(see 16)		Galleria Cinema...................... **41** A3	
Dutch Embassy.......................**7** B2	**SLEEPING**		
Egyptian Embassy.....................**8** A1	Canary Hotel.........................**26** E2	**SHOPPING**	
French Embassy....................... **9** C2	Caravan Hotel........................**27** D1	Al-Alaydi Jordan Craft Centre...**42** E3	
German Embassy.....................**10** A2	Grand Hyatt Amman **28** D2	Al-Burgan.............................**43** E2	
Goethe Institut.......................**11** C2	Hisham Hotel.........................**29** C2	Artisana................................**44** E2	
Iranian Embassy......................**12** C2	Jordan InterContinental		
Iraqi Embassy.........................**13** E3	Hotel...........................**30** D2	**TRANSPORT**	
Jacob's Pharmacy.....................**14** D2	Select Hotel..........................**31** F1	Abdali Bus Station...............(see 49)	
Jordan National Bank...............**15** D2	Shepherd Hotel......................**32** E3	Airport Express Bus **45** E1	
Jordan National Bank...............**16** A3		Emirates...............................**46** C1	
Lebanese Embassy...................**17** B4	**EATING**	Firas/Alamo Car Rental............**47** F3	
Ministry of Foreign Affairs........**18** C2	Blue Fig Café......................... **33** A4	Gulf Air.................................**48** E1	
Ministry of Tourism &	Fakhr el-Din......................... **34** E3	Hijazi....................................**49** E1	
Antiquities............................ **19** D2	Haboob Grand Stores **35** E3	Minibuses to Dead Sea & Wadi	
Post Office............................(see 30)		as-Seer......................... **50** D3	
Saudi Arabian Consulate...........**20** F3	**DRINKING**	Royal Jordanian......................**51** E1	
Standard Chartered Bank.........**21** F3	Caffe Moka........................... **36** A3	Royal Jordanian.................(see 30)	
		Turkish Airlines...................... **52** D2	

Ghazal, thought to be the world's oldest examples of sculpture.

Darat al-Funun (House of Arts; Map p368; ☎ 4643251; www.daratalfunun.org; Nimer bin Adwan St; admission free; ☒ 10am-7pm Sat-Wed, 10am-8pm Thu) is a superb, tranquil complex dedicated to contemporary art. It features a small art gallery, an art library, artists' workshops and a regular programme of exhibitions, lectures, films and public discussion forums. It also has a great café (p374).

The attraction at the **King Hussein Mosque** (Map p368; Hashemi St, Downtown) is the surrounding backstreet souqs rather than the building. This is definitely the best place in Amman to explore on foot. The first mosque was built on this site in AD 640 by Omar, the second caliph of Islam. The current mosque was built by King Abdullah I in 1924.

King Abdullah Mosque (Map p370; ☎ 5672155; Suleiman al-Nabulsi St; admission JD2; ☒ 8-11am & 12.30-2pm Sat-Thu, 8-10am Fri) can house up to 7000 worshippers, with room for 3000 more in its courtyard. It welcomes non-Muslim visitors but women must cover their hair. Admission includes entry to a small Islamic museum.

The small but excellent **Jordan National Gallery of Fine Arts** (Map p370; ☎ 4630128; www.national gallery.org; Hosni Fareez St; admission JD1; ☒ 9am-5pm Sun-Thu) exhibits contemporary Jordanian works, including painting, sculpture and pottery.

Car enthusiasts might like the **Royal Automobile Museum** (☎ 5411392; www.royalautomuseum .jo; King Hussein Park; admission JD3; ☒ 10am-7pm Wed-Mon), which has a display of 70 classic cars and motorbikes from King Hussein's personal collection. It's in the northwestern suburbs, north of 8th Circle.

Al-Pasha Hammam (Map p368; ☎ /fax 4633002; www.pashaturkishbath.com; Al-Mahmoud Taha St; ☒ 9am-2am, last booking midnight) is the perfect antidote to Amman's hills and bustle. The full service (JD15) includes a steam bath, sauna, Jacuzzi, body scrub, 40-minute massage and two soft drinks, all in a superb building architecturally faithful to Turkish *hammam* tradition. Bring a swimming costume.

AMMAN FOR CHILDREN

The **Haya Cultural Centre** (Map p366; ☎ 5665195; Ilya Abu Madhi St; admission free; ☒ 9am-6pm Sat-Thu) is designed for children and has a playground and interactive eco-museum.

Luna Park (Map p366; Khaled bin al-Walid Rd; admission JD1; ☒ 10am-10pm) has rides and amusements. There's another branch at King Abdullah Gardens (Map p366).

TOURS

For information on organised day trips from Amman, see p408.

SLEEPING
Budget

Downtown Amman has many cheap hotels. Budget places listed below have shared bathroom facilities unless stated otherwise; all promise hot water and some even deliver.

JORDAN

THE AUTHOR'S CHOICE

Palace Hotel (Map p368; ☎ 4624326; www
.palacehotel.com.jo; Al-Malek Faisal St; s/d/tr with
shared bathroom incl breakfast JD6/8/12, s/d/tr with
private bathroom JD11/14/21; 🖳) Definitely
the best budget and lower midrange in
the area. There's a wide variety of rooms
from midrange options with satellite TV
to cheaper rooms with (spotless) shared
bathrooms. All rooms are very clean and
some have balconies. The great management runs the best value local tours (see
p408) and there's a laundry service, daily
newspaper and free baggage storage.

Cliff Hotel (Map p368; ☎ 4624273; fax 46238078;
Al-Amir Mohammed St; dm/s/d JD3/5/6) A long-
standing shoestring favourite with friendly
staff in the heart of Downtown. Rooms are
generally tidy and simple although some of
the mattresses feel as old as Amman itself.
Hot showers cost 500 fils.

Farah Hotel (Map p368; ☎ 4651443; farahhotel@
hotmail.com; Cinema al-Hussein St; dm JD4, mattress on
roof JD2.500, s/d JD7/9; 🖳) This is a backpacker-
savvy place which gets generally good reports from travellers. The rooms are a bit
dingy and the shared bathrooms are little
more than a shower head above a squat
toilet, but the staff are friendly and eager
to help.

Mansour Hotel (Map p368; ☎ 4621575; Al-Malek
Faisal St; s/d JD5.500/8.800) An old-school place
that's central but quieter than most because
it's a little back from the busy main road.
Toilets are Arab-style squatters. Hot showers cost 500 fils.

Sydney Hostel (Map p368; ☎ 4641122; sydney
_hostel@yahoo.com; 9 Sha'ban St; dm/s/d/tr JD4/10/15/
20) A short walk from Downtown's bustle.
Rooms here are clean and comfortable with
hot-water bathrooms, a small balcony and
satellite TV. There's only one dorm room.

Midrange

Al-Saraya Hotel (Map p368; ☎ 4656791; www.saraya
hotel.com; Al-Jaza'er St; s/d/tr JD14/18/22; 🖳) One of
few midrange options in Downtown and luck-
ily a good one, with clean, spacious rooms.
The owner, Fayez, is super friendly. It's at the
eastern end of Raghadan bus station.

Select Hotel (Map p370; ☎ 4637101; www.select
-amman.com; 52 Al-Ba'ouniyah St; s/d with breakfast

JD12/18; 🖳 🕾) This is an excellent upper-
end budget hotel. It's quiet and well run,
with a family feel. Ask for one of the four
rooms with a balcony.

Canary Hotel (Map p370; ☎ 4638353; canary_h@hot
mail.com; 17 Al-Karmali St; s/d/ste JD18/22/28; 🖳) This
place has a welcoming vibe and is walk-
ing distance from Abdali bus station. The
rooms are comfortable rather than luxurious, although the (smallish) bathrooms
sparkle. The best deal here is the four-bed
family suite.

Caravan Hotel (Map p370; ☎ 5661195; caravan@
go.com.jo; Al-Ma'moun St; s/d JD15/18) Almost opposite the King Abdullah Mosque, the
Caravan is a similarly good and reliable
B&B-style place with pleasant rooms, some
bigger than others.

Shepherd Hotel (Map p370; ☎ /fax 4639197;
shepherdhtl@joinnet.com.jo; Zayd bin Harethah St; s/d
JD30/40; 🖳) Lots of readers recommend this
place. The comfortable rooms are great
value and prices are somewhat negotiable.
The hotel restaurant is good and there's a
bar and terrace.

Hisham Hotel (Map p370; ☎ 4644028; www.hisham
hotel.com; Mithqal al-Fayez St; s/d JD30/40; P 🕾 🖳)
Junior diplomats and journalists like this excellent choice in the leafy embassy district,
with lots of personal touches and comfortable, spacious rooms. Prices are negotiable.
The garden restaurant is great in summer.

Top End

Howard Johnson Alqasr Plaza Hotel (Map p366;
☎ 5689671; www.alqasr-hojo.com; 3 Arroub St; s/d incl
breakfast & tax JD60/70; 🖳 🗙) This is the closest
thing to a boutique-style hotel in Amman,
with an excellent range of chic restaurants
and bars, free access to a local gym and
good service.

Grand Hyatt Amman (Map p370; ☎ 4651234;
www.amman.hyatt.com; Al-Hussein bin Ali St, 3rd Circle;
s/d JD106/116; 🖳 🕾 🗙) It's quite a com-
plex with seven restaurants, JJ's nightclub,
an indoor and outdoor pool, high-speed
Internet, and a cinema next door.

Jordan InterContinental Hotel (Map p370;
☎ 4641361; www.amman.intercontinental.com; Al-Kulliyah al-Islamiyah St; d JD77; 🖳 🕾 🗙) Midway
between 2nd and 3rd Circles; it's suitably
luxurious and has a Royal Jordanian office,
a good bookstore, a post office, a deli, a
24-hour gym, an indoor and outdoor pool,
and wireless Internet.

EATING

Amman's budget restaurants are concentrated in Downtown and, to a lesser extent, Jebel Amman. More upmarket restaurants are found in Shmeisani and Abdoun.

Kunafa-holics are spoiled for choice in Downtown. Get your sugar hit at Jabri Restaurant, Jerusalem (Al-Quds) Restaurant, or, best of all, Habibah, all next to each other on Al-Malek al-Hussein St (Map p368). There's an insanely busy takeaway branch of Habibah further southeast, down an alleyway off Al-Malek al-Hussein St.

Of the larger supermarkets, **Safeway** has a few outlets, one around 500m southwest of the Sports City junction (Map p366; ☎ 5685311; Nasser bin Jameel St; ☯ 24hr), and another just southwest of 7th Circle (Map p366; ☎ 5815558). More central but smaller is **Haboob Grand Stores** (Map p370; ☎ 4622221; Al-Kulliyah al-Islamiyah St; ☯ 7am-midnight), between 1st and 2nd Circles.

Budget

There are plenty of felafel and shwarma stalls in Downtown, but be warned that most shut by 9pm.

Palestine Juice (Map p368; Al-Malek Faisal St; ☯ 7am-11pm; small/large drink 500 fils/JD1) This is a good juice stand which serves refreshing carrot or orange juice, or banana with milk.

Hashem Restaurant (Map p368; Al-Amir Mohammed St; mains around JD1; ☯ 24hr) Overflowing into the alley, this near legendary restaurant is very popular with locals for quality felafel, chips, hummus, fuul, tea, and nothing else.

Cairo Restaurant (Map p368; ☎ 4624527; Al-Malek Talal St; mains from JD1; ☯ 6am-10pm) By far the best budget meal in Downtown. The *shish tawooq* (grilled chicken; JD1.750) is excellent, or combine a tomato-y kofta and a yogurt for another great meal.

Jerusalem (Al-Quds) Restaurant (Map p368; ☎ 4630168; Al-Malek al-Hussein St; mains from JD2; ☯ 7am-10pm) Specialising in sweets and pastries, this place has a restaurant serving Jordanian standards. The menu is in Arabic so you're at the mercy of the grumpy staff.

Batata (Map p368; ☎ 4656768; Abu Bakr as-Siddiq St; fries 600 fils-JD1.500; ☯ noon-10pm Sat-Thu, 6pm-late Fri) Does one thing and does it well; in this case French fries (and nothing else), with a choice of eight sauces (100 fils).

R&B Shawerma (Map p368; ☎ 4645347; Abu Bakr as-Siddiq St; shwarmas 700 fils-JD1.500; ☯ noon-midnight) This is not your average shwarma

place; it has cheese, chicken and Chinese varieties in three sizes, and good fries.

Books@cafe (Map p368; ☎ 4650457; Omar bin al-Khattab St; mains from JD2.500; ☯ 10am-midnight) For a slice of coffeehouse chic, this trendy place serves genuine Italian pizzas and good salads, plus a special brunch on Fridays (JD5). The food is excellent. Hot drinks are a steep JD1 to JD1.250 although the 'hot strawberry' may just be worth it.

Wild Jordan Café (Map p368; ☎ 4633542; Othman bin Affan St; mains JD4.500-7.500; ☯ 11am-midnight; 🖥 ✉) Another cool and contemporary place worth checking out, along with its shop and RSCN tourism projects. The fresh and zesty smoothies, organic salads and wraps are great and the views over Amman superb. The Friday and Saturday breakfast specials have a devoted following.

There are a few decent fast food places such as **Bifa Billa** (Map p368; Cinema al-Hussein St; mains from 500 fils; ☯ noon-midnight), which does good burgers and shwarmas, and **Fast Meal** (Map p368; ☎ 4650037; Hashemi St; mains from JD1.250; ☯ 7.15am-2.30am), serving up superb juice smoothies.

Midrange

Amman has a number of excellent restaurants if you're willing to pay a little more.

Taiwan Tourismo (Map p366; ☎ 5924670; Abdul Rahman Alawi St; dishes from JD2; ☯ noon-3.30pm &

JORDAN

6.30-11.30pm) Authentic Chinese food if you have a craving, with great General Tso's chicken or toffee bananas.

La Terrasse (Map p366; ☎ 5662831; 11 August St; mezze JD1.250, mains JD5-9; ☾ noon-1am) Decent European cuisine, strong on steaks, are served in a pleasant setting. The live Arabic music most nights after 10pm makes it popular with well-to-do local families.

Fakhr el-Din (Map p370; ☎ 4652399; www.fakhr eldin.com; 40 Taha Hussein St; mezze JD1-2; mains JD4-5.500; ☾ 12.30-3.30pm & 7.30-11.30pm) Highly recommended Lebanese food is served in a classy setting. Good for a splurge.

Top End
The classy and expensive places are often in the suburbs, such as Shmeisani. Most top-end places add a whopping 26% tax to the quoted prices.

Tannoureen Restaurant (Map p366; ☎ 5515987; Shatt al-Arab St; mains JD4.500-9; ☾ 12.30-4.30pm & 7.30-11.30pm) This restaurant is good for Lebanese food, especially mezze (try the spinach and pine-nut pie), but it also does Western grills and fish. Bookings are required.

DRINKING
Cafés
Some of the cafés in Downtown are great places to watch the world go by, smoke a nargileh, meet locals and play cards or backgammon.

Al-Rashid Court Café (Map p368; ☎ 4652994; Al-Malek Faisal St; tea or coffee 400 fils, nargileh JD1.250; ☾ 10am-midnight Sat-Thu, 1-11pm Fri) Also known as the Eco-Tourism Café. The 1st-floor balcony here is *the* place to pass an afternoon and survey the chaos of the Downtown area. It's also one of the best places for the uninitiated to try a nargileh. The entrance is hidden down a side alley.

Darat al-Funun Café (Map p368; ☎ 4643251; www .daratalfunun.org; Nimer bin Adwan St; admission free; drinks 300 fils ☾ 10am-7pm Sat-Wed, 10am-8pm Thu) Definitely the most peaceful place to escape from Downtown traffic. Darat al-Funun (p371) overlooks the silent ruins of a Byzantine church.

Tche Tche Café (Map p370; ☎ 5932020; www.tche tchecafe.com; Abdoun Circle; ☾ 10am-11pm) Far from traditional, this bright, buzzy teahouse is full of Jordanian women smoking the nargileh, sipping fruit smoothies and nodding to Arabic pop. Come early to get a seat.

Caffe Moka (Map p370; ☎ 5926285; Al-Qahira Rd; ☾ 7.30am-11pm) This place serves great pastries (from 500 fils) and delicious cakes (from JD1.200).

A dozen or more cafés can be found around Hashemite Sq, which is a great place for people-watching in summer.

The place to be seen in Amman at night is Abdoun Circle (Map p370), where there are plenty of popular cafés overflowing with young, wealthy Ammanis. The fashion changes frequently in this part of Amman so just walk around and take your pick.

Bars
Living Room (Map p370; ☎ 4655988; www.romero -jordan.com; Mohammed Hussein Haikal St; ☾ 1pm-1am) Part lounge, part sushi bar, the Living Room is so coolly understated that it's easy to miss. The full bar, sofas and fine music make it a great place to hang out.

Blue Fig Café (Map p370; ☎ 5928800; www.bluefig .com; Prince Hashem bin al-Hussein St; starters from JD1.650, mains JD4-8; ☾ 8.30am-1am) This is a great place to spend an afternoon or evening, with a trendy crowd, draught beer, good cocktails, and a pleasant atmosphere. The Blue Fig Café (p373) has live music most Wednesday and Saturday nights.

There are several earthy local bars Downtown, visited almost exclusively by men and tucked away in the alleys near the Cliff Hotel. **Jordan Bar** (Map p368; ☎ 079-5796352; off Al-Amir Mohammed St; ☾ 10am-midnight) and **Salamon Bar** (Map p368; ☎ 079-5902940; off Al-Amir Mohammed St; ☾ noon-midnight) are both tiny local dives full of smoke with cheap beer on tap.

ENTERTAINMENT
There is plenty of nightlife in Amman, although little that's salubrious in the Downtown area. Shmeisani, Abdoun and, to a lesser extent, Jebel Amman have numerous trendy cafés, bars and a few nightclubs that stay open late.

Nightclubs
Nai (Map p366; ☎ 5689671; Arroub St; ☾ 6pm-2am) Currently one of the hottest places in town, Nai is a super-cool Ottoman-style lounge-club-cum-mezze bar. Mondays and Thursdays bring international DJs and a cover charge (JD10; bookings advised) and there's an Arabic band the first Thursday of the month.

JORDAN

Cinemas

Programmes for these modern cinemas are advertised in the two English-language newspapers, the *Jordan Times* and the *Star*. Tickets cost JD5.

Century Cinemas (Map p370; ☎ 4613200; www .century-cinemas.com; 3rd Circle) In the Zara Centre behind the Grand Hyatt.

Cine Le Royal (Map p370; ☎ 4603022; Le Royal Hotel, 3rd Circle)

Galleria Cinema (Map p370; ☎ 5934793; Abdoun Circle)

SHOPPING

Amman is one of the better places to shop for souvenirs in Jordan, with everything from tourist kitsch to high-quality handicraft boutiques, many of which are run to benefit vulnerable communities and environmental groups.

The following are among the better places in Amman, and are generally open 9am to 6pm Saturday to Thursday. Prices are fixed.

Al-Alaydi Jordan Craft Centre (Map p370; ☎ /fax 4644555; www.alaydijordan.1colony.com; off Al-Kulliyah al-Islamiyah St) A large selection.

Al-Burgan (Map p370; ☎ 4652585; www.alburgan .com) Behind Jordan InterContinental Hotel.

Artisana (Map p370; ☎ /fax 4647858; Mansour Kraishan St; ⊗ 9.30am-6pm Sat-Thu)

Jordan River Foundation (Map p368; ☎ 4613081; www.jordanriver.jo; Bani Hamida House, Fawzi al-Malouf St; ⊗ 8.30am-7pm Sat-Thu, 10am-6pm Fri) An emphasis on home design. Off Abu Bakr as-Siddiq St.

Wild Jordan Centre (Map p368; ☎ 4633587; Othman bin Affan St; ⊗ 9am-7pm) Eco-inspired nature products made in Jordan's nature reserves.

GETTING THERE & AWAY
Air

The only domestic air route is between Amman and Aqaba. For details see p406. For a list of airlines serving Amman see p404.

Bus

The three main bus stations in Amman are Abdali bus station (Map p370), for transport to the north and west; Wahadat bus station for the south; and Raghadan station (Map p368) for Amman and nearby towns.

Tickets for the following private buses should be booked at least one day in advance. The **domestic JETT office** (Map p366; ☎ 5664146; Al-Malek al-Hussein St), about 500m northwest of the Abdali bus station, is the best option for buses to Aqaba (JD4.300, four hours) with

five buses daily. Services to Petra were not running at the time of research.

Trust International Transport (Map p366; ☎ 5813428; Mataar al-Malekah Alya Rd) also has seven daily buses to Aqaba (JD5, four hours) but the location is inconvenient, way out near 7th Circle. **Hijazi** (Map p370; ☎ 4625664) has frequent and comfortable buses to Irbid (870 fils, 1½ hours) from Abdali station.

From Abdali station (which is scheduled to be relocated in the next few years), minibuses leave regularly for the following destinations:

Destination	Cost (fils)	Duration (hr)
Ajlun	500	2
Deir Alla (for Pella)	500	1
Irbid	600	2
Jerash	400	1¼
Madaba	270	1
Ramtha	500	2
Salt	200	¾

From Wahadat station, minibuses depart regularly for the following destinations:

Destination	Cost (JD)	Duration (hr)
Aqaba	3.500	5
Karak	0.800	2
Ma'an	1.100	3
Shobak	1.500	2½
Tafila	1.100	2½

For Petra (actually Wadi Musa) minibuses and service taxis depart when full from Wahadat station between 7am and 4pm. The local fare is JD1.800 but minibus drivers almost always charge foreigners JD3.

For the Dead Sea, minibuses leave from the small station opposite the **Al-Muhajireen Police Station** (Map p370; cnr of Al-Ameerah Basma bin Talal Rd & Ali bin Abi Taleb Rd). You may find a direct service to Suweimeh (600 fils) or even Amman Beach; if not, head to Shuneh al-Janubiyyeh (South Shuna; 500 fils, 45 minutes) and change for Suweimeh (200 fils). From there you'll have to hitch.

The newly renovated Raghadan station in Downtown hadn't reopened at time of research but you can expect it to hold service taxis (for nearby suburbs), local city buses and, probably, minibuses to Madaba, Salt and Wadi as-Seer.

Car

All the major hotels have car rental offices. The largest selection of rental companies is at King Abdullah Gardens (Map p366). See p407 for details.

Service Taxi

Most service taxis depart from the same stations as the minibuses. You'll find that departures are more frequent in the morning than in the afternoon.

From Abdali bus station, there are service taxis to Irbid (JD1), Ramtha (JD1) and Salt (450 fils). Service taxis to the King Hussein Bridge (for Israel and the Palestinian Territories) cost JD2.

From Wahadat bus station, there are departures to Karak (JD1.400, two hours), Wadi Musa/Petra (JD3, three hours), Ma'an (JD1.200, three hours) and also to Aqaba (JD5, five hours). A chartered service taxi to Petra should cost JD15.

Train

See p406 for information on the train between Amman and Damascus.

GETTING AROUND
To/From the Airport

Queen Alia International Airport is 35km south of the city centre.

The **Airport Express bus** (Map p370; ☎ 0880-022006, 4451531) runs between the airport and the upper end of Abdali bus station, passing through 4th, 5th, 6th and 7th Circles en route. The service (JD1.500, 45 minutes) runs every half hour or so between 8am and midnight. The last buses to the airport leave at 10pm and midnight; the first bus leaves at 6am.

A taxi costs JD15 from the airport to Amman, or JD10 in the opposite direction.

Private Taxi

The flag fall in a standard taxi is 150 fils, and cross-town journeys rarely cost more than JD1.500. Make sure your driver uses the meter, although most will do so automatically.

Service Taxi

Most fares on service taxis cost 130 fils and you pay the full amount regardless of where you get off. Some of the more useful routes include the following (Map p368):

No 2 From Basman St, for 1st and 2nd Circles.
No 3 From Basman St, for 3rd and 4th Circles.
No 6 From Cinema al-Hussein St, for Abdali station and JETT offices.
No 7 From Cinema al-Hussein St, past Abdali station and King Abdullah Mosque to Shmeisani.
No 27 From Italian St for Wahadat station.
No 35 From Quraysh St for Al-Muhajireen Police Station.

AROUND AMMAN

WADI AS-SEER & IRAQ AL-AMIR
عراق الأمير & ادي السير

The narrow, pretty and fertile valley of Wadi as-Seer is quite a contrast to the bare and treeless plateau to the east of Amman. The caves of **Iraq al-Amir** (Caves of the Prince) and the ruins of **Qasr al-Abad** (Palace of the Slave) are a further 10km down the valley from the largely Circassian (Muslims from the Caucasus who emigrated to Jordan in the 19th century) town of Wadi as-Seer.

The caves are arranged in two tiers – the upper forms a long gallery along the cliff face. The small but impressive ruins of Qasr al-Abad, thought to have been a 2nd-century-BC villa or minor palace, can be found about 700m further down the valley. The palace was built out of some of the biggest blocks of any ancient structure in the Middle East – the largest measures 7m by 3m.

Minibuses leave Amman regularly for Wadi as-Seer (130 fils, 30 minutes) from the station opposite the Muhajireen Police Station (on the corner of Al-Ameera Basma bin Talal Rd and Ali bin Abi Taleb Rd). From the town of Wadi as-Seer, take another minibus (100 fils) – or walk about 10km, mostly downhill – to the caves.

JERASH & THE NORTH

The relatively densely populated north of Jordan consists of lovely rolling hills, olive groves and classical ruins that sometimes seem transported direct from Tuscany. The two main sites of Jerash and Ajlun are generally visited as day trips from Amman, whereas Umm Qais is accessible from Irbid. You can visit all as part of an overland trip north to Syria.

JERASH
جرش
☎ 02

The beautifully preserved Roman city of **Jerash** (☎ 6351272; adult/student/child JD5/2.500/2.500; ☾ 8am-4pm Oct-Apr, 8am-7pm May-Sep), 51km north of Amman, is deservedly one of Jordan's major attractions. Excavations have been ongoing for 85 years but it is estimated that 90% of the city is still unexcavated. In its heyday the ancient city, known in Roman times as Gerasa, had a population of around 15,000.

Allow at least three hours to see everything in Jerash. The best times to visit are before 10am or after 4pm, but this is tricky if you are relying on public transport.

In July and August, Jerash hosts the **Jerash Festival** (www.jerashfestival.com.jo), featuring local and overseas artists, music and drama performances inside the ancient city and displays of traditional handicrafts.

History

Although there have been finds to indicate that the site was inhabited in Neolithic times, the city really only rose to prominence from the time of Alexander the Great (333 BC).

In the wake of the Roman general Pompey's conquest of the region in 64 BC, Gerasa became part of the Roman province of Syria and, soon after, a city of the Decapolis (the commercial league of cities formed by Pompey after his conquest). Gerasa reached its peak at the beginning of the 3rd century AD, when it was bestowed with the rank of Colony, after which time it went into a slow decline as trade routes shifted.

By the middle of the 5th century AD, Christianity was the region's major religion and the construction of churches proceeded at a startling rate. With the Sassanian invasion from Persia in 614, the Muslim conquest in 636 and a devastating earthquake in 747, Jerash's heyday passed and its population shrank to about a quarter of its former size.

Sights & Activities

At the extreme south of the site is the striking **Hadrian's Arch**, also known as the Triumphal Arch, which was built in AD 129 to honour the visit of Emperor Hadrian. Behind the arch is the **hippodrome**, which hosted chariot races watched by up to 15,000 spectators. In summer 2005, **chariot races** (☎ 6342471; www.jerashchariots.com) were revived here for the first time in 1500 years.

The **visitors centre** is worth checking out for its reconstructions of many buildings in Jerash (and for its toilets). The **South Gate**, originally one of four along the city wall and built in AD 130, leads into the city proper.

The **Oval Plaza** (Forum) is one of the most distinctive images of Jerash, unusual because of its oval shape and huge size (90m long and 80m at its widest point). Some historians attribute this to the desire to gracefully link the main north–south axis (the *cardo maximus*) with the Temple of Zeus. Fifty-six Ionic columns surround the paved limestone plaza.

On the south side of the Forum, the **Temple of Zeus** was built in about AD 162 over the remains of an earlier Roman temple; it's currently being restored. The next door **South Theatre** was built in the 1st century AD and could seat 5000 spectators. From the upper stalls, there are excellent views of ancient and modern Jerash, particularly the Forum, and the acoustics are still wonderful.

To the northeast of the Forum lies the **cardo maximus** (the city's main thoroughfare), also known as the **colonnaded street**, which stretches for 800m from the Forum to the **North Gate**. The street is still paved with the original stones, and the ruts worn by thousands of chariots can be clearly seen.

Halfway along the colonnaded street is the elegant **nymphaeum**, the main fountain of the city. The nymphaeum is followed by the imposing **Temple of Artemis**, reached via a fine propylaeum or monumental gateway, and a staircase. The Temple of Artemis was dedicated to the patron goddess of the city.

Further to the north is the **North Theatre**, built originally in AD 165 and now wonderfully restored.

The small **museum** (☎ 6312267; admission free; ☾ 8.30am-6pm Oct-Apr, 8.30am-5pm May-Sep) contains a good collection of artefacts from the site.

Sleeping & Eating

Surprisingly, there is still no hotel in Jerash, but it's an easy day trip from Amman.

Olive Branch Resort (☎ 6340555; www.olivebranch.com.jo; s/d JD15/25; ⚡) Around 7km from Jerash, off the Ajlun road, this secluded place has modern, comfortable rooms with satellite TV and good bathrooms, as well as great views, a games room and a good restaurant. You can also camp for JD4, or JD5 if you didn't bring your own tent. A taxi from Jerash costs JD2 one way.

JERASH

INFORMATION
Jerash Festival Ticket
    Office...................................**1** B5
Main Ticket Office (Site
    Entrance)...........................**2** B6
Ticket Checkpoint..................**3** B5
Tourist Police.........................**4** B5
Visitors Centre.......................**5** B5

SIGHTS & ACTIVITIES
Agora (Macellum)..................**6** B4
Cathedral...............................**7** B3
Church of Bishop Genesius..**8** A3
Church of Bishop Isaiah......**9** B2
Church of St Cosmos & St
    Damianus..........................**10** A3
Church of St George...........**11** A3
Church of St John the
    Baptist...............................**12** A3
Church of St Peter & St
    Paul....................................**13** A3
Church of St Theodore.......**14** B3
Eastern Baths.......................**15** C3
Hadrian's Arch (Triumphal
    Arch)..................................**16** B5
Hippodrome..........................**17** B5
Market....................................**18** C4
Mortuary Church..................**19** A3
Mosque...................................**20** C4
Museum..................................**21** B4
North Gate.............................**22** C2
North Theatre........................**23** B2
Northern Tetrapylon...........**24** B2
Nymphaeum...........................**25** B3
Oval Plaza (Forum)..............**26** B4
Propylaeum (Gateway to the
    Temple of Artemis)..........**27** B3
Propylaeum Church.............**28** B3
South Gate.............................**29** B4
South Theatre........................**30** A4
Southern Tetrapylon............**31** B3
Synagogue Church...............**32** A2
Temple of Artemis...............**33** B3
Temple of Zeus.....................**34** B4
Umayyad Houses...................**35** B3
Upper Temple of Zeus.........**36** B4
Western Baths.......................**37** C2

EATING
Al-Khayyam Restaurant....**38** C4
Janat Jerash Restaurant....**39** C4
Jerash Rest House................**40** B5

DRINKING
Drinks Shop.........................**41** B5

SHOPPING
Souvenir Shops.................(see **2**)

TRANSPORT
Buses to Amman..............**42** B6

Jerash Rest House (☎ 6351437; khader@jerashrest .com; buffet JD5, mains JD3-7, plus 26% tax; ☒ noon-5pm) It has decent à la carte meals but most opt for the lunch buffet.

Lebanese House (☎ 6351301; mains JD2.500-5; ☒ noon-11pm) Overlooking orchards a 10-minute walk from Jerash centre, this is a local favourite, with good Lebanese-style dishes and pleasant outdoor seating.

You'll find cheaper meals opposite the visitors centre, including at **Al-Khayyam Restaurant** (grills JD2.500) or the **Janat Jerash Restaurant** (Al-Qayrawan St; mains JD2.500). Both have nice terraces.

Getting There & Away

Buses and minibuses run frequently between Amman's Abdali bus station and Jerash (400 fils, 1¼ hours). From Jerash, minibuses travel regularly to Irbid (500 fils, 45 minutes) and Ajlun (300 fils, 30 minutes) until mid-afternoon. If you're still in Jerash after about 5pm, be prepared to hitch back to Amman because most buses stop running soon after that. A taxi to Amman costs JD10.

Jerash's new bus station is a 15-minute walk west of the site, at the second set of traffic lights. If you don't fancy the walk you can often jump on buses headed to Amman from the junction southeast of the main ticket office.

AJLUN   عجلون
☎ 02

Ajlun (or Ajloun) is another popular and easy day trip from Amman, and can be combined with a trip to Jerash if you leave early. The main attraction is the nearby **Qala'at ar-Rabad** (admission JD1; ☒ 8am-4pm Oct-Apr, 8am-7pm May-Sep), 3km west of town. The castle was built by the Arabs as protection against the Crusaders, and is a fine example of Islamic military architecture. It commands unparalleled views of the Jordan Valley and was one in a chain of beacons and pigeon posts that allowed messages to be transmitted from Damascus to Cairo in a single day. The castle is an uphill walk (2.5km) from the town centre. Occasional minibuses (100 fils) and private taxis (JD1 one way) go to the castle from Ajlun.

Sleeping & Eating

Qalet al-Jabal Hotel (☎ 6420202; www.jabalhotel .com; s/d JD24/32) About 1km before the castle, this is probably the pick of the hotels near

Ajlun, though it's a bit overpriced. The outdoor terrace is fantastic.

Ajlun Hotel (☎ /fax 6420542; s/d JD24/32) This cheaper option is about 500m down the road from the castle and isn't bad, though only the top floors take advantage of the fine views.

There are a few good felafel and shwarma places on the town's central roundabout.

Getting There & Away

Minibuses travel regularly from Ajlun to Jerash (300 fils, 30 minutes) and Irbid (320 fils, 45 minutes). From Amman direct minibuses (500 fils, two hours) leave a few times a day from the Abdali bus station. You'll have difficulty finding anything going in either direction after 5pm.

IRBID   إربد
☎ 02 / pop 500,000

Irbid, Jordan's second largest city, is a university town and one of the more lively and progressive of Jordan's large towns. It's also a good base for exploring the historic site of Umm Qais, Pella and even Jerash. There's little to see in town apart from the excellent **Museum of Archaeology & Anthropology** (☎ 7271100; admission free; ☒ 10am-1.45pm & 3-4.30pm Sun-Thu) in the grounds of Yarmouk University. In the energetic area around the university, the streets are lined with restaurants and Internet cafés. In the late afternoon in particular, you'll find students out strolling.

Sleeping & Eating

The cheapest hotels are in the city centre in the blocks immediately north of King Hussein St. Most have shared bathrooms.

Al-Ameen al-Kabir Hotel (☎ 7242384; al_ameen _hotel@hotmail.com; Al-Jaish St; dm/s/d JD2/5/8) This is by far the best cheapie: friendly management, simple but well-tended rooms, and clean shared bathrooms (with hot showers).

Omayed Hotel (☎ /fax 7245955; King Hussein St; s/d with private bathroom & satellite TV JD15/20) This is a cut above the rock-bottom cheapies in both price and quality. The frumpy rooms are spacious, clean and most have nice views. The staff are friendly and it's probably the only budget place where women will feel comfortable.

Al-Joude Hotel (☎ 7275515; joude@go.com.jo; off University St; s/d/tr incl buffet breakfast JD25/35/45, ste JD60) This is Irbid's finest hotel, near the university, with a classy ambience, pleasing rooms and friendly staff.

Al-Saadi Restaurant (☎ 7242354; King Hussein St; mains from JD2.500; ◷ 8.30am-9.30pm) This is one of the better places in the centre and it also does breakfast (500 fils to JD1.500).

Omayed Restaurant (☎ 7240106; King Hussein St; mains JD2-4; ◷ 8am-9.30pm) Another good choice with pretty decent food, nice décor and superb views over the city. Take the lift to the 3rd floor.

News Café (Al-Joude Hotel; pizza JD2.500) A warm and inviting place for Irbid's cool set to hang out and enjoy milkshakes, pizza and other snacks, along with a slow puff on a nargileh.

There are dozens of restaurants to suit most budgets along University St.

Getting There & Away

Minibuses run from Irbid's north bus station to Umm Qais (250 fils, 45 minutes).

From the large south bus station, air-conditioned Hijazi buses leave regularly for Amman's Abdali station (900 fils, 1½ hours) until 7pm. Alternatively there are minibuses (600 fils, two hours) and plenty of service taxis (JD1). Minibuses also leave the south station for Ajlun (320 fils, 45 minutes) and Jerash (500 fils, 45 minutes).

From the west bus station (*mujama ala gharb al-jadid*), about 2km west of the centre, minibuses go frequently to Al-Mashari'a (400 fils, 45 minutes) for the ruins at Pella.

Getting Around

Service taxis and minibuses going to the south bus station can be picked up on Radna al-Hindawi St, three blocks east of the Al-Ameen al-Kabir Hotel. For the north station head to Prince Nayef St. For the west station take a bus from Palestine St, just west of the roundabout. The standard taxi fare from *il-balad* (the centre) to *al-jammiya* (the university) is 500 fils.

UMM QAIS أم قيس
☎ 02

Tucked in the far northwest corner of Jordan, and about 25km from Irbid, are the ruins of **Gadara** (☎ 7500072; admission JD1; ◷ 8am-5pm Oct-Apr, 8am-6pm May-Sep), the site of both an ancient Roman city and an Ottoman-era village. The hill-top site offers spectacular views over the Golan Heights in Syria, the Sea of Galilee (Lake Tiberias) in Israel, the Palestinian Territories, which are to the north; and the Jordan Valley to the south.

Sights

From the parking lot and ticket office you'll soon come to the nicely restored **West Theatre**, the nearby colonnaded courtyard and **Byzantine church**. You'll soon hit the **decumanus maximus**, Gadara's main road. West are the overgrown **baths**.

As you head back east, past the Jerash Rest House to the exit, pop into the **museum** for some fine mosaics, statues and other artefacts from the site.

Sleeping & Eating

Umm Qais Hotel (☎ 7500080; s/d with shared bathroom JD6/12, with private bathroom JD8/16) If you want to spend the night in town, this is a comfortable place on the main street, about 400m west of the Umm Qais ruins. The rooms are clean, quiet and sunny, and the management is friendly. It also has a small **restaurant**, or guests can use the small kitchen.

Umm Qais Resthouse (☎ 7500055; www.romero-jordan.com; starters 600-800 fils, mains JD3-4.500; ◷ 10am-7pm year-round, until 10pm Jun-Sep) Inside the ruins, this restaurant is an atmospheric place to linger, with tables commanding spectacular views.

Getting There & Away

Minibuses leave Irbid's north bus station for Umm Qais (250 fils, 45 minutes) on a regular basis. To continue to Pella on public transport you'll have to backtrack to Irbid.

PELLA (TABAQAT FAHL) بيلا
☎ 02

Near the village of Al-Mashari'a are the ruins of the ancient city of Pella, 2km east (and uphill) of the road. The ruins require considerable imagination but the setting is superb.

Pella was flourishing during the Greek and Roman periods, and, like Jerash and Amman, was one of the cities of the Decapolis. The city also came under the rule of the Ptolemaic dynasty, Seleucids and Jews, with the latter largely destroying Pella in 83 BC. Christians fled to Pella from Jerusalem to escape persecution from the Roman army in the 2nd century AD. The city reached its peak during the Byzantine era and there were subsequent Islamic settlements until the site was abandoned in the 14th century.

Of most interest are the ruins atop the hill on your right as you enter through the main gate. These include an **Umayyad settlement** with shops, residences and storehouses, the small **Mamluk mosque** (14th century) and the **Canaanite temple** which was constructed around 1270 BC and was dedicated to the Canaanite god Baal.

Also of interest is the **Byzantine church**, which was built atop an earlier Roman civic complex, and the **east church**, up the hill to the southeast.

Sleeping & Eating

Pella Countryside Hotel (☎ 079-5574145; fax 6560899; s/d half board JD20/25) There's a lovely family feel at this hotel. The seven well-kept rooms each come with a private bathroom and it's a nice place to kick back.

Pella Rest House (☎ 079-5574145; mains JD6, beer JD2.500) This quality place commands exceptional views over Pella and towards the Jordan Valley; Israel and the Palestinian Territories are visible to the right of the communications towers, the West Bank to the left. The chicken and fresh St Peter's fish (from the Jordan River) are worth trying.

Getting There & Away

From Irbid's West bus station minibuses go frequently to Al-Mashari'a (400 fils, 15 minutes). Pella is a steep 2km walk up from the highway which can be punishing in summer. Unlicensed minibuses (100 fils) run reasonably regularly up to the main entrance of Pella, but check the price first as overcharging is common.

THE DEAD SEA & AROUND

There are several reasons to visit the Dead Sea region, not least for a float in the sea itself (p329), especially if you're not visiting the Israeli side. Bethany is an important archaeological site that pinpoints a major event in the life of Jesus to a remarkably specific physical location on the banks of the Jordan River. For something completely different, Wadi Mujib offers some of Jordan's wettest and wildest adventure opportunities.

Public transport is unreliable on the Dead Sea Hwy and this is one place to consider renting a car or taxi for the day. Most budget travellers visit the Dead Sea as part of a day trip from Amman or Madaba.

BETHANY-BEYOND-THE-JORDAN المغطس

Known in Arabic as Al-Maghtas (Baptism Site), this important site is claimed by Christians to be the place where Jesus was baptised by John the Baptist, where the first five apostles met and where the prophet Elijah ascended to heaven in a chariot. It wasn't until the 1994 peace treaty with Israel that the remains of churches, caves and baptism pools were unearthed. Pope John Paul II authenticated the site in March 2000.

Sights

Entry to the **site** (foreigner/Jordanian/child under 12 JD5/1/free; 🕒 8am-3pm winter & Ramadan, 8am-5pm summer) includes a mandatory guided tour, due to the nature of the border zone. The shuttle bus makes a brief stop at Tell Elias, where the prophet Elias is said to have ascended to heaven after his death, and then normally continues to the **Spring of John the Baptist**, one of several places where John is believed to have baptised. The main archaeological site is the church complex next to the likely **site of Jesus's baptism**. The trail continues to the muddy **Jordan River**, where you could be baptised if you had the foresight to bring your own priest.

Tours often return via the **House of Mary the Egyptian**, and a two-room **hermit cave**. On the way back you can ask to be dropped at the archaeological site of **Tell Elias** (Elijah's Hill), which includes a 3rd-century church, the cave of John the Baptist, baptism pools and the Byzantine **Rhotorius Monastery**.

Getting There & Away

Take any minibus to Suweimeh, en route to the Dead Sea. About 5km before the town, the road forks; the baptism site is well signposted to the right. From here you'll need to walk or hitch the 5km to the visitors centre.

A taxi from Madaba to the site, taking in the Dead Sea and Mt Nebo en route costs around JD20.

THE DEAD SEA البحر الميت
☎ 05

The Dead Sea is at the lowest point on earth and has such high salinity (due to evaporation) that you just bob about on the surface like a cork. (For more on the Dead Sea see p327).

The most luxurious way to swim on the Jordanian side of the Dead Sea is at one of the upmarket resorts, where you'll pay from JD10 (Dead Sea Spa Hotel) to JD20 (Mövenpick Resort & Spa) for access to their private beaches and swimming pools.

Most budget visitors (foreigners and Jordanians) head for **Amman Beach** (☎ 3560800; foreign adult/child JD4/2, Jordanian JD1; ☒ 24hr), a clean public beach with good facilities, 2km south of the hotels. Locals generally swim fully clothed, though foreigners shouldn't feel uncomfortable here in a modest swimming costume.

A free alternative is the popular **Herodus Spring**, about 10km south of the hotel strip. Fresh (but undrinkable) water runs down its narrow canyon – ideal for washing afterwards. There's little privacy here so dress modestly.

Try to avoid Fridays and public holidays, when the hotels and public areas are very busy. Always take lots of water as the humidity and heat (over 40°C in summer) can be dehydrating and there's little shade. You need to shower after a dip in the Dead Sea to wash off the uncomfortable coating of encrusted salt. Don't shave before bathing!

Sleeping & Eating

About 5km south of Suweimeh is a strip of opulent pleasure palaces that offer the latest in spa luxury.

Dead Sea Marriott (☎ 3560360; www.mariotthotels .com/qmdjv; r from JD93, poolview/poolside extra JD10/20, weekend stay extra JD10; ☒ ☒ ☒) A stylish and ostentatious resort with a poolside bar, good spa, lots of restaurants and good kids facilities, including a jungle playground and family pool.

Mövenpick Resort & Spa (☎ 3561111; www.moe venpick-deadsea.com; standard/superior/deluxe r JD120/140/ 160; ☒ ☒ ☒) The resort to beat, with Moroccan kasbah–style luxury accommodation, tennis courts, the gorgeous Zara spa, nine bars and restaurants and a poolside bar.

Dead Sea Spa Hotel (☎ 3561000; www.jordan deadsea.com; s/d US$100/120, ste from US$220; ☒ ☒) About 200m south of the Mövenpick, this is a definite notch down in quality but it's still nice if you haven't seen the neighbours. It has a medical spa, a decent beach and a big pool with water slides.

Getting There & Away

The budget hotels in Amman sometimes organise day trips to Madaba, Mt Nebo and the Dead Sea if there are enough people. From Amman (see p375), minibuses run to Suweimeh, from where you need to hitch. Hitching back to Amman from Amman Beach is relatively easy.

From Madaba, minibuses leave from the bus/minibus station to South Shuna (350 fils, 45 minutes), from where you can change for Suweimeh (250 fils, 30 minutes). The Mariam Hotel (p385) in Madaba can often organise a day trip by taxi to take in Bethany-Beyond-the-Jordan and Amman Beach for around JD20 (JD18 without Bethany), with an hour stop at each site.

WADI MUJIB NATURE RESERVE

محمية الموجب

Wadi Mujib Nature Reserve (215 sq km) was established by the Royal Society for the Conservation of Nature (RSCN) for the captive breeding of the Nubian ibex, but it also forms the heart of an exciting ecotourism project.

First stop is the **visitors centre** (☎ 03-2313059; admission JD1), by the Dead Sea Hwy. The easiest activity on offer is the **Siq Trail**, a lovely 2km splash up into the gorge, ending at a dramatic waterfall; imagine hiking up Petra's Siq, with a river running through it. Bring a swimming costume, towel, and shoes that can get wet.

The most exciting option is the **Maqui Trail** (per person JD40; ☒ 1 Apr-31 Oct), a guided half-day trip which involves a hike up into the wadi, a visit to some lovely swimming pools and then a descent (often swimming) through the *siq*, finally rappelling down the 18m waterfall (not appropriate for non-swimmers or those with a fear of heights). It's not cheap, and you need to have a minimum of five people, but it's definitely one of the most exhilarating things you can do in a day in Jordan.

Other options include the **Ibex Trail** (JD8), a half-day guided hike that leads up to the Nubian ibex enclosure.

The reserve operates a nearby **camp** (s/d/tr per person JD20/17/16) right on the shores of the Dead Sea. Day use of the camp costs JD5. You can't pitch your own tent. Accommodation and guided treks should be booked in advance with **Wild Jordan Centre** (☎ 06-

4616523; www.rscn.org.jo) in Amman. For more details on the reserve see its website.

There's no public transport to the reserve so you need to rent a car or take a taxi from Amman, Madaba or Karak.

THE EASTERN DESERT

The landscape east of Amman quickly turns to a featureless stone desert, known as the *badia*, cut by twin highways running to Iraq and Saudi Arabia. The main reason to go out there is to visit a string of lonely 'desert castles', of which the most impressive are Qusayr Amra and Qasr al-Kharana. Most travellers visit the region on a day trip from Amman.

UMM AL-JIMAL أم الجمال

The strange, ruined basalt city of **Umm al-Jimal** (admission free; ☼ daylight hr), only 10km from the Syrian border, is thought to have been founded around the 2nd century AD and to have formed part of the defensive line of Rome's Arab possessions. It continued to flourish into Umayyad times as a city of 3000 inhabitants but was destroyed by an earthquake in AD 747. Much of what remains is urban (as opposed to monumental) architecture, including houses, reservoirs, various **churches**, a **Roman barracks** and the impressive **Western Church**. It's great fun to explore for a couple of hours, though little is labelled.

It's possible to see Umm al-Jimal in a day trip from Amman. Take a local minibus from Raghadan station to Zarqa (150 fils, 20 minutes), a minibus from there to Mafraq (350 fils, 45 minutes) and then another minibus 20km on to the ruins (200 fils, 20 minutes).

THE DESERT CASTLES قصور الصحراء

Most of the so-called 'desert castles' were built or adapted by the Damascus-based Umayyad rulers in the late 7th and early 8th centuries as desert retreats or hunting lodges, rather than actual castles. The most popular ruins can be visited in a loop from Amman via Azraq. It is just feasible to travel this loop in one long day using a combination of public transport and hitching, but most travellers join a tour (JD10 per person) organised by one of Amman's budget hotels. This is a good place to have a private car (it's approximately JD35 return for a pri-

vate taxi from Amman). Grab a copy of the free *Desert Castles* brochure from the Jordan Tourism board (p403) before heading off.

Visitors centres have just been built at many of the castles and you can expect an admission fee of around JD2 to follow soon.

Qasr al-Hallabat & Hammam as-Sarah حمام الصرح & قصر الحلابات

Crumbling Qasr al-Hallabat was originally a Roman fort built as a defence against raiding desert tribes. During the 7th century it was converted into a monastery and then the Umayyads fortified it into a country estate. The site consists of the square Umayyad fort and a partially restored mosque.

Some 2km down the road heading east is the **Hammam as-Sarah**, an Umayyad bathhouse and hunting lodge. It has been well restored and you can see the underground channels for the hot, cool and tepid bathrooms.

From Amman's Raghadan station, take a minibus to Zarqa (150 fils, 20 minutes), where you can get another to Hallabat (250 fils, 30 minutes). The bus should drive right past the two sites.

Azraq الأزرق
☎ 05 / pop around 6000

The oasis town of Azraq ('blue' in Arabic) lies 103km east of Amman. For centuries an important meeting of trade routes, the town is still a junction of truck roads heading northeast to Iraq, and southeast to Saudi Arabia. South Azraq was founded early last century by Chechens fleeing Russian persecution, while North Azraq is home to a minority of Druze, who fled French Syria in the 1920s.

SIGHTS
Azraq Wetland Reserve
Azraq is home to the **Azraq Wetland Reserve** (☎ 3835225; admission JD2, combination ticket with Shaumari Wildlife Reserve JD3; ☼ 9am-sunset), which is administered by the RSCN and is good for bird watching. The Azraq Basin was originally 12,710 sq km (an area larger than Lebanon), but over-pumping of ground water sucked the wetlands dry in the 1970s and 1980s. The RSCN is trying to rehabilitate a small section (12 sq km) of the wetlands.

Qala'at Al-Azraq قصر الأزرق
This brooding black basalt **castle** (admission free; ☼ daylight hr) dates back to the Roman

emperor Diocletian (300 AD) but owes its current form to the beginning of the 13th century. It was originally three storeys high, but much of it crumbled in an earthquake in 1927. The Umayyads maintained it as a military base, as did the Ayyubids in the 12th and 13th centuries. In the 16th century the Ottoman Turks stationed a garrison here.

After the 16th century, the only other recorded use of the castle was during WWI when Sherif Hussein (father of King Hussein) and TE Lawrence made it their desert headquarters in the winter of 1917, during the Arab Revolt against the Ottomans. You can still visit Lawrence's room, directly above the southern entrance.

Shaumari Wildlife Reserve محمية الشومري
This **reserve** (admission JD2, combination ticket with Azraq Wetland Reserve JD3; ☾ 8am-4pm), 10km south of Azraq, was established in 1975 to reintroduce endemic wildlife such as Arabian oryxes (87 now in the reserve), blue-necked and red-necked ostriches (now 40), gazelles (six) and Persian onagers (wild asses; seven). You can spot these animals in their enclosures from a viewing platform.

For more on the Arabian oryx see p81.

SLEEPING & EATING
Zoubi Hotel (☎ 3835012; r JD10) This is the best budget accommodation in town, with comfortable, old-fashioned rooms. It's behind the Refa'i Restaurant, 800m south of the T-junction where the Amman road intersects with the roads to Saudi Arabia and Iraq.

Azraq Resthouse (☎ 3834006; fax 3835215; s/d/tr incl breakfast JD17.500/21.500/28.500) This semiresort is surprisingly good value with plush rooms, satellite TV and a pleasant swimming pool. The turn-off is 2km north of the T-junction.

Azraq Palace Restaurant (☎ /fax 4397144; buffet JD6; ☾ noon-4pm & 6-11pm) This is probably the best place to eat in town and the place most groups stop for lunch. For a light lunch choose the salad-only buffet.

A string of budget truck-stop restaurants lines the 1km stretch of road south of the main T-junction.

GETTING THERE & AWAY
Minibuses (650 fils, 1½ hours) run from the post office (north of the castle in northern Azraq) to the old station in Zarqa, which is well connected to Amman and Irbid.

Qusayr Amra قصر عمرا
Heading back towards Amman on Hwy 40, the road passes **Qusayr Amra** (admission free; ☾ 7am-7.30pm Oct-Apr, 8am-4.30pm May-Sep), the best preserved of the desert castles and a Unesco World Heritage site. Amra was part of a larger complex (qusayr means 'little palace') that served as a caravanserai, with baths and a hunting lodge, possibly predating the Umayyads. The highlight here isn't the plain exterior but rather the gorgeous internal **frescoes**. The excellent **visitors centre** at the entrance is worth a stop for a detailed explanation of the frescoes and a relief map of the site. There's no public transport (though plenty of traffic) along the busy Hwy 40 so you'll need to take a tour or hitch.

Qasr al-Kharana قصر الحرانه
This well-preserved castle or caravanserai is 16km southwest of Qusayr Amra, standing as a lonely sentinel on the edge of the bleak badia. It was built either by the Romans or Byzantines, although what you see today is the result of renovations carried out by the Umayyads in AD 710. Around 60 labyrinthine rooms surround the central courtyard and there are good views from the roof. Again, you'll need to hitch to reach this site.

KING'S HIGHWAY

There are three routes south of Amman to Aqaba: the Desert Hwy, the Dead Sea Hwy and the King's Hwy. The first has the most traffic but the last is by far the most interesting of the three, passing through the historic centres of Madaba, Karak, Shobak and Petra, and the wonderful landscapes of Wadi Mujib and Dana Nature Reserve.

Unfortunately, public transport along the King's Hwy is patchy and stops altogether at the Wadi Mujib Gorge for 30km between Dhiban and Ariha; you'll have to hitch or take a private vehicle for at least part of the way. The Palace Hotel (p372) in Amman and the Mariam Hotel (opposite) in Madaba can organise transport along the highway.

MADABA مأديا
☎ 05
This easy-going town is best known for its superb, historically significant Byzantine-era mosaics. Madaba is the most important

Christian centre in Jordan, and has long been an example of religious tolerance.

Madaba is worth considering as an alternative place to stay to Amman: Madaba is far more compact, has excellent hotels and restaurants, and is less than an hour by regular public transport from the capital. Madaba is also a good base for exploring the Dead Sea, Bethany and other sites such as Mt Nebo, Machaerus (Mukawir) and Hammamat Ma'in.

Information

Madaba's **visitors centre** (☎ 3253536; Abu Bakr as-Seddiq St; ◷ 8am-5pm Oct-Apr, 8am-7pm May-Sep) is helpful, with a few brochures and toilets.

Among Madaba's better Internet cafés are **Friends Internet** (per hr JD1; ◷ 11am-midnight) and **Waves Internet** (Talal St; per hr JD1; ◷ 24hr).

All the town's half-dozen banks can change money and have ATMs.

Sights

Madaba's most famous site is the **Mosaic Map** in the 19th-century Greek Orthodox **St George's Church** (Talal St; admission JD1; ◷ 8am-6pm Sat & Mon-Thu, 10.30am-6pm Fri & Sun). Unearthed in 1864, the mosaic was once a clear map with 157 captions (in Greek) of all major biblical sites from Lebanon to Egypt. The mosaic was constructed in AD 560 and once contained more than two million pieces, but only a third of the whole now survives.

For the following places, admission is on a combination ticket (JD2), which covers all three sites.

The **Archaeological Park** (☎ 3246681; Hussein bin Ali St; ◷ 8am-5pm Oct-Apr, 8am-7pm May-Sep) contains exceptional mosaics from all around the Madaba area. The large roofed structure in front of you as you enter contains the **Hippolytus Hall**, a former Byzantine villa with some superb classical mosaics (the upper image shows a topless Aphrodite sitting next to Adonis and spanking a naughty winged Eros). The other half of the structure is the 6th-century **Church of the Virgin Mary**. There are also remains of a Roman road.

The **Church of the Apostles** (Al-Nuzha St; ◷ 9am-5pm Oct-Apr, 8am-7pm May-Sep) contains a remarkable mosaic dedicated to the 12 apostles. The central portion shows a vivid representation of the sea, surrounded by fish and a comical little octopus.

Housed in several old Madaba residences, **Madaba Museum** (☎ 3244056; Al-Baiqa St; ◷ 8am-4pm Oct-Apr, 8am-7pm May-Sep) contains a number of ethnographic exhibits and some more good mosaics.

Sleeping

Madaba Hotel (☎ /fax 3240643; Al-Jame St; s/d with shared bathroom from JD7/12, with private bathroom JD8/15) The only budget option but a good one, with clean, simple rooms and a friendly family feel. The shared hot-water bathrooms are spotless and there's a ground-floor lounge and kitchen. Breakfast costs JD1.

Mariam Hotel (☎ 3251529; www.mariamhotel .com; Aisha Umm al-Mumeneen St; s/d/tr JD18/22/26; 🖥 🍴 🅿 🐾) Our bet for the best place in town, with spotless rooms, a new pool and some of the most comfortable beds in Jordan. It's two blocks northeast of the Al-Mouhafada Circle. Charl, the super-friendly owner can organise a taxi to/from Amman's Queen Alia airport for around JD10.

Salome Hotel (☎ 3248606; salomeh@wanadoo .jo; Aisha Umm al-Mumeneen St; s/d/tr JD15/20/25; 🖥 🅿 🐾) Next door to the Mariam, and run by the same family, this place is equally comfortable. It offers discounts of up to 15% off in the low season.

Black Iris Hotel (☎ 3250171; www.blackirishotel .com; Al-Mouhafada Circle; s/d/tr/q JD15/20/27/32) This is another good value and friendly family-run place that offers good value and comes warmly recommended by readers.

Lulu's Pension (☎ 3243678; fax 3247617; Hamraa al-Asd St; s/d/tr with shared bathroom JD10/20/30, s/d/tr with private bathroom & balcony JD15/25/35) Comfortable rooms and a warm welcome from this family B&B.

Moab Land Hotel (☎ /fax 3251318; moabland hotel@wanadoo.jo; Talal St; s/d from JD20/25, ste from JD30) This place is centrally located directly opposite St George's Church. It's warm and cosy, with friendly staff and a great top-floor terrace. Discounts of up to 15% are available in the low season.

Eating

Most of Madaba's restaurants serve alcohol and there are liquor stores dotted around town. For cheap felafel, shwarma and chicken places try opposite the bus station.

Coffee Shop Ayola (☎ 3251843; Talal St; snacks around JD1; ◷ 8am-11pm) Almost opposite St George's Church, this is a cosy, relaxed snack bar. It serves delicious toasted sandwiches (JD1), all types of coffee (500 fils to JD1) and cans of cold beer (JD1.500).

Haret Jdoudna (☎ 3248650; Talal St; mains JD4-7, pizzas JD2-4, plus 26% tax; ☒ 9am-midnight) This charming, upmarket complex of craft shops, café, bar, pizzeria and restaurant is set in one of Madaba's restored old houses. The food is a notch above the standard, with good *fatteh* (chicken with yogurt and hummus) and *sawani* (meat or vegetables cooked on trays in a wood-burning oven). Live music kicks in from 9pm, making it the only place in town with any nightlife.

Getting There & Away
The new bus station is 2km east of the King's Hwy.

Minibuses travel frequently between Madaba and Amman's Raghadan, Wahadat and, less often, Abdali bus stations (270 fils, one hour). The last bus back to Amman is around 9pm.

It is possible to travel to Karak on a daily university minibus (JD1.500, two hours) from the main bus/minibus station, although it travels via the less interesting Desert Hwy.

The Mariam Hotel can arrange transport to Petra via the King's Hwy (JD13 per person, minimum three people) and also to the Dead Sea (JD18 to JD20). There is no public transport to Karak along the King's Hwy.

AROUND MADABA
Mt Nebo   جبل نيبو
Mt Nebo, on the edge of the East Bank plateau and 9km from Madaba, is where Moses is said to have seen the Promised Land. He then died (aged 120!) and was buried in the area, although the exact location of the burial site is the subject of conjecture.

The entrance to the **complex** (admission JD1; ☒ 7am-5am Oct-Apr, 7am-7pm May-Sep) is clearly visible on the Madaba – Dead Sea road. The first church was built on the site in the 4th century AD but most of the **Moses Memorial Church** you'll see today was built in the 6th century. The impressive main floor mosaic measures about 9m by 3m, and is very well preserved, as are the other mosaics dotted around the sanctuary.

From the **lookout**, the views across the valleys to the Dead Sea, Jericho, the Jordan Valley and the spires of Jerusalem are

superb but often hazy. The new **museum** is worth a quick look before leaving.

From Madaba, shared taxis run to the village of Fasiliyeh, 3km before Mt Nebo (150 fils a seat). For 500 fils the driver will drop you at Mt Nebo. A return taxi, with about 30 minutes to look around, shouldn't cost more than JD4 per vehicle.

Hammamat Ma'in (Zarqa Ma'in)
حمامات ماعين (زرقاء ماعين)
The hot-springs resort of **Hammamat Ma'in** (admission per person JD5, per vehicle JD5; ☒ 6am-midnight), sometimes known as Zarqa Ma'in, lies 27km southwest of Madaba, reached via a scenic road that drops steeply into the Zarqa Ma'in valley. The top-end hotel and chalet complex was being renovated at the time of research but the swimming pools and hot waterfall are still open to the public.

A taxi from Madaba costs about JD6 one way, or JD15 for a return journey, including around an hour's waiting time at the springs.

MACHAERUS (MUKAWIR)
مكاريوس (مكاور)
Just beyond the village of Mukawir is the spectacular 700m-high hilltop perch of **Machaerus** (admission free; ☒ daylight hr), the castle of Herod the Great. The ruins themselves are only of moderate interest but the setting is breathtaking and commands great views out over the surrounding hills and the Dead Sea.

Machaerus is known to the locals as Qala'at al-Meshneq (Gallows Castle). The ruins consist of the palace of Herod Antipas, a huge cistern, the low-lying remains of the baths and defensive walls. Machaerus is renowned as the place where John the Baptist was beheaded by Herod Antipas, the successor to Herod the Great, at the request of the seductive dancer Salome. The castle is about 2km past the village and easy to spot.

From Madaba, minibuses (350 fils, one hour) go to the village of Mukawir four or five times a day (the last around 5pm). Unless you have chartered a taxi from Madaba, you'll need to walk the remaining 2km (downhill most of the way). However, your minibus driver may, if you ask nicely and sweeten the request with a tip, take you the extra distance.

WADI MUJIB   وادي الموجيب

Stretching across Jordan from the Desert Hwy to the Dead Sea is the vast and beautiful Wadi Mujib, sometimes known as the 'Grand Canyon of Jordan'. This spectacular valley is about 1km deep and over 4km from one edge to the other. Don't confuse the canyon here with Wadi Mujib Nature Reserve (p382) by the Dead Sea.

Dhiban, on the northern side of the canyon, is where almost all transport south of Madaba stops. The only way to cross the mighty Mujib from Dhiban to Ariha (about 30km) is to charter a taxi for JD5 each way. Hitching is possible, but expect a long wait.

KARAK   الكرك
☎ 03

The evocative ancient Crusader castle of Karak (or Kerak) became a place of legend during the 12-century battles between the Crusaders and the Muslim armies of Salah ad-Din (Saladin). Although among the most famous, the castle at Karak was just one in a long line built by the Crusaders, stretching from Aqaba in the south to Turkey in the north. The fortifications still dominate the modern walled town of Karak.

The **castle** (admission JD1; ⊙ 8am-5.30pm) is entered through the **Ottoman Gate**, at the end of a short bridge over the dry moat. The path leading up to the left from inside the entrance leads to the **Crusader Gallery** (stables). At the end of the gallery, a long passageway leads southwest past the **soldiers' barracks** and **kitchen**. Emerging from the covered area, you will see the overgrown **upper court** on your right, and going straight ahead you will go past the castle's main **Crusader church**. At the far southern end of the castle is the impressive **Mamluk keep**, in front of which some stairs lead down to the **Mamluk palace**, which was built in 1311 using earlier Crusader materials. More stairs lead down to the delightful underground **marketplace**, which leads back to the entrance.

Sleeping & Eating
Towers Castle Hotel (☎ 2352489; fax 2354293; Al-Qala'a St; dm/s/d with shared bathroom JD3/8/12, s/d with private bathroom from JD9/16, new r JD12/18) The great location near the castle gates and the friendly reception staff make this the best option. There's a wide range of rooms, most bright and clean, and many with great views.

Al-Kemmam Hotel (☎ 079-5632365; Al-Maydan St; dm/s/d JD3/5/6) This men-only dosshouse in the modern town centre is the cheapest option if you are broke.

Al-Fid'a Restaurant (☎ 079-5037622; Al-Mujamma St; mains JD2.500-3.500; ⊙ 8am-10pm) This is a popular place and excellent value with main course, dips and salad for JD3.

Ram Peace Restaurant (☎ 353789; Al-Mujamma St; mezze JD1, mains JD3; ⊙ 8am-10pm) This place is similarly good, with some pleasant outdoor seating and friendly staff.

Kir Heres Restaurant (☎ 2355595; Al-Qala'a St; mains JD5-7; ⊙ 9am-10pm) If you want to step up a notch, this classy restaurant has a pleasant ambience, good food and attentive service.

Turkey Restaurant (☎ 079-5730431; Al-Umari St; mains JD1.500; ⊙ 7am-9.30pm) One of several local restaurants by the central statue of Salah ad-Din, offering roast chicken, hummus and other standard local fare.

Getting There & Away
From the bus/minibus station at the bottom of the hill just south of town, reasonably regular minibuses go to Amman's Wahadat station (800 fils, two hours) via the Desert Hwy. Minibuses also run fairly frequently to Tafila (750 fils, 1½ hours), the best place for connections to Qadsiyya (for Dana Nature Reserve) and Shobak. To Wadi Musa (for Petra), take a minibus to Ma'an (JD1.500, two hours) and change there. Minibuses to Aqaba (JD2, three hours) run about four times a day, mostly in the morning.

TAFILA   الطفيله

Tafila is a busy transport junction and you may have to change transport here. Minibuses run frequently from Karak (700 fils, one hour) across the dramatic gorge of Wadi Hasa. There are also direct minibuses to/from the Wahadat station in Amman (JD1.100, 2½ hours) via the Desert Hwy, Aqaba (JD1.200, 2½ hours) via the Dead Sea Hwy, Ma'an (JD1, one hour) via the Desert Hwy, and down the King's Hwy to Shobak and Qadsiyya (for Dana Nature Reserve; 350 fils, 30 minutes).

DANA NATURE RESERVE
محمية دانا الطبيعية
☎ 03

RSCN-run **Dana Nature Reserve** (adult/student JD5/2.500) is one of Jordan's hidden gems and its most impressive ecotourism project. The gateway to the reserve is the charming 15th-century stone village of **Dana**, which clings to a precipice overlooking the valley and commands exceptional views. It's a great place to spend a few days hiking and relaxing.

The reserve consists of a series of wadis which descend through dramatic sandstone bluffs into the Rift Valley of Wadi Araba to the west. The red rock escarpments and valleys protect a surprisingly diverse ecosystem, and the reserve is also home to almost 100 archaeological sites, including the 6000-year-old copper mines of Khirbet Feinan.

The **visitors centre** (☎ 2270497; dhana@rscn.org.jo; www.rscn.org.jo; ⏰ 8am-8pm) in the Dana Guest House can advise on hiking routes, most of which require a reserve guide (JD15/30 half/full day).

Hiking routes include the Dana Village Trail (Steppe Trail; three hours, 8km) to Rummana camp site, the Waterfalls Trail (2½ hours, 2.5km) and the short but steep Nabataean Tomb Trail (two hours, 2.5km). The last two hikes require a shuttle to the trailhead (JD6). The main unguided (and thus cheapest) option is the **Wadi Dana Trail** (14km) to Feinan Lodge, which switchbacks steeply down into the gorge (coming back is a real killer!).

Sleeping & Eating

Dana Hotel (☎ 2270537; sdqe@nets.com.jo; s/d with shared bathroom JD5/10, with private bathroom JD8/12) This hotel, ethically run by the Sons of Dana Cooperative, is the best option in the village, with simple but stylish rooms and helpful management. Prices include breakfast and excellent meals (JD4) are served in the rooftop Bedouin tent.

Dana Guest House (☎ 2270497; dhana@rscn.org.jo; s JD34, d/tr with balcony JD43/53, q with bunk beds JD57, s/d with bathroom JD53/57) The RSCN runs this sleek, stylish and highly recommended lodge. The balconies have truly breathtaking views. Book meals (JD7) in advance.

Dana Tower Hotel (☎ 2270226; dana_tower2@hotmail.com; dm/s/d with shared bathroom JD1.500/3/6, s/d with private bathroom JD4/8, full board per person JD8) This funky, slightly grungy place is popular with younger backpackers and it's a sociable option, though the unsightly building sits uncomfortably with the rest of the village.

Rummana Campground (s/d/tr/q tent per person JD18/15/14/13; ⏰ 1 Mar-31 Oct) This lovely but pricey camp site 11km from Dana has several hiking trails nearby. You can hike here in three hours from Dana village or arrange transport with the RSCN (JD6). Book meals (JD7) in advance or bring your own food. This site is reached via a turn-off on the King's Hwy around 5km north of Qadsiyya. Prices include park entry fee and students can get a 20% discount.

Feinan Lodge (Wadi Feinan; per person US$80) This unique ecolodge is only accessible on foot from Dana (four hours) or by 4WD from the Dead Sea Hwy. At night the monastic-style lodge is lit solely by hundreds of candles. Bring a torch and mosquito repellent.

Getting There & Away

Minibuses run reasonably often throughout the day between Tafila and Qadsiyya (350 fils, 30 minutes). The turn-off to Dana village is just north of Qadsiyya; from here it's a 2.8km (steep downhill) walk to Dana village. A single bus departs from Qadsiyya daily at 6.30am for Amman's Wahadat station (JD1.500, three hours), returning from Amman at around 11am.

The Dana Tower Hotel claims that it will pick up travellers for free from Qadsiyya or even Petra if you ring in advance and stay at the hotel. A taxi to Petra or Karak costs around JD15.

SHOBAK   شوبك

The commanding **Shobak Castle** (admission free; ⏰ daylight hr) is another renowned but little-visited crusader fortress. Some readers prefer it to the more frequented Karak Castle.

Excavation on the castle's interior is ongoing and has revealed a market, two crusader churches, and, at the northern end of the castle, a semicircular keep whose exterior is adorned with Quranic inscriptions, possibly dating from the time of Saladin. The court of Baldwin I is also worth a look. The real highlight is the underground **escape tunnel** that winds down seemingly forever into the bowels of the earth, finally resurfacing way outside the castle at the base of the hill. Bring a torch and nerves of steel. A visitors centre has just been completed so expect admission fees to follow soon.

Occasional minibuses link Shobak village with Amman's Wahadat station (JD1.500, 2½ hours) and there are irregular minibuses to Karak from Aqaba via the Shobak turn-off (ask the driver before setting out). Either way you'll still need a taxi for the last 3km or so to the fort.

PETRA & THE SOUTH

Southern Jordan has a totally different feel from the north and holds some of the country's most dramatic desert landscapes. Petra and Wadi Rum are both unmissable sights and Aqaba is a popular last stop before catching the ferry to Egypt.

PETRA & WADI MUSA البترا & وادي موسى
☎ 03

If you can only go to one place in Jordan, make it Petra. Hewn from towering rock walls, the imposing façades of the great temples and tombs of Petra are an enduring testament to the grandeur of the Nabataean vision. The Nabataeans – Arabs who controlled the frankincense trade routes of the region in pre-Roman times – chose as their city a hidden valley concealed from the outside world and transformed it into one of the Middle East's most memorable sites.

Orientation

The village that has sprung up around Petra is Wadi Musa (Moses' Valley), a mass of hotels, restaurants and shops stretching about 5km from Ain Musa, the head of the valley, down to the main entrance to Petra. The village centre is at the Shaheed roundabout, with its shops, restaurants and budget hotels, while other hotels are strung out all along the main road for the remaining 2km to the entrance to Petra.

Information

The Petra **visitors centre** (Map p390; ☎ 2156020; fax 2156060; ⊙ 6am-9pm), just before the entrance to Petra, has a helpful information counter, several souvenir shops and toilets. The tourist police centre is opposite and there is a small post office behind the visitors centre.

The Housing Bank (Visa; Map p392) and Jordan Islamic Bank (Visa and MasterCard; Map p392), up from the Shaheed roundabout, are good places to change money and both have ATMs. There are a couple of banks (but no ATMs) at the lower end of town near Petra. There are a couple of Internet cafés in Wadi Musa near the Shaheed roundabout.

Sights

The spectacular rose-stone city of **Petra** (Map p390) was built in the 3rd century BC by the Nabataeans, who carved palaces, temples, tombs, storerooms and stables from the sandstone cliffs. From here they commanded the trade routes from Damascus to Arabia and great spice, silk and slave caravans passed through, paying taxes and protection money. In a short time, the Nabataeans made great advances – they mastered hydraulic engineering, iron production, copper refining, sculpture and stone-carving. Archaeologists believe that several earthquakes, including a massive one in AD 555, forced the inhabitants to abandon the city.

ENTRY

The **ticket office** (Map p390; ⊙ 6am-4.30pm Oct-Apr, 6am-5.30pm May-Sep) is in the visitors centre. Admission fees are JD21/26/31 for a one-/two-/three-day pass (subsequent days are free with the three-day pass). There's a student discount of 50% with an ISIC card. Multiday tickets are nontransferable and signatures are checked. Children under 15 years are free.

THE SITE

You approach Petra through an incredibly narrow 1.2km-long defile known as the **Siq**. This is not a canyon but rather one block that has been rent apart by tectonic forces. Just as you start to think there's no end to the Siq,

---

SUGGESTED PETRA ITINERARIES

You really need two full days to do Petra justice. The best advice is to start early; the tour buses start arriving around 8am and the enchanting Siq is best experienced away from the crowds. Al-Kazhneh (Treasury) has its best light around 9am, and Al-Deir (Monastery) and the Royal Tombs are at their best in the late afternoon.

In a **full day** (eight hours) you could cover the main sights mentioned in 'The Site' (above) and then hike up to Al-Deir. If you have a **second day**, perhaps enter Petra via stunning Wadi Muthlim, climb to the High Place of Sacrifice starting near the Theatre and then descend to the city centre via the western side of the hill. A **third day** would allow you to hike to Umm al-Biyara and explore a little off the beaten track.

JORDAN

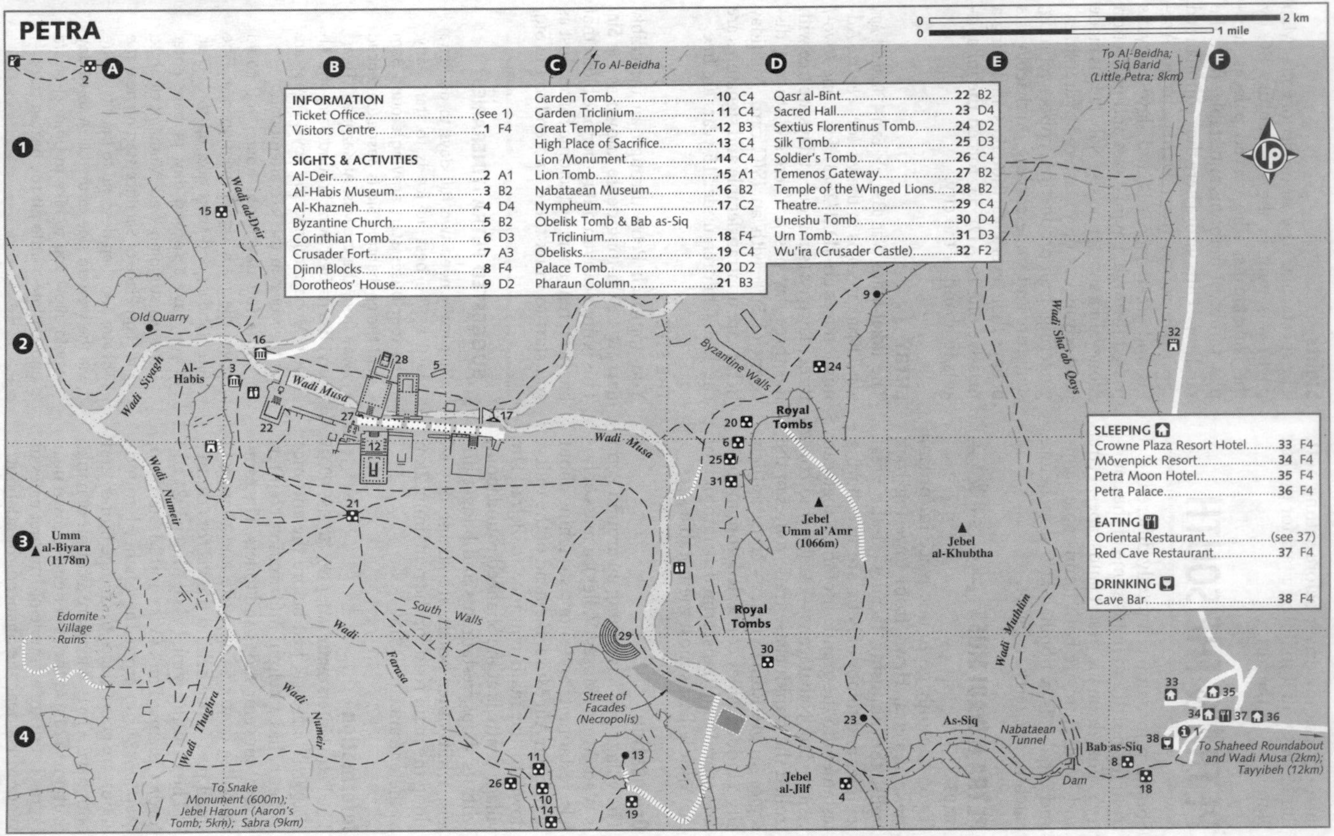

PETRA
0 2 km
0 1 mile
INFORMATION
Ticket Office.....(see 1)
Visitors Centre.....1 F4
SIGHTS & ACTIVITIES
Al-Deir.....2 A1
Al-Habis Museum.....3 B2
Al-Khazneh.....4 D4
Byzantine Church.....5 B2
Corinthian Tomb.....6 D3
Crusader Fort.....7 A3
Djinn Blocks.....8 F4
Dorotheos' House.....9 D2
Garden Tomb.....10 C4
Garden Triclinium.....11 C4
Great Temple.....12 B3
High Place of Sacrifice.....13 C4
Lion Monument.....14 C4
Lion Tomb.....15 A1
Nabataean Museum.....16 B2
Nympheum.....17 C2
Obelisk Tomb & Bab as-Siq Triclinium.....18 F4
Obelisks.....19 C4
Palace Tomb.....20 D2
Pharaun Column.....21 B3
Qasr al-Bint.....22 B2
Sacred Hall.....23 D4
Sextius Florentinus Tomb.....24 D2
Silk Tomb.....25 D3
Soldier's Tomb.....26 C4
Temenos Gateway.....27 B2
Temple of the Winged Lions.....28 B2
Theatre.....29 C4
Uneishu Tomb.....30 D4
Urn Tomb.....31 D3
Wu'ira (Crusader Castle).....32 F2
SLEEPING
Crowne Plaza Resort Hotel.....33 F4
Mövenpick Resort.....34 F4
Petra Moon Hotel.....35 F4
Petra Palace.....36 F4
EATING
Oriental Restaurant.....(see 37)
Red Cave Restaurant.....37 F4
DRINKING
Cave Bar.....38 F4
To Al-Beidha
To Al-Beidha; Siq Barid (Little Petra; 8km)
Wadi ad-Deir
Old Quarry
Al-Habis
Wadi Siyagh
Wadi Musa
Byzantine Walls
Royal Tombs
Wadi Sha'ab Qays
Wadi Numeir
Umm al-Biyara (1178m)
Edomite Village Ruins
South Walls
Wadi Farasa
Wadi Thughra
Jebel Umm al'Amr (1066m)
Jebel al-Khubtha
Wadi Muthlim
Street of Facades (Necropolis)
As-Siq
Nabataean Tunnel
Bab as-Siq
Dam
Jebel al-Jilf
To Snake Monument (600m); Jebel Haroun (Aaron's Tomb; 5km); Sabra (9km)
To Shaheed Roundabout and Wadi Musa (2km); Tayyibeh (12km)

you catch breathtaking glimpses ahead of the most impressive of Petra's sights, the **Al-Khazneh** (Treasury). Carved out of iron-laden sandstone to serve as a tomb, the Treasury gets its name from the misguided local belief that an Egyptian Pharaoh hid his treasure in the top urn. The Greek-style pillars, alcoves and plinths are masterpieces.

Further into the site is the **Street of Facades**, the highlight of which is the weather-worn 7000-seat **theatre**. Further north above the path are the **Royal Tombs**, standing elegantly in various stages of erosion.

The main path turns west along the **colonnaded street**, which was once lined with shops, passing the rubble of the **nymphaeum** en route to the elevated **Great Temple**, staring across the wadi to the **Temple of the Winged Lions**. At the end of the colonnaded street is the imposing and (unusually for Petra) free-standing **Qasr al-Bint**. The path turns north towards the **Al-Habis Museum** and the start of the winding path that climbs to the monastery.

HIGH PLACES

Although all of Petra's high places are worth visiting, **Al-Deir** (the Monastery) shouldn't be missed. It's reached by a long rock cut staircase leading north from the museum (a 45-minute walk). Al-Deir has a similar façade to the Khazneh, but is far bigger and the views from the nearby cliff-tops are stunning, especially towards Jebel Haroun in the late afternoon. On the way up, look out for the **Lion Tomb**.

The **High Place of Sacrifice** is reached by stairs (45-minute climb) from off the **Street of Facades** and affords stunning views. Descend on the other side of the mountain via the **Garden Tomb**, **Soldier's Tomb** and **Garden Triclinium**.

Other more challenging hikes include those to **Umm al-Biyara** (a steep hour each way) and the day return hike to **Jebel Haroun** (topped with the tomb of the biblical/islamic prophet Aaron/Haroun).

The exciting scramble through the **Wadi Muthlim** slot canyon from the Siq to near the Royal Tombs (45 minutes) is highly recommended, but don't try it if there has been any recent rain as flash floods are possible.

Sleeping

Prices for hotels in Wadi Musa fluctuate wildly, depending on the season and amount of business. Discounts are common.

BUDGET

Unless otherwise noted, all the following hotels are in Wadi Musa village, close to the central Shaheed Roundabout.

Mussa Spring Hotel (☎ 2156310; musaspring _hotel@yahoo.co.uk; rooftop bed JD2, dm JD3-4, s/d with shared bathroom JD7.500/11, s/d with private bathroom JD8.500/15) A pleasant place far removed from the clamour of the village centre. There are daily free shuttles to/from the gate at Petra, 5km away. Some rooms are small.

Al-Anbat Hotel II (Map p392; ☎ 2156265; alanbath@ joinit.com.jo; s/d JD12/14) This hotel has generally quiet, well-furnished rooms with clean private bathrooms and (unreliable) satellite TV, which makes it good value in the heart of Wadi Musa.

Cleopetra Hotel (Map p392; ☎ /fax 2157090; cleo petrahotel@hotmail.com; s/d with private bathroom & breakfast JD10/14) The Cleopetra has small but reasonable rooms and BBC World in the lobby. It's a sociable place to hang out in the evenings.

Valentine Inn (Map p392; ☎ 2156423; valentine inn@hotmail.com; dm JD2-3, s/d with shared bathroom JD6/8, s/d with private bathroom JD8/10; 🖳) The good news here is that for men the Valentine Inn is the biggest backpacker hangout in Wadi Musa. It's well attuned to a range of budget travel needs, from travel information, laundry, a great veggie dinner buffet (JD3) and Internet access to transport to Amman along the King's Hwy and more. The rooms are decent but nothing special and the dorms are very cramped. Unfortunately, many travellers, particularly women, have complained of pushy, rude staff and a 'bad vibe'.

MIDRANGE

Amra Palace Hotel (Map p392; ☎ 2157070; www.amra palace.com; half-board JD25/40; 🐾) This well-run hotel has very comfortable rooms with satellite TV. The heated outdoor pool, Jacuzzi, summer terrace and excellent Turkish bath (JD15 per person) push this a notch above anything else in Wadi Musa.

Al-Anbat Hotel I (☎ 2156265; www.alanbat.com; s/d JD13/16; 🖳 🐾 🅿) Good value and very well-run three-star resort on the road between Ain Musa and Wadi Musa. Facilities include a Turkish bath (JD12 for guests) and a small pool (in summer). Campers (JD3 per person) can use a designated area with showers and a kitchen.

JORDAN

El-Rashid Hotel (Map p392; ☎ 2156800; s/d from JD10/15) Uninspiring but comfortable rooms at Shaheed roundabout right in the centre of town. The newly renovated rooms are more spacious.

Petra Moon Hotel (Map p390; ☎ 2156220; petra moonhotel@yahoo.com; s/d JD15/20) This is up behind the Mövenpick Resort and convenient for the entrance to Petra. The rooms are spacious and comfortable, and the staff helpful. The price drops if you spend more than two nights.

Petra Palace (Map p390; ☎ 2156723; www.petra palace.com.jo; s/d/tr JD31/46/60; 🖳 🖪) This place, about 500m from the Petra entrance, is superb value. Some of the luxury rooms open on to a terrace with a swimming pool and

there's a good restaurant and bar. Renovations planned for 2006 will bring new rooms and another pool, as well as possible noise and disruption. Credit cards are accepted.

TOP END

Sofitel Taybet Zaman Hotel & Resort (☎ 2150111; fax 2150101; s/d US$146/184, discounted to US$105) One of Jordan's unique hotels, the Taybet Zaman was built into a reconstructed traditional Ottoman stone village, near Tayyibeh, 10km from Petra. Rooms are superstylish and luxurious; if we had the money we'd live here. A taxi from Petra will cost about JD10 one way.

Crowne Plaza Resort Hotel (Map p390; ☎ 2156266; cprpetra@nets.jo; www.crowneplaza.com; s/d from JD80/90; 🖪) A great location and online discounts make this a good option. The heated swimming pool is useful outside summer and there's a lovely terrace. Email the hotel for special rates.

Mövenpick Resort (Map p390; ☎ 2157111; www .moevenpick-petra.com; s/d JD92/112; 🖪) The most luxurious place in town, close to the gate into Petra, with a lovely Moroccan-style bar, good restaurants and a roof garden.

Eating

Central Wadi Musa, is dotted with grocery stores where you can stock up for a picnic at Petra.

Al-Afandi Quick Restaurant (Map p392; meals from JD1) Just off Shaheed roundabout, Al-Afandi is a simple and friendly shwarma place and one of the few places in town that doesn't habitually overcharge foreigners.

Al-Wadi Restaurant (Map p392; ☎ 2157163; mains JD3-4; 🕑 7am-11pm) One of two good places right on Shaheed roundabout. It does pasta and pizza, as well as a range of vegetarian dishes and local Bedouin specialities such as *gallaya* (meat, rice and onions in a spicy tomato sauce) and *mensaf* (Bedouin lamb dish).

Al-Arabi Restaurant (Map p392; ☎ 2157661; mains from JD1; 🕑 6am-midnight) Almost next door, this is a bright place with helpful staff and simple but good meals.

Red Cave Restaurant (Map p390; ☎ 2157799; mains from JD2.500; 🕑 9am-10pm) This is cavernous, cool and friendly, and the menu has a good selection of Bedouin specialities, including *maqlubbeh*.

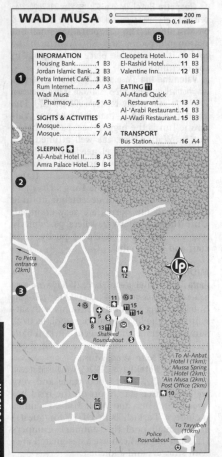

WADI MUSA 0 ___ 200 m 0 ___ 0.1 miles

INFORMATION		Cleopetra Hotel........10 B4
Housing Bank............1 B3		El-Rashid Hotel.........11 B3
Jordan Islamic Bank...2 B3		Valentine Inn............12 B3
Petra Internet Café....3 B3		
Rum Internet............4 A3		EATING 🍴
Wadi Musa		Al-Afandi Quick
Pharmacy..............5 A3		Restaurant.........13 A3
		Al-'Arabi Restaurant..14 B3
SIGHTS & ACTIVITIES		Al-Wadi Restaurant..15 B3
Mosque.....................6 A3		
Mosque.....................7 A4		TRANSPORT
		Bus Station..............16 A4
SLEEPING 🛏		
Al-Anbat Hotel II......8 A3		
Amra Palace Hotel....9 B4		

To Petra entrance (2km)

To Al-Anbat Hotel I (1km); Mussa Spring Hotel (2km); 'Ain Musa (2km); Post Office (2km)

Shaheed Roundabout

Police Roundabout

To Tayyibeh (10km)

Oriental Restaurant (Map p390; ☎ 2157087; mains JD4-5, pizzas from JD2.500; ☯ 11am-9.30pm) A popular place that does Lebanese main courses alongside Western-style pasta and pizza.

Entertainment
There's not a lot to do in the evening, other than recover from aching muscles and plan your next day in Petra. Most hotels screen *Indiana Jones and the Last Crusade* nightly until everyone is sick of it.

Cave Bar (Map p390; ☎ 2156266; beer from JD2.500, plus 26% tax; ☯ 8am-midnight) If you've never downed a pint in a 2000-year-old Nabataean rock room (and we're guessing you haven't) then a drink here is a must. Some seats are actually in the side tombs, which is a bit creepy. There's live Bedouin music from 9pm (not Saturday).

Getting There & Away
Minibuses generally leave from the bus station in central Wadi Musa (Map p392). Minibuses run about three times a day when full between Amman (Wahadat station) and Wadi Musa (JD3, three hours), along the Desert Hwy. Minibuses and service taxis leave Wadi Musa regularly throughout the day for Ma'an (JD1, 45 minutes), from where there are connections everywhere. Minibuses also leave Wadi Musa for Aqaba (JD3, two hours) at about 6.30am, 8am and 4pm – ask around the day before.

For Wadi Rum (JD3, 1½ hours), there is a daily minibus at about 6am; get your hotel to make a 'reservation' the day before. Be wary of any 'bus boys' who try to charge you JD1 for 'luggage' and attempt to book you on a substandard tour. Alternatively, take a minibus to Aqaba, get off at the crossroads at Rashidiya, and hitch a ride from there to Wadi Rum.

Getting Around
The standard, non-negotiable taxi fare from Petra to central Wadi Musa is JD1.

WADI RUM   وادي رم
☎ 03
Wadi Rum has some of the most extraordinary desert scenery you'll ever see, and is a definite highlight of any visit to Jordan. This area, made famous by the Arab Revolt and TE Lawrence in the early 20th century, not to mention the film *Lawrence of Arabia*,

which was partly filmed here, has lost none of its forbidding majesty. Its myriad moods, dictated by the changing angle of the sun, make for a memorable experience. Unless you're really pushed for time, linger for a few days here, slowing down to the timeless rhythm of desert life, enjoying the night skies and spectacular sunrises and sunsets.

Information
Admission to **Wadi Rum Protected Area** (per person/vehicle JD2/5) is strictly controlled and all vehicles, camels and guides must be arranged either through or with the approval of the **visitors centre**, 7km before the village of Wadi Rum.

Most people visit the desert as part of a 4WD trip arranged on arrival at the visitors centre; half-/full-day excursions cost around JD20/45. Prices are regulated, but do not include overnight stays in a Bedouin camp (around JD25 extra).

Baggy trousers or skirts and modest shirts or blouses will, besides preventing serious sunburn, earn you more respect from the conservative Bedouin, especially out in the desert.

Sights
The enormous, dramatic **Jebel Rum** (1754m) towers above Rum Village. Of the sites closest to Rum Village (distances from the Rest House in brackets), there's a 1st-century-BC **Nabataean temple** (400m) and good views from **Lawrence's Spring** (3km), named after TE Lawrence because he wrote about it in his book *Seven Pillars of Wisdom*.

Further afield, the main highlights accessible by 4WD include:

Barrah Siq (14km) A long picturesque canyon that's great to traverse on foot or by camel.

Burdah Rock Bridge (19km) View this impressive 80m-high bridge from the desert floor or, better, scramble up to it with a guide (one hour).

Jebel Khazali (7km) Narrow *siq* with rock inscriptions.

Lawrence's House/Al-Qsair (9km) Remote location and supreme views of the red sands.

Sand Dunes/Red Sands (6km) Superb red sand dunes on the slopes of Jebel Umm Ulaydiyya.

Sunset & Sunrise Points (11km) Superb views from near Umm Sabatah.

Umm Fruth Rock Bridge (13km) Smaller and more visited than Burdah.

Wadak Rock Bridge (9km) Magnificent views across the valley.

THE BEDOUIN

All over the eastern and southern deserts of Jordan, you'll see the black goat-hair tents (*beit ash-sha'ar* – literally 'house of hair') of the Bedouin. The *bedu* (the name means nomadic) today number several hundred thousand, but few can still be regarded as truly nomadic. Some have opted for city life, but most have, voluntarily or otherwise, settled down to cultivate crops.

A few retain the old ways; they camp for a few months at a time in one spot and graze their herds of goats, sheep or camels. When the sparse fodder runs out, it is time to move on again, which allows the land to regenerate.

The Bedouin family is a close-knit unit. Women do most of the domestic work, including fetching water, baking bread and weaving clothes. Men are traditionally providers and warriors, though the traditional intertribal raids that for centuries were the staple of everyday Bedouin life are now a memory. Tents and houses are divided into a haram (forbidden area) for women and another section for the men, where guests are entertained. Men generally wear white robes. Women tend to dress in more colourful garb and rarely veil their tattooed faces.

Although camels, once the Bedouin's best friend, are still in evidence, they are now often replaced by the Land Rover or Toyota pick-up – Wilfred Thesiger would definitely not approve! Other concessions to modernity are radios (sometimes even TVs), plastic water containers and, occasionally, a kerosene stove.

The Bedouin are renowned for their hospitality; it is part of their creed that no traveller is turned away. This is part of a desert code of survival. Once taken in, a guest will be offered the best of the available food and plenty of tea and coffee. The thinking is simple: today you're passing through and they have something to offer; tomorrow they may be passing your camp and you may have food and drink – which you would offer them before having any yourself. Such a code of conduct made it possible for travellers to cross the desert with some hope of surviving in such a hostile natural environment. Whether this code can continue in the face of mass tourism is uncertain.

Activities

You don't have to shell out for a pricey 4WD tour if you don't want to. Ask at the visitors centre for information on the great 2½-hour loop **hike** from the visitors centre to the Seven Pillars of Wisdom and up **Makharas Canyon** (take the left branch of the wadi), curving around the northern tip of Jebel Umm al-Ishrin back to the visitors centre.

With a guide you can make the excellent **rock scramble** through the **Rakhabat Canyon**, crossing through Jebel Umm al-Ishrin.

A **camel** ride offers a great way to traverse the desert. A two-hour trip to the Alameleh Inscriptions, for example, costs JD7. Full-day camel hire costs JD20 per day – see the rates posted at the visitors centre.

For ideas on more adventurous trips see www.bedouinroads.com.

Sleeping & Eating

Most travellers who stay overnight prefer to sleep out in the desert.

Rest House (☎ 2018867; mattress in 2-person tent per person JD3) Has frayed and torn tents out the back, with access to a toilet and shower

block. The tents aren't very secure so keep your valuables with you at all times. The Rest House is at the entrance to Rum village, where the bus drops you off.

Sunset Camp (☎ 2032961, 079-5502421; www.mohammedwadirum.8m.com) This desert camp, around 12km from Rum village, has been recommended by many travellers. A half-/full-day jeep excursion, with accommodation and meals, costs from JD20/27 per person.

Redwan Paradise (☺ 6am-1am) A local café, 500m south of the Rest House, that serves tea, hummus and felafel for around JD1.

The **restaurant** (☺ 8am-9pm) at the Rest House offers good value meals like *shish tawooq* with French fries, and salads and dips for JD3.600.

Getting There & Away

At the time of research, there was at least one minibus a day to Aqaba (JD1.500, one hour) at 7am, and maybe another at 8am. From Sunday to Thursday, you should also find one leaving around 12.30pm and possibly again at 3pm. To Wadi Musa (JD3, 1½ hours), there is a daily minibus at 8.30am.

If you are headed to Ma'an, Karak or Amman, the minibuses to either Aqaba or Wadi Musa can drop you at the Desert Hwy (JD1, 20 minutes), from where it's easy enough to hail onward transport.

AQABA   العقبة

☎ 03

The balmy winter climate and idyllic setting on the Gulf of Aqaba make this Jordan's aquatic playground, attracting visitors from across Jordan and even Saudi Arabia. In summer it gets scorching.

The diving and snorkelling south of Aqaba is the region's main attraction, and Aqaba itself is a relaxed place with a good range of hotels and restaurants.

Information

BOOKSHOPS

Redwan Bookshop (☎ 2013704; redwanbook@hot mail.com; Zahran St; ۞ 7.30am-12.30pm & 4-9pm) Extensive selection of newspapers, hard-to-find Jordanian titles and Lonely Planet guidebooks.

Yamani Library (☎ /fax 2012221; Zahran St; ۞ 9am-2.30pm & 6-10pm)

INTERNET ACCESS

Gate Net (☎ 2017677; Aqaba Gateway; per hr 750 fils, after midnight 500 fils; ۞ 24hr)

MONEY

There are plenty of banks (with ATMs) and moneychangers around town – see Map p396 for locations.

POST

General post office (Al-Yarmuk St; ۞ 7.30am-7pm Sat-Thu, 7.30am-1.30pm Fri)

TOURIST INFORMATION

Tourist office (☎ /fax 2013363; Prince Mohammed St; ۞ 8am-2.30pm Sun-Thu) Next to the Aqaba Museum (head for the huge Jordanian flag). Staff offer little more than a limited range of brochures.

VISA EXTENSIONS

Aqaba Special Economic Zone Authority (ASEZA; ☎ 2091000; www.aqabazone.com) Behind Safeway, by the Central Bank of Jordan. You need to register here if you got a free visa on arrival in Aqaba and are planning to stay in Jordan for more than 48 hours (see p403).

Police station (☎ 2012411; Ar-Reem St; ۞ 7am-9pm Sat-Thu) Opposite the bus station.

A three-month extension is usually available on the spot

and is free. It's best to go earlier in the day (8am to 3pm). Aqaba is the only reliable place to get your visa extended outside Amman.

Sights

Along the Corniche, and squeezed between the marina and the Mövenpick Resort, is the site of **Ayla** (Old Aqaba), which is the early medieval port city. The ruins are limited, but they are worth a quick look if you're in the area.

Of more interest is **Aqaba Castle** (adult/student JD1/0.150, incl Aqaba Museum; ۞ 8am-4pm Sat-Thu, 10am-3pm Fri Oct-Apr, 8am-7pm daily May-Sep), built originally by the Crusaders and expanded by the Mamluks in the early 16th century. The Ottomans occupied the castle until WWI when it was substantially destroyed by shelling from the British. The Hashemite Coat of Arms above the main entrance was raised soon afterwards as the Arab Revolt swept through Aqaba.

Nearby is the small but interesting **Aqaba Museum** (adult/student JD1/0.150, incl Aqaba Castle; ۞ 8am-4pm Sat-Thu, 10am-3pm Fri Oct-Apr, 8am-7pm daily May-Sep).

Activities

SWIMMING & HAMMAMS

The café-lined public beaches of Aqaba are aimed at sunset strollers rather than swimmers.

Barracuda Beach (☎ 2109891; admission JD5, towel hire JD1; ۞ 9am-7pm) is a private stretch of nice sandy beach, equipped with hammocks, loungers, a bar, restaurant, pool and lots of water sports.

The **Mövenpick Resort** (☎ /fax 2034020; www .movenpick-aqaba.com; King Hussein St; 🖳 ✖) charges JD16/19 for weekday/weekend use of its beach, three pools, health club and sauna; however, the Mövenpick (p398) is by far the best in town and includes JD5 worth of drink vouchers.

Aqaba Turkish Baths (☎ 2031605; King Hussein St; ۞ 9am-9pm) offers the full works – massage, steam bath and scrubbing – for JD8. Readers have recommended this place highly.

DIVING & SNORKELLING

There are some superb sites for diving and snorkelling in the Gulf of Aqaba, south of the town centre and ferry-passenger terminal. Aqaba's dive agencies are very professional. Dives cost from JD17 to JD25 with equipment. Night dives and PADI courses are available.

Aqaba International Dive Centre (☎ /fax 2031213; diveaqaba@yahoo.com; King Hussein St).

Arab Divers (☎ 2031808; arabdivers@hotmail.com; King Hussein St) Next to Nairoukh 2 Hotel.

Dive Aqaba (☎ 2034849; www.diveaqaba.com; As-Sadah St) Opposite Golden Tulip Hotel.

Red Sea Diving Centre (☎ 2022323; www.redsea divecentre.com; off King Hussein St)

Royal Diving Club (☎ 2017035; www.rdc.jo) Twelve kilometres south of the city.

For snorkelling, all the places listed above rent out flippers, mask and snorkel for JD3 to JD5 per day. Some offer snorkelling boat trips for around JD20 per person.

Sleeping
BUDGET

Bedouin Garden Village (☎ 079-5602521; bedwin jamal@yahoo.com; per person camping JD2-3, s/d JD15/20, large room JD20/30; ☒) Beach or dive bums will like this place, located about 10km south of the town centre. Accommodation is cramped and a bit overpriced (and there's no air-con) but you can camp or park a camper van for cheap. You can also get meals for JD5.

Jordan Flower Hotel (☎ 2014378; Zahran St; s/d with shared bathroom JD7/8, with private bathroom JD10/11) This place is simple, but the best of a group of three neighbouring cheapies. Rooms vary so look at a few.

Al-Kholil Hotel (☎ /fax 2030152; Zahran St; s/d JD10/12) One of the better places in the area.

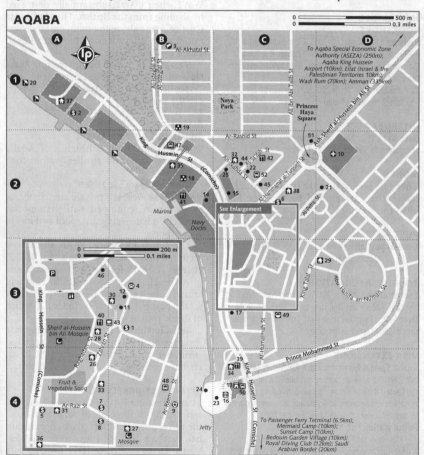

It's worth paying an extra JD2 for a balcony as these make the rooms.

Amira Hotel (☎ /fax 2018840; s/d incl breakfast JD12/18) Best of a trio of similar places next to each other. There are clean bathrooms, small balconies and quiet rooms.

Al-Naher al-Khaled Hotel (☎ 2012456; zv51@hot mail.com; Ar-Razi St; s/d from JD8/10) Rooms are pleasant and bright, with TV and a hot-water bathroom. Off-season rates are a bargain. The windows don't quite fit properly so rooms can be noisy.

Other camps, such as the **Mermaid Camp** (☎ 079-5567761) and **Sunset Camp** (☎ 077-7786023; reefdiverjo@yahoo.com) are due to relocate next door to (maybe) create a Dahab-style budget beach community.

MIDRANGE

The following places have a fridge, air-con, satellite TV, telephone and hot water, and prices include breakfast.

Al-Zatari Hotel (☎ 2022970; fax 2022974; King Talal St; s/d/tr from JD18/28/35) Well run and highly recommended. It has well-appointed rooms with balconies and a nice coffee shop. Front-facing rooms are worth a couple of extra dinar as they are bigger and have better views.

Nairoukh 2 Hotel (☎ 2012980; nairoukh2hot@hot mail.com; King Hussein St; s/d JD15/22, JD19/27.500 Apr, May, Oct, Nov) Good value close to the centre with modern rooms, helpful staff and some great views of the gulf.

Moon Beach Hotel (☎ /fax 2013316; King Hussein St; s without seaview JD12, s/d with seaview JD17/30) Removed from (but in easy walking distance of) the bustle of central Aqaba. The rooms at the Moon Beach are lovely and the five new rooms come with beach views. Credit cards are accepted.

Crystal Hotel (☎ 2022001; fax 2022006; Ar-Razi St; s/d JD20/30) A comfortable and spacious option, if a little sterile, that feels like a 'real' hotel, with a plush marble lobby to boot. The corner doubles are the best. The official rates of JD40/55 rarely apply.

Al-Shula Hotel (☎ 2015153; alshula@wanadoo.jo; Raghadan St; s/d JD15/20) The Al-Shula is right in the heart of the action. Some of the rooms are smaller than others, but those on the west side have excellent views of Eilat. Add JD5 to the rooms in high season. Don't let the lobby fool you; it's a lot grander than the rooms.

Shweiki Hotel (☎ 2022657; fax 2022659; Al-Hammamat al-Tunisieh St; s/d/tr JD16/24/28) Another good-value option. Rooms are spacious with good bathrooms and some come with nice coastal views. The rooms without a balcony are a little cheaper; all rates are open to discussion.

Golden Tulip (☎ 2031901; www.goldentulip.com; An-Nahda St; s/d JD50/60; 🛜 🗙) A modern and fresh four-star choice, with an interior atrium, a rooftop plunge pool and a good location. The 110 rooms are all nicely decorated and come with balconies. Rooms are often discounted to JD30/40 for singles/doubles.

JORDAN

TOP END
Mövenpick Resort (☎ /fax 2034020; www.movenpick
-aqaba.com; King Hussein St; d standard/sea view/superior
JD78/85/96; 🔋 🗶) Aqaba's finest, with lovely
interiors, fine gardens and a huge pool and
beach complex.

Radisson SAS Hotel (☎ 2012426; aqaba@radisson
.com.jo; King Hussein St; s/d JD60/65, sea view add JD10;
🔋 🗶) A comfortable rather than opulent
four-star option, with a small beach, kids
entertainment centre and a beach bar-grill.

Eating

Aqaba's speciality is its fish, particularly
the *sayadieh* – fish, delicately spiced, served
with rice in an onion and tomato (or tahini)
sauce.

Syrian Palace Restaurant (☎ /fax 2014788; Raghadan St; mains JD2-6; 🕒 10am-midnight) This place
offers good local and Syrian food at moderate prices.

Al-Tarboosh Restaurant (☎ 2018518; Raghadan
St; pastries around 200 fils; 🕒 7.30am-midnight) This
hole-in-the-wall pastry shop does a great
range of meat, cheese and veggie pastries
that are heated up in a huge oven.

National Restaurant (☎ 2012207; Zahran St; mains
from JD2.500; 🕒 7.30am-midnight) Under Al-Kholi
Hotel. This is a busy place and deservedly
so. The meat and chicken dishes come with
salads and hummus and are a great deal.

Al-Safara'ah Restaurant (King Hussein St; mains
from JD1; 🕒 11am-10pm) One of two good open-
air grills by the entry to the southern end of
the public beach. Good shwarma meals and
grilled chicken dishes make this the best
value place in town.

Royal Yacht Club Restaurant (☎ 2022404; www
.romero-restaurant.com; mains JD6-12; 🕒 noon-11.30pm)
Situated in the Royal Yacht Club, and with
views of the marina, this is an upmarket
and romantic place to grab a drink and
watch the sunset. The food is Italian.

Silk Road Restaurant (☎ 2033556; As-Sa'dah St;
mains JD3-12.500; 🕒 noon-4pm & 6pm-2am) This is
one of Aqaba's finest restaurants, with a
lovely atmosphere and delicious seafood.

Drinking

Al-Fardos Coffee Shop (just off Zahran St; coffee 500 fils) A
traditional outdoor café where local men sip
coffee, play backgammon and watch Arabic
music videos. Foreign women are welcome.

Baranda Lounge (☎ 077-7232444; Aqaba Gateway;
beer JD3; 🕒 until 3am) This 'bar and a lounge' is

the coolest place in town with a lovely terrace that catches the sea breezes at night.

Getting There & Away

For information about crossing the border
to/from Israel and the Palestinian Territories, see p405.

AIR
Royal Jordanian (☎ 2014477; www.rja.com.jo;
Ash-Sherif al-Hussein bin Ali St; 🕒 9am-5pm Sun-Thu)
Tickets to Amman cost JD39 one way.

BUS & MINIBUS
JETT (☎ 2015223; King Hussein St) operates buses
(JD4.300, four hours) five times daily to
Amman between 7am and 5pm.

Trust International Transport (☎ 2039480; An-
Nahda St) has six daily buses to Amman (JD5,
four hours) and three daily buses to Irbid
(JD8, 5½ hours).

Minibuses to Wadi Musa (for Petra), (JD3,
two hours) leave when full between 7am and
2pm; you may have to wait up to an hour for
one to leave. Otherwise, get a connection in
Ma'an (JD1.500, 80 minutes).

Two minibuses go to Wadi Rum (JD1.500,
one hour) at around 6.30am and 11am. If
nothing is going for a while, catch a minibus towards Ma'an, get off at the turn-off
to Wadi Rum and take a minibus (JD1) or
hitch a ride to Rum village.

All these minibuses leave from the main
bus/minibus station on Ar-Reem St. Minibuses to Karak (JD2, three hours), via Safi
and the Dead Sea Hwy, are the exception,
leaving from the small station next to the
mosque on Al-Humaimah St.

There is talk of moving the bus station to
the northern outskirts of Aqaba.

SEA
For details of boat services between Aqaba
and Nuweiba in Egypt, see p406.

SERVICE TAXIS
Service taxis run to Amman (three to four
hours) for JD5 a seat. Chartering a taxi costs
at least JD25 one way to Petra (1½ hours)
and to Wadi Rum (one hour) return.

Getting Around

Minibuses (250 fils) leave from near the
entrance to Aqaba castle on King Hussein
St for the Royal Diving Club via the south-

ern beach camps, dive sites and the ferry terminal for boats to Egypt.

JORDAN DIRECTORY

ACCOMMODATION
Jordan offers a range of generally good-value accommodation. A bed in a shared room in a cheap hotel will cost around JD3 to JD5 and you can sometimes sleep on the hotel roof in summer for around JD2.500.

There is a good choice of midrange and top-end hotels in Amman, Aqaba and Wadi Musa (Petra), and usually at least one or two in other towns. A double costs from around JD20, although discounts are often available when things are quiet. The RSCN (p364) offers some of the country's most interesting accommodation options in nature reserves.

ACTIVITIES
Diving and snorkelling are popular pastimes in the Gulf of Aqaba – see p395 for more details.

Hiking is a great way to get off the beaten track, with Dana Nature Reserve, Wadi Rum Protected Area and Wadi Mujib Nature Reserve particularly worth the effort. Wadi Mujib in particular offers some great canyoning and rappelling. Wadi Rum is the Middle East's premier climbing destination.

For details of outdoor activities in Jordan's nature reserves check out the **Royal Society for the Conservation of Nature** (RSCN; www.rscn.org.jo).

BOOKS
Lonely Planet offers a detailed *Jordan* guide.

Seven Pillars of Wisdom, by TE Lawrence, describes Lawrence's epic adventures in Jordan before, during and after WWI (he wrote a substantial portion of the book in Amman). It's dense going at times.

Annie Caulfield's *Kingdom of the Film Stars: Journey into Jordan* is an entertaining, personal account of the author's relationship with a Bedouin man in Jordan.

Petra: Lost City of the Ancient World, by Christian Augé and Jean-Marie Dentzer, is an excellent and very portable background introduction to Petra.

Tony Howard and Di Taylor's books *Walking in Jordan* and *Walks & Scrambles in Rum* describe dozens of hikes in Jordan, from wadi walks to climbing routes up Jebel Rum.

BUSINESS HOURS
Government offices are open from 8am to 2pm Saturday to Thursday. Banks are open from 8.30am to 12.30pm and 4pm to 6pm Saturday to Thursday. Private businesses keep similar hours but are more flexible. Everything closes Friday lunchtime for weekly prayers.

PRACTICALITIES

- The daily *Jordan Times* (200 fils) and weekly *Star* (500 fils) are the two English-language newspapers and are worth a read.
- Major international daily newspapers and magazines, such as the *International Herald Tribune* (JD1.250), *Newsweek* (JD2.700), *Guardian Weekly* (JD1.500) and *Le Monde* (JD1.500) are available in bookshops in Amman, Madaba and Aqaba.
- Radio Jordan transmits in English on 855kHz and 96.3kHz FM in Amman, and 98.7kHz FM in Aqaba. It's mostly a pop music station. You can find the BBC World Service on 103.1 FM in Amman and 1323kHz AM across the country.
- Jordan TV broadcasts on three channels: two in Arabic, and one (Channel 2) almost exclusively in French and English. Satellite stations such as the BBC CNN, MTV and Al-Jazeera can be found in most midrange and luxury hotels, as well as the homes of most wealthy Jordanians.
- Jordan's electricity supply is 220V, 50 AC. Sockets are mostly of the European two-pronged variety, although some places use European three-pronged sockets.
- Jordan uses the metric system for weights and measures.

COURSES

Jordan isn't a bad place to study Arabic, though living costs are a little higher than in Egypt or Syria.

University of Jordan Language Center (☎ 06-535500, ext 3436; www.ju.edu.jo; University of Amman) Offers two-month summer courses (July to August) in Modern Standard Arabic for JD500, as well as four-month spring and autumn semesters for JD750. Tuition is 20 hours a week and there are six levels of proficiency.

Yarmouk University (☎ 02-7271111; www.yu.edu.jo; Irbid) Fourteen-week spring and autumn semesters cost US$1500; subsequent courses and an intensive 10-week summer course are cheaper.

CUSTOMS

You can import 200 cigarettes and up to 1L of wine or spirits into Jordan duty free. There are no restrictions on the import and export of Jordanian or foreign currencies.

DANGERS & ANNOYANCES

Jordan is very safe to visit and travel around, remarkably so considering the political turmoil surrounding it. There is very little crime or anti-Western sentiment.

There are fears that this could change. Al-Qaeda and, specifically, Abu Musab al-Zarqawi, himself a Jordanian, were blamed for the November 2005 hotel suicide bombings in Amman, which killed dozens of people. You can expect security checks throughout the country to be increased in the wake of the attacks.

DISABLED TRAVELLERS

Jordanians happily help anyone with a disability but cities are crowded, traffic is chaotic and visiting most attractions, such as the vast archaeological sites of Petra and Jerash, involves long traverses of uneven ground.

Some travellers with a disability have reported having little difficulty getting around most of Petra on a combination of donkey, horse and carriage.

The Royal Diving Club (p396) south of Aqaba, is a member of the **Access to Marine Conservation for All** (AMCA; www.amca-international .org) initiative to enable people with disabilities to enjoy scuba diving and snorkelling.

DISCOUNT CARDS

Student discounts of 50% are available at numerous tourist sites, including Petra, if you have an international student card such as ISIC, not just an ID card from a university.

EMBASSIES & CONSULATES
Jordanian Embassies & Consulates

Following are the Jordanian embassies and consulates in major cities around the world. For addresses of Jordanian embassies and consulates in neighbouring Middle Eastern countries, see the relevant country chapter.

Australia (☎ 02-6295 9951; www.jordanembassy.org .au; 20 Roebuck St, Redhill, Canberra, ACT 2603)

Canada (☎ 613-238 8090; 100 Bronson Ave, Suite 701, Ottawa, Ontario ON K1R 6G8)

France (☎ 01 46 24 23 78; 80 Blvd Maurice Barres, 92200 Neuilly-Seine, Paris)

Germany (☎ 030-36 99 60 0; www.jordanembassy .de; Heerstrasse 201, 13595 Berlin) There's a consulate in Hanover.

Netherlands (☎ 070-416 7200; www.jordanembassy .nl; Badhuisweg 79, 2587 CD, The Hague)

UK (☎ 020-7937 3685, 0870-005 6952; www.jordan embassyuk.org; 6 Upper Phillimore Gardens, London, W8 7HB)

USA New York (☎ 212-832 0119; 866 Second Ave, 4th fl, New York, NY 10017); Washington DC (☎ 202-966 2664; www.jordanembassyus.org; 3504 International Dr NW, Washington DC 20008)

Embassies & Consulates in Jordan

Foreign embassies and consulates are in Amman (Egypt also has a consulate in Aqaba). They mostly open from 9am to 11am Sunday to Thursday for visa applications and from 1pm to 3pm for visa collections.

Australia (Map p366; ☎ 06-5807000; www.jordan .embassy.gov.au; 3 Youssef Abu Shahhout, Deir Ghbar)

Egypt Amman (Map p370; ☎ 06-5605175; fax 06-5604082; 22 Qortubah St, btwn 4th & 5th Circles, Jebel Amman); Aqaba (Map p396; ☎ 03-2016171; cnr Al-Isteglal & Al-Akhatal Sts; ☒ 8am-3pm Sun-Thu)

France (Map p370; ☎ 06-4641273; www.ambafrance -jo.org; Al-Mutanabbi St, Jebel Amman)

Germany (Map p370; ☎ 06-5930367; fax 06-5685887; 31 Bin Ghazi St, btwn 4th and 5th Circles, Jebel Amman)

Iran (Map p370; ☎ 06-4641281; 28 Tawfiq Abu Al-Huda St, Jebel Amman)

Iraq (Map p370; ☎ 06-4623175; fax 06-4619172; Al-Kulliyah al-Islamiyah St, near 1st Circle, Jebel Amman)

Israel (Map p366; ☎ 06-5524686; Maysaloon St, Shmeisani)

Lebanon (Map p370; ☎ 06-5922911; fax 06-5929113; Al-Neel St, Abdoun)

Netherlands (Map p370; ☎ 06-5930525; www.nether landsembassy.com.jo; 22 Ibrahim Ayoub St, Jebel Amman)

New Zealand (Map p368; ☎ 06-4636720; fax 06-4634349; 4th fl, Khalas Bldg, 99 Al-Malek al-Hussein St, Downtown)
Saudi Arabia (Map p370; ☎ 06-5920154; fax 06-5921154; 1st Circle, Jebel Amman)
Syria (Map p370; ☎ 06-5920648, 5920684; Al-Salloum St, near 4th Circle, Jebel Amman)
Turkey (Map p370; ☎ 06-4641251; 36 Al-Kulliyah al-Islamiyah St, Jebel Amman)
UK (Map p370; ☎ 06-5923100; www.britain.org.jo; Wadi Abdoun, Abdoun)
USA (Map p366; ☎ 06-5920101; http://usembassy-amman.org.jo; 20 Al-Umawiyeen St, Abdoun)

FESTIVALS & EVENTS

Jordan's best-known cultural event is the **Jerash Festival** (www.jerashfestival.com.jo), a programme of traditional music concerts and plays held in the spectacular Roman ruins of Jerash and Amman in July and August.

GAY & LESBIAN TRAVELLERS

There is some confusion over the legal status of homosexuality in Jordan. Most sources state that gay sex is not illegal and that the age of consent for both heterosexuals and homosexuals is 16.

There is a subdued underground gay scene in Amman, so if you're keen to explore it make very discreet inquiries. Public displays of affection by heterosexuals are frowned upon, and the same rules apply to gays and lesbians, although two men or two women holding hands is a normal sign of friendship.

Although the gay and lesbian scene is very much underground, there are a few places in Amman that are gay-friendly, such as the multipurpose Books@cafe (see p373) and Blue Fig Café (see p373), which pull in a young, mixed gay and straight crowd.

HOLIDAYS

In addition to the main Islamic holidays described on p647, Jordan observes the following holidays:
New Years Day 1 January
King Abdullah's Birthday 30 January
Arab League Day 22 March
Labour Day 1 May
Independence Day 25 May
Army Day & Anniversary of the Great Arab Revolt 10 June
King Hussein's Birthday 14 November
Christmas Day 25 December

INTERNET ACCESS

There are Internet cafés in almost every town in Jordan, with costs averaging JD1 per hour.

Connecting to the Internet from your hotel room is possible, although usually only at top-end and a few midrange hotels. **AOL** (local access number ☎ 06-5606241; www.aol.com) offers a local access number as part of its global roaming services.

INTERNET RESOURCES

For a comprehensive list of general Middle East websites see p24. Specific websites about Jordan include:
Jordan Jubilee (www.jordanjubilee.com) The best single website about Jordan, it offers loads of extra detail on Petra and Wadi Rum, among other practical tips.
Jordan Tourism Board (www.see-jordan.com) Good site with links to a range of Jordan-related websites.
Madaba (www.madaba.freeservers.com) Excellent description of Madaba's attractions and other nearby sites.
Ministry of Tourism and Antiquities (www.tourism.jo) Lots of tourist information.
Nabataea.Net (http://nabataea.net) 'Everything you wanted to know about the Nabataean empire.'
RSCN/Wild Jordan (www.rscn.org.jo) Ecotourism adventures in Jordan's nature reserves.

LANGUAGE

Arabic is the official language of Jordan. English is widely spoken, however, and in most cases is sufficient to get by. For a list of Arabic words and phrases, see the Language chapter, p679.

LAUNDRY

There are good laundries (mostly dry cleaners) in Amman and Aqaba, although it's often easier to get your hotel to arrange it. Be prepared to pay JD3 for a 5kg load of washing – it comes back smelling better and folded more neatly than you could ever have hoped.

MAPS

The Jordan Tourism Board's free *Map of Jordan* will suffice for most people.

The Royal Geographic Centre of Jordan's 2005 *Map of Petra* (JD3) is worth getting if you intend to do any hiking there.

Jordan by Kümmerly & Frey is good, and probably the best if you're driving around Jordan. GEO Project's *Jordan* (1:730,000) includes an excellent map of Amman.

JORDAN

MONEY

The currency in Jordan is the dinar (JD) – known as the *jay-dee* among hip young locals – which is made up of 1000 fils. You will often hear *piastre* used, which is 10 fils. Often when a price is quoted, the ending will be omitted, so if you're told that something is 25, it's a matter of working out whether it's 25 fils, 25 piastre or 25 dinars! Although it sounds confusing, most Jordanians wouldn't dream of ripping off a foreigner, so just ask for clarification.

It's not difficult to change money in Jordan; most hard currencies are accepted. Below are the rates for a range of currencies when this book went to print.

Country	Unit	Dinar (JD)
Australia	A$1	0.515
Canada	C$1	0.601
Egypt	E£1	0.121
euro zone	€1	0.830
Israel & the Palestinian Territories	NIS1	0.149
Japan	¥100	0.609
New Zealand	NZ$1	0.487
Syria	S£10	0.134
UK	UK£1	1.226
USA	US$1	0.704

ATMs

It is possible to survive in Jordan almost entirely on cash advances as ATMs abound in all but the smallest towns. This is certainly the easiest way to travel (just don't forget your pin number!).

Banks that accept both Visa and Master-Card include the Arab Bank and Jordan Gulf Bank, while the Housing Bank for Trade & Finance, Cairo-Amman Bank and Jordan Islamic Bank have numerous ATMs for Visa. The Jordan National Bank and HSBC ATMs allow you to extract dinars from your MasterCard and are Cirrus compatible.

If an ATM swallows your card, call ☎ 06-5669123 (Amman).

Credit Cards

Credit cards are widely accepted in midrange and top-end hotels and restaurants and a few top-end shops but check whether a commission (of up to 5%) is added. In general you'll find it most useful to use your credit card to get cash from ATMs.

Moneychangers

There are plenty of moneychangers in Amman, Aqaba and Irbid, which are useful because they keep longer hours than the banks. Many only deal in cash but some take travellers cheques, usually for a commission. Always check the rates at banks or in the English-language newspapers before changing.

Syrian, Lebanese, Egyptian, Israeli and Iraqi currency can all be changed in Amman, usually at reasonable rates though you may have to shop around. Egyptian and Israeli currency is also easily changed in Aqaba.

Tipping

Tips of 10% are generally expected in the better restaurants and loose change is usually appreciated by low-paid workers in cheaper places. A service charge of 10% is automatically added to most midrange and top-end restaurants.

Travellers Cheques

Travellers cheques are easily cashed by banks and some moneychangers, though commissions vary considerably so shop around. American Express travellers cheques seem to be the most widely accepted.

PHOTOGRAPHY

Reputable brands of film are widely available in Jordan, as are camera batteries and digital memory cards. Prices are similar to what you'd pay at home. Slide film is becoming increasingly hard to find (JD5 to JD8 for 36-exposures).

POST

Normal-sized letters and postcards cost 325 fils to the Middle East, 475 fils to the UK and Europe and 625 fils to the USA and Australia.

Parcel post is ridiculously expensive but efficient. A 1kg parcel to Australia costs around JD11.600, with each subsequent kilogram JD6.200. To the UK and Europe, the first kilogram is JD12.350 and each kilogram thereafter JD3.400. To the US and Canada, it costs JD12.800 per 1kg, and JD7 for each additional kilogram.

For typically reliable but expensive express mail services try **FedEx** (Map p366; ☎ 06-5511460; fax 5531232; Nasser bin Jameel St, Amman) and **DHL** (Amman Map p366; ☎ 06-5857136; info@amm-co

.jo.dhl.com; behind C-Town Shopping Centre, 7th Circle, Amman; Aqaba Map p396; ☎ 03-2012039; Al-Petra St).

SOLO TRAVELLERS

There's not much of a backpacker scene in Jordan, except in Wadi Musa and, to a small extent, Amman. The tours run by the budget hotels in Amman are a good way to share travel expenses and meet other travellers.

Single rooms are generally much smaller than doubles so always try to negotiate a double room for a single price.

TELEPHONE

The local telephone system is quite reliable. For directory assistance, call ☎ 121. Local calls cost around 100 fils. The easiest place to make a local call is your hotel.

Overseas calls are cheapest at private telecommunication centres, which often consist of little more than a guy with a sign and a mobile phone! These international calls range from 150 fils to 500 fils per minute. Local phonecards are more expensive for international calls.

Mobile Phones

Jordan is covered by the GSM cellular network. Mobile telephones can be rented from companies such as **Mobilcom** (☎ 5857777; www.mobilecom.jo) or contact **Fastlink** (☎ 06-5512010; www.fastlink.com.jo). Rates for signing up can start at JD60 including 20 minutes mobile-to-mobile time or 50 minutes mobile-to-land time. If you have your own phone and purchase a local sim card, expect to pay around JD25 to get started.

Phone Codes

Jordan's country code is ☎ 962, followed by the local area code (minus the zero), then the subscriber number. For local area codes, see the start of each city or town section.

TOILETS

Many hotels and restaurants, except those in the budget category, have Western-style toilets. In most others you'll be using squat toilets with either a hose or water bucket provided for flushing.

There is also usually a receptacle for toilet paper – use it or the toilet's contents will return to you as an overflow on the floor. Public toilets are to be avoided except in cases of extreme emergency.

TOURIST INFORMATION

Jordan runs a good network of visitors centres inside the country. You can get most information from the website of the **Jordan Tourism Board** (www.see-jordan.com). The following offices abroad will post you a package of brochures and maps if you contact them in advance:

France (☎ 01-55 60 94 46; gsv@article.com; 122 rue Paris, 92100 Boulogne-Billancourt, Paris)

Germany (☎ 069-9231 8870; jordan@adam-partner.de; Weser Str 4, 60329 Frankfurt)

UK (☎ 020-7371 6496, brochure hotline ☎ 0870-7706933; info@jordantourismboard.co.uk; 115 Hammersmith Rd, London, W14 0QH)

USA (toll-free ☎ 1-877-SEEJORDAN, 703-2437404; www.seejordan.org; Suite 102, 6867 Elm St, McLean, VA 22101)

VISAS

Visas are required by all foreigners entering Jordan. These are issued at both the border and airport on arrival (JD10) or can be easily obtained from Jordanian embassies or consulates outside the country. The cost is usually around US$20/40 for single-/multiple-entry visas, two photos are typically required, and the visa is issued within 24 hours. The only reason to apply for a visa from a Jordanian embassy or consulate is if you wish to obtain a multiple-entry visa, as these are not issued at the border, or if you plan to arrive from Israel and the Palestinian Territories via the King Hussein Bridge, where visas are not issued.

One exception worth knowing about is that if you arrive in Aqaba by sea from Nuweiba in Egypt (and, in theory, by land from Eilat in Israel) your visa should be free because Aqaba has been designated as a Special Economic Zone set up for free trade. You will have to register at the ASEZA office in Aqaba (see p395) if you plan to stay in Jordan for more than 15 days.

Tourist visas are now generally valid for a stay of up to a month from the date of entry. If you want to stay more than a month you must register with the police in Amman (p369) or Aqaba (p395), who will give you an extension for a stay of up to three months.

Check your visa, as until mid-2005 foreigners had to register with police within two weeks and regulations may change again. For details of visas for other Middle Eastern countries, see the table on p653.

JORDAN

WOMEN TRAVELLERS

Most women who travel around Jordan experience no problems, although there have been some reports of varying levels of sexual harassment. Women will feel uncomfortable on any of the public beaches in Aqaba. Many restaurants usher female customers into their family areas where single men are not permitted. Women travellers should avoid hitching. For both men and women, dress should be modest; baggy trousers or skirts and modest shirts or blouses are acceptable in most circumstances.

Attitudes to women vary greatly throughout the country. In the upmarket districts of Amman, women are treated the same as they would be in any Western country, whereas in rural areas more traditional attitudes and dress codes prevail.

WORK

Work is not really an option for most foreigners passing through Jordan. Those hoping to work with Palestinian refugees might have luck with the public information office of the **United Nations Reliefs & Works Agency** (UNRWA; Map p366; ☎ 06-5609100, ext 165; jorpio@unrwa.org; Al-Zubeid Bldg, Mustapha bin Abdullah St, Shmeisani, Amman); contact them at least three months in advance.

The only other alternative is occasional vacancies for English teachers at the **British Council** (Map p370; ☎ 4636147; www.britishcouncil .org.jo) or the **American Language Center** (☎ 06-5523901; www.alc.edu.jo) but you need to have solid teaching experience.

TRANSPORT IN JORDAN

GETTING THERE & AWAY
Entering the country

For information on Jordanian visas and entry requirements, see Visas, p403.

Air

The main international airport is **Queen Alia International Airport** (☎ 4452000), 35km south of Amman. Flights to Sharm el-Sheikh and occasional charters to Paris serve the smaller Aqaba airport.

Royal Jordanian (Map p366 ☎ 5678321; www.rja .com.jo; 9th fl, Housing Bank Centre, Shmeisani, Amman) is the excellent and reliable national carrier, but from the main European capitals you

can generally get cheaper deals with other airlines. In Amman there are more convenient offices in the Jordan InterContinental Hotel on **Al-Kulliyah al-Isalamiyah St** (Map p370; ☎ 4644267) and along **Al-Malek al-Hussein St** (Map p370; ☎ 5663525), uphill from the Abdali bus station.

The Amman contact details of other airlines flying to/from Jordan are as follows:
Air France (Map p366; airline code AF; ☎ 5666055; www.airfrance.com) Hub: Charles de Gaulle International Airport, Paris.
British Airways (Map p366; airline code BA; ☎ 5828801; www.ba.com) Hub: Heathrow Airport, London.
Emirates (Map p370; airline code EK; ☎ 4615222; www .emirates.com) Hub: Dubai.
Gulf Air (Map p370; airline code GF; ☎ 4653613; www .gulfairco.com) Hub: Bahrain.
KLM (Map p368; airline code KL; ☎ 4655267; www.klm .com) Hub: Schipol Airport, Amsterdam.
Kuwait Airways (Map p366; airline code KU; ☎ 5685246; www.kuwait-airways.com) Hub: Kuwait City.
Lufthansa Airlines (Map p366; airline code LH; ☎ 5601744; www.lufthansa.com) Hub: Frankfurt.
Middle East Airlines (Map p368; airline code ME; ☎ 4603500; www.mea.com.lb) Hub: Beirut.
Qatar Airways (Map p366; airline code QR; ☎ 5656682; www.qatarairways.com) Hub: Doha.
Turkish Airlines (Map p370; airline code TK; ☎ 4659102; www.turkishairlines.com) Hub: İstanbul.

One-way regional airfares from Amman include: Baghdad (JD380), Beirut (JD100), Cairo (JD135), Damascus (JD70), İstanbul (JD180) and Tel Aviv (JD80).

Land

Middle Eastern politics being what it is, all border crossing information should be considered highly perishable – things can alter at short notice so always check the situation before setting out.

IRAQ

Minibuses and service taxis leave from Amman's Abdali bus station for Baghdad but the lack of security along the highway (via

---

> **DEPARTURE TAX**
>
> At the time of research, the departure tax from Jordan was JD5. If you are in the country for less than 72 hours, you are usually exempt from the tax.

Fallujah) made this an extremely dangerous option at time of research.

ISRAEL & THE PALESTINIAN TERRITORIES

Since the peace treaty between Jordan and Israel was signed in 1994, three border crossings opened to foreigners (detailed following). Border crossings may be closed on the Israeli holiday of Yom Kippur and on the main days of Islamic New Year and Eid al-Fitr.

Trust International Transport (p375) has bus services from Amman to Nazareth (JD18), Haifa (JD18) and Tel Aviv (JD21) daily except Saturday. Trust also offers services from its offices in Irbid to Tel Aviv (JD21) and Nazareth (JD14).

It is also worth noting that one-month Israeli visas are issued at the Wadi Araba (Rabin) and Sheikh Hussein Bridge crossings, but those issued at the King Hussein Bridge are usually for three months.

King Hussein Bridge Crossing

Also known as Jisr al-Malek Hussein or Allenby Bridge, this **border crossing** (🕑 8am-2.30pm Sun-Thu, 8am-11.45pm Fri & Sat) offers travellers the most direct route between Amman and Jerusalem or Tel Aviv. Public transport doesn't run during the Jewish Shabbat (sunset Friday to sunset Saturday).

Due to the ongoing intifada (uprising) in the Palestinian Territories, no Jordanian buses were offering services across the King Hussein Bridge at the time of research, using the other crossings to avoid the West Bank. Instead you must take a service taxi from Amman's Abdali bus station to the King Hussein Bridge (JD2 per seat, 45 minutes) or the sole daily JETT bus (JD6.500, one hour) at 6.30am. Once at the crossing, service buses shuttle you across the border (JD2). The ride to the Israel and Palestinian Territories side, although extremely short, can seem to last an eternity with repeated stops for passport and bag checks. At the time of research, it was not possible to walk, hitch or take a private car across. There are money-changing facilities on your way to the border.

If you wish to return to Jordan while your Jordanian visa is still valid, you need only keep the stamped exit slip and present it on returning via the same crossing (it won't work at the other crossings). At the Israeli border post, you may have to plead with officials to stamp the Jordanian exit slip rather than your passport, especially if you intend going on to Syria and/or Lebanon – if you are, there must be no evidence of any trip to Israel in your passport, including any evidence at all that you have used any of Jordan's border crossings with Israel and the Palestinian Territories. For more information see p353.

To get to Jerusalem from the border, you can catch *sherut* (shared taxis) to Damascus Gate or take a cheaper bus to Jericho and then a *sherut* on to Damascus Gate. Be warned, much of the public transport in the West Bank was not running when we were there recently.

Sheikh Hussein Bridge Crossing

Also known as Jisr Sheikh Hussein or Jordan Bridge, this northernmost **border crossing** (🕑 6.30am-10pm Sun-Thu, 8am-8pm Fri & Sat) into Israel is the least used of the three crossings. It links northern Jordan with Beit She'an in Galilee.

Service taxis and minibuses leave the Irbid's west bus station for the border (750 fils, 45 minutes). From the bridge it's a 2km walk (or hitch) to the Israeli side from where you take a taxi to the Beit She'an bus station for onward connections inside Israel.

Wadi Araba (Arava) Crossing

This handy **border crossing** (🕑 6.30am-10pm Sun-Thu, 8am-8pm Fri & Sat) in the south of the country links Aqaba to Eilat; it's known as the Rabin crossing to the Israelis. To get there from Aqaba you'll probably have to take a taxi (JD5). Once at the border you just walk across. On the other side, central Eilat is only 2km away. Bus 16 runs from the crossing to Eilat's central bus station or you can take a taxi (50NIS).

SYRIA
Bus

The border crossings between Jordan and Syria are at Ramtha/Der'a and Jabir/Nasib.

Air-conditioned JETT buses make the journey between Amman (Abdali) and Damascus (JD5, seven hours) twice a day in either direction and there's a daily afternoon service to Aleppo (JD7.500). Book a day in advance for either.

JORDAN

If you want to travel directly between Damascus and Amman, it's worth taking the direct bus or service taxi but it is also possible to take a bus from Irbid's South bus station to Ramtha (250 fils), another minibus or service taxi to the border and then transport to Der'a and Damascus beyond. This main reason to travel this way is if you want to stop off en route at Ezra'a and Bosra ash-Sham in Syria, or Jerash and Umm Qais in Jordan.

The Palace Hotel (p372) in Amman offers a useful minibus tour from Amman to Damascus, with stops in Jerash, Bosra and Shaba. You'll need a minimum of four passengers and the price should be around JD20 per person.

Service Taxi
The enormous yellow *servees* (shared taxis) leave regularly throughout the day from the lower (eastern) end of the Abdali bus station for Damascus (JD6). They generally cross at Jabir. From Irbid's south bus station, service taxis go to Damascus (JD4.500).

Train
A biweekly train service still leaves Amman for Damascus (JD3) along the Hejaz Railway on Monday and Thursday at 8am, but few travellers go this way as the dawdling service takes all day, with a change of trains at the border. The quaint old station is on King Abdullah I St, about 2.5km east of Raghadan bus station in Amman. The **ticket office** (☎ 06-4895413) is really only open from 7am on the morning of departure, although you may find someone around at other times. To get to the station, take a service taxi from Raghadan bus station, or a private taxi (around 800 fils).

Sea
There are two boat services from Aqaba to Nuweiba in Egypt. With both, departure times can be subject to change so call the **passenger terminal** (☎ 2013240; www.abmaritime .com.jo/english) before travelling and arrive at least 90 minutes before departure. It's no problem to buy your tickets at the ferry port on the morning of departure (you'll need your passport).

The fast boat (one hour) leaves daily except Saturday and costs US$36/JD26.

There is also a slower (three hours or more) ferry service which officially leaves at noon but often doesn't get going until 5pm or later. Some days it doesn't leave at all. Tickets cost US$25/JD18.

Children aged two to 12 pay about half price for both services. Fares from Nuweiba are significantly more expensive and must be paid for in US dollars.

There is a sporadically run twice-weekly catamaran trip between Aqaba and Sharm el-Sheikh (officially US$45, three hours) but this wasn't operating at the time of research.

There are money exchange facilities at the terminals at Nuweiba and Aqaba, primarily for buying visas on arrival. The Jordanian side offers a decent exchange rate but avoid travellers cheques, which attract a huge commission. You can get an Egyptian visa on arrival at Nuweiba but be sure to ask for a full visa, not one that covers Sinai only. Passports are collected on the boat in both directions and handed back on arrival at immigration.

GETTING AROUND
Air
Jordan is such a small country that there is only one domestic air route, between Amman and Aqaba (JD39 one way).

Royal Jordanian operates flights to Amman's Queen Alia International Airport on Fridays and Saturdays. **Royal Wings** (www .royalwings.com.jo), a subsidiary of Royal Jordanian, flies daily between Aqaba and Amman's Marka airport (airport code ADJ), a smaller civil airport in the eastern suburbs of Amman. You can buy tickets for either airline at any travel agency or Royal Jordanian office.

Bicycle
Cycling is an option in Jordan but not necessarily a fun one. In summer the desert is not a good place to indulge in strenuous activity, and cyclists on the King's Hwy have reported stone-throwing by groups of young children. Cycling north or south can be hard work as there is a strong prevailing western wind that can wear you down. Anywhere from the East Bank plateau down to the Dead Sea or Jordan Valley makes for exhilarating descents, but coming the other way will really test your calf muscles. Bring plenty of spare parts (see p666).

Bus

The national bus company JETT operates the most comfortable bus service from Amman to Aqaba (and King Hussein Bridge border crossing). Services to Petra and Hammamat Ma'in are not running at present but may resume as tourism picks up again (see p375 for details).

Other reliable companies with regular services from Amman include Trust International Transport and Afana (both to Aqaba), and Hijazi (to Irbid).

Just about all towns in Jordan are connected by 20-seat minibuses, although the King's Hwy and eastern Jordan are less well served. These minibuses leave when full so you may spend an hour or more waiting for the seats to fill up. Overcharging tourists is rare except on routes to and from Wadi Musa (for Petra), where drivers will probably try to charge you extra for 'luggage'.

Car & Motorcycle

Hiring a car is an ideal way to get the most out of Jordan. Distances are generally short and you'll have freedom to explore off the beaten track. Road conditions are generally good outside Amman.

DRIVING LICENCE

International Driving Permits (IDPs) are not needed. If you're driving, keep your driving licence, rental or ownership papers, and car registration in an easily accessible place.

FUEL & SPARE PARTS

Petrol is available along the Desert and King's Hwys and in most sizable towns. Expect to pay about 350/450 fils for a litre of regular/super, though prices are rising weekly. Best of luck if you're looking for unleaded. Diesel is about 150 fils a litre.

Motorcyclists should be aware that there are precious few mechanics in Jordan able to deal with the average modern motorcycle and its problems.

HIRE

The following are some of the more reliable agencies. Charges, conditions, drop-off fees, insurance costs and waiver fees in case of accident vary considerably so shop around. Daily rates run at around JD25 to JD30, weekly rates at JD140 to JD200. You can

normally drop off the rental car in another city (eg Aqaba), for a fee of around JD20.

Always read your contract carefully before signing; remember that many places require a minimum three days hire and all require a deposit of up to JD400 payable upon pick-up and refunded upon the return of the car.

Avis (Map p366; ☎ 5699420, 24hr ☎ 777-397405; www.avis.com.jo; King Abdullah Gardens, Amman) Offices at King Hussein Bridge and Aqaba, and branches at the airport, Le Royal Hotel and Jordan InterContinental Hotel. The biggest car hire company in Jordan.

Budget (Map p366; ☎ 5698131; budget@go.com.jo; 125 Abdul Hameed Sharaf St, Amman)

Europcar (Map p366; ☎ 5655581, 800-22270; www.europcar.jo; Isam Al-Ajlouni St, Amman) Branches at Radisson SAS, King Abdullah Gardens and in Aqaba (Map p396).

Firas/Alamo Car Rental (Map p370; ☎ 4612927, 079-5846454; alamo@nets.com.jo; 1st Circle, Amman)

Hertz (Map p366; ☎ 5624191, 24hr line at airport ☎ 4711771; www.hertz.com; King Abdullah Gardens, Amman) Offices at the airport, Grand Hyatt Amman, Sheraton and In Aqaba (Map p396).

Reliable Rent-a-Car (Map p366; ☎ 5929676, 079-5521358; www.reliable.com.jo; 19 Fawzi al-Qawegli St, Amman) Cars JD20 to JD25. Offers free drop-off and pick-up in Madaba or the airport, will deliver the car to you anywhere in Amman and will even drive you to the edge of town if you are nervous about Amman traffic. Contact Mohammed Hallak.

INSURANCE

All car rentals come with some kind of insurance but you should find out how much your excess is (ie the maximum you will have to pay in case of an accident). This may be as high as JD350. For JD5 to JD10 extra per day you can buy Collision Damage Waiver (CDW) which takes your deductible down to zero, or sometimes JD100.

ROAD RULES

Vehicles drive on the right-hand side of the road in Jordan, at least in theory. The general speed limit inside built-up areas is 50km/h or 70km/h on multilane highways in Amman, and 90km/h to 110km/h on the highways. Note that indicators are seldom used, rules are occasionally obeyed, the ubiquitous horn is a useful warning signal and pedestrians must take their chances. Wearing a seat belt is now compulsory.

JORDAN

Keep your passport, drivers licence, rental agreement and registration papers handy, especially along the Dead Sea Hwy, where there are quite a few police checkposts.

Hitching

For information on hitching see p670.

Local Transport

BUS

Local city buses are generally packed, routes are confusing and the chances of being pickpocketed are higher. Take a service taxi instead.

TAXI

Private (yellow) taxis are quite cheap although only those in Amman use the meters.

White *servees* are a little more expensive than minibuses and don't cover as many routes, but they're generally faster and take less time to fill up (there are generally only four seats). Inside cities like Amman, service taxis offer extensive coverage and are a good alternative to walking or taking private taxis. For more details, see p376 and p376.

Tours

The Cliff, (p372) Farah (p372) and Palace (p372) hotels in Amman offer useful day trips from the capital. The most popular ones run to the desert castles (JD10 per person); to Jerash, Ajlun and Umm Qais (JD13 per person); and along the King's Hwy to Petra, via Madaba, Mt Nebo, Mujib Gorge, Karak and Shobak (JD15 to JD25 per person). We've received varying reports about the quality of such tours so it's worth asking other travellers before deciding. The tours are really just transport so don't expect much from the guide.

One option that has been recommended by readers is the tour that leaves Amman at 8.30am and travels to Petra (9½ hours) via Madaba, Wadi Mujib, Karak, Shobak and Dana with time spent at each of the various sites. The Mariam Hotel (p385) in Madaba can arrange a similar itinerary.

There are a few tour companies with a good reputation for comprehensive (but more expensive) tours around Jordan; try **International Traders** (☎ 06-5607075) in Amman and Aqaba or alternatively call **Petra Moon** (☎ 03-2156665; eid@petramoon.com) in Wadi Musa.

Lebanon

Coolly combining the ancient with the ultramodern, Lebanon is one of the most captivating countries in the Middle East. From Tyre's Phoenician findings and Roman Baalbek's tremendous temple to Beirut's BO18 and Bernard Khoury's modern movement, the span of Lebanon's history leaves many visitors spinning.

With all of the Middle East's best bits – warm and welcoming people, mind-blowing history and considerable culture, Lebanon is also the antithesis of many people's imaginings of the Middle East: mostly mountainous with skiing to boot, it's also laid-back, liberal and fun. While Beirut is fast becoming the region's party place, Lebanon is working hard to recapture its crown as the 'Paris of the Orient'.

The rejuvenation of the Beirut Central District is one of the largest, most ambitious urban redevelopment projects ever undertaken. Travellers will find the excitement surrounding this and other developments and designs palpable – and very infectious.

Finally, Lebanon's cuisine is considered the richest of the region. From hummus to *hommard* (lobster), you'll dine like a king. With legendary sights, hospitality, food and nightlife, what more could a traveller want?

FAST FACTS

- **Area** 10,400 sq km
- **Capital** Beirut
- **Country code** ☎ 961
- **Language** Arabic
- **Money** Lebanese lira (LL) – known locally as the 'Lebanese pound'; US$1 = LL1502; €1 = LL1774
- **Official name:** Republic of Lebanon
- **Population** 4.4 million

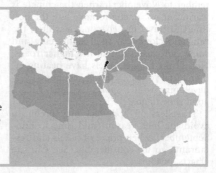

LEBANON

HIGHLIGHTS

- **Baalbek** (p451) Arguably the Middle East's top Roman site and one of the world's most wonderful. Spend a day sizing up this ancient Sun City.
- **Tyre** (p446) With its long, dramatic and colourful history, Tyre has ruins to spare. Take a tour of this terrific World Heritage site.
- **Byblos** (p434) A Crusader castle, Roman ruins, a picturesque port, and enticing souqs – Byblos has it all. Take your time to explore it.
- **Beirut** (p417) Rapidly becoming *the* party town of the Middle East. Don't skip some of the funkiest nightlife and best dining in the region.
- **Tripoli** (p437) Grab a glimpse of Lebanon's other side, its Islamic monuments and history, then sample some of the best sweets in the region.
- **Aanjar** (p453) Meander the main street and marvel at the well-preserved ruins of the Middle East's only Umayyad fortified city.

CLIMATE & WHEN TO GO

Lebanon has a Mediterranean climate – hot and dry in summer (June to August), cool and rainy in winter (December to February).

In summer humidity is very high along the coast and daytime temperatures average 30°C, with night temperatures not much lower. Winter is mild, with daytime temperatures averaging 15°C. In the mountains, summer days are moderately hot (26°C on average) and the nights cool. Winters are cold, with snowfall above 1300m.

Spring (March to May) and autumn (September to November), when the climate is warm but not uncomfortable, are the best times to travel in Lebanon. In winter, the rain and cloud can spoil sightseeing and snow can close some of the higher roads. Not all the budget hotels have heating either. But if you fancy trying Lebanon's ever-developing winter sports (see p642) it's a good time to go.

Travellers on a budget may prefer to avoid the high season (mid-June to mid-September), when prices of hotels and restaurants go up considerably. See Climate Charts, p643.

HOW MUCH?

- Cup of coffee LL1500
- Newspaper LL2000
- One-minute phone call to the UK LL3000
- Internet connection per hour LL3000
- Average museum admission LL5000

LONELY PLANET INDEX

- Litre of petrol LL1300
- Litre of bottled water LL600
- Bottle of local beer in bar/restaurant LL3000
- Souvenir T-shirt LL5000
- Sandwich LL2000

HISTORY

Until it gained independence in 1946, Lebanon formed part of the region known as Syria. As it shared that country's history, see p508 for pre-Independence events.

Post-Independence & Civil War

Lebanon emerged with Syria from the break-up of the Ottoman Empire following WWI. Between the wars, the country was under a French mandate and then it became fully independent in 1946. Its strategic Middle Eastern location and relatively stable, West-leaning government made it a major trade and banking centre, with many Western multinationals basing their Middle Eastern head offices in Beirut.

But Lebanon had a fatal flaw in its national make-up: power and control rested with the right-wing Christian part of the population, while Muslims (almost half the population) felt they were excluded from real government. Add large numbers of displaced and restive Palestinians and the result was a recipe for conflict. In 1975 civil war broke out between a predominantly Muslim leftist coalition (allied with Palestinian groups) and Christian right-wing militias. In April 1976 Syrian forces intervened at the request of the Lebanese president, Suleiman Franjieh, to halt the defeat of the Christian forces. An uneasy peace was foisted upon the two sides by the Syrians.

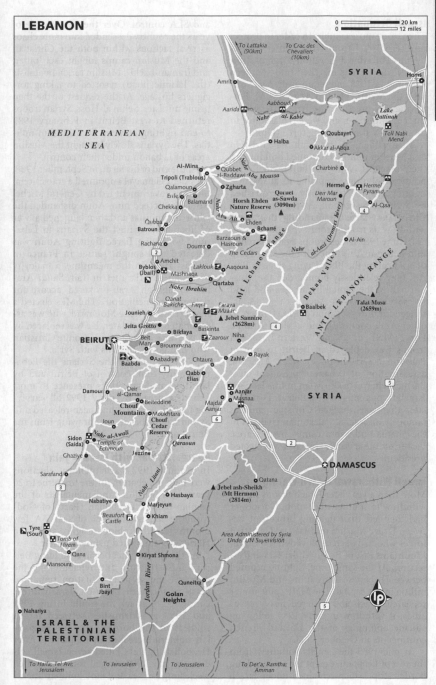

LEBANON

0   20 km
0   12 miles

SYRIA

MEDITERRANEAN
SEA

To Lattakia
(90km)

To Crac des
Chevaliers
(10km)

Homs

Amrit

Aarida

Nahr al-Kabir

Lake
Qattinah

Tell Nabi
Mend

Halba

Qoubayet

Akkar al-Atiqa

Charbiné

Al-Mina

Qubbet
al-Baddawi Abu Moussa

Hermel

Hermel
Pyramid

Tripoli (Trablous)

Qalamoun

Zgharta

Qornet
as-Sawda
(3090m)

Deir Mar
Maroun

Erife

Balamand

Horsh Ehden
Nature Reserve

Al-Qaa

Chekka

Qubba

Ehden

Batroun

Bcharré

Al-Ain

Rachana

Barzaoun &
Hasroun

Douma

The Cedars

Nahr al-Aasi (Orontes River)

Nahr Abu Ali

Amchit

Lebanon Range

Byblos
(Jbail)

Laklouk

Aaqoura

Mashnaqa

Qartaba

Nahr Ibrahim

Bekaa Valley

Qanat
Bakiche

Faqra

Faraya
Mzaar

Baalbek

Talat Musa
(2659m)

Jounieh

Jeita Grotto

Bikfaya

Jebel Sannine
(2628m)

ANTI-LEBANON RANGE

BEIRUT

Beit
Mary

Baskinta

Broummana

Zaarour

Niha

Baabda

Aabadiyé

Chtaura

Zahlé

Rayak

Qabb
Elias

Damour

Deir
al-Qamar

SYRIA

Beiteddine

Aanjar

Chouf
Mountains

Majdal
Aanjar

Masnaa

Joun

Moukhtara

Chouf
Cedar
Reserve

Lake
Qaraoun

Sidon
(Saida)

Nahr al-Awali

Temple of
Echmoun

Jezzine

DAMASCUS

Ghaziyé

Sarafand

Qatana

Nahr Litani

Hasbaya

Nabatiye

Jebel ash-Sheikh
(Mt Hermon)
(2814m)

Marjeyun

Beaufort
Castle

Khiam

Tyre
(Sour)

Tomb of
Hiram

Area Administered by Syria
Under UN Supervision

Qana

Mansoura

Bint
Jbayl

Kiryat Shmona

Nahariya

Quneitra

Golan
Heights

Jordan River

ISRAEL & THE
PALESTINIAN
TERRITORIES

To Haifa, Tel Aviv;
Jerusalem

To Jerusalem

To Jerusalem

To Der'a; Ramtha;
Amman

Israeli Occupation

Then came more trouble. In order to protect northern Israel from cross-border attacks by the Palestine Liberation Organisation (PLO), the Israelis marched into southern Lebanon in 1978 and set up a surrogate militia, the South Lebanon Army (SLA). Following UN pressure, the Israelis withdrew three months later and were replaced by an interim UN peacekeeping force (Unifil).

Meanwhile in Beirut, both the Christian and Muslim militias continued building up their arsenals. With the failure to find a political solution acceptable to all parties, fighting erupted frequently, only quashed by Syrian intervention. At the same time, Christians started demanding that Syria withdraw its troops from Lebanon.

In June 1982 Israeli troops again marched into Lebanon, this time with the stated aim of eradicating the PLO. Laying siege to Beirut, they relentlessly bombarded the Muslim half of the capital by air, sea and land for seven weeks. In August the USA arranged for the evacuation of PLO fighters to other Arab countries, and a Multinational Force (MNF) of US and Western European troops was deployed in Beirut to protect Palestinian and Muslim civilians. After the assassination of Lebanese president-elect Bashir Gemayel (a Christian militia leader), Israeli troops entered west Beirut. Two days later the Israeli-backed Christian militias famously massacred Palestinian civilians in the Shatila and Sabra camps in this area. Bashir's brother Amin Gemayel was elected president.

Israeli Withdrawal & Civil War Again

More than a year later Israeli troops finally withdrew to southern Lebanon. No sooner had they left than fighting broke out between Druze Muslim militias and Christian forces who had been deployed in the Chouf Mountains east of Beirut under Israeli protection. At the same time, fighting erupted between Lebanese army units and Muslim militia in the capital. The MNF came under repeated attack and suffered heavy casualties; it withdrew in early 1984 following suicide bombings of the US and French contingents in October 1983.

In mid-1985 the Israelis withdrew from the rest of Lebanon, except for a 60km-long border strip, which remained under Israeli

and SLA control. Over the next couple of years the country descended into more chaos as rival factions within both the Christian and the Muslim camps fought each other, and Iranian-backed Muslim fundamentalists (the Islamic Jihad) resorted to taking foreigners hostage. At the request of the then prime minister, Selim al-Hoss, Syrian troops returned to west Beirut in February 1987 to end fighting between rival Muslim militias. The Syrians slowly brought the Muslim areas of Lebanon under their control.

At the end of his term, in September 1988, President Gemayel appointed a transitional military government led by General Michel Aoun to succeed him. Aoun disbanded the Christian militias and then launched a 'war of liberation' against the Syrians in Lebanon. Following fierce fighting Aoun was defeated and sought refuge in France in August 1991. In the meantime, a majority of Lebanese MPs met in Taif, Saudi Arabia, to sign an Arab-brokered 'accord for national reconciliation'. The MPs elected a new president, René Mouawad, who was assassinated 17 days later. He was replaced by Elias Hrawi, a moderate Maronite Christian who had good relations with Syria.

With the help of the Syrians the Lebanese army took control of Beirut and by late 1991 had spread its presence to most Lebanese areas. By early 1992 all surviving foreign hostages had been released and Syrian troops began withdrawing from the Beirut area.

Peace...& War with Israel Again

In August 1992 parliamentary elections were held in Lebanon for the first time in 20 years, and Muslim fundamentalists of the Iranian-backed Hezbollah (Party of God) won the largest number of seats. A few months later the cabinet resigned and Rafiq Hariri was appointed prime minister.

As the new cabinet began rebuilding Beirut's infrastructure and rehabilitating the country, the security situation remained tense in southern Lebanon. Israeli forces continued to attack the south during 1991 and 1992 as skirmishes between Israeli soldiers in the border strip and Hezbollah fighters increased in frequency. After Hezbollah fighters killed seven Israeli soldiers in July 1993, Israeli forces launched week-long air, sea and land bombardments on some 80 villages in southern Lebanon, killing 113 people and causing more than 300,000 civilians to leave for safer areas.

Trouble flared up again in April 1996 when Israel mounted a wave of air strikes on Hezbollah positions in the southern suburbs of Beirut and southern Lebanon. After Hezbollah responded, the Israelis launched another campaign, 'Operation Grapes of Wrath'. Their action attracted wide condemnation when media reported that 102 refugees sheltering in a UN base at Qana had been massacred when the base was bombed by the Israelis.

Lebanon Today

In late May 2000, the Israelis and the SLA withdrew from Lebanon, leading to great rejoicing throughout the region. Nevertheless, relations between the two countries remain tense, and many Lebanese fear that their country will once again be dragged into the volatile and seemingly irresolvable conflict between the Israelis and the Palestinians.

In February 2005, a tragic event acted as a catalyst for a major historical upheaval. The former prime minister and popular benefactor, Rafiq Hariri, was killed in a car bomb in Beirut. Though Damascus denied any involvement, the Syrians were popularly blamed and huge anti- (and some pro-) Syrian demonstrations followed. The public reaction in turn triggered both the withdrawal of Syrian forces from Lebanon (ending a 29-year military presence) and the eventual downfall of the government later that year. Following elections in May and June 2005, an anti-Syrian alliance led by Saad al-Hariri, (the son of the assassinated Rafiq Hariri) won a majority in Parliament – and for the first time in 15 years, members opposed to Syrian influence outnumbered the pro-Syrians. Fouad Siniora (a Hariri ally) is currently prime minister, and, although the Syrian-backed Emile Lahoud remains as president, pressure is mounting on him to resign. For the first time also, a member of Hezbollah joined the new cabinet. The government has pledged to continue the reform and development initiated by Rafiq Hariri.

In the meantime, political jockeying and continuing Syrian interest in the country, allied with deeply rooted corruption and ever-simmering sectarian tensions still far from guarantee a smooth path forward for the country. Even if the natural Lebanese optimism continues regardless.

THE CULTURE
The National Psyche

In Beirut you are your car. Show, status and fun are the chief concerns of many Beirutis. Even outside the famously frenetic capital, people work hard and play hard – sleeping fewer hours per night and notching up more minutes on their mobiles than any other nation in the Middle East.

While a collective amnesia has seemingly seized the country, rude reminders of the civil war are never far beneath the surface. Every inhabitant has lost a loved one, and every corner reveals a scar. Under the glitz and glamour lurks a public debt of US$32 billion, unemployment at a massive 24%; and an unusually high incidence of depression.

But let's not poop the party. The Lebanese are still intent on fun and travellers will be swept along by the particular brand of Lebanese hedonism. 'Guests are a gift of God', they say in Lebanon, and the country's hospitality is legendary.

Daily Life

Family is the core unit in Lebanon. Several generations often live together; the old are cared for and the young stay at home until they get married and can afford their own house. Lebanese Christians tend to marry later than Muslims and have fewer children. Muslims now outnumber Christians.

Though Lebanese society – and particularly Lebanese Christian society – is probably the most liberal in the Middle East, certain limits still apply. Excessive drinking, promiscuity and drugs are all taboo.

VARIETY IS THE SPICE OF LIFE

Lebanon is a republic with a president (elected for a six-year, nonrenewable term), a cabinet and a unicameral National Assembly of 128 members. Under a power-sharing National Covenant agreed to in 1943, the president is a Maronite Christian, the prime minister a Sunni Muslim, the deputy prime minister a Greek Orthodox, the speaker of parliament a Shiite Muslim and the armed forces chief of staff a Druze!

Education is highly valued by both men and women in Lebanon. With high unemployment and a struggling economy, making a living is a key concern. Many seek employment abroad. More than 10 million Lebanese now live abroad (2½ times Lebanon's population), and the brain drain continues.

Population

Lebanon has an estimated population of 4.4 million. With nearly 90% living in urban areas (almost 1.5 million in Beirut alone), it is one of the most densely populated countries in the Middle East. An estimated 400,000 Palestinian refugees live in the country – representing nearly 9% of the population.

RELIGION

Lebanon is home to numerous official religious groups including five Muslim and 11 Christian denominations. Prior to the civil war, Christians and Muslims were about equal in numbers; today (due to the Christian exodus and a higher birth rate among Muslims) the latter make up around 70% of the population.

Muslim denominations include the Shiites (the majority) who are largely found in the south, the Bekaa Valley and southern suburbs of Beirut; the Sunnis in Beirut, Tripoli and Sidon; and the Druze in the Chouf Mountains. The Maronite Christians (the largest Christian group) live in the Mt Lebanon region.

ARTS

In summer, many towns and villages hold their own traditional dance and music festivals (see p456). Baalbek's international music festival is the most famous of these. The nation's capital hosts its own festivals for cinema, theatre and music, as well as being home to a number of lively contemporary galleries.

Literature

In the 10th century, the region was known for its classical Arabic poetry. Credited with reviving the classical tradition was Khalil Gibran, Lebanon's most famous poet (p442). A writer, painter and philosopher, he won international acclaim with the publication of *The Prophet* in 1923. An-

other multiaward winner is the Lebanese-Palestinian poet, Mahmoud Darwish.

Lebanon's buoyant publishing industry has produced a number of famous novelists and poets including the widely published Amin Maalouf (*The Rock of Tanios* is considered his masterpiece), the London-based Tony Hanania and the feminist Hanan al-Shaykh.

Cinema & TV

Although Lebanon boasts three major film festivals, four film schools and six TV stations, the industry languishes far behind the heady production days of the mid-70s to '80s, when up to 200 films a year were made. The civil war has inspired many directors including Ziad Duweyri, Mai Masri, Jean Chamoun and Ghassam Shalhab. Other names to look out for include Georges Nasser, Maroun Baghdadi and Andre Gedeon. Some films are available on video (in French) from Naufal Booksellers in Beirut.

Music

Lebanon has an ancient musical tradition. Much music today successfully combines Eastern and Western influences. In the bars of Rue Monot or Gemmayzeh in Beirut, listen out for the oriental trip hop, lounge, Arab deep house, jazz, acid *and* traditional music.

Lebanon contributes its fair share of pop stars, including the megastar Fairouz (p77), Marcel Khalife, Najwa Karam, Haifa and Nancy, to name but a few.

In the larger towns, traditional and contemporary music can be heard in certain bars (see the Entertainment sections in those towns).

Architecture

Almost all the great civilisations have marched through the region that comprises modern-day Lebanon, and most of these civilisations left spectacular traces. Unfortunately, much has been destroyed by the years of war and also by uncontrolled redevelopment.

Nevertheless, the rebuilding of Beirut's Central District has sparked a new energy and vitality. Undoubtedly the most innovative and prolific contemporary architect in the country is Bernard Khoury (see the boxed text, opposite).

> **BERNARD KHOURY – BEIRUT'S ENFANT TERRIBLE**
>
> After studying architecture at the Rhode Island School of Design and later at Harvard, Bernard Khoury went home to Lebanon. Bursting to rebuild his beloved Beirut, he found that his daring designs were discarded in favour of nostalgia and picture-perfect French-Mandate and Ottoman reproductions. After returning in disgust to New York, he was tempted back again in 1997. Since then, his buildings, including the famous nightclub BO18 and the restaurants Yabani and Centrale, have won him international fame and acclaim. Look out for one of his latest projects, the high-profile restoration of the Beirut City Centre Building (BCCB).

Painting

Long-accomplished in calligraphy and decorative arts (like the rest of the Arab world), Lebanon didn't open its first fine art school until 1937, the *Academie Libanais des Beaux-Arts*. Today, the American University of Beirut has a Department of Fine Arts.

In the 1950s and '60s the artistic community thrived in Lebanon. Interrupted by the war years, it has re-established itself and flourishing galleries can be found in Beirut. Well-known 20th-century artists include Mohammed Rawas, Moustafa Farroukh and Hassan Jouni. Contemporary artists of note include female sculptor Salwa Raodash Shkheir.

Theatre & Dance

Though funding and venues are limited, Beirut's theatre scene is active and innovative. Some playwrights to look out for are Jalal Khoury, Roger Assaf and Issam Mahfouz.

Lebanese dance blends Turkish and Egyptian styles. The region's most famous dance is the *dabke,* an energetic folk dance that's performed at social occasions, particularly weddings. Belly dancing (known locally as *raks sharki*) is still popular in Lebanon.

ENVIRONMENT
The Land

Though Lebanon is one of the smallest countries in the world, its terrain is surprisingly varied and diverse. Four main geographical areas run almost parallel to each other from north to south. They are (from west to east): the coastal plain, the Mt Lebanon Range, the Bekaa Valley and the Anti-Lebanon Range.

The Mt Lebanon range includes Lebanon's highest summit, Qornet as-Sawda (3090m) and the famous Cedars of Lebanon. The Anti-Lebanon Range marks the border between Lebanon and Syria. Its highest summit is Jebel ash-Sheikh (Mt Hermon), at 2814m.

Wildlife
ANIMALS

Lebanon is an important migratory staging ground and boasts a large number of birds. Off the coast alone, more than 135 species have been recorded. In the Bekaa Valley, migrating storks can be seen in April.

Unfortunately uncontrolled hunting has taken a major toll on wildlife. Wolves, wild boars, gazelles and ibexes are now all endangered and are very rarely seen. With conservation efforts, some species are thought to be returning.

PLANTS

Trees are poems that the earth writes upon the sky. We fell them down and turn them into paper that we may record our emptiness.

Extract from Sand & Foam, *1926, by Khalil Gibran*

Although Lebanon has suffered appalling deforestation, it is still the most densely wooded country in the Middle East (though that's not difficult!). In the mountains, many varieties of pine, juniper, oak, beech and cypress can be found. In spring, wild flowers carpet the hills and mountains, including the indigenous Lebanese violet. In Beirut a large palm-replanting scheme is under way.

Unfortunately, Lebanon's most famous plant (and the one emblazoned on its flag) the cedar tree, has been reduced from once-great forests to a few lonely patches at Bcharré (p442) and in the Chouf Mountains. Though some replantation is afoot, it will take centuries to restore them to their former glory.

Environmental Issues

Ravaged by more than two decades of war, anarchy, unfettered construction and weak state control, Lebanon's environment remains very fragile. The only areas to have escaped destruction are – ironically – known mined areas.

The complete lack of basic service industries or infrastructure during the war meant that solid waste was dumped throughout the country. Most water sources are still polluted. Air pollution is another serious, ongoing problem particularly in Beirut. Lebanon now has 1.5 million cars within its cramped confines.

In the past 10 years, new water treatment plants have at last been built, a Ministry of Environment has been created (albeit weak and lacking influence) and various environmental organisations set up (both by locals and NGOs). The coastline is also slowly being cleaned up. Though signs are more positive than they have been for years, the Lebanese government has still to prove its commitment and concern.

FOOD & DRINK

One of the best things about a holiday in Lebanon is the food. Lebanese cuisine has a reputation as being the best in the Middle East. The proof's in the pudding (literally), so try it.

MIND YOUR MEZZE MANNERS

Just like its food, Lebanese eating etiquette is more sophisticated that it might look.

- Use only your right hand; tuck away the left.
- Take food from your side of the table; stretching to the other side is considered impolite.
- Avoid letting your fingers come into contact with the dips; use bread like a spoon.
- Don't dip the same piece of bread twice.
- Gobbling, taking large portions, or filling your mouth too full is seen as uncivilised.
- Try not to devastate the dishes; keep them tidy.
- Leaving a little food behind on your plate after eating is good manners.

LEBANON'S GOLDEN GRAPES

Lebanon is one of the world's oldest wine-producing regions. Its most famous and successful region, the Bekaa Valley, boasts excellent wine-growing conditions including reliable sunshine (for 240 days of the year), steep slopes and chalky soils.

All the main grape varieties are found, including Chardonnay, Cabernet Sauvignon, Merlot and Syrah. Wine consumption both inside and outside Lebanon is rising fast and Lebanon's wines are being taken seriously at last. The country now earns more than US$7 million annually from sales, producing over seven million bottles, nearly half of which are exported.

When you're in the country don't miss an opportunity to taste the golden grapes. Worth a visit are Château Ksara (the oldest commercial vineyard), Château Kefraya (the largest producer) and Château Musar (the most successful on the international markets and winner of various viticultural medals). Worth sampling are Château Musar (1998), Château Ksara chardonnay (1999) and Le Château Kefraya (1999).

Fresh ingredients, including numerous types of fruit, vegetables and pulses, are plentiful in Lebanon. Unfortunately, seafood is prohibitively expensive and not always of a very high quality. Populations of both fish and seafood were decimated during the civil war.

Arabic or 'Turkish' coffee is popular in Lebanon. Freshly squeezed vegetable and fruit juices are quite widely available. Try the *jellab* (a delicious drink made from raisins and served with pine nuts) and *ayran* (a yoghurt drink). Sohat, Sabil and Tannourini are considered the three best brands of Lebanese mineral water.

Alcohol is widely available in Lebanon – you'll find everything from local beers and wines to imported whisky and vodka. The most popular alcoholic drink is arak, which is mixed with water and ice and usually accompanies meals. Good local brands include Ksarak and Le Brun. The best local beer is Almaza; it lives up to its name ('diamond' in Arabic).

See p84 for other typical drinks and dishes.

LEBANON

BEIRUT   بيروت

☎ 01 / pop 1,251,739

Beirut is Lebanon's heart and soul as well as the nation's capital. Double-faced – all banks, boutiques and patisseries at one end; ruined, ragged and the refuge of poverty-stricken Palestinians at the other – it's also vital and resolute. Out of the ashes and scars of the civil war, the city is rising phoenix-like in an exciting rebirth. Beirut is beavering hard to regain its former status as 'the jewel of the Middle East'. It's also fast becoming the party capital of the Middle East. Visitors to Beirut shouldn't miss the chance to sample the capital's now legendary nightlife and superb cuisine. And a nose around the National Museum is a must.

HISTORY

Beryte, as Beirut was originally known, was a modest port during Phoenician times (2nd millennium BC). Later, it became famous in Roman times for its School of Law, one of the first three in the world, which made it a cultural centre right up until the 6th century AD. Following a long period of decline, it regained its importance as a trading centre and gateway to the Middle East in the 19th century, and its port became the largest on the eastern Mediterranean coast. The city soon became a major business, banking and publishing centre and remained so until the civil war put paid to its supremacy.

Since the war ended, rehabilitation of the city's infrastructure has been the major focus of both the local and national governments.

ORIENTATION

Beirut is an easy city to navigate as there are conspicuous landmarks all over town.

Hamra, with its many hotels and restaurants, the Ministry of Tourism and a commercial area, is the preferred base for many travellers. To the immediate north and east is Ras Beirut, home of the American University of Beirut (AUB). To the southwest are the seaside suburbs of Manara and Raouché, where you'll find a host of seaside cafés.

The Corniche runs along the coast east from Raouché to Ain al-Mreisse. Further east, past Minet al-Hosn, home of the Phoenicia Intercontinental Hotel, is the newly rebuilt Beirut Central District, also called Downtown or Solidere, the symbolic heart of the city. Further southeast, Gemmayzeh and Achrafiye are where Beirutis flock to sample the restaurants, bars and nightclubs on offer.

Maps

The tourist office and some of the car hire companies produce quite useful city maps of Beirut.

INFORMATION
Bookshops

Beirut has a good range of foreign-language bookshops (which keep standard opening hours unless indicated otherwise).

Books & Pens (Maliks; Map p422; ☎ 741 975; Rue Jeanne d'Arc, Hamra; ☽ 8am-10pm Mon-Fri, 8am-8pm Sat) This stationers/bookshop stocks a decent selection of international newspapers and magazines, including the *International Herald Tribune* (with the local *Daily Star* inset) for LL2000.

Librairie Antoine (Map p422; ☎ 341 470; Rue Hamra, Hamra) If you're out of holiday reading, this place stocks literature (including Lebanese) in English, French and Spanish. Also has a good children's section.

Naufal Booksellers (Map p422; ☎ 354 898; Rue Sourati, Hamra) One of the best for books on Lebanon and the region (in French and English), including coffee-table books, guidebooks, maps, Arabic phrasebooks and Middle Eastern cookbooks. Also stocks Lebanese documentaries and feature films, and postcards.

Virgin Megastore (Map pp418-19; ☎ 999 666; Opera Bldg, Place des Martyrs, Downtown; ☽ 9.30am-midnight Sun-Thu, 9.30am-1am Fri & Sat) New shop with the best collection of books and maps on Lebanon (on its 1st floor) as well as a wide range of children's books and, on the 2nd floor, local and regional music. The *Guide* (see p419) is sold here. Also sells tickets for some of Lebanon's festivals (such as the Beiteddine Festival).

Emergency
Ambulance (☎ 140)
Fire brigade (☎ 175)
Police (☎ 112)
Tourist police (☎ 350 901)

Internet Access

There's no shortage of Internet cafés in Beirut.

Pass Par Tout (Map p422; ☎ 367 149; Rue Omar ben Abdel Aziz, Ras Beirut; per 30min LL1500; ☽ 11am-2am)

LEBANON

BEIRUT

Ⓐ   **Ⓑ**   **Ⓒ**   **Ⓓ**

① INFORMATION
Australian Embassy.................(see 1)
UK Embassy..............................**1** D4
Dutch Embassy.........................**2** F4
Egyptian Embassy.....................**3** B5
French Embassy........................**4** F6
General Security Office.............**5** F6
Italian Embassy........................**6** F4
Main Post Office.......................**7** E4
Solidere Information
  Office.....................................**8** E3
Virgin Internet......................(see 9)
Virgin Megastore......................**9** E4

② SIGHTS & ACTIVITIES
Al-Omari Mosque.....................**10** E3
Beirut Luna Park......................**11** A4
Beirut Swimming Club.............**12** C3
Beirut-by-Bike Cycling Club
  Solidere.............................**13** D3
Bicycles Jeep...........................**14** D3
Cardo Maximus.......................**15** E4
Cyclo Sport.............................**16** E4
Espace Starco..........................**17** D3

Grand Serail.............................**18** D4
Hoops Sports Center.............(see 14)
Mohammed al-Amin
  Mosque...............................**19** E4
National Museum.....................**20** F6
Parliament Building..................**21** E4
Planet Discovery......................**22** D3
Ramlet al-Bayda.......................**23** B5
Roman Baths...........................**24** D4
St George's Cathedral..............**25** E4
Sursock Museum......................**26** F4

SLEEPING 🛏
Hotel Albergo..........................**27** E5
Hotel Monroe..........................**28** D3
Lord's Hotel.............................**29** A4
Pension al-Nazih......................**30** E4
Pension Florida.....................(see 31)
Pension Mhanna...................(see 31)
Pensions Home Valery.............**31** C3
Phoenicia Intercontinental.......**32** D3
Regis Hotel..............................**33** C3
Riviera Hotel...........................**34** A3
Talal's New Hotel....................**35** E4

EATING 🍴
Abdel Wahab..........................**36** E5
Al Dente..............................(see 27)
Al-Balad..................................**37** D4
Al-Mijana................................**38** E5
Al-Rawda................................**39** A4
Al-Sultan Brahim.....................**40** D3
Barbar.....................................**41** D4
Bay Rock Café.........................**42** A4
Gemmayzeh Café.....................**43** F4
La Posta Gourmet....................**44** E4
La Tabkha................................**45** F4
Le Chef...................................**46** F4
Le Coffee House......................**47** E5
Le Rouge.................................**48** F4
Le Sushi Bar............................**49** E5
L'O..(see 45)
Manara Palace Café.................**50** A3
Pasta di Casa..........................**51** C3
Pâtisserie Ahmad Aouni Hallab
  & Fils.................................**52** A4
Paul..**53** E5
Tribeca...................................**54** E5
Yabani....................................**55** E5

MEDITERRANEAN SEA

St George
Bay

Corniche

Ave de Paris

Stadium

Ave du Parc

Rue Minet el-Hosn

MINET
AL-HOSN

Rue Ahmad Chaouqi

Rue Ain al-Mreisse

Mosque Ayn
al-Mreisse

AIN AL-MREISSE

Rue Fakhr ed-Dine

American University
of Beirut (AUB)

RAS
BEIRUT

Rue Bliss

Omar ed-Daouk

Rue Riad
el-Solh

Old Lighthouse

HAMRA

Rue Clemenceau

Rue de Rome

Église St Elie

Club Militaire
Central

Rue Hamra

MANARA

Ave du Général de Gaulle

United
Nations
Building

Rue Emile Eddé

See Hamra & Ras Beirut Map (p422)

Rue Spears

Lebanese
American
University

Sanayeh
Public
Garden

Rue Chatila

Rue Madame Curie

Rue Dunant

SANAYEH

Pigeon
Rocks

RAOUCHÉ

VERDUN

Rue Verdun

Rue Mar Elias

Rue Mnear

Rue Selim Salam

Rue Bashir

Blvd Saeb Salam

MAZRAA

SHOPPING 🛍
Maison de l'Artisan..................**68** C3

TRANSPORT
Aeolus Travel..........................**69** F4
Avis.....................................(see 32)
Beirut Pullman Terminal Office..**70** F4
Budget Rent a Car................(see 63)
Buses to Beit Mary &
  Broummana........................**71** F6
Charles Helou Bus Station......(see 70)
Cola Transport Hub.................**72** D6
Europcar..................................**73** C3
Kurban Tours.......................(see 32)

RAMLET
AL-BAYDA

Ave Rafic al-Hariri

UNESCO

Blvd Saeb Salam

Rue de la République

To Saida (42km);
Tyre (80km)

To Beirut International
Airport (5km)

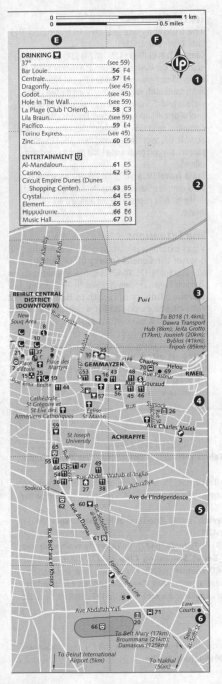

DRINKING 🍸
37°..(see 59)
Bar Louie..56 F4
Centrale..57 E4
Dragonfly...(see 45)
Godot...(see 45)
Hole In The Wall..................................(see 59)
La Plage (Club l'Orient)........................58 C3
Lila Braun...(see 59)
Pacifico...59 E4
Torino Express.....................................(see 45)
Zinc..60 E5

ENTERTAINMENT 🎭
Al-Mandaloun.......................................61 E5
Casino...62 E5
Circuit Empire Dunes (Dunes
   Shopping Center)..............................63 B5
Crystal..64 E5
Element...65 E4
Hippodrome..66 E6
Music Hall...67 D3

Claiming the quickest connections in town, it's also friendly and helpful – albeit rather smoky and dingy.

PC Club (Map p422; ☎ 745 338; Rue Mahatma Gandhi, Hamra; per 30min LL1500; 🕙 9am-5am Mon-Sat, 10am-5am Sun) Popular Internet café that's open later than most.

Virgin Internet (Map pp418-19; ☎ 999 777; 4th fl, Opera Bldg, Place des Martyrs, Downtown; 🕙 10am-midnight Mon-Thu & Sat, 10am-1am Fri, 11am-midnight Sun) At the time of writing, customers had free use of the Internet, and could bring their own laptops.

Web Café (Map p422; ☎ 03-283 456; Rue Khalidy, Hamra; per hr LL4000; 🕙 9am-midnight Mon-Sat, noon-midnight Sun) If you want to check your mail whilst listening to music and sipping a beer (LL3000 to LL4000), then head here. There's also a restaurant.

Laundry

Hotel and dry cleaners can do laundry, but it's expensive (around LL2000 for a small load). There was only one self-service laundromat in Beirut at the time of research.

Laundromatic (Map p422; ☎ 03-376 187; Rue Sidani; load under/over 4.5kg LL3000/4500, detergent free, dryer per 10min LL1500; 🕙 9am-8pm Mon-Sat, 12-4pm Sun) Service wash (extra LL1000) and ironing service (LL1000 per item) also available.

Media

According to the Reporters Sans Frontiers *Worldwide Press Freedom Index 2005*, Lebanon has the freest press in the Middle East. Its daily and weekly newspapers aren't afraid to criticise politicians and their policies, though more sensitive issues (such as the continuing Syrian influence) remain taboo.

There are six Arabic dailies and one weekly; one French daily, **L'Orient Le Jour** (www.lorientlejour.com), and one English daily, the **Daily Star** (www.dailystar.com; LL2000).

The *Guide* (LL5000) is a useful glossy monthly which reviews the latest hotspots (including bars, cafés and restaurants) and details forthcoming gigs, concerts, shows, exhibitions, festivals, and events for kids.

Medical Services

There are several good hospitals with outpatient clinics in Beirut.

American University of Beirut Hospital (Map p422; ☎ 374 374; Rue du Caire, Ras Beirut; 🕙 8am-5pm Mon-Fri except holidays) Considered the best hospital in the Middle East; English and French spoken. If you're at death's door outside hours, head for the Emergency Unit, which is open 24/7; it's on the right-hand side of the

420 BEIRUT •• Information

building as you enter the AUBMC down Rue du Caire. The hospital also provides a current list of pharmacies open 24 hours, and can recommend qualified dentists.

Money

There are ATMs all over the city.

Amir Exchange (Map p422; ☎ 341 265; Rue Hamra, Hamra; ⌚ 8am-8pm Mon-Sat). One of the very few moneychangers accepting travellers cheques (preferably dollars), it charges US$2 to US$3 per US$100. Bring your passport and original purchaser's receipt.

Sogetour (Map p422; ☎ 747 111; www.sogetour.com.lb; 1st fl, Block A, Gefinor Center, Rue Maamari, Ras Beirut; 2% commission; ⌚ 8.30am-4pm Mon-Fri, 8.30am-1pm Sat) The best place to change Amex US-dollar travellers cheques.

Post

Main post office (Map pp418-19; ☎ 629 629; Rue Riad el-Solh, Downtown; ⌚ 8am-5pm Mon-Fri, 8am-1.30pm Sat)

Tourist Information

Tourist Information Office (Map p422; ☎ 343 073; www.lebanon-tourism.gov.lb; ground fl, Ministry of Tourism Bldg, Rue Banque du Liban, Hamra; ⌚ 8am-6pm Mon-Thu, 8am-11am & 1.30-6pm Fri, 8am-1.30pm Sat) Enter from Rue Banque du Liban. Staff are helpful and also give out quite informative brochures (in six European languages). Well worth picking up is the series published in 2005, *Archaeological Promenade*, on Tyre, Sidon, Tripoli, Baalbek and Beiteddine.

Tourist police office (Map p422; ☎ 752 428; fax 343 504; opposite Tourist Information Office; ⌚ 24hr) For complaints or problems (including robbery), contact this office.

Travel Agencies

The following are just two of the many Beiruti travel agencies:

Campus Travel (Map p422; ☎ 744 588; www.campus-travel.net; Rue Makhoul, Ras Beirut) A student travel agency offering discounts (between 5% and 10%) on flights (particularly to Europe, the US and the Gulf) to students (with ISIC cards), young people under 26 (with proof of date of birth) and teachers. Booklets offering discounts of up to 45% on books, clothes, cafés etc are also available. ISIC cards can be bought there (US$11, with passport, passport photo and a letter from your university/college).

Tania Travel (Map p422; ☎ 739 679; www.tania travel.com; Rue Sidani, Hamra; ⌚ 8am-6pm Mon-Sat) On the 1st floor opposite the old Jeanne d'Arc theatre.

Visa Extensions

Visas extensions can be obtained on the 2nd floor of the **General Security Office** (maktab amn al-aam; Map pp418-19; ☎ 429 061; www.general-security.gov.lb; Rue de Damas; ⌚ 8am-2pm Mon-Fri, 8am-1pm Sat), beside the Ministry of Health in Beirut. Tourist visas can be extended for a minimum of one month and a maximum of three months.

Bring two photocopies of passport details (including the original visa) and one passport-sized photo. The procedure generally takes five to seven days for a tourist visa, and between 14 and 20 days for a business visa.

BEIRUT IN...

Two Days

Kick off the day with some caffeine at the **Al-Kahwa café** (p426) before notching the **National Museum** (opposite) on your list of sights.

Try mouthwatering mezze for lunch at **Al-Balad** (p425), then size up startling, sparkling **Solidere** (opposite) and its sights. Later, stroll down the **Corniche** (p422) and sip a sundowner at sunset at the **Bay Rock Café** (p426).

Take tapas and drinks in fashionable **Gemmayzeh** (p428), fine-dine at its **restaurants** (p425), then bar-crawl again or head for **Rue Monot** (p428).

Hit the hangover with breakfast at **Paul** (p427) or **Tribeca** (p427), followed by swimming and sunbathing at **Ramlet al-Bayda** (p422) or the **Beirut Swimming Club** (p422). Later, shop for souvenirs at **Maison de l'Artisan** (p430) or **La CD-Thèque** (p430). For dinner, seek out seafood at **Al-Sultan Brahim** (p425), then bag a bar seat at superslick **Centrale** (p428). For live jazz, head for **Blue Note** (p428), or for live local lutes try **Gemmayzeh Cafe** (p427). Before bed, hit the booming Beiruti institution, **BO18** (p429).

Four Days

On day three take a day trip to **Tyre** (p446). On day four, bus to **Baalbek** (p451) and back, then live it up one last time in **Casino** (p429) or **Al-Mandaloun** (p429).

SURE SAFETY

While Lebanon has seen unrest, demonstrations and political assassination in recent times, there's little reason to be unduly alarmed about travel here. One top tip is to watch the news (as the Lebanese do); events in Israel and the rest of the Middle East can impact fast upon this little country.

DANGERS & ANNOYANCES

The biggest danger – and annoyance – in Beirut is the traffic. Rules both on and off the road are nonexistent, and pedestrians should take particular care when crossing the road.

Don't forget to carry your passport with you at all times. Police checkpoints outside the capital will request them.

SIGHTS & ACTIVITIES

Beirut's sights and activities are spread fairly evenly in a west–east direction, starting from the Corniche, through Hamra and Ras Beirut into the new Downtown area, before jumping south to the National Museum and Hippodrome.

Museums
NATIONAL MUSEUM

Light, bright and well laid out, this excellent **museum** (Map pp418-19; ☎ 612 295/7; www.beirut nationalmuseum.com; cnr Rue de Damas & Ave Abdallah Yafi; adult/student/child LL5000/1000/1000, guide US$15; ☼ 9am-5pm Tue-Sun except some public holidays) has an impressive, but not overwhelming, collection of archaeological artefacts. It gives a great overview of Lebanon's history and the civilisations that made their home here, and is a useful primer before a trip around the country or a neat round-off after one. Explanatory panels and captions in English and French assist. Allow at least an hour.

Highlights include some beautifully observed Phoenician marble statues of baby boys (from Echmoun, 5th century BC), lovely 3rd- and 4th-century-AD mosaics, Byzantine gold jewellery (found in a jar under the floor of a villa in Beirut) and the famous, much-photographed Phoenician gilded bronze figurines from Byblos. A plan is distributed free with tickets.

The museum screens a free 12-minute video in its **theatrette** (ground fl; ☼ every hr 9am-4pm) in English or French on demand, detailing how curators saved the collection during the civil war.

To get there, walk south from Sodeco Sq along Rue de Damas for 15 minutes, or hail a taxi and ask for the Musée or the Hippodrome.

AMERICAN UNIVERSITY OF BEIRUT (AUB) MUSEUM

The **AUB museum** (Map p422; ☎ 340 549; ddc.aub.edu lb/projects/museum/; AUB campus; admission free; ☼ 10am-4pm Mon-Fri except university & public holidays), just inside the university's main gate, was founded in 1868 and is one of the oldest in the Middle East. On display is a collection of Lebanese and Middle Eastern artefacts dating back to the early Stone Age, a fine collection of Phoenician glass and Arab coins from as early as the 5th century BC, and a large collection of pottery dating back to 3000 BC.

SURSOCK MUSEUM

The exhibitions of contemporary Lebanese art vary in quality at this private **museum** (Map pp418-19; ☎ 334 133; Rue Sursock, Achrafiye; admission free; ☼ 10am-1pm & 4-7pm), which opens only when there are exhibitions scheduled (phone first to check). But the area is still worth a wander if only to admire the beautiful Ottoman- and French Mandate–era mansions and the luxurious villas including this one (which is owned by the Sursock family).

Beirut Central District (Downtown/Solidere)

In the 1970s the Beirut Central District (now usually called Downtown or Solidere) was exalted as the Paris of the Middle East. In the 1980s it was the centre of a war zone, and in the 1990s it became the focus of a colossal rebuilding program.

Today, with much of the construction work finished, the spotlessly clean and traffic-free streets are so unlike the rest of the city that it has an almost surreal feel. Indeed, the whole area, though impressive, has been criticised for it Disneyesque flavour, with ersatz Ottoman and French Mandate–era architecture almost indistinguishable from the restored real thing.

Nevertheless, the area has undeniably succeeded and is now an upmarket and fashionable part of the city.

The **Solidere Information Office** (Map pp418-19; ☎ 980 650; www.solidere.com; Bldg 149, Rue Saad Zaghloul; admission free; ⊗ 8.30am-1.30pm & 2.30-6pm Mon-Fri) has well-crafted display models and information panels outlining the redevelopment. Staff can suggest walking-tour routes. At nearby **Place des Martyrs**, take a peek at the before-and-after exhibition of photographs of the area.

If you devise your own walking tour, don't miss the **Al-Omari Mosque** (Map pp418-19), built in the 12th century as the Church of John the Baptist of the Knights Hospitaller and converted into a mosque in 1291, and the new and impressive **Mohammed al-Amin Mosque** (Map pp418-19), which is currently under construction. Funded by the ex-PM

Rafiq Hariri who was largely responsible for the bid to rebuild Downtown (but killed by a car bomb in early 2005), it has a particular place in the heart of Beirutis. **St George's Cathedral** (Map pp418-19; ☎ 561 980; services 7.15am & 6.60pm Mon-Thu & Sat, 9am & 11am Sun) is a Maronite church dating from the Crusades. Well-preserved and well-restored are the **Roman baths** (Map pp418-19) and the **cardo maximus** (Map pp418-19), the evocative remains of a Roman-era market area, and the **Grand Serail**, a majestic Ottoman-era building now housing government offices including the PM's.

Corniche

The Corniche (seafront) is a favourite promenade spot, especially in late afternoon and

HAMRA & RAS BEIRUT

0 _____ 300 m
0 _____ 0.2 miles

INFORMATION		
American University of Beirut	Royal Garden Hotel..............20 C4	Chez André.........................32 C4
Hospital............................1 D3	Seaside Furnished Flats..........21 D2	De Prague..........................33 C4
Amir Exchange.....................2 C4	University Hotel.................22 C3	Pickwick Pub..................(see 19)
Books & Pens.......................3 B3		
Campus Travel......................4 C3	EATING 🍴	ENTERTAINMENT 🎭
Gefinor Center......................5 D3	Al-Kahwa..........................23 B3	Théâre al-Medina..............34 D4
Laundromatic.......................6 B3	Barbar.............................24 C4	
Librairie Antoine...................7 B4	Bliss House........................25 C3	SHOPPING 🛍
Naufal Booksellers.................8 C3	Casablanca.........................26 D2	La CD-Thèque.....................35 C3
Pass Par Tout.......................9 C3	Co-op.............................27 B4	Nargileh Seller....................36 B4
PC Club.............................10 B3	Idriss Supermarket................28 C3	Yahya Express Photofinishing
Sogetour...........................11 D3	Pepita..............................29 C2	Specialist.........................37 C4
Tania Travel........................12 B3	Snack Hamadeh.....................30 D4	
Tourist Information Office		TRANSPORT
(Ministry of Tourism)........13 D4	DRINKING 🍸	City Car...........................38 A4
Tourist Police Office........(see 13)	Blue Note..........................31 C3	Middle East Airlines........(see 11)
Web Café...........................14 B3		
SIGHTS & ACTIVITIES		
American Language Center.......15 C3		
American University of Beirut....16 B2		
AUB Museum........................17 C3		
SLEEPING 🛏		
Cedarland Hotel...................18 C3		
Marble Tower Hotel................19 B3		

RAS BEIRUT

MEDITERRANEAN SEA

Ave de Paris

Stadium

American University of Beirut (AUB)

AIN AL-MREISSE

Rue George Post

Rue Van Dyck

Rue Rustom Bacha

Rue Omar ed-Daouk

AUB Main Gate

Rue Bliss

Rue Khalidy

Rue Makhoul

Rue Clemenceau

Rue Sidani

Rue Maamari

HAMRA

Rue Adonis

Rue Tannoukhiyine

Rue de Kuwait

Rue Makdissi

Rue Souraty

Rue de Rome

Rue Hamra

Rue Labban

Hamra Mosque

Rue Baalbek

Eglise Sts Pierre & Paul

Rue Banque du Liban

Rue Emile Eddé

Eglise Catholique St François

Rue Spears

Sanayeh Public Garden

THE NEW BEIRUT

The rebuilding of Beirut's Central District is one of the largest and most ambitious urban redevelopment projects in the world. This area was blown to pieces in the civil war and its rebuilding is not just practical but also strongly symbolic. The project covers 1.8 million sq metres of land, plus over 608,000 sq metres reclaimed from the sea.

Phase One saw the arrival of upmarket shops and some of the hippest restaurants and cafés in town. Phase Two, under way at the time of writing, involves a new marina and building on reclaimed land.

A bonus has been the unearthing of many archaeological finds issuing from just about every period of Beirut's history.

early evening (in time for the sunset) and on weekends. This is Beirut at its best – a few hours of people-watching here will be one of the best things you do in Lebanon.

If you fancy a dip, the only public beach is the rather litter-strewn and predominantly male **Ramlet al-Bayda** (Map pp418–19), the strips of sand fringing this part of town, from which it gets its name. A better option is one of the many private beach clubs. Though they're less about swimming and more about seeing and being seen, they're convenient, well equipped (many with pleasant pools, bars, snack bars, dressing areas etc) and well maintained. The **Beirut Swimming Club** (Map pp418-19; ☎ 365 999; Corniche, Ain al-Mreisse; adult/child Sun-Thu LL15,000/10,000, Fri & Sat LL20,000/10,000; �%8am-7pm) has a lovely pool and terrace directly above the seafront.

BEIRUT FOR CHILDREN

Beirut and the Beirutis welcome children and there are numerous activities for them. *Family Fun in Lebanon* (LL18,000), by Charlotte Hamaoui and Sylvia Palamoudian, is a useful guide.

The **Espace Starco** (Map pp418-19; Downtown) area has a **fun park** (admission free, rides LL3000-5000; �%erratic, usually noon-7pm) with activities including go-carts, pony riding and a trampoline. In the park's far eastern corner you can hire decent-quality children's (and adults') bikes from **Bicycles Jeep** (Map pp418-19; ☎ 03-539 603; �%3-10pm Mon-Sat, 9am-10pm Sun) and, opposite, the excellent **Beirut-by-Bike**

Cycling Club Solidere (Map pp418-19; ☎ 03-435 524; jawadsbeity@hotmail.com; �%8am-8pm), which occasionally organises bike-gymkhanas for kids. Bikes in both places cost LL4000 per hour, or US$10/30/70 per day/week/month. In 2007 the company will probably move to another location in Solidere. Behind Bicycle Jeeps is **Hoops Sports Center** (Map pp418-19; ☎ 371 713), which offers various ball sports. **Beirut Luna Park** (Map pp418-19; ☎ 03-889 659; Ave du Général de Gaulle; admission free, rides all LL500; �%10am-midnight) has around 10 different rides plus a big wheel.

Planet Discovery (Map pp418-19; ☎ 980 650; Espace Starco; Rue Omar ed-Daouk; adult & child LL5000; �%9am-3pm Mon-Thu, 9am-7pm Fri, 10.30am-7pm Sat) is a French-sponsored science museum for children aged three to 15 with a playhouse, toys, puzzles and interactive displays. On some Fridays (at 4pm and 5pm) and Saturdays (3pm, 4pm and 5pm) there are puppet or magic shows (LL5000 on top of admission).

TOURS

Various tour companies including **Kurban Tours** (Map pp418-19; ☎ 01-363 848; www.kurbantravel.com; Phoenicia Intercontinental, Minet al-Hosn; �%8am-6pm Mon-Sat) offer three-hour city tours for around US$22 per person.

The **Beirut-by-Bike Cycling Club Solidere** (left) offers various excellent (free) guided tours by bike including 'Beirut Historical Background' from 7pm to 9pm Tuesday and Thursday, 'Pedal For Fun' (a 15km to 45km day excursion outside Beirut) every second Sunday in the month and 'Ladies on Bikes' from 7pm to 9pm every Thursday.

FESTIVALS & EVENTS

Beirut International Marathon (www.beirutmarathon.org) Held in early October, it includes wheelchair events.
Mid East Film Festival Beirut (www.beirutfilmfoundation.org) Also held in October, showcases films from both Lebanon and the rest of the Middle East.

SLEEPING
Budget

Cheap accommodation isn't easy to find in Beirut. The Ain al-Mreisse is the more pleasant location, but the area around Charles Helou is closer to Rue Monot, one of the city's main nightclub and eating strips.

Pension al-Nazih (Map pp418-19; ☎ 564 868; www.pension-alnazih.8m.com; Rue Chanty; dm/s/d with TV & fan

US$6/10/15, d with bathroom, TV & air-con US$25; 🖥 😸)
Located near the bus station, the hotel is a
friendly, spotless and homely place. Some
rooms have small balconies. There are free
hot showers and laundry facilities (US$3 a
load). To find it, turn off Ave Charles Helou
into Rue Chanty. Lonely Planet has heard
from one female traveller that she was as-
saulted in her room at this pension.

Talal's New Hotel (Map pp418–19; 🕾 562 567;
zsal72tnh@yahoo.com; Ave Charles Helou; dm/s/d/tr some
with private shower & TV, fridge & balcony US$6/14/18/21;
🖥 😸) Though rooms are small, simple
and reasonably clean, the hotel's best assets are its facilities: there's free access to the
kitchen and Internet, free hot showers and
laundry facilities (US$2 per load).

Regis Hotel (Map pp418–19; 🕾 361 845; Rue Khoda
off Rue ibn Sina, Ain al-Mreisse; s/d/tr with bathroom, TV &
fridge US$20/25/30; 😸 🖥) Though next to an
old bomb site and looking a little war-weary
itself, it's a friendly place and the rooms are
pretty clean. Some have access to a large,
common balcony; ask for one with direct
sea views.

Long on the beaten path of Beirut backpackers are four pensions in the same
building, located next to the Wash Me car
wash. To find them, head for the rear of the
building, past some lifts, to Block C where
you'll find more lifts. As they're all much
of a muchness, and rooms are only reasonably clean, they're best reserved for those
on their last Lebanese lira.

Pension Home Valery (Map pp418–19; 🕾 362 169;
homevalery@hotmail.com; 2nd fl, Saab Bldg, Rue Phoenicia off
Rue ibn Sina, Ain al-Mreisse; beds in 2-bed/3-bed dm US$6, s/d
US$8/12; 🖥) is probably the friendliest and best
managed. Guests have free use of the kitchen.
All rooms have fan; the salon has air-con.
Internet access costs LL6000 per hour. On
the 3rd floor is the confusingly same-named
Pension Home Valery (🕾 364 906; pensionvalery3rdflr@
hotmail.com). Prices, facilities and cleanliness are
similar. The **Pension Mhanna** (🕾 365 216; 5th fl) is
slightly cheaper but more basic. The **Pension
Florida** (🕾 374 629; 5th fl; s US$6, d US$13-15, tr US$17)
is not bad either, with its large and pleas-
ant common balcony where you can sleep.
There's also use of the kitchen.

Midrange

Seaside Furnished Flats (Map p422; 🕾 363 200; www
.beirutflats.com; Rue George Post, Ain al-Mreisse; studio
flat with/without TV US$69/49.50; 😸 🅿 🖥) With

an enviable position by the sea, these fully
furnished, one-bedroom flats represent
great value. Rooms are basic but clean and
spacious with a big balcony, fully-equipped
kitchen, bathroom and lounge. Ask for a
sea view (from 3rd to 8th floor). Long-stay
rates are US$750 per month. Internet access
costs LL5000 per hour.

Cedarland Hotel (Map p422; 🕾 340 233; info@
cedarlandhotel.com; Rue Omar ben Abdel Aziz, Hamra; s/d
with bathroom, TV & fridge US$37/42, ste US$53-150;
breakfast US$5; 😸) A reasonably priced and
friendly spot; rooms here are light and
pleasant and have access to a kitchenette
(on each floor) and a washing machine. Ask
for a room with balcony with side views
(3rd floor and above).

Marble Tower Hotel (Map p422; 🕾 354 586, 346
260; www.marbletower.com.lb; Rue Makdissi, Hamra; s/d
with bathroom, TV & buffet breakfast US$55/66, ste US$100-
120; 😸) Well named for its miles of mar-
ble, the hotel is most popular for its central
Hamra location. Recently renovated rooms
are attractive and comfy and represent great
value; rooms at the back don't have balconies, but are quieter. Attached to the hotel
is the Pickwick Pub (admission free, open
4pm to 4am), which also serves food.

University Hotel (Map p422; 🕾 365 390; www.uni
versity-hotel.net; 19 Rue Bliss, Ras Beirut; s with bathroom,
TV & minibar US$25-30, d with bathroom, TV & minibar
US$35-40; 😸) Diagonally opposite the AUB
(just off the street, above McDonald's), this
hotel is a popular student choice. Rooms
are small but very clean and good value. Fif-
teen rooms have balconies with sea views.

Royal Garden Hotel (Map p422; 🕾 350 010;
rogarden@dm.net.lb; Rue Emile Eddé, Hamra; d with
bathroom US$66; 😸) Although its located on
one of Beirut's busiest streets, its facilities

(swimming pool, health club and bar) make it an attractive option.

Lord's Hotel (Map pp418–19; ☎ 740 382/3; fax 740 385; off Ave du Général de Gaulle, Corniche, Manara; s/d with bathroom TV, fridge & breakfast US$40/50; ✖) Though a little frayed around the edges, the hotel's great location close to the seafront makes it a good summer choice. Prices are modest (though they may soon increase). Ask for a room with direct sea views; we recommend room 408.

Top End

Riviera Hotel (Map pp418–19; ☎ 373 210; www.riviera hotel.com.lb; the Corniche, Manara; s/d with sea views & breakfast US$150/170, with rear views & breakfast US$130/150 plus 10% tax; ✖ ☎ ▢) With the best hotel beach club in Beirut (offering two swimming pools, a diving school, facilities for jet-skiing, water-skiing etc), good restaurants, and room balconies with gorgeous views, this is the place in summer. Nonguests can use the Riviera Yacht Club (adults during week/weekend US$10/13, children US$6/7, open 8am to 8pm between March and mid-October, depending on the weather), with its Olympic-sized pool and children's pool (complete with lifeguards and crèche) both set attractively by the seafront.

Phoenicia Intercontinental (Map pp418–19; ☎ 369 100; www.intercontinental.com; Rue Fakhr ed-Dine, Minet el-Hosn; s US$310-330, d US$490-520, ste US$945-14,000; 1-/3-bed/penthouse apt US$1000/2750/10,000; ☎ ✖ ▢) Long the queen of the pre-civil war days, the Phoenicia's now back with a vengeance. A small escalator helps guest who can't make the red-carpeted stairs. Five high-quality restaurants including Caffè Mondo (Italian), Eau de Vie (French) and Wok Wok (Asian) also reside here.

Hotel Monroe (Map pp418–19; ☎ 371 122; www.mon roebeirut.com; Rue Fakhr ed-Dine, Minet al-Hosn; s/d with bathroom US$150/165, ste US$300-400, plus 10% tax; ☎ ✖ ▢) Hippest on the block is this perfect 1960s recreation. Ask for a room with direct sea views. Unlike many hotels, the Monroe's pool is open year-round.

EATING

Beirutis love to eat out and their capital is famous for its eating establishments. There's a great range of cuisine at a wide variety of places and prices. And almost every month a new places bursts on the scene. The biggest problem is the choice.

Beirutis often dress for dinner and eat quite late (most won't arrive before 9.30pm). Reservations are advised (essential at weekends or during the high season). Most restaurants also do hotel delivery.

Restaurants
LEBANESE/MIDDLE EASTERN

Al-Sultan Brahim (Map pp418–19; ☎ 989 989; Rue Omar ed-Daouk, Downtown; ✓ noon-midnight; ✖) Considered the best fish restaurant in Lebanon, Al-Sultan has been run by the same family for 35 years and has kept its reputation and quality. The menu is small but select; choose your own fish (and method of cooking) from the day's catch as you enter the restaurant. The set menu (lunch/dinner US$35) with its choice of mezze, fish main plus open bar is good value. Choose between the cool and civilised restaurant and the terrace and parasols outside.

Al-Mijana (Map pp418–19; ☎ 328 082; Rue Abdel Wahab el-Inglizi, Achrafiye; ✓ 9am-3.30pm & 7.30pm-midnight; ✖) In the restored house of an aristocrat with a shady, peaceful garden, this old-timer's known for its Lebanese food. If you're looking for a final splurge or a last romantic evening, this might fit the bill. We recommend the three-course set menu (including 11 mezze) plus open bar for US$35.30.

Al-Balad (Map pp418–19; ☎ 985 375, Rue Ahdab, off Place d'Étoile, Downtown; ✓ 11am-midnight Mon-Fri, 11am-1am Sat; ✖) With traditional Lebanese cooking prepared to its own special recipes,

---

THE AUTHOR'S CHOICE

Le Chef (Map pp418–19; ☎ 445 373; Rue Gouraud, Gemmayzeh; 2-course meal LL10,000; ✓ 7am-7pm Mon-Sat) Beloved for years by both locals and visitors to Beirut, this cheap and cheerful place serves up 'good food at good prices in a good atmosphere', as one regular patron put it. Huge plates of home-style Arabic and Western food are served. Daily specials – from couscous to shepherds pie – are listed in French and Arabic but the helpful waiters are always happy to translate or make recommendations; ask for the entertaining waiter Charbel. No credit cards accepted, but there's an ATM nearby. At the time of writing, the restaurant was planning to open in the evenings too.

LEBANON

this is one of the best places for mezze (from LL3300 to LL9900). Try the delicious and slightly spicy red hummus.

Abdel Wahab (Map pp418-19; ☎ 200 552; Rue Abdel Wahab el-Inglizi; Achrafiye; ☾ noon-1am; ✖) This restaurant has an impressive Orientalist-meets-modernist interior and a growing following. The 'set plateaux' (plates) – hors d'oeuvre for LL13,000, or mezze, grill and salad for LL12,000 to LL17,500 – offer value for money. From May to October, the pleasant terrace on the 1st floor opens.

La Tabkha (Map pp418-19; ☎ 579 000; Rue Gouraud, Gemmayzeh; mains with salad LL12,000; ☾ noon-midnight Mon-Sat, 11am-5pm Sun; ✖) One of the best options for vegetarians, there's also an all-you-can-eat veggie 'antipasti' buffet served daily for US$6.50.

ASIAN

Le Sushi Bar (Map pp418-19; ☎ 338 555; Rue Abdel Wahab el-Inglizi, Achrafiye; sushi per 2 pieces LL5000-7000, set menu LL32,500-38,500; ☾ noon-3.30pm & 7-11.30pm; ✖) Credited with the launch of the sushi craze in Beirut, this restaurant has also featured in *Vogue Paris*' feature '100 Best Restaurants in the World'. Decorated 'au japonais' (with bamboo especially imported), its sushi is known for its quality and freshness. The 'Imperial Selection' dishes (such as marinated scallop) are to die for, but so also are the prices (LL17,000 to LL36,000). Reservations for dinner are a must (48 hours ahead on weekends).

Yabani (Map pp418-19; ☎ 211 113; Rue de Damas, Achrafiye; average meal with wine LL65,000, set lunch LL36,300; ☾ 10.30am-3.30pm & 8.30pm-midnight Mon-Sat, 8.30pm-midnight Sun; ✖) Designed by Bernard Khoury, it's innovative, exciting and fun. Guests take the glass elevator down to the restaurant sunk like a bowl in the ground. The sushi is excellent – salmon is flown in twice weekly from Scotland, apparently.

FRENCH

Le Rouge (Map pp418-19; ☎ 442 366; Rue Gouraud, Gemmayzeh; mains from LL9000; pizzas from LL6000; ☾ 10am-11.30pm; ✖) This contemporary-style French restaurant has good bistro food at excellent prices. Reservations advised.

INTERNATIONAL

L'O (Map pp418-19; ☎ 03-199 005; Rue Gouraud, Gemmayzeh; ☾ noon-4pm & 8pm-midnight Mon-Sat, 8pm-midnight Sun; ✖) Cool, contemporary – and

packed – this restaurant has an award-winning chef who offers superb 'fusion cuisine' such as seared duck breast with sweet potato mash and balsamic reduction.

Casablanca (Map p422; ☎ 369 334; Rue Ain al-Mreisse, Ain al-Mreisse; brunch LL28,000, set-menu lunch LL33,000, dinner LL55,000; ☾ 12.30-3.30pm & 8pm-midnight Tue-Sun; ✖) In a renovated Ottoman villa overlooking the Corniche, the restaurant's an old favourite among the well-heeled. The speciality is seafood and its 'international cuisine' is high-class – like its clients. Reserve a table with a sea view. Enter the restaurant from the side street opposite the Lalipco petrol station.

ITALIAN

Al Dente (Map pp418-19; ☎ 202 440, 333 333; 137 Rue Abdel Wahab el-Inglizi, Achrafiye; starters LL11-38,000, mains LL14,500-38,000; ☾ noon-3pm & 8.30-11pm Sun-Fri, 8.30-11pm Sat; ✖) Suitably grand and resplendent as befits its home in the Hotel Albergo, this restaurant has also been called the 'best Italian restaurant in the Middle East'. The food is excellent.

Pasta di Casa (Map pp418-19; ☎ 363 368; Rue Clemenceau, Ras Beirut; mains around LL12,000; ☾ noon-midnight; ✖) With its rafters, checked curtains and tablecloths, you'd be forgiven for thinking you were in Italy. If you're kebabed-out, this family-run place is a good choice. Pasta is homemade. Credit cards are not accepted.

Cafés

Bay Rock Café (Map pp418-19; ☎ 796 700; Ave du Général de Gaulle, Raouché; set 'tourist menu' per person US$16.50; ☾ 7am-3am, summer 24hr; ✖) Spectacularly situated overlooking Pigeon Rocks (one of the icons of Beirut), this café is an essential port of call. Food is on the pricey side but is good quality and fresh. The outdoor terrace is great place for breakfast (from LL4400) or a sundowner. Live music can be heard nightly from midnight to 3am, and belly dancers usually perform from 2am to 2.30am at weekends.

Al-Kahwa (Map p422; ☎ 362 232; Al-Kanater Bldg, Rue Bliss, Ras Beirut; ☾ 9am-1am; ✖) With its Moorish interior, this place combines style and friendliness with decent and well-priced food (Western and Lebanese). It's a popular hangout of AUB students during the day. At night, locals come for a game of backgammon or to smoke a nargileh. If you fancy trying the latter (LL10,000 to LL12,000), this is a great place to do it. There are also veggie options (pizza LL6000, pasta LL8000 and baked potatoes LL3000).

Pepita (Map p422; ☎ 370 096; Ave de Paris, Corniche, Ras Beirut; sundaes LL4000-12,000, milkshakes LL4500, ice creams from LL1000; ⊙ 6am-2am; ⊠) A branch of the famous Tal al-Moulouk, this is a heaven for sweet-tooths. With its spectacular array of pastries, delicious ice cream and a pleasant terrace, it makes the perfect pit stop when walking the length of the Corniche.

Gemmayzeh Cafe (Map pp418-19; ☎ 580 817; Rue Gouraud, Gemmayzeh; beer LL3500-4000, grills LL10,000; ⊙ 24hr except 2-8am Mon; ⊠) Something of a Beiruti institution, the café resembles an old Parisian bistro. Its special attraction is its live Arabic music. Shows (10.30pm to midnight) take place every night except Tuesday.

Tribeca (Map pp418-19; ☎ 339 123; Rue Abdel Wahab el-Inglizi, Achrafiye; ⊙ 7am-1am; ⊠) Beloved by academics and journalists, the cosy but contemporary Tribeca prides itself on its coffee and homemade bagels (LL1250). It's a terrific place for breakfast (serving everything from omelettes to pancakes with peanut butter and jelly).

Paul (Map pp418-19; Ave Georges Haddad, Gemmayzeh; mains LL12,000-26,500; ⊙ 8am-midnight; ⊠) A French franchise and really a restaurant, it's another great place for breakfast with its home-baked croissants and cakes. There's an attractive if rather trafficky little terrace.

Manara Palace Café (Map pp418-19; ☎ 364 949; the Corniche, Manara; mains around LL11,000; ⊙ 24hr; ⊠) With its lovely terrace slap bang on the waterfront and fresh fish at good prices, this is popular with Lebanese families particularly at weekends. There's also a small children's park. At night, from 10pm to 2am, there's live Arabic music (admission free).

Al-Rawda (Map pp418-19; ☎ 743 348; Corniche, Manara; grills LL8500; ⊙ 7.30am-midnight summer, 8am-8pm winter; ⊠) The only place in Beirut with a shaded garden right on the seafront, this is a peaceful and tranquil little haven serving quite good food at reasonable prices.

Le Coffee House (Map pp418-19; ☎ 211 115; Rue Monot; sandwiches & snacks from LL7500, mains LL13,500-26,000, kids menu LL7500-9000; ⊙ 9am-midnight Sun-Thu, 9am to 1am Fri & Sat; ⊠) Located opposite Crystal, with its large and lovely terrace this stylish café is an oasis in madding Monot. Try the 'Compose Your Own Salad' speciality.

Pâtisserie Ahmad Aouni Hallab & Fils (Map pp418-19; ☎ 789 999; Ave du Général de Gaulle, Raouché; cake & ice cream from LL1000-1500; ⊙ 5.30am-11.30pm/1am winter/summer; ⊠) Also recommended, this has a terrace opposite the seafront.

Quick Eats

Barbar (Map p422; Rue Omar ben Abdel Aziz, Hamra; ⊙ 24hr; ⊠) A phenomenally popular chain selling everything from mezze and shwarma to BBQ chicken wings and vegetarian pizza, as well as pastries, ice cream and fantastic fresh juice. There's an indoor seating area. There's also a branch on Rue Spears, Hamra (Map pp418-19, open 24 hours).

Bliss House (Map p422; Rue Bliss, Ras Beirut; ⊙ 7am-5am, ⊠) Cheaper than Barbar, and always packed with AUB students, Bliss has three shop fronts offer decent-quality fast food at good prices including shwarma (LL3000), kebabs (LL3000 to LL3500), fresh juice (LL2000 to LL3250) and ice cream (LL1750 to LL2000).

Snack Hamadeh (Map p422; Rue de Rome, Hamra; ⊙ 7am-7pm Mon-Sat) This tiny family-run food stall does a roaring trade with fat-cat businessmen who seek out the home-baked and delicious Lebanese pizzas (LL250 to LL2000).

Self-Catering

Supermarkets such as **Co-op** (Map p422; ☎ 712 879 Rue Makdissi, Hamra; ⊙ 8am-10pm) and **Idriss Supermarket** (Map p422; ☎ 745 255; Rue Sourati, Hamra; ⊙ 7am-9pm Mon-Sat, 2-9pm Sun) offer a wide range of fresh and quality produce and products (including baby food and infant's dried milk).

At the Co-op, there's also a bread, cheese and patisserie counter and, next door, a liquor store. For a treat or a deluxe picnic, check out **La Posta Gourmet** (Map pp418-19; ☎ 990 707; Rue Gouraud, Gemmayzeh; ⊙ 10am-9pm Mon-Sat), a fabulous Italian delicatessen selling more than 55 varieties of cheese and charcuterie, prepared dishes, olives etc.

DRINKING

Beirut has an embarrassment of riches when it comes to bars. Though numerous, they're not cheap and you'll find yourself paying for the 'after-hour' entertainment dearly. A local beer will generally set you back from LL7000 to LL9000 and a cocktail costs LL9500 to LL14000 or more. Between

LEBANON

7pm and 8pm many bars have happy hour, when drinks are up to 50% cheaper. For more information on the hottest areas to hang out, see opposite).

Achrafiye

Centrale (Map pp418-19; ☎ 915 925; Rue Mar Maroun, Achrafiye; ☾ kitchen 8pm-12.30am, bar 8pm-2am; ☒) Designed by Beiruti architect Bernard Khoury, this is arguably the capital's most stylish place. If you can't afford the excellent French cuisine in its industrial-chic interior, head for the lively barrel-shaped bar on the top floor with its roof that opens. To find it, look for the leafy alleyway near the ruined archway, about 20m east of the Eglise St Maron.

Pacifico (Map pp418-19; Rue Monot, Achrafiye; admission free; ☾ 7pm-1.30/2.30am; ☒) Styling itself on '1920s and '30s Havana after Prohibition', this club prides itself on its food (Cuban-Mexican) and lengthy cocktail list (more than 200 listings) as much as its atmosphere. It's frequented by expats.

Lila Braun (Map pp418-19; Rue Monot, Achrafiye; admission free; ☾ 8pm-2am Mon-Fri, 8pm-4am Sat & Sun; ☒) 'In' at the time of writing and hopping up the hip stakes is this well-designed '80s-style bar. The entrance is opposite Pacífico, through an unmarked hallway.

37° (Map pp418-19; Rue Monot, Achrafiye; ☾ 7pm-3am; ☒) Less pretentious and very popular with students and graduates for its bargain beers (LL5000), this pub gives students with an ISIC card a 20% discount on drinks. It's a few metres down from Lila Braun.

Hole In The Wall (Map pp418-19; Rue Monot, Achrafiye; beer LL5000; ☾ 6pm-2/3am; ☒) Particularly popular with expats, this place has been described as 'an unofficial tourist office with alcohol'!

Corniche

La Plage (Map pp418-19; Corniche, Ain al-Mreisse; beer from LL4500; ☾ 10am-midnight Apr-Sep; ☒) Though not cheap, this is a great place for a sundowner either in the Orientalist interior or outside on the terraces (amid the boats, cigars and yachting shoes). Part of the Club l'Orient, eating here entitles you to free use of the Beirut Swimming Club next door.

Gemmayzeh

The following bars are all cheek-by-jowl along Rue Gouraud in the newly fashionable

quarter of Gemmayzeh. Beer (from LL4000) spirits (from LL7000) and cocktails (from LL9500) are no bargain, but there's usually a 'happy hour' from 5pm to 8pm.

Bar Louie (Map pp418-19; admission free, with live band LL8000; ☾ 11am-2.30am; ☒) Has a particularly lively atmosphere and plays jazz, Latin and Blues music. Bands usually play five times a week (not Wednesdays and Saturdays) from 10pm to 12.30am.

Also recommended are **Dragonfly** (Map pp418-19; ☾ noon-1am Mon-Sat), **Torino Express** (Map pp418-19; ☾ 8am-2am Mon-Sat) and **Godot** (Map pp418-19; ☾ 8am-2am Mon-Fri).

Hamra

Blue Note (Map p422; ☎ 743 857; Rue Makhoul, Hamra; ☾ noon-1am Mon-Sat; ☒) A restaurant-cum-jazz bar plastered with photos of musicians who've performed here, this is one of the best places to hear jazz and blues in Lebanon. Local – and sometimes international – bands perform at least every Thursday, Friday and Saturday. Admission (LL8800 for local bands; LL19,800 for international) is only charged on evenings when music is live. Beer costs upwards of LL4290 and wine/cocktails will set you back LL9350 or more. Reserve at weekends.

Chez André (Map p422; Rue Hamra, Hamra; admission free; ☾ 8am-4am Mon-Sat) A favourite watering hole of the international set of the '70s, this tiny bar is something of an institution and is much beloved by local academics, artists and journalists. Try the house speciality: a dark and dangerous cocktail called 'Dracula'. It's inside the arcade on Rue Hamra.

De Prague (Map p422; Rue Makdissi, Hamra; admission free; ☾ noon-1am Mon-Sat; ☒) Relatively new to the scene, this place is cool but also laid-back and friendly.

Sodeco

Zinc (Map pp418-19; Rue Seifeddine al-Khatib, Sodeco; beer LL8000; ☾ 8.30pm–2am Mon-Sat; ☒) Another popular restaurant-cum-bar-cum-club set in an old Ottoman house; the atmosphere is friendlier than some, and there's a pleasant outdoor garden.

ENTERTAINMENT

Beirut now claims to be the party capital of the Middle East. A visit may well convince you and a night on the town is not to be missed. The typical Beiruti night out consists of a dinner with friends at a good restaurant (with optional apéritif at the restaurant or elsewhere beforehand) from around 9.30pm to 11pm, followed by some bar hopping to around 1am or 2am, followed by a stint at an 'after hours' nightclub such as BO18, which should take you nicely to breakfast! During the summer months, the vibrant Maameltein nightclub strip in Jounieh 21km north of Beirut jerks into life. The *Guide* should keep you in the loop.

Many clubs also serve as restaurants and bars. Beirutis like to come to eat at these places between 9pm and 11pm, then get up to drink and dance (when the tables are cleared away). If you want to eat also, a reservation is essential; otherwise you can just turn up for a drink at the bar. Generally the music matches the moment: soft music for the diners, gradually vamped up in readiness for the full-on dance music after midnight. Note that the dress code is smart.

Nightclubs

Element (Map pp418-19; ☎ 212 100; cnr Rue Université St Joseph & Rue de Damas, Achrafiye; admission free, beer LL7800; ☾ 8.30pm-4am; ☒) Designed like an underground bunker, the look is industrial-chic. Though it's one of the top spots, drinks aren't prohibitive and the atmosphere is still friendly and fun. Locals in the know come on Sunday; at weekends it's heaving. Under-21s are not permitted entry.

THE AUTHOR'S CHOICE

BO18 (Map pp418-19; ☎ 580 018; Beirut-Jounieh Hwy, La Quarantaine; admission free, beer LL11,000; ☾ 9pm-5am or later) Next to Forum de Beyrouth, just past the old train station, this is the most famous nightclub in Lebanon. Designed by Lebanese architect Bernard Khoury, it looks more like a bomb shelter than a nightclub. Its roof opens through an ingenious system of truck hydraulics, and seats fold away to form tables on which to dance. It lies about 1.5km from the edge of Downtown; a taxi will take you there for LL10,000 to LL15,000. It's an 'after hours place': most people come from 2am onwards. Uniquely, no food is served and bookings are not accepted. The clientele's age range is generally 18 to 30.

Crystal (Map pp418-19; ☎ 332 523; 243 Rue Monot, Achrafiye; admission free, beer LL12,000; ☾ kitchen 9pm-1am Tue-Sun, bar 9pm-5am; ☒) This is a very popular place that has set its sights firmly on the rich and the very rich, and caters to them with both food and wine (including Petrus for LL5,500,000) but when the tables are cleared the club gets going! Despite an interior that's plush and rather hideous, the music and atmosphere are oh-so-cool and also fun. Peak time is 1am onwards.

Al Mandaloun (Map pp418-19; ☎ 611 411; Rue Seifeddine al-Khatib, Achrafiye; admission free, beer LL18,000; ☾ 9pm-3/4am Mon-Sat; ☒) Popular particularly with a 30-something Arab clientele, this is where the wealthy, the glitzy and the ritzy hang out. Music is mixed Arab and international and from 1.30am live music replaces the DJ. Monday is considered the best night.

Casino (Map pp418-19; ☎ 656 777; Sodeco Sq; admission free, cover charge incl meal & 2 drinks US$45 Fri & Sat; drinks with/without meal LL15,000/12,000, mains LL17,000-30,000; ☾ 11.30pm-5am Tue-Sun; ☒) Another restaurant-cum-nightclub, this was one of the top three hottest places to be seen when we visited.

Cinemas

Circuit Empire Dunes (Map pp418-19; ☎ 792 123; www.circuit-empire.com; Dunes Shopping Center, Rue Verdun, Verdun; tickets afternoon/evening shows LL5500/7500; ☾ 2.30pm, 5pm, 8pm, 10pm; ☒) One of the largest and most modern cinemas.

Theatre

Unfortunately, the old-timer Théâtre de Beyrouth was closed at the time of research.

Théâtre al-Medina (Map p422; ☎ 753010; masmad@cyberia.net.lb; Saroulla Bldg, Rue Hamra, Hamra; tickets depending on seat & performance LL10,000-30,000; top seats extra LL5,000; ☾ 8.30-10/11pm Tue-Sun mid-Sep–end Jul; ☒) The theatre hosts well-staged plays and musicals (some in English and French), concerts and recitals. From September to May, there is sometimes children's theatre; the rest of the year it operates as a cinema. It's found behind the Kabab-Ji restaurant on Rue Hamra. Book at least one day in advance.

Live Music

Music Hall (Map pp418-19; ☎ 361 236; Starco Center, Downtown; admission free, beer LL11,000; ☾ 10.30pm-

LEBANON

3/4am Thu-Sat; 😎) This converted theatre has fabulous and diverse live music shows from 11.30pm (with short breaks when a DJ takes over). The entrance is at the rear of the Starco Center.

Some cafés, bars and nightclubs also put on live music. See p426 and p429.

Spectator Sport

Hippodrome (Map pp418-19; ☎ 632 515; Ave Abdallah Yafi; admission LL5000-15,000; 🕑 most weekends) This racing venue is one of the few places you can legally bet in the Middle East; the Lebanese love it.

SHOPPING

Maison de l'Artisan (Map pp418-19; ☎ 368 461; Rue Minet el-Hosn, Ain al-Mreisse) Run by the Ministry of Social Affairs, the house was set up to support local artists, and at the same time guarantee a certain standard. The range of products includes rugs, lanterns, pots, candles, slippers and musical instruments, though few are outstandingly original or of high quality.

Yahya Express Photofinishing Specialist (Map p422; ☎ 735 305; Rue Emile Eddé, Hamra) This shop develops film (LL4000 to LL5000) and also burns CDs of images from a memory card (LL5000).

La CD-Thèque (Map p422; ☎ 746 078; Rue Sourati, Hamra) The newest branch of 'the best music shop in Lebanon' sells a good variety of CDs (US$12 to US$17) including a selection by local artists.

Nargileh Seller (Map p422 ; cnr Rue Antoine Gemayel & Rue Baalbek; 🕑 10am-11pm Mon-Sat, 12-11pm Sun) If you're looking for something beautiful as well as functional, then head for this little specialist shop. To purchase a complete nargileh set costs around LL20,000 to LL90,000.

GETTING THERE & AWAY

For information about transport between Syria and Beirut, see p458.

Buses, minibuses and service taxis to destinations north of Beirut leave from Charles Helou bus station (Map pp418–19) and the Dawra (AKA Dora) transport hub. To the south and southeast they leave from the Cola transport hub. See p461 and the relevant town and city sections for further details.

For information on car hire, see p461.

GETTING AROUND
To/From the Airport

Beirut international airport lies approximately 5km south of Beirut. The red-and-white LCC bus 1 will take you from the airport roundabout (1km from the terminal) to Rue Sadat (off Rue Bliss at western end) in Hamra; bus 5 will take you to Charles Helou bus station. The blue-and-white OCFTC buses 7 and 10 also stop at the airport roundabout en route to the city centre; bus 10 goes to Charles Helou bus station and bus 7 goes to Raouché, from where you can take bus 9 to Hamra. Fares are LL500. The buses operate between 5.30am and 6pm daily and the maximum wait is generally about 10 minutes.

The yellow airport taxis are notoriously expensive, often charging US$25 for the trip into town. It's possible to bargain this down to as little as US$10, but only if the supply of taxis greatly outstrips demand. A cheaper option is to walk 1km to the highway and hail a service taxi into town for LL2000.

From Beirut to the airport, the usual fare is LL10,000 (though they may ask twice this).

Car & Motorcycle

To park, head for the larger supermarkets, shopping malls, restaurants and business centres. Many have underground or valet parking (around LL1500 to LL2000). Street parking is also possible if you can find a spot, but note that if you park in a no-parking zone (signposted), you may be towed away.

Buses

Beirut is well serviced by its network of buses. They operate on a 'hail-and-ride' system: just wave at the driver and the bus will stop. There are no timetables, but buses come frequently in the day, and services stop early in the evening.

The bus routes most useful to travellers are listed below. A trip will almost always cost LL500.

LCC BUSES
No 1 Hamra–Khaldé Rue Sadat (Hamra), Rue Emile Eddé, Hotel Bristol, Rue Verdun, Cola roundabout, Airport roundabout, Kafaat, Khaldé.
No 2 Hamra–Antelias Rue Sadat (Hamra), Rue Emile Eddé, Radio Lebanon, Sassine Sq, Dawra, Antelias.
No 3 Ain al-Mreisse–Dawra Ain al-Mreisse, Club Militaire Central, Raouche, Verdun, Museum, Dawra.

No 4 Wardieh–Sfeir Radio Lebanon, Riad el-Solh Sq, Place des Martyrs, Fouad Chehab, Yessoueieye, Sfeir.
No 5 Charles Helou–Hay as-Saloum Place des Martyrs, Fouad Chehab, Yessoueiye, Airport roundabout, Hay as-Saloum.
No 6 Dawra–Byblos Antelias, Jounieh, Jbail (Byblos).
No 7 Museum–Baabda Museum, Beit Mary, Broummana, Baabda.
No 13 Charles Helou–Cola Place des Martyrs, Riad el-Solh Sq, Cola roundabout.

OCFTC BUSES
No 1 Club Militaire Central–Khaldé Club Militaire Centrale, Unesco, Summerland, Khaldé.
No 4 Dawra–Jounieh Dawra, Dbayé, Kaslik, Jounieh
No 5 Ministry of Information–Sérail Jdeideh Ministry of Information, Sodeco, Bourj Hammoud, Sérail Jdeideh.
No 7 Club Militaire Central–Airport Club Militaire Central, Summerland, Bourj Brajné, Airport.
No 8 Ain al-Mreisse–Sérail Jdeideh Ain al-Mreisse, Charles Helou, Dawra, Sérail Jdeideh.
No 9 Club Militaire Central–Sérail Jdeideh Club Militaire Central, Rue Bliss, Rue Adbel Aziz, Rue Clemenceau, Rue Weygand, Taharis Sq, Sassine Sq, Hayek roundabout, Sérail Jdeideh.
No 10 Charles Helou–Airport Charles Helou, Shatila, Airport roundabout.
No 15 Ain al-Mreisse–Nahr al-Mott Ain al-Mreisse, Raouché, Museum, Nahr al Mott.
No 16 Charles Helou–Cola Charles Helou, Downtown, Cola.
No 23 Club Militaire Central–Dawra Club Militaire Central, Ain al-Mreisse, Charles Helou, Dawra.
No 24 Museum–Hamra Museum, Barbir, Hamra.

Taxi & Service Taxi
Private taxi companies usually have meters and can quote you an approximate fare on the phone. Within Beirut, taxis charge anywhere from LL2000 to LL10,000, depending on your destination.

Service taxis cover the major routes in Beirut. The fare is LL1000 on established routes within the city and LL2000 to outlying suburbs.

AROUND BEIRUT

BEIT MARY & BROUMMANA
بيت مرعي & برومانا
☎ 04
Set in pine forests some 800m above and 17km east of Beirut, Beit Mary offers panoramic views over the capital. The town

dates back to Phoenician times and is home to Roman and Byzantine ruins, including some fine **floor mosaics** in a Byzantine church dating from the 5th century. They lie scattered in the enclosure off the road. Nearby and also worth a visit is the 17th-century Maronite monastery of **Deir al-Qalaa**, built on top of the hill with the remains of a Roman temple; three very large columns can be viewed around the back.

The smart **Al-Bustan Hotel** (☎ 870 400; Beit Mary www.albustanhotel.com; s/d US$210/230; ste US$250-550 plus 26% tax; ⌨ ☒ P) hosts an annual music and arts festival (p456) from mid-February to mid-March (dates vary).

About 1km northeast of Beit Mary is Broummana, a bustling town full of hotels, eateries, cafés, shops and nightclubs. In summer it's extremely popular with Beirutis escaping the heat of the city and has a carnival-like atmosphere, particularly on weekends.

Near Broumanna there are two exceptionally good restaurants worth a visit in themselves.

Restaurant Mounir (☎ 873 900; Main St; mezze LL5000; grills LL8000; ☻ noon-midnight; ☒) serves food on a pleasant terrace with spectacular views over Beirut and the Mediterranean. Book in advance and request a table with a view. To get here from Broumanna, make your way towards Beit Mary, turn right into the downhill street and follow the 'Mounir' sign to the bottom of the street.

Though its mountain views don't quite match Restaurant Mounir's sea views, **Kasr Fakhredine** (☎ 960 407; mezze average LL4000-5000; grills LL9000-10,000; ☻ 10am-midnight; ☒) outdoes Mounir on the food front. Believed by some to serve the best classic Lebanese food in the country (some of which comes from its own fruit and vegetable garden), it's *the* place to splurge in Lebanon, though prices are very reasonable for the quality. There's also a good wine list. Ask for a table for the window. The large and attractive terrace is open from mid-May to the beginning of October. The restaurant lies off the main road, around 50m beyond the centre of Broumanna if coming from Beirut.

Service taxis from the National Museum or Dawra usually charge LL2000 to either

Beit Mary or Broummana. The LCC bus 7 (LL500, 40 minutes) departs from just east of the museum.

JEITA GROTTO مغارة جعيتا
☎ 09

For many the **Jeita grotto** (☎ 220 841; www.jeita grotto.com; adult/child 4-11 LL18,150/10,175, parking LL2200; ☯ 9am-6pm Mon-Fri, 9am-7pm Sat & Sun Jul-Aug, 9am-6pm Tue-Fri, 9am-7pm Sat & Sun May-Jun & Sep-Oct, 9am-5pm Tue-Sun Nov-April, closed for 4 weeks late Jan-early Feb) is one of the highlights of Lebanon. Even for those spoiled by other cave experiences, this one is impressive. It's well worth a visit.

The award-winning development is well designed, well managed and well looked after. A cable car transports visitors up to the caves where they can wander the cathedral-like Upper Cavern, before watching an informative 20-minute film (9.30am, 1.30pm and 5.30pm in English, 11.30am and 3.30pm in French) and finally enjoying a brief boat ride through the Lower Cavern. A visit (including the film) takes around 1½ hours.

There's a **restaurant** (set combo LL6500; ☯ 9am-5pm/7pm winter/summer) that serves reasonably priced mains (LL12,000) and snacks (pizzas and burgers from LL6500), with a shaded terrace overlooking the river. A snack bar serves sandwiches for LL2000 to LL4000.

Note that for one to three months in winter the Lower Cavern may be closed due to high water levels. Arrive early to avoid the crowds; it's the most visited attraction in Lebanon.

Jeita lies 18km northeast of Beirut. To get there, catch a minibus (LL1000) or LCC 6/OCFTC bus 4 (LL500) from Dawra and ask the driver to drop you at the Jeita turn-off on the Beirut–Jounieh Hwy, where taxis congregate. Negotiate a return price with the driver (who will wait) as taxis from the grotto back to the highway/Dawra are exorbitant (US$10/20). A taxi from Beirut costs LL25,000, a return trip from Jeita (including a 1½ hour wait) will cost US$20 to US$25.

JOUNIEH جونيه
☎ 09 / pop 96,315

Once a sleepy fishing village, Jounieh, 21km north of Beirut, is now a high-rise strip mall hemmed in by the sea on one side and the mountains on the other. Famous as the home of noisy nightclubs and glitzy shops, on summer weekends and nights, half of Beirut's population seems to decamp here and the atmosphere, though crazy, is great fun.

Orientation & Information
The town is roughly divided into three parts: Maamelten, home to most of the nightclubs, the famous casino and some of Lebanon's best restaurants; Centre Ville with its hotels, supermarket and banks; and Kaslik, an upmarket area full of boutiques fleecing the fashionable.

There's no Internet café in Maamelt-ein, only in Kaslik. **Rodolfo** (☎ 636 177; Rue Maameltein, Kaslik; coffee LL2500; pizza LL8000-14,000; ☯ 10am-4am; ☒), the new Italian café-restaurant, has free Internet access if you buy something. No banks in Jounieh change travellers cheques, though they do have ATMs.

Activities
TELEFERIQUE
A **teleferique** (cable car; ☎ 914 324; adult/child return LL7500/3500; ☯ 10am-7pm Tue-Sun autumn & winter, 10am-10pm daily summer) runs from Maameltein up to the mountaintop Basilica of Our Lady of Lebanon. The views are spectacular.

To get there, walk from Centre Ville to the clock-tower roundabout; the teleferique is about 10 minutes further on. It closes in bad weather. Note that operational times change marginally from week to week; ring ahead if necessary. Summer is classed as 24 June to 21 October.

WATER SPORTS
Restaurant al-Bihar (☎ 930 862; Rue Maameltein; ☯ 8am-3am), next to restaurant Makhlouf, offers jet skis (US$80 per hour), water-skiing (US$15 per 15 minutes) and parapenting (US$30 per ride).

Sleeping
BUDGET
Les Jardins du Liban (☎ 224 123; www.jardinsdu liban.com; Rue Maameltein; s/d with bathroom & TV US$35/40; ☒ **P**) Though it lies 150m from the main Jounieh–Beirut road in central Jounieh (follow the lane that leads down

the hill), it's well worth the trek. Homely and comfy, the hotel also represents great value for money.

MIDRANGE

La Medina (☎ 930 875; www.lamedinahotel.com; Rue Maameltein; s/d with bathroom, TV, minibar & breakfast US$60/92; ✖ ☒) Rooms are on the small (and kitsch) side but are reasonably comfortable. Ask for a room with a balcony (which are larger); some – such as Nos 123 to 125 – overlook the pool and the sea. The hotel has two little private sandy beaches, a pool open in the summer (nonguests US$8/5 for adults/children), a restaurant and free Internet access.

Holiday Suites (☎ 933 907; www.holidaysuites .com; Rue Mina; s/d/ste with bathroom from US$65/75/95 plus 19% tax; ☒) Rooms are comfortable and most have lovely balconies with direct sea views. It also has a restaurant and facilities for jet-skiing (US$40 to US$60 per hour).

TOP END

Four Stars Hotel (☎ 855 601; www.thefourstarshotel lebanon.com; Rue Maameltein; s/d/ste with bathroom & breakfast from US$110/154/242; ✖ ☒) This new hotel has three restaurants, a private marina, pool and, soon, diving and watersports facilities. Rooms are comfortable and well furnished; those with direct sea views are more expensive. Nonguests can use the pool (open mid-May to mid-September) for US$15/7 per adult/child at weekends and US$10/5 on weekdays. Towels/deckchairs are US$2/7.

Eating

Chez Sami (☎ 910 520; Rue Maameltein; 500g fish LL24,000-37,000, meals excl drinks US$30; ✖ noon-midnight) Considered one of the best seafood restaurants in Lebanon, it's simple but stylish and offers great seaside views and a lovely terrace (open in summer). There's no fish menu, you just pick what you fancy directly from the day's catch as you come in. A plate of fresh fried calamari/crab costs LL12,000/17,000.

Manuella Restaurant (☎ 832 480; Rue Maameltein; mezze LL3000-7300, seafood LL44,000-55,000, grills LL9000; ✖ noon-3am) Though the restaurant's rather kitsch (head for the conservatory-cum-terrace at the back), the food makes up for the décor.

Makhlouf (☎ 645 192; Rue Maameltein; shwarma LL3500, mains LL11,000, large fresh juice from LL3000, all plus 10% tax; ✖ 24hr) A branch of the popular Lebanese chain, it's always packed with locals and has a lovely shaded outdoor terrace right above the sea. Food is simple but fresh and tasty.

For sushi, try **Sushi Bento** (☎ 919 193; Rue Maameltein; sushi LL1500-2750, set menus LL16,000-28,000, noodle dishes from LL5000; ✖ 11am-11pm; ☒).

A good place to prepare for a beach picnic is **Fahed Supermarket** (☎ 832 705; ✖ 8.30am-8.30pm Mon-Sat, 9am-1.30pm Sun), in downtown Jounieh.

For sweets, you can't go wrong with **Pâtisserie Rafaat Hallab** (☎ 635 531; Rue Maameltein; cakes & ice cream LL1000-1500; ✖ 7am-midnight mid-May–Sep), which sells all the usual deliciously sticky pastries and ice cream.

Entertainment

Jounieh is famous for its nightlife. Your best bet is to walk down Rue Maameltein and choose the bars and nightclubs with the biggest crowds around their entrances. Beware the 'super nightclubs' with tacky dance shows and female escorts.

Casino du Liban (☎ 855 888; www.cdl.com .lb; Rue Maameltein; ✖ slot-machine area noon-5am, gaming rooms 4pm-5am, restaurants 8pm-4am, show 10-11pm Tue-Sat) The most famous nightspot in Jounieh is less glamorous than you might imagine: for the most part it consists of lots of gaming machines and middle-aged couples trying their luck. Guests must be over 21 and wear smart casual gear (no jeans or sports shoes); a suit and tie are required if you want to play the roulette wheels.

Getting There & Away

The OCFTC bus 4 runs from Dawra to Centre Ville, stopping at Kaslik on the way. Also leaving from Dawra is the LCC bus 6 to Byblos, which stops at Maameltein en route. Both services charge LL750 and take approximately 30 to 40 minutes. The trip from Jounieh to Byblos on bus 6 costs LL750 to LL1000. Minibuses to/from Dawra charge LL1000, service taxis LL2000 and private taxis LL10,000 to LL15,000. Taxis to/from Jounieh to Hamra cost LL15,000 during the day and LL20,000 at night. A taxi to Byblos will cost LL10,000 and a service taxi LL2000.

NORTH OF BEIRUT

BYBLOS (JBAIL)   بيبلوس
☎ 09 / pop 20,784

With its ancient port (now a pretty fishing harbour), Roman site, Crusader castle and restored souq, travellers inevitably fall for Byblos. Lying 42km from Beirut, it's a great place to visit overnight or on a day trip.

There's an annual arts festival in Byblos (see p456).

History

Excavations have shown that Byblos (biblical name Gebal) was probably inhabited as early as 7000 years ago. In the 3rd millennium BC it became the most important trading port on the eastern Mediterranean under the Phoenicians. In exchange for gold, alabaster, papyrus rolls and linen, it sent cedar wood and olive oil to Egypt.

The city was renamed Byblos by the Greeks, who ruled from 333 BC. The city was named after the Greek word *bublos*, meaning papyrus, which was shipped from Egypt to Greece via Byblos' port.

The Romans under Pompey took over Byblos in 64 BC, constructing temples, baths, colonnaded streets and public buildings. In AD 1104 the city fell to the Crusaders, who built the castle and moat with stone and columns taken from the Roman temples.

Subsequent centuries under Ottoman and Mamluk rule saw Byblos' international reputation as a trading port wane, as Beirut's waxed. It soon settled into life as the small-time fishing town it is today.

Orientation

The old town stretches from just outside the perimeter of the ruins to the old port and fortified tower. A hotel and restaurants are clustered around the port; the souq is situated just outside the entrance to the ruins.

Information

INTERNET ACCESS
CD Master (☎ 540 032; off Rue Jbail; per hr L2000; ☽ 9am-1am Mon-Sat, 2pm-1am Sun) Directly behind the Standard Chartered Bank on Rue Jbail.

MONEY
Lebanese Inter-Market Company Exchange (☎ 541 623; Rue Jbail; ☽ 8am-6pm Mon-Sat) About 100m

north of Hawaii Cocktail, Juice & Glace on Rue Jbail. Changes travellers cheques and all major currencies (US$5 commission per transaction).

The following banks have ATMs (but none change travellers cheques):
Banque Libanaise pour le Commerce (BLC; ☎ 540 150; Rue Jbail) Can change US dollars or euros.
Byblos Bank (☎ 542 198; Rue Jbail)

POST
Post office (☎ 540 003; Rahban St; ☽ 7.30am-5pm Mon-Fri, 8am-1pm Sat) Look for the Coral Petrol Station on Rue Jbail; it lies around 30m east of the station on a side street. Walk up the hill and it's around 20m on your right, on the 2nd floor.

TOURIST INFORMATION
Tourist office (☎ 540 325; ☽ 9am- 5pm Mon-Sat, 10am-1pm Sun occasionally) Near the souvenir shops just north of the entrance to the archaeological site. Provides free brochures and information on Byblos.

Sights
RUINS
This ancient archaeological site (☎ 540 001; adult/student & child LL6000/1500; ☽ 8am-sunset) is entered through the restored 12th-century Crusader castle that dominates the sturdy 25m-thick city ramparts (which date from the 3rd and 2nd millennia BC). There are some glorious views of Byblos from the castle ramparts and from this vantage point you're also able to get a very clear idea of the layout of the ancient city. Due east of the castle are the remains of the older Persian castle. From the Crusader castle, turn left past the remains of the city gate and follow the path until you reach the Amorite L-shaped Temple of Resheph dating from the third millennium BC. From here, move on to check out the intriguing Obelisk Temple from the early 2nd millennium BC, where offerings of human figures encrusted in gold leaf were discovered (now the famous Phoenician figurines in the National Museum).

Following the path southwest, go past the King's Well, a spring that supplied the city with water until the end of the Hellenistic era, to some of the earliest remains on the site, the early Bronze Age residence, and building foundations, as well as on the left, the enclosures and houses from the chalcolithic period (4th millennium BC) and the Neolithic and chalcolithic huts (4th and 5th millennia BC).

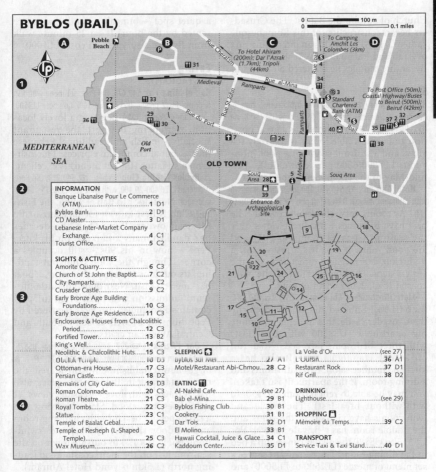

BYBLOS (JBAIL)

MEDITERRANEAN SEA

OLD TOWN

Old Port

Throughout this area, large burial jars were found here containing bodies in the foetal position. Past the better-preserved **Ottoman-era house** and the site of the adjacent **Amorite quarry** is the oldest temple at Byblos, the **Temple of Baalat Gebal** (the Mistress of Byblos) dating from 2800 BC. This was the largest and most important temple constructed at Byblos and was rebuilt a number of times in the two millennia that it survived.

During the Roman period the temple was replaced by a Roman structure and there are the remains of a **Roman colonnade** leading to it. To the northwest of the temple towards the sea is the **Roman theatre**, which has been restored and relocated near the cliff edge, with great views across the sea. Behind this

are nine **royal tombs**, which were cut in vertical shafts deep into the rock in the 2nd millennium BC; some of the sarcophagi found are now housed in the National Museum, including that of King Ahiram, whose sarcophagus has one of the earliest Phoenician alphabet inscriptions in the world.

A one- to two-hour guided tour of the sites (guides speak English, French, Italian, Spanish and German) costs LL20,000 for a group.

CHURCH OF ST JOHN THE BAPTIST (EGLISE ST JEAN MARC)
Diagonally facing the overpriced and underwhelming **Wax Museum** (☎ 540 463; adult/child under 13 LL6000/4000; ♡ 9am-5/6pm) is the

Church of St John the Baptist. The Crusaders began construction of this Romanesque cathedral in AD 1115. It's an interesting mix of Arab and Italian designs. The remains of Byzantine mosaics lie scattered all around.

Sleeping

Byblos Sur Mer (☎ 548 000; www.byblossurmer.com.lb; Rue du Port; s/d with bathroom, TV & balcony US$75/88, ste US$119-136; 🗙 🗷) The hotel has a great position and comfortable rooms with lovely sea views and a seafront swimming pool (nonguests LL8000/6000 per adult/child), open mid-May to the end of September).

Hotel Ahiram (☎ 540 440; ahiram@inco.com.lb; s/d with bathroom, minibar & breakfast plus 10% tax US$40/60; 🗙) As rooms vary, check out several. The best have balconies with direct views over the seafront (such as room No 305) and are good value. It also has a restaurant, a nightclub, a terrace and direct access to the sea via steps. The hotel lies just off the main coastal road, 200m north of town.

Motel/Restaurant Abi-Chmou (☎ /fax 540 484; Nassib Eid Bldg) Situated diagonally opposite the Crusader castle, this motel is really one big apartment (US$200 with breakfast) with three bedrooms (six beds) that run off a large communal area. It also has a kitchen, another salon, two bathrooms and a dining room. If the apartment isn't taken, you may be able to rent a room (US$50/40 with/without breakfast). The triple and twin rooms have views over the ruins and the double room has a private shower. For US$15 to US$20 the owner can set up a bed in the dining room. The restaurant serves a set menu of mezze (LL2500 to LL5000) and main courses (LL7000 to LL18,000).

Camping Amchit Les Colombes (☎ 622 401; Amchit; camp site US$3, 1-/2-person bungalow without air-con US$20, 3-/4-person chalet with/without air-con US$30; 🗙) Lebanon's only camping ground is in Amchit, 3km north of Byblos. Set on a promontory overlooking the sea, it's a pleasant spot with good views and amenities, including hot showers, kitchen with gas burners, and electrical points for caravans (220V). The fully furnished chalets (with kitchen with gas cooker and fridge; same price with or without air-con) and bungalows (tiny and basic A-frame huts with two single beds and a Portaloo-type shower and toilet) are not well maintained, however. Note that this is really a place for Byblos' young to find

a quiet spot – bungalows and chalets are rented by the hour! It's a 25-minute walk from Byblos; a service taxi costs LL1000.

Eating

RESTAURANTS

Bab el-Mina (☎ 540 475; Old Port; set menu with fish & drinks for 2 people US$30 plus 10% tax, beer LL3500; 🕑 11am-midnight; 🗙) Boasting a lovely location overlooking the port, the restaurant specialises in fish and traditional Lebanese mezze, but at competitive prices. The Fisherman's Platter (the set menu) is excellent.

Byblos Fishing Club (Pepés; ☎ 540 213; Old Port; set menus LL26,400-29,400, with wine LL31,350; 🕑 11am-midnight) Next door to Bab el-Mina, the Fishing Club is best known for its charismatic Mexican owner, Pepé. Over the decades he's dandled many a film star on his knee. Pepé – now in his 90s – still occupies a corner. Though the food's not outstanding, its outdoor terrace and eccentric 'boat bar' merit a visit. Next door, the little museum (admission free; open 11am to 5pm) contains Phoenician artefacts recovered by Pepé himself, as well as some South and Central American crafts.

Dar l'Azrak (☎ 737 379; 3-course meal US$25; 🕑 11.30am-midnight/1am winter/summer; 🗙 🅿) A large new establishment considered the best restaurant in Byblos, this place also has terraces with lovely seaside views. It specialises in seafood. Stairs lead down to a small pebbly beach (with changing room and outdoor shower) and natural 'swimming pool'. It's 1.7km outside town on the seafront just off the main coastal road leading north (1.5km beyond Hotel Ahiram).

El Molino (☎ 541 555; Rue du Port; meal with 2 margaritas about LL35,000, beer LL4000; 🕑 noon-midnight Tue-Sun; 🗙) This place offers Mexican food and a fun atmosphere at night; at lunchtime it can be quiet. Some tables have sea views.

Rif Grill (☎ 545 822; off Rue Jbail; burgers LL2500-3500, platters LL12,000; 🕑 11.30am-1.30am; 🗙) Modern, quite stylish and 'in', Rif Grill serves up reasonable Western food for its 20- and 30-something clientele. Burgers, pizzas (LL6000 to LL8000) and salads (around LL4000) are all served.

Cookery (☎ 544 500; Rue al-Mina; 🕑 7.30am-midnight) Popular locally, this recently renovated restaurant has a great selection of delicious sandwiches (LL5000 to LL12,000), pizzas (LL7500 to LL14,000) and mains

(LL8000 to LL16,000). It's probably the best choice for veggies.

L'Oursin (fish plate with drinks US$30-40; 🕑 noon-midnight Apr-Oct) Situated on a jetty on the seafront. Reservations are essential for Saturday night and Sunday midday.

The restaurants at the Byblos Sur Mer hotel include **La Voile d'Or** (mains LL17,000, pasta LL3850-11,000; 🕑 6am-midnight; 🛇), which has a good reputation.

CAFÉS

Al-Nakhil Café (hamburger, fries & Pepsi LL7500; 🕑 9am-midnight summer only) Set on the jetty and also forming part of the Byblos Sur Mer hotel, this place serves tasty fast food at palatable prices – with a pleasant seafront table and parasol thrown into the bargain.

Dar Tois (☎ 330 352; Rue Jbail; cakes & ice cream LL1500-2500; 🕑 6am-10pm) A bright and cheerful patisserie that's a good place for breakfast.

QUICK EATS

There are several good, cheap fast-food places on and around Rue Jbail.

Restaurant Rock (near Byblos Bank, Rue Jbail; felafel & kebabs LL1500-3250, mezze LL3000, beer LL1000; 🕑 8am-1am) Probably the top spot for fast food, this is clean, popular and reasonably priced. It claims to serve the best felafel and kebabs in town.

Kaddoum Center (Rue Jbail; 🕑 8am-2am; 🛇) Next door to Restaurant Rock and more upmarket, it has fruit juices (LL1500 to LL4500) and milkshakes (LL4500) as well as burgers and sandwiches (LL4000 to LL11,000).

Hawaii Cocktail, Juice & Glace (☎ 541 500; Rue Jbail; snacks 2000-5500; 🕑 8am-3am; 🛇) Also good for fruit juices, ice cream and Western snacks such as nachos and chicken wings, it has a large, pleasant terrace overlooking Rue Jbail.

Drinking

Lighthouse (☎ 03-455 718; Port; 🕑 6pm-midnight Tue-Sun) Opening at the time of research, this promises to become a popular pub-bar (also serving food) that transforms itself into a nightclub with DJ after 10pm. It's beside the steps leading up to Bab el-Mina restaurant.

Shopping

Mémoire du Temps (☎ 547 083; www.memoryoftime.com; souq; 🕑 9am-7.30pm) Styling itself as a museum-cum-shop, Mémoire has a stunning collection of fossils (some of which

are not for sale) for US$5 upwards. Certificates of authenticity are supplied. The second Mémoire du Temps at the entry of the souq near Motel/Restaurant Abi-Chmou is a good bookshop that also sells some old artefacts.

Getting There & Away

The service-taxi stand in Byblos is near the Banque Libanaise pour le Commerce. A service taxi to/from Beirut (the hub in Beirut is Dawra) costs LL3000 (about eight services between 7am and 6pm). The LCC bus 6 (LL500, around one hour) and minibuses (LL1000) also leave from Dawra and travel regularly along the coast road between Beirut and Byblos, stopping on Rue Jbail. It's a scenic and very pleasant trip.

TRIPOLI (TRABLOUS) طرابلس
☎ 06 / pop 229,398

Tripoli, 85km north of Beirut, is Lebanon's second largest city and is the main port and trading centre for northern Lebanon. Famous for its medieval Mamluk architecture, including a large souq area considered the best in Lebanon, it's a great point from which to explore the northern part of the country. Tripoli is also famous as the sweets capital of Lebanon. The main speciality is *haliwat al-jibn*, a sweet made from cheese and served with syrup.

History

Like other Phoenician cities along the eastern Mediterranean coast, Tripoli's early expansion reflected its success as a trading post. Its name, taken from the Greek word *tripolis* (three cities), derives from the 8th-century arrival of traders from the three ports of Sidon, Tyre and Arwad (off Tartus in Syria).

Conquered in turn by the Seleucids, Romans, Umayyads, Byzantines and Fatimids, it was invaded by the Crusaders in 1102 and ruled by them for 180 years. In 1289 the Mamluk sultan Qalaun took control and embarked upon an ambitious building programme; many of the mosques, souqs, madrassas and khans in the old city date from both the Crusader and Sultan Qalaun's eras. The Turkish Ottomans took over the city in 1516 and ruled quite peacefully until 1920, when it became part of the French mandate of Greater Lebanon.

LEBANON

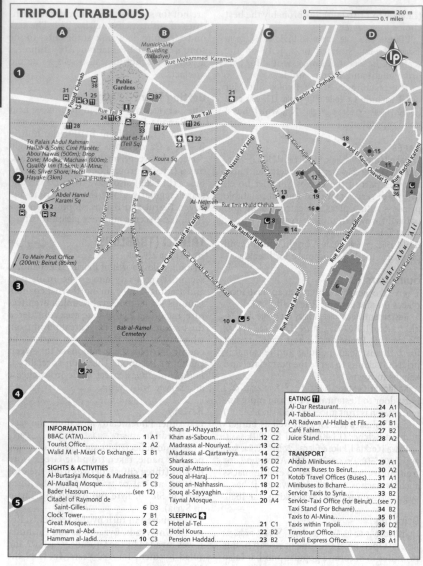

TRIPOLI (TRABLOUS)

INFORMATION		
BBAC (ATM)	1	A1
Tourist Office	2	A2
Walid M el-Masri Co Exchange	3	B1

SIGHTS & ACTIVITIES		
Al-Burtasiya Mosque & Madrassa	4	D2
Al-Muallaq Mosque	5	C3
Bader Hassoun	(see 12)	
Citadel of Raymond de		
Saint-Gilles	6	D3
Clock Tower	7	B1
Great Mosque	8	C2
Hammam al-Abd	9	C2
Hammam al-Jadid	10	C3

Khan al-Khayyatin	11	D2
Khan as-Saboun	12	C2
Madrassa al-Nouriyat	13	C2
Madrassa al-Qartawiyya	14	C2
Sharkass	15	C2
Souq al-Attarin	16	C2
Souq al-Haraj	17	D1
Souq an-Nahhassin	18	D2
Souq al-Sayyaghin	19	C2
Taynal Mosque	20	A4

SLEEPING		
Hotel al-Tel	21	C1
Hotel Koura	22	B2
Pension Haddad	23	B2

EATING		
Al-Dar Restaurant	24	A1
Al-Tabbal	25	A1
AR Radwan Al-Hallab et Fils	26	B1
Café Fahim	27	B2
Juice Stand	28	A2

TRANSPORT		
Ahdab Minibuses	29	A1
Connex Buses to Beirut	30	A2
Kotob Travel Offices (Buses)	31	A1
Minibuses to Bcharré	32	A2
Service Taxis to Syria	33	B2
Service-Taxi Office (for Beirut)	(see 7)	
Taxi Stand (For Bcharré)	34	B2
Taxis to Al-Mina	35	B1
Taxis within Tripoli	36	D2
Transtour Office	37	B1
Tripoli Express Office	38	A1

Orientation

There are two main parts to Tripoli: the city proper, which includes modern Tripoli and the old city; and Al-Mina, the port area, a promontory 3km to its west. The geographical centre of town is Saahat et-Tall (pronounced 'at-tahl'), a large square by the clock tower where you'll find the service taxi and bus stands, as well as most of the cheap hotels.

The old city sprawls east of Saahet et-Tall, while the modern centre is west of the square, along Rue Fouad Chehab. In Al-Mina you'll find the Corniche, shops and some of the city's best restaurants and cafés.

Information

INTERNET ACCESS

There are Internet cafés scattered around the new part of town.

Drop Zone (☎ 03-151 719; City Complex, Rue Riad al-Solh; per hr 10am-2pm LL1000, other times LL2000; 🕑 8.30am-1am/2am; 🔀)

Modka (☎ 423 788; City Complex, off Rue Riad al-Solh; per hr LL1000; 🕑 9am-midnight) Next to Drop Zone but newer and cheaper and with a juice bar serving good fruit juices (LL1000 to LL3000).

MONEY

Most of the large banks have ATMs, such as the BBAC on Rue Tall.

Walid M el-Masri Co Exchange (☎ 430 115; Rue Tall; 🕑 8am-8pm Mon-Sat, 8am-1pm Sun) US-dollar travellers cheques can be changed here for US$2 per cheque (up to a maximum of US$100).

POST

Main post office (Rue Fouad Chehab; 🕑 8am-5pm Mon-Fri, 8am-noon Sat) Around 400m south of Abdel Hamid Karami Sq.

Post office branch (Rue ibn Sina; 🕑 8am-5pm Mon-Fri, 8am-noon Sat) In Al-Mina.

TOURIST INFORMATION

Tourist office (☎ 433 590; www.lebanon-tourism.gov .lb; Abdel Hamid Karami Sq; 🕑 8am-5/6pm winter/ summer Mon-Sat) Staff members are friendly and helpful and speak English and French. English- and French-speaking guides cost US$25/50 for three-hour/full-day tour for one to three people (prices are negotiable).

Sights

If you want to enter the mosques, remember to wear appropriate clothing: legs and arms must be covered and women must also cover their hair. Most mosques have kaftans (gowns) that you can borrow for a small tip. In general, mosques are open from about 10am to 11am/noon, from 1pm to 4.30pm, from 5.15pm to 7pm and from 7.30pm to 9pm (closing for prayer). Leave shoes *inside* the mosque (occasionally petty thieves snatch those left outside), and watch your valuables in the souqs.

THE OLD CITY

Dating from the Mamluk era (14th and 15th centuries), the Old City is a maze of narrow alleys, colourful souqs, hammams, khans, mosques and madrassas. It's a lively and fascinating place where craftspeople, including tailors, jewellers, soap makers and coppersmiths, continue to work as they have done for centuries. The **Souq al-Sayyaghin** (the gold souq), **Souq al-Attarin**, the medieval **Souq al-Haraj** and **Souq an-Nahhassin** (the brass souq) are well worth a wander.

The **Great Mosque**, built on the site of a Crusader cathedral and incorporating some of its features, has a magnificent entrance and minaret. Opposite the mosque's northern entrance is the **Madrassa al-Nouriyat**, which has distinctive black-and-white stonework and a beautiful inlaid mihrab. This madrassa is still in use today. Attached to the east side of the Grand Mosque is the **Madrassa al-Qartawiyya**, converted between 1316 and 1326 from the former St Mary's church. Its elegant black-and-white façade and honeycomb-patterned half-dome above the portal are well worth a look.

You have to look up to see the **Al-Muallaq Mosque**, which is suspended over the street. This simple 14th-century building is a fair distance south of the Grand Mosque and very close to the **Hammam al-Jadid**, the palatial ruin of an 11th-century bathhouse with coloured-glass windows studded in the cupolas that cast shafts of light down into the rooms. A neighbouring **shop** (🕑 9am-5/7pm winter/summer) holds the key.

The **Khan as-Saboun** (Soap Khan) is in the centre of the medina, just off the gold souq. Built in the 16th century, it was first used as an army barracks, though it's been functioning as a market for centuries. In the 18th century, when Tripoli's soap industry was world famous, the khan was at its centre. Today, it's occupied by various shops including **Bader Hassoun** (☎ 03-438 369), which sells soap.

To the west of the Khan as-Saboun is the 300-year-old **Hammam al-Abd** (🕑 8am-11pm), the city's only functioning bathhouse. Unfortunately, it's only open to men – the full treatment costs LL16,000. To find it, turn into the passageway marked 'Sona-Massage'.

One of the most beautiful buildings in the old city is the **Khan al-Khayyatin**, formerly a Crusader hospital during a beautifully restored 14th-century tailors' souq lined with small workshops. To the northwest of the khan is **Khan al-Misriyyin**, which is believed to date from the 14th century when it was used by Egyptian merchants. On the first floor of the dilapidated khan, you can find

Sharkass (Mahmoud al-Sharkass; ☎ 425 857; bar of soap LL1000-3000, boxes of 3 LL4000, 1kg natural/perfumed soap LL6000/8000; ☽ 10am-5/7pm winter/summer). Making soap since 1803, the family produces good-quality, authentic Tripoli soap; you're welcome to look around. Note that the shop is on the 1st floor (not the one with the same name on the ground). Close to the souq is the **Al-Burtasiya Mosque & Madrassa**, with its particularly fine mihrab inside.

To the south of the souqs on the outskirts of the old city, but well worth the walk, is the restored **Taynal Mosque**. This dates from 1336 and has a magnificent inner portal.

CITADEL OF RAYMOND DE SAINT-GILLES

Towering above Tripoli, this **Crusader fortress** (adult/student & child over 10 LL8000/4000; ☽ 8am-sunset) was originally built during the period from AD 1103 to AD 1104. It was burnt down in AD 1297 and partly rebuilt the following century by a Mamluk emir.

The most impressive part of the citadel is the imposing entrance, with its moat and three gateways (one Ottoman, one Mamluk, one Crusader). Guided tours are available and prices depend on group size: generally LL5000/15,000/20,000 for one person/small group/large group.

Sleeping

There's plenty of budget accommodation in Tripoli but almost no midrange or top-end options.

BUDGET

Hotel Koura (☎ /fax 425 451, 03-326 803; off Rue Tall; dm/s US$7/15, d with bathroom & breakfast US$20, s/d with bathroom, air-con & breakfast US$35/40; ✖) This is a spotless small hotel with a central shared lounge run by a charming brother and sister. Rooms are simple but quite well furnished, with decent bathrooms.

Pension Haddad (☎ 03-507 709; www.pension haddad.8m.com; off Rue Tall; dm/s/d with fan US$7/10/15; breakfast/dinner LL3000/6000, laundry per shirt/trousers LL500/1000) A family-run place, its rooms are reasonably clean and cosy and have character even if the paint's peeling and there are only two common bathrooms. Free tea is offered and there's a warm welcome.

Hotel Hayke (☎ 601 311; Rue ibn Sina; s/d/tr with breakfast US$10/20/30) Located in Al-Mina, this is a friendly, family-run hotel offering pretty basic but fairly hygienic rooms (with rather

thin mattresses). The advantage here is the location: ask for a room on the second floor with a sea view. Rooms 7 and 8 have the best views. It's next door to the post office, 150m from the mosque on a road running parallel to the Corniche. The entrance is at the back of the building.

Hotel al-Tel (☎ 628 407; Rue Tall; s/d with fan LL15,000/30,000, d with fan & bathroom LL35,000, d with air-con & bathroom LL45,000; ✖) Quite cosy and with moderately clean rooms, this is an option if the Koura, Haddad or Hayke are full. Six rooms have balconies. TV is available on request.

TOP END

Quality Inn (☎ 211 255; www.qualityinntripoli.com; s/d/ste with bathroom, TV, minibar & breakfast plus 26% tax LL120,000/150,000/225,000; ✖ 🖭) It offers good facilities (three restaurants, two pools, a Jacuzzi and sauna); however, rooms at Quality Inn are comfortable but nothing special. There are no balconies and rooms look on to the exhibition space next door. The pools (nonguests US$10) are open from June to September. Credit cards accepted. The hotel lies beside a fairground located between the old city and Al-Mina, around 1.7km northwest of Abdel Hamid Karami Sq.

Eating

RESTAURANTS

Silver Shore (☎ 601 384; the Corniche, Al-Mina; meals around US$30 plus drinks; ☽ 8am-7pm; ✖) Considered the best seafood restaurant in northern Lebanon, it serves only fish. Try the special-recipe hot sauce dish.

Al-Dar Restaurant (☎ 432 121; Rue Tall; mezze LL2500-5500, mains LL7000-8500; ☽ 9am-7/9pm winter/summer; ✖) This new restaurant in a 19th-century Ottoman house is probably the best place in town for simple but enjoyable and inexpensive food. Upstairs there's a pleasant restaurant, and downstairs a takeaway section (with a few tables) where the food is even cheaper (shwarma/kebabs LL2000).

'46 (☎ 212 223; the Corniche, Al-Mina; mains LL16,500; ☽ 10am-midnight Tue-Sun; ✖) With large windows overlooking the seafront and a nautically themed interior, this place is known for its fish (LL18,000 to LL26,000) as well as its pasta dishes (LL9,000 to 15,000). There's live piano or instrumental music every Saturday night. Credit cards are accepted.

Abou Nawas (☎ 611 412; 1st fl Masri & Kabara Bldg, Nadim al-Jisr St; 3-course meal with half-bottle of wine US$20; ⊗ 10am-midnight Mon-Sat; ✗) Lying diagonally opposite the Ciné Planète Complex, this restaurant is an opulent Orientalist fantasy complete with murals, chandelier and festoon curtains. The food is classic Lebanese and high quality – but at reasonable prices. To find it, look for the stylised red logo outside, which resembles a Chinese lantern. Credit cards are accepted.

Machawi (☎ 433 344; Rue Riad al-Solh; shwarma LL2000, mains LL5000; ⊗ 11am-11pm; ✗) A clean and quite stylish place furnished with its own ovens, it serves simple but excellent food at great prices.

CAFÉS

Palais Abdul Rahman Hallab & Sons (☎ 444 445; Rue Riad al-Solh; coffee from LL1250, juice LL2500, cakes/ice cream from LL1500; ⊗ 5am-midnight; ✗) Founded in 1881, this is probably the best Hallab patisserie in Lebanon and certainly the best place to sample Tripoli's famous sweets. Everything is made on the premises, including the Hallab chocolate and ice cream, and you can visit the vast kitchens and the experimental 'laboratory'. On the 2nd floor there's a restaurant (with set menus for LL6500 to LL12,000 that change daily). Credit cards are accepted.

Café Fahim (☎ 444 516; Rue Tall; coffee/soft drink LL1500, nargileh LL1000-3000; ⊗ 6am-10pm) An atmospheric if rather male-orientated place, with its vaulted interior and local men smoking nargileh and playing backgammon. It's opposite the clock tower.

AR Radwan Al-Hallab et Fils (☎ 444 433; Rue Tall; plate of mixed pastries LL2500; ⊗ 6am-11pm; ✗) Another good patisserie.

There's also a juice stand on Rue Fouad Chehab.

QUICK EATS

There are several fast-food places located around Saahat et-Tall.

Al-Tabbal (Rue Tall; shwarma LL2000; ⊗ 8am-1.30am; ✗) Probably the best fast-food option, it has a menu chalked up in English above the till and clean tables to sit at.

Entertainment

Tripoli is not renowned for its nightlife, but it does have a cinema complex, **Ciné Planète** (☎ 442 471; City Complex, Rue Riad al-Solh; tickets LL5500, half price on Mon & Wed; ⊗ programmes 3pm, 5.30pm, 8pm, 10.30pm; ✗), which shows latest-release English-language movies, with Arabic subtitles.

Getting There & Away

TO/FROM BEIRUT

Three companies run coach services from Beirut to Tripoli (as well as various individually owned microbuses). **Connex** (☎ 611 232; www.connexliban.com) has 20 buses daily (LL2000, 1½ hours via Jounieh and Byblos, 7.30am to 8pm). **Tripoli Express** (☎ 03-327 625) has 17 smaller buses daily (LL2000, 1¼ hours, 7am to 8.30pm) via Jounieh (LL2000, 20 minutes) and Byblos (LL2000, 50 minutes). **Kotob** (☎ 444 986), which runs 10 older buses daily, is the cheapest option and takes longer (LL1500, two hours, every 15 minutes from 5.30am to 6pm), stopping to let passengers off and on at Jounieh (LL1500, 30 minutes), Byblos (LL1500, one hour) and Batroun (LL1500, 1½ hours). All three services leave from Zone C of Charles Helou bus station in Beirut.

From Tripoli, **Connex** (☎ 400 037) runs buses every 10 to 20 minutes to Beirut (LL2000, 1½ hours, 5.30am to 6pm) and express services on 'luxury coaches' (LL2500, 1¼ hours, every hour on the hour 7am to 4pm); **Tripoli Express** (☎ 444 986) runs smaller buses (LL2000, 1½ hours, every 10 to 15 minutes from 5am to 6pm); and **Kotob** (☎ 444 986) service runs between 5am and 5.30pm (LL1000, every 15 minutes) and follows a similar route.

Ahdab (☎ 437 799) runs minibuses from Tripoli to Beirut every 15 minutes from 5am until 8pm (before/after 2pm LL1000/ 1500, 1½ to two hours).

Service taxis leave about every half hour to Beirut (LL1000 between 5am and 4pm, LL1500 between 4pm and 5pm, about 1½ hours) travelling via Jounieh (LL1000 to LL1500, 40 minutes) and leave from just outside the clock tower. For Byblos (LL1000 to LL1500, 30 minutes) take the Beirut bus.

TO BCHARRÉ, CEDARS & BAALBEK

Minibuses from Tripoli to Bcharré (LL2000, 1¼ hours, three to four buses daily between 9am and 5pm) leave from outside the Marco Polo travel agency about 25m from the tourist office on Abdel Hamid Karami Sq. From Bcharré, they leave hourly from

6am until 2pm. For the Cedars, organise a taxi at Bcharré, which costs LL4000.

A service taxi from Tripoli to Bcharré costs LL4000 (from 6am to 5pm daily) and one to the Cedars costs LL10,000; service taxis leave from Al-Koura Sq.

When there is no snow or ice and the mountain road is open, it is possible to take a taxi from Bcharré to Baalbek (around US$50, 1½ hours).

For information on buses from Tripoli to Syria, Turkey, Jordan and Saudi Arabia, see p459.

Getting Around

Service taxis cost LL500 within the old and new parts of Tripoli; LL1000 to outlying parts of the city; and LL500 to LL1000 to Al-Mina. Foreigners are often asked double; try negotiating.

BCHARRÉ   بشرى
☎ 06

The trip to Bcharré takes you through some of the most beautiful scenery in Lebanon. The road winds along the mountainous slopes, continuously gaining in altitude and offering spectacular views of the Qadisha Valley. A Unesco World Heritage site, the valley is home to several old monasteries and hermits' dwellings, and offers good trekking. Villages of red-tile-roofed houses perch atop hills or cling precariously to the mountainsides; the Qadisha River, with its source just below the Cedars, runs along the valley bottom; and Lebanon's highest peak, Qornet as-Sawda (3090m), towers overhead. It's a truly magnificent area.

Bcharré is the main town in the Qadisha Valley. Famous as the birthplace of Khalil Gibran, and the stronghold of the right-wing Maronite Christian Phalange party, it's a very relaxing place to spend a couple of days.

Orientation & Information

The town is dominated by the St Saba Church in the main street. There are a few shops on the main street, as well as the **L'Intime Internet Café** (☎ 03-732 091; per hr LL2000; ☼ 9am-midnight), which is about 20m from the church.

Sights & Activities
GIBRAN MUSEUM

In keeping with his wishes, the famous poet and artist Khalil Gibran (1883–1931) was buried in a 19th-century monastery built into the rocky slopes of a hill overlooking Bcharré. The **museum** (☎ 671 137; adult/student LL3000/2000; ☼ 10am-6pm daily summer, 9am-5pm Tue-Sun winter), which has been set up in this monastery, houses a large collection of Gibran's paintings, drawings and gouaches, and also some of his manuscripts. His coffin is in the monastery's former chapel, which is cut into the rock. The museum is really only for avid fans of Gibran but those who are unfamiliar with the poet but want to get to know his work will appreciate the selection of books for sale.

CEDARS OF BCHARRÉ

From Bcharré it's about a 4km climb along a tortuous road to the last remaining forest of **cedars** (☎ 672 562; suggested donation LL1500-5000; ☼ 9am-6pm May-Oct) in Lebanon, here since biblical times. Known locally as Arz ar-Rab (Cedars of the Lord), they populate the slopes of Jebel Makmel at an altitude of more than 2000m. Once covering most of Lebanon's high summits, the forest has been reduced over the centuries to little more than a small wood. The forest is classified as a national monument; in summer, you can walk through it on marked trails.

A taxi from outside the St Saba Church in Bcharré costs LL10,000/20,000 one way/return (including a one-hour wait). At the time of research, there was also a regular minibus service (leaving every hour from 7am to 7pm from outside the St Saba Church) transporting soldiers back and forth to the Cedars. You can hop on for LL1000. The main entrance to the forest is off the main road opposite the first group of souvenir stalls. There's another entrance on the other side of the forest where there's also the **Restaurant al-Kalaa** (☎ 03-892 856).

SKIING

The skiing season commences around mid-December and ends in March or April, depending on the weather. There are ski-hire shops (full equipment hire US$8) and accommodation in the village below the forest. The resort is slowly developing; three new chair lifts have been built; by the end of 2006 there will be a new gondola and a large hotel, and a whole new skiing area is due to open higher up the mountain at the end of 2008.

Near the Cedars, **Cedar of Lebanon Ski Resort** (☎ 06-678 078; www.cedarsoflebanon.info, www.skileb .com; Sat, Sun & holidays half-/full-day LL25,000/40,000, Mon-Fri LL25,000, child any time LL25,000/18,000; ☺ 8.30am-3pm Mon-Fri, 8.30am-4pm Sat & Sun during ski season) is open in winter for both downhill and cross-country skiing.

QADISHA GROTTO

This small **grotto** (admission LL4000; ☺ caves 8am-6pm summer, closed mid-Dec to mid-May) extends around 500m into the mountain and has some great limestone formations. Though not as extraordinary as Jeita Grotto, its spectacular setting makes it well worth a visit.

The grotto is a 7km walk from Bcharré; follow the signs to the L'Aiglon Hotel and then take the footpath opposite. It's then a 1.5km walk to the grotto. The caves (illuminated) take around 30 to 40 minutes to visit. Occasionally after rain the caves are closed due to dangerous water levels. The small **restaurant** (☺ noon-midnight or later) opens in summer.

Sleeping & Eating

There are just two hotels in Bcharré. At the Cedars of Bcharré, there are more options, of which we recommend Hotel St Bernard.

Hotel St Bernard (☎ 678 100; www.hotelstbernard .com; s/d/ste with bathroom & breakfast US$60/100/120) Designed like a chalet with a cosy log fire in the large lounge, it has comfortable rooms (with balconies on the 1st floor) and there's a good restaurant (mains LL12,000) that has a terrace with views over the forest. The hotel lies off the main road; follow the signs.

Palace Hotel (☎ 671 005; fax 671 460; Bcharré; s with bathroom & TV US$20-30, d/tr with bathroom & TV US$40/48, breakfast US$4.50) Located just below the main road, about 100m west of St Saba Church, the hotel offers very clean, tranquil and good value rooms. Rooms on the 2nd floor have balconies with views over the valley.

Hotel Chbat (☎ 672 672; www.hotelchbat.com; Rue Gibran, Bcharré; s/d/tr with bathroom, TV & breakfast US$50/75/90, apt with salon for 1/2 people summer US$80/ 105, winter US$90/120; ℗) More Swiss-looking than Lebanese this chalet-style hotel has comfortable rooms with balconies. There's also a pool (open from mid-May to mid-September; LL5000 per day for nonguests), a gymnasium, a restaurant (serving home-made food) and a large lounge and terrace.

The owners can propose guided walks through the Qadisha Valley. If you have time, do explore this beautiful valley.

Makhlouf Elie Restaurant (☎ 672 585; Main St, Bcharré; 2-course set menu with coffee & soft drink US$7, sandwich LL2000-3000; ☺ 9am-midnight) The main boon of this restaurant opposite the fire station is its outdoor terrace with great views overlooking the valley. The food is standard Lebanese fast food.

Restaurant River Roc (☎ 671 169; Bchharé; mezze LL2000, grills LL4500-7000; ☺ 10am-1am) Though there's a large and lovely terrace commanding great views of the valley, the food doesn't quite live up to the setting. It lies on the main road to Tripoli about 2km uphill from the centre.

Pâtisserie Ô Delices (☎ 850 784; Bcharré; ☺ 9am-8pm/10pm winter/summer) This family-run patisserie offers around a dozen delicious and inexpensive homemade Lebanese and Western-style cakes (LL1000 to LL2000) as well as fruit juices and ice cream. It lies on the main road 50m east of the village church.

Drinking

La Noche (☎ 671 200; beer LL2000; ☺ 4pm-1am daily mid-Jun–mid-Sep, Fri-Sun winter) The new – and only¹ – pub lies at the bottom of the hill on the road leading up to Hotel Chbat.

Getting There & Away

The bus and service-taxi stop is outside the St Saba Church in the centre of town. Buses/service taxis leave daily from 6/7am to 5pm every hour for Tripoli (LL3000/ 5000, about one hour) and to Beirut via Byblos every hour (LL5000/10,000, about two hours) During the dry season (July to November), you may find a taxi to Baalbek, which costs about US$40.

SOUTH OF BEIRUT

SIDON (SAIDA)   صيدا

☎ 07 / pop 163,554

Sidon is a small port city lying 45km south of Beirut. With Beirut's ever-widening sprawl, it's becoming quite difficult to distinguish the two. Sidon far precedes Beirut, however. Dating back some 6000 years, it was once a prominent and wealthy Phoenician city.

A succession of invaders passed through Sidon's portals, including Persians, Greeks,

Romans, Byzantines, Arabs (who gave it the name Saida), Crusaders and Mamluks. With its attractive Crusader Sea Castle and fine mosques, khans and vaulted souqs, it makes a great day trip from Beirut. Sidon is also famous for its sweets and soap.

Orientation & Information

Saahat an-Nejmeh, a huge roundabout, marks the centre of town. You'll also find the bus and service-taxi stands here. On Rue Riad as-Solh, which runs south off Saahat an-Nejmeh, there are banks and moneychangers. The old city, the harbour, the Sea Castle and the one hotel are west of Saahat an-Nejmeh and Rue Riad as-Solh.

Banque Audi (☎ 720 411; Riad as-Solh; ☼ 8.30am-2pm Mon-Thu, 8.30am-12.30pm Fri, 8.30am-noon Sat) About 300m south of Nejmeh Sq. Has an ATM and can also change travellers cheques.

Bob Net (☎ 03-865 706; Dalaa St; per hr LL1000; ☼ 8.30am-2am) Around 200m from the Dalaa hospital, it's the best Internet café in town (though connections are slow).

Foundation Hariri (☎ 727 344; ☼ 9am-4pm Mon-Sat) Also inside the Khan al-Franja, this proactive organisation gives excellent information on Sidon and Tyre, as well as providing (free) guided tours of the khan (if staff are not busy).

Post office (☎ 722 813; Rue Riad as-Solh; ☼ 8am-5pm Mon-Fri, 8am-noon Sat)

Tourist office (☎ 727 344; ☼ 8.30am-2pm Mon-Sat) Operates inside the Khan Franja.

Sights & Activities

Though Sidon's beaches look pleasant, they are not clean and are probably best avoided.

THE OLD CITY

Old Sidon lies behind the buildings fronting the harbour, just across from the wharf. It's a fascinating labyrinth of vaulted souqs, tiny alleyways and old buildings dating back to the Middle Ages.

In the **souqs** you'll find shops selling everything from electrical appliances to orange water; you'll also see craftspeople – many of whom live above their stalls – at work. You can also get good-quality fruit here at bargain prices (LL500 for a kilogram of tangerines – though you may be asked more).

Highlights include the **Khan al-Franj** (Inn of the Foreigners; admission free), a graceful limestone khan built by Fakhreddine (Fakhr ad-Din al-Maan II) in the 17th century. Beauti-

fully restored, it consists of vaulted galleries surrounding a large rectangular courtyard with a central fountain. Just behind the Khan al-Franj is the **Bab as-Saray Mosque**, the oldest in Sidon, dating from 1201. Unfortunately it was closed to visitors at the time of research. Another gem is the **Palace Debbané** (Al-Moutran St, Souq; admission free; ☼ 9am-6pm Sat-Thu) entered from the souq via a tall staircase marked with a sign. Built in 1721, this former Ottoman aristocrat's building has intricate Mamluk decoration, including tile work and cedar wood ceilings. There are plans to open a Sidon historical museum here in the future.

Further inside the old city is the **Great Mosque al-Omari** (admission free), said to be one of the finest examples of Islamic religious architecture of the 13th century. It was constructed around a church built by the Crusaders. Severely damaged by the Israeli bombings of 1982, it underwent a long restoration.

SEA CASTLE

Erected in the early 13th century by the Crusaders, the **Sea Castle** (Qasr al-Bahr; admission LL4000; ☼ 9am-6pm, closes 4pm winter) sits on a small island that was formerly the site of a temple dedicated to Melkart, the Phoenician Hercules. It is connected to the mainland by an Arab fortified stone bridge. Like many other coastal castles, it was largely destroyed by the Mamluks to prevent the Crusaders returning to the region. Fortunately, Fakhreddine II had it restored in the 17th century. Sometimes freelance guides hang around outside. They charge LL10,000 for four people; negotiate if there are fewer of you.

SOAP MUSEUM

Located in an old soap factory that dates from the 17th century, this **museum** (☎ 733 353; Rue al-Moutran; admission free; ☼ 9am-6pm Sat-Thu) shows that soap can be scintillating!

Sidon (alongside Tripoli) has been famous in the Middle East for its soap since the 17th century. The museum's exhibits and interpretive installations are well done. Look for the fantastic drying towers (where the soap bars are left to dry for up to a year) and the delightful bird-shaped soap moulds. Guides (speaking English and French) give interesting 15- to 20-minute free tours (but you should tip LL5000 to LL10,000). Other features include a 12-minute video with subtitles in English, a good coffee shop and souvenir shop selling Sidon's speciality, *sanioura* (a kind of Middle Eastern shortbread), as well as other delicacies including rose water syrup, Turkish delight and, of course, soap.

Sleeping
BUDGET
At the time of research, budget sleeping options were almost nonexistent in Sidon. However, a new place, Hotel al-Kalaa is expected to open in 2006, diagonally opposite the Sea Castle.

Couvent Latin (Katia; ☎ 03-442 141; Couvent de Terre Sainte et Paroisse Latine; s/d with bathroom US$15/25) Located inside the convent, the little hotel boasts a pleasant open courtyard. Rooms are reasonably clean. The friendly family offers to take guests around the souq. Ask for directions at the Milk Time Café in the souq, which is about 30m from the Soap Museum's souq-side entrance.

Hotel d'Orient (☎ 720 364; Rue Shakrieh, Souq, Old City; dm/s with fan US$5/7, d with fan US$10-12) Grim and grimy, this is really only an option for those on their last Lebanese lira. It lies diagonally opposite the As-Shakrieh Mosque on Rue Shakrieh.

MIDRANGE
Yacoub Hotel (☎ 737 733; www.yacoubhotel.com; btwn Rue al-Moutrah & Rue Shakrieh; s/d with bathroom, TV & breakfast US$30/50, ste with bathroom, TV & breakfast US$60-80) This newly converted 200-year-old building offers spotless, comfortable and attractive rooms at good prices. It's friendly and well managed with a salon where hot drinks can be had. There are two entrances; the easiest to find is from the courtyard opposite the Catholic cathedral of St Nicholas around 150m from the soap museum.

Eating
Palamera (☎ 729 543; Riad as-Solh; pizzas LL6000-9000, pasta LL8000-12,000; �a noon-midnight Tues-Sun; ☒) Serving an eclectic mix of Italian, Chinese and Mexican, this place also has a kind of conservatory at the back that opens in summer. It's about 100m from the Soap Museum.

Rest House (☎ 722 469; mezze LL4000-6000, grills LL12,000; �a noon-10pm) On the seafront, 200m southeast of the Sea Castle (over which it looks), this government-owned restaurant

has indoor and outdoor eating areas and serves good fish, though it's not cheap.

Patisserie Kanaan (☎ 720 271; Rue Riad as-Solh; �a 5.30am-10pm; ☒) This modern, clean and air-conditioned place, just south of the Nejmeh roundabout, has an excellent selection of Arab sweets and ice cream (LL1250 for a cornet). It's great for a coffee (from LL2250), a cake (LL1250) or breakfast.

Patisserie Al-Fardos (☎ 721 878; Nejmeh Sq; �a 5am-10pm) This patisserie is cheaper than Kanaan, with coffee from LL1000 and a good selection of Arab pastries including *sanioura* (LL1000 for six).

There are lots of sandwich stalls and cheap cafés around Saahat an-Nejmeh and the harbour. A good choice is **Abou Rami** (☒ 7.30am-9.15pm Sat-Thu), a felafel shop opposite the Sea Castle which also has some outdoor tables and chairs.

Getting There & Away
TO/FROM BEIRUT
Buses and service taxis from Beirut to Sidon leave from the Cola bus station. To Sidon, OCFTC buses (LL750, one hour, every 10 minutes from 6am to 8pm) leave from the southwest side of the Cola roundabout. **Zantout** (in Beirut ☎ 03 223 414), the best private company for the south, also runs 36 buses daily from 6am to 9pm (LL750, one hour), 14 of which are express (LL1500, 30 minutes). Minibuses (without air-con) to/from Sidon leave every 10 to 15 minutes from 6.30am to 8.30pm and cost LL1000/1500 for day/ evening trips. Service taxis to Sidon, which congregate near the buses, cost LL2500.

Zantout (☎ 722 783) runs regular buses from Sidon to Beirut from 5am to 8pm daily (LL1500, 30 minutes) departing from the Lebanese Transport Office on Saahat an-Nejmeh; OCFTC buses (LL750, one hour, every 10 minutes from 5am to 6.30pm) also leave from here.

TO TYRE
The Zantout bus from Sidon to Tyre (LL750, 45 minutes to one hour, nine to 10 buses from 6am to 7.30pm) leaves from the Lebanese Transport Office at the southern end of the town on Rue Fakhreddine, the continuation of Rue Riad as-Solh, near the Castle of St Louis. A service taxi from Sidon to Tyre costs LL3000 and a minibus (leaving from Saahat an-Nejmeh) costs LL1000.

LEBANON

ECHMOUN

About 4km northeast of Sidon, **Echmoun** (admission free; ⏰ 8.30am-6pm) is Lebanon's only Phoenician site boasting more than mere foundations. There are remains of temples and shops as well as interesting mosaics (though most are damaged).

The temple complex devoted to Echmoun, god of the city of Sidon, was begun in the 7th century BC. Other buildings were added later by the Persians, Romans and Byzantines. The highlight of the site is undoubtedly the throne of Astarte, guarded by winged lions.

From Sidon you can take a taxi (one way/return LL5000/8000), service taxi (LL1000 to LL2000) or minibus (LL500) to the turn-off on the highway at the funfair, then walk the 1.5km to the ruins.

TYRE (SOUR)   صور
☎ 07 / pop 135,204

Famous for its extraordinary Roman ruins (it's a Unesco World Heritage site), Tyre offers much more besides. It has picturesque harbours, fascinating souqs and, according to some, the cleanest beaches in Lebanon – or the least polluted, according to others! It also makes a good base for further exploration of the south. After suffering dreadfully during the civil war and Israeli incursions, Tyre is now showing signs of renewal.

History

Tyre's origins are still under investigation by historians. Herodotus dates it to approximately 2750 BC. Ruled by the Egyptians and then the famous King Hiram (who sent cedar wood and skilled workers to Jerusalem so that the Hebrew King Solomon could build the Temple of Jerusalem) it prospered. Later it was colonised by the Assyrians, Neo-Babylonians, Greeks, Seleucids, Romans, Byzantines, Arabs, Crusaders, Mamluks and Ottomans and lost much of its early prosperity. Today it is home to a number of Palestinian refugee camps, but it is trying to regain its position as one of Lebanon's major cities.

Orientation & Information

The old part of Tyre lies on the peninsula jutting out into the sea. The modern town is on the left-hand side as you arrive from Beirut. Behind the port is the Christian quarter, with its tiny alleys and old houses with shaded courtyards.

There's still no tourist information office in Tyre (though one should open in 2007), but two freelance **guides** (group LL20,000) are usually available at the archaeological sites. Individuals or pairs can negotiate a price. Look also for the very informative guidebook (LL10,000) written by a Lebanese archaeologist, Ali Khalil Badawi, and recently translated into English (and, in the future, French) on offer at the sites. A brochure about the sites is available at the tourist office in Beirut.

Banks with ATMs and the **post office** (☎ 740 565) are near the service-taxi stand in the town centre. Internet cafés include the following:

Alfanet (☎ 347 047; off Rue Abu Deeb; per hr LL1500; ⏰ 10.30am-1am; 🖳) Just north of the main roundabout.

Swiss.Net (☎ 03-446 154; Rue Nabih Berri; per hr LL1000; ⏰ 9am-midnight) Cheaper but a bit slower.

Sights

Tyre's excavated ruins are in three parts. The **Al-Mina Archaeological Site** (Area 1; ☎ 740 115; adult/student/child LL6000/3500/3500; ⏰ 8.30am-30min before sunset) covers a large area leading down to the ancient Egyptian **submerged harbour** created in the 3rd millennium BC. It features a '**mosaic street**' paved with impressive geometrical Roman and Byzantine mosaics. On each side of the street are rows of large columns, made of green marble imported from Greece.

Look out also for the unusually large public **bath** from the 2nd or 3rd century AD and an unusual 4th-century **rectangular arena**, which served as a central meeting place and would have held up to 2000 spectators.

The second site, known as **Area 2**, is a five-minute walk to the north of the first site. On our last visit it was fenced off and closed to the public but it should reopen by mid-2007. You can see the ruins of a **crusader cathedral**, including massive granite columns, from the road.

The **Al-Bass Archaeological Site** (Area 3; ☎ 740 530; adult/student/child LL6000/3500/3500; ⏰ 8.30am-30min before sunset) lies 2km from the Al-Mina site. Just past the entrance is a **funerary complex**, with hundreds of ornate stone and marble sarcophagi from the Roman period lining the road. Some are intricately carved with the names of the occupants or reliefs drawn from the *Iliad*. The Byzantines re-

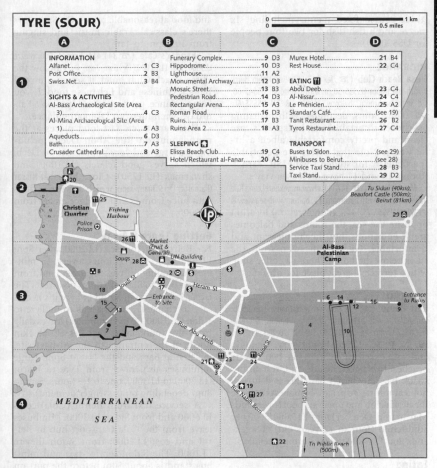

TYRE (SOUR)

0 —————— 1 km
0 —————— 0.5 miles

INFORMATION	
Alfanet	1 C3
Post Office	2 B3
Swiss.Net	3 B4

SIGHTS & ACTIVITIES	
Al-Bass Archaeological Site (Area 3)	4 C3
Al-Mina Archaeological Site (Area 1)	5 A3
Aqueducts	6 D3
Bath	7 A3
Crusader Cathedral	8 A3
Funerary Complex	9 D3
Hippodrome	10 D3
Lighthouse	11 A2
Monumental Archway	12 D3
Mosaic Street	13 B3
Pedestrian Road	14 D3
Rectangular Arena	15 A3
Roman Road	16 D3
Ruins	17 B3
Ruins Area 2	18 A3

SLEEPING	
Elissa Beach Club	19 C4
Hotel/Restaurant al-Fanar	20 A2
Murex Hotel	21 B4
Rest House	22 C4

EATING	
Abou Deeb	23 C4
Al-Nissar	24 C4
Le Phénicien	25 A2
Skandar's Café	(see 19)
Tanit Restaurant	26 B2
Tyros Restaurant	27 C4

TRANSPORT	
Buses to Sidon	(see 29)
Minibuses to Beirut	(see 28)
Service Taxi Stand	28 B3
Taxi Stand	29 D2

used some, etching a quick cross and a new name on them. The well-preserved **Roman road** from the 1st century AD is made of big blocks of paving stone and lined in many parts with marble columns. The road stretches in a straight line for about 1.6km from the impressive 20m-high **monumental archway**, which probably dates from the time of Emperor Hadrian (2nd century AD). To the south of the Roman road and on a raised level is a **pedestrian road** which was originally roofed (arches remain). Further along, there's a U-shaped **hippodrome** built in the 2nd century AD for chariot racing. One of the largest of the Roman period, it could hold more than 20,000 spectators. At the far end of the road, there are the remains of Roman **aqueducts**, parts of which are held up by arcades.

Sleeping
BUDGET
Hotel/Restaurant al-Fanar (☎ 741 111; www.alfanar resort.com; s/d with bathroom & breakfast without sea view US$25/40, with sea view US$35/50; ⚡) With its feet almost in the water, the location is the principal plus here. Run by a charming family, it's also homely, peaceful and welcoming, with rooms that are simple but clean. There are two little terraces, a pub (beer LL3000) in the cellar and, outside, a tiny beach. The restaurant (open from noon to 10pm or later) overlooks the lighthouse and serves homemade food and fish dishes

(three-course fixed menus including six mezze and a fish dish for two/four people for US$30/50).

MIDRANGE

Elissa Beach Club (☎ /fax 347 551; Rue Nabih Berri; s with bathroom US$35-50, d with bathroom US$47-60, s/d with bathroom, balcony, minibar & TV US$55/60; ⊠) The rooms, decorated with matching psychedelic curtains and bedspreads, are clean and pretty comfortable albeit a little weary. Note that prices are negotiable (particularly for students with ISIC cards). Rooms 10 and 11 have direct sea views.

Murex Hotel (☎ 347 111; www.murexhotel.com; Rue Nabih Berri; s/d with bathroom, TV, balcony with sea view & breakfast US$65/75; ⊠) With a central location opposite the sea, the rooms and balconies aren't enormous, but they're pleasant and comfortable. Guests can swim from the steps below the hotel. There's a coffee shop with a terrace; a great place for breakfast.

TOP END

Rest House (☎ 742 000; www.resthouse-tyr.com.lb; Istiraha St; r with bathroom, TV, terrace/balcony & breakfast US$70, with sea view US$90, ste US$120-200 plus 10% tax; ⊠ 🅿 ⊠) Large, bright, airy, tranquil, and with excellent facilities like two private beaches, two pools, health club, restaurant, snack bar and beach bar, this is a luxury hotel at midrange prices. Nonguests can use the beach club and open-air pool (open mid-May to mid-October) for LL15,000/8000 per adult/child (four to 12 years old) at weekends and LL11,000/6000 during weekdays.

Eating

Le Phénicien (☎ 740 564; Old Port; mezze LL3000-5500, fish LL40,000-70,000, beer LL3000; ⊠ noon-11pm winter, noon-2am summer; ⊠) Considered the best in town, its speciality is fish. The pleasant outdoor terrace overlooks the fishing harbour.

Tanit Restaurant (☎ 347 539; mezze LL4000, mains LL15,000, beer LL3000; ⊠ 10am-midnight or later) The atmospheric Tanit is popular with locals for its bar as well as its food, which ranges from mezze to stir-fries and steaks. The restaurant lies around the corner from the fishing harbour.

Tyros Restaurant (☎ 741 027; Rue Nabih Berri; mezze LL4500, grills LL6500-7500, beer LL2500; ⊠ 8am-midnight Mon-Fri, 8am-4am Sat & Sun; ⊠) This enormous, tentlike place is popular with the locals for its great atmosphere, a huge mezze menu

and food at reasonable prices. On Saturdays there's classical Arabic music and singing from 10.30pm to 4am.

Skandar's Café (☎ 344 414; beer LL3000, mezze LL3000, grill LL10,000; ⊠ 6am-2am; ⊠) Below the Elissa Beach Club hotel, it serves a mix of Italian, Chinese and Lebanese food. If you fancy a dance, get here after 11pm on a Saturday, when there's a DJ in attendance.

There are a few fast-food places at the roundabout on Rue Abou Deeb, including the large and very popular Abou Deeb, which serves good felafels (LL1000) and shwarmas (LL1750). Close by is **Al-Nissar** (Ramel St; ⊠ 9.30am-3am), which serves delicious fruit juice from LL2000 and ice cream from LL1000.

Getting There & Away

For Beirut, microbuses (LL2000, after 8pm LL3000, one to 1½ hours, every 15 minutes depending on passenger demand from around 5am to 8om or 10om) go direct. The larger buses stop in Sidon (where it's necessary to change). The first bus from Tyre to Sidon (LL1000, 30 to 45 minutes) leaves daily from the roundabout that lies about 1km north of the entrance to the Al-Bass site, the first at 6am and the last at 8pm. Large minibuses also travel from Tyre to Beirut (LL2000 to LL3000, one to 1½ hours, 5am to 8pm depending on passenger demand).

A service taxi from Beirut (Cola) costs LL6000 and from Sidon LL3000. Minibuses leave from the Cola transport hub in Beirut and cost LL2000; from Sidon they're LL1000. The Sidon service-taxi and minibus stand is about 50m before the port on the northern coastal road.

CHOUF MOUNTAINS   جبال الشوف

These spectacular mountains, southeast of Beirut, are the southernmost part of the Mt Lebanon Range. In places they're wild and beautiful; in others they're dotted with small villages and terraced for easy cultivation.

Information

Reel (☎ 511 195; Deir al-Qamar; per hr LL2000; ⊠ 9am-2am) Provides Internet access.

Sights

BEITEDDINE PALACE (BEIT AD-DIN)   بيت الدين

The main attraction in the Chouf is the **Beiteddine Palace** (Beit ad-Din; ☎ 05-500 077; adult/

student LL7500/5000; 9am-6pm Tue-Sun Apr-Oct, 9am-3.45pm Nov-May), 50km southeast of Beirut. Sitting majestically atop a hill and surrounded by terraced gardens and orchards, the palace was built by Emir Bashir over a period of 30 years, starting in 1788.

Meaning 'House of Faith', it was built over and around a Druze hermitage. During the French mandate it was used for local administration, but after 1930, was declared a historic monument. In 1943 it became the president's summer residence. The palace was extensively damaged during the Israeli invasion; it's estimated that up to 90% of the original contents were lost during this time. When fighting ended in 1984, the palace was taken over by the Druze militia, who ordered its restoration and declared it a 'Palace of the People'. In 1999 the Druze returned it to the government.

Although conceived by Italian architects, the palace incorporates all the traditional forms of Arab architecture. The gate opens on to a 60m-wide courtyard (Dar al-Baraniyyeh) walled on three sides only; the fourth side has great views out over valleys and hills.

A double staircase on the western side leads into a smaller central courtyard (Dar al-Wousta) with a central fountain. Beyond this courtyard is the third – and last – courtyard (Dar al-Harim). This was the centre of the family quarters, which also included a beautiful *hammam* and huge kitchens.

Underneath the Dar al-Wousta and Dar al-Harim are the former stables, now home to an outstanding collection of 5th- and 6th-century **Byzantine mosaics**. Found at Jiyyeh, 30km south of Beirut, they were brought to Beiteddine in 1982. Don't miss them.

In the right-hand wing of the building, there's a **museum** exhibiting Roman and Byzantine artefacts, some guns, jewellery and old clothes.

There's no information available on site so it's worth picking up a free brochure at Beirut's tourist office beforehand. Guided tours are no longer available.

The palace hosts an annual music festival in July (see p456).

DEIR AL-QAMAR   دير القمر
☎ 05

This picturesque town, 5km downhill from Beiteddine, was the seat of Lebanon's emirates during the 17th and 18th centuries.

> **MODERN MYTHS**
>
> Around 2½km from Deir al-Qamar, you'll pass a strange folly in the shape of a castle known as **Musée Moussa** (☎ 500 106; admission LL7500; 8am-5pm winter, 8am-6pm summer). Built in 1945 in response to a seemingly impossible condition of marriage requiring that 'every stone must be different', the unrequited lover built his castle yet never got his queen. Inside are montages showing traditional Lebanese life as well as an extensive collection of armoury.

The main square has some fine examples of Arab architecture, including the **Mosque of Fakhreddine** built in 1493; a **silk khan** built in 1595, now housing the French Cultural Centre; the Municipality housed in an 18th-century palace, which was once a tribunal; and **Fakhreddine's Palace**, built in 1620 and now an underwhelming **wax museum** (☎ 512 777; adult/student LL6000/4000; 8.30am-sunset) featuring Lebanon's historical personalities. Inside there's a **terrace café** (mezze/steak LL3000/12,000; 9am-midnight) and, in the basement in summer, a **disco** (admission free; 8pm-2am).

Sleeping & Eating
BEITEDDINE
There's nowhere to stay in Beiteddine village, and few places to eat.

Mir Amin Palace (☎ 05-501315; www.miraminpalace.com; s/d/junior ste with bathroom, TV & breakfast US$123/155/300 plus 10% tax;) On the hill overlooking both the palace and Beiteddine village is this five-star establishment, built by Emir Bashir for his eldest son. It's one of the most beautifully set, tranquil and luxurious hotels in Lebanon. In the low season (end of September to end of March) discounts of up to 40% are offered, making it a bargain. Internet access is available at LL5000 per hour. If you can't stay here, come for a drink (beer LL4400) or meal (three courses and open bar per adult/child US$25/12.50, open Monday to Saturday). The pool (open from early May to the end of October) is open to nonguests (per adult/child LL15,500/10,100).

Le Moulin (☎ 05-501 050; mezze LL3250-7000, grill LL8000-12,000; 10am-11pm Sun-Fri, Sat 10am-5am summer only;) Around 1.5km from Mir Amin Palace at the base of the hill, this renovated water mill has an attractive vaulted cellarlike

LEBANON

interior and outdoor terrace. On Saturday from 9pm to 3am there's live Arab music.

In the village, there are a couple of fast-food places, such as **Snack Vieux Moulin** (shish kebabs LL3000), open all year.

DEIR AL-QAMAR

There's nowhere to stay in the town itself.

La Bastide (☎ 505 320; bastideir@hotmail.com; d with bathroom & breakfast winter/summer US$50/60) Follow the main road up the hill going east to Beiteddine and, perched just off the main road about 1.5km past the town, is this old house with lovely views from the terrace across to Beiteddine, and comfortable rooms (most with balconies). Drinks and snacks are available.

Al-Midane (☎ 03-763 768; ☽ 10am-10pm winter, 10am-2am or later in summer) With its large terrace right on the main square, this is a great place for a drink (beer LL3000) or a meal (mezze LL3000 to LL7500, grills LL12,000 to LL18,000). The food is a mix of Italian, French and Lebanese. You can also eat inside the stunning 600-year-old vault in the building behind.

Snack Antoun (sandwiches, pizzas & burgers LL3000; ☽ 8.30am-8.30pm) In the little arcade that runs off the road just above the mosque, this place serves snacks and good coffee in a tiny 'garden'. The charming and characterful old proprietor, Mr Antoun, is so pleased to have company (even non-Arab-speaking) he rarely allows customers to pay!

Getting There & Away

If you want to visit Beiteddine, go to the northwest junction of the big roundabout at Cola (look for the derelict building) and ask for the bus to Niha (LL1500, 1½ hours, every hour from 8.15am until early evening). On the bus, tell the driver you're going to Beiteddine; you'll be dropped off at a roundabout with a statue of two soldiers. Take the road opposite the Al-Dalwa restaurant and walk approximately 200m (don't take the first turn right). A bit further on and around a bend is the road leading to the Mir Amin Palace Hotel, and from there it's a short walk downhill to Beiteddine. If this all sounds too complicated, you can pay LL5000 for a service taxi direct from Cola to Beiteddine.

From Beiteddine, it's a 6km downhill walk to Deir al-Qamar. (A service taxi for this trip costs LL2500 to LL3000.)

Travellers wanting to go to Deir al-Qamar first can catch OCFTC bus 18 from Cola to Damour then take a service taxi from Damour (from LL500). A service taxi from Cola to Deir al-Qamar costs LL4000.

To get away, travellers can usually catch one of the buses or service taxis on their way to/from Beirut.

Note that service taxis on the Beirut–Deir al-Qamar route are infrequent, and rare after dark.

BEKAA VALLEY
وادي البقاع

The Bekaa Valley is famous for its magnificent archaeological sites at Baalbek and Aanjar as well as for being the homeland of Hezbollah (Party of God). Heavily cultivated over millennia (it was one of Rome's 'breadbaskets'), it has suffered from both deforestation and soil erosion and now is a relatively deprived area.

The valley's major transport hub is the town of Chtaura, situated on the Beirut–Damascus Hwy.

ZAHLÉ   زحله
☎ 08 / pop 78,145

Zahlé is renowned within Lebanon for its open-air riverside restaurants and general holiday feel. Very busy during the hot weather, it's like a ghost town in winter when most restaurants close. In summer, it makes a nice lunch stop en route from Beirut to Baalbek and is a good base for exploring the valley. Most travellers choose to stay either in Baalbek or in Aanjar.

Information

Most of the town's banks, ATMs and exchange bureaus are on Rue Brazil, the main street. No banks change travellers cheques.

Dataland Internet (☎ 891 009; Rue Brazil; per hr LL2000; ☽ 11am-11pm Mon-Sat, noon-2pm & 5-11pm Sun) Opposite the clock tower. Offers the fastest connections in town.

Post office (☎ 822 127; Rue Brazil) About 750m from highway turn-off, on the right.

Tourist Information Office (☎ 802 566; 3rd fl Chamber of Commerce Bldg; ☽ 8.30am-1.30pm Mon-Sat) Just off Rue Brazil, signposted about 750m from the highway turn-off.

Sleeping & Eating

Hotel Monte Alberto (☎ 810 912; www.monteal
berto.com; s/d with bathroom, TV, balcony & breakfast
US$50/60; 🔌) Located high above town, the
hotel commands amazing views. Its rooms
are simple but spotless and comfortable.
There's a large restaurant (with a rotating
section in the corner) and a lovely summer
terrace landscaped into the mountainside.

Hotel Akl (☎ 820 701; Rue Brazil; s/d US$15/20, s/d
with bathroom US$25/33) Though the character-
filled hotel is dilapidated, rooms are clean
with balconies and loads of light. Rear rooms
overlook the river. Management is friendly.

Grand Hotel Kadri (☎ 813 920; www.grandhotel
kadri.com; Rue Brazil; s/d with bathroom, TV & breakfast
US$105/125 plus 10% tax; 🔌 P) Facilities include
a health club, tennis court, nightclub and
two restaurants but, like all hotels on the
strip, it can be noisy. The swimming pool
(mid-June to mid-September) is open to
nonguests for US$10/5 per adult/child up
to 12 years old.

Arabi Hotel (☎ 821 214; Rue Bardouni; sarabi@inco
.com.lb; d/ste with bathroom, TV, balcony & breakfast Apr-
Oct US$66/132; 🕙 closed Nov-Mar; 🔌) Located on
the Bardouni river at the heart of the outdoor eating scene, its rooms are quite noisy
and rather overpriced. Its terrace restaurant
(meals US$20 to US$40) is famous in Zahlé.

Next door to the Arabi Hotel is the new
restaurant **Mazaj** (☎ 800 800; mains LL9000-16,000;
🕙 noon-midnight Sun & Mon, noon-6am Sat; 🔌) With
two separate menus, one Lebanese and
the other international, it's a good place
for bickering couples unable to agree! We
recommend the mezze. On Saturday from
around 10.30pm to 6am, it transforms into
a club with live music.

Getting There & Away

Only minibuses run from Beirut to Zahlé
(LL3000, around one hour, approximately
every 15 minutes from 4am to 1am) leaving
from the southwest side of the roundabout
at the Cola transport hub. Service taxis
(LL6000) leave from the same spot. Both
will drop you off at the highway turn-off,
which is over 1km from the centre of town
(or for LL1000 extra you can ask the service
taxi to drop you off at the centre).

To get to Baalbek from Zahlé by government bus, take OCFTC bus 4 or 5 (LL500,
30 minutes) from the bus stop just below
the car park midway along Rue Brazil. A

> **VISIT TO THE VINEYARD**
>
> A few kilometres south of Zahlé lies one
> of Lebanon's most prestigious vineyards,
> **Château Ksara** (☎ 813 495; Ksara; admission
> free; 🕙 9am-7pm, 9am-4pm Mon-Sat winter).
> Lebanon's oldest winery was founded by
> the Jesuits in 1857. Underground, a network
> of more than 2km of tunnels was discov-
> ered, dating from Roman times. These nat-
> ural 'cellars' made perfect storage. A visit
> includes a 10-minute film about the winery
> and a tasting of the Château's red, white
> and rosé wines, followed by a short tour
> (in English and French) of the cellars.

service taxi to Baalbek will cost LL2000 and
take around 30 minutes; you'll find one at
the main taxi stand on a square off Rue
Brazil. Minibuses run regularly to Baalbek
(LL2000, 30 minutes) from around 6am
to 11pm from the bus stop; they also run
regularly during the same hours to Beirut
(LL3000 to LL4000, about one hour) and
to Chtaura (LL1000) for Anjar.

BAALBEK   بعلبك

☎ 08 / pop 30,916

Known as the 'Sun City' of the ancient world,
Baalbek is the most impressive ancient site in
Lebanon and arguably the most impressive
Roman site in the Middle East. Its temples,
built on an extravagant scale that outshone
anything in Rome, enjoyed a reputation as
one of the wonders of the world. Today,
the World Heritage–listed site is Lebanon's
number one tourist attraction.

Each July, Lebanon's most famous arts
festival is held here (see p456).

History

The town of Baalbek, 86km northeast of
Beirut, was originally named after the Phoenician god Baal. The Greeks later called it
Heliopolis (City of the Sun), and the Romans made it a major worship site for their
god Jupiter.

Orientation & Information

The ruins lie just off the main Beirut road,
with the Palmyra opposite. The banks, various eateries and Al-Shams Hotel also lie on
Rue Abdel Halim Hajjar. Intersecting with
the latter is Ras al-Ain Blvd, where Pension

Shouman, the service-taxi office and riverside restaurants are found.

Jamal Bank (☎ 370 563; Rue Abdel Halim Hajjar; ⏲ 8.30am-2pm Mon-Thu, 8.30-12.30 Fri, 8.30-noon Sat) Has an ATM and changes travellers cheques.

Network Center (☎ 370 192; off Rue Abdel Halim Hajjar; per hr LL1000; ⏲ 10am-9pm) The only place in town offering Internet access.

Sights

A good time to visit the site of the **ruins** (☎ 370 645; adult LL12,000; ⏲ 8.30am-30min before sunset) is early morning or – even better – late in the afternoon, outside the tour bus time when it's also cooler. Allow a few hours to wander through the museum and the ruins and consider taking food and drink with you;

none is available at the site. Guides speaking English, French, Italian, Spanish or German can be organised at the ticket office and cost US$17 for one to 10 people and US$20 for a group of 11 to 20, for one hour.

In the car park near the ticket office there is a **museum** (admission included with site ticket; same opening hours) housed in a large vaulted tunnel. As well as displaying some beautiful artefacts, there are well-designed, interesting and informative illustrated panels chronicling Baalbek's history through a series of themes. It's well worth a visit.

From the ticket office, you'll enter the ruins via a **forecourt** and monumental staircase leading up to the **propylaeum**. Next to this is the **hexagonal court**, where a raised threshold

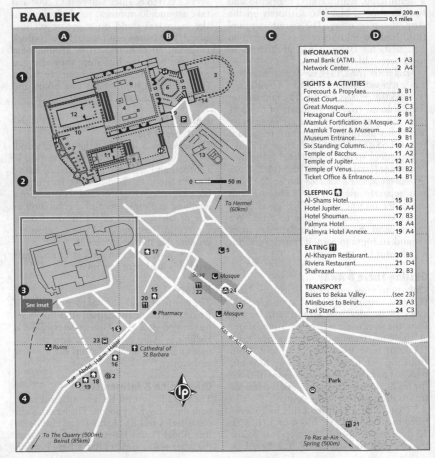

BAALBEK

0 — 200 m
0 — 0.1 miles

0 — 50 m

To Hermel
(60km)

To The Quarry (500m);
Beirut (85km)

To Ras al-Ain
Spring (500m)

See Inset

Souq

Pharmacy

Mosque

Mosque

Ruins

Cathedral of
St Barbara

Park

Ras al-Ain Blvd

Rue Abdel Halim Hajjar

INFORMATION		
Jamal Bank (ATM)	1	A3
Network Center	2	A4

SIGHTS & ACTIVITIES		
Forecourt & Propylaea	3	B1
Great Court	4	B1
Great Mosque	5	C3
Hexagonal Court	6	B1
Mamluk Fortification & Mosque	7	A2
Mamluk Tower & Museum	8	B2
Museum Entrance	9	B1
Six Standing Columns	10	A2
Temple of Bacchus	11	A2
Temple of Jupiter	12	A1
Temple of Venus	13	B2
Ticket Office & Entrance	14	B1

SLEEPING		
Al-Shams Hotel	15	B3
Hotel Jupiter	16	A4
Hotel Shouman	17	B3
Palmyra Hotel	18	A4
Palmyra Hotel Annexe	19	A4

EATING		
Al-Khayam Restaurant	20	B3
Riviera Restaurant	21	D4
Shahrazad	22	B3

TRANSPORT		
Buses to Bekaa Valley	(see 23)	
Minibuses to Beirut	23	A3
Taxi Stand	24	C3

separates the propylaea from the sacred enclosure. Beyond this is the **Great Court** (Sacrificial Courtyard), which leads to the remains of the **Temple of Jupiter**, completed around AD 60. Its remaining six columns are a massive and spectacular reminder of the size and majesty of the original structure.

Adjacent to the Temple of Jupiter is the **Temple of Bacchus**, known in Roman times as the 'small temple'. This was, in fact, dedicated to Venus/Astarte rather than to Bacchus. Completed around AD 150, it's amazingly well preserved and is quite ornate. In the southeastern corner of the temple stands the attractive 15th-century **Mamluk tower**. The **museum** it houses was closed when last visit. Behind the temple on its western flank are the remains of the **Mamluk fortifications** and **mosque**.

When you leave the site, check out the exquisite **Temple of Venus** near the entrance. It's closed to visitors but you can have a good look by wandering around the perimeter fence.

Sleeping

Palmyra Hotel (☎ 376 011; fax 370 305; Rue Abdel Halim Hajjar; s/d/tr with bathroom US$38/53/63) A relic itself, the Palmyra has seen guests as diverse as Jean Cocteau and the shah of Iran grace its portals. Rooms are simple but comfortable though the bathrooms are showing their age. Ask for a room with views over the ruins; best are Nos 25, 27 and 28. A few doors down in a lovely old building is the Palmyra's annexe (double room in low/high season US$75/100) furnished like a beautiful private home with very comfortable rooms. Breakfast costs US$5.

Hotel Jupiter (☎ 376 71; Rue Abdel Halim Hajjar; s with/without shower US$15/10, d with shower US$20) Entered via an arcade northeast of the Palmyra Hotel, it has large, light but basic rooms with fans off a central courtyard. There's also a restaurant. Hani, the helpful (and talkative) owner, is a mine of local knowledge.

Hotel Shouman (☎ 03-796 077; Ras al-Ain Blvd; dm/s/d LL10,000/20,000/25,000) Close to the ruins, three of the rooms here enjoy great views. There are comfortable beds and a simple but clean shared bathroom. Enter via a stone staircase; the pension is on the 1st floor.

Al-Shams Hotel (☎ 373 284; Rue Abdel Halim Hajjar; dm/d US$6/7) Three rooms have balconies (two with views over the ruins), there's free

kitchen access and 24-hour hot water, but rooms (with shared bathroom) are basic and only moderately clean. Breakfast is US$3.

Eating

Shahrazad (Shearazade; ☎ 371 851; Souq, off Rue Abdel Halim Hajjar; chicken shwarma sandwich/kebab LL3000/7000; ☺ 8am-midnight) Frequented by locals, this place is best known for the fabulous views of the ruins from its large windows. Food is simple but tasty and good value. If you haven't yet done justice to Lebanese mezze, here's your chance: there's a mezze menu (a selection of 13) for US$8.

Riviera Restaurant (☎ 370 296; Ras al-Ain Blvd; mezze LL2000; ☺ 8am-midnight) In summer, this restaurant en route to the spring serves basic but tasty food in its outdoor eating area.

There are quite a few cheap eateries on Rue Abdel Halim Hajjar; the best is the very popular **Al Khayam Restaurant** (☺ 10am-midnight) at the beginning of the street, which serves delicious felafels (LL750) and shwarma (LL1500) and has a few tables.

Further up Rue Abdel Halim Hajjar are several shops selling delicious sweets and meat pastries.

Getting There & Away

The only public transport options from Beirut to Baalbek are minibuses and service taxis. From the Cola transport hub, a minibus to Baalbek costs LL5000 (1½ hours); a service taxi costs LL7000. The bus stop in Baalbek is opposite the Palmyra Hotel and the service-taxi office is in the souq area.

For information about how to get to Baalbek from Zahlé, see p451. For information about how to get to Baalbek from Tripoli or Bcharré, see p441.

Minibuses from Baalbek go direct to Beirut (LL5000, 1½ hours, 24 hours a day subject to demand); to Damascus (LL7500, two hours) go direct mornings only (from 8am to noon); in the afternoon change at Chtaura (LL3000, 20 to 30 minutes, 24 hours). If you can't find a minibus to Beirut, you can take a bus to Chtaura (LL2000), then a service taxi from there (US$4 per person).

AANJAR   عنجر
☎ 08 / pop 3240

The best-preserved Islamic archaeological site in Lebanon, **Aanjar** (☎ 621 780; admission LL6000; ☺ 8am-sunset), is the only significant

Umayyad site in Lebanon. It was discovered by archaeologists as recently as the 1940s.

The Umayyads ruled briefly but energetically from AD 660 to 750 and Aanjar is thought to have been built by the sixth Umayyad caliph, Walid I (r AD 705–715). It was an important inland commercial centre, located on intersecting trade routes. The walled and fortified city was built along symmetrical Roman lines; the layout is in four equal quarters, separated by two 20m-wide avenues, the **cardo maximus** and the **decumanus maximus**. There is a **tetrapylon**, a four-column structure, where the two streets intersect; it's interesting due to its alternating layers of large blocks and narrow bricks, a typically Byzantine effect.

In the city's heyday, its main streets were flanked by palaces, baths, mosques, shops (600 have been uncovered) and dwellings. The **remains** of these can be seen today. Perhaps the most impressive are those of the **great palace**, one wall and several arcades of which have been reconstructed.

Local guides are usually available (around US$6/10 for couples/groups) at the site, and very useful free tourism brochures (with map) are distributed with tickets.

If you need to overnight here, you can stay at the very comfortable **Challalat** (Mona Lisa; ☎ /fax 620 753; s/d/ste with bathroom, TV & balcony LL60,000/90,000/120,000; ☒) a new hotel and the only one in town at the time of writing. It also has a restaurant.

To eat, head for the excellent and extremely popular **Shams Restaurant** (☎ 620 567; Beirut-Damascus Hwy; mezze LL2500, grill LL6000; ☯ 10am-midnight), serving superb fresh fish and seafood, among other dishes, at excellent prices. It's around 200m down from the ruins on the main road and also has a lovely terrace.

Aanjar is 21km from Chtaura on the Beirut–Damascus Hwy. You can catch a service taxi (LL1000) or bus 12 (LL500) from Chtaura, which will drop you at the turn-off with the 'Welcome to Aanjar' sign, leaving you with a 2km walk. Take the road on the left-hand side, walk for approximately 10 minutes and turn left at the road opposite the Shams restaurant. Follow that road until you reach the entrance to the ruins. Alternatively, hire a taxi to take you all the way to the site from Chtaura, have the cab wait an hour while you admire the site, then return. This costs around LL15,000. For Beirut, go to Chtaura first.

From Beirut a bus leaves at 2pm (LL2000 to LL3000, 1½ hours, Monday to Saturday). From Aanjar, there's a bus daily at 6am.

LEBANON DIRECTORY

ACCOMMODATION
Accommodation in Lebanon is not the bargain it is elsewhere in the Middle East. Budget-category dorm beds/singles start at around US$6/10, doubles around US$12 to US$15; midrange at US$35/45 for singles/doubles. Top-end hotels start at US$95/125 for singles/doubles. Hotels quote room rates in both Lebanese lira and US dollars, but you can often pay in either.

Note that during the low season (December to March) and excluding holidays, discounts of up to 40% or 50% are often available; always ask. During the high season (May to September), book well in advance.

ACTIVITIES
Lebanon offers a good range of activities. Water sports, including water-skiing, boating and jet-skiing (in Beirut and Jounieh among other places) and diving (including Beirut) are all possible. Diving is a rapidly growing activity with some interesting wrecks to ex-

---

PRACTICALITIES

- The *Daily Star* provides good coverage of local news in English, the daily *L'Orient Le Jour* in French. The monthly magazine, the *Guide*, is useful for upcoming events, openings and exhibitions in Beirut. You can usually find it in Beirut's Virgin Megastore.

- The BBC World Service can be received on both 1323kHz and 72kHz; popular locally are Radio One, Light FM and Nostalgie. The major local TV channels are the government-run broadcaster Tele-Liban, and five commercial channels: New TV, MTV, Future TV, NBN and LBC.

- European two-round-pin plugs are needed to connect to Lebanon's electricity supply (220VAC, 50Hz).

- Lebanon uses the metric system for weights and measures.

plore. A recommended website to check out for diving in Lebanon is that of the **Atlantis Diving College** (www.atlantisdivingcollege.com).

Lebanon is also one of the few countries in the Middle East to offer skiing. The main resorts include **Faraya Mzaar** (☎ 09-341 034/5), the **Cedars** (☎ 06-671 073/2), **Faqra** (☎ 01-257 220) and **Lalouq** (☎ 01-200 019). See p442 for more information on skiing at the Cedars.

Biking is another growing sport. **Cyclo Sport** (Map pp418-19; ☎ 446 792; cyclspor@cyberia .net.lb; Rue Gouraud, Gemmayze, Beirut; ☑ 9am-11pm) can suggest itineraries and routes and also hires out bikes for LL4000/15,000/30,000 per hour/day/month. You can also buy a bike (from LL150,000 to LL2,500,000) and resell it here when you leave.

Caving is possible in various places including the Jeita Grotto (p432); Paragliding is practised at some of the ski resorts, and trekking possibilities are almost limitless in Lebanon, including in the Qadisha Valley near the Cedars.

BOOKS
As well as this book, Lonely Planet publishes a comprehensive guide, *Syria & Lebanon*.

For ancient history, *The Phoenicians* by Donald Harden is comprehensive and authoritative. For prewar travel accounts, try *The Hills of Adonis* by Colin Thubron.

For the civil war *The Formation of Modern Lebanon* by Meir Zamir, and *Pity the Nation: Lebanon at War* by Robert Fisk are both recommended.

New publications include *Transit Beirut – New Writing & Images* (edited by Malu Halasa and Roseanne Saad Khalaf), which includes short stories by local authors; *Bliss Street* by Kris Kenway, a breathless account of a love affair between a local girl and a mobile-phone salesman detained in Lebanon by accident; and *Teta, Mother & Me – An Arab Woman's Memoir* by Jean Said Makdisi (the sister of Edward Said), which tells the stories of three generations of women. Much of it is set in Beirut.

For those planning a longer sojourn in Beirut, the new *At Home in Beirut. A Practical Guide to Living in the Lebanese Capital* (LL25,000) by Charlotte Hamaoui and Sylvia Palamoudian is comprehensive and useful. Similar in vein is *Family Fun in Lebanon* (LL18,000) by the same authors.

All these books are available in Beirut.

BUSINESS HOURS
Unlike the rest of the Middle East, Lebanon's 'weekend' (when government offices and schools close) is Sunday, not Friday. During religious holidays (such as Ramadan) and the summer, hours may vary. The following is a general guide only:
Banks Open 8.30am to 2pm Monday to Friday (a few open to 4pm) and Saturday morning.
Government offices Open 8am to 2pm from Monday to Saturday, except Friday when they open 8am to 11am. Some offices close at noon on Saturday.
Museums and monuments Most close on Monday.
Private offices Open from 9am/10am to 2pm and 4pm to 8pm/9pm Monday to Friday and some on Saturday morning too.
Restaurants Between noon and midnight daily. Some close on Sunday. Cafés open from around 7am (or earlier) to around 7pm.
Shops Open from 9am/10am to 6pm/7pm from Monday to Friday and Saturday morning. Some also open for a few hours on Sunday.

COURSES
Many students come to Beirut to study Arabic. The following centres provide courses for foreigners:
American Language Center (Map p422; ☎ 366-002; www.a/c.edu.lb; 1st fl, Choueiry Bldg, Rue Bliss, Beirut; 25 hr per week for 1 month; US$250; ☑ 9am-6pm Mon-Sat)
American University of Beirut (Map p422; ☎ 01-374 444; www.aub.edu/lb/cames)

For details about student visas see p458, and for hotels that offer long-term accommodation see p423.

DANGERS & ANNOYANCES
The main danger in Lebanon is land mines. UN experts estimate that more than 100,000 remain. Don't wander off tracks. Driving carries its own risk (see p461).

EMBASSIES & CONSULATES
Lebanese Embassies & Consulates
Following are the Lebanese embassies and consulates in major cities around the world. Irish and New Zealand nationals should apply to the UK consulate for visas. For addresses of Lebanese embassies in neighbouring Middle Eastern countries, see the relevant country chapter. Note: there is no Lebanese embassy in either Israel or Syria.
Australia Canberra (☎ 02-6295 7378; fax 6239 7024; 27 Endeavour St, Red Hill, Canberra, ACT 2603); Melbourne (☎ 03-9529 4588; toun@alphalink.com.au;

117 Wellington St, Windsor, Victoria 3181); Sydney (☎ 02-9361 5449; Level 5, 70 William St, Kings Cross, Sydney, NSW 2010) The Melbourne and Sydney branches only issue visas to Victorian and NSW residents, respectively.

Canada Montreal (☎ 514-276 2638, consuliban@qc .aira.com; 40 Chemin Côte Ste Catherine, H2V-2A2-PQ, Montreal153); Ottawa (☎ 613-236 5825; fax 613-232 1609; 640 Lyon St, K1S 3Z5 Ottawa, Ontario)

Egypt (☎ 02-361 0623; fax 361 0463; Sharia Ahmad Nasim, Giza, Cairo)

France (☎ 01 40 67 75 75; fax 01 40 67 16 42; 3 Rue Coperic, 75016 Paris)

Germany (☎ 4930-474 98 60; fax 474 986 66; Berlinerstrasse 126-127, 13187 Berlin)

Jordan (☎ 5929111; fax 5922333; Sharia Mohammed Ali Bdeir, Abdoun, Amman)

Netherlands (☎ 0703-65 89 06; fax 0703-62 0779; Frederick Straat 2, 2514 LK The Hague)

UK (☎ 020-7229 7265; fax 020-7243 1699; 21 Palace Gardens Mews, London W8 4RA)

USA Los Angeles (☎ 213-467 1253; fax 213-467 2935; Ste 510, 7060 Hollywood Blvd, Los Angeles, CA 90028); New York (☎ 212-744 7905; lebconny@aol.com; 9 East 76th St, New York, NY 10021); Washington (☎ 202-939 6300; emblebanon@aol.com; 2560 28th St, Washington, DC 20008)

Embassies in Lebanon

Opening hours are generally from 8am or 9am to 12.30pm or 1pm Monday to Friday. Some, such as the Jordanian embassy, are also closed on Friday. Nationals of Ireland and New Zealand should contact the UK embassy. Note: there is no Syrian or Israeli embassy in Lebanon; however, most nationalities will have no problem obtaining a Syrian visa on the Syrian border (see p653).

Australia (Map pp418-19; ☎ 01-374 701; austemle@cyberia.net.lb; Serail Hill, Downtown, Beirut)

Canada (☎ 04-521 163; beirut@dfait-maeci.gc.ca; 1st fl, Coolrite Bldg, Autostrade, Jal ad-Dib) Around 10km outside Beirut.

Egypt (Map pp418-19; ☎ 01-862 932; fax 01-863 751; Rue Thomas Edison, off Rue Verdun, Ramlet al-Bayda)

France (Map pp418-19; ☎ 01-616 730; ambafrance@ cyberia.net.lb; Rue de Damas) Near the National Museum.

Germany (☎ 04-914 444; germanemb@german embassy.org.lb; Mtaileb, Rabieh) About 20km outside Beirut.

Italy (Map pp418-19; ☎ 01-340 225; Place d'Etoile, Downtown)

Jordan (☎ 05-922 500; fax 922 502; Rue Elias Helou, Baabda) Around 7km outside Beirut.

Netherlands (Map pp418-19; ☎ 01-204 663; nlgovbei@sodetel.net.lb; 9th fl, ABM Amro Bldg, Ave Charles Malek, Achrafiye)

UK (Map pp418-19; ☎ 01-990 400; Serail Hill, Downtown, Beirut)

US (☎ 04-417 774; fax 407 112; Awkar, facing the Municipality, PO Box 70-840 Antelias) About 25km outside Beirut.

FESTIVALS & EVENTS

Many towns and villages host their own small festivals which range from local fairs to full-on folkloric performances. The five major arts festivals are listed here.

February

Al-Bustan Festival (www.albustanfestival.com) An annual festival held for five weeks in Beit Mary (North of Beirut). Daily events feature opera, chamber music and orchestral concerts.

July & August

Baalbek Festival (www.baalbeck.org.lb) Lebanon's most famous arts festival; held at the Roman ruins. Features opera, jazz, poetry and pop, and theatre productions.

Beiteddine Festival (www.beiteddine.org.lb) Music, dance and theatre held in the beautiful courtyard of the Beiteddine Palace.

Byblos International Festival (www.byblosfestival .org) Held in August among the ruins of Byblos's ancient harbour – includes pop, classic, opera and world music.

October

Beirut International Marathon (www.beirut marathon.org) Also includes wheelchair events.

Mid East Film Festival Beirut (www.beirutfilm foundation.org) High-profile film festival with a growing reputation as the best in the Middle East.

GAY & LESBIAN TRAVELLERS

There's a thriving (if clandestine) gay scene in Beirut, which is regarded as the most liberal capital in the Middle East. Nevertheless, homosexuality is illegal under Lebanese law; gay travellers should be discreet, particularly in predominantly Muslim areas. For further information, check out: www.gaymiddleeast .com, www.travelandtranscendence.com and www.bintelnas.org.

HOLIDAYS

New Year's Day 1 January

Feast of Mar Maroun 9 February – feast of the patron saint of the Maronites

Easter March/April – Good Friday to Easter Monday inclusive

Qana Day 18 April – commemorates the massacre at the UN base at Qana

Labour Day 1 May
Martyrs' Day 6 May
Day of Resistance and Liberation 25 May –
celebrates the Israeli withdrawal from South Lebanon in 2000
Assumption 15 August
All Saints Day 1 November
Independence Day 22 November
Christmas Day 25 December

Also observed are the Muslim holidays
(p647) of Eid al-Fitr, Eid al-Adha, Prophet's
Birthday, Islamic New Year and Ashura.

MONEY

Lebanon's currency is the Lebanese lira (LL)
(known locally as the Lebanese pound).
There are a few coins (piastres) of LL50, 100
and (more commonly) 250 and 500 pieces
still in circulation, as well as notes of 50, 100,
250, 500, 1000, 5000, 10,000, 20,000, 50,000
and 100,000.

US dollars are accepted everywhere and
are as good as interchangeable with the
Lebanese lira. Often, smaller amounts are
quoted in Lebanese lira, and larger amounts
(with fewer 0s!) are quoted in US dollars
(the etiquette also followed in this chapter).
Many places give change in either currency.

Country	Unit	Lebanese lira (LL)
Australia	A$1	1101
Canada	C$1	1268
euro zone	€1	1774
Israel & the		
Palestinian Territories	NIS1	320
Japan	¥100	1283
New Zealand	NZ$1	1027
Syria	S£1	29
UK	UK£1	2620
USA	US$1	1502

US dollars are widely accepted, but travellers
cheques (in any currency) are not. The best
way to access cash is through the ATMs found
in all larger towns. ATMs accept credit cards
or co-branded home banking cards for Cirrus, Diners Club, Maestro, MasterCard, Visa
and Visa-Electron and dispense cash in both
Lebanese lira and US dollars.

Budget hotels and restaurants do not accept credit cards. Tipping is widely expected
in Lebanon particularly in the better hotels
and restaurants and by drivers of hired cars
or guides; around 10% is a good bench-

mark. There is no black market in Lebanon,
but there are plenty of moneychangers that
sometime offer better rates that the banks.
Check commission, which can range from
3% to 5%, and shop around.

PHOTOGRAPHY

Film (from around LL6500) and video tapes
are widely available in Lebanon. Colour
transparency film (from around LL15,000)
is available in Beirut and some of the larger
towns (though Fujichrome Velvia as well as
black-and-white transparencies and film are
harder to find). It costs around LL4500/16,000
to process negative/transparency film.

Memory cards can be bought in Beirut,
but prices are on the high side. A few places
in Beirut are beginning to burn CDs of digital
photos (see p430). In Beirut, various shops
stock the spare parts of (and can repair)
the mainstream camera brands, including
Nikon, Canon, Olympus and Pentax.

TELEPHONE
Mobile Phones

Mobile-phone coverage extends throughout most of the country (bar a few remote,
mountainous areas). Obtaining a mobile in
Lebanon costs from US$250, but some car-
hire agencies hire them out for around US$6
per day, plus a deposit and call charges (see
Hire, p461).

Phone Codes

The country code for Lebanon is ☎961,
followed by the local area code (minus the
zero), then the subscriber number. Local
area codes are given at the start of each
city or town section in this chapter. The
area code when dialling a mobile phone is
☎03. The international access code (to call
abroad from Lebanon) is ☎00.

Phonecards

Telephone cards have now rendered the old
government *centrales* or telecom centres
redundant. Cards come in two types: the
Telecard for LL10,000 or LL30,000, which
you can only use in card-operated public
phone booths, or the prepaid Kalam card
for LL15,000 or LL45,000, which you can
use to call from any phone, public or private
(by employing a code). Cards can be bought
in any *centrale* or anywhere the 'OGERO'
sign is displayed. Calls to Australia and New

Zealand cost LL1400, to Ireland LL1500, and to France, Germany, Italy, Netherlands, Spain and the US LL1100. Rates are a couple of hundred lira cheaper off-peak (10pm to 7am).

VISAS

People of all nationalities require a visa for Lebanon bar Gulf countries (but not Yemen). Nationals of Australia, Austria, Belgium, Canada, Cyprus, Denmark, Finland, France, Germany, Greece, Gulf Cooperative Council (GCC) countries, Ireland, Italy, Japan, Luxembourg, Malaysia, Monaco, Netherlands, New Zealand, Norway, Portugal, South Korea, Spain, Sweden, Switzerland, the UK and the USA can get a tourist or business visa on arrival at Beirut International Airport, or at the border with Syria.

Lebanon denies entry to travellers with evidence of a visit to Israel in their passport (see p353). Look out for the question 'Have you ever visited Israel or Occupied Palestine?' on some visa application forms – a 'yes' will put paid to your application.

Note that visa rules and regulations can – and do – change in Lebanon; always check the latest information with your embassy/consulate.

At the airport, visa stamps are sold at a window on the right (open 24 hours), just before passport control. Visas for 48-hour transit and one-month visas are issued free of charge; a three-month visa costs US$34. Note that the 'three-month' visa requires you to extend this before the end of your first month (see p420). Visas (including multiple-entry visas, which are useful if you're planning to go in and out of Lebanon from Syria) can also be obtained in advance at any Lebanese embassy or consulate. For addresses of Lebanese embassies in the Middle East see the relevant country chapters.

If you're coming by road (bus or private transport), see the information under Border Crossings, p660.

Those wishing to study in Lebanon can apply for a student one-year residence visa (LL250,000) with a letter from the school, two passport photos and two copies of your passport details.

For details of visas for other Middle Eastern countries, see p653.

WOMEN TRAVELLERS

Compared to many parts of the Middle East, Lebanon seems very liberal and laidback; women should have few problems with either undue attention or safety. Revealing clothes are common in Beirut and Jounieh, but outside the main centres long-sleeved, loose clothing is still preferable. This is particularly the case in the south and the Bekaa Valley, which is a predominantly Shiite area. For further advice for female travellers see p654.

TRANSPORT IN LEBANON

GETTING THERE & AWAY

You can travel to Lebanon by air, by land from Syria and, from May to October, by boat from Limassol in Cyprus.

Entering Lebanon

Entering the country at the airport or border crossings is neither complicated nor bureaucratic. All that's required is a valid passport and a visa. You can't enter Lebanon if there is evidence in your passport of a visit to Israel.

Passport

Make sure you carry your passport at all times. Many Lebanese checkpoints require them.

Air

Beirut international airport (BEY; ☎ 01-628 000; www.beirutairport.gov.lb) is Lebanon's only airport. The national carrier, **Middle East Airlines** (MEA; Map p422; in Beirut ☎ 01-622 225; www.mea.com.lb), has an extensive network including flying from Beirut to and from Australia, Europe and the Middle East. The airline has a pretty good safety record.

Several airlines have their offices in the Gefinor Center in Ras Beirut including MEA.

DEPARTURE TAX

Airline passengers departing from Beirut International Airport must pay a steep US$37/50 for economy/business class. It's *usually* included in the ticket price, but check.

The following international airlines service Beirut:

Air France (airline code AF; in Beirut ☎ 01-200 700; www.airfrance.com) Hub: Charles de Gaulle Airport, Paris.

British Airways (airline code BA; in Beirut ☎ 01-747 777; www.britishairways.com) Hub: Heathrow Airport, London.

Cyprus Airways (airline code CY; in Beirut ☎ 01-200 886; www.cyprusairways.com) Hub: Larnaca Airport, Larnaca.

EgyptAir (airline code MS; in Beirut ☎ 01-980 165; www.egyptair.com.eq) Hub: Cairo International Airport, Cairo.

Emirates (airline code EK; in Beirut ☎ 01-739 042; www.emirates.com) Hub: Dubai Airport, Dubai.

Gulf Air (airline code GF; in Beirut ☎ 01-323 332; www.gulfairco.com) Hub: Bahrain Airport, Bahrain.

Lufthansa (airline code LH; in Beirut ☎ 01-347 006; www.lufthansa.com) Hub: Frankfurt Airport, Frankfurt.

Malaysia Airlines (airline code MH; in Beirut ☎ 01-741 344; www.mas.com.my) Hub: Sepang International, Kuala Lumpur.

Middle East Airlines (airline code ME; Map p422; in Beirut ☎ 01-737 000; www.mea.com.lb) Hub: Beirut International Airport, Beirut.

Royal Jordanian Airline (airline code RJ; in Beirut ☎ 01-379 990; www.rja.com.jo) Hub: Queen Alia Airport, Amman.

Syrian Arab Airlines (airline code RB; in Beirut ☎ 01-375 632; www.syrian-airlines.com) Hub: Damascus Airport, Damascus.

Turkish Airlines (airline code TK; in Beirut ☎ 01-741 391; www.turkishairlines.com) Hub: Ataturk Airport, İstanbul.

Airline tickets bought in Lebanon are expensive. Examples of return flights (not including tax) to neighbouring countries: Amman (US$210), Cairo (US$246), İstanbul (US$185) and Larnaca in Cyprus (US$95). MEA does not fly currently to Baghdad (Iraq), Damascus (Syria), Tehran (Iran) and Tripoli (Libya).

Land
BORDER CROSSINGS
The only way into Lebanon by land is through Syria; the border with Israel is closed and will be for the foreseeable future. You can't get a visa for Syria in Lebanon, but you can at the border crossings (see Visas at the Border, p553 for details). There is no departure tax when leaving by land.

Syria
There are four places in Lebanon where you can cross the border with Syria: at Masnaa (for Damascus), Abboudiye (for Aleppo), Al-Qaa (at the northern end of the Bekaa Valley) and Aarida (on the coastal road from

Tripoli to Lattakia) which are open all year. Visas can be obtained at these Lebanese/Syrian border crossings.

Crossing the borders is pretty quick and painless; you'll need to fill out an entry and exit form for each country (taking about 10 minutes), hand over your yellow entry card (which you received on entering the country) and provide details of your accommodation in either country. Ensure you have a reservation at a hotel with the name and number at hand; they may well check. Otherwise you may be charged business visa rates.

If coming from Syria to Lebanon you deal with **Lebanese border immigration** (☎ 08-620 016/620 017; 1-month tourist/2-day business visa free, 15-day/1-month business visa LL25,000/50,000; ☼ 24hr). Note that payment can only be made in Lebanese pounds, and that immigration allows tourists to spend a maximum of four days in Syria on a single-entry visa (as opposed to multiple entry).

Crossing from Lebanon to Syria, **Syrian border immigration** (☎ 011-391 4029/391 4208; ☼ 24hr) issues a two-week tourist visa (but up to one month is permitted) for citizens of Australia and New Zealand (US$30), Ireland (US$50), France, Italy, Spain and the Netherlands (US$52); Germany (US$28); and the US (US$16).

To/From Turkey
The Turkish embassy in Beirut will only issue visas to Lebanese nationals. However, Western nationals wanting to travel from Lebanon to Turkey will have no trouble obtaining a Turkish visa at the Syrian–Turkish border (or at Turkey's international airports). Depending on your nationality, they cost US$20 to US$45.

BUS & SERVICE TAXI
Buses to Syria from Beirut leave from the **Charles Helou bus station** (Map pp418-19). **Beirut Pullman Terminal office** (Map pp418-19; ☎ 573 322; ☼ 24hr) sells tickets. The buses aren't luxurious, but they're clean and have allocated (numbered) seats. Reservations are not necessary in winter, but in summer they're wise; book at least one day in advance.

For Syria, buses go to Damascus (LL7500, three to four hours, every hour from 6am to 8pm daily), Aleppo (Halab; LL11,000, 6½ hours, every 30 minutes from 7am to 1.30am) and Lattakia (LL9000, four hours, three times a day at 10.30am, 2.30pm and 5.30pm). These services run every day of the week. For Turkey, buses travel to İstanbul (LL26,000, 36 hours, 10.30pm daily), and for Egypt, to Cairo (LL60,000, 24 hours, 3am Friday and Sunday). All buses go via Damascus and involve a change of bus in each country (on to local services).

A service taxi from Charles Helou will cost you US$10 to Damascus (2¼ hours) and US$12 to Aleppo (five hours). Don't worry about finding a seat in one of these – the Syrian drivers are famous for pouncing on potential customers the minute they enter the bus station! Service taxis also go to Amman in Jordan (US$25, five hours, 10 daily).

Tripoli (in northern Lebanon) also has an international bus service. **Kotob** (Map p438; ☎ 06-444 986) buses leave for Aleppo in Syria (LL7500, almost five hours, every hour from 9am to 1pm) and to Lattakia (LL7500, two hours, 3pm). They go to Damascus (LL10,000, three hours) via Beirut on Tuesday, Thursday and Saturday. Daily **Transtour** (Map p438; ☎ 06-445 514; Rue Mohammed Karameh, Tripoli) buses leave for Aleppo (LL8000, five hours, every 30 minutes) from 8.30am to 11pm via Homs (LL5000, 2½ hours). There are two Transtour services daily to Damascus (LL8000, 4½ hours), leaving at 5am and 3pm.

Kotob also go to Amman in Jordan (LL37,500, five to seven hours). Transtour runs one daily bus at 11pm to İstanbul in Turkey (LL75,000, 32 hours) as well as Sunday services (at 9am and 11pm) to about 10 other destinations in Turkey and Eastern Europe (ask at the office), a daily bus at 5am to Amman (LL38,000, eight hours) and a bus every Sunday at 5am to Cairo, Egypt (LL98,000, 32 to 36 hours).

Service taxis from Tripoli to Syria travel to Homs (LL7500), to Hama (LL9000) and to Aleppo (LL15,000). They leave when full from Saahat et-Tall. Service taxis from Tripoli don't go to Damascus.

CAR & MOTORCYCLE

If you're bringing your car into Lebanon, you must have an International Driving Permit and a *carnet de passage* (see p662). Note also that a steep charge (payable in cash) is levied for foreign-registered vehicles at the border (refundable on departure). There are petrol stations on both sides of the border (fill up in Syria by preference;

it's cheaper) as well as quite good garages that can provide spares and repairs. At the time of writing, diesel vehicles were banned from entering Lebanon; check for the latest information with your embassy before setting off. For information on road rules etc see opposite.

Sea

There is no regular public sea transportation from Lebanon. Boats connect Beirut to other countries but the majority are middle-market cruise ships operating during summer months only (mid-March to end of October). You *may* be able to get a passage with them. For more information and schedules contact **Aeolus Travel** (Map pp418-19; ☎ 564 666; www.aeoloslb.com; Rue Pasteur, Rmeil; ☺ 8am-5pm Mon-Fri, 8.30am-1pm Sat). It's located opposite the Subaru car showroom.

The company works with Louis Cruise Lines, Salamis Lines, Silver Sea and Aida Cruises, which generally follow the route: Beirut–Limassol (Cyprus)–Greek Islands–Limassol–Beirut. It takes between nine and 12 hours from Beirut to Limassol and prices (usually for two-person packages) include a three-star cabin and full board. Discounts of between 10% and 50% are available either for advance or last-minute bookings. In the peak season (July to August) prices are highest. At present there are no boats to Italy, Egypt or Turkey (go first to Cyprus and change).

GETTING AROUND

There are no air services or trains operating within Lebanon, but the country is so small (you can drive from one end to the other in half a day) that you don't really need them. Additionally the bus, minibus and service taxi network is extensive, reasonably efficient and cheap.

Bicycle

Lebanon's steep terrain and the state of many urban roads demand a rugged, all-terrain-type bicycle. There are no designated bike lanes or routes and cars treat bicycles with contempt and derision. Beware of travelling in summer months, when heat exhaustion is a real danger. Other hazards and annoyances include the heavily congested roads and the pure anarchy on them (see opposite). See also p455 and p423 for further information and for bike hire and purchase.

Bus

Buses travel between Beirut and all of Lebanon's major towns. There are three main bus pick-up and drop-off points in Beirut:

Charles Helou bus station (Map pp418-19) Just east of downtown, for destinations north of Beirut (including Syria).

Cola transport hub (Map pp418-19) In fact a bustling intersection. Generally serves the south, and the Bekaa Valley.

Dawra transport hub Lying east of Beirut and covering the same destinations as Charles Helou, it's usually a port of call in and out of the city.

Charles Helou is the only formal station and is divided into three signposted zones:

Zone A For buses to Syria.

Zone B For buses servicing Beirut (where the route starts or finishes at Charles Helou).

Zone C For express buses to Jounieh, Byblos and Tripoli.

Zones A and C have ticket offices where you can buy tickets for your journey. In the other stations (Cola and Dawra) ask any driver for your bus (if they don't find you first).

Some buses in Lebanon are poorly maintained and go too fast; accidents do happen. In general, however, they're reasonably safe, comfortable and reliable and are very cheap by Lebanese standards. The networks are extensive. There's just one class and bus passes are not available. A typical journey from Beirut to Tripoli (85km north of Beirut) costs LL2000, ie about LL24 a kilometre.

There's also a growing number of independently owned microbuses which cover the same routes but are slightly more expensive that the regular buses, but they're comfortable and frequent. Tickets are bought on the microbuses.

See the relevant town and city sections for further details about getting there by bus.

Car & Motorcycle

You should think carefully before deciding to drive in Lebanon (see Road Hazards, p462).

DRIVING LICENCE

In theory, you require an International Driving Permit (IDP), but in practice a home driving licence should suffice for most nationalities. Note that, if you plan to drive *into* Lebanon, you will need an IDP.

FUEL & SPARE PARTS

Petrol (including unleaded) and spare parts for most makes of car are easily available.

HIRE

Most of the big rental agencies are in Beirut. If you can afford one, a hired car is probably the best way to see some of Lebanon's most beautiful scenery. To reduce the cost, try and find a small group.

To hire a car in Lebanon, drivers must be over 21 years old (in some places, over 23), have been in possession of a licence for at least three years, have adequate insurance cover and own a credit card or have a large amount of cash (to cover the deposit). You can't take hired cars over the border to Syria.

Car hire starts at approximately US$25 to US$30 per day for a Renault Clio, rising to US$500 per day for a Porsche Boxer convertible. For car hire up to three days, there's a mileage limit of 150km per day; for three days or more it's usually unlimited. Drivers and guides both cost from US$20 per day extra (but note that you must pay for their accommodation, and food is expected).

In the low season and if hiring a car for five days or more, discounts of up to 40% are sometimes available. During the high season (15 June to 15 September, Christmas, Easter and the major Lebanese holidays) cars can be hard to come by; reserve at least two weeks in advance.

Car hire companies in Beirut, some of which have branches open 24 hours at the airport, include the following:

Avis (Map pp418-19; ☎ 01-363 848; www.avis.com .lb; Kurban Tours, Phoenicia Intercontinental, Rue Fakhr ed-Dine, Minet el-Hosn, Beirut; ☑ 9am-6pm)

Budget Rent a Car (Map pp418-19; ☎ 01-740 741; www.budget-rental.com; Dunes Shopping Center, Rue Verdun, Verdun, Beirut; ☑ 8am-6pm Mon-Sat)

City Car (Map p422; ☎ 01-803 308; www.citycar.com .lb; Al-Oraifi Bldg, Rue Kalaa, Ras Beirut; ☑ 8am-7pm Mon-Sat, 9am-noon Sun)

Europcar Ain al-Mreisse (Map pp418-19; ☎ 01-363 636; www.lenacar.com; Nsouli Bldg, Rue Ain al-Mreisse, Ain al-Mreisse, Beirut; ☑ 9am-6pm Mon-Sat); airport branch (☎ 01-629 888; ☑ 24hr)

INSURANCE

Though prices may include insurance, you may still be liable for the first US$300 or more in case of damage; check. Though there's an option to pay for extra cover, even that probably won't save you much in the long run.

LEBANON

ROAD HAZARDS

Despite the attempts of traffic police to organise the flow of cars, very few drivers follow road regulations. Many Lebanese purchase their licences for as little as US$100. Some intersections in Beirut do have traffic lights, but they are usually treated as give-way signs at best. Look out also for road-mending projects (which are often unmarked).

In the cities, watch the service taxis that stop without warning in the middle of the road to let passengers in or out. On the highways, lanes are ignored.

In the mountains many roads are narrow, with hairpin bends, and it's not unusual for drivers to recklessly overtake on hidden bends.

Keep an eye out for pedestrians, who often walk in the middle of the roads or streets or haphazardly cross highways and roads. Accidents are frequent.

In the winter (particularly from December to February) snow on the higher roads (such as from Masnah to Syria) can cause problems, and some roads (such as from Bcharré to the Cedars) are closed from November to mid-June. Chains can be rented from garages or ski resorts (LL10,000 per day).

ROAD RULES

None! In fact the first rule of driving in Lebanon is: forget rules. Officially, the Lebanese system is based on French road law, which includes the priority from the right rule (in which oncoming traffic has to give way to traffic coming from the right except on major highways). Don't be tempted to drink, however. Breathalysers are sometimes used in the event of an accident, and if over the limit you may get yourself into serious trouble. Don't forget also that you *must* stop at military checkpoints. Driving is on the right.

Local Transport

BUS

Some towns, including Beirut, have both government and privately owned buses that operate a hail and ride system. Fares are generally LL500 for all except the most distant destinations.

TAXI & SERVICE TAXI

Taxis are usually elderly Mercedes with red licence plates and a taxi sign on the roof.

For travellers considering day trips from Beirut, hiring them is not a bad option, as they are comfortable, solid in case of accidents and have seat belts, a rare thing in Lebanon.

Most routes around Lebanese towns and cities are covered by service taxis, or 'shared taxis' (see p672). You can hail them at any point on their route and also get out wherever you wish by saying *'anzil huun'* (drop me off here). Be sure to ask *'servees?'* before getting in as (if it's an empty car) the driver may try to charge you a private taxi fare.

The fixed fare for service taxis for routes around towns is generally LL1000, and to outlying parts LL2000. Outside towns, the fares range from LL2000 to LL8000, depending on the destination. Try to pay at the earliest opportunity during your trip and keep some LL1000 notes handy for this.

If you do want to engage the car as a private taxi, make sure the driver understands exactly where you want to go and negotiate the fare before you get in (fares are suggested in relevant sections). If you're planning several journeys, it may be cheaper to hire a car for a half or full day. You'll need to negotiate hard; expect to pay around US$50 for a whole day.

Tours

Several Lebanese operators organise tours within Lebanon, and to Syria and Jordan from Lebanon. They cover most of Lebanon's highlights, are reasonably priced and usually include lunch, guide (in English or French), entrance fees and pick-up/drop-off at your hotel, and are comfortable (transport is in air-con coaches or minibuses). A day trip costs from US$30 per person for shorter trips and US$50 to US$60 for longer trips.

Tour operators:

Kurban Tours (Map pp418-19; ☎ 01-363 848; www .kurbantravel.com; Phoenicia Intercontinental, Minet al-Hosn; ☼ 8am-6pm Mon-Sat)

Nakhal (☎ 01-382 444; www.nakhal.com; Sami as-Solh St, Ghorayeb Bldg; ☼ 7am-6pm Mon-Fri, 7am-2pm Sat) Lies around 550m south of the Law Courts on Sami as-Solh St.

Tania Travel (Map p422; ☎ 01-739 679; www.tania travel.com; Rue Sidani, Hamra; ☼ 8am-6pm Mon-Sat) On the 1st floor opposite the old Jeanne d'Arc theatre.

Libya

Libya is everything you could want a Middle Eastern destination to be.

First and foremost, it's a crossroads of history, continents and ancient empires, home to the Mediterranean's richest store of Roman and Greek cities – Sabratha, Cyrene and, above all, Leptis Magna – each of which is overlaid by remnants of Byzantine splendour. It's a place where history comes alive through the extraordinary monuments on its shores. Every corner of cosmopolitan Tripoli resonates with a different period of history. It's where the Sahara meets the Mediterranean.

Libya is also home to the Middle East's most exceptional and accessible desert scenery. The Sahara engulfs over 90% of the country, offering up vast sand seas the size of small European countries. Visit the enchanting oasis towns of Ghadames and Ghat where the caravans once showcased the riches of Africa. Marvel at palm-fringed lakes surrounded by sand dunes in the desert's heart. Be bewitched by extinct volcanoes, such as Waw al-Namus, where black sand encircles multicoloured lakes. Go deeper into the desert and experience Jebel Acacus, one of the world's finest open-air galleries of prehistoric rock art.

One important point to note is that visits to Libya can only be made as part of an organised tour. While independent travellers may prefer the chance to go it alone, remember that Libya is a vast country and on a tour you'll be able to cover so much more territory than you otherwise could. Remember also that organised groups can be as small as a party of one and with most tour companies you can design your own itinerary.

Until recently, Libya was the Middle East's best-kept secret. Now riding an exciting wave of optimism and openness, Libya is a place that will live long in the memory.

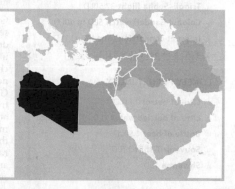

FAST FACTS

- **Area** 1,759,540 sq km
- **Capital** Tripoli
- **Country code** ☎ 218
- **Languages** Arabic, Berber
- **Money** Libyan dinar (LD); US$1 = 1.27LD; €1 = 1.50LD
- **Official name** Great Socialist People's Libyan Arab Jamahiriya (GSPLAJ)
- **Population** 5,499,074

HIGHLIGHTS

- **Leptis Magna** (p479) One of the world's best-preserved Roman cities with exceptional baths complexes, theatres, forums and a stunning seaside location.
- **Jebel Acacus** (p498) Striking mountain range, home to the indigenous Tuareg and some magnificent 12,000-year-old rock art.
- **Ghadames** (p491) A labyrinthine, palm-fringed old city and the most enchanting caravan post in the Sahara.
- **Tripoli** (p473) Delightful whitewashed medina replete with Ottoman mosques and houses and the world-class Jamahiriya Museum.
- **Waw al-Namus** (p498) Remote volcanic crater, off the beaten track in the heart of the Sahara, with black sand and red, green and blue lakes.

CLIMATE & WHEN TO GO

Libya is at its best in November and from February to April. Because of the lack of natural barriers, both the Sahara and the Mediterranean Sea affect the country's climate. In summer it's generally very hot with average temperatures on the coast of around 30°C, often accompanied by high humidity. Don't even think of going into the desert from late May until October, when temperatures can reach a sweltering 55°C. At other times, desert nights can drop below freezing. Also see Climate Charts, p643.

HOW MUCH?

- **Museum admission** 3LD
- **Tripoli–Sebha flight** 37.50LD
- **Colonel Gaddafi watch** 5LD to 40LD
- **Internet connection (one hour)** 1LD
- **4WD hire per day** 90LD

LONELY PLANET INDEX

- **Litre of petrol** 0.11LD
- **Litre of bottled water** 1LD
- **Bottle of beer** 1.50LD
- **Souvenir T-shirt** 11LD
- **Shwarma** 1LD

HISTORY

Throughout history Libya has been blighted by its geography, lying in the path of invading empires and someone else's war.

The Great Civilisations of the Mediterranean

From 700 BC Lebdah (Leptis), Oea (Tripoli) and Sabratha formed links in a chain of safe Phoenician (Punic) ports stretching from the Levant to Spain. Traces of the Phoenician presence remain at Sabratha and Leptis Magna.

On the advice of the Oracle of Delphi, in 631 BC Greek settlers established the city of Cyrene in the east of Libya. Within 200 years the Greeks had built four more cities of splendour as part of the Pentapolis (Five Cities), which included Ptolemais (Tolmeita) and Apollonia. But with Greek influence on the wane, the last Greek ruler, Ptolemy Apion, finally bequeathed the region of Cyrenaica to Rome in 75 BC.

Meanwhile in the west, the fall of the Punic capital at Carthage (in Tunisia) prompted Julius Caesar to formally annex Tripolitania in 46 BC. The Pax Romana saw Tripolitania and Cyrenaica become prosperous Roman provinces – Tripolitania was a major source of Rome's olive oil. Such was Libya's importance that a Libyan, Septimus Severus, became Rome's emperor (r AD 193–211; see p480). A massive earthquake in AD 365 sealed the fate of the Libyan colonies.

The Garamantes Empire of the Fezzan

While Europe's empires were battling over the Mediterranean littoral, an enlightened and longer-surviving indigenous empire, the Garamantes, held sway over southern Libya.

A legendary, warlike, nomadic people, the Garamantes nonetheless built sophisticated settlements and for centuries mastered the desert's most precious resource – water – by utilising hundreds of *foggara* (underground channels). The community, a loosely connected confederation of tribes centred on Garama (now Germa), is credited with introducing writing, horses, wheeled-transport and camels to the Sahara and also controlled many of the ancient caravan routes across the Sahara. By AD 500 the last of the Garamantes people disappeared from Garama and from history when underground water supplies dried up.

Islamic Libya

In AD 533 Byzantine armies captured Libya for Emperor Justinian. With tenuous and unpopular Byzantine control over Libya restricted to a few poorly defended coastal strongholds, the Arab horsemen of the Islamic armies encountered little resistance and by 643 had taken Tripoli and Cyrenaica.

From 800 the Abbasid-appointed emirs of the Aghlabid dynasty took their custodianship of Libya seriously, repairing Roman irrigation systems, restoring order and bringing a measure of prosperity to the region.

After Libya's flirtation with Sunnism, the Shiite Fatimid rulers in Cairo sent two tribes from the Arabian Peninsula into the Maghreb. The Bani Salim settled in Libya, particularly in Cyrenaica, while the Bani Hilal, numbering up to 200,000 families, spread across North Africa. The destruction of Cyrene and Tripoli by this unstoppable mass migration was the most effective conquest Libya had seen. The Berber tribespeople were displaced from their traditional lands and the new settlers finally cemented the cultural and linguistic Arabisation of the region.

Ottoman & Italian Rule

Tripoli was occupied by the Ottomans in 1551. The soldiers sent by the sultan to support the Ottoman pasha (governor) grew powerful and calvary officer Ahmed Karamanli seized power in 1711. His Karamanli dynasty would last 124 years, ruling from Tripoli's Al-Saraya al-Hamra. The Ottoman Turks finally reined in their erstwhile protégés in 1835 and resumed direct control over much of Libya.

The Sanusi Movement, led by Islamic cleric Sayyid Mohammed Ali as-Sanusi, called on the Cyrenaican people to resist Ottoman rule. The Grand Sanusi established his headquarters at Al-Jaghbub (and then later Al-Kufra) while his *ikhwan* (followers) set up *zawiyas* (religious colleges or monasteries) across North Africa and brought some stability to regions not known for their submission to central authority.

With Ottoman control tenuous at best, the Italian government sensed an opportunity. On 3 October 1911 the Italians attacked Tripoli claiming somewhat disingenuously to be liberating Libya from Ottoman rule. The Ottoman sultan had more important concerns and ceded Libya to the Italians.

In 1922 Mussolini announced the *Riconquista* of Libya. In response the legendary Sanusi sheikh Omar al-Mukhtar became the leader of the uprising against Italian rule in Cyrenaica. He was still fighting at the age of 73, before being captured and hanged in Benghazi in front of his followers in 1931.

Italy's Libya policy plumbed new depths of oppression. More than 100,000 people ended up in concentration camps in eastern Libya where up to 80,000 died in squalid conditions. Some 95% of Libyan livestock was also killed. The wholesale massacring of civilians fleeing Al-Kufra was the final outrage of a ruthless occupation. A quarter of Libya's population died during the almost three decades of Italian occupation.

By 1934 Italian control extended into the Fezzan, and in 1938 to 1939 Mussolini sought to fully colonise Libya, introducing 30,000 Italian settlers, which brought their numbers to more than 100,000 (proportionally more than the French settlers in neighbouring Algeria).

With the onset of WWII, devastating fighting broke out in the area around Tobruk. By January 1943 Tripoli was in British hands and by February the last German and Italian soldiers were driven from Libya.

In November 1949 the UN General Assembly approved the formation of an independent state. On 24 December 1951 the independent United Kingdom of Libya, with King Idris as its monarch, was finally proclaimed by the National Assembly.

Gaddafi's Libya

Libya's fortunes were transformed by the discovery of oil in 1959 at Zelten in Cyrenaica. By early 1960, 35 wells had been sunk nationwide and international oil companies clamoured to obtain exploration rights in Libya, much as they do today. Over the decade that followed, Libya was transformed from an economic backwater into one of the world's fastest-growing economies.

With regionwide political trends coalescing around the devastating 1967 Arab-Israeli War and the charisma of Egyptian president Gamal Abdel Nasser, it came as no great surprise when a Revolutionary Command Council, led by a little-known but charismatic 27-year-old Mu'ammar Gaddafi, seized power in Libya on 1 September 1969.

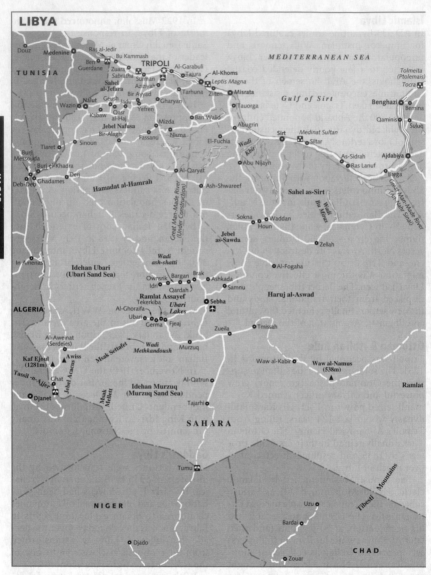

LIBYA

Riding on a wave of anti-imperialist anger, the new leader closed British and American military bases, expanded the armed forces and closed all newspapers, churches and political parties. Some 30,000 Italian settlers were deported and their assets expropriated. The new government injected massive funds into agriculture and

long-overdue development programmes with a concomitant rise in the standard of living of ordinary Libyans.

In the mid-1970s Colonel Gaddafi retreated into the desert for a period of reflection. He re-emerged clutching his Third Universal Theory, spelled out in *The Green Book*. Central to its philosophy was the

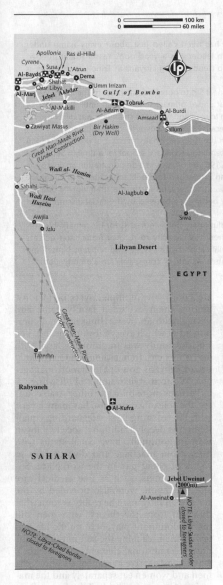

The US accused Libya of involvement in a string of terrorist attacks across Europe and on 15 April 1986, the US navy fired missiles into Tripoli and Benghazi. Up to 100 people were killed in Tripoli and around 30 in Benghazi. Two of Gaddafi's sons were injured and his adopted daughter, Hanna, was killed.

After Libyan agents were charged with the 1988 bombing of Pan Am flight 103 over the Scottish town of Lockerbie and the 1989 explosion of a French UTA airliner over the Sahara, UN sanctions came into effect. Finally, in early 1999, a deal was brokered and the suspects were handed over for trial by Scottish judges in The Hague. The sanctions, which had cost Libya over US$30 billion in lost revenues and production capacities, were immediately lifted.

Libya Today

When Colonel Gaddafi's urbane, Western-educated and media-savvy son Seif al-Islam al Gaddafi told the Davos 2005 World Economic Forum that 'the old times are finished', you could almost hear the collective sigh of relief from Libyans. Libya today is like a country awakening from a nightmare. Years of tortuous negotiations yielded a solution of sorts to the Lockerbie crisis with Libya agreeing to pay billions of dollars in compensation to families of the victims. Libya's announcement on 19 December 2003 that it would abandon its chemical and nuclear weapons programmes finally ended its international isolation. Suddenly, Libya was the West's best friend, held up as an example to so-called rogue states across the region.

World leaders have since flocked to Libya, the US has announced plans to re-open its embassy in Tripoli and Western businesspeople are clamouring for lucrative oil contracts. The Libyan government has promised far-reaching economic reforms as part of its plans to overhaul Libya's moribund economy.

The only shadow over Libya's future is uncertainty over who will lead Libya after Colonel Gaddafi. Two of his sons – Seif al-Islam and Al-Saadi, who plays soccer for Perugia in Italy – are the most likely candidates. Libyans prefer to hold fast to Colonel Gaddafi's public rejection of a dynasty and his statement that 'all Libyans will be president'.

aim of political participation by all Libyans rather than a representative system. Less savoury were the Revolutionary Committees who became famous for assassinating political opponents throughout Europe. Their takeover of the Libyan People's Bureau in 1984 confirmed Libya's increasing international isolation.

LIBYA

MU'AMMAR GADDAFI – MAN OR MYTH?

Libya's self-proclaimed 'Leader of the Masses' has been called just about every name under the sun. Ronald Reagan decided that the Libyan leader was a 'mad dog'. Yasser Arafat dubbed him the 'knight of the revolutionary phrases'. To trendy young Libyans in Tripoli, their leader is known simply as 'the man'.

Colonel Gaddafi was born in 1942 in the desert near Sirt to poor Bedouin parents. The future leader of the revolution was a serious, pious child who attended primary school in Sirt until the age of 14 and became the first member of his family to learn to read and write. His childhood was difficult, with reports that he was ridiculed by his classmates because of his impoverished background.

Stung by these experiences, and caught up in the Arab nationalist fervour of the day, Gaddafi was politically active from an early age. After attending secondary school for a time in Sebha, he was expelled because of his political activities. In 1961 he organised a demonstration against Syria for breaking the unity agreement with Egypt and proceeded to a military academy in Benghazi, from which he graduated in 1965. In 1966 he went to England for further training – a difficult experience for the young Libyan and he quickly became embittered by the racial discrimination and prejudice he suffered.

Apart from his alternately eccentric and revolutionary behaviour, it is for his remarkable survival skills that Gaddafi will be most remembered. His capacity to recover from bitter defeats (domestic opposition, the war with Chad and vilification by the West) and reinvent himself (eg as the saviour of Africa) is central to his endurance. As are, of course, his female bodyguards.

THE CULTURE
The National Psyche
In some ways, Libyans are everything that Colonel Gaddafi isn't – reserved, famed for their tolerance, and discreet. They are self-sufficient and wonderful improvisers, characteristics fostered during the long years of sanctions. They are open to outsiders, as devoid of hostility to the West as they are hospitable, and summed up the Libyan saying: 'if you have a good heart, one spoon can feed 100 people'. Libyans are also deeply attached to their land, proud of it and even loathe to leave it, especially at such an exciting time in their history. Libyans never forget where they came from, whether it be their home village or the dark years of isolation. Surprisingly knowledgeable about the world, they remain refreshingly untouched by it. You'll often hear Libyans say, 'we are a simple people', which is true only to the extent that the old ways of decency and generosity survive. But above all, for the first time in decades, Libyans are optimistic, convinced that the future is theirs.

Daily Life
Life revolves around the family, a bond that took on added significance during the years of international isolation when Libyan society turned inwards in search of company and support. Grafted onto the immedi-

ate family are multiple layers of identity, among them extended family, tribe and village, with an overarching national component of which every Libyan is proud. The nuclear family was traditionally large with numerous children, although some, mainly urban, Libyans now opt for a more manageable Western-style number of offspring.

Perhaps more than any other Arab country, the role of women also has many layers, with far-reaching laws safeguarding equality in this deeply traditional society. Libyan women nominally have equal status with men, from marriage and divorce laws to rights of equal pay in the workplace. Social safety nets, such as free medical care and education, were also provided by the state to all Libyans. The reality is somewhat different from the theory, with men still the predominant players of public life and few women reaching the summit of any industry. Traditional elements also remain – when guests arrive at someone's home, the men and women eat separately and the majority of women outside Tripoli and Benghazi wear traditional headscarves.

Population
With its vast territory inhabited by less than three people per square kilometre, Libya's population density is one of the lowest in the world. Over 70% of people live in urban

centres (some put the figure closer to 90%), in stark contrast to Libya's pre-oil days, when less than 25% lived in cities. Libya also has an overwhelmingly youthful population, with almost half under 15 years of age.

Libya's demographic mix is remarkably homogenous – 97% are of Arab or Berber origin, with many claiming mixed Arab and Berber ancestry due to intermarrying between the two communities.

The Tuareg (singular: Targi) are the indigenous people of the Sahara, the bearers of a proud desert culture whose members stretch across international boundaries into Algeria, Niger, Mali and Mauritania. The nation's 17,000 Tuareg are concentrated in the southwestern desert, particularly in the oases around Ghadames and Ghat, and have strong historical cross-border links.

Southeastern Libya is home to another nomadic community, the Toubou, thought to number about 2600. They were strongly influenced by the Sanusi Movement during the 19th century. Their homeland is the Tibesti Mountains and the area around Murzuq.

For more information, see p48.

Religion

More than 95% of Libya's population is Sunni Muslim with most following the Maliki school of Quranic interpretation. Founded by Malik ibn As, an Islamic judge who lived in Medina from AD 715 to 795, it is based on the practice that prevailed in Medina at the time. The Maliki strand of thought preaches the primacy of the Quran (as opposed to later teachings) and tolerance. In this sense, orthodox Islam in modern Libya bears strong similarities to the Sanusi teachings.

ARTS
Literature

Libya has a strong literary tradition that has always been highly politicised. At first it was associated with resistance against the Italian occupation (Suleiman al-Baruni, Al-Usta Omar, Ahmed Qunaba and Alfagi Hassan) and later with the 1960s preoccupation with imperialism and the massive social change that Libya was experiencing (Khalifa Takbali and Yusuf al-Sharif).

After the 1969 revolution, writers were required to align themselves closely to the government. Ahmed Ibrahim al-Fagih and Mohammed al-Zawi, in particular, became the foremost intellectuals of this generation, although for outsiders their work blurs the line between fiction and propaganda.

Libya's best-known writer throughout the Arab world is Ibrahim al-Kouni whose works reveal a fascination with the desert. He has published eight volumes of short stories and a number of novels, including *The Magians* and *The Bleeding of the Stone*; the latter is a stirring ecological desert fable and is available in Fergiani's Bookshop (p471) in Tripoli.

A younger generation of Libyan writers has now emerged. Of the novelists, Khalifa Hussein Mustapha has come to prominence, while poetry is increasingly the

---

LIBYA'S FINEST ARCHITECTURE

- Leptis Magna (p479) – the finest surviving monuments to Roman civilisation in North Africa
- Cyrene (p485) – superbly located Greek and Roman city in the foothills of the Jebel Akhdar (Green Mountains)
- old city of Ghadames (p491) – arguably the best-preserved caravan town in the entire Sahara
- Ghat's medina (p498) – an enchanting, crumbling and compact mud-brick medina deep in the Sahara
- Tripoli's medina (p473) – the Ottoman heart of Libya's cosmopolitan capital, with richly decorated mosques and whitewashed homes
- Qasr al-Haj (p489), Nalut (p490) and Kabaw (p490) – fairy-tale and cavelike Berber fortified granaries
- Mausoleum & Mosque of Sidi Abdusalam (p481), Zliten – Libya's most dazzling example of modern Islamic architecture
- Old Town Hall (p482), Benghazi – the most elegant and decrepit example of colonial Italy's architectural largesse

preserve of voices such as Gillani Trebshan and Idris at-Tayeb. The voice of women is slowly coming to the fore in the short stories of Lutfiah Gabaydi and the poetry of Mariam Salame and Khadija Bsikri.

Music

One of the most famous traditional music forms in Libya is the celebratory *mriskaawi*, which came from Murzuq and forms the basis for the lyrics of many Libyan songs. *Malouf*, with its origins in Andalusia, involves a large group of seated revellers singing and reciting poetry of a religious nature or about love. Groups capable of performing the *malouf* are highly sought-after.

Libya's best-known singer of modern music is Mohammed Hassan whose music carries the heartfelt passion of Arab music elsewhere; it's the subject matter (always Libyan topics), rather than the style, that marks him as distinctively Libyan. Another male singer of note is Mohammed Sanini. Libya's best-loved female singer is Salmin Zarou.

One name to watch out for in the future is Ayman al-Aathar (see Arab Pop Idol, p78).

ENVIRONMENT
The Land

Libya is the fourth-largest country in Africa, twice the size of Egypt and over half the size of the EU. Northwestern Libya (Tripolitania) contains the fertile Sahel al-Jefara (Jefara Plain), along Tripoli's narrow strip of Mediterranean coast. The plain rises to the formerly volcanic hills of the Jebel Nafusa with an average elevation of 600m to 900m.

LIBYA'S GEOGRAPHY: THE STATS

- length of Libya's Mediterranean coastline: 1770km
- proportion of country covered by desert: 95%
- proportion of Libya covered by sand dunes: 20%
- proportion of country covered by forest: 1%
- proportion of country suitable for agriculture: 1%
- number of permanent rivers or watercourses: zero

The hills give way to a series of east–west depressions that lead into the Fezzan.

In the Sahara, the *idehan* (sand seas) are interspersed with oases, lakes and wadis. The most dominant features of the Libyan Sahara include *hamada* (plateaus of rock scoured by wind erosion) and mountain ranges, such as the Jebel Acacus in the southwest and the larger massifs of the Tibesti along the border with Chad.

In Cyrenaica in the east, the low-lying terrain of the Sahara is separated from the northeastern coastline of Libya by the fertile Jebel Akhdar (Green Mountains), which drop steeply into the Mediterranean from a height of around 600m.

Wildlife

The prehistoric rock-paintings of the southern Sahara suggest that leopards, elephants and giraffes once roamed the region. Even 2500 years ago, elephants, lions, horned asses and bears were reported in Cyrenaica. Not surprisingly, none remains and Libya has few surviving species of mammal.

In desert regions, there are still gazelles in remote areas, and nocturnal fennecs (small foxes with large ears) can be glimpsed if you're lucky, as can the occasional wolves. Lizards, snakes and scorpions are also quite common. The shy waddans – large goatlike deer – can sometimes be seen hiding on the rocky ledges of the Jebel Acacus.

Environmental Issues

Some say the last decent, regular rainfalls in Libya stopped 8000 years ago. Underground water reserves have been Libya's only reliable water sources, with reservoirs of fresh, underground water preserved for millennia in porous rocks between impermeable layers. Colonel Gaddafi's brainchild in tapping these vast underground reserves is the Great Man-Made River, which pipes water from under the desert to Libya's thirsty coastal cities. Depending on your perspective, the project is either visionary or grossly irresponsible – the reserves are expected to last only for around 50 years. No-one knows the environmental side effects and supplies will be exhausted at around the same time that Libya is expected to run out of oil. For further details see p83.

Compounding concerns over the depletion of Libya's resources and the damage caused to the environment is the fact that Libya depends completely on fossil fuels for its power needs. Some new tourist developments are being designed with solar power as the energy source, but this doesn't go far in terms of addressing Libya's energy imbalance.

Another major environmental problem for Libya is rubbish – lots of it. The fields littered with black plastic bags on the outskirts of most towns can somewhat diminish Libya's aesthetic appeal for many visitors.

FOOD & DRINK
If you're on a tight budget, the staple tourist diet consists of couscous and chicken in Tripolitania and the Fezzan, with rice replacing couscous in Cyrenaica. For a little variety, there are also macaroni-based dishes inspired by the Italians; vegetable stews and potatoes might be a recurring theme if you're lucky.

Tripoli, Benghazi and a few other cities have some wonderful restaurants serving dishes of great variety. Particular highlights are the seafood dishes at specialist fish restaurants in Tripoli.

Many restaurants will assume that you will have a banquet-style meal, which consists of soup, salad, a selection of meat (or fish)

dishes, rice or couscous, a few vegetables and tea or coffee. In this book, the prices given for meals refer to these banquets.

Vegetarians should always specify their requirements as soon as they arrive in the restaurant. Tour companies should also be told in advance to help with planning. Remember that vegetarianism is rare in Libya, but most restaurants are obliging and keen to make sure you don't leave hungry.

For drinks, soft drinks and bottled mineral water will be your staples, along with coffee or tea. Nonalcoholic beer is also widely available.

TRIPOLI   طرابلس

☎ 021 / pop 1.15 million

Set on one of North Africa's best natural harbours, Tripoli exudes a distinctive Mediterranean charm infused with a decidedly Arab-Islamic flavour. Tripoli (Al-Tarablus in Arabic) is Libya's largest and most cosmopolitan city. With such a rich mosaic of historical influences – from Roman ruins and artefacts to the Ottoman-era medina – few travellers leave disappointed.

HISTORY
Tripoli has worn many guises throughout history. The Oea of Roman antiquity yielded to an Islamic city and by the end of the 17th century, Tripoli was Libya's only city of size with over 30,000 inhabitants. The disparate civilisations that have occupied Tripoli have all left their mark in this sophisticated modern city that beats with an ancient heart.

ORIENTATION
The city's most recognisable landmark is the castle, Al-Saraya al-Hamra, at the eastern corner of the medina beside the central Martyrs Sq (Green Sq). The main shopping and business streets radiate from the square.

INFORMATION
Bookshops
Fergiani's Bookshop (☎ 4444873; fergi_u@hotmail.com; Sharia 1st September; 🕑 10am-2pm & 5-9pm Sat-Thu) An excellent selection of hard-to-find English-language books on Libya, good postcards and a smaller number of books in French and Italian.
Fergiani 2 (☎ 3330192; fergiani_b2@hotmail.com; 🕑 10am-2pm & 5-9pm Sat-Thu)

THE BEST OF LIBYAN FOOD

It's a pity that few Libyan restaurants serve the delicious home-cooked foods that Libyans themselves eat at home. Here we recommend the local specialities that you may find on a restaurant menu (and where you may find them).

bourdim – meat slow-cooked in a sand pit; try this at Mat'am al-Najar or Mat'am al-Khayma (p479), both near Al-Khoms

fitaat – lentils, mutton and buckwheat pancakes cooked together in a tasty sauce in a low oven and eaten with the hands from a communal bowl – it's served in some of the old houses of Ghadames (see the boxed text, p494)

osban – a sheep's stomach cleaned out and filled with rice, herbs, liver, kidney and other meats, and steamed or boiled in a sauce; eat this at Mat'am ash-Sharq (p475) in Tripoli

rishda – delicately spiced vermicelli-style pasta noodles with chickpeas, tomatoes and caramelised onions can also be tried at Mat'am ash-Sharq (p475) in Tripoli

TRIPOLI

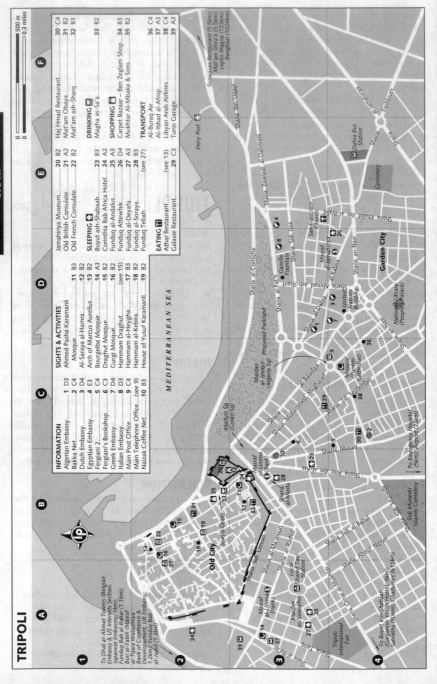

MEDITERRANEAN SEA

To Dhat al-Ahmat Towers (Belgian
Embassy) & US Interests Section;
Japanese Embassy (3km);
Funduq Bab al-Bahar (1.1km);
Burj al-Fateh (Masraf
al-Tijara Watamniya -
Bank of Commerce &
Developement; UK Embassy;
1.2km); Funduq Bab
al-Jadid (1.3km)

Old City

Martyrs Sq
(Green Sq)

Maidan
al-Jezair
(Algeria Sq)

Proposed Parkland

Ferry Port

Dahra Bus
Station

Cemetery

Seawaves Restaurant (5.5km);
Mat'am Shira'a (5.5km);
Leptis Magna (123km);
Benghazi (1024km)

San Francisco
Church

Gazelle
Fountain

United
Nations
Building

National Library
(People's Palace)

Garden City

Mosque
(Former
Catholic
Cathedral)

To Emergency Hospital
(5km); Airport (23km)

To Buyut ash-Shabaab
(Gargaresh Youth Hostel; 4km);
Sabratha (80km); Ghadames (611km)

Tripoli
International
Fair

Sidi Munedir
Islamic Cemetery

LIBYA

Emergency

Emergency Hospital (☎ 121)

Internet Access

Bakka Net (cnr Sharias Mizran & Haity; per hr 1LD; ☒ 8.30am-midnight Sat-Thu, 5pm-midnight Fri)
Naizak Coffee Net (☎ 0913216723; off Sharia 1st September; ☒ 9am-2am)

Money

The most easily accessible *masraf* (banks) are in the streets between Martyrs Sq and Maidan al-Jezayir (Algeria Sq). Masraf al-Tijara Watanmiya (Bank of Commerce & Development) has a branch on the ground floor of the Dhat al-Ahmat Tower 1 and the 1st floor of the Burj al-Fateh where you can obtain cash advances on your Visa card.

Post & Telephone

Main post office (Maidan al-Jezayir; ☒ 8am-10.30pm Sat-Thu) Has a reasonably efficient poste restante service.
Main telephone office (Maidan al-Jezayir; ☒ 8am-midnight) Inside the main hall there's a useful fax restante service (fax 3331199 or 3340040; 1LD), which is signed as 'Flash Fax'.

DANGERS & ANNOYANCES

Few travellers encounter any difficulties in Tripoli and the most arduous task you're likely to encounter is finding your way in a city where most of the street signs are written in Arabic. If in doubt, ask a local to help out. One potential hazard is crossing those same streets.

SIGHTS & ACTIVITIES
Jamahiriya Museum & Al-Saraya al-Hamra (Tripoli Castle)

One of the Mediterranean's finest classical art collections is found in Tripoli's **Jamahiriya Museum** (☎ 3330292; Martyrs Sq; adult/child 3/1LD, camera/video 5/10LD; ☒ 9am-1pm Sun-Tue). Built in consultation with Unesco, it's extremely well designed and provides a comprehensive overview of all periods of Libyan history.

If time is limited, you may want to restrict yourself to those galleries that provide context to the places you're most likely to visit. Most of the galleries are located on the ground floor, which covers, among other subjects: **Saharan rock art** (Gallery 4); the **Garamantian empire** of Wadi al-Hayat (Gallery 5); artefacts from **Cyrene** and **Greek Libya** (Galleries 7 and 8); and the excep-

TRIPOLI IN...

Two Days

You could easily spend a day exploring the medina, factoring in shopping time in the medina's southeastern corner. Not to be missed are the exceptional **mosques** (p474), the **Old British** and **French Consulates** (p474) and the **House of Yusuf Karamanli** (p474). Just outside the medina's walls, the **Jamahiriya Museum** (left) and **Al-Saraya al-Hamra** (left) could collectively occupy an entire morning. For the remainder of the second day, linger in a **teahouse** (p476) smoking nargileh, explore the attractive white Italianate architecture southeast of Martyrs Sq and seek out Tripoli's excellent **restaurants** (p475).

Four Days

If you have four days, you could do everything in the two-day itinerary and spend a day each at the outstanding Roman ruins of **Sabratha** (p477) and **Leptis Magna** (p479). Both are an easy day trip from the capital.

tional displays covering Roman **Leptis Magna** and **Sabratha** (Gallery 9). On the 2nd floor, the sections on **Islamic architecture** (Galleries 15 to 19) and the **Libyan ethnographic exhibits** (Gallery 20), with some fine sections on Ghadames, are also excellent.

The museum's only drawback is that most of the exhibits are labelled only in Arabic, although there are informative general descriptions in English. Taking a **guide** (50LD) will enhance your visit. If he's not already booked up, Dr Mustafa Turjman, who works with the **Department of Antiquities** (☎ 3333042), is outstanding.

The museum once formed part of the 13,000-sq-metre **Al-Saraya al-Hamra** (Tripoli Castle or Red Castle; ☎ 3330292; Martyrs Sq; adult/child 3/1LD, camera/video 5/10LD; ☒ 9am-1pm Tue-Sun), which represented the seat of power in Tripolitania from the 7th until the 20th centuries. Tripoli Castle has a separate entrance.

Medina

Tripoli's whitewashed medina is an evocative place where modern Libya barely encroaches. The first fortified wall around the medina was built in the 4th century, while

LIBYA

further ramparts and reinforcements were added by subsequent occupiers to safeguard the city from seaborne attack. The layout follows the blueprint of the old Arab city and although much modified, its design has changed little. Most of the public buildings, houses and 38 mosques in the medina date from the Turkish period.

The **Arch of Marcus Aurelius**, the only intact remnant of the ancient Roman city of Oea, was completed in AD 163 to 164. It stood at the main crossroads of the Roman city and provided an entrance from the harbour. One reason for the preservation of the arch is that an ancient prophecy foretold terrible punishments for anyone who removed a stone.

The 19th-century **Gurgi Mosque**, the last mosque built in Tripoli under the Turks, has one of the most beautiful interiors in the city with imported marble pillars from Italy, ceramic tilework from Tunisia and intricate stone carvings from Morocco.

Near the mosque, the **Old British Consulate** (Sharia Hara Kebir; admission 2LD, camera/video 2/5LD; 9am-5.30pm Sat-Thu) housed Her Majesty's representatives from the second half of the 18th century until 1940. As well as diplomatic representation, the consul's representatives used their position to launch expeditions into the Sahara with an eye on lucrative trade routes. With a marble-paved courtyard and elegant Moorish archways, it's one of old Tripoli's most attractive buildings.

In the same area, the **Old French Consulate** (Zenghet el-Fransis; admission 2LD, camera/video 2/5LD; 9am-5.30pm Sat-Thu), dating from 1630, is set around a compact, high-walled courtyard complete with some fine tilework and wooden doors around the perimeter. Not far away, the 16th-century **Draghut Mosque**

has elegantly rendered pillars and arches (15 in the prayer hall alone).

Just south of the Roman Column Crossroads, in the centre of the medina, the 19th-century **House of Yusuf Karamanli** (admission 2LD, camera/video 2/5LD; 9am-5.30pm Sat-Thu) has another fine courtyard and ethnographic exhibits from the period.

The largest mosque in the medina, with a beautiful octagonal minaret, the richly decorated **Ahmed Pasha Karamanli Mosque** was opened in the 1730s. The intricate carvings around the five doorways and 30 domes suggest a high level of Moroccan and Andalusian influence.

Hammams

All of Tripoli's best *hammams* (bathhouses) are in the medina. Charges are 1LD for a steam bath, 2LD for a massage and 5LD for the full scrubbing works. Try **Hammam Draghut** (Draghut Mosque; women 7am-5pm Mon, Wed & Thu, men 7am-5pm Tue, Sat & Sun), **Hammam al-Kebira** (women 7am-5pm Mon, Wed & Thu, men 7am-5pm Tue, Sat & Sun) or **Hammam al-Heygha** (women 7am-5pm Mon, Thu, Sat & Sun, men 7am-5pm Tue & Wed, Fri).

SLEEPING

All prices for midrange and top-end hotels listed here include a private bathroom and breakfast unless otherwise stated.

Budget

Buyut ash-Shabaab (Central Youth Hostel; 4445171; fax 3330118; Sharia Amr ibn al-Ass; dm HI nonmembers/members 4/6LD) The location is ideal and the shared bathrooms are fine, but otherwise this hostel is a pretty basic place.

Buyut ash-Shabaab (Gargaresh Youth Hostel; 4776694; fax 4474755; off Sharia Gargaresh; dm HI nonmembers/members 4/6LD) It's a long way from Tripoli's sights, but this well-run hostel is marginally better than its more central counterpart. It's 5km south of the town centre in the lively district of Gargaresh.

Funduq Bab al-Jadid (3350670; fax 3350670; Sharia al-Corniche; s/d with private bathroom 30/40LD;) With a good seafront location, this popular place is outstanding. It has small but spotless and well-appointed rooms.

Funduq al-Soraya (4443817; fax 3330821; off Sharia Omar al-Mukhtar; s/d 25/40LD;) One of the closest hotels to Martyrs Sq, Funduq al-Soraya has simple, drab but comfortable

THE AUTHOR'S CHOICE
Funduq al-Andalus (☎ 3343777; www.anda
lushotel.com; Sharia al-Kindi; s/d 50/60LD; ☒) It
can be hard to choose between the new
private hotels, but our favourite is Funduq
al-Andalus, which is just the sort of place
that Tripoli, and indeed Libya has been
crying out for. It has all the necessary bells
and whistles – satellite TV, air-conditioning,
minibar – but the decoration is more stylish than most and the service is attentive.
The location, a 10-minute walk to Martyrs
Sq and the medina, is also ideal.

rooms. The location is unbeatable and staff
are friendly.

Midrange
Funduq al-Deyafa (☎ 4448182; diafatip@hotmail.com;
Sharia al-Raza; s/d 40/50LD; ☒) A good choice in
the area, Funduq al-Deyafa is as friendly as
Funduq al-Andalus, but the rooms lack character. Bathtubs in most rooms is a plus. It's a
well-run place that's worth every dinar.
    Funduq Tebah (☎ 3333575; www.tebah-ly.com;
Sharia al-Raza; s/d 40/50LD; ☒) Similarly impressive, this place has very tidy rooms with
exactly the kind of attention to detail that
government hotels lack.
    Funduq Attewfek (☎ 4447253; fax 3340316; Sharia
Qusban; s/d 55/65LD; ☒ ▯) A stone's throw
from San Francisco Church and an easy
15-minute walk into the centre, Funduq At-
tewfek has spacious if simple rooms with
balconies (some overlook the church), a
laundry service, Internet access and a good
buffet breakfast. This is also one of the few
hotels to accept Visa card.

Top End
Corinthia Bab Africa Hotel (☎ 3351990; tripoli@
corinthia.com; Souq al-Thulatha; d €225-250, junior ste
€275-450; ▣ ☒ ▯ ▣) A towering temple of
glass and elegance, this is Libya's classiest
hotel. The rooms are enormous and luxurious, the restaurants of the highest order
and the service everything you'd expect for
the price. The hotel has a business centre,
conference facilities, two swimming pools,
a gymnasium, an exclusive spa and plans
for wi-fi Internet connection in every room.
Credit cards are also accepted. All of which
adds up to Libya's premier address.

Funduq Bab al-Bahar (☎ 3350676; fax 3350711;
Sharia al-Corniche; s/d/ste 60/75/120LD; ☒) Seen in
the light of the Corinthia's emergence, the
Bab al-Bahar is anything but the five stars it
claims to be. The rooms are fine and most
afford good views over the town or Mediterranean, but the service is woeful. That notwithstanding, it's a favourite of tour groups
and probably not bad value for money.

EATING
Medina
Athar Restaurant (☎ 4447001; meals 17-20LD; ☽ lunch
& dinner) This excellent place, next to the Arch
of Marcus Aurelius, has a wonderful location and some of the outdoor tables (almost impossible to snaffle on a summer's
evening) are among the most pleasant in
Tripoli. The food is high quality and ranges
from more traditional couscous or *tagen* (a
lightly spiced lamb dish with a tomato-and-
paprika-based sauce) to mixed grills and
fish. Visa cards are accepted.
    Mat'am ash-Sharq (Mat'am al-Bourai; ☎ 091315
7772; Sharia al-Halqa; meals from 10LD; ☽ lunch & dinner)
Above one of the liveliest thoroughfares in
the medina, this bright and busy restaurant
has basic décor, but excellent food. Its speciality is the delicious *rishda* (noodles with
chickpeas and onions) and, for the more
adventurous, *osban* (sheep's stomach filled
with liver, kidney and other meat, rice and
herbs, and steamed or boiled in a sauce),
which is a Libyan favourite.

East of Martyrs Square
The area sprawling east of Martyrs Sq is
awash with restaurants.

THE AUTHOR'S CHOICE
Mat'am Obaya (Obaya Seafood Restaurant;
☎ 0925010736; Souq al-Turk 114; ☽ lunch Sat-
Thu) This is the sort of place that Lonely
Planet authors hesitate to include in a book
for fear that they can't get a table next time
they visit. It's small with no pretensions to
luxury, but there's no finer seafood in Libya
and all of it's home-cooked. The stuffed calamari is the tastiest restaurant dish you'll
find and the *shola* fish with sauce is not far
behind. Expect to pay no more than 10LD
for one of these main dishes, the octopus
salad and a drink. Exceptional.

LIBYA

Galaxie Restaurant (☎ 4448764; galaxie_libya@ yahoo.com; Sharia 1st September 135; meals 14-18LD; ☺ lunch & dinner) One of the best restaurants in this area, Galaxie is tastefully decorated and does the usual dishes with a touch more imagination than similar places elsewhere. The *jara* (a meat stew) is excellent but needs to be ordered three hours in advance. Shwarma and sandwiches are available downstairs.

Haj Hmad Restaurant (☎ 0913136367; Sharia Haity; meals from 8LD; ☺ lunch & dinner) Haj Hmad is a great place to enjoy traditional Libyan dishes heavy on internal organs, feet and heads. But there are plenty of nonoffal dishes (including fish and beans) to choose from and it's popular with locals – always a good sign.

For a totally different eating experience, head 5.5km east of the port along the road to Tajura where there's a ramshackle fish market. Choose the fish or other seafood that you want, buy it and then take it to one of the basic restaurants where they'll grill it for you for a small fee (around 1.50LD). The most pleasant place to eat your meal is **Seawaves Restaurant** (☎ 0925061406); you could also try **Mat'am Shira'a** (☎ 0913206971). If you're going there under your own steam, ask the taxi driver for the Marsa or Al-Hufra area; it's opposite the turn-off to Sharia 11 June.

DRINKING
Magha As-Sa'a (Clock Tower Coffee Shop; ☎ 0925032511; Maydan al-Sa'a; ☺ 7am-2am) Opposite the Ottoman clock tower in the medina is Tripoli's outstanding traditional teahouse. You can sit outside, but make sure you check out the ground-floor room with its eclectic and distinctly musical theme – an old electric guitar, archaic jukebox and gramophone.

SHOPPING
The souqs of the medina are definitely the most atmospheric places in Libya to shop.

Carpet Bazaar – Ben Zeglam Shop (☎ 0913212 660; Souq al-Attara; ☺ 10am-2pm & 5-8.30pm Sat-Thu) This is one shop that stands out in terms of quality, price and range for Libyan (mostly Berber) items, such as pottery, Tuareg jewellery, knives and boxes, flat-weave kilim cushions and larger rugs. The owner, Ahmeda Zeglam, is a delight.

Nearby, behind the clock tower, the Souq al-Ghizdir (Copper Souq) is a great place to see and hear the artisans at work and there are plenty of items for sale. At the northwestern end of the Copper Souq, you'll find **Mukhtar Al-Mbaka & Sons** (☎ 3331057; Souq al-Turk 12-16; ☺ 9am-8pm) where traditional Libyan silver items are on offer from Mukhtar himself who can explain the history of each piece.

GETTING THERE & AWAY
Air
Libyan Arab Airlines (☎ 3331143; Sharia Haity) flies from Tripoli International Airport and **Al-Buraq Air** (☎ 4444811; Sharia Mohammed Megharief) flies from Metiga Airport, 10km east of Tripoli. They both operate domestic flights.

Bus & Shared Taxi
Long distances buses and shared taxis for most cities around Libya depart from the area near Tunis Garage at the western end of Sharia al-Rashid.

GETTING AROUND
Tripoli International Airport is located some 25km south of the city. A private taxi costs 10LD, but if you're leaving after mid-

DOMESTIC FLIGHTS FROM TRIPOLI			
Destination	**Airline**	**One-way/return (LD)**	**Frequency**
Benghazi	Libyan Arab Airlines	37.50/75	2 daily
	Al-Buraq Air	42.50/85	2 daily
Ghadames	Libyan Arab Airlines	26.50/53	2 weekly*
Ghat	Libyan Arab Airlines	56/112	2 weekly
Houn	Libyan Arab Airlines	28/56	2 weekly
Lebreq (near Al-Bayda)	Libyan Arab Airlines	56/112	3 weekly
Sebha	Libyan Arab Airlines	37.50/75	1 daily

* The Tripoli–Ghadames service is not regular despite appearing in airline schedules.

night, the drivers will ask for more. Elsewhere in the city, a trip rarely costs more than 2LD.

SABRATHA   صبراتة

☎ 024 / pop 102,037

The ruins of the ancient Roman city of Sabratha, 80km west of Tripoli, are among the highlights of any visit to Libya, especially as it is home to one of the finest theatres of antiquity.

HISTORY

There was a Punic settlement here from the 4th century BC, but Sabratha's Punic character was altered with the arrival of Greek (Hellenistic) settlers in the 2nd century BC. After a violent earthquake in the 1st century AD, the city's architects turned towards Rome for inspiration, resulting in the Roman character so strongly evident today. Sabratha's heyday was during the reigns of the four Roman emperors Antoninus Pius (AD 138–61), Marcus Aurelius Antoninus (AD 161–80), Lucius

Aelius Aurelius Commodus (AD 180–92) and Septimus Severus (AD 193–211). Although it never competed in significance or grandeur with Leptis Magna, it was given the coveted title of *colonia* (colony) in the 2nd century AD. Sabratha was destroyed in AD 365 by an earthquake.

INFORMATION

Guides (50LD) are compulsory for entrance to the **ancient city** (☎ 622214; admission 3LD, camera/video 5/10LD; ✆ 8am-6.30pm). **Dr Mustapha Turjman** (in Tripoli ☎ 021-3333042) is highly recommended.

SIGHTS

The **Roman Museum** (admission 3LD, camera/video 5/10LD; ✆ 8am-6pm Tue-Sun) contains a number of wonderful mosaics and frescoes. It's located close to the site entrance. The nearby **Punic Museum** (admission 3LD, camera/video 5/10LD; ✆ 8am-6pm Tue-Sun) probably appeals only to those with a specialist's interest in the city's earliest history.

Heading northwest into the monumental heart of Sabratha, the 24m-high **Mausoleum B** (Mausoleum of Bes) is one of the few

SABRATHA

MEDITERRANEAN SEA

0   100 m
0   0.1 miles

Old Port

Seaward or Ocean Baths

Christian Basilica

To Amphitheatre (200m)

Christian Basilica

Old Road to Oea (Tripoli)

Olive press

Statue of Flavius Tullus

Decumanus

Theatre Baths

Temple of Hercules

Southern Temple to an Unknown Divinity

Byzantine Gate

Ancient Residential Quarter

Peristyle House

To Modern Sabratha (500m); Tripoli (80km)

SIGHTS & ACTIVITIES

Antonine Temple	1 B2
Basilica of Justinian	2 A2
Baths of Oceanus	3 D1
Capitoleum	4 A2
Curia	5 A2
Entrance & Ticket Office	6 C3
Forum	7 A2
Judicial Basilica	8 A2
Mausoleum B	9 B3
Punic Museum	10 B3
Roman Museum	11 B3
Temple of Isis	12 D1
Temple of Liber Pater	13 B2
Temple of Serapis	14 A2
Theatre	15 C2

LIBYA

remaining Punic structures in Sabratha. After passing through the 6th-century **Byzantine Gate**, pause at the elevated **Antonine Temple**, dedicated to the Roman emperor Antoninus Pius. The temple offers superb views from the top.

The **Judicial Basilica** (Basilica of Apuleius of Madora or House of Justice) was originally built in the 1st century AD as a Roman court. Most of what remains dates from around AD 450 when the Byzantines converted it into a basilica.

Sabratha's Roman **forum** formed the centrepiece of the ancient city and served as a market and public meeting place where the news of the city was disseminated. Overlooking the forum is the 1st-century **Capitoleum**, also known as the Temple of Jupiter or Zeus, the principal temple of the city and the soapbox of choice for the great orators of the era.

On the northern side of the forum is the **Curia** (Senate House), the meeting place of the city's magistrates and senators. East of the Curia is the **Temple of Liber Pater** (Temple of Dionysius; 2nd century AD). Dedicated to one of the most revered gods of Roman Africa, it was second only to the Capitoleum in the hierarchy of temples in Roman Sabratha.

Immediately east of the Curia are the **Temple of Serapis** and the 6th-century **Basilica of Justinian**, one of the finest churches of Byzantine Sabratha. The buildings around the Basilica of Justinian date from the 1st century AD when the city was still primarily Punic in character.

East of Sabratha's centre is the outstanding **theatre**, the jewel in Sabratha's crown. Begun in AD 190 under Commodus' reign and in use until AD 365, its auditorium once measured 95m in diameter. As such, it was the largest theatre in Africa. The three-tiered façade behind the stage is one of the most exceptional in the Roman world, with alcoves and 108 fluted Corinthian columns that rise over 20m above the stage and are adorned with exquisite carvings of Roman divinities. The front of the elevated stage is simply magnificent.

A pleasant hike off to the northeast takes you to the once-lavish **Baths of Oceanus** and the superb 1st-century **Temple of Isis**, one of Sabratha's finest and dedicated to the Egyptian goddess Isis, the protector of sailors.

GETTING THERE & AWAY

Shared taxis run regularly to/from Tripoli's Sharia al-Corniche station.

LEPTIS MAGNA & AROUND

Leptis Magna is the most impressive Roman city outside Rome and its intoxicating coastal location make this *the* must-see in Libya. The nearby coastal cities of Al-Khoms and Zliten have little to hold your interest but make for comfortable places to eat and sleep on your way east.

AL-KHOMS   الخمس
☎ 031 / pop 201,943

As the closest town to Leptis Magna, Al-Khoms makes a good base for exploring the ruins. A pleasant if unspectacular town, it's 120km east of Tripoli.

Information

Along Sharia al-Khoms, the main road through town that continues east to Leptis Magna 3km away, are private telephone offices, a sprinkling of Internet cafés, the post office and the *jawazzat* (passport office); all are close to the intersection with Sharia al-Jamahiriya.

Sleeping & Eating

Inside Leptis itself, it is possible to camp (5LD) in car park No 1 under the pine and eucalyptus trees – it's a quiet spot at night and guarded by police from the station opposite.

Buyut ash-Shabaab (Youth Hostel; ☎ 621880; dm HI members/nonmembers 3/5LD) In a quiet area 2km west of the town centre, this is a typically basic but friendly hostel.

Al-Madinah Hotel (☎ 620799; al_madinahotel@yahoo.com; s/d with private bathroom 15/2 LD; 🗙) The rooms here may be simple but they're spotless and come with TV, phone and decent bathrooms. For this price, you won't find better in Libya. Dodgy pillows are the only disappointment. It's behind the *jawazzat*.

Leptes Hotel (☎ 621252; lepdahhotel@yahoo.com; Sharia al-Khoms; s/d with private bathroom from 15/25LD; 🗙) Almost as good as the Al-Madinah Hotel, the Leptes has rooms that have more character, but which can be a bit dark and overdone. The bathrooms are excellent and it's the closest hotel to Leptis Magna. There's no elevator.

Funduq al-Andalus (☎ 626667; Tripoli-Misrata Hwy; s with shared bathroom 20LD, tw/d with private bathroom 30/40LD; 🅿) The rooms here are clean and spacious; those at the back are quieter. There is also a pleasant restaurant (meals 15LD).

Tell Libyans that you're passing through Al-Khoms and many will ask with envy whether you'll be eating at either **Mat'am al-Najar** (☎ 0913205398) or **Mat'am al-Khayma** (☎ 0913205169), 12km west of Al-Khoms on the road to Tripoli. That's because they're famous throughout the country for their *bourdim* (meat slow-cooked in a sand pit). Most meals go for around 8LD.

Inside Leptis, between the ticket office and museum, is **Mat'am Addiyafa** (☎ 621210; meals 15LD; 🕑 lunch), which has an agreeable atmosphere.

Getting There & Away
Al-Khoms is connected by regular shared taxis with Tripoli and Zliten.

LEPTIS MAGNA
لبدة
☎ 031

It must have been a great place to live. Leptis Magna (called Lebdah in Arabic) is one of the best-preserved and most evocative Roman cities in the Mediterranean. It's a testament to extravagance with abundant examples of lavish decoration, grand buildings of monumental stature, indulgent bath complexes and forums for entertainment.

History
Although founded by Punic refugees in the 7th century BC, Leptis Magna came under Roman influence in 111 BC and was raised to prominence under Emperor Augustus (r 27 BC–AD 14) when the city was laid out in Roman style and adorned with monuments of grandeur. It soon became one of the leading ports in Africa, an entrepôt for the trade in exotic animals and locally grown olives. Leptis became Africa's premier Roman city during the reign of Leptis' favourite son, Septimus Severus (see p480).

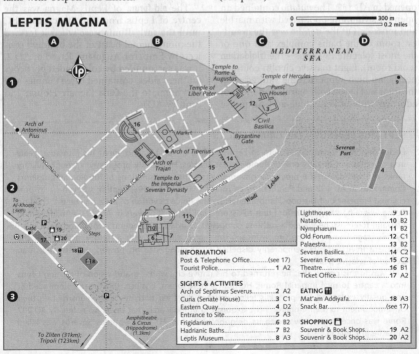

LIBYA

Information

Leptis Magna (☎ 624256; admission 3LD, guide 50LD, camera/video 5/10LD; ☯ 8am-6.30pm) is accessible through car park No 1. Note that there are separate entry fees for the **Leptis museum** (admission 3LD, guide 50LD, camera/video 5/10LD; ☯ 8am-6.30pm Tue-Sun) and **amphitheatre** (admission 3LD, guide 50LD, camera/video 5/10LD; ☯ 8am-6.30pm). It is compulsory to have a **guide** (50LD) to visit Leptis Magna. Guides we recommend include Dr Mustapha Turjman, Miftah Mansor, Mahmud at-Taib, Khalifa Wada, Mr Darnaoti and Hajj Omar.

Sights

The **Arch of Septimus Severus** is a grand introduction to the architectural opulence of Leptis. Built in AD 203 to mark the emperor's visit to his native city, its Corinthian columns and relief carvings of the great events of the Severan era are breathtaking.

The arrival of water (via aqueduct) and marble in Leptis early in the 2nd century AD prompted Emperor Hadrian to commission the superb **Hadrianic Baths**, which became one of the social hubs of the city. The baths were opened in AD 137. The *natatio* contained an open-air swimming pool paved with marble and mosaics. Off the *natatio* was the grandest room of the baths complex and one of the most splendid in Leptis – the **frigidarium** (cold room). Eight massive cipolin columns nearly 9m high supported the vaulted roof, the floor was paved with marble and the roof adorned with brilliant blue-and-turquoise

mosaics. The niches around the walls once held more than 40 statues, some of which are in the museums in Leptis and Tripoli.

East of the **palaestra** (sports ground) and Hadrianic Baths is the **Nymphaeum** (Temple of Nymphs) with its superb façade of red-granite and cipolin columns.

Septimus Severus' audacious transformation of Leptis involved reconfiguring the heart of the city, moving it away from the old forum to the new one that bore his name. The open-air **Severan Forum** measured 100m by 60m and its superb floor was covered with marble. In the great tradition of Roman city squares, Septimus Severus' forum was once surrounded by colonnaded porticoes. On the façades between the arches were Gorgon heads, of which over 70 have been found.

The **Severan Basilica**, 92m long and 40m wide, ran along the northeastern side of the Severan Forum and served as the city's House of Justice. Begun by Septimus Severus and completed by his son Caracalla in AD 216, it contains extravagantly sculpted pillars at either end honouring Liber Pater (Dionysius) and Hercules.

The **old forum** of Leptis Magna was the centre of Leptis from the 7th century BC until the early Roman era when it formed the monumental heart of the building projects by Emperor Augustus. Paved in AD 2, it was surrounded by colonnaded porticoes on three sides, contained three temples and was home to the **Curia** (Senate House; 2nd century AD).

SEPTIMUS SEVERUS – THE GRIM AFRICAN

Lucius Septimus Severus was born in Leptis Magna in AD 145 and spent his formative years in a city that was already one of Rome's great centres. He quickly progressed through military ranks and was declared a provincial governor. After the assassinations of the Roman emperors Commodus in AD 192 and Pentinax three months later in AD 193, Septimus Severus was proclaimed emperor by his troops. Emboldened by the fierce devotion of his army, he marched on Rome where he swept all before him to assume full imperial powers in AD 193. A military man first and foremost, he waged a ruthless campaign to extend the boundaries of Rome's empire. By this stage known as 'the Grim African', the feared emperor won a further victory over the Parthians in AD 202–03, temporarily dispelled all challenges to his power, and ushered in a period of relative peace.

It was in this period that he returned to his native city with a grand vision of turning Leptis into a centre to rival imperial Rome. He built a new forum, basilica, the Great Colonnaded St and greatly expanded the port. His fellow citizens did their part by hastily constructing their own monument to their emperor – the exquisite triumphal arch that bears his name. By AD 207 Rome was once again at war with its neighbours and in AD 211 Septimus Severus was killed in battle in England.

The **port**, another key element of Septimus Severus' vision, contained a **lighthouse** that was once more than 35m high and may have rivalled the more-famous Pharos of Alexandria. The reason the buildings of the **eastern quay** are still relatively intact is that the port was hardly used. Soon after its construction, the harbour silted up and it is now covered by vegetation.

The **market** is one of the most unusual and attractive of the Leptis monuments, with two reconstructed octagonal halls where stalls were set up to sell the bounty of Leptis farmers and fabric merchants. First built in 9 to 8 BC, the market was rebuilt during the reign of Septimus Severus.

Leptis' **theatre** is one of the oldest stone theatres anywhere in the Roman world and is the second-largest surviving theatre in Africa after Sabratha. Begun in AD 1 to 2, its most striking feature is the stage with its façade of three semicircular recesses surrounded by three-tiered fluted columns dating from the era of Antoninus Pius (AD 138–61). The stage was adorned with hundreds of statues and sculptures that included portraits of emperors, gods and wealthy private citizens.

The evocative **amphitheatre** once held 16,000 people and was hollowed out of a hill, 1km east of the port in the 1st century AD. The **circus**, below the amphitheatre, dates from AD 162. During the reign of Marcus Aurelius Antoninus, it was home to chariot races attended by up to 25,000 people.

The **museum** is very well organised with labels in both English and Arabic. To see the museum properly, you'll need to allow a minimum of two hours. Particularly fine galleries include Rooms 4 to 7 (Roman triumphal arches with wonderful statues and busts from Leptis), Room 8 (artefacts from the Hadrianic Baths), Room 10 (theatre) and Room 11 (Severan Forum).

Getting There & Away
Leptis Magna is just over 1km from the centre of Al-Khoms.

ZLITEN زليطن
☎ 0571 / pop 99,289
Zliten, 34km east of Al-Khoms, has an excellent hotel and a fine mosque and so it makes for a good overnight stay.

Sights
The **Mausoleum & Mosque of Sidi Abdusalam** is one of the finest modern Islamic buildings in Libya. Its distinctive green dome is surrounded by a multitude of minarets and smaller domes. The external panels of the façade contain some superb ceramics with floral and arabesque motifs. The tiled pillars are most attractive. Non-Muslims are not permitted inside the mausoleum's inner sanctum but the gilded tomb is clearly visible from the door, as are the marvellous stucco ceilings.

Sleeping & Eating
Funduq Zliten (☎ 620121; fax 620120; Sharia al-Jamahiriya; s/d/ste with private bathroom 30/40/70LD; 🅿) It's the only hotel in town but this place is very comfortable with attractively furnished rooms, satellite TV, phone, balcony, video player and comfortable beds. The staff are friendly if not always helpful and there's a reasonable restaurant (meals 18LD).

There's a handful of cheap restaurants close to the post office and between the highway and main roundabout.

Getting There & Away
Shared taxis connect Zliten with Al Khoms (or the Leptis Magna turn-off) and Tripoli.

SIRT سرت
☎ 054 / pop 128,123
Colonel Gaddafi's birthplace is a custombuilt city yearning to be the capital of Libya, if not Africa. Sadly, this supposed showpiece of the revolution is a city without soul, a lifeless place of few charms. Without any apparent attempt at irony, one sign in Arabic proudly proclaims: 'The best thing about Sirt is that it is in the centre of Libya'. The only reason for travellers to spend any time here is to break up the long journey between Benghazi and Tripoli.

Sleeping & Eating
Buyut ash-Shabaab (Youth Hostel; ☎ 61825; off Sharia al-Corniche; dm HI members/nonmembers 3/5LD) This is a friendly, down-to-earth place without pretensions to luxury. Arrive early as it's often full if you arrive late in the day. Staff can arrange simple meals from 1LD.

Funduq Bab al-Medina (☎ 60906; fax 60908; Sharia al-Jamahiriya; s/tw/d with private bathroom incl breakfast 20/30/35LD; 🅿) Sirt's only privately run hotel. It has a run-down air but the rooms aren't bad.

Funduq al-Mehari (☎ 60100; fax 61310; Sharia al-Jamahiriya; s/d with private bathroom incl breakfast 35/45LD) Funduq al-Mehari is a bit out on a limb, just north of the road, almost 6km west of the post office, but the rooms are comfortable, spacious, spotless and most travellers' hotel of choice in Sirt. If the showers are an indication of the achievements of the Great Man-Made River, then it is literally a roaring success.

There are plenty of cheap restaurants doing hamburgers and grilled chicken along Sharia al-Jamahiriya in the blocks west of the post office.

Getting There & Away

At 592km to Sebha, 561km to Benghazi and 463km to Tripoli, it's a long ride to anywhere. Buses pass through here en route to Benghazi or Tripoli.

EASTERN LIBYA

The northeastern region of Cyrenaica is home to the verdant Jebel Akhdar (Green Mountains), stunning Mediterranean coastline and superbly preserved ancient Greek cities. In the area around Ras al-Hillal, the northern ridges plunge down towards the Mediterranean to spectacular effect.

BENGHAZI بنغازي

☎ 061 / pop 650,629

Libya's second-largest city makes a comfortable base for exploring the ancient cities of eastern Libya. While it may lack the cosmopolitan charm of Tripoli and has few monuments to its ancient past, Benghazi is known for its pleasant climate and friendly people.

History

Benghazi was founded by Greek settlers from Cyrene, and the area around Benghazi is thought to be the site of the legendary garden of Hesperides, from the Greek myth of the golden apples. In the face of fierce resistance by the surrounding tribes, Benghazi became an Italian fortress in 1911. During WWII the city constantly changed hands and came under bombardment from the Allies and the Axis powers. By the time the war ended there was very little left.

Information

As with everywhere in Libya, Internet cafés are to be found on almost every street of the city centre. Most of the hotels also have Internet access, including **Funduq al-Fadheel** (per hr 1LD; ☺ 3pm-midnight) and **Funduq Tibesti** (per hr 1LD; ☺ 10am-midnight).

There are plenty of banks in the central area. The Masraf al-Tijara Watanmiya (Bank of Commerce & Development), where you can get Visa cash advances, has branches at the airport, Islamic Call Building, Funduq Uzu and Funduq Tibesti; the latter has what was for a time Libya's only internationally connected ATM.

The **main post & telephone office** (Sharia Omar al-Mukhtar) is about 300m north of the harbour, on the southeastern side of the road.

Sights

Benghazi's **Old Town Hall** runs along the western side of **Freedom Square**. It's largely derelict but strong traces of its former elegance remain in its whitewashed Italianate façade, which has some lovely arched doorways and pillars. The balcony played host to its share of important orators, among them Mussolini, Field Marshal Rommel and King Idris.

The covered **Souq al-Jreed** stretches for more than a kilometre and, like any Middle Eastern market worth its salt, it offers just about anything you could want and plenty that you don't, including 'anything you want, one dinar'. It's all displayed to the accompaniment of the music of Umm Kolthum crooning out from the latest Sony sound systems.

Sleeping

At all of the following places (except Buyut ash-Shabaab), quoted room prices include private bathroom and breakfast.

Buyut ash-Shabaab (Youth Hostel; ☎ 2234101; dm HI members/nonmembers 3/5LD) Benghazi's well-run youth hostel, behind sports stadium, is basic but most rooms are well maintained and there are a few family rooms. It's a popular place, so book ahead.

Funduq Ifriqiya (☎ 338044; fax 3386698; Sharia al-Jezayir; s/d/tr 15/20/25LD; ☒) Funduq Ifriqiya is a fine budget choice with simple but tidy rooms (with satellite TV) and you're an easy walk from the centre of town. It's little used by tour groups, an attraction in itself.

BENGHAZI

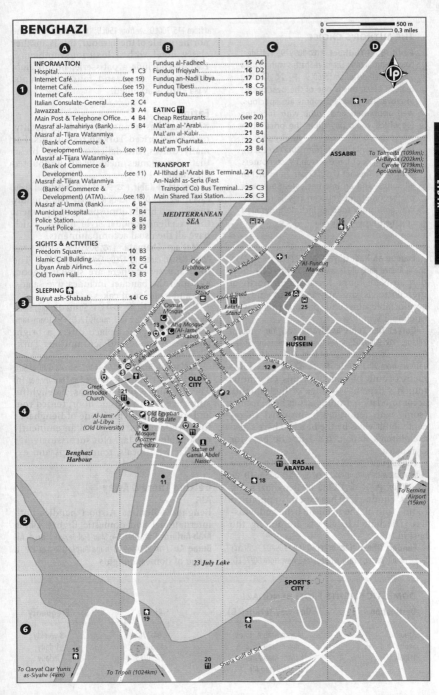

INFORMATION
Hospital............................... 1 C3
Internet Café..........................(see 19)
Internet Café..........................(see 15)
Internet Café..........................(see 18)
Italian Consulate-General............ 2 C4
Jawazzat............................... 3 A4
Main Post & Telephone Office..... 4 B4
Masraf al-Jamahiriya (Bank)........ 5 B4
Masraf al-Tijara Watanmiya
 (Bank of Commerce &
 Development)....................(see 19)
Masraf al-Tijara Watanmiya
 (Bank of Commerce &
 Development)....................(see 11)
Masraf al-Tijara Watanmiya
 (Bank of Commerce &
 Development) (ATM)..........(see 18)
Masrat al-Umma (Bank)............. 6 B4
Municipal Hospital.................... 7 B4
Police Station......................... 8 B4
Tourist Police......................... 9 B3

SIGHTS & ACTIVITIES
Freedom Square...................... 10 B3
Islamic Call Building................. 11 B5
Libyan Arab Airlines................. 12 C4
Old Town Hall........................ 13 B3

SLEEPING
Buyut ash-Shabaab...................14 C6

Funduq al-Fadheel................... 15 A6
Funduq Ifriqiyah...................... 16 D2
Funduq an-Nadi Libya.............. 17 D1
Funduq Tibesti........................ 18 C5
Funduq Uzu........................... 19 B6

EATING
Cheap Restaurants..................(see 20)
Mat'am al-'Arabi..................... 20 B6
Mat'am al-Kabir...................... 21 B4
Mat'am Gharnata..................... 22 C4
Mat'am Turki......................... 23 B4

TRANSPORT
Al-Itihad al-'Arabi Bus Terminal. 24 C2
An-Nakhl as-Seria (Fast
 Transport Co) Bus Terminal... 25 C3
Main Shared Taxi Station........... 26 C3

Scale: 0 — 500 m / 0 — 0.3 miles

MEDITERRANEAN SEA

ASSABRI

To Tolmeita (109km);
Al-Bayda (202km);
Cyrene (219km);
Apollonia (239km)

LIBYA

SIDI HUSSEIN

OLD CITY

Greek Orthodox Church
Al-Jami' al-Libya (Old University)
Benghazi Harbour
Old Egyptian Consulate
Mosque (Former Cathedral)
Statue of Gamal Abdel Nasser
RAS ABAYDAH
To Bernina Airport (15km)
23 July Lake
SPORT'S CITY
To Qaryat Qar Yunis as-Siyahe (4km)
To Tripoli (1024km)

THE AUTHOR'S CHOICE

Funduq al-Fadheel (☎ 9099795; elfadeel
hotel@hotmail.com; Sharia el-Shatt; s with city/sea
view 37/40LD, d/ste from 55/60LD; ⓟ ⊠ 🖳 🖵)
Built in 2003, this is one of the best hotels
in Libya. The pleasant rooms are spacious,
well appointed and come with facilities
for which you'd pay triple the price elsewhere: balconies, a barber, laundry service,
two restaurants (meals from 20LD to 25LD),
swimming pool, large-screen TV, computers
with wi-fi Internet (7.50LD per 24 hours) in
all suites, and an Internet café. Service is
professional and you can pay with Visa.
Welcome small touches include a detailed
city map for each guest.

Funduq an-Nadi Libya (☎ 3372333; fax 3372334;
Sharia Ahmed Rafiq al-Madawi; s/d 35/40LD; ⊠) Funduq an-Nadi Libya, located 3km north of
the centre, is similarly excellent and has
comfortable, quiet and spacious rooms with
satellite TV.

Qaryat Qar Yunis as-Siyahe (Qar Yunis Tourist
Village; ☎ 9096903; www.tourist-village.com; Sharia
Qar Yunis; s/d/ste incl breakfast from 27/38/60LD, chalet/
apt/villa from 20/25/50LD; ⓟ ⊠ 🖵 🖳) Six kilometres south of Benghazi, this enormous
tourist village has a range of high-quality
accommodation, from spacious hotel rooms
(some with renovated bathrooms) to recently built villas by the beach. There's also
a children's funfair. It's a terrific base for
Cyrenaica.

Funduq Uzu (☎ 9095160; www.uzuhotel.com; Sharia
al-Jezayir; s with/without lake view 60/50LD, d 75/65LD, ste
100-220LD; ⓟ ⊠ 🖵) One of Benghazi's top
hotels, Funduq Uzu has superbly appointed
rooms with all the requisite bells and whistles. The buffet breakfasts are among the
best in town.

Funduq Tibesti (☎ 9090017; fax 9098029; Sharia
Jamal Abdul Nasser; s with/without lake view from 80/75LD,

d from 115/100LD, ste from 150LD; ⓟ ⊠ 🖵) On the
northern side of the harbour, this is another
classy hotel with a luxurious ambience.
Facilities include a patisserie, health club,
three coffee shops and four restaurants.
Visa card is accepted.

Eating

Benghazi has a number of high-quality,
reasonably priced Turkish restaurants. For
many diners, the delicious cheese bread
that accompanies meals is an undoubted
highlight.

Mat'am al-Kabir (☎ 9081692; Sharia Jamal Abdul
Nasser; meals 18LD; ☽ lunch & dinner) The friendly
service and bright atmosphere complement
the excellent banquet-style meals, which
have all the usual accompaniments.

Mat'am Gharnata (☎ 9093509; Sharia Jamal
Abdul Nasser; meals 15-17LD; ☽ lunch & dinner) The
food and service here are similarly good,
although the banquet includes five salads,
fish and a choice of cakes.

Mat'am Turki (☎ 9091331; Sharia 23 July; sandwiches from 1LD, pizza 2-6LD, meals 12LD; ☽ 10am-1am)
This newly opened place offers a bright
and breezy mood and scrumptious Turkish food.

Mat'am al-'Arabi (☎ 9094468; Sharia Gulf of Sirt;
meals 16.50LD; ☽ lunch & dinner Sat-Thu, dinner Fri)
The upstairs eating area has a delightful
ambience, with a mosaic floor, tented roof
and soft lighting. This is one of Benghazi's
finest restaurants, but it has an eminently
reasonable price tag. Not surprisingly, it's
popular with locals, tour groups and expats alike.

Getting There & Away
AIR

Benghazi's Bernina Airport handles both
international and domestic flights. **Libyan
Arab Airlines** (☎ 9092064; Sharia al-Jezayir) and **Al-
Buraq Air** (☎ 2234469; Bernina Airport) operate a
range of domestic flights.

DOMESTIC FLIGHTS FROM BENGHAZI

Destination	One-way/return (LD)	Airline	Frequency
Al-Kufra	Libyan Arab Airlines	64/128	3 weekly
Sebha	Libyan Arab Airlines	46.50/93	1 daily
Tripoli	Libyan Arab Airlines	37.50/75	2 daily
	Al-Buraq Air	42.50/85	2 daily

BUS & SHARED TAXI

There are daily buses and shared taxis to Tripoli, Sirt, Al-Bayda, Sebha and Tobruk from Al-Funduq Market.

Getting Around

Bernina Airport is 18km east of the city. A private taxi to the airport costs 10LD. Elsewhere in town, private taxi journeys will cost 2LD.

TOLMEITA (PTOLEMAIS)   طلميثة

Palm-fringed Tolmeita, one of the five cities of the Greek Pentapolis, is an especially good place to see the transition from Greek to Roman and then Byzantine occupation. Although founded in the 4th century BC, the excavated areas of the city (10% of the original) mostly date from the 1st and 2nd centuries BC.

Information

At **Tolmeita** (admission 3LD, camera/video 5/10LD; ☾ 7.30am-5.30pm) you'll find an excellent guide, **Abdusalam Bazama** (☎ 0685-2124; 50LD).

Sights

Tolmeita climbs up the hill towards the Jebel Akhdar. Included among its highlights are the compact 5th-century **Byzantine Church**, the 4th-century **Villa of the Four Seasons** and the enchanting **Odeon**, a small theatre that was once covered by a roof and had seating for up to 500 people. The Greek **agora** (marketplace) later served as the Roman **forum** and was surrounded by temples. Along the northern side were three temples, each with four Doric columns. Northeast of the agora you'll find the **Villa of Columns** and the 5th-century **Athanasius' Fortress**.

Tolmeita's **museum** (admission 3LD, camera/video 5/10LD; ☾ 7.30am-5.30pm) is dominated by the superb Four Seasons mosaic from the villa of the same name and a wonderful Medusa mosaic from the Villa of Columns.

Eating

There's nowhere to stay in Tolmeita, but an **open-air restaurant** (meals 10LD) in the car park serves simple food and drinks.

Getting There & Away

Occasionally, you may be able to find a shared taxi to Benghazi.

AL-BAYDA   البيضاء

☎ 084 / pop 120,000

Al-Bayda is an attractive city on the northern fringe of the Jebel Akhdar and another good base for exploring the ruins of Cyrene, Apollonia and Qasr Libya.

Sleeping & Eating

Hotel Loaloat el-Jebel el-Akhdar (☎ 630968; fax 630971; Sharia el-Oroba; s/d/ste with private bathroom 30/40/70LD; ✄ ⬜) This welcome addition to the Al-Bayda hotel scene has attractive rooms, friendly management and a central location. A standard Libyan-style tourist restaurant here provides ample banquet-style meals (15LD). There's also a 24-hour Internet café (1LD per hour) next door.

Albaida Palace Hotel (☎ 633455; qaseralbida@ yahoo.com; Sharia al-Ruba; s/d with private bathroom 30/ 40LD; ✄) Now faced with competition, this erstwhile favourite of tour groups has improved – the rooms are good and the service less dysfunctional than it used to be.

Asservium (Sharia al Ruba; meals from 10LD; ☾ lunch & dinner Sat-Thu, dinner Fri) This cool place has trendy music and great outdoor seating. The upstairs terrace is a wonderful place from which to watch the world go by with a *shay* (tea, 1LD) or a nargileh (1LD).

Mat'am al-Barqa (☎ 635328; Sharia al-Ruba; meals from 15LD; ☾ lunch & dinner Sat-Thu, dinner Fri) At the eastern end of town, Mat'am al-Barqa serves good-quality banquets in pleasant surroundings.

Getting There & Away

Shared taxis run from the station at the eastern end of town to Benghazi, Tobruk and Shahat (for Cyrene).

SHAHAT (CYRENE)   شحات

☎ 084 / pop 43,376

The small village of Shahat, 17km east of Al-Bayda, is the gateway to the spectacular ancient city of Cyrene and is the best place to stay if you want to get an early start into the old city. It's easy to spend a day exploring the stunning ruins of Cyrene, where the spectacular setting is as captivating as the extraordinary monuments.

History

Founded by Greek settlers from the island of Thera (modern Santorini) in 631 BC, Cyrene was the pre-eminent city of the

LIBYA

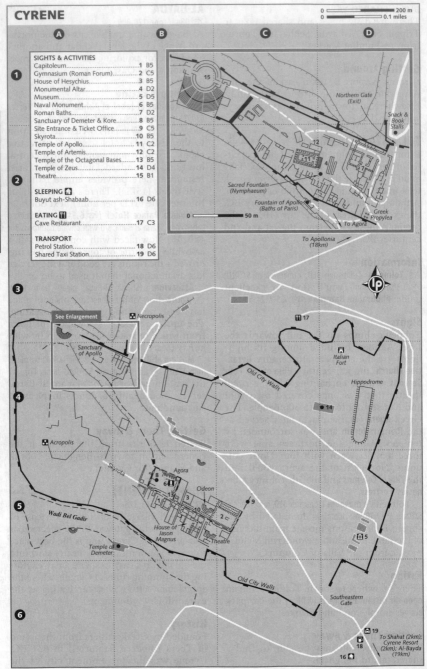

CYRENE

0 — 200 m
0 — 0.1 miles

SIGHTS & ACTIVITIES
Capitoleum..............................1 B5
Gymnasium (Roman Forum)........2 C5
House of Hesychius...................3 B5
Monumental Altar....................4 D2
Museum.................................5 D5
Naval Monument......................6 B5
Roman Baths...........................7 D2
Sanctuary of Demeter & Kore......8 B5
Site Entrance & Ticket Office.......9 C5
Skyrota.................................10 B5
Temple of Apollo....................11 C2
Temple of Artemis...................12 C2
Temple of the Octagonal Bases...13 B5
Temple of Zeus.......................14 D4
Theatre................................15 B1

SLEEPING
Buyut ash-Shabaab...................16 D6

EATING
Cave Restaurant......................17 C3

TRANSPORT
Petrol Station.........................18 D6
Shared Taxi Station...................19 D6

Greek world in the 4th century BC. It was renowned for its philosophers, astronomers, mathematicians and other scholars. After the change from Greek to Roman administration in 75 BC, Cyrene became an important Roman capital.

Information

Visiting **Cyrene** (admission 3LD, camera/video 5/10LD; ◯ 8am-6.30pm) requires a **guide** (50LD). Mahmoud Abu Shreet, Ali Mahmud, Abdul Ghader and Fadil Ali Mohamed are all recommended guides.

Sights

The large, open **gymnasium** was originally built by the Greeks in the 2nd century BC as the major sporting building of Cyrene. In the second half of the 1st century AD, it was converted by the Romans into a forum (caesareum; Forum of the Caesars). The **Skyrota**, the main road through the Greek city, is still lined with impressive columns bearing graven images of Hermes and Hercules. The **House of Hesychius** contains a fine mosaic of an angel alongside an inscription imploring God to protect the women and children of Cyrene.

The **agora** was the heart of ancient Cyrene, serving as a public square, a forum for orators, a market and a magnet for the powerful people of the day. Many civic and religious buildings were clustered around the agora, among them the **Temple of the Octagonal Bases** (2nd century AD), the striking **Naval Monument** (3rd century BC) and the unusual **Sanctuary of Demeter and Kore**, the scene of a riotous, women-only annual celebration. Outside the agora's southern wall is the **Capitoleum**, the customary temple to the Greek trinity of Zeus, Hera and Athena (or, if you were Roman, Jupiter, Juno and Minerva).

The rich collection of temples, baths and other public buildings in the **Sanctuary of Apollo** includes the 6th-century-BC **Temple of Apollo**, one of the earliest temples at Cyrene, preceded by the 22m-long **monumental altar** where animals were sacrificed. Adjacent is the **Temple of Artemis**, which may predate the Apollo temple. There are fine views down over the coastal plain from here.

Just west of the sanctuary is the spectacularly situated **theatre**, which could once seat 1000 spectators. It was originally constructed by the Greeks and probably dates from the 6th century BC, although it was much modified in subsequent centuries. The **Roman baths**, built in AD 98 to 99, contain some good mosaics and cipolin columns.

Up the hill from the rest of Cyrene is the famed 5th-century-BC **Temple of Zeus**, which was once larger than the Parthenon in Athens. Under the Romans it was used as a temple of Jupiter and it also served the Greek-Libyan hybrid deity Zeus Ammun.

Cyrene's **museum** (admission 3LD, guide 50LD, camera/video 5/10LD; ◯ 8am-6.30pm Tue-Sun), southeast of the Temple of Zeus, has wonderful statues, sculptures and other artefacts that once adorned this extraordinary Graeco-Roman city.

Sleeping & Eating

Buyut ash-Shabaab (☎ 637371; camping 5LD, dm HI members/nonmembers 3/5LD) The hostel is a stone's throw from the gate leading down to the ruins. It's clean, friendly and has been recommended by a number of travellers – the hot water is reliable.

Cyrene Resort (☎ 0851-64391; s/d with private bathroom 35/45LD; P ✕) This former Winzrik Hotel, 2km northeast of the police station, is set in the fields around Cyrene. It has pleasant rooms and an excellent café and restaurant cut into one of the caves.

Cave Restaurant (☎ 635206; elbadertours@hotmail.com; meals from 15LD; ◯ lunch) Living up to its name, this is another cave restaurant. It's an atmospheric place offering tasty food, friendly young waiters and good views down towards the coast from the terrace.

Getting There & Away

Shared taxis between Al-Bayda and Shahat arrive and leave from under the eucalyptus trees, just short of the pillars marking the gate leading down to Cyrene.

SUSA (APOLLONIA)   سوسه
☎ 084

The small town of Susa, about 20km from Shahat, is the gateway to another wonderful ancient Greek city, Apollonia, the one-time port of Cyrene. Apollonia came to rival Cyrene in significance in the late Roman period. Most of what remains today dates from the Byzantine era when Apollonia was known as the 'city of churches'.

Information

Apollonia's **ticket office** (admission 3LD, camera/video 5/10LD; ☪ 8am-7pm Oct-Apr) is on the waterfront at the northern end of Susa. Two excellent **guides** (50LD) are Ali Mahmud and Mahmoud Abu Shreet.

Sights

APOLLONIA

The ruins of Apollonia are strung out along a narrow strip of coastline and include the **Western Church** with its mixture of Roman and Byzantine columns. The marble floor of the **Central Church** is better preserved and some pillars bear traces of Byzantine crosses. Throughout the site, especially around the 2nd-century **Roman baths** and **gymnasium**, is strewn pottery from the Greek (black) and Roman (red) eras. Above the baths on the hill is the **Byzantine Duke's Palace**, once one of the biggest palaces in Cyrenaica, while northeast of here lies the **Eastern Church**, once the biggest church in Cyrenaica. Although this was among the earliest of the churches (5th century AD), some mosaics still remain. Remnants of the **port**, including cisterns, line the beach, while over the hill to the southeast is the plunging and picturesque **Greek theatre**.

APOLLONIA MUSEUM

The **museum** (admission 3LD, camera/video 5/10LD; ☪ 8am-5pm Tue-Sun) has poorly labelled exhibits. Among the highlights are the exquisite door frame from the Byzantine Duke's Palace and four mosaics found in the Eastern Church.

Sleeping & Eating

Al-Manara Hotel (☎ 63035; www.manarahotel.com; s/d/ste with private bathroom 45/60/95LD; P ✗ ⬜) One of the new breed of private hotels sweeping Libya, Al-Manara Hotel is exceptional. It has outstanding rooms, a prime location just 50m from the site entrance, fine views from most rooms, a good restaurant (meals 15LD) and professional service.

Getting There & Away

There's little if any public transport to Susa. A private taxi from Shahat will cost you 10LD one way or 25LD return (including waiting time).

TOBRUK   طبرق

☎ 087 / pop 121,052

Tobruk was the scene of some of the most important WWII battles. Its main (and only) attraction is the war cemeteries – remember that Tobruk was fought over for its strategic significance, not its aesthetic beauty.

Sights

Tobruk's **WWII cemeteries** (admission free; ☪ 9am-5pm Sat-Thu, 2-5pm Fri) are well maintained.

The **Knightsbridge (Acroma) Cemetery**, 20km west of town, is the largest in Tobruk. Contained within its walls are 3649 graves housing fallen soldiers from the UK, New Zealand, South Africa, Australia and Canada.

Between the Knightsbridge Cemetery and Tobruk is the former battlefield dressing station, which is known as the **Australian (Fig Tree) Hospital**. The now-peaceful plains surrounding Tobruk were an ideal location for a hospital, with deep natural caves (now heavily silted up) and shelter offered by fig trees just a few kilometres from the front line. It was also connected by a ridge to the battlefields of Knightsbridge.

The **Tobruk (Commonwealth) War Cemetery**, 6km south of the harbour, also has an air of simplicity and dignity and contains 2479 graves. The countries most represented include Australia, India, New Zealand, South Africa and the UK.

Most of the more than 300 soldiers buried in the **French Cemetery**, 8km south of the harbour, died in the Battle of Bir Hakim, 80km southeast of Tobruk, in May and June 1942.

The names of 6026 German soldiers are inscribed in mosaic slabs lining the inside walls of the **German Cemetery**, a forbidding sandstone fort 3.2km south of the harbour.

Sleeping & Eating

Funduq Qartaj (☎ 623043; Ring Rd; tw with shared bathroom from 20LD, tw/tr with private bathroom 30/45LD; ✗) This is a fine choice, 2km northwest of the harbour. The tidy rooms are clustered in groups of three and open out onto a shared sitting room with TV.

Funduq al-Masira (☎ 625761; fax 625769; s/d with private bathroom 35/45LD; ✗) This concrete eyesore on the southwestern corner of the harbour also happens to be Tobruk's finest hotel. It has declined in recent years and suffers from a lack of competition. The rooms, with satellite TV, are ageing but should be comfortable for a few more years.

The largest concentration of cheap restaurants is in the city centre, in the streets fanning out from the main post office. There are also a couple of outdoor sandwich shops along the western end of the harbour.

Getting There & Away
Shared taxis leave a few times per day for Al-Bayda, Benghazi, Shahat and the Egyptian border.

Getting Around
If you want to see every one of the WWII sites listed in this section, expect to pay at least 25LD for a private taxi and budget a minimum of three to four hours.

JEBEL NAFUSA & GHADAMES

The barren Jebel Nafusa (Western Mountains) protect Libya's northeastern coast from the Sahara, which stretches away deep into the heart of Africa from the mountains' southern slopes. It's a land of rocky escarpments and stone villages clinging to outcrops high above the plains. Away to the southwest, on the northern reaches of the world's greatest desert, is the enchanting oasis of Ghadames.

GHARYAN   غريان
☎ 041 / pop 135,000
Gharyan sprawls across the top of a plateau and is one of the last towns of any size before Sebha, 690km south across the desert. It's a place to rest from long desert journeys and take in its unusual underground Berber houses.

Sights
Built by the ancient Berber inhabitants of the area, Gharyan's **underground houses** consisted of living quarters at the base of a dramatic, circular pit three-storeys deep, which were reached by a tunnel leading from street level. They provided a refuge from cold winters, hot summers and invaders (the houses were invisible to all but those within a few hundred metres). The most accessible houses are close to Funduq

Rabta; ask your guide or at the hotel for directions to the *dammous*.

Gharyan is also famous throughout Libya for its pottery, and stalls line the road in from Tripoli selling everything from huge serving bowls to small storage jars at reasonable prices (not much more than 10LD).

Sleeping & Eating
Funduq Rabta (☎ 631970; fax 631972; Sharia al-Jamahiriya; s/d with private bathroom 35/45LD) This place is expensive for what you get (uninspiring, cramped and run-down rooms) but it's OK for a night. There's a mediocre restaurant (meals 15LD) that lacks atmosphere, although in Gharyan you are not exactly spoilt for choice.

Gharyan Hotel (☎ 631483; fax 631415; s/d with private bathroom 25/35LD; meals 15LD) Gharyan Hotel, located off the main highway near the town entrance, is similar to the Rabta with tired, 1970s-era décor that has been kindly left unaltered. The restaurant here is like that at Funduq Rabta – uninspiring banquet-style meals (15LD) that will fill but not excite you.

Getting There & Away
The shared taxi and micro station is 500m south of Funduq Rabta.

QASR AL-HAJ   قصر الحاج
The small village of Qasr al-Haj has one of Libya's most spectacular examples of Berber architecture. The circular and completely enclosed **fortified granary** (admission 2LD; ☾ daylight hr) is an extraordinary structure that has stored the local harvests since the 12th century. The main courtyard is breathtaking with the walls completely surrounded by 114 cavelike rooms – exactly the same number as there are suras (chapters) in the Quran.

Public transport to Qasr al-Haj is non-existent but as you'll almost certainly come here as part of a tour, that's unlikely to be a problem.

YEFREN   يفرن
☎ 0421
Yefren is one of the more appealing towns in this mountainous region, situated high on a series of rocky bluffs, overlooking the flat coastal plain and surrounded by attractive wooded areas. It's a relaxed place

LIBYA

and nothing happens here in a hurry. The deserted, old part of town dates from over 500 years ago and there are a few ruined remains scattered around the hillsides. The largest concentration of old houses is on the hilltop overlooking the town.

Sleeping & Eating

Yefren Hotel (☎ 60278; fax 021-4830117; s/d/tr with private bathroom 25/45/55LD) This place opened in early 2005 and is arguably the best base for exploring the Jebel Nafusa. The rooms (without air-con) are pleasant but the views over Yefren and the surrounding hills are spectacular, especially at sunset. It's at the western end of town (look for the green-domed mosque nearby). The meals (15LD) in the restaurant here are, like the rooms, the best you'll find for miles around.

Getting There & Away

There are shared taxis between Yefren and Tripoli (two hours) or Gharyan (one hour).

KABAW   كاباو

The pleasant Berber town of Kabaw, 9km north of the Gharyan–Nalut road, is set among rolling hills and is home to another superb *qasr*.

Sights

Known locally as the *ghurfas*, **Qasr Kabaw** is over 700 years old and one of the oldest in the region. Smaller and less uniform than the one at Qasr al-Haj, Qasr Kabaw is nonetheless captivating, with a wonderful medieval charm. None of the storage rooms

remains in use and the gate is permanently left open.

Festivals & Events

In April every year, Kabaw hosts the **Qasr Festival**. The festivities celebrate the unique heritage of the Berber people of the area, with particular emphasis on Berber folklore. Important local ceremonies, such as weddings, funerals and harvests, are re-enacted by people in traditional dress.

Eating

There are no hotels in Kabaw. The only restaurant is **Hannibal** (☎ 0912123957; ❁ lunch & dinner), which is actually 11km southeast of town, on the Gharyan–Nalut road, 2km east of the Kabaw turn-off. The soup is hearty, the chicken dishes tasty and the service willing.

Getting There & Away

There are no regular shared taxis to Kabaw.

NALUT   نالوت

☎ 0470 / pop 66,228

At the more-barren, western end of the Jebel Nafusa, the regional centre of Nalut boasts yet another exceptional Berber *qasr* and is a good place to break up the long journey from Ghadames to Tripoli.

Sights

QASR NALUT

Perched on a rocky bluff overlooking the western mountain valleys, **Qasr Nalut** (admission 1LD; ❁ daylight hr) has the most captivating setting of any in Jebel Nafusa. It's almost completely surrounded by the uninhabited

---

THE BERBER QASRS OF JEBEL NAFUSA

Berber architecture in the Jebel Nafusa is like something out of a *Star Wars* film set. Most of the fortified granary stores, known as *qasrs*, date from the 12th century and have stood the test of time remarkably well.

Despite their name ('*qasr*' means castle), these structures were rarely used as a form of defence. Instead they offered protection for the local crops necessary for the community's survival. Constructed entirely from local rock, sun-dried mud brick and gypsum, the cool storage areas, sealed with doors made of palm trunks, warded off insects, thieves and inclement weather alike. Their purpose was akin to that of a modern bank, with the system of enforced saving and stockpiling preventing the cropholders from squandering their resources.

Rooms below ground were used to preserve olive oil; the above-ground rooms customarily housed barley and wheat. You'll often see animal horns high on the ramparts; these served as amulets of good fortune. Also evident are the remains of ancient winches used for hoisting produce from ground level to the upper storage rooms.

remains of the village that cling to the edge of the steep hillside.

Qasr Nalut, built in AD 1240, has the feel of a small, fortified village. Rather than facing onto an open courtyard, the rooms are tightly packed and overlook two narrow thoroughfares without any hint of uniformity. There were 400 chambers, but the keeper always knew how much each family had in storage at any given time. The rooms were last used in 1960.

OLD TOWN

Nalut's derelict old town, surrounding the *qasr*, has crumbling stone-and-gypsum houses and three old mosques. The 1312 **Alal'a Mosque** is the oldest and has low arches, a stone mihrab and a functioning well. Two old **olive oil presses** with their impressive huge circular platforms and crushing stones are also in the vicinity.

Sleeping

Buyut ash-Shabaab (☎ 2858; Sharia Ghadames; dm HI members/nonmembers 3/5LD) Close to the petrol station, this small hostel is basic but as cheap as you'll get in Nalut and it's rarely crowded.

Funduq Winzrik (☎ 2204; s/d/ste with private bathroom 25/40/50LD) Magnificently located across the valley from the old town, Funduq Winzrik has been restored although not with much imagination. Design features include carpet on the floors, carpet on the walls, carpet on the bedside table… The rooms are spacious and simple but the bathroom plumbing is in need of attention. Meals cost from 13LD to 25LD.

Eating

There are small sandwich bars along the road in from Ghadames and just down the hill from the roundabout in the centre of town; most charge 1LD for a filled baguette and soft drink.

If you're arriving by private vehicle around lunch or dinner time, consider stopping at **Mat'am Ajweiba** (☎ 0913705327; meals 10-12LD; ☺ lunch & dinner), 8km south of town. One of the better restaurants in this part of the country, it has a pleasant dining room, good food and friendly service.

Getting There & Away

Shared taxis between Ghadames and Tripoli stop at the main roundabout.

GHADAMES غدامس
☎ 0484 / pop 16,752

The Unesco World Heritage–listed old city of Ghadames has everything that you imagine a desert oasis to have – abundant palm groves, a wonderfully preserved, labyrinthine old town and a pace of life largely unchanged for centuries. It's an extraordinary place.

History

When Romans occupied the area around Ghadames in 19 BC, it had been inhabited for almost 3000 years. The Romans fortified the town and called it Cydamus. The old city as you see it today was founded around 800 years ago and was occupied by both the Ottomans and Italians. Ghadames was bombed by the French in 1943, causing terrible damage and loss of life. In 1984 there were 6666 people living in the old town; four years later there was just one family left. The government, as part of its push for modernisation, had built new air-conditioned housing in the new part of town and put pressure on people to move.

Information

The story of Ghadames is largely an oral history and a guide is essential for exploring the old city. The standard charge is 40/60LD for a half/full day. Highly recommended guides include **At-Tayeb Mohamed Hiba** (☎ 62300; dandoomer731@yahoo.com) and **Mohamed Ali Kredan** (☎ 62190; fax 021-3601374).

Dan Do Omer Internet Café (☎ 62300; dandoomer@ yahoo.com; per hr 1LD; ☺ 9.30am-late Sat-Thu, 9.30am-1.30pm & 3.30pm-late Fri) Also offers international phone calls. It's in the heart of town near the main junction and opposite Restaurant Awwal.

Post office (☺ 8am-1pm & 5-8pm Sat-Thu) South of the New Mosque.

Sights
OLD CITY

Old Ghadames (adult/child 3/1LD, camera/video 5/10LD) is another world of covered alleyways, whitewashed houses and extensive palm gardens irrigated by wells.

The old city of Ghadames comprised loosely configured concentric areas containing residential and commercial districts and covering around 10 hectares. The city was divided into seven 'streets', each the domain of a different subsection of the Bani

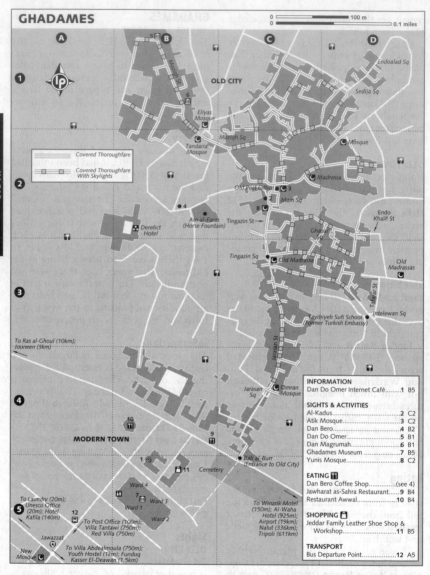

GHADAMES

INFORMATION
Dan Do Omer Internet Café........1 B5

SIGHTS & ACTIVITIES
Al-Kadus...................................2 C2
Atik Mosque..............................3 C2
Dan Bero...................................4 B2
Dan Do Omer.............................5 B1
Dan Magrumah..........................6 B1
Ghadames Museum 7 B5
Yunis Mosque............................8 C2

EATING
Dan Bero Coffee Shop.........(see 4)
Jawharat as-Sahra Restaurant.....9 B4
Restaurant Awwal....................10 B4

SHOPPING
Jeddar Family Leather Shoe Shop &
  Workshop............................11 B5

TRANSPORT
Bus Departure Point................12 A5

Walid and Bani Wazid tribes. Each 'street' was essentially a self-contained town, with a mosque, houses, schools, markets and a small communal square for public events.

The designers of the **traditional houses** of Ghadames made maximum use of vertical space and a visit to one is a must. Eye-catching with whitewashed walls and brightly painted interiors, all of the houses were connected. The rooftops were the domain of women in the same way that the public laneways below belonged to men. At least three of the old houses have been stunningly restored and opened to the public: **Dan Do Omer** (☎ 62300; dandoomer731@yahoo.com); Dan Bero (ask at Dan Bero Coffee Shop, p494) and Dan Magrumah. Talk to your guide about arranging a visit.

Apart from the houses, it's the overall experience – a town that time forgot, your way lit by shafts of natural light – that will live longest in the memory. Specific sights to watch out for include the distinctive **palm-trunk doors**; delightful **Tingazin Square**, at once intimate and picturesque; and **Ghazar Square** with its alcove niches and encircling balcony. Take in the ancient **Yunis** and **Atik Mosques** in the main square, which also houses a niche, **Al-Kadus**, from where water was drawn and distributed across Ghadames. **Maziqh Square**, with its arched alcoves, is overlooked by two fine mosques.

GHADAMES MUSEUM
The **museum** (☎ 62225; adult/child 3/1LD, camera/video 5/10LD; ☉ 9am-1.30pm Sat-Thu) has five sections devoted to everything from Roman artefacts to the more-recent ethnographic displays. Highlights include the famous embroidered slippers of Ghadames; huge copper keys and padlocks, the like of which are still used in the old city; a large selection of folk medicines; old black-and-white photos of Ghadames; and Tuareg handicrafts.

Festivals & Events
In October every year, the annual three-day **Ghadames Festival** brings the old city alive in a riot of colour and activity. Ghadamsis return to their family homes in the old town and throw open the doors for singing, dancing and public festivities including wedding and initiation ceremonies. Most of the festivities are performed in traditional dress.

Sleeping
HOSTELS & VILLAS
Youth Hostel (Buyut ash-Shabaab; ☎ 62023; dm HI members/nonmembers 3/5LD) Ghadames' youth hostel is basic, has small rooms and is plagued by problematic plumbing, but for this price you can hardly complain.

One solution to Ghadames' shortage of beds is the prevalence of villas – homes that operate like bed-and-breakfast places. All offer kitchen facilities and charge 20LD (including breakfast).

Villa Abdealmoula (☎ 62844; villa_moula@yahoo .com; ✿) Run by the energetic Othman, this is the most homely of the villas and is very well run.

Villa Tantawi (☎ 62205; ✿) Friendly place with ornate, over-the-top rooms and a resident cat.

Red Villa (☎ 0912133524; fax 021-4778225; ✿) Simple rooms but most have private bathrooms.

HOTELS
All of the following places have air-con and private bathrooms unless stated otherwise and prices include breakfast.

Funduq Kasser El-Deawan (☎ 63350; fax 041-634115; s/d/tr 30/40/50LD; ✿) Almost as far south as you can go in Ghadames (which isn't far), this new place is outstanding with its spacious, well-appointed rooms with satellite TV. There are plans for expansion.

Al-Waha Hotel (☎ 62569; fax 62568; s/d 30/40LD; ✿) The rooms here are simple and the bathrooms could do with an overhaul but

---

THE GREAT CARAVANS OF GHADAMES
Ghadames became one of the principal trading towns of the Sahara, despite not possessing any lucrative products of its own. Indeed, embroidered slippers and salt were about all Ghadames could muster. What enabled Ghadames to become one of the great entrepôt towns for goods from all over Africa was its abundance of wells in the harsh deserts of the northern Sahara. The reach of Ghadames' commerce and the sheer volume of trade that passed through its gates was so great that when caravans arrived in towns across the Sahara, they were assumed to be caravans from Ghadames.

In ancient times, goods from the interior of Africa that passed through the gates of Ghadames en route to the coast included an exotic array of precious stones, gold and silver, ivory, dates and ostrich plumes. In the other direction, glass necklaces and paper for use in religious texts from Venice, pearls from Paris and linen from Marseille passed through on their way south.

The arrival of a caravan in town was quite an event. The camels bearing great chests were unloaded and the goods almost immediately offered for sale in the markets of the town. The world that many Ghadamsis would never see for themselves was brought to life in the perfumes from Timbuktu, spices from the Maghreb and precious metals from central Africa.

THE AUTHOR'S CHOICE

The ultimate eating experience in Ghadames is lunch in one of the traditional houses (see p492) of the old town. The most frequently prepared meal is the delicious *fitaat* (lentils, mutton and buckwheat pancakes cooked together in a tasty sauce in a low oven and eaten with the hands from a communal bowl). Eating this wonderful meal amid an evocative atmosphere is a highlight. **Dan Do Omer** (☎ 62300; dandoomer 731@yahoo.com) does this to perfection; ask for At-Tayeb Mohamed Hiba.

it's comfortable and a favourite of tour companies.

Winzrik Motel (☎ /fax 82485; camping/s/d 5/30/35LD; 🏊) The closest hotel to the entrance to the old city, this comfortable place has spotlessly clean rooms that are better kept than other Winzrik hotels in Libya.

Eating

Restaurant Awwal (☎ 62429; meals 12-15LD; 🕐 lunch & dinner) The only problem with the Awwal is that it's so good most of the other restaurants in town have closed. Its chicken and lamb dishes, especially the *tagen*, are great, as is the service. There's also an enormous garden, which is an ideal place to pass a summer Ghadames evening. It's located at the main intersection.

Jawharat as-Sahra Restaurant (☎ 62015; meals 10-15LD; 🕐 lunch & dinner Sat-Thu, dinner Fri) This small place somehow survives. The chilled atmosphere is a pleasant alternative to the crowds at Awwal. It does great coffee.

Drinking

In the old city, it's hard to tear yourself away from the **Dan Bero Coffee Shop** (🕐 9am-midnight), which has a delightfully shady palm garden, friendly, laid-back owners and great tea and coffee. There is no finer place to pass a hot Ghadames afternoon.

Shopping

Brightly coloured embroidered slippers, unique to Ghadames, have been produced by the Jeddar family for centuries. They still have a shop and workshop north of the museum. The slippers aren't cheap (50LD and upwards) but make a wonderful souvenir.

Getting There & Away

There are, in theory, two weekly flights with Libyan Arab Airlines between Ghadames and Tripoli (26.50/53LD one way/return), although they don't always run. Some tour companies organise charter flights from Tripoli.

There's a daily bus and a shared taxi from Ghadames to Tripoli (via Nalut).

TO THE SAHARA

Desert tracks lead south across the Hamadat al-Hamrah, a featureless rocky plateau that separates northern Libya from the sand dunes and rocky mountain ranges of the south; all tour companies (p506) can arrange such expeditions.

The most popular route skirts the Algerian border all the way to Ghat or Al-Aweinat, both gateways to the exceptional Jebel Acacus. The journey takes a minimum of two to three days with the second day passing through the western reaches of the Idehan Ubari (Ubari Sand Sea) with its towering dunes.

FEZZAN & THE SAHARA

The Fezzan region of southern Libya is engulfed by the Sahara and is home to some of the most spectacular and diverse desert scenery in the world. The majestic dunes of the Idehan Murzuq and Idehan Ubari (Murzuq and Ubari Sand Seas) cover thousands of square kilometres, and deep valleys conceal idyllic, palm-fringed lakes. In the Jebel Acacus in the southwest, you'll find breathtaking rock formations of the once-volcanic mountains that rise starkly from the sands and conceal carvings and paintings dating back 12,000 years. Off to the southeast of the country, Waw al-Namus is an astonishing volcano featuring stunning scenery amid a horizon that never seems to end.

SEBHA سبها

☎ 071 / pop 126,387

The promise of an Internet café, a cold drink or the company of people can make Sebha feel like an oasis, at least for a few hours. Sebha is the largest settlement in the Libyan Sahara, although it's not a particularly attractive town.

Orientation & Information

It's unlikely that you will need to stray beyond the two main streets, Sharia Jamal Abdul Nasser (the extension of the road in from Murzuq and Germa) and Sharia 5 October (formerly Sharia Mohammed Megharief), which run parallel to each other through the heart of town. An **Internet café** (Sharia 5 October; per hr 1LD; ☺ 9am-midnight Sat-Thu, 5pm-midnight Fri) can be found 50m east of the Acacus Restaurant.

Sleeping

Sebha has plenty of hotels, most of which are fine if sterile and few offer service with a smile. It's about the comfort of a bed and a hot shower, but stay too long and you're likely to long for the freedom of star-spangled desert nights.

Fezzan Park (☎ 0925131967; fax 632860; 3-bed huts 30LD, ste 50LD; ☒ ☒) Arguably the best of the Sahara's camps, this appealing place is 12km southwest of Sebha off the road to Ubari. It offers the usual huts but they're airtight and pleasant, while the suites will seem like paradise after dusty desert trails. There's a swimming pool and a zoo with desert animals. The roaming ostriches are more inquisitive than dangerous. Breakfast costs 4LD.

Funduq Afriqiya (☎ 623952; fax 631550; Sharia Jamal Abdul Nasser; s/d/tr/ste with private bathroom 25/40/65/80LD; ☒) The recently renovated Funduq Afriqiya has large rooms that are unexciting but comfortable. There are some fine views over town from the upper floors.

Funduq al-Mehari (☎ 631910; fax 631914; Sharia al-Jamahiriya; s/d with private bathroom 25/40LD; ☒) Once Sebha's finest choice, this place is ageing, but not particularly gracefully, and the service can be quite indifferent. The rooms are comfortable if a tad bland.

Eating

Acacus Restaurant (☎ 634934; Sharia 5 October; meals from 6.50LD; ☺ lunch & dinner) This is an outstanding choice with excellent, friendly service. The quality of the food is first-rate and the airy dining area can seem like an oasis in this uninspiring town. Great coffee is another bonus.

Mat'am an-Nasser (☎ 628220; Sharia Jamal Abdul Nasser; meals 10LD; ☺ lunch & dinner) Although not quite as impressive, Mat'am an-Nasser is also good; the atmosphere in the upstairs air-con dining room is a bit plain, despite the eerie blue aviary. However, it produces fine food and the service is well intentioned if a little quirky at times.

Getting There & Around

Libyan Arab Airlines (☎ 623875; cnr Sharias Jamal Abdul Nasser & al-Jamahiriya; ☺ 7am-2pm Sat-Thu May-Sep & 8am-3pm Sat-Thu Oct-Apr) has nightly flights to Tripoli (37.50LD) and to Benghazi (46.50LD) as well as a twice-weekly flight to Ghat (28LD). Sebha airport is 4km southeast of the town centre. Private taxis into town shouldn't cost more than 3LD, however their drivers often demand and won't budge from 5LD.

Shared taxis connect Sebha with Tripoli and Ubari.

IDEHAN UBARI & THE UBARI LAKES
بحيرات أوبارى

The Idehan Ubari (the eastern stretch of which is known as the Ramlat Dawada) is a dramatic sea of towering sand dunes, shadowed to the south by Wadi al-Hayat (Valley of Life). While elsewhere many oases of the Sahara have been consumed by sprawling towns, the salt lakes of the Idehan Ubari still provoke that sense of awe that only water in the desert can inspire.

There are at least 11 lakes in the area. Although many have dried up and most require longer expeditions, three – pretty **Mavo**, dramatic **Gebraoun** and the enchanting **Umm al-Maa** (Mother of Water) – are easily accessible and majestically beautiful at sunset.

Swimming in the buoyant waters surrounded by sand dunes and palm trees is one of *the* great desert experiences; Gebraoun is the best lake to swim in due to the proximity of a freshwater well to wash off the sand. Camp Winzrik, on the northern shore of Lake Gebraoun, has some skis and a snowboard (5LD) available, so you can try the exhilaration of dune skiing.

Finally, if you're considering sleeping by the lake shore, remember that mosquitoes will ruin the experience – camp nearby in the sand for an undisturbed night's sleep.

GERMA
جرمة
☎ 0729

Germa is one of the largest settlements in Wadi al-Hayat and carries with it a wealth of historical associations. It's adjacent to the

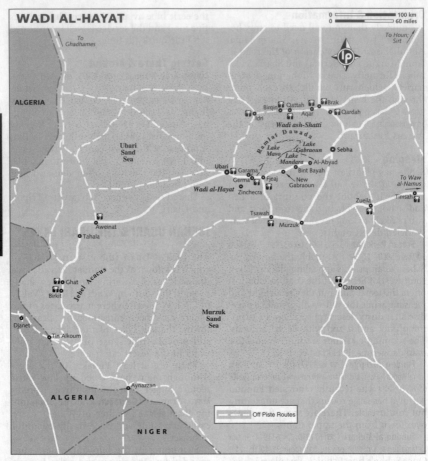

ancient city of Garama, the one-time capital of the Garamantian empire (see p464).

Sights
ANCIENT GARAMA
Garama (adult/child 3/1LD; camera/video 5/10LD; 🕑 8am-7pm May-Sep & 9am-5pm Oct-Apr) was founded in the 1st century AD. It's a city built from stone, clay and animal dung at the foot of the sand dunes. With the ruins of a **Garamantian palace**, **temple** and narrow, twisting **lanes**, there's just enough here to provide some idea of how the city must have once been.

MUSEUM
In Germa's small **museum** (Tripoli-Ghat Hwy; admission 3LD, camera/video 5/10LD; 🕑 8.30am-2pm

& 3-6.30pm Tue-Sun), there are informative English explanations that illuminate some (but not all) of the highlights of the area. Displays include the history of Garamantian civilisation, an excellent time graph of prehistoric rock art, and a dramatic satellite photo that shows the Idehan Murzuq and Idehan Ubari separated by Wadi al-Hayat.

Festivals & Events
Every year in March the town hosts the **Germa Festival**, which is a colourful occasion when inhabitants of the Wadi al-Hayat don their traditional dress and perform local dances, all contributing to a highly festive atmosphere.

Sleeping & Eating

Germa's camping grounds and hotels are generally better for showering (2LD for nonguests) and eating after emerging from the sand than for sleeping; at the camps, night-time mosquitoes are a problem. All camping grounds have kitchens that can be used for a small fee. The options include **Eirawan Camping** (☎ 2413; huts per person 10LD), which offers breakfast for 15LD and meals for 10LD, and **Timbuktu Camp** (☎ 2416), next to Eirawan Camping, which was under construction when we visited.

Funduq Dar Germa (☎ 2396; s/d with private bathroom & breakfast 30/40LD) If you're arriving in Germa from the desert, Funduq Dar Germa will feel like the Garden of Eden. The rooms are very comfortable and the squeaky-clean private bathrooms come with, wait for it, a bathtub. Not surprisingly, you'll need to book ahead. Meals cost 20LD to 25LD.

Old City Tourist Restaurant (☎ 0722-642245; tents 5LD; meals 8-12LD) Next to the gate of ancient Garama, this restaurant is laid-back and pleasant enough on a hot afternoon. You can use the kitchen (4LD) and smoke the nargileh (1LD).

Getting There & Away

Shared taxis run occasionally throughout the day to Ubari and Sebha.

UBARI   أوبارى

☎ 0722 / pop 42,975

The friendly town of Ubari has little of interest for travellers, but you're likely to pass through here en route to the Jebel Acacus. It's also the only town of any size between Al-Aweinat and Germa.

Orientation & Information

Ubari sprawls either side of the highway, but most of the facilities you'll need are along the main road. There are two **Internet cafés** (per hr 1.50LD) 50m west of the roundabout in the town centre.

Sleeping & Eating

Wat Wat Camp (☎ 642471; south of Tripoli-Ghat Hwy; tents 5LD, hut with/without breakfast 13/10LD) Reasonable huts, outdoor eating (meals 8LD to 15LD) and friendly staff are the order of the day here, but sleeping could mean a plague of mosquitoes.

Funduq Qala'a (☎ 626000; castle_obari@hotmail .com; Germa-Ghat Hwy; s/d with shared bathroom 30/40LD; 🛇) Ubari's most atmospheric choice, this converted castle has tidy rooms that are extremely comfortable for this part of the country. The castle origins can mean some rooms are a little cell-like but it's very well maintained and the courtyard's an antidote to the bleakness of the town surrounds. Meals cost 15LD.

Funduq Ubari (☎ 623095; s/d with private bathroom 30/35LD; 🛇) It's difficult to decide whether the pervading smell of disinfectant is reassuring or disconcerting. The beds also sag prodigiously and the atmosphere is that of a typical government hotel – fine, but depressing. Meals cost 15LD.

Simple food rules in Ubari with basic restaurants along the highway serving couscous, chicken and not much else.

Getting There & Away

Shared taxis run to Ghat (via Al-Aweinat) and Sebha (via Germa).

AL-AWEINAT   العوينات

☎ 0716

The pleasant and small oasis town of Al-Aweinat straddles the highway and can make an alternative staging post to Ghat en route to the Jebel Acacus. Another alternative is the challenging route from Ghadames to Al-Aweinat (see p494). **Aflaw Camp** (☎ 32040; fax 0724-2828; Tripoli-Ghat Hwy; bed in thatched hut 15LD) is well run and has a delightful open-sided dining area (meals 10LD).

GHAT   غات

☎ 0724 / pop 24,347

The ancient trading centre of Ghat is one of the most attractive of the Libyan oasis towns. There's an evocative mud-brick medina in the heart of town and a superb setting: a backdrop of stunning sand dunes, the dark ridges of the Jebel Acacus to the east and the distant peaks of the Tassili-n-Ajjer (in Algeria) to the west.

History

The medina was built at the end of the 1st century BC, but most of what's visible originated in the 12th century. First built by the Garamantians, Ghat was one in a chain of fortified oases that afforded protection to merchants as they crossed the desert in

LIBYA

their caravans. Although it never rivalled Ghadames in size, its strategic location as the only significant town in the region ensured that it played a critical role in the ebb and flow of Saharan conflicts and trade.

Sights

Ghat's compact **medina** (admission 3LD, camera/video 5/10LD) is a fine example of an ancient Saharan town. Largely deserted, it has some haunting remnants of its former role as the lifeblood of the surrounding desert. There's an ancient **well**; crumbling **mud-brick houses** with **palm-trunk doors**; a 9th-century **mosque**; and a ziggurat-like **former congress building** where public meetings once were held. Fine views can be had from a Turkish-Italian **fort** that rises above the town.

Festivals & Events

The **Acacus Festival** (December to January) features a spectacular sunset concert amid the cathedral-like Jebel Acacus, with Tuareg dancing and reenactments of traditional ceremonies in the medina to bring in the New Year.

Sleeping & Eating

Most visitors to Ghat stay in one of the camps – **Anay Camping** (☎ 2622; fax 2479), Rifa as-Sahara Camp, or Tuareg Camping – all of which have simple thatched huts, kitchens and charge 15LD per person including breakfast; you can also pitch a tent for 5LD.

Tassili Hotel (☎ 2560; s/d with private bathroom 25/30LD) Ghat's oldest hotel has seen better days and is in urgent need of a make-over. You'd be better off staying at one of the camps until it gets its act together. It does, however, have the town's only restaurant to speak of (meals 15LD).

Getting There & Away

Libyan Arab Airlines flies twice a week to Tripoli (56LD) via Sebha (28LD), but is often booked out months in advance. The airport is 25km north of town. Shared taxis only go as far as Ubari (via Al-Aweinat).

THE JEBEL ACACUS   جبل اكاكوس

The Jebel Acacus is an other-worldly landscape of dark basalt stone monoliths that rise up from the sands of the central Sahara. This is a Unesco World Heritage–listed area, which is home to some wonderful scenery.

The site features a number of unique natural rock formations enhanced by the ever-shifting sands of the desert, not to mention prehistoric rock paintings and carvings including elephants, giraffes, wedding ceremonies and dancing human figures.

The possible routes for exploring the Acacus region are endless, although the most usual starting points are Ghat and Al-Aweinat. Places you won't want to miss include the awe-inspiring 150m-high **Natural Arch**, the **Awiss** region, the fine rock art of **Wadi Anshal** and **Wadi Tanshal**, the relief of **Imenineh well**, and the prolific rock art of the beautiful **Wadi Tashwinat**.

IDEHAN MURZUQ   أدهان مرزق

For many travellers the Idehan Murzuq is the sand sea of which they have always dreamed, if only because it's less frequented than the Idehan Ubari. This incomprehensibly vast mountain range (over 35,000 sq km), made entirely of sand, is simply breathtaking with dunes rising hundreds of metres. The northern face of the sand sea rises up from the impossibly barren Murzuq Plateau; myriad wavelike ridges, sculpted by the wind, ascend to razor-sharp summits. From a distance during the heat of the day, the Idehan Murzuq shimmers pale yellow in the haze. As the sun lowers, the undulations in the midst of the dunes change into subtle yet magical plays of light and shadow.

WADI METHKANDOUSH   وادى متخندوش

Wadi Methkandoush, accessible from both Germa (150km) and the Jebel Acacus, has one of the richest concentrations of **prehistoric rock carvings** in the world. Most of the carvings in the soft sandstone date back at least 12,000 years, making this one of the oldest rock-art sites in Libya. This open-air gallery contains hundreds of carvings of animals, including wild cattle, giraffes, hippopotamuses, elephants, ostriches and rhinoceroses.

WAW AL-NAMUS   واو النامؤس

The extraordinary extinct and steep-sided volcanic crater of Waw al-Namus is a weird-and-wonderful place and one of the most remote destinations in the world. It's 300km southeast of where the paved road ends at Tmissah. The black-and-white volcanic sand

---

THE ROCK ART OF THE LIBYAN SAHARA

The rock art of the Jebel Acacus and Wadi Methkandoush have an almost whimsical beauty, combining a childlike understanding of the natural world with extremely skilful artistic ability. The local Tuareg believe that the ancient artists saw their art as a school for their descendants, a record of what they saw and how they lived.

The Sahara had a temperate climate from 10,000 BC until 2500 BC. The rock art spans the following periods, thereby depicting humankind's changing relationship with nature.

Wild Fauna or Early Hunter Period (10,000–6000 BC) Characterised by the portrayal of elephants, giraffes and Barbary sheep from the time when the Sahara was covered by the plentiful savanna.

Round Head Period (8000–6000 BC) Known for human figures with formless bodies and painted circular heads devoid of features; its later stages feature more-decorative figures adorned with headdresses and unusual clothing.

Pastoral or Bovidian Period (5500–2000 BC) Charts the gradual transition from temperate to arid climate with human figures shown in positions of dominance over the natural world (spears, domesticated cattle and ceremonies in keeping with more-settled communities).

Horse Period (1000 BC–AD 1) Horses and chariots reflect more-sophisticated transport and human movement and human figures are represented by two triangles with a circular head.

Camel Period (200 BC–present) Camels replace wild and domesticated cattle.

The wet pigment (derived from ground-and-burnt stone) necessary for the paintings was usually applied using a brush made of feathers or animal hair, a spatula made of stick or bone or the fingers of the artist. Liquid binders (egg white, milk, urine, animal fat or blood) were then added and account for the paintings' remarkable longevity. The carvings or petroglyphs were rendered using a method known as 'pecking', which involved the use of a heavy, sharp stone.

Please leave the paintings and carvings as you find them. That seemingly obvious point is lost on a small minority of travellers whose greed to take home the perfect gift has placed the rock art under threat. Wetting the rock to enhance a photograph can also cause irreparable damage.

If you want to learn more about Saharan rock art, contact the **Trust for African Rock Art** (TARA; ☎ /fax 254-2-884467; tara@swiftkenya.com), which is based in Kenya.

---

is stunning, as are the three palm-fringed lakes in which the water is red, green and blue. The crater is 7km in circumference and the summit of the rocky mountain in the centre affords stunning views. Not for nothing is Waw al-Namus known as the Crater of the Mosquitoes, so bring repellent and don't even think of camping in the crater. Also be sure to use the existing tracks down into the crater to avoid scarring the landscape for others.

Visiting here is a major undertaking and involves a two-day round trip in reliable, well-equipped vehicles. The road east from Zueila goes as far as the tiny town of Tmissah (76km). Thereafter, it is unsurfaced for about another 100km to Waw al-Kabir, an army camp with showers and basic meals. Beyond Waw al-Kabir are two army checkpoints, including one just before you arrive at Waw al-Namus; dropping off cigarettes and reading matter is much appreciated by the bored conscripts manning them. A permit is officially needed to visit Waw al-Namus, but this should be handled by your tour company and the price included in the overall cost of your tour.

You may be thinking that this is a lot of trouble and expense just to see a crater, but this is not a place you'll easily forget.

LIBYA DIRECTORY

ACCOMMODATION

Libya has an extensive network of *buyut ash-shabaab* (youth hostels), which can be pretty basic but dirt-cheap and fine for a night; a Hostelling International (HI) card entitles you to discounts of 2LD. As for camping, sleeping on the desert sand under a canopy of stars is free and unrivalled in beauty.

Funduq (government-run hotels) are frequently well situated and possess rooms of a reasonable standard, but service is often suspicious and downright dysfunctional. The crop of new private hotels is usually

PRACTICALITIES

■ International newspapers and magazines are not available in Libya.

■ Radio and TV coverage in Libya includes the BBC World Service (15.070MHz and 12.095MHz) and other European radio on short-wave, and International satellite TV channels in most hotels.

■ Libya has the PAL (B) video system as in western Europe.

■ Libya's electricity system caters for 220V to 240V AC, 50Hz; plugs are of the European continental-style two-pin type.

■ Libya uses the metric system for weights and measures.

cheaper, friendlier and much better maintained; some are outstanding. Along Libya's coastline, *qaryat as-siyahe* (tourist villages) offer proximity to the beach and a break from hotel ambience.

Throughout this chapter, budget hotels and hostels refer to places where hostel dorm beds cost 3LD up to 20/30LD for singles/doubles in a hotel. Midrange hotels and tourist villages range from 30/40LD up to 50/60LD, while top-end choices start from 70LD for a single and can scale the giddy heights of 400LD.

ACTIVITIES

Desert safaris by 4WD (and occasionally camel) enable you to experience some of the finest scenery the Sahara has to offer. All Libyan tour companies (p506) can arrange such expeditions lasting from two days up to deep desert expeditions of two weeks. At Gebraoun Lake (p495), dune skiing or sandboarding is also possible.

BOOKS

Desert Encounter, by Knud Holmboe, is a classic and sympathetic account of a journey across Libya and one of the few first-hand accounts of the Italian occupation of Libya in the early 1930s.

Difficult & Dangerous Roads: Hugh Clapperton's Travels in Sahara & Fezzan 1822–1825 is a sometimes cranky, but highly readable account of Hugh Clapperton's journeys through the Libyan Sahara.

South from Barbary, by Justin Marozzi, is an epic journey by camel from Ghadames to Al-Kufra. Although it reads a little like a *Boy's Own* adventure at times, it contains a wealth of historical detail.

African Rock Art, by David Coulson and Alec Campbell, is a beautifully illustrated study with a section on Libya's rock art.

Libya: The Lost Cities of the Roman Empire, by Robert Polidori et al, is unrivalled in its superb coverage of Libya's Greek and Roman sites, rich as it is with detailed research and great photography.

The Green Book, by Mu'ammar Gaddafi, lays out the philosophical basis that underpins Colonel Gaddafi's Libya.

Libya and the West: From Independence to Lockerbie, by the respected analyst Geoff Simons, is one of the more up-to-date (2004) explorations of Libyan history.

Libya's Qaddafi: The Politics of Contradiction, written by Mansour O el-Kikhia, is a penetrating and readable account of Libya under Colonel Gaddafi.

BUSINESS HOURS

Banks Open from 9am to 1pm Sunday to Tuesday and Thursday, 8am to 12.30pm and 3.30pm to 4.30pm or 4.30pm to 5.30pm Wednesday and Saturday.

Government offices Open from 7am to 2pm Saturday to Thursday April to September, and 8am to 3pm Saturday to Thursday October to March.

Internet cafés Open 9am to 1am Saturday to Thursday, and 3pm to 1am Friday.

Restaurants Open 12.30pm to 3pm and 6pm to 10pm Saturday to Thursday, and 6pm to 10pm Friday.

Shops Open 10am to 2pm and 5pm to 8pm Saturday to Thursday.

CHILDREN

Many Libyans live with or have close ties to their extended families and you'll find that most are terrific in dealing with children. Nappies (diapers), powders and most simple medications are available at pharmacies and grocery stores in most cities (especially Tripoli and Benghazi). The difficulty you're most likely to encounter is keeping your children entertained during the long journeys between towns.

CUSTOMS

Libyan customs checks on arrival are pretty cursory although bags are X-rayed. Don't even think of trying to bring alcohol into the country. If you're bringing your own car into the country, expect an hour or two of inspections at the border and make sure you have your carnet (see p662). Customs inspections upon departure tend to be slightly more rigorous; they're especially concerned about antiquities and fragments from the Saharan rock art of southern Libya being taken out of the country.

DANGERS & ANNOYANCES

Libya is a very safe country in which to travel and Libyans are generally a hospitable and friendly bunch. Police checkpoints can be tiresome and slow your journey but you'll rarely be asked to show identification. The only occasion on which you may encounter difficulties is if you point your camera at a restricted site (ie a government building or police station). Petty theft is extremely rare but does occur. Driving in Libya can be hazardous with the major danger being people driving at high speed.

DISABLED TRAVELLERS

As long as you're healthy, there's no reason why you shouldn't enjoy travelling in Libya. If you're going as part of a group, notify your tour company well in advance of any special requirements you may have. Most of the better hotels have entrances at ground level and functioning lifts and most group tours involve transport to all sites. Even in the desert transport is usually by 4WD rather than camel. Depending on your disability, you may find it difficult exploring some of the archaeological sites where paths are uneven and access for wheelchairs can be difficult.

EMBASSIES & CONSULATES
Libyan Embassies & Consulates

Libyan embassies are known as Libyan People's Bureaus.

Australia (☎ 02-6290 7900; 50 Culgoa Circuit, O'Malley, ACT 2606)
Austria (☎ 01-367 7639; Balaasstrasse 33, 1190 Vienna)
Belgium (☎ 02-649 15 03; Ave Victoria 28, B-1050 Brussels)
Canada (☎ 0613-230 0919; Suite 1000, 81 Metcalfe St, Ottawa K1P 6K7)
Egypt (☎ 02-735 1269; fax 02-735 0072; 7 Sharia el-Saleh Ayoub, Zamalek)

France Marseille (☎ 091 71 50 60; 424 rue Paradis, Marseille 13008); Paris (☎ 01 40 67 75 75; 3 villa Copernic, 75116)
Germany (☎ 030-20 05 96 0; Schützenstrasse 15-17, 10117 Berlin)
Italy Milan (☎ 02-86 46 42 85; Via Barrachini 7, Milan 02); Rome (☎ 06-86 32 09 51; Via Nomentana 365, Rome 00 162)
Netherlands (☎ 020-355 8886; Parkweg 15, 1285 GH, The Hague)
Spain (☎ 91 563 57 53; Calle Pisuerga 12, 28071 Madrid)
Switzerland (☎ 031-351 3076; Travelweg 2 CH-3006, Bern)
Tunisia (☎ 01-780 866; 48 Bis Rue due 1er Juin, Tunis 01)
Turkey (☎ 18100 225 12101; Miralay Sefik Dey Sok No 3, Gumussuyu, Taksim, İstanbul)
UK (☎ 020-7589 6120; 61-62 Ennismore Gardens, London SW7 1NH)
USA (☎ 212-752 5775; lbyun@undp.org; 309 East 48th St, New York 10017)

Embassies & Consulates in Libya

Both the Australian and US governments have announced plans to open embassies in Tripoli. At the time of research they were yet to open.

Belgium (☎ 021-3350115; Dhat al-Ahmat Tower 4, Level 5, Tripoli)
Egypt (Map p472; ☎ 021-6605500; Sharia al-Fat'h, Tripoli)
France (☎ 021-4774891; Sharia Beni al-Amar, Hay Andalus, Tripoli)
Germany (☎ 021-3330554; Sharia Hassan al-Mashai, Tripoli)
Italy (Map p472; ☎ 021-3334131; italconstrip@esteri.it; 1 Sharia Uaharan, Tripoli)
Japan (☎ 021-3350056; Dhat al-Ahmat Tower 4, Level 1, Tripoli)
Netherlands (Map p472; ☎ 021-4441549; 20 Sharia Galal Bayar, Tripoli)
Spain (☎ 021-3336797; Sharia al-Amir Abd al-Kader al-Jezaylr, Garden City, Tripoli)
Tunisia (☎ 021-3331051; off Sharia al-Jrabah, Bin Ashour, Tripoli)
UK (☎ 021-3351422; Burj al-Fateh, Level 24, Tripoli)
USA (c/o US Interests Section, Belgian embassy)

FESTIVALS & EVENTS

Germa Festival (p496) Held in March and showcases local ceremonies and dance.
Qasr Festival (p490) Honours the Berber traditions of the Jebel Nafusa and centres around Kabaw's evocative *qasr*. Held in April.

Ghadames Festival (p493) Held each October in the old city with celebrations of traditional culture and weddings.
Acacus Festival (p498) Held in Ghat during December and January. Celebrates the town's Tuareg heritage and includes concerts in the mountains.

HOLIDAYS

For a full list of religious holidays that are celebrated in Libya, see p647. Most government offices and some shops will be closed during the main national holidays.
Declaration of the People's Authority Day On 2 March commemorates the founding of the Jamahiriya in 1977.
Evacuation Day On 28 March celebrates the evacuation of British forces from Libyan soil.
Evacuation Day On 11 June celebrates the evacuation of other foreign military bases.
Revolution Day The biggest nonreligious holiday in the Libyan calendar occurs on 1 September.
Day of Mourning Pays tribute on 26 October to Libyans killed during the Italian occupation.

INTERNET ACCESS

Libya has joined the Internet revolution with Internet cafés present in almost every small town – look for the blue Internet Explorer sign on the window. Connections can be quite slow. The costs range from 0.75LD per hour in Tripoli to 1.50LD in more-remote places.

INTERNET RESOURCES

Some of the better Libya-specific websites:
Libya Online (www.libyaonline.com/) The most extensive directory devoted to Libyan society with a contemporary twist – everything from recipes to Libyan fashion.
Libya Our Home (http://ourworld.compuserve.com /homepages/dr_ibrahim_ighneiwa/) An expansive range of links on Libya, with sections on history, the arts, sport, human rights and travel.
Libyana (www.libyana.org) Another excellent site devoted to Libyan arts, especially music and poetry.
Society for Libyan Studies (www.britac.ac.uk/insti tutes/libya/) Useful for researchers and those interested in the archaeological work being undertaken in Libya.

LANGUAGE

Arabic is the national language of Libya and all signs are in Arabic – not even motorway signs are translated. English signs have recently been declared legal for sites and businesses that are tourist-related, but it's taking a while to catch on. Although some English or Italian is spoken in the main

cities, few people elsewhere speak a foreign language. Some French is spoken in Ghadames and Ghat.

MAPS

For desert expeditions in remote areas, the most reliable map is Michelin's Map No 953, *Africa North and West* (1:4,000,000). The best maps available in Libya include Malt International's *Map of the Socialist People's Libyan Arab Jamahiriya* (1:3,500,000) and Cartographia's *Libya* (1:2,000,000), which would be the map of choice were it not for the fact that it omits the Jebel Acacus and Waw al-Namus.

MONEY

The official unit of currency is the Libyan dinar. Notes include 0.25LD, 0.50LD, 1LD, 5LD, 10LD and, rarely, 20LD. For changing money, the bank and black-market exchange rates are all but identical. Large denomination euros, US dollars or British pounds are the preferred currencies. No banks change travellers cheques – cash is king in Libya. The following were the official bank rates at the time of publication.

Country	Unit	Libyan dinar (LD)
Australia	A$1	0.93
Egypt	E£1	0.24
Canada	C$1	1.16
euro zone	€1	1.50
Japan	¥100	1.18
New Zealand	NZ$1	0.94
UK	UK£1	2.21
USA	US$1	1.27

It's also now possible to obtain a cash advance on your Visa card (although not, at the time of writing, with any other card). The Masraf al-Tijara Watanmiya (Bank of Commerce & Development), with branches in Tripoli (p473) and Benghazi (p482), is the only bank to do this. Libya's only ATM for Visa cards at the time of writing was in the lobby of the Funduq Tibesti (p484) in Benghazi.

PHOTOGRAPHY

Digital photography has been slow to catch on in Libya. While you may find that some photo shops know what they're talking about in Tripoli, you're better off arriving fully equipped. If you want to burn photos to CDs, it is possible at some Internet cafés in Tripoli and, to a lesser extent, in Benghazi. However, this applies only to dedicated Internet cafés and not to the ubiquitous phone centres that have a few computers out the back.

POST

Almost every town in Libya has a post office that's easily recognisable by the tall telecommunications mast rising above the centre of town. It costs 0.30/0.50LD to send a postcard/letter to most places, including Europe and Australia.

SHOPPING

The best place in Libya to shop is in the souqs of Tripoli's medina (p476), where you'll find the largest selection of goods. For Tuareg items, many Tuareg in the Fezzan spread out their goods for sale on a rug alongside the lakes.

The most distinctive items for sale include high-quality flat-weave Berber cushions and rugs, colourful pottery, copper items and leatherwork. Other must-haves are Colonel Gaddafi watches, embroidered leather slippers from Ghadames (p494) and silver Tuareg jewellery.

SOLO TRAVELLERS

Travelling to Libya on your own is not generally a problem, although it can be prohibitively expensive. Even on your own, you're required to travel with a guide, which means you shoulder the full cost of transport, guiding fees etc, rather than sharing them among a group. To visit the desert requires a minimum of two 4WD vehicles (90LD each per day), in case one breaks down, which can really blow out costs.

TELEPHONE & FAX

Calls within Libya invariably receive instant connections and are quite cheap (around 0.25LD). To make an international call, go to the counter of a government telephone office, write out the number in full for the clerk who will make the connection, and then take the call in the allocated private booth. For most Western countries, the cost is 1.50LD per minute. Far cheaper is using an Internet café to telephone via the Internet. Most cafés sell 8LD cards and can help you connect. For

8LD, you will have 210/145/152 minutes to the UK/USA/Italy.

Fax

An international/local fax will rarely cost more than 2/0.50LD. The best places from which to send faxes are also the government telephone offices. The main telephone office in Tripoli offers a handy fax restante service (see p473).

Mobile Phones

You're unlikely to get coverage for your mobile phone in Libya – check with your company at home before travelling.

TOILETS

There are no public toilets in Libya, but you're never too far from a restaurant or mosque where they're usually happy to point you in the right direction. In the event of an emergency ask for *al-hammam* or *mirhab*.

TOURIST INFORMATION

Libyan government tourist offices operate as overseers of the tourism industry and tour companies, *not* providers of practical tourist information.

VISAS

To obtain a Libyan visa, you'll need an invitation from a Libyan tour company; if you've organised your tour through a non-Libyan company, they'll arrange the invitation from their Libyan affiliates. The tour company will then send you a visa number. Make sure you have an Arabic-language confirmation to smooth the process with airlines, the embassy or immigration officials. You can collect your visa either from the Libyan embassy in your home country or at your entry point to Libya but specify which you prefer when making first contact with the tour company. The process generally takes two weeks, but allowing for a month is safer. Visas are valid for 30 days from the date of entry and you must enter Libya within 30 days of the visa being issued.

A further requirement of entry into Libya is that travellers must be in possession of a minimum of 500LD in foreign currency. Those who pay all travel expenses to their tour operator or agency in advance are exempt from this requirement.

Registration

All holders of tourist visas must register with the Libyan authorities at any *jawazzat* within seven days of arrival in the country. The process will invariably be completed by the tour company responsible for you during your stay and the fee is usually included in your overall tour cost.

WOMEN TRAVELLERS

Balancing the liberal and the conservative strands of Libyan society is an inexact science, but it's one that causes few difficulties for the overwhelming number of female visitors to Libya. In general, Libya is one of the easiest countries in the Middle East for women to travel in, largely because of Libyan government policies in relation to women. Since the revolution the government's policies have contributed to a less-misunderstood view of Western women than can be found in some other countries of the region. As a result, most female travellers have reported being treated with respect, with few incidents of unpleasant behaviour. When foreign visitors are introduced to Libyan men, men will in most circumstances shake hands with Western women.

The usual dress guidelines for the region apply in Libya; see p655 for details.

TRANSPORT IN LIBYA

GETTING THERE & AWAY

For information on travelling to Libya from outside the Middle East, see p657.

Entering Libya

Coming into Libya, whether by air, sea or land, is generally a trouble-free process. If you are collecting your visa on arrival in Libya, try to ensure that your tour company has a representative waiting for you to reduce the time that they spend processing your visa.

Passport

When entering Libya, there is no longer any requirement that your passport details be translated into Arabic. Israeli citizens will not be issued with a visa under any circumstances, nor will those with Israeli stamps in their passport.

Air

Travellers will find that the Libyan capital and, to a lesser extent, Benghazi are well connected to other Middle Eastern cities by air.

For details on flights to Libya from outside the Middle East, see p657.

AIRLINES FLYING TO/FROM LIBYA

Afriqiyah Airways (airline code 8U; in Tripoli ☎ 021-3333647; www.afriqiyah.aero) Hub: Tripoli.
Air Malta (airline code KM; in Tripoli ☎ 021-3350579; www.airmalta.com) Hub: Valetta.
Al-Buraq Air (airline code UZ; in Tripoli ☎ 021-4444811; www.buraqair.com) Hub: Tripoli.
Alitalia (airline code AZ; in Tripoli ☎ 021-3350298; www.alitalia.com) Hub: Rome.
Austrian Airlines (airline code OS; in Tripoli ☎ 021-3350242; www.aua.com) Hub: Vienna.
British Airways (airline code BA; in Tripoli ☎ 021-3351281; www.britishairways.com) Hub: Heathrow Airport, London.
Emirates (airline code EK; in Tripoli ☎ 021-3350597; www.emirates.com) Hub: Dubai.
KLM Royal Dutch Airlines (airline code KL; in Tripoli ☎ 021-3350018; www.klm.com) Hub: Amsterdam Schipol Airport.
Libyan Arab Airlines (airline code LN; in Tripoli ☎ 021-3616738) Hub: Tripoli.
Lufthansa (airline code LH; in Tripoli ☎ 021-3350375; www.lufthansa.com) Hub: Frankfurt.
Royal Jordanian (airline code RJ; in Tripoli ☎ 021-4442453; www.rja.com.jo) Hub: Amman.
Swiss International Airlines (airline code LX; in Tripoli ☎ 021-3350022; www.swiss.com) Hub: Zurich.

FLIGHTS FROM LIBYA

Departures from Tripoli	Airline	One-way/return Fare (US$)
Aleppo (via Benghazi)	Al-Buraq Air	150/275
Alexandria (via Benghazi)	EgyptAir	144/173
Amman	Royal Jordanian	140/275
	Libyan Arab Airlines	140/275
Beirut	Libyan Arab Airlines	140/240
Cairo	EgyptAir	144/173
(via Benghazi)	Libyan Arab Airlines	144/173
Damascus	Syrianair	150/275
	Al-Buraq Air	150/275
	Libyan Arab Airlines	150/275
İstanbul	Turkish Airlines	180/335
	Libyan Arab Airlines	180/335

Syrianair (airline code RB; in Tripoli ☎ 021-4446716; www.syriaair.com) Hub: Damascus.
Tunis Air (airline code TU; in Tripoli ☎ 021-3336303; www.tunisair.com) Hub: Tunis.
Turkish Airlines (airline code TK; in Tripoli ☎ 021-3351252; www.turkishairlines.com) Hub: İstanbul.

Land
BORDER CROSSINGS
The most commonly used land borders for travellers are the coastal frontiers with Tunisia (Ras al-Jedir) and Egypt (Amsaad). The land borders with Sudan, Chad and Algeria were, at the time of writing, closed to non-Libyans. The remote border crossing with Niger is open, although you should make sure that you have the necessary visas (valid for land arrivals) firmly ensconced in your passport – it is a long way to backtrack if there's some kind of problem.

Egypt
The Libyan Egyptian border, 139km east of Tobruk at Amsaad and 12km west of Sallum in Egypt, is remote, often chaotic and, in summer, perishingly hot; bring your own water. Foreign travellers are often, embarrassingly, shepherded to the front of the queue. We've never heard of anyone turning down such an offer as a matter of principle.

Long-distance buses run from Benghazi to Alexandria (40LD to 50LD) and Cairo (50LD to 60LD). Shared taxis run from the taxi station in Tobruk all the way to the border (5LD). On the other side, shared taxis go to Sallum (E£3 to E£4) where you can get buses (E£12) or service taxis (E£15) to Marsa Matruh. **Al-Itihad al-Afriqi** (Map p472; ☎ 021-3342532; Sharia al-Ma'ari, Tripoli) has departures from Tripoli for Cairo (100LD, 36 hours); you'll need to book at least two days in advance.

Tours
For a full list of international tour companies who run tours to Libya and elsewhere, see p664.

GETTING AROUND
In this era of organised tours, getting around Libya couldn't be easier because all transport within the country will be organised by your tour company.

Air
Libya's domestic airline network is expanding rapidly with flights connecting Tripoli to Benghazi, Ghat, Houn, Lebreq (near Al-Bayda) and Sebha. There are also occasional flights to Ghadames with more regular flights planned. For details on prices and frequency, see the relevant city entries throughout this chapter. From Benghazi, there are also flights to Sebha and Al-Kufra (p484).

There are two airlines that fly domestically in Libya.
Al-Buraq Air (www.buraqair.com) Benghazi (☎ 061-2234469); Tripoli (☎ 021-3510016) Only operating a Tripoli–Benghazi route at the time of writing but it has plans for flights to Sebha and other Libyan destinations. It has a newer fleet than Libyan Arab Airlines, and is a little more expensive but more reliable. Operates from Tripoli's Metiga Airport.
Libyan Arab Airlines (☎ 021-3616738; Sharia Omar al-Mukhtar, Tripoli)

Bus & Shared Taxi
There are daily bus connections between the major cities, with services along the coast the most frequent. Many buses are air-conditioned, although the quality is variable. The routes are shadowed by shared taxis, which can take an age to fill.

Car & Motorcycle
If you do have your own vehicle, especially a 4WD, there are few limits on where you can go, however, the Tibesti region is one exception. You must be accompanied by at least one representative of the Libyan tour company who arranged your visa and who remains responsible for you for the duration of your stay.

Driving is on the right-hand side of the road, and Libyans generally drive as fast as they think they can get away with. For the record, all cars (including 4WDs) must stay on or below 100km/h on highways and 50km/h inside towns.

All road signs are in Arabic so familiarise yourself with the written Arabic names for your destination (see each town's individual listing throughout this chapter). Libyan roads are generally maintained in excellent condition and petrol is ridiculously cheap; you'll fill your tank for around 5LD. No matter how many times you have been waved through a checkpoint, never assume that you will be. Always slow down or stop until you get the wave from your friendly machine-gun-toting soldier.

Tours

The following companies are among those that we either recommend or have been recommended to us by travellers.

Al-Muheet Tours (in Benghazi ☎ 061-9082084; www
.almuheettours.net) The owner, Sami al-Ghibani, has a reputation for running an efficient and flexible company. Benghazi-based.

Destination Libye (in Tripoli ☎ 021-4779854; www
.dlibye.com) Good company specialising in French-language tours.

Robban Tourism Services (in Tripoli ☎ 021-4441530; www.robban-tourism.com; off Sharia as-Sarim, Tripoli) Outstanding and professional small company with flexible itineraries and good guides. Hussein Founi should be your first port of call.

Sahara Link Travel (in Tripoli ☎ 021-3343209; saharalink@hotmail.com; Sharia Kuwait, Tripoli)

Shati Zuara Travel & Tourism (☎ 091315 8229; info@shati-zuara.de; www.shati-zuara.de) Very good Libyan company with its main base in Germany.

Sukra Travel & Tourism (in Tripoli ☎ 021-3340604; www.sukra-travel.com; Sharia Mohammed Megharief, Tripoli)

Taknes Co (in Tripoli ☎ 021-3350526; fax 3350525; Funduq Bab al-Bahar, Tripoli) The owner is the helpful Ali Shebli. The postal address is PO Box 91218, Tripoli.

Wings Travel & Tours (in Tripoli ☎ 021-3331855; www.wingstours.com; Green Sq, Tripoli)

Winzrik Tourism Services (in Tripoli ☎ 021-3611123; www.winzrik.com; Sharia 7 November, Tripoli) Libya's largest and longest-standing tour company.

Syria

Here's a newsflash: contrary to what the US State Department may wish the world to think, Syria is not populated by terrorists, zealots and other bogeymen. In fact, Syrians are among the most friendly and hospitable people in the world, and most visitors to their country end up developing a lifelong infatuation with its gentle charms.

Since Bashar al-Assad took over the reins from his father in 2001, modernisation has been on the national agenda. This is no Levantine backwater – Syria is a modern, efficient and very proud nation with an administration that is becoming more liberal and outward looking by the day. It needs and deserves travellers to bear witness to this fact.

Fortunately, all this modernisation doesn't mean that Syria has lost sight of its past. The country has more than its fair share of significant historical sites, all of which are respectfully maintained by the authorities. The ancient cities of Damascus, Aleppo and Bosra are all listed on Unesco's World Heritage list, as is the sensationally beautiful ruined city of Palmyra. Mighty Crusader castles, labyrinthine medieval souqs, jewel-like Damascene houses and sacred Umayyad mosques are only some of the treats on offer; there are plenty more for those who are keen to search them out. Best of all is the fact that these monuments are often woven into the fabric of daily life – the locals worship in the mosques, shop in the souqs, drink tea in the houses and picnic in the ruins. And they're happy for travellers to join them.

Talking about picnics brings us to the *pièce de résistance* when it comes to a Syrian sojourn – the food. The national cuisine is simply superb, so come with a big appetite. You're bound to be replete in so many ways when you finally tear yourself away.

FAST FACTS

- **Area** 185,180 sq km
- **Capital** Damascus
- **Country code** ☎ 963
- **Language** Arabic
- **Money** Syrian pound (also known as the lira; S£); US$1 = S£51.91; €1 = S£61.30
- **Official name** Syrian Arab Republic
- **Population** 20 million

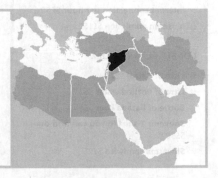

HIGHLIGHTS

- **Old City in Damascus** (p514) The jewel in Syria's crown is the most beautiful district in the Middle East.
- **Aleppo's souqs** (p538) Nothing beats getting lost in these mazelike lanes.
- **Crac des Chevaliers** (p529) The castle of every child's imagination – it never ever disappoints.
- **Palmyra** (p545) Queen Zenobia's magnificent sandstone city is the ultimate desert oasis.
- **Qala'at Samaan** (p544) Its bizarre history is equalled only by its magnificent location.

CLIMATE & WHEN TO GO

Syria has a Mediterranean climate with hot, dry summers (June to August) and mild, wet winters (December to February) close to the coast. Inland it gets progressively drier and more inhospitable. On the coast, average daily temperatures range from 29°C in summer to 10°C in winter and the annual rainfall is about 760mm. On the cultivated steppe area, temperatures average 35°C in summer and 12°C in winter. Rainfall varies from 250mm to 500mm. In the desert, the temperatures are high and rainfall is low. In summer, the days average 40°C and highs of 46°C are not uncommon. Winter can be extremely cold in mountainous areas, including Crac des Chevaliers.

Spring is the best time to visit as temperatures are mild and the winter rains have

---

HOW MUCH?

- **Cup of tea** S£25
- **Newspaper** S£5
- **One-minute phone call to the UK** S£75
- **Internet connection per hour** S£50
- **Museum admission** S£150

LONELY PLANET INDEX

- **Litre of petrol** S£25
- **Litre of bottled water** S£25
- **Bottle of Barada beer** S£60
- **Souvenir T-shirt (if you can find one)** S£500
- **Shwarma sandwich** S£25

---

cleared the haze that obscures views for much of the year. Autumn is the next best choice. The busiest tourism periods are Easter, July, August, October and Islamic religious holidays. During these times it is essential to book accommodation in advance. This chapter often quotes opening hours as 'summer' or 'winter'; summer hours generally refer to April to September and winter hours to October to March, but these aren't set in stone and can be dependent on the weather.

See Climate Charts p643.

HISTORY

Historically, Syria included the territories that now make up modern Jordan, Israel and the Palestinian Territories, Lebanon and Syria itself. Due to its strategic position, its coastal towns were important Phoenician trading posts. Later the area became an equally pivotal part of the Egyptian, Persian and Roman empires – and many others in the empire-building business, for that matter. For more details, see p37.

Syria finally ended up as part of the Ottoman domains ruled from İstanbul, and was dished out to France (along with Lebanon) when the Ottoman Empire broke up after WWI. This caused considerable local resentment, as the region had been briefly independent from the end of WWI until the French took over in 1920.

France never had much luck with its Syria-Lebanon mandate. Local opposition to its policy of carving up the country into mini-states (Grand Liban, Lebanon, Aleppo and Damascus) and minority enclaves (for the Druze and Alawite) led to revolts against French rule. Elections were held in 1928 and 1932, but moves to establish a constitution were stymied by the occupying power, which compounded its unpopularity in 1939 when it ceded the northern cities of Antioch (Antakya) and Alexandretta (Iskenderun) to Turkey in an effort to ensure Turkey's neutrality in WWII.

After the surrender of France to Germany in 1940, Syria came under the control of the Vichy government; its overthrow in 1941 paved the way for Syria's independence to be formally recognised, though it took a while for the French to acknowledge this and finalise the handover.

A nationalist government was formed under Shukri al-Kuwatli in August 1943,

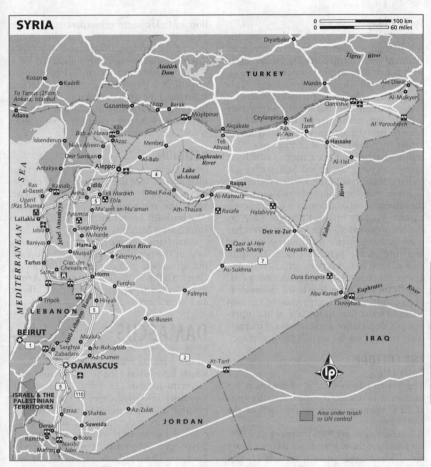

SYRIA

Area under Israeli
or UN control

but the French continued to be in denial about the waning of its influence in the region, bombing Damascus after locals had demonstrated in support of a final handover of administrative and military services to the new government. The situation was only resolved after the British intervened and oversaw the final departure of all French troops and administrators at the end of the war.

A period of political instability followed and by 1954, after several military coups, the nationalist Ba'ath Party (Ba'ath means 'renaissance') took power virtually unopposed. A brief flirtation with the Pan-Arabist idea of a United Arab Republic (with Egypt) in 1958 proved unpopular and coups in 1960, '61 and '63 saw the leadership change hands yet again. By 1966 the Ba'ath Party was back in power, but it was severely weakened by losses in two conflicts – the Six Day War with Israel in 1967 and the Black September hostilities in Jordan in 1970. At this point, Defence Minister Hafez al-Assad seized power.

Assad maintained control longer than any other postindependence Syrian government, with a mixture of ruthless suppression and guile. In 1998, he was elected to a fifth seven-year term with a predictable 99.9% of the vote. It took a failing of health to finally remove the man from power; his death was announced on 10 June 2000.

Syria Today

Following the death of Assad senior, his son Bashar acceded to power. A new government was formed in December 2001 with a mandate to push forward political, economic and administrative reforms. This has proved a challenge, particularly when it comes to reforming the country's unwieldy bureaucracy, many members of which have been recruited due to their political contacts rather than their level of competence. As a result, change isn't occurring as swiftly as many observers had hoped. Still, you've got to hand it to Assad junior – he's trying.

Improving the country's relations with the international community is proving even trickier. Publicly branded a 'rogue state' by the US president, George W Bush, Syria has recently been forced to withdraw its army and intelligence personnel from Lebanon (see p35). It has also been criticised by the US for its support of Hezbollah and for allegedly turning a blind eye to the movements of Iraqi insurgents. Though making a gallant effort to stand firm in the face of the superpower's displeasure, Syria is looking increasingly isolated on the world's political stage.

THE CULTURE
Daily Life

The Syrian labour force is estimated at 5.3 million, and unemployment currently runs at 20%. Women comprise just 20% of the workforce.

Literacy rates are 93% for males and 78% for females. School attendance is compulsory for children aged between six and 12, and there are four national public universities, which have combined enrolments of 173,000. Salaries are generally low, even among these university graduates. An average wage for a doctor, for instance, is US$400 to US$600 per month, and one of the greatest problems the country faces is the 'brain drain' that is occurring as many graduates head overseas to find better-paying work.

Families are large, and extended families often live together. Rural–urban migration over recent years now means that about half of the country's population lives in the cities.

Population

Syria has a population of around 20 million, about 90% of which is Arab. The population includes some minorities such as the Bedouin (about 100,000) and smaller groupings of Armenians, Circassians and Turks. There are also around one million Kurds.

The country has an annual population growth of 2.4%. Although this is a decline from the 3.6% growth that was seen during the 1990s, it's still very high by international standards. Fifty per cent of the population is under 20 years of age.

RELIGION

Islam is practised by about 89% of the population – 20% of this is made up of minorities such as the Shiite, Druze and Alawite, while the remainder are Sunni Muslims. The business community is mainly drawn from Sunni Muslims.

Christians account for the remaining 11% of the population and belong to various churches, including Greek Orthodox, Greek Catholic, Syrian Orthodox, Armenian Orthodox, Maronite, Roman Catholic and Protestant.

DAMASCUS   دمشق

☎ 011 / pop five million

Roads have always led to Damascus (Ash-Sham to locals). One of the oldest continuously inhabited cities in the world, its position in the verdant Ghouta oasis and its proximity to the Silk Road led to it being coveted by waves of conquering empires. Egyptians, Assyrians, Persians, Greeks, Romans, Umayyads, Mongols, Turks and French were all lured by the city's charms and left their imprint on its physical form, making Damascus one of the most architecturally significant cities in the Middle East. These days, the only foreign interlopers are travellers, who inevitably end up being seduced by its extraordinary Old City and unusual mixture of tradition and modernity.

ORIENTATION

The city centre is compact and finding your way around on foot is no problem. The main street, Sharia Said al-Jabri, begins at the Hijaz train station and runs northeast, changing its name to Sharia Bur Said. It finishes in Saahat Yousef al-Azmeh, the square that is at the heart of the modern city. The

---

DAMASCUS IN TWO DAYS

On day one, make your way to the magical **Old City** (p514) and spend your day exploring every souq, street and sensational café (two of the best coffeehouses to relax in are **An-Nafura** and **Ash-Shams**, p520). If you're a keen shopper, make sure you check out the city's most famous antique dealer, **Georges Dabdoub** (Map pp516–17), and one of its most reputable carpet dealers, **Khayat Carpets** (Map pp516–17). Both are next to the wonderful **Azem Palace** (p515). After returning to your hotel for a brief rest, move on to Central Damascus for a casual but delicious dinner at **Al Shamiat** (p519).

Day two starts at the **National Museum** (p515). After admiring the collection, saunter past the **Military Museum** (p515) and **Takiyya as-Süleimaniyya** (p515) until you reach the **Artinasat** (p515), where you may want to purchase some locally made handicrafts. Next, walk up Sharia Mousalam al-Baroudi past the historic Hijaz train station to the Old City, where you can enjoy a snack from one of the food stands near the mosque or colonise a table on the outdoor terrace at chic **Leila's Restaurant & Terrace** (p520).

After spending the rest of the afternoon revisiting the souqs you'll probably be in need of a drink with dinner, so make your way to the nearby Christian quarter and the atmospheric **Elissar** (p520).

---

streets off this square are home to most of the airline offices, the main tourist office, the central branch of the Commercial Bank of Syria (CBS) and a host of hotels and restaurants. Souq Saroujah, the home of the city's backpacker hotels, is southeast of the square.

South of Souq Saroujah is Martyrs' Sq (known to locals as Al-Merjeh), the city's 'downtown' district. Though it's currently a slightly seedy part of town, this may change with the opening of the enormous new mosque currently under construction. Further east again is the Old City, still ringed by its old Arab walls.

Maps

Avicenne Bookshop (below) publishes a *Syria* map with an inset of Damascus. It costs S£150. The tourist offices in town and at the airport stock a free *Damascus & Damascus Countryside* map.

INFORMATION
Bookshops

Avicenne Bookshop (Map pp512-13; ☎ 221 2911; 4 Sharia Attuhami; ◷ 9am-2pm & 4.30-8pm Sat-Thu summer, 9am-8pm Sat-Thu rest of year) The only decent English-language bookshop in Damascus; located southwest of the Cham Palace Hotel.

Emergency

Ambulance (☎ 110)
Fire department (☎ 113)
Police (☎ 112)

Internet Access

The following are a few of the many Internet cafés in Damascus:

Angelsnet (per hr S£50; ◷ 24hr) This friendly place is usually packed with students from the nearby Damascus University. Connections are very fast. You'll find it behind the Oumaoyeen Centre, near the Baramke garage.

Fast Link Internet (Map pp512-13; 2nd fl, Abdin Bldg, Sharia Hammam al-Ward; per hr S£60; ◷ 10am-11pm Sat-Thu, 5-11pm Fri) Fast connections and good work stations make this a worthwhile option, particularly as it's in the middle of the backpacker quarter. You'll find the street off Sharia Souq Saroujah.

High Point (Map pp516-17; per hr S£75; ◷ noon-1am) The best Internet café in town, with fast connections and free tea and coffee. Located off Sharia Bab Touma.

Zoni Internet (Map pp512-13; per hr S£60; ◷ 10.30am-11pm Sat-Thu & 1-11pm Fri) Situated on the 3rd floor of the same building as Fast Link Internet, this café offers an almost identical service, but doesn't burn CDs.

Medical Services

Al-Chami Hospital (☎ 373 4925; Sharia Jawaher an-Nehru) Northwest of the main centre of town. Accepts credit cards.

Cham Clinic (☎ 333 8742; ◷ 24hr) Conveniently located behind the Meridien Hotel. Doctors speak English.

Money

There are several branches of the Commercial Bank of Syria (CBS) around town, as well as exchange booths where you can change money fairly easily; the branch on Saahat Yousef al-Azmeh will change

CENTRAL DAMASCUS

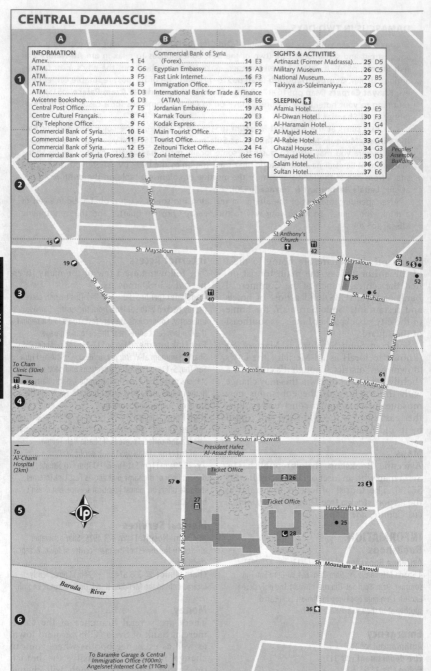

INFORMATION
Amex	1 E4
ATM	2 G6
ATM	3 F5
ATM	4 E3
ATM	5 D3
Avicenne Bookshop	6 D3
Central Post Office	7 E5
Centre Culturel Français	8 F4
City Telephone Office	9 F6
Commercial Bank of Syria	10 E4
Commercial Bank of Syria	11 F5
Commercial Bank of Syria	12 E5
Commercial Bank of Syria (Forex)	13 E6
Commercial Bank of Syria (Forex)	14 E3
Egyptian Embassy	15 A3
Fast Link Internet	16 F3
Immigration Office	17 F5
International Bank for Trade & Finance (ATM)	18 E6
Jordanian Embassy	19 A3
Karnak Tours	20 E3
Kodak Express	21 E6
Main Tourist Office	22 E2
Tourist Office	23 D5
Zeitouni Ticket Office	24 F4
Zoni Internet	(see 16)

SIGHTS & ACTIVITIES
Artinasat (Former Madrassa)	25 D5
Military Museum	26 C5
National Museum	27 B5
Takiyya as-Süleimaniyya	28 C5

SLEEPING
Afamia Hotel	29 E5
Al-Diwan Hotel	30 F3
Al-Haramain Hotel	31 G4
Al-Majed Hotel	32 F2
Al-Rabie Hotel	33 G4
Ghazal House	34 G3
Omayad Hotel	35 D3
Salam Hotel	36 C6
Sultan Hotel	37 E6

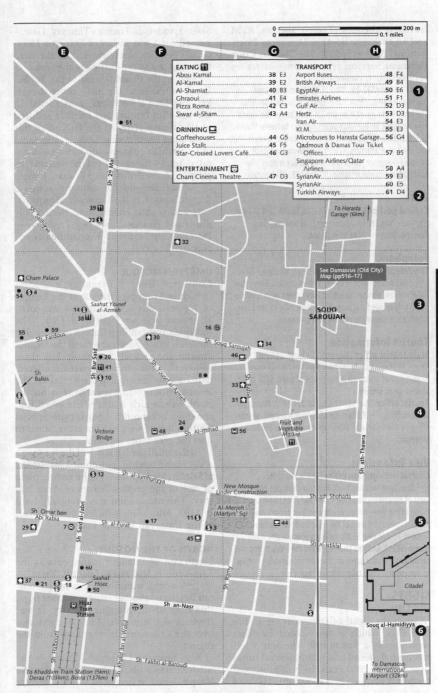

EATING 🍴		
Abou Kamal	38	E3
Al-Kamal	39	E2
Al-Shamiat	40	B3
Ghraoui	41	E4
Pizza Roma	42	C3
Siwar al-Sham	43	A4

DRINKING 🍷		
Coffeehouses	44	G5
Juice Stalls	45	F5
Star-Crossed Lovers Café	46	G3

ENTERTAINMENT 🎭		
Cham Cinema Theatre	47	D3

TRANSPORT		
Airport Buses	48	F4
British Airways	49	B4
EgyptAir	50	E6
Emirates Airlines	51	F1
Gulf Air	52	D3
Hertz	53	D3
Iran Air	54	E3
KLM	55	E3
Microbuses to Harasta Garage	56	G4
Qadmous & Damas Tour Ticket Offices	57	B5
Singapore Airlines/Qatar Airlines	58	A4
SyrianAir	59	E3
SyrianAir	60	E5
Turkish Airways	61	D4

SYRIA

travellers cheques. There's also an ATM and an exchange booth at Damascus International Airport (p522). The Thomas Cook Financial Services representative offers no services for travellers.

Amex (Map pp512-13; ☎ 221 7813; amexrep@net .sy; Sharia Balkis; ☼ 8.30am-2pm & 4.30-8pm Sat-Thu) The local Amex agent is on the 1st floor, above the Sudan Airways office on the small street running between Sharias al-Mutanabi and Fardous. It offers very limited services, and can't give advances against your credit card, cash cheques or replace stolen ones. One service it does offer cardholders is poste restante (PO Box 1373, Damascus).

Post
Central post office (Map pp512-13; Sharia Said al-Jabri; ☼ 8am-7pm Sat-Thu, 8am-1pm Fri & holidays) Just downhill from the Hijaz train station.

Telephone
City telephone office (Map pp512-13; Sharia an-Nasr; ☼ 24hr) A block east of the Hijaz train station. Given that there are card phones on almost every street corner, you're only likely to need this place if you have a fax to send (for which it's necessary to present your passport).

Tourist Information
Main tourist office (Map pp512-13; ☎ 232 3953; Sharia 29 Mai; ☼ 9.30am-8pm Sat-Thu) Just up from Saahat Yousef al-Azmeh in the centre of town. Staff don't always speak English.

Tourist office (Map pp512-13; ☎ 221 0122; Ministry of Tourism Bldg; ☼ 9.30am-8pm Sat-Thu) A second, smaller office by the Takiyya as-Süleimaniyya, near the National Museum.

Visa Extensions
Central immigration office (Sharia Filasteen; ☼ 8am-2pm Sat-Thu) You'll find this office one block west of Baramke garage. Go to the 2nd floor to begin filling in the three forms. You'll need four photos (the Kodak Express just west of the Hijaz train station can do them in 10 minutes; S£200 for eight photos), one entry stamp (S£25), and two photocopies of the entry stamp and photo page of your passport. You can get extensions of up to one month. Visas take 24 hours to process.

SIGHTS
Old City
Most of the sights of Damascus are in the Old City, which is surrounded by what was initially a **Roman wall**. The wall itself has been flattened and rebuilt several times over the past 2000 years. Its best-preserved section is between Bab as-Salaama (Gate of

Safety) and Bab Touma (Thomas' Gate – named for a son-in-law of Emperor Heraclius). For the best view, follow the road that runs along the outside of the wall.

Next to the **citadel** (closed to the public) is the entrance to the main covered market, the **Souq al-Hamidiyya**, constructed in the late 19th century and recently restored to its original state. At the far end of this wide shop-lined avenue is an arrangement of Corinthian columns supporting a decorated lintel – the remains of the **western temple gate** of the 3rd-century Roman Temple of Jupiter. Beyond the columns, across a flagged square, is the Umayyad Mosque.

If you get the chance, read the lavishly illustrated *Hidden Damascus: Treasures of the Old City* by Brigid Keenan before exploring the city.

UMAYYAD MOSQUE
Converted from a Byzantine cathedral (which had occupied the site of the Temple of Jupiter), this revered **mosque** (Map pp516-17; admission S£50) was built in AD 705. The mosque's outstanding feature is its golden mosaics, which adorn several of the façades around the central courtyard. The three minarets, although subsequently altered, date back to the original construction. The tourist entrance to the mosque is on the north side, which is also where you'll find the small ticket office. Look for the 'Special Clothes Room' sign; women are required to don the grey robes supplied.

In the small garden north of the mosque's walls is the modest, red-domed **Mausoleum of Saladin** (Map pp516–17), the resting place of one of the greatest heroes of Arab history. The mausoleum was originally built in 1193. Admission is included in the price of the Umayyad Mosque ticket.

NORTH OF THE MOSQUE
Northwest of Saladin's mausoleum is the 13th-century **Madrassa az-Zahiriyya** (Map pp516-17; ☼ 9am-5pm), within which is buried Sultan Beybars – another Islamic warrior hero, this time of the Mamluk dynasty. It was Beybars who won several decisive victories over the Crusaders, driving them from the region.

Also near the Umayyad Mosque is the modern Iranian-built Shiite **Sayyida Ruqayya Mosque**, which is dedicated to the daughter of the martyr Hussein, son of Ali. It stands out for its decoration (covered in gold and shades of blue) and striking Persian styling.

SOUTH OF THE MOSQUE

The **Azem Palace** (Map pp516-17; adult/student S£150/10; 9am-3.30pm Wed-Mon winter, 9am-5.30pm Wed-Mon rest of year, closed Fri noon-2pm summer & 11am-1pm winter), south of the Umayyad Mosque, was built in 1749 by the governor of Damascus, As'ad Pasha al-Azem. It's fashioned in the typical Damascene style of striped stonework, which is achieved by alternating layers of black basalt and limestone. The rooms of the palace are magnificent, decorated with inlaid tile work and the most exquisite painted ceilings.

Swinging back to the west, the **Madrassa an-Nuri** is the mausoleum of Saladin's predecessor, Nureddin. Just south of the Souq al-Hamidiyya, the **Bimarstan Nureddin** was built in the 12th century as a mental hospital and was for centuries renowned in the Arab world as an enlightened centre of medical treatment. Around the cool, peaceful inside courtyard are displayed the hodgepodge exhibits of the **Arab Medical & Science Museum** (Map pp516-17; adult/student S£150/10; 8am-2pm Sat-Thu).

Heading east, about two-thirds of the way along Sharia Medhat Pasha – historically known as **Straight Street** (Via Recta) – are the remains of a **Roman arch**. This roughly marks the starting point of what's referred to as the Christian quarter. **St Paul's Chapel** marks the spot where, according to the biblical tale, the disciples lowered St Paul out of a window in a basket one night so that he could flee the Jews. The old cellar of the **Chapel of Ananias** (Sharia Hanania) is reputedly (but probably not) the house of Ananias, an early Christian disciple.

National Museum

Located off Sharia Shoukri al-Quwati, the **National Museum** (Map pp512-13; 221 9938; adult/student S£150/10; 9am-4pm Wed-Mon Oct-Jan, 9am-6pm Wed-Mon Apr-Sep, closed for Fri prayers) is well worth at least one visit. Behind the imposing façade (the relocated entrance of Qasr al-Heir al-Gharbi, a desert fortress near Palmyra) is an eclectic array of exhibits. Highlights are the hypogeum, which is a reconstruction of an underground burial chamber from the Valley of the Tombs at

Palmyra; the fresco-covered synagogue recovered from Dura Europos; and the Qasr al-Heir galleries. There's a pleasant coffee shop in the courtyard (tea S£50).

Immediately east of the National Museum is the black-and-white-striped **Takiyya as-Süleimaniyya** (Map pp512–13), built in 1554 to the design of the Ottoman Empire's most brilliant architect, Mirmar Sinan. Part of the complex is now the **Military Museum** (Map pp512-13; adult/student S£5/3; 8am-2pm Wed-Mon).

East of the Takiyya is a small madrassa that now serves as the **Artisanat** (Map pp512–13), an excellent handicrafts market.

ACTIVITIES

There are a few *hammams* (bathhouses) in the Old City, all of which offer a full service of massage, bath, exfoliation and sauna with towel, soap and tea.

Hammam Bakri (Map pp516-17; 542 6606; Sharia Qanayet al-Hattab; bath only S£100, full bath S£230; women 10am-4pm Sat-Thu, men 4pm-midnight Sat-Thu) A local bath in the Christian quarter, near Bab Touma.

Hammam Nureddin (Map pp516-17; 222 9513; Souq al-Bzouriyya; bath only S£150, full bath S£350; 9am-midnight Sat-Thu) The oldest *hammam* in the city, located in the covered street that runs between the Umayyad Mosque and Sharia Medhat Pasha (Straight St). Strictly men only.

TOURS

The Al-Rabie and Al-Haramain Hotels organise popular day trips by minibus and private car. Prices depend on numbers, but as a rule are around S£500 to go to Bosra, Suweida and the Sayyida Zeinab Mosque; S£400 to visit Maalula, Seidnayya and Jebel Qassioun; and S£600 to visit Maalula and Mar Musa. Though considerably more expensive than doing the trip by public transport, this is a convenient option and worth considering.

SLEEPING
Budget

Sharia Bahsa, in the Saroujah district, is Damascus' travellers' ghetto. Here you'll find two perennial favourites, Al-Haramain and Al-Rabie, and newcomer Ghazal House. These are usually full, making booking essential, and have prices that stay the same year-round.

Al-Rabie Hotel (Map pp512-13; 231 8374; fax 231 1875; Sharia Bahsa; roof mattress S£150, dm S£250, d with

DAMASCUS – OLD CITY

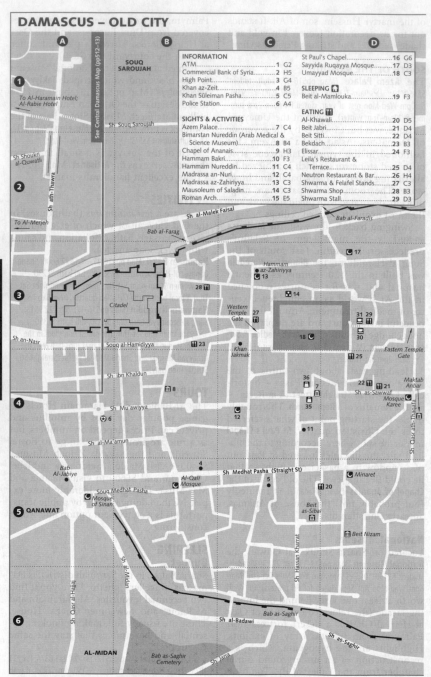

SOUQ SAROUJAH

INFORMATION
ATM	1 G2
Commercial Bank of Syria	2 H5
High Point	3 G4
Khan az-Zeit	4 B5
Khan Süleiman Pasha	5 C5
Police Station	6 A4

SIGHTS & ACTIVITIES
Azem Palace	7 C4
Bimarstan Nureddin (Arab Medical & Science Museum)	8 B4
Chapel of Ananais	9 H3
Hammam Bakri	10 F3
Hammam Nureddin	11 C4
Madrassa an-Nuri	12 C4
Madrassa az-Zahiriyya	13 C3
Mausoleum of Saladin	14 C3
Roman Arch	15 E5

St Paul's Chapel	16 G6
Sayyida Ruqayya Mosque	17 D3
Umayyad Mosque	18 C3

SLEEPING
Beit al-Mamlouka	19 F3

EATING
Al-Khawali	20 D5
Beit Jabri	21 D4
Beit Sitti	22 D4
Bekdach	23 B3
Elissar	24 F3
Leila's Restaurant & Terrace	25 D4
Neutron Restaurant & Bar	26 H4
Shwarma & Felafel Stands	27 C3
Shwarma Shop	28 B3
Shwarma Stall	29 D3

SYRIA

To Al-Haramain Hotel; Al-Rabie Hotel

Sh Souq Saroujah

Sh Shoukri al-Quwatli

Sh ath-Thawra

See Central Damascus Map (pp512–13)

To Al-Merjeh

Sh al-Malek Faisal

Bab al-Farag

Bab al-Faradis

Hammam az-Zahiriyya

Citadel

Western Temple Gate

Souq al-Hamidiyya

Sh an-Nasr

Khan Jakmak

Eastern Temple Gate

Sh ibn Khaldun

Maktab Anbar

Sh as-Sawwaf

Mosque Karee

Sh Mu'awiyya

Sh al-Ma'amun

Sh Qasr ath-Thiqla

Bab Al-Jabiye

Sh Medhat Pasha (Straight St)

Al-Qali Mosque

Souq Medhat Pasha

Mosque of Sinan

Minaret

Beit as-Sibai

QANAWAT

Beit Nizam

Sh Hassan Kharrat

Sh Qasr al-Hajar

Sh al-Midan

Bab as-Saghir

Sh al-Badawi

Sh as-Saghir

AL-MIDAN

Bab as-Saghir Cemetery

Sh Jarra

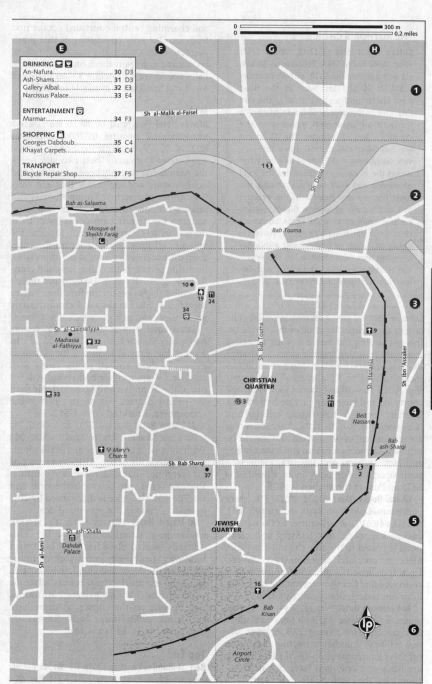

SYRIA

DRINKING 🖥 🍷
An-Nafura.................................. 30 D3
Ash-Shams................................ 31 D3
Gallery Albal.............................32 E3
Narcissus Palace........................33 E4

ENTERTAINMENT 🎭
Marmar......................................34 F3

SHOPPING 🛍
Georges Dabdoub.......................35 C4
Khayat Carpets..........................36 C4

TRANSPORT
Bicycle Repair Shop....................37 F5

SYRIA

THE AUTHOR'S CHOICE

Sultan Hotel (Map pp512-13; ☎ 222 5768; sultan.hotel@mail.sy; Sharia Mousalam al-Baroudi; s/d with bathroom US$22/30, without bathroom US$17/22; ☒ ☐) Just west of the Hijaz train station and a short walk to the Old City, this is the accommodation of choice for most archaeological missions to the country – and no wonder. The 31 rooms are basic but clean; most have tiny private bathrooms and 22 have air-con. What makes the place so exceptional is the level of service: the staff here are among the most friendly and helpful in the country and will happily reconfirm flights; organise bus, train or onward hotel bookings; or arrange car rentals or tours. There's a library of novels to borrow and a lounge/breakfast area with satellite TV, where you can sit and enjoy a tea and a chat with fellow guests. Highly recommended.

bathroom S£800, s/d without bathroom S£350/600) The best of the backpacker choices in Damascus, this enchanting old house has an attractive courtyard featuring trailing vines, an orange tree and a central fountain. Modern additions include a satellite TV and comfortable seating. A few downstairs rooms look onto the courtyard and have tiny private bathrooms. Upstairs rooms feature ornate ceilings and large windows. Rooms at the downstairs rear are reminiscent of prison cells and should be avoided. All rooms are clean and have heating and fans. Showers are downstairs; toilets – some squat – are on both floors. Breakfast is S£75 and use of the kitchen is S£25.

Ghazal House (Map pp512-13; ☎ 231 3736; ghazal _hotel@hotmail.com; Sharia Bahsa; roof mattress US$3, dm US$5, s/d US$7/12) A newcomer to Damascus' backpacker scene, this friendly and clean hotel is poised to become the most popular place in town and is getting rave reviews from travellers. It's in an old house with a courtyard and has showers out the back (24-hour hot water). Breakfast costs US$1.50.

Al-Haramain Hotel (Map pp512-13; ☎ 231 9489; alharamain_hotel@yahoo.com; Sharia Bahsa; roof mattress S£150, dm S£250, d with bathroom S£900, s/d without bathroom S£350/600) Another attractive old house off this picturesque shop-filled alley. Rooms are basic and only two have private bathrooms, but the comfortable beds, clean linen

and charming central courtyard get the nod from us. Our only reservation is that management crams too many guests into dorm rooms and even puts them on mattresses in hallways. There's a satellite TV in the small foyer and breakfast is available for S£85.

Midrange

Afamia Hotel (Map pp512-13; ☎ 222 8963; afamia@ hotel.sy.com; s/d renovated US$27/30, unrenovated US$22/25; ☒) Vying with the Sultan for the accolade of Damascus' best two-star hotel, the Afamia has recently been renovated and offers rooms and amenities that are worthy of four-star status. Plump doonas and pillows on comfortable beds are standout features; the private bathrooms (with hairdryers) are so clean they gleam. Satellite TV and air-con provide the icing on the cake. Even the unrenovated rooms are impressive, featuring private bathrooms, fans and comfortable beds. All rooms are light and there's a comfortable salon on the first floor where breakfast (US$2) is served. Extraordinarily good value, and in a great location to boot.

Salam Hotel (Map pp512-13; ☎ 221 6674; salam hotel@mail.sy; Sharia ar-Rais; s/d US$20/25; ☒ ☐) In a quiet but central location, the Salam is extremely clean and all rooms come with satellite TV and private bathroom. Ask for one at the front. It's more comfortable than the nearby Sultan, but doesn't match the atmosphere. Breakfast costs US$2.

Al-Diwan Hotel (Map pp512-13; ☎ 231 9327; 2nd fl, Sharia Souq Saroujah; s/d incl breakfast US$24/30; ☒) With its apricot colour scheme, small rooms and slightly frilly décor, Al-Diwan won't be for everyone. That said, rooms are comfortable and come with private bathrooms and satellite TV. The price is discounted by 20% in winter, making it a very good deal.

Al-Majed Hotel (Map pp512-13; ☎ 232 3300; www.almajed-group.com; s/d US$40; ☒ ☐) This centrally located place has been built by a local who spent many years working in the Gulf, and the décor and clientele reflect this fact. The extremely clean rooms all come with satellite TV and private bathrooms. Ask for one on the corner, as these have two windows and large beds. Rooms are discounted to US$30 in winter.

Top End

Beit al-Mamlouka (Map pp516-17; ☎ 543 0445/6; www.almamlouka.com; s/d/ste US$115/210/260; ☒)

This courtyard house, which dates from 1650, has been converted into a sumptuous boutique hotel. Staying in the Süleyman the Magnificent room with its painted ceiling and marble fountain is a once-in-a-lifetime experience, made even better by the hotel's high level of service and great position within the walls of the Old City. There are only eight rooms, all of which are individually and beautifully decorated.

Omayad Hotel (Map pp512-13; ☎ 221 7700; www.omayad-hotel.com; 1 Sharia Brazil; s/d US$85/95; ✗ ✗ ▣) This Art-Deco hulk down the road from the Cham Palace Hotel offers better rooms and infinitely better value for money than its neighbour. The décor has a few discordant notes, but rooms are large and extremely comfortable. The hotel is home to the luxurious Whispers Restaurant Lounge (mains S£300, open from 11am to 2am), and also has a roof terrace where you can enjoy drinks, nargilehs and spectacular views to Jebel Qassioun. Breakfast costs US$8. Book ahead.

EATING
When it comes to Damascene dining options, you'll have no trouble at all finding a place with the food, atmosphere and budget

to suit you. For a big night out try one of the historic courtyard restaurants in the Old City; if you want alcohol with your meal you'll need to venture into the Christian quarter rather than the area around the Umayyad Mosque. In Central Damascus, the best restaurants are found in the area around Saahat Yousef al-Azmeh.

The places reviewed here don't accept credit cards or serve alcohol. Exceptions are noted.

Central Damascus
The side streets off Martyrs' Sq are crowded with cheap eateries, which mostly offer shwarma and felafel, while some of the pastry shops also do good savouries. One of the city's most popular snack stands is nearby, on the corner of Saahat Yousef al-Azmeh and Sharia Fardous. It's a great place to grab a cheap shwarma or fresh juice.

Pizza Roma (Map pp512-13; ☎ 331 6434; 3 Sharia Odai bin ar-Roqaa; pizza around S£100; ✗) If you're keen on American-style pizzas, this is the most popular place in town. You'll find it west of the Cham Palace Hotel.

Al-Shamiat (Al-Shameatt; Map pp512-13; ☎ 222 7270; mezze S£25-55, fatta S£45-85, burgers S£130; ✗) This narrow neighbourhood eatery serves up excellent food for extremely reasonable prices. Try the absolutely delicious *shish tawooq* (marinated chicken grilled on skewers; S£150). Lone diners are made to feel very welcome.

Siwar al-Sham (Map pp512-13; ☎ 331 9568; Sharia Mousa Ben Nasir; mezze S£20-85, mains S£150; ✗) This family restaurant behind the Meridien Hotel is cheap and friendly. We recommend the delicious lentil soup (S£30), but feel obliged to make a derogatory comment about the totally appalling muzak (think 'Endless Love' and you'll be sufficiently warned).

Abou Kamal (Map pp512-13; ☎ 221 1159; 1st fl, Saahat Yousef al-Azmeh; mezze S£40-65, salads S£40-175; ✗) Damascene families, businessmen and ladies who lunch have been ordering from Abou Kamal's extensive and delicious menu for over 60 years. Don't let the blue velvet chairs and tuxedoed waiters frighten you – it's neither as expensive nor as stuffy as it looks.

Al-Kamal (Map pp512-13; ☎ 232 3572; Sharia 29 Mai; mezze S£40-100, mains around S£200; ◷ 11am-midnight; ✗) Next to the main tourist office and always packed at lunchtime, Al-Kamal has a Parisian-style décor and a menu that features many home-style dishes as well as truly excellent *fatta* (an oven-baked dish of chickpeas, minced meat or chicken, and bread soaked in tahini; S£85 to S£115). There's a changing daily menu – try the Saudi *kabsa* (spiced rice with chicken or lamb) at S£130.

Old City

In the small alley east of the Umayyad Mosque, just past the two coffeehouses, are a couple of very good shwarma places and a stall that does a great felafel. There's another collection of felafel and shwarma hole-in-the-wall eateries in the covered market lane that runs north off Souq al-Hamidiyya, just before you reach the mosque.

Beit Jabri (Jabri House; Map pp516-17; ☎ 541 6254; 14 Sharia as-Sawwaf; mezze S£20-125, fatta S£65-125) This informal and phenomenally popular café is set in the partially restored courtyard of a particularly beautiful Damascene house. The menu runs from breakfasts and omelettes to Oriental mezze and mains – the quality of the food is OK, but it doesn't live up to the magnificence of the surrounds. Service can be rude.

Beit Sitti (Map pp516-17; ☎ 245 9800) Next to Beit Jabri, this relative newcomer has a similar menu and prices, but its setting isn't quite as attractive. Many locals prefer it for its friendly waiters and occasional live music. To find it, follow the 'Arabic Restaurant' sign and go through the low doorway marked '4'.

Leila's Restaurant & Terrace (Map pp516-17; ☎ 9456;) In the shadow of the Umayyad Mosque, this stylish place gets the blend of Oriental style and European chic just right. Located in a beautifully restored courtyard house with a rooftop terrace and glass ceiling, it serves up some of the best food in the city. Vegetarians will love the lentil *kibbeh* (cracked-wheat croquettes; S£100) and the goat labneh (thick yogurt flavoured with garlic and sometimes with mint; S£75); carnivores will be just as pleased with the wide range of succulent grills and roasts (S£175 to S£300).

Al-Khawali (Map pp516-17; ☎ 9793; Sharia Hamrawi; mezze S£15-100, kebabs S£140;) Located in a building dating from 1368, this upmarket restaurant is patronised by the likes of President Assad. Needless to say, its food and

service are as impressive as the absolutely gorgeous surrounds. Try the Al-Khawali aubergine (S£40) and see what great mezze is all about, particularly when served with bread still warm from the house oven.

Neutron Restaurant & Bar (Map pp516-17; ☎ 544 5451; Ja'afar Ave; mezze S£45-125, fillet steaks S£275-300;) One of a growing number of licensed restaurants in the Christian quarter of the Old City, Neutron is noteworthy for its French-influenced menu, full bar and live music (every night).

Elissar (Map pp516-17; ☎ 542 4300; Sharia ad-Dawamneh, Bab Touma; mezze S£30-150, mains S£200-375;) This elegant restaurant is named after a Phoenician princess, and its décor and menu are impressive enough to claim such a pedigree. Situated in an enormous old house with tables filling the courtyard and two upper levels of terraces, it serves up refined Syrian dishes and a few European-influenced mains, washed down by selections from a good wine and arak list. Make sure you're cashed up, as it's pricey.

DRINKING

The finest places to relax in Damascus are the two historic coffeehouses, An-Nafura and Ash-Shams, nestled in the shadow of the Umayyad Mosque's eastern wall. Lingering over a tea here should be on every visitor's itinerary.

For something a bit different, **Gallery Albal** (Map pp516-17; ☎ 544 5794; Sharia Shaweesh), about a five-minute walk from the coffeehouses east along Sharia al-Qaimariyya, is a loud Western-style café with an art gallery above. It's where the city's bohemian types congregate.

There are a number of coffeehouses in atmospheric Old City buildings, and most of these also serve food. Our favourite is **Narcissus Palace** (Map pp516-17; ☎ 541 6785; mezze S£25-100), which is packed to its very attractive rafters with young people catching up over a nargileh (S£95) and tea (S£25). Music clips blare from the satellite TV, backgammon pieces clink, the fountain gently plays and the extremely friendly staff make sure everyone is happy. Great stuff.

The Star-Crossed Lovers Café, near the backpacker hotels in Souq Saroujah, is a great place to discuss regional politics and local popular culture over a tea. It also serves mega-cheap breakfasts.

ENTERTAINMENT

The most popular nightclub in town is **Marmar** (Map pp516-17; ☎ 544 6425; Sharia ad-Dawanneh; admission incl 3 drinks S£600; 🗶), a bar-restaurant at Bab Touma that morphs into a club on Thursday and Friday nights and occasionally hosts live gigs on Sundays.

The **Cham Cinema Theatre** (Map pp516-17; ☎ 223 3300; Sharia Maysaloun; tickets S£150; 🗶) regularly screens mainstream Hollywood fare in its two wide-screen auditoriums. The only way to find out what's showing is to drop by; screenings are usually at 3pm, 6pm and 9pm.

GETTING THERE & AWAY

Air

Several Syrianair offices are scattered about the city centre. A very convenient **Syrianair office** (Map pp512-13; ☎ 245 0097/8) is on Saahat Hijaz, just opposite the train station.

Most of the other airline offices are grouped across from the Cham Palace Hotel on Sharia Maysaloun, or one block south on Sharia Fardous.

Bus & Microbus

There are two main bus stations in Damascus: Harasta garage (*karajat* Harasta), offering Pullman bus services to the north and international services to Turkey; and Baramke garage (*karajat* Baramki), which has services to the south, including to Jordan, Lebanon and the Gulf. In addition there are several other minibus and microbus stations serving regional destinations.

HARASTA

Harasta garage is about 6km northeast of the city centre. All the big private-bus companies have their offices here.

Al-Kadmous runs a 24-hour service to Aleppo every hour on the hour (S£160, five hours); an hourly service to Deir ez-Zur (S£200, six hours) from 6am to 2.30am; 14 buses to Homs (S£70, two hours) between 6.15am to 8.15pm; four buses a day to Hama (S£90, 2½ hours) at 6.15am, 7am, 11.15am and 2.45pm; and hourly buses to Tartus (S£110, 3½ hours) from 5.30am to 11pm. It's the only company running services from Harasta to Palmyra (S£150, four hours); these leave hourly from 6am to 2.30am.

Al-Ahliah has services to Aleppo (S£150) every hour between 6am and 8pm. It also

has services to Lattakia (S£150, 4½ hours) at 7.45am, 10.15am, 2pm, 4.15pm and 6pm.

If you're travelling to Turkey, Hatay has Pullman services to Antakya (S£300, eight hours) and İstanbul (S£1300, 36 hours), leaving at 10pm daily. JETT buses also travel to Antakya (S£500) and İstanbul (S£1600) at 10pm daily.

To get to Harasta you can take a microbus (S£5) from outside the fruit and vegetable market on Sharia al-Ittihad, just near Al-Haramain and Al-Rabie Hotels. A taxi will cost somewhere between S£40 to S£60. Some taxi drivers will maintain that the official fare between Harasta and the centre of town is S£200, set by the bus garage. This is rubbish – insist that they turn on the meter and make sure that it shows only S£3.50 at the start of your trip.

BARAMKE

Baramke garage is located about a 15- to 20-minute walk southwest of the Hijaz train station. The bus station occupies a square block, which is organised in four quarters. As you approach from the north, local microbus services are in front to the left; buses to southern areas are behind. The front right quarter is for service taxis to Beirut and Amman; behind them is the Karnak lot.

From here Karnak runs buses to Beirut (S£175, 3½ hours) hourly from 7.30am to 12.30pm and then 2.30pm to 7.30pm), plus two buses a day to Amman (S£325, seven hours) at 7am and 3pm. These are the only buses from Syria to Jordan and they operate on a code-share basis with JETT, Jordan's national bus line. You are much better off doing this trip on a JETT bus than a Karnak one, as they're far more comfortable.

If you're travelling to Lebanon and don't want to travel with Karnak, Dreams 2000 runs a service from Baramke to Beirut (S£200, 3½ hours) in Pullman buses. These leave every hour from 6.30am to 10pm. There is no bus service from Damascus to Baalbek.

Karnak has a daily service to Jeddah (S£1200, 24 hours) at 9.30am. There are two services per week on Saturday and Wednesday at 3pm to Kuwait (S£1500, 42 hours). Tickets should be bought in advance.

OTHER BUS STATIONS

Microbuses to Deraa (for the Jordanian border) leave from the Deraa garage in the south of the city. You are much better off getting a Pullman bus from Baramke.

Service Taxi

There is a service-taxi station at Baramke. Ageing but well-loved yellow American sedans offer a 24-hour service to Amman (S£500, five hours) and Beirut (S£500, three hours). There are also infrequent service taxis to Baalbek (S£200).

Train

All trains depart from the **Khaddam train station** (☎ 634 1166), about 5km southwest of the centre. There are four daily services to Aleppo (S£140/100 in 1st/2nd class, six hours).

The Hijaz Railway offers a twice-weekly slow and uncomfortable train service to Jordan (S£200/US$4, nine to 12 hours) on Monday and Thursday at 8am; passengers must change trains at Deraa on the Syrian–Jordanian border. For details of services from Syria to Tehran and İstanbul see p543.

The historic Hijaz station was being renovated at the time of research and there are plans to construct a new, purpose-built terminal behind it. This will be the terminus of a new Damascus–Beirut railway line.

GETTING AROUND
To/From the Airport

Damascus International Airport is 32km southeast of Damascus. In the arrivals hall there's an ATM next to the Commercial Bank of Syria exchange booth. This is enabled for Cirrus, Maestro, Visa and MasterCard. The booth exchanges cash, but not travellers cheques. There's a 24-hour tourist info office, supplying free city maps.

A Karnak airport bus service runs between the airport forecourt and the southwest corner of the Baramke garage (S£25, 30 minutes). Departures are every half hour between 6am and midnight. Look for the orange-and-white bus to the right as you exit the arrivals hall.

A taxi into the city centre organised at one of the desks in the arrivals hall costs between S£400 to S£600, depending on the type of car on offer. It pays to shop around. If you're taking a taxi from the centre out to the airport, expect to pay around S£500.

Car rental companies like Hertz and Europcar have booths open from 8am to 10pm.

Bus & Taxi

Damascus is well served with a local bus and microbus network, but as the centre is so compact you'll rarely have to use it. A microbus ride within the city costs S£5.

All the taxis are yellow and there are hundreds of them. A ride within the centre of town should never cost more than S£25.

BOSRA   بصره

☎ 015

The black-basalt town of Bosra, 137km from Damascus, is an easy day trip from the capital. Once the main city of the Roman province of Arabia, it's now little more than a backwater. But what a weird and wonderful backwater it is. The gigantic Roman theatre in its centre is incongruous but magnificent, and the atmospheric and substantial ruins of the Roman city contrast to the shantytown feel of the modern settlement. It's well worth a visit.

INFORMATION

Exchange booth (☉ 8am-2pm & 4-6pm Sat-Thu) Near the entrance to the citadel. You can change cash; the Cham Palace Hotel will usually change travellers cheques.

ReefNet Cyber Cafe (☎ 795 881; ☉ irregular) Next to the Al-Dahe office on the town's main street.

Restaurant 1001 Nights (☎ 795 331; www.obeida.9f .com; per hr S£50; ☉ 24hr) Offers Internet access.

Tourist office (☉ 9am-7pm) In the square near the citadel. Staff are friendly, but don't all speak English.

SIGHTS

The **citadel** (adult/student S£150/10; ☉ 9am-6pm Mar-Nov, 9am-4pm Dec-Feb) is a unique construction – it began life as a massive Roman theatre and later had its fortifications grafted on. The theatre was built early in the 2nd century AD, when Bosra was the capital of the Roman province of Arabia. The first walls were built during the Umayyad and Abbasid periods, with further additions being made in the 11th century by the Fatimids.

The big surprise on entering the citadel is the magnificent 15,000-seat **theatre** – a rarity among Roman theatres in that it is completely freestanding rather than built into the side of a hill. It's a wonderful experience to be lost in the dark, oppressive fortress halls and then to pass through a sunlit

SYRIA

opening to find yourself suddenly looking down on a vast, steeply terraced hillside of stone seating. Bring a torch with you, as many of the passages under the theatre are dark.

Other sites located in the Old Town include various monumental gates, colonnades, Roman baths, vast cisterns and the **Mosque of Omar**, which dates to the 12th century.

SLEEPING & EATING

Restaurant 1001 Nights (☎ 795 331; www.obeida.9f .com; ☷ 24hr) Run by local entrepreneur Obeida Mokdad, this laid-back place is the travellers' hub in Bosra. You can grab a meal (breakfast S£100, set lunch/dinner S£250) or relax over a tea (S£25) or local beer (S£50). There's a 25% student discount. Obeida will also let you bunk down overnight in a room off the restaurant; there's a shower and toilet but you'll need your own sleeping bag. Note that single women may not feel comfortable doing this.

Bosra Cham Palace (☎ 790 881; chambsra@net .sy; s/d US$122/145; ☷ ☷) The Cham Palace is currently the only hostelry in town, making the hefty prices no surprise. In actual fact, it offers reasonable value for money, with well-set-up rooms, nice gardens, a large swimming pool and a licensed coffee shop (sandwiches S£150 to S£170, tea S£65, beer S£130). Its Citadelle Restaurant (three-course meal S£660) is popular with tour groups.

GETTING THERE & AWAY

Two companies run Pullman services between Bosra and Damascus (S£50, 1¾ hours): Al-Dahe and As-Soukor (often signed as Al-Skour). These have offices in the Baramke garage. Both leave from here every two hours from 8am to 10pm, and Al-Dahe has one extra service at 3pm.

From Bosra, both companies have services to Damascus every two hours from 6am to 8pm, leaving from their offices (As-Soukor's is west of the citadel, Al-Dahe's is on the main street).

Minibuses run between Bosra and Deraa (S£15) between 4.30am and 4pm. These leave when full from the front of the tourist information office. From Deraa, five Pullman bus companies run services to Damascus (S£50) from 5am to midnight.

LATTAKIA   أللاذقية

☎ 041 / pop 990,000
Laid-back Lattakia has little in common with the rest of Syria. A busy port since Roman times, it has a Mediterranean feel, an outward-looking inclination and true *joie de vivre*. Its pavement cafés are inevitably packed with locals sipping espresso, smoking nargilehs, listening to imported music and telling slightly risqué jokes. In Lattakia, young women don skintight jeans and apply their lipstick lavishly, eschewing the headscarf; young men dress in homeboy uniform, albeit with a Syrian slant. The place offers a refreshing change, particularly if you have travelled from conservative Aleppo.

INFORMATION
Internet Access
Virus Internet Cafe (☎ 465 540; Sharia Baghdad; per hr S£60; ☷ 24hr) Central location, plenty of terminals and free tea or coffee. Connections can be unreliable.
Y Net Cafe (☎ 471 604; per hr S£50; ☷ 9am-3am) A real café, with very fast connections.

Money
There are two Syriabank ATMs on Sharia Baghdad that will give cash advances on Visa and MasterCard, but neither is Cirrus and Maestro enabled. The **Commercial Bank of Syria** (Sharia Baghdad) will change travellers cheques for a flat fee of S£25.

Post
Main post office (☷ 8am-2pm Sat-Thu) Some distance out of the centre, just north of the train station, in a little alley off Sharia Suria.

Telephone
Telephone office (Sharia Seif al-Dawla; ☷ 8am-11pm) To make an international call, buy a phonecard then wait your turn for a free phone.

Tourist Information
Tourist office (☎ 416 926; Sharia 14 Ramadan; ☷ 8am-8pm Sat-Thu) Opposite the Riviera Hotel. English-speaking staff supply maps and helpful advice.

Visa Extensions
Immigration office (near Saahat Jumhuriyya; ☷ 8am-2pm Sat-Thu) Beyond the tourist office, on the far side of a large traffic roundabout.

SYRIA

www.lonelyplanet.com

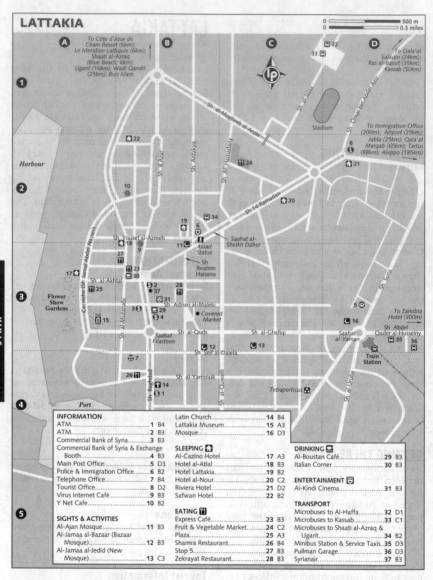

LATTAKIA

INFORMATION	
ATM..1 B4	
ATM..2 B3	
Commercial Bank of Syria.........3 B3	
Commercial Bank of Syria & Exchange	
Booth......................................4 B3	
Main Post Office.......................5 D3	
Police & Immigration Office......6 B2	
Telephone Office......................7 B4	
Tourist Office...........................8 D2	
Virus Internet Café...................9 B3	
Y Net Cafe.............................10 B2	
SIGHTS & ACTIVITIES	
Al-Ajan Mosque......................11 B3	
Al-Jamaa al-Bazaar (Bazaar	
Mosque).................................12 B3	
Al-Jamaa al-Jedid (New	
Mosque).................................13 C3	

Latin Church...........................14 B4	
Lattakia Museum.....................15 A3	
Mosque..................................16 D3	
SLEEPING	
Al-Cazino Hotel.......................17 A3	
Hotel al-Atlal..........................18 B3	
Hotel Lattakia.........................19 B2	
Hotel al-Nour.........................20 C2	
Riviera Hotel...........................21 D2	
Safwan Hotel..........................22 B2	
EATING	
Express Café...........................23 B3	
Fruit & Vegetable Market.........24 C2	
Plaza.....................................25 A3	
Shamra Restaurant..................26 B4	
Stop 5...................................27 B3	
Zekrayat Restaurant................28 B3	

DRINKING	
Al-Boustan Café......................29 B3	
Italian Corner.........................30 B3	
ENTERTAINMENT	
Al-Kindi Cinema......................31 B3	
TRANSPORT	
Microbuses to Al-Haffa............32 D1	
Microbuses to Kassab..............33 C1	
Microbuses to Shaati al-Azraq &	
Ugarit...................................34 B2	
Minibus Station & Service Taxis..35 D3	
Pullman Garage......................36 D3	
Syrianair................................37 B3	

SIGHTS & ACTIVITIES

The small **Lattakia Museum** (Sharia Jamal Abdel Nasser; adult/student S£150/10; 9am-6pm Wed-Mon Apr-Sep, 8am-4pm Wed-Mon Oct-Mar) is housed in a charming old khan near the waterfront. Though its archaeological garden is attractive, the museum's displays are rather unimpressive.

There is a good public **beach** at Shaati al-Azraq (Blue Beach), 6km north of town. Minibuses (S£5) leave from a back alley down the side of the big white school on Saahat al-Sheikh Daher. A taxi will cost S£100 one way.

Women will feel comfortable swimming at Wadi Qandil, 25km north of town, where the beach has black sand and clean water. To get here catch a microbus (S£10) from the station near the stadium. Microbuses (S£10) also leave from here going to Burj Islam, where there is clean water and a stone beach. Ask to get off at Sakhra (the Rock). Women won't feel quite as comfortable here.

SLEEPING

Hotel Lattakia (☎ 479 527; Sharia Yousef al-Azmeh; s/d with bathroom 300/350, without bathroom S£150/250; ❄) The cheapest and probably the best of the backpacker options in town, it's much better than the filthy entrance stairs would indicate. Tucked away down a narrow alley north of the Al-Ajan mosque, it has basic rooms and a kitchen that guests can use. Ten rooms on the 1st floor share two bathrooms with squat toilets; the 2nd-floor rooms have private bathrooms, comfortable beds and satellite TV. Three also have air-con.

Hotel Al-Atlal (☎ 476 121; Sharia Yousef al-Azmeh; r with/without air-con S£700/600; ❄) Popular with visiting Lebanese families, this quiet establishment has immaculate rooms with snug beds, freshly laundered sheets and private bathrooms (squat toilets). There's a pleasant common area with free tea and satellite TV. Rates are per room, and preference is given to families. Breakfast costs an extra S£50.

Safwan Hotel (☎ 093 376 900; safwanhotel@go .com; Sharia Mousa bin Nosier; mattress on roof S£100, dm S£200, s/d with bathroom S£300/500, without bathroom S£250/400) Run by Tintin-fan Mohamad and his family, the Safwan is run-down, but most rooms have satellite TV and private bathrooms, and all have clean linen (albeit on hard beds). It pays to ask to see a few before choosing. Breakfast costs S£100.

Hotel al-Nour (☎ 243 980; fax 245 340; Sharia 14 Ramadan; s/d US$21/26; ❄) A two-star place overlooking the motorway, Hotel al-Nour has beds resembling concrete slabs, private bathrooms in all rooms, and a fusty but comfortable lounge area and breakfast room. Ask for a room at the rear. Breakfast costs US$1. Rooms are 15% cheaper in winter.

Zanobia Hotel (☎ 425 703; fax 425 719; Autostrad Zera'a; s/d US$35/42; ❄) One of the better midrange choices in town, the Zanobia's major drawback is its location away from the centre. It's also a bit overpriced for what it offers: clean rooms with tiny private bathrooms and satellite TV. Breakfast costs S£125. There is a 20% discount in winter.

Al-Cazino Hotel (☎ 461 140/1; www.alcazino.com; Corniche; s/d US$40/55; ❄) In an imposing and well-located French Mandate–era building, this recently opened hotel has large and comfortable rooms with satellite TV and private bathroom. The hotel is home to the city's most popular reception venue, so it can be noisy. Winter rates are US$5 cheaper.

Riviera Hotel (☎ 211 806; riviera@net.sy; Sharia 14 Ramadan; s/d US$79/91; ❄ 🖵) The best hotel in town, the Riviera offers homely but slightly worn rooms that for this price should offer better fittings (sheets were nylon and there were no hairdryers). Service is pretty lacklustre, too. That said, private bathrooms are large and there is a restaurant and bar off the attractive downstairs lobby. Breakfast is included in the price. There's a 20% discount in winter.

EATING & DRINKING

Snack stalls are located around the Saahat al-Sheikh Daher area. For something a cut above, head for Sharia al-Mutanabi, known as the American quarter' because an American school used to be based here.

Shamra Restaurant (sandwiches S£50, pizzas S£90-130; ❄) Situated off Sharia Baghdad, this Western-style fast-food place is always packed with locals noshing on good-quality pan pizzas, salads, burgers and spring rolls. The surrounds are clean and pleasant. It's also a good place for breakfast.

Zekrayat Restaurant (☎ 460 858; ❄) The minute you walk into this bustling place you'll understand why it's the most popular restaurant in town. The attractive courtyard garden and stone-walled dining room of a historic house are jam-packed with locals puffing on nargilehs (S£75), indulging in ice-cream sundaes (S£65) or sipping fresh-fruit cocktails (S£60). But wait, there's more! It also serves up some of the best food in the country – the mouhammarah (walnut and pomegranate-syrup dip; S£25) has to be tasted to be believed and the muttabal (purée of aubergine mixed with tahini, yogurt and olive oil; S£25) is just as good. If it had served alcohol we would have moved in permanently. Go.

Express Cafe (☎ 456 200; 22 Sharia al-Mutanabi; burgers S£90-145, pasta S£110-135; ✖) An American diner in the Hard Rock Café style, this bright and noisy place offers burgers, steaks, pizza, and hot and cold sandwiches. It also does great milk shakes (S£45). There's a bar downstairs (Almaza beer S£60).

Stop 5 (☎ 477 919; 27 Sharia al-Mutanabi; mezze S£20-30, pizzas S£75-125, burger S£95; ✖) Resembles a New York bar, with shelves of spirits, posters advertising happy hours and wood-panelled walls. The food is good and management doesn't mind if you sit for a while with a drink (local beer S£40) and a snack.

Plaza (☎ 461 013; Corniche; mezze S£20-80, grills S£90-125; ✖) Families and groups of businessmen come here to graze on the wide choice of excellent mezze, washed down with arak (S£50 per glass) or local beer (S£50). You can sit in the glassed-in area at the front or the over-the-top dining hall in the rear.

There's a real coffee culture in Lattakia, and many places serve up espresso that could stand up and be counted in Italy. Try the sidewalk terraces at **Al-Boustan Café** (Sharia Baghdad; espresso S£30) or **Italian Corner** (Sharia al-Mutanabi; espresso S£35, cappuccino S£50).

ENTERTAINMENT
Al-Kindi Cinema screens Hollywood new releases and charges S£60 per ticket.

GETTING THERE & AWAY
Air
Basil al-Assad International Airport lies about 25km southeast of Lattakia. A taxi to the centre of town costs around S£250.

Syrianair flies to Damascus on Wednesday at 6pm, Saturday at 4.45pm and Sunday at 9am. A ticket costs S£560. There's also one flight per week to Cairo.

There's a local office of **Syrianair** (☎ 476 863/4; 8 Sharia Baghdad; ☾ 8am-8pm).

Bus
The Pullman garage is on Sharia Abdel Qader al-Husseiny about 200m east of the train station. Numerous private companies have their offices here.

Al-Kadmous has a 24-hour service to Damascus (S£150, four hours) leaving on the hour. Its regular minibus service to Tartus (S£30, one hour) runs between 6am and 9pm, stopping at Baniyas (S£15) en route. There are also four services daily to

Homs (S£80, two hours) at 10am, 12.30pm, 2.30pm and 11pm.

As-Salaam runs regular services to Aleppo (S£100, 3½ hours).

Al-Hassan runs a daily minibus service (S£500) to Antakya in Turkey, departing at 7.30am. If you call ☎ 352 021 it will collect you at your hotel.

Karnak buses also depart from this station, but its ticket office is just outside the station compound, on the left as you enter the access street. It runs one service per day to Damascus (S£125) at 7.15am, and one to Homs (S£75) at 6.30am. It also has a 6am service to Beirut (S£300) via Tripoli (S£200) in Lebanon.

Express Tours runs daily services to Beirut (S£300) via Tripoli (S£250). These leave at 11am and midnight.

Microbus
The main congregation of microbuses is 1.5km north of the town centre, near the sports stadium. From a huge lot, buses depart frequently for destinations such as Al-Haffa for Qala'at Saladin (opposite), and Kassab (S£25, 1½ hours) for the Turkish border.

Microbuses for Ugarit (Ras Shamra) go from a back alley down the side of the big white school on Saahat al-Sheikh Daher.

Microbuses to Baniyas (S£10, 45 minutes), Tartus (S£35, one hour), Homs (S£60, two hours) and Hama (S£60, 6.30am and then every three hours until evening) leave from the minibus station near the train station.

Taxi
Taxis charge S£25 for trips within town.

A seat in a new yellow service taxi to Lebanon costs S£300 to Tripoli and S£500 to Beirut. These leave from the minibus station near the train station. If you call ☎ 353 077 they will collect you from your hotel.

Train
The train station is about 1.5km east of the city centre on Saahat al-Yaman. There are four daily departures for Aleppo: two express services (S£135, three hours) at 7am and 6.30pm, and two slow services (S£70/50 in 1st/2nd class, four hours) at 7.50am and 3.20pm. If you're travelling to Aleppo we recommend you take a train rather than the bus, as they are extremely comfortable and the scenery is stunning.

AROUND LATTAKIA

UGARIT   رأس شمرا

The ruins at **Ugarit** (Ras Shamra; adult/student S£150/10; 9am-4pm Nov-May, 9am-6pm Jun-Oct) are a city that was once the most important on the Mediterranean coast. From about the 16th to the 13th century BC, it was a centre for trade with Egypt, Cyprus, Mesopotamia and the rest of Syria. The writing on tablets found here is widely accepted as the earliest known alphabet. The tablets are on display in the museums in Lattakia, Aleppo and Damascus, as well as the Louvre in Paris. Today, the masonry left behind shows you the layout of the streets and gives you some vague idea of where the most important buildings were.

Regular microbuses (S£5) make the trip from Lattakia to Ugarit. A taxi will charge between S£400 to S£500 to take you to the site, wait one hour and then bring you back to town.

QALA'AT SALADIN   قلعة صلاح الدين

Although Qala'at Saladin is less celebrated than Crac des Chevaliers, TE Lawrence was moved to write, 'It was I think the most sensational thing in castle building I have seen.' The sensational aspect is largely due to the site – the castle is perched on top of a heavily wooded ridge with precipitous sides dropping away to surrounding ravines. It's pretty amazing.

The **castle** (adult/student S£150/10; 9am-4pm Wed-Mon Nov-Mar, 9am-6pm Wed-Mon Apr-Oct) is located 24km east of Lattakia and is a very easy half-day trip.

Take a microbus from Lattakia to the small town of Al-Haffa (S£10, 30 minutes). These leave from the minibus station near the stadium. Taxis and local cars wait at the bus stop at Al-Haffa and will take you the further 6km to the castle. They charge anywhere between S£200 to S£500 to take you there, wait one hour and bring you back to the minibus. A taxi from Lattakia will charge S£500 to S£600 for the round trip.

QALA'AT MARQAB   قلعة مرقب

This black-basalt **castle** (adult/student S£150/10; 9am-4pm Wed-Mon Oct-Mar, 9am-6pm Wed-Mon Apr-Sep) was originally a Muslim stronghold, possibly founded in 1062. After falling into Crusader hands in the early 12th century, the fortifications were expanded. The main defensive building, the donjon, is on the southern side, as the gentler slopes made that aspect the castle's most vulnerable. After several attempts, Saladin gave up trying to take Marqab. It eventually fell to the Mamluks in 1285.

The walls and towers are the most impressive element of what is left today, and the interior of the citadel is rapidly being overrun with vegetation and rubbish. In truth, you're much better off visiting Qala'at Saladin and Crac des Chevaliers, particularly as ugly refineries mar the views to the sea here.

You'll find a restaurant and cheap tea stands near the castle's entrance.

To get there, take a microbus (S£5) from Baniyas on the coast towards Zaoube – it goes right past.

TARTUS   طرطوس

043 / pop 773,000
It's hard to see why Tartus is such a popular holiday destination among Syrians. In fact, it's difficult to describe it without using foul language (or at least a string of pejoratives). The beach is revolting – dirty sand, murky water and rubbish everywhere, including the ugly rusting hulks of cargo ships – and the Corniche (the seafront promenade) is basically a big construction site, with derelict unfinished buildings everywhere. In all, it gets the big thumbs down from us. You will do much better to stay in Lattakia.

INFORMATION

There's only one ATM in town, located on the ground floor of the office building opposite the post office. It will give advances on Visa and MasterCard, but isn't Maestro and Cirrus enabled.

Commercial Bank of Syria (Sharia Khaled ibn al-Walid; 8am-noon Sat-Thu) Doesn't change travellers cheques.

Friends Computer Center (Sharia Tarek ibn Ziad; per hr S£60; 24hr) Internet access. Walk south from the Shahin Tower Hotel, near the corner with Sharia Ahmad al-Azawi; look for the sign on the street, and the entrance is down the lane.

Immigration office (8am-2pm Sat-Thu) Just south of Sharia Jamal Abdel Nasser, one block east of the park.

SYRIA

Post office (☻ 8am-8pm Sat-Thu, to 2pm Fri) On the northeast corner of Sharia 6 Tichreen and Sharia Jamal Abdel Nasser.

Telephone office (☻ 24hr Sat-Thu, to 8pm Fri) Just north of the junction of Sharias Khaled ibn al-Walid and Ath-Thawra.

Tourist office (☎ 223 448; Sharia 6 Tichreen; ☻ 8am-2pm Sat-Thu) Inconveniently stuck out on the southeast edge of town on the main Homs highway.

SIGHTS

From the outside, the 12th-century **Cathedral of Our Lady of Tortosa** looks more like a fortress – that's no coincidence as its construction was conceived with defence in mind. It's a splendid piece of Crusader construction. Inside is the unimpressive **Tartus Museum** (adult/student S£150/10; ☻ 9am-6pm Wed-Mon Apr-Sep, 9am-4pm Wed-Mon Oct-Mar), which is only worth visiting to see the soaring arches and graceful vaulting of the cathedral's interior.

The island of **Arwad**, visible from the seafront off to the southwest, was also a Crusader stronghold. Small motor launches leave from the fishing harbour every 15 minutes from 6am and 7pm (pay on the return voyage; S£20). There are ship-building yards, dodgy fish restaurants and the remnants of sea walls on the island – plus an unfortunate amount of garbage.

SLEEPING

Hotel al-Menshieh (☎ 220 616, 220 097; Saahat Manchieh; beds per person S£200; ✗) This homely place opposite the cathedral offers the town's best budget accommodation. In a converted 2nd-floor apartment, it has 10 light-filled rooms, three of which have private bathrooms and balconies. It's quiet, comfortable and very clean. If the hotel is locked you need to go to the grocery on the corner, which is owned by the same people. If that's closed, ring the bell at the back of the brown letterbox at the front door. Breakfast costs S£125.

Daniel Hotel (☎ 220 581; daniel-hotel@shuf.com; Sharia al-Wahda; s/d S£300/600) After enjoying a free tea at check-in, you'll be shown your clean but faded room by the helpful staff. The beds here would fail any chiropractic assessment. All rooms have private bathrooms with lukewarm water.

Grand Hotel (☎ 355 600; fax 365 476; s/d US£25/30; ✗) This hulk of a building at the far end of the Corniche has an institutional feel but is very popular with holidaying Syrian families over summer. Though the place is run down, beds are comfortable and front rooms have clean private bathrooms, satellite TV and sea-facing balconies. Try negotiating the price down in the off season. Breakfast costs S£150.

EATING

The usual cheap restaurants and snack places (for felafel, shwarma, grilled chicken) are clustered around the clock tower and Sharia al-Wahda, and south down Ath-Thawra. There's also a group of cheap-eats places along Sharia Ahmed al-Azawi (south of Sharia al-Wahda), where the local kids hang out.

Tec Tac (☎ 323 600, 210 600; Sharia al-Corniche al-Bahr) One of a string of coffee shops along the seafront between the fishing harbour and old city, this place serves up pizzas (S£110 to S£135) and mezze (S£15 to S£35) to throngs of young locals, including plenty of girls sharing nargilehs (S£75). There's an extensive alcohol list.

Sea Whispers (☎ 216 800; mezze S£25, grills S£150; ✗) Cowering underneath a bizarrely shaped blue office building, this casual place is invariably packed with locals enjoying decent food accompanied by nargilehs (S£60) and cheap local beer (S£40).

Yamak (☎ 328 755; Sharia al-Amarna; fresh seafood by weight S£500-1000; ✗) Though it's light on character, this licensed restaurant on the 4th floor of the nondescript chamber of commerce building opposite the fishing harbour serves the best seafood in town. Enter from the side street.

Cave (☎ 221 016; Sharia al-Corniche al-Bahr; mains S£300-750; ✗) A vaulted 85-year-old hall burrowed into the sea wall of the old city, this place has got atmosphere in spades. The food's pretty good, too. The house speciality is seafood (pricey) but there are also grilled meat dishes. Lebanon's national beer, Almaza, costs S£100.

GETTING THERE & AWAY

Al-Kadmous has a bus station on Sharia Jamal Abdel Nasser opposite the park, just past the big roundabout. It has services to Damascus (S£110, four hours) every hour from 2am until 9pm. Buses to Aleppo (S£125, four hours) leave every hour from 4.30am until 11.30pm. Buses to Homs

(S£40, one hour) leave at 4am, 9am, noon, 1.15pm, 3pm, 6.30pm and 9.15pm. There are no services to Hama or Lebanon.

Microbuses depart for Baniyas (S£15, 30 minutes) and Homs (S£15, 1½ hours) from Sharia 6 Tichreen, east of the centre next to the usually deserted train station. Ramshackle minibuses make their way to Damascus (S£75, four hours) from here also. Minibuses to Lattakia (S£30, every 30 minutes from 6.30am to 9pm) leave from the Al-Kadmous bus stop.

A taxi ride anywhere within the centre of town costs S£25.

CRAC DES CHEVALIERS
قلعة الحصن

☎ 031

Author Paul Theroux described Crac des Chevaliers as the epitome of the dream castle of childhood fantasies. TE Lawrence simply called it 'the finest castle in the world'. Impervious to the onslaught of time, Crac des Chevaliers (in Arabic Qala'at al-Hosn) is one of Syria's must-see sights.

The first fortress known to have existed on this site was built by the emir of Homs in 1031, but it was the Crusader knights who, around the middle of the 12th century, largely built and expanded Crac into its existing form. Despite repeated attacks and sieges, the castle held firm. In fact, it was never truly breached; the Crusaders just gave it up. Numbers in the castle, which was built to hold a garrison of 2000, had fallen to around 200. Surrounded by the armies of Islam and with no hope of reprieve, Crac must have seemed more like a prison than a stronghold. Even though they had supplies to last for five years, after a month under siege the Crusaders agreed to depart the castle in return for safe conduct.

SIGHTS

The remarkably well preserved **castle** (adult/student S£150/10; ☻ 9am-6pm Apr-Oct, 9am-4pm Nov-Mar) comprises two distinct parts: the outside wall with its 13 towers and main entrance; and the inside wall and central construction, which are built on a rocky platform. A moat dug out of the rock separates the two walls.

A suggested route for exploration is to walk from the main entrance up the sloping ramp and out to the moat. Visit the baths, which you can get down to by a couple of dogleg staircases over in the corner on your left, then move on to the great hall, from where you can gain access to the three towers that punctuate the southern wall.

Continue around the wall and enter the inner fortress through the tower at the top of the access ramp into an open courtyard. The loggia, with its Gothic façade, on the western side of the yard, is the most impressive structure in the castle. Beyond the loggia is a vaulted hall and long room, with the castle's original latrines at the north end. Opposite the loggia is a chapel that was converted to a mosque after the Muslim conquest (the minbar, or pulpit, still remains). The staircase that obstructs the main door is a later addition and leads to the upper floors of the fortress, where there is a café and public toilets. From here you can make your way over to the round tower in the southwest corner, which is known as the Warden's Tower – on a clear day there are magnificent views from the roof.

SLEEPING & EATING

Crac is only an hour or so from Tartus, Homs or even Hama, so most people visit on a day trip. If you decide to stay the night, there are only two sleeping options around the castle. A decent meal is also pretty hard to come by.

Bibars Hotel (☎ /fax 741 201; akrambibars@mail.sy; Sharia Okbah Ben Nafee; s/d with air-con & view US$20/30, with fan US$10/15; ✗) This new hotel has 23 comfortable rooms, 15 featuring balconies and stunning unobstructed views of the castle. All have private bathrooms. The hotel is on the first hill west of the castle, about a 15-minute walk from the main entrance. Breakfast is included in the price. Our experience would indicate that it's best not to eat here.

Hotel La Table Ronde (☎ 740 280; fax 741 400; s/d S£250/500) About 200m south of the castle's main entrance, this run-down place has four grubby and vastly overpriced rooms with uncomfortable beds, squat toilets and basic showers. There is no heating or cooling. When we visited, the owners (who also run Bibars Hotel) were planning to renovate. You can also camp here (S£250). Breakfast costs S£75.

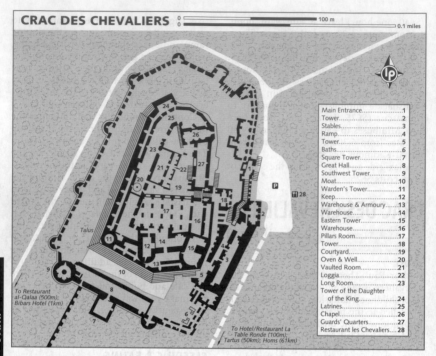

CRAC DES CHEVALIERS

Main Entrance	1
Tower	2
Stables	3
Ramp	4
Tower	5
Baths	6
Square Tower	7
Great Hall	8
Southwest Tower	9
Moat	10
Warden's Tower	11
Keep	12
Warehouse & Armoury	13
Warehouse	14
Eastern Tower	15
Warehouse	16
Pillars Room	17
Tower	18
Courtyard	19
Oven & Well	20
Vaulted Room	21
Loggia	22
Long Room	23
Tower of the Daughter of the King	24
Latrines	25
Chapel	26
Guards' Quarters	27
Restaurant les Chevaliers	28

To Restaurant al-Qalaa (500m); Bibars Hotel (1km)

To Hotel/Restaurant La Table Ronde (100m); Tartus (50km); Homs (61km)

Restaurant al-Qalaa (☎ 740 493, 093 562 236; set menu S£250-300; ◷ 8.30am-10pm Apr-Oct, 8.30am-6pm Nov-Mar) Boasting stunning views of the castle and surrounding valleys, Restaurant al-Qalaa is the best eatery in town. Look for the lone white two-storey building immediately west of the castle, on the next hilltop. The sign outside reads 'Alklaa Restaurant'. The all-you-can-eat menu comprises a wide range of mezze as well as grilled chicken or meat. In winter, ring ahead so that the friendly owner-chef can cater lunch or dinner for you. Alcohol is served (local beer S£100).

Hotel La Table Ronde has a large restaurant that serves up lunch and dinner buffets of mediocre-quality mezze and grills for S£200. **Restaurant Les Chevaliers** (☎ 740 411), directly opposite the castle, serves up carbon-copy food at the same prices. Both sell alcohol.

The licensed café in the castle serves mezze, grills and drinks. The quality isn't as impressive as the setting, but it's relatively inexpensive (mezze, grill and drink S£200). A tea costs S£25. There are fast-food stands in the village of Hosn, but none near the castle.

GETTING THERE & AWAY

Crac des Chevaliers lies approximately 10km north of the Homs–Tartus highway. The castle is on the crest of the hill, perched above the small village of Hosn, which is in turn perched above the main highway.

Microbuses (S£25) travel from Homs to Hosn daily, mostly in the morning. If you ask nicely these might drop you at the castle or at the Hotel La Table Ronde, where you can leave your luggage while you're touring the castle. Otherwise you'll have to walk up the hill from Hosn. Microbuses from Hosn to Homs leave between 7am to 3pm when full. For an extra S£25 per person (less if there are a few of you), these will pick you up from Hotel La Table Ronde. Ask its management to arrange this for you.

The only ways to get to or from Tartus are to catch a taxi (S£600 to S£700 one way), or to get on or off a Tartus–Homs minibus on the main highway (S£25). Ask to be let out at 'Qala'at al-Hosn'. The microbus serving the route between Hosn and Homs will drop you at the highway for S£25.

A taxi to Tripoli in Lebanon will cost S£1500 and take 1½ hours.

HOMS   حمص

☎ 031 / pop 1.5 million

There's little of interest in Homs, but it's one of those crossroads most travellers have to pass through at some stage. Roads head north to Hama, east to Palmyra and the Euphrates, south to Damascus and west to Tartus and the coast.

INFORMATION

The **tourist office** (🕑 8am-2pm, 3-7pm Sun-Thu, 9am-1pm Sat) is in front of the Khaled ibn al-Walid Mosque. Staff speak very little English.

There aren't too many Internet cafés in the centre of town. One of the most central is **Proxy.net Internet Café** (per hr S£70; 🕑 24hr), which has fast connections and helpful staff. To find it, walk south down Sharia Abdel Moniem Riad from the clock tower and turn right into Sharia Droubi opposite the gardens. Turn right at the T-intersection at Sharia Tarablus and right again at Sharia Hafez Ibrahim. Proxy.net is in the first street off to the left.

SIGHTS

The only building of great note in town is the **Khaled ibn al-Walid Mosque**; it's on the Hama road about 600m north of the town centre. It holds the tomb of the commander of the Muslim armies that brought Islam to Syria in AD 636. The small **Homs Museum** in Sharia Shoukri al-Quwatli opposite the gardens was closed for renovation at the time of research.

SLEEPING & EATING

An-Nasr al-Jedid Hotel (☎ 227 423; Sharia Shoukri al-Quwatli; s/d S£200/300) Entered from a side street just off Sharia al-Quwatli, this is about the best of the budget places in town – but that's not saying much. It's grubby and has very uncomfortable beds, but the sheets are relatively clean and one of the showers along the corridor can sometimes be cranked up to give out some hot water (S£50 per shower).

Hotel al-Mimas (☎ 211 066; haj885@hotmail.com; Sharia Malaab al-Baladi; s/d US$30/35; 🞨) This old-fashioned place is the only decent midrange hotel in town. Clean rooms come with big plump beds, satellite TV and basic private bathrooms. Breakfast costs an extra S£100. It's a kilometre or so southwest of the city centre.

Safir Hotel (☎ 412 400; www.safirhotels.com; Sharia Ragheb al-Jamali; s/d incl breakfast US$151/169; 🞨 🞨 🖳 🞨) A decent five-star hotel, the Safir offers recently renovated and very comfortable rooms, and excellent leisure facilities. It has a good Italian restaurant (pizza S£90 to S£150, pasta S£125 to S£175) and an eatery with an international menu and a pleasant garden outlook (mains S£300 to S£750, sandwiches S£150 to S£250, open 6am to midnight). Both are licensed and credit cards are accepted. It's near the Hotel al-Mimas.

If you are forced to eat in Homs, we suggest you eat at one of the restaurants at the Safir Hotel or grab something from one of the cheap-and-greasy restaurants in the group one block south of Sharia al-Quwatli, as there doesn't seem to be anything viable in between.

GETTING THERE & AWAY

There are two bus stations in Homs. The minibus garage is about 1.5km north of the city centre up Sharia Hama, a 15-minute walk from the Khaled ibn al-Walid Mosque on the left-hand side of the road. Microbuses also leave from here. The Pullman garage is a further 1.5km (20-minute) walk out of town on the same road (opposite side).

From the Pullman garage, Al-Ahliah runs luxury buses to Damascus (S£75, two hours) every hour from 4.15am to 11.15pm, and to Aleppo (S£85, 2½ hours) every hour from 7.15am to 10.15pm. To Tartus (S£43, one hour), there are buses at 6.45am, 10.15am, 3pm, 5.45pm and 7pm. Buses go to Hama (S£20, 30 minutes) every 30 minutes.

Al-Kadmous travels to Palmyra (S£100, two hours) at 7.30am, 2pm, 2.45pm, 3.30pm, 5.30pm, 9pm, midnight and 2am. It also runs 12 services to Damascus (S£75) per day. To Tartus (S£40) it runs services at 10.30am, 4.30pm and 7pm, and to Aleppo (S£85) there are services at 6am, 10.30am, 1pm, 4.30pm and 8.30pm.

Microbuses to Hama (S£20, 30 minutes) leave from the Hama garage, part of the minibus station. They run regularly from

6am to 10pm. Battered old minibuses and Karnak buses leave from another part of this station and travel to all parts of Syria.

See p530 for details of getting to Crac des Chevaliers.

A taxi from the Pullman garage to the centre of town costs S£50. To the Safir or Al-Mimas hotels you'll be up for S£75. Microbus service taxis run between the bus stations and the tourist office and charge S£4.

HAMA   حماه

☎ 033 / pop 1.5 million

The serenade of Hama's creaking ancient wooden *norias* (water wheels) is famous throughout the Middle East, and makes this attractive town one of the country's tourism hot spots. Best of all, it's perfectly located to be your base when visiting Crac des Chevaliers, Apamea and other sights in the area.

INFORMATION
Internet Access

Compu.Net (per hr S£50; ☯ 9am-2am Sat-Thu, noon-2am Fri) The cheapest place in town. Look for the 'CoffeeN@t' sign and go down the stairs.

Space Net (per hr S£60; ☯ 10am-midnight Sat-Thu, noon-midnight Fri) Free tea, helpful staff and the fastest connections in town.

Money

At the time of research there were no ATMs in Hama. Two branches of the **Commercial Bank of Syria** (Sharia ibn Rushd & Sharia Shoukri al-Quwatli) will change cash and travellers cheques (no commission).

Post & Telephone

The new post office is on the north side of the river. From the clock tower, walk north and cross the bridge. Turn right at the first major road and continue walking until you see the post office on the left-hand side of the road, near the Syrian Telecom Office. The phone office is off Sharia Shoukri al-Quwatli, at the side of the former post office building. You can find Easycomm card phones around town.

Tourist Information

Tourist office (☎ 511 033; Sharia Said al-A'as; ☯ 8am-8pm Sat-Thu) Located in a small building in the gardens just north of the river.

Visa Extensions

Passport office (Sharia Ziqar; ☯ 8am-2pm Sat-Thu) Situated on the north edge of town, near the new museum. It's in a modern building with 'Passport' written in English above the main entrance.

SIGHTS

Hama's main attraction is the **norias** (wooden water wheels up to 20m in diameter) that have graced the town for centuries, scooping water from the Orontes River and tipping it into mini aqueducts, where it travels to irrigation channels watering the surrounding fields.

Because both the water wheels and the blocks on which they are mounted are wooden, the friction when they turn produces a mournful groaning. The most impressive wheels are about 1km upstream from the centre of town, in the Al-Medina part of town. The four *norias* here, known as the Four Norias of Bechriyyat, are in two pairs on a weir straddling the river. About 1km west of the centre is the largest wheel of them all, known as Al-Mohammediyya.

A 4th-century AD mosaic depicting a *noria* is one of the artefacts displayed in the **Hama museum** (Sharia Ziqar; adult/student S£150/10; ☯ 9am-4pm Wed-Sun Nov-Mar, 9am-6pm Wed-Sun Apr-Oct), 1.5km north of the centre past the Omar ibn al-Khattab Mosque. Other exhibits cover the region in the Iron Age, Roman and Islamic periods. All are well presented and have informative labelling in English.

The small but lovely **Azem Palace Museum** (adult/student S£75/5; ☯ 8am-3pm Wed-Mon), in the old part of town, was once the residence of the governor, As'ad Pasha al-Azem (r 1700–42). The palace is reminiscent of the more grandiose building of the same name in Damascus, which is hardly surprising as the latter was built by al-Azem after he was transferred to the capital. The *haramlek* (women's quarters) behind the ticket office is particularly beautiful.

TOURS

Hama is conveniently situated for trips to surrounding sites including Crac des Chevaliers, Apamea and the Dead Cities. The Cairo and Riad Hotels offer a wide range of tours, but these are on the pricey side and, in the case of the Cairo at least, are in old cars reeking unpleasantly of petrol fumes. You may be better off making your way by

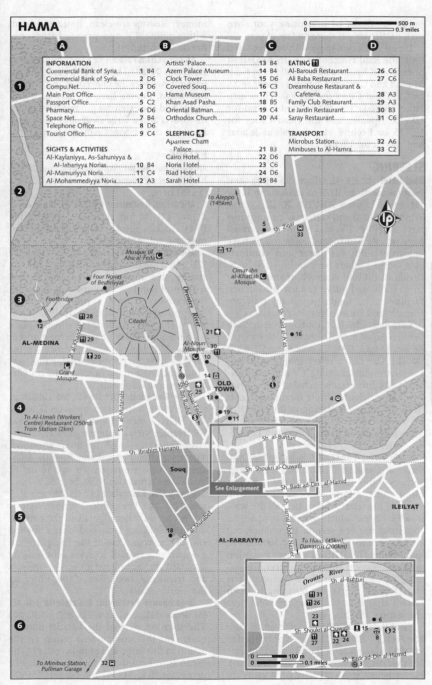

HAMA

INFORMATION
Commercial Bank of Syria........1 B4
Commercial Bank of Syria........2 D6
Compu.Net..............................3 D6
Main Post Office......................4 D4
Passport Office........................5 C2
Pharmacy................................6 D6
Space Net................................7 B4
Telephone Office......................8 D6
Tourist Office...........................9 C4

SIGHTS & ACTIVITIES
Al-Kaylaniyya, As-Sahuniyya &
  Al-Iabariyya Norias..............10 B4
Al-Mamuriyya Noria...............11 C4
Al-Mohammediyya Noria.........12 A3

Artists' Palace.........................13 B4
Azem Palace Museum..............14 B4
Clock Tower............................15 D6
Covered Souq.........................16 C3
Hama Museum........................17 C3
Khan Asad Pasha....................18 B5
Oriental Batman......................19 C4
Orthodox Church....................20 A4

SLEEPING
Apamee Cham
  Palace.................................21 B3
Cairo Hotel.............................22 D6
Noria I lotel............................23 C6
Riad Hotel..............................24 D6
Sarah Hotel............................25 B4

EATING
Al-Baroudi Restaurant.............26 C6
Ali Baba Restaurant................27 C6
Dreamhouse Restaurant &
  Cafeteria.............................28 A3
Family Club Restaurant...........29 A3
Le Jardin Restaurant...............30 B3
Saray Restaurant....................31 C6

TRANSPORT
Microbus Station....................32 A6
Minibuses to Al-Hamra............33 C2

SYRIA

public transport or organising your own taxi, particularly if there's a few of you.

If you do decide to go with an organised tour, the Riad Hotel offers tours to Qala'at Sheisar and Apamea for S£1100 per person, Musyaf and Crac des Chevaliers for S£1800, or the Dead Cities for S£1500. The Cairo Hotel will take you to Crac and Musyaf for US$25, Apamea and the Dead Cities for US$35 or Beehive Houses/Qala'at Ja'abar and Rasafa for US$60.

SLEEPING

Riad Hotel (☎ 239 512; riadhotel@SCS-net.org; Sharia Shoukri al-Quwatli; dm S£175, s/d with bathroom S£350/450, without bathroom S£250/350; ✖ ▢) Wow! Freshly painted and extremely clean rooms have satellite TV and good beds; most have private bathrooms. Some rooms have balconies onto the street and comfortable seating; others have queen-sized beds. Breakfast (S£100) is served in an attractive front room and guests can use the kitchen facilities. The English-speaking staff are friendly and knowledgeable. Fantastic.

Cairo Hotel (☎ 222 280; cairohot@scs-net.org; Sharia Shoukri al-Quwatli; mattress on the roof S£100, dm S£175, s/d with air-con S£450/600, without air-con S£350/450; ✖ ▢) The Cairo offers rooms with private bathrooms, satellite TV and comfortable beds. Breakfast is included in the price of all single/double/triple rooms and costs S£75 for travellers staying in dorm rooms or on the roof. Staff are as friendly and knowledgeable as those at the Riad. Equally fantastic.

Noria Hotel (☎ 512 414; bader@mail.sy; Sharia Shoukri al-Quwatli; s/d US$22/35; ✖) The older section of this 4th-floor hotel has spacious, clean and comfortable rooms, some with views of the water wheels. Beware the windowless ones, which are claustrophobic. Rooms in the new section are smaller, but equally comfortable. All have bathrooms and satellite TV. There's a smart reception area and a good restaurant. Service is excellent and credit cards are accepted. The owner of the Noria was planning to open Orient House, a small boutique hotel near the station, in 2006.

Sarah Hotel (☎ 515 941; basarah@scs-net.org; Sharia Abu al-Feda; s/d US$15/21) Though it only opened in 2000, this place in the city's old quarter isn't wearing too well (damp is a problem). Nevertheless, it offers pretty good value for

money. Rooms are clean, quiet and light, with satellite TV and private bathrooms. Breakfast costs US$2.

Apamee Cham Palace (☎ 525 335; fax 511 626; s/d US$122/145; ✖ ▢) The best hotel in town, offering views over the Old Town and some of the *norias*. Rooms have five-star accoutrements and the extensive grounds house tennis courts and a large swimming pool area. Breakfast costs US$6. Credit cards accepted.

EATING

Ali Baba Restaurant (Sharia Shoukri al-Quwatli) We highly recommend the excellent felafels (S£15) here.

Al-Baroudi Restaurant (☎ 224 213; Sharia Shoukri al-Quwatli) Basic but clean; we enjoyed the BBQ chicken meal (chicken, salad, hummus and soft drink S£150).

Al-Umali (Worker's) Centre (☎ 525 771/0; mezze S£50, grills S£100) In a decommissioned railway station, this unpretentious place is packed with local families, who order up big from the extensive menu. Try the *fatta haleb* (Aleppo-style *fatta* with meatballs and tomato) and you'll understand why the place is so popular. There's a garden for summer dining. No alcohol or credit cards. To get there, follow Sharia Ibrahim Hanano west until reaching a major junction; the restaurant is on the south side.

Saray Restaurant (☎ 510 830; Sharia al-Buhturi; mezze S£20-100, burgers S£100, sandwiches S£100-150; ✖) Hama's most stylish dining spot has spectacular views over the *norias* and the river from its large 1st-floor windows. There's a young crowd and friendly management who are happy for you to eat or just have a drink (tea S£50, beer S£100).

Family Club Restaurant (☎ 423 510; mezze S£25, grills S£150; ✖) The outdoor terrace here is perfect for summer nights and the cavernous indoor space is a good choice for the rest of the year. One of the few places in town serving alcohol, it serves good-quality standard dishes to large groups of families and friends. A beer costs S£100. Enter up the marble stairs.

Dreamhouse Restaurant & Cafeteria (☎ 411 687; Sharia al-Khandak; mezze S£25, grills S£150; ✖) The location west of the Citadel may be quiet, but the music videos pump up the action at this large and popular eatery. The menu is in English and includes meals like pizzas (S£90 to S£150) and burgers (S£90).

You can drink beer (S£50) or a cappuccino (S£41). Accepts credit cards.

On the river near the Apamee Cham Palace hotel, the enormous glass conservatory of Le Jardin Restaurant overlooks three of the town's *norias* and is a great, if noisy, spot to enjoy an evening beer (S£78) and nargileh (S£85).

GETTING THERE & AWAY

The Pullman garage is a 20-minute walk southwest of the town centre, just beyond the minibus station. The microbus station is on the same road, slightly closer to town.

Al-Ahliah has the most frequent departures from the Pullman garage, with services to Damascus (S£90, 2½ hours) departing regularly between 3.30am and 10pm; all stop en route in Homs (S£20, 30 minutes). Services to Aleppo (S£65, 2½ hours) leave at 6.30am, 7.15am, 8am and 8.30am, and then on the hour from 9am to 11pm. Services to Tartus (S£63, two hours) leave at 6am, 9.30am, 12.15pm, 5pm and 6.15pm. Services to Lattakia (S£100, three hours) depart at 6am, 9.30am, 12.15pm and 6.15pm.

Al-Kadmous has services to Damascus (S£90) at 7am, 9.45am, 12.30pm, 1.45pm, 4.30pm, 8.45pm and 1am. All go via Homs (S£20). There are extra services to Homs at 6.45am, 8.30am, 9.30am, 2pm, 6.15pm, 6.45pm and 11.15pm. Buses to Aleppo (S£60) leave at 8.15am, 9.30am, 11.15am, 1.30pm, 2pm, 3.30pm, 6.30pm, 7.30pm, 11.30pm and 1.30am. To Tartus (S£60), there are services at 5am, 5.45am, 7.30am, 9.30am, 11am, 2.30pm, 5.45pm, 6.45pm, 9.30pm and 12.30am. Services to Lattakia (S£60) leave at 6.30am, 9.30am, 12.30pm, 3.30pm and 7pm, as well as one air-con service per day (S£100) at 6.15am. The Al-Kadmous service from Hama to Deir ez-Zur (S£185) via Homs and Palmyra (S£85) leaves daily at 6.45am, 2pm, 6.15pm and 11.15pm.

Microbuses travel to Homs (S£18) every 10 minutes from 7am to 10pm, but you're much better off paying the little bit extra to travel with one of the luxury bus companies. Microbuses also travel to Suqeilibiyya (for Apamea) when full (S£20). There's one daily microbus to Tripoli (S£200) and Beirut (S£300).

Taxis from the bus stations to the centre of town charge S£25 during the day, S£30 at night. Minibuses from the town centre to the bus or train stations (S£3) leave from the clock tower and run between 7.30am and 10pm.

APAMEA   أفاميا

If it weren't for Palmyra's unsurpassable magnificence, the city of Apamea (a-*fam*-ia) would be considered a wonder and one of the highlights of Syria. As it is, Apamea is like a condensed version of the pink-sandstone desert city, but executed in grey granite and transposed to a high, wild grassy moor overlooking the Al-Ghab Plain. The city was founded in the 2nd century BC by Seleucus I, one of Alexander the Great's generals. It prospered until the Byzantine period but then was sacked by the Persians in AD 540 and again in 612. Barely a quarter of a century later, Syria was seized by the Muslims and Apamea fell into decline. It was all but flattened in a devastating earthquake in 1157. The **site** (adult/student S£150/10; 9am-4.30pm Oct-Mar & 9am-6.30pm Apr-Sep) is unfenced, but officials patrol it to make sure that visitors have paid the admission fee at one of the two ticket boxes. There's a pleasant but pricey small café near the southern ticket box.

Beside the site is the village of Qala'at al-Mudiq, sheltered in a medieval castle, while down below, beside the main road, is a poorly maintained **mosaic museum** (adult/student S£75/5; 8.30am-3pm Wed-Mon).

Minibuses (S£15) and microbuses (S£20) regularly run the 45km from Hama to Suqeilibiyya; from there microbuses go on to Qala'at al-Mudiq (S£10). The whole trip usually takes about an hour.

ALEPPO   حلب

021 / pop four million

Once lost in Aleppo's magical and labyrinthine souqs, you're not going to want to be found. The only thing that gets most travellers out of these fascinating and ever-busy centres of commerce is the lure of some of the country's best restaurants and the promise of an excellent night's sleep at a slew of charming boutique hotels. Called Haleb by the locals, the city is outwardly more conservative than many of

SYRIA

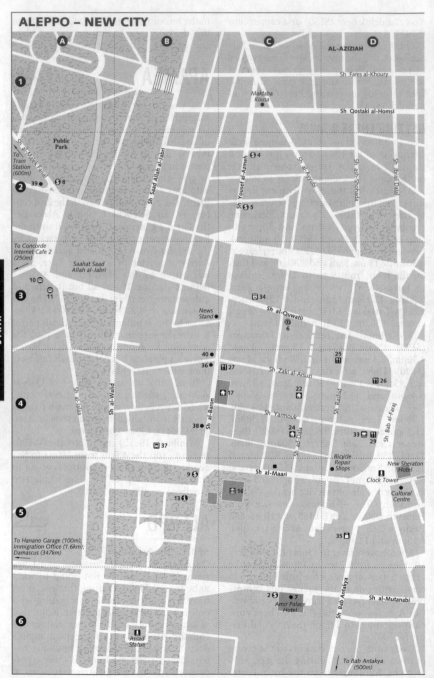

ALEPPO – NEW CITY

AL-AZIZIAH

SYRIA

Sh Fares al-Khoury
Sh Qostaki al-Homsi

Maktaba Kousa

Public Park

Sh al-Malek Faisal
To Train Station (600m)

39 ● ⑤ 8

Sh Saad Allah al-Jabri

Sh Yousef al-Azmeh

⑤ 4

Sh al-Ayoub

Sh ash-Shohada

Sh Jbrail Dalal

⑤ 5

To Concorde Internet Cafe 2 (250m)

Saahat Saad Allah al-Jabri

10 ⊗
11

News Stand ●

☑ 34
Sh al-Quwatli
@ 6

Sh al-Walid

40 ●
36 ●
ᛘ 27

Sh Zaki al-Arsuzi

25
ᛘ

ᛘ 26

Sh al-Jabba

Sh al-Baron

⌂ 17

22
⌂

Sh Rashid

Sh Bab al-Faraj

⊡ 37

Sh Yarmouk

38 ●

24
⌂

Sh ad-Dala

33 ▭ ᛘ
29

Bicycle Repair Shops ●

New Sheraton Hotel

9 ⑤

Sh al-Maari

🏛 16

◪ Clock Tower

Cultural Centre

13 ⓘ

35 ◻

To Hanano Garage (100m);
Immigration Office (1.6km);
Damascus (347km)

Sh Bab Antakya

2 ⑤ ● 7
Amir Palace Hotel

Sh al-Mutanabi

◻ Assad Statue

To Bab Antakya (500m)

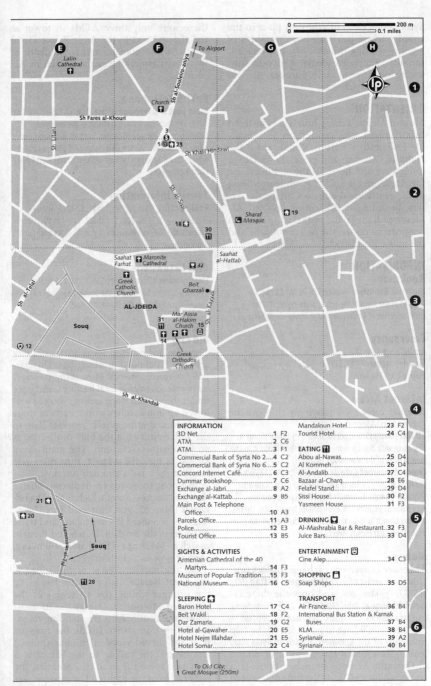

SYRIA

INFORMATION
3D Net......................................1 F2
ATM..2 C6
ATM..3 F1
Commercial Bank of Syria No 2....4 C2
Commercial Bank of Syria No 6....5 C2
Concord Internet Café................6 C3
Dummar Bookshop....................7 C6
Exchange al-Jabri.......................8 A2
Exchange al-Kattab....................9 B5
Main Post & Telephone
    Office...............................10 A3
Parcels Office..........................11 A3
Police.....................................12 E3
Tourist Office..........................13 B5

SIGHTS & ACTIVITIES
Armenian Cathedral of the 40
    Martyrs............................14 F3
Museum of Popular Tradition....15 F3
National Museum.....................16 C5

SLEEPING
Baron Hotel.............................17 C4
Beit Wakil...............................18 F2
Dar Zamaria............................19 G2
Hotel al-Gawaher.....................20 E5
Hotel Nejm Illahdar..................21 E5
Hotel Somar............................22 C4

Mandaloun Hotel.....................23 F2
Tourist Hotel...........................24 C4

EATING
Abou al-Nawas........................25 D4
Al Kommeh..............................26 D4
Al-Andalib...............................27 C4
Bazaar al-Charq........................28 E6
Felafel Stand............................29 D4
Sissi House..............................30 F2
Yasmeen House........................31 F3

DRINKING
Al-Mashrabia Bar & Restaurant..32 F3
Juice Bars...............................33 D4

ENTERTAINMENT
Cine Alep................................34 C3

SHOPPING
Soap Shops.............................35 D5

TRANSPORT
Air France...............................36 B4
International Bus Station & Karnak
    Buses..............................37 B4
KLM.......................................38 B4
Syrianair.................................39 A2
Syrianair.................................40 B4

Syria's other cities (it's the only place in the country where you'll see large numbers of women wearing the chador), but beneath the surface there are plenty of friendly fun-loving locals keen to introduce travellers to the city's many charms.

ORIENTATION

Most of Aleppo's cheap hotels are clustered in a compact zone centred on Sharias al-Quwatli and al-Baron. Restaurants, the National Museum and places to exchange money are also here. To the southeast are the citadel and the old city, while northeast of the centre are the main Christian quarters, including the charming cobbled Al-Jdeida district. To the west are the modern commercial centre, the newer suburbs and the university district.

INFORMATION
Bookshops

Dummar Bookshop (Map pp536-7; ☎ 221 4800) Located in the foyer of the Amir Palace Hotel, it stocks a small selection of English-language books about Syria.

Emergency

Ambulance (☎ 110)
Fire department (☎ 113)
Police (☎ 362 4300)

Internet Access

Internet cafés are annoyingly thin on the ground in Aleppo.

3D Net (Map pp536-7; per hr S£40; ☺ 10am-10pm) A tiny place with dial-up connection only. You'll find it in the lane in front of the Mandaloun Hotel.

Concord Internet Cafe (Map pp536-7; ☎ 212 70060; per hr S£100; ☺ 9.30am-3am) Above a pastry café on Sharia al-Quwatli. Extremely fast connections go some way towards excusing the extortionate hourly rate. There's another branch in Al-Jameleia, two blocks west of the main post office, near French Sweets.

Money

There are convenient exchange offices outside the tourist office, **Exchange al-Kattab** (Map pp536-7; ☺ 10am-5pm), and opposite the citadel, **Exchange al-Jabri** (Map pp536-7; ☺ 10am-5pm), but travellers cheques are not accepted – for these you'll have to go to one of the two branches of the **Commercial Bank of Syria** (Map pp536-7; Sharia Yousef al-Azmeh), north of Sharia al-Quwatli. At both branches there is a commission of S£25. At the time of research

there were only three ATMs in town: at the airport, next to the Amir Palace Hotel in Sharia al-Mutanabi, and in the front of the Planet Hotel on Sharia al-Telal in Al-Jdeida.

Post & Telephone

Main post & telephone office (Map pp536-7; ☎ 362 4010; ☺ 8am-5pm) You'll find this in the enormous building on the far side of Saahat Saad Allah al-Jabri. For international calls, use the Easycomm card phones dotted around town, including in front of the post office and the National Museum.

Tourist Information

Tourist office (Map pp536-7; ☎ 212 1228; Sharia al-Baron; ☺ 8.30am-7pm Sat-Thu) Located in the gardens opposite the National Museum, it doesn't stock maps and is generally unhelpful.

Visa Extensions

Immigration office (Map pp536-7; ☎ 225 5330; ☺ 8am-1.30pm Sat-Thu) In the square near the Chahba Cham Palace Hotel, on the Damascus road.

SIGHTS
Old City

The fabulous covered **souqs** of the old city are one of Aleppo's big attractions. This partially covered network of bustling passageways extends over several hectares, and once under the vaulted stone ceiling, you're swallowed up into another world. Parts of these dimly lit and atmospheric markets date to the 13th century but the bulk of the area is an Ottoman-era creation. The main souq, known as the **Souq al-Atarin**, runs east–west between the citadel and Bab Antakya.

In among the souqs are numerous khans, the most impressive of which is the **Khan al-Jumruk** (Map p539). Completed in 1574, at one time it housed the consulates and trade missions of the English, Dutch and French, as well as 344 shops. The khan is still in use, serving now as a cloth market.

On the northern edge of the souqs is the **Great Mosque** (Jamaa al-Kebir; Map p539), the younger sibling (by 10 years) of the Umayyad Mosque in Damascus. Its most impressive feature is its freestanding minaret dating from 1090. Inside the mosque is a fine carved wooden minbar (pulpit) and behind the railing to the left of it is supposed to be the head of Zacharias, the father of John the Baptist. The mosque was

ALEPPO – OLD CITY

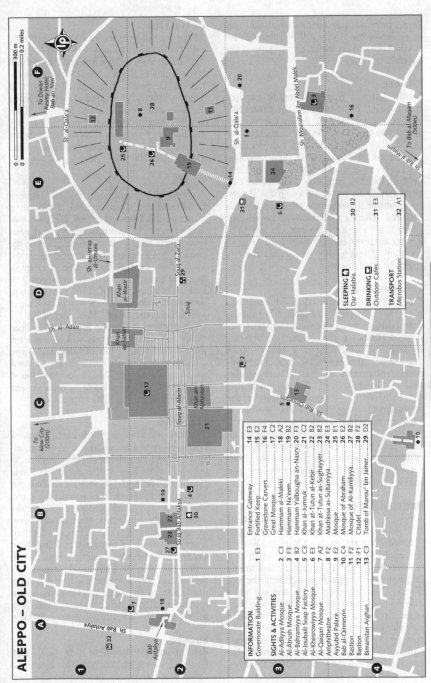

SYRIA

INFORMATION
Governorate Building............1 E3

SIGHTS & ACTIVITIES
Al-Adiliyya Mosque..............2 C3
Al-Atrush Mosque................3 F3
Al-Bahramiyya Mosque.........4 B2
Al-Joubaili Soap Factory.......5 C3
Al-Khosrowiyya Mosque........6 E3
Al-Qaiqan Mosque...............7 A2
Amphitheatre.....................8 F2
Ayyubid Palace...................9 F2
Bab al-Qinnesrin................10 C4
Bastion...........................11 F2
Bastion...........................12 F1
Bimaristan Arghan..............13 C3
Entrance Gateway..............14 E3
Fortified Keep....................15 F2
Gravestone Carvers.............16 F4
Great Mosque....................17 C2
Hammam al-Maleki.............18 A2
Hammam Na'eem................19 B2
Hammam Yalbougha an-Nasry..20 F3
Khan al-Jumruk..................21 C2
Khan at-Tutun al-Kebir.........22 B2
Khan at-Tutun as-Sughayyer...23 B2
Madrassa as-Sultaniyya........24 E2
Mosque...........................25 E1
Mosque of Abraham............26 E2
Mosque of Al-Kamiliyya........27 B2
Citadel............................28 F2
Tomb of Marou' bin Jamer....29 D2

SLEEPING
Dar Halabia......................30 B2

DRINKING
Outdoor Cafés...................31 E3

TRANSPORT
Microbus Station................32 A1

being painstakingly renovated at the time of research, but it was still possible to visit if you knocked on the door and tipped the caretaker.

CITADEL
Sitting atop a huge manmade earthen mound east of the old city, the **citadel** (Map p539; adult/student S£150/10; ☺ 9am-6pm Wed-Mon Apr-Sep, 9am-4pm Wed-Mon Oct-Mar) dominates the city skyline. On the southern side, its moat is spanned by a bridge that then climbs at a 45 degree angle up to the imposing 12th-century fortified gate. Once inside, the castle is largely in ruins, although the throne room above the entrance has been lavishly restored. There's a sparsely endowed museum (S£75) in an Ottoman-era barracks, a recently restored *hammam* (not open to the public) and terrific views over the city from the battlements.

Christian Quarter
The Christian quarter of Al-Jdeida is the most charming part of Aleppo. A beautifully maintained warren of long, narrow stone-flagged alleyways, the quarter is currently undergoing something of a rebirth, with age-old townhouses being converted into hotels, restaurants and bars. There are also several churches worth visiting, including the 15th-century **Armenian Cathedral of the 40 Martyrs** (Map pp536–7). The **Museum of Popular Tradition** (Le Musee des Traditions; Map pp536-7; adult/student S£75/5; ☺ 8am-2pm Wed-Mon), which occupies a beautiful 18th-century residence, is also worth a visit. Don't miss the guest room, with its amazing silver ceiling and snake-entwined light fitting.

National Museum
Aleppo's main **museum** (Map pp536-7; ☎ 221 2400; Sharia al-Baron; adult/student S£150/10; ☺ 9am-5.30pm Wed-Mon Apr-Sep, 9am-3.30pm Wed-Mon Oct-Mar) could be mistaken for a sports hall if it weren't for the extraordinary colonnade of giant granite figures that fronts the entrance. The wide-eyed characters are replicas of pillars that once supported the ceiling of an 8th- or 9th-century-BC temple-palace complex unearthed in the northeast of the country. Inside, the collection is predominantly made up of other finds from northern Syria – there are some beautiful pieces, but it's a pity the labelling is so poor.

ACTIVITIES
At the foot of the citadel, on the southeast side, the **Hammam Yalbougha an-Nasry** (Map p539; ☎ 362 3154; Sharia al-Qala'a; bath only S£200, full bath S£415) is one of Syria's finest working bathhouses. Originally constructed in 1491, it was most recently restored in 1985. Women are admitted from 10am to 5pm on Monday, Wednesday (in winter only), Thursday and Saturday; men are admitted on Sunday, Tuesday, Wednesday (in summer only) and Friday from 10am to 1.30am.

TOURS
A good tour guide should cost between US$40 and US$50 per day. Ask at the tourist office. **Halabia Tours** (☎ 2248497, 094 245543; www .halabia-tours.com) is recommended if you need to organise transport to other parts of the country or day tours to surrounding sights. Most of the budget hotels offer a range of day trips to attractions in the area; you'll be looking at a base rate of S£500 per person to go to Qala'at Samaan, S£600 to go to Qala'at Samaan and the Dead Cities, and S£800 for a full-day trip to Qala'at Samaan, the Dead Cities and Apamea. Costs will be higher if there are only one or two of you going. If you arrange this yourself through an operator such as Halabia, you'll be looking at around US$50 to US$70 plus tip for a minibus and an English-speaking driver for the day.

SLEEPING
The bulk of the budget hotels are in the block bounded by Sharias al-Maari, al-Baron, al-Quwatli and Bab al-Faraj. Many backpackers end up staying at the Zahrat ar-Rabie (Springflower Hostel) on Sharia ad-Dala but we don't recommend that you do the same. Rooms are tiny, dark, grubby and radically overpriced for what they offer. More worrying are the reports (verified by us) we've had from a number of female travellers about sleazy staff members using peepholes to watch guests in the shower. Do everyone a favour and stay elsewhere – hostel owners need to know that they can't overcharge on reputation alone and that sleazy behaviour on the part of staff is totally unacceptable.

Budget
Hotel al-Gawaher (Map pp536-7; ☎ /fax 223 9554; Bab al-Faraj; s/d/tr S£500/1000/1500) This hotel just off Bab al-Faraj may not be the cheapest

backpacker place in town but it's without doubt the best. Rooms come complete with clean linen, pristine bathroom, toilet paper and soap, fans and electric heaters. Some have balconies onto the street; others have windows onto the interior salons. Those on the 1st floor have satellite TV. There's 24-hour hot water, and two large and pleasantly decorated lounges where you can relax over a tea. A 10% discount is offered in the low season.

Tourist Hotel (Map pp536-7; ☎ 211 6583, 094 786206; Sharia ad-Dala; s/d with bathroom S£400/700, without bathroom S£350/650; 🖭) Run by the formidable Madam Olga and her family, this small hotel is the most comfortable of Aleppo's budget options. It's famous throughout the country for its standards of cleanliness (it's immaculate), and rooms are freshly painted, light and comfortable. Some have private bathrooms. There's 24-hour hot water, fresh linen daily and an optional breakfast (S£100).

Hotel Nejm Illahdar (Hotel Green Star; Map pp536-7; ☎ 223 9157; s S£250-300, d S£400-500, t S£700) On the 2nd floor of a building just off Bab al-Faraj, this place has been recently renovated. Cheaper rooms come with fan, balcony and shower cubicle; the more expensive have air-con, comfortable beds and full (if tiny) private bathrooms. When we visited, the cheaper rooms were a bit grubby. There's a lounge with satellite TV, as well as a fabulous rooftop terrace where breakfast (S£75) is served in summer.

Hotel Somar (Map pp536-7; ☎ 211 3198; fax 211 4669; Sharia Yarmouk; s US$17-20, d US$23; 🖭) If you have no luck scoring a room at the Tourist Hotel, the old-fashioned Somar is a decent alternative. Rooms are comfortable and have satellite TV. All come with tiny but very clean private bathrooms. Rooms at the front are the best, as those at the rear are dark. The clientele is predominantly Arab.

Midrange & Top End

Unless indicated otherwise, all of these hotels provide comfortable rooms with heating, satellite TV and private bathroom. All except the Baron accept credit-card payment. Breakfast is included in the room cost given.

Dar Halabia (Map p539; ☎ 332 3344; www.halabia -tours.com; s/d US$30/40; 🖭) The Halabia bills itself as a 'Hotel de Charme' and it's entitled

to do so. Located near Bab Antakya, it's the only hotel in the souq. It occupies three old houses and has 19 rooms, the most attractive of which are on the ground floor around the courtyard of the main building. Although lonely at night when the whole quarter is deathly silent, the hotel is quite lovely, spotlessly clean and great value. There are no TVs.

Mandaloun Hotel (Map pp536-7; ☎ 228 3008; www.mandalounhotel.com; off Sharia Al-Telal; s/d US$67/78; 🖭) Gorgeous is the first word that comes to mind when describing the well-located Mandaloun. A boutique hotel converted from two old houses, it has a magnificent and comfortable central courtyard complete with fountain and antique furniture, as well as a cosy restaurant and bar. The downstairs rooms and suites (US$100) are knockouts, with four-star amenities and extremely attractive décor. Rooms on the top floor are cramped and nowhere near as nice as their downstairs counterparts.

Beit Wakil (Map pp536-7; ☎ 221 7169; www.beit wakil.com; Sharia as-Sissi; s/d US$78/111; 🖭) In the Al-Jdeida quarter, this may well be Syria's most romantic hotel. Nineteen small rooms have an almost monastic simplicity and enormous charm. There's a particularly fine triple (US$133) on the ground floor and a stunning suite (US$145) in the house's former reception room.

Dar Zamaria (Map pp536-7; ☎ 363 6100; www .darzamaria.com; s/d US$83/111; 🗙 🖭) Another boutique hotel in an old and very lovely building in Al-Jdeida, Dar Zamaria is known throughout the city for its attractive and very popular courtyard restaurant. Though quite small and a bit dark, rooms are comfortable; light sleepers might find restaurant noise a problem.

Diwan Rasmy Hotel (☎ 331 2222; www.diwan rasmy-hotel.com; s/d US$56/72; 🖭 💻) In a maze-like part of town just near the Citadel – tell your taxi driver it's near the 'Jawazat' (former passport building) – this boutique hotel occupies two connected and beautifully renovated houses, one of which is over 500 years old. Public areas are impressive, but the room décor is a bit bland. All rooms are well equipped; ask for number 519, which boasts wonderful views of the citadel. There's a panoramic rooftop restaurant that's perfect for summer nights. Service is desultory.

Baron Hotel (Map pp536-7; ☎ 211 0880/1; hotel baron@mail.sy; Sharia al-Baron; s/d US$45/55; ☒) The Baron has a big reputation and an air of Gothic romance, but has seen better days. Public areas (including the famous bar) are looking decidedly worse for wear, and rooms (even those that have been recently renovated) have an institutional feel, uncomfortable beds and peeling paintwork.

EATING

The block bounded by Sharias al-Maari, Bab al-Faraj, al-Quwatli and al-Baron is full of cheap eateries offering the usual array of roast chicken and shwarma. A row of excellent juice stands lines up at the Bab al-Faraj end of Sharia Yarmouk, and there's an immensely popular felafel stand right on the corner here. There are tiny stalls along the length of Souq Bab Antakya/az-Zarb/al-Attarine selling cheap felafel, kebabs, hummus, pastries and fuul.

Abou al-Nawas (Map pp536-7; ☎ 211 5100; Sharia Rashid; mezze S£15-35, mains S£100-200) This long-standing favourite has a menu that stretches way beyond the basics to include the kind of dishes that are usually only ever served up at home (patrons are often invited into the kitchen to choose from the daily pots). There's an excellent value set meal for S£175, which gives you a daily dish of your choice with rice or fries, pickles, tea or coffee, and a sweet. Be clear that this is what you're ordering, because the waiters inevitably encourage you to order a more expensive main dish instead. No alcohol.

Al-Andalib (Map pp536-7; ☎ 222 4030; Sharia al-Baron; set menu S£200) The atmosphere at this rooftop restaurant one block north of the Baron Hotel is boisterous and the place is packed most evenings. It serves a huge set meal of kebabs, salads, dips and fries. There's a S£50 service charge and a limited alcohol list. Come prepared to have a good time.

Al-Kommeh (Map pp536-7; ☎ 211 3550; Sharia Zaki al-Arsuzi; mezze S£20-50, kebabs S£100-120; ☒) Just off Bab al-Faraj, this cavernous 1st-floor place serves up decent and well-priced mezze and kebabs to a constant stream of local families. The décor is ornate but the squalid toilets let down the side. The downstairs Al-Kindi Restaurant offers more of the same. Neither is licensed.

Bazaar al-Charq (Map pp536-7; ☎ 224 9120; btwn Sharia al-Mutanabi & Sharia Hammam al-Tal; ☒) Ask locals to recommend their favourite restaurant in town and the answer will inevitably be Al-Charq. An enormous place designed to resemble a bazaar, it has live music on Thursdays and Saturdays that often entices diners into singing along. The food is great, too. No alcohol is served.

Yasmeen House (Map pp536-7; ☎ 222 5562; www .yasmeenhouse.com; mezze S£45-60, grills S£150-180; ☒) Run by two friendly brothers who have spent a lot of time in Canada, Yasmeen has a more casual vibe than the nearby Beit Wakil and Sissi House. Peruse the English-language menu (with prices listed); you're sure to find something that appeals among the standard array of mezze and grills. It's licensed, but doesn't accept credit cards.

Beit Wakil (Map pp536-7; ☎ 221 7169; Sharia as-Sissi; mezze S£45-100, grills S£175; ☒) Aleppo's best restaurant is also housed in one of its most beautiful buildings. Guests sit in an atmospheric courtyard and can choose from a tempting array of mezze and local specialities such as the highly recommended *kabab karaz* (cherry kebab). It's licensed and accepts credit cards.

Sissi House (Map pp536-7; ☎ 221 9411; www.sissi house.com; mezze S£35-110, mains S£150-220; ☒) Just off Saahat al-Hattab in the Al-Jdeida quarter, this upmarket restaurant is where Aleppo's glam set hangs out. Like the restaurant at Beit Wakil, it specialises in local variations on Levantine cuisine and offers a choice of over 50 mezze dishes. The licensed menu is in Arabic and French only, and doesn't list prices. Credit cards are accepted.

DRINKING

If you're after a drink only, the upstairs bar at **Sissi House** (Map pp536-7; ☎ 221 9411; ☒) is open until late and hosts a jazz pianist every night of the week, with a singer on Saturdays. It's the most sophisticated bar in town. Nostalgia buffs may want to pop into the pricey small bar at the venerable **Baron Hotel** (Map pp536-7; ☎ 211 0880/1; Sharia al-Baron), but most visitors prefer the laid-back **Al-Mashrabia Pub & Restaurant** (Map pp536-7; ☎ 224 0249) in Al-Jdeida, where the drinks are cheaper (local beer S£75) and the décor is more atmospheric. There's also an extensive snack menu here.

The outdoor cafés on Sharia al-Qala'a, located opposite the entrance to the citadel are great places to enjoy a coffee, fresh

SYRIA

juice or nargileh and watch the world go by. Equally popular are the restaurants with pavement seating that are scattered around Sharia Georges and Mathilde Salem in Al-Aziziah.

ENTERTAINMENT

Cine Alep (Map pp536-7; Sharia al-Quwatli) screens relatively new Hollywood films in its two cinemas. Tickets cost S£150. Women should be careful if going here alone.

GETTING THERE & AWAY
Air

Aleppo's airport offers irregular connections to Turkey, Europe and other cities in the Middle East. There is a regular weekly Syrian air service to Cairo. Internally, there's a daily flight to Damascus (S£950, one hour). A taxi between the airport and the city centre will cost between S£300 to S£400 depending on the time of day and the city destination.

Bus

The main bus station, as far as most travellers are concerned, is the Hanano garage, about 800m west of the National Museum. All luxury, long-distance buses to destinations within Syria leave from here. It's a short walk to the budget hotel area around Bab al-Faraj; a taxi to the old city or Al-Jdeida will cost around S£50.

From Hanano, Al-Kadmous runs 24-hour services to Damascus on the hour (S£160, four hours) as well as 'VIP' services (S£230) at 10.30am, 5.30am, 3.30pm and 8.30pm. It also runs a regular service to Hama (S£60, 2½ hours) and Homs (S£85, three hours) from 5.30am to 10.30pm, and around-the-clock services to Deir ez-Zur (S£135, five hours).

Al-Ahliah runs one bus per day to Damascus (5am, S£150) as well as buses to Hama (S£65) and Homs (S£85) on the hour from 7am till noon and then hourly from 1.30pm until 9.30pm.

Sarraj runs a minibus service to Damascus International Airport (S£125) every 30 minutes.

Al-Salaam is one of only two companies servicing the Aleppo–Lattakia route. Its 24-hour minibuses leave on the hour (S£100, 3½ hours).

There are no direct services to Tartus or Palmyra. Change at Homs for these.

Seven or eight companies offer daily services from Hanano to Beirut (six hours) via Tripoli (five hours). These include Sarraj (S£300 both destinations), which has services at 10.30am, 1pm, 4pm, midnight, 1am and 2.30am; Ramadan (S£300 Tripoli, S£350 Beirut), at 10am and 11am; and Zetouni (S£250 Tripoli, S£300 Beirut), which has eight services daily from 10.30am to 3am.

You'll find the International Bus Station north of the tourist office. From here, there are services at 5am and 8am to Antakya (adult/student S£250/200), from where you can connect to buses servicing destinations throughout Turkey. There are also buses at 10pm and 11pm to Amman (S£450). All Karnak buses also leave from here.

Microbuses covering local routes around Aleppo leave from the sprawling microbus and minibus station just south of the Amir Palace Hotel near Bab Antakya.

Service Taxi

If you can't wait around for a bus to Antakya, a seat in a service taxi costs S£500. These leave when full from the International Bus Station.

Train

The train station is housed in an attractive old building located about a 15-minute walk from the central hotel area, north of the big public park. The telephone number for Syrian Railways in Aleppo is ☎ 221 3900.

There are two daily express services to Damascus at 4am and 5.25am (S£180) and one slow service at midnight (S£110/75 in 1st/2nd class).

To Lattakia there are two daily express trains (S£135, three hours) at 6.25am and 5.10pm, and two slow trains (S£70/50 in 1st/2nd class) at 7.50am and 3.20pm. Two daily trains travel to Deir ez-Zur (S£115/75 in 1st/2nd class) and Al-Qamishle (S£175/115 in 1st/2nd class) in the northeast at 11pm and 3am. An extra 4pm service travels to Deir ez-Zur only.

There are services to Tehran (S£3850/2750 in sleeper/1st class) on Mondays at 1.10pm, and to İstanbul (S£2815 in sleeper) on Tuesdays at 11.05am.

A taxi from the station to the Al-Jdeida, Bab Antakya or Bab al-Faraj areas should cost between S£35 and S£50.

QALA'AT SAMAAN

قلعة سمعان

Also known as the Basilica of St Simeon, the ruins of **Qala'at Samaan** (adult/student S£150/10; ✆ 9am-6pm Apr-Sep, 9am-4pm Oct-Mar) are among the most atmospheric of Syria's archaeological sites. The basilica commemorates St Simeon Stylites, one of Syria's most eccentric early Christians.

In AD 423 Simeon climbed to the top of a 3m pillar and went on to spend the next 36 years atop this and other taller pillars. He ended his days on one that was a full 18m high. After his death in 459, an enormous church was built around the most famous pillar, and pilgrims from all parts of Christendom came to pay their respects. The site today is remarkably well preserved, with the main Romanesque façade still standing and the arches of the octagonal yard still reasonably complete. Views of the surrounding countryside are simply stunning.

Qala'at Samaan is a 40-minute drive from Aleppo. Microbuses to the village of Daret' Azze (S£15, one hour) leave Aleppo every hour or so from the microbus bays and this is as close to the site as you can get by public transport. From here there are no local buses or taxis to take you the remaining 8km, so the only options are to hitch (difficult) or walk. Aleppine taxi drivers will charge S£800 to take you there, wait one hour and bring you back to town.

DEAD CITIES

These eerie and ancient ghost towns are dotted along the limestone hills that lie between the Aleppo–Hama highway in the east and the Orontes River in the west. They date from the time when this area was part of the hinterland of the great Byzantine city of Antioch, and range from single monuments to whole villages complete with houses, churches and baths. Together they represent a great archive in stone, from which historians can put together a picture of life in antiquity. Some, such as **Al-Bara**, are on intensively farmed land where vegetables, olives, grapes and apricots are grown alongside striking pyramid tombs and ruined

monasteries. In winter these sites are very muddy and can be difficult to explore.

The most evocative of the Dead Cities is undoubtedly **Serjilla**. It has the most semi-complete buildings, all sitting in a natural basin in windswept and hilly moorland. Although Serjilla has been deserted for about 15 centuries, the buildings' stone façades are remarkably well preserved and it's easy to get a feel for what the town would have looked like in its heyday. There's a spooky feel to the place, almost as if you've stumbled upon it just after the occupants have vanished. In fact, some of the buildings have been reoccupied by local shepherds, so don't be surprised if you see chickens wandering around, washing drying on bushes or smoke issuing from chimneys. Though there is a ticket box next to the car park, it is rarely open.

You are best off visiting the Dead Cities on a combined Qala'at Samaan/Dead Cities tour from Aleppo (p540) or in your own car, as they are extremely difficult to reach on public transport and are scattered over a large area. The drive from Qala'at Samaan to Serjilla takes 1½ hours.

PALMYRA

تدمر

☎ 031

In *A Scandalous Life* (Mary S Lovell's fascinating biography of that famous and highly unconventional 19th-century traveller to Syria, Lady Jane Digby) the author spends much time describing Jane's long-term infatuation with the rose-gold ancient ruins of Tadmor (Palmyra). Jane isn't the only Western traveller to have fallen victim to this desert city's charms, and these days Palmyra is Syria's prime tourist attraction.

HISTORY

Palmyra was an Assyrian caravan town for over 1000 years, after which it enjoyed a period of glory for two centuries under the Greeks. It was annexed by Rome in AD 217 and became a centre of unsurpassed wealth.

The city's most famous character was Zenobia, the half-Greek, half-Arab queen who claimed descent from Cleopatra. A woman of exceptional ability and ambition, she became ruler of Palmyra in 267 after the death (in suspicious circumstances) of her husband Odenathus. Zenobia set her sights on

Rome, but her army was soundly beaten by the forces of the Roman emperor Aurelian in 271; he torched the city two years later.

This was the beginning of the end for Palmyra. It fell to the Muslims in 634 and was finally and completely destroyed by an earthquake in 1089.

INFORMATION

Palmyra's helpful **tourist information office** (☎ 910 574; Saahat ar-Rais; ⊙ 8am-6pm Sat-Thu) is situated across from the museum. There is a **Commercial Bank of Syria exchange booth** (⊙ 8am-8pm Sun-Thu, 10am-8pm Fri & Sat) in front of the museum, but it doesn't change travellers cheques. The post office is in front of the Al-Assad Gardens, just west of the tourist office; you can make 24-hour international calls from the card phones in front of the building (cards available inside). **Hani Internet** (☎ 910 878; ⊙ 8am-midnight) at the Traditional Palmyra Restaurant charges an outrageous S£150 per hour for Internet access. The Citadel Hotel and Spring Restaurant were charging S£75 per hour when we visited, though both warned that price rises were planned.

SIGHTS
The Ruins

Bel was the most important of the gods in the Palmyrene pantheon and the **Temple of Bel** (adult/student S£150/10; ⊙ officially 8am-1pm & 4-6pm Apr-Sep, 8am-4pm Oct-Mar but often closed for longer periods over lunch) is the most complete structure and most impressive part of the ruins. Once inside, you'll see that the complex consists of two parts: a huge walled temenos (courtyard) and at its centre, the cella (the temple proper), which dates from AD 32.

Just to the left of the entrance into the temenos is a sunken passage that enters the temple from the outside wall and gradually slopes up to the level of the courtyard. This was probably used to bring sacrificial animals to the precincts. The podium of the sacrificial altar is on the left, and beside it are the foundations of a banqueting hall. The cella is unusual in that its entrance is in one of the sides rather than at an end, and is offset from the centre. Inside is a single chamber with *adytons* (large niches) at either end.

The building beside the temple was originally the residence of Palmyra's Ottoman governor. It now has a ho-hum **Ethnographic Museum** (adult/student S£75/5; ⊙ 8.30am-2.30pm).

Formerly connected to the temple by a colonnade, the **monumental arch** across the road now serves as the entrance to the site proper. There is no admission cost to this part of the ruins, though you will probably be stalked by camel owners keen to charge you S£200 for a 30-minute ride around the site.

The arch is interesting as it is actually two arches joined like a hinge to pivot the main street through a 30-degree turn. This slight direction switch, and a second one just a little further west, are in themselves evidence of the city's unique development – a crooked street like this would be quite unimaginable in any standard Roman city.

South of the main colonnaded street is the city's **theatre**, which was buried by sand until the 1950s. Since its discovery it has been extensively restored.

About one-third of the way along the colonnaded street is the reconstructed **tetrapylon**, a monumental structure that served to mark a junction of thoroughfares. From here the main street continues northwest, and another smaller pillared street leads southwest to the agora, or forum, and northeast to the **Temple of Baal Shamin**, a small shrine dedicated to the god of storms and fertilising rains.

Beyond the tetrapylon the main street continues for another 500m. This stretch has seen much less excavation and reconstruction, and is littered with tumbled columns and assorted blocks of masonry. The road ends in the impressive portico of a 3rd-century funerary temple. South of the funerary temple, along the porticoed way, is the **Camp of Diocletian**, erected after the destruction of the city by Aurelian. It was possibly on the site of what had been the palace of Zenobia, although excavations so far have been unable to prove this. The camp lay near the Damascus Gate, which led on to a 2nd-century colonnaded street that supposedly linked Emesa (Homs) and the Euphrates.

To the south, at the foot of some low hills, is a series of tall, freestanding square-based towers known as the **Towers of Yemliko**. These were constructed as multistorey burial chambers, stacked with coffins posted in pigeonhole-like niches. The niches were sealed with stone panels carved with a head-and-shoulder portrait of the deceased; you can see many of these in the special displays at the National Museum in Damascus (p515).

SYRIA

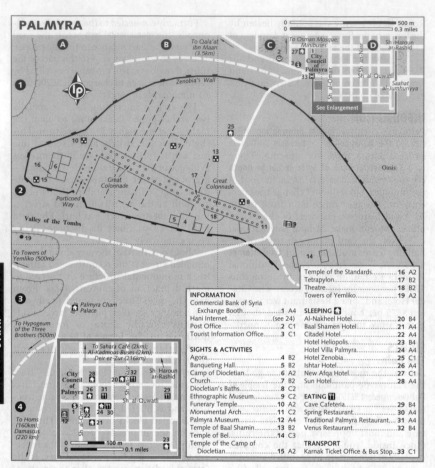

PALMYRA

To Qala'at
ibn Maan
(3.5km)

To Osman Mosque;
Minibuses

City Council
of Palmyra

Sh Haroun
ar-Rashid

Zenobia's Wall

See Enlargement

Oasis

Great Colonnade

Great Colonnade

Porticoed Way

Valley of the Tombs

To Towers of
Yemliko (500m)

Palmyra Cham
Palace

To Hypogeum
of the Three
Brothers (500m)

To Sahara Café (2km);
Al-Kadmous Buses (2km);
Deir ez-Zur (216km)

City
Council
of
Palmyra

Sh Haroun
ar-Rashid

Sh al-Quwatli

To Homs
(160km);
Damascus
(220 km)

Temple of the Standards	16	A2
Tetrapylon	17	B2
Theatre	18	B2
Towers of Yemliko	19	A2

INFORMATION

Commercial Bank of Syria Exchange Booth	1	A4
Hani Internet	(see 24)	
Post Office	2	C1
Tourist Information Office	3	C1

SLEEPING 🏠

Al-Nakheel Hotel	20	B4
Baal Shamen Hotel	21	A4
Citadel Hotel	22	A4
Hotel Heliopolis	23	B4
Hotel Villa Palmyra	24	A4
Hotel Zenobia	25	C1
Ishtar Hotel	26	A4
New Afqa Hotel	27	C1
Sun Hotel	28	A4

SIGHTS & ACTIVITIES

Agora	4	B2
Banqueting Hall	5	B2
Camp of Diocletian	6	A2
Church	7	B2
Diocletian's Baths	8	C2
Ethnographic Museum	9	C2
Funerary Temple	10	A2
Monumental Arch	11	C2
Palmyra Museum	12	A4
Temple of Baal Shamin	13	B2
Temple of Bel	14	C3
Temple of the Camp of Diocletian	15	A2

EATING 🍴

Cave Cafeteria	29	B4
Spring Restaurant	30	A4
Traditional Palmyra Restaurant	31	A4
Venus Restaurant	32	B4

TRANSPORT

| Karnak Ticket Office & Bus Stop | 33 | C1 |

It's possible to visit one of these towers, Elahbel, on a tour organised by the Palmyra Museum (adult/student S£75/5). Tours leave from the museum at 8.30am, 10am, 11.30am and 4.30pm (no 11.30am tour on Fridays; no 4.30pm tour October to March) and include a visit to the impressive **Hypogeum of the Three Brothers**, an underground burial chamber with beautiful frescoes.

Perched high on a hilltop to the west of the ruins is **Qala'at ibn Maan** (adult/student S£75/5; 🕐 noon-sunset Wed-Mon), also known as the Arab Castle. From here there are spectacular sunset views over the ruins. Though it's possible to walk here, many travellers choose to take one of the many tours sold by hotels in town (approximately S£100 per person).

Palmyra Museum

With labelling in French and Arabic only, and generally poor presentation, it's debatable whether the modest **Palmyra Museum** (adult/student S£150/10; 🕐 8am-1pm & 4-6pm Wed-Mon Apr-Sep, 8am-4pm Wed-Mon Oct-Mar) is worth a visit or not.

However, there is a very good, large-scale model of the Temple of Bel that gives an excellent idea of how the complex would have looked in its original state, as well as a couple of dynamic mosaics that were found in what are presumed to be nobles' houses, just east of the temple. There are also countless busts and carved portraits that formed part of the panels used to seal the tombs in Palmyra's many funerary towers.

SYRIA

SLEEPING

Prices vary seasonally and according to demand. This is one place where it pays to haggle.

Budget

New Afqa Hotel (☎ 910 386; mahran_afqa@hotmail .com; roof mattress S£100, s/d with air-con S£350/500, without air-con S£250/300; ✗) This excellent budget choice is run by the genial Mahran and offers basic but clean boxlike rooms, some of which have air-con and bathrooms. The welcoming reception area has satellite TV and beer. Breakfast costs S£75.

Citadel Hotel (☎ 910 537; razisaleh@hotmail.com; Sharia As'ad al-Amir; dm/s/d S£150/250/500; ✗) Facing the side of the museum, this popular place has a comfortable foyer with satellite TV and 17 clean rooms. All but the dorm rooms on the roof have small bathrooms. The pick of the rooms are the five new doubles on the top floor. Breakfast costs S£50. In winter, rooms are discounted to S£200 per person.

Sun Hotel (☎ 911 133; sunhotel_sy@hotmail.com; dm/ s/d S£150/200/400; 🖳) The freshly painted rooms at this small hotel come complete with fans and clean private bathrooms; ask for one with an exterior window. Tidy but dark dorm rooms (also with bathrooms) sleep three or four. Breakfast costs S£50, and the owner's mum is happy to cook dinner for S£100.

Al-Nakheel Hotel (☎ 910 744; mohamed1st12@ yahoo.com; s/d incl breakfast US$6/12; ✗) The guy running this small place is extremely enthusiastic and has made a real effort with the décor. It'll probably remind you of your great-aunt's house, albeit with a bit of local colour. Small clean rooms have bathrooms, rug-strewn floors and comfortable beds. One has a balcony with views over the ruins.

Baal Shamen Hotel (☎ 910 453; fax 912 970; mattress on roof S£100, s/d with bathroom S£200/300, without bathroom S£125/250; ✗) It's the cheapest of Palmyra's budget options, but this hotel isn't the best. Five rooms have air-con and clean private bathrooms, the rest are a bit musty and share bathrooms that need a good clean. There's a Bedouin tent on the roof where you can sleep on a thin mattress in summer. You'll have to eat breakfast elsewhere.

Midrange & Top End

The prices given include breakfast. All rooms offer satellite TV, heating and bathrooms. Credit cards are accepted.

Ishtar Hotel (☎ 913 073/4; ishtarhotel@hotmail .com; Sharia al-Quwatli; s/d US$15/24; ✗ 🖳) Once you're over the shock of the leopard-skin-covered furniture in the foyer of this friendly hotel you'll be won over by its understated charm. Though small, rooms are comfortable. You can drink in the foyer or in the bizarre cave-cum-basement restaurant. Prices are 30% cheaper March to November.

Hotel Villa Palmyra (☎ 910 156; villapalmyra@ mail.sy; s/d US$40/50; ✗) This new hotel offers smallish rooms with an attractive turquoise décor. There's a rooftop restaurant with great views of the ruins, as well as a downstairs bar and pub. Be very firm when negotiating room prices; the first price we were given was 50% more than what we eventually settled on.

Hotel Heliopolis (☎ 913 921/2; heliopolis-palmyra@ usa.net; s/d US$52/61; ✗) In a quiet location behind Saahat al-Jumhuriyya, this somewhat bland but well-maintained place offers the most comfortable rooms in town. There's a good restaurant on the 5th floor and a downstairs bar. Breakfast is an extra S£200.

Hotel Zenobia (☎ 910 107; zenobia-hotel@net.sy; s/d US$50/65; ✗ 🖳) Built in 1900, the Zenobia can rightfully claim to be one of the most famous hotels in the Middle East, but these days it's short on any kind of charm, period or otherwise. You're much better off staying elsewhere as the rooms are damp, grubby and run down.

EATING & DRINKING

Most places to eat are on or around the main drag, Sharia al-Quwatli. If our experience is anything to go by, you should avoid the Garden Restaurant near the ruins. When we visited, the food was mediocre and the bill involved some creative accounting.

You'll find cheap fast-food eateries selling roast chicken, felafel and shwarma on Sharia al-Quwatli, between the Traditional Palmyra Restaurant and Saahat al-Jumhuriyya. The best of these is probably Zenobia Restaurant. Grocery and fruit and veg shops are also found in this area.

Traditional Palmyra Restaurant (☎ 910 878; set meals S£250) This small place serves what is probably the best food in town, but you shouldn't expect a gourmet experience. Set meals of decent *mensaf* (lamb on a bed of rice), *kawaj* (meat or vegetables roasted in a terracotta pot) or stuffed vegetables are served with bread and tea. The atmosphere is friendly and the place has a nice feel overall, though it's pricey for what it offers. There are delicious sweet and savoury pancakes (S£100 to S£150) on the menu if you don't want the full set meal. A glass of beer costs S£75.

Venus Restaurant (☎ 913 864; 🔀) Near the Traditional Palmyra, this place has an almost identical menu. We're not sure whether this type of imitation constitutes a sincere form of flattery or a blatant infringement of commercial rights, but we did note that that its prices were considerably cheaper. The kitchen could do with a good scrub.

Spring Restaurant (☎ 910 307) The Spring has a ground-floor dining area and a dusty Bedouin tent on the roof where you can enjoy a meal and nargileh (S£75) in summer. The set *mensaf* meal is S£250, mezze range from S£25 to S£50 and grills are S£150. Students get a 20% discount.

The Ishtar Hotel's basement restaurant serves a good-value set menu of mezze, soup, *mensaf* and dessert for S£200. The Hotel Villa Palmyra serves good mezze (S£25) and has great views, but the grills (S£150) are disappointing. The similarly priced food at the Hotel Heliopolis is slightly better.

Locals can be found gossiping over cheap tea or playing cards at Cave Cafeteria near Saahat al-Jumhuriyya. Women won't feel comfortable here.

The Zenobia Hotel has an outdoor terrace overlooking the ruins, where you can relax over a pricey tea (S£50) or local beer (S£125).

GETTING THERE & AWAY

Palmyra doesn't have a bus station.

Karnak buses leave from outside its office on the main square, opposite the museum. Karnak runs one bus per day to Damascus (S£110, three hours), leaving at 12.30pm, for which you'll need to reserve a seat in advance. Make sure you get an allocated seat number. There are two services per day to Deir ez-Zur (S£80, two hours) at 3pm and 5.30pm, and two to Homs (S£75, two hours) at 7.30am and 2.30pm.

Al-Kadmous buses stop at the Sahara Café on the edge of town (2km from the museum; a taxi should cost S£25). The ticket office is in front of the café. Buses to Damascus (S£115) leave hourly from 6am to 7pm, at 9.30pm and hourly from 12.30am to 6am. Buses to Deir ez-Zur (S£85, two hours) leave hourly from 8am to 8pm. Homs (S£75) services leave at 10am, 2.30pm, 7.30pm and 2.30am.

Seven **private bus companies** (☎ 913 435) provide 24-hour services to Damascus (S£110) and Deir ez-Zur (S£90), leaving every 15 minutes from outside Restaurant Palace Palmyra on Sharia Al-Omair, northeast of the museum.

THE PROBLEM WITH PALMYRA

Palmyra's economy is largely dependent on tourism, and many locals support large extended families with the income they earn from operating the town's hotels, restaurants and shops. Since tourist numbers plummeted after September 2001, these businesses have hit hard times and competition between them has become fierce – and sometimes nasty – as a result. For example, the operators of the Spring and Venus Restaurants are envious of the success of the town's most popular tourist restaurant, the Traditional Palmyra, and regale travellers who will listen to them with rants about the competition. If they start sounding off to you, tell them you're not interested.

Competition is no less heated in the hotel scene, with the major object of disaffection being Al-Faris Hotel, located more than a kilometre outside town. If you're arriving in town by bus, you may be dropped here rather than at the official bus stop in town, but you shouldn't get off the bus here unless you want to.

Those travellers who make it past Al-Faris and into town will no doubt encounter another competition-fuelled annoyance, the hotel touts. These guys (often kids) will try to take you to one of the hotels in town paying commission. Be aware that if you turn up at a hotel with one of them an extra 10% to 20% will be added to the quoted cost of a bed or room to cover his commission. And beware of the old 'That hotel is full/dirty/closed/a brothel' spiel about somewhere that you've already booked; the truth is that these touts will say anything to steer you towards a commission-paying place.

Microbuses (S£65) and minibus service taxis (S£50) travel to Homs between 6am and sunset. They leave from outside the Osman Mosque.

Travellers find that taxis and microbuses usually charge US$100 to drive to Aleppo via As-Sukhna (Qasr al-Heir ash Sharqi), Rasafa and Qala'at Je'eber. You may be able to bargain this price down.

SYRIA DIRECTORY

ACCOMMODATION

Though there are no youth hostels in Syria, there are many excellent budget hotels. Mid-range hotels abound in the capital and at least one excellent example can be found in every major tourist hot spot. When it comes to the top end, the choices aren't as extensive. Indeed, four-star hotels are rare, with the only outstanding example being the Omayad Hotel in Damascus. The five-star scene has been dominated for many years by the lack-lustre government-run Cham chain, but this is poised to change with the opening of the Four Seasons in Damascus, the Semiramis Palmyra Palace and the Sheraton in Aleppo.

Prices cited are for rooms in the high season and include taxes. We have defined budget hotels as any that charge up to US$20 for a double room; midrange as any that charge from US$20 to US$80; and top end as those that charge US$80 plus for a room. In the low season (December to March) you should be able to get significant discounts at all hotels, including those at the top end. Conversely, during July and August it can be extremely difficult to get a room in Damascus, Hama or Lattakia as these towns are flooded with Gulf Arabs fleeing the summer heat of their countries.

Hotels rated two-star and up generally require payment in US dollars. They are increasingly accepting credit-card payments (often with a surcharge) but you shouldn't take this for granted.

BUSINESS HOURS

The following is a guide only. The official weekend is Friday and Saturday. Most museums and sites are closed on Tuesday.

Banks Generally follow the government office hours but there are quite a few exceptions to the rule. Some branches keep their doors open for only three hours

PRACTICALITIES

- As well as the three state-run Arabic daily newspapers, there is one English-language daily, the *Syria Times* (S£5). This is published under direct government control and is predictably big on anti-Zionist, pro-Arab rhetoric and short on news.

- You can pick up the BBC World Service on a range of radio frequencies, including AM 1323 in Damascus and the Europe short-wave schedule in Aleppo. See www.bbc.co.uk/worldservice for details.

- Satellite dishes are becoming common in Syria, and international English-language news services such as CNN and BBC World can be accessed in hotel rooms throughout the country.

- The country's electrical current is 220V AC, 50Hz. Wall sockets are the round, two pin European type.

- Syria uses the metric system for weights and measures.

from 9am, while some exchange booths are open as late as 7pm.

Government offices 8am to 2pm daily except Friday and holidays. Post offices are open later in the large cities and are often open on Fridays.

Private offices 10am to 2pm, and 4pm to 9pm except Friday and holidays.

Restaurants Between noon and midnight daily. Cafés tend to open earlier and close a bit later.

Shops 9am to 1.30pm and 4pm to 9pm summer; 9am to 1.30pm and 4pm to 8pm winter. Often closed on Fridays and holidays.

CHILDREN

Although Syrians are extraordinarily welcoming to children, Syria's hotels have few child-friendly facilities, and hardly any towns have easily accessible public gardens with playground equipment or shopping malls with amusement centres. This can mean that travelling with children is a bit challenging. Fortunately, restaurants are extremely welcoming to families.

Formula is readily available in pharmacies, and disposable nappies are stocked in supermarkets. Restaurants usually have highchairs. Babysitting facilities are sometimes available in top end hotels.

COURSES

If you're a would-be student of the Arabic language, there are a number of options in Damascus:

Amideast (☎ 333 2804; www.amideast.org/offices/syria; Sharia Wahab Bin Saad, Roummaneh) Offers courses (S£6000 for 40 hours) in colloquial Syrian Arabic at three levels. Small classes with a good reputation.

British Council (☎ 331 0631; www.britishcouncil.org/syria; Sharia Karim al-Khalil) Offers courses in modern standard or colloquial Syrian Arabic at three levels. The regular course comprises 28 hours of classes over seven weeks and runs between September and June. It costs S£9000. There is also an intensive course over 48 hours in July/August that costs S£20,000. You'll find it off Sharia Maysaloun.

DISCOUNT CARDS

Students get massive discounts on site admissions on presentation of an internationally recognised card such as the ISIC.

EMBASSIES & CONSULATES
Syrian Embassies & Consulates

There is no Syrian representation in New Zealand, and citizens are advised to contact the embassy or one of the Syrian honorary consulates in Australia. For the addresses of Syrian embassies and consulates in the Middle East, see the relevant chapter.

Australia Canberra (☎ 02-6286 5235; www.syrianembassyaustralia.org; 41 Culgoa Circuit, O'Malley, ACT 2606); Melbourne (☎ 03-9347 8445; fax 03-9347 8447; 57 Cardigan St, Carlton, Victoria 3053); Sydney (☎ 02-9597 7714; fax 03-9597 2226; 10 Belmore St, Arncliffe, NSW 2205)

Canada (☎ 613-569 5556; fax 613-569 3800; Suite 3114, 433 Laurier Ave, Ottawa, Ontario)

France (☎ 01 40 62 61 00; 20 Rue Vaneau, 75007 Paris)

Germany Berlin (☎ 030-220 2046; www.syrianembassy.de; Otto Grotewohl Str 3, Berlin); Bonn (☎ 228-819 9220; Andreas Hermes Str 5, D-53175 Bonn); Hamburg (☎ 40-3090 5414; fax 40-3090 5233; Brooktor 11, 20457 Hamburg)

Japan (☎ 358 68977; Akasaka Minato-ku, Tokyo 107)

Netherlands (☎ 070-346 9795; Laan van Meerdervoort 53d, The Hague)

Spain (☎ 239 4619; Plaza Platerias Martinez, Madrid)

UK (☎ 020-7245 9012; http://syria.embassyhomepage.com/syrian_embassy_london_unitedkingdom.htm; 8 Belgrave Sq, London SW1 8PH)

USA New York (☎ 212-661 1313; 820 Second Ave, New York NY 10017); Washington, DC (☎ 202-232 6313;

www.syrianembassy.us; 2215 Wyoming Ave NW, Washington, DC, 20008)

Embassies & Consulates in Syria

Most embassies and consulates are open from around 8am to 2pm and are closed on Friday, Saturday and public holidays. The following are in Damascus. Note: the Canadian embassy currently provides emergency consular services to Australians; Irish interests are looked after by the UK embassy.

Canada (☎ 011-611 669; www.dfait-maeci.gc.ca/syria; Block 12 Autostrad al-Mezze) About 4km west of city centre.

Egypt (Map pp512-13; ☎ 011-333 3561; fax 011-333 7961; Sharia al-Jala'a, Abu Roumana)

France (☎ 011-332 7992; www.amb-damas.fr; Sharia Ata Ayyubi, Salihiyya)

Germany (☎ 011-332 3800/1; Sharia Abdulmunem Al-Riad, Malki)

Iran (☎ 011-222 6459; fax 011-222 0997; Autostrad al-Mezzeh) About 4km west of the city centre.

Italy (☎ 011-333 2621, 011-333 8338; Sharia al-Ayubl)

Japan (☎ 011-333 8273; Sharia Shark Asiya al-Jala, Abu Roumana)

Jordan (Map pp512-13; ☎ 011-333 4642; jordan@visto.com; Sharia al-Jala'a, Abu Roumana)

Netherlands (☎ 011-333 6871, 011-333 7661; fax 011-333 9369; Sharia al-Jala'a, Abu Roumana)

Spain (☎ 011-613 2900/1; embespsy@mail.mae.es; Sharia Shafi, east Mezze) Behind Hotel Al-Hayat.

Turkey (☎ 011-333 1411; dakkabe@citechco.net; 58 Sharia Ziad bin Abi Soufian, Al Rawda)

UK (☎ 011-373 9241/2/3/7; Kotob Bldg, 11 Sharia Mohammed Kurd Ali, Malki)

USA (☎ 011-333 1342, 011-333 2814; http://damascus.usembassy.gov; 2 Sharia al-Mansour, Abu Roumana)

FESTIVALS & EVENTS

Visit the Syrian Ministry of Tourism website (www.syriatourism.org) for festival details.

Bosra Festival This festival of music and theatre is held every September or October in odd years. It offers the chance to be part of an audience in the town's spectacular Roman amphitheatre. Tickets cost from S£25.

Silk Road Festival Held annually in the cities where the ancient caravans once met: Palmyra, Aleppo, Bosra, Tartus, Damascus and Lattakia. A varied programme features overseas acts, concerts, sporting events and dance performances.

GAY & LESBIAN TRAVELLERS

Homosexuality is prohibited in Syria and conviction can result in imprisonment.

Cleopatra's Wedding Present, by Robert Tewdwr Moss, is an entertaining account of a gay American's travels through Syria.

HOLIDAYS
In addition to the main Islamic holidays (p647), Syria celebrates the following public holidays:

New Year's Day 1 January
Revolution Day 8 March
Al-Adha Day 15 March
Mother's Day 21 March
Easter March/April
Hijra New Year's Day 6 April
National Day 17 April
May Day 1 May
Martyrs' Day 6 May
Liberation War of October Day 6 October
Christmas Day 25 December

MONEY
The official currency is the Syrian pound (S£), also called the lira. There are 100 piastres (*qirsh*) to a pound but this is redundant as the smallest coin is one pound. Other coins come in denominations of two, five, 10 and 25. Notes come in denominations of five, 10, 25, 50, 100, 200, 500 and 1000.

Country	Unit	Syrian pound (S£)
Australia	A$1	38.06
Canada	C$1	44.27
Egypt	E£1	9.00
euro zone	€1	61.30
Japan	¥100	44.81
Jordan	JD1	72.75
Lebanon	LL10	0.35
New Zealand	NZ$1	35.87
Turkey	YTL1	38.14
UK	UK£1	90.57
USA	US$1	52.91

ATMs
There is a growing number of ATMs in Syria, particularly in Damascus, but there are still a number of towns (eg Palmyra, Hama, Homs, Bosra) that are yet to have machines. Some of the ATM machines that are on the ground give advances on Visa and MasterCard, but are not Cirrus or Maestro enabled.

Banks
The Syrian banking system was opened to private banks in 2004. New, mainly Lebanese, players such as the Banks of Syria & Overseas (BSO) and the International Bank for Trade & Finance (IBTF) are starting to provide much-needed retail services and create competition for the state-owned Commercial Bank of Syria (CBS).

Credit Cards
Major credit cards are increasingly being accepted by travel agencies, hotels and shops, but they're not yet accepted in most restaurants. This situation will change as soon as Visa and MasterCard are given permission to set up shop in Syria; at present all transactions must be processed through Jordan, and a surcharge of around 10% is invariably levied on the customer to cover this.

The contact number for Amex in Syria is ☎ 011-221 7813; for Visa, MasterCard and Diner's Club it's ☎ 011-222 1326.

Moneychangers
There's at least one branch of the Commercial Bank of Syria in every major town and most of them will change US dollars or euros. There are also a small number of officially sanctioned private exchange offices. These change cash at official bank rates, and generally don't charge any commission. The other advantage is that whereas banks usually close for the day at 12.30pm or 2pm, the exchange offices are often open until 7pm.

Tipping & Bargaining
Tipping is expected in the better restaurants and by all tour guides. Whatever you buy, remember that bargaining is an integral part of the process and listed prices are always inflated to allow for it. If you are shopping in the souqs, bargain hard – even a minimum amount of effort will almost always result in outrageous asking prices being halved.

Travellers Cheques
It is becoming increasingly difficult to cash travellers cheques in Syria. If you do find a bank that will change your cheques, you must have the bank receipt with the cheque numbers detailed on it. Exchange offices never change them.

POST
The Syrian postal service is slow but trustworthy. Letters mailed from the main cities take about a week to Europe and anything up to a month to Australia or the USA. Stamps for postcards to the UK, Europe, Australia and the USA cost S£18.

TELEPHONE

The country code for Syria is ☎ 963, followed by the local area code (minus the zero), then the subscriber number. The international access code (to call abroad from Syria) is ☎ 00. The numbers for directory assistance are ☎ 141 142 (national calls) and ☎ 143 144 (international calls).

There are two major phone companies in Syria: Syriatel and Spacetel (aka 94).

The easiest way to make calls is probably to purchase an Easycomm phonecard; alternatively you can call from card phones inside or just outside the local telephone office. Buy the necessary card either from a booth within the office or from a vendor who'll be hovering around the phones. The cards will only work at that particular phone office.

Syrian phone charges:

Australia and Asia Per minute S£90 (S£50 per minute from 2pm to 7pm).

Europe Per minute S£75 (S£40 per minute from 10pm to 3am).

Lebanon Per minute S£17.

Middle East Per minute S£35 (S£25 per minute from 9pm to 2am).

USA Per minute S£90 (S£50 per minute from 10pm to 3am).

Within Syria Per minute 300 piastres (average).

Mobile Phones

You can purchase a Syriatel 'Ya Hala' SIM card to use in your mobile phone while you're in the country. These cost S£1000, are valid for 30 days and can be recharged in S£400 units. Spacetel offers a similar card, the 'ANA'. Both cards are available at mobile-phone shops throughout the country (these are ubiquitous) and at the arrivals hall at Damascus International Airport.

Phonecards

Easycomm cards are available from mobile-phone shops and you will find Easycomm phones in most cities. You'll need a S£200 card to make calls within Syria (S£20 per minute), a S£350 card to phone Europe (S£100 per minute), a S£500 card to phone the rest of the world except the USA (S£100 per minute) and a S£1000 to call the USA (S£125 per minute).

VISAS

Most travellers must have a visa to enter Syria; the only exceptions are citizens of Arab countries. Obtain a visa before arriv-

ing at the border, preferably in your home country, well before your trip. Avoid applying in a country that's not your own or that you don't hold residency for as the Syrian authorities don't like this. At best they'll ask you for a letter of recommendation from your own embassy (often an expensive and time-consuming proposition); at worst, they'll turn you down flat. US citizens should be aware that many US embassies abroad have a policy of not issuing letters of recommendation – leading to the ridiculous situation where they issue letters stating that they don't issue letters of recommendation. If your home country doesn't have a Syrian embassy or consulate, there's no problem with you applying in another country; alternatively you can obtain a visa on arrival.

Officially, the Syrian embassy in Amman issues visas only to nationals and residents of Jordan and to nationals of countries that have no Syrian representation. So, if you are from a country such as the UK, the USA or France, all of which have a Syrian embassy, you will not be able to get a Syrian visa in Jordan. That said, we have received recent reports that citizens without Jordanian residence were obtaining single-entry Syrian visas in Amman for JD82.50.

In Turkey, you can get Syrian visas in both Ankara and İstanbul, but you'll need a letter of recommendation from your embassy. There is no Syrian embassy in Lebanon.

There are three types of visa: transit, single entry and multiple entry. Transit visas are only good for airport stays, so most travellers will need a single- or multiple-entry visa. Both are valid only for 15 days inside Syria and must be used within three months of the date of issue. Don't be misled by the line on the visa stating a validity of three months – this simply means the visa is valid *for presentation* for three months. You'll usually require two photographs and have to fill out two forms.

The cost of visas varies according to the reciprocal agreement Syria has made with your home country. For example, UK citizens pay UK£32 for a single-entry visa, US citizens US$100 and Australian citizens A$41. If you book travel arrangements through a foreign tour operator that has a working relationship with a Syrian operator, you are entitled to a free visa, collectable at the point of entry.

TRAVEL FROM ISRAEL TO SYRIA

The rule is crystal clear: if border officials see that you have an Israeli visa or stamp in your passport, or if a scan of recent stamps suggests that you have recently travelled through Israel and the Palestinian Territories, you will be refused entry to Syria (p353). However, slight changes are afoot. In a recent meeting with Dr Saadalla Agha Al Kalaa, Syria's minister for tourism, Lonely Planet was told that tour groups of eight people or more who are making their way overland from Israel to Jordan and Syria will be allowed to enter the country. Great news. Let's hope that the new rule is extended to independent travellers in the near future.

Visas at the Border

If there is no Syrian representation in your country, you can obtain a visa on arrival at borders, airports or ports. Otherwise you MUST secure a visa in advance. The only official exception is for travellers entering Syria from Lebanon; if you have a valid Lebanese visa, a Syrian visa will be issued without problem on the border – for a charge (p459). This rule also applies to holders of single-entry visas who cross over from Syria to Lebanon and then return to Syria.

Visa Extensions

If you're staying in Syria for more than 15 days you'll have to get a visa extension while in the country. This is done at an immigration office, which you'll find in all main cities. The length of the extension appears to depend on a combination of what you're willing to ask for and the reason you cite for wanting the extension, eg travel or work. They are usually only granted on the 14th or 15th day of your stay, so if you apply earlier expect to be knocked back. The specifics vary from place to place but there are always a couple of forms to complete and you need two to six passport photos. The cost is never more than US$1. For addresses and further details see the individual city sections.

WOMEN TRAVELLERS

Syria is an extraordinarily safe country in which to travel, and foreign women are generally treated with courtesy and respect.

Even so, there will still always be a certain amount of unwanted predatory male attention, particularly in Palmyra and in the area around Sharia Baron in Aleppo. To minimise the chance of any unpleasant encounters follow the advice given on clothing and behaviour on p654 and try to sit next to women on public transport.

TRANSPORT IN SYRIA

GETTING THERE & AWAY
Entering the Country

For information on Syrian visas and entry requirements, see opposite.

Air

Syria's main **international airport** (☎ 544 5983-9) is just outside Damascus and has regular connections to other cities in the Middle East, Europe, Africa and Asia on a variety of European- and Middle East–based airlines. There are other international airports at **Aleppo** (flights ☎ 421 1200, reservations ☎ 421 6900) and Lattakia, but other than one weekly Syrianair flight to Cairo from each of these, they are most frequently used for charters and domestic flights.

Syrian Arab Airlines (Syrianair; www.syriaair.com) is the national airline. It has a small fleet, which includes some recently purchased Airbuses. From Damascus, Syrianair flies to destinations including Cairo (US$158 one way) and İstanbul (US$194 one way).

Land

Syria has borders with Lebanon, Turkey, Jordan and Iraq. It also shares a border with Israel, the hotly disputed Golan Heights, but it's a definite no-go zone that's mined and is patrolled by UN peacekeepers.

IRAQ

The only open border crossing with Iraq is just south of Abu Kamal in the extreme east of the country. See p269 for details.

DEPARTURE TAX

There's an airport departure tax of S£200 payable in local currency at booths next to airport check-in counters. There's no departure tax if you leave by land.

SYRIA

JORDAN

There are two border crossings between Syria and Jordan: at Nasib/Jabir and Deraa/Ramtha. These crossings are 3km apart. If crossing by car, service taxi or bus you'll cross through the main Nasib/Jabir post, on the Amman–Damascus highway. If you're travelling by train or by local transport, you'll use Deraa/Ramtha. Microbuses from the bus station at Deraa charge S£150 per person to take you across the border to Ramtha. The best way to get to Deraa from Damascus is to catch a bus from Baramke garage.

From Damascus there are a couple of daily buses to Amman (p521), for which you need to book in advance as demand for seats is high, or you can catch a service taxi. The famous Hijaz railway trip (p522) is also a possibility.

Jordanian visas are issued at the border (p403), or can be obtained in advance from the embassy in Damascus. It's cheaper to get it at the border.

LEBANON

There are plenty of buses from Damascus to Beirut, although to travel direct to Baalbek the only option is a service taxi (see p522 for details). You can also travel by bus or service taxi to Beirut via Tripoli from Aleppo and Lattakia (p543 and p526).

See p458 for information on obtaining Lebanese visas on the border.

TURKEY

There are several border crossings between Syria and Turkey. The busiest and most convenient links Antakya in Turkey with Aleppo, via the Bab al-Hawa border station. This is the route taken by all cross-border buses including those from Damascus, Lattakia and Aleppo bound for Antakya and onward Turkish destinations. See p521, p526 and p543 for details.

An interesting alternative to the bus might be the weekly train from Aleppo to İstanbul (p543).

You can also make your way by microbus from Lattakia, on the Syrian coast, to the border post on the outskirts of the village of Kassab and on to Antakya via Yayladağı. Over in the far northeast of Syria there's another crossing at Qamishle for the southeastern Turkish town of Nusaybin.

While Turkish visas are issued at the border (p633), you must already be in possession of a valid visa to enter Syria – unless you hold a passport of a country without Syrian representation, in which case you can get your visa at the border (p552).

GETTING AROUND
Air

Syrianair has a monopoly on domestic flights in the country, and operates flights from Damascus to Aleppo, Deir ez-Zur, Lattakia and Qamishle. Under-26s can usually get discounted tickets.

Bus

Syria has a well-developed road network, and bus transport is frequent and cheap. Distances are short, so journeys rarely take more than a few hours. Carry your passport at all times as you may need it for ID checks; you'll definitely need it to buy tickets.

Several kinds of buses ply the same routes, but the most safe and comfortable way to travel is by 'luxury' Pullman bus.

KARNAK & OTHER BUSES

At the time of research the future of Karnak was under a cloud, as the state-owned bus line has been losing money ever since the national bus system was opened to private competition. A government review was looking into whether it should be closed down or not, and the feeling on the street was that it was unlikely to be around in 2006. If it is propped up, the government will need to spend a lot of money upgrading its buses, because at the moment they're very old and none too clean. Fares are usually about a third cheaper than those charged by the luxury buses but given that, you're talking a difference perhaps of less than a dollar...

There's also a third, even cheaper category of buses. These are really old rust buckets on wheels, and buying a ticket is akin to a gamble on whether the vehicle's going to make it or not. Needless to say, this is the cheapest way of covering long distances between towns. These vehicles have their own garages separate from those of the luxury buses. We suggest you steer clear.

MINIBUS & MICROBUS

Minibuses operate on many of the shorter routes, eg Hama–Homs, Tartus–Lattakia and Homs–Lattakia. They take about 20 people, are often luridly decorated and have no schedule, departing only when full. This means that on less popular routes you may have to wait quite some time until one fills up. Journey times are generally longer than with the other buses, as they set people down and pick them up at any and all points along the route – hence their common name of 'hob-hob' (stop-stop).

The term microbus is blurred, but in general refers to the little white vans (mostly Japanese) with a sliding door. These are used principally to connect the major cities and towns with surrounding small towns and villages. They are replacing the lumbering old minibuses with which they compete, and are faster and slightly more expensive. They follow set routes but along that route passengers can be picked up or set down anywhere. The fare is the same whatever distance you travel.

PULLMAN BUS

The state-owned bus company Karnak once had a monopoly on the road, but since the early 1990s it's been overtaken by private companies operating excellent services. Routes are few and operators are in fierce competition for passengers. Every city bus station (known locally as 'karajats', or garages) has a row of prefab huts serving as booking offices for the various companies. There's no central information source for departure times or prices so it's a case of walking around and finding out which company has the next bus to your destination. Fares vary little and buses are pretty much the same (large, newish, air-con). Seats are assigned at booking. A rigid no-smoking rule is imposed on most buses, and during the journey a steward will distribute cups of water. A few companies do have the edge when it comes to the cleanliness and roadworthiness of their vehicles; we particularly recommend travelling with Al-Kadmous (sometimes signed 'KT') and Al-Ahliah.

Car & Motorcycle

You'll need an International Driving Permit (IDP) if you decide to drive in Syria. Traffic runs on the right-hand side of the road. The speed limit is 60 km/h in built-up areas, 70km/h on the open road and 110km/h on major highways. The roads are generally quite reasonable, but when heading off into the backblocks you will find that most signposting is in Arabic only.

Europcar (☎ 011-212 0624/5; europcar@net.sy) has been joined by **Hertz** (☎ 011-221 6615; fax 011-222 6181) and a number of other international firms, including a gaggle of sometimes dodgy local companies. With the latter, keep your eye on insurance arrangements, which seem quite lackadaisical. Hertz's cheapest standard rate is US$49/309 per day/week for a Renault Clio, including all insurance and unlimited mileage. Europcar is more expensive, starting at US$62/412 per day/week for a Peugeot 106 (plus insurance). The local companies can be cheaper. Most of the firms have desks at the airport, and offices on or around the Cham Palace Hotel on Sharia Maysaloun in central Damascus. You'll need an IDP and a deposit of US$1000 (cash or major credit card); the minimum hire is usually three days.

Local Transport

Service taxis (shared taxis; ser-vees) only operate on the major routes and can cost three times the microbus fare – sometimes more.

Tours

Tours of some of the country's highlights can be organised in Damascus (p515), Hama (p532) and Aleppo (p540), among other places.

Train

The Syrian railway system was neglected for many decades, but is improving due to recent government investment, including the purchase of new French-made locomotives. That said, buses are still usually the better option for getting around the country. The only exception to this rule is the Lattakia–Aleppo service; this goes through spectacular countryside, starts and terminates in centrally located stations and is very comfortable.

First class is air-con with aircraft-type seats; 2nd class is the same without air-con. Student discounts are only given on 2nd-class tickets.

The main line connects Damascus, Aleppo, Deir ez-Zur, Hassake and Qamishle. A secondary line runs from Aleppo to Lattakia, along the coast to Tartus and again inland to Homs and Damascus.

Turkey

East or West? It's a never-ending debate. Turkey has one foot in Europe and one foot in Asia. It was the first Muslim former-Ottoman land to establish a republic and achieve democracy, and the first to look Westward, to Europe and North America, for cultural models. This probably explains why it has so many contradictions – secular, but Muslim; conservative, but innovative; epicurean, but austere; traditional, but modernising; open to the world, but staunchly patriotic. The wonder is that, rather than clashing, these disparate forces exert a fascinating appeal.

There's so much for travellers to bite into here: sun-drenched coastal resorts, eye-popping scenery, more classical ruins than Greece or Italy, vibrant nightlife, plus plush hotels, atmospheric pensions and excellent restaurants – all affordably priced. And, if you're a sweet tooth, you've reached paradise.

With its diverse landscapes, Turkey should also suit those seeking outdoor pursuits. Pant up Mt Ararat, Turkey's highest mountain; if you dare, paraglide over a turquoise lagoon; cruise on a wooden yacht along the southern coast; hike amid 'fairy chimneys'; sea-kayak over a sunken city; and take in a flight in a hot-air balloon over Cappadocia (Kapadokya). Then recharge your batteries in a steamy *hamam* (bathhouse) – the perfect antidote to a long, active day.

Once you've had your fill of the sybaritic delights of the western and southern coasts, head for central and eastern Anatolia. Here you'll feel a 'last frontier' atmosphere and a mounting sense of exoticism and adventure.

Perhaps the deepest impression is made by the Turks themselves. They are fabulously hospitable, and what will probably linger longest in the memory of most travellers is a warm-hearted *hoş geldiniz* (welcome).

And remember: you'll never go wrong in a country that has the best baklava in the world.

FAST FACTS

- **Area** 779,452 sq km
- **Capital** Ankara
- **Country code** ☎ 90
- **Language** Turkish
- **Money** New Turkish Lira (YTL); US$1 = YTL1.36; €1 = YTL1.60
- **Official name** Türkiye Cumhuriyeti (Turkish Republic)
- **Population** 68 million

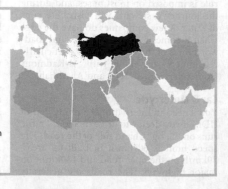

HIGHLIGHTS

- **Old İstanbul** (p566) Whether you want to haggle like a pro in the Grand Bazaar or behold architectural treasures, you'll leave Turkey's pulsating metropolis with everlasting memories.
- **Mt Nemrut** (p626) The 'thrones of the gods' offer awesome views over the Taurus range at sunset or sunrise.
- **Göreme Open-Air Museum** (p611) One of Turkey's World Heritage sites, this cluster of rock-hewn churches and dwellings is set amidst lunar landscapes.
- **Blue cruise** (p597) Those wanting to experience an idyllic sailing excursion should take in a four-day cruise from Fethiye to Olympos.
- **Anı** (p620) Give the well-trodden path a miss and soak up the former glory of this ancient Armenian capital located at the Armenian border.

CLIMATE & WHEN TO GO

The Aegean and Mediterranean coasts have mild, rainy winters and hot, dry summers. The Anatolian plateau can be boiling hot (although less humid than the coast) in summer and freezing in winter. The Black Sea coast is mild and wet in summer, chilly and wet in winter. Mountainous eastern Turkey is icy cold and snowy in winter, and only pleasantly warm in high summer.

Spring (late April to May) and autumn (late September to October) are the best times to visit; the weather is warm and dry, and there are few tourists. In the high season (July to mid-September) it can be suffocatingly hot and clammy, and major tourist destinations are crowded and overpriced.

Also see Climate Charts p643.

HISTORY
Early Anatolian Civilisations

The greatest of the early civilisations of Anatolia (Asian Turkey) was that of the Hittites, a force to be reckoned with from 2000 to 1200 BC. Their capital was at Hattuşus, north of Ankara.

After the collapse of the Hittite empire, Anatolia splintered into several small states and it wasn't until the Graeco-Roman period that parts of the country were reunited. Later, Christianity spread through Anatolia, carried by the apostle Paul, a native of Tarsus (near Adana).

> **HOW MUCH?**
> - **Cup of tea in a carpet shop** free
> - **Bus fare from İstanbul to Ankara** €15
> - **Airfare from İstanbul to Van** €80
> - **Smoking a nargileh** €3
> - **Entry to ancient sites** €1.25 to €10
>
> **LONELY PLANET INDEX**
> - **Litre of petrol** €1.40
> - **1.5L of bottled water** €0.30
> - **Bottle of Efes beer** €1
> - **Souvenir T-shirt** €4
> - **Simit** €0.20

Rome, then Byzantium

In AD 330 the Roman emperor Constantine founded a new imperial city at Byzantium (İstanbul). Renamed Constantinople, this strategic city became the capital of the Eastern Roman Empire and was the centre of the Byzantine Empire for 1000 years. During the European Dark Ages, the Byzantine Empire kept alive the flame of Western culture, although it was occasionally threatened by the powerful empires to the east (Persians, Arabs, Turks) and west (the Christian powers of Europe).

The Coming of the Turks – Seljuks & Ottomans

The beginning of the Byzantine Empire's decline came with the arrival of the Seljuk Turks and their defeat of the Byzantine forces at Manzikert, near Lake Van, in August 1071. The Seljuks overran most of Anatolia and established a provincial capital at Konya. Their domains included modern-day Turkey, Iran and Iraq.

With significantly reduced territory, the Byzantines endeavoured to protect Constantinople and reclaim Anatolia, but the Fourth Crusade (1202–04), part of a series of crusades ostensibly formed to save eastern Christendom from the Muslims, proved disastrous for them when a combined Venetian and Crusader force took and plundered Constantinople. The Byzantines eventually regained the ravaged city in 1261.

A Mongol invasion of the late 1200s put an end to Seljuk power, but small Turkish

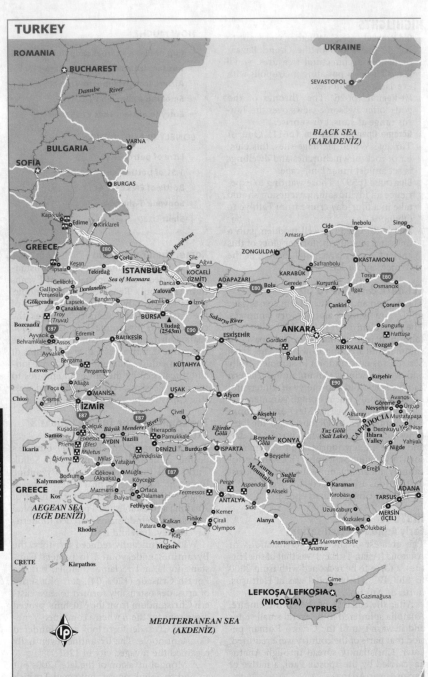

TURKEY

ROMANIA
★ BUCHAREST

UKRAINE

Danube   River

SEVASTOPOL ○

BLACK SEA
(KARADENİZ)

BULGARIA

VARNA ○

SOFIA
☆

○ BURGAS

Kapıkule
Edirne   Kırklareli

GREECE

Cide   İnebolu   Sinop
Amasra
ZONGULDAK
Safranbolu   KASTAMONU
KARABÜK
Tosya   E80
Gerede   Kurşunlu   Ilgaz   Osmancık

Keşan
Tekirdağ   Çorlu   The Bosphorus   Şile   Ağva
E80
İPSALA   Sea of Marmara   Danca   İSTANBUL   KOCAELİ
(İZMİT)   ADAPAZARI   Bolu
Gelibolu   Yalova   E80
Gallipoli   Lapseki   Gemlik   İznik
Peninsula   The Dardanelles   Bandırma
Gökçeada   Çanakkale   BURSA   Sakarya River   Çankırı   Çorum
Troy   Uludağ   ANKARA
(Truva)   (2543m)   E90   ESKİŞEHİR   Gordion   Sungurlu
Bozcaada   Edremit   BALIKESİR   KIRIKKALE   Hattuşa
Ayvacık   Behramkale   Assos   KÜTAHYA   Polatlı   Yozgat
Ayvalık   Bergama   Pergamum
Lesvos   Aliağa   KIRŞEHİR   Avanos
Foça   UŞAK   Afyon   Aksaray   Nevşehir   Ürgüp   CAPPADOCIA   Mustafapaşa
Chios   Çeşme   MANİSA   Çivril   Akşehir   Tuz Gölü   Derinkuyu   Yeşilhisar
İZMİR   (Salt Lake)   Ihlara   Niğde   Yahyalı
E87   Hierapolis   Eğirdir   Valley
Kuşadası   Selçuk   Büyük Menderes River   Nazilli   Pamukkale   Gölü   Beyşehir   KONYA
Samos   Priene   Ephesus   AYDIN   DENİZLİ   Gölü
Ikaria   Miletus   (Efes)   Aphrodisias   Burdur   ISPARTA   Ereğli
Didyma   Milas   Yatağan   Beyşehir   Suğla
Kalymnos   Bodrum   Muğla   E87   Taurus   Gölü   Karaman   ADANA
Gökova   Köyceğiz   Perge   Mountains   Kırobası   TARSUS
GREECE   (Akyaka)   Aspendos   Akseki   Uzuncaburç   MERSİN
Kos   Marmaris   Ortaca   Termessos   ANTALYA   Side   Kızkalesi   (İÇEL)
Dalyan   Dalaman   Kemer   Alanya   Silifke   Olukbaşı
AEGEAN SEA   Fethiye   Finike   Çıralı   Anamurium   Mamure Castle
(EGE DENİZİ)   Kalkan   Olympos   Anamur
Rhodes   Patara   Kaş
Megiste

CRETE   Kàrpathos

Girne
LEFKOŞA/LEFKOSIA ○
(NICOSIA)   ○ Gazimağusa
CYPRUS

MEDITERRANEAN SEA
(AKDENİZ)

LP

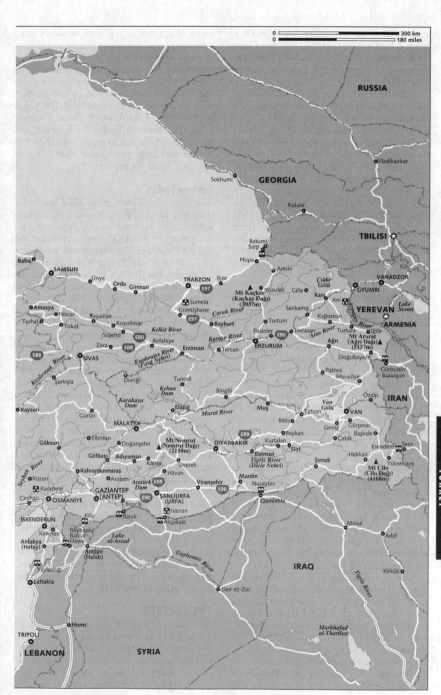

states soon arose in western Anatolia. One, headed by Osman (1258–1326), grew into the Ottoman Empire, and in 1453 Constantinople finally fell to the Ottoman sultan Mehmet the Conqueror (Mehmet Fatih).

A century later, under Süleyman the Magnificent, the Ottoman Empire reached the peak of its power, spreading deep into Europe, Asia and North Africa. Ottoman success was based on military expansion. When the march westward was stalled at Vienna in 1683, the rot set in and by the 19th century the great European powers had begun to covet the Ottomans' vast domains.

Nationalist ideas swept through Europe after the French Revolution, and in 1829 the Greeks won their independence from the Ottomans, followed by the Serbs, the Romanians and the Bulgarians. In 1913, the Ottomans lost Albania and Macedonia, the last of their European lands.

The Republic

The Turks emerged from WWI stripped of their last non-Turkish provinces: Syria, Palestine, Mesopotamia (Iraq) and Arabia. Most of Anatolia itself was to be parcelled out to the victorious Europeans, leaving the Turks virtually nothing.

At this low point, Mustafa Kemal, the father of modern Turkey, took over. Atatürk, as he was later called, made his name by repelling the Anzacs in their heroic attempt to capture Gallipoli. Rallying the tattered remnants of the Turkish army, he pushed the last of the weak Ottoman rulers aside and outmanoeuvred the Allied forces in the War of Independence, which the Turks finally won in 1923 by pushing the invading Greeks into the sea at Smyrna (İzmir). In the ensuing population exchange, over a million Greeks left Turkey and nearly half a million Turks moved in. The two countries were left with grievances that have festered for more than 80 years.

After renegotiation of the WWI treaties, a new Turkish Republic, reduced to Anatolia and part of Thrace, was born. Atatürk then embarked on a rapid modernisation programme, establishing a secular democracy, introducing the Latin script and European dress, and adopting equal rights for women – at least in theory. The capital was also moved from İstanbul to Ankara. Such sweeping changes did not come easily and

some of the battles (eg over women's head coverings) are still being fought today.

Since Atatürk's death in 1939, Turkey has experienced three military coups and considerable political turbulence. During the 1980s and '90s it was also racked by the conflict with the Kurdistan Workers Party (PKK; led by Abdullah Öcalan), which aimed to create a Kurdish state in Turkey's southeast corner. This conflict led to an estimated 36,000 deaths and huge population shifts; it also wreaked havoc on the economy.

Turkey Today

The elections of November 2002 marked a dramatic turning point in modern Turkish history. The year-old Islamic Justice & Development Party (AKP) were victorious and the AKP's leader, the charismatic ex-mayor of İstanbul, Recep Tayyip Erdoğan, became prime minister in 2003. With much determination he tackled the issues that were undermining Turkey. Inflation? Not completely curbed, but down to around 12% – almost a miracle. Growth? Up at around 5% per annum. The Armenian tragedy (the mass deportation and slaughter of hundreds of thousands of Armenians in eastern Turkey in 1915, which was consistently denied by the successive Turkish governments)? Still an impasse, but a bit less of a taboo. Kurdish separatism? Almost tamed, as the Kurdish minority have been granted greater cultural rights (the once-banned Kurdish New Year Festival of Nevruz is now a general holiday and the Turkish government started the first state broadcasts in Kurdish in 2004). And as Erdoğan strives to steer Turkey into the EU, many reforms are being brought in to meet EU criteria. There's still a long way to go, but Turkey is undeniably changing. The reward for these endeavours is that Turkey finally started on the long, obstacle-laden road to EU membership in December 2004. According to even the most optimistic experts, however, Turkey won't be granted full membership before 2020.

THE CULTURE

As a result of Atatürk's reforms, republican Turkey has largely adapted to a modern Westernised lifestyle, at least on the surface. But making sense of this country could keep visitors intrigued for months. The Turks' mentality reflects the geographical patterns of their country – one foot in Europe, one foot in Asia. This constant sway between two cultures can be really disconcerting. In İstanbul, İzmir, Antalya and coastal resorts, you'd be forgiven for thinking you're in Europe. Here, you will not feel much need to adapt in order to fit in. In smaller towns and villages, however, you may find people warier and more conservative.

The Turks have an acute sense of pride and honour. They are fiercely proud of their history and their heroes, especially Atatürk, whose portrait and statues are ubiquitous in the country. It's also a country where formality and politeness are all important. If asked 'how is Turkey?', answer 'çok güzel' (excellent).

The last trait that encompasses the national psyche is family – the extended family still plays a key role in Turkey.

SPORT

Football (soccer) is a national obsession and barely a day goes by without a match on TV. To soak up the atmosphere of the real thing, try to get a ticket for one of the three İstanbul biggies: Galatasaray, Fenerbahçe or Beşiktaş.

More-unusual sports include camel and oil wrestling. The main camel-wrestling bouts take place near Selçuk and Kuşadası from January to March, with oil wrestling near Edirne in June.

RELIGION

Turkey is 98% Muslim, overwhelmingly Sunni, with small groups of Shiites and larger groups of Alevis mainly in the east. The religious practices of Sunnis and Alevis differ markedly.

Turkey espouses a more relaxed version of Islam than many other countries in the Middle East; for instance, many men drink alcohol. But almost no-one touches pork, and many women still wear headscarves.

İstanbul still has a tiny Jewish community. There's also a small but rapidly declining community of Assyrian Orthodox Christians in the southeast.

ARTS
Literature

The most famous Turkish novelists are Yaşar Kemal, who has been nominated for the Nobel prize for literature on numerous occasions, and the journalist Orhan Pamuk.

Kemal's novels – *The Wind from the Plains*, *Salman the Solitary* and *Memed, My Hawk* among them – take traditional Turkish farming or working-class life as their subject matter. Pamuk's award-winning *Snow* was set in the remote town of Kars. Other well-known writers include Elif Şafak (*Flea Palace*) and Latife Tekin (*Tales from the Garbage Hills*).

Cinema

Several Turkish directors have won worldwide recognition, most notably the late Yılmaz Güney, whose *Yol* (The Road), *Duvar* (The Wall) and *Sürü* (The Herd) have all been released with English subtitles. Following in Güney's footsteps, Nuri Bilge Ceylan has made *Uzak* (Distant), which probes the lives of village migrants in the big city.

Music

Turkey's home-grown pop industry is one of its big success stories. After a few days in the country, you'll no doubt be familiar with the biggest stars, such as Sezen Aksu, Tarkan, Hakan Peker, Sibel Can and Mustafa Sandal. Famous Kurdish singers with a harder-hitting message include Diyar, Ferhat Tunç and Aynur Doğan.

Arabesk is another popular style of music, which has an Arabic spin. You'll probably hear or see the hugely successful Kurdish singer Ibrahim Tatlıses.

Architecture

The history of architecture in Turkey encompasses everything from Hittite stonework and grand Graeco-Roman temples to the most modern tower-blocks in İstanbul, but perhaps the most distinctively Turkish styles were those developed by the Seljuks and Ottomans. The Seljuks endowed Turkey with a legacy of magnificent mosques and *medreses* (seminaries), distinguished by their elaborate entrances. The Ottomans also left many magnificent mosques and *medreses*, as well as many more fine wood-and-stone houses.

Carpets

Turkey is famous for its beautiful carpets and kilims (woven rugs). It's thought that handwoven carpet-making techniques were introduced to Anatolia by the Seljuks in the 12th century. Traditionally, village women wove carpets for their own family's use, or for their dowry; these days, many carpets are made to the dictates of the market, but still incorporate traditional symbols and patterns.

ENVIRONMENT
The Land
The Dardanelles, the Sea of Marmara and the Bosphorus divide Turkey into Asian and European parts, but Eastern Thrace (European Turkey) makes up only 3% of the 779,452-sq-km land area. The remaining 97% is Anatolia, a vast plateau rising eastward towards the Caucasus mountains. With 7000km of coastline, snowcapped mountains, rolling steppes, vast lakes and broad rivers, Turkey is geographically very diverse.

Environmental Issues
Turkey's embryonic environmental movement is making slow progress, and you may well be shocked by the amount of discarded litter and ugly concrete buildings (or, worse still, half-finished buildings) disfiguring the west in particular.

Over the last few years the largest environmental ding-dongs have been over big dam projects. One such scheme, which would have drowned the historic town of Hasankeyf in southeastern Turkey, has thankfully been derailed, but other valleys are scheduled to vanish for the sake of a dam.

On the plus side, Turkey is slowly acquiring an interest in reclaiming its architectural heritage. Fine restoration and new buildings have gone up in Sultanahmet and in other historic places.

There's a branch of **Greenpeace Mediterranean** (Map pp564-5; ☎ 0212-292 7620; fax 292 7622; Tarlabaşı Caddesi 60) in İstanbul.

FOOD
Not without reason is Turkish food regarded as one of the world's greatest cuisines. Kebaps (kebabs) are, of course, the mainstay of restaurant meals; you'll find *lokantas* (restaurants) that sell a wide range of kebaps everywhere. Try the ubiquitous *durum döner kebap* – lamb packed on a revolving spit, sliced off and rolled up in pide bread. Laid on pide bread, topped with tomato sauce and browned butter and with yogurt on the side, döner kebap becomes *İskender kebap*, primarily a lunchtime delicacy. Equally ubiquitous are *köfte* (meatballs).

For a quick, cheap fill you could hardly do better than a Turkish pizza, a freshly cooked pide topped with cheese, egg or meat. Alternatively, *lahmacun* is a paperthin Arabic pizza topped with chopped onion, lamb and tomato sauce. One of the best snacks is *simit*, a small ring of bread decorated with sesame seeds.

Fish dishes, although excellent, are often expensive – always check the price before ordering.

For vegetarians, a meal of meze (hors d'oeuvre) can be an excellent way to ensure a varied diet. Most restaurants will be able to rustle up at least *beyaz peynir* (white sheep's-milk cheese), *sebze çorbası* (vegetable soup), börek (flaky pastry stuffed with white cheese and parsley), *kuru fasulye* (beans) and *patlıcan tava* (fried aubergine).

For dessert, try *fırın sütlaç* (baked rice pudding), *aşure* ('Noah's Ark' pudding, made from up to 40 different ingredients), baklava (honey-soaked flaky pastry stuffed with walnuts or pistachios), *kadayıf* (shredded wheat with nuts in honey) and *dondurma* (ice cream).

The famously chewy sweet called *lokum* (Turkish delight) has been made here since the 18th century; there's not a bus station in the country that doesn't sell it.

For more information on Turkish cuisine, look out for Lonely Planet's *World Food Turkey* guide. Also see p84.

DRINK
The national hot drink is *çay* (tea). It is served in tiny tulip-shaped glasses with copious quantities of sugar. If you're offered a tiny cup of traditional Turkish *kahve* (coffee), order it *sade* (no sugar), *orta* (medium sweet) or *çok şekerli* (very sweet). But these days Nescafé is fast replacing *kahve*. In tourist areas it usually comes *sütlü* (with milk).

The Turkish liquor of choice is *rakı*, a fiery aniseed drink like the Greek ouzo or Arab arak; do as the Turks do and cut it by half with water if you don't want to suffer ill effects. Turkish *şarap* (wine), both red and white, is improving in quality and is well worth the occasional splurge. You can buy Tuborg or Efes Pilsen beers everywhere, although outside the resorts you may need to find a Tekel store (the state-owned alcoholic-beverage and tobacco company) to buy wine.

Ayran is a yogurt drink, made by whipping up yogurt with water and salt. Bottled water is sold everywhere, as are all sorts of packaged fruit juices and canned soft drinks.

İSTANBUL

Asian side ☎ 0216 / **European side** ☎ 0212 / **pop 16 million**

Be prepared to run out of superlatives. İstanbul is a feast for the eyes and the senses. Some have started to dub it the 'Barcelona of the East', and no wonder. Turkey's most charismatic metropolis is bursting with energy and has an unrivalled appetite for life. There's a *movida* here, similar in many respects to that jolly mood that characterised Barcelona in the 1980s. Sure, all the monuments you could possibly dream of – lofty palaces, labyrinthine bazaars, outstanding mosques, historic *hamams* (bathhouses) – await your visit, but there's more to İstanbul than Topkapı Palace, Aya Sofya and the Blue Mosque. Sure, history is achingly prominent here but fast-modernising İstanbul is much more than an open-air museum or a heritage city. It exudes vitality and bristles with countless trendy eateries, atmosphere-laden taverns, fashionable shops, upscale discos and smart venues of all kinds. Powered by the sheer zest and vitality of its inhabitants, İstanbul is one of the most energising cities in the world.

HISTORY

Late in the 2nd century, the Roman Empire conquered the small city-state of Byzantium, which was renamed Constantinople after Emperor Constantine moved his capital there in AD 330.

The city walls kept out barbarians for centuries while the western part of the Roman Empire collapsed before invasions of Goths, Vandals and Huns. When Constantinople fell for the first time it was to the misguided Fourth Crusade in 1204.

In 1453, after a long, bitter siege, Mehmet the Conqueror marched to Aya Sofya (also known as Haghia Sofia or Sancta Sophia) and converted the church into a mosque.

As capital of the Ottoman Empire, the city experienced a new golden age. During the glittering reign of Süleyman the Magnificent (1520–66), the city was graced with many beautiful new buildings. Occupied by Allied forces after WWI, it came to be thought of as the decadent capital of the sultans, just as Atatürk's armies were shaping a new republican state.

When the Turkish Republic was proclaimed in 1923, Ankara became the new capital. Nevertheless, İstanbul remains the centre for business, finance, journalism and the arts.

ORIENTATION

The Bosphorus strait, between the Black Sea and the Sea of Marmara, divides Europe from Asia. On its western shore, European İstanbul is further divided by the Golden Horn (Haliç) into Old İstanbul in the south and Beyoğlu in the north.

The International İstanbul Bus Station is at Esenler, about 10km west of the city.

Sultanahmet is the heart of Old İstanbul and boasts many of the city's most famous sites. The adjoining area, with hotels to suit all budgets, is actually called Cankurtaran, although if you say 'Sultanahmet' most people will understand where you mean.

North of Sultanahmet, on the Golden Horn, is Sirkeci Railway Station, terminus for European train services. Ferries for Üsküdar, the Princes' Islands and the Bosphorus leave from nearby Eminönü, the bustling waterfront.

Across the Galata Bridge (Galata Köprüsü) from Eminönü is Karaköy, where cruise ships dock. Ferries also depart from Karaköy for Kadıköy and Haydarpaşa on the Asian shore.

Beyoğlu, on the northern side of the Golden Horn, was once the 'new', or 'European', city. The Tünel (an underground railway) runs uphill from Karaköy to the southern end of Beyoğlu's pedestrianised main street, İstiklal Caddesi. A tram runs all the way to Taksim Sq, at the north end of the street, and the heart of 'modern' İstanbul; it's home to many luxury hotels and airline offices.

On the Asian side, Haydarpaşa station is the terminus for trains to Anatolia, Syria and Iran. There's an intercity otogar (bus station) at Harem, a 10-minute taxi ride north.

INFORMATION
Emergency
Police (☎ 155)
Tourist police (Map pp568-9; ☎ 527 4503; Yerebatan Caddesi 6, Sultanahmet)

İSTANBUL

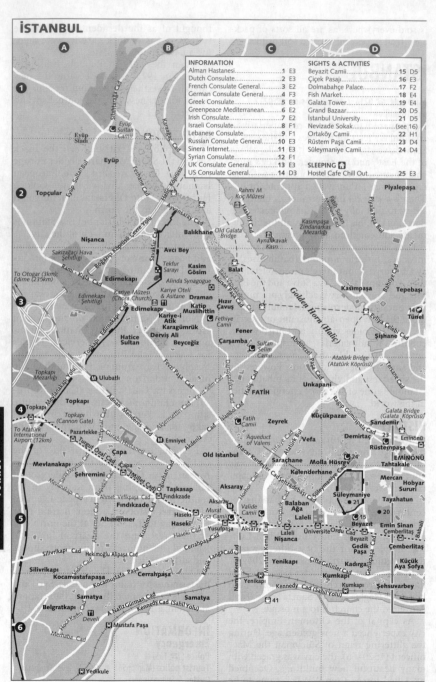

INFORMATION	
Alman Hastanesi	1 E3
Dutch Consulate	2 E3
French Consulate General	3 E2
German Consulate General	4 F3
Greek Consulate	5 E3
Greenpeace Mediterranean	6 E2
Irish Consulate	7 E2
Israeli Consulate	8 F1
Lebanese Consulate	9 F1
Russian Consulate General	10 E3
Sinera Internet	11 E3
Syrian Consulate	12 F1
UK Consulate General	13 E3
US Consulate General	14 D3

SIGHTS & ACTIVITIES	
Beyazıt Camii	15 D5
Çiçek Pasajı	16 E3
Dolmabahçe Palace	17 F2
Fish Market	18 E4
Galata Tower	19 E4
Grand Bazaar	20 D5
İstanbul University	21 D5
Nevizade Sokak	(see 16)
Ortaköy Camii	22 H1
Rüstem Paşa Camii	23 D4
Süleymaniye Camii	24 D4

SLEEPING	
Hostel Cafe Chill Out	25 E3

TURKEY

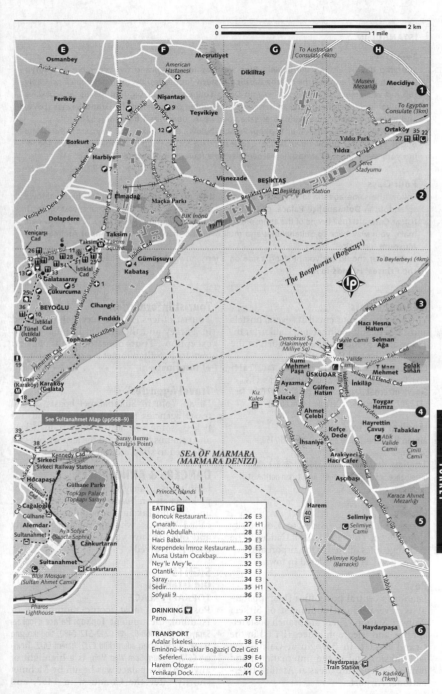

EATING 🍴
Boncuk Restaurant....................**26** E3
Çınaraltı...................................**27** H1
Hacı Abdullah...........................**28** E3
Hacı Baba.................................**29** E3
Krependeki İmroz Restaurant.....**30** E3
Musa Ustam Ocakbaşı...............**31** E3
Ney'le Mey'le...........................**32** E3
Otantik....................................**33** E3
Saray......................................**34** E3
Sedir......................................**35** H1
Sofyali 9.................................**36** E3

DRINKING 🍷
Pano.......................................**37** E3

TRANSPORT
Adalar İskelesi.........................**38** E4
Eminönü-Kavaklar Boğaziçi Özel Gezi
    Seferleri..............................**39** E4
Harem Otogar..........................**40** G5
Yenikapı Dock..........................**41** C6

TURKEY

İSTANBUL IN...

Two Days
Start the day by visiting the opulent **Blue Mosque** (opposite) and the venerable **Aya Sofya** (opposite). Next, explore the nearby **Basilica Cistern** (opposite). By this stage you'll probably run out of stamina, so make your way up Divan Yolu Caddesi to **Çiğdem** (p573) for a baklava fix. Suitably re-energised, you can delve into the jumble of streets of the **Grand Bazaar** (p570) and hone your bargaining skills. Later, take your weary bones to a **hamam** (p571).

The following day, kick off at **Topkapı Palace** (below), then make your way across the Galata Bridge to Beyoğlu. Amble down **İstiklal Caddesi** (p570) and soak up the ambience, before spending your evening in an atmosphere-laden *meyhane* (tavern) in **Nevizade Sokak** (p574).

Four Days
Follow the same agenda for days one and two, then on the third day gasp at the overblown splendour in **Dolmabahçe Palace** (p570). Follow the shore road to the east and feast on fresh fish at **Çınaraltı** (p574), one of the atmospheric waterside restaurants in Ortaköy. In the afternoon, make your way back to Sultanahmet and mull over the marvels at the **İstanbul Archaeology Museum** (opposite).

Day four should see you hitching a ride on a ferry down the mighty **Bosphorus** (p571) or to the **Princes' Islands** (p572).

Internet Access

You can check your email at several hostels and cafés in Sultanahmet and Cankurtaran. There are also lots of Internet outlets in the streets off İstiklal Caddesi.

Café Turka Internet Café (Map pp568-9; ☎ 0212-514 6551; Divan Yolu Caddesi 22/2, Sultanahmet; per hr €1.40)

Sinera Internet (Map pp564-5; ☎ 0212-292 6899; fax 517 7287; Mis Sokak 6/1, Beyoğlu; per hr €0.90)

Medical Services

Alman Hastanesi (Map pp564-5; ☎ 293 2150; Sıraselviler Caddesi 119, Taksim)

American Hastanesi (Map pp564-5; ☎ 311 2000; Güzelbahçe Sokak 20, Nişantaşı) About 2km northeast of Taksim Sq.

Money

Banks with ATMs are widespread, especially along Divan Yolu and İstiklal Caddesi. The exchange rates offered at the airport are usually as good as those offered in town.

Post

İstanbul's central post office (Map pp568-9) is several blocks southwest of Sirkeci Railway Station. There are branch post, telephone and telegraph offices (PTTs) in the Grand Bazaar, in Beyoğlu at Galatasaray and Taksim, and in the international and domestic departure areas at Atatürk International Airport.

Tourist Information

Tourist offices are not very well organised in Turkey and the ones in İstanbul are no exception. Tour operators and pension owners in Sultanahmet are the best sources of information.

Travel Agencies

Divan Yolu in Sultanahmet boasts several travel agencies that sell cheap air and bus tickets; some can also arrange train tickets and minibus transport to the airport, but you will need to shop around for the best deals.

DANGERS & ANNOYANCES

İstanbul is a fairly safe city but be wary of pickpockets on buses, in the Grand Bazaar and around Taksim Sq. Avoid following so-called 'friends' who approach you gently and offer to buy you a drink – a scam is usually involved.

SIGHTS
Old İstanbul
TOPKAPI PALACE

Possibly the most iconic monument in İstanbul, the opulent **Topkapı Palace** (Topkapı Sarayı; Map pp568-9; ☎ 0212-512 0480; Soğukçeşme Sokak, Sultanahmet; adult/child €7/2, harem €6/2, Treasury €6/2; ☒ 9am-5pm Wed-Mon) is a highlight of any trip. The palace was begun by Mehmet shortly after the Conquest in 1453, and

Ottoman sultans lived in this impressive environment until the 19th century. It consists of four massive courtyards and a series of imperial buildings, including pavilions, barracks, audience chambers and sleeping quarters. Make sure you visit the mind-blowing **harem**, the palace's most famous sight, and the **Treasury**, which features an incredible collection of precious objects.

AYA SOFYA (CHURCH OF HOLY WISDOM)
No doubt you will gasp at the overblown splendour of **Aya Sofya** (Haghia Sofia, Sancta Sophia; Map pp568-9; ☎ 0212-522 0989; Aya Sofya Meydanı, Sultanahmet; adult/child €8.50/3; ☻ 9am-4.30pm Tue-Sun), one of the world's most glorious buildings. Built as part of Emperor Justinian's (527–65) effort to restore the greatness of the Roman Empire, it was completed in AD 537 and reigned as the grandest church in Christendom until the Conquest in 1453. The exterior does impress, but the interior, with its sublime domed ceiling soaring heavenward, is truly over-the-top.

Climb up to the **gallery** to see the remaining splendid mosaics. After the Turkish Conquest and the subsequent conversion of Aya Sofya to a mosque (hence the minarets), the mosaics were covered over, as Islam prohibits images. They were not revealed until the 1930s, when Atatürk declared Aya Sofya a museum.

BLUE MOSQUE
Another striking monument in Sultanahmet, the **Blue Mosque** (Sultan Ahmet Camii; Map pp568-9; Hippodrome, Sultanahmet; donation requested; ☻ closed during prayer times), just south of Aya Sofya, is a work of art in itself. It was built between 1609 and 1619, and is light and delicate compared with its squat ancient neighbour. The graceful exterior is notable for its six slender minarets and a cascade of domes and half domes; the inside is a luminous blue, created by the tiled walls and painted dome.

HIPPODROME
In front of the Blue Mosque is the Hippodrome (Atmeydanı; Map pp568-9), where chariot races took place. It was also the scene of a series of riots during Justinian's rule. While construction started in AD 203, the Hippodrome was later added to and enlarged by Constantine.

The **Obelisk of Theodosius** (Map pp568-9) is an Egyptian column from the temple of Karnak. It features 3500-year-old hieroglyphics and rests on a Byzantine base. South of the obelisk are the remains of a **spiral column** of intertwined snakes. Erected at Delphi by the Greeks to celebrate their victory over the Persians, it was later transported to the Hippodrome, where the snakes' heads disappeared.

TURKISH & ISLAMIC ARTS MUSEUM
On the Hippodrome's western side, the **Turkish & Islamic Arts Museum** (Türk ve İslam Eserleri Müzesi; Map pp568-9; ☎ 0212-518 1805; Hippodrome 46, Sultanahmet; admission €2.50; ☻ 9.30am-5.30pm Tue-Sun) is housed in the former palace of İbrahim Paşa, grand vizier and son-in-law of Süleyman the Magnificent. The building is one of the finest surviving examples of 16th-century Ottoman secular architecture. Inside, the most spectacular exhibits are the wonderful floor-to-ceiling Turkish carpets, beautifully illuminated Qurans and the mosque fittings. Don't miss the fascinating ethnographic collection downstairs either.

BASILICA CISTERN
Across the tram lines from Aya Sofya is the entrance to the majestic **Basilica Cistern** (Yerebatan Sarnıcı; Map pp568-9; ☎ 0212-522 1259; Yerebatan Caddesi 13; admission €7; ☻ 9.30am-7.30pm Apr-Sep, 9.30am-5.30pm Oct-Mar), which was built by Constantine and enlarged by Justinian. This vast, atmospheric, column-filled cistern held water not only for regular summer use but also for times of siege.

İSTANBUL ARCHAEOLOGY MUSEUM
Down the hill from the Topkapı Palace, the **İstanbul Archaeology Museum** (Arkeoloji Müzeleri; Map pp568-9; ☎ 0212-520 7740; Osman Hamdi Bey Yokuşu; admission €3; ☻ 9.30am-5pm Tue-Sun) is a must-see for anyone interested in the Middle East's ancient past. The main building houses an outstanding collection of Greek and Roman statuary, including the magnificent sarcophagi from the royal necropolis at Sidon in Lebanon, while a separate building on the same site, the **Museum of the Ancient Orient**, houses Hittite relics and other older archaeological finds.

DIVAN YOLU CADDESI
Walk or take a tram westward along Divan Yolu from Sultanahmet, looking out on

SULTANAHMET

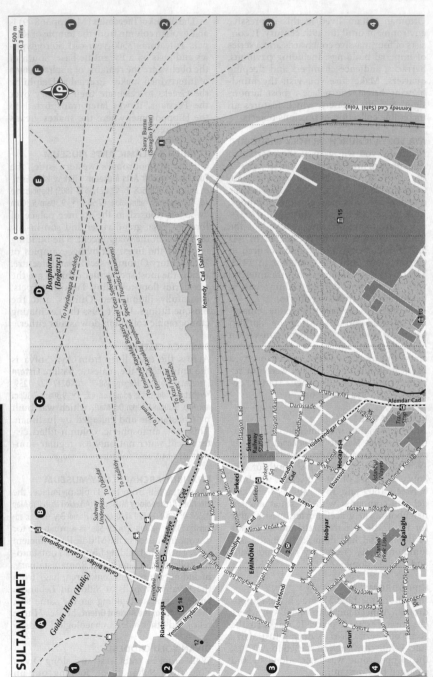

Golden Horn (Haliç)

Bosphorus (Boğazıçı)

To Havdarpaşa & Kadıköy

To Eminönü-Kavaklak Boğazıçı Özel Gezi Seferleri Bosphorus Special Touristic Excursions)

To Eminönü-Kavalak Boğazıçı (Eminönü-Kavalak)

To Kızıl Adalar (Princes Islands)

To Üsküdar

To Kadıköy

To Harem

Galata Bridge (Galata Köprüsü)

Saray Burnu (Seraglio Point)

Kennedy Cad (Sahil Yolu)

Kennedy Cad (Sahil Yolu)

Sirkeci Railway Station

Sirkeci Sq

Sirkeci

İstasyon Cad

İstasyon Arkası Sk

Darüssade

Nöbethane Cad

Taya Hatun Sk

Hüdayendigar Cad

Alemdar Cad

Tram Stop

Erdoğan Sk

İbnikemal Gonul

İstanbul Vilayet

İstanbul Konak Sk

Hükümet Konağı Sk

Ankara Cad

Ebussuut Cad

Hocapaşa

Hocapaşa Cad

Cağaloğlu

Cağaloğlu Yokuşu

Hobyar

İstanbul Erkek Lisesi

Ankara Cad

Cemal Nadir Sk

Muradiye Cad

Ankara Cad

Seyhülislam Cad

Şeftimah Pehlevi Cad

Koprücü Sk

Emirname Sk

Reşadiye Cad

Emirname Sk

Eminönü

Yalı Köşkü Cad

Mimar Kemalettin Cad

Hamidiye Cad

Mimar Vedat Sk

EMİNÖNÜ

Hurhan İslam Ticaret

Eminönü Sq

Eminönü

Arpaçılar Cad

Hocahanı Sk

Hocahanı Sk

Hocapaşa Sk

Aşirefendi Cad

Hamidiye Cad

Hamam Sk

Çifte Gelinler Sk

NebçPazar Cad

Taşçılar Çifte Cad

Çeşnici Sk

Servili

Mengene

Beziciler Sk

Tarakçı Cad

Sultan Mektebi Sk

Mederd Gökçay Sk

Bezciler Sk

Yenicami Cad

RÜSTEMPAŞA

Yenicami Meydan Sk

18

12

Subway Underpass

SURURI

Kemalpaşa

TURKEY

500 m
0.3 miles

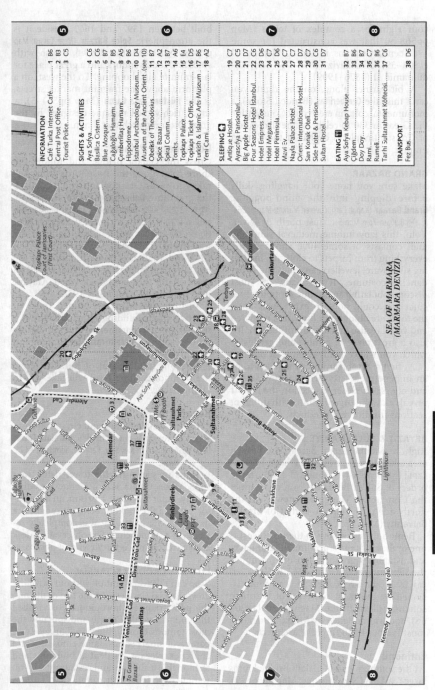

Topkapı Palace Court of Janissaries (First Court)

Cankurtaran

Cankurtaran

Kennedy Cad (Sahil Yolu)

SEA OF MARMARA (MARMARA DENİZİ)

Ishakpaşa

Yeni

Babıhümayun Cad

Soğukçeşme Sk

Alemdar Cad

Çatlçeşme Sk

Aya Sofya Meydanı

Kabasakal Cad

Sultanahmet Parkı

ATMs PTT Booth

Sultanahmet

Mimar Mehmet Ağa Cad

Arasta Bazaar

Alemdar

Yerebatan Cad

Zeynep Sultan Sk

Küçük Aya Sofya Cad

Sultanahmet

Ticketbahçe Sk

Binbirdirek

Lux Courts

PTT

Atmeydanı Sk

Molla Fenari Sk Dr Emin Paşa

Bab-ı Ali Cad

Cağaloğlu Hamamı Sk

Prof Kazım İsmail Gürkan Cad

Baş Müşahip Sk

Divan Yolu Cad

Tavukhane Sk

Tomurcuk Cad

Pharos Lighthouse

TURKEY

To Grand Bazaar

Cağaloğlu Cad

Cemide Ferhe

Babıali Cad

Türbedar Sk

Mescit Sk

Şeref Efendi Sk

Nuruosmaniye Cad

Yeniçeriler Cad

Çemberlitaş

Vezir Hanı Cad

Nakilbent Sk

Terzihane Sk

Şehit Mehmet Paşa Yokuşu

Kaleiçi Sk

Aksakal Sk

Bostan Arkası Sk

Kennedy Cad (Sahil Yolu)

your right for a complex of **tombs** (Map pp568–9) that was constructed for some 19th-century sultans, including Mahmut II (1808–39), Abdülaziz (1861–76) and Abdülhamid II (1876–1909).

A bit further along, on the right, you can't miss the **Çemberlitaş** (Banded Stone), a monumental column erected by Constantine the Great in 330 to celebrate the dedication of Constantinople as capital of the Roman Empire.

GRAND BAZAAR

Make sure you hone your haggling skills before dipping into the mind-boggling **Grand Bazaar** (Kapalı Çarşı, Covered Market; Map pp564–5; 8.30am-7pm Mon-Sat). Just north of Divan Yolu, this labyrinthine medieval shopping mall consists of some 4000 shops selling everything from carpets to clothing, including silverware, jewellery, antiques and belly-dancing costumes. It's probably the most discombobulating and manic shopping precinct you could hope to experience. Sure, the touts are ubiquitous, but come prepared and you'll realise that it's part of the fun. It's also a great place to ramble and get lost – which you will certainly do at least once.

At first sight this mini city appears to be an impenetrable latticework of tiny streets and alleys; on closer inspection the bazaar reveals a careful organisation, with different sections for different products.

BEYAZIT & SÜLEYMANIYE

Right beside the Grand Bazaar, the Beyazıt area takes its name from the graceful **Beyazıt Camii** (Map pp564–5), built in 1506 on the orders of Sultan Beyazıt II, son of Mehmet the Conqueror. The great gateway on the north side of the square is that of **İstanbul University** (Map pp564–5).

Behind the university to the northwest is one of the city's most prominent landmarks and İstanbul's grandest mosque complex, the **Süleymaniye Camii** (Map pp564–5; Prof Sıddık Sami Onar Caddesi; donation requested). It was commissioned by the most powerful of Ottoman sultans, Süleyman the Magnificent (1520–66), and was designed by Mimar Sinan, the most famous of all Imperial architects.

Eminönü

At the southern end of Galata Bridge looms large **Yeni Cami** (New Mosque; Map pp568–9),

built between 1597 and 1663. Beside it is the atmospheric **Spice Bazaar** (Mısır Çarşısı; Map pp568-9; 8.30am-6.30pm Mon-Sat), awash with spice and food vendors and a great place for last-minute gift shopping. To the west, on a platform above the fragrant market streets, is the **Rüstem Paşa Camii** (Map pp564–5), a small, richly tiled mosque designed by the great Ottoman architect Sinan.

Dolmabahçe Palace

Cross the Galata Bridge and follow the shore road along the Bosphorus from Karaköy towards Ortaköy and you'll come to the grandiose **Dolmabahçe Palace** (Map pp564-5; ☎ 0212-236 9000; Dolmabahçe Caddesi, Beşiktaş; admission selamlık €7, harem-cariyeler €5, combined ticket €9; 9am-4pm Tue, Wed & Fri-Sun), right on the waterfront. The palace was built between 1843 and 1856 as a home for some of the last Ottoman sultans. It was guaranteed its place in the history books when Atatürk died here on 10 November 1938.

Visitors are taken on guided tours of the two main buildings: the over-the-top **selamlık** (men's apartments) and the slightly more restrained **harem-cariyeler** (harem and concubines' quarters).

Any bus heading out of Karaköy along the Bosphorus shore road will take you to Dolmabahçe.

Beyoğlu

Cross the Galata Bridge and cut uphill from Karaköy towards the cylindrical **Galata Tower** (Map pp564-5; Galata Meydanı, Karaköy; admission €3.75; 9am-8pm).

In its present form the tower dates from 1348, when Galata was a Genoese trading colony. Later it became a prison, an observatory, then a fire lookout before it caught fire itself in 1835. In 1967 it was completely restored as a supper club. The observation desk is an excellent place for views and photos.

İSTIKLAL CADDESI & TAKSIM

You can't leave İstanbul without strolling down İstiklal Caddesi. At the top of the hill, this pedestrianised thoroughfare, once called the Grand Rue de Péra, is indisputably the most famous thoroughfare in Turkey. It's a parade of smart shops, large embassies and churches, elegant residential buildings and fashionable teahouses and restaurants. If you want to experience a slice of modern Turkey, there's no better place than İstiklal Caddesi. It's almost permanently crowded with locals, who patronise the atmosphere-laden *meyhaneler* (taverns) that line the side streets or indulge in shopping sprees in the hundreds of shops along its length. It's served by a picturesque restored tram that trundles up and down the boulevard.

There's a plethora of sights, but the colourful **Fish Market** (Balık Pazar; Map pp564–5) and **Çiçek Pasajı** (Flower Passage; Map pp564–5), near the Galatasaray Lisesi (a famous high school), are absolute must-sees. Just behind Çiçek Pasaji, make a foray into Nevizade Sokak; with its collection of bustling taverns heaving with chattering locals sampling meze and rakı, this is the epicentre of Beyoğlu's thriving bar scene.

At the southern end of İstiklal Caddesi, shambolic **Taksim Square**, with its huge hotels, park and Atatürk Cultural Centre, is not exactly an architectural gem but it's the symbolic heart of modern İstanbul.

Ortaköy

Ortaköy is a cute suburb east of Dolmabahçe Palace, right by the Bosphorus. Right on the water's edge, the decorative **Ortaköy Camii** (Map pp564–5) is the most prominent feature. The mosque fronts onto Ortaköy Sq, home to a pretty fountain and popular waterfront cafés and restaurants. You could easily combine a visit to Dolmabahçe Palace with a leisurely stroll in Ortaköy. To get here catch any bus heading east from Beşiktaş.

ACTIVITIES
Hamams

A visit to a *hamam* is an unforgettable experience, and we strongly recommend it. The **Çemberlitaş Hamamı** (Map pp568-9; ☎ 0212-522 7974; Vezi Hanı Caddesi 8, Çemberlitaş; bath only €9, bath & massage €14; ☽ 6am-midnight), just off Divan Yolu, was designed by the great Ottoman architect Mimar Sinan in 1584, and is one of the most atmospheric *hamams* in the city. Another wonderful place is **Cağaloğlu Hamamı** (Map pp568-9; ☎ 0212-522 2424; Yerebatan Caddesi 34, Cağaloğlu; bath only €10, bath & massage €20; ☽ men 8am-10pm, women 8am-8pm). It's pricey and pretty touristy but the service is experienced and hassle-free, and the surroundings are extraordinary.

Bosphorus Cruise

Don't leave the city without exploring the Bosphorus. Most day-trippers take the famous **Eminönü-Kavaklar Boğaziçi Özel Gezi Seferleri** (Map pp564-5; one way €2, return €4; ☽ 10.30am year-round, noon & 1.35pm Jun-Sep) ferries up its entire length. These depart from Eminönü and stop at various points before turning around at Anadolu Kavağı (the turnaround point). The shores are sprinkled with monuments and various sights, including the monumental Dolmabahçe Palace, the majestic Bosphorus Bridge, the seductive suburbs of Arnavutköy, Bebek, Kanlıca, Emirgan and Sarıyer, as well as lavish *yalıs* (waterside wooden summer residences) and numerous mosques.

THE PLEASURES OF THE BATH

After a long day's sightseeing, few things could be better than relaxing in a *hamam* (bathhouse). The ritual is invariably the same. First, you'll be shown to a cubicle where you can undress, store your clothes and wrap the provided *peştamal* (cloth) around you. Then an attendant will lead you through to the hot room where you sit and sweat for a while.

Next you'll have to make a choice. It's cheapest to wash yourself with the soap, shampoo and towel you brought with you. The hot room will be ringed with individual basins that you fill from the taps above. Then you sluice the water over yourself with a plastic scoop. But it's far more enjoyable to let an attendant do it for you, dousing you with warm water and then scrubbing you with a coarse cloth mitten. Afterwards you'll be lathered with a sudsy swab, rinsed off and shampooed.

When all this is complete you're likely to be offered a massage, an experience worth having at least once during your trip.

Bath etiquette dictates that men should keep the *peştamal* on at all times.

Traditional *hamams* have separate sections for men and women or admit men and women at separate times. In tourist areas most *hamams* are more than happy for foreign men and women to bathe together.

TURKEY

Princes' Islands (Adalar)

With good beaches, open woodland, a couple of monasteries, superb villas and transport by horse-drawn carriages, this string of nine spotless islands, especially **Büyükada** (the biggest), make an ideal escape from the noise and hustle of İstanbul. Ferries (€1.50) to the islands leave from the Adalar İskelesi dock (Map pp564–5) near Sirkeci Railway Station. Try to go midweek to avoid the crowds.

FESTIVALS & EVENTS

The **İstanbul International Music Festival** (www .iksv.org), from early June to early July, attracts big-name artists from around the world, who perform in venues that are not always open to the public (such as Aya İrini Kilisesi).

SLEEPING

İstanbul's accommodation is becoming quite pricey. For the time being, the best area to stay remains Cankurtaran, immediately southeast of Sultanahmet, where the quiet streets play host to a range of moderate hotels, mostly with stunning views from their roof terraces, as well as more-luxurious options. Unless otherwise stated, room rates include breakfast and private bathrooms; the exception is hostel dorms, which have shared bathrooms.

Budget

If your holiday budget is less offshore bank, more piggy bank, you can rest in one of the numerous hostels in Sultanahmet.

   Orient International Hostel (Map pp568-9; ☎ 0212-518 0789; www.orienthostel.com; Akbıyık Caddesi 13, Sultanahmet; dm/s/d €9/17/21; ☐) Party, party, party. The Orient has built a serious reputation in this domain, especially on Monday, Wednesday and Friday nights, when there are free belly-dancing shows. Rooms are colourful and well tended, and the rooftop terrace is a stunner.

   Sultan Hostel (Map pp568-9; ☎ 0212-516 9260; www.sultanhostel.com; Akbıyık Caddesi 21, Sultanahmet; dm €10-14, d €23-30; ☐) Next door to the Orient, the well-organised Sultan is a bit more sedate than its neighbour. Top marks go to the squeaky-clean bathrooms, quality bedding and atmospheric rooftop bar.

   Antique Hostel (Map pp568-9; ☎ 0212-638 1637; www.antiquehostel.com; Kutlugün Sokak 51, Sultanahmet; dm/s/d €10/30/40; ☐) There's a homy, rustic feel in this hostel, located in a quiet side street. There are only seven rooms and a basement dorm, ensuring calm and intimacy. It's salubrious and atmospheric.

   Big Apple Hostel (Map pp568-9; ☎ 0212-517 7931; Akbıyık Caddesi, Bayrami Fırını Sokak 12, Sultanahmet; dm €7-9; ☐) An ambitious newcomer, the Big Apple Hostel features fairly airy and comfortable dorms. No doubt it will rank among the best-value abodes in the area by the time you read this.

   Other recommendations:

Hostel Cafe Chill Out (Map pp564-5; ☎ 0212-249 4784; www.chillouthc.com; Balyoz Sokak 17-19, Beyoğlu; dm/s/d €8/10/25) In Beyoğlu, spitting distance from İstiklal Caddesi. A quirky hostel, with a colourful paint scheme and a mellow downstairs lounge-café. Unfortunately, the rooms are frustratingly tired looking and bathrooms are the most compact we've seen this side of the Euphrates.

Nayla Palace Hotel (Map pp568-9; ☎ 0212-516 3567; www.geocities.com/nayla_hotel; Kutlugün Sokak 22, Sultanahmet; s/d €26/30; ☒) In a quiet side street, this modest number offers small, clean, no-frills rooms.

Midrange

Sultanahmet and Cankurtaran harbour a smorgasbord of high-quality midrange options.

   Side Hotel & Pension (Map pp568-9; ☎ 0212-517 2282; www.sidehotel.com; Utangaç Sokak 20, Cankurtaran; s/d hotel €34/43, pension €19/32; ☒ ☐) Many travellers set up a base in this well-regarded venue, and it's easy to see why. The convivial Side features an inviting rooftop terrace and accommodation to suit all budgets. The pension rooms, with fans, provide the best value. Rooms 15 and 16 overlook the Blue Mosque and Aya Sofya. Ship out if offered rooms at the rear, as some are darkish and a bit noisy.

   Hotel Peninsula (Map pp568-9; ☎ 0212-458 6850; www.hotelpeninsula.com; Adliye Sokak 6, Cankurtaran; s/d €35/45; ☒) Particularly good value for the price, the friendly Peninsula offers comfy, spacious rooms with firm beds and crisp sheets, but it's the rooftop terrace, with hammocks for guests (an instant elixir to a hot day's sightseeing), that wins out. You can get a discount if you pay cash.

   Hotel Megara (Map pp568-9; ☎ 0212-458 4848; www.megarahotel.com; Akbıyık Caddesi 85, Sutanahmet; s/d €50/65; ☒ ☐) You could do a lot worse than book into one of these solidly furnished rooms, which are cosy and perfectly clean. The romantic rooftop restaurant is an added bonus.

Other recommendations:
Sarı Konak Oteli (Map pp568-9; ☎ 0212-638 6258; www.sarikonak.com; Mimar Mehmet Ağa Caddesi 42-46, Sultanahmet; s/d €50/70; 🗙 🖳) Rooms come with all the requisite comforts. The atmospheric courtyard at the rear is a great place to chill out.
Ayasofya Pansionlari (Map pp568-9; ☎ 0212-513 3660; www.ayasofyapensions.com; Soğukçeşme Sokak, Sultanahmet; s €70-80, d €85-100; 🗙 🖳) Feeling posh? Then kick back in style at this sybaritic venue, on a quiet pedestrianised street. The interior is seductively cosy, with velvet curtains, mirrors and armchairs with tasselled fringes.

Top End

Hotel Empress Zoe (Map pp568-9; ☎ 0212-518 2504; www.emzoe.com; Adliye Sokak 10, Cankurtaran; s/d €68/88; 🗙) This peach of a place is conjured up straight out of *The Thousand and One Nights*. Live the life of a royal in the charmingly appointed rooms or the divine suites, and soothe your chakras in the gorgeous flower-filled garden. Oh – and it doesn't cost the earth.

Four Seasons Hotel İstanbul (Map pp568-9; ☎ 0212-638 8200; www.fshr.com; Tevkifhane Sokak 1, Cankurtaran; s/d €350/385; 🗙 🖳) For glamour and style in sumptuous surroundings, the Four Seasons surpasses them all – and it's literally in the shadow of the Blue Mosque and Aya Sofya. Of course, it has all the bells and whistles your credit card will allow for, including king-size beds, enormous marble bathrooms and antique-style work desks. And did we mention that it used to be the infamous Sultanahmet prison (remember *Midnight Express*?).

EATING

Although there's a reasonable selection of places to eat in Sultanahmet, for a bigger choice you must head across town to

Beyoğlu. Start walking along İstiklal Caddesi and you'll be spoilt for choice, from takeaway döner kebap places to flashier, Westernised bar-cafés.

Sultanahmet

Tarihi Sultanahmet Köftecisi (Map pp568-9; ☎ 0212-520 0566; Divan Yolu Caddesi 12; mains €3-4) As the name suggests, *köfte* are the order of the day.

Çiğdem (Map pp568-9; ☎ 0212-526 8859; Divan Yolu Caddesi 62/A) It's difficult for even the staunchest dieter to pass by the tantalising display of treats offered by this slick pastry shop on Divan Yolu. Enjoy!

Aya Sofya Kebap House (Map pp568-9; ☎ 0212-458 3653; Küçük Aya Sofya Caddesi 23; mains €2-5) This unfussy hole in the wall lines the stomach with great pides and kebabs. The freshly squeezed orange juice is bliss.

Doy Doy (Map pp568-9; ☎ 0212-517 1588; Şifa Hamamı Sokak 13; mains €2-5) Another place well worth bookmarking. In the shadow of the Blue Mosque, Doy Doy consists of four sections, including a cosy lounge complete with cushions. The views from the breezy rooftop terrace are straight from heaven.

Other recommendations:
Rami (Map pp568-9; ☎ 0212-517 6593; Utangaç Sokak 6, Cankurtaran; mains €11-13) Damn expensive, but this restored Ottoman house is downright romantic and the food equally impressive.
Rumeli (Map pp568-9; ☎ 0212-512 0008; Ticarethane Sokak 8; mains €8-12) This stylish venue boasts an attractively rustic interior and serves up well-executed Turkish classics in romantic surroundings.

Beyoğlu

Hacı Baba (Map pp564-5; ☎ 0212-244 1886; İstiklal Caddesi 49; mains €5-9) Nosh on Ottoman delicacies in this bastion of traditional food, a short bag-haul from its rival Hacı Abdullah. The menu groans with lip-smacking dishes, and there's a vine-garlanded terrace for alfresco dining. Rejoice! You can order a beer, rakı or wine with your meal.

Sofyali 9 (Map pp564-5; ☎ 0212-245 0362; Sofyalı Sokak 9; mains €4-10) The congenial, much-lauded Sofyali 9 is reckoned to serve up the best *meyhane* food in the city. We agree.

Saray (Map pp564-5; ☎ 0212-292 3434; İstiklal Caddesi 102-104; sweets €1-2) Don't know what a *muhallebici* is? It's time to get an education. This renowned pudding shop has been serving puddings and other bait to sweet tooths since 1935. Drool over the *aşure* and the *kemal paşa* (a syrupy sweet) on display; if you can resist, you're not human.

Musa Ustam Ocakbaşı (Map pp564-5; ☎ 0212-245 2932; Küçük Parmakkapı Sokak 17; mains €5-7) A carnivore's paradise. Join the locals chattering by the big *ocak* (grill) at the back. *Afiyet olsun* (bon appétit)!

Otantik (Map pp564-5; ☎ 0212-293 8451; İstiklal Caddesi 170; dishes €3-8) Two women in traditional Anatolian costume make crispy *gözleme* (pancakes) in the window. Don't be put off by this fairly cheesy choreography – enjoy the expertly cooked Turkish dishes on offer.

Don't leave the city without spending an evening out at one of the *meyhaneler* on Nevizade Sokak in Beyoğlu. Buried in the maze of narrow streets behind the historic Çiçek Pasajı (Flower Passage) on İstiklal Caddesi, this is the most lively eating precinct in the city. The emphasis is on meze and fresh fish. Knock it all back with a glass (or two) of rakı and you'll be in seventh heaven. We recommend **Boncuk Restaurant** (Map pp564-5; ☎ 0212-243 1219; Nevizade Sokak 19; mains €3-8) and **Ney'le Mey'le** (Map pp564-5; ☎ 0212-249 8103; Nevizade Sokak 12; mains €2-8). **Krependeki İmroz Restaurant** (Map pp564-5; ☎ 0212-249 9073; Nevizade Sokak 24; mains €3-5) also has its share of devotees.

Ortaköy

Çınaraltı (Map pp564-5; ☎ 0212-261 7867; İskele Meydanı; mains €3-8) Probably the best Ortaköy waterside restaurant, with splendid views, a shady terrace, peerless people-watching opportunities and tasty fish dishes.

Sedir (Map pp564-5; ☎ 0212-327 9870; Mecidiye Köprüsü Sokak 16-18; mains €5-8) This elegant res-

taurant serves up Mediterranean fusion food, as well as salads and various snacks. Nab a seat on the terrace and enjoy the views of the decorative Ortaköy Camii. No alcohol is served.

For a quick bite on the hop, nothing beats the stands selling *kumpir* (potatoes stuffed with vegetables).

DRINKING

There's a thriving bar scene in Beyoğlu, and there's nothing better than swigging more than a few glasses of rakı in the *meyhaneler* on Nevizade Sokak. If you're after a wine bar, **Pano** (Map pp564-5; ☎ 0212-292 6664; Hamalbaşı Caddesi 26, Beyoğlu) is extremely popular at weekends, with an eclectic crowd gulping down glasses of blood-red wine. If hunger beckons, order an assortment of high-quality meze.

In summer, Akbıyık Caddesi in Sultanahmet really hops, with travellers drinking until the early hours at tables set out on the footpaths.

GETTING THERE & AWAY
Air

Most people fly into İstanbul's **Atatürk International Airport** (☎ 0212-663 2550; www.ataturkairport.com), 25km west of the city centre. Most foreign airlines have their offices north of Taksim, along Cumhuriyet Caddesi. Travel agencies can also sell tickets and make reservations. Domestic air services are operated by the main carrier, **Turkish Airlines** (☎ 0212-225 0556; www.thy.com). Onur Air, Atlasjet and Fly Air also operate domestic flights from İstanbul.

For more details on flying to/from and within Turkey, see p634 and p635.

Boat

Yenikapı (Map pp564–5), south of Aksaray Sq, is the dock for fast ferries across the Sea of Marmara to Yalova (for Bursa) and Bandırma (for İzmir).

Bus

The huge **International İstanbul Bus Station** (Uluslararası İstanbul Otogarı; ☎ 0212-658 0505; Esenler) is the city's main otogar (bus station) for intercity and international routes. It's in the western district of Esenler, 10km from Sultanahmet. The Light Rail Transit (LRT) service stops here en route from the airport; catch it to Aksaray or Yusufpaşa, then take a tram to Sultanahmet. A taxi from Sultanahmet or Taksim Sq to the bus station will cost around €8. Many bus companies offer a free *servis* (shuttle bus) to or from the otogar.

Buses leave from here for virtually anywhere in Turkey and for international destinations including Bulgaria, Greece, Iran, Kosovo, Macedonia, Nakhichevan (Azerbaijan), Romania and Syria.

If you're heading east to Anatolia, you might want to board at the smaller **Harem Otogar** (Map pp564-5; ☎ 216-333 3763), north of Haydarpaşa Railway Station on the Asian shore, but the choice of service there is more limited.

Car & Motorcyle

It makes no sense to drive around İstanbul itself and have to deal with the traffic and parking problems. However, if you're heading out of the city all the main car-hire agencies have desks in the international terminal of Atatürk International Airport.

Train

For services to Edirne, Greece and eastern Europe go to **Sirkeci Railway Station** (Map pp564-5; ☎ 0212-527 0051). International services from Sirkeci include the daily *Bosfor Ekspresi* service to Budapest (Hungary) via Sofia (Bulgaria) and Bucharest (Romania; around €50). There's also a slow daily service to Thessaloniki (Greece; around €50).

Trains from the Asian side of Turkey and from points east and south terminate at **Haydarpaşa Railway Station** (Map pp564-5; ☎ 0216-336 44/0), on the Asian shore of the Bosphorus. International services from Haydarpaşa include the *Trans-Asya Ekspresi* to Iran and the *Toros Ekspresi* to Syria.

GETTING AROUND
To/From the Airport

The fastest way to get into town from the airport is by taxi. During the day it costs about €13 to Sultanahmet (and takes about 25 minutes).

There is a quick, cheap and efficient LRT service from the airport to Aksaray (€0.70, 30 minutes). From Aksaray it's a five-minute walk to the Yusufpaşa tram stop, from where the tram makes its way down Divan Yolu to Sultanahmet.

If you are staying near Taksim Sq, the **Havaş airport bus** (☎ 0212-243 3399; €5) is your best bet. It departs from the international terminal, stops at the domestic terminal, then goes to Taksim Sq via Aksaray. Buses leave every 30 minutes or so from 5am till midnight.

Many Divan Yolu travel agencies and Sultanahmet hostels book minibus transport from the hotels to the airport for about €4 a head. Unfortunately, this option only works going *from* town to the airport and not vice versa.

Boat

The cheapest and nicest way to travel any distance in İstanbul is by ferry. The main ferry docks are at the mouth of the Golden Horn (Eminönü, Sirkeci and Karaköy) and at Kabataş, 2km northeast of the Galata Bridge, just south of Dolmabahçe Palace. Short ferry hops cost about €0.50.

Public Transport

A tram runs from Karaköy to Gülhane and Sultanahmet, and then along Divan Yolu to Çemberlitaş, Beyazıt (for the Grand Bazaar) and Aksaray (to connect to the otogar and the airport). Trams run every five minutes from 5.30am to midnight. At the time of writing, works were underway to extend the line further. Another restored tram trundles along İstiklal Caddesi to Taksim.

An LRT service connects Aksaray with the airport, stopping at 18 stations, including the otogar, along the way. It operates from around 6am till midnight.

The most useful bus for travellers is the T4 bus that runs between Sultanahmet and Taksim Sq.

There is a one-stop Tünel funicular system between Karaköy and İstiklal Caddesi in Beyoğlu (€0.40, every 10 or 15 minutes from 7am to 9pm).

Every 30 minutes, suburban trains from Sirkeci Railway Station (€0.60) run along the southern walls of Old İstanbul and west along the Marmara shore. There's a handy station in Cankurtaran for Sultanahmet.

Taxi

İstanbul has 60,000 yellow taxis, all of them with meters – even if not every driver wants to run them. From Sultanahmet to Taksim costs around €4; to the otogar around €13.

AROUND İSTANBUL

Since İstanbul is such a vast city, few places are within easy reach on a day trip. However, if you make an early start it's just possible to see the sights of Edirne in Thrace (Trakya), the only bit of Turkey that is geographically within Europe. The fast ferry link means that you can also just make it to Bursa and back in a day, although it's much better to plan to overnight there. İznik is another must-see; it's a historic walled town on the shores of a peaceful lake, and is easily accessible from İstanbul.

EDİRNE

☎ 0284 / pop 115,000

A crossroads between Turkey, Bulgaria and Greece, Edirne is much more than a large frontier town or a mere stop-off point to or from the neighbouring countries. Several splendid mosques, historic houses and lively bazaars are testimony to its past prosperity – it was briefly the capital of the Ottoman Empire – and add to its distinctive, preserved Turkish character. And we must mention the **Kırpınar Wrestling Festival** at the end of June, when the town fills with Turkish tourists – it's a spectacle definitely worth seeing.

Sights

Dominating Edirne's skyline like a massive battleship is the **Selimiye Mosque** (1569–75), the finest work of the great Ottoman architect Mimar Sinan. Its lofty dome and its four tall (71m), slender minarets create a dramatic perspective. Smack-bang in the centre of town, you can't miss the 1414 **Eski Cami** (Old Mosque), which has rows of arches and pillars supporting a series of small domes. Behind it is the **Rüstem Paşa Hanı**, a grand caravanserai built 100 years later. Another example of architectural magnificence is the **Üçşerefeli Cami**, which has four strikingly different minarets, all built at different times. Edirne's last great imperial mosque, the **Beyazıt II complex** (1481–1512), stands in splendid isolation to the north of the town.

Sleeping & Eating

Tuna Hotel (☎ 214 3340; fax 214 3323; Maarif Caddesi 17; s/d €22/30; ✺) Behind Ali Paşa Bazaar, this is possibly the friendliest and best-value place in town. All the rooms and facilities are neat

as a pin and there's a pleasant courtyard for breakfast. Bookings are recommended.

Aksarayli Pansiyon (☎ 212 6035; Alipaşa Ortakapı Caddesi; s/d €10/20) A few doors from the Tuna, this pension occupies a white, crumbling old house. The rooms, which have shoe-box bathrooms, are a tad scuffed around the edges, but at this price we're not complaining.

Karam Hotel (☎ 225 1555; fax 225 1556; Maarif Caddesi; s/d €40/50; ✺) A brave attempt at creating a boutique hotel, the Karam occupies a historic mansion complete with fine, high-ceilinged rooms with impeccable bathrooms and a welcoming courtyard restaurant.

You'll find numerous eateries in the vicinity of the bazaar, serving simple meals at unbeatable prices.

Getting There & Away

The otogar is 8.5km east of the city centre. There are regular bus services for İstanbul (€9, 2½ hours, 235km) and Çanakkale (€9, 3½ hours, 230km). If you're heading for the Bulgarian border crossing at Kapıkule (€0.50, 18km), catch a minibus from in front of the tourist office.

İZNİK

☎ 0224 / pop 20,000

A historic walled town on the shores of a peaceful lake, İznik is popular with weekending İstanbullus but largely ignored by tourists, which has helped preserve its Turkish character. Visitors in a languid mood can stroll along the lakefront or mosey around the city centre, admiring the ruins of **Aya Sofya** (admission €1.25; ✺ 9am-noon & 2-5pm) and the Seljuk-style **Yeşil Cami** (Green Mosque), built between 1378 and 1387. The minaret, decorated with green-and blue-glazed zigzag tiles, is a wonder. It's also worth sparing an hour to visit the **İznik Museum** (admission €1.50; ✺ 8.30am-noon & 1-5pm Tue-Sun), which contains examples of İznik tiles. More-active types can follow a 5km circuit around most of İznik's **walls**, which were first erected in Roman times. Four imposing **gates** still pierce the walls.

Sleeping & Eating

Kaynarca Pansiyon (☎ 757 1753; www.kaynarca.s5.com; Kılıçaslan Caddesi, Gündem Sokak 1; dm/s/d €8/12/18) The most obvious choice if funds are short. It consists of two dorms and several monastically plain rooms. Breakfast is extra (€2).

Aydin (☎ 757 7650; www.iznikhotelaydin.com; Kılıçaslan Caddesi 64; s/d €20/30) If you want to scale up the ladder, opt for Aydin, which offers colourful rooms and tiled bathrooms, as well as a pastry shop on the ground floor.

Çamlık Motel (☎ 757 1362; www.iznikcamlikmotel.com; s/d €24/45) Scrupulously clean and quietly located at the southern end of the road along the lakeshore, Çamlık is also more upmarket. There's an on-site restaurant.

When it comes to the culinary scene, nothing really stands out. Well placed for a little sustenance, **Izgara** (☎ 757 8230; Kılıçaslan Caddesi 149; mains €2-3) churns out run-of-the-mill Turkish food at moderate prices.

In summer the best places to sip a cup of tea are the open-air cafés on Şahil Yol, overlooking the lake.

Getting There & Away
There are regular buses from the otogar to Bursa (€2, 1½ hours, 82km) and less frequent services to İstanbul and Ankara.

BURSA
☎ 0224 / pop one million
Sprawling at the base of Uludağ, Turkey's biggest winter-sports centre, Bursa prides itself on having been the first capital of the Ottoman Empire. Nowadays it's a modern, prosperous, sprawling city with lots of vitality and personality. Allow at least a day to make the most of its innumerable ancient mosques, *medreses* and *hamams*. Even if you're not an architecture buff, you'll be enthralled by the design of all these monuments. And if you prefer to pamper your frail body, the thermal springs in the villagelike suburb of Çekirge are the perfect salve after a day spent exploring the city on weary feet.

The city centre, with its banks and shops, is along Atatürk Caddesi, between the Ulu Cami (Grand Mosque) to the west and the main square, Cumhuriyet Alanı, commonly called Heykel (Statue), to the east. Çekirge is around about 6km west of Heykel. Bursa's otogar is an inconvenient 10km north of the centre on the Yalova road.

Sights & Activities
About 1km east of Heykel is the supremely beautiful **Yeşil Cami** (Green Mosque; 1424) and its stunningly tiled **Yeşil Türbe** (Green Tomb; admission free; ⏰ 8.30am-noon & 1-5pm). Right in the city centre, the largest of Bursa's mosques is the 20-domed **Ulu Cami** (Grand Mosque; Atatürk Caddesi), built in 1396. Behind the Ulu Cami, Bursa's sprawling **Covered Market** (Kapalı Çarşı) is a great place to while away a few hours.

Uphill and west of the Ulu Cami, on the way to Çekirge, don't miss the 14th-century **tombs of Osman and Orhan**, the first Ottoman sultans. A kilometre beyond lies the delightful **Muradiye Complex**, with a mosque and 12 decorated tombs dating from the 15th and 16th centuries. With a shady park in front, it's a peaceful oasis in a busy city.

Whether it's winter or summer, it's worth taking a cable-car ride up the 2543m-high **Uludağ** (Great Mountain) to take advantage of the view and the cool, clear air of Uludağ National Park. From Heykel take a dolmuş (shared taxi) east to the **teleferik** (cable car; one way €2.50). Alternatively take a dolmuş from central Bursa to the hotels on Uludağ (22km). Bear in mind that the skiing facilities, while some of Turkey's best, are not up to those of the best European ski resorts.

Sleeping
There are a couple of decent options in Bursa, but also consider Çekirge, which has better options where you can escape the city's noise. Many hotels in Çekirge have private or public mineral baths. To get here, take a 'Çekirge' bus or dolmuş from Heykel or along Atatürk Caddesi.

Hotel Çeşmeli (☎ /fax 224 1511; Gümüşçeken Caddesi 6; s/d €24/42) In a tranquil side street north of Atatürk Caddesi, this is a sparklingly clean outfit, handy for everything. It's also a friendly retreat that suits solo women travellers.

Otel Safran Restaurant (☎ 224 7216; fax 224 7219; Ortapazar Caddesi, Arka Sokak 4; s/d €30/53) Opposite the Osman and Orhan tombs, this nearly-but-not-quite boutique hotel occupies a well-restored Ottoman-style mansion, with comfortable, if simply furnished, rooms.

Mutlu Hotel (☎ 236 3136; 1 Murat Caddesi 19, Çekirge; s/d €18/30; 🖭) Coming from central Bursa, one of the first places you see in Çekirge is this agreeable hotel, with cosy pine-clad rooms and private mineral baths. An excellent choice for budget-seekers.

Atlas Hotel (☎ 234 4100; fax 236 4605; Hamamlar Caddesi 35, Çekirge; s/d €25/42; 🖭) A step up in price and comfort, the Atlas is another commendable option, with its functional rooms and private mineral baths.

Eating & Drinking

Kebapçı İskender (Ünlü Caddesi 7; mains €3-5) *The* place in Turkey to sample an *İskender kebap* for which Bursa is famous. Half a block from Heykel on a pedestrian-only street, this perennial favourite has been whipping up supertasty kebaps since 1867.

Darüzziyafe (☎ 224 6439; 2 Murat Caddesi 36; mains €3-6) Near the Muradiye mosque, this is a good place to feast on well-prepared Otto-man delicacies. We were impressed by the desserts, especially the *fukara keşkülü* (a de-licious creamy pudding with pistachio and vanilla), easier to devour than to pronounce. There's a picture menu to help you choose.

Hünkar (☎ 327 8910; Yeşil Camii Yanı 17; mains €4-10) The selling point of this group-focused restaurant is its sublime position, next to the Yeşil Cami, which has such a breathtaking view over sprawling Bursa that it's hard to tear yourself away. Nab a windowside seat.

Make sure you spend an evening out at one of the fish restaurants on Sakarya Caddesi, just south of Altıparmak Caddesi. This is certainly the most atmospheric eat-ing precinct in the city.

There are a few fashionable café-teahouses east of Heykel on either side of a stream. Mahfel Mado is an oversized place where bright young things gather to enjoy the at-mosphere and chat over a glass of tea. Hayal Bahçesi, right by the stream, is a haven of calm. Sakarya Caddesi is also a hot spot, with several bars featuring live music at night.

Getting There & Away

The fastest way to get to İstanbul (€11, 2½ to three hours) is to take a bus to Yalova, then a catamaran to İstanbul's Yenikapı docks. There are buses between Yalova and Bursa.

Karayolu ile (by road) buses to İstanbul (€7) take four to five hours and drag you around the Bay of İzmit. Those designated *feribot ile* (by ferry) go to Topçular, east of Yalova, and take the car ferry to Eskihisar, a much quicker and more pleasant way to go.

AEGEAN COAST

While the scenery of the Aegean coast is not as spectacular as that of the Mediterranean, this is the part of Turkey that was once Asia Minor and it is studded with fantastic his-toric sites, including the ruins of Troy, Ephe-sus and Pergamum. This is also where you come to see the battlefield sites at Gallipoli.

ÇANAKKALE

☎ 0286 / pop 60,000

Çanakkale is the most popular base for visit-ing the famous Gallipoli battlefields, across the other side of the Dardanelles, and the ruins at Troy. For Australians and New Zea-landers, it's a mandatory stopover, especially on Anzac Day (25 April), when a dawn serv-ice commemorates the anniversary of the Allied landings on the peninsula in 1915. Unfortunately, Çanakkale is woefully inad-equate for an influx of up 12,000 visitors on one day (not to mention hundreds of buses and cars). You would be well advised to make a visit at another quieter time.

The tourist office, all the cheap hotels, Internet cafés and a range of reasonable restaurants are within a block or two of the ferry pier, near the town's landmark clock tower.

Sleeping

If you choose to visit on Anzac Day, keep in mind that rooms are expensive at that time and usually booked solid months be-fore 25 April.

Anzac House (☎ 213 5969; www.anzachouse.com; Cumhuriyet Meydanı; dm/s/d €7/10/17; 🖳) In an excel-lent location on the main drag, a short stag-ger from the docks, this backpackers' staple is a friendly and well-run operation with good facilities, including a travel agency, Internet access and laundry service. Rooms are barren but spick-and-span. Avoid the windowless ones, which are claustrophobic.

Yellow Rose Pension (☎ /fax 217 3343; Yeni Sokak 5; dm/s/d €6/9/17; 🖳) The exuberant colour scheme at this guesthouse can make your eyes water and the rooms are fairly Spartan, but the staff are friendly, there's a kitchen, and the place has a laid-back appeal. It's on a quiet side street, 50m southeast of the clock tower.

Hotel Efes (☎ 217 3256; Aralık Sokak 5; s/d €25/30; 🏵) Not your average hotel, the Efes is run by women. Located behind the clock tower, it's intimate, cosy and well tended, with lots of feminine touches.

Hotel Kervansaray (☎ 217 9011; Fetvane Sokak 13; s/d €25/43; 🏵) Too good to be true, this tastefully restored *eski konak* (old mansion) exudes Ot-toman charm and rustic elegance without

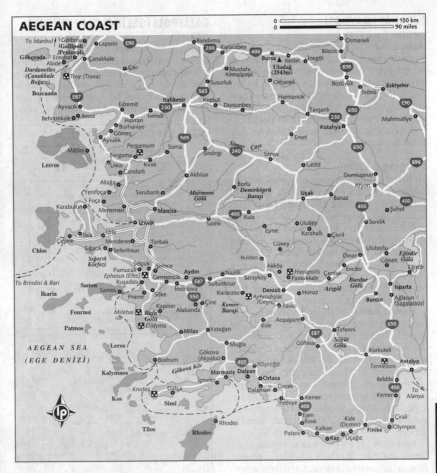

AEGEAN COAST

costing the earth. Rooms are spacious, with garnet-coloured bedcovers, and there's also a pretty garden at the back. Enjoy.

Hotel Helen (☎ 212 1818; www.helenhotel.com; Cumhuriyet Meydanı 57; s/d € 31/42; P ❉) All the creature comforts are available at this sleek, modern three-star affair. The only drawback is the busy road, so bag a room at the back.

Eating & Drinking

Gülen Pide (Cumhuriyet Meydanı; mains €3-5) This cheerful eatery is usually packed to the gills with hungry punters wolfing down delectable pide. There's also a wide range of kebaps.

Doyum Pide ve Kebap Salonu (Cumhuriyet Meydanı; mains €3-5) Another reputable staple, similar in standards and style to the nearby Gülen.

Baklavaları (Cumhuriyet Meydanı) A gem for carb-lovers, this fancy pastry shop prepares the most gooey baklava this side of the Dardanelles. We'll be back.

Sea Side (mains €3-8) After a touch of sophistication? Head for this snazzy, Westernised bar-restaurant right by the harbour. Nab a table on the terrace, scoff a plate of pasta or a salad and watch the world stroll by.

Getting There & Away

There are regular services to get to Ayvalık (€9, 3½ hours), Behramkale/Assos (€3.50, two hours), İstanbul (€13, six hours) and İzmir (€12, five hours).

There are also frequent ferry services to Eceabat (€0.50).

ECEABAT (MAYDOS)

☎ 0286 / pop 4500

Across the Dardanelles from Çanakkale, Eceabat has perked up considerably in recent years and now makes a convenient base from which to visit the Gallipoli battlefields. If Çanakkale's raffish charm and raucous nightlife are not to your liking, you'll enjoy this easy-going waterfront town.

Everything you will need is a short hop from the dock.

Sleeping & Eating

TJs Hostel (☎ 814 3122; www.anzacgallipolitours.com; Cumhuriyet Caddesi 5/A; dm/s/d €7/8/16; 🖳) In a multistorey building 100m from the main square, this enduringly popular backpackers' haunt is run by a friendly Turkish-Australian couple. The rooms are nothing flash and a tad poky, but there are heaps of services, including a book exchange, a travel agency, movies and the inevitable Vegemite toast for breakfast (about €2). There are rooftop barbecues for €6.50.

Eceabat Hotel (☎ 814 2458; www.anzacgallipoli tours.com; Cumhuriyet Caddesi; s/d €18/26; 🏊) The greyish façade of this high-rise lump on the waterfront ain't eye candy but it's much more appealing inside. It's owned by the same people as TJs, so no prizes for guessing this place is also well run. Here you'll get airy, spanking-new rooms and Ottoman-style furnishings. Facilities include air-con, double-glazing, TV, fridge and laundry service.

Aqua Hotel (☎ 814 2864; www.heyboss.com; İstiklal Caddesi; s/d €20/38; 🏊) Once a tomato-canning factory, aesthetically resurrected with super-clean, hospital-white rooms and a vast restaurant with exposed beams, stone walls and fluffy carpets. The main selling point is its location, right by the waterside. Oh, and the bar gets really zippy in high season.

Liman Restaurant (İstiklal Caddesi; mains €4-8) Settle into this popular joint south of the ferry dock, choose from the fresh fish on display and sample it grilled or fried with a salad. The terrace is an added bonus.

Getting There & Away

Long distance buses pass through Eceabat on the way from İstanbul to Çanakkale (€13, 5½ hours).

There are frequent ferry services to Çanakkale (€0.50).

GALLIPOLI (GELIBOLU) PENINSULA

☎ 0286

Gallipoli has a special significance for Australians and New Zealanders, thousands of whom come here every year. Even if you're not overly interested in military matters, you can't help but be moved by the poignancy and sheer natural beauty of the site.

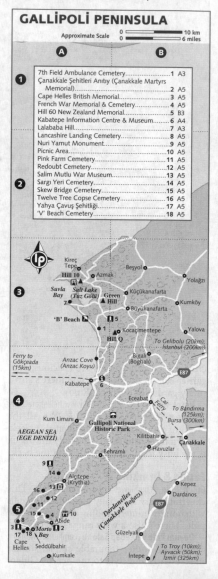

GALLIPOLI PENINSULA

Approximate Scale

7th Field Ambulance Cemetery	1 A3
Çanakkale Şehitleri Anıtıy (Çanakkale Martyrs Memorial)	2 A5
Cape Helles British Memorial	3 A5
French War Memorial & Cemetery	4 A5
Hill 60 New Zealand Memorial	5 B3
Kabatepe Information Centre & Museum	6 A4
Lalababa Hill	7 A3
Lancashire Landing Cemetery	8 A5
Nuri Yamut Monument	9 A5
Picnic Area	10 A5
Pink Farm Cemetery	11 A5
Redoubt Cemetery	12 A5
Salim Mutlu War Museum	13 A5
Sargı Yeri Cemetery	14 A5
Skew Bridge Cemetery	15 A5
Twelve Tree Copse Cemetery	16 A5
Yahya Çavuş Şehitliği	17 A5
'V' Beach Cemetery	18 A5

Always the first line of defence for İstanbul, the Dardanelles defences proved their worth in WWI. Atop the narrow, hilly Gallipoli Peninsula, Atatürk and his troops fought off a far superior but badly commanded force of Anzac and British troops. After nine months and having suffered horrendous casualties, the Allied forces were withdrawn.

For most people, a visit to the battle-fields and war graves of Gallipoli (now a national historic park) is an overwhelming experience.

Visiting the sights by public transport is not very convenient. The easiest way to see the battlefields, particularly if time is tight, is with your own transport or on a minibus tour from Çanakkale or Eceabat with **Hassle Free Tours** (☎ 213 5969; hasslefree@anzachouse.com; Anzac House, Çanakkale), **Troy-Anzac Tours** (☎ 217 5849; Saat Kulesi Meydanı 6, Çanakkale) or **TJs Tours** (☎ 814 3121; www.anzacgallipollitours.com; Eceabat) for about €20 per person. With a tour you can get the benefit of a guide who can ex-plain the battles as you go along.

Most people use Çanakkale or Eceabat as a base for exploring Gallipoli. Car fer-ries cross the straits on a frequent basis from Çanakkale to Eceabat (per person €0.50). From there you can take a dolmuş to Kabatepe on the western shore of the pe-ninsula. Ask to be dropped at the Kabatepe Information Centre & Museum.

Some travellers prefer to join an organ-ised tour from İstanbul.

TROY (TRUVA)
☎ 0286
The ruins of ancient Troy may not be as spectacular as those of Ephesus (Efes), but for anyone who has ever read Homer's *Iliad*, they have a romance few places on Earth can hope to match.

The ticket booth for the ruins of **Troy** (admission €6; ☽ 8.30am-5.30pm) is 500m before the site. The site is rather confusing for nonexpert eyes, but the most conspicuous features include the **walls** from various pe-riods; the **Bouleuterion** (Council Chamber), built around Homer's time (c 800 BC); the Roman **Odeon**, where concerts were held; the stone **ramp** from Troy II (2600–2300 BC); and the **Temple of Athena** from Troy VIII (700–85 BC), rebuilt by the Romans.

In summer, dolmuşes ply back and forth along the 32km between Troy and Çanakkale

(€1.75, 35 minutes). Walk inland from the ferry pier to Atatürk Caddesi, and turn right towards Troy; dolmuşes wait by the bridge.

The travel agencies offering tours to the Gallipoli battlefields (left) also offer tours to Troy (around €25 per person).

BEHRAMKALE & ASSOS
☎ 0286
Behramkale, 19km southwest of Ayvacık, is a colourful place with a colourful past. Pic-ture an old hilltop village hugging a superb archaeological site where you can admire the ruins of a Doric-style **Temple of Athena** (admission €3; ☽ 8.30am-dusk). The view from the ruins out to Lesvos and the dazzling waters of the Aegean are nothing short of spectacular and well worth the admission fee. Beside the entrance to the ruins, the 14th-century **Hüdavendigar Camii** is a simple, pre-Ottoman mosque.

Just before the entrance to the village, a road winds 2km down to Assos harbour. It's a cluster of half-a-dozen old stone houses-turned-hotels overlooking a picture-perfect harbour, and is the ideal place to unwind over a cup of tea.

And the catch? It's no longer a sleeping beauty and it gets overcrowded, especially over summer weekends when İstanbullus and İzmirlis pour in by the bus load. Con-sider yourself warned.

Sleeping
You can either stay in Behramkale village it-self or in the hotels around Assos harbour.

BEHRAMKALE
Tekin Pansiyon (☎ 721 7099; s/d €14/21; ☒) A brilliant-value guesthouse with ultraclean bathrooms and spotless, tiled rooms – no brownish, whiffy carpet!

Assos Konukevi (☎ 721 7081; d €55) Tucked away round the back of the village, this charming *evi* (house) is a peaceful retreat. It has three cosy, old-fashioned rooms with nice views over the ruins and an inviting courtyard.

Eris Pansiyon (☎ 721 7080; www.assos.de/eris; s €40, d €50-60; ☐) You can't miss the ivy-clad façade of this fine stone house at the back of the village. It's run by a semiretired Ameri-can couple who have lots of information on the area. The rooms are certainly tidy and functional but nothing thrilling. The highlights here are the manicured garden

TURKEY

and the breezy terrace with million-dollar views over the hills.

Also recommended:

Sidar Pansiyon (☎ 721 7047; s/d €15/25) A simple place, next door to Tekin Pansiyon, with plain but restful rooms.

Testi Han (☎ 721 7477; fax 721 7478; r €40) A fairly upmarket guesthouse, with smallish but pretty rooms and natty bathrooms. A good pick.

ASSOS

If you prefer to stay in the pricey hotels by Assos harbour, note that in high season virtually all of them insist on *yarım pansiyon* (half-board, ie breakfast and dinner). The **Nazlıhan Boutique Hotel** (☎ 721 7385; www.asso sedengroup.com; s/d with half-board from €35/50) and the **Yıldız Saray Otel** (☎ 721 7025; www.yildizsaray -hotels.com; s/d with half-board €40/60; ✖) have the most atmosphere. Be sure to ask for a room facing the sea.

Eating

There's a smattering of cheap-and-cheerful options in the old village. Check the ramshackle Köy Restaurant in the heart of the village and the Assos Restaurant next to the mosque, where a plate of belly-filling *mantı* (Turkish ravioli) or a melt-in-your-mouth *gözleme* cost a pittance.

In Assos harbour, most harbourside hotels host a restaurant. The emphasis is unsurprisingly on fresh fish. Check the cost before ordering fish and wine.

Getting There & Away

To get to Behramkale, catch an infrequent dolmuş (€1.25, 19km) from Ayvacık (not to be confused with nearby Ayvalık). Ayvacık is, in turn, linked by bus to Çanakkale (€3, two hours, 73km).

AYVALIK
☎ 0266 / pop 32,000

Ayvalık is a delightful fishing port and beach resort, and is the departure point for ferries to Lesvos (Greece). It has embraced tourism without being consumed by it. If you come from a more touristy coastal town, you'll notice the difference in atmosphere and attitudes the minute you step off the bus. The wonderful winding streets in the old quarter and the buzzy waterfront area lend themselves perfectly to a day or two's relaxed pottering.

The otogar is 1.5km north of the town centre. In summer there's an information kiosk on the waterfront south of the main square, Cumhuriyet Alanı. Offshore is **Alibey Island** (Cunda), which is lined with open-air fish restaurants and linked by ferries and a causeway to the mainland. In summer don't leave Ayvalık without taking a **cruise** around the bay – there are plenty of operators keen to get you on board (about €8).

Sleeping & Eating

Taksiyarhis Pansiyon (☎ 312 1494; www.taksiyarhis .com; Mareşal Çakmak Caddesi 71; per person €12) A delightfully quaint place in a renovated Ottoman house only five minutes' walk east of the PTT. It's a very friendly and affordable hang-out with bags of character. The rooms are nothing outstanding and the bathrooms are shared, but the general feel of cleanliness, the numerous artistic touches that adorn the communal areas, the two terraces with sprawling views and a kitchen for guests' use make it a real bargain. Book ahead if possible. Breakfast costs €4.

Bonjour Pansiyon (☎ 312 8085; Fevzi Çakmak Caddesi, Çeşme Sokak 5; s/d €15/30) Another gem of a place, shrouded with a palpable historic aura. Live like a pasha in this gorgeous house that once belonged to a French priest who was ambassador to the sultan. Rooms are spacious and high-ceilinged, and the shared bathrooms are impeccable. Some rooms in the rear building have private bathrooms. To find it, follow the signs across the road from the PTT.

Paşalı (☎ 312 5018; Vural Pasaji Arkasi 18; mains €2-4) Tables here are hot property at weekends, and no wonder. This place serves up some of the best *Akdeniz mutfak* (Mediterranean cuisine) in town, and does so in surroundings as welcoming as they are attractive. It's worth saving room for the gooey desserts. It's also a good spot for vegetarians, with various *sebzeli yemekler* (vegetables). Paşali is in a side street off Cumhuriyet Meydanı.

Canlı Balık (☎ 313 0081; Cumhuriyet Alanı; mains €6-7) Settle into this bright joint right by the harbour and enjoy a large selection of seafood. The fish is so fresh it's almost jumping off the plate. The terrace also offers peerless people-watching opportunities.

Getting There & Away

There are frequent direct buses from İzmir (€6, 1¾ hours) and Bergama (€4.50, 1¾

hours) to Ayvalık. Coming from Çanakkale
(€6, 3½ hours), some buses drop you on the
main highway to hitch to the centre.

Ayvalık Belediyesi buses run to Alibey
Island (€0.40) via the causeway. Or you
can take a boat from near the main square
(€0.60, 15 minutes).

Daily boats operate to Lesvos (Greece)
from June to September (€40/50 one way/
return). There's at least one boat a week,
even in winter. Buy your ticket at **Cunda
Denizcilik** (☎ 312 7210), near the harbour.

BERGAMA (PERGAMUM)
☎ 0232 / pop 50,000
From the 3rd century BC to the 1st century AD, Bergama (formerly Pergamum)
was one of the Middle East's richest and
most powerful small kingdoms. Today this
glorious past is a distant memory but the
extensive and well-preserved ruins on the
outskirts of the city offer an unparalleled
chance to step back in time.

There are banks with ATMs on Banka-
lar Caddesi (the main street), which is also
where you'll find the PTT. **Arkadaş Cafe** (İzmir
Caddesi; per hr €1; �9am-midnight), near Böblingen
Pension, has good Internet connections.

Sights
One of the highlights of the Aegean coast,
the well-proportioned **Asclepion** (Temple of As-
clepios; admission €6; �8.30am-5.30pm), about 3km
from the city centre, was a famous medical
school with a library that rivalled that of
Alexandria in Egypt. The ruins of the **Acropolis** (admission €6; �8.30am-5.30pm), 6km from
the city, are equally striking. The hilltop
setting is absolutely magical, and the well-
preserved ruins are magnificent – especially
the vertigo-inducing 10,000-seat **theatre** and
the marble-columned **Temple of Trajan**, built
during the reigns of Emperors Trajan and
Hadrian (2nd century) and used to worship
them as well as Zeus.

Expand your knowledge of Turkish history by visiting the excellent **Archaeology Museum** (İzmir Caddesi; admission €3; �8.30am-5.30pm
Tue-Sun), which has fine displays from both
of these sites.

Sleeping & Eating
Böblingen Pension (☎ 633 2153; fax 631 5676; Askle-
pion Caddesi 2; s/d €9/18) This family-run guesthouse is the best bet if you don't want to

strain your wallet. The rooms won't win
any prizes for decoration but it's perfectly
clean and your hosts are a mine of local
information. The evening meals (€7) are
warmly praised. It's at the start of the road
to the Asclepion.

Manolya Pension (☎ 633 4488; www.manolya
pension.8m.net; Tanpınar Sokak 11; s/d €13/26; ☒ ☐)
Don't be put off by the rather drab-looking
façade of this high-rise block – the Manolya
is a perfect place to rest your head after a
long day's sightseeing. It has a kilim-draped
lobby, clean-smelling rooms, well-sprung
mattresses and pastel colours splashed all
over the walls.

Gobi Pension (☎ 633 2518; İzmir Caddesi 18; s €12-15,
d €21 24) It's nothing to write home about but
at least it's clean and well kept. Light sleepers
should steer clear of the rooms at the front,
as the busy main drag is close by.

Sağlam 3 Restaurant (☎ 632 8897; Cumhuriyet
Meydanı 29; mains €3-4) A short bag-haul from
the PTT, the Sağlam is reckoned to cook up
the best meat dishes in town and is usually
packed. So many locals can't be wrong.

Tadim Kebap Salonu (☎ 632 1815; Denizciler Caddesi; mains €2-3) This hole-in-the-wall, close to
Kulaksız Cami, tosses up the usual suspects
at puny prices.

Özlem Pide ve Çorba Salonu (☎ 632 5156; İzmir
Caddesi 8; mains €2-4) First-rate hearty pide are
served in this bright and cheery place on
the main drag.

Getting There & Around
There are frequent buses to and from İzmir
(€4, two hours, 100km) and Ayvalık (€4.50,
1¾ hours, 50km). Check to see if your bus actually stops at Bergama's otogar. Some buses
will drop you along the highway at the turn-
off to Bergama, leaving you to hitch 7km
into town or take a taxi (€11). At the time of
writing, there were plans to build a new otogar on the outskirts of Bergama, close to the
turn-off, which would make things easier.

There's no public transport to the archaeological sites. A taxi tour of the Acropolis, the Asclepion and the museum costs
about €30.

İZMİR
☎ 0232 / pop 2,233,000
Let's face it: although it has a dramatic setting
around a bay backed by mountains, İzmir
(once known as Smyrna) lacks the charisma

TURKEY

of other big Turkish cities. Its sites are relatively underwhelming and fail to impress. For most travellers, Turkey's third-largest city is just a place to hop off a bus or train and onto a bus or dolmuş heading north or south to the coastal resorts. But, to its credit, İzmir offers a refreshing touch of sophistication, an enticing cosmopolitan atmosphere and a disarmingly liberal attitude. Give it a chance and you may find it grows on you.

Orientation & Information

The central area of İzmir is a web of *meydanlar* (squares) linked by streets that aren't at right angles to each other. Instead of names, the back streets have numbers. Ask for a free map at the tourist office.

Budget hotels cluster near Basmane train station, in a district sometimes called Çankaya. To the southwest, Anafartalar Caddesi twists and turns through the labyrinthine bazaar to the waterfront at Konak, the commercial and government centre. Atatürk Caddesi (Birinci Kordon) runs northeast from Konak along the waterfront, finishing 1.4km past Cumhuriyet Meydanı with its equestrian statue of Atatürk, the main PTT, luxury hotels and airline offices.

İzmir's otogar is 6km northeast of the town centre.

The helpful **tourist office** (☎ 484 2147; fax 489 9278; Akdeniz Caddesi 1344 Sokak 2; 🕒 8.30am-5.30pm Mon-Fri) is right on the seafront.

Sights

Since most of old İzmir was destroyed by earthquakes there's little to see here compared with other Turkish cities. However, it does boast the remains of an extensive 2nd-century-AD Roman **agora** (marketplace; admission €2; 🕒 8.30am-noon & 1-5pm), right inside the sprawling, atmospheric modern **bazaar**. It's also worth taking a bus to the hilltop **Kadifekale** (*kale* means fortress), where women still weave kilims on horizontal looms and where the views are breathtaking.

Sleeping

The area around Basmane train station – cross the road outside the station, turn left and immediately right – nurtures lots of cheapies, but most of them tend to be basic digs. It's best to stick to the places listed here.

Hotel Imperial (☎ 483 9771; 1296 Sokak 54; s/d €15/24) A sensible choice for budget travellers – if you can look past the garish fake Greek columns guarding the entrance. The rooms, while not luxurious, are perfectly adequate.

Hotel Baylan (☎ 483 1426; http://hotelbaylan.site mynet.com; 1299 Sokak No 8; s/d €21/36; P ❄) Those wanting a clean and comfortable place could do worse than check into this professionally run outfit, a few doors from the Imperial. Rooms come with all the mod cons, including TVs, telephones and minibars.

Otel Antik Han (☎ 489 2750; www.otelantikhan.com in Turkish; Anafartalar Caddesi 600; s/d €35/60; P ❄) A pleasant surprise right in the bazaar, close to the agora, this boutiquish hotel in a painstakingly restored Ottoman house oozes atmosphere. While the rooms are not luxurious, they are cosy and intimate enough. The courtyard is a great place to relax or to scribble a postcard or two over a cup of tea. There's a bar here, too.

For other hotel options, walk straight down Fevzipaşa Bulvarı from Basmane station and turn right (north). There are a few

DON'T FORGET YOUR NAZAR BONCUK

It's ubiquitous in Turkey, but you might not have noticed it. Nazar Boncuk is a Turkish 'evil-eye' charm. As in many cultures, Turks believe that the 'evil eye' can bring you bad luck. Turks use Nazar Boncuks (literally 'evil-eye beads') to ward off malicious forces associated with envious eyes. Nazar Boncuks can be seen pinned to the clothes of babies, guarding the doorways of restaurants, nailed on doors and walls... The bead reflects the evil intent back to the onlooker. With its concentric dots of colours, it somewhat resembles an eye and it is said that the typical blue colour helps protect the user.

This tradition goes back to the Arabian craftsmen who settled in İzmir during the decline of the Ottoman Empire. Today, the genuine eye beads are produced by a handful of glass masters in Görece and Kurudere near İzmir. Their methods and techniques have changed very little over the centuries.

Nazar Boncuks appear in various shapes and sizes, and make an ideal gift.

clean, quiet hotels in 1368 Sokak and its
westward continuation, 1369 Sokak.

Eating

For bargain-basement meals, especially at
lunchtime, head straight into the bazaar and
take your pick from the countless small restaurants. For something more sophisticated,
explore the tiny streets lined with restored
houses in Alsancak district. Alternatively hit
the waterfront café-bars, which offer innumerable opportunities for people-watching.

Altın Kapı (☎ 422 2709; 1444 Sokak 9/A & 14/A, Alsancak; mains €4-10) A ragingly popular venue in
Alsancak that serves well-prepared dishes to
a well-heeled crowd. It has three branches
in the street, each specialising in a type of
food (kebaps, fish dishes, Turkish meals).
Get a seat on the shady terrace.

Kırçiçeği (☎ 464 3090; Kıbrıs Şehitleri Caddesi,
Alsancak; mains €4-9) Business is brisk in this
well-regarded option, set in the bustling
pedestrianised Kibris Şehitleri Caddesi. It
serves the full array of Turkish staples, including kebaps, pide and grills. There's a
picture menu to help you choose.

Getting There & Away

AIR

Turkish Airlines offers nonstop flights to
İstanbul (€85) and Ankara (€60) from İzmir,
with connections to other destinations. Onur
Air, Atlasjet and Fly Air also fly to İzmir.

BUS

İzmir is a major transport hub. From the
otogar, frequent buses leave for Bergama
(€4, two hours), Kuşadası (€2, 1½ hours),
Selçuk (€2, one hour), and other destinations
around the country. Buses to Çeşme (€5, 1½
hours) leave from a local bus terminal in
Üçkuyular, 6.5km southwest of Konak.

TRAIN

The only train service that is really useful
for travellers is the daily *İzmir Mavi* (€12)
from Basmane station to Ankara. There are
also express trains to Selçuk/Ephesus (€2)
and Denizli (for Pamukkale; €5).

ÇEŞME

☎ 0232 / pop 100,000

With its tangle of narrow backstreets and a
dramatic Genoese fortress that dominates
the town centre, Çeşme is a joy to explore.

Unfortunately it's no longer a secret and
can get very busy during the school holidays. About 85km due west of İzmir, it's
also popular with weekending İzmirlis. Outside high season, however, you'll have
the whole place for yourself. Kick back
with a meal of seafood washed down with
a glass of rakı to really get into the spirit
of things.

The helpful **tourist office** (☎ /fax 712 6653;
İskele Meydanı 6; ☺ 9am-5pm Mon-Sat in summer),
ferry and bus ticket offices, banks with
ATMs, restaurants and hotels are all within
two blocks of the main square.

Sleeping & Eating

There's a wealth of good value, homy pensions in Çeşme. They are usually open from
May to October. Bookings are essential in
summer and at weekends.

Can Pansiyon (☎ 712 6210; 2032 Sokak; d €24) One
of the best pads in town. Away from the hub-
bub, it has had a lick of paint – in vivid hues,
a refreshing sea-breeze choice – and offers
sparkling clean accommodation. Some rooms
sport balconies to maximise the view.

Barınak Pansiyon (☎ 712 6670; 3052 Sokak 58; d
€35; ❀) Another sound choice, with light,
airy interiors, a breezy terrace and knockout
views.

06 Pansiyon (☎ 712 6047; 2037 Sokak 16; s/d €15/
25) It has no views to speak of, but is blessed
with a leafy garden.

Yalçın Otel (☎ 712 6981; www.yalcinhotel.freeser
vers.com; 1002 Sokak 10; s/d €19/25) After a bit more
privacy? Head for Yalçın Otel, perched on
the hillside overlooking the harbour. This
well-managed place features well-equipped,
value-for-money rooms, some with smashing views, and an agreeable terrace.

Heading north towards the marina there
are several harbour restaurants that specialise in fresh fish, including **Rıhtım** (☎ 712 7433;
mains €4-10). Near the fortress, **Biz Bize** (☎ 712
1746; İnkilap Caddesi; mains €4-8) is renowned for
its kebaps, while **İmren** (☎ 712 7620; İnkilap Caddesi; mains €2-5) serves up the usual suspects at
moderate prices in an attractive old building.
For a melt-in-your-mouth pide, the cognos-
centi swear there's no better place than **Fatih
Pide** (☎ 712 8121; İnkilap Caddesi; mains €2-4). Amble
down İnkilap Caddesi and you'll come across
the **Friendly Corner** (☎ 712 1751; 3025 Sokak 2; mains
€5-8), a 'rustic chic' establishment tarted up
for tourists.

Getting There & Away

There are buses from İzmir to Çeşme (€5, 1½ hours, 85km) from the western Üçkuyular terminal.

Çeşme is a transit point to the Greek island of Chios, 10km away across the water. In summer, there are daily ferries to Chios, and at least three weekly services in winter. Buy your ticket from any travel agency at the harbour.

There are also weekly or twice-weekly ferry services to Brindisi and Ancona (Italy). See p663 for more information.

SELÇUK

☎ 0232 / pop 23,100

An easy one-hour bus trip south of İzmir, Selçuk is a magnet for backpackers from all over the world. It's packed with cheap pensions and eateries aimed at independent travellers. Although very touristy in the high season, this pleasant small town has retained an unhurried pace of life and is a backwater compared with coastal playpens such as Kuşadası and Marmaris.

Why it's so popular is easy to understand: the grandiose Roman ruins of Ephesus are almost on its doorstep.

Orientation & Information

Most of the pensions are on the quieter western side of the highway (Atatürk Caddesi), behind the Ephesus Museum, but others are on the eastern side along with the otogar, restaurants and train station. There's a **tourist office** (☎ 892 6328; www.selcuk .gov.tr; ☼ 8.30am-noon & 1-5.30pm Mon-Fri year-round, 1-5pm Sat & Sun summer) in the park on the western side of the main street.

Ephesus is a 3km walk west from the otogar along a shady road – turn left (south) at the junction. There are frequent minibuses from the otogar to the junction, leaving you with just a 1km walk.

Sights

Selçuk is not only close to Ephesus, it's also blessed with superb monuments scattered around the centre. Don't miss the conspicuous **Basilica of St John** (admission €2.50; ☼ 8am-5.30pm), atop Ayasuluk Hill. It was built in the 6th century on the site where it was believed St John the Evangelist had been buried. The less impressive **Temple of Artemis** (☼ 8.30am-5.30pm), between Ephesus and Selçuk, was

once one of the Seven Wonders of the Ancient World. In its prime, it was larger than the Parthenon at Athens. Unfortunately, little more than one pillar now remains.

The excellent **Ephesus Museum** (admission €2.50; ☼ 8.30am-noon & 12.30-4.30pm), opposite the tourist office, houses a striking collection of artefacts.

Sleeping

You'll be spoilt for choice in Selçuk. Many pensions offer free lifts to Ephesus.

Homeros Pension (☎ 892 3995; www.homeros pension.com; 1048 Sokak 3; s €9-15, d €18; ✕) This pension gets glowing reports from travellers, and it's no wonder. The squeaky-clean rooms are individually decorated – the owner is a carpenter – and there's a mellow atmosphere. The breezy rooftop terrace is perfect for a tipple and guests can borrow bikes free of charge.

Hotel Bella (☎ 892 3944; www.hotelbella.com; St Jean Sokak 7; s/d €15/22; ✕ 🖳) The artistically inclined will enjoy staying at this charming hotel run by affable hosts. It features tastefully decorated rooms and an inviting rooftop terrace overlooking the basilica. The evening meals (€7) have also garnered high praise from travellers.

Hotel Akay & Amazon Pansiyon (☎ 892 3172; www .hotelakay.8m.com; 1054 Sokak 3; s in pension €8, s in hotel €20-40, d in hotel €30-60; 🅿 ✕ 🖳 🕭) This welcoming spot has three separate buildings to suit all budgets. Shoestringers will opt for the basic but pleasant pension, while wealthier travellers will stay at the conventional hotel or at the plusher boutique hotel, across the road from the pension. Facilities are excellent, and include a pool and a superb rooftop terrace blessed with lovely views.

Jimmy's (Artemis) Place Ephesus (☎ 892 1982; 1016 Sokak 19; dm/s/d €7/11/19, r deluxe €30; ✕ 🖳 🕭) Smack-bang in the centre of town, Jimmy's Place is a perennial favourite, with lots of services and comforts. Some rooms feel a bit too lived-in but overall it's perfectly adequate, and owner Jimmy is a mine of local information. There's an on-site library of information on Turkey and guests can use the pool, just one minute's walk away.

Australia & New Zealand Pension (☎ 892 1050; www.anzturkishguesthouse.com; Profesör Mitler Sokak 17; dm/s €8/11, d €21-30; ✕ 🖳) This lively pension-cum-hostel is a gregarious backpacking option, with a mixed bag of rooms set around

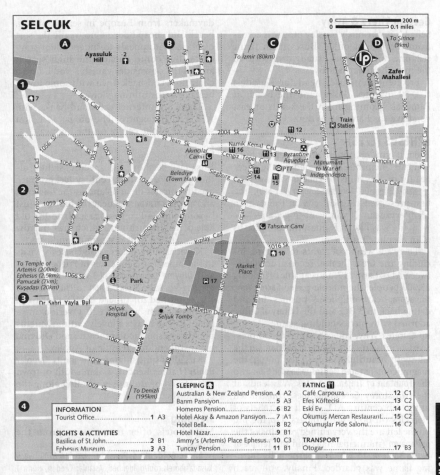

SELÇUK

0 ————— 200 m
0 ————— 0.1 miles

TURKEY

a refreshing courtyard. It's a bit cramped and lacks intimacy, but nothing beats a tasty barbecue and a cold beer on the rooftop terrace in the evening (€6). Air-con is extra.

Also recommended:

Barım Pansiyon (☎ 892 6923; 1045 Sokak 34; s/d €14/24; 💻) In an old stone house.

Hotel Nazar (☎ 892 2222; 2019 Sokak 34; www .nazarhotel.com; d €25; ❄) Was undergoing complete renovation when we visited.

Tuncay Pension (☎ /fax 892 6260; s €9, d €18-20; ❄) A friendly spot with an open courtyard.

Eating

Selçuk's culinary scene is not exactly enthralling but there are some commendable options in the centre.

Okumuş Mercan Restaurant (☎ 892 6196; PTT Karşısı Hal Binaları 43; mains €3-6) A popular place with a shady terrace; it's in the small square south of the post office.

Efes Köftecisi (☎ 892 3267; Namik Kemal Caddesi 2, mains €2-5) This cheap and cheerful eatery serves up plates of *köfte*.

Okumuşlar Pide Salonu (Namık Kemal Caddesi; mains €2-4) For pide, you won't find better than Okumuşlar Pide Salonu.

Café Carpouza (☎ 892 9264; Argenta Caddesi; mains €2-4) In the mood for an atmospheric setting? Try Café Carpouza, a well-restored house set in a verdant park north of the PTT.

Eski Ev (☎ 892 9357; 1005 Sokak 1; mains €2-5) This place boasts a relaxing *bahçe* (garden), but we found the food fairly average.

Getting There & Away

Selçuk's notoriously hassley otogar is across from the tourist office. Buses from İzmir (€2, one hour, 80km) usually drop you on the main highway nearby.

Frequent minibuses head for Kuşadası (€2, 30 minutes, 35km) and the beach at Pamucak. Coming from the south or east you have to change at Aydın.

EPHESUS (EFES)

Even if you're not an architecture buff, you can't help but be dazzled by the sheer beauty of the ruins of **Ephesus** (admission €10; ◉ 8am-4.30pm Oct-Apr, 8am-6.30pm May-Sep), the best-preserved classical city in the eastern Mediterranean. If you want to get a feel for what life was like in Roman times, Ephesus is an absolute must-see.

There's a wealth of sights to explore, including the **Great Theatre**, reconstructed between AD 41 and 117, and capable of holding 25,000 people; the marble-paved **Sacred Way**; the **agora**, heart of Ephesus' business life and dating back to 3 BC; and the **Library of Celsus**, adorned with niches holding statues. Going up Curetes Way, you can't miss the impressive Corinthian-style **Temple of Hadrian**, on the left, with beautiful friezes in the porch; the magnificent **Terraced Houses** (admission €10); and the **Fountain of Trajan**. Curetes Way ends at the two-storey **Gate of Hercules**, constructed in the 4th century AD, which has reliefs of Hercules on both main pillars. Up the hill on the left are the very ruined remains of the **prytaneum** (municipal hall) and the **Temple of Hestia Boulaea**, in which a perpetually burning flame was guarded. Finally, you reach the **odeum**, a small theatre dating from AD 150 and used for musical performances and meetings of town council.

You'll find a couple of unpretentious restaurants and *gözleme* and *ayran* stalls near the entrances.

Many pensions in Selçuk offer free lifts to Ephesus. Note that there are two entry points roughly 3km apart. A taxi from Selçuk to the main entrance should cost about €5.

KUŞADASI

☎ 0256 / pop 50,000

At first glance, Kuşadası is not exactly the most alluring seaside town in Turkey. In summer, it's bustling with package holidaymakers from Europe in search of sun, beach and cheap booze – not really the sort of place that appeals to independent travellers. But come outside the high season and all the downsides vanish – you'll find a charming, laid-back town with some lovely beaches and stunning views.

There are Internet cafés and banks with ATMs in the centre. The otogar is 1.5km southeast of the centre on the highway.

Sights

Kuşadası is short on specific sights, although there's a 16th-century **fortress** once used by pirates on an island in the harbour, and an old **caravanserai** near the harbour. Just beyond the PTT, a passage leads to the old **Kaleiçi** neighbourhood, which has narrow streets packed with restaurants and bars.

Kuşadası also makes a good base for visits to the superb ancient cities of **Priene**, **Miletus** and **Didyma** (admission to all 3 sites €1.25; ◉ 9am-8pm May-Sep, 8.30-5.30pm Oct-Apr) to the south; if you're pushed for time, a 'PMD' tour from the otogar costs around €20. Overlooking a plain, Priene boasts a lovely setting; Miletus preserves a spectacular theatre; and Didyma has a stupendous Temple of Apollo.

Kuşadası's most famous beach is **Kadınlar Denizi** (Ladies Beach), 2.5km south of town and served by dolmuşes running along the coastal road.

Sleeping

Most hotels offer free pick-up from the otogar.

Anzac Goldenbed Pension (☎ 614 8708; www .kusadasihotels.com/goldenbed; Aslanlar Caddesi, Uğrlu 1 Çıkmazı 4; s €6-15, d €21-24; ◉) Tucked away in a quiet cul-de-sac, this long-time backpackers' favourite remains a solid choice, with a wide array of rooms varying in shape and size. The rooftop terrace is a killer and has a bar overlooking the town. It's a great place to socialise or to curl up with a book. The Turkish-Aussie couple who run the place will go the extra yard to help travellers.

Liman Hotel (☎ 614 7770; www.limanhotel.com; Kıbrıs Caddesi, Buyral Sokak 4; s/d €18/25; ◉ ▣) Liman Hotel is a colourful pile, wedged between various shops right by the harbour. The spiffing location, as well as the spacious and comfy rooms with pristine bathrooms, make this a steal, and the talkative manager, dubbed 'Mr Happy', could not run the place

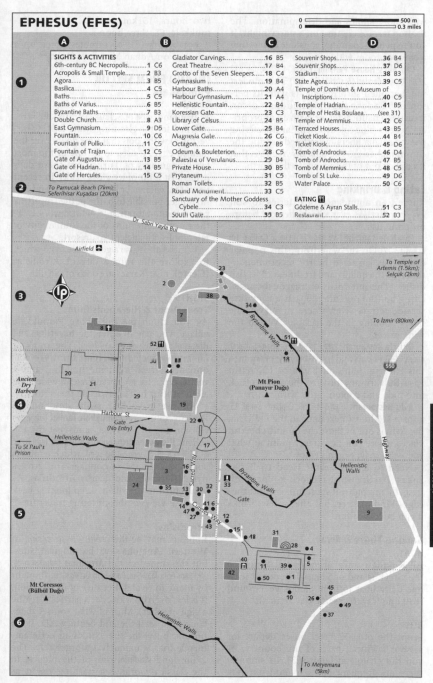

EPHESUS (EFES)

0 ────── 500 m
0 ────── 0.3 miles

SIGHTS & ACTIVITIES

6th-century BC Necropolis	**1**	C6
Acropolis & Small Temple	**2**	B3
Agora	**3**	B5
Basilica	**4**	C5
Baths	**5**	C5
Baths of Varius	**6**	B5
Byzantine Baths	**7**	B3
Double Church	**8**	A3
East Gymnasium	**9**	D5
Fountain	**10**	C6
Fountain of Pollio	**11**	C5
Fountain of Trajan	**12**	C5
Gate of Augustus	**13**	B5
Gate of Hadrian	**14**	B5
Gate of Hercules	**15**	C5
Gladiator Carvings	**16**	B5
Great Theatre	**17**	B4
Grotto of the Seven Sleepers	**18**	C4
Gymnasium	**19**	B4
Harbour Baths	**20**	A4
Harbour Gymnasium	**21**	A4
Hellenistic Fountain	**22**	B4
Library of Celsus	**24**	B5
Lower Gate	**25**	B4
Magnesia Gate	**26**	C6
Octagon	**27**	B5
Odeum & Bouleterion	**28**	C5
Palaestra of Verulanus	**29**	D4
Private House	**30**	C5
Prytaneum	**31**	C5
Roman Toilets	**32**	B5
Round Monument	**33**	C5
Sanctuary of the Mother Goddess Cybele	**34**	C3
South Gate	**35**	B5
Souvenir Shops	**36**	B4
Souvenir Shops	**37**	D6
Stadium	**38**	B3
State Agora	**39**	C5
Temple of Domitian & Museum of Inscriptions	**40**	C5
Temple of Hadrian	**41**	B5
Temple of Hestia Boulaea	(see 31)	
Temple of Memmius	**42**	C6
Terraced Houses	**43**	B5
Ticket Kiosk	**44**	B4
Ticket Kiosk	**45**	D6
Tomb of Androclus	**46**	D4
Tomb of Androclus	**47**	B5
Tomb of Memmius	**48**	C5
Tomb of St Luke	**49**	D6
Water Palace	**50**	C6

EATING 🍴

Gözleme & Ayran Stalls	**51**	C3
Restaurant	**52**	B3

To Pamucak Beach (7km);
Seferihisar Kuşadası (20km)

Dr Sabri Yayla Bul

Airfield ✈

To Temple of
Artemis (1.5km);
Selçuk (2km)

To İzmir (80km)

Byzantine Walls

Mt Pion
(Panayır Dağı) ▲

550

Highway

Ancient
Dry
Harbour

Harbour St

Gate
(No Entry)

Hellenistic Walls

To St Paul's
Prison

Sacred Way

Byzantine Walls

Gate

Hellenistic
Walls

Curetes Way

Mt Coressos
(Bülbül Dağı) ▲

Hellenistic Walls

To Meryemana
(5km)

TURKEY

with more smiles and determination. The rooftop terrace is a treat on a starry night. If you're penny-counting, consider requesting a cheaper room with no view.

Captain's House Pension (☎ 614 4754; fax 612 2216; Atatürk Caddesi 66; s/d €15/30; ☒) This modest number often surprises guests with its personality. Lacking the typical ho-hum décor, it carries a nautical theme, with an appropriate Aegean-blue colour scheme and seafaring paraphernalia liberally scattered around the communal areas. The only downside is that it's a flick out of the action, to the north.

Eating & Drinking

There's an abundance of eateries to suit every wallet. As ever, check the cost before ordering fish.

Ferah Restaurant (☎ 614 1281; Liman Caddesi 10; mains €8-12) On the waterfront, this popular eatery has garnered hearty recommendations for the quality and freshness of its fish dishes. The interior is outrageously unexciting but the restaurant boasts an inviting seaside terrace from where to survey the boats bobbing in the harbour. Watch the wine prices.

Öz Urfa Restaurant (☎ 614 6070; Cephane Sokak 9; mains €4-6) Locals and tourists alike cram into this cheerful joint, off Barbaros Hayrettin Paşa Bulvarı, any time of the day to tuck into pide and copious grills with relish.

Avlu Restaurant (☎ 614 7995; Cephane Sokak 15; mains €4-6) Almost next door to the Öz Urfa, the Avlu is one of those cheap-and-cheerful places where you can simply point at what you want, pay, eat and enjoy.

Need to let off steam? Head to Barlar Sokak (Bar St), which is chock-a-block with Irish-theme pubs. It's a scruffy-round-the-edges kind of street but after a few drinks it can be lots of fun.

Getting There & Away

BOAT

All Kuşadası travel agencies sell tickets to the Greek island of Samos. There's at least one daily boat to/from Samos year-round (€30 one way, €35 same-day return).

BUS

From the otogar, direct buses depart for several far-flung parts of the country, or you can change at İzmir (€3). In summer there are frequent buses to Bodrum (€8,

two hours, 151km) and Denizli (for Pamukkale; €8, three hours).

For Selçuk (€1, 40 minutes), pick up a minibus on Adnan Menderes Bulvarı.

INLAND FROM SELÇUK
Pamukkale
☎ 0258

Way inland, east of Selçuk, Pamukkale is renowned for the gleaming white ledges (travertines) with pools that flow down over the plateau edge. It used to be one of the most familiar images of Turkey but these days it has lost a bit of its gloss. Sadly in recent years the water supply has dried up and it is no longer possible to bathe in the travertine pools. Behind this fragile natural wonder lie the magnificent ruins of the Roman city of Hierapolis, an ancient spa resort.

Pamukkale is also a good base from which to explore the ruined city of Afrodisias (Geyre), near Karacasu south of Nazilli.

SIGHTS
Travertines & Hierapolis Ruins

As you climb the hill above Pamukkale village, you pay to enter the **travertines and Hierapolis** (admission €3; ☽ 24hr). The ruins of Hierapolis, including a huge theatre, a colonnaded street, a latrine building and a vast necropolis, are spread over a wide area; allow at least half a day to do them justice.

Afterwards you can swim amid sunken Roman columns at **Pamukkale Termal** (admission €10), on top of the ridge, and visit the excellent **Hierapolis Archaeology Museum** (admission €1.25; ☽ 8.30am-noon & 1.30-5pm), which contains some spectacular sarcophagi and friezes from Hierapolis and nearby Afrodisias. As you return to the village keep looking back for great views of the glittering travertines.

Afrodisias

Ephesus may be the *crème de la crème* of Western Anatolia's archaeological sites, but the ruined city of **Afrodisias** (admission €5; ☽ 9am-6pm May-Sep, 9am-5pm Oct-Apr) is thought by many to rival it. Because of its isolation, it is less overrun with coach parties (breathe a sigh of relief). Most of what you see dates back to at least the 2nd century AD. If it's not too busy, the site exudes an eerie ambience that is uniquely unforgettable. The 270m-long **stadium**, one of the biggest in the classical world, is a startling vision, as are the **Temple of Aphrodite** and the white-marble **theatre**.

The only downside is that access by public transport is not easy. It makes sense to sign up for a transport-only arrangement with your pension in Pamukkale (about €18).

SLEEPING & EATING

Competition between Pamukkale's many pensions is intense, and the services on offer are much better than in most other towns. Most places provide good, cheap home-cooked meals and serve wine and beer.

Kervansaray Pension (☎ 272 2209; kervansaray2@ superonline.com.tr; İnönü Caddesi; s/d €13/20; 🔀 💻 🏖) One of the best deals in town, with cheerful rooms and a friendly family atmosphere.

Beyaz Kale (Weisse Burg Pension; ☎ 272 2064; weisseburg@yahoo.com; Menderes Caddesi; s/d €12/22; 🏖) The Beyaz Kale deserves plaudits for its eight renovated rooms, its tasty meals and its rooftop restaurant.

Koray (☎ 272 2300; Fevzi Çakmak Caddesi 27; s/d €12/22; 🔀 🏖) Find heaven in this inviting place, located in the quiet south part of the village. After all that vigorous activity, re-cline by the pool or relax in the basement *hamam*. The Koray brothers offer tour services to all the surrounding sites.

Öztürk Otel-Pension (☎ 272 2116; ozturkhotel@ ozturkotel.com; İnönü Caddesi; s/d €11/20; 🔀 💻 🏖) Next to the Koray, the Öztürk is another firm favourite. There's lots of greenery around the pool.

Allgau Hotel (☎ 272 2767; allgau@superonline.com; Hasan Tahsin Caddesi; s/d €11/18; 🔀 💻 🏖) Well-tended gardens and clean-smelling rooms.

GETTING THERE & AWAY

In summer, Pamukkale has several direct buses to and from other cities. At other times of year you'll probably need to change in Denizli. Buses run between Denizli and Pamukkale every 30 minutes or so.

BODRUM

☎ 0252 / pop 32,200

If you have time for only one stop on the Aegean coast, you can hardly do better than Bodrum. With its sugar-cube houses draped in brilliantly coloured bougainvillea, its palm-lined streets and its twin bays, it has managed to cling to its original charm. By some miracle it retains a really special magic – a fusion of wind, sea, light and re-strained sophistication – that isn't dissipated even by the throngs of lager louts and the influx of charter deals in high summer.

Orientation & Information

The **otogar** (Cevat Şakir Caddesi) is 500m inland from the Adliye (Yeni) Camii, a small mosque at the centre of the town. The PTT and several banks with ATMs are on Cevat Şakir. There are Internet cafés on Üçkuyular Caddesi, all charging about €1 per hour. The **tourist office** (☎ 316 1091; fax 316 7694; Kale Meydanı; 🕑 8.30am-5.30pm) is beside the Castle of St Peter.

Sights & Activities

Bodrum's star attraction is the conspicuous **Castle of St Peter**. Built in 1402 and rebuilt in 1522 by the Crusaders, the castle houses the **Museum of Underwater Archaeology** (admission €6.25; 🕑 9am-noon & 1-5pm Tue-Sun), containing finds from the oldest Mediterranean **shipwreck** (admission €2.50; 🕑 10-11am & 2-4pm Tue-Fri) ever discovered; and a model of a Carian princess's tomb, inside the **French Tower** (admission €2.50; 🕑 10am-noon & 2-4pm Tue-Fri). Sadly there's little left of the **Mausoleum of Halicarnassus** (admission €1.50; 🕑 8am-noon & 12.30-5pm Tue-Sun), the monumental tomb of King Mausolus, which was once among the Seven Wonders of the Ancient World.

Bodrum is famous for its **scuba diving**. Look for the dive centres on the boats moored near the tourist office. Numerous yachts moored along Neyzen Tevfik Caddesi on the western bay run **day trips** (around €15) around the bay.

Sleeping

The narrow streets north of Bodrum's western harbour house pleasant family-run pensions. Those behind the western bay tend to be quieter than those on the eastern bay because they're further from the famously noisy Halikarnas Disco. Prices drop between November and March, but few places stay open in winter.

Su Otel & Cottages (☎ 316 6906; www.bodrum4u .com/suhotel; Turgutreis Caddesi, 1201 Sokak; s/d €40/80; 🔀 💻 🏖) Here, quite possibly, is Bodrum's most seductive hotel. Why do we love it so? Amiable, English-speaking owners who take pride in their hotel, sparkling bathrooms, handsome rooms set around a flower-filled courtyard, colourful walls, a

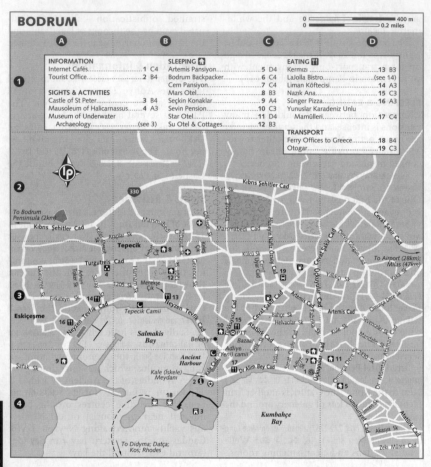

BODRUM

0 —————— 400 m
0 —————— 0.2 miles

INFORMATION
Internet Cafés.................1 C4
Tourist Office.................2 B4

SIGHTS & ACTIVITIES
Castle of St Peter..............3 B4
Mausoleum of Halicarnassus....4 A3
Museum of Underwater
  Archaeology...............(see 3)

SLEEPING
Artemis Pansiyon..............5 D4
Bodrum Backpacker............6 C4
Cem Pansiyon.................7 C4
Mars Otel....................8 B3
Seçkin Konaklar..............9 A4
Sevin Pension................10 C3
Star Otel...................11 D4
Su Otel & Cottages...........12 B3

EATING
Kermızı.....................13 B3
LaJolla Bistro...............(see 14)
Liman Köftecisi..............14 A3
Mars Otel...................15 C3
Sünger Pizza................16 A3
Yunuslar Karadeniz Unlu
  Mamülleri................17 C4

TRANSPORT
Ferry Offices to Greece........18 B4
Otogar.....................19 C3

spiffing location in a quiet side street and a jazzy atmosphere. And did we mention the splendid pool? Book ahead.

Bodrum Backpacker (☎ 313 2762; www.bodrumbackpackers.com; Atatürk Caddesi 31/B; dm/s/d €8/9/17; ▯) Shoestringers would be nuts to stay anywhere else. The staff are helpful and the tiled rooms are spotless, if a bit poky and anonymous. There are a host of facilities, such as satellite TV, bike and care hire, laundry service and the popular 'British Bar' downstairs.

Sevin Pension (☎ 316 7682; www.sevinpansiyon.8m .com; Türkkuyusu Caddesi 5; s €16-24, d €20-28; ▯ ▯) Brilliantly located right in the thick of things, the Sevin is a friendly, well-run operation with good facilities – plus there's a

pleasant courtyard draped in bougainvillea. Ask for a renovated room.

Mars Otel (☎ 316 6559; Turgutreis Caddesi, İmbat Çıkmazı 20; s/d €13/25; ▯ ▯ ▯) Come here expecting airs and graces and you'll be disappointed, but if you want a clean and serviceable room in a no-frills family-run hotel you'll do all right. The highlights here are the glistening pool and the bar. Pity about the meagre breakfast.

Other recommendations:
Artemis Pansiyon (☎ 316 1572; Cumhuriyet Caddesi 121; s/d €40/70; ▯) Boasts an ace location on the waterfront but is hardly likely to be quiet.
Cem Pansiyon (☎ 316 1757; Üçkuyular Caddesi 9; s/d €40/60; ▯) A few espadrille steps from the waterfront. Unremarkable but clean rooms.

Star Otel (☎ 316 3741; Atatürk Caddesi; s/d €26/45) When we popped into this white building behind the eastern bay, renovations were in progress and things were looking good.

Seçkin Konaklar (☎ 316 1351; Neyzen Tevfik Caddesi 246; r €45-80; ⚇ ⚏) A haven of peace and comfort, facing the marina. It has several apartments and normal rooms set around a central pool.

Eating & Drinking

Bodrum is a great place for a splurge. Ease a belt hole at the following favourites.

Liman Köftecisi (☎ 316 5060; Neyzen Tevfik Caddesi 172; mains €3-6) Rumbling tummies won't go hungry; portions are huge at this cheerful restaurant on the waterfront. As the name suggests, it specialises in *köfte*. Make sure to try the divine *Liman köfte*, with yogurt, butter, tomato sauce and bread.

Nazık Ana (☎ 313 1891; Eski Hukumet Sokak 7; mains €2-3) You don't have to shift your credit card into overdraft to eat in this quirky eatery behind the PTT. It's a self-service restaurant with appetising homemade fare, including lots of veggie-friendly options. The dining space is gaily decorated with plants, as well as artefacts and black-and-white pictures on the walls.

In warm weather, head straight for Meyhaneler Sokak (Taverna St), off İskele Caddesi. Wall-to-wall *meyhaneler* serve food, drink and live music to rapturous crowds for €9 to €12.

Other recommendations:

Sünger Pizza (☎ 316 0854; Neyzen Tevfik Caddesi 218; mains €3-5) On the waterfront, the Sünger doles out palate-blowing pizzas and Turkish classics.

Kırmızı (☎ 316 4918; Neyzen Tevfik Caddesi 44; mains €4-8) A snug place with an arty feel. It features a fusion menu of Mediterranean and Turkish dishes.

Yunuslar Karadeniz Unlu Mamülleri (☎ 316 1748; Cumhuriyet Caddesi 13) For a quick bite, nothing beats this fancy bakery in the market area. Its little sandwiches with pastrami or cheese and sausage are out of this world.

LaJolla Bistro (☎ 313 7660; Neyzen Tevfik Caddesi 174; mains €2-5) This tiny wine bar with stylish surrounds serves up good tapas as well as salads, pasta and steaks. Its terrace on the waterfront is well placed for watching the sophisticated swagger of passers-by.

Getting There & Away

Turkish Airlines, Atlasjet, Fly Air and Onur Air have flights from İstanbul to Bodrum.

By bus, there are services to more or less anywhere you could wish to go. Useful services include those to Kuşadası (€8), Marmaris (€7) and Pamukkale (€10).

In summer, daily hydrofoils (€33 same-day return) and ferries (€23 same-day return) link Bodrum with Kos (Greece); in winter, services shrink to three weekly. In summer there are also two weekly services to Rhodes (Rhodos; €45 one way, €50 same-day return); check with the ferry offices near the castle.

MEDITERRANEAN COAST

Turkey's Mediterranean coastline winds eastward for more than 1200km, from Marmaris to Antakya on the Syrian border.

From Marmaris to Fethiye, the gorgeous 'Turquoise Coast' is perfect for boat excursions, with many secluded coves and quiet bays. The rugged peninsula east of Fethiye to Antalya and the Taurus Mountains east of Antalya are wild and beautiful. Further east you pass through fewer seaside resorts and more workaday cities.

The entire coast has plenty to set your camera's flash popping. It is liberally sprinkled with impressive ruins, studded with gorgeous beaches and washed by a glittering sea, which is ideal for sports.

MARMARİS

☎ 0252 / pop 22,700

Like Bodrum, Marmaris sits on a marvellous bay at the edge of a hilly peninsula. Unlike Bodrum, however, Marmaris has succumbed to unplanned, haphazard development, which has sullied some of its appeal. It's not all bad news though – you may still want to drop by to sample the raging nightlife and amble along the manicured harbourside promenade. And if it's a boat cruise or transport to the Greek island of Rhodes you're after, this is the place.

Orientation & Information

İskele Meydanı (the main square) and the **tourist office** (☎ 412 1035; İskele Meydanı 2; ⏱ 8am-7.30pm May-Sep, 8am-noon & 1-5pm Mon-Fri Oct-Apr) are by the ferry pier, northeast of the castle near the waterfront. The post office is in the bazaar. Hacı Mustafa Sokak, also called Bar St, runs inland from the bazaar; action here keeps going until the early hours.

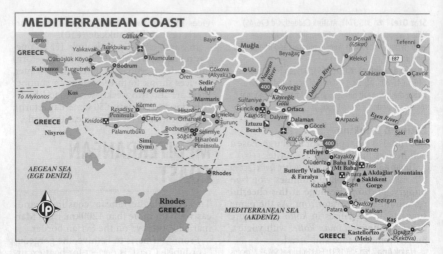

MEDITERRANEAN COAST

The otogar is 2km north of town, off the road to Bodrum.

Sights & Activities

The small **castle** (admission €0.70; ☼ 8am–noon & 1-5.30pm) houses a modest museum and offers lovely views of Marmaris.

Numerous yachts along the waterfront offer day tours of Marmaris Bay, and its beaches and islands. A day's outing usually costs around €15 per person, much less in the low season.

The most popular daily excursions are to Dalyan and Kaunos or to the bays around Marmaris, but you can also take longer, more serious boat trips along the hilly peninsula west of Marmaris to Datça and Knidos.

Marmaris is also a popular place to scuba dive, and there are several dive centres located on the waterfront.

Sleeping

Unlike Kuşadası and Bodrum, Marmaris is bereft of small, cheap pensions. Most places are closed from November to April.

Ayçe Otel (☎ 412 3136; www.aycehotel.com; 64 Sokak 11; s/d €25/33; P ✗ 🕮) No doubt the best place to rest your party-weary head is this family-run hotel. Located in a residential neighbourhood north of the tourist office, the Ayçe is one of the most commendable options in town. Rooms are fairly compact but immaculate and well furnished. The facilities are top-notch and the nifty pool is a distinct bonus.

Interyouth Hostel (☎ /fax 412 3687; Tepe Mahallesi, 42 Sokak 45; dm/d €7/17; 🖳) In the covered bazaar, right in the swing of things. Relishing being the only backpacker place in town, this hostel has piles of Spartan, boxlike but clean rooms. The shared bathrooms are in fine fettle. The staff here are as clued-up as you'd expect from an HI joint. The hostel sells cheap ferry tickets to Rhodes, hires out scooters for €18 per day and runs *gület* (traditional wooden yacht) cruises. No breakfast is served.

Marina Hotel (☎ 412 6598; Barbaros Caddesi 39; s/d €27/45; ✗) Nothing beats the Marina's location beneath the castle and the unsurpassable views from the rooftop terrace. Ignore the Barbie-esque yellow colour scheme if you can; instead, focus on the fabulously detailed wooden ceilings.

Barış Motel (☎ 413 0652; barismotel@hotmail .com; 66 Sokak 10; s/d €17/23) A short hop from the Ayçe, this modern building is nothing exciting, but it's quiet, clean, well managed and sizzling-hot value for Marmaris. There's a handful of cheaper singles with shared bathrooms (€10) – a boon for budget travellers.

Eating & Drinking

Waterfront restaurants to the south and the east of the tourist office have pleasant outdoor dining areas, but prices are inevitably higher than those inland. Check prices before ordering to avoid nasty shocks. For the cheapest fare, explore the bazaar and the

TURKEY

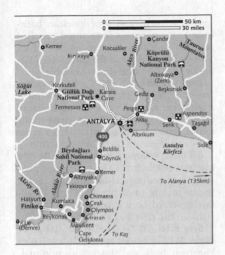

streets beyond it, looking for 'untouristy' local Turkish places selling pide, kebaps and ready-made food.

Kırçiçeği (☎ 413 7710; Yeni Yol Caddesi 15; mains €2-6) Cut inland from the Atatürk statue along Ulusal Egemenlik Bulvarı and turn right opposite the Tansaş shopping centre to find this exceedingly popular eatery. The attentive staff zip about at lunchtime and the menu runs the gamut from pide to grills, kebaps, soups and stews.

Ney Restaurant (☎ 412 0217; 26 Sokak 24; mains €6-9) Dramatically housed in a quaint old house off the waterfront, Ney has much more character than most of its nearby competitors. The food is on an equal footing. Indulge in yummy Turkish home-style cooking served in a pocket-sized dining room.

Fellini (☎ 413 0826; Barbaros Caddesi 61; mains €6-9) On the waterfront, this is the perfect place to give your palate a break from the usual kebaps. It specialises in delectable pasta and Italian-style pizzas.

Just inland from the PTT are several reputable restaurants, including **Sofra** (☎ 413 2631; 36 Sokak 23; mains €2-3; ⏰ 24hr), a sprawling place heaving with happy diners any time of the day (or night), and its competitor **Anadolu Ev Yemekleri** (☎ 413 1331; 34 Sokak 13; mains €2-3; ⏰ 24hr). These long-standers have a hearty range of dishes. Join the throng and enjoy.

Good news if you're up for a big night: Hacı Mustafa Sokak is wall-to-wall with bars and discos that keep the music pumping until around 4am.

Getting There & Away

The nearest airports to Marmaris are at Bodrum and Dalaman.

The otogar in Marmaris has frequent buses and minibuses to Bodrum (€7, four hours, 165km), İzmir (€7, 4½ hours, 320km) and Fethiye (€7, four hours, 130km).

Hydrofoils to Rhodes operate twice daily in summer (once or twice weekly in winter) for €40 one way/same-day return (one hour). Buy your ticket in any Marmaris travel agency.

KÖYCEĞIZ

☎ 0252 / pop 7600

Hard to pronounce, but definitely worth the effort of a little practise, Köyceğiz is one of southern Turkey's most peaceful villages, almost perfectly preserved from the relentless growth of hotels serving package holidaymakers. Set inside a nature reserve, it boasts a superb setting on the edge of a serene lake, which is joined to the Mediterranean Sea by the Dalyan River. The town smells sweetly of orange blossom, a reminder that it still has a farming life beyond tourism. Köyceğiz is the perfect place to kick back and unwind before heading to the more adrenaline-fuelled resorts further east.

Sleeping & Eating

Most accommodation options are off to the right (west) as you approach the mosque when coming into town. They can organise various tours on and around the lake.

Tango Pansiyon & Hostel (☎ 262 2501; www.tango pension.com; Alihsan Kalmaz Caddesi; dm/s/d €8/13/19; ❌ 💻) With a relaxed, easy-going vibe, this guesthouse-cum-hostel has a social life that gets the thumbs up from more than a few travellers in season. Rooms are luminous and marshmallow coloured, with lashings of bright colours splashed all over the walls. Other pluses include hire bikes, English movies, free pick-up from the bus station, a verdant garden, boat trips on the lake and an extensive breakfast menu (cornflakes, anyone?). The terrace is a delightful place to chill out with a beer in hand. Tango is used by the Fez Bus (p636).

Hotel Alila (☎ /fax 262 1150; Emeksiz Caddesi; s/d €22/34; ❌ 🏊) This well-situated hotel has full-frontal views of the beach and is easily Köyceğiz' fanciest place to stay. Think light-filled rooms, a pool to cool off in when it's

TURKEY

sweltering and bathrooms so scrupulously clean you could probably eat off the floor. Recommended.

Fulya Pension (☎ 262 4356; Alihsan Kalmaz Caddesi; s/d €10/19; 🏠) A short jaunt from Tango Pansiyon, this casual-feeling family-run guesthouse is another solid choice, with unremarkable but perfectly serviceable rooms at unbeatable prices.

Panorama Plaza (☎ 262 3773; www.panorama-plaza .de; Cengiz Topel Caddesi 69; s/d €23/38; 🏠 🖳 🏊) Almost 1km west of the mosque, the Panorama is run with care and efficiency, and is popular with German tour groups – not a bad sign. It offers spruce (if a wee bit impersonal) rooms with spotless bathrooms, but the killer here is the gleaming swimming pool.

İstanbul Pide & Pizza Lahmacun (☎ 262 2186; Fevzipaşa Caddesi 23; mains €1-2) Make a beeline for this little eating den in the alley of shops off the main square. It has the best pide in town, cooked before your eyes, at tiny prices.

Coliba Restaurant (☎ 262 2987; Emeksiz Caddesi; mains €3-7) West of the mosque, this is one of the most agreeable places in town, especially on a sunny day. Nab a table on the terrace and soak up the views of the lake while munching on fresh seafood.

Getting There & Away

There are frequent buses to Fethiye (€4, 1¾ hours), Marmaris (€3, one hour) and Ortaca (for Dalyan; €1, 25 minutes).

DALYAN

☎ 0252

Set on the banks of a placid river and backed by a cliff face cut with elegant Lycian tombs, Dalyan is the kind of quaint, picturesque small-scale town that looks great on postcards. Some people feel it has become a bit too touristy but it's still a superb place worth including on your itinerary.

In summer, excursion boats go out to explore the river and the lake, charging about €5 per person. A typical cruise might take in the **Sultaniye hot springs** and **mud baths** on the shores of Köyceğiz Lake, the unspoilt **İztuzu beach** and the ruined city of **Kaunos** (admission €2.50; ☽ 8.30am-5.30pm).

Sleeping & Eating

Tolga Pansiyon (☎ /fax 284 2294; Maraş Caddesi; s/d €20/35; 🏠) Quiet and understated, this lovely pension is a genuine find. It features bright,

spacious rooms and squeaky-clean bathrooms. Some rooms have wood-panelled ceilings and superb views of the river. There's lots of space in the garden for loafing by the river. Boat hire is available.

Adem's Pension (☎ 284 2030; info@ademspension .com; s/d €18/30; 🏠) This engaging pension is a winner if you can score one of the more expensive rooms, blessed with views to the tombs. Enjoy your breakfast or dinner in the well-tended garden overlooking the river.

Gül (Rose) Pansiyon (☎ 284 2467; fax 284 4803; Erkul Sokak; s/d €15/20; 🏠) This welcoming pension is exceedingly clean and tidy. Some rooms feature wood panelling and breakfast is served on a shady terrace. It's not right on the river and air-con is extra (€3).

Berg Hotel (☎ /fax 284 4024; Ada Sokak 20; s/d €33/56; 🏠) The newest option, close to Tolga Pansiyon. Slick and smart, with minimalist décor, well-chosen furnishings, pristine bathrooms and light tones.

If you don't fancy eating in your pension, try one of the riverside restaurants. Beyaz Gül Restaurant serves excellent outdoor grills in a dreamy garden setting, while Ceyhan concocts a wide array of Turkish specialities, including vegetarian options. There are also some bars on the main drag to keep you active until the wee hours.

Getting There & Away

To get to Dalyan you'll have to change bus in Ortaca (€0.50, 13km) on the main highway. At Ortaca otogar you can catch connecting buses to Köceğiz (€1, 25 minutes).

FETHIYE

☎ 0252 / pop 48,200

Despite its picture-postcard harbour backdrop, Fethiye still has much more of the feel of a living town than big resorts such as Kuşadası and Marmaris. It's an incredibly easy-going place, often visited at the beginning or end of a *gület* cruise.

Orientation & Information

Fethiye's otogar is 2km east of the centre. Atatürk Caddesi, the main street, has banks with ATMs. Most pensions are west of the centre and overlook the yacht harbour.

Tours

Be sure to sign up for the **12-Island Tour** (per person €16), which mixes swimming, cruising

BLUE VOYAGES

For many travellers a four-day, three-night cruise on a *gület* (traditional wooden yacht) between Fethiye and Kale (Demre) is the highlight of their trip to Turkey. Usually advertised as a Fethiye–Olympos voyage, the boats actually start or stop at Kale and the trip to/from Olympos (1¾ hours) is by bus. From Fethiye, boats call in at Ölüdeniz and Butterfly Valley and stop at Kaş, Kalkan and Üçağız (Kekova), with the final night at Gökkaya Bay. A less common route is between Marmaris and Fethiye, also taking four days and three nights.

Food and water is usually included in the price, but you have to buy your booze on the boat. All boats are equipped with showers, toilets and smallish but comfortable double cabins (usually six of them). In practice most people sleep on mattresses on deck.

Backpacker cruises are usually quoted in pounds sterling. Depending on the season the price is €120 to €150 per person, which is not at all cheap, so it makes sense to shop around. Here are some of our suggestions to avoid getting fleeced:

■ Do ask for recommendations from other travellers.

■ Do bargain, but don't necessarily go for the cheapest option because the crew will skimp on food and alcohol.

■ Do check out your boat (if you are in Fethiye) and ask to see the guest list.

■ Do ask whether your captain and crew speak English.

■ Don't go for gimmicks such as free water sports – they don't cost the companies anything.

■ Don't buy your ticket in İstanbul, as pensions and commission agents take a healthy cut selling tickets.

■ Don't take a boat just because it is leaving today.

We recommend owner-operated outfits, as they run a much tighter ship. During summer some larger companies may farm out unknowing tourists to lazy captains with suspect boats. Boats come and go just about every day of the week between late April and October. Competition is still between the following companies:

Almila Boat Cruise (☎ 0535-636 0076; www.beforelunch.com)
Big Backpackers (☎ 0252-614 9312; www.bluecruisefethiye.com)
Compass Yachting (☎ 0252-612 5921; www.compassyachting.com)
Interyouth Hostel (☎ 0252-412 3687; interyouth@turk.net)
Olympos Yachting (☎ 0242-892 1145; www.olymposyachting.com)

and sightseeing. Any hotel or travel agency can sign you up, or you can ask around at the harbour. The boats usually stop at six islands and cruise by the rest.

Sleeping

Most places to stay are uphill from the yacht marina along Fevzi Çakmak Caddesi. Take a Karagözler dolmuş along the harbour road to reach them or give them a call on arrival and they will pick you up from the bus station.

Ferah Pension (Monica's Place; ☎ 614 2816; ferahpension@hotmail.com; 2 Karagözler Mahallesi, Ordu Caddesi 2; dm/s/d €8/15/18; ☒ ☐) The long-standing and quality Ferah Pension is clean and well managed, and has received positive reviews from many travellers. All rooms have private bathrooms and there's one dorm room with its own bathroom. This place is as neat as a pin and the flowery courtyard is a great place to rest on a hammock. Monica's hearty home cooking (€6) gets lots of warm praise.

Duygu Pension (☎ 614 3563; www.duygupansiyon .com; 2 Karagözler Mahallesi; s/d €12/19; ☒ ☐) Almost a carbon copy of the Ferah and further along the same street, the Duygu Pension is another endearing option, with its commodious and functional rooms. There's a pervading tranquillity here and the views from the breezy terrace will take your breath away. The rooms with air-con cost an extra €6.

İrem Hotel (☎ 614 3006; fax 614 3396; 1 Karagözler Mahallesi, Fevzi Çakmak Caddesi 38; s/d €22/37;

P ⊠ ⊠) This concrete pile overlooking the bay is perfectly acceptable, with well-appointed and comfortable rooms containing not one whit of soul or character. Still, some boast superb views and there's a smallish pool if you want to take a dip.

Eating & Drinking

There's a smattering of excellent options in the centre, in or around the bazaar.

Meğri Lokantasi (☎ 614 4047; Çarşı Caddesi; mains €2-5) This casual spot in the bazaar is heavily patronised by locals at lunchtime. It serves the usual selection of kebaps and ready-made meals at bargain-basement prices.

Meğri Restaurant (☎ 614 4046; Likya Sokak 8-9; mains €5-15) More upmarket than its *lokanta*, this venue, located in the heart of the bazaar, oozes character. The large, rustic interior is enticing but the real wow is the outdoor seating. It's a great place to chill out and soak up the atmosphere. There's an extensive menu, including vegetarian options, and a very decent wine list.

Paşa Kebap (☎ 614 9807; Çarşı Caddesi 42; mains €2-6) This popular eatery near the bazaar has won accolades for its ultrafresh dishes, all served with a smile. The *kalamar salata* (squid salad) is a good bet to start, followed by a *tavuk güveç* (chicken stew).

Cafe Oley (☎ 612 9532; Eski Meğri Sokak 4; mains €3-7; 🖳) You don't expect to find this cute café-bistro in the bazaar. If you're growing weary of kebaps, this is the place to chow down on spaghetti, chicken wings and fresh salads.

In the mood for fish? Head for the fish section of the market, where several eateries, including the **Cem & Can** (☎ 614 3097), have hit on a great idea – you buy a fish at the market and they cook it. A full meal will set you back about €10.

If you fancy an evening out, the **Ottoman Bar** (☎ 612 1148; Hamam Sokak), set in a restored old house behind the bazaar, is the best place to check out the local scene. In high season it's packed to the rafters with fun-seekers of all backgrounds and nationalities, all jostling shoulders with a minimum of worries.

Getting There & Away

If you're going straight to Antalya (€9, four hours, 222km), note that the *yayla* (inland) route is quicker and much more comfortable than the *sahil* (coastal) route. There are also regular services to Marmaris (€7, four hours, 130km), Kalkan (€3.50, two hours, 81km), Kaş (€4, 2½ hours, 110km) and Olympos (€9, five hours, 219km). Minibuses to more-local destinations, including Ölüdeniz (€2, 15km), leave from behind the big white mosque (Yeni Cami) in the town centre.

ÖLÜDENİZ
☎ 0252

Over the mountains to the south of Fethiye, lovely Ölüdeniz (Dead Sea) has proved a bit too beautiful for its own good. It's now one of the most famous beach spots on the Mediterranean, with far too many hotels catering for the package-holiday market backed up behind the sands. Still, the **lagoon** (admission €1.25; 🕙 8am-8pm) itself remains tranquillity incarnate and is a gorgeous place to sun yourself. Ölüdeniz is also a mecca for **tandem paragliding**. Many companies here offer tandem paragliding flights for €65.

Sleeping & Eating

Oba (☎ 617 0158; www.obahostel.com; old bungalows s/d €15/24, villas €75; 🐾) In a congenial, spacious and leafy garden, the Oba offers accommodation to suit all budgets, including ultrabasic bungalows for the impecunious. Should you need some luxury, there's a series of chaletlike bungalows (called villas) fitted with all the mod cons – they wouldn't be out of place in Finland or Switzerland. The food comes in for good reviews too and there's an inviting Turkish corner complete with cushions for practising idleness.

Ünsal Hotel (☎ 617 0031; www.unsalhotel.com; s/d €30/45; ⊠ 🖳 ⊠) This family-run two-star venture, about 100m from the beach, prides itself on its large pool amid a verdant garden, and rightly so. It has plainly decorated, light-filled rooms with sparkling bathrooms.

There are also plenty of camping grounds a thong's throw from the beach. Most offer fixed tents and cabins with or without running water.

Getting There & Away

Frequent minibuses run between Ölüdeniz and Fethiye (€2, 20 minutes).

PATARA
☎ 0242

Blessed with a splendid 20km white-sand **beach**, Patara, by some miracle, has been successful at clinging to its original charm.

With its rural setting and unhurried pace of life, it's a great place to chill out for a few days. There are also extensive **ruins** (admission €1.25), including a triple-arched triumphal gate at the entrance to the site, with a necropolis containing several Lycian tombs nearby. All in all, it's a good combination of nature and culture.

Sleeping & Eating

All the places to stay and most of the places to eat are in Gelemiş village, 1.5km inland from the beach.

Akay (☎ 843 5055; akaypension@hotmail.com; s/d €12/18; 🌏 🖳) A good find for budget-seekers, with spotless rooms, a homely atmosphere and good Turkish meals.

Flower Pansiyon (☎ 843 5164; flowerpension@ hotmail.com; s/d €11/18; 🌏) Another welcoming option, similar in standards to the Akay.

Golden Pension (☎ 843 5008; www.goldenpension .com; s/d €15/19; 🌏 🖳) You'll strike gold at this pension, with its good facilities and prim, clean rooms. It's owned by the mayor, who is, unsurprisingly, knowledgeable about the area.

Patara View Point Hotel (☎ 843 5105; www.patara viewpoint.com; s/d €21/31; 🌏 🖳) Picture this: a tranquil setting up a hill, first-rate facilities, plain but well-equipped rooms, unabashed views over the valley and a delightful pool. This is our idea of a nice retreat.

Getting There & Away

Buses plying the Fethiye–Antalya route can drop you on the highway, 2km from the village (3.5km from the beach, signposted 'Patara'). From here dolmuşes head down to the village. In summer there are also direct dolmuşes from Kaş (€3, one hour, 42km), from Kalkan (€1.50, 25 minutes) and from Fethiye (€4).

KALKAN

☎ 0242

Kalkan is, arguably, the most picturesque and photographed of the coastal towns along the western Mediterranean. What is not in question, however, is that you'll need a sturdy set of knees, for Kalkan tumbles down a steep hillside to a marina full of open-air restaurants.

Once a quaint fishing village, it's now a rather sophisticated tourist resort, 11km east of the Patara turn-off. Its picturesque tangle

of narrow streets lined with pretty wood-and-stone houses is a real treat. With its high-quality restaurant scene and excellent pensions and hotels to suit all budgets, Kalkan is a place for sybarites. The only gripe is that Kalkan itself has no good beaches – you'll have to hire a scooter and head to Patara.

Sleeping

Türk Evi (☎ 844 3129; selmaelitez@superonline.com; Yalıboyu Mahallesi; d €25-35) Fancy something stylish without breaking the bank? This sensitively restored mansion is for you. Its nine rooms are elegantly decked out, with a subdued rustic feel and lots of feminine touches. The delightful courtyard is a great place to chill out. The only drawback may be the lack of air-con.

Daphne Pansiyon (☎ 844 3380; daphne_kalkan@ hotmail.com; Kocabaya Caddesi; s/d €25/35; 🌏) Find heaven in this tranquil retreat on the road winding down past the mosque to the harbour. The décor combines Ottoman charm (carpets and kilims) with more-modern trimmings, including air-con in all the rooms. Black-and-white photos taken by the owner add a touch of originality, plus there's the mandatory rooftop terrace.

Çelik Pansiyon (☎ 844 2126; Yalıboyu Mahallesi 9; s/d €15/20; 🌏) Tidy, unfussy and attractively priced, Çelik is best suited to the thrifty, who'll enjoy the refreshingly low-key atmosphere. Rooms 9 and 11 are the best lit and boast lofty views of the bay. Breakfast is served on a breezy terrace overflowing with purple bougainvillea (another clincher).

The White House (☎ 844 3738; fax 844 3501; s/d €21/36; 🌏) This renovated guesthouse doesn't exude much personality, but the 10 rooms are well appointed and neat as a pin. There's a great rooftop terrace for dozing in the sun. Fancy a carpet? Rejoice: the ones that adorn the walls in the corridor are for sale.

Eating

Aubergine Restaurant (☎ 844 3332; mains €8-12) Turkish cuisine with a French twist. Feast on *saumon en croute* (salmon cooked in pastry), Ottoman leg of lamb, savoury burgers or a tender fillet of wild boar. The flowery terrace right by the seafront is hard to beat, and a respectable wine list encourages a long, relaxed dinner. There's a vegetarian menu, too.

Korsan (☎ 844 3076; mains €3-7) Next to the town beach, this place is almost hidden under a veil of bougainvillea. The bird's-eye view of the bay from the rooftop terrace may aid digestion of the hearty dishes on offer.

Ottoman House (☎ 535 224 6684; mains €6-12) This much-praised restaurant attends to most tastebuds and includes good vegetarian options. The *Hünkar Beğendi* (sautéed lamb served on a bed of aubergine puree), the sultan's favourite dish, goes down a treat. Or you could sit on floor cushions on the terrace and puff a nargileh.

Paprika Cafe & Terrace Restaurant (☎ 844 1136; Yalıboyu 12/B; mains €7-10) It's slick, it's swish, it's smart. The eye-catching menu includes fresh homemade pasta, salads, meat dishes and desserts. There's occasionally live music in the evenings.

New Flower Tomato Restaurant (☎ 844 2655; mains €2-3) Look no further in Kalkan for a cheap (ie a bit greasy, but delicious) fill. It serves up ready-made meals and the proverbial kebap. It's usually packed at lunchtime.

Foto'Nun Yeri (☎ 844 3464; Yalıboyu Mahallesi; mains €2-4) Another welcoming place with cool vibes. The food is straightforward, with dishes such as *gözleme*, and the views are thrown in for free.

Getting There & Away

In summer, minibuses connect Kalkan with Fethiye (€3.50, two hours), Kaş (€2, 30 minutes) and Patara (€1.50, 25 minutes).

KAŞ

☎ 0242 / pop 8000

This little stunner is the pride of the western Mediterranean coast. It's an incredibly scenic town with a picturesque quay, a very good restaurant scene, numerous shops and a scattering of Lycian tombs. Although it's pretty touristy, it has so far managed to keep some of its small-town charm and rarely comes under siege from tour groups and souvenir sellers. For action-seekers, there are outdoor adventures galore to gorge on amid a stunning landscape. You should definitely afford Kaş a day or two if you possibly can.

Sights & Activities

Apart from enjoying the town's wonderfully mellow atmosphere and a few small pebble beaches, you can walk west a few hundred metres to the well-preserved **theatre**. Behind it you'll see the **Doric Tomb**, cut into the hillside in the 3rd century BC. It's

also well worth walking up the hill on the street to the left of the tourist office to reach the **Monument Tomb**, a Lycian sarcophagus mounted on a high base.

The most popular **boat trip** (€15) is to Kekova Island and Üçağız, a three-hour excursion that includes time to see several interesting ruins as well as stops for swimming. Other standard excursions go to the Mavi Mağara (Blue Cave), Patara and Kalkan, or to Liman Ağzı and several nearby islands. There are also overland excursions to the wonderful 18km-long Saklıkent Gorge and villages further inland.

If you want to do anything slightly active while you are in Kaş, contact **Bougainville Travel** (☎ 836 3737; www.bougainville-turkey.com; İbrahim Selin Caddesi 10). This long-established English-Turkish tour operator offers scuba diving, trekking, mountain biking and canyoning trips in the area. The sea-kayaking day trips over the Kekova sunken city (€35), suitable for all fitness levels, will be the highlight of your stay in Kaş.

Sleeping

Kaş' quietest places to stay are all on the west side of town. All places provide free pick-up from the otogar.

Anı Motel (☎ 836 1791; Süleyman Yıldırım Caddesi; www.motelani.com; dm/s/d €7/10/18; 🖳 🖵) Congenial owners are part of the reason that the Anı has such a faithful following. This backpackers' den has oodles of hippy charm and features well-arranged, if a tad sterile, rooms with pathogen-free bathrooms. Some rooms have air-con, the others are equipped with fans. If you're watching the pennies, there are also three functional dorms. In summer, the breezy rooftop terrace is a winner, with a BBQ every other day (€6), satellite TV and comfy couches that you can happily laze on.

Kaş Otel (☎ 836 1271; kasotel@yahoo.com; Hastane Caddesi 15; s €22, d €30-45; 🖳) You couldn't possibly get a better position for a dreamy night: the dazzling waters of the Mediterranean are right at your doorstep, the waves are within earshot and Meis Island looms on the horizon. The Kaş Otel has piles of sun-filled, uncluttered rooms with gleaming bathrooms; be sure to score a sea-facing room with balcony. There's also a rooftop restaurant. What more could you ask for?

Hilal Pension (☎ 836 1207; www.korsan-kas.com; Süleyman Yıldırım Caddesi; s/d €8/16; 🖳) Another cheery backpacker haunt with a homy feel and excellent facilities, including free Internet access, air-con in all the rooms, back-friendly beds, balconies and a plant-filled terrace.

Other options:

Kale Otel & Pension (☎ 836 1062; info@guletturkey .com; Amfitıyatro Sokak 8; s/d pension €35/50, hotel €50/70; 🐾) It's a wee bit overpriced, but it's still a pleasant place to mooch around, drinking tea or reading a book on the sea-facing lawn at the rear. Rooms are immaculate.

Santosa (☎ 836 1714; Süleyman Yıldırım Caddesi; s/d €15/24; 🐾) A decent fallback if the other pensions are full.

Eating

Chez Evy (☎ 836 1253; Terzi Sokak 2; mains €8-15; 🕑 dinner Tue-Sun) In the mood for something different? *Ooh la la*, this French outpost, tucked away in a side street, is really worth checking out. Savvy locals swear that the steaks here are the best this side of the Seine. Evy won't let you leave until you're patting your tummy contently.

Bahçe Restaurant (☎ 836 2370; Anıt Mezar Karşısı 31; mains €5-8) Up behind the Monument Tomb, this enchanting venue boasts a dreamy garden setting. Vegetarians will thank their lucky stars for the flavoursome meze on offer.

Çınarlar (☎ 836 2860; Şube Sokak 4; mains €3-7) This cheap-and-cheerful joint specialises in pide, pizzas and *güveç* (stew), all flawlessly cooked.

Nur Pastaneleri (☎ 836 4380; Atatürk Bulvarı) This sleek pastry shop is something of a treasure-trove for carb-lovers, with lots of ravishing baklava. Just treat yourself!

Natur-el (☎ 836 2834; Gürsoy Sokak 6; mains €5-8) Indulge in fine *ev mutfağı* (home cooking), prepared with care and served with a smile in attractive surroundings. Finish up with the calorie-busting homemade *aşure*.

Sun Café & Bar (☎ 836 1053; Hükümet Caddesi; mains €3-6) Favoured by locals for its chilled-out vibe and tasty Ottoman specialities.

Also recommended:

Oba Restaurant (☎ 836 1687; Çukurbağlı Caddesi 8; mains €2-4) A perennial favourite, up the hill past the PTT.

Sempati Restaurant (☎ 836 2418; Gürsoy Caddesi 11; mains €4-8) A rather sophisticated place, with an intimate atmosphere.

Drinking

Rejoice! There are a couple of buzzing bars in Kaş. Not the kind of boisterous places you would find in Marmaris or Kuşadası, but more-civilised venues heavy on atmosphere. Check out Harry's Bar, Mavi Bar or Hi Jazz Bar.

Getting There & Away

There are daily bus services to Kalkan (€2, 30 minutes, 29km), Olympos (€5, 2½ hours, 109km) and Patara (€3, one hour, 42km). For other destinations, connect at Fethiye (€4, 2½ hours, 110km) or Antalya (€6, four hours, 185km).

OLYMPOS & ÇIRALI
☎ 0242

Olympos is a Shangri-la for travellers. Picture fragmentary ruins scattered among wild grapevines, a secluded beach, a steep forested valley, a stream that runs through a rocky gorge and various accommodation options heavy on atmosphere. This fabulous mix – a heart-palpitatingly dramatic setting and an unrivalled ambience – is a rare treat. No wonder many people come here for a couple of days and end up staying for weeks.

Neighbouring Çıralı, 1km to the east, has another gem of a place. While Olympos has a well-established party reputation, Çıralı is the perfect place to experience the fine art of *keyif* (quiet relaxation).

The drive here is also a treat, strewn with mountain views all the way from Kaş.

Sights

Don't miss the fascinating ruins of **ancient Olympos** (admission €1.25). A skip away from the beach, it's a wild, abandoned place where ruins peek out from forested coppices, rock outcrops and riverbanks.

If you just want to spend a lazy day, nothing beats the **beach** in Olympos. Çıralı also boasts a fine stretch of clear sand.

Various pensions in Olympos and in Çıralı run evening tours (for a modest fee) to **Chimaera**, a cluster of flames that blaze spontaneously from crevices on the rocky slopes of Mt Olympos. It's located about 3km from Cirali's beach.

Sleeping & Eating
OLYMPOS

Staying in a rustic treehouse is a typical Olympos experience, though they are slowly being replaced by proper bungalows with bathrooms. Treehouses cost about €9 to €12 per person, and rooms or bungalows

TURKEY

with bathrooms cost €14 to €16 (€18 with air-con). Prices include breakfast and dinner. Most places offer a plethora of services such as laundry, satellite TV, bus tickets, Internet etc.

Kadir's (☎ 892 1250; www.kadirstreehouse.com) Easily the quirkiest place to stay in Turkey, Kadir's is an icon on the accommodation scene in the Middle East. The compound looks like a 19th-century farmhouse, with real treehouses, barnlike bungalows and rustic rooms with ramshackle charm. Its party reputation is unrivalled in the country – spend an evening in the infamously cheesy Bull Bar and you'll know what we mean. It can organise various activities, including sea-kayaking and rock climbing.

Türkmen (☎ 892 1249; www.olymposturkmentree houses.com) Rivalling Kadir's with its party reputation, ambitious Türkmen is a sprawling place. The accommodation options run the whole gamut from basic dorms to cabins, treehouses and comfortable bungalows with air-con. It's very well organised – too much so for some tastes.

Şaban (☎ 892 1265; www.sabanpansion.com) Tired of late-night revelling? Try this peaceful option, opposite Türkmen. It features spacious grounds, tidy bungalows and lounging areas. The home-style Turkish cooking (€6) gets good reports.

Also recommended:

Bayram's (☎ 892 1243; www.bayrams.com; ⊠) Relaxed, friendly and unfussy. The more-expensive bungalows have air-con.

Varuna Pension (☎ 892 1347; ⊠) A slightly more upscale option with newish bungalows and conventional rooms with private bathrooms.

ÇIRALI

There are no treehouses here but some good midrange options and the crowds are much more sedate – a good place if you need to escape the mayhem in Olympos. Most places provide good meals but if you want to eat out you'll find a line-up of restaurants at the northern end of the beach – nothing beats a grilled fish and a cold beer on the beach at sunset.

Sima Peace (☎ 825 7245; www.simapeace.com; s/d €20/30; ⊠) Run by the exuberant Aynur Kurt, this guesthouse is a good find, with four wooden chalets set amid a well-tended garden and four mundane rooms in the main building. You won't forget the resi-

dent parrot. Aynur's hearty home cooking (dinner €10) is not to be missed. It's 200m off the beach.

Myland (☎ 825 7044; www.mylandnature.com; s/d €45/65; ⊠ ▣) Take your weary bones to this peaceful retreat for the ultimate in zen – there are meditation and yoga sessions. Accommodation is in prim bungalows set around a pretty garden and guests praise the food (organic meals around €8). Bikes are available.

Also recommended:

Yıldız Pension (☎ 825 7160; www.yildizpansiyon.com; s/d €30/35; ⊠) A family-run guesthouse at the northern end of the beach. It consists of 13 plain but well-equipped rooms and four pine-clad bungalows.

Barış Pansiyon (☎ 825 7080; s/d €24/40; ⊠) A delightful place set among citrus orchards and neat gardens, a Frisbee throw from the beach.

Getting There & Away

Buses and minibuses plying the Fethiye–Antalya road will drop you at a roadside restaurant from where minibuses go on to Çıralı and Olympos (€2, about 8km) in summer. In the low season you may need to phone a pension to collect you, or take a taxi.

You can also get to Çıralı from Olympos by walking 1km along the beach.

ANTALYA

☎ 0242 / pop 509,000

A bustling, modern and liberal town, Antalya has more than just its lovely harbour setting to boast about; it also avoids that soullessness that tends to overcome resorts that live only for tourism. It's fun to amble along narrow cobbled lanes in Kaleiçi, the old restored Ottoman town that spreads back from a beautiful marina and the sea-facing Karaalioğlu Parkı.

Pebbly Konyaaltı beach spreads out to the west of town, sandy Lara beach to the east. Both are solidly backed with package-holiday hotels – you'd do best to wait until Olympos for a swim.

Antalya is also a good base for visiting the exciting ancient cities on its outskirts.

Orientation & Information

The otogar is 4km north of the centre on the D650 highway to Burdur. The city centre is at Kale Kapısı, a major intersection marked by a clock tower. To get into Kaleiçi, head south down the hill from the clock tower

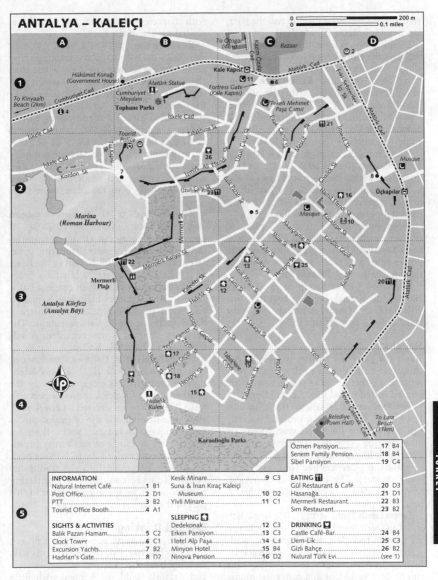

ANTALYA – KALEIÇI

0 — 200 m
0 — 0.1 miles

To Otogar (4km)

Kazım Özalp Cad

Bazaar

Atatürk Cad

Eski Sebzeciler İç Sk

Kale Kapısı

Hükümet Konağı (Government House)

Cumhuriyet Cad

Atatürk Statue

Cumhuriyet Meydanı

Tophane Parkı

Fortress Gate (Kale Kapısı)

Tekeli Mehmet Paşa Camii

To Kınıaltı Beach (2km)

İskele Cad

İskele Cad

Tourist Police

İskele Cad

Kordon Sk

İzmirli Ali Efendi

Üzun Çarşı Sk

Tabakhane Sk

Uzun Çarşı Sk

Paşa Camii Sk

Mescit Sk

Atatürk Cad

Civelek Sk

Namik Efendi

Mosque

Üçkapılar

Marina (Roman Harbour)

Mermerli Sk

Üzun Çarşı Sk

Balık Pazarı Sk

Mosque

Kocatepe Sk

Akarçeşme Sk

Muze Sk

Hesapçı Sk

Kandiler Geçidi

Kandiler Sk

Kandiler Sk

Mermerli Banyo Sk

Mermerli Plajı

Antalya Körfezi (Antalya Bay)

Kırlan Sk

Küçük Minare Sk

Kaledibi Sk

Hıdırlık Sk

Cami Sk

Finn Sk

Zeytin Çıkmazı

Tuzcular

Zafer Çıkmazı

Zeytin Geçidi

Hesapçı Geçidi

Tabakhane Sk

Hıdırlık Sk

Tabakhane Sk

Yeni Kapı Sk

Tabakhane Sk

Hesapçı Sk

Hıdırlık Kulesi

Park Sk

Fevzi Çakmak Cad

Belediye (Town Hall)

To Lara Beach (11km)

Karaalioğlu Parkı

INFORMATION			SLEEPING 🏠		
Natural Internet Café	1	B1	Dedekonak	12	C3
Post Office	2	D1	Erken Pansiyon	13	C3
PTT	3	B2	Hotel Alp Paşa	14	C3
Tourist Office Booth	4	A1	Minyon Hotel	15	B4
			Ninova Pension	16	D2
SIGHTS & ACTIVITIES			Özmen Pansiyon	17	B4
Balık Pazarı Hamam	5	C2	Senem Family Pension	18	B4
Clock Tower	6	C1	Sibel Pansiyon	19	C4
Excursion Yachts	7	B2			
Hadrian's Gate	8	D2	EATING 🍴		
Kesik Minare	9	C3	Gül Restaurant & Café	20	D3
Suna & İnan Kıraç Kaleiçi			Hasanağa	21	D1
Museum	10	D2	Mermerli Restaurant	22	B3
Yivli Minare	11	C1	Sırrı Restaurant	23	B2
			DRINKING 🍷		
			Castle Café-Bar	24	B4
			Dem-Lik	25	C3
			Gizlı Bahçe	26	B2
			Natural Türk Evi	(see 1)	

or cut in from Hadrian's Gate (Hadriyanüs Kapisi), just off Atatürk Caddesi.

There's a small **tourist office booth** (☎/fax 241 1747; Cumhuriyet Caddesi; ⊗ 8am-5pm) about 600m west of Kale Kapısı. The post office is around the corner in Güllük Caddesi. **Natural Internet Café** (☎ 243 8763; Tophane Parkı; per hr €1; ⊗ 9am-11pm) has good connections.

Sights & Activities

Around the harbour is the lovely historic district called **Kaleiçi**, whose walls once re-pelled raiders. It's a charming hill full of twisting alleys, atmosphere-laden court-yards, souvenir shops and lavishly restored mansions, while cliffside vantage points on either side of the harbour provide stunning

TURKEY

views over a beautiful marina and the soaring Bey Mountains (Beydağları).

Heading down from the **clock tower** you will pass the **Yivli Minare** (Grooved Minaret), which rises above an old mosque. Further into Kaleiçi, the quirky **Kesik Minare** (Truncated Minaret) is built on the site of a ruined Roman temple.

Just off Atatürk Caddesi, the monumental **Hadrian's Gate** was erected during the Roman emperor Hadrian's reign (AD 117–38).

Don't miss the excellent **Suna & İnan Kıraç Kaleiçi Museum** (Kocatepe Sokak 25; admission €1.25; ⏰ 9am-noon & 1-6pm Thu-Tue), in the heart of Kaleiçi. It houses a fine collection of Turkish ceramics, together with rooms set up to show important events in Ottoman family life.

Need some hush and a cool place to rest your sightseeing-abused feet? Nothing beats **Karaalioğlu Parkı**, a large, attractive and flower-filled park that's good for a stroll, or the equally inviting **Tophane Parkı**.

Excursion yachts tie up in the Roman Harbour in Kaleiçi, offering **boat trips** that visit the Gulf of Antalya islands and some beaches for a swim (from €15).

Sleeping

There are pensions aplenty in Kaleiçi. Architecture buffs, this area will appeal to your sense of aesthetics: most places to stay are housed in renovated historic buildings.

Sibel Pansiyon (☎ 241 1316; fax 241 3656; Fırın Sokak 30; s/d €16/26; ✖) This is a peaceful, sweetly run retreat with spick-and-span rooms set in a pair of renovated Ottoman houses. Your multilingual host, Sylvie, goes all out to make this place feel like your own home (only cleaner). The plant-filled courtyard, where breakfast is served, is a real plus. A peach of a place.

Senem Family Pension (☎ 247 1752; fax 247 0615; Zeytin Geçidi Sokak 9; s/d €19/25; ✖) A safe haven for women travellers, with luminous, well-scrubbed rooms and an inviting terrace affording heavenly views over the bay. It's run by Mrs Seval Ünsal, a congenial mama who goes out of her way to make your stay a happy one.

Erken Pansiyon (☎ 247 6092; fax 247 6092; Hıdırlık Sokak 5; s/d €15/21; ✖) Another good runner up, with natty bathrooms and well-furnished rooms. It's housed in a *konak* (mansion).

Dedekonak (☎ 248 5264; Hıdırlık Sokak 13; s/d €15/25; ✖) This stately mansion is a bargain,

with character-filled rooms and a lovely secluded garden at the back.

Ninova Pension (☎ 248 6114; fax 248 9684; Hamit Efendi Sokak 9; s/d €25/40; ✖) Those wanting a cosy and comfortable base could do worse than check in here. Parquet floors, wooden ceilings, fine rugs and crisp white linen make the rooms distinctive. An added bonus is the stone-walled garden shaded by orange trees.

Özmen Pansiyon (☎ 241 6505; www.ozmenpension .com; Zeytin Çıkmazı 5; s €12-15, d €20-25; ✖ 🖳) This backpacker staple has undergone a quality renovation and is now perfectly serviceable, with airy rooms and modern bathrooms. Enjoy the views from the attractive rooftop terrace.

Hotel Alp Paşa (☎ 247 5676; reservation@alppasa .com; Hesapçı Sokak 30; s/d €55/75; ✖ 🖳 🛋) If you're keen to play out Ottoman fantasies during your stay, consider pampering yourself in this swish establishment in the heart of the Kaleiçi. It sports 70 blissfully decorated rooms and suites with opulent bathrooms. Other luxuries include a *hamam*, a courtyard swimming pool and whirlpool baths in the more-expensive rooms. The on-site restaurant is well regarded. A sultan's life is a hard life, isn't it?

Minyon Hotel (☎ 247 1147; www.minyonhotel.com; Tabakhane Sokak 31; d €75-80; ✖ 🖳 🛋) The attention to detail in this elegant place, in the southern part of Kaleiçi, shows impeccable taste. The owner has created an enveloping ambience through the use of period pieces and antiques, including mosaic flooring, and the full comforts of modernity (minibar, bathrooms with all the frills) have been seamlessly integrated into the traditional design. You can cool off in the glittering pool too, when temperatures swelter in this part of the city.

Eating & Drinking

Many pensions serve good meals at decent prices. Otherwise, Eski Sebzeciler İçi Sokak, an alley near the junction of Cumhuriyet and Atatürk Caddesis, is lined with little restaurants and pastry shops where you can feast on goodies such as chicken, beef and baklava at unbeatable prices. Many eateries have outdoor tables.

Mermerli Restaurant (☎ 248 5484; Mermerli Banyo Sokak 25; mains €5-8) Perched above the eastern end of the harbour, this restaurant can't be beaten for sunset views of the bay and Bey

Mountains. It serves up the usual array of grills and salads.

Gül Restaurant & Café (☎ 247 5126; Kocatepe Sokak 1; mains €5-7; ☾ closed lunch Sun) Cosy and intimate, the Gül offers well prepared meat dishes. An unexpected bonus is the garden at the back.

Hasanağa (☎ 242 8105; Mescit Sokak 15; mains €5-9) Located in a quiet backstreet, this enduring Antalya icon doesn't disappoint. The menu covers enough territory to please most palates, and vegetarians are well catered for with a respectable selection of tasty meze. The leafy garden at the back has atmosphere by the bucket load. Musicians appear most nights, getting the rakı drinkers singing along.

Sırrı Restaurant (☎ 241 7239; Uzun Çarşı Sokak 25; mains €4-7) One of the most interesting places to eat, even if the food hardly rises to gourmet standards. You'll love the Ottoman décor and the outdoor tables in a garden strung with lights.

There are innumerable bars in Kaleiçi and around the yacht harbour. It's well worth seeking out the atmospheric **Gizli Bahçe** (☎ 247 4601; Karadayı Sokak 5), tucked away in a side street just outside of Kaleiçi; the lively **Dem-Lik** (☎ 247 1930; Zafer Sokak 6), filled with Turkish students; the dynamic **Castle Café-Bar** (☎ 242 3188), right on the cliff's edge behind the tower Hıdırlık Kulesi; and the mellow **Natural Türk Evi** (Tophane Parkı).

Getting There & Away
Antalya's airport is 10km east of the city centre on the Alanya highway. Turkish Airlines offers frequent flights to/from İstanbul and Ankara. Onur Air and Atlasjet also have flights to/from Antalya.

From the otogar, buses head for Alanya (€4, 2¾ hours), Göreme (€13, around 10 hours), Konya (€9, five hours), Olympos (€2, 1½ hours) and Manavgat/Side (€3, 1¼ hours).

AROUND ANTALYA
Between Antalya and Alanya there are several magnificent Graeco-Roman ruins to explore. You can't help but be dazzled by the sheer beauty of the ruins at **Perge** (admission €6; ☾ 8am-5.30pm), east of Antalya and just north of Aksu. The site has a 12,000-seat stadium and a 15,000-seat theatre. Another stunning place is **Aspendos** (admission €6), 47km east of Antalya. Here you'll see Turkey's best-preserved ancient theatre, dating from the

2nd century AD and still used for performances during the Antalya Festival every June/July. **Termessos** (admission €2.50; ☾ 8am-5pm), high in the mountains off the Korkuteli road, to the west of Antalya, has a spectacular setting but demands some vigorous walking and climbing to see it all. Unless a coach party turns up, these places are eerily deserted.

The only gripe is that it's not convenient to get to these sights by public transport. The easiest way to see them is with your own transport or on a tour from Antalya. A full-day tour to Perge and Aspendos should not cost more than €35 per carload, and a half-day tour to Termessos should cost about €25. Ask at your pension or hotel in Antalya. There are plenty of agencies in Antalya hiring out cars for €25 per day.

SIDE
☎ 0242 / pop 18,000
Come prepared. In summer, Side is a huge destination, and you won't feel as if you've fallen upon an undiscovered gem. During the day the heart of the town is awash with carpet shops and souvenir sellers catering to coach-party holidaymakers. Unless you like the 'Hello, I do a special price for you' sales pitch, it'll quickly drive you insane. But by late afternoon, when the crowds have left, Side reverts to a charming, relatively low-key coastal town – it's the perfect time to enjoy its fantastic ruins and sandy beaches.

You'll find several banks with ATMs on the main drag.

Sights
Side's impressive ancient structures include a huge **theatre** (admission €6.50; ☾ 8am-5pm) with 15,000 seats, one of the largest in Anatolia; a Roman bath, now a **museum** (admission €3; ☾ 8.30am-5.15pm), with an excellent small collection of statues and reliefs; and seaside **temples** to Apollo and Athena, dating from the 2nd century AD. It's also blessed with sandy **beaches**.

Sleeping & Eating
Beach House Hotel (☎ 753 1607; Küçük Plaj; s/d €18/33) Gets the thumbs up for its plain but serviceable sea-facing rooms – some with a balcony. Perched right on the beach, it also offers free sun beds.

Emir Pansion Cafe (☎ 753 4859; Köseoğlu Otel Yanı; d €20) Another nifty option, it has luminous, clean rooms with slick bathrooms. Feeling peckish? The café on the ground floor serves up various inexpensive munchies.

Moonlight Restaurant (☎ 753 1400; Barbaros Caddesi 49; mains €5-12) This alluring restaurant overlooking the sea offers indoor and outdoor seating for tucking into tasty dishes. On balmy summer evenings, the seaside tables, with waves almost lapping your toes, are a winner. It specialises in fish, so check the prices carefully.

The harbour is wall-to-wall with restaurants chock-full of tourists. Most serve average cuisine whipped up for tourists (yawn). Be careful to get the price on any seafood and wine you order.

Getting There & Away

In summer, Side has direct bus services to Ankara, İzmir and İstanbul. Otherwise, frequent minibuses connect Side with Manavgat otogar (€0.30), 4km away, from where buses go to Antalya (€3, 1¼ hours), Alanya (€3, 1¼ hours) and Konya (€11, 5½ hours).

ALANYA

☎ 242 / pop 110,100

Ask any independent traveller: Alanya has little to entice backpackers. Because of its swathe of sandy beaches stretching 22km east from the town, Alanya has swollen out of recognition with package holidaymakers and frolicking sun-seekers from Europe. It's not all that bad, however. The waterfront promenade is worth a stroll and the magnificent Seljuk fortress perched high on a hill above the town is a magnet for architecture buffs.

The otogar is on the coastal highway (Atatürk Caddesi), 3km west of the centre. You'll find numerous banks with ATMs in the centre.

Sights & Activities

Alanya's crowning glory is the Seljuk **fortress** on top of the promontory. It was built in 1226. From here you get unimpeded views over the city and the coast. The octagonal **Kızıl Kule** (Red Tower; admission €2; ☾ 8am-noon & 1.30-5.30pm), down by the harbour, was also built in the year 1226.

If you're an active type, it's possible to **scuba dive** in the bay. There are several dive operators uphill above the harbour.

Various boats offer **excursions** around the promontory (about €15). Tours visit several caves as well as a beach.

Sleeping

Sadly, Alanya is bereft of cheap accommodation options, as pensions have been superseded by faceless concrete lumps. But there are a couple of exceptions above the harbour.

Hotel Temiz (☎ 513 1016; fax 519 1560; İskele Caddesi 12; s/d €18/30; 🖳) This friendly place is definitely *temiz* (clean) and offers 32 spruce and well-maintained rooms with stout bedding and gleaming bathrooms. The rooms at the front boast terrific views of the bay but those at the back are certainly quieter.

Eating & Drinking

These days, you'll have to head well inland to the bazaar and beyond to get a cheap bite to eat. Otherwise, the waterfront restaurants are worth frequenting for evening meals if your credit line can stand it.

Ravza (☎ 513 3983; Yeni Çarşı Zambak Sokak; mains €2-5) Brisk, buzzing, filling and excellent value: this popular eatery, off the seafront, bounces with ebullient waiters. It's been doling out well-executed pide and kebaps since 1955.

Mahperi (☎ 512 5491; Rıhtım Caddesi; mains €6-14) A veteran on the Alanya dining scene, this local favourite on the seafront serves up an expansive (and expensive) selection of lip-smacking specialities, including seafood, grills, salads and pasta.

Ottoman House (☎ 511 1421; Damlataş Caddesi 31; mains €10-12) This old Ottoman house is high on atmosphere, with a neat garden and cosy upstairs rooms. Undecided tastebuds can go for a big plate of meze.

Çello (İskele Caddesi) On the same street as the Hotel Temiz. Looking slightly sinister with its dimly lit interior, Çello is actually anything but. Featuring a much more amiable atmosphere than its kitsch counterparts on the harbour, it has Turkish live bands every evening.

Getting There & Away

There are frequent buses from Alanya to Antalya (€4, 2¾ hours) and to Adana (€11, 10 hours), stopping in Anamur (€4, three hours).

Akfer Denizcilik (☎ 511 5565) runs ferries to Girne (Northern Cyprus) three times a week from April to October (€83 return, including tax).

THE EASTERN COAST

East of Alanya, the coast sheds some of its touristic freight. About 7km east of **Anamur**, it would really be a shame to miss the wonderful **Mamure Castle** (Mamure Kalesi; admission €1.25; ☉ 8am-6pm), built right on the beach by the emirs of Karaman in 1230. The ghostly ruins of Byzantine **Anamurium** (admission €1.25; ☉ 8am-8pm), 8.5km west of the town, are also worth a stop.

Anamur is a good base to break your journey. In the harbour district, **Hotel Bella** (☎ 0324-816 4751; Kürşat Caddesi 5; tayfun98@hotmail .com; s/d €15/27; 🖭) has benefited from an overhaul, and offers clean rooms and excellent facilities. It's professionally managed by Anamur local Tayfun Eser, who is fluent in English. He also runs **Eser Pansiyon** (☎ 0324-814 2322; eser@eserpansiyon.com; s/d €14/22; 🖭), almost next door. If you want to be next to the otogar, **Hotel Dedehan** (☎ 0324-814 7522; Otogar Yanı; s/d €11/18; 🖭) is a decent pad, but expect some noise seeping in from the main drag or from the mosque across the street. If hunger beckons, opt for **Kaptan Mustafanin Yeri** (☎ 0324-816 6957; İnönü Caddesi; mains €2-4), on the waterfront, or **Astor** (☎ 0324-814 7405; İskele Meydanı; mains €2-5), a delightful restaurant decorated with folksy flair. The Astor *köfte* go down a treat, but the fish dishes are equally tasty.

Kızkalesi (Maiden's Castle), 185km east of Adana, is a growing holiday resort with a striking Crusader castle offshore.

ANTAKYA (HATAY)

☎ 0326 / pop 140,700

The biblical Antioch, Antakya (confusingly, also called Hatay) was vilified as the Roman Empire's most depraved city. Undeterred, St Peter dropped by to preach here and you can visit the ancient **Church of St Peter** (St Pierre Kilisesi; admission €3; ☉ 8.30am-noon & 1.30-4.30pm Tue-Sun), 3km east of the centre. The magnificent Roman mosaics in the **Antakya Archaeology Museum** (☎ 214 6168; Gündüz Caddesi; admission €3; ☉ 8.30-11.30am & 1.30-5pm Tue-Sun) more than justify an overnight stop on the way to Syria.

Hotel Saray (☎ 214 9001; fax 214 9002; Hürriyet Caddesi; s/d €12/17) is the best budget option in town. **Atahan Hotel** (☎ 214 2140; Hürriyet Caddesi 28; s/d €16/20; 🖭) is conveniently located in the town centre. If you want to kick back

in style, the **Antik Beyazıt Otel** (☎ 216 2900; bbey azit@antikbeyazitoteli.com; Hükümet Caddesi 4; s/d €60/75; 🖭) fits the bill. It's in a French colonial building dating from the 1920s.

The otogar has direct buses to most western and northern points. There are also frequent services to Gaziantep (€6, four hours) and Şanlıurfa (€10, seven hours).

There are direct buses across the border to Aleppo and Damascus in Syria (p635).

CENTRAL ANATOLIA

For people needing a break from the tourist trails of the southern Aegean and the western Mediterranean, central Anatolia is the perfect antidote. Here, amid the mildly undulating steppe, you find some of modern Turkey's most important towns, including Ankara, the country's capital. For curious travellers, central Anatolia is a godsend: you won't see coach parties here, and the resorts are nonexistent, which adds to the sense of adventure.

And culture? Lovers of fine Seljuk architecture will be enthralled by Konya and Sivas; those who prefer the Ottoman style should stop off in Safranbolu and Amasya, two hidden treasures blessed with uniquely unforgettable architecture.

ANKARA

☎ 0312 / pop four million

It's often said that the capital of Turkey is devoid of charm, but one visit to the citadel and the Museum of Anatolian Civilisations will help you change your mind. Sure, the relative austerity and orderliness of the Turkish capital are not to everybody's taste, but you'll soon discover that Ankara boasts beguiling sights and has its inviting quarters. So pack an open mind and investigate the possibilities.

Orientation & Information

Ankara's *hisar* (citadel) crowns a hill 1km east of Ulus Meydanı (Ulus Sq), the heart of Old Ankara and near most of the inexpensive hotels. The newer Ankara lies further south, around Kızılay Meydanı (Kızılay Sq) and Kavaklıdere.

Atatürk Bulvarı is the main north–south axis. Ankara's mammoth otogar is 6.5km southwest of Ulus Meydanı and 6km west of Kızılay Meydanı. The train station is about 1.4km southwest of Ulus Meydanı.

The helpful **tourist office** (☎ /fax 231 5572; Gazi Mustafa Kemal Bulvarı 121, Maltepe) is opposite Maltepe Ankaray station. The main **PTT** (Atatürk Bulvarı) is just south of Ulus Meydanı. There are Internet facilities and branches of the main banks with ATMs in Ulus.

Sights

With the world's richest collection of Hittite artefacts, the state-of-the-art **Museum of Anatolian Civilisations** (Anadolu Medeniyetleri Müzesi; ☎ 324 3160; Hisarparkı Caddesi; admission €6; ⏱ 8.30am-5.15pm) is the *crème de la crème* of the museums in Turkey, and Ankara's premier attraction. Just up the hill, it's also well worth exploring the side streets of the **citadel**, by far the most stunning part of Ankara. Inside it, local people still live as if in a traditional Turkish village.

About 500m north of Ulus Meydanı, it's worth taking a look at the surprisingly well preserved remains of the **Roman baths** (admission €1.25; ⏱ 8.30am-12.30pm & 1.30-5.30pm Tue-Sun), dating back to the 3rd century. To the east you'll find Roman ruins, including the **Column of Julian** (AD 363) in a square that is ringed by government buildings, and the **Temple of Augustus & Rome**.

If you're an Atatürk devotee, you can't leave the city without having paid your respects to the founder of modern Turkey at the **Anıt Kabir** (Mausoleum of Atatürk; admission free; ⏱ 9am-noon & 1.30-5pm), 2km west of Kızılay Meydanı.

Sleeping & Eating

All places listed below are in Ulus or in the citadel, which are convenient for the main attractions.

Hotel Oğultürk (☎ 309 2900; www.ogulturk.com; Rüzgarlı Eşdost Sokak 6; s/d €30/45; [P] [✖]) Just off Rüzgarlı Sokak on the right, the Oğultürk is a reliable three-star affair, featuring good-sized rooms and a cheerful lobby with a mellow Turkish corner and a small fountain. It's professionally managed and good for lone women.

Hotel Spor (☎ 324 2165; fax 312 2153; Rüzgarlı Plevne Sokak 6; s/d €25/30; [P] [✖]) A block west, and just off Rüzgarlı Sokak, the modernish Spor wins no prize for character but features well-equipped (if smallish) rooms with impeccable bathrooms and a surpris-

ingly scrumptious (by Turkish standards) breakfast buffet.

Angora House Hotel (☎ 309 8380; fax 309 8381; Kalekapısı Sokak 16-18; s/d €45/70; [✖]) Step through the door into this treasure-trove of a *konak* and you'll never want to leave. It's blessed with an ace location inside the citadel, a short bag-haul from the Museum of Anatolian Civilisations. The six rooms are individually decorated and ooze rustic charm, with wood-beamed ceilings, antique furniture and brick walls. Rooms 20 and 22 boast fine views.

Kebabistan (Sanayi Caddesi, Ulus İşhanı 6/A; mains €3-5) Off Atatürk Caddesi, this place perches above the courtyard of a huge block of offices and shops. Indulge in hearty kebaps and succulent pide. It's often packed out, and justifiably so.

Urfali Hacı Mehmet (☎ 439 6068; Turan Güneş Bulvarı; mains €2-5) Just near the PTT, this long-running institution is a godsend for vegetarians and those who've grown weary of kebaps. Where else in Turkey could you find a menu groaning with 20 varieties of salad? It also concocts excellent pide.

Zenger Paşa Konağı (☎ 311 7070; Ankara Kale, Üstü Doyran Sokak 13; mains €3-8) Set in an old house in the citadel, this quirky restaurant has several dining rooms stuffed with a mind-boggling array of ethnographic artefacts. The food gets good reports, with the usual array of Turkish staples. Nab a table near the window to enjoy the sensational views of the city. There's live music every evening.

Kale Restaurant (☎ 311 4344; Ankara Kale, Doyran Sokak 5-7; mains €6-12) Another place strong on atmosphere, but much less cluttered than the Zenger Paşa. The Kale also occupies a wonderfully converted *konak*, with a soothing courtyard, splendid views and high-quality food. Finish off your meal with one of the delicious calorie-laden desserts.

Getting There & Away

AIR

Ankara's Esenboğa airport, 33km north of the city centre, is the hub for Turkey's domestic flight network. There are daily nonstop flights to most Turkish cities with Turkish Airlines. Atlasjet and Flyair also operate flights to/from Ankara.

BUS

Ankara's huge otogar (Ankara Şehirlerarası Terminali İşletmesi; AŞTİ) is the vehicu-

---

SAFRANBOLU & AMASYA: RELAX IN (OTTOMAN) STYLE

Bored with the ubiquitous concrete eyesores that disfigure almost every city centre in Turkey? Make a beeline for Safranbolu and Amasya, 90km off the road from İstanbul to Ankara and 175km off the road from Ankara to Sivas respectively. These two picture-postcard towns are slightly off the beaten track, but beckon the savvy with their unique setting and historic atmosphere. Both retain much of their original Ottoman style. For Safranbolu, there are a few direct buses from Ankara, while Amasya is conveniently reached from Sivas. Budget in a couple of days to savour both cities and their treasures.

Safranbolu is such an enchanting city that it was declared a Unesco World Heritage site, on a par with Florence, Italy. It boasts a wonderful old Ottoman quarter bristling with 19th-century half-timbered houses. Most of them have been restored, and as time goes on, more and more are being saved from deterioration and turned into hotels or museums.

Blissfully located on riverbanks hemmed in by a cliff, Amasya is probably Turkey's best-kept secret. One of the prettiest towns in all Turkey, it harbours numerous historic sites, including the rock-hewn tombs of the kings of Pontus, a lofty citadel, impressive Seljuk buildings and a profusion of picturesque Ottoman wooden houses scattered among the city centre.

Good news: both Safranbolu and Amasya are endowed with excellent accommodation. There's a profusion of delightful B&Bs, all set in skilfully restored Ottoman mansions. Enjoy!

---

lar heart of the nation, with coaches going everywhere all day and night. They depart for İstanbul (€15, six hours) at least every 15 minutes.

TRAIN

There are useful services to Adana, İstanbul, Kayseri, Sivas and a few other cities, but the long haul services can be excruciatingly slow.

SİVAS

☎ 0346 / pop 252,000

Once an important crossroads on the long-distance caravan route to Persia and Baghdad, Sivas has many marvellous Seljuk buildings to prove it, all handily situated right in the centre of town. The quintessential Turkish town, it has a very special significance for Turks: in 1919 Atatürk convened the second congress of the War of Independence here.

The **tourist office** (☎ 221 3535; Hükümet Meydanı; 9am-5pm) is in the *valılık* (provincial government headquarters) building on the main square. Don't miss the buildings in the adjoining park: the **Çifte Minare Medrese** (Seminary of the Twin Minaret) with a grand Seljuk-style gateway; the fabulous **Şifaiye Medresesi**, a medical school that's one of the city's oldest buildings; the **Bürüciye Medresesi**; the 1197 **Ulu Cami** (Great Mosque); and the glorious **Gök Medrese** (Blue Seminary).

There's a clutch of cheap hotels 700m southeast of Konak Meydanı, at the junction of Atatürk Caddesi and Kurşunlu Sokak. If you're after more creature comforts, opt for the **Otel Madımak** (☎ 221 8027; Eski Belediye Sokak 2, s/d €23/35), near the PTT, or the renovated **Sultan Otel** (☎ 221 2986; rezervation@sultanotel.com; Eski Belediye Sokak 18; s/d €35/50), which has modern, well-equipped rooms and satellite TV.

If you're after a quick, no-frills bite, head for the small street behind the PTT, which is packed with pint-sized cheap restaurants. Nimet and Örnek Lokanta are regarded as the best joints for a savoury kebap any time of the day.

There are services to go to Amasya (€10, 3½ hours), Ankara (€13, six hours) and Erzurum (€17, seven hours), among others.

Sivas is a main rail junction. The *Doğu Ekspresi* goes through Sivas to Erzurum and Kars daily; the *Güney Ekspresi* (from İstanbul to Diyarbakır) goes on alternate days.

KONYA

☎ 0332 / pop 762,000

Be savvy: don't skip Konya. South of Ankara, this booming town was the capital of the Seljuk Turks and showcases some of the best Seljuk architecture in Turkey. It's also a highly significant spiritual centre; it was here that the 13th-century poet Mevlana Rumi inspired the founding of the whirling dervishes, one of Islam's most important mystical orders. You can see the whirling dervishes perform in Konya during the **Mevlana Festival** held on 10 to 17 December.

TURKEY

Orientation & Information

The town centre stretches from Alaettin Tepesi, the hill topped by the Alaettin Mosque (1221), along Mevlana Caddesi to the tomb of Mevlana, now called Mevlana Müzesi. The otogar is 14km north of the centre; free *servis* take half an hour for the trip into town.

The **tourist office** (☎ 351 1074; Mevlana Caddesi 21; ☺ 8.30am-5pm Mon-Sat) is across the square from the Mevlana Müzesi. You'll find numerous banks with ATMs and Internet cafés in the centre, as well as the PTT.

Sights

Ditch your bags on arrival and leg it straight to the wonderful **Mevlana Museum** (admission €3; ☺ 9am-5pm Tue-Sun, 10am-5.30pm Mon), off Mevlana Caddesi. The former lodge of the whirling dervishes, it is topped by a brilliant turquoise-tiled dome – one of the most inspiring images of Turkey. Although it's virtually under siege from pilgrims, there's a palpable mystique here.

It's also well worth visiting two outstanding Seljuk buildings near the Alaettin Tepesi: **Karatay Müzesi** (admission €1.25; Alaettin Bulvarı; ☺ 9am-noon & 1-5.30pm), once a Muslim theological seminary, now a museum housing a superb collection of ceramics; and **İnceminare Medresesi** (Seminary of the Slender Minaret; admission €1.25; Alaettin Bulvarı; ☺ 9am-noon & 1.30-5.30pm), now the Museum of Wooden Artefacts & Stone Carving. The former features a splendid marble entrance, the latter boasts an extraordinarily elaborate doorway.

Sleeping & Eating

Otel Mevlana (☎ 354 0334; Cengaver Sokak 2; s/d €21/36; ℗ ✖) A good deal, one block off Mevlana Caddesi, to the south. This hotel has been updated and features unexciting but serviceable rooms with satisfactory beds and TVs. Try to get a 10% discount.

Otel Derya (☎ 352 0154; Ayanbey Caddesi 18; s/d €21/33; ℗ ✖) The newish Derya is a good-value business hotel with glistening bathrooms. It's conveniently positioned, a short bag-haul from Mevlana Müzesi.

Hotel Ulusan (☎ 351 5004; ulusanhotel@mynet .com; Çarşı PTT Arkası; s/d €9/16; ☐) Signposted behind the PTT, this is a nice surprise, with perfectly presentable rooms.

Aydın Et Lokantası (☎ 351 9183; Mevlana Caddesi, Şeyh Ziya Sokak 5; mains €2-5) In a city swarming with unimpressive kebap joints, this outfit bucks the trend and features a welcoming interior, with tables set around a fake tree that rises from a fish pond – tacky, but pleasantly soothing. The ultrafresh pide is a winner, as is the *fırın kebap* (slices of tender, oven-roasted mutton served on puffy bread).

Meşhur Tandır Kebapçısı (☎ 351 4485; Naci Fikret Sokak 4; mains €2-4) A fine spot for an informal meal, just near the tourist office. The menu doesn't try to set records in culinary innovation, sticking to classics such as pide and kebaps.

Şifa (☎ 352 0519; Mevlana Caddesi 29; mains €2-5) A bright, spacious and bustling *lokanta* on the main drag, noted for its variety of ready-made meals and savoury *fırın kebap*.

Getting There & Away

There are daily flights to and from İstanbul with Turkish Airlines.

From the otogar there are frequent buses to Nevşehir, some of which continue to Göreme (€8, 3½ hours). There are also frequent buses between Konya and Pamukkale (€12, seven hours).

You can get to Konya by train from İstanbul.

CAPPADOCIA (KAPADOKYA)

Deep in the heart of the country lies a world of lunar landscapes and surreal scenery, of ancient churches and cave dwellings, of picture-postcard villages and big cities steeped in tradition. One of Turkey's most tourist-friendly areas, Cappadocia boasts an exceptional blend of cultural sights, activities and geological wonders. Compared to the southern and eastern coasts, tourist development here has retained a more human scale.

Cappadocia's heavenly backdrop consists of soft volcanic tuff that has been sculpted over millennia into fantastic shapes by water and erosion. The end result is fascinating: huge stone mushrooms (dubbed 'fairy chimneys' by locals), soft ridges and deep valleys, acute edges and mild undulations. Early Christians carved chambers, vaults and labyrinths into the chimneys, for use as churches, stables and homes.

Cappadocia is a place that never fails to make onlookers' jaws drop in awe.

CENTRAL CAPPADOCIA

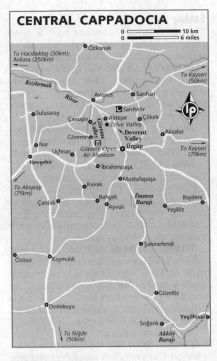

cliffs, and surrounded by vineyards. Unsurprisingly it's a magnet for backpackers from all over the world. It is chock-a-block with pensions, restaurants and tour agencies, and the amazing Göreme Open-Air Museum is on its doorstep – Göreme really does seem to have it all.

All the services useful to travellers are in the centre, including the otogar, two ATMs, the PTT and Internet cafés.

Sights & Activities

Cappadocia's number one attraction is the **Göreme Open-Air Museum** (admission €7.50, Karanlık Kilise €3.50; ☼ 8am-5.30pm Apr-Oct, 8am-4.30pm Nov-Mar). It's pricey but it's worth every lira. Medieval frescoes can be seen in the rock-hewn monastery, nunnery and churches. Some date from the 8th century, though the best are from the 10th to 13th centuries. The stunning **Karanlık Kilise** (Dark Church) is one of the most famous and fresco-filled of the churches. The **Tokalı Kilise** (Buckle Church), which is across the road from the main entrance, is equally impressive and has fabulous frescoes.

There are a number of **hiking** options around Göreme village. It's surrounded by a handful of gorgeous valleys that are easily explored on foot, allowing about one to three hours for each of them. Most pension owners will be happy to guide you on the trails for a minimal fee.

Tours

The following agencies offer good daily tours (costing around €45) of local highlights, including Ihlara Valley.

Neşe Tour (☎ 0384-271 2525; www.nesetour.com; Avanos Yolu, Göreme)

Ötüken Voyage (☎ 0384-271 2588; www.otuken travel.com; Avanos Yolu, Göreme)

Zemi Tour (☎ 0384-271 2576; Bilal Eroğlu Caddesi, Göreme)

Kirkit Voyage (☎ 0384-511 3259; www.kirkit.com; Atatürk Caddesi, Avanos) and **Argeus** (☎ 0384-341 4688; www.argeus.com.tr; İstiklal Caddesi 7, Ürgüp) are experienced travel agencies with varied programmes including horse-riding and cycling tours. **Middle Earth Travel** (☎ 0384-271 2528; www.middleearthtravel.com; Göreme) also offers a programme of walking tours and activities such as abseiling.

GÖREME

☎ 0384 / pop 2000

One of Turkey's most familiar images, Göreme village is a magical place set amid towering tuff cones and honeycombed

---

CAPPADOCIA FROM ABOVE

If you've never taken a flight in a hot-air balloon, Cappadocia is one of the best places in the world to do it. Flight conditions are especially favourable here, with balloons operating most mornings from the beginning of April to the end of November. The views are simply unforgettable and it's a magical experience. It costs about €180 to €200 per person, or €120 for the cheaper 45-minute flight. It's pricey but definitely worth blowing your budget on.

The following two agencies have good credentials.

Göreme Balloons (☎ 0384-341 5662; www.goremeballoons.com; Sivritas Mahallesi 4, Ürgüp) Based in Ürgüp and Göreme.

Kapadokya Balloons (☎ 0384-271 2442; www.kapadokyaballoons.com; Adnan Menderes Caddesi, Göreme)

Sleeping

Göreme has some of Turkey's best-value pensions, which often offer guests the chance to try out the troglodyte lifestyle by sleeping in a cave.

Elif Star Caves (☎ 271 2479; www.elifstar.com; Uzundere Caddesi; d €30) This welcoming place is run with care and efficiency by a Turkish-English couple. The seven cave rooms are well appointed and as clean as a whistle. And if you really need an English breakfast, this one's for you!

Kemal's Guest House (☎ 271 2234; www.kemals guesthouse.com; Zeybek Sokak 3; dm/d €6/24; ▤) Barbara and Kemal, a Dutch-Kurdish couple, run this attractive pension, located stumbling distance from the otogar.

Flintstones (☎ 271 2555; flintstonescave@hotmail .com; dm €6, s €8-10, d €15-18; ▤ ▧) Along the road leading to the Pigeon Valley, this is a secluded place offering accommodation (caves, dorms and standard rooms) to suit all budgets. The best assets here are the swimming pool and the laid-back, chummy atmosphere.

Köse Pension (☎ 271 2294; dawn@kosepension .com; per person dm €4, huts €5, d with shared/private bathroom €7/11; ▤ ▧) Another solid choice, run by a friendly Scottish-Turkish couple. There's a stadium-sized basic roof dorm, two quirky adjoining huts, and unspectacular, no-frills bedrooms with balconies. But the real drawcards here are the swimming pool and good home-cooked food for vegetarians and meat-eaters (€5). Pity about the rather dull location, near the PTT.

Canyon View (☎ 271 2333; www.canyonviewhotel .com; s €25, d €30-50; ▤) Stay at this nearly-but-not-quite boutique hotel right up in the old village and you won't believe your bill – it's excellent value. The nine rooms – some caves, some vaulted – are all decked out with flair, and the architecture is perfectly in tune with the local environment.

Also recommended:

Paradise Pension (☎ 271 2248; www.paradise pension.com; Müze Caddesi; dm €3, s €7-12, d €13-18; ▤) On the road to the Göreme Open-Air Museum.

Walnut House (☎ 271 2235; www.walnuthouse.info; Zeybek Sokak; s/d €14/20; ▤) A stately mansion, a few steps away from the otogar.

Kelebek (☎ 271 2531; www.kelebekhotel.com; r €25-50, ste €65-100) Pamper yourself in this smart boutique hotel, snugly situated in the heights of Göreme. The suites, in a lovely separate building, are exceedingly atmospheric.

Eating

Most of Göreme's pensions provide good, cheap meals but you could also take advantage of some fine eateries in town.

Alaturca (☎ 271 2882; Müze Caddesi; mains €6-10) Tired of kebap joints? Then consider splashing out a bit in this gastronomic venue. It specialises in traditional Ottoman cuisine with a contemporary twist. Hmm.

Orient (☎ 271 2346; Adnan Menderes Caddesi; mains €5-11) Another much-lauded spot, serving excellent fare in rustic, yet elegant, surrounds.

Dibek (☎ 271 2209; Hakki Paşa Meydanı; mains €5-7) Housed in an attractive old stone house, the Dibek oozes atmosphere with its traditional, cosy design. There are few more pleasant experiences than sitting on floor cushions around low wooden tables while noshing on a plate of *mantı*.

SOS Restaurant & Café (☎ 271 2872; Bilal Eroğlu Caddesi; mains €2-6) Another place well worth bookmarking. Come here for the tasty ready-made meals served in friendly surroundings. The pots lining the front are for the *testi kebap* (a delicious meat and vegetable dish cooked in a sealed pot, which is broken to serve).

Also recommended:

Café Utopia (☎ 271 2487; Harım Sokak; mains €5-15) A funky place, with a cosy décor and a rather sophisticated ambience. You can't help but feel you're paying more for the setting and the views than for the food.

Silk Road (Müze Caddesi; mains €2-4) A tiny place, which is also puny on prices. Grab a seat on the terrace and chow down on decent munchies.

Cappadocia Kebap House (Müze Caddesi; mains €2) This no-nonsense den churns out good sandwiches.

Göreme Restaurant (Müze Caddesi; mains €3-5) A genuinely relaxed eatery that serves up Turkish staples in a cosy setting, with kilims and cushions.

Getting There & Away

There are daily long-distance buses to all sorts of places from Göreme otogar.

Minibuses travel from Ürgüp to Avanos (€0.75) via the Göreme Open-Air Museum, Göreme village and Zelve every two hours. In summer, there's also a half-hourly municipal bus running from Avanos to Nevşehir (€0.75) via Göreme and Uçhisar.

UÇHİSAR

☎ 0384 / pop 3851

Between Göreme and Nevşehir is picturesque, laid-back yet stylish Uçhisar, built around a **rock citadel** (admission €1.25; ☼ 8am-sunset) that offers panoramic views from its summit. There are some excellent places to stay; the following spots are brilliant value and afford formidable views over the valley. They are all located on the same street.

Kilim Pansiyon (☎ 219 2774; www.sisik.com in Turkish; Eski Göreme Yolu; s/d €15/27)

La Maison du Reve (☎ 219 2199; www.lamaison dureve.com; Tekelli Mahallesi 17; s/d €18/28)

Les Terrasses d'Uçhisar (☎ 219 2792; www.terrasses pension.com; Eski Göreme Yolu; s/d €26/29)

In summer, there's a half-hourly municipal bus running from Avanos to Nevşehir via Göreme and Uçhisar (€0.75).

ZELVE VALLEY

Make sure to visit the excellent **Zelve Open-Air Museum** (admission €3.50; ⏰ 8.30am-5.30pm), off the road from Göreme to Avanos. It is less visited than the Göreme Valley, though it too has rock-cut churches, a rock-cut mosque and the chance to indulge in some serious scrambling. On the way back be sure to stop off to see some of the finest fairy chimneys at **Paşabağı**. This beguiling, much-photographed spot is a popular place to come to watch the sunset.

AVANOS

☎ 0384 / pop 15,900

On the northern bank of the Kızılırmak (Red River), Avanos is known for its pottery. Less touristy than Göreme, it's another potential base for exploring the Cappadocian valleys. You'll find banks with ATMs, the PTT and a couple of Internet cafés along the main drag.

Sleeping & Eating

Kirkit Pension (☎ 511 3148; www.kirkit.com; s/d €22/33) An excellent base, set in converted old stone houses off the main drag. This home away from home offers impeccable rooms with spick and span bathrooms. Other perks include an on-site restaurant and a reputable travel agency.

Venessa Pansiyon (☎ 511 3840; www.katpatuka .org/venessa; Hafızağa Sokak 20; d €30) Another savvy option. Set in a beautifully restored old house decked out with collectables – and its own private underground city.

Sofa Hotel (☎ 511 5186; www.sofa-hotel.com; Orta Mahallesi 13; s/d €25/40) Near the northern end of the bridge, this quirky place is full of nooks and crannies, and has 31 character-filled rooms set in several old houses.

Dayının Yeri (☎ 511 6840; Atatürk Caddesi 23; mains €2-5) This central place gets the thumbs up for its ultrafresh meat dishes and is usually full of happily chomping locals and tourists.

Bizim Ev (☎ 511 5525; Orta Mahallesi; mains €3-6) One of the fancier eateries in town, Bizim Ev exudes bucket loads of charm, thanks to its delightful setting (a vaulted dining room), exemplary service, some dazzling wine and well-prepared food.

Getting There & Away

Minibuses travel from Ürgüp (€0.75) to Avanos via the Göreme Open-Air Museum, Goreme village and Zelve every two hours. In summer, there's also a half-hourly municipal bus running from Avanos to Nevşehir (€0.75) via Göreme and Uçhisar.

ÜRGÜP

☎ 0384 / pop 14,600

With the most irresistible collection of boutique hotels in Turkey, Ürgüp is the perfect place to splash out. Do yourself a favour and live like a sophisticated sultan for a couple of days in one of these top-notch lodgings.

Although Ürgüp is no longer a well-kept secret, it is still a lovely place to discover, with honey-coloured stone buildings and old houses left over from the days (pre-1923) when the town still had a large Greek population. It is ideally positioned, about 7km east of Göreme Valley. For wine buffs, it also boasts Cappadocia's best wineries.

There are Internet cafés, banks with ATMs, hotels and restaurants around Cumhuriyet Meydanı, the main square.

Sleeping & Eating

Elkep Evi Pansiyon 1, 2 & 3 (☎ 341 6000; www.elkepevi .com; Esbelli Mahallesi; s/d €50/75) All we can say is… oh yeah! The most affordable boutique hotel in Ürgüp is perfect for an indulgent holiday. It boasts three separate sections containing a total of 21 cave rooms, each with a small rock-cut terrace. It's elegant, atmospheric and not to be missed. The breakfast room's terrace has unsurpassable views.

Hotel Elvan (☎ 341 4191; fax 341 3455; Dutlu Cami Mahallesi, Barbaros Hayrettin Sokak 11; s/d €16/27) A homely atmosphere and motherly welcome await you at this unpretentious but immaculate guesthouse. Excellent value.

TURKEY

Asia Minor Hotel (☎ 341 4645; www.cappadocia house.com; İstiklal Caddesi; s/d €25/35) This is a great deal: the hardwood floor, balconies and manicured garden create a tasteful, comfortable ambience.

Sun Pension (☎ 341 6165; İstiklal Caddesi; s/d €8/16) Tucked away behind the *hamam*, this simple pension is run by an elderly couple. It's a good bet if you can get a room on the upper floors, especially rooms 201 to 208, which are brighter and more modern. Avoid by all means the tiny and sombre cave rooms set around the courtyard. Breakfast costs €3.

Razziya Evi (☎ 341 5089; www.razziyaevi.com; Cingilli Sokak 24; s/d €25/40) One of the best-value options in Ürgüp, this appealing *evi* is located across the other side of town, southwest of the main square. It has only seven generously sized rooms (some are cave rooms) for greater intimacy. An added benefit is the *hamam* (€5).

Esbelli Evi (☎ 341 3395; www.esbelli.com; Esbelli Mahallesi; s/d €65/80; 🖵) Yet another darling in Ürgüp's luxury clique, Esbelli Evi was the first boutique hotel in town and still attracts its fair share of aficionados with a refined yet informal environment and a cocoon-like ambience.

For plump wallets, other recommended boutique hotels in the Esbelli district include **Kayadam Cave House** (☎ 341 6623; www .kayadam.com; Esbelli Sokak 6; s/d €60/75) and **Selçuklu Evi** (☎ 341 7460; www.selcukluevi.com; Esbelli Mahallesi; r €60-80), both designed to spoil you rotten. Pure fairy-tale romance!

Eating & Drinking

Şömine Restaurant (☎ 341 8442; Cumhuriyet Meydanı; mains €3-8) The widely acclaimed Şömine, right on the main square, has indoor and outdoor tables and serves up a broad variety of Turkish staples in fairly classy surroundings.

Ocakbaşı (☎ 341 3277; Güllüce Caddesi 44; mains €3-7) This is practically an institution. Despite a no-nonsense décor, the Ocakbaşı is consistently rated as one of the best restaurants in Ürgüp. It's a carnivore's paradise, with superb grills, but vegetarians can tuck into equally good meze.

Kardeşler (Cumhuriyet Meydanı; mains €2-4) This quirky eatery on the main square, is famed for its *tandır* (stew cooked in a clay pot, then wrapped in bread).

Şu & Ne Kahvaltı Ve Börek Salonu (☎ 341 2818; Cumhuriyet Meydanı; mains €1-2) A small eatery popular with local women, who come here for some *dedikodu* (gossip), a cup of tea and excellent snacks.

Şükrüoğlu (Cumhuriyet Meydanı) This is the place towards which all heads turn; it's a sleek pastry shop crammed with bait for the sweet toothed. Find heaven here!

Prokopi Bar (Cumhuriyet Meydanı) A cosy lounge-bar on the main square.

Getting There & Away

There are daily long-distance buses to all sorts of places from Ürgüp's otogar.

Minibuses travel to Avanos (€0.75) via the Göreme Open-Air Museum, Göreme village and Zelve every two hours.

MUSTAFAPAŞA

☎ 0384 / pop 2500

Mustafapaşa is the sleeping beauty of Cappadocia, a peaceful village with pretty old stone-carved houses, a few minor rock-cut churches and several good places to stay. If you want to get away from it all, this is the place to base yourself.

For backpackers, **Monastery Pension** (☎ 353 5005; www.monasteryhotel.com; Mehmet Şakirpaşa Caddesi; s/d €12/24) is a lovely find. It has 12 neat rooms – some vaulted, some caved – with tiled bathrooms. Some are a bit claustrophobic, so ask to see a few. The pleasant leafy balcony is perfect for kicking back with a book. Meals are available on request (€7).

Another good option, the family-run **Hotel Pacha** (☎ 353 5331; www.pachahotel.com; Sinaso Meydanı; s/d €21/30) is a notch up in standard, with immaculate yet nondescript rooms. More atmospheric is the terrace, with its kilims and artefacts. The home-cooked dinners (about €7), as only a Turkish mama can make them, get rave reviews from travellers.

The quirkiest place in town is probably **Old Greek House** (☎ 353 5306; www.oldgreekhouse.com; Şahin Caddesi; s/d €30/40), a wonderful Ottoman-Greek house with an attractive courtyard. Some rooms have original 19th-century frescoes. Guests praise the meals (€10).

Six buses a day (less on Sunday) travel between Ürgüp (€0.50) and Mustafapaşa.

IHLARA VALLEY

☎ 0382

A beautiful canyon full of rock-cut churches dating back to Byzantine times, **Ihlara Valley** (Ihlara Vadisi; admission €3; ⏰ 8am-7pm Apr-Oct, 8.30am-

5pm Nov-Mar) is a definite must-see. It's still less touristy than Göreme, if only because access is more time-consuming. People come here to follow the course of the stream, Melendiz Suyu, which flows for 16km from the wide valley at Selime to a narrow gorge at Ihlara village. The easiest way to see this gorgeous valley is on a day tour from Göreme (p611), which allows a few hours to walk through the central part of the gorge.

KAYSERİ

☎ 0352 / pop 536,000

In the shadow of Mt Erciyes, Kayseri is a mind boggling city that mixes religious conservatism with a phenomenal sense of business and innovation. Much of Kayseri's charm lies in this contradiction and in the juxtaposition of old and new. Venerable mosques and the bustling bazaar district, awash with traditional shops and pungent smells, rub up against contemporary Kayseri in the pedestrianised streets in the centre, where hip-looking university students can be seen courting in slick pastry shops.

Don't miss Kayseri. Even if you're not an architecture buff, you'll be enthralled by the mosques, tombs and old seminaries sprinkled around the city centre, behind the faceless high-rises.

Orientation & Information

The basalt-walled citadel at the centre of the old town, just south of Cumhuriyet Meydanı (the huge main square) is a good landmark. The train station is at the northern end of Atatürk Bulvarı, 500m north of the old town. The otogar is 800m northwest of the centre.

You'll find banks with ATMs in the centre. To check your email, head to **Hollywood Internet Café** (Sivas Caddesi 15; per hr €1; ☺ 9am-11pm), east of the old town.

Sights

The fabulous walls of the **citadel** were constructed out of black volcanic stone by Emperor Justinian in the 6th century and extensively repaired in the 13th and 15th centuries. Just southeast of the citadel is the wonderful **Güpgüpoğlu Konağı**, a fine stone mansion dating from the 18th century, which now houses a mildly interesting museum.

Among Kayseri's distinctive features are important building complexes founded by Seljuk queens and princesses, such as the impressive **Mahperi Hunat Hatun Complex**, east of the citadel. Opposite is the **Ulu Cami** (Great Mosque), a good example of early Seljuk style. Other must-sees are the **Çifte Medrese** (Twin Seminaries). These adjoining religious schools, in Mimar Sinan Parkı north of Park Caddesi, date back to the 12th century.

Scattered about Kayseri are several conical **Seljuk tombs**.

Sleeping & Eating

Hotel Titiz (☎ 221 4203; fax 221 4204; Maarif Caddesi 7, Zengin Sokak 5; s/d €17/25) One of the best ventures if you're on a budget; it's also very conveniently positioned inside the city walls.

Hotel Gönen (☎ 222 2778; fax 231 6584; Nazmi Toker Caddesi 15; s/d €19/30) Another reliable stand-by, a short hop from the Titiz.

Hotel Almer (☎ 320 7970; www.almer.com.tr; Kavuncu Caddesi 15; s/d €30/42; P) With its glass-fronted façade and faux-marble reception, this well-organised high-rise on Düvenönü Meydanı certainly impresses. Rooms are soulless but comfortable and fair sized.

Beyaz Saray (☎ 221 0444; Millet Caddesi 8; mains €3-5), near the citadel, is always packed to the rafters with happy punters enjoying succulent kebaps, as is the ever-popular **İskender Kebap Salonu** (☎ 222 0903; Millet Caddesi 5; mains €3-5) across the road. Afterwards, finish up with a delectable baklava at **Divan Pastanesi** (☎ 222 3974; Millet Caddesi), immediately opposite.

Getting There & Away

Turkish Airlines and Onur Air have flights from Kayseri's Erkilet airport to İstanbul.

On an important north–south and east–west crossroads, Kayseri has lots of bus services. Destinations include Sivas (€7, three hours) and Ürgüp (€3, 1¼ hours).

By train, there are useful services to Adana, Ankara, Diyarbakır, Kars and Sivas.

THE BLACK SEA & NORTHEASTERN ANATOLIA

Travel no further: you've found what you're looking for. A place where resorts are non-existent, where you can really feel a sense of wilderness and adventure, and where superb archaeological sites and hidden treasures are set amidst eerie landscapes – welcome to the Black Sea coast and eastern Turkey.

If you're heading overland for Iran or Syria you will certainly need to transit parts of these fascinating areas; bear in mind that the weather can be bitterly cold and snowy in winter, especially in eastern Turkey.

Turkey's Black Sea coast is a distinctive part of the country. With plenty of rain, even in summer, it's the garden of Turkey. It is steep and craggy, damp and lush, and isolated behind the Pontic Mountains for most of its length. The coast west from Sinop to the Bosphorus is little visited, although the quaint seaside town of **Amasra**, with its Roman and Byzantine ruins and small, cheap hotels, is worth a look. **Sinop**, three hours northwest of Samsun, is a fine little backwater, with beaches on both sides of the peninsula, as well as a few historic buildings and several cheap hotels.

While **Samsun** has little of interest to detain tourists, there are excellent beaches around the cheerful resort town of **Ünye**, on a wide bay 85km east of Samsun. About 80km further to the east, **Ordu** is a bustling seaside city with a pleasant seafront boulevard. **Giresun** is famous for its hazelnuts and cherries.

From the Black Sea coast, it's fairly straightforward to get to northeastern Anatolia. This remote section of the country exerts a magnetic power, even for the Turks. Here the flavours of the neighbouring Caucasus, Central Asia and Iran are already palpable. It's a perfect blend of nature and culture, with many palaces, castles, mosques and churches dotted around the steppe.

TRABZON

☎ 0462 / pop 485,000

Modern Trabzon is vibrant, sprawling, energising and fairly cosmopolitan. It is by far the most engaging urban centre along the Black Sea coast, with lots of old Byzantine buildings and the amazing Sumela Monastery right on its doorstep. Trabzon held out against the Seljuks and Mongols and was the last town to fall to the Ottoman Turks. Today it still feels very different from other Turkish towns, not least because its trading focus is on Russia and the Caucasus.

Orientation & Information

Modern Trabzon is centred on Atatürk Alanı (also known as Meydan Parkı). About

3km to the east is the otogar for long-distance buses. The airport is 5.5km east of the centre of town. You'll find several banks with ATMs as well as a PTT booth and Internet cafés on or just off Atatürk Alanı.

The helpful **tourist office** (☎ /fax 326 4760) is off the southern side of Atatürk Alanı, near Hotel Nur. The **Georgian consulate** (☎ 326 2226; fax 326 2296; Gazipaşa Caddesi 20) is off the northern side of the square. There's also the **Russian consulate** (☎ 326 2600; fax 326 2101; Şh Refik Cesur 6, Ortahisar), which is west of the centre in Ortahisar district, past the bazaar.

Sights

Without doubt, Trabzon's star attraction is the 13th-century **Aya Sofya** (admission €1.25; ⏰ 9am-6pm Tue-Sun Apr-Oct, 9am-5pm Tue-Sun Nov-Mar), 4km west of town and reachable by dolmuş from Atatürk Alanı. Marvel at the vividly coloured frescoes and mosaic floors.

Another draw is the **Atatürk Köşkü** (Atatürk Villa; admission €1.25; ⏰ 8am-7pm May-Sep, 8am-5pm Oct-Apr). This beautiful 19th-century mansion is set high above the town and is accessible by bus from the northern side of Atatürk Alanı.

The lively **bazaar** is to the east, accessible by the pedestrianised Kunduracılar Caddesi from Atatürk Alanı, which cuts through the tightly packed streets of the ancient bazaar.

You could also poke around the atmospheric **old town**, a 20-minute walk west of Atatürk Alanı. With its timber houses and stone bridges, it still looks medieval.

SUMELA MONASTERY

Of all the dreamy spots in eastern Turkey that make you feel like you're floating through another time and space, **Sumela Monastery** (admission €3; ⏰ 9am-6pm Jun-Aug, 9am-4pm Sep-May), 46km south of Trabzon, wins the time-travel prize by a long shot. Carved out of a sheer rock cliff like a swallow's nest, this Byzantine monastery features superb frescoes (partially damaged by vandals). Some of them date from the 9th century.

From May to August, Ulusoy buses depart for Sumela (€9, 45 minutes) from outside the Ulusoy ticket office by Atatürk Alanı. You can also visit on a tour (€6) from Trabzon.

Sleeping

Hotel Nur (☎ 323 0445; fax 323 0447; Cami Sokak 15; s/d €24/36; ❄) Location, location, location!

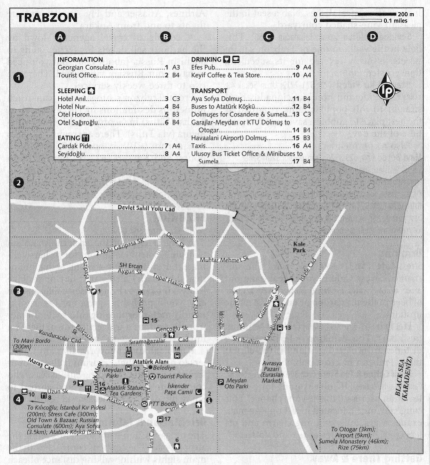

TRABZON

0 — 200 m
0 — 0.1 miles

INFORMATION
Georgian Consulate..........................1 A3
Tourist Office...................................2 B4

SLEEPING
Hotel Anıl.......................................3 C3
Hotel Nur.......................................4 B4
Otel Horon.....................................5 B3
Otel Sağıroğlu.................................6 B4

EATING
Çardak Pide....................................7 A4
Seyidoğlu.......................................8 A4

DRINKING
Efes Pub...9 A4
Keyif Coffee & Tea Store.................10 A4

TRANSPORT
Aya Sofya Dolmuş..........................11 B4
Buses to Atatürk Köşkü...................12 B4
Dolmuşes for Cosandere & Sumela..13 C3
Garajlar-Meydan or KTU Dolmuş to
Otogar.......................................14 B4
Havaalanı (Airport) Dolmuş.............15 B3
Taxis...16 A4
Ulusoy Bus Ticket Office & Minibuses to
Sumela.......................................17 B4

Next to the tourist office, just steps away from Atatürk Alanı, this is the best haunt for frugal travellers. Rooms (especially singles) are a little boxy, but never less than spotlessly clean.

Otel Horon (☎ 326 6455; fax 321 6628; Sıramağazalar Caddesi 125; s/d €42/53; P ﷽) Sure, the greyish façade of the Horon could do with a makeover, but inside it's much more enticing. Enjoy the cosy rooms with prim bathrooms, as well as the rooftop restaurant-bar commanding stellar views of the city.

Otel Sağıroğlu (☎ 323 2899; Taksim İşhanı Sokak 1; s/d €39/56; P ﷽) Located off Atatürk Alanı, this impossible-to-miss yellow high-rise sports excellent rooms kitted out with the full array of amenities, including TV,

minibar, stout bedding and the obligatory rooftop restaurant.

Hotel Anıl (☎ 326 7282; Güzelhisar Caddesi 12; s/d €15/24) The Anıl is not exactly the most suitable place for a honeymoon, but it does the trick for shoestringers. The rooms are decent enough, though the bathrooms are a tad skanky. The English-speaking staff can organise trips to Sumela (€9).

Eating
Rumbling tummies should head for Atatürk Alanı and the two main drags (Uzun Sokak and Maraş Caddesi) to the west, where there's a choice of cheap-and-cheerful *lokantas*.

Çardak Pide (☎ 321 7676; Uzun Sokak 4; mains €2-3) Patrons pour in at lunchtime for a pide fix.

It also serves meat dishes. Nab a seat in the pleasant vine-shaded courtyard.

Seyidoğlu (Uzun Sokak; lahmacun €0.50) This hole in the wall, on one of Trabzon's main streets, is justly revered for its succulent, thin-crusted *lahmacun*.

İstanbul Kır Pidesi (☎ 321 2212; Uzun Sokak 48; mains €1-2) Pide and börek aficionados head straight to this popular joint, regarded as the best place to gobble a savoury börek any time of the day.

Also recommended:

Mavi Bordo (☎ 323 3325; Trabzonspor Sadri Şener Sosyal Tesisleri; mains €3-7) A sassy newcomer, making a brave attempt at creating a spiffy-yet-minimalist décor. Pizzas, pasta, ice creams and other munchies are on offer.

Kılıçoğlu (☎ 321 4525; Uzun Sokak 42) Hands down the best pastry shop in town. One lick of the *fıstıklı* (pistachio) ice cream and you'll be hooked.

Drinking

Stress Cafe (☎ 321 3044; Uzun Sokak) The misnamed Stress Cafe is your ideal hang-out after a day's sightseeing. Relax over a glass of beer in the tea garden or enjoy live music upstairs.

Efes Pub (☎ 326 6083; Maraş Caddesi 5) Mmmm, fresh beer. This drinking hole, just spitting distance from Atatürk Alanı, is the closest thing Trabzon has to a pub.

Keyif Coffee & Tea Store (☎ 326 8026; Uzun Sokak, Canbakkal İş Merkezi) If you're pining for a milky tea or an espresso, this is your chance! This congenial outfit, located in a shopping mall, exudes a gracious, winning charm and offers over 200 varieties of tea and coffee.

Getting There & Away

Turkish Airlines, Onur Air, Atlasjet and Fly Air fly to and from İstanbul. Turkish

---

SAFETY IN THE EAST

The security situation in southeastern Turkey has improved considerably since the capture of the Kurdistan Workers Party (PKK) leader Abdullah Öcalan in 1999. Although it's always wise to keep your ear to the ground, at the time of writing there was little reason to think travellers would suffer anything worse than delays at checkpoints along the way. The only spot that was still considered unsafe at the time of research was the Şirnak area.

Airlines, Atlasjet and Fly Air also operate flights to and from Ankara.

A couple of travel agencies down by the harbour sell tickets for ferries going to Sochi in Russia (about €50), but you need to have your Russian visa sorted. There are two to three weekly services.

From Trabzon's otogar, you can reach numerous destinations in Turkey as well as Tbilisi (Tiflis) in Georgia and Erivan in Armenia (via Tiflis). There are regular services to Erzurum (€10, six hours), Kars (€16, 10 hours) and Kayseri (€22, 12 hours). From May to late August, Ulusoy runs buses to Sumela (€7), departing from outside the Ulusoy ticket office by Atatürk Alanı.

ERZURUM
☎ 0442 / pop 362,000

The largest city on the eastern Anatolian plateau, Erzurum is famous for its harsh climate, but it has some striking Seljuk buildings that justify a stay of a day or so. Like Konya, it's said to be a conservative, austere city; you'll probably agree, but Erzurum is rapidly metamorphosing into a vibrant metropolis and, as a university town, there's a fluid, lively energy to the city.

It also comes as a surprise to many travellers to discover that Erzurum is also a popular base in winter for skiing enthusiasts, who come from all over Turkey and abroad to enjoy the nearby **Palandöken** ski resort.

Orientation & Information

The otogar is 2km from the centre along the airport road. The centre is compact, with the main sights within walking distance of each other. You'll find lots of banks with ATMs, the PTT and Internet cafés on or around Cumhuriyet Caddesi, the main drag.

The **Iranian consulate** (☎ 316 2285; fax 316 1182; ☺ 8am-noon & 2.30-5pm Mon-Thu & Sat), just off Atatürk Bulvarı, can arrange visas in 10 days.

Sights

The well-preserved walls of the 5th-century **citadel** loom over a maze of narrow streets, offering good views of the town and the bleak surrounding plains.

Another must-see is the beautifully symmetrical **Çifte Minareli Medrese** (Twin Minaret Seminary; Cumhuriyet Caddesi), a famous example of Seljuk architecture dating from 1253.

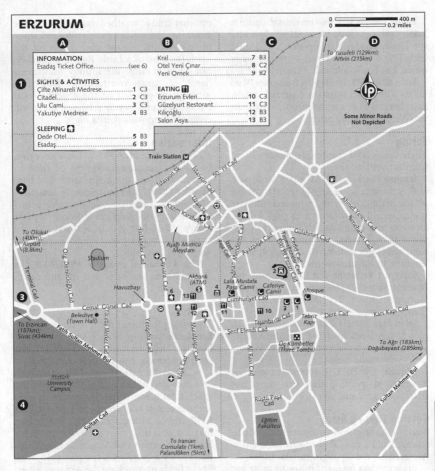

ERZURUM

0 _____ 400 m
0 _____ 0.2 miles

INFORMATION	
Esadaş Ticket Office.............(see 6)	

SIGHTS & ACTIVITIES	
Çifte Minareli Medrese............1 C3	
Citadel......................2 C3	
Ulu Cami....................3 C3	
Yakutiye Medrese..............4 B3	

SLEEPING	
Dede Otel...................5 B3	
Esadaş.....................6 B3	

Kral......................7 B3	
Otel Yeni Çınar..............8 C2	
Yeni Örnek.................9 B2	

EATING	
Erzurum Evleri..............10 C3	
Güzelyurt Restorant.........11 C3	
Kılıçoğlu...................12 B3	
Salon Asya.................13 B3	

Some Minor Roads
Not Depicted

To Yusufeli (129km);
Artvin (215km)

To Oltual
(400m);
Airport
(8.8km)

To Erzincan
(187km);
Sivas (434km)

To İranian
Consulate (1km);
Palandöken (5km)

To Ağrı (183km);
Doğubayazıt (285km)

TURKEY

The eye-catching carved portal is flanked by twin brick minarets decorated with small blue tiles.

Next to the Çifte Minareli is the **Ulu Cami** (Great Mosque; Cumhuriyet Caddesi), built in 1179. Unlike the elaborately decorated Çifte Minareli, the Ulu Cami is restrained but elegant.

Further west along Cumhuriyet Caddesi is a square with an Ottoman mosque and, at the western corner, the **Yakutiye Medrese** (Cumhuriyet Caddesi), a seminary built by the local Mongol emir in 1310 and now a museum.

Sleeping

Otel Yeni Çınar (☎ 213 6690; Ayazpaşa Caddesi 18; s/d €11/16) A cross between a genteel guesthouse and a standard motel – veering towards

the former – the Yeni Çınar is a colourful, friendly and well-run operation with no-frills clean rooms. It's in the market. The only flaw is the deserted, dimly lit street at night. No breakfast is served.

Dede Otel (☎ 233 9041; Cumhuriyet Caddesi 8, s/d €15/19) If the Yeni Çınar is full, this is an OK runner-up, brilliantly located in the heart of the action. Despite the rosy walls, the interior is fairly characterless, but the rooms are more than adequate. Breakfast is supremely disappointing.

Yeni Örnek (☎ 233 0053; Kazım Karabekir Caddesi 25; s/d €12/24) About 400m north of Cumhuriyet Caddesi, the newish Örnek won't make it into the style mags, but it's a good place to rest your head after a long day's travelling.

Esadaş (☎ 233 5425; www.erzurumesadas.com.tr in Turkish; Cumhuriyet Caddesi 7/A; s/d €25/36) Opposite the Dede, Esadaş has top-notch facilities, including a restaurant and a bus company office, but few would call it homely.

Kral (☎ 234 6400; fax 234 6474; Erzincankapı 18; s/d €25/36) This hotel boasts a central location and cheerful rooms with far more style than you'd expect for the price.

Eating

There are several reasonable choices along Cumhuriyet Caddesi.

Erzurum Evleri (☎ 214 0635; Yüzbaşı Sokak; mains €2-4) A stunner set in an old wooden house off the main drag. With its several intimate rooms lavishly decorated with rugs, kilims, artefacts and cushions, it's the perfect antidote to sightseeing fatigue. You can eat some snacks or indulge in a nargileh while listening to the mellow music.

Güzelyurt Restorant (☎ 234 5001; Cumhuriyet Caddesi 51; mains €3-7) The most renowned restaurant in town. Try the *mantarlı güveç* (lamb-and-mushroom casserole).

Salon Asya (☎ 234 9222; Cumhuriyet Caddesi 27; mains €2-4) A block away or so from Güzelyurt, Salon Asya dishes up excellent kebaps and ready-made meals.

Kılıçoğlu (☎ 235 3233; Cumhuriyet Caddesi 20) A smart pastry shop that also turns out snacks, burgers and pizzas.

Getting There & Away

Turkish Airlines has two weekly flights to İstanbul and a daily flight to Ankara. Onur Air operates a daily flight to İstanbul.

Erzurum has frequent buses to most big towns in eastern Turkey, including Doğubayazıt (€10, 4½ hours), Trabzon (€10, six hours) and Kars (€7, 3½ hours).

Erzurum has rail connections with İstanbul and Ankara via Kayseri and Sivas, and with Kars via the same cities.

KARS

☎ 0474 / pop 76,000

Arriving in Kars, about 260km northeast of Erzurum, is discombobulating. From the mix of influences – Azeri, Turkmen, Kurdish and Russian – you'd be forgiven for thinking that you're in Central Asia. Kars may look a bit austere and rough around the edges, but that's part of its charm. How you feel about Kars, however, probably depends

on what kind of weather you see it in. In the sunshine, the stately pastel-coloured stone buildings look almost chirpy, giving the town the look of a Little Russia in Turkey. But when it rains, the muddy backstreets hardly encourage you to linger. Don't forget to gorge yourself on the delicious local *bal* (honey) and *peynir* (cheese); these will certainly keep your spirits high.

Information

Most banks (and ATMs), Internet cafés, hotels and restaurants are on or close to Atatürk Caddesi, the main street. The **tourist office** (☎ 212 6817; Lise Caddesi; 8am-noon & 1-5pm Mon-Fri) can help you organise a taxi to Ani, but your best bet is to contact **Celil Ersoğlu** (☎ 212 6543, 0532-226 3996; celilani@hotmail.com), who acts as a private guide and speaks very good English.

The **Azerbaijani consulate** (☎ 223 6475; fax 2238741; Erzurum Caddesi) is just off the canal, to the north.

Sights

The most prominent point of interest is the **Kars Castle** (admission free; 8am-5pm), which has smashing views over the town and the steppe. Actually, most people come to Kars to visit the dramatic ruins of **Ani** (admission €3; 8.30am-5pm), 45km east of town. Set amid spectacular scenery, the site exudes an eerie ambience. Ani was completely deserted in 1239 after a Mongol invasion, but before that it was a thriving city and a capital of both the Urartian and Armenian kingdoms. Fronted by a hefty wall, the ghost city now lies in fields overlooking the Arpaçay River, which forms the border with Armenia. The ruins include several notable churches and a cathedral built between the years 987 and 1010.

Sleeping & Eating

Güngören Oteli (☎ 212 5630; Halit Paşa Caddesi, Millet Sokak 4; s/d €17/26) This two-star venture is one of the best picks in town, with a friendly atmosphere, colourful amply sized rooms and a welcoming lobby. A good restaurant and *hamam* in the basement are perks.

Hotel Temel (☎ 223 1376; fax 223 1323; Yenipazar Caddesi 9; s/d €15/27) A serious competitor to the Güngören, the Temel is another reliable choice. Bright blues and yellows colour the nifty rooms.

Kent Otel (☎ 223 1929; Hapan Mevkii 12; s/d €10/16) Smack-bang in the centre, this bare-boned alternative is suitable for hardened travellers. There are private rooms with clean sheets, stout bedding and a sink. The shared bathrooms could do with a fresh paint job but are passable. No breakfast is served.

Ocakbaşı Restoran (☎ 212 0056; Atatürk Caddesi 276; mains €2-4) For carnivores, nothing beats this bustling place, which rustles up hearty portions of kebaps, grills and pide. It has two adjoining rooms, including a troglodyte-themed one.

Şirin Anadolu Mutfağı (☎ 213 3379; Karadağ Caddesi 55; mains €2-5) Fill up from an eclectic range of tasty yet predictable kebaps, salads and pide at bargain-basement prices, and enjoy the quirky décor – the big *ocak* is set in a mock grotto.

Antep Pide & Lahmacun Salonu (☎ 223 0741; Atatürk Caddesi 121; mains €1-2) For the best pide or *lahmacun* in town, don't miss this inexpensive little spot.

Doğuş Pastanesi ve Simit Sarayı (☎ 212 3583; Faik Bey Caddesi) The aptly named Simit Sarayı (Simit Palace) puts out some delicious *simits* and other goodies to a hungry crowd of students of both sexes.

Getting There & Away

There are a few daily minibuses to Erzurum (€7, 3½ hours) and one daily minibus to Van (€16, six hours). If you're heading for Doğubayazıt, you'll have to take a minibus to Iğdır, then another to Doğubayazıt.

For Ani take the taxi dolmuşes organised by Kars tourist office or Celil Ersoğlu, a private guide. It costs about €12 per person, provided there's a minimum of six people. If not, the full fare is €38 return plus waiting time.

DOĞUBAYAZIT

☎ 0472 / pop 36,000

Doğubayazıt is a dusty frontier town blessed with a fabulous backdrop; picture a soaring dormant volcano – Mt Ararat (Ağrı Dağı; 5137m), Turkey's highest summit – capped with ice and shrouded in clouds, towering above a sweeping grass plain. A biblical aura emanates from this fantastic mountain: Noah and his flock are said to have landed on Mt Ararat when the 40 days and 40 nights finally ended. It's a nice story but one that innumerable mountaineers have failed to confirm.

Doğubayazıt is also the main kicking-off point for the overland trail through Iran (the border is a mere 35km away).

Information

Everything is within a five-minute stroll of the centre. You'll find banks (including Nişantaş Döviz and TC Ziraat Bank) with ATMs, Internet cafés (including Omega Internet Café) and the PTT, but no tourist office. Instead, various travel agencies, including **East Turkey Expeditions** (☎ 0536-702 8060; www.eastturkey.com), will be able to help with your queries. They can also help with getting a visa to Iran in five days (about €80).

Sights & Activities

Your jaw will drop in amazement the minute you see **İshak Paşa Palace** (İshak Paşa Sarayı; admission €3; ☼ 8am-5.30pm Apr-Oct, 8.30am-5pm Nov-Mar). Perched romantically among rocky crags, 6km east of town, this palace-fortress is the epitome of a *Thousand and One Nights* castle. Built between 1685 and 1784, it blends elements of Seljuk, Ottoman, Georgian, Persian and Armenian architecture.

Travel agencies in Doğubayazıt offer tours to sights around the town, taking in İshak Paşa Palace, a couple of interesting geological formations (including a giant meteor crater), hot springs and a Kurdish village for about €25 per person.

Now that the troubles in the east have died down, it is once again possible to climb **Mt Ararat**, although you need a permit and a guide. At the time of research you needed to apply at least one month in advance. You can apply through any reputable travel agency in Turkey.

Sleeping & Eating

Hotel Tahran (☎ 312 0195; Büyük Ağrı Caddesi 124; s/d €8/12; ▯) The Tahran is a godsend for savvy budgeters, with modestly sized but spotless rooms with tiled bathrooms. Another draw is Celal, the ebullient, English-speaking young owner, who does his best to make you feel at ease. You can read, watch satellite TV or check your emails for free in a communal room. It's also a great option for women travellers.

Hotel Erzurum (☎ 312 5080; Dr İsmail Beşikçi Caddesi; s/d €4/6) For true budget-seekers, this place is hard to beat. Rooms are Spartan and cell-like, but tidy enough. Bathrooms

TURKEY

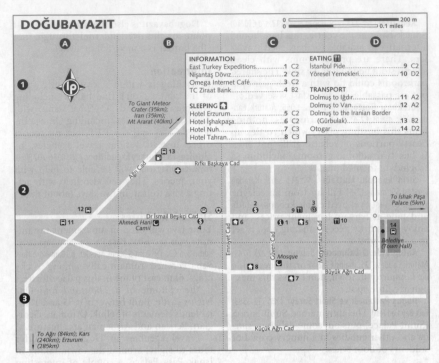

DOĞUBAYAZIT

0 — 200 m
0 — 0.1 miles

INFORMATION
East Turkey Expeditions..............1 C2
Nişantaş Döviz........................2 C2
Omega Internet Café..................3 C2
TC Ziraat Bank.......................4 B2

SLEEPING
Hotel Erzurum........................5 C2
Hotel İşhakpaşa......................6 C2
Hotel Nuh............................7 C3
Hotel Tahran.........................8 C3

EATING
İstanbul Pide........................9 C2
Yöresel Yemekleri...................10 D2

TRANSPORT
Dolmuş to Iğdır.....................11 A2
Dolmuş to Van.......................12 A2
Dolmuş to the Iranian Border
  (Gürbulak)........................13 B2
Otogar..............................14 D2

To Giant Meteor
Crater (35km);
Iran (35km);
Mt Ararat (40km)

To İshak Paşa
Palace (5km)

Ağrı Cad
Rıfkı Başkaya Cad
Dr İsmail Beşikçi Cad
Ahmedi Hani
Cami
Emniyet Cad
Güven Cad
Meryemana Cad
Mosque
Büyük Ağrı Cad
Belediye
(Town Hall)
Küçük Ağrı Cad

To Ağrı (84km); Kars
(240km); Erzurum
(285km)

are shared, but they're kept in damn good nick. The young owner, Metin, is a good source of local information and can help you organise a trek to Mt Ararat (although it's dubious whether he can get a proper permit in three days, as he claims).

Hotel İşhakpaşa (☎ 312 7036; fax 312 7644; Emniyet Caddesi 10; s/d €9/13) Don't be put off by the ratty carpets in the rooms. The tiled bathrooms are in good working condition, the back-friendly beds are graced with crisp linen and all rooms have balconies and TVs.

Hotel Nuh (☎ 312 7232; www.hotelnuh.8m.com; Büyük Ağrı Caddesi; s/d €24/40; **P**) A short bag-haul from the otogar, the Nuh offers characterless but functional good-sized rooms, and a rooftop restaurant affording superb vistas of Ararat.

Yöresel Yemekleri (☎ 312 4026; Dr İsmail Beşikçi Caddesi; mains €2-4) Don't miss this quirky restaurant on the 1st floor. The décor is bland, but what makes it distinctive is the staff; for once, it's predominantly female. An association of Kurdish women whose husbands are imprisoned prepares savoury *yöresel* (traditional) meals at bargain-basement prices.

İstanbul Pide (☎ 312 2324; Dr İsmail Beşikçi Caddesi 77; mains €2) A cheerful, welcoming joint famous for its mouthwatering pide and börek.

Getting There & Away

There are about four daily minibuses to Van (€6, 2½ hours). To get to Kars, change minibus at Iğdır (€2.50, 45 minutes).

For services to Iran, see p634.

VAN
☎ 0432 / pop 447,000

One of the easternmost cities in Turkey, Van is not the dusty, exotic, rough-around-the-edges place you would expect in such a remote location. It's more a sprawling modern town with lots of good vibes, thanks to a sizable student population.

Everything you'll need (hotels, restaurants, banks, the PTT and the bus-company offices) lie on or around Cumhuriyet Caddesi, the main commercial street.

Sights

Van's main claim to fame is its 3000-year-old **castle** (admission €1.25; ⏰ 9am-dusk), about 3km west of the city centre. Another must-see is the 10th-century church on **Akdamar Island** in Van Gölü (Lake Van), an easy half-day trip from Van. It's a poignant piece of Armenian architecture in a fantastic setting, and has frescoes and reliefs depicting biblical scenes. To get here you need to take a dolmuş to Akdamar harbour (€2, 44km), or catch a minibus to Tatvan and ask to be let off at the Akdamar harbour. From there pick up a boat. An inclusive ticket for the crossing and admission to the island costs €3.

A day excursion southeast of Van takes you to the spectacular **Hoşap Castle** (admission €1.25), a Kurdish castle perched on top of a rocky outcrop. From Van, catch a minibus heading to Başkale and ask to be let off at Hoşap (€3).

Sleeping

Otel Aslan (☎ 216 2469; Özel İdare İş Merkezi Karşısı; s €7-11, d €11-15) Space is tight at this little no-nonsense joint, so the rooms can be something of a squeeze, but the atmosphere makes it a pleasant haven from the nearby market. The tiled shared bathrooms are well scrubbed. No breakfast is served.

Büyük Asur Oteli (☎ 216 8792; fax 216 9461; Cumhuriyet Caddesi, Turizm Sokak 5; s/d €14/24; P) This looks drab and severe from the outside, but the lobby has floor cushions you can snuggle into. The well-maintained rooms are painted in vaguely refreshing shades of green. It's an excellent choice and has a helpful manager who speaks English.

Otel Akdamar (☎ 214 9923; fax 212 0868; Kazım Karabekir Caddesi; s/d €25/34) Ignore the outside of this concrete monstrosity fronting busy Kazım Karabekir Caddesi, because inside the renovated rooms are spruce and roomy and the facilities are excellent. It's a reliable stand-by if you're after some creature comforts.

Eating & Drinking

Besse (☎ 215 0050; Sanat Sokak; mains €3-6) If you're in search of a bit of sophistication, Besse fits the bill perfectly. It's done out in soothing yellow tones and features parquet flooring and dim lights. Foodwise, the focus is on tasty meat dishes.

Akdeniz Tantuni (☎ 216 9010; Cumhuriyet Caddesi; mains €2-3) This modest eatery features surprisingly pleasant surrounds. Enjoy your chicken sandwich while sitting around low wooden tables.

Simit Sarayı (Cumhuriyet Caddesi; mains €1-2) You can't miss this bustling *simit* shop, on the main drag, which entices by aroma alone. If you can resist these damn-heavenly little things, you're masochistic.

Kebabistan (☎ 214 2273; Sinemalar Sokak; mains €2-4) A carnivore's paradise, with expertly cooked kebaps. Its second branch, across the street, specialises in pide.

Saçi Beyaz (☎ 212 2693; Kazım Karabekir Caddesi) Right in the centre, the pleasant, shaded terrace is a real oasis for those wanting to unwind over a cup of tea or a delectable *dondurma*.

Safa 3 (☎ 215 8121; Kazım Karabekir Caddesi 29; soups €1.50) The quirky Safa 3 serves up soups around the clock. Adventurous diners can try the *İşkembe çorbası* (tripe soup). Hardened overlanders can check out the supposedly palate-pleasing *kelle* (mutton's head). *Afiyet olsun!*

Barabar Türk Evi (☎ 214 9866; Sanat Sokak) This popular haunt, upstairs in a concrete building near Besse, attracts a feisty young crowd in the evening, here to enjoy Kurdish live music and that oh-so-refreshing beer.

Getting There & Away

There are daily flights to/from Ankara and İstanbul with Turkish Airlines. Atlasjet operates daily flights to/from İzmir and İstanbul.

There are also regular daily bus services to Diyarbakır (€14, seven hours) and several morning dolmuşes to Doğubayazıt (€6, 2½ hours). For services to Iran, see p634.

DIYARBAKIR

☎ 0412 / pop 350,400

Diyarbakır prides itself on being *the* bastion of Kurdish identity, culture and tenacity. Indeed, it won't take long to feel that the atmosphere is noticeably different from the rest of the country. Some travellers think it's a bit rough around the edges, others regard it as a veiled, self-contained city that doesn't easily bare its soul. Whatever your perspective, Diyarbakır is not bereft of charm. The mazelike old town – encircled by impressive basalt walls pierced by four main gates – the Arab-style mosques with black-and-white bands of stone, the hustle and bustle of the bazaar, the women with their colourful Kurdish headscarves and the men with their baggy *şalvar* (traditional baggy pants) all conjure up an air of exoticism.

Orientation & Information

Most services useful to travellers are in Old Diyarbakır, on or around Gazi Caddesi, including the PTT, Internet cafés and banks with ATMs. The **tourist office** (☎ 228 1706; Dağ Kapı; ☼ 8am-5pm Mon-Fri) is housed in a tower within the walls. The otogar is 3.5km northwest of the centre. The train station is 1.5km west of the centre.

Sights

Diyarbakır's single most conspicuous feature is the 6km circuit of basalt **walls**, probably dating from Roman times. The walls make a striking sight whether you're walking along the top or the bottom.

Of Diyarbakır's many mosques, the most impressive is the **Ulu Cami** (Gazi Caddesi), built in 1091 by an early Seljuk sultan. The **Nebi Camii** (Gazi Caddesi), at the main intersection of Gazi and İzzet Paşa/İnönü Caddesis, has a quirky detached minaret sporting a stunning combination of black-and-white stone.

Sleeping

Aslan Palas Oteli (☎ 228 9224; fax 223 9880; Kıbrıs Caddesi 21; s €8-10, d €13-16; ☒) A good pick for the cash conscious, with unadorned but cleanish rooms featuring back-friendly beds and tiled bathrooms. The cheapest rooms have shared bathrooms. Those at the back are a tad sombre but less noisy. No breakfast is served.

Hotel Aslan (☎ 224 7096; fax 224 1179; Kıbrıs Caddesi 23; s/d €13/19; ☒) Not to be confused with the Aslan Palas Oteli next door, the Aslan is not exactly a home away from home but fits the bill if you're penny-counting. Rooms are on the small side but serviceable. Breakfast is extra (€2).

Hotel Kaplan (☎ 229 3300; fax 224 0187; Yoğurtçu Sokak 14; s/d €16/25; ☒) Tucked in an alleyway off Kıbrıs Caddesi, the Kaplan is a pleasant surprise, with nondescript yet comfortable good-sized rooms. Aim for one of the brighter top-floor rooms.

Balkar Otel (☎ 228 6306; İnönü Caddesi 38; s/d €19/30; P ☒) A step up in quality, the Balkar is a typical middling three-star, with well-looked-after rooms and prim bathrooms. Added bonuses include a lift and a hearty breakfast.

Eating & Drinking

A stroll along Kıbrıs Caddesi reveals plenty of informal places to eat and tantalising pastry shops.

Aslan Yemek Salonu (Kıbrıs Caddesi; mains €2-4) Almost next door to Hotel Aslan, this famous local joint is packed like a rock concert at lunch, when it dishes up tasty grills and superfresh ready-made meals.

Şarmaşık Ocakbaşı (Kıbrıs Caddesi 31; mains €2-4) You can't go wrong at this cheap and cheerful eatery specialising in savoury kebaps.

Küçe Başı Et Lokantası (☎ 229 5661; Kıbrıs Caddesi 11; mains €2-7) Head to the room at the back for more atmosphere – it's designed like a rustic barn or a fake cavern, depending on your perspective. Order innovative dishes (ie not kebaps) such as *güveç* or *kiremit* (meat cooked in a clay pot) – the picture menu really helps. Add a salad and a Turkish coffee, and you can walk away happy and buzzing for €7.

Güllüoğlu (☎ 228 2404; Kıbrıs Caddesi 35) Don't leave Diyarbakır without sampling some delectable *kadayıf* in this slick pastry shop. It's also a good spot for breakfast.

Getting There & Away

Diyarbakır is connected with İstanbul and Ankara by daily Turkish Airlines flights. Onur Air also flies to Diyarbakır from İstanbul.

Several buses a day link Diyarbakır with Şanlıurfa (€6, three hours) and Van (€14, seven hours), among others. For Mardin (€4), take a minibus from a separate terminal near Dağ Kapı.

MARDIN
☎ 0482 / pop 55,000

About 100km south of Diyarbakır, Mardin is a real gem and should definitely be on your itinerary. This beautiful ancient town, crowned with a castle, overlooks the vast Mesopotamian plains extending to Syria. It's pure joy to explore the streets of honey-coloured stone houses that trip down the side of the hillside, giving the town something of the feel of old Jerusalem.

Mardin has started to become popular with Turkish travellers. Get here before it becomes too touristy!

Sights

Strolling through the rambling **bazaar**, keep your eyes open for the ornate **Ulu Cami**, a 12th-century Iraqi Seljuk structure.

Mardin Museum (Mardin Müzesi; admission €1.25; ☼ 8am-6pm), prominently positioned on

Cumhuriyet Meydanı, is housed in a superbly restored mansion dating from the late 19th century. Back on Cumhuriyet Caddesi, head east and keep your eyes peeled for the three-arched façade of an ornately carved **house**.

Continue east, looking for steps on the left (north) that lead to the **Sultan İsa Medresesi** (☻ daylight), which dates from 1385 and is the town's prime architectural attraction.

Opposite the post office, you can't miss the minaret of the 14th-century **Şehidiye Camii**. It's superbly carved, with colonnades all around and three small domes superimposed on the summit.

Also worth visiting is the 15th-century **Forty Martyrs Church** (Kırklar Kilisesi; 217 Sağlık Sokak), with the martyrs depicted above the doorway of the church as you enter. If it's closed, try to find the caretaker.

The **Kasımiye Medresesi** (1469), 800m south of Yeni Yol, the main drag, is another mustsee. It sports a sublime courtyard walled in by arched colonnades, as well as a magnificent carved doorway.

Sleeping & Eating

Otel Bilen (☎ 213 0315; fax 212 2575; s/d €32/47; **P** **❀**) In the new part of Mardin (Yenişehir), 2km northwest of Cumhuriyet Meydanı. Nothing flash, but the rooms are serviceable. Try to negotiate a discount if it's not busy.

Erdoba Konakları (☎ 212 7677; www.erdoba.com.tr; Cumhuriyet Caddesi 135; s/d €45/68; **❀**) In the heart of the old town, this hotel comprises two finely restored historic mansions, which have graciously decorated rooms and splendid views over the Mesopotamian plain. It also houses a vaulted restaurant.

Turistik Et Lokantası (☎ 212 1647; Cumhuriyet Meydanı; mains €3-6) A long-standing institution, the Turistik features indoor and outdoor areas with superb views over the plains and has an extensive menu to suit all palates.

Cercis Murat Konağı (☎ 213 6841; Cumhuriyet Caddesi 517; mains €4-6) If you're after some kind of sophistication, the Cercis fits the bill. It occupies a traditional Syrian Christian home with two finely decorated rooms and a terrace affording stunning views. The food is as elaborate as the classy décor.

Getting There & Away

There are frequent bus services between Mardin and Diyarbakır (€4, 1½ hours).

ŞANLIURFA (URFA)

☎ 0414 / pop 839,800

Women cloaked in black chadors elbowing their way through the odorous crush of the bazaar streets; moustachioed gents in *şalvar* swilling tea and click-clacking backgammon pieces in a shady courtyard; pilgrims feeding sacred carp in the shadows of a medieval fortress – welcome to Şanlıurfa, one of the most exotic cities in Turkey. It's here that you begin to feel you've reached the Orient, yet there's also a distinctly Middle Eastern flavour, courtesy of its proximity to Syria. Şanlıurfa also boasts a glut of historic buildings, and you could easily spend several days here without getting bored. It's a magical place, and a definite must-see.

Orientation & Information

Along different stretches the city's main thoroughfare is called Atatürk, Köprübaşı, Sarayönü and Divan Yolu Caddesis. Gölbaşı park is about 1km south of the centre. The otogar is about 1km to the west.

Most banks with ATMs and Internet cafés are on or around Sarayönü Caddesi. For tourist information, contact **Harran-Nemrut Tours** (☎ 215 1575; ozcan_aslan_teacher@hotmail.com; Köprübaşı Şanmed Hastanesi). The owner speaks very good English.

Sights

The former **Edessa** is a delightful city that claims to harbour the **cave** where the patriarch Abraham (İbrahim) was born. It's in the Gölbaşı park, surrounded by a complex of mosques. Pilgrims come to pay their respects, then feed fat sacred carp in a pond nearby. After doing likewise, you can explore the wonderful **bazaar**. It's a jumble of streets, some covered, some open, selling everything from sheepskins and pigeons to jeans and handmade shoes.

The **kale** (fortress; admission €1.25; ☻ 8am-8pm) on Damlacık hill, from which Abraham was supposedly tossed, is Urfa's most striking feature. It looks magnificent when floodlit and can be reached via a flight of stairs or a tunnel cut through the rock. Come up here for unobstructed views over Urfa.

It's also worth visiting the numerous **mosques** dotted in the centre.

About 50km to the south, **Harran** is one of the oldest continuously occupied settlements in the world. Its ruined walls and

Ulu Cami, crumbling fortress and beehive houses are powerful, evocative sights.

Getting to Harran is straightforward and most people visit from Urfa on a day trip. Minibuses (€3, one hour) leave from Urfa's otogar approximately every hour.

Sleeping

İpek Palas (☎ 215 1546; Köprübaşı Şanmed Hastanesi Arkası 4; s €12-19, d €20-30; ❸) Right in the swing of things, but in a tranquil side street, this well-run hotel boasts rooms that have been done up recently. They're nothing flashy, but it's a good choice for women travellers and the shared bathrooms are well tended.

Hotel Doğu (☎ 215 1228; Sarayönü Caddesi 131; s/d €10/13) The Doğu is not exactly the perfect cocoon for a romantic getaway, but it's a reliable pad for backpackers, with bare but clean rooms. Be prepared for a sweaty night in summer – there's no air-con.

Hotel Bakay (☎ 215 8975; Asfalt Yol Caddesi 24; s/d €15/25; ❸) A bustling, friendly establishment with lived-in appeal. Some rooms are darker than others, so ask to see a few. It's popular with Turkish families – a good sign for women travellers.

Beyzade Kokak (☎ 216 3535; Sarayönü Caddesi; s/d €20/31; ❸) It's too good to be true: a short stagger from the main drag, this utterly charming 19th-century stone building features a soothing courtyard that's the perfect spot to debrief over a cup of tea. There are also several comfy Ottoman-style lounges – and just look at the rates! The rooms themselves are, surprisingly, less impressive but are well equipped. It also has a reputable restaurant with live music in the evening.

Also recommended:

Hotel Güven (☎ 215 1700; Sarayönü Caddesi 133; s/d €18/30; ❸) A safe choice that won't hurt that shrinking wallet, a few doors from the Doğu.

Hote El-Ruha (☎ 215 4411; www.hotelelruha.com; Balıklıgöl; s/d €60/80; ❸ 💻) Brand-spanking-new when we popped in (you could still smell the paint), this is Urfa's first boutique hotel.

Eating & Drinking

Zahter Kahvaltı & Kebap Salonu (Köprübaşı Caddesi 3; mains €2-3) The best place for a hearty breakfast. Here you'll enjoy gooey honey and cream on flat bread, washed down with a large glass of tea or *ayran*.

Altınşiş (☎ 215 4646; Sarayönü Caddesi; mains €2-5) The Altınşiş is a popular eatery where you can delve into a range of Turkish fare and ready-made meals.

Çardaklı Köşk (☎ 217 1080; Vali Fuat Caddesi, Tünel Çıkışı 1; mains €3-5) Set up in a superb old Urfa house, the Çardaklı has several rooms arranged around the courtyard. The food is not that inspirational – the reals draws are the atmosphere and the view over Gölbaşı.

Birlik Pastanesi (☎ 313 1823; Köprübaşı Caddesi) Almost next door to the Zahter, this is an ideal stop for those who want to sate a sweet tooth. Try the *kadayıf* and you'll instantly feel happy with life.

Kızılay Cafe Restaurant (☎ 215 8553; Sarayönü Caddesi; mains €2-4) Off the main drag, this is a great place to chill out and soak up the atmosphere.

Zerzembe (☎ 216 4499; Karameydanı Otopark İçi; mains €2-3) It serves up some nibbles, but it's the setting that's the pull here rather than the cuisine. In a converted depot, the interior is embellished with rugs, pottery, carpets and other knick-knacks.

The various tea gardens in the Gölbaşı park all serve simple grills.

Getting There & Away

Turkish Airlines has direct flights to Ankara and İstanbul.

Fairly frequent buses connect Şanlıurfa with Gaziantep (€5, 2½ hours) and Diyarbakır (€7, three hours).

Minibuses to Akçakale, at the Syrian border, and Harran leave from the minibus terminal beside the otogar.

MT NEMRUT

Mt Nemrut (Nemrut Dağı; 2150m) is one of the great must-see attractions of eastern Turkey. Two thousand years ago, right on top of the mountain and pretty much in the middle of nowhere, an obscure Commagene king chose to erect his **memorial sanctuary** (admission €3.50). The fallen heads of the gigantic decorative statues of gods and kings, toppled by earthquakes, form one of Turkey's most enduring images.

There are a few possible bases for visiting Mt Nemrut. To the north is Malatya, where the tourist office organises daily minibus tours (€30, early May to late September), with a sunset visit to the heads, a night at a hotel near the summit and a second, dawn visit. Or, visit the mountain from the south via Kahta. This is the most straightforward option, but Kahta is notoriously hassley. At least by taking this route you do get to see other interesting sites along the way.

Two-day tours (€40, minimum four people) or sunset/sunrise tours (€40, minimum four people) to Nemrut are also available from **Harran-Nemrut Tours** (☎ 0414-215 1575; ozcan_aslan_teacher@hotmail.com; Köprübaşı Şanmed Hastanesi) in Şanlıurfa.

Some people take a three-day tour (€130 per person) from Göreme in Cappadocia but it's a tedious drive. These take in other places in the east too.

Sleeping
MALATYA
Malatya Büyük Otel (☎ 0422-325 2828; fax 323 2828; Halep Caddesi; s/d €18/30) Definitely the best choice in the town centre and handy for shopping in the bazaar.

Hote Yeni Sinan (☎ 0422-321 2907; Atatürk Caddesi 6; s/d €15/24) Very central. Clean, if simple, rooms.

Aygün Hotel (☎ 0422-325 5657; PTT Caddesi 7; s/d €10/18) A welcoming place with well-scrubbed, if smallish, rooms with shared bathrooms.

KAHTA
In high summer the nicest places to stay, especially if you have your own transport, are not in Kahta itself but on the slopes of the mountain.

Karadut Pension (☎ 0416-737 2169; camp sites per person €3, d €22) Five small but neat rooms.

Hotel Kervansaray (☎ 0416-737 2190; fax 737 2085; s/d €23/28; 🖳) This place also has great views, and piles on the home comforts too.

In Kahta itself:

Hotel Nemrut (☎ 0416-725 6881; fax 725 6880; Mustafa Kemal Caddesi; s/d €21/39; 🍽) A characterless but well-regarded hotel.

Pension Kommagene (☎ 0416-725 9726; fax 725 5548; Mustafa Kemal Caddesi; camp sites per person €3, s/d from €12/17; 🍽) At the start of the Nemrut road. A better choice than the Anatolia.

Hotel Mezopotamya (☎ 0416-725 7705; fax 725 5385; Mustafa Kemal Caddesi 18; s/d €10/16; 🍽) This hotel gets good reports from tour operators used to working in Kahta.

GAZİANTEP (ANTEP)
☎ 0342 / pop one million

Although well off the tourist trail, Gaziantep offers an altogether Turkish experience and an untapped potential as a travel destina-

tion. For most travellers it comes as a surprise to discover a fast-growing, pulsing and atmospheric city with a soul. If you're a sweet tooth, you'll be in seventh heaven – Gaziantep is said to be the baklava capital of the world.

Orientation & Information
The throbbing heart of Gaziantep is the intersection of Atatürk Bulvarı/Suburcu Caddesi and Hürriyet/İstasyon Caddesis, marked by a large statue of Atatürk. Most hotels, banks with ATMs, and sights are within walking distance of the main intersection. The otogar is about 6km from the town centre. The train station is 800m north.

The **tourist office** (☎ 230 5969; 100 Yıl Atatürk Kültür Parkı İçi; 🕑 8am-noon & 1-5pm Mon-Fri) is in a park, to the northwest.

Sights
The unmissable **kale** (citadel; admission free; 🕑 8am-noon & 1-5pm Tue-Sun) offers superb vistas over the city. Not far from the citadel is a buzzing **bazaar**, where you can see artisans at work. Scattered in the centre are numerous old **stone houses**, some of which are skilfully restored.

It would be a shame to skip the **Gaziantep Museum** (İstasyon Caddesi; admission €1.25; 🕑 8am-noon & 1-5pm). It holds portions of the fabulous mosaics unearthed at the rich Roman site of Belkıs-Zeugma.

Sleeping
Yunus Hotel (☎ 221 1722; fax 221 1796; Kayacık Sokak 16; s/d €13/22; P 🍽) The well-run Yunus has comfortable rooms and gleaming bathrooms. Its peerless location, in a tranquil side street but close to the action, makes this an excellent base for exploring the city.

Hotel Uğurlu (☎ 220 9690; www.hotelugurlu.com; Kayacık Sokak 14; s/d €18/25; P 🍽) Next door to the Yunus, this is another reassuring choice with no surprises up its sleeve.

Hotel Veliç (☎ 221 2212; fax 221 2210; Atatürk Bulvarı 23; s/d €22/36; P 🍽) The bland façade is not attractive but the rooms are much more inviting, with squeaky-clean bathrooms and springy carpets. The breakfast room on the upper floor affords stunning views. The catch? The singles are pocket sized.

Anadolu Evleri (☎ 220 9525; www.anadoluevleri .com; Köroğlu Sokak 6; r €70-100; 🍽) After the rigors of eastern Anatolia, pamper yourself

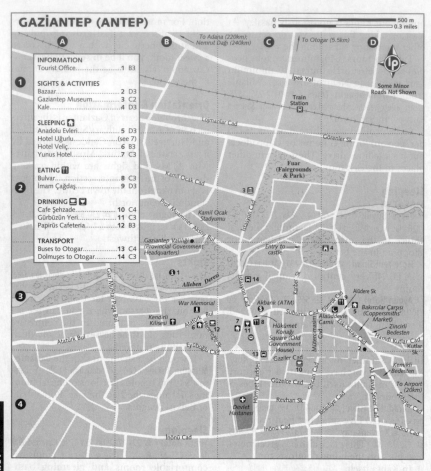

GAZİANTEP (ANTEP)

INFORMATION		
Tourist Office	1	B3
SIGHTS & ACTIVITIES		
Bazaar	2	D3
Gaziantep Museum	3	C2
Kale	4	D3
SLEEPING		
Anadolu Evleri	5	D3
Hotel Uğurlu	(see 7)	
Hotel Veliç	6	B3
Yunus Hotel	7	C3
EATING		
Bulvar	8	C3
İmam Çağdaş	9	D3
DRINKING		
Cafe Şehzade	10	C4
Gürbüzün Yeri	11	C3
Papirüs Cafeteria	12	B3
TRANSPORT		
Buses to Otogar	13	C4
Dolmuşes to Otogar	14	C3

in this gorgeous boutique hotel, located in a beautifully restored stone house close to the bustling bazaar. The rooms ooze charm and character, with exposed beams, period furniture, mosaic floors, painted ceilings and carefully displayed artefacts. The owner speaks perfect English and is well clued-up.

Eating & Drinking

İmam Çağdaş (☎ 220 4545; Kale Civarı Uzun Çarşı; mains €1-5) Just thinking about İmam Çağdaş' gorgeously gooey *fıstıklı baklava* titillates our tastebuds. This Gaziantep institution (established in 1887) also serves up savoury kebaps and melt-in-your-mouth *lahmacun* in a separate building across the street.

Bulvar (☎ 220 7011; Suburcu Caddesi, İstasyon Kavşağı 2/A; mains €2) Famous for its delicious *tavuk döner* (chicken sandwich), this central, no-frills place is always packed with hungry punters grabbing a supercheap meal.

Cafe Şehzade (☎ 231 0350; Gaziler Caddesi 47; snacks €2-3; ⏰ 8.30am-8pm) The food, mostly snacks, is nothing to write home about, but the setting is absolutely lovely. Where else could you sip a cup of tea in an eight-centuries-old converted *hamam*?

Gürbüzün Yeri (Hürriyet Caddesi; juices €1) Feeling weak? This tiny juice bar right in the centre has the antidote, with superb freshly squeezed juices. Try the *muzlu süt* (a mixture of milk, honey, banana, hazelnuts and pistachios) and you'll be hooked forever.

Papirüs Cafeteria (☎ 220 3279; Noter Sokak 10) Housed in a historic mansion off Atatürk Caddesi, this treasure-trove is perfect for unwinding after a bout of sightseeing. It has piles of character, and features a leafy courtyard and several rooms with ancient frescoes and old furniture. It lures in students looking for a pleasant spot to flirt and relax.

Getting There & Away

Turkish Airlines has flights to Ankara and İstanbul. Onur Air also flies to İstanbul.

From the otogar you can reach many destinations in Turkey, including Şanlıurfa (€6, 2½ hours) and Antakya (€6, four hours).

TURKEY DIRECTORY

ACCOMMODATION
Camping

Camping facilities are dotted about Turkey, although not perhaps as frequently as you might hope. Some hotels and pensions will also let you camp in their grounds and use their facilities for a small fee.

Hostels

Given that pensions are so cheap, Turkey has no real hostel network. Some are real hostels with dormitories, others are little different from the cheapest pensions.

PRACTICALITIES

- For the news in English, pick up the *Turkish Daily News*. Fez Travel's free magazine *Fark Etmez*, available at the big tourist gathering points, is full of tips for travellers.

- TRT3 (Türkiye Radyo ve Televizyon) on 88.2MHz, 94MHz and 99MHz provides short news broadcasts in English, French and German every two hours.

- Digiturk offers more than 300 different TV channels (including CNN, Fox News and BBC World).

- Electrical current is 220V AC, 50Hz. Wall sockets are the round, two-pin European type.

- Turkey uses the metric system for weights and measures.

Pensions & Hotels

Most tourist resorts offer simple family-run pensions where you can get a good, clean bed for around €10 a night. They are often cosy and represent better value than full-blown hotels. These places usually offer a choice of simple meals (including breakfast), book exchanges, laundry services, international TV services and so on, and it's these facilities that really distinguish them from traditional small, cheap hotels. Most pensions also have staff who speak English.

In most cities there is a variety of old and new hotels, which range from the heart-sinkingly basic to full-on luxury. The cheapest nonresort hotels (around €15 a night) are mostly used by working Turkish men travelling on business and are not always suitable for lone women, unless they can face the stares whenever they enter the lobby. Moving up a price bracket, one- and two-star hotels may cost €20 to €30 for a double room with shower, but these hotels are less oppressively masculine in atmosphere, even when the clientele remains mainly male.

If you fancy top-notch accommodation at reasonable prices, Turkey is the place to do it. Boutique hotels are all the rage in the country. Increasingly, old Ottoman mansions and other historic buildings are being refurbished or completely rebuilt as hotels equipped with all the mod cons and bags of character. The best boutique hotels are located in İstanbul, Cappadocia, Safranbolu and Amasya, but almost every city boasts at least one or two character-filled establishments.

Note that along the coast the vast majority of hotels and pensions close from mid-November to mid-March.

Unless otherwise stated, breakfast and private bathrooms are included in the room rates quoted in this book, with the exception of dorms in İstanbul, which all have shared bathrooms.

Treehouses

Olympos, on the coast southwest of Antalya, is famous for its 'treehouses', wooden shacks of minimal comfort in forested settings near the beach. Increasingly, these basic shelters are being converted into chalets with much more comfort.

RESIST THE TOUTS!

In smaller tourist towns such as Fethiye, Pamukkale and Selçuk, touts for the pensions may accost you as you step from your bus and string you whatever line they think will get you to their lair most quickly. Of course they are after commission from the owner. Taxi drivers often like to play this game too. For everyone's sake, do your best to avoid letting them make your choices for you.

ACTIVITIES

Popular activities include hiking and trekking in the Kaçkar Mountains and in the Ala Dağlar, near Niğde. Another popular area is the Lycian Way, a 30-day, 509km walk around the coast and mountains of Lycia, starting at Fethiye and finishing near Antalya. The spectacular valleys of Cappadocia make another excellent area for hiking. If you're a serious hiker you could even consider conquering the 5137m-high Mt Ararat (p621) near Doğubayazıt, but you need a permit.

All sorts of water sports, including diving, water-skiing, rafting and kayaking, are available in the Aegean and Mediterranean resorts. The best diving is offered off Kaş, Bodrum and Marmaris. You can also try tandem paragliding at Ölüdeniz.

Skiing is becoming more popular, with the best facilities at Uludağ, near Bursa; on Mt Erciyes, near Kayseri; and at Palandöken, near Erzurum. However, even at these sites the facilities would not meet the standards of the better European resorts.

Those of a lazier disposition may want to take a *gület* trip along the coast, stopping off to swim in bays along the way (see Blue Voyages, p597). The laziest 'activity' of all consists of paying a visit to a *hamam*, where you can get yourself scrubbed and massaged for a fraction of what it would cost in most Western countries.

BUSINESS HOURS

Government and business offices, and banks usually open from 8.30am to noon and 1.30pm to 5pm Monday to Friday. Main post offices in large cities are open every day. Smaller post offices may be closed on Saturday afternoon and all day Sunday. During the hot summer months

the working day in some cities begins at 7am or 8am and finishes at 2pm. The working day also gets shortened during the holy month of Ramazan.

In tourist areas food, souvenir and carpet shops are often open virtually around the clock. Elsewhere, grocery shops and markets are usually open from 6am or 7am to 7pm or 8pm Monday to Saturday. It's increasingly rare for shops to close for lunch except in the most out-of-the-way places.

Friday, the Muslim Sabbath, is a normal working day in Turkey. The day of rest, a secular one, is Sunday.

CUSTOMS

Two hundred cigarettes and 50 cigars or 200g of tobacco, and five 100cc or seven 70cc bottles of alcohol can be imported duty-free.

It's strictly illegal to buy, sell or export antiquities. Customs officers spot-check luggage and will want proof that you have permission from a museum before letting you leave with an antique carpet.

DANGERS & ANNOYANCES

Although Turkey is one of the safest countries in the region, you must take precautions. Wear a money belt under your clothing and be wary of pickpockets on buses, in markets and in other crowded places. Keep an eye out for anyone suspicious lurking near ATMs.

In İstanbul, single men are sometimes lured to a bar (often near İstiklal Caddesi) by new Turkish 'friends'. The man is then made to pay an outrageous bill, regardless of what he drank. Drugging is also becoming a serious problem, especially for lone men. Sometimes the person in the seat next to you on the bus buys you a drink, slips a drug into it and then makes off with your luggage. So be a tad wary of who you befriend, especially when you're new to the country.

More commonly, the hard-sell tactics of carpet sellers can drive you to distraction. Be warned that 'free' lifts and suspiciously cheap accommodation often come attached to near-compulsory visits to carpet showrooms.

Travelling in the southeast is now safe, provided you don't venture into the mountains south of Hakkari or into the Şirnak area. For more information, see p618.

EMBASSIES & CONSULATES
Turkish Embassies & Consulates

Following are the Turkish embassies and consulates in major cities around the world. For addresses of Turkish embassies in neighbouring Middle Eastern countries, see the relevant country chapters.

Australia (☎ 02-6295 0227; www.turkishembassy.org
.au; 60 Mugga Way, Red Hill ACT 2603)
Canada (☎ 613-789 4044; www.turkishembassy.com;
197 Wurtemburg St, Ottawa, Ontario KIN 8L9)
France (☎ 01 53 92 71 11; www.tcparbsk.com; 184
Boulevard Malesherbes, 75017 Paris)
Germany (☎ 49-228 34 40 93; www.tcberlinbe.de;
Johann-Georg Str 12, 10709 Berlin)
Ireland (☎ 01-668 5240; turkembassy@eircom.net;
11 Clyde Rd, Ballsbridge, Dublin 4)
Netherlands (☎ 70-360 4912; turkijc@dataweb.nl;
Jan Evenstraat 2514 BS, The Hague)
New Zealand (☎ 4-472 1290; turkem@xtra.co.nz;
15-17 Murphy St, Level 8, Wellington)
UK (☎ 0207-393 0202; info@turkishembassy-london
.com; 43 Belgrave Sq, London SW1X 8PA)
USA (☎ 202-612 6700; www.turkishembassy.org; 2525
Massachusetts Ave, NW Washington, DC 2008)

Embassies & Consulates in Turkey

Foreign embassies are in Ankara but many countries also have consulates in İstanbul. In general they are open from 9am to noon Monday to Friday.

Australia Ankara (☎ 0312-446 1180; www.embaustralia
.org.tr; Nenehatun Caddesi 83, Gaziosmanpaşa); İstanbul
(☎ 0212-257 7050; fax 257 7054; Tepecik Yolu 58, Etiler)
Bulgaria (☎ 0312-426 2071; fax 427 3178; Atatürk
Bulvarı 124, Kavaklıdere, Ankara)
Canada (☎ 0312-459 9200; fax 459 9361; Nenehatun
Caddesi 75, Gaziosmanpaşa, Ankara)
Egypt Ankara (☎ 0312-426 1026; fax 427 0099; Atatürk
Bulvarı 126, Kavaklıdere); İstanbul (☎ 0212-263 6038; fax
257 4428; Cevdet Paşa Caddesi 173, Bebek)
France Ankara (☎ 0312-455 4545; fax 455 4527;
Paris Caddesi 70, Kavaklıdere); İstanbul (Map pp564-5;
☎ 0212-334 8730; fax 249 9168; İstiklal Caddesi 8,
Taksim)
Germany Ankara (☎ 0312 455 5100; fax 427 8926;
Atatürk Bulvarı 114, Kavaklıdere); İstanbul (Map pp564-5;
☎ 0212-334 6100; fax 249 9920; İnönü Caddesi 16-18,
Taksim)
Greece Ankara (☎ 0312-436 8860; fax 446 3191;
Ziya-ur-Rahman (Karagöz) Caddesi 9-11, Gaziosmanpaşa);
İstanbul (Map pp564-5; ☎ 0212-245 0597; fax 252 1365;
Turnacıbaşı Sokak 32, Galatasaray)
Iran Ankara (☎ 0312-468 2820; fax 468 2823; Tahran
Caddesi 10, Kavaklıdere); Erzurum (☎ 0442-316 2285;

fax 316 1182; off Atatürk Bulvarı); İstanbul (☎ 0212-513
8230; fax 511 5219; Ankara Caddesi 1/2, Cağaloğlu)
Iraq (☎ 0312-468 7421; fax 468 4832; Turan Emeksiz
Sokak 11, Gaziosmanpaşa, Ankara)
Ireland Ankara (☎ 0312-446 6172; fax 446 8061; Uğur
Mumcu Caddesi, MNG Binasi B-Bl 88/3, Gaziosmanpaşa);
İstanbul (Map pp564-5; ☎ 0212-246 6025; fax 248 0744;
Cumhuriyet Caddesi 26/A, Harbiye)
Israel Ankara (☎ 0312-446 3605; fax 446 8071;
Mahatma Gandhi Caddesi 85, 06700 Gaziosmanpaşa);
İstanbul (Map pp564-5; ☎ 0212-225 1040; fax 317 6555;
Valikonağı Caddesi 73/4, Nişantaşı)
Jordan Ankara (☎ 0312-440 2054; fax 440 4327;
Mesnevi Dede Korkut Sokak 18, Çankaya); İstanbul (☎ 0212-
325 6862; fax 325 6565; Sümbül Sokak 51, İçlevent)
Lebanon Ankara (☎ 0312-446 7485; fax 446 1023;
Kıkulesi Sokak 44, Gaziosmanpaşa); İstanbul (Map pp564-5;
☎ 0212-236 1365; fax 227 3373; Teşvikiye Caddesi 134/1,
Teşvikiye)
Netherlands Ankara (☎ 0312-409 1800; fax 409 1898;
Turan Güneş Bulvarı 7, Caddesi 3, Yıldız); İstanbul (Map
pp564-5; ☎ 0212-393 2121; fax 292 5031; İstiklal
Caddesi 393, Beyoğlu)
New Zealand Ankara (☎ 0312-467 9056;
newzealand@superonline.com.tr; İran Caddesi
13/4, Kavaklıdere); İstanbul (☎ 0212-251 3895;
nzhonconist@hatem-law.com.tr; İnönü Caddesi 92/3)
Russia Ankara (☎ 0312-439 2122; fax 438 3952; Karyağdi
Sokak 5, Çankaya); İstanbul (Map pp564-5; ☎ 0212-292
5101; İstiklal Caddesi 443, Beyoğlu); Trabzon (☎ 0462-326
2600; fax 326 2101; Şh Refik Cesur 6, Ortahisar)
Syria Ankara (☎ 0312-440 9657; fax 438 5609; Sedat
Simavi Sokak 40, Çankaya); İstanbul (Map pp564-5;
☎ 0212-232 6721; fax 230 2215; Maçka Caddesi 59/5,
Teşvikiye)
UK Ankara (☎ 0312-455 3344; fax 455 3351; Şehit Ersan
Caddesi 46/A, Çankaya); İstanbul (Map pp564-5; ☎ 0212-
334 6400; fax 245 4989; Meşrutiyet Caddesi 34, Tepebaşı,
Beyoğlu)
USA Ankara (☎ 0312-455 5555; fax 467 0019; Atatürk
Bulvarı 110, Kavaklıdere); İstanbul (Map pp564-5;
☎ 0212-335 9000; fax 323 2037; Kaplıcalar Mevkii 2,
İstiniye)

FESTIVALS & EVENTS

Following are some of the major annual festivals and events in Turkey:
Anzac Day The great battle at Gallipoli is commemorated with a dawn ceremony (25 April).
International İstanbul Music Festival Held from early June to early July.
Kırkpınar Oil Wrestling Championship Huge crowds watch oil-covered men wrestling in a field near Edirne in June.
Mevlana Festival The dervishes whirl in Konya from 10 to 17 December.

Nevruz Kurds and Alevis celebrate the ancient Middle Eastern spring festival on 21 March. Banned until recently, Nevruz is now an official holiday.

GAY & LESBIAN TRAVELLERS

Although not uncommon in a culture that traditionally separates men and women, overt homosexuality is not socially acceptable except in a few small pockets in İstanbul, Bodrum and other resorts. In İstanbul there is an increasing number of openly gay bars and nightclubs, mainly around the Taksim Sq end of İstiklal Caddesi. Some *hamams* are known to be gay meeting places.

For more information, contact Turkey's own gay and lesbian support group, **LAMBDA İstanbul** (www.lambdaistanbul.org).

HOLIDAYS

As well as the major Islamic holidays (p647), Turkey observes the following national holidays:

New Year's Day 1 January
Children's Day 23 April
Youth & Sports Day 19 May
Victory Day 30 August
Republic Day 29 October
Anniversary of Atatürk's Death 10 November

INTERNET ACCESS

Wherever you go, you'll never be far from an Internet café. Lots of hotels, pensions, tour operators and carpet shops are also hooked up. Fees are usually around €1 for an hour. In the big cities, ADSL connections tend to dominate.

LANGUAGE

Turkish is the official language and almost everyone understands it. It's been written in the Latin script since Atatürk rejected Arabic in 1928. In southeastern Anatolia, most Kurds speak Turkish, but in remote places you'll hear Kurmancı and Zazakı, the two Kurdish dialects spoken in Turkey. South of Gaziantep you'll also certainly hear Arabic being spoken alongside Turkish.

For words and phrases in Turkish, see p679.

MAPS

Turkish tourist offices supply an excellent free *Tourist Map* (1:850,000). IGN's *Carte Touristique Turquie* (1:750,000) is also a good reference.

MONEY

The new *(yeni)* Turkish lira (YTL) was introduced in January 2005 and will have completely replaced the Turkish lira (TL) by the time you read this. Notes are in denominations of one, five, 10, 20, 50 and 100 new Turkish lira. The new Turkish lira is divided into 100 new *kuruş*.

Inflation was more or less under control when we visited but check exchange rates shortly before your visit. Prices in this book are quoted in more stable euros.

Below are the exchange rates for a range of currencies when this book went to print.

Country	Unit	New Turkish lira (YTL)
Australia	A$1	1.00
Canada	C$1	1.15
euro zone	€1	1.59
Japan	¥100	1.16
New Zealand	NZ$1	0.93
Syria	S£10	0.26
UK	UK£1	2.37
USA	US$1	1.36

ATMs

ATMs readily dispense Turkish lira to Visa, MasterCard, Cirrus, Maestro and Eurocard holders; there's hardly a town that lacks a machine. Provided that your home banking card only requires a four-digit personal identification number (PIN), it's perfectly possible to get around Turkey with nothing else. But remember to draw out money in the towns to tide you through the villages, and keep some cash in reserve for the inevitable day when the ATM decides to throw a wobbly.

Note that some overseas banks charge an arm and a leg for the conversion so check before you leave home.

Cash

US dollars and euros are the easiest currencies to change, although many banks and exchange offices will change other major currencies such as UK pounds and Japanese yen. You may find it difficult to exchange Australian or Canadian currency except at banks and offices in major cities.

Credit Cards

Visa and MasterCard are widely accepted by hotels, restaurants, carpet shops and so on, although they are not accepted by pensions and local restaurants outside the main tourist areas. You can also get cash advances on these cards. Amex cards are rarely useful.

Moneychangers

It's easy to change major currencies in most exchange offices, some PTTs, shops and hotels, although banks may make heavy weather of it. Places that don't charge a commission usually offer a worse exchange rate instead.

Although Turkey has no black market, foreign currencies are readily accepted in shops, hotels and restaurants in main tourist areas.

Tipping

Turkey is fairly European in its approach to tipping and you won't be pestered by demands for baksheesh as elsewhere in the Middle East. Leave waiters and bath attendants around 10% of the bill. It's usual to round off metered taxi fares.

Travellers Cheques

Our advice: don't bring them! Banks, shops and hotels often see it as a burden to change travellers cheques, and will probably try to get you to go elsewhere. In case you do have to change them, try Akbank.

POST

Postcards to Europe cost €0.45, to Australia and New Zealand €0.55, and to the USA €0.50. Letters to Europe cost €0.50, to Australia and New Zealand €0.60, and to the USA €0.55.

Turkish *postane* (post offices) are indicated by black-on-yellow 'PTT' signs.

Most post offices in tourist areas offer a poste restante service.

TELEPHONE & FAX

Türk Telekom payphones can be found in many major public buildings and facilities, public squares and transportation termini. International calls can be made from all payphones.

Türk Telekom centres have faxes, but require lots of paperwork and often insist on retaining your original! It's easier to use your hotel fax, although you should always check the cost first.

Mobile Phones

The Turks just love *cep* (mobile) phones. But calling a mobile costs roughly three times the cost of calling a land line, no matter where you are. Mobile phone numbers start with a four-figure code beginning with ☎ 04 or ☎ 05. If you set up a roaming facility with your home phone provider you should be able to connect your own mobile to the Turkcell or Telsim network. At the time of writing, US-bought mobile phones couldn't be used in Turkey.

Phone Codes

The country code for Turkey is ☎ 90, followed by the local area code (minus the zero), then the seven-digit subscriber number. Local area codes are given at the start of each city or town section. Note that İstanbul has two codes: ☎ 0212 for the European side and ☎ 0216 for the Asian side. The international access code (to call abroad from Turkey) is ☎ 00.

Phonecards

All Türk Telekom's public telephones require telephone cards, which can be bought at telephone centres or, for a small mark-up, at some shops. If you're only going to make one quick call, it's easier to look for a booth with a sign saying '*köntörlü telefon*', where the cost of your call will be metered.

TOILETS

Most hotels and public facilities have familiar Western toilets, but you'll also sometimes see traditional squat toilets. Always carry toilet paper and don't forget to place it in the bin provided to avoid inadvertently flooding the premises.

Almost all public toilets require payment of about €0.30.

VISAS

Nationals of the following countries don't need to obtain a visa to visit Turkey for up to three months: Denmark, Finland, France, Germany, Israel, Japan, New Zealand, Sweden and Switzerland. Although nationals of Australia, Austria, Belgium, Canada, Ireland, Italy, the Netherlands, Norway, Portugal, Spain, the UK and the USA need a visa, this is just a stamp in the passport that you buy on arrival at the airport or at an overland border rather than at an embassy in advance. Make sure you join the queue to buy your visa before joining the one for immigration. How much you pay depends on your nationality; at the time of writing British citizens paid UK£10, Australians and Americans US$20, and Canadians US$60 or €45. You *must* pay in hard currency cash.

The standard visa is valid for three months and, depending on your nationality, usually allows for multiple entries.

For details of visas for other Middle Eastern countries, see p653 and the Visas sections in the Directory of the other country chapters.

In theory a Turkish visa can be renewed once after three months, but the bureaucracy and costs involved mean that it's much easier to leave the country (usually to a Greek island) and then come back in again on a fresh visa.

WOMEN TRAVELLERS

Some women travel around virtually unmolested while others report constant harassment. Whatever your own experience and feeling, your best bet is to dress modestly and be sensitive to the society's customs. Cover the upper legs and arms and avoid shorts or skimpy T-shirts, except in the resorts. Provided you stick to these recommendations, most men will treat you with kindness and generosity. Wearing a wedding ring and carrying a photo of your 'husband' and 'child' will help immeasurably, as can wearing dark glasses to avoid eye contact.

Unrelated men and women are usually separated on buses and there are separate sections in most restaurants for women and families (although in tourist areas they won't mind where you sit).

TRANSPORT IN TURKEY

GETTING THERE & AWAY
Entering the Country
For information on Turkish visas and entry requirements, see p633.

Air
Turkey's most important airport is İstanbul's **Atatürk International Airport** (code IST; ☎ 0212-663 2550; www.ataturkairport.com), 25km

west of the city centre. The cheapest fares are almost always to İstanbul, and to reach other Turkish airports, even Ankara, you usually have to transit in İstanbul. Other international airports are at Adana, Ankara, Antalya, Bodrum, Dalaman and İzmir.

Turkey's national carrier is **Turkish Airlines** (Türk Hava Yolları, THY; ☎ 0212-444 0849, 225 0556; www.thy.com), which has direct flights from İstanbul to most capital cities around the world, including Beirut, Cairo, Damascus, Dubai, Jeddah, Kuwait, Riyadh, Tehran and Tripoli in the Middle East. It has a good safety record.

Other airlines flying to and from Turkey:
Air France (airline code AF; in İstanbul ☎ 0212-310 1919; www.airfrance.com) Hub: Charles de Gaulle International Airport, Paris.
American Airlines (airline code AA; in İstanbul ☎ 0212-219 2930; www.aa.com) Hub: O'Hare Airport, Chicago.
Azerbaijan Airlines (airline code AHY; in İstanbul ☎ 0212-245 1852) Hub: Baku airport.
British Airways (airline code BA; in İstanbul ☎ 0212-234 1300; www.britishairways.com) Hub: Heathrow Airport, London.
Emirates Airlines (airline code EK; in İstanbul ☎ 0212-293 5050; www.emirates.com) Hub: Dubai International Airport.
Iran Air (airline code IR; in İstanbul ☎ 0212-225 0255) Hub: Tehran Mehrabad Airport.
KLM (airline code KL; in İstanbul ☎ 0212-230 0311; www.klm.com) Hub: Amsterdam Schipol Airport.
Lufthansa (airline code LH; in İstanbul ☎ 0212-315 3434; www.lufthansa.com) Hub: Frankfurt Airport.
Olympic Airlines (airline code OA; in İstanbul ☎ 0212-247 3701; www.olympicairlines.com) Hub: Athens International Airport.
Qantas Airways (airline code QF; in İstanbul ☎ 0212-219 8223; www.qantas.com) Hub: Sydney Airport.
Singapore Airlines (airline code SIA; in İstanbul ☎ 0212-232 3706; www.singaporeair.com) Hub: Singapore Changi Airport.

Land
Turkey shares borders with Armenia, Azerbaijan, Bulgaria, Georgia, Greece, Iran, Iraq and Syria. There are plenty of ways to get into and out of the country by rail or bus. For details see p660.

IRAN
Gürbulak/Bazargan, 35km east of Doğubayazıt, is the main crossing point for Iran. It's pretty hassle-free. The second border

post at Esendere/Sero, southeast of Van, keeps shorter hours than the one near Doğubayazıt.

From Van, there are at least two daily buses to Orumiyeh (€15, 311km) in Iran. From Doğubayazıt, minibuses run approximately every half-hour to Gürbulak (€2). The crossing may take up to an hour. From the Iranian side of the border, you can pick up a shared taxi on to Maku, from where regular buses make the four-hour run to Tabriz. From İstanbul, there are several direct bus services to Tabriz and Tehran each week (about €45), but the ride is tedious.

By train, the *Trans-Asya Espresi* leaves İstanbul every Wednesday and arrives two nights later in Tehran (about €65).

IRAQ

As long as the situation in Iraq is unsafe, we strongly advise you against crossing the border into Iraq.

SYRIA

There are several border posts between Syria and Turkey, with the border at Reyhanlı/Bab al-Hawa, 50km east of Antakya, by far the busiest and most convenient. Other border posts include Yayladağı (south of Antakya), Kilis (south of Gaziantep), Akçakale (south of Şanlıurfa) and Nusaybin (east of Mardin).

From Antakya, there are direct buses across the border to the Syrian cities of Aleppo (Haleb; €6, four hours, 105km) and Damascus (€8, eight hours, 465km). Although you have to wait for everyone on the bus to complete border formalities, it's much easier than doing it on your own.

Alternatively you can catch a dolmuş south to the border post at Yayladağı, from where you can pick up a taxi or hitch a few kilometres further to the border. Once across, you're just 2km from the Syrian village of Kassab, from where regular micro-buses make the 45-minute run to Lattakia.

From Mardin, there are regular minibuses to Nusaybin (€3). From Gaziantep, you can take a minibus to Kilis (€3).

You can also buy tickets direct from İstanbul to Aleppo (€30, 24 hours) or Damascus (€35, 33 hours), but the trip's long and painful.

A train for Damascus (via Aleppo, about €70) leaves İstanbul's Haydarpaşa Railway Station every Thursday.

Sea

Turkey has passenger shipping connections with Greece, Italy and northern Cyprus. For details see p663.

GETTING AROUND
Air

The state-owned **Turkish Airlines** (Türk Hava Yolları, THY; in İstanbul ☎ 0212-444 0849, 0212-225 0556; www.thy.com) connects all the country's major cities and resorts, albeit inconveniently, via its two main hubs, İstanbul and Ankara.

The most useful destinations for travellers include Ağrı (for Doğubayazıt), Ankara, Antalya, Bodrum, Dalaman (for Marmaris), Diyarbakır, Erzurum, Gaziantep, İstanbul, İzmir, Kars, Kayseri, Konya, Mardin, Şanlıurfa, Sivas, Trabzon and Van. A one-way fare usually costs between €75 and €90. You can buy tickets through travel agencies or directly through the airlines.

Domestic flights are also available with the following airlines:

Atlasjet (in İstanbul ☎ 0216-444 0387; www.atlasjet .com) Flies from İzmir to Antalya, İstanbul, Konya, Kars, Trabzon and Van, and from İstanbul to Ankara, Antalya, Bodrum, İzmir, Kars, Trabzon and Van. One-way fares cost about €55.

Fly Air (in İstanbul ☎ 0212-444 4359; www.flyair .com.tr) Flies from İstanbul to Antalya, Bodrum, İzmir and Trabzon, and from Ankara to Trabzon. One-way fares cost about €50.

Onur Air (in İstanbul ☎ 0212-662 9797; www.onur air.com.tr) Flies from İstanbul to Antalya, Bodrum, Dalaman, Diyarbakır, Erzurum, Gaziantep, İzmir, Kayseri, Kars and Trabzon, among others. One-way fares cost about €50.

Bus

Turkish buses go just about everywhere you could possibly want to go, and what's more they do so cheaply and comfortably (around €40 to cross the whole country).

A town's otogar (bus station) is often on the outskirts, but the bigger bus companies usually have free *servis* (shuttle minibuses) to ferry you into the centre and back again. Most otogars have an *emanet* (left-luggage room) that will charge a small fee, or you can sometimes leave luggage at the bus company's ticket office. Besides intercity buses, the otogar often handles dolmuşes that operate local routes.

All Turkish bus services are officially smoke-free.

FEZ BUS

A hop-on, hop-off bus service, the **Fez Bus** (Map pp564-5; in İstanbul ☎ 0212-516 9024; www.feztravel .com; Aybıyık Caddesi 15, Sultanahmet, İstanbul) links the main tourist resorts of the Aegean and the Mediterranean with İstanbul and Cappadocia. The big bonuses of using the Fez Bus are convenience (you never have to carry your bags), flexibility (the passes are valid all year and you can start anywhere on the circuit) and atmosphere (it's fun and energetic, with a strong party vibe). The downsides? You spend most of your time with other travellers rather than with locals, and it can rapidly become boring once you've had your fill of the backpacker fraternity. And it doesn't work out to be cheaper than doing it yourself with point-to-point buses.

A Turkish Delight bus pass, costing €190, allows you to travel from İstanbul to Çanakkale, Selçuk, Köyceğiz, Fethiye, Olympos, Cappadocia and then back to İstanbul.

Car & Motorcycle

In the major cities, plan to leave your car in a parking lot and walk – traffic is terrible.

DRIVING LICENCE

An international driving permit (IDP) may be handy if your driving licence is from a country likely to seem obscure to a Turkish police officer.

FUEL

There are plenty of modern petrol stations in the west, many open 24/7. In the east, they are a bit less abundant but you won't have trouble finding one. Be warned: petrol is deadly pricey (about €1.30 per litre at the time of writing).

HIRE

Hiring a car is quite expensive (often around €40 to €50 per day with unlimited mileage, less for a longer period). All the main car-hire companies are represented in the main towns and resorts. It's better to stick to the well-established companies (such as Avis, Budget, Europcar, Hertz and Thrifty) as they have bigger fleets and better emergency backup.

INSURANCE

You *must* have third-party insurance, valid for the entire country.

ROAD RULES

Drink-driving is a complete no-no. Maximum speed limits, unless otherwise posted, are 50km/h in towns, 90km/h on highways and 130km/h on an *otoyol* (motorway). Driving is fairly hazardous because of fast, inappropriate driving and overladen trucks.

Local Transport

With a few exceptions you probably won't use public buses in large cities. In İstanbul, the underground metro and the tram are a quick and efficient way of getting around.

Taxis are plentiful. They have meters – just make sure they're switched on.

Train

Turkish State Railways (TCDD; www.tcdd.gov.tr in Turkish) runs services across the country, but it has a hard time competing with the long-distance buses for speed and comfort. Don't plan a trans-Turkey train trip in one go as the country is large and the trains depressingly slow. For example, the *Vangölü Ekspresi* from İstanbul to Lake Van (Tatvan), a 1900km trip, takes almost two days. The bus takes less than 24 hours, the plane less than two hours. Only between Ankara and İstanbul is train travel really fast and pleasant.

Middle East Directory

CONTENTS

This chapter provides a general overview of essential things you need to know about the Middle East, covering, in alphabetical order, everything from Accommodation and Activities to Women Travellers and Work. Each individual country chapter also has a Directory section that includes more specific information about these headings as they relate to each country. Please consult both when searching for information.

ACCOMMODATION

In most countries of the Middle East, you'll find accommodation that ranges from cheap and nasty to plush and palatial; most places sit comfortably somewhere in between. Throughout this book, accommodation is ordered according to the author's preference within each price category (budget, midrange and top end). The way these price categories are defined varies according to the conditions on the ground within each country. The amount you can expect to pay and the amenities you can expect within each category are explained under Accommodation in the Directory section of each individual country chapter.

Generally, Iran, Syria and Egypt have the cheapest accommodation, while Libya, Turkey, Jordan, Israel and the Palestinian Territories and Lebanon will cost a little more. However, travel through the Middle East is now such a well-worn path that in most major destinations covered by this book you'll find at least one high-quality place to suit your budget, whether you're travelling on a shoestring or an expense account.

Camping

Camping in the Middle East is possible, but it's always better to stick to officially sanctioned camp sites because many areas that are military or restricted zones aren't always marked as such and erecting a tent on an army firing range won't be a highlight of your trip. There are official camping grounds in Egypt, Iran, Israel and the Palestinian Territories and Lebanon. In Libya there are no official sites but it's generally no problem to camp anywhere in the Sahara desert or in the Jebel Nafusa (Western Mountains) provided you're travelling with an accredited tour company (see p506).

Hostels

There are youth hostels in Egypt, Israel and the Palestinian Territories and Libya. It's not usually necessary to hold a Hostelling International card to stay at these places, but it will get you a small discount.

Hotels

Standards vary between countries but price generally reflects quality.

In hotels at the bottom end of the price scale, rooms are not always clean. In fact, let's be honest: they can be downright filthy, and shared showers and toilets often bear traces of the previous inhabitants. Very cheap hotels are just dormitories where you're crammed into a room with whoever else fronts up.

Some of the cheapest places are probably too basic for many tastes; they're rarely suitable for women travelling alone.

That said, there are some places that stand out and while they may have no frills, nor do their bathrooms give any indication of the good health or otherwise of previous occupants. Some places even treat you like a king even if you pay the price of the pauper. The happy (and most common) medium somewhere between these two extremes is usually a room devoid of character, but containing basic, well-maintained facilities.

In the midrange, rooms have private bathrooms, usually (but not always) with hot water, fans to stir the air, a bit more space to swing a backpack and (sometimes) TVs promising international satellite channels.

Hotels at the top end of the range have clean, self-contained rooms with hot showers and toilets that work all the time, not to mention satellite TV, shampoo and regularly washed towels in the bathrooms, air-con to provide a refuge from the Middle Eastern sun and a few luxuries to lift the spirits.

For further details and other types of accommodation see the Accommodation sections in the Directory of each individual country chapter.

ACTIVITIES

The Middle East's rich variety of terrain – from deserts to beaches and snow-capped mountains – offers ample opportunities to get beyond the museums-and-old-stones routine.

Cycling & Mountain Biking

The Middle East offers some fantastic, if largely undeveloped, opportunities for cyclists and mountain bikers. Unlike in Europe, you're likely to have many of the trails to yourself. However, the heat can be a killer (avoid June to September) and you'll need to be pretty self-sufficient as spare parts can be extremely scarce. However, mountain biking is popular in Israel and the Palestinian Territories, Jordan and to some extent in Lebanon (eg mountain biking in the Mt Lebanon Range). Many people particularly enjoy cycling the flatter roads of Syria. One of the highlights of travelling in this way is that locals in more out-of-the-way places will wonder what on earth you're doing – an ideal way to break the ice and meet new friends.

See p666 for details about cycling around the Middle East, including practicalities and organisations to contact.

Desert Safaris & Drives

Visitors to the Middle East either fall in love with the desert or feel crushed by the heat and solitude of the region's vast empty spaces. If you belong to the former group, as most travellers seem to, Jordan and Libya are worth seeking out as an antidote to the clamour of Middle Eastern cities. Apart from anything else, they promise desert scenery that will leave you spellbound.

The easiest place to experience such landscapes – largely because it's accessible from

---

TOP FIVE DEEP DESERT EXPERIENCES

If the solitude and perfect ridge lines of sand dunes, mountains rising up from the middle of nowhere, palm-fringed oases and sunsets uncluttered by the clamour of modern life are your thing, the Middle East is hard to beat. The following are our places not to miss.

- Wadi Rum (p393), Jordan – the richest desert colours as shown to you by the Bedouin who've made this land their own

- Jebel Acacus (p498), Libya – prehistoric rock paintings, Tuareg nomads and stunning rock formations in the Sahara's heart

- Idehan Ubari (p495), Libya – some of the most beautiful sand dune scenery in the world with stunning palm-fringed lakes in abundance

- Waw al-Namus (p498), Libya – extraordinary volcanic crater with black sand and multi-coloured lakes in one of the earth's most remote corners

- Siwa Oasis (p148), Egypt – mud-brick fortress and an old-world charm on the fringe of a desert that reaches deep into Africa

---

RESPONSIBLE DIVING

Please consider the following tips when diving to help preserve the ecology and beauty of reefs.

- Never use anchors on the reef, and take care not to ground boats on coral.

- Avoid touching or standing on living marine organisms or dragging equipment across the reef. Polyps can be damaged by even the gentlest contact. If you must hold on to the reef, only touch exposed rock or dead coral.

- Be conscious of your fins. Even without contact, the surge from fin strokes near the reef can damage delicate organisms. Take care not to kick up clouds of sand, which can smother organisms.

- Practise and maintain proper buoyancy control. Major damage can be done by divers descending too fast and colliding with the reef.

- Take great care in underwater caves. Spend as little time within them as possible as your air bubbles may be caught within the roof and thereby leave organisms high and dry. Take turns to inspect the interior of a small cave.

- Resist the temptation to collect or buy corals or shells or to loot marine archaeological sites (mainly shipwrecks).

- Ensure that you take home all your rubbish and any litter you may find as well. Plastics in particular are a serious threat to marine life.

- Do not feed fish.

- Minimise your disturbance of marine animals. *Never* ride on the backs of turtles.

---

major travel routes and is compact enough to explore within short time frames – is Wadi Rum (p393) in Jordan with its orange sand, improbable rocky mountains and echoes of TE Lawrence. There are plenty of operators there who organise anything from afternoon camel treks to 4WD safaris and hikes lasting several days.

Libya offers the chance to lose yourself amid some of the finest landscapes anywhere in the world's largest and most evocative desert the Sahara. As visits to Libya are only possible as part of an escorted tour (p503), the hassle of planning your own expedition is usually taken care of by your guide who can arrange shorter camel or 4WD safaris of a few days or 4WD expeditions lasting up to two weeks.

In Egypt, you'll find that there are plenty of small Bedouin operators who lead groups into the Sinai interior (p158) on overnight, two- or three-day camel treks. It is also possible to head off into the less-visited Western Desert (p145) as part of a 4WD safari.

Israel's Negev Desert is less attractive than deserts elsewhere, but there are some fun truck tours organised by Desert Eco Tours (see p334) in Eilat.

Diving

The Red Sea is a revelation for those who've never dived before and even for many who have – it's one of the world's top diving sites and a wholly different world from any you may have experienced before. Seemingly around every underwater corner is a dazzling array of colourful coral and fish life, supported by an extensive reef system and the occasional shipwreck. The best place to experience the Red Sea is from one of the resorts on southern Sinai (p158) or south along Egypt's Red Sea coast (p153). Eilat (p332) in Israel and Aqaba (p395) in Jordan also have dive centres, but if you're travelling on to Egypt, it's worth the wait.

Most clubs in these places offer every possible kind of dive course. The average open-water certification course for beginners, either with CMAS, PADI or NAUI, takes about five days and usually includes several dives. The total cost varies between US$275 and US$400 depending on the operator and location. A day's diving (two dives), including equipment and air fills, costs US$50 to US$100. An introductory dive is around US$60. Full equipment can be hired for about US$20 per day.

For more details see the Activities sections in each country's Directory.

MIDDLE EAST DIRECTORY

Hammams

One of the great sensual indulgences of the Middle East, the *hammam* (*hamam* in Turkey) is better known in the West as a "Turkish bath". There's nothing quite like a robust massage on tiled slabs, a sweltering steam-room session, or hot tea taken afterwards while swathed in towels, all under vaulted domes that have changed little in centuries (the architecture is invariably exceptional). Even if you've showered beforehand you'll never consider yourself clean again until you've had a *hammam*. For years afterwards you'll remember your masseur as you would a scary teacher who taught you some of the more invigorating lessons in life.

The Middle East's best *hammams*:

Çemberlitaş Hamamı (p571) İstanbul, Turkey.
Cağaloğlu Hamamı (p571) İstanbul, Turkey.
Hammam Yalbougha an-Nasry (p540) Aleppo, Syria.
Hammam Nureddin (p515) Damascus, Syria.
Al-Pasha Hammam (p371) Amman, Jordan.
Al-Shifa (p342) Nablus, Israel and the Palestinian Territories.
Hammam Draghut (p474) Tripoli, Libya.

For a rundown on the complete *hammam* experience see p571.

Hiking & Climbing

Jordan is a trekkers' and climbers' paradise, most notably in the spectacular landscapes around Wadi Rum (p393), Petra (p389) and

---

RESPONSIBLE HIKING

To help preserve the ecology and beauty of the Middle East, consider the following tips when hiking.

Erosion

- Hillsides and mountain slopes, especially at high altitudes, are prone to erosion. Stick to existing tracks and avoid short cuts.
- If a well-used track passes through a mud patch, walk through the mud so as not to increase the size of the patch.
- Avoid removing the plant life that keeps topsoils in place.

Fires & Low-Impact Cooking

- Don't depend on open fires for cooking. The cutting of wood for fires in popular trekking areas can cause rapid deforestation. Cook on a lightweight kerosene, alcohol or Shellite (white gas) stove and avoid those powered by disposable butane gas canisters.
- If you are trekking with a guide and porters, supply stoves for the whole team. In alpine areas, ensure that all members are outfitted with enough clothing so that fires are not a necessity for warmth.
- If you patronise local accommodation, select those places that do not use wood fires to heat water or cook food.
- Fires may be acceptable below the tree line in areas that get very few visitors. If you light a fire, use an existing fireplace. Don't surround fires with rocks. Use only dead, fallen wood. Remember the adage 'the bigger the fool, the bigger the fire'. Use minimal wood, just what you need for cooking. In huts, leave wood for the next person.
- Ensure that you fully extinguish a fire after use. Spread the embers and flood them with water.

Human Waste Disposal

- Contamination of water sources by human faeces can lead to the transmission of all sorts of nasties. Where there is a toilet, please use it. Where there is none, bury your waste. Dig a small hole 15cm (6in) deep and at least 100m (320ft) from any watercourse. Cover the waste with soil and a rock. In snow, dig down to the soil.

the steep valleys of Dana Nature Reserve (p387) and Wadi Mujib (p387). Maktesh Ramon (the Middle East's largest crater; p331) and the canyons and pools of En Avdat in Israel and the Palestinian Territories' Negev Desert are great trekking areas, but those who don sturdy boots and head to the higher, cooler Upper Galilee and Golan regions (p324) will also be amply rewarded.

North of Tehran it's possible to climb Mt Damavand (5671m; p198), the highest peak in the Middle East. The surrounding Alborz Mountains also offer some marvellous trekking and mountaineering.

In Turkey some fine trails pass through the Kaçkar Mountains, the Ala Dağlar (near Niğde), the mountains of Lycia, Cappadocia and Mt Ararat (5137m) near Doğubayazıt. For more information see p630.

See the Activities section in the relevant country chapters for further details.

Sailing

With its whitewashed villages, idyllic ports and mountainous backdrop, Turkey's Mediterranean coast is ideal for yacht cruising, especially given its proximity to the Greek Islands. Possibilities include everything from day trips to two-week luxury charters. Kuşadası, Bodrum and Marmaris are the main centres, with more resorts developing yachting businesses all the time. You can hire crewless bareboats or flotilla boats, or take a cabin on a boat hired by an agency.

■ Ensure that these guidelines are applied to a portable toilet tent if one is being used by a large trekking party. Encourage all party members, including porters, to use the site.

Rubbish

■ Carry out *all* your rubbish. Don't overlook easily forgotten items, such as silver paper, orange peel, cigarette butts and plastic wrappers. Empty packaging should be stored in a dedicated rubbish bag. Make an effort to carry out rubbish left by others.

■ Never bury your rubbish: digging disturbs soil and ground cover and encourages erosion. Buried rubbish will likely be dug up by animals, who may be injured or poisoned by it. It may also take years to decompose.

■ Minimise waste by taking minimal packaging and no more food than you will need. Take reusable containers or stuff sacks.

■ Sanitary napkins, tampons, condoms and toilet paper should be carried out despite the inconvenience. They burn and decompose poorly.

Washing

■ Don't use detergents or toothpaste in or near watercourses, even if they are biodegradable.

■ For personal washing, use biodegradable soap and a water container (or even a lightweight, portable basin) at least 50m (160ft) away from the watercourse. Disperse the waste water widely to allow the soil to filter it fully.

■ Wash cooking utensils 50m (160ft) from watercourses with a scourer, sand or snow, not detergent.

Wildlife Conservation

■ Do not engage in or encourage hunting.

■ Never buy items made from endangered species.

■ Don't attempt to exterminate any animals you may find in huts. In wild places, they are likely to be protected native animals.

■ Discourage the presence of wildlife by not leaving food scraps behind you. Place gear out of reach and tie packs to rafters or trees.

■ Do not feed the wildlife as this can lead to animals becoming dependent on hand-outs, to unbalanced populations and to diseases.

DESERT HIKING

While the Middle East offers a host of hiking opportunities, the conditions are quite different to those most visitors are accustomed to. For this reason, you have to be careful in picking the right time of year for your visit so that you don't expire by lunchtime on the first day.

In the summer, hiking can be extremely dangerous, and in 40°C heat most hikers will go through 1L of water every hour. Even in the cooler months, your main issue will be water, and hikers should have available at least 4L per person per day (an excellent way to carry water is in 2L plastic soft drink bottles, which are available in many places).

The most effective way to conserve water isn't necessarily to drink sparingly, as this tends to psychologically focus attention on water availability, and may lead to an unhealthy hysteria. Before setting off in the morning, flood your body's cells with water. That is, drink more water than you feel you can possibly hold! After a few hours, when you grow thirsty, do the same again from the supply you're carrying. Believe it or not, with this method you'll actually use less water and feel less thirsty than if you drink sparingly all day long.

Another major concern is the desert sun, which can be brutal. Wear light-coloured and light-weight clothing; use a good sunscreen (at least UV Protection Factor 30); and never set off without a hat or Arab-style head covering to shelter your neck and face from the direct sun. You'll also value a light, semitransparent veil to protect your eyes, nose, mouth and ears from blowing sand and dust.

If the heat's a major problem, it's best to rise before the sun and hike until the heat becomes oppressive. You may then want to rest (in the shade) through the heat of midday and begin again after about 3pm. During warmer months, it may also be worthwhile timing your hike with the full moon, which will allow you to hike at night.

Because many trails follow canyons and wadis, it's also important to keep a watch on the weather. Rainy periods can render normally dry wadis impassable, and those with large catchment areas can quickly become raging – and uncrossable – torrents of muddy water, boulders and downed trees. Never camp in canyons or wadis and always keep to higher ground whenever there's a risk of flash flooding.

Ask anywhere near the docks for information. For more information, see the boxed text, p597.

A slow cruise up the Nile aboard a felucca (p130) is one of the Middle East's most leisurely and enjoyable experiences.

Skiing & Snowboarding

Although snow sports hardly spring to mind when considering the Middle East,

SAND ON YOUR SKIS

Hurtling down a steep-sided sand dune with a lake at the bottom and surrounded by stunning desert scenery is the kind of activity that you won't tell your mother about until after you've done it, but it's also one experience that you'll never forget. It's possible at Lake Gebraoun (p495) in Idehan Ubari in Libya. There are also a few 'sand-boards' available to maintain the interest of those for whom silent contemplation of the landscape just doesn't cut it.

there are some places where they're possible. In the 1970s Beirut was famous for the fact that you could swim in the Mediterranean waters of the Lebanese capital in the morning and then ski on the slopes of Mt Makmel, northeast of Beirut, in the afternoon. This is again an option as Beirut regains its sophisticated soul. For more information on skiing in Lebanon, see p442 and p454. A somewhat different but no less improbable experience awaits in the Alborz Mountains, north of Tehran, where Iran's slowly reemerging middle class take to the slopes (sometimes in chadors).

Water Sports

At any Red Sea resort worth its salt – from the expensive package tour resorts of Sharm el-Sheikh (Egypt) to the chilled, backpacker-friendly Dahab (Egypt) – you can indulge your passion for a variety of water sports from sailing to water-skiing. Eilat (p334) in Israel is possibly the Middle East's water sports capital, although places like Sharm el-Sheikh (p158) and Hurghada (p153) in

Egypt, Aqaba (p395) in Jordan, Beirut and Jounieh (p454) in Lebanon and many of Turkey's Mediterranean beach resorts all offer ample opportunities for year-round snorkelling, water-skiing and windsurfing. For the region's best windsurfing spot though, head to Moon Beach in Sinai.

For more details see the Activities sections in each country's Directory.

BUSINESS HOURS

With just a few exceptions, the end-of-week holiday throughout the Middle East is Friday. In Israel and the Palestinian Territories it's Saturday (Shabbat), while in Lebanon and Turkey it's Sunday. In countries where Friday is the holiday, most embassies and offices are also closed on Thursday (in Libya they close Saturday), although in areas where there are lots of tourists, many private businesses and shops are open on Thursday mornings and many stores will reopen in the evening on Friday.

In many countries, shops and businesses have different opening hours for different times of the year – they tend to work shorter hours in winter and open earlier in summer to allow for a longer lunchtime siesta – and during Ramadan (the month-long fast for Muslims), almost everything shuts down in the afternoon.

Open Sesame

Where possible, throughout this book we give the opening times of places of interest. The information is usually taken from notices posted at the sites. However, often the reality on the ground is that sites open pretty much as and when the gate guard feels like it. On a good day he'll be there an hour early, on a bad day he won't turn up at all. Who can blame him when in out-of-the-way places he may never see a visitor for days anyway? With the exception, perhaps, of those countries with a more Western concept of timekeeping (Israel and the Palestinian Territories and Turkey, for example), all opening hours must be prefaced, therefore, with a hopeful *in sha' Allah* (God willing).

CHILDREN

Your children have a decided advantage over the rest of us – unlike any vaguely news-savvy adult, most children are yet to have their perceptions of the Middle East distorted by stereotypes and selective news reporting. Taking the kids can add another dimension to a trip to the Middle East, although there are a few provisos that should be borne in mind. Firstly it's a good idea to avoid travel in the summer as the extreme heat can be quite uncomfortable and energy sapping. With infants another problem may be cleanliness. It is impractical to carry more than about a half dozen washable nappies around with you, but disposable ones are not always that easy to come by – although in Egypt, Israel and the Palestinian Territories, Lebanon and Turkey there should be no problem. Powdered milk is widely available, as is bottled water. As for hotels, you'll almost certainly want something with a private bathroom and hot water, thereby precluding most budget accommodation. The good news is that children are made a big fuss of in the Middle East. Many locals have grown up in large families and children will help break the ice and open doors to closer contact with local people.

Another way to deepen your child's experience of the Middle East is to find books on topics you're likely to encounter – from child-friendly history that helps your children understand archaeological sites to local fables as told to children.

For an itinerary through the Middle East that has been specially designed with kids in mind, see p34, while for more comprehensive advice on the dos and don'ts of taking the kids in your luggage, see Lonely Planet's *Travel with Children* by Cathy Lanigan.

CLIMATE CHARTS

The low-lying coast lands of the Red Sea and the Gulf are hot in the extreme throughout the year, with humidity continuously exceeding 70%; summer can be unbearable. Along the southern coasts of the Black and Caspian Seas the mild climate resembles that of central Europe.

For every 100m of ascent the temperature drops by 0.5°C to 0.7°C: many high plateaus are quite hot during the summer days but still freezing cold at night. Mountains with snow caps are to be seen in Turkey, Iran and even as far south as Lebanon and northern Israel and the Palestinian Territories. Winters are regularly snowy in the nonarid highlands of Turkey and Iran. Libya is fiercely

MIDDLE EAST DIRECTORY

hot in summer with desert temperatures above 50°C and high humidity on the Mediterranean coast. Desert nights across the region, especially in Libya, Iran and Jordan, can fall below freezing in winter.

Most of the Middle East is arid or semiarid, including the greater part of Egypt, Libya and most of Jordan, Iraq and Iran. In many regions annual rainfall hardly reaches 100mm. In southern Egypt and Libya, years

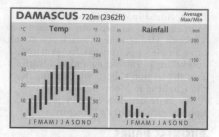

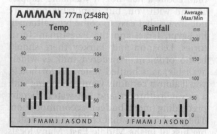

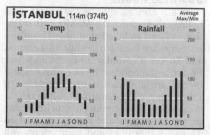

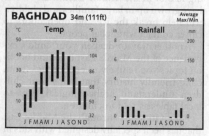

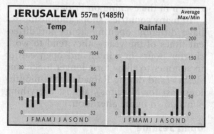

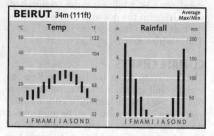

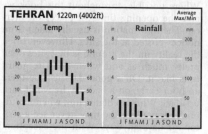

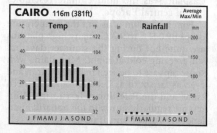

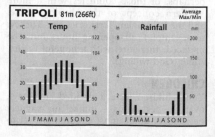

often pass without rain. Dasht-e Kavir (Great Salt Desert) of Iran is the largest area in the world with absolutely no vegetation.

The coastal areas of Turkey, Syria and Lebanon, and northeastern Iraq and northwestern Iran, get ample rain. Annual rainfall can reach 600mm in some areas, while in others it can go up to 2000mm. Further south there tends to be less rain, although, occasionally, southeastern Iran is affected by the Indian monsoon system.

For more information on how the climate affects travel, see p22.

COURSES
Various institutes and colleges in Egypt, Jordan and Lebanon offer short intensive courses in Arabic and there are many places in İstanbul to study Turkish. It's also possible to take up Hebrew and biblical studies in Israel. See the Courses section in the Directory of each country chapter for details.

CUSTOMS
Customs regulations vary from country to country, but in most cases they aren't that different from what you'd expect in the West – a couple of hundred cigarettes and a couple of bottles of booze. The exceptions are, of course, in dry countries like Iran and Libya where it is strictly forbidden to take alcohol into the country.

Electronics sometimes arouse interest too, particularly in Egypt, Syria and Iran. Items such as laptop computers and especially video cameras may be written into your passport to ensure that they leave the country with you and are not sold. If you are carrying this sort of thing, it's better not to be too obvious about it.

In Iran video and even audio cassettes may be scrutinised and taken off you for examination; books and magazines will also be given a careful going through for any pornographic or other incendiary material. Even something as innocuous as *Newsweek* may be confiscated because, for example, a woman in an ad is deemed to be wearing a dress that's too low cut. The simple rule is don't take in any print material that you're not prepared to lose.

In Libya that unusual desert stone you picked up in the Sahara may be confiscated, as the Libyan authorities are understandably concerned that antiquities or prehistoric rock art not be smuggled out of the country – the definition is broadly defined so best not to test its limits.

DANGERS & ANNOYANCES
Don't believe everything you read about the Middle East. Yes, there are regions where travellers would be ill-advised to visit. But alongside the sometimes disturbing hard facts is a vast corpus of exaggeration, stereotyping and downright misrepresentation.

The Middle East's reputation for danger is built on news of political turmoil, the Arab-Israeli conflict and the emergence of Islamic fundamentalism in many countries. Don't let this deter you. The trouble spots are usually well defined, and as long as you keep track of political developments, you're unlikely to come to any harm (see the boxed texts p646 and below).

In general, theft is not really a problem in the Middle East and robbery (mugging) even less of one, but don't let the relative safety lull you. Take the standard precautions. Always keep valuables with you or

IS IT SAFE?

Safety is a very subjective subject. Perceptions of the Middle East are shaped for most people by ever-present news stories of conflict, killings and bombings. It's a lopsided picture. Imagine somebody whose image of the USA was built solely on the 9/11 attacks or who refused to visit Spain or the UK as a result of terrorist attacks in Madrid and London in recent years. Just as the USA, the UK and Spain are rarely typecast as dangerous destinations, so day-to-day life in the Middle East very rarely involves shootings, explosions and other elements of terror. Remember that good news is rarely, if ever, reported. There are trouble spots (most notably at the time of writing Iraq, and the Palestinian territories of the West Bank and Gaza Strip), but these are well-defined areas that are easily avoided.

Incidents such as the terrorist bombing in Sharm el-Sheikh in July 2005, in which almost 100 people died, are clearly major causes for concern, but these are definitely the exception, rather than the norm. The sad fact about modern terrorism is that you may face similar dangers anywhere in the world and that you're probably no more at risk in the Middle East than you may be in your home country. As one holidaymaker was reported saying in the wake of the Sharm el-Sheikh bombings, 'Actually, I live in central London, I don't really want to go home!'

In our experience most people in the Middle East are perfectly able to distinguish between the policies of Western governments and individual travellers. You may receive the occasional question ('Why does the West support Israel?'), but you'll almost never be held personally accountable, except perhaps in deeply troubled Iraq. Once in Tehran we stood, obviously Westerners, with cameras and pasty complexions, and watched a crowd march by chanting 'Death to America! Death to Britain!' – several marchers grinned, waved and broke off to come over and ask how we liked Iran.

So, while right now we'd advise against visits to Gaza City, Hebron or Baghdad, rarely should events in the news make you reconsider your travel plans. Keep abreast of current events and if you need to phone your embassy for travel advice then do, but otherwise, just go.

locked in a safe – never leave them in your room or in a car or bus. Use a money belt, a pouch under your clothes, a leather wallet attached to your belt, or internal pockets in your clothing. Keep a record of your passport, credit card and travellers cheque numbers separately; it won't cure problems, but it will make them easier to bear.

However, beware of your fellow travellers; there are more than a few backpackers who make their money go further by helping themselves to other people's.

DISABLED TRAVELLERS

Generally speaking, scant regard is paid to the needs of disabled travellers in the Middle East. Steps, high kerbs and other assorted obstacles are everywhere, streets are often badly rutted and uneven, roads are made virtually uncrossable by heavy traffic, and many doorways are low and narrow. Ramps and specially equipped lodgings and toilets are an extreme rarity. The happy exception is Israel and the Palestinian Territories; see p348 for details. Elsewhere, you'll have to plan your trip carefully and will

probably be obliged to restrict yourself to luxury-level hotels and private, hired transport. For this reason, Libya, where escorted tours are mandatory, may be a good choice of destination.

If it all sounds difficult, remember that where Middle Eastern governments have singularly failed to provide the necessary infrastructure, local officials, guides and hotel staff almost invariably do their best to help in any way they can.

Before setting out for the Middle East, disabled travellers should consider contacting any of the following organisations who can help with advice and assistance:

Accessible Travel & Leisure (☎ 01452-729739; www.accessibletravel.co.uk; Avionics House, Naas Lane, Gloucester GL2 2SN) Claims to be the biggest UK travel agency dealing with travel for the disabled and encourages people with a disability to travel independently. It also runs tours to Egypt.

Holiday Care (☎ 0845 124 9971; www.holidaycare .org.uk; 2nd fl, Imperial Bldgs, Victoria Rd, Horley, Surrey RH6 7PZ) Information on hotels with disabled access, where to hire equipment and tour operators dealing with the disabled.

Royal Association for Disability & Rehabilitation (RADAR; ☎ 020-7250 3222; www.radar.org.uk; Unit 12, 250 City Rd, London EC1V 8AF) Publishes a useful guide called *Holidays & Travel Abroad: a Guide for Disabled People*.

DISCOUNT CARDS

An International Student Identity Card (ISIC) can come in useful in the Middle East. Egypt, Israel and the Palestinian Territories and Turkey have various student discounts on flights and rail travel, and reduced admissions at museums, archaeological sites and monuments of anything between 25% to 33% for cardholders. A student card also gets the holder 50% off admissions to museums and cultural sites in Iran, while in Syria it slashes admissions to almost all historical sites to about a 10th of the normal foreigners' price. Bear in mind that a student card issued by your own university or college may not be recognised elsewhere: it really should be an ISIC.

EMBASSIES & CONSULATES

It's important to realise what your own embassy can and can't do to help you if you get into trouble. Generally speaking, it won't be much help in emergencies if the trouble you're in is remotely your own fault. Remember that you are bound by the laws of the country you're in. Your embassy will not be sympathetic if you end up in jail after committing a crime locally, even if such actions are legal in your own country.

In genuine emergencies you might get some assistance, but only if other channels have been exhausted. For example, if you need to get home urgently, a free ticket home is exceedingly unlikely – the embassy would expect you to have insurance. If all your money and documents are stolen, it might assist with getting a new passport, but a loan for onward travel is out of the question.

For the addresses and contact details of embassies and consulates abroad and in the Middle East, see the Directory sections in the individual country chapters.

GAY & LESBIAN TRAVELLERS

Except in Egypt, Lebanon, Turkey and Israel and the Palestinian Territories, homosexuality is illegal in all Middle Eastern countries. Penalties include fines and/or imprisonment, and in Iran the death penalty may be invoked. That doesn't mean that gays aren't active but it does mean that gay identity is expressed only in trusted, private spheres.

Even in those countries in which homosexuality is not prohibited by law, it remains fairly low-key, with a few exceptions (İstanbul in Turkey and Tel Aviv in Israel both have vibrant gay scenes). However, in general as a Westerner, you're unlikely to encounter prejudice or harassment as long as you remain discreet, although this may not be the case if you become involved with a local.

For a good rundown on the prevailing legal and social situation in most countries of the Middle East – including news updates, the legal situation and postings by locals and by gay visitors – visit www.gaymiddleeast .com or www.globalgayz.com.

For more information on gay-friendly bars and hotels see the *Spartacus International Gay Guide* and Gay & Lesbian Travellers sections in the individual Egypt, Israel and the Palestinian Territories, Jordan, Lebanon and Turkey chapters.

HOLIDAYS

All Middle Eastern countries, save Israel, observe the main Islamic holidays listed below. Countries with a major Shiite population also observe Ashura, the anniversary of the martyrdom of Hussein, the third imam of the Shiites. Most of the countries in this book also observe both the Gregorian and the Islamic New Year holidays. Every country also has its own national days and other public holidays – for details refer to the individual country chapters.

Eid al-Adha (Kurban Bayramı in Turkey) This feast marks the time that Muslims make the pilgrimage to Mecca.

Eid al-Fitr (Şeker Bayramı in Turkey) This feast marks the end of Ramadan fasting; the celebrations last for three days.

Islamic New Year Also known as Ras as-Sana, it literally means 'the head of the year'.

Lailat al-Mi'raj This is the celebration of the Ascension of the Prophet Mohammed.

Prophet's Birthday This is also known as Moulid an-Nabi, 'the feast of the Prophet'.

Ramadan (Ramazan in Iran and Turkey) This is the ninth month of the Muslim calendar, when Muslims fast during daylight hours. Foreigners are not expected to follow suit, but it is impolite to smoke, drink or eat in public during Ramadan. As the sun sets each day, the fast is broken with *iftar* (the evening meal prepared to break the fast). See also p55 for further details.

ISLAMIC HOLIDAYS

Hejira year	New Year	Prophet's Birthday	Lailat al-Mi'raj	Ramadan begins	Eid al-Fitr	Eid al-Adha	Ashura
1426	10 Feb 2005	19 Apr 2005	31 Aug 2005	3 Oct 2005	2 Nov 2005	10 Jan 2006	19 Feb 2005
1427	31 Jan 2006	11 Apr 2006	20 Aug 2006	24 Sep 2006	24 Oct 2006	31 Dec 2006	9 Feb 2006
1428	20 Jan 2007	31 Mar 2007	9 Aug 2007	13 Sep 2007	13 Oct 2007	20 Dec 2007	29 Jan 2007
1429	10 Jan 2008	20 Mar 2008	30 Jul 2008	2 Sep 2008	2 Oct 2008	9 Dec 2008	19 Jan 2008
1430	31 Dec 2008	9 Mar 2009	19 Jun 2009	23 Aug 2009	21 Sep 2009	29 Nov 2009	8 Jan 2009

Actual dates may occur a day later, but not earlier, depending on western hemisphere moon sightings.

Islamic Calendar

All Islamic holidays fall according to the Muslim calendar, while secular activities are planned according to the Christian system, except in Iran, where the Iranian solar calendar is used.

The Muslim year is based on the lunar cycle and is divided into 12 lunar months, each with 29 or 30 days. Consequently, the Muslim year is 10 or 11 days shorter than the Christian solar year, and the Muslim festivals gradually move around our year, completing the cycle in roughly 33 years.

Year zero in the Muslim calendar was when Mohammed and his followers fled from Mecca to Medina (AD 622 in the Christian calendar). This Hejira (migration) is taken to mark the start of the new Muslim era, much as Christ's birth marks year zero in the Christian calendar.

INSURANCE

Travel insurance covering theft, loss and medical problems is highly recommended. Some policies offer travellers lower and higher medical-expense options; the higher ones are chiefly for countries such as the USA, which have extremely high medical costs. There is a wide variety of policies available, so check the small print.

Some policies specifically exclude 'dangerous activities', which can include scuba diving, motorcycling and even trekking.

For further details on health insurance see p673, and for car insurance, see p669.

INTERNET ACCESS

From the small town of Ubari in Libya's Sahara desert to the centuries-old laneways of Jerusalem, the Middle East is well and truly connected to the Internet, although most connections may be a lot slower than you're used to. Most travellers make constant use of Internet cafés that proliferate in most countries and free Web-based email such as **Yahoo** (www.yahoo.com) or **Hotmail** (www.hotmail.com).

Hooking up your own laptop is still difficult throughout most of the region, although in Israel and the Palestinian Territories and Turkey you'll encounter less of a problem doing so. If you're travelling with a notebook or hand-held computer, be aware also that your modem may not work once you leave your home country. The safest option is to buy a reputable 'global' modem before you leave home, or buy a local PC-card modem if you're spending an extended time in any one country. You should also carry with you a universal AC adaptor that will enable you to plug your appliance in anywhere without frying the innards in case the power supply voltage differs from that at home.

For more information on travelling with a portable computer, see www.teleadapt.com.

AOL (www.aol.com) and **CompuServe** (www.compuserve.com) have dial-in nodes only in Egypt, Israel and the Palestinian Territories and Turkey. If you access an Internet account at home through a smaller ISP or an office or school network, the best option is either to open an account with a global ISP or to rely on Internet cafés and other public access points to collect your mail.

If you're relying on Internet cafés, you'll need three pieces of information with you to access your Internet mail account: your incoming (POP or IMAP) mail server name, account name and password. Your

ISP or network supervisor can provide these. With this information, you should be able to access your Internet mail account from any Net-connected machine worldwide, provided it runs some kind of software (remember that Netscape and Internet Explorer both have mail modules). It pays to be familiar with this process before you leave home.

MONEY

Details on each country's currency, places to change money and advice on specific exchange rates are given in the Directory of the individual country chapters. Throughout this general section we have quoted prices in US dollars (US$) as these rates are more likely than local currencies (which may go up and down) to remain stable.

ATMs

Most of the larger banks in the region (with the exception of those in Iran, Iraq, Syria and Libya) now have ATMs linked up to one of the international networks (eg Master-Card/Cirrus, Visa/Plus or GlobalAccess systems). In countries such as Egypt, Israel and the Palestinian Territories, Lebanon and Turkey it's possible to completely avoid having to bring wads of cash and/or travellers cheques – just bring your plastic. Major credit and credit/debit cards, especially Visa and MasterCard, are readily accepted (Libya is an exception, although times are changing) and many machines will also take bank-issued cash cards (which you use at home to withdraw money directly from your bank account). Make sure you remember your PIN (personal identification number), and it's also a good idea to check out what sort of transaction fees you're likely to incur from both your own bank and the banks whose machines you'll be using while you travel. See the Money section in the individual country chapters for more details.

Black Market

There is still black-market activity in some Middle Eastern countries, notably Iran and, to a lesser extent, Libya. If you do play the black market don't do it on the street – a dealer with a front, a travel agency or tailor shop, for example, is safest. If possible, ask a trusted local for advice. Big notes are worth

much more than small ones – you'll get a lot less for 100 US$1 bills (or even five US$20 bills) than you will for one US$100 bill.

Cash

Check around when looking to exchange your cash as rates do vary. A good general rule is to never change more than you have to in cash at borders or airports. Also be on the lookout for hidden extras such as commission. Official moneychangers rather than banks often offer the best deals. Throughout the Middle East avoid accepting torn or particularly tatty notes as you may have difficulty disposing of them. If you do find yourself with a bill that looks like it has been used to clean the floor, a bank alone will usually exchange it without complaints.

Bank-to-bank transfers are possible but, unless your home bank has links with a banking group in the country you're travelling in, it's a very complicated, time-consuming and expensive business, especially when you get outside the major capitals. Unless you're going to be in that one place for at least a couple of weeks don't attempt it. A cash advance on a credit card is much simpler. Alternatively Western Union Money Transfer has representatives in quite a few Middle East countries including Egypt, Israel and the Palestinian Territories and Turkey.

The safest place to carry your money is right next to your skin. A money belt, pouch or an extra pocket inside your jeans will help to keep things with their rightful owner. Remember that if you lose cash you've lost it forever – insurance companies simply won't believe that you had US$1000 in cash – so don't go overboard on the convenience of cash versus the safety of cheques or the replaceability of credit cards. A good idea is to put aside a separate emergency stash, say US$50, for use if everything else disappears.

Credit Cards

Iran and Libya aside (where your plastic is next to useless), credit cards are fairly widely accepted in the Middle East, although in Syria and Jordan their use is often restricted to top-end hotels. Israel and the Palestinian Territories, Lebanon and Turkey, on the other hand, are fully plastic societies where almost everything can be paid for by credit card, right down to your morning coffee. Visa, MasterCard and Amex are the most popular. It's possible to get cash advances on credit cards in several countries in the region including Egypt – see the Money section in those individual country chapters for more details.

Tipping

Tipping is expected in varying degrees in all Middle Eastern countries. Called 'baksheesh', it's more than just a reward for having rendered a service. Salaries and wages are much lower than in Western countries, so baksheesh is regarded as an often essential means of supplementing income. To a cleaner in a one- or two-star hotel who may earn the equivalent of US$50 per month, the accumulated daily dollar tips given by guests can constitute the mainstay of his or her salary.

For Western travellers who aren't used to continual tipping, demands for baksheesh for doing anything from opening doors to pointing out the obvious in museums can be quite irritating. But it is the accepted way. Don't be intimidated into paying baksheesh when you don't think the service warrants it, but remember that more things warrant baksheesh here than anywhere in the West.

One tip: carry lots of small change with you but keep it separate from bigger bills, so that baksheesh demands don't increase when they see that you can afford more.

In Libya and elsewhere where you're likely to be using the same guide or driver for a longer expedition, tips at the end of a journey are usually more generous, depending on the length of the expedition and the helpfulness of the guide.

Travellers Cheques

Most travellers carry a mix of cash and travellers cheques. Cash is quicker to deal with, can be exchanged at almost any place and gets better rates, but it cannot be replaced. Travellers cheques are accepted everywhere in the Middle East except for Iraq, Iran and (sometimes) Libya. If your travellers cheques are lost or stolen you get a refund. When you buy your cheques make sure you are clear about what to do when the worst happens – most companies give you a 24-hour international phone number to contact. Well-known brands of cheque, such as Amex and Thomas Cook, are better to deal with as they're the most widely accepted; both companies have offices in the Middle East.

It's worth carrying a mix of high and low denomination notes and cheques so that if

---

SHOPPING FOR THAT SPECIAL SOMETHING

For the kitsch connoisseur the Middle East is an absolute dream. How about one of the following?

Blinking Jesus There's a lot of kitsch available at Christian sites in Israel, but it's perhaps best represented by the 3-D postcards portraying a very Swedish-looking Jesus whose eyes open and close, depending on the angle of view.

Ephesus clock A plastic version of a Roman gate with arch stones for nine o'clock through to three o'clock. However, the time (in the open portal) between three and nine o'clock is anybody's guess.

Inflatable Arafat Just put your lips to the back of his head and blow for a life-size, pear-shaped, air-filled bust of everybody's favourite keffiyeh-wearing world leader. Gathering dust on shelves in Gaza City.

King Tut galabiyya Perfect for lounging around the house, a short-sleeved, brightly coloured robe that is usually too short and festooned with a giant iron-on reproduction of the famous funerary mask.

King Tut hologram lamp White plaster bust of the famous boy-king that appears to float like a hologram when plugged in. Available in Cairo's Khan al-Khalili for a mere US$50.

Mother-of-pearl telephone A real telephone, but in a wooden casing with inlaid mother-of-pearl (actually plastic) patterning. Not only is it hideous but it's about the shape and size of a typewriter. Available in the Souq al-Hamidiyya, Damascus.

Now-you-see-him-now-you-don't Khomeini plate A plate that you tilt one way to get a stern Ayatollah, then tilt another way for a cheery President Khatami. Available at the Holy Shrine of Imam Khomeini, south of Tehran.

Priapus from Ephesus A small replica of the (in)famous, generously endowed statue on display at the museum here. Attach to the wall for a splendid coat hook.

Pyramid paperweight A clear resin pyramid with a golden sphinx inside. When you shake it golden 'snow' rains down. Or maybe it's acid rain. Available in Egypt anywhere tourists congregate.

you're about to leave a country, you can change just enough for a few days and not have too much local currency to get rid of.

PHOTOGRAPHY & VIDEO
Film & Equipment
If you're shooting digital, the situation is patchy across the Middle East. You're unlikely to have difficulties tracking down batteries and memory cards in the major cities of Turkey, Lebanon, Jordan, Israel and the Palestinian Territories and Egypt, but elsewhere you'd be well advised to take your own supply. When it comes to burning photos onto CDs, the more savvy Internet cafés in capital cities can usually provide what you need, although, again, don't count on such cafés being easy to find in Iran, Iraq, Syria or Libya.

Most types of film are available in the Middle East, although they may not be easily found outside of the big cities and if you have a favourite brand don't count on finding it when you most need it. Colour-print processing is usually quite adequate, while B&W and slide processing is not that good and less often available.

Film prices are usually similar, if not more expensive, to prices in Western countries, so you may want to bring your own supply. In some countries, film may have been stored for ages in less-than-ideal conditions, so always check the 'use by' date.

Cameras and lenses collect dust quickly in desert areas. Lens paper and cleaners can be difficult to find in some countries, so bring your own. A dust brush is also useful.

Photographing People
As a matter of courtesy, don't photograph people without asking their permission first. Children will almost always say yes, but adults may say no. In the more conservative Muslim countries, such as Iran, you should not photograph women. In countries where you can photograph women, show them the camera and make it clear that you want to take their picture. Digital cameras have the advantage of being able to show people their photo immediately after you've taken it.

Restrictions
In most Middle Eastern countries, it is forbidden to photograph anything even vaguely military in nature (bridges, train stations, airports and other public works). The definition of what is 'strategic' differs from one country to the next, and signs are not always posted, so err on the side of caution and ask your friendly neighbouring police officer for permission if in doubt.

Photography is usually allowed inside religious and archaeological sites, unless there are signs indicating otherwise. As a rule, however, do not photograph inside mosques during a service. Many Middle Easterners are sensitive about the negative aspects of their country, so exercise discretion when taking photos in poorer areas.

Also, be aware that certain countries, such as Iran, are very suspicious of video cameras and may not let you take one into the country. In Libya you pay more for your camera and video to enter museums and archaeological sites than you do to get in yourself.

See the Photography & Video section in the Directory of the individual country chapters for further details.

Technical Tips
In most Middle Eastern countries, early morning and late afternoon are the best times to take photographs. During the rest of the day, sunlight can be too bright and the sky too hazy, causing your photos to look washed out. There are a few remedies for this: a polarising filter will cut glare and reflection off sand and water; a lens hood will cut some of the glare; Kodachrome film, with an ASA of 64, and Fujichrome 50 ASA and 100 ASA are good slide films to use when the sun is bright.

Many religious sites and other buildings are not lit inside and you'll need long exposures (several seconds), a powerful flash or faster film. A tripod can be very useful, too.

POST
Postal services are quite reliable in most places in the Middle East, although in rural areas services can range from slow to nonexistent – it definitely pays to send your mail from the main centres. For details such as rates and prices, see the Post section in the Directory of the individual country chapters.

Receiving Mail
If you need to receive mail, you can use poste restante services. In this way, you can

have letters sent to a post office (usually in a capital city or major town) for you to collect. Letters should be addressed as follows: Your NAME, Poste Restante, General Post Office, City, Country.

To collect your mail, go to the main post office in that town and show your passport. Letters sometimes take a few weeks to work through the system, so have them sent to a place where you're going to be for a while, or to a place you'll be passing through more than once.

Some hotels and tour companies operate a mail-holding service.

Sending Mail

Letters sent from a major capital take about a week to reach most parts of Europe, and anything between a week and two weeks to reach North America or Australasia. If you're in a hurry, either DHL or FedEx have offices in almost every capital city in the Middle East.

SOLO TRAVELLERS

Travelling on your own is a great way to make new friends and to ensure that you have the freedom to follow your own itinerary. The opportunity to meet locals is greatly enhanced by travelling on your own rather than in a larger group. The downside is that hotel rooms generally cost more for individual travellers (a single room is rarely half the price of a double room). Otherwise there are few drawbacks from travelling solo as most Middle Eastern trails are pretty well worn, ensuring that you're never too far away from a new travel buddy if you're in need of company. Women travellers should read p654.

TELEPHONE

In most countries of the Middle East, the cheapest way to make international calls is at your friendly local Internet café for a fraction of the cost of calling on a normal land line. Staff at Internet cafés are generally pretty tech-savvy and can sell you the relevant card (there are often a number of brands to choose from) and show you how to use it.

If you're not likely to be in a country long enough to use up all the money on the card – although even a couple of calls via the Internet can be cheaper than one call in the old way – most cities and large towns have public telephone offices (either part of the post office, or privately run; the latter usually have three-minute minimums) where you can make international calls and send faxes. Costs for international calls start at about US$3 per minute, and only a few countries offer reduced rates at night. The other problem is the waiting time between placing your call with the operator and actually getting through, which can be minutes or hours depending on the locality and time of day.

If cash is tight, many travellers make an international call and then make their (long-suffering) parents call them back later at their hotel. If that's the case, the least you can do is buy them a calling card back home before you leave so that they don't dread every time they hear from you.

Mobile Phones

Throughout the Middle East the use of mobile phones is widespread (not to say obsessive) and every country has its own networks. Some of these networks run on the GSM system, like Europe, so if your phone works on GSM and your account allows you to roam, then you'll be able to use your mobile (this is the case in Egypt) – always check with your carrier at home before setting out. In other places – few Western phones function in Libya and Iran – you'll have to buy prepaid SIM cards. Beware though: the cost of using a mobile in some countries is up to three times as high as a call on a land line. For further details on whether you'll be able to use your mobile phone in a specific country, see the Directory section of each individual country chapter.

Phonecards

Card phones offering international direct dial are possible in most Middle Eastern countries, including Egypt, Israel and the Palestinian Territories, Jordan, Syria and Turkey. But, even though this service is expanding, the cards can drain money for very few minutes' conversation. Probably best to use local cards for local calls only.

TIME

Egypt, Israel and the Palestinian Territories, Jordan, Lebanon, Libya, Syria and Turkey are two hours ahead of GMT/UTC, Iraq is three hours ahead, and Iran is 3½ hours ahead. For a comprehensive guide to time zones in the region, see p698. Of the countries covered by this book, only Jordan and Libya do not operate daylight-saving hours.

Time is something that Middle Eastern people always seem to have plenty of; something that should take five minutes will invariably take an hour. Trying to speed things up will only lead to frustration. It is better to take it philosophically than try to fight it.

TOILETS

Outside the midrange and top-end hotels and restaurants of the Middle East (where Western-style loos are the norm), visitors will encounter more than their fair share of Arab-style squat toilets (which incidentally, according to physiologists, encourage a far more natural position than the Western-style invention!).

It's a good idea to carry an emergency stash of toilet paper with you for the times when you're caught short outside the hotel as most of these toilets have a water hose and bucket for the same purpose.

TOURIST INFORMATION

Most countries in the region have tourist offices with branches in big towns and at tourist sights. One exception is Libya where tourist information from the government is a closely guarded secret. However, even where there is a tourist office, don't expect much. Usually the most the offices can produce is a free map; help with booking accommodation or any other service is typically beyond the resources of the often nonetheless amiable staff. The exception to this are some of the offices in Israel and the Palestinian Territories, which are in fact very useful. You'll usually get better results relying on the knowledge and resourcefulness of your hotel reception. Tourist office locations are given in the individual town and city sections.

VISAS

You can either get them before you go, along the way, or increasingly frequently, at the airport or border – for more information see Visas in the Directory of the relevant country chapter.

The advantage of predeparture collection is that it doesn't waste travelling time and 'difficult' embassies are sometimes less difficult when you are in your own country – apart from anything else they can usually explain things in your own language and that seemingly meaningless but utterly essential document they require is much easier to find back home. There's also never any guarantee that the Iranians and, sometimes, the Syrians, are going to grant you a visa; if you apply from home first, you at least know where you stand before setting

---

MIDDLE EASTERN VISAS

The following table is intended as an overview only – for all the complications of visa costs and exactly how and where to get your visas, see the Visas section in the Directory of each individual country chapter.

Country	Visa required?	Visa available on arrival?	Special requirements	Visa available in the Middle East?
Egypt	yes (unless just visiting Sinai)	at airports & seaports only	none	yes, in all capitals plus Aqaba & Eilat
Iran	yes	no	must not have visited Israel	see p248
Iraq	yes	no	must not have visited Israel	unlikely
Israel	no	n/a	none	n/a
Jordan	yes	yes (except at King Hussein Bridge)	none	yes, in all capitals
Lebanon	yes	yes	must not have visited Israel	yes (not in Syria)
Libya	yes	yes (with prior authorisation)	must not have visited Israel	rarely
Syria	yes	no*	must not have visited Israel	only in some countries (eg Turkey & Egypt)
Turkey	see p633	yes	none	n/a

* If your home country has no Syrian embassy you may obtain your visa at the border.

off. If you are turned down in your home country, there's usually nothing to stop you trying again while on the road.

Some embassies request a letter from an employer or, if you're applying abroad, a letter of introduction from your embassy, while if the Israeli officials don't like the look of you they may ask to see that you have a sufficient amount of money to cover your stay. Some embassies also ask to see a 'ticket out', which means that before you can obtain a visa to get into a country you must have a ticket to prove that you intend leaving again.

WOMEN TRAVELLERS

Some women imagine that travel to the Middle East is taboo; many think of it as difficult and dangerous. In reality there's no reason why women can't enjoy the region as much as their male counterparts. In fact, some seasoned women travellers consider their gender a help not a hindrance in the Middle East.

Sexual harassment is a problem worldwide. The Middle East is no exception. While mild harassment (such as stares and muttered comments) can be common in some countries (notably Egypt, Israel and the Palestinian Territories and Turkey), physical harassment is rare. In fact, incidents of sexual assault or rape are far lower in the region than in the West. Sexual harassment in many Middle Eastern countries is a serious crime; local women are rarely harassed. The fact that travellers are is more to do with perceptions than with a predatory attitude per se. The best way to tackle the stereotypes is visibly to debunk them: in other words, do as the locals do and dress and behave more modestly than you might at home. And above all, keep your sense of humour!

Expatriate women and those who have travelled extensively throughout the region maintain that the most important thing is to retain your self-confidence and sense of humour.

Treatment of foreign women tends to be at its best in strictly Islamic societies such as Iran (providing of course you adhere to the prevailing social mores; see the boxed text, p249), and at its worst in Egypt, Israel and the Palestinian Territories and Turkey, where sexual harassment can be a real holiday-souring experience.

For more information on the situation for women travellers in specific countries, see the Women Travellers section in the Directory of each individual country chapter.

Attitudes Towards Women

Some of the biggest misunderstandings between Middle Easterners and Westerners occur over the issue of women. Half-truths and stereotypes exist on both sides: many Westerners assume all Middle Eastern women are veiled, repressed victims, while a large number of locals see Western women as sex-obsessed and immoral.

For many Middle Easterners, both men and women, the role of a woman is specifically defined: she is mother and matron of the household. The man is the provider. However, as with any society, generalisations can be misleading and the reality is far more nuanced. There are thousands of middle- and upper-middle-class professional women in the Arab World who, like their counterparts in the West, juggle work and family responsibilities. Among the working classes, where adherence to tradition is strongest, the ideal may be for women to concentrate on home and family, but economic reality means that millions of women are forced to work (but are still responsible for all domestic chores).

The issue of sex is where differences between Western and Middle Eastern women are most apparent. Premarital sex (or, indeed, any sex outside marriage) is taboo, although, as with anything forbidden, it still happens. Nevertheless, it is the exception rather than the rule – and that goes for men as well as women. However, for women the issue is potentially far more serious. With the possible exception of the upper classes, women are expected to be virgins when they get married and a family's reputation can rest upon this point. In such a context, the restrictions placed on a young girl – no matter how onerous they may seem to a Westerner – are intended to protect her and her reputation from the potentially disastrous attentions of men.

The presence of foreign women presents, in the eyes of some Middle Eastern men, a chance to get around these norms with ease and without consequences. That this is even possible is heavily reinforced by distorted impressions gained from Western

TIPS FOR WOMEN TRAVELLERS

Top of the list is to dress modestly. The woman wearing short pants and a tight T-shirt on the street is, in some locals' eyes, confirmation of the worst views held of Western women. Generally, if you're alone or with other women, the amount of harassment you'll get will be directly related to how you dress: the more skin exposed, the more harassment you'll get. In order to avoid giving out the wrong signals, attracting unwanted attention or misunderstandings, the following tips may prove useful:

- Dress modestly.
- Wear a wedding ring, which will make you appear less 'available'.
- If you are unmarried but travelling in male company say you are married rather than girlfriend/boyfriend or just friends.
- Don't say that you are travelling alone or just in the company of another female friend; always say that you are with a group.
- Avoid direct eye contact with local men; dark sunglasses help. There are, however, times when a cold glare is an effective riposte to an unwanted suitor.
- Don't respond to any obnoxious comments – act as if you didn't hear them.
- Be careful in crowds and other situations where you are crammed between people, as it is not unusual for crude things to happen behind you.
- Don't sit in the front seat of taxis unless the driver is a woman.
- On public transport, sit next to a woman if possible.
- Be very careful about behaving in a flirtatious or suggestive manner; it could create more problems than you ever imagined.
- If you need help for any reason (directions etc), ask a woman first. That said, local women are less likely than men to have had an education that included learning English – you'll find this a major drawback in getting to meet and talk with them.
- If dining alone, try and eat at Western-style places or those more used to tourists. Ask to be seated in the 'family' section, if there is one.
- It's perfectly acceptable for a woman to go straight to the front of a queue or to ask to be served first before any men that may be waiting – you have to have some advantages!
- Going to the nearest public place, such as the lobby of a hotel, usually works in getting rid of any hangers-on. If they still persist, however, asking the receptionist to call the police usually frightens them off.

TV and by the comparatively liberal behaviour of foreign women in the country. As one hopeful young man in Egypt remarked when asked why he persisted in harassing every Western woman he saw, 'For every 10 that say no, there's one that says yes.'

What to Wear

Except in Iran, travelling in the Middle East is not as prescriptive clothes-wise as you'd imagine. Nevertheless, it still pays to do as the locals do and err on the side of caution. And dressing modestly has the following advantages: you'll get a much warmer reception from the locals (who will really appreciate your willingness to respect their culture and customs), you'll attract less unwanted attention, and you may well feel more comfortable (long baggy clothes will not just keep you cooler, they'll also protect you from the fierce Middle Eastern sun). Dressing 'modestly' really means covering your upper legs and arms, shoulders and cleavage. A scarf is also useful, both to cover your neckline and to slip over your head when you want to look even more inconspicuous or when the occasion requires it (such as when visiting a mosque).

As with anywhere, take your cues from those around you: if you're in a rural area and all the women are in long, concealing dresses, you should be conservatively dressed.

In the very traditional society of Iran, although it is not necessary for foreign women to wear the chador (the one-piece cloak associated with Muslim countries), it is essential for them to cover all parts of the body except the hands, feet and face (from hairline to neckline), and to ensure that the outer layer of clothing gives no hint of the shape of the body. For more on this, see the boxed text, p249.

WORK

It's quite possible to pick up work in the Middle East in order to extend your stay and eke out your savings – but you have to know where to look and what you're looking for. Forget places such as Iran, Syria or Libya: realistically, your best options are Egypt, Israel and the Palestinian Territories and Turkey, ie the places where other foreigners gather in numbers.

For information about working on a kibbutz or a moshav, see p354.

Copy-editing

In the Middle East there are literally dozens of English-language newspapers and magazines published. Unless you have the proper training and experience you're unlikely to be offered any work in the way of journalism but there's often a need for people with good English-language skills who can copy-edit. The amount of work available and money to be made obviously depends on whether the paper or magazine is daily, weekly or monthly – whatever the case, you aren't going to make much, but it may be enough to cover the cost of your accommodation. The only way to find such work is to pick up the newspapers and phone.

Teaching English

Teaching centres – both of the respectable kind and cowboy outfits – can be found throughout the Middle East region. Cowboy outfits are often desperate for teachers, and they will take on people whose only qualification is that their mother tongue is English. In general, the pay is minimal and you'll probably have to stay on a tourist visa, which it will be up to you to renew. However, numerous long-term travellers

finance their stays this way, particularly in Cairo and İstanbul.

Your chances of getting a job are greatly improved if you have a certificate in CELTA (Certificate in English Language Teaching to Adults). This is what used to be known as TEFL and, basically, it's your passport to work abroad. To get the qualification you'll need to attend a one-month intensive course, which you can do in your home country via an English-language training centre. In the UK contact **International House** (IH; ☎ 020-7491 2598; www.ihlondon.com; 106 Piccadilly Circus, London W1J 7NL), which runs more than a dozen courses a year and has 110 affiliated schools in 30 countries worldwide, including Egypt (Cairo) and Turkey (İstanbul). Once you've completed the course, you can apply for any advertised positions.

Alternatively, you could fly out to Cairo and do the CELTA course at Cairo's International Language Institute, Heliopolis (which can be contacted through International House). The cost of the course is generally a little more than half the equivalent of doing it in the UK. Depending on the price of your flight, this may be a cheaper way to do it than at IH in London.

The other big employer of English-language teachers is the British Council. Its overseas teaching centres very rarely take on people who just turn up at the door as most recruiting is done in the UK. Contact the **Information Centre** (☎ 0161-957 7755; fax 957 7762; www.britishcouncil.org) well in advance of your departure date and check its website, which has a list of upcoming vacancies and British Council addresses in the Middle East.

Qualified teachers should also check www.eslcafe.com for regular job postings.

Working at a Backpackers

In Israel (Jerusalem, Tel Aviv and Eilat) and various places in Turkey (particularly İstanbul, Selçuk, Bodrum, Fethiye and Cappadocia), it's usually possible to pick up work in a hostel, typically cleaning rooms or looking after reception. It doesn't pay much, but it does usually get you a free room, a meal or two a day plus some beer money. The only way to find this kind of work is to ask around.

Transport in the Middle East

CONTENTS

GETTING THERE & AWAY

This section tells you how to reach the Middle East by air, land and sea from other parts of the world, and outlines the routes for onward travel from the region. For details of travel once you are in the region between one country and its neighbours see the Getting There & Away section at the end of the relevant country chapter.

ENTERING THE MIDDLE EAST

For the requirements of entering particular countries, see the Transport section of each individual country chapter.

Please note that neither Israeli citizens nor anyone with an Israeli stamp in their passport will be allowed to enter Iran, Iraq, Lebanon, Syria or Libya. For advice on how to get around this decades-old Middle Eastern conundrum, see the boxed text, p353.

AIR

All the major European, Middle Eastern and some Asian airlines serve the principal cities of the Middle East, although the cheapest (and most frequent) flights head for Cairo, İstanbul and Tel Aviv. Outside these three,

THINGS CHANGE...

The information in this chapter is particularly vulnerable to change. Check directly with the airline or a travel agent to make sure you understand how a fare (and ticket you may buy) works and be aware of the security requirements for international travel. Shop carefully. The details given in this chapter should be regarded as pointers and are not a substitute for your own careful, up-to-date research.

most of the Middle East is still seen primarily as a business destination, a fact reflected in the expense of flying there.

What this means in practice is that when booking a flight to the Middle East, you shouldn't automatically aim for the airport nearest to where you are going. For instance, your first destination might be Jordan, but you may find tickets to Tel Aviv significantly cheaper, even taking into account the cost of the overland trip to Amman.

Airlines

The following airlines all fly into the Middle East:

Afriqiyah Airways (airline code 8U; www.afriqiyah .aero) Hub: Tripoli.

Air Canada (airline code AC; www.aircanda.com) Hub: Pearson International Airport, Toronto.

Air France (airline code AF; www.airfrance.com) Hub: Charles de Gaulle International Airport, Paris.

Alitalia (airline code AZ; www.alitalia.com) Hub: Rome.

American Airlines (airline code AA; www.aa.com) Hub: O'Hare Airport, Chicago.

Austrian Airlines (airline code OS; www.aua.com) Hub: Vienna.

British Airways (airline code BA; www.britishairways .com) Hub: Heathrow Airport, London.

EgyptAir (airline code MS; www.egyptair.com.eg) Hub: Cairo.

El Al (airline code LY; www.elal.co.il) Hub: Tel Aviv.

Emirates (airline code EK; www.emirates.com) Hub: Dubai.

Ethiopian Airlines (airline code ET; www.flyethiopian .com/new/) Hub: Addis Ababa.

Gulf Air (airline code GF; www.gulfairco.com) Hub: Bahrain.

Iran Air (airline code IR; www.iranair.com) Hub: Tehran Mehrabad Airport.

Iran Aseman (airline code EP; www.iaa.ir) Hub: Tehran.

Kenya Airways (airline code KQ; www.kenya-airways .com) Hub: Nairobi.

KLM Royal Dutch Airlines (airline code KL; www.klm .com) Hub: Amsterdam Schipol Airport.

Kuwait Airways (airline code KU; www.kuwait-airways .com) Hub: Kuwait City.

Kyrgyz Airways (airline code KT) Hub: Bishkek.

Libyan Arab Airlines (airline code LN) Hub: Tripoli.

Lufthansa (airline code LH; www.lufthansa.com) Hub: Frankfurt.

Mahan Air (airline code W5; www.mahanairlines.com) Hub: Tehran.

Middle East Airlines (airline code ME; www.mea.com .lb) Hub: Beirut.

Olympic Airlines (airline code OA; www.olympicairlines .com) Hub: Athens.

Point-Afrique (www.point-afrique.com in French) Hub: Paris.

Qantas Airways (airline code QF; www.qantas.com) Hub: Sydney Airport.

Qatar Airways (airline code QR; www.qatarairways.com) Hub: Doha.

Royal Jordanian (airline code RJ; www.rja.com.jo) Hub: Amman.

Singapore Airlines (airline code SIA; www.singaporeair .com) Hub: Singapore Changi Airport.

Sudan Airways (airline code: SD; www.sudanair.com) Hub: Khartoum.

Swiss International Airlines (airline code LX; www .swiss.com) Hub: Zurich.

Syrianair (airline code RB; www.syriaair.com) Hub: Damascus.

Tunis Air (airline code TU; www.tunisair.com) Hub: Tunis.

Turkish Airlines (airline code TK; www.turkishairlines .com) Hub: İstanbul.

Turkmenistan Airways (airline code T5) Hub: Ashghabat.

Uzbek Airways (airline code HY; www.airways.uz) Hub: Tashkent.

Tickets

Buying cheap air tickets in the Middle East isn't easy. Usually the best deal you can get is an airline's official excursion fare and no discount on single tickets unless you qualify for a youth or student fare. Some travel agencies in the Middle East will knock the price down by up to 10% if you're persistent, but may then tie you into fixed dates or flying with a less popular airline.

The nearest thing you'll find to a discount-ticket market in the Middle East is offered by some travel agencies in Israel and the Pal-estinian Territories, particularly in Tel Aviv (p299), and in İstanbul (p566), especially in Sultanahmet.

As well as discounts on tickets to Western Europe and North America, the İstanbul agencies often have cheap deals on flights to places such as Moscow, Mumbai/Delhi and Singapore/Bangkok.

Travel agencies recommended for online bookings:

American Express Travel (www.itn.net)

Cheap Tickets (www.cheaptickets.com)

Expedia.com (www.expedia.com)

Lowestfare.com (www.lowestfare.com)

Orbitz (www.orbitz.com)

STA Travel (www.statravel.com)

Travelocity (www.travelocity.com)

Africa

The widest choice of African destinations is offered by EgyptAir, but, despite the proximity, there is nothing cheap about flying from the Middle East into Africa. In fact, for most African capitals a ticket bought in London will be cheaper than one bought in the Middle East. The best bet is to buy your African ticket with a stopover in the Middle East.

As an idea of prices, Cairo to Addis Ababa (Ethiopian Airlines and EgyptAir) is around US$600/850 one way/return; Nairobi (Kenya Airways) is US$635 one way; and Khartoum (EgyptAir and Sudan Airways) is US$400/490 one way/return.

Another alternative is Afriqiyah Airways, which connects Tripoli with 11 sub-Saharan African capitals, including Bamako (Mali), Accra (Ghana), Lagos (Nigeria) and Khartoum (Sudan).

Australia & New Zealand

EgyptAir has a regular service from Sydney via Southeast Asia to Cairo, from where there are connections to almost all other Middle Eastern destinations. However, the aircraft and in-flight service are much better with Gulf Air and Emirates, both of which fly out of Sydney and Melbourne to Abu Dhabi, Bahrain and Dubai, with connections onward from there to most other Middle Eastern capitals. Return fares to the Middle East start from around A$1450. Gulf Air's round-the-world (RTW) fare could be good value if you also want to visit London and stop over in Asia.

If you're heading for Tel Aviv, Qantas Airways and El Al via Asia are the best. Other options include Alitalia via Milan, Lufthansa Airlines via Frankfurt or KLM Royal Dutch Airlines via Amsterdam.

Both **STA Travel** (☎ 1300 733 035; www.statravel .com.au) and **Flight Centre** (☎ 133 133; www.flight centre.com.au) have offices throughout Australia. For online bookings, try www.travel .com.au.

In New Zealand both **Flight Centre** (☎ 0800 243 544; www.flightcentre.co.nz) and **STA Travel** (☎ 0508 782 872; www.statravel.co.nz) have branches throughout the country. The site www.travel .co.nz is recommended for online bookings.

Central Asia & the Caucasus

There is a small but rapidly growing number of flights from the Middle East to Central Asian and Caucasus destinations. There are regular flights between İstanbul and Almaty (Kazakhstan), Bishkek (Kyrgyzstan), Baku (Azerbaijan), Tashkent (Uzbekistan) and Ashghabat (Turkmenistan) with either Turkish Airlines or the national airlines of each country. There are also flights to these destinations from Tehran with either Iran Air or Iran Aseman, as well as services from Mashhad to Ashghabat, Bishkek and Dushanbe.

From Tel Aviv, Uzbekistan Airways flies to Tashkent.

Europe

Although London is the travel discount capital of Europe, there are several other cities where you'll find a range of good deals, particularly Frankfurt. Generally there's not much variation in air fare prices for departures from the main European cities. All the major airlines are usually offering some sort of deal and travel agencies generally have a number of special offers, so shop around.

Look out for cheap charter flight packages from western Europe to destinations in Turkey, Egypt and Israel. Some of the flight-plus-accommodation packages offered by travel agencies can work out to be cheaper than a standard flight, although often the dates can be very restrictive.

Afriqiyah Airways flies to Tripoli from London Gatwick, Brussels, Paris and Geneva, while Mahan Air offer flights to Tehran from Birmingham and Düsseldorf. Another option is to fly with Point-Afrique from Paris or Marseilles to the Libyan oasis town of Ghat (late October to early May only).

MAINLAND EUROPE

Most European carriers fly into the major cities of the Middle East (usually several times a week); the most frequent connections are with Paris, Frankfurt, Rome and Athens. Unless you're travelling on a charter flight, expect to pay around €500 as a minimum, but you could pay a whole lot more.

Recommended agencies on the mainland:
Airfair (☎ 020 620 5121; www.airfair.nl; Netherlands)
Barcelo Viajes (☎ 902 116 226; www.barceloviajes .com; Spain)
CTS Viaggi (☎ 06 462 0431; www.cts.it; Italy)
Expedia (www.expedia.de; Germany)
Nouvelles Frontières (☎ 0825 000 747; www .nouvelles-frontieres.fr; France)
STA Travel (☎ 01805 456 422; www.statravel.de; Germany)
Voyageurs du Monde (☎ 01 40 15 11 15; www.vdm .com; France)

UK

You can get to the Middle East on direct flights from almost any European city of any size. For the past few years fares to the region have remained fairly steady and the cheapest return fares you can expect to find (including all taxes) are around UK£235 to İstanbul, UK£250 to Cairo or Tel Aviv and UK£275 to Damascus.

As far as Middle East flights are concerned, there are few dedicated specialists and the best bet is to call **STA Travel** (☎ 020-7361 6142; www.statravel.co.uk) and **Trailfinders** (☎ 020-7938 3939; www.trailfinders.co.uk), both of which have branches throughout the UK.

If you're looking to fly into Egypt then it's also worth calling **Soliman Travel** (☎ 020-7244 6855; www.solimantravel.com), a reputable Egypt specialist that often manages to undercut the competition.

USA & Canada

There are more flights from the USA than from Canada, but still not that many: Royal Jordanian flies between New York/Chicago and Amman; EgyptAir flies between New York/Los Angeles and Cairo; while El Al connects Tel Aviv to a number of US cities as well as Montreal. Expect to pay around US$1400 for a return ticket.

Otherwise, it may work out cheaper to go via Europe or even fly to London and buy a ticket from a bucket shop there; the latter option would depend on the fare to London and the time you would have to spend in London waiting for a flight out.

Council Travel (☎ 800-226 8624; www.ciee.org; 205 E 42 St, New York, NY 10017), America's largest student travel organisation, has around 60 offices in the USA. Call the head office for the office nearest you or visit its website. **STA Travel** (☎ 800-777 0112; www.statravel.com) has offices in many major US cities; call the toll-free 800 number for office locations or visit its website.

Travel CUTS (☎ 800-667 2887; www.travelcuts.com) is Canada's national student travel agency and has offices in all major cities.

LAND
Border Crossings
Border crossings in the Middle East can be slow and it can take hours to pass through immigration and customs formalities, especially if you bring your own car. Make certain that you have all the required documentation with you. Showing patience, politeness and good humour is likely to speed up the process. For further information see Visas, p653; Bring Your Own Vehicle, p668; as well as the Transport sections of each individual country chapter.

If travelling independently overland to or from the Middle East – whether hitching, cycling, driving your own car or riding by train or by bus – you can approach the region overland from Africa, the Caucasus, Central Asia, Europe or Pakistan.

AFRICA
Travel between Africa and the Middle East was extremely problematic at the time of writing. The Nile ferry connecting Aswan in Egypt to Wadi Halfa in Sudan is running, but much of Sudan is unsafe for travel. Most East African overlanders skip Sudan by flying from Egypt to Addis Ababa in Ethiopia; but, recent clashes on the Eritrean–Ethiopian border have now placed a big question mark over the validity of this option.

Many travellers fly to Tunisia (for which there are numerous cheap flights) and then cross the Tunisia–Libya border by land at the Ras al-Jedir border post (the only border crossing open to travellers). There are numerous buses and shared taxis between Tripoli and Tunis, although most travellers take a Tunisian shared taxi from Sfax or Ben Guerdane as far as the border where their Libyan tour company will meet them and arrange onward travel.

Some hardy souls make the long desert crossing into Niger via the Libyan border post at Tumu. Other than overloaded and downright dangerous trucks carrying African immigrants, there is no regular public transport between the two countries, and the journey to Agadez in Niger – which involves crossing the Sahara desert – is only for the well equipped and well prepared. Visas are not available at the border in either direction, so make sure you have one before setting out.

Libya's borders with Algeria, Chad and Sudan are not open to foreigners.

THE CAUCASUS
Armenia & Georgia
The main border crossing from Turkey into Georgia is at Sarp on the Black Sea coast, near Hopa, but you can also cross at Posof, near Ardahan. The Sarp border crossing is open 24 hours a day, but Posof closes at night.

From Trabzon otogar there are daily bus services to Tiflis (Tbilisi, Georgia, €25, 20 hours) and on to Erivan (Armenia, €30, 25 hours) via the Sarp border crossing. You can also take a minibus from Trabzon to Sarp (€7) and on the other side of the border you can take a taxi to Batumi (about €15).

A certain amount of extortion seems to be a fact of life at these borders, especially when coming back into Turkey.

In Turkey, the train line from Ankara to Erzurum runs as far as Kars but at the time of writing the Turkish–Armenian border was closed to foreign travellers.

The border between Armenia and Iran is open at Agarak (Armenia) and Norduz (Iran), about an hour by private taxi (IR60,000) from Jolfa, in northwestern Iran. The border is theoretically open 24 hours and Armenian visas are available there for US$30, or US$20 for a three-day transit visa; Iranian visas are not. It's faster and more fun to take public transport to either side of the border, but buses do run between Tabriz (IR150,000) or Tehran (IR250,000) in Iran and Yerevan, the capital of Armenia, several times weekly.

Azerbaijan

Some of the buses from Trabzon to Tbilisi continue to Baku (US$75, plus a US$10 'tip' payable on the bus if you're going to Tbilisi, US$25 for Baku). It's a fairly gruelling journey with a three- to four-hour delay at Sarp on the border with Turkey and Georgia – mainly because the Georgians and Azerbaijanis buy up and take home half of Turkey. Trabzon to Tbilisi takes the best part of 19 hours.

You can also cross from Turkey to the Azerbaijani enclave of Nakhichevan via the remote Borualan/Sadarak border post, 105km southeast of Iğdır. Once in Nakhichevan, you'll have to fly across Armenian-occupied Nagorno-Karabakh to reach Baku, the Azerbaijani capital. From Iğdır, there are about seven daily minibuses to the border (€4, three hours).

You can enter Iran with little hassle at the twin towns of Astara between 8.30am and 6.30pm – visas are *not* available at the border (for the address of the Azerbaijani embassy in Tehran see p244). Astara is accessed via hops from Rasht in the west or Ardabil and Tabriz to the south. Alternatively, direct buses between the Azerbaijan capital of Baku and Tabriz (IR150,000, eight hours) or Tehran (IR150,000, 16 hours) leave the Iranian cities nightly, but the border wait can be long.

CENTRAL ASIA
Afghanistan

Crossing the Afghan border (open 7.30am to 4.30pm) is easy at Dogharon, southeast of Taybad in northeastern Iran. Most travellers take the direct bus between the Mashhad terminal and Herat (IR55,000, eight to 12 hours), the major city in northeastern Afghanistan. This service is prone to lengthy delays at the border but is safer and easier. Alternatively, take a bus to Taybad (three hours), a savari the 20km to the border, walk across and find something going to Herat. Visas are available in two days in Mashhad (see p244), but note that Afghanistan is definitely not for the faint-hearted or inexperienced.

Turkmenistan

There are two main crossings between Iran and Turkmenistan. Visas are not available on arrival in either direction. The Bajgiran border is easiest, with regular savaris (long-distance taxis, IR20,000 per person, 3½ hours) leaving from 100m north of Azadi Sq in Mashhad, and regular buses from the terminal running via Quchan. You'll have to change transport at the border (open 24 hours, but best between 8am and 6pm), and on the Turkmen side it's a short but costly hop to the capital, Ashghabat.

The relatively quiet border (open from 8am to 5pm) at Sarakhs (Iran) and Saraghs (Turkmenistan) is easy to reach by bus, savari or train from Mashhad although the train times can be annoying. From the Turkmen side, occasional buses and savaris run to Mary (three to four hours).

Travelling in either direction you must obtain a visa in advance.

EUROPE

One train a day heads from İstanbul to Bucharest (17 hours) and then on to Budapest (31 hours), with connections elsewhere in Europe. There have been reports of long delays and hassle, especially for women, at the Bulgarian border.

Despite the romantic appeal of train journeys, getting to Turkey overland is usually cheaper and faster by bus. Several Turkish bus lines, including Ulusoy, Varan and Bosfor, offer reliable and quite comfortable services between İstanbul and major European cities such as Frankfurt, Munich and Vienna for around US$80 one way. These services travel via Greece and the ferry to Italy, thereby avoiding any hassle at the Bulgarian border.

Bulgaria & Other Eastern European Countries

The main border crossing between Bulgaria and Turkey is at busy Kapitan-Andreevo/Kapıkule, 18km west of Edirne. It's open 24 hours.

From İstanbul, there are regular bus services to Sofia and Plovdiv (about €25), transiting the border post at Kapıkule. Or you can head for the Bulgarian border crossing at Kapıkule from Edirne (€0.50).

If you plan on leaving the Middle East via Bulgaria, nationals of the USA and the EU are admitted without a visa for stays of less than 30 days. Travellers of other nationalities (including Aussies, Kiwis and Canadians) need a transit visa, which is issued at the border for US$68.

A few bus services are offered from İstanbul otogar (bus station) to Macedonia (€30), Kosovo (€35) and Romania (€30). These all pass via the Kapıkule border post.

From İstanbul's Sirkeci Railway Station, there's the daily *Bosfor Ekspresi* service to Budapest via Sofia and Bucharest.

Greece

The crossing points between western Thrace in Greece and eastern Thrace in Turkey are at Kipi/İpsala, and Kastanies/Pazarkule, near Edirne.

At least six weekly buses travel from Athens' Peloponnese train station to İstanbul (around US$85; 22 hours). You can also pick up the bus in Thessaloniki (around US$60) and at Alexandroupolis (US$25). Alternatively, you can make your own way to Alexandroupolis and take a service from the intercity bus station to the border town of Kipi (US$3, thrice daily). You can't walk across the border but it's easy enough to hitch (you may be able to get a lift all the way to İstanbul). Otherwise, take a bus to İpsala (5km east beyond the border) or Keşan (30km east beyond the border), from where there are many buses to the capital.

Greece's sole rail link with Turkey is the daily Thessaloniki–İstanbul service. The train leaves İstanbul late in the evening, arriving in Thessaloniki late the next afternoon; in the reverse direction, it leaves Thessaloniki late in the evening. Although the 1400km trip is supposed to take 16

hours, delays of more than five or six hours at the border are common, especially on the eastbound leg, and the train can get uncomfortably crowded and hot. Only 2nd-class seats (US$40) are available.

PAKISTAN

The only proper crossing for foreigners is between Mirjaveh (Iran) and Taftan (Pakistan). It's pretty smooth as long as your papers are in order and you don't take the train, which might see you stranded at the border for ever as your fellow passengers are exhaustively searched. This would be a fate worse than death, as Taftan has been described, not unfairly, as hell on earth. It's best to take a bus (IR5500) or savari (about IR15,000) between Zahedan (p236) and the border, and a bus for the mind-numbingly long trip between Taftan and Quetta. Bargain hard! The border opens from about 7am to 4.30pm Iranian time.

Car & Motorcycle

Anyone who is planning to take their own vehicle with them needs to check in advance what spare parts and petrol are likely to be available (see p669). A number of documents are also required (see also the boxed text, below):

Green card Issued by insurers. Insurance for some countries is only obtainable at the border.

International Driving Permit (IDP) Although most foreign licences are acceptable in Middle Eastern countries, an IDP issued by your local automobile association is highly

---

CARNETS

A carnet de passage is like a passport for your car, a booklet that is stamped on arrival at and departure from a country to ensure that you export the vehicle again after you've imported it. It's usually issued by an automobile association in the country where the vehicle is registered. Most countries of the Middle East require a carnet although rules change frequently.

The sting in the tail with a carnet is that you usually have to lodge a deposit to secure it. If you default on the carnet – that is, you don't have an export stamp to match the import one – then the country in question can claim your deposit, which can be up to 300% of the new value of the vehicle. You can get around this problem with bank guarantees or carnet insurance, but you still have to fork out in the end if you default.

Should the worst occur and your vehicle is irretrievably damaged in an accident or catastrophic breakdown, you'll have to argue it out with customs officials. Having a vehicle stolen can be even worse, as you may be suspected of having sold it.

The carnet may also need to specify any expensive spare parts that you're planning to carry with you, such as a gearbox, which is designed to prevent any spare-part importation rackets. Contact your local automobile association for details about all necessary documentation at least three months in advance.

recommended, and is required for entry with a vehicle at some border crossings.

Vehicle registration documents In addition to carrying all ownership papers, check with your insurer whether you're covered for the countries you intend to visit and whether third-party cover is included.

SEA

Ferries shuttle reasonably regularly between southern Europe and Israel, Turkey and Egypt. There are other less frequented routes connecting Egypt with Sudan and the Arabian Peninsula.

As well as the services listed below, some cruise liners call at Middle Eastern ports such as Suez, Alexandria, Tripoli, Benghazi or Tobruk, but these are beyond the scope of this book. A good travel agent should be able to tell you what's available in the season you are travelling.

Unless stated otherwise, all services run in both directions and all fares quoted below are single. A slight discount may apply on return tickets as well as student, youth or child fares on some lines. Schedules tend to change at least annually according to demand; fares, too, often fluctuate according to season, especially on the Mediterranean routes.

Although vehicles can be shipped on most of the following routes, bookings may have to be made some time in advance. The charge usually depends on the length or volume of the vehicle and should be checked with the carrier. As a rule, motorcycles cost almost nothing to ship while bicycles are free.

You're unlikely to regret taking an adequate supply of food and drink with you on any of these ships; even if it is available on board you're pretty stuck if it doesn't agree with you or your budget.

Between Greece, Cyprus and Israel & the Palestinian Territories

Twice-weekly car and passenger ferry services connect Haifa and Piraeus (the port for Athens), with a stop at Limassol (Cyprus). For more information about sailing times and fares, contact **Rosenfeld Shipping** (☎ 04-861 3671; reservations@rosenfeld.net) in Israel.

At the time of writing, boats depart from Haifa at 8pm Monday and Thursday and arrive in Limassol (US$160/285/225/125 for passenger/jeep/car/motorcycle) around 10 hours later, with a further 12-hour jour-

ney on to Piraeus (US$250/460/385/277). Fares include port taxes, war-risk taxes and all breakfasts and dinners; return fares are about 20% less than two one-way fares.

Between Italy, Greece & Turkey

Private ferries link Turkey's Aegean coast and the Greek islands, which are in turn linked by air or boat to Athens. Services are usually daily in summer, several times a week in spring and autumn and perhaps just once a week in winter.

From Çeşme, situated about 85km west of İzmir, **Marmara Lines** (www.marmaralines.com; per person from €110; 2½ days) ferries run twice weekly to Brindisi via Corfu and Patras in Greece (once weekly in winter).

Marmara Lines also connects Ancona in Italy from Çeşme between April and November (from €200, 2½ days).

Daily boats operate from Ayvalik to Lesvos (Greece) from June to September (€40/50 one way/return). There's at least one boat a week, even in winter. Çeşme is a transit point to the Greek island of Chios, 10km away across the water. In summer, there are daily ferries to Chios (€35/40 one way/return), and at least three weekly services in winter. Buy your ticket from any travel agency at the harbour.

All Kuşadası travel agencies sell tickets to the Greek island of Samos. There's at least one daily boat to/from Samos year-round (€30 one way, €35 same-day return). In summer, daily hydrofoils (€33 same-day return) and ferries (€23 same-day return), link Bodrum with Kos (Greece); in winter services shrink to three times weekly. In summer, there are also two weekly services to Rhodes (Rhodos, €45 one way, €50 same-day return); check with the ferry offices near the castle. From Marmaris, hydrofoils to Rhodes operate twice daily in summer (once or twice weekly in winter) for €40 one way/same-day return (one hour). Buy your ticket in any Marmaris travel agency.

Between Cyprus & Turkey

From Alanya, there are ferries to Girne (Northern Cyprus) three times a week from April to October for a return fare of €83 including tax.

If you have a multiple-entry visa for Turkey you should be able to cross over to Northern Cyprus and back again without buying a new one. However, if your visa has expired, you should anticipate long queues at immigration.

Between Russia & Turkey

Travelling from Trabzon, there are two to three weekly ferry services to Sochi (from €50 one way).

Between Cyprus & Egypt

From Port Said, boats to Limassol in Cyprus depart twice weekly from May to November. A ticket costs US$120 one way. For information and tickets, visit one of the many shipping agencies in Port Said. These include **Canal Tours** (☎ 066-332 1874, 012 798 6338; canaltours@bec.com.eg).

Between Sudan, Saudi Arabia & Egypt

Telestar Tours (in Cairo ☎ 02-794 4600, in Suez ☎ 062-332 6251) runs a ferry between Port Sudan and Suez three times per week. Tickets cost E£300 one way.

The **Nile River Valley Transport Corporation** (in Aswan ☎ 097-303 348, in Cairo ☎ 02-575 9058) runs one passenger ferry per week from Aswan to Wadi Halfa. One-way tickets cost E£383.50 for 1st class with bed in a cabin; E£236 for an airline seat and E£164.50 for deck class. At the time of research the ferry was departing on Monday at around noon. The trip takes between 16 and 24 hours. Passengers should arrive at about 8.30am to allow time to clear customs and fight for a decent seat.

To board the ferry, you must have a valid Sudanese visa in your passport.

Telestar Tours also runs an irregular ferry service between Suez and Jeddah (about 36 hours). Tickets cost E£300/400/500/600 for deck/3rd/2nd/1st class (or the US dollar equivalent). The ferry also carries cars. Note that getting a berth during the haj is virtually impossible.

There's also a thrice weekly fast ferry (adult/child E£300/200, three hours) between Hurghada and Duba in Saudi Arabia. You must be at the port three hours before departure. For information, contact an agent for **International Fast Ferries Co** (in Hurghada ☎ 065-344 7571; www.internationalfastferries .com) or enquire at the Hurghada port.

You will not be allowed to board any of these services unless you have a valid Saudi visa in your passport.

Between Iran & the Arabian Peninsula

Iran's Valfajre 8 Shipping Company has regular but unpredictable ferries between several Gulf ports. For travellers, the Bandar-e Abbas–Dubai (US$55 in 1st class, one way) fast boat service is the most convenient, though flying is easier and cheaper. Slow boat services between Bushehr and Kuwait (US$64), Qatar (US$43) and Bahrain (US$45) could also be useful. For schedules and prices, see www.vesc.net.

TOURS

International tour companies offer a host of tour possibilities for visiting the Middle East – everything from a package tour by the beach to a more gruelling six-week overland expedition.

Remember also that Libya can only be visited as part of an organised tour; for a list of companies offering tours to Libya see p506.

For tour companies specialising in individual countries, see the Transport section of the relevant country chapter.

Australia & Elsewhere

In Australia and elsewhere, most of the companies that offer tours to the Middle East do so as agents for the UK packages; check out the websites that are listed under the UK companies for the local affiliate closest to you.

In Australia, there are also a few interesting home-grown outfits:

Passport Travel (☎ 03-9867 3888; www.travelcentre .com.au) Middle East specialist (especially Libya, Egypt and Jordan) with a focus on arranging itineraries for individuals or groups.

Ya'lla Tours (☎ 03-9510 2844; yallamel@yalltours.com .au) Wide variety of package and private arrangement tours to the Middle East.

An innovative Netherlands-based company is **Idrisi Travel** (☎ 0492-340632; info@idrisitravel .co.uk), which specialises in walking and archaeology with tours to Jordan and Libya.

UK

Adventure Company (☎ 0870 794 1009; www .adventurecompany.co.uk) Small-group 'adventure' tours with structured itineraries to Egypt and Jordan.

Crusader Travel (☎ 020-8744 0474; www.crusader travel.com) Diving and adventure tours from Egypt, Israel and the Palestinian Territories and Turkey.

Dragoman (☎ 0870 499 4475; www.dragoman.com)
The largest of the overland companies takes in Turkey,
Syria, Jordan, Libya and Egypt, not to mention just about
everywhere else on the planet.
Economic Expeditions (☎ 020-7262 0177; www
.economicexpeditions.com) İstanbul to Cairo, or vice versa.
Exodus (☎ 020-8675 5550; www.exodus.co.uk)
Overland and adventure trips covering Egypt, Iran, Jordan,
Lebanon, Libya, Syria and Turkey.
Explore Worldwide (☎ 0870 333 4001; www.explore
worldwide.com) Small group exploratory holidays that take
in Egypt, Iran, Jordan, Lebanon, Syria and Turkey.
Imaginative Traveller (☎ 0800 316 2717; www
.imaginative-traveller.com) Highly professional, established
outfit with a vast range of tours offered to Egypt, Iran,
Jordan, Syria and Turkey.
Kumuka (☎ 020 7937 8855; www.kumuka.com)
Masses of routes offered including dedicated explorations
of Egypt, Jordan or Syria.
Oasis Overland (☎ 01963 363 400; www.oasisover
land.co.uk) Turkey, Syria, Jordan and Egypt.
On the Go (☎ 020-7371 1113; www.onthegotours
.com) Egypt and Turkey specialist with the odd detour into
Jordan.

GETTING AROUND

This chapter should be used for general
planning. If you want to travel, for instance,
between Turkey and Israel and the Palestinian Territories, this chapter will give you an
overview of the options: air, land or sea, train
versus bus, and so on. Then, if you decide to
go by bus from İstanbul to Damascus, from

Damascus to Amman, and Amman to Jerusalem you should begin by going to the Getting There & Away section at the back of the
Turkey chapter for further details on buses to
Syria. The destination-specific sections will
tell where the border crossing points are.

Once in Syria, consult that chapter's Getting There & Away section for the best way
to continue to Amman in Jordan. Simple.

One particular point to note: at the time
of writing, Libya could only be visited as
part of an organised tour. Although public
transport exists throughout Libya, most of
your transport will be organised by your
tour company once you reach the border.

AIR

With no regional rail network to speak of
and distances that make the bus a discom-
forting test of endurance, flying is certainly
the most user-friendly method of transport
in the Middle East. Tickets are more flexible
than buses or trains, schedules more rigidly
adhered to, refunds easier to get and information more readily available.

Flying isn't a safe option for getting to or
from Iraq, nor is flying possible between Israel and the Palestinian Territories and most
other Middle Eastern countries, except for
Egypt, Jordan and Turkey. But, these exceptions aside, almost every Middle Eastern
capital is linked to each of the others.

If you're in a capital city, it's usually worth
buying your ticket through a reputable travel
agency. It can give you all the available

**TRANSPORT IN THE
MIDDLE EAST**

MIDDLE EAST AIR ROUTES

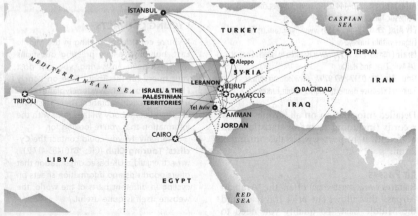

choices without you having to visit several different airline offices. The price you pay will usually be the same, if not less.

Travel agency addresses are found in the Information sections of individual cities.

Airlines in the Middle East

Flights are usually operated by state airlines, most of which are reasonable, although an increasing number of charter and private airlines fly around the Middle East.

Of the national airlines, when it comes to service, punctuality and safety, El Al (Israel), Royal Jordanian, Turkish Airlines and Middle East Airlines (Lebanon) are probably the pick of the bunch, while Iran Air and Syrianair have reasonably solid if unspectacular reputations. Libyan Arab Airlines will get you from A to B but not much else and don't expect to arrive on time, while EgyptAir is probably best avoided.

Many of the private airlines that now operate – including Afriqiyah Airways, Mahan Air and Iran Aseman – connect Middle Eastern capitals and provincial centres to cities beyond the Middle East that are not covered by national airlines.

For a full list of airlines flying to and from the Middle East, see p657. Many of these airlines also fly domestically within the Middle East.

Some others:

Al-Buraq (☎ 021-4444811; www.buraqair.com; Libya) Connects Tripoli to Benghazi, Damascus and Aleppo.

Arkia (☎ 03-699 2222; www.arkia.co.il; Israel) Connects Tel Aviv, Eilat and Haifa and has international charters to Jerusalem.

Atlasjet (☎ 0216-444 0387; www.atlasjet.com; Turkey) Domestic Turkish services.

Fly Air (☎ 0212-444 4359; www.flyair.com.tr; Turkey) Flights within Turkey.

Israir (☎ 03-795 5777; www.israir.co.il; Israel) Connects Tel Aviv, Eilat and Haifa.

Onur Air (☎ 0212-662 9797; www.onurair.com.tr; Turkey) Extensive domestic flights within Turkey.

Detailed information on all airlines' safety records (including reams of statistics) can be found at http://www.airsafe.com/index .html.

Air Passes

Emirates (www.emirates.com) offers the 'Arabian Airpass' that allows cut-price travel around the Middle East. To qualify you need to buy a flight to Dubai. Onward flight 'coupons' (a minimum of two, maximum of six) are then available to cities such as Cairo, Amman, Beirut, Damascus or Tehran. The coupons are valid for three months from when the first coupon is redeemed. Prices are based upon zones, with the above cities coming within Zone 3 (US$120).

BICYCLE

Although the numbers doing it are small, cycling round the Middle East is a viable proposition, provided that cyclists are self-sufficient and able to carry litres of extra water.

Most of the people we spoke to reckoned that the most enjoyable cycling was in Turkey and Syria (this is backed up by letters from readers). Although hilly, the scenery in Turkey is particularly fine and accommodation is fairly easy to come by, even in the smallest villages. This is definitely not the case elsewhere, and in Syria in particular you have to expect to spend the odd night in a tent. In Turkey if you get tired of pedalling it's also no problem to have your bike transported in the luggage hold of the big modern buses.

One big plus about cycling through the region is the fact that cyclists are usually given fantastic welcomes – a trademark of the Middle East anyway – showered with food and drink. Cyclists in Syria frequently receive invitations from people along the way to come home, meet the family, eat and stay over. Even the police are helpful and friendly. There are a couple of exceptions – along Jordan's King's Hwy and in Sinai kids

---

CYCLING CONTACTS

If you're considering cycling in the Middle East, but have a few pressing questions that first need answering, you can post your query on the Thorn Tree on Lonely Planet's website (www.lonelyplanet.com) under the Activities branch. There's a strong likelihood somebody will respond with the information that you're looking for.

Alternatively, you could contact the **Cyclists' Touring Club** (CTC; ☎ 01483-417 217; www.ctc.org.uk), a UK-based organisation that offers good tips and information sheets on cycling in different parts of the world; the website itself is quite useful.

throw stones at cyclists (maybe because of the cycling shorts, we don't know) – but these are minor blips of annoyance.

Aside from such isolated cases, by far the major difficulty cited by all cyclists was the heat. This is at its worst from June to August and cycling in these summer months is definitely not recommended. May to mid-June and September through October are the best times. Even then you're advised to make an early morning start and call it a day by early afternoon.

There are bicycle repair shops in most major towns and the locals are excellent 'bush mechanics' with all but the most modern or sophisticated equipment.

The following additional tips may help:

- Carry a couple of extra chain links, a chain breaker, spokes, a spoke key, two inner tubes, tyre levers and a repair kit, a flat-head and Phillips-head screwdriver, and Allen keys and spanners to fit all the bolts on your bike.
- Check the bolts daily and carry spares.
- Fit as many water bottles to your bike as you can – it gets hot.
- Make sure the bike's gearing will get you over the hills.
- Confine your panniers to a maximum weight of 15kg.
- Carrying the following equipment in your panniers is recommended: a two-person tent (weighing about 1.8kg) that can also accommodate the bike where security is a concern; a sleeping bag rated to 0°C and an inflatable mattress; a small camping stove; cooking pot; utensils; a water filter (two microns) and a compact torch.
- Wear cycling shorts with a chamois bum and cleated cycling shoes.
- Don't worry about filling the panniers with food as it is plentiful and fresh along the route.

BOAT

Practicality is the essence of Middle East ferry services, not luxury. Even in 1st class you shouldn't expect your voyage to be a pleasure cruise, while deck class often means just that. In summer conditions may be a little too hot for many people. While food and drink of some sort may be available on board, many passengers prefer to take their own.

Vehicles can usually be shipped on the services listed below, but advance arrangements may have to be made. For the latest information, get in touch with the head office or local agency of the respective company some time in advance.

Two ferry services operate between Nuweiba in Egypt and Aqaba in Jordan. The fast-ferry service from Egypt (adult/child US$55/39) takes one hour, while the slow ferry (adult/child US$41/29) makes the journey in 2½ to three hours. From Jordan, the adult prices for the fast/slow ferry are US$36/25.

There is also, in theory at least, a twice-weekly catamaran trip between Aqaba and Sharm el-Sheikh (officially US$45, three hours), but this wasn't operating at the time of research.

For more information on these ferry services, see p406 and p177.

BUS

Buses are the most reliable, comfortable and (for longer journeys, at least) popular means of land transport in the Middle East. Throughout most of the region buses will take you to almost anywhere of any size; on many routes there may be no other form of public transport.

The cost and comfort of bus travel vary enormously throughout the region. One most typical nuisance, however, is the Middle Eastern bus drivers' fondness for loud videos (a fondness presumably shared by local passengers); sleep is almost always impossible. Another potential source of discomfort is that in most Middle Eastern countries the concept of a 'nonsmoking bus' is that these are things that other regions have.

Most Middle Eastern countries can be reached by taking a direct international bus from other parts of the region. For example, Damascus has several daily bus services to İstanbul (30 hours), Ankara (14 hours), Beirut (four hours) and Amman (seven hours), while Aleppo also has daily services to İstanbul (22 hours), Ankara (10 hours) and Beirut (six to seven hours). From Tehran, there are regular services to Ankara (28 hours), İstanbul (35 hours) and twice-weekly services to Damascus. From Amman it's also possible to travel to the King Hussein Bridge (for Israel and the

Palestinian Territories; 45 minutes), Cairo (a daily bus-ferry combination; 16 hours) or even Baghdad (14 hours), although the latter journey is chronically unsafe. There are also services from Cairo to Jerusalem and from Cairo to Tel Aviv via Sinai (at least 10 hours).

For further details of these services see the Getting There & Away sections of the relevant cities and the Transport sections of the individual country chapters.

Even in those countries without any international bus services it's usually possible to get to at least one neighbouring country by using domestic services, making your own way across the border and picking up another domestic service or taxi in the next country. This method is usually cheaper and it avoids one of the big problems of international services: waiting for the vehicle to clear customs at each border, which can mean delays of several hours. However, if you're planning on using domestic buses make sure that there will be onward transport on the other side of the border.

Reservations
It's always advisable to book bus seats in advance at the bus station, which is usually the only ticket outlet and source of reliable information about current services. Reservations are a must over the Muslim weekend (Friday) as well as during public holidays (see p647).

CAR & MOTORCYCLE
Bringing your own car to the Middle East will give you a lot more freedom but it's certainly not for everyone. For more information on the paperwork required for bringing your vehicle to the Middle East, see p662.

Throughout the Middle East, motorcycles are fairly popular as a means of racing around in urban areas, but they are little used as long-distance transport. If you do decide to ride a motorcycle through the Middle East, try to take one of the more popular Japanese models if you want to stand any chance of finding spare parts. Even then, make sure your motorcycle is in very good shape before setting out. Motorcycles can be shipped or, often, loaded as luggage on to trains.

Bring Your Own Vehicle
The advantages of having your own vehicle are many:
- You aren't tied to schedules.
- You can choose your own company, set your own pace, take the scenic route, declare your vehicle a smoking or non-smoking zone and you won't be at the mercy of dishonest taxi drivers or have to fight for a place on a bus.
- You can avoid all the hassles that go with carrying your world on your back.
- Fuel is much cheaper than at home.

That said, it's difficult to imagine a route through the Middle East that would justify the expense and hassle of bringing a car and getting it out again. Indeed, for the vast majority of short-term visitors to the Middle East, the advantages of being attached to one vehicle are far outweighed by the disadvantages. Primary among these are:
- The expense of getting hold of a carnet de passage.
- The often hair-raising driving in unfamiliar territory.
- The variability in the quality of the roads themselves.
- The sheer distance to travel between places of interest.
- The mountains of paperwork and red tape before you leave home – documents usually take a month or more to obtain, and just finding out the current regulations can be difficult. It's best to get in touch with your automobile association (eg AA or RAC in the UK) at least three months in advance.
- The millstone-around-the-neck worry of serious accident, breakdown or theft.
- The difficulty of establishing a feasible route through the Middle East. This can be hard enough if you're relying on public transport, but at least there's nearly always the alternative of flying if a particular overland route proves too difficult or dangerous. This is hardly an option if you have a car with you, and air freighting even a motorcycle isn't cheap. Selling or dumping a temporarily imported vehicle in the Middle East is more or less ruled out by customs regulations.

To circumvent the latter disadvantage, it's at least theoretically possible to have your car put under customs seal in one country and to return for it later, but this is a hassle to arrange, requires backtracking and somewhat negates the point of bringing a vehicle in the first place. Car ferries can get around some of these problems, but shipping a car isn't cheap, often requires an advance booking and won't help you out in every eventuality. Note that the rules and conventions covered here may not apply if you stay more than three months in any one country, or if you're going for any purpose other than tourism.

Driving Licence

If you plan to drive, get an IDP from your local automobile association. An IDP is compulsory for foreign drivers and motorcyclists in Egypt, Iran, Iraq and Syria. Most foreign (or national) licences are acceptable in Israel and the Palestinian Territories, Lebanon, Libya and Turkey, and for foreign-registered vehicles in Jordan. However, even in these places an IDP is recommended. IDPs are valid for one year only.

Fuel & Spare Parts

Mechanical failure can be a problem as spare parts — or at least official ones – are often unobtainable. Fear not, ingenuity often compensates for factory parts; your mechanic back home will either have a heart attack or learn new techniques when you show them what's gone on under your hood in the Middle East.

Generally, Land Rovers, Volkswagens, Range Rovers, Mercedes and Chevrolets are the cars for which spare parts are most likely to be available, although in recent years Japan has been a particularly vigorous exporter of vehicles to the Middle East. In countries such as Iran, Syria and Iraq, spare parts for US vehicles may be very hard to find. One tip is to ask your vehicle manufacturer for a list of any authorised service centres it has in the countries you plan to visit. The length of this is likely to be a pretty good reflection of how easy it is to get spare parts on your travels.

Usually two grades of petrol are available; if in doubt get the more expensive one. Petrol stations are few and far between on many desert roads. Away from the main towns, it's advisable to fill up whenever you get the chance. Locally produced maps often indicate the locations of petrol stations. Diesel isn't readily available in every Middle Eastern country, nor is unleaded petrol. On the plus side, petrol is wonderfully cheap in many countries, especially Iran and Libya.

Hire

Car hire is possible in all Middle Eastern countries, and international hire companies such as **Hertz** (www.hertz.com), **Avis** (www.avis.com) and **Europcar** (www.europcar.com) are represented in many large towns. Local companies are usually cheaper, but the cars of international companies are often better maintained and come with a better back-up service if problems arise. Local companies (eg those offering 4WD vehicles in Libya) sometimes carry the advantage of including a driver for a similar cost to hiring the car alone. A good place to find competitive rates is **Imakoo Cars** (www.imakoocars.co.uk/directory-in.php/middle-east/), a clearing house for cheap rates of international companies with services in Lebanon, Turkey, Israel and the Palestinian Territories, Jordan, Syria, Iran and Iraq.

Reputable tour agencies can also be a good source of cars, offering competitive rates, decent cars and often a driver thrown in for little extra – usually the best option for short-term travellers. Some agencies can arrange vans, minibuses and buses for groups, but most deal only in cars; very few rent out motorcycles or bicycles.

To hire a car, you'll need any or all of the following: a photocopy of your passport and visa; deposit or credit card imprint; and your driving licence or IDP. The minimum age varies between 21 and 25; the latter is most common, particularly with international companies.

Always make sure whether insurance is included in the hire price, familiarise yourself with the policy, and don't hire a car unless it's insured for every eventuality.

Before hiring a self-drive vehicle, ask yourself seriously how well you think you can cope with the local driving conditions and whether you know your way around well enough to make good use of one. Also compare the cost with that of hiring a taxi for the same period.

Insurance

Insurance is compulsory in most Middle Eastern countries, apart from being highly advisable. Given the large number of minor accidents, not to mention major ones, fully comprehensive insurance (as opposed to third-party) is strongly advised, both for your own and any hire vehicle. Car-hire companies customarily supply insurance, but check the cover and conditions carefully.

Make certain that you're covered for off-piste travel, as well as travel between Middle Eastern countries (if you're planning cross-border excursions). A locally acquired motorcycle licence is not valid under some policies.

In the event of an accident, make sure you submit the accident report as soon as possible to the insurance company or, if hiring, the car-hire company.

Road Conditions

The main roads are good or at least reasonable in most parts of the Middle East, but there are plenty of unsurfaced roads and the international roads are generally narrow and crowded. Conditions across the Middle East vary enormously, but in almost all cases, they'll be worse than you're used to back home. Turkey, Jordan and Israel and the Palestinian Territories probably have the best roads, but those in Iran, Lebanon, Syria and Libya adhere to the following rule: worse than they should be but probably better than you'd expect. Some of Egypt's roads are fine; others are bone-jarringly bad.

Road Hazards

One of your enduring (and hopefully not too painful) memories of the Middle East will undoubtedly be the driving standards: the driving is appalling by Western norms. Fatalism and high speed rule supreme. Many regulations are, in practice, purely cautionary. Car horns, used at the slightest provocation, take the place of caution and courtesy. Except in well-lit urban areas, try to avoid driving at night, as you may find your vehicle is the only thing on the road with lights.

In desert regions, particularly in Egypt and Libya, beware of wind-blown sand and wandering, free-range camels; the latter can be deadly at night.

Remember that an accident in the more remote parts of the region isn't always handled by your friendly insurance company. 'An eye for an eye' is likely to be the guiding principle of the other party and their relatives, whether you're in the wrong or not. Don't hang around to ask questions or gawp. Of course we're not saying that you shouldn't report an accident, but it may be more prudent to head for the nearest police station than to wait at the scene.

Road Rules

You're unlikely even to know what the speed limit is on a particular road, let alone be forced to keep to it – the rules exist more in theory than they are enforced in reality. As a rule only non–Middle Easterners wear motorcycle helmets or car safety belts in most countries of the region, but that doesn't mean you shouldn't if one is available.

A warning triangle is required for vehicles (except motorcycles) in most Middle Eastern countries; in Turkey two triangles and a first-aid kit are compulsory.

In all countries, driving is on the right-hand side of the road (although many motorcyclists seem to consider themselves exempt from this convention) and the rules of when to give way (at least officially) are those which apply in Continental Europe.

HITCHING

Although many travellers hitchhike, it is never an entirely safe way of getting around and those who do so should understand that they are taking a small but potentially serious risk. There is no part of the Middle East where hitching can be recommended for unaccompanied women travellers. Just because we explain how hitching works doesn't mean we recommend you do it.

Hitching as commonly understood in the West hardly exists in the Middle East (except Israel and the Palestinian Territories). Although in most countries you'll often see people standing by the road hoping for a lift, they will nearly always expect (and be expected) to offer to pay. Hitching in the Middle Eastern sense is not so much an alternative to the public transport system as an extension of it, particularly in areas where there is no regular public transport. The going rate is often roughly the equivalent of the bus or shared taxi fare, but may be more if a driver takes you to an address or place off their route. You may well be offered free lifts from time to time, but you won't get very far if you set out deliberately to avoid paying for transport.

Hitching is not illegal in any Middle Eastern country and in many places it is extremely common. However, while it's quite normal for Middle Easterners, Asians and Africans, it isn't something Westerners are expected to do. In many Middle Eastern countries, Westerners who try to set a precedent of any kind often attract considerable (and sometimes unwelcome) attention. While this can work to your advantage, it can also lead to suspicion from the local police.

Throughout the Middle East a raised thumb is a vaguely obscene gesture. A common way of signalling that you want a lift is to extend your right hand, palm down.

TRAIN

No Middle Eastern country has an extensive railway network and there are few international services. Most railway lines in the region were built primarily for strategic or economic reasons, and many are either no longer in use or only carry freight. However, where there is a choice (such as in Iran and Egypt) the trains are usually much more comfortable than the buses and compare favourably in price. On the other hand, they are less frequent and usually slower, while many stations are some distance out of the town centres they serve.

In general, tickets are only sold at the station and reservations are either compulsory or highly recommended.

The only functioning international passenger services within the region travel between the following cities:

Amman–Damascus A twice-weekly train connects the capitals of Jordan and Syria. It's a slow diesel train with ancient carriages – see p406 and p522 for further details.

Damascus–İstanbul There is a once-weekly service between these cities (via Aleppo) – see p543 and p635 for details.

Tehran–Damascus The Tehran–İstanbul train splits at Van and carriages divert to Damascus – see p251 and p634 for further details.

Tehran–İstanbul This is a weekly train running via Sero, the border and Ankara – see p251 and p634 for more information.

LOCAL TRANSPORT
Bus

In most cities and towns, a minibus or bus service operates. Fares are very cheap, fast, regular and run on fixed routes with, in some cases, fixed stops. However, unless you're very familiar with the town, they can be difficult to get to grips with (few display their destinations and fewer still do so in English and they are often very crowded). Unless you can find an English-speaking local to help you out, your best bet is to stand along the footpath of a major thoroughfare heading in the direction you want to go and call out the local name (or the name of a landmark close to where you're heading) into the drivers' windows when they slow down.

Few countries have public minibuses to/ from the airport, but top-end hotels and travel agencies (if you're taking a tour) can usually send a complimentary minibus if they're given sufficient advance notice.

Taxi

In the West, taxis are usually considered a luxury. In the Middle East they are often unavoidable. Some cities have no other form of urban public transport, while there are also many rural routes that are only feasible in a taxi or private vehicle.

Taxis are seemingly everywhere you look and, if you can't see one, try lingering on the footpath next to a major road and one will soon find you. Within no time, plenty of taxis will appear as if from nowhere and will soon toot their horns at you just in case you missed them, even if you're just trying to cross the street.

The way in which taxis operate varies widely from country to country, and often even from place to place within a country. So does the price. Different types of taxis are painted or marked in different ways, or known by different names, but, often, local people talking to foreigners in English will just use the blanket term 'taxi.' If you want to save money, it's important to be able to differentiate between the various kinds.

Details of local peculiarities are given in the Getting Around sections at the end of the country chapters.

REGULAR TAXI

Regular taxis (variously known as 'agency taxis', 'telephone taxis', 'private taxis' or 'special taxis') are found in almost every Middle Eastern town or city. Unlike shared taxis, you pay to have the taxi to yourself, either to take you to a preagreed destination or for a specified period of time. In some

TIPS FOR CATCHING TAXIS

On the whole, taxi drivers in the Middle East are helpful, honest and often humorous. Others – as in countries all over the world – find new arrivals too tempting a target for minor scams or a spot of overcharging. Here are a few tips:

- Not all taxi drivers speak English. Generally, in cities used to international travellers they will (or know enough to get by), but not otherwise. If you're having trouble, ask a local for help.
- Always negotiate a fare (or insist that the meter is used if it works) before jumping in. Town taxis occasionally have meters, which sometimes work and are even used from time to time. This book quotes local rates but, if in doubt, inquire at your point of departure.
- Don't rely on street names (there are often several versions and the driver may recognise your pronunciation of none of them). If you're going to a well-known destination (such as a big hotel), find out if it's close to a local landmark (check the Lonely Planet map if there is one) and give the driver the local name for the landmark. Even better, get someone to write down the name in Arabic or whatever the local language is.
- Make sure you're dropped off at the right place.
- Avoid using unlicensed cab drivers at airports.

places there's no other public transport, but in most, regular taxis exist alongside less expensive means of getting around (although these usually shut down overnight). They are primarily of use for transport within towns or on short rural trips, but in some countries hiring them for excursions of several hours is still cheap. They are also often the only way of reaching airports or seaports.

SHARED TAXI

A compromise between the convenience of a regular taxi and the economy of a bus, the shared taxi – the workhorse of the Middle Eastern road – picks up and drops off passengers at points along its (generally fixed) route and runs to no particular schedule. It's known by different names – collect, collective or service taxi in English, *servees* in Arabic, *sherut* in Hebrew, *dolmuş* in Turkish and just *taksī* in Farsi (Persian). Most shared taxis take up to four or five passengers, but some seat up to about 12 and are indistinguishable for most purposes from minibuses.

Shared taxis are much cheaper than private taxis and, once you get the hang of them, can be just as convenient. They are dearer than buses, but more frequent and usually faster, because they don't stop so often or for so long. They also tend to operate for longer hours than buses. They can be

used for urban, intercity or rural transport, but not necessarily all three in a particular place.

Fixed-route taxis wait at the point of departure until full or nearly full. Usually they pick up or drop off passengers anywhere en route, but in some places they have fixed halts or stations. Sometimes each service is allocated a number, which may be indicated on the vehicle. Generally, a flat fare applies for each route, but sometimes it's possible to pay a partial fare.

Shared taxis without routes are supreme examples of market forces at work. If the price is right you'll quickly find a taxi willing to take you almost anywhere, but if you're prepared to wait a while, or to do your journey in stages, you can get around for almost nothing. Fares depend largely on time and distance, but can also vary slightly according to demand.

Beware of boarding an empty one, as the driver may assume you want to hire the vehicle for your exclusive use and charge you accordingly. It's advisable to watch what other passengers pay and to hand over your fare in front of them. Passengers are expected to know where they are getting off. 'Thank you' in the local language is the usual cue for the driver to stop. Make it clear to the driver or other passengers if you want to be told when you reach your destination.

Health

CONTENTS

Prevention is the key to staying healthy while travelling in the Middle East. Infectious diseases can and do occur in the Middle East, but these are usually associated with poor living conditions and poverty and can be avoided with a few precautions. The most common reason for travellers needing medical help is as a result of accidents – cars are not always well maintained and poorly lit roads are littered with potholes. Medical facilities can be excellent in large cities, but in remoter areas may be more basic.

BEFORE YOU GO

A little planning before departure, particularly for pre-existing illnesses, will save you a lot of trouble later. See your dentist before a long trip; carry a spare pair of contact lenses and glasses (and take your optical prescription); and carry a first-aid kit with you.

It's tempting to leave it all to the last minute – don't! Many vaccines don't ensure immunity for two weeks, so visit a doctor four to eight weeks before departure. Ask your doctor for an International Certificate of Vaccination (otherwise known as the yellow booklet), which will list all the vaccinations you've received. This is mandatory for countries that require proof of yellow fever vaccination upon entry, but it's a good idea to carry it wherever you travel.

Travellers can register with the **International Association for Medical Advice to Travellers** (IMAT; www.iamat.org). Its website can help travellers to find a doctor with recognised training. Those heading off to very remote areas may like to do a first-aid course, (Red Cross and St John Ambulance can help) or attend a remote medicine first-aid course, such as those offered by the **Royal Geographical Society** (www.rgs.org).

Bring medications in their original, clearly labelled containers. A signed and dated letter from your physician describing your medical conditions and medications, including generic names, is also a good idea. If carrying syringes or needles, be sure to have a physician's letter documenting their medical necessity.

INSURANCE

Find out in advance if your insurance plan will make payments directly to providers or reimburse you later for overseas health expenditures (in many Middle Eastern countries doctors expect payment in cash). It's also worth ensuring that your travel insurance will cover repatriation home or to better medical facilities elsewhere. Your insurance company may be able to locate the nearest source of medical help, or you can ask at your hotel. In an emergency, contact your embassy or consulate. Your travel insurance will not usually cover you for anything other than emergency dental treatment. Not all insurance covers emergency aeromedical evacuation home or to a hospital in a major city, which may be the only way to get medical attention for a serious emergency.

RECOMMENDED VACCINATIONS

The World Health Organization (WHO) recommends that all travellers, regardless of the region they are travelling in, should be covered for diphtheria, tetanus, measles, mumps, rubella and polio, as well as hepatitis B. While making preparations to travel, take the opportunity to ensure that all of your routine vaccination cover is complete.

The consequences of these diseases can be severe and outbreaks do occur in the Middle East.

MEDICAL CHECKLIST

Following is a list of other items you should consider packing in your medical kit.

- antibiotics (if travelling off the beaten track)
- antidiarrhoeal drugs (eg loperamide)
- acetaminophen/paracetamol (eg Tylenol) or aspirin
- anti-inflammatory drugs (eg ibuprofen)
- antihistamines (for hay fever and allergic reactions)
- antibacterial ointment (eg Bactroban) for cuts and abrasions
- steroid cream or cortisone (allergic rashes)
- bandages, gauze, gauze rolls
- adhesive or paper tape
- scissors, safety pins, tweezers
- thermometer
- pocket knife
- DEET-containing insect repellent for the skin
- permethrin-containing insect spray for clothing, tents and bed nets
- sun block
- oral-rehydration salts
- iodine tablets (for water purification)
- syringes and sterile needles (if travelling to remote areas)

INTERNET RESOURCES

There is a wealth of travel health advice on the Internet. For further information, the website of **Lonely Planet** (www.lonelyplanet.com) is a good place to start. The **WHO** (www.who.int /ith/) publishes a superb book, *International Travel and Health*, which is revised annually and is available online at no cost.

TRAVEL HEALTH WEBSITES

It's usually a good idea to consult your government's travel health website before departure, if one is available.
Australia (www.dfat.gov.au/travel/)
Canada (http://www.hc-sc.gc.ca/english/index .html)
United Kingdom (www.doh.gov.uk/travel advice/)
United States (www.cdc.gov/travel/)

Another website of general interest is **MD Travel Health** (www.mdtravelhealth.com), which provides complete travel health recommendations for every country, updated daily, also at no cost. The website of the **Centers for Disease Control & Prevention** (www.cdc.gov) is a very useful source of traveller health information.

FURTHER READING

Recommended references include *Traveller's Health* by Dr Richard Dawood (Oxford University Press), *International Travel Health Guide* by Stuart R Rose, MD (Travel Medicine Inc), and *The Travellers' Good Health Guide* by Ted Lankester (Sheldon Press), an especially useful health guide for volunteers and long-term expatriates working in the Middle East.

IN TRANSIT

DEEP VEIN THROMBOSIS (DVT)

Deep vein thrombosis occurs when blood clots form in the legs during plane flights, chiefly due to prolonged immobility. The longer the flight, the greater the risk. Most blood clots are reabsorbed uneventfully, but some may break off and travel through the blood vessels to the lungs, where they may cause life-threatening complications.

The chief symptom of DVT is swelling or pain of the foot, ankle or calf, usually but not always on just one side. When a blood clot travels to the lungs, it may cause chest pain and difficulty breathing. Travellers with any of these symptoms should immediately seek medical attention.

To prevent the development of DVT on long flights you should walk about the cabin, perform isometric compressions of the leg muscles (ie contract the leg muscles while sitting), drink plenty of fluids, and avoid alcohol and tobacco.

JET LAG & MOTION SICKNESS

Jet lag is common when crossing more than five time zones, and results in insomnia, fatigue, malaise or nausea. To avoid jet lag try drinking plenty of fluids (nonalcoholic) and eating light meals. Upon arrival, seek exposure to natural sunlight and readjust your schedule (for meals, sleep etc) as soon as possible.

Antihistamines such as dimenhydrinate (Dramamine) and meclizine (Antivert, Bonine) are usually the first choice for treating motion sickness. Their main side-effect is drowsiness. A herbal alternative is ginger, which works like a charm for some people.

IN THE MIDDLE EAST

AVAILABILITY & COST OF HEALTH CARE

The health care systems in the Middle East are varied. Medical care can be excellent in Israel, with well trained doctors and nurses, but can be patchier elsewhere. Reciprocal arrangements with countries rarely exist and you should be prepared to pay for all medical and dental treatment.

Medical care is not always readily available outside major cities. Medicine, and even sterile dressings or intravenous fluids, may need to be bought from a local pharmacy. Nursing care may be limited or rudimentary as this is something families and friends are expected to provide. The travel assistance provided by your insurance may be able to locate the nearest source of medical help, otherwise ask at your hotel. In an emergency, contact your embassy or consulate. Also see Medical Services in the Information section of the capital city in each country chapter.

Standards of dental care are variable and there is an increased risk of hepatitis B and HIV transmission via poorly sterilised equipment. And keep in mind that your travel insurance will not usually cover you for anything other than emergency dental treatment.

For minor illnesses such as diarrhoea, pharmacists can often provide valuable advice and sell over-the-counter medication. They can also advise when more specialised help is needed.

INFECTIOUS DISEASES

Diphtheria

Diphtheria is spread through close respiratory contact. It causes a high temperature and severe sore throat. Sometimes a membrane forms across the throat requiring a tracheostomy to prevent suffocation. Vaccination is recommended for those likely to be in close contact with the local population in infected areas. The vaccine is given as an injection alone, or with tetanus, and lasts 10 years.

Hepatitis A

Hepatitis A is spread through contaminated food (particularly shellfish) and water. It causes jaundice, and although it is rarely fatal, can cause prolonged lethargy and delayed recovery. Symptoms include dark urine, a yellow colour to the whites of the eyes, fever and abdominal pain. Hepatitis A vaccine (Avaxim, VAQTA, Havrix) is given as an injection: a single dose will give protection for up to a year, while a booster 12 months later will provide a subsequent 10 years of protection. Hepatitis A and typhoid vaccines can also be given as a single dose vaccine (hepatyrix or viatim).

Hepatitis B

Infected blood, contaminated needles and sexual intercourse can all transmit hepatitis B. It can cause jaundice, and affects the liver, occasionally causing liver failure. All travellers should make this a routine vaccination. (Many countries now give hepatitis B vaccination as part of routine childhood vaccination.) The vaccine is given singly, or at the same time as the hepatitis A vaccine (hepatyrix). A course will give protection for at least five years, and can be given over four weeks or six months.

HIV

Countries in the Middle East covered by this book that require a negative HIV test as a visa requirement for some categories of visas include Egypt, Iran, Iraq, Jordan, Lebanon and Libya.

Leishmaniasis

Spread through the bite of an infected sand fly, leishmaniasis can cause a slowly growing skin lump or ulcer. It may develop into a serious life-threatening fever usually accompanied by anaemia and weight loss. Infected dogs are also carriers of the infection. Sand fly bites should be avoided whenever possible. Leishmaniasis is present in Iran, Iraq, Israel and the Palestinian Territories, Jordan, Lebanon, Syria and Turkey.

Leptospirosis

Leptospirosis is spread through the excreta of infected rodents, especially rats. It can

HEALTH

cause hepatitis and renal failure that may be fatal. It is unusual for travellers to be affected unless living in poor sanitary conditions; the greatest risk is in Turkey. It causes a fever and jaundice.

Malaria
The prevalence of malaria varies throughout the Middle East. Many areas are considered to be malaria free, while others have seasonal risks. The risk of malaria is minimal in most cities; however, check with your doctor if you are considering travelling to any rural areas. It is important to take antimalarial tablets if the risk is significant. For up-to-date information about the risk of contracting malaria in a specific country, contact your local travel health clinic.

Anyone who has travelled in a country where malaria is present should be aware of the symptoms of malaria. It is possible to contract malaria from a single bite from an infected mosquito. Malaria almost always starts with marked shivering, fever and sweating. Muscle pains, headache and vomiting are common. Symptoms may occur anywhere from a few days to three weeks after the infected mosquito bite. The illness can start while you are taking preventative tablets if they are not fully effective, and may also occur after you have finished taking your tablets.

Poliomyelitis
Generally spread through contaminated food and water, polio is present, though rare, throughout the Middle East. It is one of the vaccines given in childhood and should be boosted every 10 years, either orally (a drop on the tongue), or as an injection. Polio may be carried asymptomatically, although it can cause a transient fever and, in rare cases, potentially permanent muscle weakness or paralysis.

Rabies
Spread through bites or licks on broken skin from an infected animal, rabies (present in all countries of the Middle East) is fatal. Animal handlers should be vaccinated, as should those travelling to remote areas where a reliable source of postbite vaccine is not available within 24 hours. Three injections are needed over a month. If you have not been vaccinated you will need a course of five injections starting within 24 hours or as soon as possible after the injury. Vaccination does not provide you with immunity, it merely buys you more time to seek appropriate medical help.

Rift Valley Fever
This haemorrhagic fever, which is found in Egypt, is spread through blood or blood products, including those from infected animals. It causes a 'flu-like' illness with fever, joint pains and occasionally more serious complications. Complete recovery is possible.

Schistosomiasis
Otherwise known as bilharzia, this is spread through the freshwater snail. It causes infection of the bowel and bladder, often with bleeding. It is caused by a fluke and is contracted through the skin from water contaminated with human urine or faeces. Paddling or swimming in suspect freshwater lakes or slow running rivers should be avoided. There may be no symptoms. Possible symptoms include a transient fever and rash, and advanced cases of bilharzia may cause blood in the stool or in the urine. A blood test can detect antibodies if you have been exposed and treatment is then possible in specialist travel or infectious disease clinics. Be especially careful in Egypt, Iraq and Syria.

Tuberculosis (TB)
Tuberculosis is spread through close respiratory contact and occasionally through infected milk or milk products. BCG vaccine is recommended for those likely to be mixing closely with the local population. It is more important for those visiting family or planning on a long stay, and those employed as teachers and health-care workers. TB can be asymptomatic, although symptoms can include coughing, weight loss or fever months or even years after exposure. An X-ray is the best way to confirm if you have TB. BCG gives a moderate degree of protection against TB. It causes a small permanent scar at the site of injection, and is usually only given in specialised chest clinics. As it's a live vaccine it should not be given to pregnant women or immunocompromised individuals. The BCG vaccine is not available in all countries.

Typhoid

Typhoid is spread through food or water that has been contaminated by infected human faeces. The first symptom is usually fever or a pink rash on the abdomen. Septicaemia (blood poisoning) may also occur. Typhoid vaccine (typhim Vi, typherix) will give protection for three years. In some countries, the oral vaccine Vivotif is also available.

Yellow Fever

Yellow fever vaccination is not required for any areas of the Middle East. However, the mosquito that spreads yellow fever has been known to be present in some parts of the Middle East. It is important to consult your local travel health clinic as part of your predeparture plans for the latest details. For this reason, any travellers from a yellow fever endemic area will need to show proof of vaccination against yellow fever before entry. This normally means if arriving directly from an infected country or if the traveller has been in an infected country during the last 10 days. We would recommend, however, that travellers carry a certificate if they have been in an infected country during the previous month to avoid any possible difficulties with immigration. There is always the possibility that a traveller without an up-to-date certificate will be vaccinated and detained in isolation at the port of arrival for up to 10 days, or even repatriated. The yellow fever vaccination must be given at a designated clinic, and is valid for 10 years. It is a live vaccine and must not be given to immunocompromised or pregnant travellers.

TRAVELLER'S DIARRHOEA

To prevent diarrhoea, avoid tap water unless it has been boiled, filtered or chemically disinfected (with iodine tablets). Eat only fresh fruits or vegetables if cooked or if you have peeled them yourself and avoid dairy products that may contain unpasteurised milk. Buffet meals are risky, as food should be piping hot; meals freshly cooked in front of you in a busy restaurant are more likely to be safe.

If you develop diarrhoea, be sure to drink plenty of fluids, preferably an oral rehydration solution containing salt and sugar. A few loose stools don't require treatment but, if you start having more than four or five stools a day, you should start taking an antibiotic (usually a quinolone drug) and an antidiarrhoeal agent (such as loperamide). If diarrhoea is bloody, persists for more than 72 hours, is accompanied by fever, shaking chills or severe abdominal pain you should seek medical attention.

ENVIRONMENTAL HAZARDS

Heat Illness

Heat exhaustion occurs after heavy sweating and excessive fluid loss with inadequate replacement of fluids and salt. It is particularly common in hot climates when taking unaccustomed exercise before full acclimatisation. Symptoms include headache, dizziness and tiredness. Dehydration is already happening by the time you feel thirsty – aim to drink sufficient water so that you produce pale, diluted urine. The treatment of heat exhaustion consists of fluid replacement with water or fruit juice or both, and cooling by cold water and fans. The treatment of the salt-loss component consists of salty fluids as in soup or broth, and adding a little more table salt to foods than usual.

Heat stroke is much more serious. This occurs when the heat-regulating mechanism in the body breaks down. An excessive rise in body temperature leads to sweating ceasing, irrational and hyperactive behaviour, and eventually loss of consciousness and death. Rapid cooling by spraying the body with water and fanning is an ideal treatment. Emergency fluid and electrolyte replacement by intravenous drip is usually also required.

Insect Bites & Stings

Mosquitoes may not carry malaria but can cause irritation and infected bites. Using DEET-based insect repellents will prevent bites. Mosquitoes also spread dengue fever.

Bees and wasps only cause real problems to those with a severe allergy (anaphylaxis). If you have a severe allergy to bee or wasp stings you should carry an adrenaline injection or similar.

Sand flies are located around the Mediterranean beaches. They usually only cause a nasty itchy bite but can carry a rare skin disorder called cutaneous leishmaniasis. Bites may be prevented by using DEET-based repellents.

HEALTH

Scorpions are frequently found in arid or dry climates. They can cause a painful bite, which is rarely life threatening.

Bed bugs are often found in hostels and cheap hotels. They lead to very itchy lumpy bites. Spraying the mattress with an appropriate insect killer will do a good job of getting rid of them.

Scabies are also frequently found in cheap accommodation. These tiny mites live in the skin, particularly between the fingers. They cause an intensely itchy rash. Scabies is easily treated with lotion available from pharmacies; people who you come into contact with also need treating to avoid spreading scabies between asymptomatic carriers.

Snake Bites

Do not walk barefoot or stick your hand into holes or cracks. Half of those bitten by venomous snakes are not actually injected with poison (envenomed). If bitten by a snake, do not panic. Immobilise the bitten limb with a splint (eg a stick) and apply a bandage over the site, firm pressure, similar to a bandage over a sprain. Do not apply a tourniquet, or cut or suck the bite. Get the victim to medical help as soon as possible so that antivenin can be given if necessary.

Water

Tap water is not safe to drink in the Middle East. Stick to bottled water, boil water for 10 minutes, or use water-purification tablets or a filter. Do not drink water from rivers or lakes; this may contain bacteria or viruses that can cause diarrhoea or vomiting.

TRAVELLING WITH CHILDREN

All travellers with children should know how to treat minor ailments and when to seek medical treatment. Make sure the children are up to date with routine vaccinations, and discuss possible travel vaccines well before departure as some vaccines are not suitable for children aged under one year.

In hot, moist climates any wound or break in the skin may lead to infection. The area should be cleaned and then kept dry and clean. Remember to avoid contaminated food and water. If your child is vomiting or experiencing diarrhoea, lost fluid and salts must be replaced. It may be helpful to take rehydration powders for

reconstituting with boiled water. Ask your doctor about this.

Children should be encouraged to avoid dogs or other mammals because of the risk of rabies and other diseases. Any bite, scratch or lick from a warm blooded, furry animal should immediately be thoroughly cleaned. If there is any possibility that the animal is infected with rabies, immediate medical assistance should be sought.

WOMEN'S HEALTH

Emotional stress, exhaustion and travelling through different time zones can all contribute to an upset in the menstrual pattern. If using oral contraceptives, remember some antibiotics, diarrhoea and vomiting can stop the pill from working and lead to the risk of pregnancy – remember to take condoms with you just in case. Condoms should be kept in a cool, dry place or they may crack and perish.

Emergency contraception is most effective if taken within 24 hours after unprotected sex. The **International Planned Parent Federation** (www.ippf.org) can advise about the availability of contraception in different countries. Tampons and sanitary towels are not always available outside of major cities in the Middle East.

Travelling during pregnancy is usually possible but there are important things to consider. Have a medical check-up before embarking on your trip. The most risky times for travel are during the first 12 weeks of pregnancy, when miscarriage is most likely, and after 30 weeks, when complications such as high blood pressure and premature delivery can occur. Most airlines will not accept a traveller after 28 to 32 weeks of pregnancy, and long-haul flights in the later stages can be very uncomfortable. Antenatal facilities vary greatly between countries in the Middle East and you should think carefully before travelling to a country with poor medical facilities or where there are major cultural and language differences from home. Taking written records of the pregnancy, including details of your blood group, are likely to be helpful if you need medical attention while away. Ensure your insurance policy covers pregnancy, delivery and postnatal care, but remember insurance policies are only as good as the facilities available.

Language

CONTENTS

ARABIC

Arabic is the official language of all Middle Eastern countries except Iran, Israel and Turkey. While English (and to a lesser extent, French – mainly in Lebanon and Syria) is widely spoken in the region, any effort to communicate with the locals in their own language will be well rewarded. No matter how far off the mark your pronunciation or grammar might be, you'll often get the response (usually with a big smile), 'Ah, you speak Arabic very well!'. Unlike English, the language is written from right to left, and it's a very good idea to at least familiarise yourself with the alphabet (p680).

Learning the basics for day-to-day travelling doesn't take long at all, but to master the complexities of Arabic would take years of constant study. In the absence of a viable phrasebook that encompasses all the varieties of spoken Arabic, Lonely Planet's *Egyptian Arabic Phrasebook* will prove very useful – depite its occasional limitations – thanks in no small way to the predominance of Egyptian TV programmes being broadcast throughout the Middle East.

TRANSLITERATION

It's worth noting here that transliterating from Arabic script into English is at best an approximate science. The presence of a number of sounds unknown in European languages, and the fact that the script is 'incomplete' (most vowel sounds are not written), combine to make it nearly impossible to settle on one method of transliteration. A wide variety of spellings are therefore possible for words when they appear in Roman script.

The matter is further complicated by the wide variety of dialects and the imaginative ideas Arabs themselves often have on appropriate spelling in, say, English. Words spelt one way in Egypt may look very different in Syria, which is heavily influenced by French. Not even the most venerable of Western Arabists have been able to come up with an ideal solution.

PRONUNCIATION

Pronunciation of Arabic can be tongue-tying for someone unfamiliar with the intonation and combination of sounds. Much of the vocabulary in this language guide would be universally understood throughout the Arab world, although some of it,

---

SPELLING THAT NAME

While we have tried to standardise all spellings in this book there are some instances in which flexibility seemed to be more appropriate than consistency. For example, if two alternative transliterations for the same thing exist in different countries, we may go with both if it's clear that these are the spellings any visitor to those countries will find on local maps and road signs.

Differences in spelling also arise through the same word having several variants in the different languages of the region – 'square' in Arabic is traditionally transliterated as *midan*, but in Turkish it's written *maydan* and in Persian *meidun* (or *meidun-é*; 'the square of'). Here lies great potential for confusion, as in the case with *hamam*, which is Turkish for the famed 'bathhouse', but Arabic for 'pigeon'; if you're looking for a good steam-cleaning, in Arabic you ask for a *hammam*, with the two syllables sounded distinctly.

We have also been forced to modify some spellings because of regional differences in Arabic pronunciation. The most obvious example of this occurs with the hard Egyptian sounding of the letter *jeem*, like the 'g' in 'gate', whereas elsewhere in the Arab world it's a softer 'j' as in 'jam' – hence we have used both *gadid* and *jadid* (new), and *gebel* and *jebel* (mountain).

THE STANDARD ARABIC ALPHABET

Final	Medial	Initial	Alone	Transliteration	Pronunciation
ا			ا	aa	as in 'father'
ب	ب	ب	ب	b	as in 'bet'
ت	ت	ت	ت	t	as in 'ten'
ث	ث	ث	ث	th	as in 'thin'
ج	ج	ج	ج	j (g/zh)	as in 'jet'; (g or as the 's' in 'measure' in Egypt)
ح	ح	ح	ح	H	a strongly whispered 'h', like a sigh of relief
خ	خ	خ	خ	kh	as the 'ch' in Scottish *loch*
د	د		د	d (z)	as in 'dim' (as z in Egypt)
ذ	ذ		ذ	dh	as the 'th' in 'this'; also as d or z
ر	ر		ر	r	a rolled 'r', as in the Spanish word *caro*
ز	ز		ز	z	as in 'zip'
س	س	س	س	s	as in 'so', never as in 'wisdom'
ش	ش	ش	ش	sh	as in 'ship'
ص	ص	ص	ص	ṣ	emphatic 's'
ض	ض	ض	ض	ḍ	emphatic 'd'
ط	ط	ط	ط	ṭ	emphatic 't'
ظ	ظ	ظ	ظ	ẓ	emphatic 'z'
ع	ع	ع	ع	'	the Arabic letter *'ayn*; pronounce as a glottal stop – like the closing of the throat before saying 'Oh-oh!' (see Other Sounds, p681)
غ	غ	غ	غ	gh	a guttural sound like Parisian 'r'
ف	ف	ف	ف	f	as in 'far'
ق	ق	ق	ق	q	a strongly guttural 'k' sound; also often pronounced as a glottal stop
ك	ك	ك	ك	k	as in 'king'
ل	ل	ل	ل	l	as in 'lamb'
م	م	م	م	m	as in 'me'
ن	ن	ن	ن	n	as in 'name'
ه	ه	ه	ه	h	as in 'ham'
و			و	w	as in 'wet'
				oo	long, as in 'food'
				ow	as in 'how'
ي	ي	ي	ي	y	as in 'yes'
				ee	as in 'beer', only softer
				ai/ay	as in 'aisle'/as the 'ay' in 'day'

Vowels Not all Arabic vowel sounds are represented in the alphabet. For more information on the vowel sounds used in this language guide, see Vowels (p681).

Emphatic Consonants To simplify the transliteration system used in this book, the emphatic consonants have not been included.

especially where more than one option is given, reflects regional dialects. For best results, pronounce the transliterated words slowly and clearly.

Vowels

Technically, there are three long and three short vowels in Arabic. The reality is a little different, with local dialect and varying consonant combinations affecting their pronunciation. This is the case throughout the Arabic-speaking world. At the very least, five short and three long vowels can be identified:

a	as in 'had'
e	as in 'bet'
i	as in 'hit'
o	as in 'hot'
u	as in 'push'
aa	as in 'father' or as a long pronunciation of the 'a' in 'had'
ee	as the 'ea' in 'eagle'
oo	as the 'oo' in 'food'

Consonants

Pronunciation for all Arabic consonants is covered in the Arabic alphabet table (p680). Note that when double consonants occur in transliterations, both are pronounced. For example, el-hammaam (toilet, bathhouse), is pronounced 'el-ham-mam'.

Other Sounds

Arabic has two sounds that are very tricky for non-Arabs to produce, the 'ayn and the glottal stop. The letter 'ayn represents a sound with no English equivalent that comes even close. It is articulated from deep in the throat, as is the glottal stop (which is not actually represented in the alphabet), but the muscles at the back of the throat are gagged more forcefully – it has even been described as the sound of someone being strangled!

In many transliteration systems 'ayn is represented by an opening quotation mark, and the glottal stop by a closing quotation mark. To make the transliterations in this language guide (and throughout the rest of the book) easier to use, we have not distinguished between the glottal stop and the 'ayn, using the closing quotation mark to represent both sounds. You should find

that Arabic speakers will still understand you through the context of your topic of conversation.

CONVERSATION & ESSENTIALS

Arabs place great importance on civility, and it's rare to see any interaction between people that doesn't begin with profuse greetings, inquiries into the other's health and other niceties.

Arabic greetings are more formal than greetings in English, and there is a reciprocal response to each. These sometimes vary slightly, depending on whether you're addressing a man or a woman. A simple encounter can become a drawn-out affair, with neither side wanting to be the one to put a halt to the stream of greetings and well-wishing. As an ajnabi (foreigner), you're not expected to know all the ins and outs, but if you come up with the right expression at the appropriate moment, they'll love it.

The most common greeting is salaam 'alaykum (peace be upon you), to which the correct reply is wa alaykum as-salaam (and upon you be peace). If you get invited to a birthday celebration or are around for any of the big holidays, the common greeting is kul sunu wu intum bi-kher (I wish you well for the coming year).

After having a bath or a haircut, you will often hear people say to you na'iman, which roughly means 'heavenly' and boils down to an observation along the lines of 'nice and clean now!'.

Arrival in one piece is always something to be grateful for. Passengers will often be greeted with al-hamdu lillah 'al as-salaama, meaning 'thank God for your safe arrival'.

Hi.	marhaba
Hello. (literally 'welcome')	ahlan wa sahlan/ahlan
Hello. (response)	ahlan beek or ya hala
Goodbye.	ma'a salaama/ Allah ma'ak
Good morning.	sabah al-khayr
(response)	sabah an-noor
Good evening.	masaa al-khayr
(response)	masaa an-noor
Good night.	tisbah 'ala khayr
(response)	wa inta min ahlu
Yes.	aywa/na'am
No.	la

Please. (request)	*min fadlak* (m)/
	min fadlik (f)
Please. (polite, eg	*law samaht* (m)/
in restaurants)	*law samahtee* (f)
Please. (come in/	*tafadal* (m)/*tafadalee* (f)/
go ahead)	*tafadalu* (pl)
Thank you.	*shukran*
Thanks a lot.	*shukran jazeelan*
You're welcome.	*'afwan or ahlan*
How are you?	*kayf haalak?* (m)/
	kayf haalik? (f)
Fine. (literally	*al-hamdu lillah*
'thanks be to God')	
Pleased to meet	*fursa sa'ida*
you. (departing)	
Pardon/Excuse me.	*'afwan*
Sorry!	*'assif!*
Congratulations!	*mabrook!*
What's your name?	*shu-ismak?* (m)/*shu-ismik?* (f)
My name is ...	*ismee ...*
Where are you from?	*min wayn inta?*
Do you speak ...?	*btah-ki ...?/hal tatakallam ...?*
I speak ...	*ana bah-ki .../ana atakallam ...*
English	*ingleezi*
French	*faransi*
German	*almaani*
I understand.	*ana af-ham*
I don't understand.	*ma bif-ham/la af-ham*
What does this mean?	*yaanee ay?*
I want an interpreter.	*ureed mutarjem*
I (don't) like ...	*ana (ma) bahib/ana (la) uhib ...*
No problem.	*mish mushkila*
Never mind.	*ma'alesh*

Questions like 'Is the bus coming?' or 'Will the bank be open later?' generally elicit the inevitable response *in sha' Allah* (God willing) an expression you'll hear over and over again. Another less common one is *ma sha' Allah* (God's will be done), sometimes a useful answer to probing questions about why you're not married yet!

HEALTH

I'm ...	*'andee ...*
asthmatic	*azmit raboo*
diabetic	*is sukkar*
I'm allergic ...	*'andee Hasasiyya ...*
to antibiotics	*min mudād Haiowi*
to aspirin	*min asbireen*
to nuts	*min mukassarāt*
to penicillin	*min binisileen*

antiseptic	*mutahhir*
diarrhoea	*is-haal*
doctor	*duktoor/tabeeb*
headache	*sudaa'*
hospital	*mustashfa*
medicine	*dowa*
pharmacy	*agzakhana/saydaliyya*

ACCOMMODATION & SERVICES

Do you have ...?	*fee'andakum ...?*
a room	*ghurfa*
a single room	*ghurfa mufrada*
a double room	*ghurfa bee sareerayn*
a shower	*doosh*
hot water	*mayy harr*
a toilet	*twalet/mirhad/hammaam*
air-con	*kondishon/takyeef*
electricity	*kahraba*
Where is (the) ...?	*wayn ...?*
bank	*al-masraf/al-bank*
hotel	*al-funduq*
market	*as-sooq*
Mohammed St	*sharia Mohammed*
mosque	*al-jaami'/al-masjid*
museum	*al-mat'haf*
passport & immi-	*maktab al-jawaazaat*
gration office	*wa al-hijra*
police	*ash-shurtaal-bolees*
post office	*maktab al-bareed*
restaurant	*al-mat'am*
tourist office	*maktab as-siyaaHa*
How much?	*qaddaysh/bikam?*
How many?	*kam wahid?*
How much money?	*kam fuloos?*
money	*fuloos/masaari*
big	*kabeer*
small	*sagheer*
good	*kwayyis*
bad	*mish kwayyis/mu kwayyis*
cheap	*rakhees*
expensive	*ghaali*
cheaper	*arkhas*

LANGUAGE

bus/train station	terminal/istgah
ticket	belit
ticket office	daftar-e belit forushi
open/closed	baz/ta'til
left	dast-e chap
right	dast-e rast
far (from ...)	dur (az ...)
near (to ...)	nazdik (-e ...)
straight ahead	mostaghim

HEBREW

Written from right to left, Hebrew has a basic 22-character alphabet – but from there it starts to get very complicated. Like English, not all these characters have fixed phonetic values and their sound can vary from word to word. You just have to know that, for instance, Yair is pronounced 'Ya-ear' and doesn't rhyme with 'hare' or 'fire'.

As with Arabic, transliteration of Hebrew script into English is at best an approximate science. The presence of sounds not found in English, and the fact that the script is 'incomplete' (most vowels are not written) combine to make it nearly impossible to settle on one consistent method of transliteration. Numerous spellings are therefore possible for words when they appear in Roman script, and that goes for place and people's names as well.

For a more comprehensive guide to Hebrew than can be given here, get a copy of Lonely Planet's *Hebrew Phrasebook*.

CONVERSATION & ESSENTIALS

Hello.	shalom
Goodbye.	shalom
See you later.	lehitra'ot
Good morning.	boker tov
Good evening.	erev tov
Goodnight.	layla tov
Thank you (very much).	toda (raba)
Please.	bevakasha
You're welcome.	al lo davar
Yes.	ken
No.	lo
Excuse me.	slikha
Wait.	regga
What?	ma?
When?	matai?
Where is ...?	eifo ...?

| Do you speak English? | ata medaber/medaberet anglit? (m/f) |

ACCOMMODATION & SERVICES

bill	kheshbon
hotel	malon
room	kheder
toilet	sherutim
How much is it?	kama ze ole?
money	kesef
bank	bank
post office	do'ar
letter	mikhtav
stamps	bulim
envelopes	ma'atafar
air mail	do'ar avir
pharmacy	bet mirkakhat
shop	khanut
cheap	zol
expensive	yakar
right (ie correct)	nakhon

TIME, DAYS & NUMBERS

What is the time?	ma hasha'a?
seven o'clock	hasha'a sheva
minute	daka
hour	sha
day	yom
week	shava'a
month	khodesh
year	shana
Monday	yom sheni
Tuesday	yom shlishi
Wednesday	yom revi'i
Thursday	yom khamishi
Friday	yom shishi
Saturday	shabbat
Sunday	yom rishon

Hebrew uses standard Western numerals for written numbers.

0	efes
1	akhat
2	shta'im
3	shalosh
4	arba
5	khamesh
6	shesh
7	sheva
8	shmone
9	tesha
10	eser

| open | maftooh |
| closed | maghlooq/musakkar |

TIME & DAYS

What is the time?	adaysh as-saa'a?
It's 5 o'clock.	as-sa'a khamsa
When?	mata/emta?
yesterday	imbaarih/'ams
today	al-yom
tomorrow	bukra/ghadan
minute	daqiqa
hour	sa'a
day	yom
week	usbu'
month	shaher
year	sana
Monday	al-itneen yom
Tuesday	at-talaata yom
Wednesday	al-arba'a yom
Thursday	al-khamees yom
Friday	al-jum'a yom
Saturday	as-sabt yom
Sunday	al-ahad yom

MONTHS

The Hejira calendar year has 12 lunar months and is 11 days shorter than the Western (Gregorian) calendar year, so important Muslim dates will fall 11 days earlier each (Western) year.

There are two Gregorian calendars used in the Arab world. In Egypt and the Gulf States, the months have virtually the same names as in English (eg January is *yanaayir*, October is *octobir*), but in Lebanon, Jordan and Syria, the names are quite different. Talking about, say, June as 'month six' is the easiest solution, but for the sake of completeness, the months from January are:

January	kaanoon ath-thaani
February	shubaat
March	aazaar
April	nisaan
May	ayyaar
June	huzayran
July	tammooz
August	'aab
September	aylool
October	tishreen al-awal
November	tishreen ath-thani
December	kanoon al-awal

The Hejira months also have their own names:

1st	moharram
2nd	safar
3rd	rabee' al-awwal
4th	rabee' ath-thaani
5th	jumada al-awwall
6th	jumada al-akheera
7th	rajab
8th	sha'baan
9th	ramadaan
10th	shawwaal
11th	zool-qe'da
12th	zool-hijja

NUMBERS

0	sifr	٠
1	waaHid	١
2	itneen	٢
3	talaata	٣
4	arba'a	٤
5	khamsa	٥
6	sitta	٦
7	saba'a	٧
8	tamaniya	٨
9	tis'a	٩
10	ashra	١٠
11	Hida'ash	١١
12	Itna'ash	١٢
13	talata'ash	١٣
14	arbatash	١٤
15	khamistash	١٥
16	sittash	١٦
17	sabi'tash	١٧
18	tamanta'ash	١٨
19	tisita'ash	١٩
20	'ishreen	٢٠
21	waaHid wa 'ishreen	٢١
22	itneen wa 'ishreen	٢٢

30	talateen	۳۰
40	arbi'een	٤۰
50	khamseen	٥۰
60	sitteen	٦۰
70	saba'een	۷۰
80	timaneen	۸۰
90	tis'een	۹۰
100	imia	۱۰۰
200	imiatayn	۲۰۰
1000	'alf	۱۰۰۰
2000	'alfayn	۲۰۰۰
3000	thalath-alaf	۳۰۰۰

TRANSPORT

How many kilometres?	kam kilometre?
airport	al-mataar
bus station	mahattat al-baas
train station	mahattat al-qitaar
car	as-sayaara
1st class	daraja awla
2nd class	daraja thani
here/there	hena/henak
left	yasaar
right	shimal/yameen
straight ahead	'ala tool

FARSI

Farsi (Persian) is the national language of Iran. Although the vast majority of Iranians can speak it, it's the first language for only about 60% of the population. The most predominant minority languages are Azeri, Kurdish, Arabic, Baluchi and Lori.

PRONUNCIATION
Vowels & Diphthongs

a	as the 'u' in 'must'; smetimes long, as in 'far'
e	as in 'bed'
i	as in 'marine'
o	as in 'mole'
u	as in 'rule'

Consonants

The letters **b**, **d**, **f**, **j**, **k**, **l**, **m**, **n**, **p**, **s**, **sh**, **t**, **v** and **z** are pronounced as in English.

ch	as in 'chip'
g	as in 'go'
y	as in 'yak'
zh	as in 'Zhivago'
r	slightly trilled as in Italian caro

h	always pronounced; like r, it doesn't lengthen the preceding vowel
kh	as the 'ch' in Scottish loch
gh	a soft guttural sound like the noise made when gargling
'	a weak glottal stop, like the double 't' in the Cockney pronunciation of 'bottle'

Double consonants are always pronounced as two distinct sounds. Stress generally falls on the last syllable of a word.

CONVERSATION & ESSENTIALS

Hello.	salam
Peace be upon you.	salam aleikom
Goodbye.	khodafez/khoda hafez (more polite)
Good morning.	sobh bekheir
Good night/Good evening.	shab bekheir
Please. (request, literally 'kindly')	lotfan
Please. (when offering something, eg 'please help yourself')	befarmayin
Thank you.	mersi/tashakkor/motashakkeram
Don't mention it.	ghabel nabud
Excuse me/I'm sorry.	bebakhshid
Yes.	bale
No.	nakheir/na (less formal)
OK.	dorost
Where are you from?	shoma ahl-e koja hastid?
Do you speak ...?	shoma ... baladid?
English	engelisi
French	feranse
German	almani

HEALTH

I have ...	... daram
asthma	asm
diabetes	diyabet
I'm allergic ...	be ... hassasiyat daram
to antibiotics	antibiyutik
to aspirin	asperin
to peanuts/nuts	badum zanini/ajil
to penicillin	penisilin
antiseptic	zedd e ufuni konande
diarrhoea	es-hal
doctor	doktor
hospital	bimarestan
medicine	daru
pharmacy	darukhune

ACCOMMODATION & SERVICES

hotel	hotel/mehmunkhune
cheap hotel/ guesthouse	mosaferkhune
Do you have ... for tonight?	emshab ... darid?
a room	otagh
a single room	otagh-e ye nafari
a double room	otagh-e do nafari
a cheaper room	otagh-e arzuntar
a better room	otagh-e behtar
How much is the room per night?	otagh shabi chand e?
Excuse me, where is the ...?	bebakhshid, ... koja st?
consulate	konsulgari
embassy	sefarat
mosque	masjed
post office	postkhune
restaurant	restoran/chelo kababi/salon-e gheza
street/avenue	kheyabun
toilet	tuvalet
town centre	markaz-e shahr
How many?	chand ta?
How much is it?	chand e?
cheap	arzun
expensive	gerun

TIME, DAYS & NUMBERS

When?	kei?
At what time?	chi vaght?
(at) ... o'clock	sa'at-e ...
today	emruz
tonight	emshab

SIGNS – FARSI	
Entrance	ورود
Exit	خروج
Open	باز
Closed	بسته
No Entry	ورود ممنوع
No Smoking	دخانیات ممنوع
Prohibited	ممنوع
Hot	گرم
Cold	سرد
Toilets	توالت
Men	مردانه
Women	زنانه

tomorrow	farda
(in the) morning	sobh
(at) night, evening	shab
Monday	doshambe
Tuesday	seshambe
Wednesday	chaharshambe
Thursday	panjshambe
Friday	jom'e
Saturday	shambe (1st day of Muslim week)
Sunday	yekshambe

1	yek	۱
2	do	۲
3	se	۳
4	chahar	٤
5	panj	٥
6	shesh	٦
7	haft	۷
8	hasht	۸
9	noh	۹
10	dah	۱۰
11	yazdah	۱۱
12	davazdah	۱۲

TRANSPORT

Where is the ... (to Tabriz)?	... (betabriz) kojast?
bus	otobus
train	ghetar
boat	ghayegh
ship/ferry	kashti
taxi (any kind)	taksi
car (or taxi)	mashin
minibus	minibus
airport	forudgah
jetty/dock/harbour	eskele

LANGUAGE

open	maftooh
closed	maghlooq/musakkar

TIME & DAYS

What is the time?	adaysh as-saa'a?
It's 5 o'clock.	as-sa'a khamsa
When?	mata/emta?
yesterday	imbaarih/'ams
today	al-yom
tomorrow	bukra/ghadan
minute	daqiqa
hour	sa'a
day	yom
week	usbu'
month	shaher
year	sana

Monday	al-itneen yom
Tuesday	at-talaata yom
Wednesday	al-arba'a yom
Thursday	al-khamees yom
Friday	al-jum'a yom
Saturday	as-sabt yom
Sunday	al-ahad yom

MONTHS

The Hejira calendar year has 12 lunar months and is 11 days shorter than the Western (Gregorian) calendar year, so important Muslim dates will fall 11 days earlier each (Western) year.

There are two Gregorian calendars used in the Arab world. In Egypt and the Gulf States, the months have virtually the same names as in English (eg January is *yanaayir*, October is *octobir*), but in Lebanon, Jordan and Syria, the names are quite different. Talking about, say, June as 'month six' is the easiest solution, but for the sake of completeness, the months from January are:

January	kaanoon ath-thaani
February	shubaat
March	aazaar
April	nisaan
May	ayyaar
June	huzayran
July	tammooz
August	'aab
September	aylool
October	tishreen al-awal
November	tishreen ath-thani
December	kanoon al-awal

SIGNS – ARABIC

Entrance	مدخل
Exit	خروج
Open	مفتوح
Closed	مغلق
Prohibited	ممنوع
Information	معلومات
Hospital	مستشفي
Police	شرطة
Men's Toilet	حمام للرجال
Women's Toilet	حمام للنساء

The Hejira months also have their own names:

1st	moharram
2nd	safar
3rd	rabee' al-awwal
4th	rabee' ath-thaani
5th	jumada al-awwall
6th	jumada al-akheera
7th	rajab
8th	sha'baan
9th	ramadaan
10th	shawwaal
11th	zool-qe'da
12th	zool-hijja

NUMBERS

0	sifr	•
1	waaHid	١
2	itneen	٢
3	talaata	٣
4	arba'a	٤
5	khamsa	٥
6	sitta	٦
7	saba'a	٧
8	tamaniya	٨
9	tis'a	٩
10	ashra	١٠
11	Hida'ash	١١
12	itna'ash	١٢
13	talata'ash	١٣
14	arbatash	١٤
15	khamistash	١٥
16	sittash	١٦
17	sabi'tash	١٧
18	tamanta'ash	١٨
19	tisita'ash	١٩
20	'ishreen	٢٠
21	waaHid wa 'ishreen	٢١
22	itneen wa 'ishreen	٢٢

LANGUAGE

30	talateen	٣٠
40	arbi'een	٤٠
50	khamseen	٥٠
60	sitteen	٦٠
70	saba'een	٧٠
80	timaneen	٨٠
90	tis'een	٩٠
100	imia	١٠٠
200	imiatayn	٢٠٠
1000	'alf	١٠٠٠
2000	'alfayn	٢٠٠٠
3000	thalath-alaf	٣٠٠٠

TRANSPORT

How many kilometres?	kam kilometre?
airport	al-mataar
bus station	mahattat al-baas
train station	mahattat al-qitaar
car	as-sayaara
1st class	daraja awla
2nd class	daraja thani
here/there	hena/henak
left	yasaar
right	shimal/yameen
straight ahead	'ala tool

FARSI

Farsi (Persian) is the national language of Iran. Although the vast majority of Iranians can speak it, it's the first language for only about 60% of the population. The most predominant minority languages are Azeri, Kurdish, Arabic, Baluchi and Lori.

PRONUNCIATION
Vowels & Diphthongs

a	as the 'u' in 'must'; smetimes long, as in 'far'
e	as in 'bed'
i	as in 'marine'
o	as in 'mole'
u	as in 'rule'

Consonants

The letters b, d, f, j, k, l, m, n, p, s, sh, t, v and z are pronounced as in English.

ch	as in 'chip'
g	as in 'go'
y	as in 'yak'
zh	as in 'Zhivago'
r	slightly trilled as in Italian caro
h	always pronounced; like r, it doesn't lengthen the preceding vowel
kh	as the 'ch' in Scottish loch
gh	a soft guttural sound like the noise made when gargling
'	a weak glottal stop, like the double 't' in the Cockney pronunciation of 'bottle'

Double consonants are always pronounced as two distinct sounds. Stress generally falls on the last syllable of a word.

CONVERSATION & ESSENTIALS

Hello.	salam
Peace be upon you.	salam aleikom
Goodbye.	khodafez/khoda hafez (more polite)
Good morning.	sobh bekheir
Good night/Good evening.	shab bekheir
Please. (request, literally 'kindly')	lotfan
Please. (when offering something, eg 'please help yourself')	befarmayin
Thank you.	mersi/tashakkor/motashakkeram
Don't mention it.	ghabel nabud
Excuse me/I'm sorry.	bebakhshid
Yes.	bale
No.	nakheir/na (less formal)
OK.	dorost
Where are you from?	shoma ahl-e koja hastid?
Do you speak ...?	shoma ... baladid?
English	engelisi
French	feranse
German	almani

HEALTH

I have ...	... daram
asthma	asm
diabetes	diyabet
I'm allergic ...	be ... hassasıyat daram
to antibiotics	antibiyutik
to aspirin	asperin
to peanuts/nuts	badum zanini/ajil
to penicillin	penisilin
antiseptic	zedd e ufuni konande
diarrhoea	es-hal
doctor	doktor
hospital	bimarestan
medicine	daru
pharmacy	darukhune

EMERGENCIES – FARSI

Help!	komak!
I'm sick.	mariz am
I wish to contact my	mikham ba sefarat/
embassy/consulate.	konsulgari khod am
	tamas begiram
Go away!	gom sho!
Shame on you!	khejalat bekesh!
(said by a woman to a man bothering her)	
Call ...!	... khabar konin!
a doctor	ye doktor
the police	polis o

SIGNS – FARSI

Entrance	ورود
Exit	خروج
Open	باز
Closed	بسته
No Entry	ورود ممنوع
No Smoking	دخانیات ممنوع
Prohibited	ممنوع
Hot	گرم
Cold	سرد
Toilets	توالت
Men	مردانه
Women	زنانه

ACCOMMODATION & SERVICES

hotel	hotel/mehmunkhune
cheap hotel/	mosaferkhune
guesthouse	
Do you have ... for	emshab ... darid?
tonight?	
a room	otagh
a single room	otagh-e ye nafari
a double room	otagh-e do nafari
a cheaper room	otagh-e arzuntar
a better room	otagh-e behtar
How much is the	otagh shabi chand e?
room per night?	
Excuse me, where	bebakhshid, ... koja st?
is the ...?	
consulate	konsulgari
embassy	sefarat
mosque	masjed
post office	postkhune
restaurant	restoran/chelo kababi/salon-e
	gheza
street/avenue	kheyabun
toilet	tuvalet
town centre	markaz-e shahr
How many?	chand ta?
How much is it?	chand e?
cheap	arzun
expensive	gerun

TIME, DAYS & NUMBERS

When?	kei?
At what time?	chi vaght?
(at) ... o'clock	sa'at-e ...
today	emruz
tonight	emshab

tomorrow	farda
(in the) morning	sobh
(at) night, evening	shab
Monday	doshambe
Tuesday	seshambe
Wednesday	chaharshambe
Thursday	panjshambe
Friday	jom'e
Saturday	shambe (1st day of Muslim week)
Sunday	yekshambe

1	yek	١
2	do	٢
3	se	٣
4	chahar	٤
5	panj	٥
6	shesh	٦
7	haft	٧
8	hasht	٨
9	noh	٩
10	dah	١٠
11	yazdah	١١
12	davazdah	١٢

TRANSPORT

Where is the ...	... (betabriz) kojast?
(to Tabriz)?	
bus	otobus
train	ghetar
boat	ghayegh
ship/ferry	kashti
taxi (any kind)	taksi
car (or taxi)	mashin
minibus	minibus
airport	forudgah
jetty/dock/harbour	eskele

LANGUAGE

bus/train station	terminal/istgah
ticket	belit
ticket office	daftar-e belit forushi
open/closed	baz/ta'til
left	dast-e chap
right	dast-e rast
far (from ...)	dur (az ...)
near (to ...)	nazdik (-e ...)
straight ahead	mostaghim

HEBREW

Written from right to left, Hebrew has a basic 22-character alphabet – but from there it starts to get very complicated. Like English, not all these characters have fixed phonetic values and their sound can vary from word to word. You just have to know that, for instance, Yair is pronounced 'Ya-ear' and doesn't rhyme with 'hare' or 'fire'.

As with Arabic, transliteration of Hebrew script into English is at best an approximate science. The presence of sounds not found in English, and the fact that the script is 'incomplete' (most vowels are not written) combine to make it nearly impossible to settle on one consistent method of transliteration. Numerous spellings are therefore possible for words when they appear in Roman script, and that goes for place and people's names as well.

For a more comprehensive guide to Hebrew than can be given here, get a copy of Lonely Planet's *Hebrew Phrasebook*.

CONVERSATION & ESSENTIALS

Hello.	shalom
Goodbye.	shalom
See you later.	lehitra'ot
Good morning.	boker tov
Good evening.	erev tov
Goodnight.	layla tov
Thank you (very much).	toda (raba)
Please.	bevakasha
You're welcome.	al lo davar
Yes.	ken
No.	lo
Excuse me.	slikha
Wait.	regga
What?	ma?
When?	matai?
Where is ...?	eifo ...?

| Do you speak English? | ata medaber/medaberet anglit? (m/f) |

ACCOMMODATION & SERVICES

bill	kheshbon
hotel	malon
room	kheder
toilet	sherutim
How much is it?	kama ze ole?
money	kesef
bank	bank
post office	do'ar
letter	mikhtav
stamps	bulim
envelopes	ma'atafar
air mail	do'ar avir
pharmacy	bet mirkakhat
shop	khanut
cheap	zol
expensive	yakar
right (ie correct)	nakhon

TIME, DAYS & NUMBERS

What is the time?	ma hasha'a?
seven o'clock	hasha'a sheva
minute	daka
hour	sha
day	yom
week	shava'a
month	khodesh
year	shana
Monday	yom sheni
Tuesday	yom shlishi
Wednesday	yom revi'i
Thursday	yom khamishi
Friday	yom shishi
Saturday	shabbat
Sunday	yom rishon

Hebrew uses standard Western numerals for written numbers.

0	efes
1	akhat
2	shta'im
3	shalosh
4	arba
5	khamesh
6	shesh
7	sheva
8	shmone
9	tesha
10	eser

LANGUAGE

11	*eakhat-esre*
12	*shteim-esre*
20	*esrim*
21	*esrim ve'akhat*
30	*shloshim*
31	*shloshim ve'akhat*
50	*khamishim*
100	*me'a*
200	*matayim*
300	*shalosh mayat*
500	*khamaysh mayat*
1000	*elef*
3000	*shloshet elefim*
5000	*khamayshet elefim*

TRANSPORT

Which bus goes to ...?	*eize otobus nose'a le ...?*
Stop here.	*atsor kan*
airport	*sde te'ufa*
bus	*otobus*
near	*karov*
railway	*rakevet*
station	*tukhana*

TURKISH

Ottoman Turkish was written in Arabic script, but this was phased out when Atatürk decreed the introduction of Latin script in 1928. In big cities and tourist areas, many locals know at least some English and/or German. In the southeastern towns, Arabic or Kurdish is the first language.

For a more in-depth look at the language, including a comprehensive list of useful words and phrases, get a copy of Lonely Planet's *Turkish Phrasebook*.

PRONUNCIATION

The letters of the new Turkish alphabet have a consistent pronunciation; they're reasonably easy to master, once you've learned a few basic rules. All letters except ğ (which is silent) are pronounced, and there are no diphthongs.

Vowels

A a	as in 'shah'
E e	as in 'fell'
İ i	as 'ec'
I ı	as 'uh'
O o	as in 'hot'
U u	as the 'oo' in 'moo'

| Ö ö | as the 'ur' in 'fur' |
| Ü ü | as the 'ew' in 'few' |

Note that ö and ü are pronounced with pursed lips.

Consonants

Most consonants are pronounced as in English, but there are a few exceptions:

Ç ç	as the 'ch' in 'church'
C c	as English 'j'
Ğ ğ	not pronounced – it draws out the preceding vowel
G g	as in 'go'
H h	as in 'half'
J j	as the 's' in 'measure'
S s	as in 'stress'
Ş ş	as the 'sh' in 'shoe'
V v	as the 'w' in 'weather'

CONVERSATION & ESSENTIALS

Hello.	*Merhaba.*
Goodbye/Bon Voyage.	*Allaha ısmarladık/Güle güle.*
Please.	*Lütfen.*
Thank you.	*Teşekkür ederim.*
That's fine/You're welcome.	*Bir şey değil.*
Excuse me.	*Affedersiniz.*
Sorry. (Excuse me/ Forgive me.)	*Pardon.*
Yes.	*Evet.*
No.	*Hayır.*
How much is it?	*Ne kadar?*
Do you speak English?	*Ingilizce biliyor musunuz?*
Does anyone here speak English?	*Kimse Ingilizce biliyor mu?*
I don't understand.	*Anlamıyorum.*
Just a minute.	*Bir dakika.*
Please write that down.	*Lütfen yazın.*

HEALTH

I'm ...	*... var.*
asthmatic	*astımım*
diabetic	*şeker hastalığı*

I'm allergic to ...	*... alerjim var.*
to antibiotics	*antibiyotiklere*
to nuts	*çerezlere*
to peanuts	*fıstığa*
to penicillin	*penisiline*

LANGUAGE

EMERGENCIES – TURKISH

Help!/Emergency!	İmdat!
I'm ill.	Hastayım.
Could you help us, please?	Bize yardım edebilirmisiniz lütfen?
Call a doctor!	Doktor çağırın!
Call the police!	Polis çağırın!
Go away!	Gidin!/Git!/Defol!
I'm lost.	Kayboldum.

antiseptic	antiseptik
diarrhoea	ishali
hospital	hastane
medicine	ilaç
nausea	mide bulantım
pharmacy	eczane

ACCOMMODATION & SERVICES

Where is a cheap hotel?	Ucuz bir otel nerede?
What is the address?	Adres ne?
Please write down the address.	Adresiyazar mısınız?
Do you have any rooms available?	Boş oda var mı?

I'd like ...	... istiyorum.
a bed	bir yatak
a single room	tek kişilik oda
a double room	İkikişilik oda
a room with a bathroom	banyolu oda
to share a dorm	yatakhanede bir yatak

How much is it per night?	Bir gecelik nekadar?
May I see it?	Görebilir miyim?
Where is the bathroom?	Banyo nerede?

I'm looking for the/a ...	... arıyorum.
bank	bir banka
city centre	şehir merkezi
... embassy	... büyükelçiliğini
hotel	otelimi
market	çarşıyı
police	polis
post office	postane
public toilet	tuvalet
telephone centre	telefon merkezi
tourist office	turizm danışma bürosu

TIME, DAYS & NUMBERS

What time is it?	Saat kaç?
today	bugün
tomorrow	yarın
in the morning	sabahleyin
in the afternoon	öğleden sonra
in the evening	akşamda

Monday	Pazartesi
Tuesday	Salı
Wednesday	Çarşamba
Thursday	Perşembe
Friday	Cuma
Saturday	Cumartesi
Sunday	Pazar

January	Ocak
February	Şubat
March	Mart
April	Nisan
May	Mayıs
June	Haziran
July	Temmuz
August	Ağustos
September	Eylül
October	Ekim
November	Kasım
December	Aralık

0	sıfır
1	bir
2	iki
3	üç
4	dört
5	beş
6	altı
7	yedi
8	sekiz
9	dokuz
10	on
11	on bir
12	on iki
13	on üç
14	on dört
15	on beş
16	on altı
17	on yedi
18	on sekiz
19	on dokuz
20	yirmi
21	yirmibir
22	yirmiiki
30	otuz
40	kırk
50	elli

LANGUAGE

SIGNS – TURKISH

Giriş	Entrance
Çıkış	Exit
Danışma	Information
Açık	Open
Kapalı	Closed
Polis/Emniyet	Police
Polis Karakolu/	Police station
Emniyet Müdürlüğü	
Yasak(tır)	Prohibited
Tuvalet	Toilet

60	altmış
70	yetmiş
80	seksen
90	doksan
100	yüz
200	ikiyüz
1000	bin
2000	ikibin
1,000,000	bir milyon

TRANSPORT

Where is the bus/ tram stop?	Otobüs/tramvay durağınerede?

I want to go to (İzmir).	(İsmir)'e gitmek istiyorum.
Can you show me on the map?	Haritada gösterebilir misiniz?
Go straight ahead.	Doğru gidin.
Turn left.	Sola dönün.
Turn right.	Sağa dönün.
near	yakın
far	uzak

When does the ... leave/arrive?	... ne zaman kalkar/gelir?
ferry/boat	feribot/vapur
city bus	şehir otobüsü
intercity bus	otobüs
train	tren
tram	tramvay

next	gelecek
first	birinci/ilk
last	son
timetable	tarife
train station	istasyon

I'd like a ... ticket.	... bileti istiyorum.
one-way	gidiş
return	gidiş-dönüş

Glossary

Here, with definitions, are some unfamiliar words and abbreviations you may meet in the text or on the road in the Middle East. This glossary contains English, Arabic (Ar), Egyptian (E), Farsi (Far), Hebrew (Heb), Jordanian (J), Lebanese (Leb), Libyan (Lib) and Turkish (T) words.

Abbasid dynasty – Baghdad-based successor dynasty to the *Umayyad dynasty*; ruled from AD 750 until the sacking of Baghdad by the Mongols in 1258
abd (Ar) – servant or slave
abeyya (Ar) – woman's full-length black robe
abra (Ar) – small motorboat
abu (Ar) – father or saint
acropolis – high city; hilltop citadel of a classic Hellenic city
agal (Ar) – headropes used to hold a *keffiyeh* in place; also *'iqal*
agora – open space for commerce and politics in a classic Hellenic city
ahl al-kitab (Ar) – 'people of the book'; the position of special respect traditionally accorded to Jews and Christians in the *Quran*
ahwa – see *qahwa*
aile salonu (T) – family room for use by couples, families and single women in a Turkish restaurant
ain (Ar) – spring or well; also *ayn*, *ein*
akhbar (Ar) – great
Al-Ahram (E) – the Pyramids at Giza
arasta (T) – row of shops beside a mosque
arg (Far) – citadel
Ashkenazi – a Jew of German or eastern European descent
ateshkade (Far) – Zoroastrian fire temple
ayn – see *ain*
Ayyubid dynasty – Egyptian-based dynasty (1169–1250) founded by *Saladin*
azan – call to prayer

bab (Ar) – gate
badia (J) – stone or basalt desert
bagdir – see *barjeel*
bait – see *beit*
bakala (Ar) – corner shop
baksheesh – alms or tip
balad (Ar) – land or city
barjeel (Ar) – wind towers; *badgir* in Iran
basbut – see *bazbort*
bawwab (Ar) – doorman

bazbort – passport; also *basbut*, *pispot*
beit (Ar) – house; also *bait*
beit ash-sha'ar – Bedouin black goat-hair tent
bey (T) – junior officer in Ottoman army; a term of respect that corresponds to Mr
bijous – service taxi
Book of the Dead – ancient Egyptian theological compositions or hymns that were the subject of most of the colourful paintings and reliefs on tomb walls
bukhnoq (Ar) – girl's head covering
burg – see *burj*
burj (Ar) – tower; *burg* in Egypt
burnous (Lib) – white robe worn by women; it exposes only one eye
buyut ash-shabaab (Lib) – youth hostel

calèche (E) – horse-drawn carriage
caliph – Islamic ruler
Camel Period – the period of Saharan rock art from 200 BC to the present
cami(i) (T)– mosque
Canopic jars – pottery jars that held the embalmed internal organs and viscera of the mummy; these were placed in the burial chamber near the sarcophagus
capitol – decorated top part of a column in Roman or Greek architecture
caravanserai – see *khan*
cardo – road running north–south through a Roman city
carnet de passage – permit allowing entry of a vehicle to a country without incurring taxes
çarşı (T) – market or bazaar
cartouche – oblong figure enclosing the hieroglyphs of royal or divine names
centrale – telephone office
chador (Ar) – black, one-piece, head-to-toe covering garment; worn by many Iranian women
cipolin – white marble with veins of green or grey
curia – senate house or municipal assembly in ancient Rome

dalla (Ar) – traditional coffeepot
dammous (Lib) – underground Berber houses in Libya
Decapolis – league of 10 cities, including Damascus, in the northeast of ancient Palestine
decumanus – road running east–west through a Roman city
deir (Ar) – monastery or convent
dervish – Muslim mystic; see also *Sufi*
Diaspora – Jewish dispersion or exile from the Land of Israel; the exiled Jewish community worldwide

ein – see *ain*
eivan – rectangular hall opening onto a mosque's courtyard
emam (Far) – see *imam*
emir – literally 'prince'; Islamic ruler, military commander or governor
Eretz Yisrael – the Land of Israel, commonly used by Israel's right wing to refer to their preferred borders for the Jewish State, which includes the Gaza Strip, the West Bank and sometimes Jordan and/or the Sinai
evi (T) – house

fadl (Ar) – large metal platters for serving food
falaj (Ar) – irrigation channel
Fatimid dynasty – Shiite dynasty (908–1171) from North Africa, later based in Cairo, claiming descent from Mohammed's daughter Fatima; founders of Al-Azhar, the oldest university in the world
felafel – deep-fried balls of chickpea paste with spices served in a piece of flat bread with tomatoes or pickled vegetables; *ta'amiyya* in Egypt
fellaheen (E) – peasant farmers or agricultural workers who make up the majority of Egypt's population; literally 'ploughman' or 'tiller of the soil'
foggara (Lib) – underground channels leading to water in the Sahara
funduq (Lib) – hotel
fuul – paste made from fava beans

galabiyya (E) – see *jalabiyya*
gebel (E) – see *jebel*
ghibli (Lib) – hot, dry wind of northern Libya
gület (T) – traditional wooden yacht

haj – annual Muslim pilgrimage to Mecca; one of the five pillars of Islam
hamada – plateaus of rock scoured by wind erosion in the Sahara
hamam (T) – see *hammam*
Hamas – militant Islamic organisation that aims to create an Islamic state in the pre-1948 territory of Palestine; acronym (in Arabic) for Islamic Resistance Movement
hammam (Ar) – bathhouse; *hamam* in Turkish
hantour – horse and carriage
haram – anything that is forbidden by Islamic law
hared – (plural haredim) member of an ultra-orthodox Jewish sect; also *hasid* (plural hasidim)
hasid – see *hared*
hejab (Ar) – woman's headscarf, worn for modesty; *hegab* in Egypt
Hejira – Mohammed's flight from Mecca to Medina in AD 622; the starting point of the Muslim era and the Muslim era itself
hisar (Ar) – fortress, citadel; *kale* in Turkish
hızlı feribot (T) – fast car ferries

Horse Period – the period of Saharan rock art from 1000 BC to AD 1
hypostyle hall – hall in which the roof is supported by columns

idehan – a vast area of shifting sand dunes in the Libyan Sahara known as sand seas
imam – prayer leader or Muslim cleric; *emam* in Farsi
intifada – Palestinian uprising against Israeli authorities in the West Bank, Gaza and East Jerusalem; literally 'shaking off'
'iqal – see *agal*
iqama – residence permit
iskele(si) (T) – landing-place, wharf or quay
iwan – vaulted hall, opening into a central court in a *madrassa* or a mosque

jalabiyya – full-length robe worn by men, *galabiyya* in Egypt
jamaa – see *masjid*
jamahiriya (Lib) – republic or 'state of the masses' in post-Revolutionary Libya
jammour – crescent atop a minaret
janissaries – professional soldiers who ruled Ottoman Libya
jawazzat (Lib) – passport office
jebel (Ar) – hill, mountain; *gebel* in Egypt
jihad – literally 'striving in the way of the faith'; holy war

ka – spirit or 'double' of a living person that gained its own identity with the death of that person; the survival of the ka, however, required the continued existence of the body, hence mummification
Kabaa – the rectangular structure at the centre of the Grand Mosque in Mecca (containing the Black Stone) around which *haj* pilgrims circumambulate; also *Qaaba*
kababi (Far) – basic kebab shop
kale(si) (T) – see *hisar*
kanyon (Heb) – shopping plaza
keffiyeh (Ar) – chequered scarf worn by Arabs
khan – travellers' inn, usually constructed on main trade routes, with accommodation on the 1st floor and stables and storage on the ground floor; also *caravanserai, wikala* in Egypt
khedive – Egyptian viceroy under Ottoman suzerainty (1867–1914)
khor – rocky inlet
khutba (Ar) – sermon delivered by an *imam*, especially at Friday noon prayers
kibbutz – (plural kibbutzim) Jewish communal settlement run cooperatively by its members
kibbutznik – member of a *kibbutz*
kilim – woven rug
knanqah – *Sufi* monastery
Knesset – Israeli parliament

komite – Iranian religious police
konak (T) – mansion
Koran – see *Quran*
kosher – food prepared according to Jewish dietary law
köy(ü) (T) – village
kufic – type of highly stylised old Arabic script

Likud – Israeli right-wing political party
liman(ı) (T) – harbour
lokanta (T) – restaurant

madhhab – 'school' of Islamic law and interpretation
madrassa – Muslim theological seminary; modern Arabic word for school; *medrese(si)* in Turkey
mafraj (Ar) – literally 'room with a view'; top room of a tower house
mahalle(si) (T) – neighbourhood, district of a city
mahattat servees – taxi depot
majlis – formal meeting room or parliament
maktab amn al-aam (Leb) – general security office where visas are extended
Mamluk – slave-soldier dynasty that ruled out of Egypt from 1250 to 1517
manzar (Ar) – attic; room on top of a tower house
mashrabiyya – ornate carved wooden panel or screen; feature of Islamic architecture
masjid (Ar) – mosque; also *jamaa*
masraf (Ar) – bank
mastaba – Arabic word for 'bench'; mud-brick structure above tombs from which the pyramids were developed
medina – city or town, especially the old quarter of a city
medrese(si) (T) – see *madrassa*
menorah – eight-pronged candelabra; an ancient Jewish symbol associated with the Hanukkah festival
Mesopotamia – ancient name for Iraq from the Greek meaning 'between two rivers'
meydan(ı) – see *midan*
meyhane (T) – (plural meyhaneler) tavern
midan (Ar) – town or city square; *meydan(ı)* in Turkish (plural meydanlar)
midrahov (Heb) – pedestrian mall
mihrab – niche in a mosque indicating direction of Mecca
minbar – pulpit used for sermons in a mosque
mosaferkhuneh (Far) – cheap hotel
moshav (Heb) – cooperative settlement, with private and collective housing and industry
moulid (Ar) – festival celebrating the birthday of a local saint or holy person
muezzin – cantor who sings the call to prayer
mullah – Muslim scholar, teacher or religious leader

nargileh (Ar) – water pipe used to smoke tobacco; *qalyan* in Iran, *sheesha* in Egypt
Nilometer – pit descending into the Nile containing a central column marked with graduations; the marks were used to measure and record the level of the river, especially during the inundation
norias – water wheels

obelisk – monolithic stone pillar with square sides tapering to a pyramidal top; used as a monument in ancient Egypt
Omayyad dynasty – see *Umayyad dynasty*
OPEC – Organisation of Petroleum Exporting Countries
otogar (T) – bus station

pansiyon – pension, B&B or guesthouse
pasha – Ottoman governor appointed by the sultan in Constantinople
Pastoral Period – the period of Saharan rock art from 5500 to 2000 BC, also known as the Bovidian Period
Pentapolis – ancient federation of five cities (Barce, Cyrene, Eusperides, Tocra and Apollonia) in Greek Libya
pispot – see *bazbort*
PLO – Palestine Liberation Organization
PTT (T) – Posta, Telefon, Telğraf; post, telephone and telegraph office
Punic – ancient Phoenician people with capital at Carthage
pylon – monumental gateway at the entrance to a temple

qa'a (Ar) – reception room
Qaaba – see *Kabaa*
qahwa (Ar) – coffee, coffeehouse; *ahwa* in Egypt
qalyan (Far) – see *nargileh*
qaryat as-siyahe (Lib) – tourist village
qasr – castle or palace; also used to describe fortified Berber granary stores in Libya
Quran – the holy book of Islam; also *Koran*

rakats (Ar) – cycles of prayer during which the *Quran* is read and bows and prostrations are performed
Ramadan – ninth month of the lunar Islamic calendar during which Muslims fast from sunrise to sunset
ras (Ar) – cape, headland or head
Riconquista – 1922 policy of reconquest of Libya by the Italians under Mussolini
Round Head Period – the period of Saharan rock art from 8000 to 6000 BC

sabil (Ar) – public drinking fountain
sabkha – soft sand with a salty crust; low-lying area or salt pan
sadu – Bedouin-style weaving
sahn (Ar) – courtyard of a mosque
Sala – the Muslim obligation of prayer, ideally to be performed five times a day; one of the five pillars of Islam
Saladin – (Salah ad-Din in Arabic) Kurdish warlord who retook Jerusalem from the Crusaders; founder of the *Ayyubid dynasty*

Sanusi Movement – organised Islamic opposition to Ottoman and the Italian occupation of Libya

Sawm – the Muslim month of *Ramadan*

şehir (T) – city or municipality

şehiriçi (T) – minibus

serdab – a secret chamber in an ancient Egyptian tomb

serir – basins, formed by *wadis*, in which salt is left after water has evaporated

settler – term used to describe Israelis who have created new communities on territory captured from the Arabs during the 1967 War

Shabbat – Jewish Sabbath observed from sundown on Friday to one hour after sundown on Saturday

Shahada – Islam's basic tenet and profession of faith: 'There is no god but Allah, and Mohammed is the Prophet of Allah'; one of the five pillars of Islam

shai (Ar) – tea

sharia – Islamic law

sheesha (E) – see *nargileh*

sheikh – venerated religious scholar; also shaikh

sherut (Heb) – shared taxi with a fixed route

shwarma – grilled meat sliced from a spit and served in pita-type bread with salad; also *doner kebab* and *döner kebap* in Turkish

siq (Ar) – narrow passageway or defile such as the one at Petra

soor (Ar) – wall

souq – market or bazaar

stele – (plural stelae) stone or wooden commemorative slab or column decorated with inscriptions or figures

Sufi – follower of any of the Islamic mystical orders that emphasise dancing, chanting and trances in order to attain unity with God; see also *dervish*

sultan – absolute ruler of a Muslim state

sura – chapter in the *Quran*

ta'amiyya (E) – see *felafel*

Tamashek – Tuareg language

tawaabi – stamps

tawle – backgammon

TC – Türkiye Cumhuriyeti (Turkish Republic); designates an official office or organisation

tell – ancient mound created by centuries of urban rebuilding

tirma – Iranian silk

toman (Far) – unit of 10 rials

Torah – five books of Moses, the first five Old Testament books; also called the Pentateuch

Tripolis – literally 'Three Cities'; referred to Leptis Magna, Oea and Sabratha in Roman Libya

Umayyad dynasty – first great dynasty of Arab Muslim rulers, based in Damascus (661–750); also *Omayyad dynasty*

velayat-e faqih (Far) – Iranian 'supreme leader'

wadi – dried up river bed; seasonal river

wikala (E) – see *khan*

Wild Fauna Period – the period of Saharan rock art from 10,000 to 6000 BC

willayat – village

Zakat – the Muslim obligation to give alms to the poor; one of the five pillars of Islam

zawiya (Ar) – small school dedicated to the teaching of a particular *sheikh*

ziggurat (Far) – rectangular temple tower or tiered mound built in *Mesopotamia* by the Akkadians, Babylonians and Sumerians

zurkane – wrestling ground

Behind the Scenes

THE LONELY PLANET STORY

The story begins with a classic travel adventure: Tony and Maureen Wheeler's 1972 journey across Europe and Asia to Australia. There was no useful information about the overland trail then, so Tony and Maureen published the first Lonely Planet guidebook to meet a growing need.

From a kitchen table, Lonely Planet has grown to become the largest independent travel publisher in the world, with offices in Melbourne (Australia), Oakland (USA) and London (UK). Today Lonely Planet guidebooks cover the globe. There is an ever-growing list of books and information in a variety of media. Some things haven't changed. The main aim is still to make it possible for adventurous travellers to get out there – to explore and better understand the world.

At Lonely Planet we believe travellers can make a positive contribution to the countries they visit – if they respect their host communities and spend their money wisely. Every year 5% of company profit is donated to charities around the world.

THIS BOOK

This 5th edition of *Middle East* was researched and written by Anthony Ham (coordinating author), Andrew Burke, Jean-Bernard Carillet, Michael Kohn, Frances Linzee Gordon, Virginia Maxwell and Bradley Mayhew. Staff writer Will Gourlay wrote the chapter Islam & the West. Roshan Muhammed Salih wrote the boxed texts 'Occupied or Liberated? Iraq Post-Saddam' (p258) and 'Prospects for an Iraqi Phoenix' (p257). The Health chapter was adapted from material written by Dr Caroline Evans. The past two editions of this book were researched and written by teams of authors led by Andrew Humphreys.

This guidebook was commissioned in Lonely Planet's Melbourne office and produced by the following:

Commissioning Editors Lynne Preston and Kerryn Burgess with assistance from Will Gourlay and Stefanie Di Trocchio
Coordinating Editor Helen Christinis
Coordinating Cartographer Amanda Sierp
Coordinating Layout Designer Christine Wieser
Managing Cartographer Shahara Ahmed
Assisting Editors Jeanette Wall, Cahal McGroarty, Margedd Heliosz, Janice Bird, Melissa Faulkner, Sarah Hassall, Justin Flynn, Lucy Monie, Laura Stansfeld, Liz Heynes
Assisting Cartographers Marion Byass, Anneka Imkamp, Jody Whiteoak, Lyndell Stringer, Joshua Geoghegan, Helen Rowley
Assisting Layout Designer Wibowo Rusli
Cover Designer James Hardy
Indexer Kate Evans

Project Managers Charles Rawlings-Way, Sarah Sloane, Nancy Ianni
Language Content Coordinator Quentin Frayne

Thanks to Karen Companez, Jacqui Saunders and Shahara Ahmed for checking the script, and to Suzannah Shwer for her guidance.

THANKS
ANTHONY HAM

First and foremost, an enormous thank you to Hakim Sallah Ashour, a dear friend without whom the Libya chapter could not have been written and who, on successive trips to Libya, has shown me all that is good about Libya. Other long-standing Libyan friends who deserve special thanks are Hussein Founi, Mu'awiya Wanis, Dr Mustapha Turjman, Ahmeda Zeglam, Mohammed Ali Kredan, At-Tayeb Mohammed Hiba and Othman al-Hama and his friends in Al-Bayda. Among the many new friends I made on this trip, Najib was a wonderful driver and memorable desert companion. Thanks also to Othman in Ghadames, Khamis in Tripoli and various places along the road, Ali Shebli, Hakim's delightful family, Mejrema Reuter and Alison McQuitty.

At Lonely Planet, a big thank you to Will Gourlay, Lynne Preston, Shahara Ahmed and to Kerryn Burgess who was an insightful commissioning editor with whom it was a pleasure to work. Thanks also to the editors and cartographers, Helen Christinis, Margedd Heliosz and Amanda Sierp, for their hard work. I was also extremely lucky to have such exceptional coauthors – Andrew, Jean-Bernard, Virginia, Frances, Will, Bradley and Michael – who brought such wisdom and experience to bear upon the book.

In Australia heartfelt thanks to Jan, Ron, Lisa, Damien, Quetta, Rachael, Greg, Alex and Greta for making the visit back home so warm. Thanks also to all my lovely friends and family in Madrid.

And to Marina, who tolerates my absences, welcomes me home with such warmth and endlessly reminds me that home is wherever she is – *gracias mi amor.*

ANDREW BURKE

There are many friends and acquaintances in Iran whom I owe a *kheyli mamnun*. In Tehran Maryam Julazadeh and Chris Taylor provided wonderful hospitality, advice and friendship that was greatly appreciated. Thanks also go to Hamid Musavi in Tehran, the Fallahi family in Esfahan; Ali and Hadi in Yazd; Towhid and his fire-jumping family in Mashhad; Maziar Ali Davoud and family in serene Garmeh; the ever-resilient Panjalizadeh Akbar and the clan in Bam, where Ziba Sharafi, Aydin, Atussa, Ali Soljhoo, Morteza and Bezhad were also good fun and a great help. Ali Karooney, Masoud Nematollahi and Zahra in Shiraz were wonderful, as were the Akhavan brothers in Kerman. Thanks also to Nasser and Mansour Khan and Hossein Ravaniyar in Tabriz; and the colonel who released me and then invited me to dinner in Howraman-e Takht.

Thanks to fellow travellers Ted, Frederic Galante, Sebastien Cabour, Tito Dupret, Pablo Strubell, Scott Jacobson and Anne. At Lonely Planet, my appreciation goes to Kerryn Burgess, Will Gourlay and the ever-patient editors in Melbourne, and to coordinating author Anthony Ham. Last but definitely not least, love and thanks to my wife Anne, who is always there when I get home.

JEAN-BERNARD CARILLET

First off, I'd like to express my deepest gratitude to the Diler family for their support and warmhearted welcome in Turkey, and especially to Tovi, Ahmet, Osman and Yassine. Thanks to them, I felt at home in Cappadocia and in İstanbul. I'm also grateful to Musa, Mehmet, Ihlan and Kenan, who helped me a lot and kept spirits high. In eastern Turkey, I'm grateful to Remzi Bozbay, Özcan Aslan, Celil Ersoğlu and Zafer Onay. In İstanbul, big thanks to Veronique Duwa and Inanç who showed me their favourite places in the city, and to Pat Yale, whose expertise and acute eyes were invaluable – not to mention the good meals and the laughs.

At Lonely Planet headquarters, I'm grateful to Lynne Preston and Kerryn Burgess, who were a pleasure to work with. Thanks also to Anthony Ham, the coordinating author, whose patience and equanimity are unrivalled.

And, last but not least, *teşekkür ederiz* to all the Turkish and Kurdish people I met on the road and who enlivened my trip. You can't go wrong in such a hospitable country.

MICHAEL KOHN

Opening thanks to Lynne Preston for assigning me the Israel & the Palestinian Territories chapter, and also in Melbourne, Kerryn Burgess for handling my weekly blogs. Cheers also to fellow authors Anthony Ham for his coordinating efforts and Bradley Mayhew for coordinating dinner in Amman.

In Israel, I could not have had better hosts than Gal Kaplan and Einav Sharav, who lent a voice and opinion to my never-ending questions. Cheers to the staff at the Coffee Bean where much of this chapter was written. Gil Shafer and his family were great hosts during Pesach. Dave Gilbert provided guiding duties in Gush Katif. In Jerusalem, cheers to Chris at the Citadel Youth Hostel and Danny Flax at the Allenby Guesthouse. Special thanks to the Davis and Golshevesky families for wonderful Shabbat dinners, as well as Shabbat companions Ari, Dave and Nathan. Viva Press at the *Jerusalem Post* lent insight for the arts and entertainment sections. Thanks also to Alexis in Mizpe Ramon, Russell Kibel in Eilat, Brian Ambrosio in Gaza, the gang at Faisal's in East Jerusalem, Ohad Sharav in Tel Aviv and border buddies Dave and Chris. At home, *shalom* and *ahava* to Baigal.

FRANCES LINZEE GORDON

Many thanks to Philip Elias, AUB Medical Center; Charles Khalil of Liban Post; Aram Tchafarian and Assadour Andekian, guides at Anjar; Dr Ing Nabil Haddad and Presette Geha, Jeita Grotto; Hamid Fakhry, Bcharré; Salwa Abdo, Bourane Merheby and Moustafa Doussouki.

Many, many thanks to Marie and Pierre Jabbour of Hotel Koura for a warm welcome and help with research in Tripoli; Michel Saidah for the lowdown on Beirut's bars; Mourad Loutfi of Hotel Albergo for expert restaurant recommendations; Khaled Abour, Bassam Mer'abi, Rice Ghaiteh and Hassan of City Car for information and help with research; and Ambassador James Watt and his wife, Amal, for insights into Lebanese politics and Beirut.

Finally, thanks to the ever-unsung team at Lonely Planet and particularly to Shahara Ahmed, managing cartographer; Kerryn Burgess, commissioning editor for the Middle East; and Anthony Ham, coordinating author, all of whom did a great job shepherding us!

VIRGINIA MAXWELL

In Syria I'd like to thank the staff and management of the Sultan Hotel in Damascus; Hassane Salloum of the Omayad Hotel Damascus; Bader and Anas from the Cairo/Noria Hotels in Hama; Sawsan Jouzy of the Syrian Ministry of Tourism; and Bridget Palmer in Damascus.

In Egypt many thanks to Hisham Youssif of the Berlin Hotel in Cairo; Mourad Gamil Abd Rabu from the tourist office in Luxor; Salah Muhammad from Noga Tours in Cairo; and Caroline Evanoff, Mary Fitzpatrick, Siona Jenkins and Anthony Sattin.

Discoveries on the road were shared with my favourite travelling companions, Max and Peter.

My fellow authors were all generous with their time and expertise. Coordinating author Anthony Ham was wonderful to work with, as were commissioning editors Lynne Preston and Kerryn Burgess, managing cartographer Shahara Ahmed, editor Helen Christinis and cartographer Mandy Sierp. *Shukran!*

BRADLEY MAYHEW

Firstly, I'd like to offer my thanks to Charl Twal, Sami and Hamid at the Palace Hotel and Mohammed Hallak of Reliable Rent-a-Car, without whom my research would have been so much less fun. Ruth of **Jordan Jubilee** (www.jordanjubilee.com) was very helpful, as she is to all travellers to Jordan.

Several people helped with tips and pointers, including Majdi Twal, Walid Nassar, Eid Nawafleh at Petra Moon, Lotus Abu Karaki for info on tourism projects and Yamaan Safadi for an overview on trekking options. Thanks to David Symes for help in getting things rolling.

Many people at the RSCN were generous with their time and information; particular thanks go to Ghada al-Sous, Abeer Smadi and Chris Johnson at the Wild Jordan office and to the guys at Wadi Mujib and Dana (Bassam al-Saudi at Rummana and Abel Razzak Khwalabeh at Dana). *Salaam* to Ahmad al-Wazani in Irbid.

OUR READERS

Many thanks to the many travellers who used the last edition and wrote to us with helpful hints, useful advice and interesting anecdotes.

A Janet Adams, Bruce Allen, Ray Allen, Lena al-Shammari, Diane Anorpong, Eva Appelman, William Apt, George Assouad, Wendy Atkinson, Helene Aoki, A Attieg, Claude Avezard **B** Julie Barss, Geoff Barton, Cliff & Jenny Batley, Shane Bauer, Luca Belis, Diane Bellafronot, Anat Bernstein, Jim Berry, Alain Bertallo, Jan Beukema, Claude Birais, Jon Bird, Jonathan Bird, Adi Birger, Julia Bishop,

Chivon Blanton, Yury Bolotov, Debbie Bonnell, Kim Boreham, Lucila Bracco, Gail Brooks, Richard Brooks, Saso Bucai, Sean Burberry, Rowland Burley **C** Andre C, Julie Capsalis, Jenny Carter-Manning, Yaelle Caspi, Shona Chamberlin, Jean-Francois Chariot, David Chaudoir, Janet Collier, Shirley Constapel, Giles Cory, Robert Crothers, Pete Cull, Nicola & Richard Curzon **D** Anita Dalley, Suzie Davidson-Kelly, Henry Dawson, Karsten Dax, Judy & Martin Dean, Winn P Dean, Romain Desrousseaux, David Dillenberger **E** Gustav Ellingsen, Jos Emmerik, Carla Eua **F** Guido Faes, John Lee Fagence, Efrat Farber, Bernard Farjounel, Hanne Finholt, Eleanor Ford, Derek Foster, Susan-Mary Foster, Ralph Fuchs **G** Heiko Gabriel, Maja Galic, David Gasda, Austin Gayer, Lia Genovese, Justn & Lucy George, Marion Golany, Miguel Alvim Gonzalez Nancy Greig, Daniel Groeber, Andrea Gryak, Peder Gustafsson, Benghazi Gross **H** Marcella Hallemeesch, Leen B Hanenberg, Patricia Havekost, Jan Havranek, Jennifer Hayes, Eva Hendrickx, Kerry Hennigan, Dana Hlavnova, Markus Hochuli, Anders Hofseth, Erik Hoogcarspel, Julia Hopkins, Abbas Hormati, Graham Hurst, Jan F Huson, Cathie Hutchison **I** Ioana Ispas, Alene Ivey **J** Malgorzata Januszko, Rok Jarc, Rasmus Bak Jespen, Christian Jongeneel, Jack Jordan, Sandra Jouravlev, Matthias Junken **K** Andre Kahlmeyer, Wouter Karst, Hiran Karunaratna, Stewart Kennedy, Muhammed Abdul Khalid, Sameen Ahmed Khan, Eldad Klaiman, Paul Koetsawang, Andrzej Komorowski, Grigory Kubatyan **L** Louise Lambert, Janice Law, Ralph Lawson, Charlotte Ledoux, Mike Lee, Sonny Lee, Brian Lema, Matthew Lerner, Chris Little, Joey Locke, Colin Lovell **M** David Mackertich, Dov Maislish, Astrid & Heidi Marshall, Winston & Jacquelyn Marshall, Michael Martin, Jacopo Mascheroni, Fotis

---

SEND US YOUR FEEDBACK

We love to hear from travellers – your comments keep us on our toes and help make our books better. Our well-travelled team reads every word on what you loved or loathed about this book. Although we cannot reply individually to postal submissions, we always guarantee that your feedback goes straight to the appropriate authors, in time for the next edition. Each person who sends us information is thanked in the next edition – and the most useful submissions are rewarded with a free book.

To send us your updates – and find out about Lonely Planet events, newsletters and travel news – visit our award-winning website: **www.lonelyplanet.com/feedback**.

Note: We may edit, reproduce and incorporate your comments in Lonely Planet products such as guidebooks, websites and digital products, so let us know if you don't want your comments reproduced or your name acknowledged. For a copy of our privacy policy, go to www.lonelyplanet.com/privacy.

Matsoukas, Cedric McCallum, Judith McCormick, Jenn McCready, Mike McGee, Richard McHale, Laurence Michalak, Phyllis Mifsud, Stephen G Miller, Brian Moody, Ronan Moore **N** AlGhamdi Nasser, Yael Neeman-Schubert, Roderick Neilsen, Anne Neiwirth, Birgit & Dietrich Nelle, Alexander Nitzsche, Joachim Norum **O** Sarah Ohring, Susan Orr, Julie & Sener Otrugman **P** Brigette Palmer, Kathy Palmer, Jeffrey Papajcik, Charlie Parker, Steven Parkinson, Sara Partington, Carlo & Emanuela Paschetto, Hubert Peres, Simon Peters, Anna Piller, Wendy Plasman, Dan Pletzer, Isabel Posthuma, Liam Pounder, Guillermo Pascual Pouteau, Matthew Pritt, Laszlo Privoczki **Q** Antonio Quaglieri **R** Ambrogio Radaelli, Loretta Rafter, Martin Reeve, Torben Retboll, Michael Reynolds, Scott Riley, Edu Romero, Wouter Rutten **S** Khalifa Saleh, Nahla Saleh, Christophe Sap, Carla Santos, Rex Saunders, Matt Shacklady, Sherin Sharawy, Tony Sharpe, Mark Sheard, Philippe Sibelly, Char Simons, Adrienne Simpson, Bahir Skinner, Bronwyn Spiteri, Mark Stallard, Joseph T Stanik, Ben Stein **T** Naureen Tadros, Sylvie Tigroudja, Iva Igracki & Momir Turudic, Cressida Trew, Miquel Trujillo, Jonathan Tsou, Greg Tuck, Katie Turner-Samuels, Warren Tute **U** Paul Ullman **V** Petra van der Klaauw, Dimitri van Uytfange, Nerea Varela, Arjan Veersma, Chris Verrill, Jeff Vize **W** Christine Wagner, Joy Wan, Fionna Ward, Joshua Welbaum, Denise Werner, Rivkah Westerman, Johan Westman, Ernest Willyard, Danielle Wolbers, Tino Wolter, Leah Wong, Alison Woodcock, Sylvie & Matt Waudby Yang, Martin Wright, Alex Wuth **Z** Sarah Zabic, Edme Zalinski, Jerrin Zumberg, Rosanne Zammit

ACKNOWLEDGMENTS

Many thanks to the following for the use of their content:

Globe on back cover: ©Mountain High Maps® 1993 Digital Wisdom, Inc.

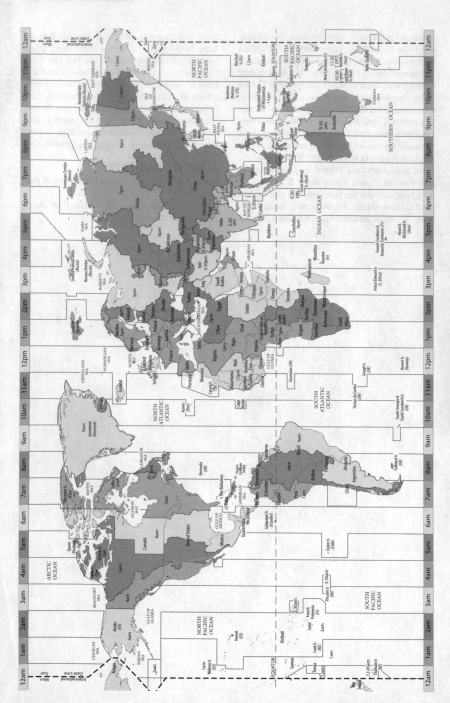

Index

INDEX

INDEX

000 Map pages
000 Photograph pages

INDEX

000 Map pages
000 Photograph pages

INDEX

INDEX

MAP LEGEND

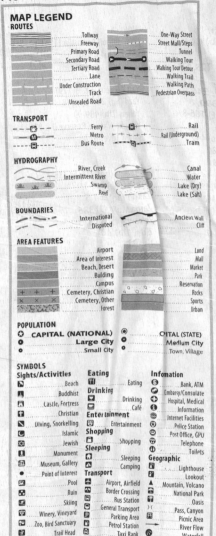

ROUTES

Tollway
Freeway
Primary Road
Secondary Road
Tertiary Road
Lane
Under Construction
Track
Unsealed Road

One-Way Street
Street Mall/Steps
Tunnel
Walking Tour
Walking Tour Detour
Walking Trail
Walking Path
Pedestrian Overpass

TRANSPORT

Ferry
Metro
Bus Route

Rail
Rail (Underground)
Tram

HYDROGRAPHY

River, Creek
Intermittent River
Swamp
Reef

Canal
Water
Lake (Dry)
Lake (Salt)

BOUNDARIES

International
Disputed

Ancient Wall
Cliff

AREA FEATURES

Airport
Area of Interest
Beach, Desert
Building
Campus
Cemetery, Christian
Cemetery, Other
Forest

Land
Mall
Market
Park
Reservation
Rocks
Sports
Urban

POPULATION

○ **CAPITAL (NATIONAL)**
○ **Large City**
● Small City

◉ **CAPITAL (STATE)**
◉ **Medium City**
● Town, Village

SYMBOLS

Sights/Activities

Beach
Buddhist
Castle, Fortress
Christian
Diving, Snorkelling
Islamic
Jewish
Monument
Museum, Gallery
Point of Interest
Pool
Ruin
Skiing
Winery, Vineyard
Zoo, Bird Sanctuary
Trail Head

Eating

Eating

Drinking

Drinking
Café

Entertainment

Entertainment

Shopping

Shopping

Sleeping

Sleeping
Camping

Transport

Airport, Airfield
Border Crossing
Bus Station
General Transport
Parking Area
Petrol Station
Taxi Rank

Information

Bank, ATM
Embassy/Consulate
Hospital, Medical
Information
Internet Facilities
Police Station
Post Office, GPO
Telephone
Toilets

Geographic

Lighthouse
Lookout
Mountain, Volcano
National Park
Oasis
Pass, Canyon
Picnic Area
River Flow
Waterfall

LONELY PLANET OFFICES

Australia
Head Office
Locked Bag 1, Footscray, Victoria 3011
☎ 03 8379 8000, fax 03 8379 8111
talk2us@lonelyplanet.com.au

USA
150 Linden St, Oakland, CA 94607
☎ 510 893 8555, toll free 800 275 8555
fax 510 893 8572
info@lonelyplanet.com

UK
72–82 Rosebery Ave,
Clerkenwell, London EC1R 4RW
☎ 020 7841 9000, fax 020 7841 9001
go@lonelyplanet.co.uk

Published by Lonely Planet Publications Pty Ltd
ABN 36 005 607 983

© Lonely Planet Publications Pty Ltd 2006

© photographers as indicated 2006

Cover photographs: Man smoking sheesha, Luxor, Egypt, Peter Adams/Photolibrary (front); Urn Tomb at Petra, Anthony Ham/Lonely Planet Images (back). Many of the images in this guide are available for licensing from Lonely Planet Images: www.lonelyplanetimages .com.

Printed through Colorcraft Ltd, Hong Kong
Printed in China

INDEX